THE SCOUTING REPORT: 1996

Produced by
The Baseball Workshop

Gary Gillette
Editor

Stuart Shea
Associate Editor

Pete Palmer, David W. Smith
Contributing Editors

Statistics by
The Baseball Workshop

HarperPerennial
A Division of HarperCollinsPublishers

Most of the player photos in this book were provided by the 28 individual
Major League Baseball teams and are used with their permission. Some of the
photos were provided by minor-league teams, including the Albuquerque Dukes,
Columbus Clippers, Edmonton Trappers, Indianapolis Indians, Knoxville
Smokies, Las Vegas Stars, Ottawa Lynx, and Toledo Mud Hens.

THE SCOUTING REPORT: 1996. Copyright © 1996 by The Baseball Workshop.
All rights reserved. Printed in the United States of America. No part of this book
may be used or reproduced in any manner whatsoever without written permission
except in the case of brief quotations embodied in critical articles and reviews. For
information address HarperCollins Publishers, Inc., 10 East 53rd Street,
New York, NY 10022.

HarperCollins books may be purchased for educational, business, or sales
promotional use. For information, please write: Special Markets Department,
HarperCollins Publishers, Inc., 10 East 53rd Street, New York, NY 10022.

FIRST EDITION

ISSN 0743-1309
ISBN 0-06-273360-5

96 97 98 RRD 5 4 3 2 1

Contributors

A book of this scope involves the hard work and contributions of many people. Some of their names are on the title page, some are not. The roll call of contributors for the major-league players:

Stuart Shea, The Baseball Workshop. Stuart contributed to the scouting reports on a majority of the teams and also edited much of the book.

David W. Smith, President of Retrosheet. David prepared the data for all of the graphs in the book and also contributed to the scouting reports for Baltimore and Los Angeles.

Pete Palmer, baseball historian and co-editor of *Total Baseball*. Pete edited and prepared most of the 1994 and career statistics in the book.

Leo Gordon, Steve Lysogorski, and Brigg Hewitt. Freelancers and correspondents who work for The Baseball Workshop during the season. Leo contributed to the Texas and Toronto scouting reports, Steve to the Detroit scouting reports, and Brigg to the San Diego reports.

The *Top Prospects* and *Others to Watch* sections for each team were written by analysts at Howe Sportsdata International in Boston, Mass. Howe is the official statistician for all of the recognized minor leagues—and some of the new independent leagues, also. Their staff keeps track of minor-league games and players on a round-the-clock basis during the season. Howe is the source for almost all of the minor-league information and statistics in this book (and in almost every other book and periodical currently in print). *The Scouting Report: 1995* contributors at Howe:

Jim Keller, who wrote or edited most of the prospects reports and helped design the prospects sections.

Chris Pollari, who prepared the biographical information and the minor-league statistics for each player.

Brian Joura, Paul LaRocca, and Vin Vitro, who wrote many of the scouting reports on the prospects.

Last, but certainly not least, several veteran major-league scouts—all of whom chose to remain anonymous—but whose scouting reports and opinions form much of the foundation for this book.

Acknowledgments

Many other people besides the writers and editors helped out in various ways with the production of this book. My sincere thanks to the dozens of Baseball Workshop stringers who contribute during and after the baseball season. This book couldn't be done without the information they provide.

The seven active major-league scouts who were interviewed extensively about the ballplayers. For understandable reasons, they have chosen to remain anonymous, but their contributions are critical in evaluating active players. It is one of the true pleasures of my job to be able to talk baseball at length with these scouts.

I would also like to acknowledge the contributions of Jim Keller, Chris Pollari, and Jay Virshbo of Howe Sporstdata International—the only place to go for minor-league information.

Steve Stovall of Mountain Lion and Margaret Trejo of Trejo Production.

Robert Wilson, former minor-league player and my editor at HarperCollins in New York.

Good friends, baseball experts, and esteemed colleagues Eddie Epstein, now Director of Baseball Operations for the San Diego Padres, and Steve Mann, author and baseball labor-management expert.

Vicki Gillette and Cecilia Garibay, who help out every day of every year.

This book is dedicated to my mother, Jean Gillette, who has had little time for baseball in her busy life. Her given name, Regina, is Latin for *queen*—my grandmother knew what she was doing when she named my mother.

Gary Gillette, Editor

Contents

Introduction vi
User's Guide vii

American League Players 1

    Baltimore Orioles 2
    Boston Red Sox 26
    California Angels 51
    Chicago White Sox 75
    Cleveland Indians 96
    Detroit Tigers 119
    Kansas City Royals 139
    Milwaukee Brewers 162
    Minnesota Twins 186
    New York Yankees 208
    Oakland Athletics 231
    Seattle Mariners 252
    Texas Rangers 275
    Toronto Blue Jays 299

National League Players 321

    Atlanta Braves 322
    Chicago Cubs 345
    Cincinnati Reds 367
    Colorado Rockies 391
    Florida Marlins 415
    Houston Astros 437
    Los Angeles Dodgers 462
    Montreal Expos 485
    New York Mets 507
    Philadelphia Phillies 528
    Pittsburgh Pirates 552
    St. Louis Cardinals 575
    San Diego Padres 598
    San Francisco Giants 622

Other Veteran Players 645
Off-Season Player Moves 659
Index 665

About The Baseball Workshop 673
The Scouting Report Spring Training Update 674

Introduction

Welcome to the 1996 edition of *The Scouting Report*. If you're a veteran reader of the book, you should be able to skip most of this introduction. If you're new to the book, this Introduction and the following User's Guide should help you better understand how the book is organized, what statistics are shown, and what the scouting terms used throughout the book mean.

The first thing to note about *The Scouting Report: 1996* is the number of players covered. The book thoroughly covers more than 750 major-league players and it also covers hundreds of the top minor-league prospects. This means that you will find detailed analysis and statistics of almost 350 top prospects (a dozen or so per team) in the book. In addition to these top prospects, you will find brief sketches of another 425 or so lesser prospects and veteran minor-leaguers (approximately 15 per team) in this year's edition.

The second thing to note about *The Scouting Report: 1996* is that it includes exactly what the title of the book implies: *scouting reports* on players. As the editor of the book, I am concerned that *The Scouting Report* deliver to the readers the type of information that professional baseball scouts provide to the teams that employ them. Therefore, I hire veteran major-league scouts and pay them to provide scouting reports for all major-league players. While the information taken from these scouting reports has been written and edited by baseball writers and analysts, the inside information about a pitcher's fastball or a hitter's swing has been taken directly from the reports filed by active professional scouts.

Because of this direct connection to baseball scouts, you will find a lot of scouting lingo included in the book. At first, these descriptions of players and their abilities may seem unusual, because baseball scouts have a unique vocabulary which has been developed over decades of watching players at all levels. When a scout says that a pitcher has a *plus* fastball, he is deliberately using a specific term to indicate a professional judgment he has made. A *plus* fastball is different than a *good* fastball, and that distinction is very important. I have deliberately chosen to incorporate much of the language and terminology of scouts into the book. I think that it helps to better understand how the scouts size up the players, and I think that the colorful language of the scouts makes the books more readable and enjoyable. For more explanation of the scouting terms used in the book, see the definitions which are included after this introduction.

The third thing to note about *The Scouting Report: 1996* is that the minor-league prospect reports have been written by analysts from Howe Sportsdata International in Boston. Howe Sportsdata is the official statistician for all of the recognized minor leagues—there's no one better at covering the minor leagues, and no one knows more about the thousands of minor-league players and prospects, than the people at Howe. Their contributions make the this a much better book.

The last thing to note about *The Scouting Report: 1996* is the inclusion of comprehensive statistics for all players and analytical graphs for regular players. The career batting and pitching statistics show important categories like Caught Stealing and On-Base Average that earlier editions of the book didn't show. Perhaps more importantly, situational statistics are shown for all 750 major-league players, not just for the regulars, and these situational breakdowns have On-Base and Slugging Averages for batters and against pitchers, as well as walks and strikeouts for pitchers. In addition, two graphs are shown for all regular batters and pitchers, making comparisons between them and other players easier and quicker.

Whether you're a new reader of *The Scouting Report*, or a long-time fan, I hope you like this new edition. Comments and suggestions are always welcome.

Gary Gillette, Editor
The Baseball Workshop

User's Guide

The Teams
This year's book is organized in a similar manner as previous editions. All players are grouped according to their 1995 major-league team or organization, except for those players who had been traded or signed by a new team shortly after the end of the season in October. The teams are shown alphabetically by league, with the American League teams at the front of the book and the National League teams following the AL teams. If you don't know where to find a player, just look in the Player Index at the back of the book.

Major-League Players
As in past editions, regular players for each major-league team get full page reports and non-regular players get half-page reports. The regular players are shown alphabetically for each team first, then the non-regulars are shown alphabetically after the regulars.

Top Minor-League Prospects
After the major-league players for each team comes two pages of alphabetical reports on that team's top minor-league prospects. Approximately one dozen top prospects are shown here, some of whom have played briefly in the majors before, many of whom have yet to make their big-league debut. Most of these prospects played in the high minors (i.e., Double-A or Triple-A) in 1995, but some of the brightest prospects in the low minors are also included.

Others To Watch
After the top prospects section for each team comes one page of brief additional reports on prospects entitled "Others to Watch." The players shown in this section are a mixture of lesser prospects, veteran minor-leaguers who might get called upon in an emergency, and former top prospects coming back from serious injuries. In a normal year, you would hear about a few of these players when they did something noteworthy in the minors or when they were called up to the majors to fill an unexpected gap caused by a rash of injuries.

Other Veteran Players
This brief section contains alphabetical lists by 1995 team of all players who played in the major leagues in 1995 who are not covered elsewhere in the book because it seems unlikely that they will play in the major leagues in 1996. This section includes veteran players who were released during the 1995 season and not picked up by another team, veteran players released during the off-season and who may not be signed by a new team, injured players who probably won't return during 1996, players who have signed to play in Japan in 1996, players who have officially retired, and fringe players who played small roles in 1995 and who probably won't make it back to the majors in 1996.

Player Index
This comprehensive index alphabetically lists all major-league players and all minor-league prospects covered in the book and shows on which page you can find them. Major-league players are shown in boldface type, top prospects in small caps, and others to watch are shown in italics.

THE SCOUTING REPORTS
The scouting reports for regular major-league players are one full page. The left-hand column of the report contains 300–400 words of analysis about that player, taken from 1995 scouting reports and from his 1995 and career statistics. The subdivisions for these player reports have been changed from previous editions of *The Scouting Report*. All player reports are now divided into three sections: Scouting Report, How He Performed in '95, and What to Expect in '96. The contents of these sections should be clear from the headers.

The right-hand column for each regular player shows a picture of that player, his biographical data, his 1995 and career official statistics, and his 1995 situational statistics. The right-hand column also shows two analytical graphs for each regular player. Of course, the statistics and graphs are different for batters and pitchers.

The scouting reports for non-regular major-league players are one-half page (one column). The player's picture and biographical information is

USER'S GUIDE

shown, followed by his 1995 and career official statistics, followed by his 1995 situational statistics. Both the career and situational statistics are the same as for regular players. Underneath the statistics are 150–200 words of analysis about that player, divided the same way as for regular players.

Biographical Information
The biographical information included is the same for all players. After the player's name is shown his 1995 position(s), how he bats and throws, his height and weight, his age as of Opening Day 1996 (April 1), his date of birth, when he was drafted, and how many major-league seasons he has played.

Position
Pitchers are divided into Starting Pitchers (SP) and Relief Pitchers (RP). If a pitcher both started at least five games and relieved in at least five games in 1995, his position will show either SP/RP or RP/SP, depending on how he was most often used. Non-pitchers have all positions listed (including DH), separated by a slash, shown in order of the frequency played in 1995. Positions shown after double slashes are those at which the player appeared in fewer than 10 games.

Opening Day Age
The player's age as of April 1, 1996.

Bats and Throws
Right-handed is indicated by an R; left-handed by an L. Switch-hitters are indicated by a B (i.e., Bats Both).

Drafted
Draft information is shown for the team which first drafted *and* signed a player, along with the year he was signed, the pick number for that team (usually the same as the round), and the overall pick number in the draft. If a player was signed as a non-drafted free agent, the team which first signed him and the date he signed is shown. Examples: Joe Carter (Drafted: CHN81 1/2) was the first pick of the Chicago Cubs in 1981, and he was the second player drafted that year. Cal Ripken (Drafted: BAL78 4/78) was the fourth selection of the Orioles in 1978; he was the 78th player drafted that year. Note that most Latin American players have not been eligible to be drafted in the past, so the fact that they signed as amateur free-agents should not be interpreted negatively.

ML Seasons
The number of different seasons in which the player has appeared in at least one major-league game. A player who appeared in 150 games in one season would have one ML Season; a player who appeared in 10 games in 1992, 2 games in 1993, and 5 games in 1995 would have three ML Seasons. Note that this number is not the same as Major League Service (MLS), which is calculated in days spent on a major-league roster, regardless of how much he played.

Statistics
Traditional official batting statistics shown are Games (G), At-Bats (AB), Runs (R), Hits (H), Doubles (2B), Triples (3B), Home Runs (HR), Runs Batted In (RBI), Stolen Bases (SB), Caught Stealing (CS), Walks (BB), Strikeouts (SO), Batting Average (BA), and On-Base Average (OBA).

Traditional official pitching statistics shown are Games (G), Games Started (GS), Games Finished (GF), Saves (SV), Wins (W), Losses (L), Earned Run Average (ERA), Innings Pitched (IP), Hits (H), Runs (R), Earned Runs (ER), Home Runs (HR), Walks (BB), and Strikeouts (SO).

Eight situational statistics breakdowns are also shown for all players. The situational breakdowns are the same for all pitchers and batters; of course, the statistical categories are different. Because doubles and triples can't be shown for the situational breakdowns, Slugging Percentage (SLG) is shown for batters and against pitchers in all situations.

Home statistics show performance in all home games; Road statistics show performance in all away games.

April–June (Apr–Jun) statistics are shown for the 1995 season for first half statistics; July–October (Jul–Oct) statistics are shown for second half statistics. In a normal 162-game season, these breakdowns are closer to the halfway mark than the

USER'S GUIDE

All-Star break is. October statistics include only regular-season games, but note that the California-Seattle playoff game to determine who won the AL West title is officially counted as a regular-season game by MLB.

Left/Right breakdowns are shown for both batters and pitchers. For batters, LHP indicates performance versus Left-Handed Pitchers; RHP indicates performance versus Right-Handed Pitchers. For pitchers, LHB indicates the performance of Left-Handed Batters against that pitcher; RHB indicates the performance of Right-Handed Batters against that pitcher.

Scoring Position (ScPos) statistics for batters show performance when there is a runner or runners in scoring position (i.e., on second base and/or third base). Scoring Position statistics for pitchers show how batters performed against that pitcher in those situations.

Clutch statistics for batters show performance in clutch situations, defined as in the late innings of close games. A clutch situation is an at-bat in the seventh inning or later in a game in which the score at that time is tied, or the batter's team is one run ahead, or the batter's team has the tying run on base, at bat, or on deck. This clutch definition is parallel to the definition of a save situation. For pitchers, clutch statistics show the performance of batters facing them in late and close situations.

GRAPHS

Each regular player report includes two graphs. With the exception of the batted ball graphs for batters, these graphs are designed to give a quick visual comparison of that player to other players in his league and show how much he was above or below the league average in key areas. The bars on these graphs show a batter's or pitcher's 1995 statistics as a percentage of the league average. League averages in each category are printed at the top of the graphs; the actual numbers for each batter or pitcher for 1995 are shown below the graphs. The only exception to the comparisons to league averages in these graphs is one statistic in the relief pitcher graphs.

Batters. The top graph for batters compares their 1995 statistics to the league average in five important categories: Batting Average, On-Base Average, Runs (R/500), Home Runs (HR/500), and Runs Batted In (RBI/500). Because playing time for different batters will vary substantially, the last three categories are averaged to a per-500 At-Bat basis.

The two graphs at the bottom of the column for batters (Where He Hits the Ball) show the parts of the field where he is most likely to hit the ball versus Left-Handed Pitchers (vs. LHP) and Right-Handed Pitchers (vs. RHP). A few batters who were almost always platooned and didn't face one type of pitcher very often will only have one batted-ball graph. All analysis of batted balls is done by considering the way the batter hits (left or right) and the handedness of the pitcher (left or right) and by comparing his individual pattern to that of all major-league hitters. In the graph, the field is divided into twelve sectors; shaded sectors show where that batter hit 75% or more of his batted balls last season. Note that all batted balls—grounders, liners, pop-ups, and fly balls—are included. The only batted balls excluded are foul balls and bunts.

Pitchers. The top graph compares their statistics to the league average in five important categories: Hits per Nine Innings (H/9), Home Runs per Nine Innings (HR/9), Walks per Nine Innings (BB/9), Strikeouts per Nine Innings (SO/9), and Strikeout-to-Walk Ratio (SO/BB). The bottom graph for pitchers compares their statistics to the league averages for other starting pitchers or for other relief pitchers in his league. Each type of graph uses five important indicators of a pitcher's performance to show how effective a pitcher was in his primary role.

Starting Pitchers. The second graph shows their Earned Run Average as a Starter (SERA), their Quality Start Percentage (QS%), their Innings Pitched per Game Started (IP/GS), their Percentage of times pitching into the 7th Inning (7INN%), and finally by their Run Support per 9 Innings (RS/9).

Relief Pitchers. The second graph shows their Earned Run Average as a Reliever (RERA), their Innings Pitched per Game in Relief (IP/GR), their

USER'S GUIDE

Percentage of games entered in the 9th Inning or later (9INN%), their Inherited Runners Scored Percentage (IRS%), and their Save Percentage (SV%). Note that the percentage of times entering the game in the 9th or later is not normalized to league average—it is used to show the difference between setup pitchers and closers.

SCOUTING TERMS

The basis for all the scouting reports on major-league players was an interview with at least one (and frequently several) active major-league scouts who had scouted that player during the 1995 season. In each interview, we asked the scout to rate that player in multiple areas, using the rating system explained in this User's Guide. All players were rated in each relevant category, but average ratings for players in some categories will sometimes be left out of a report for space considerations.

While different major-league teams have different rating systems, they all attempt to judge players in key areas of potential and ability ("tools" and "skills"). Whether a team is using a 20-80 rating scale, a 0–60 rating scale, or a completely different rating scale, they are always making those judgments compared to an average major-league player. Even when judging minor-leaguers, they are evaluating them compared to a big-league standard: Who cares if a guy has an average Double-A fastball? If a scout thinks that a player will develop better skills in a certain area, he will say something like, "He has slightly below-average power now but will develop plus power as he matures."

When a scout turns in a report on a player, he will rate him in each category according to the scale his team uses: for example, on a 20-80 scale, 50 is the average for each tool or skill for a major-leaguer. Teams get multiple reports from multiple scouts and can review these in detail—we have only a half-page or page to communicate some of the same information to you. Frankly, the difference between a "55" fastball and a "54" fastball isn't meaningful unless you have several reports from different games over a season for that pitcher. So, knowing that a pitcher has a "55" fastball on a particular report isn't going to tell you much—that's why we convert these numerical ratings to the plus/minus scale used in the book.

Rating Scale
Excellent or Outstanding
Good or Well Above-average
Plus or Above-average
Average-Plus or Slightly Above-average
Average
Average-Minus or Slightly Below-average
Minus or Below-average
Poor or Well Below-average
Very Poor (very rare for major-leaguers)

Note that the categories of Average-Plus and Average-Minus mean what they say: *slightly* above or below the norm. This typically means that the pitch, tool, or skill in question is rated average but the player will be above- or below-average in that area sometimes, but not consistently. Remember, however, that a major-league average skill is nothing to dismiss—being average at the peak of a highly competitive profession is pretty damn good. Throughout all of this, we have consciously chosen to be conservative in our ratings and have chosen to work with veteran scouts who aren't overawed by flashes of ability: if a player or pitcher can't consistently demonstrate plus ability, they don't get a plus rating in that area. Pitchers and players, just like everyone else, have good days and bad days. Young players, especially, will have varying levels of performance on different days, for they have frequently not developed the consistency that a veteran player has. Yet even Frank Thomas sometimes goes 0-for-5 with three strikeouts; Greg Maddux sometimes allows four runs in three innings. If all you had was a snapshot from one game, you wouldn't get very reliable reports.

What we are trying to assess in *The Scouting Report* is a player's overall ability: what he can reasonably be counted on to do on a sustained basis over a season. Player's abilities can and do change as they mature, gain experience, get stronger and faster—and also as they age, are injured, and get slower and weaker. Even as their abilities change, players' performances can change even more than their level of ability would indicate. Every baseball fan knows that there are fast runners who are poor basestealers, that there are hitters with tremendous power who rarely connect, that there are pitchers who throw very hard but don't know what zip code

USER'S GUIDE

home plate is in, and that there are fielders who aren't very quick but who play the hitters perfectly.

Position Player Reports

Position players were rated for their hitting, their baserunning speed, their arm strength, their throwing accuracy, their range, and their hands. Unless noted otherwise in the text, these ratings are for their primary position. Basestealing prowess is frequently not noted in the player report, since a player's basestealing stats are usually an excellent indicator of how good a thief he is. Similarly, a batter's power is frequently not noted in the report, since his extra-base and home run stats give a good picture of most hitters' power. If a player bunts a lot, that will be included, and if he is especially good or bad at it, this will be mentioned.

It is critical to remember that scouts are rating players on their tools or abilities, but that many players fail to take advantage of their abilities. A fielder with a strong arm, for instance, might have a slow release, might make inaccurate throws, or might throw to the wrong base frequently—all of which mitigates the effect of his plus arm strength. A hitter with plus power might chase too many bad pitches, making his power production (i.e., how often he gets extra-base hits) much less than it could be. A fielder with good range might position himself poorly, thus getting to fewer batted balls than he could, or he could make a deliberate choice to position himself in a way which cuts down on the number of plays he makes. For example, many veteran outfielders with declining range will play very deep so that balls don't get hit over their head. This means they cut down on the number of doubles and triples hit by them, but it also means they see many more fly balls drop in front of them for singles.

When the phrases "up and over the plate" or "down and over" are used, that means the hitter likes to swing at offerings either high or low and on the outer half of the plate. Basically, these hitters want to extend their arms when they swing. When "up and in" or "down and in" are used, this indicates the batter prefers pitches high or low from the middle of the plate inward. Because of the lower strike zone, a "high-ball" hitter now refers to anything but a dead low-ball swinger, since few hitters swing at pitches much higher than the belt these days. The phrase "plate discipline" refers to the hitter's ability to lay off bad pitches and swing mostly at good pitches; hitters who are too "aggressive" will frequently "get themselves out" by swinging at bad pitches.

Generally, "power" and "bat speed" are interchangeable terms. The more speed one generates in one's swing, the better chance one has of getting around on a pitch and pulling it for distance. In rating a hitter's power, several terms are used. "Pull" means that a hitter will take pitches to the same side of the field that he is hitting from (a righthanded hitter to left field, a lefty to right field). Most hitters can pull inside, off-speed pitches; some hitters can pull good fastballs; a select few can pull the best fastball, even when it's not inside. Many hitters get themselves into trouble by trying to pull everything, even pitches too far outside or too fast for them to handle. Other hitters, who have some pull power but know their limitations, will take outside pitches to the opposite field (i.e., they "use the whole field"). Players who lack bat speed/power normally concentrate on simply putting the bat on the ball; they are usually called "contact" hitters. These hitters tend to swing early in order to catch up to good fastballs, meaning they hit to the opposite field much of the time. Many players are "straightaway" hitters, meaning they lack pull power and hit most pitches back up the middle. "Alley power" refers to the ability to hit for doubles and triples in the outfield gaps.

Pitcher Reports

Pitcher were rated on their fastball, curveball, slider, change-up, and any other pitches they might throw. Each pitch was given a quality rating from the scale shown above. In addition, pitchers' control, their ability to hold baserunners, and their fielding were rated. For NL pitchers, their 1995 and, typically, their career hitting stats are also given.

For fastballs, the quality rating directly indicates their velocity; for breaking pitches and change-ups, it indicates how effective that pitch is. That's because the velocity of a fastball is much more important than the velocity of a breaking pitch. If the report says that a pitcher will "show" a certain pitch, or says that he uses it just "for show," that indicates the pitcher doesn't use that pitch much in a

USER'S GUIDE

game—especially not in important situations—he just occasionally shows it to a hitter to keep it in their mind. Normally, a show pitch will be thrown out of the strike zone.

Angle of delivery. The typical angle of delivery for each pitcher's motion was also included in their report. The categories used are: overhand, high three quarters, three quarters, low three quarters, side-arm, and underhand. Note that many pitchers will vary their angle of delivery for different types of pitches or even from pitch to pitch. Sometimes, this is deliberately done to confuse hitters; sometimes this variance is unintentional. Other notes about a pitcher's motion (e.g., "high leg kick" or "throws across his body") may also be included in the report.

Fastball. The rating for each pitcher's fastball is the typical velocity he can sustain for six or more innings (if he's a starter) or for two or more innings (if he's a reliever). No pitcher throws as hard as he physically can on every pitch: he would tire out too quickly, unless he's a closer and knows that if he gets one or two batters out, the game is over. While many big-league pitchers survive—and some even thrive—without plus fastballs, it remains true that the faster the pitch, the harder it is to hit. It's also generally true that the faster the fastball is, the greater the contrast is between it and that pitcher's breaking and off-speed stuff. Most pitchers have a "comfort zone" into which the velocity on their fastball will fall most of the time. However, almost all pitchers will occasionally reach back for that little extra on the ball in important situations. Therefore, a pitcher with an above-average fastball will sometimes throw a well above-average heater, and a pitcher with an average fastball will sometimes show plus velocity.

In addition to the velocity rating of the fastball, the typical movement on a pitcher's fastball was noted in the reports. All fastballs are harder to hit when they're not straight—when they "sink," "bore in," "tail," or "ride." Righthanders' fastballs will commonly "bore in" to righthanded hitters, meaning they will move inside toward the hitter as they get to the plate. Lefthanders' fastballs typically "tail" away from righthanded hitters and into lefthanded hitters near the plate. Usually, this "boring" or "tailing" action is more pronounced higher and less noticeable when thrown low. A "riding" fastball is a fastball which is thrown high and "rides up" as it approaches the plate. A "cut fastball" or "cutter" acts like a hard slider with a small break; in fact, many broadcasters confuse cutters and sliders. Scouts sometimes can't tell if a pitcher is using a cutter or slider—they're that close. Most pitchers throw primarily two-seam fastballs and will try to keep their fastball low in the strike zone. If they throw their fastball up in the zone, it will usually be thrown to the inside or outside edge of the plate. Almost all active pitchers throw two-seam fastballs, either exclusively or most of the time. These low two-seam fastballs are commonly called *sinkers*.

Because of the lower strike zone which now prevails in the major leagues, few pitchers currently throw four-seam fastballs—the classic "rising fastball" of legendary power pitchers like Sandy Koufax. Throwing the ball with an across-seam grip so that each rotation of the ball shows four seams to the hitter creates more turbulence underneath the ball as it travels—thus causing the ball to sink less than if thrown with two seams. (No pitch, no matter how hard, actually rises, but a pitch which doesn't sink as much as expected gives the hitter the impression that it rises.)

Because most pitches above the belt are now called balls by the umpires, the high fastball has gone out of fashion: a fastball without exceptional velocity at the belt can be hit a long way by almost all major-league hitters. Only pitchers who throw hard use the four-seamer much anymore, and very few of the hard throwers use it exclusively. Most will mix high, four-seam fastballs with low, two-seam fastballs. The most important reason for this is that a pitch thrown low in the strike zone is harder to hit when it sinks—if a low pitch stays straight or "rises" higher in the zone, it's much easier to hit.

The reason that we don't quote miles-per-hour velocity often in *The Scouting Report* is that such speed numbers are often misunderstood. The primary reason for the confusion is that there are two different types of radar guns used to measure pitch speed, and they will give different velocity readings on the same pitch. The most common brands of radar guns used by baseball scouts are the JUGS

USER'S GUIDE

Gun and the RAGUN (pronounced RAY-GUN). The JUGS gun, used by more big-league teams and by almost all television broadcast crews, is faster than the RAGUN by 3–5 mph on most pitches. Because the faster gun is much more common now, velocities quoted in the book are from the JUGS gun.

What's the difference? One gun measures the velocity of the pitch soon after it comes out of the pitcher's hand, the other measures the velocity close to the plate on the same pitch. Additional confusion about pitch speeds comes because pitch speeds will vary for the same pitcher from game to game, from inning to inning, and from pitch to pitch. Knowing that a pitcher threw a 93-mph fastball in the third inning doesn't tell you much. That could have been the fastest pitch he threw all game, and he might have averaged only 91 mph over seven innings. It could also have been a pitch which was a bit slower than his typical offering, with that pitcher averaging 95 mph for the game—and the difference between sustained fastball velocity of 91 compared to 95 is huge. Most big-league pitchers can throw a fastball in the 90s, if you're measuring them with a JUGS gun. However, some can only throw 90–91, some throw 93–94, some can get it up there at 98–100 mph. The number of pitchers who can sustain a velocity in the 90s over seven innings is substantially smaller than the number who can pop one fastball at 90 mph, however. Remember that different organizations and different scouts evaluate velocities slightly differently; the scale below is conservative in rating velocity.

Typical Consistent Fastball Ratings on JUGS Gun:
Outstanding 97 mph or greater
Good 94–96 mph
Plus 91–93 mph
Average 88–90 mph (includes average-plus and average-minus)
Minus 85–87 mph (more common for lefthanders)
Poor 82–84 mph (rare in the majors)
Very Poor 81 or less mph (very rare)

Breaking and Off-Speed Pitches. Breaking balls can be effective at many different speeds, and the deception involved in throwing a change-up can be even more important than its speed. The velocity on breaking pitches varies according to the pitch and to the pitcher, so the rating for a breaking or off-speed pitch is a judgment combining its break, its velocity, and its deception.

Slider. A typical slider will be about 10 mph less than that same pitcher's fastball. A "hard" slider will be closer to fastball velocity; a "soft" slider will be closer to curveball velocity. Most sliders break primarily downward and only a little bit laterally; if a pitcher has an unusually flat slider, it will normally be noted in his report. The best sliders have sharp, quick, late breaks that fool hitters into thinking they are fastballs up until the last moment. A very few pitchers will throw an off-speed slider at substantially lower velocity than their regular slider.

Curveball. The velocity on curveballs varies more than on sliders. Typically, a curve will be about 15 mph slower than a pitcher's fastball. Most curveballs break both down and away from the same-side hitter (i.e., a righthanded pitcher's curve will normally break down and away from a righthanded batter). If a pitcher's curve is unusually flat or normally breaks straight down without much lateral movement, it will be noted in the report. Many pitchers throw slow curves (also called change-up curveballs if that same pitcher throws a harder curve) that will be even slower than a typical curve. These slower curveballs are normally noted if the pitcher also throws a harder curve.

Change-up. Almost all pitchers throw some sort of change-of-pace pitch to throw off hitters' timing. The most common exceptions to this rule are hard-throwing short relievers, who face only a few batters each appearance, who can frequently overpower hitters, and who know that most hitters can't time their fastball when they only see them for one at-bat. A typical change-up is thrown with a fastball motion: the more the change looks like a fastball coming out of the pitcher's hand, the more likely it is that the hitter will swing too soon and be out in front of the slower-than-expected pitch. That's why the deception involved with throwing a change is as important as its slow velocity. Because change-ups are relatively slow, they will also sink more than a fastball. Many pitchers will "turn over" their change-up: this means that they turn their wrist inward and down when releasing the pitch, imparting a spin like a screwball and causing the

USER'S GUIDE

pitch to dip down and away from the opposite-side hitter. Such turned-over change-ups are favorites of lefthanded pitchers, who will use them frequently on the outside corner to righthanded hitters.

Two variations on the standard change-up are the *circle change* and the *palmball*. Both of these pitches are change-ups thrown with different grips: the circle change grip keeps the pitcher's index finger off the ball so that it spins like a screwball upon release, while the palmball grip keeps the ball back in the pitcher's hand so the fingertips don't impart backspin upon release. A circle change will act like a good turned-over change-up; a palmball will act like a slow sinker or forkball. Since scouts can tell the movement on a pitch without necessarily knowing how the pitcher is gripping the ball, what one scout calls a "turned-over" change will be called a "circle" change by another scout. Many scouts also will simply say that a pitcher "palms" his change rather than calling it a palmball.

Splitfinger Fastball and Forkball. There is plenty of confusion about the difference between these two pitches. The reason is that they're very similar—in fact, some coaches insist that they are interchangeable. Other pitchers and coaches, however, use the two names to distinguish between two slightly different types of grips. Either way, these pitches get less backspin than fastballs because the fingertips are not gripping the ball so, ideally, they are released without much backspin, "tumbling" rather than spinning. The better the "tumble," the better the drop and the better the pitch.

To try to avoid confusion, we have not used the two terms interchangeably in the book. If a scouting report for a pitcher notes that he throws a forkball, then it means that it's 10 mph or more slower than his fastball and that he normally will use it like a change-up. In fact, many pitchers who throw forkballs don't throw a straight change much. When a scouting report notes that a pitcher throws a splitfinger fastball (also called a *splitter* or *splitfinger pitch*), it means that he's throwing it harder than a change-up and closer to his fastball velocity. Essentially, a good splitfinger is like an excellent sinking fastball—only somewhat slower with more sink.

Slurve. Many pitching coaches and scouts use the term "slurve" to describe a breaking pitch midway between a slider and a curve. Because some pitchers' curves and sliders are hard to tell apart, the term is fairly common now. We've chosen to avoid using this term much and describe such curves or sliders in detail instead (e.g., "soft slider with a big break" or "hard curve with a small break").

Sinker. As noted in the discussion of fastballs above, most pitches that are called sinkers are really two-seam fastballs thrown low. Some pitchers throw what's called a "heavy" sinker or a "true" sinker, meaning that they apply downward pressure on the inside of the ball upon release and let the pitch slide out of their hand without much backspin so that the ball sinks more than normal. Such sinkers will typically move down and in to the same-side hitter.

Screwball. Very few active pitchers will throw a screwball (mostly lefties with minus fastballs), but a fair number of pitchers give an inward wrist turn upon release of their fastball or change-up to give it "screwball" action. Sometimes these pitches are called screwballs.

Holding Runners. The ability to hold baserunners close and to prevent them from stealing is a combination of many factors: how quick or slow a pitcher delivers the pitch to home, how easy it is for a runner to "read" a pitcher's motion, how good a pitcher's pickoff move is, how much attention he pays to baserunners, how often he throws over to first—and, of course, how good the catcher is. Having a good pickoff move doesn't necessarily mean runners can't steal on a pitcher. Moreover, the number of attempted steals on pitchers who pitch a small number of innings is so few (usually a dozen or less) that the success or failure rate is subject to large variances due to chance.

Fielding. Most pitchers get very few chances in the field, and most chances they get are easy ground balls back to the mound. Therefore, fielding ratings for pitchers are largely subjective and vary quite a lot from scout to scout.

American League

BALTIMORE ORIOLES

SCOUTING REPORT
Manny hits with an open stance, which gives him time to hit high fastballs effectively with some pop. However, he struggles with breaking balls and anything off-speed. Although he was an overaggressive hitter in the minors, he has improved his strike-zone judgment. He can bunt, but could do so more often. Alexander is a plus baserunner and basestealer.

In the field, Manny has plus range and good hands with a strong arm and above-average accuracy.

HOW HE PERFORMED IN '95
Finally getting a chance to play, Alexander showed impressive speed and defense and some potential as an offensive player. After a rough start in the field, where he made five errors in the first six weeks, Alexander settled down and committed just five more all season, and only one in his final 41 contests.

Formerly a shortstop, Manny ended up splitting time at second base with Bret Barberie in '95 and adapted fairly well. He doesn't know the position like Barberie does, and had a lot of trouble on balls hit up the middle.

The double-play pivot was another source of trouble for Alexander, but he is expected to improve with experience and could become a very good second baseman. Moving from shortstop to second is viewed by many as a tough adjustment.

Alexander hit very effectively in June and July but sagged badly in August, collecting just nine hits in 51 at-bats with only two RBI. After suffering a strained groin on September 8 in Cleveland, Manny missed the rest of the season.

While Alexander didn't have a great year at the plate, he did cut his strikeouts and increase his walks from his previous levels. He may never be a top-flight offensive performer, but if he keeps improving a little each year, Manny could be valuable.

WHAT TO EXPECT IN '96
So there's this young guy who spends years trying to push Cal Ripken out of a job—but Ripken just keeps on playing. So the team finally moves the kid over to second base and, after half a year of playing there, the club decides to sign free-agent Roberto Alomar. Obviously, Alexander will play a reserve role in the future in Baltimore absent a trade to a team without two established stars in the middle of the infield.

MANNY ALEXANDER

Positions: 2B//SS/3B/DH
Bats: R **Throws:** R
Ht: 5'10" **Wt:** 150
Opening Day Age: 25
Born: 3/20/1971
Drafted: BAL 2/4/88
ML Seasons: 3

Overall Statistics

	G	AB	R	H	2B	3B	HR	RBI	SB	CS	BB	SO	BA	OBA
95 BAL	94	242	35	57	9	1	3	23	11	4	20	30	.236	.299
Career	101	247	37	58	9	1	3	23	11	4	20	33	.235	.297

1995 Situational Statistics

	AB	HR	RBI	BA	OBA	SLG		AB	HR	RBI	BA	OBA	SLG
Home	121	2	11	.207	.262	.289	LHP	84	2	5	.250	.308	.357
Road	121	1	12	.264	.336	.347	RHP	158	1	18	.228	.295	.297
Apr-Jun	115	1	10	.261	.309	.330	ScPos	61	0	18	.246	.313	.262
Jul-Oct	127	2	13	.213	.291	.307	Clutch	31	0	2	.258	.281	.258

How He Compares to Other Batters

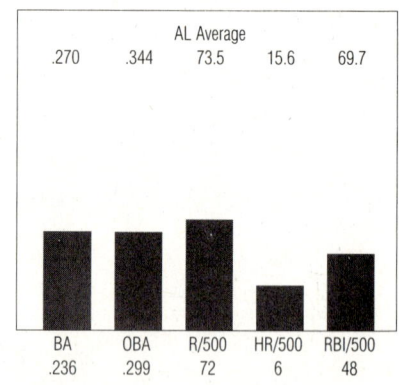

Where He Hits the Ball

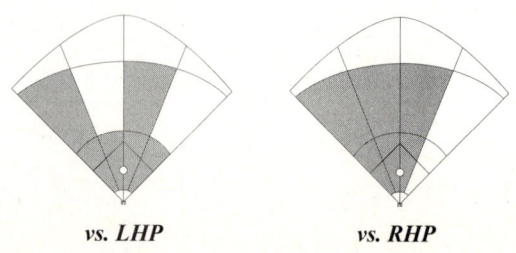

vs. LHP   vs. RHP

BALTIMORE ORIOLES

BRADY ANDERSON

Position: OF
Bats: L **Throws:** L
Ht: 6'1" **Wt:** 170
Opening Day Age: 32
Born: 1/18/1964
Drafted: BOS85 10/257
ML Seasons: 8

SCOUTING REPORT
Anderson hits with home run power, has a good batting eye, and can handle high pitches both inside and out over the plate but sometimes struggles with low pitches. Although normally a plus bunter, Brady slumped in this category in '95.

Scouts feel Anderson is the AL's best left fielder. His fielding and range are well above-average, and making big catches has become a specialty for him. However, Brady has a minus arm with average accuracy.

He has plus speed and baserunning ability, will take the extra base, leg out hits, and steal bases as well.

HOW HE PERFORMED IN '95
Since his early struggles in Boston, Brady has been viewed as a disappointment. However, he has enjoyed four straight quality seasons. Over those four campaigns he has batted .271, .263, .263, and .262 with good power. In that same span, Anderson's on-base averages have been between .356-.373.

All some people can do is talk about what Brady can't do. He's not good enough to play center field; he doesn't make enough contact; he won't hit .300; he should hit lower in the order. Why anyone would focus on Anderson's negatives is a mystery. What the record shows is a good left fielder with power and speed who hits very consistently and walks close to 90 times a season.

Lefthanders have begun to spook him; although he doesn't bail out, Brady simply isn't producing much against portsiders. While he didn't duplicate his amazing 31-for-32 stolen base performance of '94, Anderson ran frequently and effectively. His speed helped him in many ways, including making him the hardest man in the AL to double up in '95.

With a weak arm, Brady nailed just one runner last year. He showed average range when used in center field, but doesn't have the ability to play the position on an everyday basis. Left field is his domain.

One more thing of note: Brady is the player who made sideburns fashionable in baseball again.

WHAT TO EXPECT IN '96
Brady has the track record of a player who will be productive until his late thirties. Baltimore said they didn't want Brady to lead off in '96 but, unless the Birds find someone who can get on base more often and steal bases more effectively, it wouldn't make sense to move Anderson from the top spot.

Overall Statistics

	G	AB	R	H	2B	3B	HR	RBI	SB	CS	BB	SO	BA	OBA
95 BAL	143	554	108	145	33	10	16	64	26	7	87	111	.262	.371
Career	945	3271	512	817	164	44	72	346	187	53	459	593	.250	.349

1995 Situational Statistics

	AB	HR	RBI	BA	OBA	SLG		AB	HR	RBI	BA	OBA	SLG
Home	277	10	33	.260	.361	.451	LHP	178	3	15	.213	.320	.331
Road	277	6	31	.264	.380	.437	RHP	376	13	49	.285	.394	.497
Apr-Jun	226	9	30	.265	.359	.473	ScPos	124	4	48	.282	.420	.460
Jul-Oct	328	7	34	.259	.379	.424	Clutch	74	2	12	.216	.326	.378

How He Compares to Other Batters

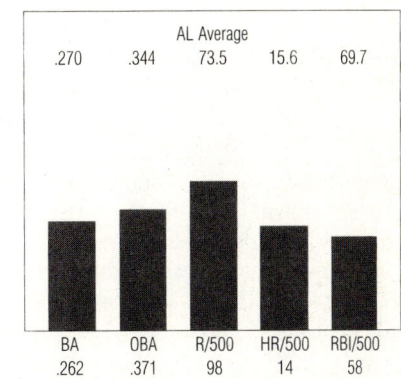

Where He Hits the Ball

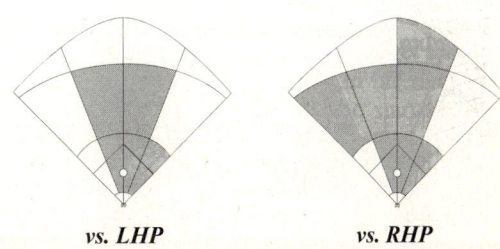

vs. LHP   vs. RHP

BALTIMORE ORIOLES

SCOUTING REPORT
Baines stands off the plate and dives into the pitch. Quick reflexes mean that he does not get hit by pitches; he has been plunked only 12 times in a 16-year major-league career.

Baines is a good fastball hitter and leaps on bad breaking balls. His smooth stroke hammers low pitches on the outer part of the plate. He lacks the ability, however, to catch the best high fastballs. Over the years, Harold has become a more patient hitter and no longer gets himself out by being over-aggressive. He has very poor speed and has stolen exactly one base in the last nine years. Baines has been hobbled by six knee operations and hasn't played defense for three years.

HOW HE PERFORMED IN '95
The veteran DH enjoyed another productive season, but it wasn't a typical year for Harold. He did many things last year that he usually does not. Despite a rep for problems with lefthanders, Baines stood in unusually well this year against them, showing some power as well. Although he has habitually been a much stronger hitter in the second half of the year, Harold batted .333 with five home runs last May, and hit .274 or more in every month. For the first time in six years, he hit more homers on the road than in his home park.

Perhaps oddest of all, Harold more than doubled his walks from his '94 total and reduced his strikeouts. This could be a warning sign for the future, as some veteran players will lose their ability to turn on a fastball and compensate by taking far more pitches than usual. However, Baines hit so well in '95 that he didn't appear to have problems with any pitchers.

He's not going to become a brand-new player at age 37. Most of the gains Baines showed are probably seasonal fluctuations. However, most players don't have years like this at Harold's age, no matter what reason—it was just a fine season for the classy Baines.

WHAT TO EXPECT IN '96
The White Sox have signed him to DH in 1996. Baines may not be capable of doing what he did for Chicago in the mid-1980s, but at the very least he will bring some elegance to a franchise sorely in need of a transfusion. Expect him to play every day against righthanders, but to sit against most left-handers.

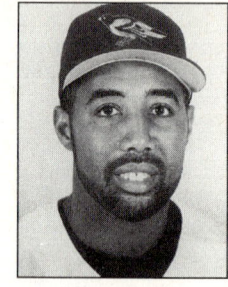

HAROLD BAINES

Position: DH
Bats: L **Throws:** L
Ht: 6'2" **Wt:** 195
Opening Day Age: 37
Born: 3/15/1959
Drafted: CHA77 1/1
ML Seasons: 16

Overall Statistics

	G	AB	R	H	2B	3B	HR	RBI	SB	CS	BB	SO	BA	OBA
95 BAL	127	385	60	115	19	1	24	63	0	2	70	45	.299	.403
Career	2183	7871	1033	2271	387	48	301	1261	30	30	804	1163	.289	.352

1995 Situational Statistics

	AB	HR	RBI	BA	OBA	SLG		AB	HR	RBI	BA	OBA	SLG
Home	172	7	22	.291	.418	.488	LHP	62	3	5	.290	.353	.452
Road	213	17	41	.305	.390	.582	RHP	323	21	58	.300	.412	.557
Apr-Jun	147	9	26	.306	.412	.537	ScPos	92	5	39	.239	.393	.457
Jul-Oct	238	15	37	.294	.397	.542	Clutch	51	4	7	.314	.410	.608

How He Compares to Other Batters

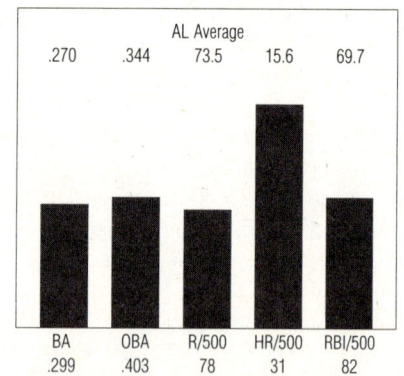

Where He Hits the Ball

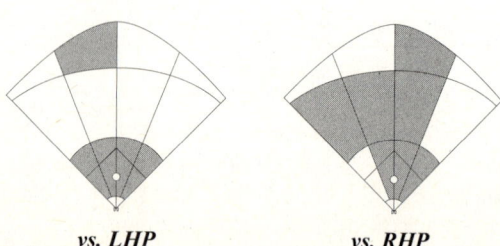

vs. LHP   vs. RHP

BALTIMORE ORIOLES

SCOUTING REPORT
Despite the criticism he endured in the Big Apple, Bonilla is a bona fide power hitter—very strong with good power from both sides of the plate who has excellent plate discipline. He is a low-ball hitter both ways, with an unusual stance in which he lifts his front foot before striding into the pitch. While a good fastball hitter, he can also hit breaking pitches reasonably well: he's so strong that he can muscle pitches into the outfield for a hit even if he's fooled.

He is a minus runner, slow out of the box, but is better when he gets going on the basepaths. He does not attempt to steal.

At third base, where he ended the '95 season, Bobby has a slightly above-average arm with good hands and adequate range, although he doesn't have a quick first step. He isn't a good third baseman, but he's far from the worst and would probably be better if he didn't get shifted from position to position so often to accommodate his team. With Baltimore, he started 38 games in right field before shifting to third base in September. With the Mets in '95, he started 41 games at third (where he played regularly in '94), 29 in left, and nine at first base. From 1987-89, he primarily played third base for the Pirates; from 1990-93, he played mostly in the outfield for the Bucs and the Mets. He's not that bad in the field to deserve being moved around so much.

HOW HE PERFORMED IN '95
While enjoying a good season offensively for the Mets (.325, 25 2B, 18 HR, 53 RBI in 80 games), Bonilla became trade bait due to his large contract and the Mets' desire to go with youth late in the season.

The Orioles took the bait and acquired Bobby Bo for outfield prospects Alex Ochoa and Damon Buford at the end of July. Bobby continued to hit well after being traded and seemed to relax after escaping the pressure-cooker atmosphere in New York.

WHAT TO EXPECT IN '96
The Orioles embarked on an off-season reconstruction of their disappointing team. Bonilla is a key component of their plans to win the AL East in '96 and should thrive in his new environment. Look for a .280-.300 average with 30-plus homers and 100-plus RBIs this season—and maybe more.

BOBBY BONILLA

Positions: 3B/OF/1B
Bats: B **Throws:** R
Ht: 6'3" **Wt:** 230
Opening Day Age: 33
Born: 2/23/1963
Drafted: PIT 7/11/81
ML Seasons: 10

Overall Statistics

	G	AB	R	H	2B	3B	HR	RBI	SB	CS	BB	SO	BA	OBA
95 NYN/BAL	141	554	96	182	37	8	28	99	0	5	54	79	.329	.388
Career	1434	5191	809	1472	306	49	217	849	36	44	644	846	.284	.360

1995 Situational Statistics

	AB	HR	RBI	BA	OBA	SLG		AB	HR	RBI	BA	OBA	SLG
Home	278	14	47	.335	.380	.554	LHP	164	8	29	.366	.420	.610
Road	276	14	52	.322	.395	.598	RHP	390	20	70	.313	.374	.562
Apr-Jun	227	12	35	.313	.373	.564	ScPos	145	4	63	.310	.416	.490
Jul-Oct	327	16	64	.339	.398	.584	Clutch	93	2	9	.269	.358	.398

How He Compares to Other Batters

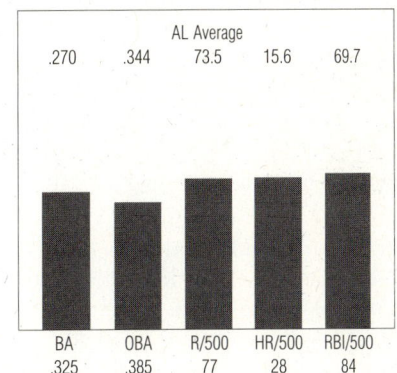

Where He Hits the Ball

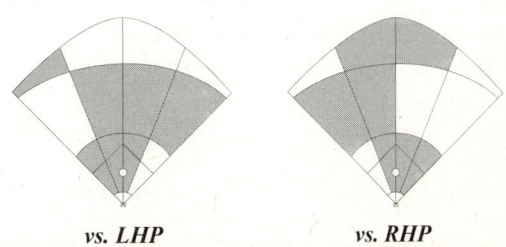

vs. LHP   vs. RHP

THE SCOUTING REPORT: 1996

BALTIMORE ORIOLES

KEVIN BROWN

Position: SP
Bats: R **Throws:** R
Ht: 6'4" **Wt:** 195
Opening Day Age: 31
Born: 3/14/1965
Drafted: TEX86 1/4
ML Seasons: 9

SCOUTING REPORT

Kevin is a classic sinkerball pitcher, delivering from three-quarters to low three-quarters with a hard, sinking fastball with good velocity and excellent movement into righthanded hitters. He uses a hard, average-plus slider to righthanded hitters and a cut fastball with a nasty late break in on the hands of lefthanded hitters.

When his sinker and cutter are working, he doesn't throw much else, but Brown will also show a curveball and change-up occasionally. His control is superior (he finished fourth in the AL with only 2.5 walks per nine innings in '95) and he allows very few long balls due to his heavy sinker (second in the AL with barely one homer per 18 innings in '95).

A good fielder who is quick off the mound when pouncing on bunts and frequent grounders, he has a slightly below-average move to first but holds runners close. Only ten ran on him in 26 starts in '95; seven safely.

HOW HE PERFORMED IN '95

Making a comeback from his career-worst performance (7-9, 4.82 ERA) in '94, Brown re-established himself as one of the most durable and consistent starting pitchers in the AL. He has now made 25 or more starts in each of the past seven seasons, including the strike-shortened '94 campaign, even though he was disabled for a month after dislocating his right index finger trying to grab a liner on June 22.

He had some bad stretches, but some excellent ones as well, and there were times when Brown was dominating. He keeps the ball down effectively and strikes out enough guys to get by. If asked to be a #3 starter, he's more than capable of turning in a very good performance. Getting out of Arlington Stadium, where he had always pitched well, might have augured danger, but Kevin pitched well in his new home in '95. Of course, both are grass fields and he has a slight but significant advantage on them over his career.

WHAT TO EXPECT IN '96

Brown was a free agent after the '95 season with the ability to command a good contract from any number of teams. He should be a big plus for any team which signs him for the next several seasons, chewing up starts and innings with good-to-excellent performance.

Overall Statistics

	G	GS	GF	SV	W	L	ERA	IP	H	R	ER	HR	BB	SO
95 BAL	26	26	0	0	10	9	3.60	172.1	155	73	69	10	48	117
Career	213	212	1	0	88	73	3.78	1451.0	1477	702	610	95	476	859

1995 Situational Statistics

	W	L	ERA	SV	IP	BB	SO		AB	HR	RBI	BA	OBA	SLG
Home	6	5	3.56	0	93.2	18	66	LHB	364	5	34	.247	.311	.343
Road	4	4	3.66	0	78.2	30	51	RHB	278	5	25	.234	.291	.338
Apr-Jun	5	6	3.91	0	76.0	16	61	ScPos	131	2	47	.237	.329	.344
Jul-Oct	5	3	3.36	0	96.1	32	56	Clutch	68	1	6	.294	.385	.397

How He Compares to Other Pitchers

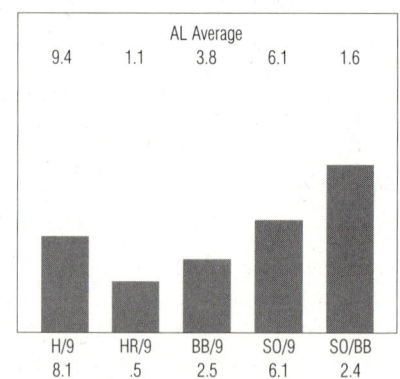

AL Average: 9.4 1.1 3.8 6.1 1.6

H/9 HR/9 BB/9 SO/9 SO/BB
8.1   .5   2.5   6.1   2.4

How He Compares to Other Starting Pitchers

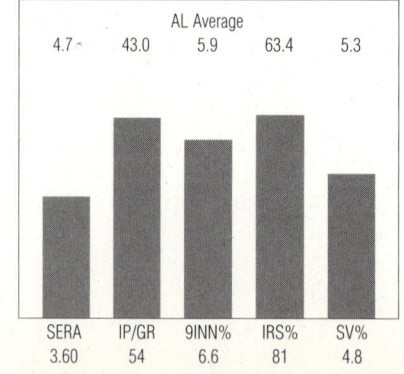

AL Average: 4.7 43.0 5.9 63.4 5.3

SERA IP/GR 9INN% IRS% SV%
3.60   54   6.6   81   4.8

BALTIMORE ORIOLES

SCOUTING REPORT

Scott throws from a three-quarter angle with average-plus control. When he's on, he breaks a lot of bats and induces weak ground balls with an average-plus fastball that sinks effectively and runs into righthanders. At times, he will also cut his fastball. When the heater is working, Scott will rely on it almost exclusively. Erickson also throws an average-plus slider which he occasionally changes speeds on. Finally, he has a change-up used mostly for show.

He had acquired a reputation in Minnesota as a six-inning pitcher who didn't know how to finish games and, early in '95 his good stuff didn't last past the early innings. However, after being traded to Baltimore, Scott's durability improved.

Scouts rate him as average with the glove and at holding runners. Ten men stole bases against Erickson in 15 tries during '95.

HOW HE PERFORMED IN '95

By the time Erickson had been traded, a deal had been rumored for years, with the only impediment to the trade away from Minnesota being that nobody really wanted him.

Finally, the pitching-desperate Orioles came calling in July 7, liberating him from the Metrodome, and stuck him in the rotation for the second half. Surprisingly, Scott pitched very well for his new team. Just 4-6 with a 5.95 ERA in 87.2 innings with the Twins, Erickson turned it around with Baltimore, going 9-4 with a 3.89 ERA after the deal.

Part of the turnaround was due to getting off artificial turf, where Scott allowed over six runs in game over eight starts, but some of the improvement was due to pitching for a better team. He received nearly seven runs of support per game last season, third-best in the AL. All seven of Erickson's complete games came during his 16 starts for the Orioles, during which he received more than 7.5 runs of support.

WHAT TO EXPECT IN '96

If Erickson's second-half improvement is real, he will be a steal for the Orioles. However, that doesn't mean the Twins shouldn't have dealt him; he had been a poor pitcher for two and a half seasons and was very unhappy in Minnesota. Scott hasn't lost anything off his pitches, and is still young enough to have several more good seasons, but isn't ever going to be a 20-game winner again.

THE SCOUTING REPORT: 1996

SCOTT ERICKSON

Position: SP
Bats: R **Throws:** R
Ht: 6'4" **Wt:** 220
Opening Day Age: 28
Born: 2/2/1968
Drafted: MIN89 4/112
ML Seasons: 6

Overall Statistics

	G	GS	GF	SV	W	L	ERA	IP	H	R	ER	HR	BB	SO
95 MIN/BAL	32	31	1	0	13	10	4.81	196.1	213	108	105	18	67	106
Career	172	169	2	0	70	64	4.19	1088.0	1146	556	506	90	402	588

1995 Situational Statistics

	W	L	ERA	SV	IP	BB	SO		AB	HR	RBI	BA	OBA	SLG
Home	6	5	5.15	0	85.2	31	55	LHB	474	10	61	.289	.347	.416
Road	7	5	4.55	0	110.2	36	51	RHB	284	8	34	.268	.334	.437
Apr-Jun	3	6	6.44	0	79.2	27	43	ScPos	181	7	78	.293	.355	.470
Jul-Oct	10	4	3.70	0	116.2	40	63	Clutch	26	0	2	.385	.429	.500

How He Compares to Other Pitchers

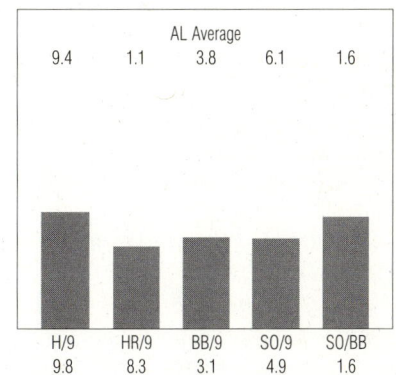

How He Compares to Other Starting Pitchers

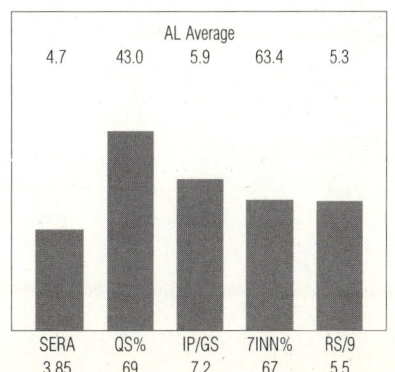

BALTIMORE ORIOLES

SCOUTING REPORT

Curtis is an outstanding runner, his speed ranking among the best in baseball. He is a terrific basestealer and will take the extra base. In addition, he has plus range in center field and is an above-average fielder. While Goodwin has only average arm strength and accuracy, that rating ranks him higher than many other center fielders.

Hitting is the problem. While Goodwin is a good bunter and does bunt often, he has a terrible problem with overaggressive swinging and he strikes out often despite his ability to slap the ball around. Curtis likes mistakes up and over the plate, but once pitchers realized he'd swing at anything, there was no need to give him anything good. Another drawback is lack of power: he has six home runs in five professional seasons.

HOW HE PERFORMED IN '95

After being called up from Triple-A on June 2, Curtis started out hot. He batted .359 for the Orioles that month but struck out 21 times. Predictably, the word spread that he'd hack at anything, and Goodwin consequently batted just .229 in July, .214 in August, and .180 in September. He ran wild on major-league catchers and pitchers, stealing 22 out of 26 attempts in only 87 games.

A broken bone in his left index finger suffered in mid-September added to Curtis' late-season misery. By year's end, his star had dimmed somewhat, despite the fact that wasn't really doing anything differently than he had in the minors. Even in the minors, Goodwin never walked more than 52 times a season, a generally fatal flaw for a leadoff hitter.

Despite his problems at bat, Goodwin played well in the outfield, getting to a lot of balls. However, he threw out just one runner on the bases in 79 games.

WHAT TO EXPECT IN '96

Curtis is still very young, and could conceivably become the star leadoff man the Orioles want him to be—if he learns how to work the pitchers by forcing them to throw pitches that he can hit in the strike zone.

The opportunities for Goodwin to use his speed on the bases will be few if he doesn't improve. Unless he can do the things successful leadoff hitters do, he won't be able to make up for his shortcomings by being fast. He's got far too much potential to end up as a pinch runner and defensive substitute.

CURTIS GOODWIN

Positions: OF//DH
Bats: L **Throws:** L
Ht: 5'11" **Wt:** 180
Opening Day Age: 23
Born: 9/30/1972
Drafted: BAL91 12/316
ML Seasons: 1

Overall Statistics

	G	AB	R	H	2B	3B	HR	RBI	SB	CS	BB	SO	BA	OBA
95 BAL	87	289	40	76	11	3	1	24	22	4	15	53	.263	.301
Career	87	289	40	76	11	3	1	24	22	4	15	53	.263	.301

1995 Situational Statistics

	AB	HR	RBI	BA	OBA	SLG		AB	HR	RBI	BA	OBA	SLG
Home	143	0	13	.294	.327	.357	LHP	77	1	6	.247	.284	.325
Road	146	1	11	.233	.277	.308	RHP	212	0	18	.269	.307	.335
Apr-Jun	103	0	6	.359	.405	.388	ScPos	67	0	20	.239	.270	.284
Jul-Oct	186	1	18	.210	.242	.301	Clutch	38	0	4	.132	.195	.184

How He Compares to Other Batters

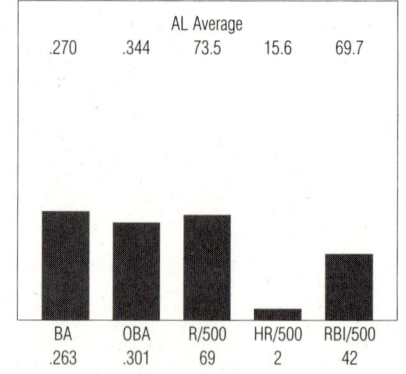

Where He Hits the Ball

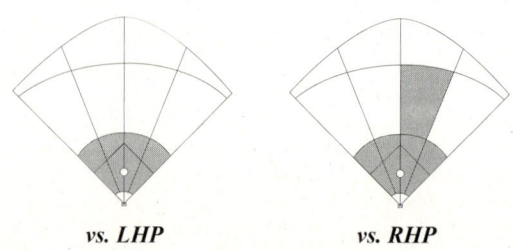

vs. LHP   vs. RHP

BALTIMORE ORIOLES

SCOUTING REPORT
At his best—which was not '95—Chris is a very good fastball hitter with good power in all areas of the zone. He is fair against breaking balls but is patient and will take the walk. He especially likes high pitches from the middle in which he can pull. The term *bunt* isn't in his dictionary.

Behind the plate, Hoiles has soft hands and average range. His arm is weak, but Chris has a quick release and makes very accurate throws. He is very slow on the bases.

HOW HE PERFORMED IN '95
Hoiles, coming off a '94 campaign that made him an offensive force, suffered a rotten start to the '95 season. His April-May average was .213; during June, he played 23 games and only hit in eight of them, batting a subterranean .134.

However, a June 30 pinch-homer seemed to ignite Chris' season, as he went on to hit .333 in July and .296 over the last two months, slugging seven of his home runs in August. While Hoiles has established a clear pattern of hitting better in the second half, his '95 performance stretched that to a much greater extreme than usual.

Righthanders give Hoiles trouble, but he still draws plenty of walks against them and shows decent power. He's amazing against lefthanders, slugging 20 home runs in 186 at-bats against them over the last two years.

On defense, Chris came to the majors with a poor reputation (largely based on poor arm strength) but has improved dramatically. Orioles' pitchers had a fine 3.93 ERA with him behind the plate and Hoiles' .996 fielding percentage led AL catchers. However, he threw out just 22 of 86 (26%) potential basestealers, a very high number of attempts.

WHAT TO EXPECT IN '96
The Tigers traded Hoiles in 1988 after three minor-league seasons in which he had shown outstanding offensive skills. While Fred Lynn, whom the Orioles traded for Hoiles, now broadcasts big-league games, Chris is still winning them on the field. He's probably never going to duplicate his outstanding '93 performance, but Hoiles is a good offensive player with some defensive value as well. He may end up sitting more against righties due to the emergence of lefthanded-hitting Greg Zaun—especially if Chris starts '96 as badly as he did last year.

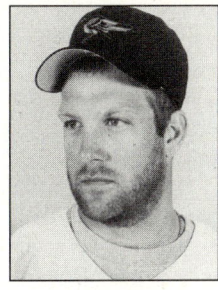

CHRIS HOILES

Positions: C//DH
Bats: R **Throws:** R
Ht: 6'0" **Wt:** 195
Opening Day Age: 31
Born: 3/20/1965
Drafted: DET86 19/489
ML Seasons: 7

Overall Statistics

	G	AB	R	H	2B	3B	HR	RBI	SB	CS	BB	SO	BA	OBA
95 BAL	114	352	53	88	15	1	19	58	1	0	67	80	.250	.373
Career	571	1826	270	481	82	2	99	271	4	5	289	383	.263	.368

1995 Situational Statistics

	AB	HR	RBI	BA	OBA	SLG		AB	HR	RBI	BA	OBA	SLG
Home	183	9	25	.251	.374	.437	LHP	100	12	27	.300	.418	.720
Road	169	10	33	.249	.373	.485	RHP	252	7	31	.230	.355	.357
Apr-Jun	147	8	21	.177	.301	.347	ScPos	91	4	35	.275	.410	.473
Jul-Oct	205	11	37	.302	.424	.541	Clutch	55	3	9	.218	.368	.418

How He Compares to Other Batters

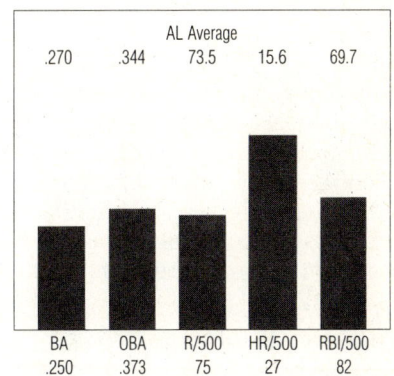

Where He Hits the Ball

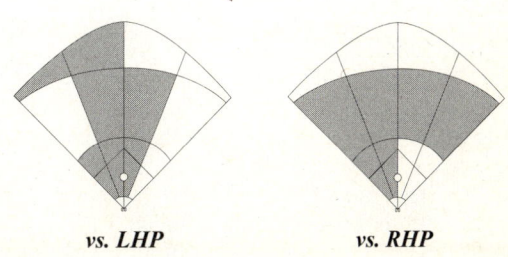

vs. LHP   vs. RHP

THE SCOUTING REPORT: 1996

BALTIMORE ORIOLES

DOUG JONES

Position: RP
Bats: R **Throws:** R
Ht: 6'3" **Wt:** 195
Opening Day Age: 38
Born: 6/24/1957
Drafted: MIL78* 3/59
ML Seasons: 11

SCOUTING REPORT

Doug is the quintessential junkballer, surviving on a plus change-up, good command and control, guile, grit, determination—and just plain luck. He delivers from three-quarters down to sidearm; his fastball has poor velocity, although he has good command of the pitch and can speed it up a tad when he wants to set up his change. He actually throws more fastballs than most think, partly because he's not afraid to use it and partly because he has to set up his change-up.

His out pitches are a circle change and a straight change, both plus pitches with late sinking action, and Doug will use them on either side of the plate. He also has an average-minus, small-breaking slider he doesn't use much. Obviously, Jones has serious problems when he can't get pitches precisely where he wants them.

Defensively, Jones is average off the mound but a bit slow to first base with runners on. He holds runners very close though and is hard to run on, resulting in only two runners trying to steal against him in the past two seasons.

HOW HE PERFORMED IN '95

Jones had an ugly ERA in '95 but didn't pitch as badly as it looked. He had some awful outings in May and August, which were enough to make his seasonal numbers look bad. He's not really capable of shouldering a classic closer's load, but his control and ability to freeze hitters make him valuable. If he can't regain his effectiveness against righthanded hitters, however, he won't be pitching much longer.

WHAT TO EXPECT IN '96

In recent seasons, Jones has been about equally effective against lefties and righties. That doesn't mean he's been consistent, however: in '94, he was battered by lefties and shut down righties; in '95, the opposite was true. This inconsistency is troubling, as it indicates a decline in his skills and because it makes it hard for any manager to use him effectively if he doesn't know how Jones will perform.

The Orioles obviously knew that they weren't going to beat the Yankees with Jones as their closer in '96, so they went out and signed Randy Myers over the winter. While Jones has some life left in his arm and in his change-up, relying on him to close games at this point is a scary idea for any team.

Overall Statistics

	G	GS	GF	SV	W	L	ERA	IP	H	R	ER	HR	BB	SO
95 BAL	52	0	47	22	0	4	5.01	46.2	55	30	26	6	16	42
Career	526	4	447	239	43	58	3.12	721.1	730	291	250	42	159	579

1995 Situational Statistics

	W	L	ERA	SV	IP	BB	SO		AB	HR	RBI	BA	OBA	SLG
Home	0	4	7.77	10	22.0	9	26	LHB	106	1	17	.226	.299	.302
Road	0	0	2.55	12	24.2	7	16	RHB	86	5	17	.360	.409	.616
Apr-Jun	0	2	4.13	11	24.0	6	21	ScPos	54	1	28	.352	.435	.481
Jul-Oct	0	2	5.96	11	22.2	10	21	Clutch	89	3	23	.292	.351	.449

How He Compares to Other Pitchers

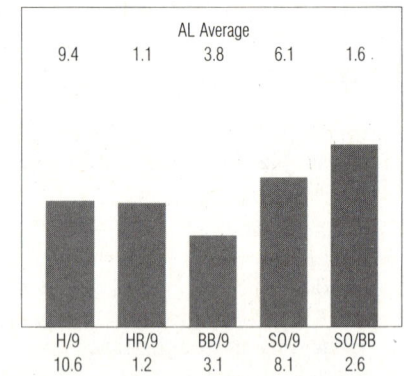

How He Compares to Other Relief Pitchers

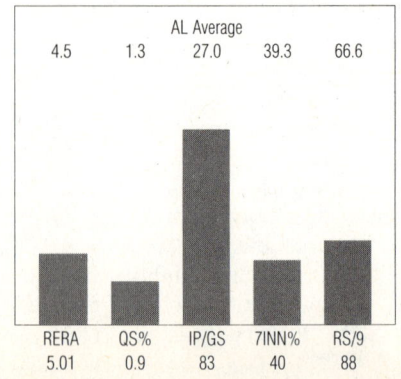

BALTIMORE ORIOLES

JEFF MANTO

Positions: 3B/DH//1B
Bats: R **Throws:** R
Ht: 6'3" **Wt:** 210
Opening Day Age: 31
Born: 8/23/1964
Drafted: CAL85 16/355
ML Seasons: 4

SCOUTING REPORT

A dead fastball hitter with good power, Manto likes fastballs medium to low in the zone. He is a flyball hitter with an uppercut swing who has had lots of trouble with breaking pitches and off-speed stuff in the past. However, he started looking for them in certain situations late last season as he adjusted to big-league pitching.

Jeff has very poor speed and hasn't attempted many stolen bases in the past five seasons. Even though he hit the ball hard, his poor speed kept his doubles total down in '95.

In the field, Jeff has minus hands and range with a plus, strong, accurate arm. He has adequate range at third base, can also play first base, and can serve as an emergency catcher, shortstop, or second baseman.

HOW HE PERFORMED IN '95

Prior to '95, Manto had accumulated only 222 major-league at-bats in ten years as a professional, along with a reputation as a career Triple-A player. What happened? Not much, other than he got a chance to play regularly and show what he could do. He hit pretty much everywhere he played in the minors but never was given enough time in the bigs to get into a groove.

Jeff went north with the Orioles as a reserve and didn't even appear in a game until May 4, an indication of what was expected of him. He made his first start on May 17 for the struggling Leo Gomez, banged out four hits, and started 37 straight games thereafter until he went on the DL with a pulled hamstring. He hit five home runs, four consecutively, in three games in early June.

After returning to action, Manto didn't hit nearly so well and eventually lost his job at third to Bobby Bonilla in September. He did make some adjustments and finish the year hitting reasonably well, however.

WHAT TO EXPECT IN '96

Manto just crushed lefthanders in '95, which means he should have a job as at least a platoon player, designated hitter, and pinch-hitter for several years. He will have to overcome lots of skepticism about his age, his defensive reputation, and his surprising '95 performance. It's long past the time when Jeff could turn in a solid major-league career but, if given another chance to play regularly in '96, he will prove that his power hitting was not a fluke.

Overall Statistics

	G	AB	R	H	2B	3B	HR	RBI	SB	CS	BB	SO	BA	OBA
95 BAL	89	254	31	65	9	0	17	38	0	3	24	69	.256	.325
Career	174	476	58	110	21	1	21	65	2	4	59	112	.231	.324

1995 Situational Statistics

	AB	HR	RBI	BA	OBA	SLG		AB	HR	RBI	BA	OBA	SLG
Home	131	12	24	.260	.331	.565	LHP	90	7	15	.322	.413	.644
Road	123	5	14	.252	.319	.415	RHP	164	10	23	.220	.273	.409
Apr-Jun	146	12	30	.281	.314	.568	ScPos	58	3	19	.207	.303	.379
Jul-Oct	108	5	8	.222	.339	.389	Clutch	45	2	5	.156	.224	.289

How He Compares to Other Batters

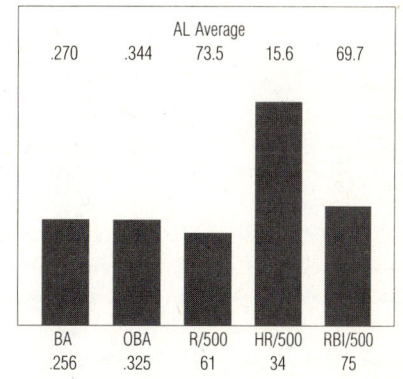

Where He Hits the Ball

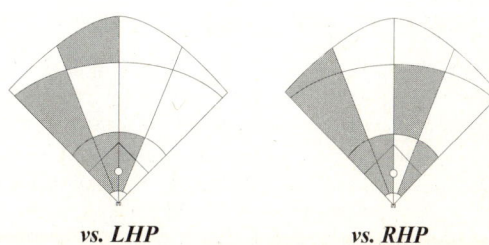

vs. LHP   vs. RHP

THE SCOUTING REPORT: 1996

BALTIMORE ORIOLES

SCOUTING REPORT
The stereotypical veteran finesse lefthander trying to hang on for a few more years, Jamie has the stereotypical minus fastball of this group of pitchers, delivered from three quarters down to sidearm. To be able to survive without being able to throw hard—Moyer will cut his fastball to move it away when facing lefthanded hitters and will turn it over to keep it away from righthanded hitters. His breaking pitches, a curveball he uses when he needs to get a strike and a flat slider, are both slightly below-average, but his change-of-pace is a plus pitch. He has good deception when he delivers the change-up and will turn it over as well.

Quick off the mound as a fielder, Moyer is slightly above-average at holding runners. Combined with the weak throwing performance of the Orioles' catchers last year, that resulted in 11 of 14 basestealers who ran on Moyer making it safely.

HOW HE PERFORMED IN '95
After spending all of the '93 and '94 seasons in the Birds' rotation, Moyer started '95 in the bullpen. He moved back into the Orioles' rotation at the end of May, not because he was pitching well but because the team needed him: the talented but erratic Arthur Rhodes had proved unable as a starter and was optioned and Sid Fernandez was disabled. Baltimore later bit the bullet and bought out the remaining millions on Sid Fernandez' big contract and released the big guy, leaving Jamie in the rotation for most of the rest of the season.

Jamie didn't pitch well, especially late in the year. Lefthanded hitters have hit him like a rag doll lately and righthanders hit him with power—not an auspicious combination, since one of the ways finesse southpaws hang on is by squelching lefthanded hitters.

WHAT TO EXPECT IN '96
Moyer is affable and willing to fill any role he's asked, but that doesn't mean he can pitch effectively in the big leagues any longer—his ERA has risen from 3.43 in 1993 to 4.77 in 1994 to 5.21 last year. At age 33, there's real doubt about his ability to fool major-league hitters much longer. His most likely role will be middle relief; if he starts many games, it's not going to be pretty.

JAMIE MOYER

Position: SP/RP
Bats: L **Throws:** L
Ht: 6'0" **Wt:** 170
Opening Day Age: 33
Born: 11/18/1962
Drafted: CHN84 6/135
ML Seasons: 9

Overall Statistics

	G	GS	GF	SV	W	L	ERA	IP	H	R	ER	HR	BB	SO
95 BAL	27	18	3	0	8	6	5.21	115.2	117	70	67	18	30	65
Career	216	177	12	0	59	76	4.51	1116.2	1195	608	559	131	388	677

1995 Situational Statistics

	W	L	ERA	SV	IP	BB	SO		AB	HR	RBI	BA	OBA	SLG
Home	3	5	6.08	0	60.2	15	28	LHB	108	2	11	.306	.367	.407
Road	5	1	4.25	0	55.0	15	37	RHB	334	16	51	.251	.296	.449
Apr-Jun	2	3	4.58	0	39.1	17	22	ScPos	73	6	45	.356	.383	.671
Jul-Oct	6	3	5.54	0	76.1	13	43	Clutch	28	2	4	.214	.267	.429

How He Compares to Other Pitchers

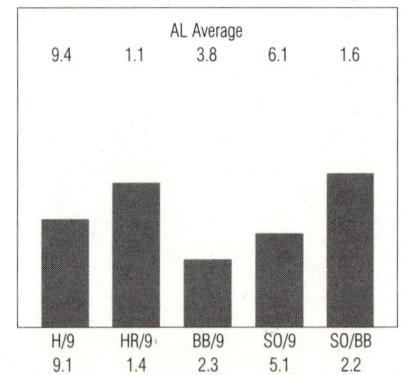

How He Compares to Other Starting Pitchers

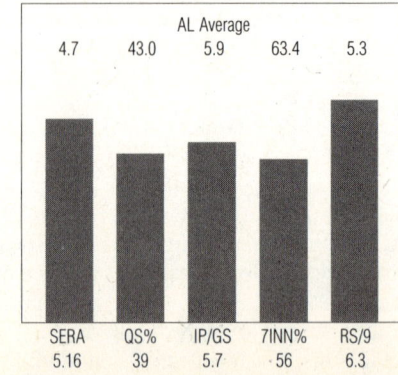

BALTIMORE ORIOLES

SCOUTING REPORT
Mike is a high three-quarter to overhand pitcher with good pitches, good command and control, good baseball sense, a good attitude and—most importantly—good results. His fastballs (four-seam and two-seam) have above-average velocity with good running and sinking movement, and he will cut his fastball for a different look. His primary breaking pitch is a plus knuckle curveball with good bite; he can change speeds on it, too. His straight change-of-pace is also a plus pitch, with good deception in its delivery, good movement and a forkball-type break.

Mussina is very quick to the plate, has a good move to the bag, and makes it hard for runners to steal on him. Only ten tried larceny with him on the mound during 222 innings in '95, and only four made it safely. To complete the package, he is a good fielder off the mound.

HOW HE PERFORMED IN '95
Mussina was just one of several Orioles who performed outstandingly despite the team's poor record. He led the AL in wins and shutouts, finished second in starts, innings pitched and complete games, and ranked fourth in ERA. He held opposing hitters to the third lowest average overall, squelching lefties better than any other pitcher—a remarkable accomplishment for a righthander.

As is Mike's pattern, he pitched his best ball late in the season, but he had more trouble than usual in the early months. This slow start kept him from making the AL All-Star Team for the first time in four years. However, even when Mussina is struggling, he keeps the ball around the plate, which means plenty of homers but not many walks. It's an effective combination.

WHAT TO EXPECT IN '96
Mussina has a stratospheric career won-lost percentage of .703 now—the best among active pitchers—and is poised to take his place among the best pitchers in the game. He is second among active pitchers (to a closer, Tom Henke) in baserunners allowed per nine innings, no mean feat. At 27, he has all the markers of a great pitcher entering his prime years. He may not be a Greg Maddux, but he's a pretty damn good Mike Mussina.

MIKE MUSSINA

Position: SP
Bats: R **Throws:** R
Ht: 6'2" **Wt:** 185
Opening Day Age: 27
Born: 12/8/1968
Drafted: BAL90 1/20
ML Seasons: 5

Overall Statistics

	G	GS	GF	SV	W	L	ERA	IP	H	R	ER	HR	BB	SO
95 BAL	32	32	0	0	19	9	3.29	221.2	187	86	81	24	50	158
Career	125	125	0	0	71	30	3.22	894.1	802	334	320	86	205	556

1995 Situational Statistics

	W	L	ERA	SV	IP	BB	SO		AB	HR	RBI	BA	OBA	SLG
Home	11	3	3.38	0	117.0	23	87	LHB	483	9	32	.209	.261	.331
Road	8	6	3.18	0	104.2	27	71	RHB	344	15	42	.250	.285	.459
Apr-Jun	7	5	4.65	0	81.1	19	44	ScPos	146	4	47	.212	.264	.384
Jul-Oct	12	4	2.50	0	140.1	31	114	Clutch	73	3	10	.260	.308	.479

How He Compares to Other Pitchers

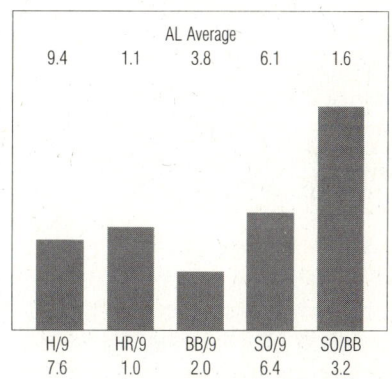

How He Compares to Other Starting Pitchers

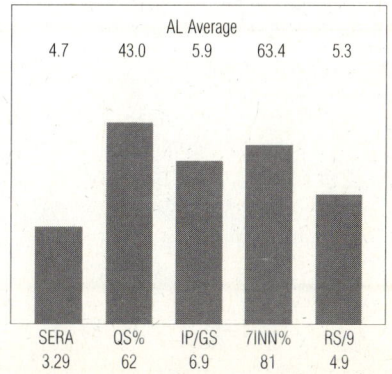

BALTIMORE ORIOLES

SCOUTING REPORT

Rafael is the least-recognized great hitter in baseball, by a wide margin. Why isn't this guy known as one of the best players in the league? He is a very productive power hitter who can slug the ball against both lefties and righties and he's very consistent: he hasn't experienced a serious slump since April of '93.

A relative rarity among hitters, Palmeiro can crush the best fastballs but also can hit breaking balls and off-speed stuff well. He is a pull hitter and likes fastballs down and from the middle of the plate in. Although he isn't patient enough to walk as often as many other big power hitters, he has good strike-zone judgment and walks almost as often as he strikes out.

On the basepaths, Palmeiro is a smart runner but now has poor speed and does not steal often anymore. He hasn't sacrificed in two years.

At first base, Rafael has quick, soft hands and plus range, although his first step is not good. He has an average arm for a first sacker. He made only four errors in '95 and led the league in assists at first base with 119.

HOW HE PERFORMED IN '95

His impressive '95 season—the best overall of his ten-year career—included leading the Birds in home runs and runs batted in while finishing second in the league in total bases, third in extra-base hits, fourth in home runs, fifth in slugging average, ninth in hits, and tenth in RBIs. While Rafael did well in Camden Yards in '94 in his first season with the Orioles, he thrived at home in '95, hitting almost 50 points and slugging almost 100 points higher there.

WHAT TO EXPECT IN '96

Now in his 30s, Palmeiro doesn't seem to be slowing down that much as his age advances. As his physical skills decline, he is able to compensate with the wisdom which comes with experience. He should be able to continue his top-rank power hitting for several more seasons—and, if Baltimore makes it to the post-season for a change, maybe he'll finally get the recognition he deserves.

Five years ago, who'd have thought that he'd be a far better hitter than his ex-Mississippi State teammate Will Clark? Now, who'd even think of trading Rafael for Will straight up?

RAFAEL PALMEIRO

Position: 1B
Bats: L **Throws:** L
Ht: 6'0" **Wt:** 180
Opening Day Age: 31
Born: 9/24/1964
Drafted: CHN85 1/22
ML Seasons: 10

Overall Statistics

	G	AB	R	H	2B	3B	HR	RBI	SB	CS	BB	SO	BA	OBA
95 BAL	143	554	89	172	30	2	39	104	3	1	62	65	.310	.380
Career	1300	4857	758	1455	296	27	194	706	60	24	494	541	.300	.365

1995 Situational Statistics

	AB	HR	RBI	BA	OBA	SLG		AB	HR	RBI	BA	OBA	SLG
Home	265	21	58	.336	.417	.634	LHP	202	14	37	.292	.347	.545
Road	289	18	46	.287	.344	.536	RHP	352	25	67	.321	.398	.605
Apr-Jun	226	13	42	.305	.378	.553	ScPos	146	10	63	.274	.393	.527
Jul-Oct	328	26	62	.314	.381	.604	Clutch	74	5	16	.257	.337	.500

How He Compares to Other Batters

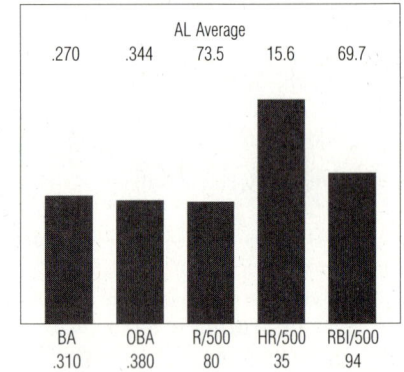

Where He Hits the Ball

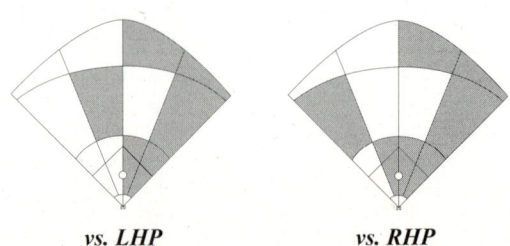

vs. LHP   vs. RHP

BALTIMORE ORIOLES

SCOUTING REPORT
At the plate, the Iron Man is a low-ball, guess hitter with above-average power. With less than two strikes in the count, he looks for pitches he can drive into the gaps or over the fence. With two strikes, he changes his stroke and is good at protecting the plate. Ripken knows the strike zone well but isn't overly patient anymore, so his walk totals have declined in recent years. He has minus speed as a baserunner but won't run into many outs.

Cal's legendary, excellent positioning and knowledge of the other team's hitters and his team's pitchers means he still gets to plenty of ground balls that other shortstops wouldn't reach. His arm remains strong with good accuracy, allowing him to play deep enough to compensate for his lack of lateral range. He has very good, soft hands and led the league in fielding percentage in '95; he also holds the major-league record with 95 consecutive error-free games at short and is carrying a 70-game errorless streak over to '96.

HOW HE PERFORMED IN '95
It's hard to say anything that hasn't already been said about Ripken's astonishing streak and magical 1995 season. His consecutive games steak now stands at 2,153 and probably will top 2,500 before it ends. The hoopla—both before and after—surrounding his breaking of Lou Gehrig's record was enormous.

Cal has not attained the national stature of many other professional athletes in recent years because of his personality. He has been recognized around the game of baseball for his excellent play, but he is uncomfortable in the limelight. That is too bad, for the national attention he received was well-deserved.

WHAT TO EXPECT IN '96
Ripken is now an icon as well as a very good player. He's a more than adequate shortstop—especially for his age—provides more power than most middle infielders, takes a few walks, and hits for a decent average. He is prone to slumps, but season to season he puts up good totals. Slow, but strong and steady—his star has rarely blazed brilliantly in his career, but it has shone with a bright, constant light.

Someday, Baltimore's starting lineup will be announced and Cal Ripken's name won't be in it. That someday isn't very likely to arrive in 1996—or 1997.

CAL RIPKEN

Position: SS
Bats: R **Throws:** R
Ht: 6'4" **Wt:** 215
Opening Day Age: 35
Born: 8/24/1960
Drafted: BAL78 4/78
ML Seasons: 15

Overall Statistics

	G	AB	R	H	2B	3B	HR	RBI	SB	CS	BB	SO	BA	OBA
95 BAL	144	550	71	144	33	2	17	88	0	1	52	59	.262	.324
Career	2218	8577	1272	2371	447	42	327	1267	34	32	901	955	.276	.345

1995 Situational Statistics

	AB	HR	RBI	BA	OBA	SLG		AB	HR	RBI	BA	OBA	SLG
Home	271	10	53	.288	.342	.465	LHP	154	7	26	.286	.354	.487
Road	279	7	35	.237	.305	.380	RHP	396	10	62	.253	.311	.396
Apr-Jun	232	7	34	.284	.332	.466	ScPos	153	5	69	.281	.344	.431
Jul-Oct	318	10	54	.245	.318	.390	Clutch	75	1	8	.147	.195	.253

How He Compares to Other Batters

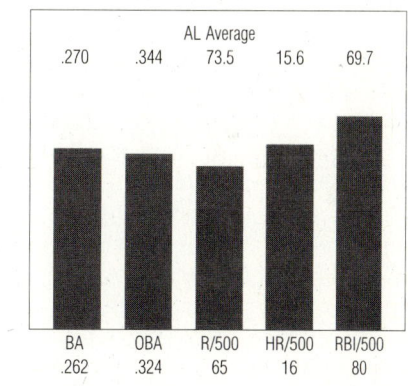

Where He Hits the Ball

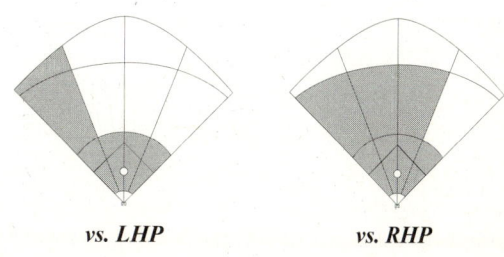

vs. LHP   vs. RHP

THE SCOUTING REPORT: 1996

BALTIMORE ORIOLES

BRET BARBERIE

Positions: 2B//DH/3B
Bats: B **Throws:** R
Ht: 5'11" **Wt:** 185
Opening Day Age: 28
Born: 8/16/1967
Drafted: MON88 7/180
ML Seasons: 5

Overall Statistics

	G	AB	R	H	2B	3B	HR	RBI	SB	CS	BB	SO	BA	OBA
95 BAL	90	237	32	57	14	0	2	25	3	3	36	50	.241	.351
Career	464	1405	159	387	73	6	15	131	16	12	159	257	.275	.360

1995 Situational Statistics

	AB	HR	RBI	BA	OBA	SLG		AB	HR	RBI	BA	OBA	SLG
Home	119	1	12	.244	.395	.336	LHP	79	0	8	.152	.274	.228
Road	118	1	13	.237	.300	.314	RHP	158	2	17	.285	.390	.373
Apr-Jun	102	0	2	.265	.342	.343	ScPos	55	1	23	.291	.391	.400
Jul-Aug	135	2	23	.222	.357	.311	Clutch	39	0	1	.256	.356	.282

SCOUTING REPORT

Bret is a line-drive hitter with good strike-zone judgment, but he strikes out too much and seems to have stagnated as a hitter. Once a top prospect and the sixth overall pick in the NL expansion draft a few years ago, he's not fast anymore after multiple knee problems and doesn't steal.

Barberie now has average range and is capable turning the double play but does not have soft hands. His arm is average for the position.

HOW HE PERFORMED IN '95

After hitting a strong .292 in the first half, Bret was a real disappointment, hitting so badly in the second half that lost his job late in the season to light-hitting Manny Alexander. He didn't hit a lick when batting righthanded last year, which will lead to a platoon role if not corrected.

WHAT TO EXPECT IN '96

Bret wasn't considered a good bet to return to Baltimore in '96 and his career as a starter is probably over. Utility duty is his probable future, although he is still young enough to step up his performance and play regularly again—if he gets another chance.

KEVIN BASS

Positions: OF/DH
Bats: B **Throws:** R
Ht: 6'0" **Wt:** 183
Opening Day Age: 36
Born: 5/12/1959
Drafted: MIL77 2/29
ML Seasons: 14

Overall Statistics

	G	AB	R	H	2B	3B	HR	RBI	SB	CS	BB	SO	BA	OBA
95 BAL	111	295	32	72	12	0	5	32	8	8	24	47	.244	.303
Career	1571	4839	609	1308	248	40	118	611	151	73	357	668	.270	.323

1995 Situational Statistics

	AB	HR	RBI	BA	OBA	SLG		AB	HR	RBI	BA	OBA	SLG
Home	142	2	14	.232	.299	.310	LHP	115	3	13	.252	.301	.365
Road	153	3	18	.255	.307	.359	RHP	180	2	19	.239	.305	.317
Apr-Jun	145	4	26	.317	.377	.462	ScPos	76	0	25	.276	.296	.342
Jul-Aug	150	1	6	.173	.230	.213	Clutch	58	2	7	.293	.317	.414

SCOUTING REPORT

Once a good all-around player in the NL, Bass is now a poor regular and only an adequate reserve outfielder. He retains some speed, but did not steal well in '95.

A good fastball hitter from both sides of the plate, liking low pitches when hitting lefthanded and high pitches when hitting righthanded, Bass has lost most of his power. Unfortunately for him, he isn't going to see a lot of fastballs in the AL unless he improves against breaking pitches and off-speed stuff. Defensively, Kevin has a minus arm and poor hands and showed below-average range in right field last season.

HOW HE PERFORMED IN '95

Bass hit well in early in '95, which meant he kept playing late in the year when he was struggling badly. At the All-Star break, he was hitting .301 with four home runs and 27 runs batted in. Afterward, he sank to .171 with only one additional homer and only five RBIs.

WHAT TO EXPECT IN '96

At age 37, Kevin will be lucky to ever get 200 at-bats again. The best he can hope for now is a role off the bench with a team not very deep in fly-chasers.

BALTIMORE ORIOLES

ARMANDO BENITEZ

Position: RP
Bats: R **Throws:** R
Ht: 6'4" **Wt:** 180
Opening Day Age: 23
Born: 11/3/1972
Drafted: BAL 4/1/90
ML Seasons: 2

Overall Statistics

	G	GS	GF	SV	W	L	ERA	IP	H	R	ER	HR	BB	SO
95 BAL	44	0	18	2	1	5	5.66	47.2	37	33	30	8	37	56
Career	47	0	19	2	1	5	4.84	57.2	45	34	31	8	41	70

1995 Situational Statistics

	W	L	ERA	SV	IP	BB	SO		AB	HR	RBI	BA	OBA	SLG
Home	0	1	6.57	1	24.2	15	31	LHB	67	2	6	.239	.420	.403
Road	1	4	4.70	1	23.0	22	25	RHB	107	6	27	.196	.321	.393
Apr-Jun	0	3	4.74	1	24.2	23	26	ScPos	63	5	29	.206	.354	.476
Jul-Aug	1	2	6.65	1	23.0	14	30	Clutch	54	5	19	.222	.403	.519

SCOUTING REPORT

Benitez is a big, young pitcher with a well above-average fastball and not enough experience to get out major-league hitters—yet. He comes from three-quarters or lower and can throw low fastballs into righthanded hitters or ride his heater up with good life. When in trouble, though, he will throw a straight pitch down the middle which can get whacked out of the park. He also has a plus slider but doesn't use it much. Because he doesn't pay enough attention to baserunners, all five who ran on him last year were successful. He is an average fielder.

HOW HE PERFORMED IN '95

Armando had real problems adjusting in '95, experiencing severe control and attitude problems. He held hitters to an excellent .213 average, but allowed plenty of walks and homers. Righthanders didn't hit him for average, but they hit his mistakes hard (six homers in only 107 at-bats). Although he was leading the AL in appearances in early June, Benitez eventually was optioned twice to Triple-A before returning for good.

WHAT TO EXPECT IN '96

He's going to be a good closer, but he might need more time at Triple-A to mature and regain his confidence.

TERRY CLARK

Position: RP
Bats: R **Throws:** R
Ht: 6'2" **Wt:** 190
Opening Day Age: 35
Born: 10/18/1960
Drafted: SL79 22/675
ML Seasons: 4

Overall Statistics

	G	GS	GF	SV	W	L	ERA	IP	H	R	ER	HR	BB	SO
95 ATL/BAL	41	0	13	1	2	5	3.59	42.2	43	17	17	3	20	20
Career	61	18	15	1	8	13	4.87	151.2	185	86	82	11	57	68

1995 Situational Statistics

	W	L	ERA	SV	IP	BB	SO		AB	HR	RBI	BA	OBA	SLG
Home	1	3	3.96	0	25.0	12	12	LHB	68	1	12	.309	.397	.456
Road	1	2	3.06	1	17.2	8	8	RHB	90	2	12	.244	.324	.378
Apr-Jun	0	1	1.93	0	14.0	7	7	ScPos	62	0	20	.242	.351	.323
Jul-Aug	2	4	4.40	1	28.2	13	13	Clutch	73	2	13	.274	.333	.452

SCOUTING REPORT

Terry delivers an average two-seam fastball with a little movement from three-quarters, also employing an average, soft curve and an average-minus change. His best pitch is a hard, plus slider with a short break. He is an average fielder but allowed all five runners who attempted to steal on him to do so successfully.

HOW HE PERFORMED IN '95

After being outrighted by Atlanta, Clark signed with the Orioles and surfaced from Triple-A again in June. Although he has been pitching professionally since the Carter administration, he had pitched only five games in the big leagues since his 1988 major-league debut (15 starts, 5.07 ERA) with California.

The thoroughly average righthander did a thoroughly average job in middle relief for the Birds, getting righthanded hitters out with his slider but getting hit hard by lefthanders.

WHAT TO EXPECT IN '96

There are literally 50 pitchers at Triple-A who could have duplicated Clark's performance in a non-critical role. Based on his '95 record, he'll get another chance in middle relief in '96. Whether that's in Triple-A or the majors is an open question.

THE SCOUTING REPORT: 1996

BALTIMORE ORIOLES

LEO GOMEZ

Positions: 3B//DH/1B
Bats: R **Throws:** R
Ht: 6'0" **Wt:** 180
Opening Day Age: 30
Born: 3/2/1966
Drafted: BAL 12/13/85
ML Seasons: 6

Overall Statistics

	G	AB	R	H	2B	3B	HR	RBI	SB	CS	BB	SO	BA	OBA
95 BAL	53	127	16	30	5	0	4	12	0	1	18	23	.236	.336
Career	475	1554	197	380	73	2	62	203	3	6	202	305	.245	.334

1995 Situational Statistics

	AB	HR	RBI	BA	OBA	SLG		AB	HR	RBI	BA	OBA	SLG
Home	57	3	9	.228	.348	.456	LHP	44	2	6	.273	.389	.432
Road	70	1	3	.243	.325	.300	RHP	83	2	6	.217	.305	.337
Apr-Jun	81	0	4	.198	.275	.235	ScPos	25	1	8	.200	.290	.360
Jul-Aug	46	4	8	.304	.431	.609	Clutch	18	0	1	.278	.278	.333

SCOUTING REPORT
A good power hitter with an undeservedly bad defensive reputation, Gomez is now on the cusp. He is a low fastball hitter with good bat speed and pull power, but a poor runner with no speed.

At third base, Leo is not nearly so bad as he is said to be. He has decent range and an average arm and doesn't make many errors—but he doesn't look smooth.

HOW HE PERFORMED IN '95
Leo suffered through a terrible '95 season. He started off ice-cold, losing his job at third to Jeff Manto. Then, just as he was starting to hit (11-for-36 with all four of his home runs), he had surgery on his right foot July 31 and missed the rest of the season.

WHAT TO EXPECT IN '96
Gomez is viewed as a disappointment and might be finished as an everyday player now that Bobby Bonilla is established in Baltimore. After two seasons of hitting lefties hard, he could easily end up as a platoon player for the rest of his career. He clearly can hit with power, however, and might make a big comeback if given a chance (i.e., 400 at-bats) somewhere.

JEFFREY HAMMONDS

Positions: OF//DH
Bats: R **Throws:** R
Ht: 6'0" **Wt:** 195
Opening Day Age: 25
Born: 3/5/1971
Drafted: BAL92 1/4
ML Seasons: 3

Overall Statistics

	G	AB	R	H	2B	3B	HR	RBI	SB	CS	BB	SO	BA	OBA
95 BAL	57	178	18	43	9	1	4	23	4	2	9	30	.242	.279
Career	158	533	73	149	35	3	15	73	13	2	28	85	.280	.314

1995 Situational Statistics

	AB	HR	RBI	BA	OBA	SLG		AB	HR	RBI	BA	OBA	SLG
Home	86	2	12	.279	.323	.407	LHP	53	0	7	.208	.254	.245
Road	92	2	11	.207	.237	.337	RHP	125	4	16	.256	.290	.424
Apr-Jun	135	4	20	.267	.291	.422	ScPos	43	2	20	.326	.340	.581
Jul-Aug	43	0	3	.163	.245	.209	Clutch	24	0	2	.083	.148	.083

SCOUTING REPORT
Hammonds has the tools to be an good major-league player. He had outstanding speed before his knee surgery and was a good percentage basestealer, although he didn't run often. A very good high fastball hitter with a quick bat, he likes pitches middle-in even though he isn't a dead pull hitter.

In right field, Jeffrey has above-average range with a below-average arm which is not especially accurate.

HOW HE PERFORMED IN '95
After reconstructive knee surgery in the off-season, Hammonds started off slowly and spent some time at Double-A in May trying to get back on track. He hit reasonably well after his return until July, when he went into a terrible slump which ended with his being placed on the DL. He returned in September for only three at-bats before the season's end.

WHAT TO EXPECT IN '96
This will be a critical year for the young outfielder. If healthy, he can win a starting job and start gaining the experience he needs to mature into a good hitter. If not, he will be passed by, although, as the fourth pick in the '92 draft, he will get plenty of time to develop.

BALTIMORE ORIOLES

JEFF HUSON

Positions: 3B/2B//DH/SS
Bats: L **Throws:** R
Ht: 6'3" **Wt:** 180
Opening Day Age: 31
Born: 8/15/1964
Drafted: MON 8/18/85
ML Seasons: 7

Overall Statistics

	G	AB	R	H	2B	3B	HR	RBI	SB	CS	BB	SO	BA	OBA
95 BAL	66	161	24	40	4	2	1	19	5	4	15	20	.248	.315
Career	528	1304	177	306	46	11	7	104	48	18	151	168	.235	.314

1995 Situational Statistics

	AB	HR	RBI	BA	OBA	SLG		AB	HR	RBI	BA	OBA	SLG
Home	71	0	7	.282	.346	.310	LHP	24	0	2	.208	.240	.208
Road	90	1	12	.222	.290	.322	RHP	137	1	17	.255	.327	.336
Apr-Jun	1	0	1	1.000	1.000	1.000	ScPos	36	0	17	.278	.386	.333
Jul-Aug	160	1	18	.244	.311	.313	Clutch	18	0	3	.167	.286	.222

SCOUTING REPORT

The skills which got Huson to the majors were speed and defense; unfortunately, due to several injuries, he is now an average-minus speed, is not a good basestealer, and is a slightly above-average fielder. He has an average arm for second base with decent range and sure hands, and he filled in capably at third base defensively when asked in '95, making 24 starts there. He can also play shortstop, his original position.

Jeff is a fastball hitter without power, looking for mediocre heaters he can handle out over the plate. He does not bunt for hits as one might expect a player of his type to, nor is he a good sacrifice bunter.

HOW HE PERFORMED IN '95

Starting the season at Triple-A Rochester, Huson came to the Orioles in late June and played both second and third for the Birds.

WHAT TO EXPECT IN '96

Jeff has nothing special to recommend him now that he can't run well anymore. He will be called upon by teams who are desperate for an infielder who won't kick the ball around when it is hit to him, but he is unlikely to contribute much other than not making errors.

RICK KRIVDA

Position: SP
Bats: R **Throws:** L
Ht: 6'1" **Wt:** 180
Opening Day Age: 26
Born: 1/19/1970
Drafted: BAL91 23/602
ML Seasons: 1

Overall Statistics

	G	GS	GF	SV	W	L	ERA	IP	H	R	ER	HR	BB	SO
95 BAL	13	13	0	0	2	7	4.54	75.1	76	40	38	9	25	53
Career	13	13	0	0	2	7	4.54	75.1	76	40	38	9	25	53

1995 Situational Statistics

	W	L	ERA	SV	IP	BB	SO		AB	HR	RBI	BA	OBA	SLG
Home	0	2	4.26	0	31.2	11	17	LHB	52	0	3	.308	.327	.442
Road	2	5	4.74	0	43.2	14	36	RHB	234	9	33	.256	.330	.453
Apr-Jun	0	0	0.00	0	0.0	0	0	ScPos	63	4	29	.238	.257	.556
Jul-Aug	2	7	4.54	0	75.1	25	53	Clutch	14	0	1	.214	.214	.357

SCOUTING REPORT

A finesse lefthander, Krivda comes overhand with a well below-average fastball that is straight, so he cuts it to lefthanders and turns it over to righthanders. He has a slightly above-average curve with a sharp downward break and a plus change which he throws with great arm action.

Rick has good poise and is a decent fielder with an average move. Five of 10 basestealers were nabbed with him pitching in Baltimore in '95.

HOW HE PERFORMED IN '95

Krivda, a good but not great prospect, got a few starts with the big club in the second half last year but had a tough time. He wasn't horrible and did a decent job against righthanders, but walks and extra base hits—the bane of young pitchers—took their toll.

WHAT TO EXPECT IN '96

The Orioles have some good starting pitching prospects, including Rocky Coppinger and Jimmy Haynes, so Krivda could get pushed out of the way. A new manager and a new GM who want to shake up the team could be bad news for him. Rick has a chance to be successful in the majors, but he could easily spend most of his time in Triple-A.

THE SCOUTING REPORT: 1996

BALTIMORE ORIOLES

MARK LEE

Position: RP
Bats: L **Throws:** L
Ht: 6'3" **Wt:** 198
Opening Day Age: 31
Born: 7/20/1964
Drafted: DET85 15/392
ML Seasons: 4

Overall Statistics

	G	GS	GF	SV	W	L	ERA	IP	H	R	ER	HR	BB	SO
95 BAL	39	0	7	1	2	0	4.86	33.1	31	18	18	5	18	27
Career	116	0	21	2	5	5	3.82	127.1	129	58	54	16	54	84

1995 Situational Statistics

	W	L	ERA	SV	IP	BB	SO		AB	HR	RBI	BA	OBA	SLG
Home	1	0	4.60	1	15.2	6	12	LHB	49	2	9	.204	.344	.347
Road	1	0	5.09	0	17.2	12	15	RHB	77	3	8	.273	.337	.506
Apr-Jun	0	0	3.38	1	10.2	9	8	ScPos	41	2	13	.220	.382	.415
Jul-Aug	2	0	5.56	0	22.2	9	19	Clutch	41	3	10	.293	.396	.610

SCOUTING REPORT

Lee delivers from high three-quarters with a straight, average-minus fastball. He also will throw a soft, average-minus slider and occasionally a minus change-up. Mark is a decent fielder but easy as pie to run on: eight enemy basestealers ran on him in only 33 innings, all safely. This is a serious problem for a southpaw reliever.

HOW HE PERFORMED IN '95

On June 23, Lee struck out Mike Greenwell of Boston with two runners on base to record his first save in the majors since April, 1991, when he was with the Brewers. That 1991 save was also his only big-league save, pretty much describing his career.

Since '91, he had spent three years at Triple-A with three different organizations before signing with the Orioles for '95 as a minor-league free agent.

WHAT TO EXPECT IN '96

With 11 years of professional experience, Lee has good poise and knows what his role is: to get left-handed hitters out with runners on base. Since he held lefties to a .204 average in '95, he'll probably be back. He could do the same again in the majors or kick around Triple-A for this 12th year.

BEN MCDONALD

Position: SP
Bats: R **Throws:** R
Ht: 6'7" **Wt:** 212
Opening Day Age: 28
Born: 11/24/1967
Drafted: BAL89 1/1
ML Seasons: 7

Overall Statistics

	G	GS	GF	SV	W	L	ERA	IP	H	R	ER	HR	BB	SO
95 BAL	14	13	1	0	3	6	4.16	80.0	67	40	37	10	38	62
Career	155	142	5	0	58	53	3.89	937.0	838	434	405	100	334	638

1995 Situational Statistics

	W	L	ERA	SV	IP	BB	SO		AB	HR	RBI	BA	OBA	SLG
Home	2	2	2.56	0	38.2	18	32	LHB	150	6	16	.200	.280	.360
Road	1	4	5.66	0	41.1	20	30	RHB	149	4	20	.248	.351	.362
Apr-Jun	2	4	4.40	0	61.1	30	44	ScPos	70	0	20	.186	.298	.229
Jul-Aug	1	2	3.38	0	18.2	8	18	Clutch	13	0	1	.385	.429	.462

SCOUTING REPORT

McDonald is an overhand pitcher with a now-average fastball (due to injury), a cut fastball, a hard curve, and an occasional change. He is an average fielder but runners have always liked to steal on him, with five of 14 caught in '95.

HOW HE PERFORMED IN '95

Ben spent much of the year with a sore right shoulder, and the fact that he won a very large arbitration award in June did not make him especially popular with management, either. It was not a good way to enter free agency, despite the fact that he pitched reasonably well when healthy.

After two stints on the DL, Ben made two appearances in September, the last a start in which he pitched six innings of one-hit ball.

WHAT TO EXPECT IN '96

McDonald has never fulfilled the promise expected of him. While the Orioles wanted him back, they weren't going to break the bank for a pitcher with a 58-53 career record. If healthy, he could easily post 20 wins. While his career has been disappointing to date, he's got the stuff and experience to be a star and is still young enough to start regularly for many years. If...

BALTIMORE ORIOLES

MIKE OQUIST

Position: RP
Bats: R **Throws:** R
Ht: 6'2" **Wt:** 170
Opening Day Age: 27
Born: 5/30/1968
Drafted: BAL89 14/323
ML Seasons: 3

Overall Statistics

	G	GS	GF	SV	W	L	ERA	IP	H	R	ER	HR	BB	SO
95 BAL	27	0	2	0	2	1	4.17	54.0	51	27	25	6	41	27
Career	47	9	7	0	5	4	5.08	124.0	138	73	70	13	75	74

1995 Situational Statistics

	W	L	ERA	SV	IP	BB	SO		AB	HR	RBI	BA	OBA	SLG
Home	1	1	3.67	0	27.0	19	13	LHB	76	3	10	.250	.389	.408
Road	1	0	4.67	0	27.0	22	14	RHB	131	3	25	.244	.358	.412
Apr-Jun	1	0	4.17	0	36.2	25	21	ScPos	72	1	28	.181	.308	.292
Jul-Aug	1	1	4.15	0	17.1	16	6	Clutch	9	0	1	.333	.571	.333

SCOUTING REPORT

Mike delivers from three-quarters with an average-minus fastball which he turns over to lefthanded hitters. Unfortunately, his fastball is too straight and he has only a minus straight change with no movement, an average-minus curve with poor bite, and an average-minus slider to fall back on when hitters time his #1. He is an average fielder with an adequate move; four of six basestealers were successful against him in '95.

HOW HE PERFORMED IN '95

To say he didn't succeed in Baltimore in '95 is a bit of an understatement. Oquist made the team in the spring and worked 27 games in long relief before being outrighted in August, walking way too many hitters for a pitcher without good stuff (41 in 54 innings). His 4.17 ERA was deceptively good.

WHAT TO EXPECT IN '96

He may need a full year at Triple-A to regain his confidence and to find an out pitch which will retire big-league hitters. In the minors, Oquist pitched pretty well prior to '95, challenging hitters despite a lack of great stuff. He's not too old to improve, but time is getting short.

JESSE OROSCO

Position: RP
Bats: R **Throws:** L
Ht: 6'2" **Wt:** 185
Opening Day Age: 38
Born: 4/21/1957
Drafted: MIN78* 2/41
ML Seasons: 16

Overall Statistics

	G	GS	GF	SV	W	L	ERA	IP	H	R	ER	HR	BB	SO
95 BAL	65	0	23	3	2	4	3.26	49.2	28	19	18	4	27	58
Career	819	4	413	133	71	68	2.96	1021.1	825	385	336	79	432	920

1995 Situational Statistics

	W	L	ERA	SV	IP	BB	SO		AB	HR	RBI	BA	OBA	SLG
Home	1	3	3.60	3	30.0	15	32	LHB	77	1	9	.143	.212	.234
Road	1	1	2.75	0	19.2	12	26	RHB	89	3	16	.191	.336	.360
Apr-Jun	1	1	3.00	0	18.0	8	24	ScPos	67	0	20	.179	.337	.269
Jul-Aug	1	3	3.41	3	31.2	19	34	Clutch	97	4	13	.155	.255	.330

SCOUTING REPORT

Jesse has now spent the past eight seasons in the majors as a designated lefthander, a job he has done well. He delivers from low three-quarters with an average-minus fastball that has good movement and which he will cut at times. He also uses a soft curve with a lateral break and a hard slider to retire his lefthanded marks; he can turn over his change to righthanded hitters.

A plus fielder, Orosco has a slightly above-average move to first but is relatively easy to run on because of his motion. Seven of nine basestealers were successful running on him last year.

HOW HE PERFORMED IN '95

The '95 season was a comeback of sorts for Orosco considering his weak '94 performance with Milwaukee. He held lefties to a .143 average and led the AL in appearances, working mainly as a one-out guy. He even shut down righty hitters, mostly by walking them to avoid giving them a pitch to hit.

WHAT TO EXPECT IN '96

Given his age and narrow specialty, Orosco can't be counted on to maintain this level of performance in '96. He should still have a couple of years left in his limited role, however.

BALTIMORE ORIOLES

ARTHUR LEE RHODES

Position: RP/SP
Bats: L **Throws:** L
Ht: 6'2" **Wt:** 190
Opening Day Age: 26
Born: 10/24/1969
Drafted: BAL88 3/34
ML Seasons: 5

Overall Statistics

	G	GS	GF	SV	W	L	ERA	IP	H	R	ER	HR	BB	SO
95 BAL	19	9	3	0	2	5	6.21	75.1	68	53	52	13	48	77
Career	69	59	3	0	17	24	5.70	344.0	344	223	218	47	188	273

1995 Situational Statistics

	W	L	ERA	SV	IP	BB	SO		AB	HR	RBI	BA	OBA	SLG
Home	1	3	6.18	0	39.1	24	40	LHB	75	2	7	.160	.232	.267
Road	1	2	6.25	0	36.0	24	37	RHB	209	11	42	.268	.388	.483
Apr-Jun	2	2	6.92	0	39.0	28	40	ScPos	83	2	30	.205	.320	.337
Jul-Aug	0	3	5.45	0	36.1	20	37	Clutch	22	4	9	.318	.483	.864

SCOUTING REPORT

Rhodes delivers from three quarters and has a slightly above-average fastball that is sneaky fast and runs a little bit. His change is average but his breaking pitches are average-plus: a hard slider and a curve, both with sharp breaks.

Arthur's move to first base is minus and he is easy to run on: 12 runners ran in only 75 innings in '95, four were caught. He is an average fielder.

HOW HE PERFORMED IN '95

Rhodes had a 7.16 ERA as a starter in '95 and lost his spot in the rotation. He pitched better in relief, working often as a long man, and fanned ten hitters in 4.2 innings of relief on August 20. His future, though, is as a starting pitcher.

WHAT TO EXPECT IN '96

The Orioles need Rhodes to harness his considerable talent soon. Location continues to be a problem for Arthur, who pitches from behind in the count constantly and allows way too many homers and walks because of that. If his velocity isn't impaired by his shoulder surgery, he retains the potential to be a good pitcher. Without velocity and without good control, there's not much to look for in the immediate future.

GREG ZAUN

Position: C
Bats: B **Throws:** R
Ht: 5'10" **Wt:** 170
Opening Day Age: 24
Born: 4/14/1971
Drafted: BAL89 18/427
ML Seasons: 1

Overall Statistics

	G	AB	R	H	2B	3B	HR	RBI	SB	CS	BB	SO	BA	OBA
95 BAL	40	104	18	27	5	0	3	14	1	1	16	14	.260	.358
Career	40	104	18	27	5	0	3	14	1	1	16	14	.260	.358

1995 Situational Statistics

	AB	HR	RBI	BA	OBA	SLG		AB	HR	RBI	BA	OBA	SLG
Home	49	1	3	.224	.321	.306	LHP	29	1	2	.241	.353	.379
Road	55	2	11	.291	.391	.473	RHP	75	2	12	.267	.360	.400
Apr-Jun	17	0	2	.235	.278	.294	ScPos	24	0	10	.292	.320	.333
Jul-Aug	87	3	12	.264	.373	.414	Clutch	11	0	0	.455	.571	.545

SCOUTING REPORT

Greg is an average receiver across the board but calls a good game for a young catcher who had no big-league experience prior to '95. He's agile behind the plate and throws decently.

A switch-hitter, Zaun is a plus fastball hitter with some pop in his bat. He has adequate speed on the basepaths for a catcher but doesn't steal much.

HOW HE PERFORMED IN '95

Starting the season with Triple-A Rochester, Zaun was recalled in on June 19 when the Orioles cut Matt Nokes loose. Greg played sparingly except for the last half of July when starter Chris Hoiles was disabled. He threw out only six of 24 would-be basestealers, though, but should improve somewhat in that area.

WHAT TO EXPECT IN '96

He's an able player and did very well last season as a solid backup. In fact, he's still young enough that he might end up getting a shot at starting duty someday if he improves a little bit more. Zaun is likely to usurp more of Hoiles' at-bats against righthanders in '96, which would benefit both catchers—giving Chris more rest and Greg more experience.

BALTIMORE ORIOLES: TOP PROSPECTS

JOE BOROWSKI

Bats: R Throws: R Opening Day Age: 24
Ht: 6-2 Wt: 225 Born: 5/4/1971
Position: P Drafted: 1989 #32 CHA

YR TEAM	LG/CLASS	G	GS	GF	SV	W	L	ERA	IP	H	HR	BB	SO	O/BA
93 Frederick	CARO/A	42	2	27	11	1	3	3.61	62.1	61	5	37	70	.258
93 Bowie	EAST/AA	9	0	5	0	3	0	0.00	17.2	11	0	11	17	.180
94 Bowie	EAST/AA	49	0	37	14	3	4	1.91	66.0	52	3	28	73	.213
95 Baltimore	AL/MAJ	6	0	3	0	0	0	1.23	7.1	5	0	4	3	.192
95 Rochester	INT/AAA	28	0	22	6	1	3	4.04	35.2	32	3	18	32	.256
95 Bowie	EAST/AA	16	0	14	7	2	2	3.92	20.2	16	2	7	32	.211

The 24-year-old reliever had a great year in 1994, and made it to Baltimore in '95. After struggling early in Triple-A, Borowski went to Bowie, regained his form and returned to Rochester in mid-July where he posted a 2.40 ERA the rest of the way. His success continued in Baltimore where he allowed just one run in 7.1 innings. The fitness-conscious Borowski throws three pitches, including a fastball in the mid-80's and a good slider. He has been especially tough on righties over the last two years, holding them to a .206 clip. He has also held first batters to a .135 (10-74) average over the same period.

CARLOS CHAVEZ

Bats: R Throws: R Opening Day Age: 23
Ht: 6-1 Wt: 200 Born: 8/25/1972
Position: P Drafted: 1992 #17 BAL

YR TEAM	LG/CLASS	G	GS	GF	SV	W	L	ERA	IP	H	HR	BB	SO	O/BA
93 Albany	SAL/A	20	0	13	3	1	3	5.29	34.0	33	3	18	28	.252
93 Bluefield	APPY/R	14	13	0	0	6	3	3.73	82.0	80	15	37	71	.256
94 Albany	SAL/A	5	0	3	0	1	0	2.89	9.1	9	0	7	4	.265
94 Bluefield	APPY/R	13	13	0	0	7	5	2.94	85.2	58	11	32	92	.193
95 Rochester	INT/AAA	1	0	0	0	0	0	10.80	1.2	3	0	3	1	.429
95 Bowie	EAST/AA	1	0	0	0	0	0	0.00	2.0	0	0	1	2	.000
95 Frederick	CARO/A	43	1	16	6	5	5	2.55	81.2	62	4	40	107	.207

Chavez is a strikeout pitcher who has gotten better while climbing the organizational ladder. After leading the Appalachian League in strikeouts in 1994, Chavez moved to the pen and pitched at three different levels last year. He spent most of 1995 at Frederick, where he led all Carolina League relievers in SO/9 IP ratio (12.06). The El Paso, TX native doesn't impress scouts with his velocity, but he has a wicked slider and will throw the change-up.

DANNY CLYBURN

Bats: R Throws: R Opening Day Age: 21
Ht: 6-3 Wt: 217 Born: 4/6/1974
Position: OF Drafted: 1992 #3 PIT

YR TEAM	LG/CLASS	G	AB	R	H	2B	3B	HR	RBI	SB	BA	OBA
93 Augusta	SAL/A	127	457	55	121	21	4	9	66	5	.265	.327
94 Salem	CARO/A	118	461	57	126	19	0	22	90	4	.273	.300
95 High Desert	CAL/A	45	160	20	45	3	1	12	37	2	.281	.359
95 Win-Salem	CARO/A	59	227	27	59	10	2	11	41	2	.260	.309
95 Frederick	CARO/A	15	45	8	9	4	0	0	4	1	.200	.294

Pittsburgh's second-round pick in 1992, Clyburn has already been traded twice in his brief career. He was sent to the Reds for Jacob Brumfield prior to the 1995 season and then dealt to the Orioles in the Brad Pennington deal. The 21-year-old has a tremendous build and has awesome power, but rarely walks, strikes out too often and is a defensive liability in left field.

ROCKY COPPINGER

Bats: R Throws: R Opening Day Age: 22
Ht: 6-5 Wt: 245 Born: 3/19/1974
Position: P Drafted: 1993 #19 BAL

YR TEAM	LG/CLASS	G	GS	GF	SV	W	L	ERA	IP	H	HR	BB	SO	O/BA
94 Bluefield	APPY/R	14	13	1	0	4	3	2.45	73.1	51	5	40	88	.198
95 Rochester	INT/AAA	5	5	0	0	3	0	1.04	34.2	23	2	17	19	.192
95 Bowie	EAST/AA	13	13	0	0	6	2	2.69	83.2	58	7	43	62	.192
95 Frederick	CARO/A	11	11	0	0	7	1	1.57	68.2	46	3	24	91	.189

Coppinger was one of the best starting pitchers in the minor leagues in 1995 and won the organization's Triple Crown for pitchers. He had the fifth best ERA in the minors, had the fourth most wins and the second best average against among starters (.191). He pitched at three levels and was dominant at each one. Coppinger had three games with ten or more strikeouts, including a two-hit shutout with 15 K's for Frederick. The big 21-year-old (6-foot-5, 245 pounds) throws an overpowering fastball, a good breaking ball, and an improving slider. The El Paso native is a durable fly-ball pitcher who is very tough on righthanded hitters.

TOMMY DAVIS

Bats: R Throws: R Opening Day Age: 22
Ht: 6-1 Wt: 195 Born: 5/21/1973
Position: 3B Drafted: 1994 #1 BAL

YR TEAM	LG/CLASS	G	AB	R	H	2B	3B	HR	RBI	SB	BA	OBA
94 Albany	SAL/A	61	216	35	59	10	1	5	35	2	.273	.331
95 Bowie	EAST/AA	9	32	5	10	3	0	3	10	0	.313	.353
95 Frederick	CARO/A	130	496	62	133	26	3	15	57	7	.268	.327

The Southern Mississippi product was Baltimore's first pick in 1994. He is a pure hitter with good power who the Orioles hope can develop into a Bagwell-type player. He has quick, strong wrists which spray the ball to all fields, and his 15 homers ranked fourth in the organization for '95. In the field, Davis made 37 errors at the hot corner and was moved to first base in the playoff finals. He has a good arm, but is still working to improve his footwork around the bag.

JIMMY HAYNES

Bats: R Throws: R Opening Day Age: 23
Ht: 6-4 Wt: 185 Born: 9/5/1972
Position: P Drafted: 1991 #7 BAL

YR TEAM	LG/CLASS	G	GS	GF	SV	W	L	ERA	IP	H	HR	BB	SO	O/BA
93 Frederick	CARO/A	27	27	0	0	12	8	3.03	172.1	139	13	61	174	.217
94 Bowie	EAST/AA	25	25	0	0	13	8	2.90	173.2	154	16	46	177	.238
94 Rochester	INT/AAA	3	3	0	0	1	0	6.75	13.1	20	3	6	14	.333
95 Baltimore	AL/MAJ	4	3	0	0	2	1	2.25	24.0	11	2	12	22	.136
95 Rochester	INT/AAA	26	25	0	0	12	8	3.29	167.0	162	16	49	140	.257

Haynes followed a great 1994 season with another solid year in '95. The lanky righthander has outstanding stuff, including a good fastball and great curve which helped him lead his league in strikeouts for the second straight year. He also paced the International League in wins and placed fifth in ERA. As impressive as he was in Triple-A, Haynes was even better in four major league appearances, surrendering only 11 hits in 24 innings and holding big leaguers to a .136 average. Over the last two years the 23-year-old has been tougher on lefties (.219 average) than righties (.275) and is very tough to steal on.

THE SCOUTING REPORT: 1996

BALTIMORE ORIOLES: TOP PROSPECTS

CALVIN MADURO

Bats: R Throws: R Opening Day Age: 21
Ht: 6-0 Wt: 175 Born: 9/5/1974
Position: P Drafted: NDFA 9-7-91 BAL

YR TEAM	LG/CLASS	G	GS	GF	SV	W	L	ERA	IP	H	HR	BB	SO	O/BA
93 Bluefield	APPY/R	14	14	0	0	9	4	3.96	91.0	90	4	17	83	.253
94 Frederick	CARO/A	27	26	1	0	9	8	4.25	152.1	132	18	59	137	.233
95 Bowie	EAST/AA	7	7	0	0	0	6	5.09	35.1	39	3	27	26	.289
95 Frederick	CARO/A	20	20	0	0	8	5	2.94	122.1	109	16	34	120	.240

The youngster from Aruba had a fantastic year in the Carolina League in 1995, averaging about a strikeout per inning and displaying good control. He won his last seven decisions for Frederick (2.23 ERA), including a three-hit shutout with 11 strikeouts before being returned to Double-A in late August. Maduro finished second in the organization in strikeouts and placed sixth in the Carolina League in ERA. He has good command of an average fastball, using the curve and changeup as his out pitches.

SCOTT McCLAIN

Bats: R Throws: R Opening Day Age: 23
Ht: 6-3 Wt: 209 Born: 5/19/1972
Position: 3B Drafted: 1990 #23 BAL

YR TEAM	LG/CLASS	G	AB	R	H	2B	3B	HR	RBI	SB	BA	OBA
93 Frederick	CARO/A	133	427	65	111	22	2	9	54	10	.260	.370
94 Bowie	EAST/AA	133	427	71	103	29	1	11	58	6	.241	.347
95 Rochester	INT/AAA	61	199	32	50	9	1	8	22	0	.251	.329
95 Bowie	EAST/AA	70	259	41	72	14	1	13	61	2	.278	.344

McClain turned down a college football scholarship to play baseball. The 23-year-old has shown improvement each year, setting career highs in several offensive categories in '95. He has a compact power stroke, which helped him place second in the system in homers and RBI, and also shows a good eye at the plate. In the field, McClain is well above average with sure hands and a good arm.

BILLY OWENS

Bats: S Throws: R Opening Day Age: 24
Ht: 6-1 Wt: 210 Born: 4/12/1971
Position: 1B Drafted: 1992 #3 BAL

YR TEAM	LG/CLASS	G	AB	R	H	2B	3B	HR	RBI	SB	BA	OBA
93 Albany	SAL/A	120	458	64	136	23	2	11	66	3	.297	.364
93 Frederick	CARO/A	17	60	8	21	4	0	0	8	0	.350	.375
94 Frederick	CARO/A	86	324	50	74	16	0	13	52	1	.228	.322
94 Bowie	EAST/AA	43	145	13	33	7	1	4	19	1	.228	.276
95 Rochester	INT/AAA	9	28	2	4	0	0	0	1	0	.143	.172
95 Bowie	EAST/AA	122	453	57	122	27	0	17	91	2	.269	.329

The 24-year-old from the University of Arizona may be the best power prospect in the system. He is a switch-hitter with more pop from the left side. He has power to all fields and led the organization in RBI. Owens showed great improvement from the previous season, boosting his average 49 points and setting a career best in slugging. He is a slow runner and an adequate first baseman at best.

BILLY PERCIBAL

Bats: R Throws: R Opening Day Age: 22
Ht: 6-1 Wt: 170 Born: 2/2/1974
Position: P Drafted: NDFA 8-2-91 BAL

YR TEAM	LG/CLASS	G	GS	GF	SV	W	L	ERA	IP	H	HR	BB	SO	O/BA
93 Bluefield	APPY/R	13	13	0	0	6	3	3.81	82.2	71	7	33	81	.225
94 Albany	SAL/A	28	28	0	0	13	9	3.56	169.1	160	9	90	132	.247
95 Bowie	EAST/AA	2	2	0	0	1	0	0.00	14.0	7	0	7	7	.156
95 High Desert	CAL/A	21	20	0	0	7	6	3.23	128.0	123	10	55	105	.254

A former infielder in the Dominican Republic, Percibal took his great arm to the mound when he signed with the O's in 1992. Since then, he has compiled a 29-16 career record with a 3.68 ERA. He throws a 90 mph fastball and a good slider. In 1995, Percibal ranked third in the organization in ERA, but was shut down with a sore elbow in mid-August.

MARK SMITH

Bats: R Throws: R Opening Day Age: 25
Ht: 6-3 Wt: 205 Born: 5/7/1970
Position: OF Drafted: 1991 #1 BAL

YR TEAM	LG/CLASS	G	AB	R	H	2B	3B	HR	RBI	SB	BA	OBA
93 Rochester	INT/AAA	129	485	69	136	27	1	12	68	4	.280	.341
94 Rochester	INT/AAA	114	437	69	108	27	1	19	66	4	.247	.311
94 Baltimore	AL/MAJ	3	7	0	1	0	0	0	2	0	.143	.143
95 Baltimore	AL/MAJ	37	104	11	24	5	0	3	15	3	.231	.314
95 Rochester	INT/AAA	96	364	55	101	25	3	12	66	7	.277	.328

The 1991 first-round pick entered pro ball with a reputation as a fine hitter who could generate power. He was selected to the International League All-Star squad last year, showing extra-base punch, and he played just about every day for Baltimore the last month of the season. Although the 25-year-old put up decent numbers in 1995, he still has not hit as well or with as much power as expected. Smith has decent speed and is an adequate left fielder.

GARRETT STEPHENSON

Bats: R Throws: R Opening Day Age: 24
Ht: 6-4 Wt: 185 Born: 1/2/1972
Position: P Drafted: 1992 #18 BAL

YR TEAM	LG/CLASS	G	GS	GF	SV	W	L	ERA	IP	H	HR	BB	SO	O/BA
93 Albany	SAL/A	30	24	3	1	16	7	2.84	171.1	142	6	44	147	.221
94 Frederick	CARO/A	18	17	0	0	7	5	4.02	107.1	91	13	36	133	.226
94 Bowie	EAST/AA	7	7	0	0	3	2	5.15	36.2	47	2	11	32	.315
95 Bowie	EAST/AA	29	29	0	0	7	10	3.64	175.1	154	23	47	139	.232

Stephenson has a similar build, motion and repertoire as that of top prospect Jimmy Haynes, but his fastball only tops out at about 87 mph. The 23-year-old keeps hitters off balance with a looping curve and plus changeup. He finished second in the Eastern League in innings pitched, third in strikeouts and first in hit batsmen and home runs allowed last season. In 1994, Stephenson led Carolina League starters in SO/9 IP (10.87) and he finished second in the South Atlantic League in wins the previous year.

BALTIMORE ORIOLES: OTHERS TO WATCH

JUAN BAUTISTA — Bats: R Throws: R Ht: 6-1 Wt: 185
Born: 6/24/1975 Drafted: NDFA 1-22-92 BAL Position: SS

YR TEAM	LG/CLASS	G	AB	R	H	2B	3B	HR	RBI	SB	BA	OBA
95 Bowie	EAST/AA	13	38	3	4	2	0	0	1	.105	.209
95 High Desert	CAL/A	99	374	54	98	13	4	11	51	22	.262	.306

Yet another shortstop from the Dominican pipeline, Bautista is on medication for a form of anemia, but showed good pop with the bat and swiped 22 bases.

HARRY BERRIOS — Bats: R Throws: R Ht: 5-11 Wt: 205
Born: 12/2/1971 Drafted: 1993 #8 BAL Position: OF

YR TEAM	LG/CLASS	G	AB	R	H	2B	3B	HR	RBI	SB	BA	OBA
95 Bowie	EAST/AA	56	208	32	51	13	0	5	21	12	.245	.332
95 Frederick	CARO/A	71	240	33	50	5	2	10	28	10	.208	.309

After hitting .342 with 19 homers and 105 RBI and stealing 56 bases in 1994, Berrios couldn't handle Double-A breaking balls.

ERIC CHAVEZ — Bats: R Throws: R Ht: 5-11 Wt: 212
Born: 9/7/1970 Drafted: NDFA 6-13-92 BAL Position: 3B

YR TEAM	LG/CLASS	G	AB	R	H	2B	3B	HR	RBI	SB	BA	OBA
95 Bowie	EAST/AA	14	51	5	10	2	0	2	4	0	.196	.268
95 High Desert	CAL/A	74	254	38	59	15	0	14	37	4	.232	.314

The 25-year-old is a power hitter, but his .232 average was a career low and he missed time with a stress fracture in his right leg.

KEVIN CURTIS — Bats: R Throws: R Ht: 6-2 Wt: 210
Born: 8/19/1972 Drafted: 1993 #15 BAL Position: 1B

YR TEAM	LG/CLASS	G	AB	R	H	2B	3B	HR	RBI	SB	BA	OBA
95 High Desert	CAL/A	112	399	70	117	26	1	21	70	8	.293	.389

The Long Beach State product had a productive year, slugging .521 and placing among the organization leaders in average, homers and RBI.

JOHN DETTMER — Bats: R Throws: R Ht: 6-0 Wt: 185
Born: 3/4/1970 Drafted: 1992 #11 TEX Position: P

YR TEAM	LG/CLASS	G	GS	GF	SV	W	L	ERA	IP	H	HR	BB	SO	O/BA
95 Texas	AL/MAJ	1	0	0	0	0	0	27.00	0.1	2	0	0	0	.667
95 Okla City	AMAS/AAA	5	0	3	0	0	0	2.08	8.2	10	1	4	10	.313
95 Rochester	INT/AAA	21	11	3	1	4	7	4.68	82.2	98	9	16	46	.292

Dettmer doesn't throw hard, but he has a good curveball, excellent control, and a 39-14 career minor league record with a 2.95 ERA.

CESAR DEVAREZ — Bats: R Throws: R Ht: 5-10 Wt: 175
Born: 9/22/1969 Drafted: NDFA 2-6-88 BAL Position: C

YR TEAM	LG/CLASS	G	AB	R	H	2B	3B	HR	RBI	SB	BA	OBA
95 Baltimore	AL/MAJ	6	4	0	0	0	0	0	0	0	.000	.000
95 Rochester	INT/AAA	67	240	32	60	12	1	1	21	2	.250	.270

One of the top catching prospects in the system, the Dominican native has a great arm which nailed 47.4% of would-be basestealers.

RICK FORNEY — Bats: R Throws: R Ht: 6-4 Wt: 210
Born: 10/24/1971 Drafted: 1991 #26 BAL Position: P

YR TEAM	LG/CLASS	G	GS	GF	SV	W	L	ERA	IP	H	HR	BB	SO	O/BA
95 Rochester	INT/AAA	3	3	0	0	0	0	3.94	16.0	19	2	6	12	.302
95 Bowie	EAST/AA	23	19	2	0	7	7	5.75	97.0	110	14	42	73	.287

Forney had won 27 games between '93 and '94, but he struggled in 1995 primarily due to elbow problems.

CHRIS LEMP — Bats: R Throws: R Ht: 6-0 Wt: 175
Born: 7/23/1971 Drafted: 1991 #9 BAL Position: P

YR TEAM	LG/CLASS	G	GS	GF	SV	W	L	ERA	IP	H	HR	BB	SO	O/BA
95 Rochester	INT/AAA	3	0	1	0	0	1	11.25	4.0	7	1	3	4	.412
95 Bowie	EAST/AA	18	0	16	4	2	4	5.40	20.0	28	0	7	14	.341
95 Frederick	CARO/A	41	0	36	19	2	3	2.38	45.1	44	4	17	50	.256

The 24-year-old led the organization in saves and his 62 appearances ranked fifth highest in the minors.

T.R. LEWIS — Bats: R Throws: R Ht: 6-0 Wt: 180
Born: 4/17/1971 Drafted: 1989 #5 BAL Position: 1B

YR TEAM	LG/CLASS	G	AB	R	H	2B	3B	HR	RBI	SB	BA	OBA
95 Rochester	INT/AAA	22	78	12	23	7	0	4	19	1	.295	.356
95 Bowie	EAST/AA	86	309	57	91	19	1	5	44	12	.294	.371

Lewis, a career .294 hitter over seven minor league seasons, has been made into an outfielder due to persistent shoulder problems.

MIGUEL MEJIA — Bats: R Throws: R Ht: 6-1 Wt: 155
Born: 3/25/1975 Drafted: NDFA 1-22-92 BAL Position: OF

YR TEAM	LG/CLASS	G	AB	R	H	2B	3B	HR	RBI	SB	BA	OBA
95 High Desert	CAL/A	37	119	14	32	6	1	0	12	16	.269	.348
95 Bluefield	APPY/R	51	181	50	54	6	3	3	30	36	.298	.361

Another product from San Pedro de Macoris, Mejia led the organization with 36 steals, including a minor-league high of five in one game.

SHERMAN OBANDO — Bats: R Throws: R Ht: 6-4 Wt: 215
Born: 1/23/1970 Drafted: NDFA 9-17-87 NYA Position: OF

YR TEAM	LG/CLASS	G	AB	R	H	2B	3B	HR	RBI	SB	BA	OBA
95 Baltimore	AL/MAJ	16	38	0	10	1	0	0	3	1	.263	.293
95 Rochester	INT/AAA	85	324	42	96	26	6	9	53	1	.296	.356

A native of Panama, Obando hits for average and power and could make the major league team as an extra outfielder.

BRIAN SACKINSKY — Bats: R Throws: R Ht: 6-4 Wt: 220
Born: 6/22/1971 Drafted: 1992 #2 BAL Position: P

YR TEAM	LG/CLASS	G	GS	GF	SV	W	L	ERA	IP	H	HR	BB	SO	O/BA
95 Rochester	INT/AAA	14	11	0	0	3	3	4.60	62.2	70	6	10	42	.287

Sackinsky, a second-round pick from Stanford, throws a fastball, slider and changeup, but was shut down in July with bone spurs in his elbow.

B.J. WASZGIS — Bats: R Throws: R Ht: 6-2 Wt: 210
Born: 8/24/1970 Drafted: 1991 #10 BAL Position: C

YR TEAM	LG/CLASS	G	AB	R	H	2B	3B	HR	RBI	SB	BA	OBA
95 Bowie	EAST/AA	130	438	53	111	22	0	10	50	2	.253	.365

Waszgis is not much defensively, but he is a good offensive talent who knocked in 100 runs in 1994.

JIM WAWRUCK — Bats: L Throws: L Ht: 5-11 Wt: 185
Born: 4/23/1970 Drafted: 1991 #5 BAL Position: OF

YR TEAM	LG/CLASS	G	AB	R	H	2B	3B	HR	RBI	SB	BA	OBA
95 Rochester	INT/AAA	39	149	21	45	12	3	1	23	5	.302	.361
95 Bowie	EAST/AA	56	212	29	59	7	1	6	30	7	.278	.345

The lefthanded hitter is a good athlete and a .299 career batter over five seasons.

BOSTON RED SOX

RICK AGUILERA

Position: RP
Bats: R **Throws:** R
Ht: 6'5" **Wt:** 200
Opening Day Age: 34
Born: 12/31/1961
Drafted: NYN83 5/58
ML Seasons: 11

SCOUTING REPORT
The hard-throwing veteran reduced the use of his slider last season and worked primarily with two pitches. Aguilera relied mostly on his average-plus sinking fastball, which he uses aggressively and runs in on righthanders. Rick's out pitch remains his plus—and occasionally outstanding—splitter, which has excellent tumble. His control of both pitches was above-average. Aguilera's fielding is average; he doesn't hurt himself with the glove. However, seventeen runners tried to steal against Rick in 1995, and all 17 were successful. This extremely poor record is in sharp contrast to his low career totals.

HOW HE PERFORMED IN '95
One of the important things that the trade for Aguilera did was stabilize the Boston bullpen. While some teams can get along with a "bullpen by committee," most teams require a closer. Every reliever feels more comfortable with a clear job description.

The 1995 Red Sox' designated closer at the start of the season, Ken Ryan, could not do the job. Neither Stan Belinda nor Rheal Cormier could assume that responsibility when asked, and not having that essential missing piece to the bullpen puzzle forced all the relievers into uncomfortable roles.

Order was restored when Boston acquired Aguilera. Belinda and Cormier returned to set-up jobs, and the veteran closer Aguilera handled the ninth inning in his usual effective way. He ended up with 20 of the team's 39 saves despite appearing in only 30 games with the BoSox, and made a huge contribution along the way to their winning the divisional crown. His was at his best in August, playing a key role in several close games during Boston's big division-winning month. Rick was far more effective against lefthanders, who slugged almost 200 points lower than right-handed batters.

WHAT TO EXPECT IN '96
Rick Aguilera was extremely unhappy about leaving Minnesota, then discovered Boston was not so awful a place. However, the Red Sox did not offer him arbitration after the season, so he moved back to Minnesota. The Twins intend that Rick will begin the 1996 season in the starting rotation, which is a risky move considering Aguilera's injury history and the fact that Aggie hasn't started a game in more than six years.

Overall Statistics

	G	GS	GF	SV	W	L	ERA	IP	H	R	ER	HR	BB	SO
95 MIN/BOS	52	0	51	32	3	3	2.60	55.1	46	16	16	6	13	52
Career	469	70	351	211	59	56	3.25	922.0	868	382	333	82	257	739

1995 Situational Statistics

	W	L	ERA	SV	IP	BB	SO		AB	HR	RBI	BA	OBA	SLG
Home	2	2	1.30	14	27.2	3	29	LHB	117	2	13	.205	.244	.282
Road	1	1	3.90	18	27.2	10	23	RHB	87	4	8	.253	.305	.448
Apr-Jun	1	1	1.96	11	23.0	6	26	ScPos	52	2	17	.192	.303	.346
Jul-Oct	2	2	3.06	21	32.1	7	26	Clutch	127	2	17	.197	.259	.276

How He Compares to Other Pitchers

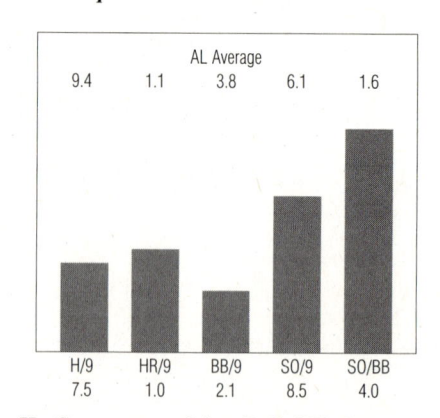

	H/9	HR/9	BB/9	SO/9	SO/BB
AL Average	9.4	1.1	3.8	6.1	1.6
	7.5	1.0	2.1	8.5	4.0

How He Compares to Other Relief Pitchers

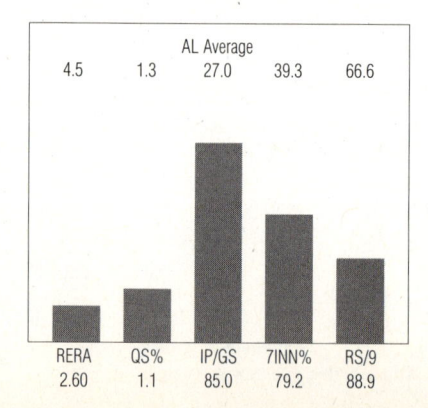

	RERA	QS%	IP/GS	7INN%	RS/9
AL Average	4.5	1.3	27.0	39.3	66.6
	2.60	1.1	85.0	79.2	88.9

BOSTON RED SOX

LUIS ALICEA

Position: 2B
Bats: B **Throws:** R
Ht: 5'9" **Wt:** 165
Opening Day Age: 30
Born: 7/29/1965
Drafted: SL86 1/23
ML Seasons: 6

SCOUTING REPORT
Luis is a basic singles spray hitter but has enough pop to keep outfielders fairly honest, with line drive power and the occasional home run. As do most switch-stickers, Alicea prefers low pitches hitting lefthanded and high pitches righty. He has only average speed, but is a smart runner and seems faster. Unfortunately, he has been a poor basestealer all his career, with the exception of an 11-for-12 performance in 1993. Defense is his forte, and with his plus range he often makes flashy plays, with a quick, accurate release and good footwork. His throwing is nothing special, but definitely adequate for his position. His one defensive weakness is hard hands; most of his errors are on dropped balls.

HOW HE PERFORMED IN '95
At age 30, Luis made the most of his chance to be a regular. Boston needed a second baseman with excellent range to support its groundball pitching staff and to reach all the balls normally handled by a first baseman (but not by Mo Vaughn). Alicea did a fine job vacuuming the outfield grass behind first base, and showed his plus range to advantage. He did not neglect the center of the diamond either, leading all league middle infielders in double plays.

Alicea changed leagues in '95, and took some time to adjust at the plate. After a dismal April, his average improved every month during the season; he also learned the AL strike zone and compiled a good on-base percentage. His RBI total was credible considering he usually batted ninth behind the team's weak-hitting catchers. Oddly, Luis was much more effective in road games, totaling a .400 on-base percentage away from Fenway.

"Little ball" wasn't his strength last year: as usual, he was a poor percentage base stealer. Alicea laid down 13 sacrifices last year, but rarely bunted for hits.

WHAT TO EXPECT IN '96
There was speculation that the Red Sox would seek a second baseman with more pop for '96, although Boston General Manager Dan Duquette had pronounced himself satisfied with Alicea. Luis could improve further in '96, since there will be no early-season "learning period" to pull down his average. However, he's no longer that young, and will probably only be a regular for a couple of more seasons. After that, he could stick around for years as a reserve.

Overall Statistics

	G	AB	R	H	2B	3B	HR	RBI	SB	CS	BB	SO	BA	OBA
95 BOS	132	419	64	113	20	3	6	44	13	10	63	61	.270	.367
Career	569	1616	197	412	73	26	17	175	31	23	200	244	.255	.340

1995 Situational Statistics

	AB	HR	RBI	BA	OBA	SLG		AB	HR	RBI	BA	OBA	SLG
Home	208	0	17	.255	.332	.327	LHP	99	2	12	.293	.388	.384
Road	211	6	27	.284	.400	.422	RHP	320	4	32	.262	.361	.372
Apr-Jun	169	2	16	.243	.358	.320	ScPos	110	1	37	.245	.370	.318
Jul-Oct	250	4	28	.288	.374	.412	Clutch	68	0	3	.191	.236	.250

How He Compares to Other Batters

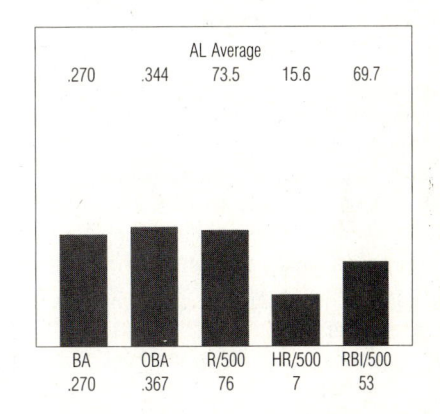

AL Average: .270 .344 73.5 15.6 69.7

BA	OBA	R/500	HR/500	RBI/500
.270	.367	76	7	53

Where He Hits the Ball

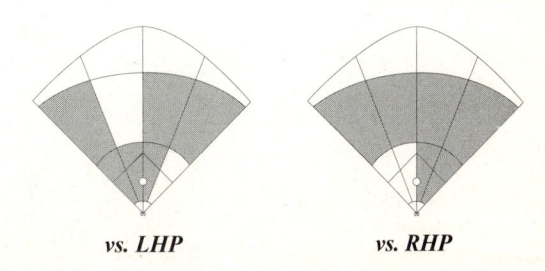

vs. LHP   vs. RHP

THE SCOUTING REPORT: 1996

BOSTON RED SOX

JOSE CANSECO

Positions: DH//OF
Bats: R **Throws:** R
Ht: 6'3" **Wt:** 240
Opening Day Age: 31
Born: 7/2/1964
Drafted: OAK82 14/392
ML Seasons: 11

SCOUTING REPORT

Jose is a classic streaky power hitter who can carry a team on his back for a couple of weeks, then can look awful for an equally long period. Like many big guys, he likes the ball out over the plate where he can flatten it with his nearly unparalleled bat speed. When healthy, he can be one of the most effective hitters in baseball. A series of maladies, however, have reduced his once-fast legs to the slow side of average and have bitten into his offensive productivity.

Canseco is not a good fielder, to understate the case, and it's not likely he now improve much due to his age, his injuries, and disuse in recent seasons.

HOW HE PERFORMED IN '95

Some of Canseco's best numbers for Boston were compiled before last season even began. His signing created local excitement that inoculated Boston from the bad karma that hurt ticket sales in many other big-league cities. Boston's attendance started strong, largely thanks to the buzz about Jose, and the team's early success guaranteed no fall-off in ticket sales during the season.

Ironically, despite all the hype, Canseco was not a factor in the first half. He lived up to his injury-prone reputation—even when only serving as the designated hitter—and as a result April, May, and June were lost. He began to heal—and hit—in July. In August, the month Boston won the division, Jose batted .356 with 14 doubles, nine home runs, and 23 runs batted in, slugging over .700 in the process!

As a result of painful leg and groin injuries, he ran station-to-station for most of 1995, going full speed only in situations where the extra base was important.

WHAT TO EXPECT IN '96

Canseco is a gamble for any general manager. When he is healthy he is devastating, but one never knows how many games he'll play in a season. The Red Sox rolled the dice last December and re-signed Jose for two years, paying him a great deal of guaranteed money. The odds are not in their favor. Despite his leg problems, Canseco is being projected as Boston's primary right fielder for this season. If he plays right everyday, it will be a defensive adventure for both him and the Red Sox pitchers.

Overall Statistics

	G	AB	R	H	2B	3B	HR	RBI	SB	CS	BB	SO	BA	OBA
95 BOS	102	396	64	121	25	1	24	81	4	0	42	93	.306	.378
Career	1245	4711	796	1275	229	12	300	951	153	67	560	1267	.271	.351

1995 Situational Statistics

	AB	HR	RBI	BA	OBA	SLG		AB	HR	RBI	BA	OBA	SLG
Home	199	10	44	.337	.401	.553	LHP	93	12	21	.280	.409	.699
Road	197	14	37	.274	.354	.558	RHP	303	12	60	.314	.367	.512
Apr-Jun	81	3	15	.235	.351	.407	ScPos	101	6	58	.337	.419	.564
Jul-Oct	315	21	66	.324	.385	.594	Clutch	47	3	13	.404	.500	.681

How He Compares to Other Batters

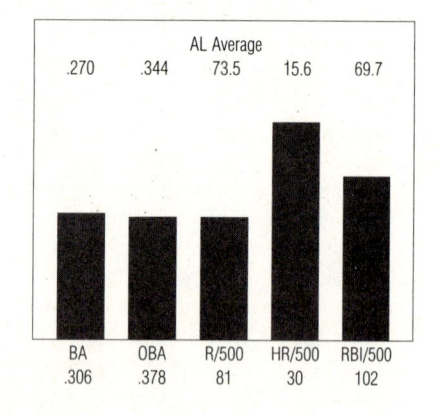

AL Average: .270 .344 73.5 15.6 69.7

BA	OBA	R/500	HR/500	RBI/500
.306	.378	81	30	102

Where He Hits the Ball

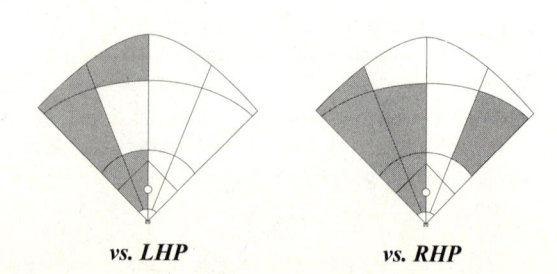

vs. LHP   vs. RHP

THE SCOUTING REPORT: 1996

BOSTON RED SOX

ROGER CLEMENS

Position: SP
Bats: R **Throws:** R
Ht: 6'4" **Wt:** 215
Opening Day Age: 33
Born: 8/4/1962
Drafted: BOS83 1/19
ML Seasons: 12

SCOUTING REPORT

The Rocket has lost some thrust off his fastball, but it is still a plus pitch and one of the better heaters around. He can throw both the four-seamer up in the zone and a two-seam sinker. To accompany the fastball, Roger has four other above-average deliveries: a curveball that rolls off the table, a hard slider, a forkball, and a newly-developed change-up. Thrown with plus control, this is a formidable array for any pitcher. Combined with Clemens' attitude and experience, it can be devastating.

Roger now throws from a high three-quarters angle or lower, and sometimes even comes sidearm to frighten righthanded hitters. Clemens is an indifferent fielder, but holds runners well with frequent step-offs. Fifteen baserunners tried to steal against him last year, and only eight were successful.

HOW HE PERFORMED IN '95

This was a transition year, when Roger was finally forced to recognize that his days as a pure power pitcher are over. He started spring training out of shape, and promptly hit the DL. While he returned, the velocity didn't, and a change of style was called for. June and July were rough months, as Clemens worked on new pitches while battling a stiff elbow. The low point came on July 23, when he allowed eight runs in an inning and a third against the Twins. His ERA had risen to 5.81 by then.

But Clemens came back. A lot of the credit should go to his former teammate Al Nipper, who was brought in as the Sox pitching coach during the July struggles. He forced Clemens to develop a change-up, a pitch that became more effective as his velocity returned. As the elbow improved, Roger also used his curve more, which gave batters another thing to worry about. From August 24 on, Roger went 6-1, resuming his role as staff ace.

WHAT TO EXPECT IN '96

This should be an interesting year. The real limiting factor to Clemens' success now is physical. His arm has thrown a lot of pitches over the years, and the big question is whether it can be forced to continue to perform. Roger worked through the mental stuff in 1995 and knows exactly what he has to do to win. Can the body do what the mind wills? Bet on the Rocket.

Overall Statistics

	G	GS	GF	SV	W	L	ERA	IP	H	R	ER	HR	BB	SO
95 BOS	23	23	0	0	10	5	4.18	140.0	141	70	65	15	60	132
Career	349	348	0	0	182	98	3.00	2533.1	2143	939	845	175	750	2333

1995 Situational Statistics

	W	L	ERA	SV	IP	BB	SO		AB	HR	RBI	BA	OBA	SLG
Home	6	3	4.56	0	71.0	27	73	LHB	303	7	32	.257	.349	.380
Road	4	2	3.78	0	69.0	33	59	RHB	241	8	30	.261	.343	.411
Apr-Jun	2	1	3.53	0	35.2	14	31	ScPos	123	3	45	.293	.396	.390
Jul-Oct	8	4	4.40	0	104.1	46	101	Clutch	25	1	3	.240	.406	.440

How He Compares to Other Pitchers

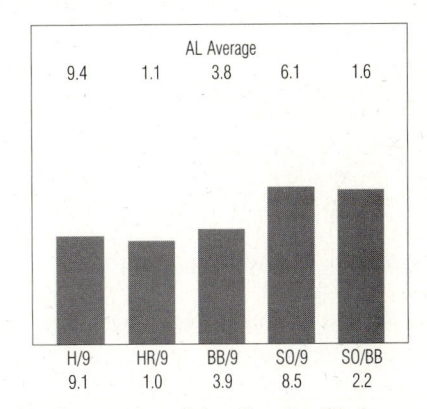

AL Average: 9.4 / 1.1 / 3.8 / 6.1 / 1.6

H/9	HR/9	BB/9	SO/9	SO/BB
9.1	1.0	3.9	8.5	2.2

How He Compares to Other Starting Pitchers

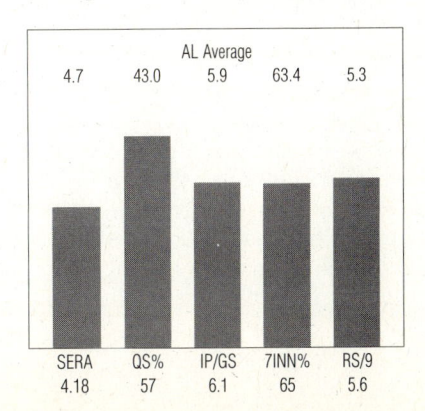

AL Average: 4.7 / 43.0 / 5.9 / 63.4 / 5.3

SERA	QS%	IP/GS	7INN%	RS/9
4.18	57	6.1	65	5.6

THE SCOUTING REPORT: 1996

BOSTON RED SOX

MIKE GREENWELL

Positions: OF//DH
Bats: L **Throws:** R
Ht: 6'0" **Wt:** 200
Opening Day Age: 32
Born: 7/18/1963
Drafted: BOS82 6/72
ML Seasons: 11

SCOUTING REPORT
Like many lefthanded batters, Greenwell makes his living off of low, inside pitches. Mike still makes good contact, but he now pulls the ball less frequently and less effectively than in years past, although he has matured enough to take outside pitches to the opposite field. He continues to handle lefthanders fairly well, and is very good with runners in scoring position. Greenwell plays hard and often plays through injuries.

He lacks lateral range in the outfield, but comes in on balls very well. His speed is now just average, and his throwing, which had been weak due to 1994 shoulder surgery, is back to average.

HOW HE PERFORMED IN '95
Mike changed his hitting style in 1995, a move that resulted in a better batting average but fewer walks and less power. Greenwell's new technique involved hacking at the first pitch he could reach, which resulted in many short at-bats.

Mike generally batted sixth last season, the proper slot for a player of his skills. Greenwell is a pure line-drive hitter, but his lack of speed turns most of his hits into singles unless they are hit down the line or deep in the gap. He rarely takes an extra base anymore.

Greenwell's defense in Fenway was outstanding. His shoulder finally healed, and Mike registered 11 assists with surprisingly strong, accurate throws, using his ability to charge balls and almost certainly benefitting from runners' assumptions that his shoulder was still weak. He also helped his pitchers by turning "Green Monster" doubles into singles time after time.

Outside Fenway, Mike was a liability in the outfield. An inability to go back well on fly balls and a late-season spate of dropped line drives made everything hit to the left side of the outfield a nail-biter for Sox fans.

WHAT TO EXPECT IN '96
Greenwell is signed through this year, which will likely be his last in Boston. Mike—aging, slow, and with a mediocre on-base percentage—is not General Manager Dan Duquette's type of player. Look for more middling production from Greenwell as Boston marks time while assembling a more talented roster.

Overall Statistics

	G	AB	R	H	2B	3B	HR	RBI	SB	CS	BB	SO	BA	OBA
95 BOS	120	481	67	143	25	4	15	76	9	5	38	35	.297	.349
Career	1192	4328	622	1313	255	37	123	682	76	43	442	337	.303	.370

1995 Situational Statistics

	AB	HR	RBI	BA	OBA	SLG		AB	HR	RBI	BA	OBA	SLG
Home	235	6	39	.319	.373	.489	LHP	142	5	22	.268	.329	.423
Road	246	9	37	.276	.325	.431	RHP	339	10	54	.310	.357	.475
Apr-Jun	226	6	31	.301	.360	.451	ScPos	137	3	60	.314	.364	.467
Jul-Oct	255	9	45	.294	.338	.467	Clutch	69	2	9	.304	.377	.449

How He Compares to Other Batters

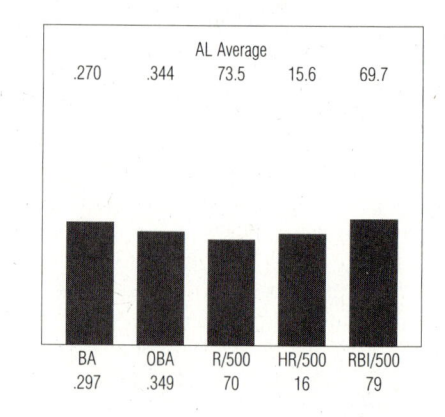

AL Average: .270 .344 73.5 15.6 69.7

BA	OBA	R/500	HR/500	RBI/500
.297	.349	70	16	79

Where He Hits the Ball

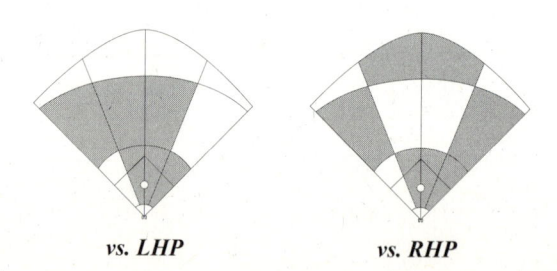

vs. LHP   vs. RHP

THE SCOUTING REPORT: 1996

BOSTON RED SOX

ERIK HANSON

Position: SP
Bats: R **Throws:** R
Ht: 6'6" **Wt:** 210
Opening Day Age: 30
Born: 5/18/1965
Drafted: SEA86 2/36
ML Seasons: 8

SCOUTING REPORT
The healthy Erik Hanson throws three pitches with average control from a three-quarter angle. A middling fastball which he spots well is greatly enhanced by an above-average change, which he throws with the same motion as his fastball.

His most feared pitch is a large curve with a sharp break, which is virtually unhittable. However, after his injury last season took away the ability to use the bender, Erik was forced to develop a new offering. He did, adding to his repertoire a cut fastball that moved like a slider and is a plus pitch. The veteran knows how to combine these pitches into a baffling array.

He is one of the few Boston pitchers who fields his position effectively, with great reflexes and fine range. However, eleven of eighteen enemy baserunners were successful stealing in 1995. Hanson's open delivery is easy for smart runners to read.

HOW HE PERFORMED IN '95
A history of injuries and a poor 1994 season with Cincinnati minimized interest in the 30-year-old Hanson, who started the spring among the homeless at Camp Homestead. However, a good workout convinced Boston management that Hanson might be able to help.

The move paid off beyond the Red Sox' wildest expectations. Hanson was the team's only consistently good starter. He only led the starting staff in starts and winning percentage, but he gave his team a chance to win nearly every time out.

His record is more amazing considering that a June elbow injury rendered Erik unable to rely consistently on that devastating curve. He gamely bore down with just his fastball, change, and the little cutter he quickly developed after the elbow trouble. Hanson's combination of pitches was particularly effective against left-handed batters. Hanson's ERA was about two runs higher in July–September than it was when he still had his curve.

WHAT TO EXPECT IN '96
Erik was expected back with the Red Sox for another year. The elbow problem should be healed, and he'll start the season 100%. Boston is hopeful of another full year of quality work, and will always get gutsy, competitive play from Hanson even if he isn't fully healthy. In seven years, he has never had a bad season in the majors.

Overall Statistics

	G	GS	GF	SV	W	L	ERA	IP	H	R	ER	HR	BB	SO
95 BOS	29	29	0	0	15	5	4.24	186.2	187	94	88	17	59	139
Career	196	193	1	0	76	64	3.81	1276.2	1273	586	541	100	367	980

1995 Situational Statistics

	W	L	ERA	SV	IP	BB	SO		AB	HR	RBI	BA	OBA	SLG
Home	5	3	4.37	0	92.2	29	58	LHB	409	7	43	.215	.266	.303
Road	10	2	4.12	0	94.0	30	81	RHB	317	10	40	.312	.369	.492
Apr-Jun	7	1	2.91	0	77.1	18	70	ScPos	180	3	64	.233	.259	.356
Jul-Oct	8	4	5.19	0	109.1	41	69	Clutch	51	1	1	.157	.246	.216

How He Compares to Other Pitchers

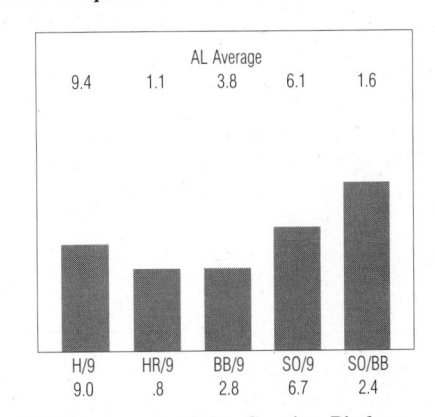

AL Average: H/9 9.4 | HR/9 1.1 | BB/9 3.8 | SO/9 6.1 | SO/BB 1.6

Hanson: H/9 9.0 | HR/9 .8 | BB/9 2.8 | SO/9 6.7 | SO/BB 2.4

How He Compares to Other Starting Pitchers

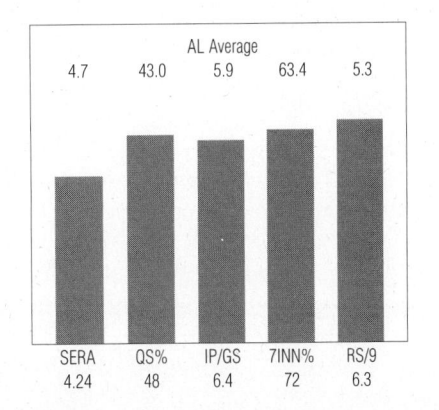

AL Average: SERA 4.7 | QS% 43.0 | IP/GS 5.9 | 7INN% 63.4 | RS/9 5.3

Hanson: SERA 4.24 | QS% 48 | IP/GS 6.4 | 7INN% 72 | RS/9 6.3

THE SCOUTING REPORT: 1996

BOSTON RED SOX

MIKE MACFARLANE

Positions: C//DH
Bats: R **Throws:** R
Ht: 6'1" **Wt:** 200
Opening Day Age: 31
Born: 4/12/1964
Drafted: KC85 4/97
ML Seasons: 9

SCOUTING REPORT
Macfarlane's offense declined precipitously last season. He tried to pull everything and as a result could not handle outside pitches. Mike has a sweeping swing which he can't adjust once it's started, and in '95 this swing produced a lot of groundouts and strikeouts. Macfarlane stands very close to the plate, and does not have the ability to move out of the way of inside pitches; as a result, he gets plunked quite a bit. Tired knees have made Macfarlane one of the slowest runners in baseball. He's now a cinch to be pinch-run for in late-game situations. Perhaps Mike's biggest asset is his catching experience. He calls a good game and handles pitchers well, but his battered body can no longer make the plays a more flexible catcher is capable of.

HOW HE PERFORMED IN '95
In 1993–94, the Red Sox had weak-hitting catchers, so the front office decided to seek more production from the position. Mike Macfarlane looked like the answer, with a career average over .250 and respectable power. Unfortunately, Mike never got it going in Boston, hovering around .200 all season. He hit for power early on, but manager Kevin Kennedy rarely rested Mike the first three months of the season, and soon an exhausted Macfarlane began to sag. He feasted on lefthanders in '95, hitting eight homers in less than one third the at-bats he had against righties, but barely cleared the Mendoza line against righthanders. This is a substantial change from his career pattern and, if it continues, will reduce him to a platoon player.

Macfarlane's mechanics behind the plate are sound, despite limited mobility. His hands are well-above average, and he handled Tim Wakefield's difficult knuckler reasonably well. However, catching multiple Wakefield games resulted in wild pitch and passed ball rates far above the AL average. Mike showed an average-plus arm, retiring 35% of opposition base stealers.

WHAT TO EXPECT IN '96
Macfarlane will be playing with Kansas City again in '96, not with Boston. After the season the club stated its dissatisfaction with both his offense and his defense and cut him loose. The Royals, where he played for eight seasons before going free-agent after '94, were glad to have him and his power back for '96.

Overall Statistics

	G	AB	R	H	2B	3B	HR	RBI	SB	CS	BB	SO	BA	OBA
95 BOS	115	364	45	82	18	1	15	51	2	1	38	78	.225	.319
Career	808	2522	313	633	154	13	91	360	8	11	215	508	.251	.326

1995 Situational Statistics

	AB	HR	RBI	BA	OBA	SLG		AB	HR	RBI	BA	OBA	SLG
Home	186	7	24	.242	.330	.419	LHP	90	8	15	.300	.388	.644
Road	178	8	27	.208	.308	.388	RHP	274	7	36	.201	.297	.325
Apr-Jun	161	10	29	.211	.344	.422	ScPos	106	4	38	.160	.262	.311
Jul-Oct	203	5	22	.236	.298	.389	Clutch	50	4	8	.280	.351	.600

How He Compares to Other Batters

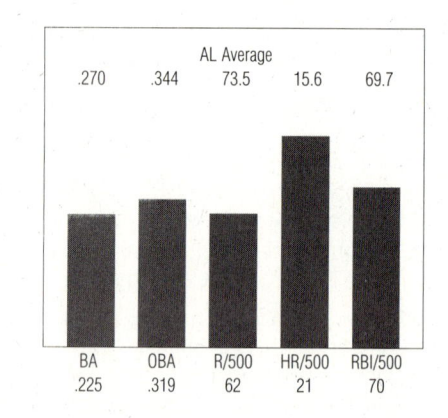

AL Average
BA	OBA	R/500	HR/500	RBI/500
.270	.344	73.5	15.6	69.7
.225	.319	62	21	70

Where He Hits the Ball

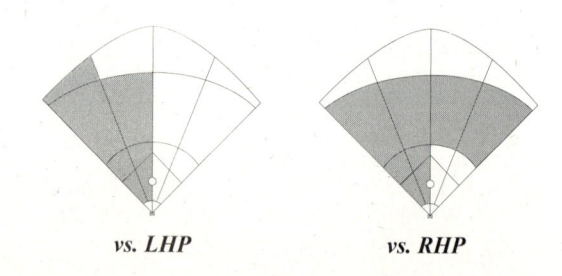

vs. LHP   vs. RHP

BOSTON RED SOX

TIM NAEHRING

Positions: 3B//DH
Bats: R **Throws:** R
Ht: 6'2" **Wt:** 190
Opening Day Age: 29
Born: 2/1/1967
Drafted: BOS88 8/199
ML Seasons: 6

SCOUTING REPORT

Tim is tough to defend against when hitting, spraying hard line drives to all parts of the park. He likes to hammer pitches that are high and over the plate and, although he has minus power, he will occasionally yank an inside pitch over the Green Monster as well. He stands back in the box and can wait on a breaking ball, sporting a superb batting eye and good hands.

The biggest weakness in Naehring's offensive game is slow legs. He's no threat to steal and hits low in the order due to his lack of speed. However, he is a heads-up runner who takes an extra base when he can exploit a good opportunity.

HOW HE PERFORMED IN '95

After five years, Tim finally got his chance at third base when Boston shipped out incumbent Scott Cooper. Naehring made the deal look good by having a fine '95 season while Cooper sagged badly in St. Louis. At age 28, Naehring posted his first season in the majors with more than 300 at-bats and only his second season with more than 200 at-bats.

He got off to his usual fast start at bat, ranking among the league leaders in batting average during the first half. However, nagging injuries helped to curb Naehring's production after the All-Star break. Tim did lead the Red Sox' regulars in walk rate by a large margin and compiled the highest on-base percentage on the club.

Neahring was terrific on defense last season, showing above-average range, a good first step, and a strong arm. He has worked hard to improve defensively, and served a vital role in an infield that backed up a staff of primarily groundball pitchers.

WHAT TO EXPECT IN '96

Look for a repeat of the '95 season from Naehring, if he has finally shaken his habit of getting hurt after a good start at the plate. He should be even better defensively after a full year of experience at third base, and is overall a very productive regular. All he needed was a full season to establish himself and, once he did that, Tim showed he was capable of helping a good team win. A year shy of 30, he could easily play regularly for several years.

Overall Statistics

	G	AB	R	H	2B	3B	HR	RBI	SB	CS	BB	SO	BA	OBA
95 BOS	126	433	61	133	27	2	10	57	0	2	77	66	.307	.415
Career	361	1183	139	329	70	3	23	145	2	5	149	209	.278	.363

1995 Situational Statistics

	AB	HR	RBI	BA	OBA	SLG		AB	HR	RBI	BA	OBA	SLG
Home	207	5	31	.348	.453	.517	LHP	102	3	11	.275	.439	.402
Road	226	5	26	.270	.379	.385	RHP	331	7	46	.317	.406	.462
Apr-Jun	185	4	30	.351	.440	.503	ScPos	118	3	48	.305	.436	.475
Jul-Oct	248	6	27	.274	.397	.407	Clutch	69	1	6	.319	.390	.420

How He Compares to Other Batters

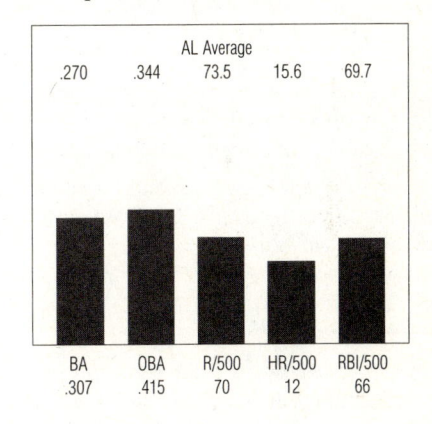

	BA	OBA	R/500	HR/500	RBI/500
AL Average	.270	.344	73.5	15.6	69.7
	.307	.415	70	12	66

Where He Hits the Ball

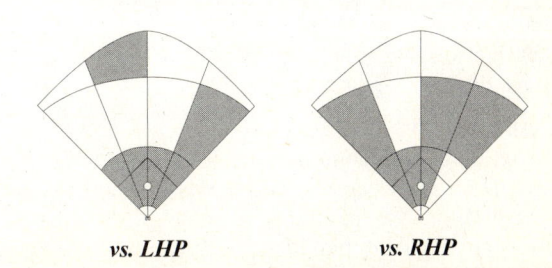

vs. LHP   vs. RHP

THE SCOUTING REPORT: 1996

BOSTON RED SOX

TROY O'LEARY

Positions: OF//DH
Bats: L **Throws:** L
Ht: 6'0" **Wt:** 175
Opening Day Age: 26
Born: 8/4/1969
Drafted: MIL87 14/331
ML Seasons: 3

SCOUTING REPORT

Despite his fine '95 hitting numbers, O'Leary did not look especially good at the plate. He likes to swing at offerings low in the zone, but will often chase pitches so low they collect dirt. Despite limited power, he tries to pull everything, which makes him an easy mark for lefthanded pitching.

Troy has shown poor plate discipline in the majors, although he was better in this regard during his tenure in the minors. He may not have enough sock to play an outfield corner, as last year was only the second time he ever reached double figures in home runs. He is not often asked to bunt, but O'Leary isn't bad at sacrificing.

Slightly below-average speed is evident in his station-to-station baserunning. While Troy's throwing arm is below par, he does have reasonably accurate aim.

HOW HE PERFORMED IN '95

O'Leary escaped obscurity in Milwaukee to become an everyday player for Boston in '95. Plucked off the waiver wire last spring by Red Sox GM (and former Brewers' scouting director) Dan Duquette, who had originally drafted him back in 1987, Troy joined a club thin in outfield depth. Seizing this opportunity, O'Leary hit so well that he soon became the team's everyday right fielder.

Troy does not hit lefties well, and manager Kevin Kennedy soon realized this. Ultimately, only one-eighth of his at-bats came against lefthanded pitching. Hitting mostly with favorable match-ups, O'Leary's average stayed over .300 the entire season and he kicked in some power.

O'Leary is too slow to play center, and he can barely handle the big right field at Fenway. His defense and throwing were shaky at first, but steadily improved in the second half. If Troy does not continue to hit for a high average, he may not be able to stay in the lineup, considering his marginal defense. He may be a spare part who happened to have his career year early.

WHAT TO EXPECT IN '96

Troy must continue to improve if he wants to keep his name in the box scores. While he performed very well in '95, he is weak in some critical areas. Boston will likely find some outfield talent during the off-season to challenge for both the center and right field positions, making a formal platoon is a real possibility for O'Leary.

Overall Statistics

	G	AB	R	H	2B	3B	HR	RBI	SB	CS	BB	SO	BA	OBA
95 BOS	112	399	60	123	31	6	10	49	5	3	29	64	.308	.355
Career	158	506	72	153	35	7	12	59	6	4	39	85	.302	.353

1995 Situational Statistics

	AB	HR	RBI	BA	OBA	SLG		AB	HR	RBI	BA	OBA	SLG
Home	209	5	26	.349	.390	.555	LHP	52	0	5	.231	.310	.250
Road	190	5	23	.263	.317	.421	RHP	347	10	44	.320	.362	.527
Apr-Jun	167	4	27	.347	.384	.527	ScPos	95	3	39	.284	.358	.484
Jul-Oct	232	6	22	.280	.335	.466	Clutch	64	1	5	.297	.348	.469

How He Compares to Other Batters

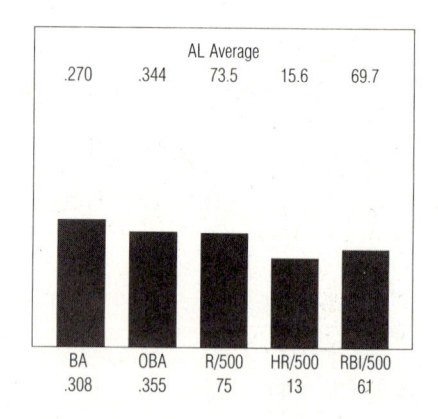

AL Average: .270 .344 73.5 15.6 69.7

BA	OBA	R/500	HR/500	RBI/500
.308	.355	75	13	61

Where He Hits the Ball

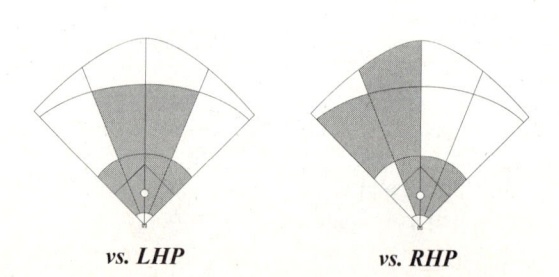

vs. LHP   vs. RHP

BOSTON RED SOX

LEE TINSLEY

Position: OF
Bats: B **Throws:** R
Ht: 5'10" **Wt:** 185
Opening Day Age: 27
Born: 3/4/1969
Drafted: OAK87 1/11
ML Seasons: 3

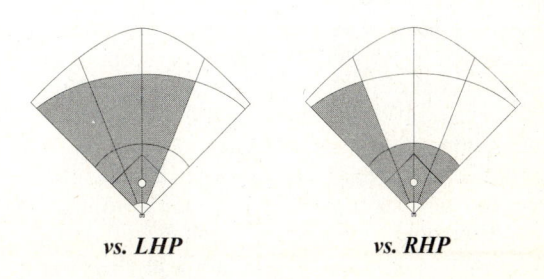

SCOUTING REPORT

Tinsley is a line-drive hitter who has minus power for his position. He's better against righthanders and prefers high pitches from the left side, unusual for a switch-hitter. He can get around on balls in his zone and pull them, but a big swing means lots of strikeouts as well. Lee's less effective from the right side and often hits to the opposite field.

Although he was touted as being fast and is a decent stealer, Tinsley does not get a good break out of the batter's box and disappointed by failing to fully utilize his speed on offense. He is an outstanding sacrifice bunter.

On defense Lee has above-average hands and range but plays a rather deep center; he allows more bloop hits than a more confident fielder with his speed should. His throwing is average.

HOW HE PERFORMED IN '95

After several deals fell through last spring, Lee became Boston's starting center fielder by default. The Red Sox knew that the speedy Tinsley could cover ground and, since he had never hit much, no offense was expected.

His early offense (.337 through May 31) was a total surprise. Lee took over as the leadoff hitter and played well. Righthanders weren't much of a mystery to him all year. However, everyone knew he was playing over his head and reality set in before the All-Star break, as the average declined and the strikeouts began to pile up. Soon, a three-sided platoon began with Tinsley, Willie McGee and Troy O'Leary. As Tinsley's hitting continued to fall off, so did his playing time. Lee hit bottom at the end of the season, when he was benched for waiver acquisition Dwayne Hosey.

In 97 games in center, Tinsley threw out just four runners and committed five errors to field a not-so-nifty .979. However, Lee showed excellent range and made his share of outstanding plays.

WHAT TO EXPECT IN '96

By the end of '95, Tinsley had defined himself more than ever as a reserve outfielder. He has some real skills but swings an inconsistent bat that his team can't afford to carry every day. Since he's still young and cheap, Tinsley should have a role with the Red Sox, but isn't likely to start unless several other players bomb out completely.

Overall Statistics

	G	AB	R	H	2B	3B	HR	RBI	SB	CS	BB	SO	BA	OBA
95 BOS	100	341	61	97	17	1	7	41	18	8	39	74	.284	.359
Career	189	504	90	132	22	1	10	57	31	8	60	119	.262	.342

1995 Situational Statistics

	AB	HR	RBI	BA	OBA	SLG		AB	HR	RBI	BA	OBA	SLG
Home	170	4	26	.288	.349	.418	LHP	88	3	9	.250	.320	.386
Road	171	3	15	.281	.367	.386	RHP	253	4	32	.296	.372	.407
Apr-Jun	168	5	22	.292	.346	.440	ScPos	83	1	32	.301	.398	.386
Jul-Oct	173	2	19	.277	.370	.364	Clutch	46	1	8	.348	.423	.500

How He Compares to Other Batters

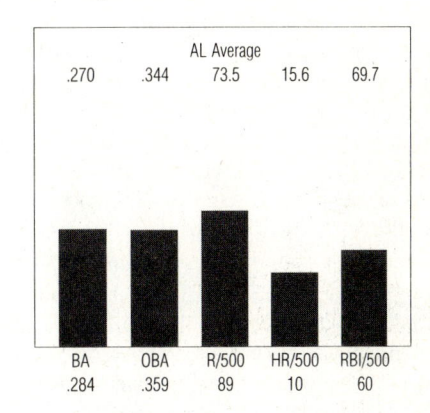

AL Average: .270 .344 73.5 15.6 69.7

	BA	OBA	R/500	HR/500	RBI/500
	.284	.359	89	10	60

Where He Hits the Ball

vs. LHP   vs. RHP

THE SCOUTING REPORT: 1996

BOSTON RED SOX

JOHN VALENTIN

Position: SS
Bats: R **Throws:** R
Ht: 6'0" **Wt:** 170
Opening Day Age: 29
Born: 2/18/1967
Drafted: BOS88 5/121
ML Seasons: 4

SCOUTING REPORT

The Boston shortstop is a classic #2 hitter, with good bat control, strong hit-and-run skills, and the ability to put the bat on the ball anywhere it's placed. Valentin, however, exceeds the specs of the job by adding excellent strike zone judgment (and, therefore, a high on-base percentage) and plenty of power. He is one tough out.

John's defense has improved to adequate. He displays slightly above-average range and makes some excellent stops. He has problems concentrating on routine plays, though, and ended up with 18 errors in '95. A decent arm and good double play skills make him a passable major-league defender, and his offensive output makes the Red Sox willing to compromise a bit.

One of the few Bostonians with any speed, John led the none-too-mobile Red Sox in stolen bases. He only occasionally bunts, and then only to sacrifice. However, his other hitting skills are so good that he doesn't need to lay the ball down often.

HOW HE PERFORMED IN '95

This was the year Valentin became the top offensive shortstop in baseball. He followed up his excellent '94 output with an off-season weight program that paid off in increased power. John's home run total tripled from 9 to 27, and he also smacked a team-high 37 doubles. He just missed batting .300 and came very close to a .400 on-base percentage, driving in over 100 runs for the first time.

John was consistent all season, batting between .274 and .319 in all but one month. He slugged at least four homers in each full month and helped generate plenty of big innings. finishing with Mo Vaughn first and second on the team in runs and RBI. Valentin is noted for his hard work; he's made large improvements in his play each season in his major-league career.

WHAT TO EXPECT IN '96

The club may eventually move John to third base and let one of their shortstop prospects (Nomar Garciaparra is the top youngster in the system) improve the infield defense. Valentin, however, will resist such a move as long as he can, and there is no one to challenge him at shortstop for 1996. He is a good example, a steady player, and overall ranks as one of the most underrated players in all of baseball.

Overall Statistics

	G	AB	R	H	2B	3B	HR	RBI	SB	CS	BB	SO	BA	OBA
95 BOS	135	520	108	155	37	2	27	102	20	5	81	67	.298	.399
Career	421	1474	232	431	116	7	52	242	27	10	192	199	.292	.377

1995 Situational Statistics

	AB	HR	RBI	BA	OBA	SLG		AB	HR	RBI	BA	OBA	SLG
Home	251	11	40	.319	.431	.554	LHP	132	6	35	.356	.465	.568
Road	269	16	62	.279	.367	.513	RHP	388	21	67	.278	.376	.521
Apr-Jun	224	12	35	.290	.392	.531	ScPos	150	8	76	.327	.402	.587
Jul-Oct	296	15	67	.304	.404	.534	Clutch	62	3	15	.339	.434	.581

How He Compares to Other Batters

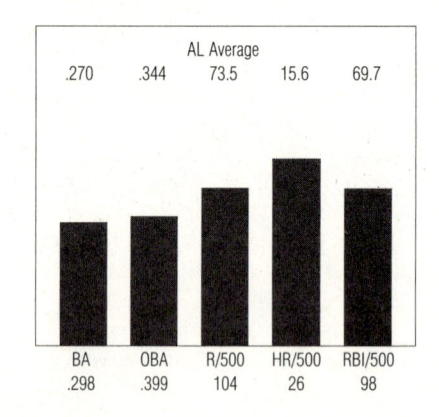

	BA	OBA	R/500	HR/500	RBI/500
AL Average	.270	.344	73.5	15.6	69.7
	.298	.399	104	26	98

Where He Hits the Ball

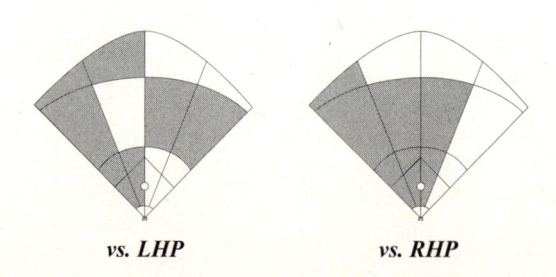

vs. LHP   vs. RHP

BOSTON RED SOX

MO VAUGHN

Positions: 1B//DH
Bats: L **Throws:** R
Ht: 6'1" **Wt:** 225
Opening Day Age: 28
Born: 12/15/1967
Drafted: BOS89 2/23
ML Seasons: 5

SCOUTING REPORT

Vaughn's tremendous strength lets him go with the pitch and hit home runs to any field. He prefers low pitches he can drop the bat onto. His power stroke can't be adjusted once it's begun, so Vaughn swings and misses a lot. Mo started the season hanging over the plate, then backed off when pitchers began throwing everything in on his hands. Mo is a decent baserunner. He breaks out of the batter's box slowly due to a full follow-through on his big swing, but accelerates well. He is faster than he looks and surprised some teams by taking a few extra bases.

Vaughn's fielding has progressed from disastrous to mere liability. He ability to catch throws has improved to mediocre, but his own throwing is still frightening, especially to Red Sox pitchers who have to try to handle his hard, wild pegs on the run. He has very limited range and kicks his share of ground balls. On pickoff attempts he steps toward the pitcher to take the throw, obviating any chance of actually catching the runner.

HOW HE PERFORMED IN '95

The tremendously popular Vaughn won the BBWAA Mr. Congeniality Award for '95 (formerly known as the MVP award) over Cleveland's Albert Belle. He took home the trophy with limitless patience, good humor, and more than a bit of power hitting. Vaughn's season showed slight improvement but no dramatic breakthroughs. In late-inning situations, the opposition generally got Vaughn out when they needed to. Although he has adjusted to most pitchers, there are still holes in the big guy's swing—he's an aggressive hitter who can be tempted to hack at balls he can't handle, and this tendency increases in game situations. But when Mo makes contact, he hits the ball very hard.

The only ugly mark on the year was a big shiner Mo suffered when he was involved in a bar fight in July 13. Despite this incident, Vaughn maintained popularity with both fans and the press.

WHAT TO EXPECT IN '96

Look for continuing improvement. Mo has vowed to cut down on the strikeouts this year, and more experience will increase his hitting effectiveness. Being sandwiched between John Valentin and Jose Canseco should help the '95 MVP compile some more big hitting numbers. At age 28, a monster power season (50-homers) is a real possibility.

Overall Statistics

	G	AB	R	H	2B	3B	HR	RBI	SB	CS	BB	SO	BA	OBA
95 BOS	140	550	98	165	28	3	39	126	11	4	68	150	.300	.388
Career	590	2057	312	587	115	7	111	398	24	15	277	502	.285	.377

1995 Situational Statistics

	AB	HR	RBI	BA	OBA	SLG		AB	HR	RBI	BA	OBA	SLG
Home	266	15	52	.301	.395	.549	LHP	174	6	31	.253	.330	.402
Road	284	24	74	.299	.382	.599	RHP	376	33	95	.322	.414	.654
Apr-Jun	227	19	47	.282	.390	.564	ScPos	149	8	84	.336	.461	.597
Jul-Oct	323	20	79	.313	.387	.582	Clutch	67	2	7	.164	.300	.269

How He Compares to Other Batters

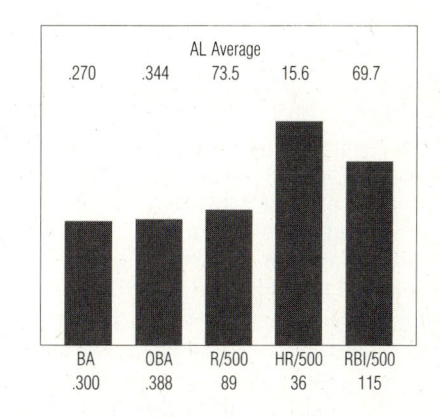

AL Average: .270 | .344 | 73.5 | 15.6 | 69.7

BA	OBA	R/500	HR/500	RBI/500
.300	.388	89	36	115

Where He Hits the Ball

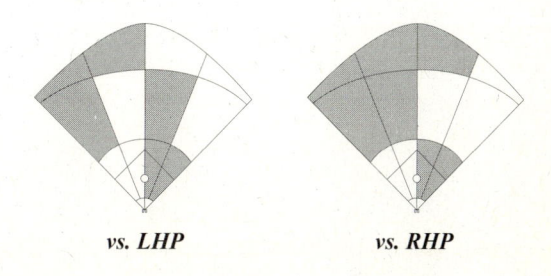

vs. LHP | vs. RHP

BOSTON RED SOX

TIM WAKEFIELD

Position: SP
Bats: R **Throws:** R
Ht: 6'2" **Wt:** 195
Opening Day Age: 29
Born: 8/2/1966
Drafted: PIT88 8/200
ML Seasons: 3

SCOUTING REPORT

Wakefield throws his knuckleball at two slightly different speeds, making the pitch even more baffling for batters. Both of the knucklers rate as plus pitches. He has a nothing curve he throws to cause additional mental anguish, and a straight ball (too slow to be a fastball) he uses when he needs a strike. This non-fastball, a minus pitch, is much more effective when the knuckler is working.

Tim's fielding is a bit below average. Considering he has an interminable delivery and most of his pitches couldn't break a pane of glass, Wakefield did a remarkable job controlling the opposition running game: 21 runners tried to steal against him but just 13 were successful.

HOW HE PERFORMED IN '95

Tim was the other compelling human interest story of last season. He didn't come from Japan and lead the NL in strikeouts, but he did resurface from minor-league obscurity, rescue an injured Red Sox' pitching staff in May, rack up a 14-1 record and 1.65 ERA through mid-August, and then suddenly lose his touch to go 2-7 the rest of the season. Quite a year.

Wakefield's long hot streak is amazing considering just how delicate that touch must be. Throwing a live knuckleball is not enough: it has to be thrown for strikes. For a knuckler to be a strike it has to move late; too much movement makes it a ball. Too little movement makes it a bleacher souvenir. Wakefield managed this balancing act for his first 17 starts. When he got behind in the count he threw his fastball to get a strike. He had luck with this pitch during his streak and, when the knuckler was working, he did not have to throw his fastball very often.

As August went on, however, Wakefield began to have trouble getting the knuckler over. Batters learned to take a couple of balls and hammer the "get-me-over" pitch. Tim led the staff in home runs allowed and his ERA nearly doubled in the final six weeks.

WHAT TO EXPECT IN '96

The future depends on whether Wakefield can get the genie back into the bottle. He's being mentored by the Niekro brothers, but only he can actually throw strikes. If he can't do it, Pawtucket beckons. Tim is likely to have more good times, and more bad times, before he's through.

Overall Statistics

	G	GS	GF	SV	W	L	ERA	IP	H	R	ER	HR	BB	SO
95 BOS	27	27	0	0	16	8	2.95	195.1	163	76	64	22	68	119
Career	64	60	1	0	30	20	3.59	415.2	384	185	166	39	178	229

1995 Situational Statistics

	W	L	ERA	SV	IP	BB	SO		AB	HR	RBI	BA	OBA	SLG
Home	8	4	2.90	0	93.0	27	60	LHB	373	13	35	.239	.304	.405
Road	8	4	2.99	0	102.1	41	59	RHB	344	9	32	.215	.295	.334
Apr-Jun	5	1	1.61	0	61.1	16	35	ScPos	160	5	45	.181	.246	.306
Jul-Oct	11	7	3.56	0	134.0	52	84	Clutch	68	1	4	.235	.325	.309

How He Compares to Other Pitchers

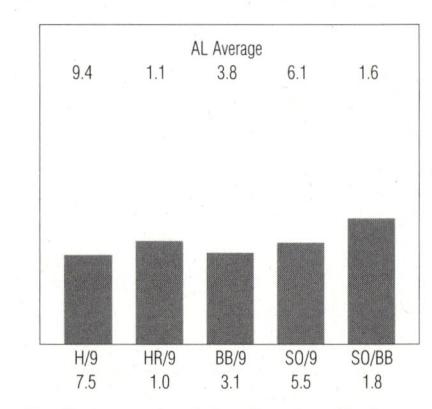

AL Average
9.4 1.1 3.8 6.1 1.6

H/9 HR/9 BB/9 SO/9 SO/BB
7.5 1.0 3.1 5.5 1.8

How He Compares to Other Starting Pitchers

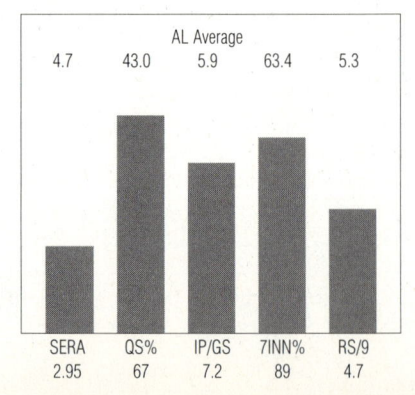

AL Average
4.7 43.0 5.9 63.4 5.3

SERA QS% IP/GS 7INN% RS/9
2.95 67 7.2 89 4.7

BOSTON RED SOX

STAN BELINDA

Position: RP
Bats: R **Throws:** R
Ht: 6'3" **Wt:** 185
Opening Day Age: 29
Born: 8/6/1966
Drafted: PIT86 10/238
ML Seasons: 7

Overall Statistics

	G	GS	GF	SV	W	L	ERA	IP	H	R	ER	HR	BB	SO
95 BOS	63	0	30	10	8	1	3.10	69.2	51	25	24	5	28	57
Career	345	0	182	72	30	19	3.70	406.2	332	179	167	39	164	342

1995 Situational Statistics

	W	L	ERA	SV	IP	BB	SO		AB	HR	RBI	BA	OBA	SLG
Home	5	0	2.91	3	43.1	20	32	LHB	111	3	12	.207	.308	.333
Road	3	1	3.42	7	26.1	8	25	RHB	138	2	21	.203	.277	.297
Apr-Jun	5	0	2.06	5	35.0	11	28	ScPos	77	2	29	.273	.348	.403
Jul-Oct	3	1	4.15	5	34.2	17	29	Clutch	188	4	30	.223	.306	.335

SCOUTING REPORT

Belinda's almost-sidearm delivery is effective against batters on both sides of the plate. He has three above-average pitches: a fastball which he can run in on righties, a big curveball, and a quick slider. He also uses a splitter, which is less formidable. His mastery of these pitches is not consistent, and he has occasional bad outings.

Just three runners tried to steal bases with Belinda pitching, two successfully. His fielding is average.

HOW HE PERFORMED IN '95

Belinda made a strong comeback this year. While he's not capable of closing, Stan excelled as a set-up pitcher for Rick Aguilera after the latter's acquisition, pitching the seventh or eighth inning. He was Kevin Kennedy's top situational righty reliever all year.

A key to his success was not giving in to hitters when behind in the count. Belinda allowed more walks this way, especially to lefthanders, but held opponents on both sides of the plate to low averages.

WHAT TO EXPECT IN '96

There's no reason to expect Stan's role to change. He should again play a strong supporting role to whomever is the Boston closer.

RHEAL CORMIER

Position: RP/SP
Bats: L **Throws:** L
Ht: 5'10" **Wt:** 185
Opening Day Age: 28
Born: 4/23/1967
Drafted: SL88 8/158
ML Seasons: 5

Overall Statistics

	G	GS	GF	SV	W	L	ERA	IP	H	R	ER	HR	BB	SO
95 BOS	48	12	3	0	7	5	4.07	115.0	131	60	52	12	31	69
Career	135	80	9	0	31	28	4.11	553.2	602	282	253	56	106	325

1995 Situational Statistics

	W	L	ERA	SV	IP	BB	SO		AB	HR	RBI	BA	OBA	SLG
Home	4	4	4.60	0	58.2	15	36	LHB	108	1	9	.259	.316	.352
Road	3	1	3.51	0	56.1	16	33	RHB	338	11	44	.305	.351	.462
Apr-Jun	3	1	4.01	0	42.2	12	24	ScPos	108	2	34	.250	.314	.361
Jul-Oct	4	4	4.11	0	72.1	19	45	Clutch	85	0	5	.259	.292	.271

SCOUTING REPORT

Cormier throws from high three quarters, delivering a slightly below-average fastball that tails and sinks. He will also turn it over for extra effect. Rheal also throws a hittable soft slider and a utility-grade change-up. Lacking both velocity and a good breaking ball, Cormier must have pinpoint control to survive for any length of time as a big leaguer.

Rheal is average at holding runners and in fielding his position. Three of five enemy basestealing attempts were successful against Cormier in '95.

HOW HE PERFORMED IN '95

The Boston bullpen was thin on southpaws early in the season, and Cormier enjoyed success as the club's best gambit against key opposition left-handed batters in the first half.

As the Red Sox picked up more portsided hurlers later in the season, Rheal's job assignment changed to spot starter-middle reliever. He was a failure in both roles and ended the season on a down note.

WHAT TO EXPECT IN '96

Cormier should be successful if a club uses him properly. He seems to thrive when utilized in short bursts and loses effectiveness after going once through the lineup.

BOSTON RED SOX

CHRIS DONNELS

Positions: 3B//1B/2B
Bats: L **Throws:** R
Ht: 6'0" **Wt:** 185
Opening Day Age: 29
Born: 4/21/1966
Drafted: NYN87 1/24
ML Seasons: 5

Overall Statistics

	G	AB	R	H	2B	3B	HR	RBI	SB	CS	BB	SO	BA	OBA
95 HOU/BOS	59	121	17	32	2	2	2	13	0	0	12	24	.264	.328
Career	283	596	62	142	27	4	7	53	5	1	75	119	.238	.322

1995 Situational Statistics

	AB	HR	RBI	BA	OBA	SLG		AB	HR	RBI	BA	OBA	SLG
Home	72	0	6	.236	.300	.292	LHP	18	1	1	.111	.200	.278
Road	49	2	7	.306	.370	.469	RHP	103	1	12	.291	.351	.379
Apr-Jun	50	1	4	.200	.255	.260	ScPos	31	0	11	.258	.333	.323
Jul-Oct	71	1	9	.310	.380	.437	Clutch	25	0	3	.240	.310	.320

SCOUTING REPORT

Chris is a patient hitter who will hit high pitches from righthanders with some power, but is really a line-drive specialist who has to be platooned. He is a minus runner.

He plays first and third base with average tools all around. He was used a few years ago at second base, but Donnels lacks the mobility to cut it there.

HOW HE PERFORMED IN '95

The Red Sox picked up Donnels to back up the infield cornermen and add lefty hitting off the bench. He had one hit in his first 20 AL at-bats, but improved in the second half. Most of his playing time came filling in for Tim Naehring at third base.

Donnels continued his career trend as a straight platoon batter, with little success against lefthanders. He's tolerable in the field, making the routine plays but not adding much more.

WHAT TO EXPECT IN '96

Chris is a proven bench player who can hit righthanders, and will find a job in '96 with some big-league team looking for a low-cost backup.

VAUGHN ESHELMAN

Position: SP/RP
Bats: L **Throws:** L
Ht: 6'3" **Wt:** 205
Opening Day Age: 26
Born: 5/22/1969
Drafted: BAL91 4/108
ML Seasons: 1

Overall Statistics

	G	GS	GF	SV	W	L	ERA	IP	H	R	ER	HR	BB	SO
95 BOS	23	14	4	0	6	3	4.85	81.2	86	47	44	3	36	41
Career	23	14	4	0	6	3	4.85	81.2	86	47	44	3	36	41

1995 Situational Statistics

	W	L	ERA	SV	IP	BB	SO		AB	HR	RBI	BA	OBA	SLG
Home	2	0	4.95	0	36.1	20	20	LHB	49	0	5	.367	.436	.490
Road	4	3	4.76	0	45.1	16	21	RHB	267	3	33	.255	.329	.356
Apr-Jun	3	2	6.43	0	42.0	23	23	ScPos	71	2	36	.324	.370	.479
Jul-Oct	3	1	3.18	0	39.2	13	18	Clutch	11	0	0	.273	.333	.273

SCOUTING REPORT

Eshelman has a good three-quarter motion, average control, and a good arsenal for a lefthander. The curve is the basis of Vaughn's game. When he gets the bender to work, it's plus, but results were mixed in '95. His fastball is below-average, so the curve's behavior is crucial. An average change-up compliments his two main pitches. Eshelman's fielding is acceptable and he held runners quite well for a rookie last season. Only two tried to steal against him last year, and both were nabbed.

HOW HE PERFORMED IN '95

Eshelman looked like the steal of the year in early May. The Rule V pick from Baltimore won his first three starts in dominating fashion. Unfortunately, control troubles made the middle of the season a washout, as he lost his spot in the starting rotation. Boston hid him on the DL and then shunted him to the bullpen. Vaughn got somewhat straightened out in August and became a spot starter, used in short appearances with decent if unspectacular results.

WHAT TO EXPECT IN '96

Vaughn will get another chance with the Red Sox this year to join the starting rotation. He'll need to improve to keep the job, however.

BOSTON RED SOX

BILL HASELMAN

Positions: C/DH//1B/3B
Bats: R **Throws:** R
Ht: 6'3" **Wt:** 205
Opening Day Age: 29
Born: 5/25/1966
Drafted: TEX87 2/23
ML Seasons: 5

Overall Statistics

	G	AB	R	H	2B	3B	HR	RBI	SB	CS	BB	SO	BA	OBA
95 BOS	64	152	22	37	6	1	5	23	0	2	17	30	.243	.322
Career	175	404	55	95	21	2	11	50	3	3	33	72	.235	.296

1995 Situational Statistics

	AB	HR	RBI	BA	OBA	SLG		AB	HR	RBI	BA	OBA	SLG
Home	73	3	10	.247	.341	.397	LHP	42	0	5	.238	.365	.286
Road	79	2	13	.241	.303	.392	RHP	110	5	18	.245	.303	.436
Apr-Jun	51	1	6	.294	.361	.392	ScPos	42	2	18	.262	.393	.429
Jul-Oct	101	4	17	.218	.301	.396	Clutch	23	2	3	.261	.333	.522

SCOUTING REPORT

Haselman is a decent hitter. Standing deep in the box, he wraps the bat to generate power. He likes pitches high and over the plate, extending his arms and using his good bat speed.

Bill is fast for a catcher (meaning that he is almost an average runner) and at times pinch-ran for Mike Macfarlane. He possesses an average arm that is erratic at times, throwing out just seven of 27 attempted basestealers in 1995. His hands are average-minus.

HOW HE PERFORMED IN '95

Haselman is a fine backup catcher. He's competent behind the plate and a respectable offensive player, and filled the DH spot eleven times last season. While he's probably not going to be a regular, Bill has power, will take the walk, and hangs in against righthanders.

Bill was underutilized in the early part of the year, but got more playing time as as the season progressed and management discovered his positive qualities.

WHAT TO EXPECT IN '96

Haselman is expected back with the Red Sox in the same role and will likely get around 150 at-bats again.

DAVE HOLLINS

Positions: 1B//DH/OF
Bats: B **Throws:** R
Ht: 6'1" **Wt:** 195
Opening Day Age: 29
Born: 5/25/1966
Drafted: SD87 6/146
ML Seasons: 6

Overall Statistics

	G	AB	R	H	2B	3B	HR	RBI	SB	CS	BB	SO	BA	OBA
95 PHI/BOS	70	218	48	49	12	2	7	26	1	1	57	45	.225	.391
Career	541	1774	316	457	87	13	67	274	14	11	268	350	.258	.363

1995 Situational Statistics

	AB	HR	RBI	BA	OBA	SLG		AB	HR	RBI	BA	OBA	SLG
Home	105	5	13	.181	.326	.362	LHP	67	3	4	.254	.425	.478
Road	113	2	13	.265	.445	.425	RHP	151	4	22	.212	.376	.358
Apr-Jun	149	4	18	.248	.414	.396	ScPos	64	1	18	.188	.349	.266
Jul-Oct	69	3	8	.174	.337	.391	Clutch	36	1	3	.139	.262	.222

SCOUTING REPORT

Once a starter with plus power from the left side of the plate, an inability to swing hard has made those long balls mostly a memory. He is patient and will often get plunked to reach base.

An average but smart runner, Dave has a strong but famously wild throwing arm at third. He is now only capable of playing a mediocre first base, which he's still learning.

HOW HE PERFORMED IN '95

Trading Mark Whiten for Hollins was one of Dan Duquette's only '95 deals that didn't pay off. While Whiten hit well for Philadelphia, Dave arrived in with a recurring hamate bone problems that ended his year after only five games in Sox' garb. The lingering problem has hampered Hollins' ability for two years.

WHAT TO EXPECT IN '96

Signed by the Twins over the winter, Hollins is expected to be 100% to start this season. It remains to be seen how much of Dave's decline was due to the diabetic condition discovered in '95. It's not a good sign that the power-strapped Phillies had deemed him unnecessary, but the hustling, hard-driving Hollins could have a surprise in store.

THE SCOUTING REPORT: 1996

BOSTON RED SOX

DWAYNE HOSEY

Positions: OF//DH
Bats: B **Throws:** R
Ht: 5'10" **Wt:** 175
Opening Day Age: 29
Born: 3/11/1967
Drafted: CHA87 13/323
ML Seasons: 1

Overall Statistics

	G	AB	R	H	2B	3B	HR	RBI	SB	CS	BB	SO	BA	OBA
95 BOS	24	68	20	23	8	1	3	7	6	0	8	16	.338	.408
Career	24	68	20	23	8	1	3	7	6	0	8	16	.338	.408

1995 Situational Statistics

	AB	HR	RBI	BA	OBA	SLG		AB	HR	RBI	BA	OBA	SLG
Home	33	1	3	.303	.395	.515	LHP	25	1	3	.400	.464	.720
Road	35	2	4	.371	.421	.714	RHP	43	2	4	.302	.375	.558
Apr-Jun	0	0	0	.000	.000	.000	ScPos	15	0	3	.200	.250	.267
Jul-Oct	68	3	7	.338	.408	.618	Clutch	6	0	0	.500	.571	.667

SCOUTING REPORT

The switch-hitting Hosey likes low pitches left-handed, but tends to pull off the ball. From the right side, he attacks high pitches. Using a closed stance, he wraps his bat, which tends to slow it down and negate his power. He is a slightly above-average runner, but Dwayne was not a good basestealer in the minors.

His defense is good enough for center field, with good range, average hands, average accuracy and slightly below-average arm strength.

HOW HE PERFORMED IN '95

Unable to break into the majors despite strong performances in Triple-A, Hosey finally made it last season. Claimed on waivers from the Royals August 31, Dwayne made 15 starts in center and one more in right, hitting the tar out of the ball and helping the BoSox win the East. Though Hosey threw out just one runner last year, he patrolled center field like a gazelle.

WHAT TO EXPECT IN '96

Hosey was weighing a winter offer to play in Japan, but decided to stay with the Red Sox. He could win the center field job this spring, but most scouts feel he projects as a fourth outfielder.

JOE HUDSON

Position: RP
Bats: R **Throws:** R
Ht: 6'1" **Wt:** 175
Opening Day Age: 25
Born: 9/29/1970
Drafted: BOS92 26/758
ML Seasons: 1

Overall Statistics

	G	GS	GF	SV	W	L	ERA	IP	H	R	ER	HR	BB	SO
95 BOS	39	0	11	1	0	1	4.11	46.0	53	21	21	2	23	29
Career	39	0	11	1	0	1	4.11	46.0	53	21	21	2	23	29

1995 Situational Statistics

	W	L	ERA	SV	IP	BB	SO		AB	HR	RBI	BA	OBA	SLG
Home	0	0	1.95	1	27.2	11	17	LHB	71	1	14	.324	.424	.423
Road	0	1	7.36	0	18.1	12	12	RHB	105	1	14	.286	.359	.352
Apr-Jun	0	0	6.35	0	5.2	2	4	ScPos	60	1	26	.333	.431	.433
Jul-Oct	0	1	3.79	1	40.1	21	25	Clutch	55	1	5	.309	.387	.400

SCOUTING REPORT

Joe uses a deceptive, three-quarter to low three-quarter motion, and hides the ball well, partly due to a hook in his delivery. He mixes an average-plus sinker with a very hard, plus slider. Hudson is developing a change as well, but it needs work. A fast worker, he lacks rhythm and consistency and is just fair in the field. Three men tried to steal against him, two successfully.

HOW HE PERFORMED IN '95

Hudson, a rookie in his fourth pro season, came to the Red Sox bullpen pretty green. He was immediately tested by being used in pressure situations. Despite spotty results, the sinkerballer was used extensively as a late-inning "hold" specialist. He seemed to grow into the role for awhile, but then struggled with control and had an awful September.

WHAT TO EXPECT IN '96

Joe will be back in the Sox bullpen. He needs to have excellent pitch placement to be effective, since he is a pure lowballer. If he can put the ball where he wants it consistently, he'll be a late-inning man again.

BOSTON RED SOX

CHRIS JAMES

Positions: DH/OF//2B
Bats: R **Throws:** R
Ht: 6'1" **Wt:** 195
Opening Day Age: 33
Born: 10/4/1962
Drafted: PHI 10/30/81
ML Seasons: 10

Overall Statistics

	G	AB	R	H	2B	3B	HR	RBI	SB	CS	BB	SO	BA	OBA
95 KC/BOS	42	82	8	22	4	0	2	8	1	0	7	14	.268	.326
Career	946	3040	343	794	145	24	90	386	27	17	193	490	.261	.307

1995 Situational Statistics

	AB	HR	RBI	BA	OBA	SLG		AB	HR	RBI	BA	OBA	SLG
Home	39	0	5	.256	.318	.282	LHP	62	1	7	.290	.352	.403
Road	43	2	3	.279	.333	.488	RHP	20	1	1	.200	.238	.350
Apr-Jun	4	0	0	.250	.250	.250	ScPos	15	0	6	.267	.435	.267
Jul-Oct	78	2	8	.269	.330	.397	Clutch	14	0	0	.286	.333	.286

SCOUTING REPORT
A minus runner with below-average tools in the outfield, Chris appears to be strictly a DH at this point. He is a good fastball hitter, especially when the pitch is up and over the plate, but breaking balls still fool James. When he makes contact, Chris hits the ball sharply. He does not bunt.

HOW HE PERFORMED IN '95
Boston fans questioned why the club would pick up a marginal veteran like James, let alone play him. The explanation is the old-boy network, New England-via-Texas-style: in a spot role, Chris hit seven homers in 133 at-bats for Kevin Kennedy in '94 when he managed the Rangers.

It's hard to see how James has hung around for so long; he can hit lefthanders a little, but can't run and is too slow to play the outfield. There are plenty of guys like this.

WHAT TO EXPECT IN '96
James no longer belongs on the roster of a contending team, unless he is viewed as a player-coach. He should demonstrate this fact pretty early in the '96 season.

REGGIE JEFFERSON

Positions: DH//1B/OF
Bats: B **Throws:** L
Ht: 6'4" **Wt:** 210
Opening Day Age: 27
Born: 9/25/1968
Drafted: CIN86 3/72
ML Seasons: 5

Overall Statistics

	G	AB	R	H	2B	3B	HR	RBI	SB	CS	BB	SO	BA	OBA
95 BOS	46	121	21	35	8	0	5	26	0	0	9	24	.289	.333
Career	277	846	99	230	39	4	27	111	1	3	59	175	.272	.323

1995 Situational Statistics

	AB	HR	RBI	BA	OBA	SLG		AB	HR	RBI	BA	OBA	SLG
Home	42	1	10	.333	.396	.500	LHP	7	0	0	.286	.375	.286
Road	79	4	16	.266	.298	.468	RHP	114	5	26	.289	.331	.491
Apr-Jun	94	4	20	.287	.330	.479	ScPos	34	3	21	.353	.400	.706
Jul-Oct	27	1	6	.296	.345	.481	Clutch	13	0	1	.154	.200	.154

SCOUTING REPORT
A sharp swinger against righthanders, Reggie has power but is susceptible to breaking balls. He does not walk often. Although he is nominally a switch-hitter, Jefferson is so weak against lefties that he rarely sees them. He is very slow and does not steal or bunt.

He is best suited for designated hitting due to below-average defensive skills, but Reggie can play first base when needed.

HOW HE PERFORMED IN '95
Jefferson served as the Red Sox' first lefthanded bat off the bench and also assumed some spot DH duties. He was a real asset when he was available. Unfortunately, Reggie missed two months of the season with injuries and the club never did find a solid replacement. When he came back in mid-September, he easily hit his way past weak competition and made the postseason roster.

WHAT TO EXPECT IN '96
After proving his value as a role player last year, Jefferson should do well in '96 as a platoon DH and pinch-hitter. Though only 27, full-time work is not in his future.

THE SCOUTING REPORT: 1996

BOSTON RED SOX

MIKE MADDUX

Position: RP
Bats: L **Throws:** R
Ht: 6'2" **Wt:** 180
Opening Day Age: 34
Born: 8/27/1961
Drafted: PHI82 5/119
ML Seasons: 10

Overall Statistics

	G	GS	GF	SV	W	L	ERA	IP	H	R	ER	HR	BB	SO
95 PIT/BOS	44	4	7	1	5	1	4.10	98.2	100	49	45	5	18	69
Career	318	41	99	19	29	28	3.87	644.0	633	309	277	39	200	430

1995 Situational Statistics

	W	L	ERA	SV	IP	BB	SO		AB	HR	RBI	BA	OBA	SLG
Home	2	1	3.57	0	40.1	7	22	LHB	183	2	23	.295	.333	.432
Road	3	0	4.47	1	58.1	11	47	RHB	204	3	27	.225	.258	.338
Apr-Jun	2	1	5.23	0	31.0	7	22	ScPos	121	3	45	.273	.315	.438
Jul-Oct	3	0	3.59	1	67.2	11	47	Clutch	37	0	3	.324	.359	.486

SCOUTING REPORT
Maddux succeeds with finesse and deception. For finesse, he uses a slightly below-average fastball, which bores in on righthanders, and an average slider that sometimes flattens out and gets hammered. Mike's plus change-up benefits from fine arm action that deceives hitters and induces groundouts. He works quickly from three-quarters and is tough when ahead in the count. He is an average fielder with an average-minus move to first, and nine baserunners stole against Maddux in 12 tries.

HOW HE PERFORMED IN '95
Released by Pittsburgh in May, Maddux revived his career by sliding comfortably into long relief with the Red Sox. He was tough on righthanders, showing superb control. His walk rate was the lowest on the club, and he got ground balls consistently. His biggest problem was reduced effectiveness pitching from the stretch; Mike was quite hittable with men on base. This tendency pushed Maddux from middle relief to his long role.

WHAT TO EXPECT IN '96
Look for Mike to resume his 1995 position in long relief. He doesn't have the stamina to win a job in the rotation, but he can deliver a consistent three or four innings.

WILLIE MCGEE

Position: OF
Bats: B **Throws:** R
Ht: 6'1" **Wt:** 175
Opening Day Age: 37
Born: 11/2/1958
Drafted: NYA77* S1/15
ML Seasons: 14

Overall Statistics

	G	AB	R	H	2B	3B	HR	RBI	SB	CS	BB	SO	BA	OBA
95 BOS	67	200	32	57	11	3	2	15	5	2	9	41	.285	.311
Career	1704	6500	877	1933	299	87	68	723	325	111	377	1010	.297	.335

1995 Situational Statistics

	AB	HR	RBI	BA	OBA	SLG		AB	HR	RBI	BA	OBA	SLG
Home	105	1	8	.286	.315	.400	LHP	85	2	9	.341	.352	.529
Road	95	1	7	.284	.307	.400	RHP	115	0	6	.243	.281	.304
Apr-Jun	0	0	0	.000	.000	.000	ScPos	48	0	12	.208	.226	.271
Jul-Oct	200	2	15	.285	.311	.400	Clutch	25	1	2	.280	.296	.440

SCOUTING REPORT
McGee's declining skills are obvious: he now strikes out a lot and has no better than average speed or arm strength. At the plate, he still looks for low balls batting left and high balls while batting right. He remains a good bunter, especially in sacrifice situations. Willie has good hands in the outfield but has lost some of his formerly plus range.

HOW HE PERFORMED IN '95
The veteran outfielder returned from a serious achilles tendon injury for a decent half-season in Boston. He had lost too much speed to be an effective center fielder, and didn't hit righthanded pitching well. Willie continued to hit lefthanders, however.

The heel injury hurt McGee's offense as well as his defense. He ran hard but couldn't steal bases or beat out infield hits. This, combined with his walk total, made him a marginal offensive performer.

WHAT TO EXPECT IN '96
The Red Sox like Willie's attitude and said they wanted him back as a coach. Unless he tries to hang on in a minor role with another club, his playing days appear to be over.

BOSTON RED SOX

KEN RYAN

Position: RP
Bats: R **Throws:** R
Ht: 6'3" **Wt:** 200
Opening Day Age: 27
Born: 10/24/1968
Drafted: BOS 6/16/86
ML Seasons: 4

Overall Statistics

	G	GS	GF	SV	W	L	ERA	IP	H	R	ER	HR	BB	SO
95 BOS	28	0	20	7	0	4	4.96	32.2	34	20	18	4	24	34
Career	124	0	78	22	9	9	3.66	137.2	127	62	56	9	75	120

1995 Situational Statistics

	W	L	ERA	SV	IP	BB	SO		AB	HR	RBI	BA	OBA	SLG
Home	0	2	8.31	3	17.1	14	19	LHB	66	1	11	.258	.395	.333
Road	0	2	1.17	4	15.1	10	15	RHB	61	3	8	.279	.380	.475
Apr-Jun	0	4	4.97	7	29.0	23	32	ScPos	41	1	15	.268	.423	.390
Jul-Oct	0	0	4.91	0	3.2	1	2	Clutch	76	4	13	.289	.419	.474

SCOUTING REPORT
A plus fastball isn't enough in the major leagues if it doesn't have some movement, and Ken's heater is often too straight. He has a plus curve and an average slider, but he has mastered neither the art of pitching nor his control yet.

Basestealers were 4-for-4 against Ken in '95, indicating no improvement from his poor record in this area; he is not good with the glove off the hill, either.

HOW HE PERFORMED IN '95
Ryan opened the season as Boston's closer, but was shelled back to the minors after two nightmarish months. Ryan didn't adjust well to the pressure of closing games—he often seemed to tense up and overthrow everything, especially high in the strike zone. He'd get behind in the count and either walk the hitter or throw a fat pitch attempting to get a strike.

WHAT TO EXPECT IN '96
The Red Sox are close to giving up on Ryan, who had such great promise just a year ago. He may well be traded before the season—and a fresh start may be just what Ken needs to realize his potential.

AARON SELE

Position: SP
Bats: R **Throws:** R
Ht: 6'5" **Wt:** 205
Opening Day Age: 25
Born: 6/25/1970
Drafted: BOS91 1/23
ML Seasons: 3

Overall Statistics

	G	GS	GF	SV	W	L	ERA	IP	H	R	ER	HR	BB	SO
95 BOS	6	6	0	0	3	1	3.06	32.1	32	14	11	3	14	21
Career	46	46	0	0	18	10	3.32	287.1	272	124	106	21	122	219

1995 Situational Statistics

	W	L	ERA	SV	IP	BB	SO		AB	HR	RBI	BA	OBA	SLG
Home	1	1	2.25	0	12.0	3	9	LHB	60	2	5	.317	.408	.517
Road	2	0	3.54	0	20.1	11	12	RHB	67	1	5	.194	.270	.254
Apr-Jun	3	1	3.06	0	32.1	14	21	ScPos	33	0	7	.152	.275	.152
Jul-Oct	0	0	0.00	0	0.0	0	0	Clutch	0	0	0	.000	.000	.000

SCOUTING REPORT
The young righthander delivers an average sinking fastball, a plus curve and slow curve, and a plus change-up from overhand. Because of his motion, his curves drop straight down, freezing hitters. He knows how to pitch and moves the ball around well.

Only one runner tried to steal against Aaron last year, as he is unusually hard to run on for a big righty. He made three miscues as a fielder in just ten chances, continuing his spotty fielding record.

HOW HE PERFORMED IN '95
After a promising '94, Sele had a lost season in 1995. He went down on May 23 with tendinitis in his pitching shoulder and never recovered despite season-long rehabilitation. In September, the club gave up on the rehab, sent Aaron home, and told him to rest the shoulder.

WHAT TO EXPECT IN '96
The lack of improvement over the summer makes Aaron's prospects for this season questionable. It's unlikely Sele will be part of the rotation in April. However, he's young enough and doesn't depend on overpowering hitters to be successful, so the long-term prognosis should be good.

BOSTON RED SOX

ZANE SMITH

Position: SP
Bats: L **Throws:** L
Ht: 6'2" **Wt:** 195
Opening Day Age: 35
Born: 12/28/1960
Drafted: ATL82 3/63
ML Seasons: 12

Overall Statistics

	G	GS	GF	SV	W	L	ERA	IP	H	R	ER	HR	BB	SO
95 BOS	24	21	0	0	8	8	5.61	110.2	144	78	69	7	23	47
Career	344	275	16	3	96	109	3.68	1836.0	1876	880	751	115	562	964

1995 Situational Statistics

	W	L	ERA	SV	IP	BB	SO		AB	HR	RBI	BA	OBA	SLG
Home	5	3	4.39	0	67.2	14	28	LHB	73	0	17	.342	.347	.452
Road	3	5	7.53	0	43.0	9	19	RHB	382	7	49	.312	.347	.432
Apr-Jun	2	4	4.72	0	53.1	11	22	ScPos	120	1	57	.350	.394	.475
Jul-Oct	6	4	6.44	0	57.1	12	25	Clutch	10	0	1	.100	.100	.100

SCOUTING REPORT

Smith still throws an average-plus splitter and change, but his curve has flattened out and his signature pitch, a sinking fastball, is now of batting-practice quality. Zane knows how to pitch but no longer has a big-league arm. He throws from a low three-quarter angle with average control, without the bite his pitches once had. Nine of 13 bases-tealing attempts were successful against Smith, who has an average-minus move to first and is slow to the plate. His fielding is below-average.

HOW HE PERFORMED IN '95

Zane, Boston's projected fifth starter, gave up plenty of line drives last summer despite his reputation as a ground-ball specialist. He got pounded all year and ended with the highest ERA of any regular Red Sox pitcher. The only reason he didn't walk many batters was because some pitch would get crushed before Smith got far into the count. He served effectively as Boston's argument for four-man pitching rotations.

WHAT TO EXPECT IN '96

Smith's endless chances prove the rule that any formerly successful lefthanded pitcher can find a job. Some desperate club is probably pick him up for '96, hoping to get lucky.

MATT STAIRS

Positions: OF//DH
Bats: L **Throws:** R
Ht: 5'9" **Wt:** 175
Opening Day Age: 28
Born: 2/27/1968
Drafted: MON 1/17/89
ML Seasons: 3

Overall Statistics

	G	AB	R	H	2B	3B	HR	RBI	SB	CS	BB	SO	BA	OBA
95 BOS	39	88	8	23	7	1	1	17	0	1	4	14	.261	.298
Career	58	126	11	31	10	1	1	24	0	1	11	22	.246	.307

1995 Situational Statistics

	AB	HR	RBI	BA	OBA	SLG		AB	HR	RBI	BA	OBA	SLG
Home	45	0	12	.289	.333	.444	LHP	3	0	0	.333	.333	.333
Road	43	1	5	.233	.261	.349	RHP	85	1	17	.259	.297	.400
Apr-Jun	9	0	2	.333	.333	.444	ScPos	31	0	16	.355	.344	.484
Jul-Oct	79	1	15	.253	.294	.392	Clutch	16	1	6	.313	.313	.625

SCOUTING REPORT

Stairs has earned a reputation as a professional hitter. He's confident at the plate, takes good swings, and puts the ball in play. His quick bat can handle low pitches on either side of the strike zone, and Matt has line-drive pull power.

Despite a beer-keg body, Stairs is a tolerable outfielder who compensates somewhat for lack of speed or throwing ability by getting a good jump on the ball. Slow legs make him less than an asset on the basepaths.

HOW HE PERFORMED IN '95

A six-year minor-league veteran, Stairs spent much of '95 with the Red Sox. Used as a backup left fielder and pinch-hitter, Matt hit well the first time around the league but had a rough September. He played more left field than right, showing very poor range at both spots. The Red Sox left Stairs off the postseason roster.

WHAT TO EXPECT IN '96

Matt is a fringe player who must scramble to make the roster and may end up unfairly typecast as a 26th man. He did not show enough last season to count on a job anywhere this year, but he can hit better than a lot of roster fillers.

BOSTON RED SOX

MIKE STANTON

Position: RP
Bats: L **Throws:** L
Ht: 6'1" **Wt:** 190
Opening Day Age: 28
Born: 6/2/1967
Drafted: ATL87 13/324
ML Seasons: 7

Overall Statistics

	G	GS	GF	SV	W	L	ERA	IP	H	R	ER	HR	BB	SO
95 ATL/BOS	48	0	22	1	2	1	4.24	40.1	48	23	19	6	14	23
Career	326	0	135	55	19	21	3.94	310.2	294	155	136	25	122	233

1995 Situational Statistics

	W	L	ERA	SV	IP	BB	SO		AB	HR	RBI	BA	OBA	SLG
Home	1	0	3.80	0	21.1	6	13	LHB	52	0	4	.212	.250	.231
Road	1	1	4.74	1	19.0	8	10	RHB	108	6	24	.343	.408	.574
Apr-Jun	1	1	5.40	0	16.2	6	11	ScPos	49	1	22	.306	.364	.429
Jul-Oct	1	0	3.42	1	23.2	8	12	Clutch	55	3	8	.273	.322	.473

SCOUTING REPORT

Using an overhand short-arm delivery, Stanton brings home a four-seam fastball that is usually quick, but lost some velocity in '95. Mike was out of shape and could not overpower hitters like he needs to. Below-average control and a poor change-up made his fastball's decline really hurt, and Stanton's average slider was not enough to make an effective late-game repertoire. However, he regained some strength late in the year.

He fields and holds runners well. Only two runners tried to steal against him last year, and both were tossed out.

HOW HE PERFORMED IN '95

Stanton was the last of a series of '95 Boston bullpen lefties. Most of these guys had two things in common: they were cheap, and they weren't very good. Mike was the best of the lot. After a poor August, Stanton found himself in September, then had one terrific playoff appearance.

WHAT TO EXPECT IN '96

A strong finish makes an optimistic view of Stanton's prospects for this year reasonable. He still has the potential to be a fine lefthanded set-up pitcher with his high-velocity deliveries if he's strong and in-shape.

THE SCOUTING REPORT: 1996

BOSTON RED SOX: TOP PROSPECTS

SHAYNE BENNETT
Bats: R Throws: R Opening Day Age: 24
Ht: 6-5 Wt: 200 Born: 4/10/1972
Position: P Drafted: 1993 #25 BOS

YR TEAM	LG/CLASS	G	GS	GF	SV	W	L	ERA	IP	H	HR	BB	SO	O/BA
93 Red Sox	GULF/R	2	1	1	1	0	0	1.29	7.0	2	1	1	4	.083
93 Ft.Laudrdle	FSL/A	23	0	18	6	1	2	1.72	31.1	26	1	11	23	.232
94 Sarasota	FSL/A	15	8	4	3	1	6	4.47	48.1	46	1	27	28	.251
95 Trenton	EAST/AA	10	0	6	3	0	1	5.06	10.2	16	0	3	6	.390
95 Sarasota	FSL/A	52	0	43	24	2	5	2.56	59.2	50	3	21	69	.223

In 1995 Bennett emerged as the top closer prospect in the system. He throws a fastball in the low 90's and last year added a nearly unhittable forkball. The 23-year-old Australian was the top Football player in that country and became a dominant force in the Florida State League, saving 24 games. He earned a late promotion to Double-A where one bad outing distorted his ERA. Bennett's 62 appearances ranked fifth in the minors.

BRENT COOKSON
Bats: R Throws: R Opening Day Age: 27
Ht: 5-11 Wt: 200 Born: 9/7/1969
Position: OF Drafted: 1991 #17 OAK

YR TEAM	LG/CLASS	G	AB	R	H	2B	3B	HR	RBI	SB	BA	OBA
93 San Jose	CAL/A	67	234	43	60	10	1	17	50	14	.256	.372
94 Shreveport	TEX/AA	62	207	32	67	21	3	11	41	4	.324	.377
94 Phoenix	PCL/AAA	14	43	7	12	0	1	1	6	0	.279	.367
95 Omaha	AMAS/AAA	40	137	28	55	13	0	4	20	0	.401	.475
95 Phoenix	PCL/AAA	68	210	38	63	9	3	15	46	3	.300	.374
95 Kansas City	AL/MAJ	22	35	2	5	1	0	0	5	1	.143	.189

Boston will be Cookson's fourth organization in his five-year minor league career; this is perhaps due to his fiery temper. Although he is not a great athlete, the Long Beach State product is a professional hitter with power to all fields. The 26-year-old has a .292 career average, and had his best year in 1995. He hit for average and power for Phoenix, then batted over .400 in 40 games for Omaha after being traded to the Royals. His .585 slugging percentage was sixth-best in the minors, and his overall .340 batting average was 11th best.

NOMAR GARCIAPARRA
Bats: R Throws: R Opening Day Age: 23
Ht: 6-1 Wt: 175 Born: 7/23/1973
Position: SS Drafted: 1994 #1 BOS

YR TEAM	LG/CLASS	G	AB	R	H	2B	3B	HR	RBI	SB	BA	OBA
94 Sarasota	FSL/A	28	105	20	31	8	1	1	16	5	.295	.356
95 Trenton	EAST/AA	125	513	77	137	20	8	8	47	35	.267	.338

The former first-round pick from Georgia Tech is Boston's shortstop of the future. Defensively, he is ready for the major leagues right now. He has outstanding range, soft hands and a good arm, drawing comparisons to Mark Belanger. Offensively, the 22-year-old is a contact hitter with good power to right center field. He is also an outstanding baserunner, swiping a Trenton franchise-record 35 bases in '95. In addition to his physical skills, he is also intelligent and has good baseball instincts.

DAVID GIBRALTER
Bats: R Throws: R Opening Day Age: 20
Ht: 6-3 Wt: 215 Born: 6/19/1975
Position: 1B Drafted: 1993 #7 BOS

YR TEAM	LG/CLASS	G	AB	R	H	2B	3B	HR	RBI	SB	BA	OBA
95 Michigan	MID/A	121	456	48	115	34	1	16	82	3	.252	.293

The former first-round pick from Georgia Tech is Boston's shortstop of the future. Defensively, he is ready for the major leagues right now. His outstanding range, soft hands, and good arm draw comparisons to those of Mark Belanger. Offensively, the 22-year-old is a contact hitter with good power to right-center. He is also an outstanding baserunner, swiping a Trenton franchise record 35 bases in '95. He has physical skills, intelligence, and good baseball instincts.

JOSE MALAVE
Bats: R Throws: R Opening Day Age: 25
Ht: 6-2 Wt: 195 Born: 5/31/1971
Position: OF Drafted: NDFA 8-2-89 BOS

YR TEAM	LG/CLASS	G	AB	R	H	2B	3B	HR	RBI	SB	BA	OBA
93 Lynchburg	CARO/A	82	312	42	94	27	1	8	54	2	.301	.374
94 New Britain	EAST/AA	122	465	87	139	37	7	24	92	4	.299	.369
95 Pawtucket	INT/AAA	91	318	55	86	12	1	23	57	0	.270	.337

An outstanding 1994 season (capped by a selection to Howe Sportsdata's Minor League All-Star team) established Malave as the top hitting prospect in the organization. A career .295 hitter, the Venezuelan native has a quick bat and strong hands and is equally adept at hitting fastballs and breaking balls. Due to a bad elbow and poor conditioning, Malave didn't play until May, but made up for lost time by slamming 19 of his 23 homers after July 1st, finishing third in the International League in round-trippers. However, he took advantage of the league's best hitters' park at Pawtucket, batting .327 with 15 home runs there. As a left fielder, Malave has a good arm, but occasionally misjudges fly falls.

RYAN McGUIRE
Bats: L Throws: L Opening Day Age: 24
Ht: 6-1 Wt: 195 Born: 11/23/1971
Position: 1B Drafted: 1993 #3 BOS

YR TEAM	LG/CLASS	G	AB	R	H	2B	3B	HR	RBI	SB	BA	OBA
93 Ft.Laudrdle	FSL/A	58	213	23	69	12	2	4	38	2	.324	.400
94 Lynchburg	CARO/A	137	489	70	133	29	0	10	73	10	.272	.371
95 Trenton	EAST/AA	109	414	59	138	29	1	7	59	11	.333	.414

The former UCLA All-American, who spent the first half of the '95 season in left field because of logjam at first base, has been likened to a young Don Mattingly. McGuire, a line-drive contact hitter, is excellent defensively. He has hit .305 over his three-year career with more walks than strikeouts and some feel that the organization's sweetest swing will develop more power in the future. The 23-year-old, who finished second in the Eastern League in batting, was the league's Player of the Month in July. He also hit .391 in the playoffs.

BOSTON RED SOX: TOP PROSPECTS

GLENN MURRAY

Bats: R Throws: R Opening Day Age: 25
Ht: 6-2 Wt: 200 Born: 11/23/1970
Position: OF Drafted: 1989 #2 MON

YR TEAM	LG/CLASS	G	AB	R	H	2B	3B	HR	RBI	SB	BA	OBA
93 Harrisburg	EAST/AA	127	475	82	120	21	4	26	96	16	.253	.340
94 Pawtucket	INT/AAA	130	465	74	104	17	1	25	64	9	.224	.310
95 Pawtucket	INT/AAA	104	336	66	82	15	0	25	66	5	.244	.329

Murray is the best pure power hitter in the system, clubbing 76 homers over the last three years. He also has excellent speed, although his stolen base totals have dropped each of the last four years. The 24-year-old led the International League in HR/AB ratio (1/13.44) last year and placed second with 25 homers despite missing some time with a wrist injury, but did hit 15 of his homers at hitter-friendly McCoy Stadium. Murray isn't in the majors yet due to a .234 career average and 100-plus strikeouts in each of the last five years.

MATT MURRAY

Bats: L Throws: R Opening Day Age: 26
Ht: 6-6 Wt: 235 Born: 9/26/1970
Position: P Drafted: 1988 #3 ATL

YR TEAM	LG/CLASS	G	GS	GF	SV	W	L	ERA	IP	H	HR	BB	SO	O/BA
93 Macon	SAL/A	15	15	0	0	7	3	1.83	83.2	70	3	27	77	.229
94 Durham	CARO/A	15	15	0	0	6	7	3.79	97.1	93	20	22	76	.253
94 Greenville	SOU/AA	12	12	0	0	3	4	5.08	67.1	89	7	31	48	.322
95 Richmond	INT/AAA	19	19	0	0	10	3	2.78	123.0	108	6	34	78	.235
95 Greenville	SOU/AA	5	5	0	0	4	0	1.53	29.1	20	0	8	25	.198
95 Boston	AL/MAJ	2	1	0	0	1	1	18.90	3.1	11	1	3	1	.524
95 Atlanta	NL/MAJ	4	1	1	0	0	2	6.75	10.2	10	3	5	3	.256

After pitching just twice in 1991–92 because of elbow surgery and struggling in 1994, Murray thought about quitting. But the 25-year-old started out last season winning his first 11 decisions, including nine consecutive starts, and posting a 1.11 ERA. By late July he led the minor leagues' in victories, but won just three more games the rest of season and struggled the last month. The Braves traded the Massachusetts native to the Red Sox at the end of August as part of the Mike Stanton deal. The 6-foot-6 righthander does not overwhelm hitters, but throws 88-91 mph with a slider and changeup.

TROT NIXON

Bats: L Throws: L Opening Day Age: 22
Ht: 6-1 Wt: 195 Born: 4/11/1974
Position: OF Drafted: 1993 #1 BOS

YR TEAM	LG/CLASS	G	AB	R	H	2B	3B	HR	RBI	SB	BA	OBA
94 Lynchburg	CARO/A	71	264	33	65	12	0	12	43	10	.246	.357
95 Trenton	EAST/AA	25	94	9	15	3	1	2	8	2	.160	.214
95 Sarasota	FSL/A	73	264	43	80	11	4	5	39	7	.303	.404

After his first professional season was cut short by a back problem, Nixon began 1995 in extended spring training rehabbing the injury. He reported to Sarasota in late April, reached base in 39 straight games and was showing his sweet swing, speed, strong throwing arm and athleticism when promoted to Trenton in early August. The 21-year-old struggled in Double-A, but the Sox are confident he is 100% recovered from his back injury.

RAFAEL ORELLANO

Bats: L Throws: L Opening Day Age: 23
Ht: 6-2 Wt: 160 Born: 4/28/1973
Position: P Drafted: NDFA 11-7-92 BOS

YR TEAM	LG/CLASS	G	GS	GF	SV	W	L	ERA	IP	H	HR	BB	SO	O/BA
93 Utica	NYP/A	11	0	7	2	1	2	5.79	18.2	22	4	7	13	.301
94 Sarasota	FSL/A	16	16	0	0	11	3	2.40	97.1	68	5	25	103	.197
94 Red Sox	GULF/R	4	3	0	0	1	0	2.03	13.1	6	0	4	10	.130
95 Trenton	EAST/AA	27	27	0	0	11	7	3.09	186.2	146	18	72	160	.213

After two outstanding years, Orellano has established himself as the best lefthanded pitching prospect in the organization. He is durable despite a slender build and hurled 187 innings last year, sixth-best in the minor leagues. The 22-year-old from Puerto Rico has above-average velocity and an outstanding changeup and keeps the ball down. He led the Eastern League in strikeouts (160), placed fifth in ERA (3.09), held opponents to a .213 average and fanned better than one out of every four lefthanded batters. Orellano also started and won the Double-A All-Star game.

DONNIE SADLER

Bats: R Throws: R Opening Day Age: 21
Ht: 5-7 Wt: 160 Born: 6/17/1975
Position: SS Drafted: 1994 #10 BOS

YR TEAM	LG/CLASS	G	AB	R	H	2B	3B	HR	RBI	SB	BA	OBA
94 Red Sox	GULF/R	53	206	52	56	8	6	1	16	32	.272	.349
95 Michigan	MID/A	118	438	103	124	25	8	9	55	41	.283	.397

The Texas native is the fastest player in the organization, stealing 32 bags in 1994 and 41 in '95. He drew 79 walks in '95, indicating that he could be an effective top-of-the-order hitter. Sadler led the Midwest League with 103 runs, the fifth-most in the minors. Although he is only 5-foot-7, the 20-year-old hits with pop to all fields. Sadler is also a good defensive shortstop with range and a strong arm.

JEFF SUPPAN

Bats: R Throws: R Opening Day Age: 21
Ht: 6-1 Wt: 200 Born: 1/2/1975
Position: P Drafted: 1993 #2 BOS

YR TEAM	LG/CLASS	G	GS	GF	SV	W	L	ERA	IP	H	HR	BB	SO	O/BA
93 Red Sox	GULF/R	10	9	1	0	4	3	2.18	57.2	52	0	16	64	.237
94 Sarasota	FSL/A	27	27	0	0	13	7	3.26	174.0	153	10	50	173	.236
95 Pawtucket	INT/AAA	7	7	0	0	2	3	5.32	45.2	50	9	9	32	.278
95 Trenton	EAST/AA	15	15	0	0	2	2	2.36	99.0	86	5	26	88	.232
95 Boston	AL/MAJ	8	3	1	0	1	2	5.96	22.2	29	4	5	19	.312

Suppan is the best upper-level pitching prospect in the system. He has drawn comparisons to Greg Maddux because of his build, poise and pitching knowledge. The 20-year-old has four pitches which he can throw for strikes. Suppan moved quickly up the organizational ladder, making his major league debut in only his second full season, but had a terrible time holding runners on base both at the major league and minor league levels. In 1994, Suppan led the Florida State League in wins and strikeouts.

BOSTON RED SOX: OTHERS TO WATCH

CHRIS ALLISON   Bats: R Throws: R   Ht: 5-10 Wt: 165
Born: 10/22/1971   Drafted: 1994 #8 BOS   Position: 2B

YR TEAM	LG/CLASS	G	AB	R	H	2B	3B	HR	RBI	SB	BA	OBA
95 Michigan	MID/A	87	298	46	94	8	4	0	22	36	.315	.429

Allison, a contact hitter, has excellent speed and a .321 average over two seasons.

GREG BLOSSER   Bats: L Throws: L   Ht: 6-3 Wt: 205
Born: 6/26/1971   Drafted: 1989 #1 BOS   Position: OF

YR TEAM	LG/CLASS	G	AB	R	H	2B	3B	HR	RBI	SB	BA	OBA
95 Pawtucket	INT/AAA	17	50	5	10	0	0	1	4	0	.200	.268
95 Trenton	EAST/AA	49	179	25	44	13	0	11	34	3	.246	.292

A former first-round pick, Blosser has a lot of power, but cannot hit lefties and was dropped from the 40-man roster.

RANDY BROWN   Bats: R Throws: R   Ht: 5-11 Wt: 160
Born: 5/1/1970   Drafted: 1989 #30 BOS   Position: SS

YR TEAM	LG/CLASS	G	AB	R	H	2B	3B	HR	RBI	SB	BA	OBA
95 Pawtucket	INT/AAA	74	212	27	53	6	1	2	12	5	.250	.294

Brown, another replacement player, is a solid defensive shortstop but not much of a hitter.

MICHAEL COLEMAN   Bats: R Throws: R   Ht: 5-11 Wt: 210
Born: 8/16/1975   Drafted: 1994 #17 BOS   Position: OF

YR TEAM	LG/CLASS	G	AB	R	H	2B	3B	HR	RBI	SB	BA	OBA
95 Michigan	MID/A	112	422	70	113	16	2	11	61	29	.268	.338

A blend of speed and power, Coleman is one of the best pure athletes in the system.

JARED FERNANDEZ   Bats: R Throws: R   Ht: 6-2 Wt: 225
Born: 2/2/1972   Drafted: NDFA 6-23-94 BOS   Position: P

YR TEAM	LG/CLASS	G	GS	GF	SV	W	L	ERA	IP	H	HR	BB	SO	O/BA
95 Trenton	EAST/AA	11	10	0	0	5	4	3.90	67.0	64	4	28	40	.253
95 Utica	NYP/A	5	5	0	0	3	2	1.89	38.0	30	2	9	23	.219

Fernandez, a knuckleballer, emerged from nowhere as a prospect in 1995.

BRENT HANSEN   Bats: R Throws: R   Ht: 6-2 Wt: 195
Born: 8/4/1970   Drafted: 1992 #18 BOS   Position: P

YR TEAM	LG/CLASS	G	GS	GF	SV	W	L	ERA	IP	H	HR	BB	SO	O/BA
95 Pawtucket	INT/AAA	14	14	0	0	7	5	4.29	92.1	90	12	23	50	.254
95 Trenton	EAST/AA	11	11	0	0	4	5	3.26	77.1	70	5	17	52	.239

Hansen is a sinker/slider pitcher who is not overpowering but posted decent numbers in 1995.

MIKE HARDGE   Bats: R Throws: R   Ht: 5-11 Wt: 183
Born: 1/27/1972   Drafted: 1990 #7 MON   Position: 2B

YR TEAM	LG/CLASS	G	AB	R	H	2B	3B	HR	RBI	SB	BA	OBA
95 Pawtucket	INT/AAA	29	91	9	23	3	0	1	5	1	.253	.313
95 Trenton	EAST/AA	40	127	18	31	4	1	0	12	5	.244	.300

Hardge, a good glove man with speed, is not much of a hitter.

SCOTT HATTEBERG   Bats: L Throws: R   Ht: 6-1 Wt: 185
Born: 12/14/1969   Drafted: 1991 #3 BOS   Position: C

YR TEAM	LG/CLASS	G	AB	R	H	2B	3B	HR	RBI	SB	BA	OBA
95 Pawtucket	INT/AAA	85	251	36	68	15	1	7	27	2	.271	.376
95 Boston	AL/MAJ	2	2	1	1	0	0	0	0	0	.500	.500

The lefthanded swinger is a contact hitter who has big trouble throwing out baserunners.

BRIAN LOONEY   Bats: L Throws: L   Ht: 5-10 Wt: 180
Born: 9/26/1969   Drafted: 1991 #11 MON   Position: P

YR TEAM	LG/CLASS	G	GS	GF	SV	W	L	ERA	IP	H	HR	BB	SO	O/BA
95 Pawtucket	INT/AAA	18	18	0	0	4	7	3.49	100.2	106	9	33	78	.265
95 Boston	AL/MAJ	3	1	0	0	0	1	17.36	4.2	12	1	4	2	.545

Acquired from the Expos before last season, the southpaw pitched well for Pawtucket and has a career 3.05 ERA over five seasons.

RON MAHAY   Bats: L Throws: L   Ht: 6-2 Wt: 185
Born: 6/28/1971   Drafted: 1991 #21 BOS   Position: OF

YR TEAM	LG/CLASS	G	AB	R	H	2B	3B	HR	RBI	SB	BA	OBA
95 Pawtucket	INT/AAA	11	44	5	14	4	0	0	3	1	.318	.375
95 Trenton	EAST/AA	93	310	37	73	12	3	5	28	5	.235	.332
95 Boston	AL/MAJ	5	20	3	4	2	0	1	3	0	.200	.273

Kevin Kennedy liked what he saw of Mahay as a replacement player, and called him up for a few games early in the season.

WALT McKEEL   Bats: R Throws: R   Ht: 6-2 Wt: 200
Born: 1/17/1972   Drafted: 1990 #2 BOS   Position: C

YR TEAM	LG/CLASS	G	AB	R	H	2B	3B	HR	RBI	SB	BA	OBA
95 Trenton	EAST/AA	29	84	11	20	3	1	2	11	2	.238	.298
95 Sarasota	FSL/A	62	198	26	66	14	0	8	35	6	.333	.407

McKeel, a good defensive catcher with a strong arm, had his best year at the plate in 1995.

LOU MERLONI   Bats: R Throws: R   Ht: 5-10 Wt: 188
Born: 4/6/1971   Drafted: 1993 #10 BOS   Position: 2B

YR TEAM	LG/CLASS	G	AB	R	H	2B	3B	HR	RBI	SB	BA	OBA
95 Trenton	EAST/AA	93	318	42	88	16	1	1	30	7	.277	.373

Merloni is a good defensive player who plays three infield positions and hits for average.

CARL PAVANO   Bats: R Throws: R   Ht: 6-5 Wt: 225
Born: 1/8/1976   Drafted: 1994 #12 BOS   Position: P

YR TEAM	LG/CLASS	G	GS	GF	SV	W	L	ERA	IP	H	HR	BB	SO	O/BA
95 Michigan	MID/A	22	22	0	0	6	6	3.44	141.1	118	7	52	138	.227

Pavano has the makings of a classic power pitcher with size, heat, and strikeouts.

BILL SELBY   Bats: L Throws: R   Ht: 5-9 Wt: 190
Born: 6/11/1970   Drafted: 1992 #12 BOS   Position: 3B

YR TEAM	LG/CLASS	G	AB	R	H	2B	3B	HR	RBI	SB	BA	OBA
95 Trenton	EAST/AA	117	451	64	129	29	2	13	68	4	.286	.350

Although he is only 5-foot-9, the lefthanded hitter has good power and does not strike out much.

J.J. THOBE   Bats: R Throws: R   Ht: 6-6 Wt: 200
Born: 11/19/1970   Drafted: 1992 #7 CLE   Position: P

YR TEAM	LG/CLASS	G	GS	GF	SV	W	L	ERA	IP	H	HR	BB	SO	O/BA
95 Ottawa	INT/AAA	55	0	25	5	5	8	3.27	88.0	79	8	16	36	.241
95 Montreal	NL/MAJ	4	0	2	0	0	0	9.00	4.0	6	0	3	0	.333

Thobe, formerly of the Expos' system, had shoulder problems that dropped his velocity by nearly 10 mph to the lower-80's, but he has a good sinker and very good control.

CALIFORNIA ANGELS

JIM ABBOTT

Position: SP
Bats: L **Throws:** L
Ht: 6'3" **Wt:** 200
Opening Day Age: 28
Born: 9/19/1967
Drafted: CAL88 1/8
ML Seasons: 7

SCOUTING REPORT

Abbott comes to the plate from a high three-quarter angle, usually throwing his average-minus sinking fastball away from lefthanded batters and cutting it on the fists of righthanders. Often the pitch is straight if it's thrown high. Jim's also utilizes an average-plus slider and a relatively slow curve. Infrequently, Jim will throw a splitfinger pitch. Control of all of his pitches rates slightly above-average, but if he can't locate the ball, Abbott doesn't have the stuff to survive.

A fine athlete, Abbott is an above-average fielder, despite the disadvantage of having to remove his glove to throw the ball. His move to first is average, and 15 of 24 stolen base attempts were successful in '95.

HOW HE PERFORMED IN '95

Abbott had a up-and-down '95, starting the year with the White Sox. Although he had some control trouble, he was Chicago's only helpful starting pitcher in the first half. Jim's July 27 trade to the Angels was very unpopular in the Windy City. The Angels hoped that working again with Marcel Lachemann (his old pitching coach) would settle Abbott down. However, Jim continued to struggle to find his rhythm. After the trade, he had a 7.54 ERA in six starts at Anaheim, but a 1.51 ERA in seven road appearances. The team's late-season slump meant that Abbott didn't get much run support, and he didn't pitch well enough to overcome that. Righthanders hit .293 against Jim after the trade.

While he wasn't that bad, Abbott's inconsistency made him a wild card down the stretch. His final totals for the Angels were a 5-4 record and 4.15 ERA, after starting 6-4, 3.36 for Chicago. The Angels would have liked him to step forward to try to halt their end-of-the-year-slide.

WHAT TO EXPECT IN '96

Abbott remains a popular figure in Southern California. Whether that translates to remaining with the Angels is another matter. The club doesn't want to part with the money Jim is asking for—the same scenario that led to Abbott leaving the Angels after the '92 season.

If he remains with the Angels, Jim will likely be a project of Lachemann's. Should he leave, Abbott will probably continue to struggle to find a consistent rhythm and be a .500 pitcher.

Overall Statistics

	G	GS	GF	SV	W	L	ERA	IP	H	R	ER	HR	BB	SO
95 CHA/CAL	30	30	0	0	11	8	3.70	197.0	209	93	81	14	64	86
Career	211	211	0	0	78	82	3.77	1418.1	1463	665	594	115	488	779

1995 Situational Statistics

	W	L	ERA	SV	IP	BB	SO		AB	HR	RBI	BA	OBA	SLG
Home	3	6	5.02	0	86.0	30	36	LHB	147	2	14	.279	.333	.361
Road	8	2	2.68	0	111.0	34	50	RHB	617	12	65	.272	.329	.378
Apr-Jun	4	3	3.33	0	75.2	23	35	ScPos	182	2	63	.275	.330	.346
Jul-Oct	7	5	3.93	0	121.1	41	51	Clutch	63	4	9	.270	.324	.476

How He Compares to Other Pitchers

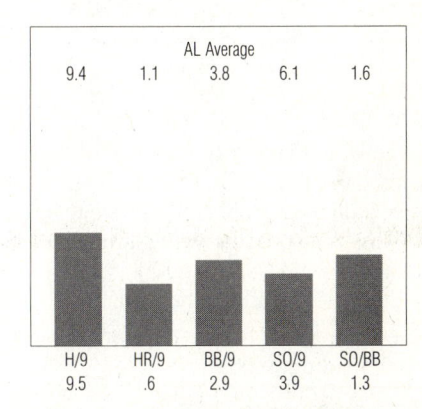

AL Average: H/9 9.4, HR/9 1.1, BB/9 3.8, SO/9 6.1, SO/BB 1.6

H/9 9.5, HR/9 .6, BB/9 2.9, SO/9 3.9, SO/BB 1.3

How He Compares to Other Starting Pitchers

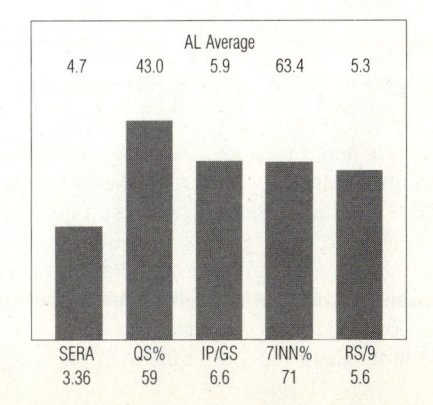

AL Average: SERA 4.7, QS% 43.0, IP/GS 5.9, 7INN% 63.4, RS/9 5.3

SERA 3.36, QS% 59, IP/GS 6.6, 7INN% 71, RS/9 5.6

THE SCOUTING REPORT: 1996

CALIFORNIA ANGELS

GARRET ANDERSON

Positions: OF//DH
Bats: L **Throws:** L
Ht: 6'3" **Wt:** 190
Opening Day Age: 23
Born: 6/30/1972
Drafted: CAL90 3/125
ML Seasons: 2

SCOUTING REPORT

Anderson has a quick bat and makes good contact. An inside fastball devotee, he can turn on the ball with some power but uses the whole field well. However, Garret is an impatient hitter and tends to bail out on breaking balls thrown by lefthanders. He is still young enough to improve.

While not a true basestealing threat, Anderson has average speed and will run some routine singles into doubles.

In the field, Garret displays slightly below-average range and average hands. He has enough speed to play center, but a weak (although reasonably accurate) arm makes him a left fielder.

HOW HE PERFORMED IN '95

Anderson was a key part to the Angels' improbable run at the AL West title. Hurt by the lack of a proper spring training, Garret started the year in Vancouver. However, he was called up in late May and inserted into left field, batting sixth, as Tony Phillips changed positions, moving to third base.

From there, Garret blossomed quickly, becoming a solid Rookie of the Year candidate. He started quickly, hitting .313 in June, but really turned it on with a .410 July, slugging seven home runs and batting in 31. From that peak, he struggled. Pitchers realized he would swing at anything, and deprived of a steady diet of fastballs, Garret fanned 22 times in August and then hit only .269 in September. Anderson was not productive against lefthanded pitching and, if he doesn't hit .321 every year, he'll need to draw more walks to be valuable.

In left field, he threw out seven runners but made five errors, fielding .978.

WHAT TO EXPECT IN '96

Garret had never hit 16 homers in a season before at any level. Pitchers are sure to try and exploit the holes in his swing again this year, and Anderson's challenge will be to make the necessary adjustments.

The Angels may be tempted to move Garret up in the batting order this year due to the expected departure of Phillips. Although he doesn't get on base often enough to be a good leadoff man, Anderson did bat .384 with eight homers in 86 at-bats leading off an inning in '95. Although he has some things to work on, Anderson has established himself as a fixture in left field for some time to come.

Overall Statistics

	G	AB	R	H	2B	3B	HR	RBI	SB	CS	BB	SO	BA	OBA
95 CAL	106	374	50	120	19	1	16	69	6	2	19	65	.321	.352
Career	111	387	50	125	19	1	16	70	6	2	19	67	.323	.353

1995 Situational Statistics

	AB	HR	RBI	BA	OBA	SLG		AB	HR	RBI	BA	OBA	SLG
Home	184	7	34	.332	.367	.505	LHP	115	5	23	.252	.285	.417
Road	190	9	35	.311	.337	.505	RHP	259	11	46	.351	.382	.544
Apr-Jun	56	2	11	.268	.359	.500	ScPos	111	3	52	.288	.336	.414
Jul-Oct	318	14	58	.330	.350	.506	Clutch	41	0	6	.220	.256	.293

How He Compares to Other Batters

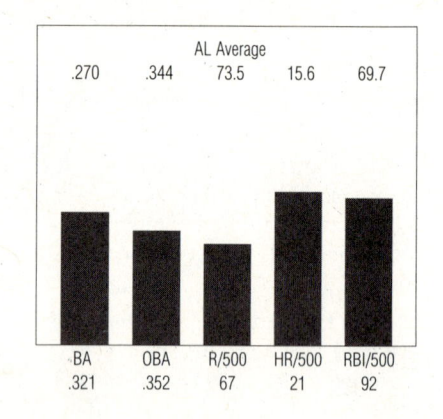

AL Average
.270   .344   73.5   15.6   69.7

BA	OBA	R/500	HR/500	RBI/500
.321	.352	67	21	92

Where He Hits the Ball

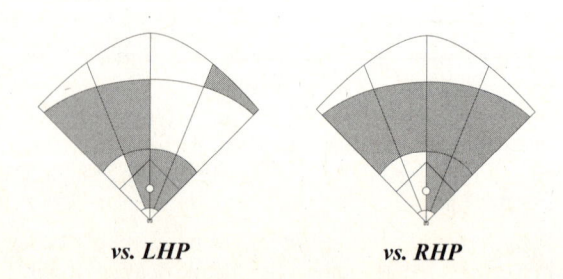

vs. LHP   vs. RHP

THE SCOUTING REPORT: 1996

CALIFORNIA ANGELS

CHILI DAVIS

Position: DH
Bats: B **Throws:** R
Ht: 6'3" **Wt:** 195
Opening Day Age: 36
Born: 1/17/1960
Drafted: SF77 11/270
ML Seasons: 15

SCOUTING REPORT

Davis is still a quality power hitter who also hits for good average. A switch-hitter, he has shown an improvement in the last few seasons batting righthanded and now hits lefthanders more effectively, both for average and extra bases.

Chili has big-field power and likes the ball low and over the plate from both sides. He is still a good breaking-ball hitter and will cream a mediocre fastball, but he can be jammed with good, hard inside pitches. When he can't hit a pitch, however, Davis is likely to take it: he will take the walk gladly and has recently cut down his strikeouts.

Davis is exclusively a designated hitter at this point, although he might play first base or left field in an emergency. Once a good runner and base thief, Chili is now a slow, station-to-station runner who can't steal effectively.

HOW HE PERFORMED IN '95

Davis kept on rolling along in '95, providing the timely hitting needed to keep the Angels in games they didn't deserve to win. He started the year strong, as did many Angels: Davis batted .379 in May with six homers. On June 20, he strained a left hamstring and was disabled the following day. Chili missed a month's worth of action but after being activated on July 24, picked up where he left off.

Chili, unlike some of his teammates, kept hitting at the end of the year. He batted .292 in August, September and October with seven home runs and 33 runs batted in. Davis and Tim Salmon tried to carry the team through their late-season struggles, but they couldn't lift the whole club out of its downward spiral all by themselves.

WHAT TO EXPECT IN '96

Since being re-acquired by the Angels in '93, Davis has provided the power and average they expected. In the past three years, he has put up impressive numbers; while he is getting up in years, there is no reason he can't continue to be productive in the future. Signed through '97, Chili should remain with California through the end of his career.

Overall Statistics

	G	AB	R	H	2B	3B	HR	RBI	SB	CS	BB	SO	BA	OBA
95 CAL	119	424	81	135	23	0	20	86	3	3	89	79	.318	.429
Career	1970	7087	1026	1934	348	29	270	1100	127	91	936	1385	.273	.355

1995 Situational Statistics

	AB	HR	RBI	BA	OBA	SLG		AB	HR	RBI	BA	OBA	SLG
Home	212	11	50	.358	.470	.585	LHP	129	6	30	.349	.427	.543
Road	212	9	36	.278	.388	.443	RHP	295	14	56	.305	.430	.502
Apr-Jun	181	9	38	.359	.464	.569	ScPos	112	10	69	.295	.409	.580
Jul-Oct	243	11	48	.288	.403	.473	Clutch	47	1	3	.277	.393	.383

How He Compares to Other Batters

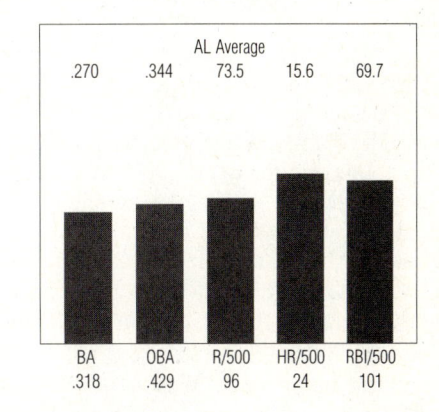

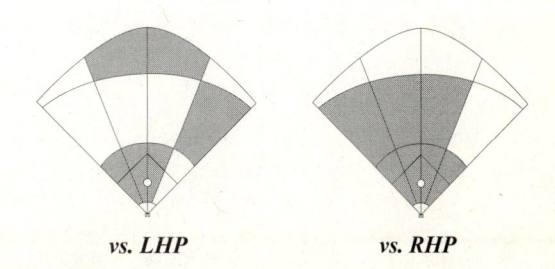

AL Average: .270 .344 73.5 15.6 69.7

BA	OBA	R/500	HR/500	RBI/500
.318	.429	96	24	101

Where He Hits the Ball

vs. LHP   vs. RHP

THE SCOUTING REPORT: 1996

CALIFORNIA ANGELS

GARY DISARCINA

Position: SS
Bats: R **Throws:** R
Ht: 6'1" **Wt:** 170
Opening Day Age: 28
Born: 11/19/1967
Drafted: CAL88 5/143
ML Seasons: 7

SCOUTING REPORT

DiSarcina made a big improvement at the plate in '95. He became more disciplined, approaching at-bats more intelligently than in the past. Using a straightaway stance, he goes after pitches up and over the plate. Because he makes contact consistently, Gary is a good hit-and-run man; he can also lay down the bunt when asked. However, he draws few walks and has minus power and must hit around .300 to be a good offensive player. DiSarcina is an intelligent baserunner, but has just average speed and is not a big threat to steal.

Gary has always been strong defensively, with good, soft hands. He has average range and quick reflexes and is willing to dive for balls. Additionally, DiSarcina has slightly above-average arm strength with plus accuracy. Many feel he is a Gold Glove-caliber shortstop.

HOW HE PERFORMED IN '95

DiSarcina's offensive improvement was pivotal to California's rise. Like most of his teammates, he started quickly, and as a result Gary made the AL All-Star team for the first time.

Unfortunately, he tore a ligament in his left thumb on August 4, and the injury created a hole that the Angels could not fill. Some felt that DiSarcina's absence was the big reason for the team's slide out of first place, although the departure of a singles-hitting shortstop doesn't really explain an entire club going into the tank. With California foundering, DiSarcina returned to the lineup on September 17. However, he may have tried to come back from the injured rolls too quickly—Gary was solid defensively, but batted just .206.

DiSarcina had another good season in the field. He went 54 straight games without committing an error, making just six on the year. His .986 fielding percentage ranked second among AL shortstops. Despite his career-best average (previous high: .260), Gary batted ninth the whole year, and probably is still best suited for that spot.

WHAT TO EXPECT IN '96

DiSarcina has always been solid defensively and, last year, he moved into the top echelon of big-league shortstops. The injury isn't considered career-threatening, but there is some concern that Gary's quick return might have set back his rehabilitation. If the thumb is fully healed, DiSarcina will continue to stabilize the California infield.

Overall Statistics

	G	AB	R	H	2B	3B	HR	RBI	SB	CS	BB	SO	BA	OBA
95 CAL	99	362	61	111	28	6	5	41	7	4	20	25	.307	.344
Career	532	1799	219	459	84	10	14	164	25	25	79	155	.255	.292

1995 Situational Statistics

	AB	HR	RBI	BA	OBA	SLG		AB	HR	RBI	BA	OBA	SLG
Home	182	1	19	.302	.332	.423	LHP	97	2	14	.289	.314	.495
Road	180	4	22	.311	.355	.494	RHP	265	3	27	.313	.354	.445
Apr-Jun	216	3	30	.329	.372	.495	ScPos	88	0	35	.318	.370	.455
Jul-Oct	146	2	11	.274	.301	.404	Clutch	49	0	7	.245	.315	.347

How He Compares to Other Batters

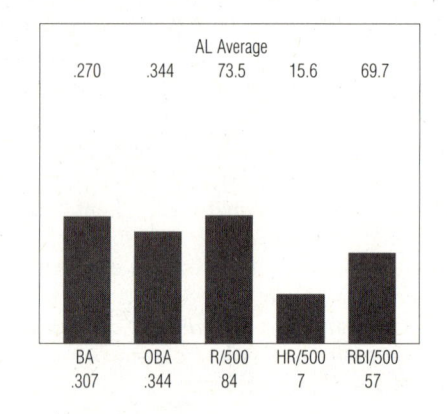

AL Average: .270 .344 73.5 15.6 69.7

BA .307 | OBA .344 | R/500 84 | HR/500 7 | RBI/500 57

Where He Hits the Ball

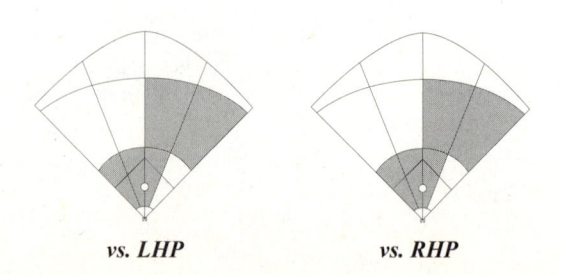

vs. LHP   vs. RHP

54   THE SCOUTING REPORT: 1996

CALIFORNIA ANGELS

DAMION EASLEY

Positions: 2B/SS
Bats: R **Throws:** R
Ht: 5'11" **Wt:** 155
Opening Day Age: 26
Born: 11/11/1969
Drafted: CAL88 30/767
ML Seasons: 4

SCOUTING REPORT
Easley is a high-fastball hitter, lashing at pitches over the plate. He is a good contact hitter but lacks power and struggles with breaking balls and off-speed deliveries. Although Damion takes big swings and has been trying to learn to pull inside pitches, the experiment is still in progress.

Easley has slightly above-average speed. Despite his good legs, however, he is not a frequent nor a particularly good basestealer. Damion's speed was better before suffering from shin splints in 1993-94.

Defensively, Damion has a average-plus arm with average accuracy; it's more than good enough for third base. Easley plays second now, where he has average-plus range but slightly below-average hands and has problems backhanding ground balls and turning the double play.

HOW HE PERFORMED IN '95
Damion has been given every chance to win a full-time job for the Angels, at third base from 1992-94 and, last year, at second base. However, injuries have derailed him and Easley has not proven himself offensively or defensively.

Easley was handed the second base job last April despite a poor spring training. He started slowly, hitting just .228 in May and bottoming out with a .135 mark during June. From then on, Damion's spot in the lineup was on a day-to-day basis. He didn't show power, continued to slide against righthanders, and failed to walk enough to take advantage of his speed.

Damion did improve somewhat in the second half, and ended up playing 25 games at shortstop because of Gary DiSarcina's injury in August. However, Easley failed to impress at the new spot and it will be surprising if he plays anywhere but second base in the future.

WHAT TO EXPECT IN '96
Given his struggles of late, it seems likely that his .313 average of '93 was not a true level of ability and that Easley will struggle to remain on a major-league roster.

Easley's future on the Angels is problematic. It's clear the team wants to play him somewhere, because they feel he has good tools. However, after two years of lackluster hitting and glovework, '96 might be Damion's last chance.

Overall Statistics

	G	AB	R	H	2B	3B	HR	RBI	SB	CS	BB	SO	BA	OBA
95 CAL	114	357	35	77	14	2	4	35	5	2	32	47	.216	.288
Career	322	1054	123	256	48	5	13	99	24	18	97	156	.243	.314

1995 Situational Statistics

	AB	HR	RBI	BA	OBA	SLG		AB	HR	RBI	BA	OBA	SLG
Home	170	1	16	.206	.283	.288	LHP	118	2	13	.246	.302	.381
Road	187	3	19	.225	.293	.310	RHP	239	2	22	.201	.281	.259
Apr-Jun	168	3	18	.196	.279	.292	ScPos	109	2	32	.183	.225	.294
Jul-Oct	189	1	17	.233	.297	.307	Clutch	24	0	2	.250	.333	.375

How He Compares to Other Batters

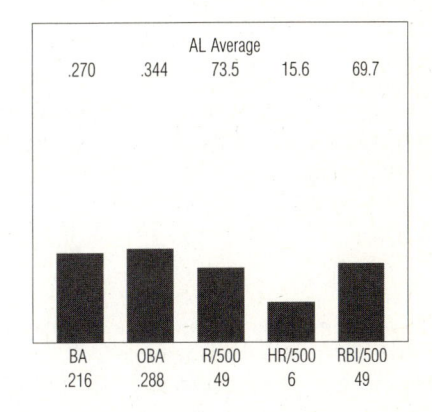

AL Average: .270 .344 73.5 15.6 69.7

BA .216 | OBA .288 | R/500 49 | HR/500 6 | RBI/500 49

Where He Hits the Ball

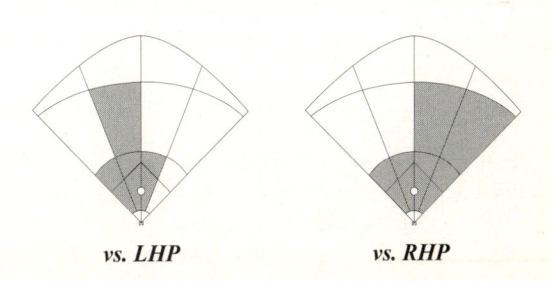

vs. LHP   vs. RHP

THE SCOUTING REPORT: 1996

CALIFORNIA ANGELS

JIM EDMONDS

Position: OF
Bats: L **Throws:** L
Ht: 6'1" **Wt:** 190
Opening Day Age: 25
Born: 6/27/1970
Drafted: CAL88 6/169
ML Seasons: 3

SCOUTING REPORT

Using a big uppercut swing, Edmonds hits pitches up and over the plate with good straightaway power. However, Jim has trouble with breaking pitches, striking out often, and struggles against lefthanded pitchers. He has a wide stance and doesn't stride much, which contributes to his problems against lefties.

Edmonds experienced a sharp rise in productivity last season, and it took pitchers some time to adjust. Now that they have changed their pattern and will give him more off-speed stuff, Jim is not likely to hit for as much power in the future as he did in '95. He has average speed but gets a good jump and can get around the bases well. Edmonds is no threat to steal, however.

Although he doesn't have the textbook physique for the position, Jim is a good center fielder with plus hands. He has plus range, with an excellent jump on balls hit over his head, and goes to the wall very well. His arm has slightly below-average strength, but Jim throws with a bit above-average accuracy.

HOW HE PERFORMED IN '95

For two months last summer, Edmonds carried the Angels' offense on his back and was one of the best hitters in all of baseball. He was just about impossible to get out and displayed surprising power. He hit a lusty .366 in June and then ripped pitchers for a .325 average in July, smacking ten home runs.

Unfortunately, his back began to ache late in the season and, after hitting nine more homers in August, Jim slumped in September. However, bad back and all, Edmonds continued to play hard every day. California management feels Jim may need more days off in the future so that he can maintain strength and stamina late in the season.

In center field, Edmonds made just one error and led the team with eight outfield assists. He continued to show good mobility.

WHAT TO EXPECT IN '96

Despite his late-season fade, Edmonds has to be considered one of the top center fielders in the American League. He provides fine defensive skills and made a huge contribution at bat. Jim will be the Angels' center fielder for years to come.

Overall Statistics

	G	AB	R	H	2B	3B	HR	RBI	SB	CS	BB	SO	BA	OBA
95 CAL	141	558	120	162	30	4	33	107	1	4	51	130	.290	.352
Career	253	908	160	256	47	6	38	148	5	8	83	218	.282	.344

1995 Situational Statistics

	AB	HR	RBI	BA	OBA	SLG		AB	HR	RBI	BA	OBA	SLG
Home	270	16	58	.300	.375	.552	LHP	164	7	29	.293	.359	.482
Road	288	17	49	.281	.329	.521	RHP	394	26	78	.289	.349	.558
Apr-Jun	227	11	44	.304	.361	.502	ScPos	160	9	73	.262	.317	.481
Jul-Oct	331	22	63	.281	.346	.559	Clutch	60	1	7	.167	.265	.233

How He Compares to Other Batters

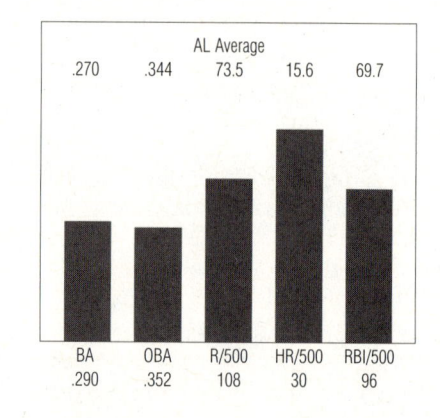

AL Average: .270 / .344 / 73.5 / 15.6 / 69.7

BA	OBA	R/500	HR/500	RBI/500
.290	.352	108	30	96

Where He Hits the Ball

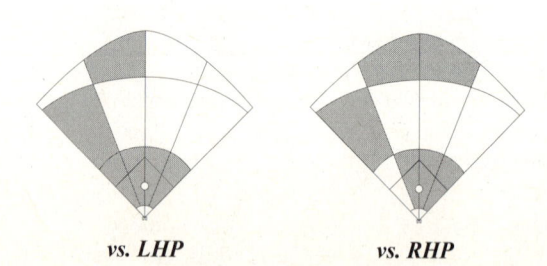

vs. LHP   vs. RHP

THE SCOUTING REPORT: 1996

CALIFORNIA ANGELS

JORGE FABREGAS

Position: C
Bats: L **Throws:** R
Ht: 6'3" **Wt:** 205
Opening Day Age: 26
Born: 3/13/1970
Drafted: CAL91 2/34
ML Seasons: 2

SCOUTING REPORT
Fabregas, once an infielder, is still learning how to use his considerable skills behind the plate. He is improving but still leaves something to be desired. Despite a minus arm, Jorge has improved his release and throws with plus accuracy. He has average range and hands.

A largely untested hitter with only one professional season of more than 400 plate appearances, Fabregas has been platooned since coming to the majors. He stands off the plate, using an inside-out swing to take high, over-the-plate pitches to left field. Although he has minus power, Jorge compensates for this by putting his bat on the ball consistently. He doesn't walk much. As befits a catcher, Fabregas has minus speed, but he is a good bunter.

HOW HE PERFORMED IN '95
Fabregas began the year with the Angels but was sent out on May 6. Injuries to other catchers pulled him back to Anaheim in June and he remained with the big club the rest of the season. Although he could have used more time at Triple-A and is not a very good player yet, the Angels didn't have anyone else available to fill in when Greg Myers and Andy Allanson got hurt. California has tried several catchers in the last two years with various degrees of success; each of them does one thing well, with none close to being a whole package.

Fabregas could conceivably hit .280 in the majors but is still learning to play behind the plate. Even though he's considered the best offensive receiver the Angels have, he struggles against lefthanded pitchers and doesn't provide any punch.

Despite some other problems, Jorge actually threw quite well in '95, nailing 36% (20 of 55) of larcenous runners. He allowed eight passed balls in just 63 games, a well above-average rate, and needs to learn more about game-calling.

WHAT TO EXPECT IN '96
With the Angels catching as unsettled as it's been in recent years, Fabregas will have the inside track to the starting job in '96. He may end up a platoon player; at worst would probably shuttle between the bench and Triple-A. If he can further improve his defensive skills, Fabregas will continue to play. However, despite being a first-round pick in '91, Jorge hasn't shown he is ready for full-time duty at this point.

Overall Statistics

	G	AB	R	H	2B	3B	HR	RBI	SB	CS	BB	SO	BA	OBA
95 CAL	73	227	24	56	10	0	1	22	0	2	17	28	.247	.298
Career	116	354	36	92	13	0	1	38	2	3	24	46	.260	.306

1995 Situational Statistics

	AB	HR	RBI	BA	OBA	SLG		AB	HR	RBI	BA	OBA	SLG
Home	109	1	11	.266	.328	.321	LHP	39	0	6	.179	.214	.205
Road	118	0	11	.229	.270	.288	RHP	188	1	16	.261	.315	.324
Apr-Jun	90	1	11	.289	.323	.389	ScPos	64	0	21	.250	.310	.281
Jul-Oct	137	0	11	.219	.282	.248	Clutch	30	0	1	.267	.290	.267

How He Compares to Other Batters

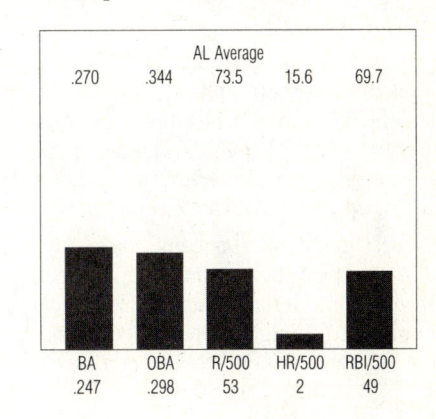

AL Average: .270 .344 73.5 15.6 69.7

BA .247   OBA .298   R/500 53   HR/500 2   RBI/500 49

Where He Hits the Ball

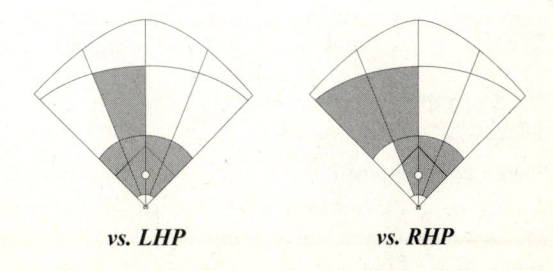

vs. LHP   *vs. RHP*

THE SCOUTING REPORT: 1996

CALIFORNIA ANGELS

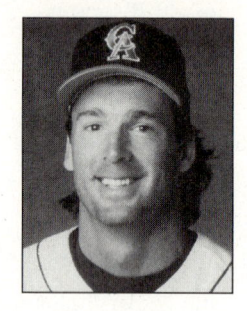

CHUCK FINLEY

Position: SP
Bats: L **Throws:** L
Ht: 6'6" **Wt:** 220
Opening Day Age: 33
Born: 11/26/1962
Drafted: CAL85* S1/4
ML Seasons: 10

SCOUTING REPORT
A tall, lanky lefthander, Finley comes to the plate with a full, straight windup and a high three-quarter delivery. He sometimes comes in overhand as well, and will even fire an occasional sidearm pitch to a lefthanded batter.

Chuck's primary pitch is his plus splitter which he will use in any situation. He also throws a slightly below-par fastball that tails away from righthanded batters. His third offering is a slightly above-average curve, and he will also show a forkball which is not as hard as his splitter.

When Finley's splitfinger pitch is dropping, he gets plenty of strikes on pitches below the knees. However, he has control problems at times. Chuck has a quick delivery; however, 26 men tried to steal against him in '95, 21 successfully. He is an adequate fielder but made four errors last year, tying for the lead among AL pitchers.

HOW HE PERFORMED IN '95
It was an up-and-down season for Finley in '95, whose inconsistency is starting to worry Angels' management. At times, Chuck seems incapable of putting together back-to-back quality starts. While never considered a control pitcher, his walk rate has increased in each of the last three years and he flung a career-high 13 wild pitches in '95. Although he was more effective than usual against lefthanders, he paid for mistakes against righties.

Chuck's best games of '95 came early. He had a 3.15 ERA on July 1, but from then on pitched quite badly, contributing in large part to the Angels' late-season collapse. Though his team scored six and a half runs per game for Finley, he was barely a .500 pitcher.

Despite leading the AL in complete games in '93, in games starts in '94, and making 32 more starts last season, Finley has been hampered by nagging foot and leg injuries over the last three seasons. That says something for Chuck's willingness to take the ball and also indicates that he may not have been healthy enough to perform to his full capability.

WHAT TO EXPECT IN '96
Finley is at a crossroads. He's not the pitcher he was a couple of years ago. While Chuck is still capable of pitching well, he is no longer dominant and must be free from injury and receive good run support to guarantee a good season.

Overall Statistics

	G	GS	GF	SV	W	L	ERA	IP	H	R	ER	HR	BB	SO
95 CAL	32	32	0	0	15	12	4.21	203.0	192	106	95	20	93	195
Career	309	252	24	0	114	98	3.58	1836.1	1744	817	731	164	756	1369

1995 Situational Statistics

	W	L	ERA	SV	IP	BB	SO		AB	HR	RBI	BA	OBA	SLG
Home	9	5	3.55	0	106.1	51	121	LHB	113	1	15	.248	.312	.292
Road	6	7	4.93	0	96.2	42	74	RHB	658	19	82	.249	.337	.403
Apr-Jun	6	6	3.15	0	88.2	37	86	ScPos	187	9	78	.278	.372	.471
Jul-Oct	9	6	5.04	0	114.1	56	109	Clutch	44	2	4	.227	.277	.409

How He Compares to Other Pitchers

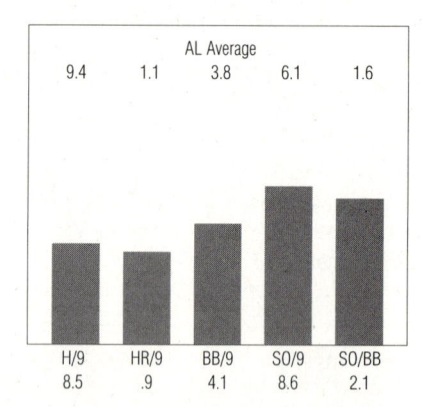

AL Average: 9.4 | 1.1 | 3.8 | 6.1 | 1.6

H/9	HR/9	BB/9	SO/9	SO/BB
8.5	.9	4.1	8.6	2.1

How He Compares to Other Starting Pitchers

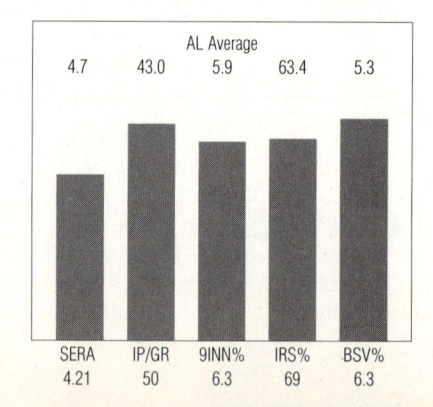

AL Average: 4.7 | 43.0 | 5.9 | 63.4 | 5.3

SERA	IP/GR	9INN%	IRS%	BSV%
4.21	50	6.3	69	6.3

CALIFORNIA ANGELS

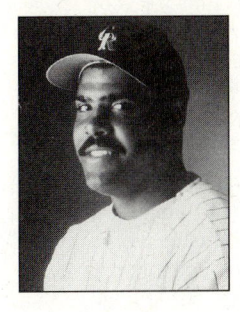

MIKE HARKEY

Position: SP/RP
Bats: R **Throws:** R
Ht: 6'5" **Wt:** 220
Opening Day Age: 29
Born: 10/25/1966
Drafted: CHN87 1/4
ML Seasons: 7

SCOUTING REPORT

Harkey uses no windup, getting the power in his delivery with a high leg kick. He will vary his delivery from low three-quarter to high three-quarter, throwing across his body.

Serious shoulder injuries have sapped most of the punch from Mike's fastball, which is now slightly below-average. Harkey will sink the fastball and run it in on the fists of righthanders. His best pitch is a slightly above-average slider with a big, hard break. A circle change and a curve are thrown just for show. Working with mediocre stuff and slightly below-average control, Harkey tends to pay for his mistakes.

Coming to home slowly, Mike is minus when holding runners: 24 tried to steal against him in '95, 18 successfully. Harkey's fielding rates just average.

HOW HE PERFORMED IN '95

Beginning the season with Oakland, his third club in three years, Mike won a job in the rotation in spring training. He made 12 starts before the Athletics designated him for assignment July 12. Apparently, even Tony LaRussa and Dave Duncan couldn't figure out how to make Harkey effective, and the veteran righty cleaned out his locker with a 6.27 ERA and a 4-6 record.

The Angels, looking for pitching help when Mike Bielecki went down with a shoulder injury, claimed Mike on waivers July 19. He pitched slightly better for California, compiling a 4-3 mark and a 4.55 ERA, but Harkey was less effective as a starter the more he pitched and did his best work as a long reliever in September.

Poor spurts of control and poor stuff combined to make gopher balls a big problem for Harkey, especially against lefthanders. He wasn't getting anybody out consistently. Shifting leagues can be a tough adjustment, but Mike had the benefit of pitching in two friendly parks for pitchers and still had one of his worst years.

WHAT TO EXPECT IN '96

Mike has now had three straight seasons with ERAs well over 5.00. He'll certainly find someone to give him a chance in '96, but it's doubtful that Harkey can serve even as a creditable fifth starter in the majors at this point. It's been a long time since he was a promising young talent.

Overall Statistics

	G	GS	GF	SV	W	L	ERA	IP	H	R	ER	HR	BB	SO
95 OAK/CAL	26	20	1	0	8	9	5.44	127.1	155	78	77	24	47	56
Career	121	104	4	0	35	36	4.49	641.1	708	348	320	72	220	310

1995 Situational Statistics

	W	L	ERA	SV	IP	BB	SO		AB	HR	RBI	BA	OBA	SLG
Home	6	7	5.08	0	88.2	32	39	LHB	281	16	41	.306	.382	.530
Road	2	2	6.28	0	38.2	15	17	RHB	233	8	29	.296	.337	.476
Apr-Jun	4	4	6.07	0	56.1	27	25	ScPos	121	4	45	.273	.357	.438
Jul-Oct	4	5	4.94	0	71.0	20	31	Clutch	6	1	2	.167	.375	.667

How He Compares to Other Pitchers

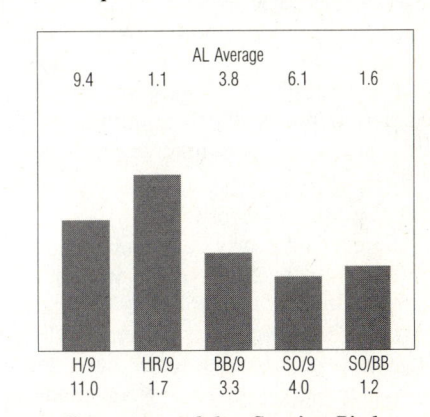

AL Average: 9.4 | 1.1 | 3.8 | 6.1 | 1.6

H/9: 11.0 | HR/9: 1.7 | BB/9: 3.3 | SO/9: 4.0 | SO/BB: 1.2

How He Compares to Other Starting Pitchers

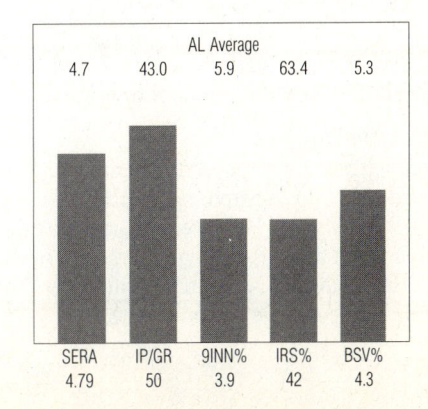

AL Average: 4.7 | 43.0 | 5.9 | 63.4 | 5.3

SERA: 4.79 | IP/GR: 50 | 9INN%: 3.9 | IRS%: 42 | BSV%: 4.3

THE SCOUTING REPORT: 1996

CALIFORNIA ANGELS

MARK LANGSTON

Position: SP
Bats: R **Throws:** L
Ht: 6'2" **Wt:** 190
Opening Day Age: 35
Born: 8/20/1960
Drafted: SEA81 3/35
ML Seasons: 12

SCOUTING REPORT

Mark comes to the plate with a big leg kick, a full windup, and an overhand to high three-quarter delivery. The motion alone makes him intimidating, but his stuff is pretty good too.

He uses each of his three pitches equally. His four-seam fastball is now average and doesn't blow by hitters like it used to. Mark's plus curve has a big downward break. He also uses deceptive arm action to deliver an above-average circle change that fades away from righthanded batters. Langston became more of a breaking-ball pitcher in '95, using his fastball to set up his other offerings instead of as an out pitch.

Langston is slightly below-average at holding runners at first, largely due to the big leg kick which makes him slow to home. He compensates for that by throwing over often. Of the 16 trying to steal against Mark last year, 12 were gunned down. A good athlete with quick hands, he fields his position well.

HOW HE PERFORMED IN '95

Langston bounced back from a subpar '94 to resume his role as the Angels' ace. He cut down on the long ball, though for the second consecutive year he allowed more hits than innings pitched. While he is not the strikeout pitcher he used to be, Mark is pitching smarter.

That said, Langston's record was better than he pitched. He received nearly seven and a half runs from the Angels' offense per start, and had a 3-1 mark in June despite a 5.94 ERA. The numbers show how much he enjoyed pitching in the spacious Big A. Lack of consistency caught up to Mark in September; he had his worst month just when the Angels needed him the most and went 2-4, allowing six runs a game. Through the whole year, he pitched just well enough to win, but when the Angels' offense finally abandoned him in the late going, Mark couldn't come through.

WHAT TO EXPECT IN '96

Because he has slowly evolved into more than just a strikeout pitcher, Langston is better than he was a couple of years ago. However, he rarely can go more than seven innings and has lost a foot or more on his fastball. Mark is signed through 1997 and California will continue to count on him.

Overall Statistics

	G	GS	GF	SV	W	L	ERA	IP	H	R	ER	HR	BB	SO
95 CAL	31	31	0	0	15	7	4.63	200.1	212	109	103	21	64	142
Career	383	380	1	0	166	141	3.81	2648.2	2370	1241	1120	265	1145	2252

1995 Situational Statistics

	W	L	ERA	SV	IP	BB	SO		AB	HR	RBI	BA	OBA	SLG
Home	9	2	3.81	0	101.2	38	76	LHB	127	3	11	.291	.343	.409
Road	6	5	5.47	0	98.2	26	66	RHB	651	18	86	.269	.326	.416
Apr-Jun	6	1	4.72	0	82.0	25	53	ScPos	173	3	70	.329	.374	.491
Jul-Oct	9	6	4.56	0	118.1	39	89	Clutch	52	1	9	.385	.467	.558

How He Compares to Other Pitchers

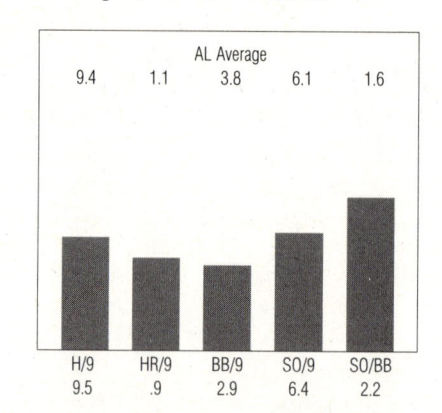

AL Average: 9.4 / 1.1 / 3.8 / 6.1 / 1.6

H/9: 9.5
HR/9: .9
BB/9: 2.9
SO/9: 6.4
SO/BB: 2.2

How He Compares to Other Starting Pitchers

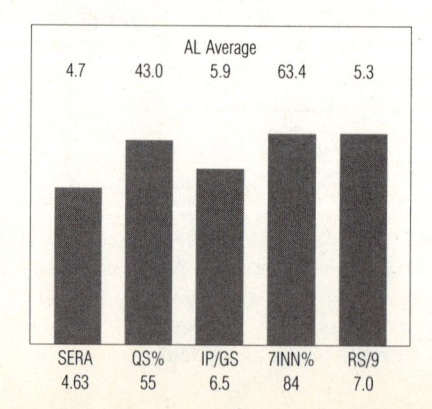

AL Average: 4.7 / 43.0 / 5.9 / 63.4 / 5.3

SERA: 4.63
QS%: 55
IP/GS: 6.5
7INN%: 84
RS/9: 7.0

CALIFORNIA ANGELS

TROY PERCIVAL

Position: RP
Bats: R **Throws:** R
Ht: 6'3" **Wt:** 200
Opening Day Age: 26
Born: 8/9/1969
Drafted: CAL90 5/179
ML Seasons: 1

SCOUTING REPORT
Percival pitches from a stretch position at all times, throwing from three quarters. He has a big leg kick, but has improved his positioning and ability to get off the mound quickly because he no longer recoils after delivering the pitch.

His excellent four-seam fastball rides in hard on righthanders. It's one of the best heaters in the league, and Troy throws fastballs almost 90 percent of the time. Percival's other pitch is a plus, very hard slider that he has problems controlling. He also shows a curve.

Troy had spotty control in the minors, but has improved. A very aggressive pitcher, he works very quickly. Below-average at holding runners because he lacks a good move to first, Percival is quick to the plate. Eight runners stole against him in nine tries last season. He is an average-minus fielder.

HOW HE PERFORMED IN '95
Percival was the best pitcher, day in and day out, that the Angels had in 1995. He rarely had a bad outing, setting up many of Lee Smith's saves. Averaging well over a strikeout per inning, Troy was virtually unhittable through the middle of the summer. During June, July, and August, Percival allowed only three runs in 35 games.

The only big worry for Troy at this point is a recurrence of the elbow problems that caused him to miss most of the '93 season. However, since having an operation on the medial collateral ligament of the elbow, Percival has been a more effective pitcher. Despite his good health, it must be noted that he had never pitched as many games or innings in a season as he did during '95.

WHAT TO EXPECT IN '96
Percival pitches best with a day of rest. However, it's likely that by the middle of this season he will have assumed at least co-closer duties with Big Lee. Troy throws very hard, has overpowering strikeout ability, and possesses the classic late-inning, "give me the ball" mentality.

At age 26 with one full season of big-league experience, Percival has been anointed the Angels' closer of the future. He could turn out to be one of the best relievers in baseball in the next few years.

Overall Statistics

	G	GS	GF	SV	W	L	ERA	IP	H	R	ER	HR	BB	SO
95 CAL	62	0	16	3	3	2	1.95	74.0	37	19	16	6	26	94
Career	62	0	16	3	3	2	1.95	74.0	37	19	16	6	26	94

1995 Situational Statistics

	W	L	ERA	SV	IP	BB	SO		AB	HR	RBI	BA	OBA	SLG
Home	1	1	1.67	0	37.2	12	55	LHB	116	2	7	.172	.262	.267
Road	2	1	2.23	3	36.1	14	39	RHB	136	4	14	.125	.200	.228
Apr-Jun	1	0	2.51	0	28.2	12	37	ScPos	60	0	13	.200	.269	.217
Jul-Oct	2	2	1.59	3	45.1	14	57	Clutch	155	5	17	.168	.222	.277

How He Compares to Other Pitchers

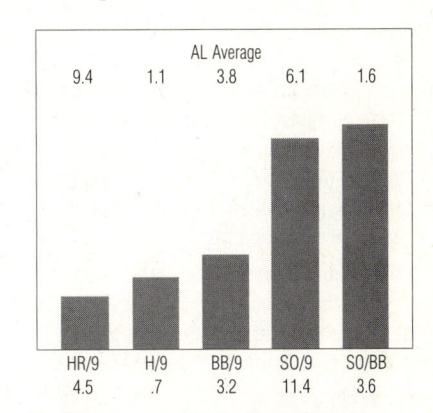

AL Average: HR/9 9.4, H/9 1.1, BB/9 3.8, SO/9 6.1, SO/BB 1.6
Percival: HR/9 4.5, H/9 .7, BB/9 3.2, SO/9 11.4, SO/BB 3.6

How He Compares to Other Relief Pitchers

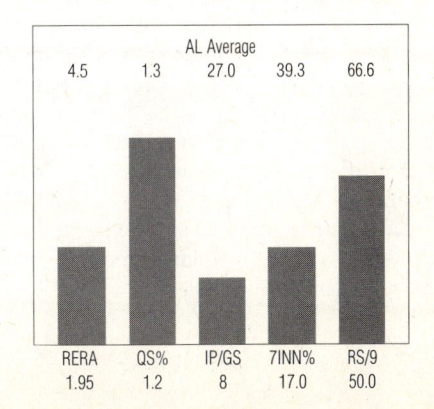

AL Average: RERA 4.5, QS% 1.3, IP/GS 27.0, 7INN% 39.3, RS/9 66.6
Percival: RERA 1.95, QS% 1.2, IP/GS 8, 7INN% 17.0, RS/9 50.0

THE SCOUTING REPORT: 1996

CALIFORNIA ANGELS

TONY PHILLIPS

Positions: 3B/OF//DH
Bats: B **Throws:** R
Ht: 5'10" **Wt:** 160
Opening Day Age: 36
Born: 4/25/1959
Drafted: MON78* S1/10
ML Seasons: 14

SCOUTING REPORT

Phillips was used at almost every position in his years with Detroit but played only left field and third base for the Angels. His arm strength and accuracy at both spots rank below-average; his range now is average at third but plus in left. Tony's hands are a little below-par.

He's a switch hitter with a big stride and a wide stance and tends to wave the bat around in the box. As a lefthanded batter, Tony can hit to all fields; as a righthanded batter he will pull the ball with power. Mostly a line-drive hitter, Phillips has a good batting eye and has now drawn 100 walks three times in the last four years. When he is pressing at the plate, Tony will chase some bad pitches.

Although Tony still possesses slightly above-average speed, he has never been an effective basestealer. He is, however, an extremely intense player who argues with umpires constantly and will not accept a lack of effort from his teammates or himself.

HOW HE PERFORMED IN '95

Tony's '95 mirrored the Angels rise and fall. He began the year in left field as the Angels tried out third basemen, but moved to the hot corner with the emergence of Garret Anderson and suddenly caught fire. He hit .352 in July, and slugged four to six homers in each full month of the season, establishing by eight a career high in four-baggers.

Phillips' bat helped propel the Angels to incredible heights, but as he wore down, the team wore down with him. He batted just .199 through the last two months, even though he continued to hit for power and take walks.

WHAT TO EXPECT IN '96

The Angels were not pleased with Tony's end-of-the-year slide, voicing concern that Phillips, who turns 37 this spring, lacks the stamina now to be an everyday player. However, after the club decided not to re-sign him, they then signed Tim Wallach (38 years old) and Jack Howell (35 years old) to replace Tony. Rather than a questions of age or stamina, California's decision to dump Phillips appeared based on purely financial considerations. You get what you pay for.

Overall Statistics

	G	AB	R	H	2B	3B	HR	RBI	SB	CS	BB	SO	BA	OBA
95 CAL	139	525	119	137	21	1	27	61	13	10	113	135	.261	.394
Career	1696	5860	975	1557	257	41	121	629	139	92	974	1105	.266	.370

1995 Situational Statistics

	AB	HR	RBI	BA	OBA	SLG		AB	HR	RBI	BA	OBA	SLG
Home	267	13	31	.255	.378	.446	LHP	132	7	13	.280	.441	.500
Road	258	14	30	.267	.410	.473	RHP	393	20	48	.254	.377	.445
Apr-Jun	219	10	30	.274	.410	.466	ScPos	117	6	37	.222	.374	.402
Jul-Oct	306	17	31	.252	.383	.454	Clutch	58	2	6	.259	.419	.379

How He Compares to Other Batters

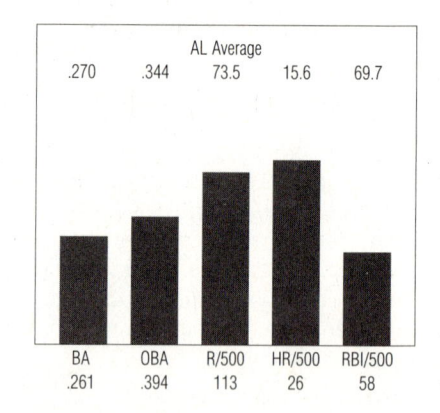

AL Average: .270 .344 73.5 15.6 69.7

BA .261 | OBA .394 | R/500 113 | HR/500 26 | RBI/500 58

Where He Hits the Ball

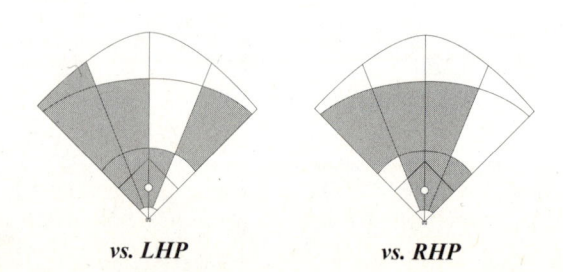

vs. LHP   vs. RHP

THE SCOUTING REPORT: 1996

CALIFORNIA ANGELS

TIM SALMON

Positions: OF//DH
Bats: R **Throws:** R
Ht: 6'3" **Wt:** 200
Opening Day Age: 27
Born: 8/24/1968
Drafted: CAL89 3/69
ML Seasons: 4

SCOUTING REPORT

A consummate power hitter, Salmon slams pitches hard to all fields but has more punch when pulling the ball. He has improved his plate discipline and is now a good contact hitter when the situation warrants it. Tim has also improve against breaking pitches, but still prefers fastballs down and on the inner half of the plate.

The strong, athletic Salmon has a slightly above-average arm with plus accuracy and is rarely run against. He also displays plus range in right field and catches what he gets to. Despite his size and build, Tim has decent speed and is a smart runner.

HOW HE PERFORMED IN '95

Salmon was the Angels' best player in '95, and is probably going to be their best player for several more years. He was the only player on the team to put together a consistent season day after day, month after month.

He hit .262 in May, which isn't bad, but batted at least .330 in every other month, spending most of August and September trying to singlehandedly carry the club to the pennant. Although it didn't work, Tim rightfully received a good deal of consideration for the AL MVP award.

Salmon had been a reverse-platoon hitter in his first two seasons, hitting just .241 against lefthanders with little power, but simply mashed southpaws last season. This alone was a big part of his leap in production during '95, and Tim has now become a truly lethal hitter.

From his post in right field, Salmon nailed eight men on the bases last season. He got to a lot of balls and made just four errors, fielding .988.

WHAT TO EXPECT IN '96

He will be hard-pressed to match his '95 performance, but he doesn't have to do that in order to be a fine player. The Angels will make every effort to try to keep Tim with the team for the indefinite future. He is the kind of player championship teams are built around.

Salmon's importance to the Angels cannot be overstated. He provides explosive offense and solid defense in as exciting a package as most California fans have seen. In a year or two, he'll probably rank as the best player the Angels have ever had.

Overall Statistics

	G	AB	R	H	2B	3B	HR	RBI	SB	CS	BB	SO	BA	OBA
95 CAL	143	537	111	177	34	3	34	105	5	5	91	111	.330	.429
Career	408	1504	279	444	88	6	90	276	12	15	238	371	.295	.394

1995 Situational Statistics

	AB	HR	RBI	BA	OBA	SLG		AB	HR	RBI	BA	OBA	SLG
Home	258	15	47	.291	.405	.531	LHP	139	11	31	.338	.456	.647
Road	279	19	58	.366	.453	.652	RHP	398	23	74	.327	.420	.575
Apr-Jun	219	15	38	.301	.432	.571	ScPos	145	9	72	.331	.442	.621
Jul-Oct	318	19	67	.349	.428	.610	Clutch	59	5	15	.356	.472	.678

How He Compares to Other Batters

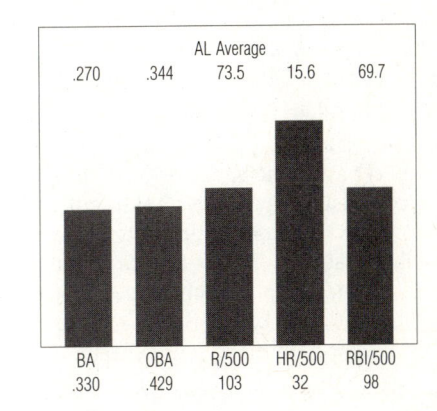

AL Average: BA .270, OBA .344, R/500 73.5, HR/500 15.6, RBI/500 69.7

Salmon: BA .330, OBA .429, R/500 103, HR/500 32, RBI/500 98

Where He Hits the Ball

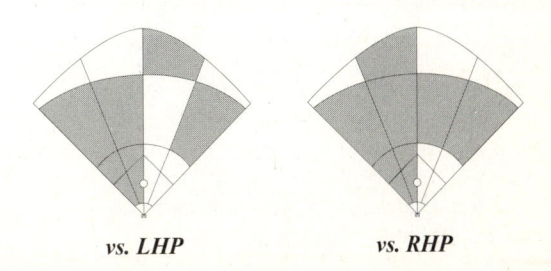

vs. LHP   vs. RHP

THE SCOUTING REPORT: 1996

CALIFORNIA ANGELS

LEE SMITH

Position: RP
Bats: R **Throws:** R
Ht: 6'6" **Wt:** 225
Opening Day Age: 37
Born: 12/4/1957
Drafted: CHN75 2/28
ML Seasons: 15

SCOUTING REPORT
Big Lee throws from three quarters, though he will come from low three-quarters from the stretch position. Once in possession of one of baseball's most ferocious heaters, Smith now has only an average fastball, throwing both a two-seam sinker and a four-seamer. When he needs to, however, Lee can reach back and summon some extra velocity. He has a slightly above-average hard slider; Smith's out pitch is a slightly above-average splitter. Lee has fine control and now succeeds when he keeps the ball away from hitters.

Ranked below-average at holding runners, Smith is slow to home from the stretch. However, just four of nine trying to steal last year were successful. Due to several knee surgeries, Lee is slow off the mound and is a minus fielder.

HOW HE PERFORMED IN '95
Smith was extremely fortunate to end up with his 37 saves. As he had in '94, he started hot and didn't give up an earned run in his first 13 games, collecting 12 saves in that span. Beginning in June, however, he was colder than ice cream. Smith could barely get a batter out in the next two months, totaling an ERA over 8.00 in that period, but still racked up 12 more saves!

A typical Smith appearance during the summer involved lots of baserunners, one or two runs scoring, but—miraculously—the Angels holding their lead. Tagged for a .283 average by first batters faced, Lee often pitched just well enough to escape many self-made jams. Most Angels' pitchers take full advantage of their home park, and Smith was no exception; he was especially rocky on the road.

After the slump, Smith was again effective in August and September as the Angels tried futilely to cling to the division lead.

WHAT TO EXPECT IN '96
With the emergence of young Troy Percival, Smith's role on the Angels for '96 is not easily defined. Lee clearly considers himself a closer, and is still able to do the job, but California is likely to shift at least some of the responsibility from the closer of the past to the closer of the future. The all-time leader in saves by a large margin, Lee is close to the end but still has something left to give.

Overall Statistics

	G	GS	GF	SV	W	L	ERA	IP	H	R	ER	HR	BB	SO
94 BAL	41	0	39	33	1	4	3.29	38.1	34	16	14	6	11	42
Career	891	6	713	434	68	82	2.93	1163.0	1006	416	378	80	427	1152

1994 Situational Statistics

	W	L	ERA	SV	IP	BB	SO		AB	HR	RBI	BA	OBA	SLG
Home	0	2	3.00	15	30.0	5	18	LHP	72	4	11	.306	.366	.542
Road	1	2	3.54	18	33.2	6	24	RHP	70	2	5	.171	.205	.271
Apr–Jun	1	1	1.55	27	48.1	5	33	ScPos	40	1	9	.200	.209	.275
Jul–Oct	0	3	8.68	6	15.1	6	9	Clutch	119	5	15	.218	.280	.370

How He Compares to Other Pitchers

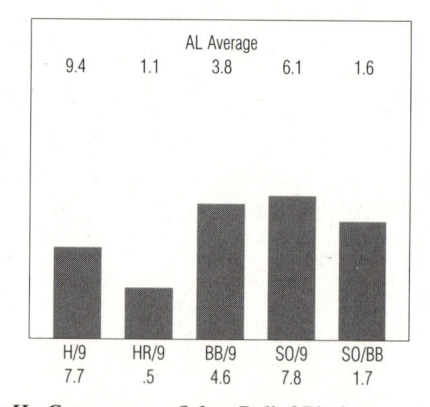

AL Average: H/9 9.4, HR/9 1.1, BB/9 3.8, SO/9 6.1, SO/BB 1.6

Smith: H/9 7.7, HR/9 .5, BB/9 4.6, SO/9 7.8, SO/BB 1.7

How He Compares to Other Relief Pitchers

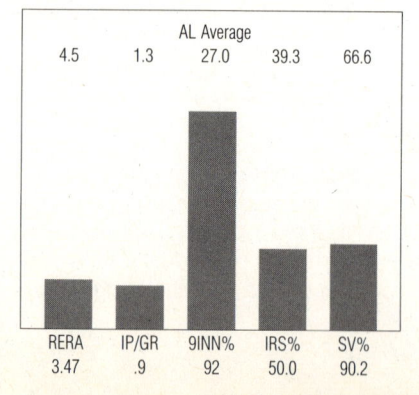

AL Average: RERA 4.5, IP/GR 1.3, 9INN% 27.0, IRS% 39.3, SV% 66.6

Smith: RERA 3.47, IP/GR .9, 9INN% 92, IRS% 50.0, SV% 90.2

CALIFORNIA ANGELS

J. T. SNOW

Position: 1B
Bats: B **Throws:** L
Ht: 6'2" **Wt:** 200
Opening Day Age: 28
Born: 2/26/1968
Drafted: NYA89 4/129
ML Seasons: 4

SCOUTING REPORT

Defense has never been the problem for J.T., who is one of the best first basemen in the American League. His range is not good, but he goes back very well on pop flies. He will also dive for balls, especially those down the line. Snow has good, soft hands and is very adept at receiving throws at first base. His throwing skills also rate above par.

Offense has always been the trouble spot in J.T.'s game, but he showed growth last year. The switch-hitting Snow has more power lefthanded but improved dramatically from the right side in '95. He prefers high pitches from both sides of the dish, hitting straightaway from the left and pulling the ball more often batting righthanded. While he has gotten better at making contact, J.T. must go to the opposite field more while batting lefthanded. Not fast on the basepaths, he is a smart runner and an effective sacrifice bunter, although he grounded into 16 double plays last season.

HOW HE PERFORMED IN '95

Snow may have finally put his game together last year. A two-year disappointment to the Angels since they acquired him from the Yankees in '93, he wasn't traded after the '94 season only because California couldn't find any takers.

Because the Angels had no one else, J.T. became the starting first baseman at the beginning of '95. He got off to the fabulous start he needed to avoid a trip to Vancouver, batting .287 in May with seven homers. Except for August, when his average skidded to .234 as nearly all the Angels' hitters had problems, Snow was productive at the plate, hitting for average and power and showing surprising stick against lefthanders.

The Angels were heartened by his last month. When the club was failing, Snow was fairly productive. However, he will have to prove that last season was not just a career year.

WHAT TO EXPECT IN '96

J.T.'s '95 performance pulled his career out of the fire and has secured him a job for the near future. There are still nagging doubts in the organization as to whether he can put up consistent numbers, but another performance like last year would likely turn even the staunchest non-believers in sunny southern California into Snow worshipers.

Overall Statistics

	G	AB	R	H	2B	3B	HR	RBI	SB	CS	BB	SO	BA	OBA
95 CAL	143	544	80	157	22	1	24	102	2	1	52	91	.289	.353
Career	340	1200	163	309	45	3	48	191	5	2	131	232	.257	.332

1995 Situational Statistics

	AB	HR	RBI	BA	OBA	SLG		AB	HR	RBI	BA	OBA	SLG
Home	270	14	60	.304	.374	.496	LHP	161	5	28	.267	.351	.404
Road	274	10	42	.274	.331	.434	RHP	383	19	74	.298	.353	.491
Apr-Jun	228	10	43	.294	.355	.474	ScPos	170	11	86	.294	.381	.547
Jul-Oct	316	14	59	.285	.351	.459	Clutch	67	5	14	.224	.316	.463

How He Compares to Other Batters

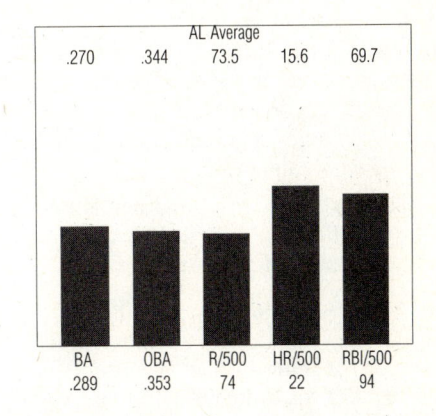

AL Average: .270 | .344 | 73.5 | 15.6 | 69.7

BA	OBA	R/500	HR/500	RBI/500
.289	.353	74	22	94

Where He Hits the Ball

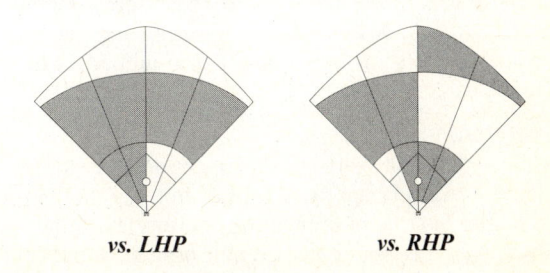

vs. LHP   vs. RHP

THE SCOUTING REPORT: 1996

CALIFORNIA ANGELS

MIKE ALDRETE

Positions: 1B/OF//DH
Bats: L **Throws:** L
Ht: 5'11" **Wt:** 185
Opening Day Age: 35
Born: 1/29/1961
Drafted: SF83 6/174
ML Seasons: 9

Overall Statistics

	G	AB	R	H	2B	3B	HR	RBI	SB	CS	BB	SO	BA	OBA
95 OAK/CAL	78	149	19	40	8	0	4	24	0	0	19	31	.268	.349
Career	867	2039	261	542	98	9	35	251	19	17	300	362	.266	.359

1995 Situational Statistics

	AB	HR	RBI	BA	OBA	SLG		AB	HR	RBI	BA	OBA	SLG
Home	74	2	11	.230	.322	.351	LHP	6	0	0	.000	.333	.000
Road	75	2	13	.307	.376	.453	RHP	143	4	24	.280	.350	.420
Apr-Jun	47	1	7	.213	.321	.383	ScPos	35	0	18	.343	.469	.400
Jul-Oct	102	3	17	.294	.362	.412	Clutch	26	0	5	.385	.485	.385

SCOUTING REPORT

Aldrete has to hit his way into a ball game these days due to his minus speed and mediocre defense. A good line-drive, contact hitter, he has little power but good strike-zone judgment. He likes pitches up and uses the whole field well.

He can play first base with good hands but minus range. In the outfield, Mike displays minus range and arm strength but throws accurately.

HOW HE PERFORMED IN '95

Mike began the year with the Athletics, filling in at first base for the injury-prone Mark McGwire. He was batting .272 for Oakland before an August 24 trade sent him to the Angels.

Expected to give California the solid lefthanded bat off the bench they felt they needed, Aldrete batted just 24 times for the Angels, collecting six hits. He continued to show better power than he had earlier in his career.

WHAT TO EXPECT IN '96

The veteran was surprised by the trade and did not leave Oakland happily. While Aldrete is still productive, his role is limited to spot duty and pinch-hitting at this point. He can still provide some offense, but is strictly a platoon hitter.

BRIAN ANDERSON

Position: SP
Bats: L **Throws:** L
Ht: 6'1" **Wt:** 190
Opening Day Age: 23
Born: 4/26/1972
Drafted: CAL93 1/3
ML Seasons: 3

Overall Statistics

	G	GS	GF	SV	W	L	ERA	IP	H	R	ER	HR	BB	SO
95 CAL	18	17	0	0	6	8	5.87	99.2	110	66	65	24	30	45
Career	40	36	3	0	13	13	5.46	212.2	241	134	129	38	59	96

1995 Situational Statistics

	W	L	ERA	SV	IP	BB	SO		AB	HR	RBI	BA	OBA	SLG
Home	4	3	3.24	0	58.1	14	24	LHB	79	6	19	.342	.354	.633
Road	2	5	9.58	0	41.1	16	21	RHB	311	18	38	.267	.329	.498
Apr-Jun	1	1	4.87	0	20.1	6	5	ScPos	79	4	33	.253	.312	.481
Jul-Oct	5	7	6.13	0	79.1	24	40	Clutch	7	1	1	.429	.556	1.000

SCOUTING REPORT

Anderson has a deep leg kick and a three-quarter to low three-quarter delivery, bringing home a slightly below-average fastball, which is straight when high. Brian cuts the fastball and runs it away from righthanders. He throws an average turned-over change-up, an average slider and will show a curve. Short on stuff, Brian can't succeed without good command. Anderson is one of the league's best at holding runners. However, the leg kick hurts him, and eight of 11 basestealing attempts were successful in '95. He is a slightly better-than-average fielder.

HOW HE PERFORMED IN '95

The '93 #1 pick was expected to be in the rotation all season. He missed most of May with a strained biceps tendon, but pitched effectively in July (4-1, 3.44 ERA). From there, it was all downhill. He crumbled in August, going 1-5 with an 8.92 ERA, allowing 51 hits—including 11 homers—in 35.1 innings. Brian's collapse hurt the Angels tremendously and he pitched just twice in September.

WHAT TO EXPECT IN '96

Anderson will probably begin the year in the rotation because the team doesn't have anybody to replace him, but he needs help.

CALIFORNIA ANGELS

MIKE BIELECKI

Position: SP/RP
Bats: R **Throws:** R
Ht: 6'3" **Wt:** 200
Opening Day Age: 36
Born: 7/31/1959
Drafted: PIT79 S1/8
ML Seasons: 12

Overall Statistics

	G	GS	GF	SV	W	L	ERA	IP	H	R	ER	HR	BB	SO
95 CAL	22	11	2	0	4	6	5.97	75.1	80	56	50	15	31	45
Career	257	173	33	1	63	63	4.29	1098.1	1117	576	524	99	442	652

1995 Situational Statistics

	W	L	ERA	SV	IP	BB	SO		AB	HR	RBI	BA	OBA	SLG
Home	1	3	6.16	0	30.2	15	16	LHB	172	9	23	.238	.307	.424
Road	3	3	5.84	0	44.2	16	29	RHB	121	6	27	.322	.393	.521
Apr-Jun	3	5	5.24	0	55.0	23	28	ScPos	53	5	34	.377	.433	.698
Jul-Oct	1	1	7.97	0	20.1	8	17	Clutch	1	0	1	.000	.333	.000

SCOUTING REPORT

Bielecki has a distracting, rocking motion, with a slight hesitation and a high three-quarter delivery. He must spot his straight, average-minus fastball, but can so effectively. Mike's slightly above-average forkball is his out pitch. He will also occasionally throw an average curve. An agile athlete, Bielecki is a slightly above-average fielder and has an average move to first. Eight men attempted steals in '95 against him, six successfully.

HOW HE PERFORMED IN '95

 Bielecki came to the Angels after spending '94 in Atlanta. He put up solid numbers early in the season, giving the Angels quality innings as a spot starter and long reliever.

Unfortunately, he began to slump, registering ERAs over six in both June and July, before going down July 18 with an aching shoulder. He didn't pitch again for California until September and was bad when he did come back.

WHAT TO EXPECT IN '96

The Angels wanted to retain Bielecki for '96. It's hard to see how he can last a whole season, however, considering that he will be 37 in July and has not shown that his shoulder can assume a heavy load.

SHAWN BOSKIE

Position: SP
Bats: R **Throws:** R
Ht: 6'3" **Wt:** 205
Opening Day Age: 29
Born: 3/28/1967
Drafted: CHN86* 1/10
ML Seasons: 6

Overall Statistics

	G	GS	GF	SV	W	L	ERA	IP	H	R	ER	HR	BB	SO
95 CAL	20	20	0	0	7	7	5.64	111.2	127	73	70	16	25	51
Career	147	90	15	0	30	43	4.79	586.1	627	336	312	74	195	301

1995 Situational Statistics

	W	L	ERA	SV	IP	BB	SO		AB	HR	RBI	BA	OBA	SLG
Home	3	3	5.01	0	50.1	11	23	LHB	246	8	37	.285	.339	.467
Road	4	4	6.16	0	61.1	14	28	RHB	206	8	31	.277	.306	.481
Apr-Jun	6	1	4.42	0	77.1	13	31	ScPos	108	5	51	.324	.358	.574
Jul-Oct	1	6	8.39	0	34.1	12	20	Clutch	26	0	1	.154	.185	.231

SCOUTING REPORT

Boskie uses a high windup and a high three-quarter delivery, throwing a straight, but slightly above-average fastball. Shawn also throws an average slider, a below-par circle change and, infrequently, a curve.

He must keep the ball away to be effective but has just average control. Slightly above-average at holding runners, Boskie has a quick delivery; just four men tried to steal against him, three successfully. He is a average fielder.

HOW HE PERFORMED IN '95

Another of the Angels' reclamation projects, Shawn started '95 as the fourth starter. He began the year pitching effectively, but in mid-July he went out with arm trouble, which kept him from inactive until September.

Once he returned, Boskie could barely get anybody out, going 1-5 with a 7.98 ERA in his last seven starts—another Angels' pitcher who started strong and fell apart at the end.

WHAT TO EXPECT IN '96

The late-season collapse is a concern, especially after an arm injury. In the unlikely event he can return to his early '95 form, Shawn will start. If not, the Angels have plenty of middle relievers.

CALIFORNIA ANGELS

MIKE BUTCHER

Position: RP
Bats: R **Throws:** R
Ht: 6'1" **Wt:** 200
Opening Day Age: 30
Born: 5/10/1965
Drafted: KC86 S2/36
ML Seasons: 4

Overall Statistics

	G	GS	GF	SV	W	L	ERA	IP	H	R	ER	HR	BB	SO
95 CAL	40	0	13	0	6	1	4.74	51.1	49	28	27	7	31	29
Career	115	0	42	9	11	4	4.47	137.0	130	75	68	14	82	96

1995 Situational Statistics

	W	L	ERA	SV	IP	BB	SO		AB	HR	RBI	BA	OBA	SLG
Home	1	1	6.14	0	22.0	12	10	LHB	83	2	12	.337	.440	.482
Road	5	0	3.68	0	29.1	19	19	RHB	108	5	22	.194	.294	.398
Apr-Jun	5	1	7.59	0	21.1	15	13	ScPos	51	4	30	.216	.394	.510
Jul-Oct	1	0	2.70	0	30.0	16	16	Clutch	38	3	5	.395	.425	.684

SCOUTING REPORT

Butcher doesn't use a windup; therefore, his three-quarter delivery takes a lot of effort. He has average control of three pitches and is very aggressive but must keep the ball down to be effective.

Mike's fastball is average. His best pitch is an average-plus slider, and he also throws a below-average curve. Mike is just average at holding runners; three of four basestealing attempts against him failed in '95. He is a slightly below-average fielder.

HOW HE PERFORMED IN '95

Butcher had one good month in '95 and four bad ones. He struggled through May and June but allowed only one run in 13.2 innings during July. After a 4.70 ERA in August, he was designated for assignment on September 8 and outrighted to Triple-A ten days later.

WHAT TO EXPECT IN '96

A major area of concern is Butcher's performance against lefthanders: he's always been good against righties, but was far worse against portsiders last year than before. Mike can rarely pitch on consecutive days and was very ineffective at home. He will need to work hard to impress someone this spring.

DAVE GALLAGHER

Positions: OF//DH
Bats: R **Throws:** R
Ht: 6' " **Wt:** 180
Opening Day Age: 35
Born: 9/20/1960
Drafted: CLE80 S1/8
ML Seasons: 9

Overall Statistics

	G	AB	R	H	2B	3B	HR	RBI	SB	CS	BB	SO	BA	OBA
95 PHI/CAL	73	173	13	53	13	0	1	12	0	0	18	21	.306	.370
Career	794	2081	273	564	100	10	17	190	20	24	187	251	.271	.331

1995 Situational Statistics

	AB	HR	RBI	BA	OBA	SLG		AB	HR	RBI	BA	OBA	SLG
Home	82	1	7	.354	.430	.524	LHP	83	0	6	.301	.385	.398
Road	91	0	5	.264	.313	.286	RHP	90	1	6	.311	.354	.400
Apr-Jun	104	1	10	.317	.368	.413	ScPos	39	0	9	.179	.313	.231
Jul-Oct	69	0	2	.290	.372	.377	Clutch	19	0	3	.263	.391	.316

SCOUTING REPORT

He can still play all three outfield spots but Gallagher has declining defensive tools. His arm is minus with average accuracy, his range is just average, and his hands rate slightly below that.

Dave now has minus speed and doesn't steal. He has little power, but makes contact, bunts well, and can be used to hit-and-run. Although he doesn't walk much, he doesn't strike out, either.

HOW HE PERFORMED IN '95

Gallagher came to the Angels in a late-season trade from the Phillies. Neither he nor fellow August acquisition Mike Aldrete got many pinch-hitting chances, because the Angels were not close in many late-season games.

While not effective and not used much with his new team as it plummeted out of first place, Dave was productive earlier in '95 in Philadelphia, playing anywhere he was asked and batting .318.

WHAT TO EXPECT IN '96

Gallagher plays steady defense, hits for average and leads by example with a good work ethic. He is a popular player who will play a few more years as an outfield reserve.

CALIFORNIA ANGELS

JOHN HABYAN

Position: RP
Bats: R **Throws:** R
Ht: 6'1" **Wt:** 195
Opening Day Age: 32
Born: 1/29/1964
Drafted: BAL82 3/78
ML Seasons: 10

Overall Statistics

	G	GS	GF	SV	W	L	ERA	IP	H	R	ER	HR	BB	SO
95 SL/CAL	59	0	16	0	4	4	3.44	73.1	68	34	28	2	27	60
Career	329	18	93	12	25	23	3.70	508.1	503	235	209	43	172	347

1995 Situational Statistics

	W	L	ERA	SV	IP	BB	SO		AB	HR	RBI	BA	OBA	SLG
Home	3	2	3.18	0	39.2	15	31	LHB	105	1	9	.267	.336	.362
Road	1	2	3.74	0	33.2	12	29	RHB	168	1	18	.238	.306	.351
Apr-Jun	2	1	2.70	0	36.2	14	35	ScPos	79	0	21	.228	.319	.304
Jul-Oct	2	3	4.17	0	36.2	13	25	Clutch	70	1	9	.357	.438	.500

SCOUTING REPORT

Habyan, a prototypical sinker-slider pitcher, works from the stretch with a three-quarter motion. His average-minus fastball sinks and his slider is average. Infrequently, John will show a curve.

His control is average, but Habyan's competitive fire burns brightly and he will take the ball at any time. John is average at holding runners and fielding: nine tried to steal against him in '95, five successfully.

HOW HE PERFORMED IN '95

He came to the Angels in July after posting a 2.88 ERA in 31 games for St. Louis. Working as a bridge from the starters to Troy Percival, he pitched well at first, but contributed to a dismal Anaheim August with a 7.94 ERA and 19 hits in 11 innings.

Although Habyan bounced back in the last month, he was not used in crucial situations. John was acquired to get tough righthanded batters out, but AL righties hit nearly .300 off him.

WHAT TO EXPECT IN '96

Habyan was two different pitchers in '95: solid with the Cardinals and ineffective for the Angels. He will pitch often again in the middle in '95, but only if he can get righthanded hitters out again.

REX HUDLER

Positions: 2B/OF//DH/1B
Bats: R **Throws:** R
Ht: 6'1" **Wt:** 180
Opening Day Age: 35
Born: 9/2/1960
Drafted: NYA78 1/18
ML Seasons: 10

Overall Statistics

	G	AB	R	H	2B	3B	HR	RBI	SB	CS	BB	SO	BA	OBA
95 CAL	84	223	30	59	16	0	6	27	12	0	10	48	.265	.310
Career	607	1302	182	335	71	7	35	117	91	38	58	231	.257	.292

1995 Situational Statistics

	AB	HR	RBI	BA	OBA	SLG		AB	HR	RBI	BA	OBA	SLG
Home	112	4	10	.268	.325	.438	LHP	92	4	16	.272	.337	.489
Road	111	2	17	.261	.293	.396	RHP	131	2	11	.260	.290	.366
Apr-Jun	78	2	12	.231	.259	.385	ScPos	62	2	23	.306	.362	.500
Jul-Oct	145	4	15	.283	.335	.434	Clutch	37	0	1	.189	.211	.216

SCOUTING REPORT

Hudler can play three infield positions as well as serve in the outfield. He has average-plus range at second base and left field (his primary spots) with average-minus hands. His throwing arm isn't strong but has average accuracy.

A contact hitter, Rex will swing at almost anything and rarely walks. He has some power. Hudler is not a good breaking-ball hitter, preferring fastballs up and over the plate. A very aggressive player, Hudler's bulldog attitude helps make up for his obvious deficiencies. Blessed with average-plus speed, Rex is an intelligent runner and had his best-ever basestealing performance in '95.

HOW HE PERFORMED IN '95

Hudler's hustling, super-aggressive play stood out on a team viewed by many as too laid-back at times. With Damion Easley struggling, he got 37 starts at second base, but Rex is basically an utility player. He hit well at times but, like most of his teammates, played very badly in August (.195, 1 RBI in 40 at-bats).

WHAT TO EXPECT IN '96

Rex has found a niche on the Angels and will remain on the team, providing versatility and a hard-nosed attitude.

THE SCOUTING REPORT: 1996

CALIFORNIA ANGELS

MIKE JAMES

Position: RP
Bats: R **Throws:** R
Ht: 6'4" **Wt:** 215
Opening Day Age: 28
Born: 8/15/1967
Drafted: LA87 43/1064
ML Seasons: 1

Overall Statistics

	G	GS	GF	SV	W	L	ERA	IP	H	R	ER	HR	BB	SO
95 CAL	46	0	11	1	3	0	3.88	55.2	49	27	24	6	26	36
Career	46	0	11	1	3	0	3.88	55.2	49	27	24	6	26	36

1995 Situational Statistics

	W	L	ERA	SV	IP	BB	SO		AB	HR	RBI	BA	OBA	SLG
Home	0	0	3.27	0	22.0	11	12	LHB	84	5	13	.262	.361	.524
Road	3	0	4.28	1	33.2	15	24	RHB	122	1	17	.221	.312	.270
Apr-Jun	0	0	4.87	1	20.1	7	12	ScPos	55	1	23	.236	.323	.345
Jul-Oct	3	0	3.31	0	35.1	19	24	Clutch	37	0	9	.297	.350	.351

SCOUTING REPORT

James, a quick worker, uses an odd short-arm delivery with a slight hesitation. Pitching from the stretch, his three-quarter delivery brings home an average-plus slider that has power but a small break. It's Mike's best offering. He also has an average fastball and shows a curve. To be successful, James needs good control: in '95, it was slightly below-par. He gets the key strikeout but may just as easily walk the next batter.

Mike comes home quickly and uses a slide step to hold runners effectively—only one runner tried to steal against him in '95. Quick off the mound, he is a plus fielder.

HOW HE PERFORMED IN '95

James was a part of the Angels' early success, pitching well in middle relief. During 20 games in July and August, Mike allowed just three runs. However, he may have been used too much early on, and he fell apart in September. James allowed ten walks and nine hits in just 7.2 innings and was a forgotten man by the end of the season.

WHAT TO EXPECT IN '96

James can be helpful in middle relief in '96 but won't graduate beyond that role.

GREG MYERS

Positions: C/DH
Bats: L **Throws:** R
Ht: 6'1" **Wt:** 200
Opening Day Age: 29
Born: 4/14/1966
Drafted: TOR84 2/74
ML Seasons: 8

Overall Statistics

	G	AB	R	H	2B	3B	HR	RBI	SB	CS	BB	SO	BA	OBA
95 CAL	85	273	35	71	12	2	9	38	0	1	17	49	.260	.304
Career	486	1379	135	340	66	3	32	158	3	8	94	224	.247	.293

1995 Situational Statistics

	AB	HR	RBI	BA	OBA	SLG		AB	HR	RBI	BA	OBA	SLG
Home	128	6	22	.250	.312	.461	LHP	75	0	9	.240	.280	.320
Road	145	3	16	.269	.296	.379	RHP	198	9	29	.268	.313	.455
Apr-Jun	97	3	19	.278	.345	.443	ScPos	72	0	25	.264	.329	.333
Jul-Oct	176	6	19	.250	.279	.403	Clutch	34	2	6	.265	.286	.500

SCOUTING REPORT

Myers is a first-ball, fastball hitter who displays some power on inside pitches. He likes to pull the ball, especially against righties, and rarely puts the ball in play to the left side of the diamond.

Like most catchers, he's slow. Defensively, Myers' skills have deteriorated. He has an average arm but average-minus throwing accuracy. Additionally, Greg has slightly below-average mobility and hands; however, Angels' pitchers enjoy throwing to him.

HOW HE PERFORMED IN '95

After a fast start, Myers was hobbled by injuries most of the rest of the year, spending three stints on the disabled list. He rebounded in August but, like many Angels, struggled through September.

Sharing duties with another lefthanded batting catcher, Jorge Fabregas, caused Greg to play against lefthanded pitchers, whom he really can't hit.

WHAT TO EXPECT IN '96

He's a one-dimensional offensive player with minimal power against righthanded pitchers. For this reason, he shouldn't play regularly. Signed by Minnesota this year, he'll try to help solve the Twins' power shortage.

CALIFORNIA ANGELS

SPIKE OWEN

Positions: 3B/SS/2B
Bats: B **Throws:** R
Ht: 5'10" **Wt:** 170
Opening Day Age: 34
Born: 4/19/1961
Drafted: SEA82 1/6
ML Seasons: 13

Overall Statistics

	G	AB	R	H	2B	3B	HR	RBI	SB	CS	BB	SO	BA	OBA
95 CAL	82	218	17	50	9	3	1	28	3	2	18	22	.229	.288
Career	1544	4930	587	1211	215	59	46	439	82	62	569	519	.246	.324

1995 Situational Statistics

	AB	HR	RBI	BA	OBA	SLG		AB	HR	RBI	BA	OBA	SLG
Home	96	0	13	.229	.282	.292	LHP	44	0	8	.205	.271	.273
Road	122	1	15	.230	.293	.328	RHP	174	1	20	.236	.293	.322
Apr-Jun	123	1	17	.228	.301	.325	ScPos	62	0	26	.306	.368	.387
Jul-Oct	95	0	11	.232	.270	.295	Clutch	50	0	9	.280	.345	.340

SCOUTING REPORT

Owen plays every infield position except first. He has average-plus range and average hands, with an average, accurate arm.

A switch-hitter, Spike bats lefthanded with an open stance, using a straightaway stance righthanded. He has minus power but makes contact much more consistently now. Owen will bunt for hits and, at age 36, still has slightly above-average speed.

HOW HE PERFORMED IN '95

The '95 season was quite a come down for Spike, who had batted a lofty .310 the season before. He filled in throughout the infield, proving adequate defensively, but struggled offensively.

With Gary DiSarcina hurt, Owen made eight starts at shortstop, but is no longer up to the task. He once hit lefthanded pitchers well, but has deteriorated in this regard.

WHAT TO EXPECT IN '96

Spike is valuable because he can play multiple positions without hurting the team badly at any of them. The Angels have several players like this. Although Owen is likely to get a job somewhere this season because of his versatility, he must produce more offense to justify playing 80 games a season.

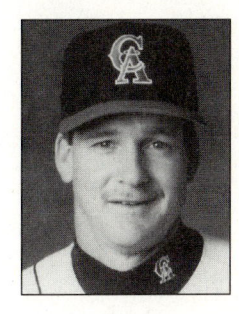

BOB PATTERSON

Position: RP
Bats: R **Throws:** L
Ht: 6'2" **Wt:** 195
Opening Day Age: 36
Born: 5/16/1959
Drafted: SD82 21/524
ML Seasons: 10

Overall Statistics

	G	GS	GF	SV	W	L	ERA	IP	H	R	ER	HR	BB	SO
95 CAL	62	0	20	0	5	2	3.04	53.1	48	18	18	6	13	41
Career	371	21	132	19	34	30	4.14	483.0	490	232	222	53	136	355

1995 Situational Statistics

	W	L	ERA	SV	IP	BB	SO		AB	HR	RBI	BA	OBA	SLG
Home	3	1	2.48	0	29.0	9	21	LHB	85	2	11	.200	.250	.329
Road	2	1	3.70	0	24.1	4	20	RHB	110	4	13	.282	.331	.436
Apr-Jun	4	2	2.39	0	26.1	8	23	ScPos	61	0	17	.279	.338	.361
Jul-Oct	1	0	3.67	0	27.0	5	18	Clutch	74	1	10	.243	.296	.351

SCOUTING REPORT

Patterson pitches from a full windup and comes to the plate from a three-quarter to high three-quarter angle. He has average-plus control and needs to works the corners effectively to succeed.

Bob's minus fastball tails into lefthanded batters. He throws an average slow curve with a big break and a subpar straight change that he will turn over. Patterson has a plus pickoff move: seven tried to steal against him in '95, but four were thrown out. He is an average fielder.

HOW HE PERFORMED IN '95

Patterson was the only southpaw in the Angels' bullpen for most of the year and pitched well until slumping seriously in August and September. At age 37, he appeared in a career-high 62 contests. Usually brought in to get one or two key lefties out, Bob has proven effective in that role. He was able to pitch well on short rest.

WHAT TO EXPECT IN '96

The veteran has pitched beyond club expectations for the last two years, and Patterson will continue to get work in late-inning situations where lefthanded hitters are coming up until he proves he can't pitch anymore.

THE SCOUTING REPORT: 1996

CALIFORNIA ANGELS: TOP PROSPECTS

GEORGE ARIAS
Bats: R Throws: R Opening Day Age: 24
Ht: 5-11 Wt: 190 Born: 3/12/1972
Position: 3B Drafted: 1993 #7 CAL

YR TEAM	LG/CLASS	G	AB	R	H	2B	3B	HR	RBI	SB	BA	OBA
93 Cedar Rapids	MID/A	74	253	31	55	13	3	9	41	6	.217	.308
94 Lake Elsnor	CAL/A	134	514	89	144	28	3	23	80	6	.280	.356
95 Midland	TEX/AA	134	520	91	145	19	10	30	104	3	.279	.359

Arias has put together two straight exceptional seasons after a standout collegiate career at Arizona. A California League All-Star in '94, Arias was named to the Texas League All-Star squad in '95. He led the league in homers, RBI, runs and total bases, was second in slugging (.527), extra-base hits, and triples, and third in hits. The former Wildcat slugger has a great work ethic and improved both offensively and defensively last year, becoming a more disciplined hitter and improving his throwing. Arias has the potential to become an outstanding defensive third baseman and a true major league power hitter.

MATT BEAUMONT
Bats: L Throws: L Opening Day Age: 23
Ht: 6-3 Wt: 210 Born: 4/22/1973
Position: P Drafted: 1994 #4 CAL

YR TEAM	LG/CLASS	G	GS	GF	SV	W	L	ERA	IP	H	HR	BB	SO	O/BA
94 Boise	NWST/A	12	10	0	0	3	3	3.52	64.0	52	2	22	77	.223
95 Lake Elsnor	CAL/A	27	26	0	0	16	9	3.29	175.1	162	15	57	149	.248

In his first full pro season, the former Ohio State Buckeye led the Angels' farm system in wins and was second in ERA and strikeouts while earning California League Pitcher of the Year honors. After a great start, he struggled in July but rebounded to win his last six starts. Beaumont's fastball could get into the 90's as he fills out, and he also throws a good curve and a changeup. He seems to have a good feel for pitching, setting hitters up well and working both sides of the plate.

JASON DICKSON
Bats: L Throws: R Opening Day Age: 23
Ht: 6-0 Wt: 190 Born: 3/30/1973
Position: P Drafted: 1994 #6 CAL

YR TEAM	LG/CLASS	G	GS	GF	SV	W	L	ERA	IP	H	HR	BB	SO	O/BA
94 Boise	NWST/A	9	7	1	1	3	1	3.86	44.1	40	3	18	37	.237
95 Cdr Rapids	MID/A	25	25	0	0	14	6	2.86	173.0	151	12	45	134	.233

Dickson is one of the Angels' top lower-level pitching prospects. The Canadian righthander led the Angels' farm system in ERA and also led the Midwest League in complete games. He tied for second in the league in wins while ranking third in innings and fifth in strikeouts. The Northeast Oklahoma A&M product won his last six decisions of the season, including a four-hit shutout of Clinton on July 25 in which he fanned 15 batters. Dickson's rising fastball is a legitimate 90-mph pitch. He changes speeds well and has the command to throw any of his pitches for a strike at any point in the count.

DARIN ERSTAD
Bats: L Throws: L Opening Day Age: 22
Ht: 6-2 Wt: 195 Born: 6/4/1974
Position: OF Drafted: 1995 # CAL

YR TEAM	LG/CLASS	G	AB	R	H	2B	3B	HR	RBI	SB	BA	OBA
95 Lake Elsnor	CAL/A	25	113	24	41	7	3	5	24	3	.363	.392
95 Angels	ARIZ/R	4	18	2	10	1	0	0	1	1	.556	.579

Erstad was the number one overall pick in last June's draft after an All-American career at Nebraska. A terrific athlete, he was the punter on the Cornhuskers' national championship football squad. The 21-year-old has outstanding tools and projects to be above-average in all phases of the game. He has a great attitude and excellent work habits and got his pro career off to a solid start, batting .389 and slugging .611 with five homers and 25 RBI in just 131 at-bats at two stops last summer. Erstad is a good defensive outfielder and has excellent speed and the ability to hit for both average and power.

TODD GREENE
Bats: R Throws: R Opening Day Age: 25
Ht: 5-10 Wt: 195 Born: 5/8/1971
Position: C Drafted: 1993 #12 CAL

YR TEAM	LG/CLASS	G	AB	R	H	2B	3B	HR	RBI	SB	BA	OBA
93 Boise	NWST/A	76	305	55	82	15	3	15	71	4	.269	.356
94 Lake Elsnor	CAL/A	133	524	98	158	39	2	35	124	10	.302	.378
95 Vancouver	PCL/AAA	43	168	28	42	3	1	14	35	1	.250	.308
95 Midland	TEX/AA	82	318	59	104	19	1	26	57	3	.327	.365

Greene, one of the top power prospects in the game, slugged 40 home runs last summer, the most in the minor leagues since Danny Tartabull hit 43 in 1985. The 24-year-old was originally an outfielder, but converted to catching in 1994. He has an average arm with a decent release, but last season threw out just 23.5% of opposing base-stealers. The Georgia Southern product has stiff hands and poor footwork behind the plate, but he has shown improvement, cutting his passed ball total from a minor league-high 44 in '94 to 15 last year. As a hitter, he is aggressive, has tremendous power and has hit .294 over his career. He does not draw many walks and had trouble against lefties last season, batting over 100 points lower against them than against righties. Had he stayed in the Texas League all season, he would have been in line for his third straight MVP award.

JULIAN HEREDIA
Bats: R Throws: R Opening Day Age: 27
Ht: 6-1 Wt: 160 Born: 9/22/1969
Position: P Drafted: NDFA 11-18-88 CAL

YR TEAM	LG/CLASS	G	GS	GF	SV	W	L	ERA	IP	H	HR	BB	SO	O/BA
93 Midland	TEX/AA	46	1	19	0	5	3	3.12	89.1	77	10	19	89	.231
94 Midland	TEX/AA	45	2	10	1	5	3	3.23	97.2	87	10	37	109	.240
95 Vancouver	PCL/AAA	51	0	37	10	5	3	3.63	74.1	69	8	23	65	.242

The skinny Dominican has been an impressive set-up man over the last three years in the upper levels of the California farm system. He registered nine wins and 20 saves in 1992 in Class-A, but the Angels moved him to middle relief because they had better closer prospects. Heredia deals from the side and throws strikes; his impressive stuff garners plenty of popups. The 26-year-old is 37-18 with a 3.13 ERA, a .233 average against, and a strikeout per inning in his six-year career.

CALIFORNIA ANGELS: TOP PROSPECTS

PETE JANICKI

Bats: R Throws: R   Opening Day Age: 25
Ht: 6-4 Wt: 190   Born: 1/26/1971
Position: P   Drafted: 1992 #1 CAL

YR TEAM	LG/CLASS	G	GS	GF	SV	W	L	ERA	IP	H	HR	BB	SO	O/BA
93 Palm Sprgs	CAL/A	1	1	0	0	0	0	10.80	1.2	3	0	2	2	.375
94 Midland	TEX/AA	14	14	0	0	2	6	6.94	70.0	86	4	33	54	.303
94 Lake Elsnor	CAL/A	3	3	0	0	1	2	6.75	12.0	17	2	4	12	.333
95 Vancouver	PCL/AAA	9	9	0	0	1	4	7.03	48.2	64	8	23	34	.323
95 Lake Elsnor	CAL/A	20	20	0	0	9	4	3.06	123.1	130	7	28	106	.266

After a fine career at UCLA, Janicki was the eighth overall pick in the 1992 draft. He didn't pitch in '92 after breaking his elbow, and re-broke the same elbow in his first and only start of '93. The 25-year-old struggled with his control and was hit hard in '94 before missing the final two months with tendinitis. Finally healthy, he pitched well last season, allowing two earned runs or fewer in 11 of 17 starts at Lake Elsinore, but he was less consistent in Triple-A. Once he gave up ten runs and twice he allowed seven runs, pitching a total of 12.2 innings in the three games. Janicki has good control of a 90-mph fastball and also throws a good split-finger pitch.

PHIL LEFTWICH

Bats: R Throws: R   Opening Day Age: 27
Ht: 6-5 Wt: 205   Born: 5/19/1969
Position: P   Drafted: 1990 #1 CAL

YR TEAM	LG/CLASS	G	GS	GF	SV	W	L	ERA	IP	H	HR	BB	SO	O/BA
93 Vancouver	PCL/AAA	20	20	0	0	7	7	4.64	126.0	138	8	45	102	.277
93 California	AL/MAJ	12	12	0	0	4	6	3.79	80.2	80	5	27	31	.259
94 California	AL/MAJ	20	20	0	0	5	10	5.68	114.0	127	16	42	67	.283
94 Lake Elsnor	CAL/A	1	1	0	0	1	0	0.00	6.0	3	0	1	4	.167
95 Vancouver	PCL/AAA	6	5	0	0	2	0	3.19	36.2	28	4	9	25	.215
95 Angels	ARIZ/R	4	4	0	0	1	1	0.45	20.0	13	0	2	32	.181

Leftwich pitched well in his first major league stint in '93, but struggled with control and a leg injury in '94 before undergoing arthroscopic shoulder surgery over the winter. He returned to the mound in July last year and seemed to have regained his arm strength. The 26-year-old has a 90-mph fastball, but his heater doesn't move much and his changeup doesn't fool many hitters. Leftwich has come up with a pretty good breaking pitch and figures to be healthy for spring training.

EDUARDO PEREZ

Bats: R Throws: R   Opening Day Age: 27
Ht: 6-4 Wt: 215   Born: 9/11/1969
Position: 3B   Drafted: 1991 #1 CAL

YR TEAM	LG/CLASS	G	AB	R	H	2B	3B	HR	RBI	SB	BA	OBA
93 Vancouver	PCL/AAA	96	363	66	111	23	6	12	70	21	.306	.360
93 California	AL/MAJ	52	180	16	45	6	2	4	30	5	.250	.292
94 California	AL/MAJ	38	129	10	27	7	0	5	16	3	.209	.275
94 Vancouver	PCL/AAA	61	219	37	65	14	3	7	38	9	.297	.394
94 Angels	ARIZ/R	1	3	0	0	0	0	0	0	0	.000	.250
95 Vancouver	PCL/AAA	69	246	39	80	12	7	6	37	6	.325	.386
95 California	AL/MAJ	29	71	9	12	4	1	1	7	0	.169	.302

After a stellar career at Florida State, Tony Perez' son was the Angels' first-round pick in the '91 draft. He was rushed through the system and reached the majors in 1993, but Perez has bounced back and forth between the majors and Triple-A the past two seasons. Perez has also struggled to find a position, moving from the outfield to third base to first and back to third. His long swing generates good bat speed and some power, but he has had trouble making contact and needs to learn the strike zone. His future with the Angels is in serious doubt, due to a .221 major league average and the presence of George Arias.

CHRIS PRITCHETT

Bats: L Throws: R   Opening Day Age: 26
Ht: 6-4 Wt: 185   Born: 1/31/1970
Position: 1B   Drafted: 1991 #3 CAL

YR TEAM	LG/CLASS	G	AB	R	H	2B	3B	HR	RBI	SB	BA	OBA
93 Midland	TEX/AA	127	464	61	143	30	6	2	66	3	.308	.386
94 Midland	TEX/AA	127	460	86	142	25	4	6	91	5	.309	.421
95 Vancouver	PCL/AAA	123	434	66	120	27	4	8	53	2	.276	.365

The UCLA product is an outstanding defensive first baseman and has a .294 career average and excellent strike zone judgment. Pritchett ranked fourth in the Pacific Coast League in walks last year after leading the Texas League in '94. While he does not have the home run power expected of a first baseman, he has a good RBI bat and gap power that produces doubles.

MARQUIS RILEY

Bats: R Throws: R   Opening Day Age: 25
Ht: 5-10 Wt: 170   Born: 12/27/1970
Position: CF   Drafted: 1992 #5 CAL

YR TEAM	LG/CLASS	G	AB	R	H	2B	3B	HR	RBI	SB	BA	OBA
93 Palm Sprgs	CAL/A	130	508	93	134	10	2	1	42	69	.264	.373
94 Midland	TEX/AA	93	374	68	107	12	4	1	29	32	.286	.353
94 Vancouver	PCL/AAA	4	14	3	3	0	0	0	1	1	.214	.353
95 Vancouver	PCL/AAA	120	477	70	125	6	6	0	43	29	.262	.330

Riley has outstanding speed and uses it to steal bases, beat out infield hits, and cover ground in the outfield. The 25-year-old has learned to switch-hit and could become a good leadoff hitter if he can hit the ball on the ground more often and draw more walks. He is a great defensive center fielder with a decent arm. Riley ranked third in the Pacific Coast league in stolen bases last year and was successful on 74.3% of his attempts, also third best in the league.

SHAD WILLIAMS

Bats: R Throws: R   Opening Day Age: 25
Ht: 6-0 Wt: 185   Born: 3/10/1971
Position: P   Drafted: 1991 #18 CAL

YR TEAM	LG/CLASS	G	GS	GF	SV	W	L	ERA	IP	H	HR	BB	SO	O/BA
93 Midland	TEX/AA	27	27	0	0	7	10	4.71	175.2	192	16	65	91	.283
94 Midland	TEX/AA	5	5	0	0	3	0	1.11	32.1	13	1	4	29	.121
94 Vancouver	PCL/AAA	16	16	0	0	4	6	4.60	86.0	100	14	30	42	.287
95 Vancouver	PCL/AAA	25	25	0	0	9	7	3.37	149.2	142	16	48	114	.250

The Fresno City College righthander had a solid season, placing second in the Pacific Coast League in ERA and strikeouts while ranking third among the league's starters in batting average against (.250) and strikeouts per nine innings (6.86). He lost a no-hit bid with two outs in the ninth inning in one start and allowed three runs or fewer 19 times, an excellent total for the PCL. However, it should be noted that Williams was much better in Vancouver, the best pitchers' park in the league, posting a 2.65 ERA there. While Williams is not a hard thrower, he spots his fastball well and has a good changeup and slider.

THE SCOUTING REPORT: 1996

CALIFORNIA ANGELS: OTHERS TO WATCH

ROB BONANNO   Bats: R Throws: R   Ht: 6-0 Wt: 195
Born: 1/5/1971   Drafted: 1994 #10 CAL   Position: P

YR TEAM	LG/CLASS	G	GS	GF	SV	W	L	ERA	IP	H	HR	BB	SO	O/BA
95 Midland	TEX/AA	3	3	0	0	1	1	9.45	13.1	24	5	6	6	.393
95 L Elsinore	CAL/A	17	17	0	0	8	4	3.05	112.0	112	10	16	72	.260

The Florida righthander was second in the California League in ERA last year with an outstanding SO/BB ratio.

JOVINO CARVAJAL   Bats: S Throws: R   Ht: 6-1 Wt: 160
Born: 9/2/1968   Drafted: NDFA 9-18-86 NYA   Position: RF

YR TEAM	LG/CLASS	G	AB	R	H	2B	3B	HR	RBI	SB	BA	OBA
95 Vancouver	PCL/AAA	41	163	25	53	3	3	1	10	10	.325	.341
95 Midland	TEX/AA	79	348	58	109	13	5	2	23	39	.313	.347

The 27-year-old Dominican has excellent speed and led the farm system in steals while batting a career-high .317.

MARK DALESANDRO   Bats: R Throws: R   Ht: 6-0 Wt: 185
Born: 5/14/1968   Drafted: 1990 #17 CAL   Position: C

YR TEAM	LG/CLASS	G	AB	R	H	2B	3B	HR	RBI	SB	BA	OBA
95 Vancouver	PCL/AAA	34	123	16	41	13	1	1	18	2	.333	.366
95 California	AL/MAJ	11	10	1	1	1	0	0	0	0	.100	.100

Dalesandro, a utility-type player, can catch, play first, third or the outfield, and has a decent bat off the bench.

JON DECLUE   Bats: R Throws: L   Ht: 6-2 Wt: 198
Born: 9/17/1970   Drafted: NDFA 1-10-94 CAL   Position: P

YR TEAM	LG/CLASS	G	GS	GF	SV	W	L	ERA	IP	H	HR	BB	SO	O/BA
95 Visalia	CAL/A	21	14	3	0	6	5	3.50	103.0	95	11	27	90	.246
95 L Elsinore	CAL/A	9	4	0	0	5	1	3.57	40.1	50	5	5	22	.313

DeClue, signed as a free agent out of Florida Southern, is not overpowering, but had one of the best breaking pitches in the California League.

KEN EDENFIELD   Bats: R Throws: R   Ht: 6-1 Wt: 165
Born: 3/18/1967   Drafted: 1990 #20 CAL   Position: P

YR TEAM	LG/CLASS	G	GS	GF	SV	W	L	ERA	IP	H	HR	BB	SO	O/BA
95 Vancouver	PCL/AAA	33	0	4	0	7	2	3.45	60.0	56	2	25	44	.251
95 California	AL/MAJ	7	0	3	0	0	0	4.26	12.2	15	1	5	6	.300

A sinker/slider type pitcher, Edenfield is a veteran righthander who has put up good Triple-A numbers the past two seasons.

RYAN HANCOCK   Bats: R Throws: R   Ht: 6-2 Wt: 220
Born: 11/11/1971   Drafted: 1993 #2 CAL   Position: P

YR TEAM	LG/CLASS	G	GS	GF	SV	W	L	ERA	IP	H	HR	BB	SO	O/BA
95 Midland	TEX/AA	28	28	0	0	12	9	4.56	175.2	222	17	45	79	.317

The former BYU quarterback blew his knee out in college and hasn't regained the velocity he once had, but led the Texas League in innings and tied for third in wins.

TIM HARKRIDER   Bats: S Throws: R   Ht: 6-0 Wt: 180
Born: 9/5/1971   Drafted: 1993 #8 CAL   Position: SS

YR TEAM	LG/CLASS	G	AB	R	H	2B	3B	HR	RBI	SB	BA	OBA
95 Midland	TEX/AA	124	460	66	134	22	4	2	39	3	.291	.358

Harkrider is a switch-hitter with speed, is good defensively, and has been one of the toughest hitters in the minors to strike out.

DAVID HOLDRIDGE   Bats: R Throws: R   Ht: 6-3 Wt: 195
Born: 2/5/1969   Drafted: 1987 #2 CAL   Position: P

YR TEAM	LG/CLASS	G	GS	GF	SV	W	L	ERA	IP	H	HR	BB	SO	O/BA
95 Vancouver	PCL/AAA	11	0	6	1	0	2	4.61	13.2	18	0	7	13	.310
95 Midland	TEX/AA	14	0	11	1	1	0	1.78	25.1	20	1	8	23	.222
95 L Elsinore	CAL/A	12	0	8	0	3	0	0.98	18.1	13	0	5	24	.200

The strong-armed journeyman righthander was once traded straight up for Lance Parrish (in 1988).

KOREY KELING   Bats: R Throws: R   Ht: 6-5 Wt: 210
Born: 11/24/1968   Drafted: 1991 #16 CAL   Position: P

YR TEAM	LG/CLASS	G	GS	GF	SV	W	L	ERA	IP	H	HR	BB	SO	O/BA
95 Vancouver	PCL/AAA	3	3	0	0	0	2	4.08	17.2	18	1	6	16	.261
95 Midland	TEX/AA	29	12	7	1	8	5	3.46	122.1	113	7	52	101	.244

The 27-year-old soft-tosser out of Oklahoma was much more effective out of the bullpen, going 4-0 with a 1.31 ERA in 17 relief outings for Midland.

KEITH MORRISON   Bats: R Throws: R   Ht: 6-4 Wt: 190
Born: 11/22/1969   Drafted: 1989 #39 ATL   Position: P

YR TEAM	LG/CLASS	G	GS	GF	SV	W	L	ERA	IP	H	HR	BB	SO	O/BA
95 Vancouver	PCL/AAA	28	26	1	0	14	9	4.93	160.2	178	16	40	84	.284

The 26-year-old righthander was a workhorse last year, finishing second in the Pacific Coast League in wins and fourth in innings, but does not possess any outstanding pitches.

ORLANDO PALMEIRO   Bats: L Throws: R   Ht: 5-11 Wt: 155
Born: 1/19/1969   Drafted: 1991 #34 CAL   Position: OF

YR TEAM	LG/CLASS	G	AB	R	H	2B	3B	HR	RBI	SB	BA	OBA
95 Vancouver	PCL/AAA	107	398	66	122	21	4	0	47	16	.307	.371
95 California	AL/MAJ	15	20	3	7	0	0	0	1	0	.350	.381

A good outfielder who has hit .318 the last two years at Triple-A, Palmeiro made the most of his cup of coffee last year.

LUIS RAVEN   Bats: R Throws: R   Ht: 6-4 Wt: 230
Born: 11/19/1968   Drafted: NDFA 7-20-88 CAL   Position: 1B

YR TEAM	LG/CLASS	G	AB	R	H	2B	3B	HR	RBI	SB	BA	OBA
95 Vancouver	PCL/AAA	37	135	18	33	11	1	5	26	3	.244	.318
95 Midland	TEX/AA	21	86	9	23	2	1	5	15	1	.267	.304
95 L Elsinore	CAL/A	6	24	5	10	2	1	2	6	1	.417	.533

Raven, a defensive liability, smacked 31 home runs in 1994, but struggled with both the bat and injuries last year.

JEFF SCHMIDT   Bats: R Throws: R   Ht: 6-5 Wt: 210
Born: 2/21/1971   Drafted: 1992 #2 CAL   Position: P

YR TEAM	LG/CLASS	G	GS	GF	SV	W	L	ERA	IP	H	HR	BB	SO	O/BA
95 Midland	TEX/AA	20	20	0	0	4	12	5.83	100.1	127	12	48	46	.312

Schmidt, a possible major league closer, has a good fastball and hard slider and was successful in relief in '94, but was pounded as a starter last year.

BEN VANRYN   Bats: L Throws: L   Ht: 6-5 Wt: 195
Born: 8/9/1971   Drafted: 1990 #5 MON   Position: P

YR TEAM	LG/CLASS	G	GS	GF	SV	W	L	ERA	IP	H	HR	BB	SO	O/BA
95 Vancouver	PCL/AAA	11	5	2	0	2	0	3.07	29.1	29	1	9	20	.264
95 Chattanooga	SOU/AA	5	3	0	0	1	9.24	12.2	22	2	6	6	.367
95 Midland	TEX/AA	19	0	8	1	1	2.78	32.1	33	4	12	24	.277

The tall lefthander dominated the Texas League in 1993, but has been unable to regain that form and is working in his fourth organization.

CHICAGO WHITE SOX

WILSON ALVAREZ

Position: SP
Bats: L **Throws:** L
Ht: 6'1" **Wt:** 175
Opening Day Age: 26
Born: 3/24/1970
Drafted: TEX 9/23/86
ML Seasons: 6

SCOUTING REPORT
Wilson Alvarez comes at hitters from a three-quarter angle, bringing an average-plus fastball that he occasionally cuts or turns over. His curve is also slightly above average, with a sharp, lateral break. He rarely uses his mediocre straight change; when Alvarez wants to change up, he simply throws his curve extra-slow.

During his career, Wilson has been below-average at holding runners on base, but he picked off five men in 1995 and 10 of 18 enemy basestealers were caught. He is an average fielder with good hands, but isn't quick off the mound. Alvarez didn't make an error last season.

HOW HE PERFORMED IN '95
More than perhaps any other member of the Sox staff, the big lefthander did not appear physically ready to pitch at the beginning of the 1995 season. However, he had a fine second half, continuing to confound the expectations of fans and management.

Wilson got out of the gate poorly and had a 5.45 ERA before the All-Star break. He (like some other Sox pitchers) looked out of shape and couldn't get anything but a "hit me" fastball over the plate. However, in the second half, Alvarez lowered his ERA by two full runs and completed three games in 16 starts. He permitted opponents to hit just .220 in the second half, but he still walked way too many hitters: 48 in his last 100 innings.

Also quite troubling was Alvarez' inability to get lefthanders out; they hit 62 points higher in 1995 than the season before. Luckily he didn't face that many portsiders.

WHAT TO EXPECT IN '96
The White Sox are unhappy with Alvarez' inconsistency, and they may not put up with it much longer. While his raw talent is perhaps the best of any pitcher on the Chicago staff, Wilson simply isn't going to win consistently in the major leagues unless he can hit the strike zone consistently. In the words of Joe McCarthy, a pitcher who hasn't control hasn't anything.

Overall Statistics

	G	GS	GF	SV	W	L	ERA	IP	H	R	ER	HR	BB	SO
95 CHA	29	29	0	0	8	11	4.32	175.0	171	96	84	21	93	118
Career	129	103	4	1	43	33	3.81	701.0	639	339	297	74	373	479

1995 Situational Statistics

	W	L	ERA	SV	IP	BB	SO		AB	HR	RBI	BA	OBA	SLG
Home	7	2	4.80	0	84.1	46	56	LHB	109	2	18	.294	.376	.422
Road	1	9	3.87	0	90.2	47	62	RHB	554	19	70	.251	.343	.413
Apr-Jun	1	5	5.32	0	69.1	41	40	ScPos	145	3	54	.255	.354	.366
Jul-Oct	7	6	3.66	0	105.2	52	78	Clutch	31	1	5	.355	.524	.581

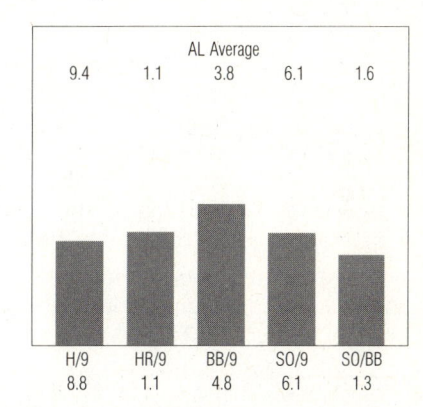

How He Compares to Other Pitchers

AL Average: 9.4 / 1.1 / 3.8 / 6.1 / 1.6

H/9	HR/9	BB/9	SO/9	SO/BB
8.8	1.1	4.8	6.1	1.3

How He Compares to Other Starting Pitchers

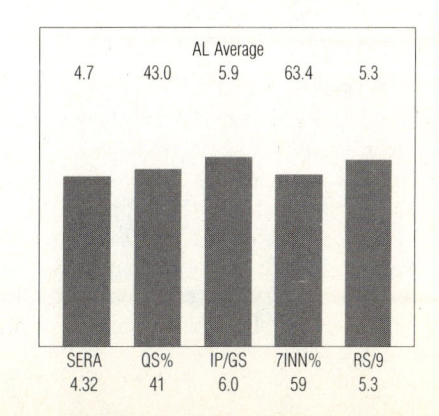

AL Average: 4.7 / 43.0 / 5.9 / 63.4 / 5.3

SERA	QS%	IP/GS	7INN%	RS/9
4.32	41	6.0	59	5.3

THE SCOUTING REPORT: 1996

CHICAGO WHITE SOX

JASON BERE

Position: SP
Bats: R **Throws:** R
Ht: 6'3" **Wt:** 185
Opening Day Age: 24
Born: 5/26/1971
Drafted: CHA90 37/952
ML Seasons: 3

SCOUTING REPORT
Hard-throwing righthander Jason Bere delivers from a three-quarter to high three-quarter angle, often struggling with his release point and other mechanics. Poor control plagues him.

Jason consistently turns over or sinks his high-velocity fastball to give it extra movement. Unfortunately, he can't control the pitch. His curve is slightly above average, but isn't consistently sharp. He likes to try to "backdoor" the curve. The "fosh" change-up he uses doesn't move much, but his deceptive arm action fools batters into swinging at what they think is a fastball.

He has a below-average pickoff move and is very slow to home, which allows runners to move at will. Bere is an average fielder.

HOW HE PERFORMED IN '95
Among eligible pitchers, Jason Bere's 7.19 1995 ERA ranked third-worst in the entire league, better than only two veterans at the end of their careers: Mike Moore and Danny Darwin. This is not good company to be in.

Was Bere really that bad? Yes. All the negative elements of his game—wildness, a protracted delivery, and problems with portsiders—doomed him in 1995. He tied for the league lead in losses and trailed only Al Leiter in walks. A whopping total of 36 runners (easily the highest total in the majors) stole against him in 41 tries, and lefty swingers batted 80 points higher than they had in 1994.

White Sox broadcaster Tom Paciorek felt that Jason's control troubles stemmed from an improper release point on his fastball. There was no speculation of any injury, and Bere's velocity was still good; he finished sixth-best in the AL with 7.19 strikeouts per game. However, he just couldn't get the ball where he wanted it and averaged only five innings per start.

WHAT TO EXPECT IN '96
The White Sox badly need Bere, their projected number two starter, to settle down and produce. Unfortunately, the problems he has experienced aren't easily dismissed, and they appeared to play havoc with his mental game as 1995 progressed. He created very high expectations given how good he was in 1993 and 1994, yet he was truly awful last year. Worse, the roller coaster ride may not yet be finished.

Overall Statistics

	G	GS	GF	SV	W	L	ERA	IP	H	R	ER	HR	BB	SO
95 CHA	27	27	0	0	8	15	7.19	137.2	151	120	110	21	106	110
Career	75	75	0	0	32	22	4.80	422.0	379	245	225	50	267	366

1995 Situational Statistics

	W	L	ERA	SV	IP	BB	SO		AB	HR	RBI	BA	OBA	SLG
Home	3	6	7.70	0	66.2	53	46	LHB	286	9	47	.304	.441	.462
Road	5	9	6.72	0	71.0	53	64	RHB	259	12	53	.247	.342	.421
Apr-Jun	4	6	5.10	0	72.1	49	65	ScPos	164	7	82	.323	.430	.530
Jul-Oct	4	9	9.51	0	65.1	57	45	Clutch	32	0	2	.188	.278	.250

How He Compares to Other Pitchers

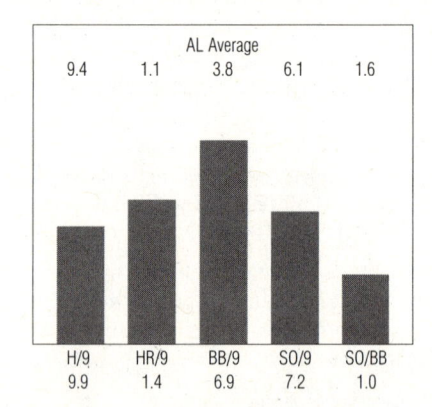

	H/9	HR/9	BB/9	SO/9	SO/BB
AL Average	9.4	1.1	3.8	6.1	1.6
	9.9	1.4	6.9	7.2	1.0

How He Compares to Other Starting Pitchers

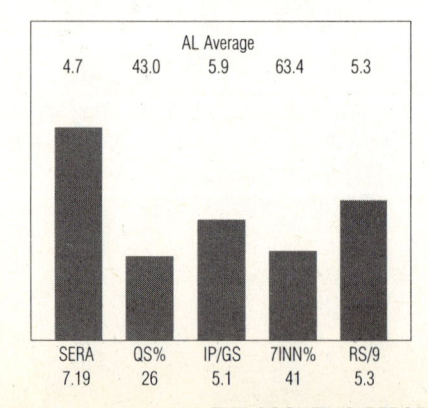

	SERA	QS%	IP/GS	7INN%	RS/9
AL Average	4.7	43.0	5.9	63.4	5.3
	7.19	26	5.1	41	5.3

CHICAGO WHITE SOX

RAY DURHAM

Position: 2B
Bats: B **Throws:** R
Ht: 5'8" **Wt:** 170
Opening Day Age: 24
Born: 11/30/1971
Drafted: CHA90 6/132
ML Seasons: 1

SCOUTING REPORT
Ray Durham is a very good fastball hitter from both sides of the plate, and he has some pop. Breaking balls, especially those thrown by righthanders, fool him.

Like most switch-hitters, Ray likes the ball low while hitting lefty and high while hitting from the right side. He is an above-average baserunner with above-average speed, but he seldom bunts.

Durham's range at second is slightly better than average in all directions and he chases pop flies well. Ray's throwing arm is average in strength and accuracy. His hands are average at all times except when he goes up the middle, when he becomes rather shaky.

HOW HE PERFORMED IN '95
Rookie Durham provided a spark to a moribund 1995 Sox squad, showing skill and poise at bat and in the field. He immediately made an impact, hitting .361 in May, but had some problems making contact, fanning 18 times in his first 42 at-bats. In June, Durham had a 4-for-43 slump, but made adjustments and finished the year strong.

While he does switch-hit, Ray was far more effective against lefthanders in his rookie season.

Sox manager Gene Lamont made Durham his leadoff hitter because of his speed, but Ray didn't walk nearly often enough for that role and soon dropped to the seventh spot. He had 11 steals by mid-June, but he didn't run as often after the demotion in the batting order. Durham could easily steal 30-40 bases a season, and it's not inconceivable that he might someday return to the top of the order. Although he tried to sacrifice and bunt for hits often last year, he is not yet an accomplished bunter.

In the field, Durham committed fifteen errors but made some fine plays and turned the double play well. He is expected to show continued improvement.

WHAT TO EXPECT IN '96
Durham will be Chicago's regular second baseman for several years at a minimum. His defense is good and will get better. However, Ray must work on his command of the strike zone to be truly valuable. With increased knowledge of how to work a count and the ability to lay off bad pitches, both his power and on-base percentage will increase.

Overall Statistics

	G	AB	R	H	2B	3B	HR	RBI	SB	CS	BB	SO	BA	OBA
95 CHA	125	471	68	121	27	6	7	51	18	5	31	83	.257	.309
Career	125	471	68	121	27	6	7	51	18	5	31	83	.257	.309

1995 Situational Statistics

	AB	HR	RBI	BA	OBA	SLG		AB	HR	RBI	BA	OBA	SLG
Home	230	1	20	.235	.291	.330	LHP	149	3	17	.315	.373	.490
Road	241	6	31	.278	.326	.436	RHP	322	4	34	.230	.277	.335
Apr-Jun	202	2	25	.287	.344	.396	ScPos	137	2	44	.255	.312	.365
Jul-Oct	269	5	26	.234	.281	.375	Clutch	81	0	8	.210	.293	.247

How He Compares to Other Batters

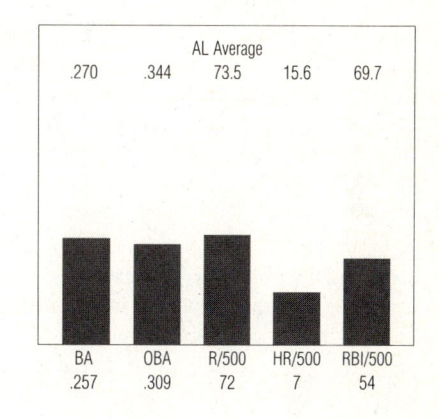

AL Average: .270 .344 73.5 15.6 69.7

BA	OBA	R/500	HR/500	RBI/500
.257	.309	72	7	54

Where He Hits the Ball

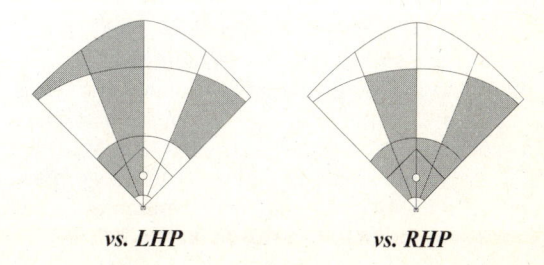

vs. LHP   vs. RHP

THE SCOUTING REPORT: 1996

CHICAGO WHITE SOX

ALEX FERNANDEZ

Position: SP
Bats: R **Throws:** R
Ht: 6'2" **Wt:** 200
Opening Day Age: 26
Born: 8/13/1969
Drafted: CHA90 1/4
ML Seasons: 6

SCOUTING REPORT

While he has no one outstanding pitch, Fernandez has three offerings better than the major-league average. His fastball is live and has some hop. (He recently added a cut fastball to his repertoire.) Alex's curve, which he backdoors well, has some bite. He also has a hard slider.

While his change-up is just average, it does have some movement. His control is average, and in the first half of 1995 was well below that.

Alex is quick off the mound, and his fielding is average-plus. His pickoff move is just average, but only 6 of 11 runners stole successfully against him.

HOW HE PERFORMED IN '95

From opening day, when he allowed eight runs on five hits and five walks, Alex didn't seem right. A June arbitration likely preyed on his mind, and talk that he was out of shape gathered speed when Fernandez couldn't string two good starts together through the All-Star break. At midsummer, Alex was 4-6 with a 5.69 ERA, having allowed 95 hits and 37 walks in 87 innings.

From that point, Fernandez turned his season around. Development of the "cutter" helped, and he walked just 28 walks over his final 115 2/3 innings. Fernandez won his last seven decisions and finished with fine seasonal totals. The signing of a new contract likely helped, but Fernandez' stuff went from decent to outstanding as the season progressed.

Fernandez paced Sox starters in every major category and ranked eighth in the AL in innings and tenth in fewest walks per game. He throws some home runs, but the 19 round-trippers Fernandez allowed in 1995 are his lowest total since 1991. Alex, still a power pitcher, fits the mold by excelling in night games and cold weather.

WHAT TO EXPECT IN '96

Fernandez is viewed as the team's ace and should be for several years. With outstanding stuff, durability, and a strong right arm, Fernandez remains capable of 20-win seasons. However, inconsistency is a problem for the stocky righthander. Whether Alex's problems stem from poor mechanics or psychological concerns, he must pitch well for Chicago to return to postseason play.

Overall Statistics

	G	GS	GF	SV	W	L	ERA	IP	H	R	ER	HR	BB	SO
95 CHA	30	30	0	0	12	8	3.80	203.2	200	98	86	19	65	159
Career	164	162	1	0	63	53	3.86	1088.1	1058	516	467	114	354	751

1995 Situational Statistics

	W	L	ERA	SV	IP	BB	SO		AB	HR	RBI	BA	OBA	SLG
Home	8	3	3.39	0	114.0	30	92	LHB	414	11	51	.278	.338	.437
Road	4	5	4.32	0	89.2	35	67	RHB	369	8	38	.230	.279	.339
Apr-Jun	4	4	5.14	0	75.1	33	61	ScPos	172	5	69	.267	.347	.413
Jul-Oct	8	4	3.02	0	128.1	32	98	Clutch	65	1	8	.262	.367	.385

How He Compares to Other Pitchers

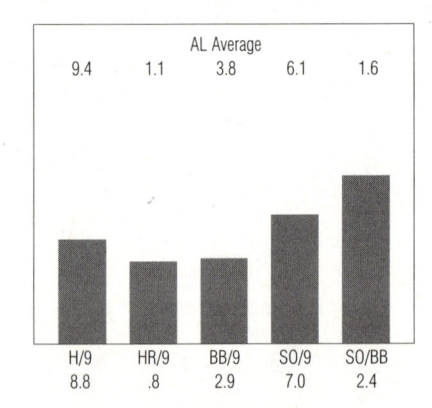

AL Average: H/9 9.4, HR/9 1.1, BB/9 3.8, SO/9 6.1, SO/BB 1.6

H/9 8.8, HR/9 .8, BB/9 2.9, SO/9 7.0, SO/BB 2.4

How He Compares to Other Starting Pitchers

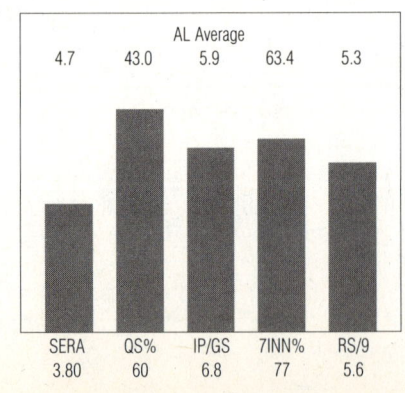

AL Average: SERA 4.7, QS% 43.0, IP/GS 5.9, 7INN% 63.4, RS/9 5.3

SERA 3.80, QS% 60, IP/GS 6.8, 7INN% 77, RS/9 5.6

CHICAGO WHITE SOX

OZZIE GUILLEN

Positions: SS//DH
Bats: L **Throws:** R
Ht: 5'11" **Wt:** 150
Opening Day Age: 32
Born: 1/20/1964
Drafted: SD 12/17/80
ML Seasons: 11

SCOUTING REPORT

Fielding is, and has always been, Guillen's key strength. Although some of his mobility was reduced by 1992 knee surgery, he still has above-average range, especially when he goes into the hole. His arm is slightly above average in strength but very accurate.

As a hitter, Guillen gets around well enough on low fastballs but ends up twisted into a pretzel when he tries to go after a high heater. He also makes good contact and can foul off several 3-2 fastballs in a row. On the minus side of the offensive ledger, though, Ozzie doesn't hit breaking pitches particularly well, has no power to speak of, and is one of the least patient hitters in the majors. He rarely bunts despite his speed.

HOW HE PERFORMED IN '95

For awhile, it looked like another typical Guillen season: he was hitting over .300 in June, and at the All-Star break was still batting .285. Unfortunately, Ozzie hit just .218 the rest of the way and by year's end was one of the worst offensive players in the majors. The only thing he adds to the attack are singles, and when he doesn't do that, he not doing anything at the plate.

There were extenuating circumstances to consider, however. Guillen's close friend, former major-league infielder Gus Polidor, was killed in late April, and Ozzie has as much as adopted Polidor's children. Later, when it was apparent that the Sox were out of contention, several of the team's veterans didn't seem to show much enthusiasm.

In the field, Ozzie showed his usual combination of heads-up play and concentration lapses. He didn't get to his usual number of ground balls. The confident Guillen is still a good shortstop but may not be as good as he thinks he is.

Guillen has never been much of a basestealer, and his 1995 performance was no better than usual. He no longer stretches many singles into doubles or doubles into triples.

WHAT TO EXPECT IN '96

He's signed through 1997, and despite alternatives who are might be better (Craig Grebeck, rookie Chris Snopek), the popular "Ozzeroo" will be there again this season. It's likely his bat will snap back somewhat, and he's not hurting the team in the field.

Overall Statistics

	G	AB	R	H	2B	3B	HR	RBI	SB	CS	BB	SO	BA	OBA
95 CHA	122	415	50	103	20	3	1	41	6	7	13	25	.248	.270
Career	1451	5078	572	1357	195	54	16	468	152	93	161	409	.267	.288

1995 Situational Statistics

	AB	HR	RBI	BA	OBA	SLG		AB	HR	RBI	BA	OBA	SLG
Home	216	1	27	.287	.313	.366	LHP	101	0	8	.198	.204	.248
Road	199	0	14	.206	.224	.266	RHP	314	1	33	.264	.291	.341
Apr-Jun	163	0	22	.294	.322	.368	ScPos	111	0	37	.261	.284	.324
Jul-Oct	252	1	19	.218	.236	.286	Clutch	84	0	6	.179	.198	.250

How He Compares to Other Batters

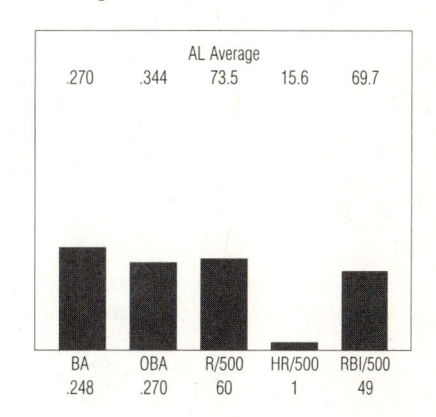

AL Average: .270 .344 73.5 15.6 69.7

BA	OBA	R/500	HR/500	RBI/500
.248	.270	60	1	49

Where He Hits the Ball

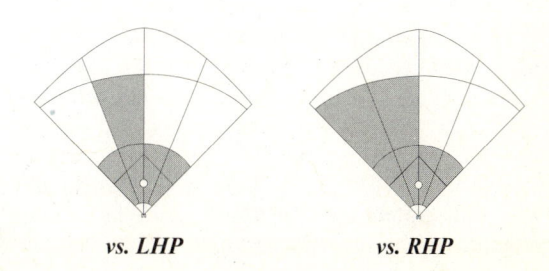

vs. LHP   vs. RHP

THE SCOUTING REPORT: 1996

CHICAGO WHITE SOX

SCOUTING REPORT

Roberto Hernandez, a classic power reliever, throws from a high three-quarters to overhand motion. He has a hard, well above-average fastball that he occasionally cuts. When it's in the strike zone, it tends to be straight, but he's capable of blowing away any hitter in the league if he keeps the pitch slightly off the plate.

His hard slider is just average because it often bounces in the dirt. However, Roberto's splitfinger fastball is above average, coming in with good velocity and a very good late break. He doesn't have a quality off-speed pitch, though.

His move to first is slightly below average, and his fielding is average. Four of six runners stole successfully against Hernandez in 1995.

HOW HE PERFORMED IN '95

Hernandez came in for his share of the blame in the disaster that was the 1995 White Sox season, some of which was merited. He blew a total of 10 save opportunities, suffered another June slump, and allowed a career-high nine home runs.

In a three-week period last June, Roberto allowed seven earned runs in five innings to lift his seasonal ERA to 5.68. He also gave up five homers in his first 19 innings. Roberto had suffered a terrible two-week stretch in June 1994, and he was again at a loss to explain his June swoons. For the rest of the year, he was much more effective, allowing just 14 runs in his last 40.2 innings.

No one strikes out nearly 13 batters per nine innings in the major leagues without outstanding stuff, and Hernandez has some of the best pure pitches of any reliever in baseball. Of course, control has been a problem at times for him.

WHAT TO EXPECT IN '96

Despite his bouts of inconsistency, Hernandez is often overpowering. The entire Sox bullpen sagged in 1995, and things are sure to be better in 1996. With young Bill Simas in line for setup duty and some save opportunities, Roberto should get more help in the late innings and his performance should improve. He had plenty of streaks last year in which he was completely dominating, and if the Sox didn't want him anymore, 25 other teams would.

ROBERTO HERNANDEZ

Position: RP
Bats: R **Throws:** R
Ht: 6'4" **Wt:** 220
Opening Day Age: 31
Born: 11/11/1964
Drafted: CAL86 1/16
ML Seasons: 5

Overall Statistics

	G	GS	GF	SV	W	L	ERA	IP	H	R	ER	HR	BB	SO
95 CHA	60	0	57	32	3	7	3.92	59.2	63	30	26	9	28	84
Career	227	3	195	96	18	18	3.24	272.0	236	110	98	25	94	279

1995 Situational Statistics

	W	L	ERA	SV	IP	BB	SO		AB	HR	RBI	BA	OBA	SLG
Home	2	1	2.90	21	31.0	9	40	LHB	129	5	20	.279	.384	.450
Road	1	6	5.02	11	28.2	19	44	RHB	108	4	20	.250	.308	.398
Apr-Jun	2	3	4.62	12	25.1	13	35	ScPos	80	4	32	.225	.340	.412
Jul-Oct	1	4	3.41	20	34.1	15	49	Clutch	183	7	31	.279	.359	.437

How He Compares to Other Pitchers

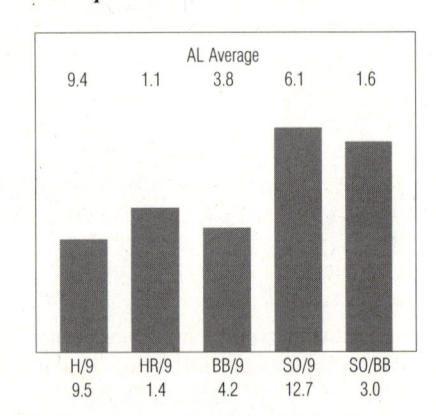

AL Average: H/9 9.4, HR/9 1.1, BB/9 3.8, SO/9 6.1, SO/BB 1.6

Hernandez: H/9 9.5, HR/9 1.4, BB/9 4.2, SO/9 12.7, SO/BB 3.0

How He Compares to Other Relief Pitchers

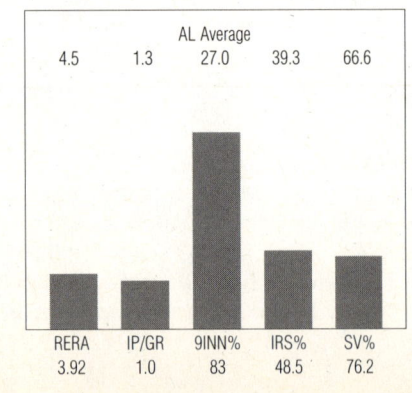

AL Average: RERA 4.5, IP/GR 1.3, 9INN% 27.0, IRS% 39.3, SV% 66.6

Hernandez: RERA 3.92, IP/GR 1.0, 9INN% 83, IRS% 48.5, SV% 76.2

CHICAGO WHITE SOX

LANCE JOHNSON

Position: OF
Bats: L **Throws:** L
Ht: 5'10" **Wt:** 160
Opening Day Age: 32
Born: 7/6/1963
Drafted: SL84 6/139
ML Seasons: 9

SCOUTING REPORT

The White Sox' best defensive player, Johnson is a plus center fielder, with hands and range both rated well above-average by scouts. Lance's arm is average in accuracy, which partially compensates for his poor arm strength.

He is a good low fastball hitter and makes contact as well as anybody in the league. Johnson has added some power of late. However, despite well above-average speed and baserunning ability, he does not bunt that often. When he does, Lance usually attempts to drag bunt. Unfortunately, he is not very effective at it.

HOW HE PERFORMED IN '95

Johnson, nicknamed "One Dog," disgusted by baseball's labor problems, had considered retiring to run One Dog Records, his jazz and R&B record label. He did elect to play in 1995, but didn't get his turntable cranked up until mid-season. Johnson has always hit better in the late months, but was hitting under .250 last June.

Lance batted .364 in July and stayed hot the rest of the way, leading the AL in hits. He showed unexpected punch, eclipsing his previous career total of seven home runs. A late rush at his fifth straight triples crown fell just one three-bagger short of the league title. In addition, he was the AL's hardest hitter to strike out for the second consecutive year.

Lance, the leadoff hitter for much of 1995, is not ideally suited to the role despite his excellent speed and basestealing ability: his career high in walks is not-impressive 36. However, he kicked in plenty of offense last season and could have contributed more by hitting lower in the order with more men on base. In center field, he's one of the best at chasing down fly balls. He rarely makes errors and last year threw out eight runners.

WHAT TO EXPECT IN '96

Johnson had improved his game a little every year, and he improved it a lot in 1995. Another step forward would make him an obvious All-Star, but given his age, it's more likely that Johnson will stabilize and, within a couple of years, begin to decline. Until then, he's very valuable. The White Sox let him go last winter rather than pay him what he was worth, and they will probably miss his offense even if his replacement, Darren Lewis, takes up the defensive slack.

Overall Statistics

	G	AB	R	H	2B	3B	HR	RBI	SB	CS	BB	SO	BA	OBA
95 CHA	142	607	98	186	18	12	10	57	40	6	32	31	.306	.341
Career	978	3618	487	1031	108	78	17	334	232	72	214	264	.285	.324

1995 Situational Statistics

	AB	HR	RBI	BA	OBA	SLG		AB	HR	RBI	BA	OBA	SLG
Home	311	2	28	.289	.324	.379	LHP	171	1	13	.287	.328	.351
Road	296	8	29	.324	.358	.473	RHP	436	9	44	.314	.346	.454
Apr-Jun	224	0	14	.250	.293	.290	ScPos	127	2	45	.323	.369	.480
Jul-Oct	383	10	43	.339	.369	.504	Clutch	90	1	10	.289	.316	.356

How He Compares to Other Batters

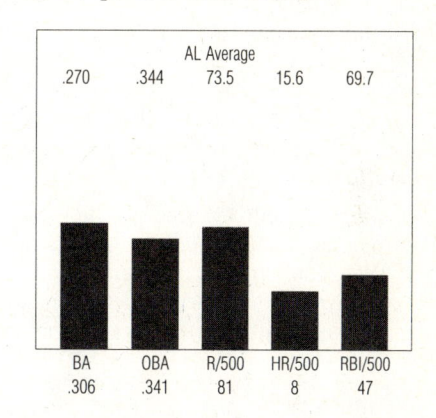

AL Average: .270 / .344 / 73.5 / 15.6 / 69.7

BA	OBA	R/500	HR/500	RBI/500
.306	.341	81	8	47

Where He Hits the Ball

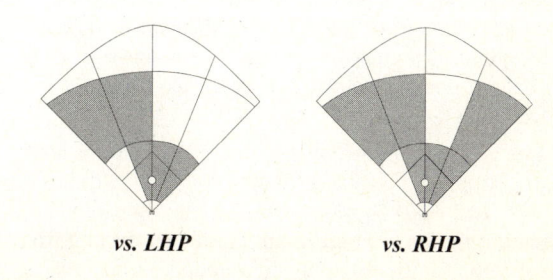

vs. LHP   vs. RHP

THE SCOUTING REPORT: 1996

CHICAGO WHITE SOX

RON KARKOVICE

Position: C
Bats: R **Throws:** R
Ht: 6'1" **Wt:** 215
Opening Day Age: 32
Born: 8/8/1963
Drafted: CHA82 1/14
ML Seasons: 10

SCOUTING REPORT

"Officer Kark" is well-celebrated for his ability to apprehend errant baserunners. His arm is well above-average in strength and accuracy and he is agile behind the dish.

He still doesn't hit off-speed pitches well, though, and usually tries to pull everything. However, he has worked on taking breaking balls to right field. Ron is a flyball hitter who strikes out often, and he generates most of his offense against mediocre fastballs. He is very slow, to put it mildly. However, he does sacrifice well and beat out five bunt singles last season.

HOW HE PERFORMED IN '95

Karkovice's 1995 performance wasn't great, but wasn't as bad as the raw numbers look. He's still one of the league's best all-around catchers.

Karkovice usually finishes high among AL catchers in caught stealing percentage, but his 1995 total of 32% (28 of 88) didn't even rank in the top five. This aberration was completely due to Jason Bere: 36 of 41 enemy basestealers were successful against the slow-delivering wild child in 1995, the highest total in the league and a truly terrible mark. No other Sox hurler was stolen against more than eight times or run on more than 17, indicating both Karkovice's strong arm and the level of respect he engenders among baserunners.

Ron always knocks out his share of homers. He loves Detroit, having smacked 10 of his career homers at Tiger Stadium. His five grand slams rank him second on the Sox' all-time list. Amazingly, one of those was an inside-the-park job at Minnesota in 1990.

WHAT TO EXPECT IN '96

The pattern is very clear on Karkovice: low average, some power, fine throwing arm, very slow, very good at handling pitchers. His defense is clearly enough to keep him in the lineup, and he has genuine home run pop, but his low on-base percentage doesn't help the offense. This will be his free-agent season.

The Sox had eight rookie pitchers last year, several in key roles and most of them unready for the majors, and Karkovice was tested in his ability to handle the staff. There should be fewer greenhorns in 1996, but the Sox will still depend on Karkovice to police their staff as well as enemy runners.

Overall Statistics

	G	AB	R	H	2B	3B	HR	RBI	SB	CS	BB	SO	BA	OBA
95 CHA	113	323	44	70	14	1	13	51	2	3	39	84	.217	.306
Career	777	2104	282	471	95	6	80	279	24	14	198	624	.224	.295

1995 Situational Statistics

	AB	HR	RBI	BA	OBA	SLG		AB	HR	RBI	BA	OBA	SLG
Home	150	5	26	.207	.292	.353	LHP	104	2	14	.231	.303	.346
Road	173	8	25	.225	.317	.416	RHP	219	11	37	.210	.307	.406
Apr-Jun	135	6	23	.230	.316	.430	ScPos	99	5	42	.232	.344	.434
Jul-Oct	188	7	28	.207	.298	.356	Clutch	48	4	10	.229	.288	.521

How He Compares to Other Batters

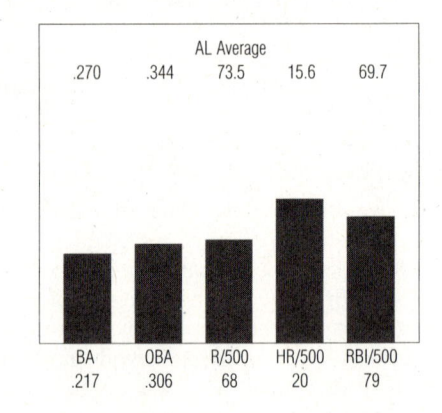

AL Average: .270 .344 73.5 15.6 69.7

BA	OBA	R/500	HR/500	RBI/500
.217	.306	68	20	79

Where He Hits the Ball

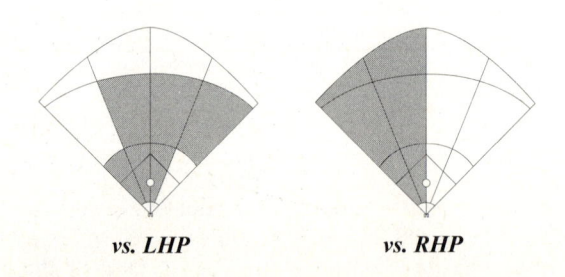

vs. LHP   vs. RHP

CHICAGO WHITE SOX

DAVE MARTINEZ

Positions: OF/1B//DH/P
Bats: L **Throws:** L
Ht: 5'10" **Wt:** 150
Opening Day Age: 31
Born: 9/26/1964
Drafted: TOR 8/23/84
ML Seasons: 10

SCOUTING REPORT

Dave began his career as a speedy center fielder, but now plays mainly right field and first base. He is now average defensively in every respect in the pasture, but he does have above-average range at first base.

He is still an average-plus runner but doesn't steal many bases anymore. Dave hits breaking balls pretty well, and fastballs better than that. He has a compact swing with some pop and hits the ball to all fields, but generates little power. Lefthanders confound him, so Martinez doesn't often get to bat against them. He bunted effectively last year, beating out seven hits and laying down nine sacrifices.

HOW HE PERFORMED IN '95

"Dear Applicant: We are pleased that you have chosen to play right field for the Chicago White Sox in 1995. Please understand, as Mr. Burks and Mr. Jackson have before you, that you are in our employ for this season only and that your on-field performance will have only incidental bearing on future employment. Thank you for your interest, and good luck in 1995."

If Dave Martinez didn't get a letter like this, he might as well have. Every year for the past three seasons, the Sox have signed a different right fielder, and Martinez was signed to fill the vacant slot in 1995. However, when the team tanked early, Dave ended up playing all over the diamond, playing each outfield position and appearing 47 times at first base when Frank Thomas moved to DH.

Dave's .307 batting average was a career high. However, he didn't do much else for the White Sox, and his bat doesn't make him especially valuable playing power positions like first base or right field, which demand big offensive production.

WHAT TO EXPECT IN '96

While Martinez enjoyed a good comeback season in 1995, his presence in the lineup indicates that the Sox have a void of impact-quality regular players. A first baseman/right fielder who drives in only 37 runs isn't scaring anybody. Dave received a two-year contract last winter, indicating that the White Sox regard his talents highly, but also indicating that the team is short of quality regulars at too many positions.

Overall Statistics

	G	AB	R	H	2B	3B	HR	RBI	SB	CS	BB	SO	BA	OBA
95 CHA	119	303	49	93	16	4	5	37	8	2	32	41	.307	.371
Career	1143	3334	429	897	136	45	53	319	124	58	294	527	.269	.329

1995 Situational Statistics

	AB	HR	RBI	BA	OBA	SLG		AB	HR	RBI	BA	OBA	SLG
Home	136	2	18	.279	.365	.419	LHP	33	0	1	.212	.297	.212
Road	167	3	19	.329	.375	.449	RHP	270	5	36	.319	.380	.463
Apr-Jun	82	3	9	.244	.311	.439	ScPos	71	2	30	.338	.427	.465
Jul-Oct	221	2	28	.330	.392	.434	Clutch	44	1	7	.318	.400	.568

How He Compares to Other Batters

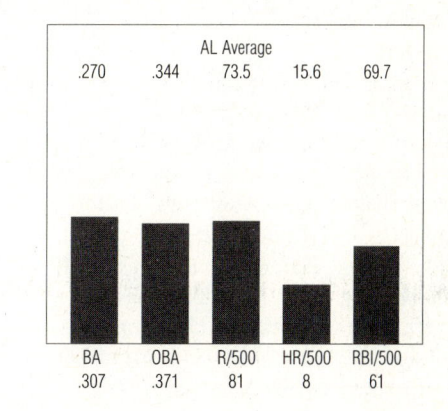

AL Average: .270 | .344 | 73.5 | 15.6 | 69.7

BA	OBA	R/500	HR/500	RBI/500
.307	.371	81	8	61

Where He Hits the Ball

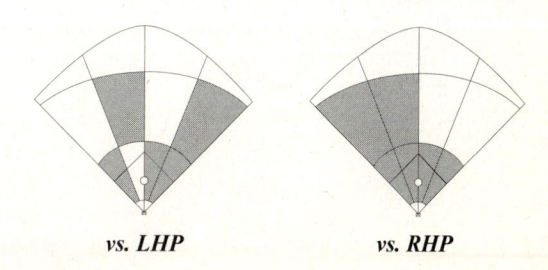

vs. LHP   vs. RHP

THE SCOUTING REPORT: 1996

CHICAGO WHITE SOX

LYLE MOUTON

Positions: OF//DH
Bats: R **Throws:** R
Ht: 6'4" **Wt:** 240
Opening Day Age: 26
Born: 5/13/1969
Drafted: NYA91 5/126
ML Seasons: 1

SCOUTING REPORT
The big, strong outfielder with the Frank Thomas-like physique is a good fastball hitter with some power. He likes to look for breaking pitches, especially hanging curves, that he can pull. However, he tends to have some problems making contact. Lyle is a below-average runner with below-average speed.

Mouton is not helpful in the outfield yet. His hands, arm strength, and arm accuracy are all average, and his range is below average. He does hustle at all times and is unafraid of hitting the outfield walls when chasing fly balls.

HOW HE PERFORMED IN '95
While the 1995 White Sox certainly missed Jack McDowell's presence in their underachieving starting rotation, the payment for the deal with the Yankees was a pleasant surprise. Lyle Mouton started the year at Triple-A Nashville, and he hit well enough to get a call to Chicago in early June. After a couple of weeks, he returned to Triple-A, but he was recalled for good on July 20. For the season, he batted .296 with eight homers at Nashville.

Mouton took over a regular outfield spot for the moribund White Sox, splitting time between left and right over the last two months. He did a fine job at the plate, showing some power and standing in very well against righthanded pitching.

Lyle does have a problem with strikeouts, however, and there is some concern that pitchers will exploit his relative lack of patience this season. He needs to generate more power to be valuable, since he doesn't add speed and has weak overall defensive skills.

WHAT TO EXPECT IN '96
Mouton will come to spring training with the inside track on a starting position in the White Sox outfield. If he can develop some additional discipline at the plate and make more consistent contact, Mouton has a good chance to be a very productive hitter and a solid everyday player.

Overall Statistics

	G	AB	R	H	2B	3B	HR	RBI	SB	CS	BB	SO	BA	OBA
95 CHA	58	179	23	54	16	0	5	27	1	0	19	46	.302	.373
Career	58	179	23	54	16	0	5	27	1	0	19	46	.302	.373

1995 Situational Statistics

	AB	HR	RBI	BA	OBA	SLG		AB	HR	RBI	BA	OBA	SLG
Home	82	4	12	.354	.436	.573	LHP	78	2	10	.295	.378	.449
Road	97	1	15	.258	.318	.392	RHP	101	3	17	.307	.369	.495
Apr-Jun	16	1	2	.188	.381	.375	ScPos	50	1	22	.280	.403	.440
Jul-Oct	163	4	25	.313	.372	.485	Clutch	22	2	5	.364	.417	.773

How He Compares to Other Batters

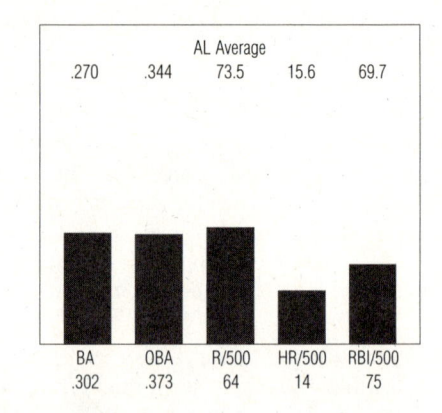

AL Average
.270 .344 73.5 15.6 69.7

BA .302 | OBA .373 | R/500 64 | HR/500 14 | RBI/500 75

Where He Hits the Ball

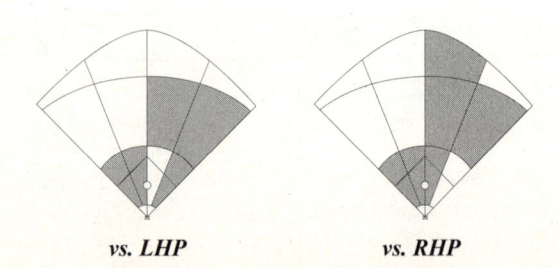

vs. LHP   vs. RHP

CHICAGO WHITE SOX

TIM RAINES

Positions: OF/DH
Bats: B **Throws:** R
Ht: 5'8" **Wt:** 178
Opening Day Age: 36
Born: 9/16/1959
Drafted: MON77 5/106
ML Seasons: 17

SCOUTING REPORT

Tim hits fastballs well from both sides of the plate, but is sometimes fooled by off-speed pitches and lunges at them too often. He likes the ball low both lefthanded and righthanded. Tim knows the strike zone well, and he is a patient, well-disciplined hitter who is productive from both sides of the plate.

Despite retaining plus speed, Raines does not bunt often (or effectively), a tendency shared by most of his White Sox teammates. He no longer steals bases at will, but he is a very intelligent baserunner.

At one time in his career, Tim was a center fielder and a better left fielder. Currently used exclusively in left, he has average-plus (but declining) range and a weak, though reasonably accurate, arm. His hands are average.

HOW HE PERFORMED IN '95

Because he has developed some power and no longer steals many bases, Raines is no longer considered leadoff-slot material by Chicago. Apparently, the Sox management must feel a high stolen base total is more important than good on-base percentage, because there is no other explanation for using Ray Durham or Lance Johnson in the top spot when Raines is available.

"Rock" was healthy all season and hit much better than his mediocre 1994 performance would have predicted. He walked often, added some power, and continued to steal bases effectively if not often. When Raines was caught stealing on September 2nd, it marked the first time he had been thrown out since 1993. His 40 straight steals set an American League record.

Tim appeared 22 times as a designated hitter last year, which may soon be the best place for him.

WHAT TO EXPECT IN '96

The White Sox were considering trading Raines over the winter. They have no one better to replace him and were primarily considering making a deal in order to shave the team's payroll. The hustling and productive Raines, a possible future Hall of Famer, deserves better than that, and so do the White Sox' fans. Raines' 1995 season provided ample reason to believe that he can continue to contribute offensively for several more years.

Overall Statistics

	G	AB	R	H	2B	3B	HR	RBI	SB	CS	BB	SO	BA	OBA
95 CHA	133	502	81	143	25	4	12	67	13	2	70	52	.285	.374
Career	2053	7766	1374	2295	371	109	146	829	777	136	1134	809	.296	.385

1995 Situational Statistics

	AB	HR	RBI	BA	OBA	SLG		AB	HR	RBI	BA	OBA	SLG
Home	239	6	31	.297	.399	.448	LHP	140	3	16	.279	.395	.414
Road	263	6	36	.274	.350	.399	RHP	362	9	51	.287	.365	.425
Apr-Jun	213	8	29	.305	.366	.484	ScPos	128	1	52	.289	.412	.383
Jul-Oct	289	4	38	.270	.379	.377	Clutch	89	3	12	.213	.290	.360

How He Compares to Other Batters

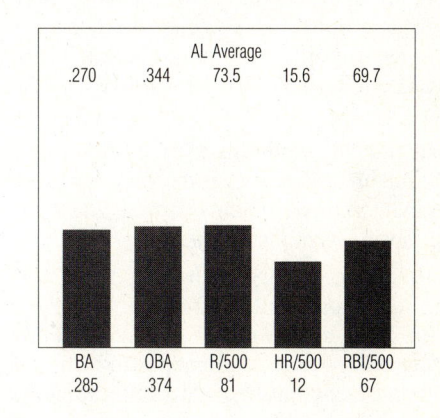

AL Average				
.270	.344	73.5	15.6	69.7

BA	OBA	R/500	HR/500	RBI/500
.285	.374	81	12	67

Where He Hits the Ball

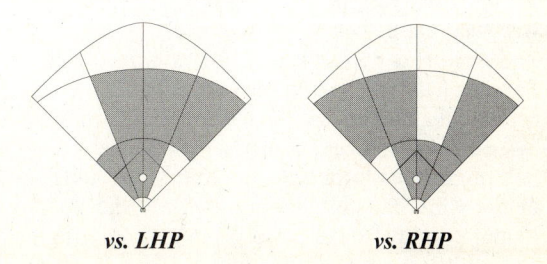

vs. LHP   vs. RHP

THE SCOUTING REPORT: 1996

CHICAGO WHITE SOX

FRANK THOMAS

Positions: 1B/DH
Bats: R **Throws:** R
Ht: 6'5" **Wt:** 240
Opening Day Age: 27
Born: 5/27/1968
Drafted: CHA89 1/7
ML Seasons: 6

SCOUTING REPORT

For some reason, AL hurlers consistently pitch to Frank Thomas' strength, working him down and away even though he steps into the ball and is a tremendous low-ball hitter. Of course, it's easier to shrug off a home run pitch hit by Frank Thomas than one hit by a mere mortal.

Frank likes pitches from the middle of the plate out where he can extend his powerful arms, and he has big power to right field as well as excellent pull power. It may be best to pitch him up and in.

Thomas is a poor runner with no speed. His fielding at first is below average, due to minus fielding, range, and throwing skills.

HOW HE PERFORMED IN '95

While Frank Thomas' star might have been eclipsed a bit last season by other players having outstanding seasons, his performance was far from perfunctory or disappointing. "The Big Hurt" did again in 1995 what he does better than almost anyone—reach base and hit for power. Thomas ended the year second in the league in on-base percentage and third in slugging percentage, becoming the only player in major-league history to collect 100 RBI and 100 walks in five consecutive seasons.

Thomas did this while his team collapsed around him. Frank hit .296 or higher in every month except September, when he "slumped" to a .242 mark but still clubbed seven home runs.

By mid-season, with the White Sox out of the race, Terry Bevington shifted Thomas to designated hitter in order to improve the team's defense and get other players into the lineup. Frank is still not good defensively, but has improved and could become at least adequate in another year or so. That's important to consider if the DH rule is finally abolished in the next few years.

WHAT TO EXPECT IN '96

The only real mystery for 1996 is what position Thomas will play. He did not enjoy being a designated hitter, and he feels he has something to prove by becoming a decent first baseman. However, the Sox might shift Robin Ventura to first if rookie infielder Chris Snopek hits his way into the lineup. Ventura could also be traded, leaving Thomas in the running to re-assume his regular first base position. Either way, Thomas should continue to be one of baseball's best hitters for another decade or so.

Overall Statistics

	G	AB	R	H	2B	3B	HR	RBI	SB	CS	BB	SO	BA	OBA
95 CHA	145	493	102	152	27	0	40	111	3	2	136	74	.308	.454
Career	789	2764	565	893	185	8	182	595	16	13	661	443	.323	.450

1995 Situational Statistics

	AB	HR	RBI	BA	OBA	SLG		AB	HR	RBI	BA	OBA	SLG
Home	247	15	49	.296	.444	.530	LHP	126	16	35	.389	.521	.849
Road	246	25	62	.321	.465	.683	RHP	367	24	76	.281	.431	.523
Apr-Jun	199	18	46	.312	.481	.643	ScPos	126	4	61	.333	.510	.516
Jul-Oct	294	22	65	.306	.436	.582	Clutch	74	7	11	.257	.441	.541

How He Compares to Other Batters

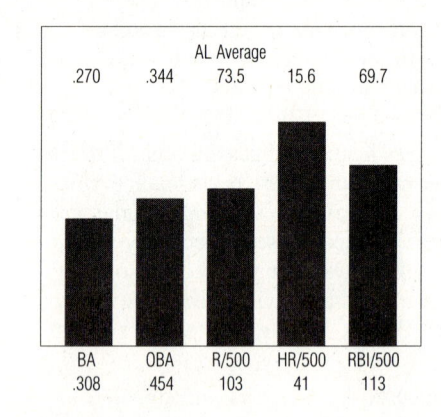

AL Average
.270 .344 73.5 15.6 69.7

BA .308 | OBA .454 | R/500 103 | HR/500 41 | RBI/500 113

Where He Hits the Ball

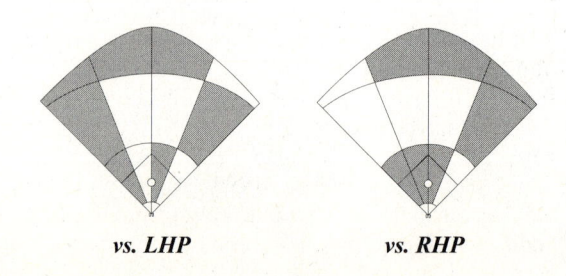

vs. LHP | vs. RHP

CHICAGO WHITE SOX

SCOUTING REPORT

Robin Ventura has good power and a smooth stroke. He hits fastballs well but breaking balls still freeze him at times. He likes pitches low in the strike zone so that he can generate some pop by lifting the ball into the air. He is very slow and is well below-average on the basepaths. For obvious reasons, he does not bunt often.

Ventura is an above-average third baseman. He has a plus arm, both in strength and accuracy, covers an average amount of ground, and has good hands despite his early-season troubles last year.

HOW HE PERFORMED IN '95

Ventura has smoothed out many of the kinks in his offense and is a much more consistent hitter now than he used to be. Lefthanders no longer spook him and he's less prone to slumps. Robin walks often, always has high on-base percentages, and can clear the bases with homers and doubles. He was very consistent in 1995, hitting .268 or better with good power and at least 10 walks in each full month.

The real nightmare for Ventura last season was in the field. He made eight errors in his first eight games, most of which were simple lapses of concentration. However, he rebounded and committed just 11 miscues the rest of the year, showing good range to his left and throwing well. However, he did play 18 times at first base, mostly in the second half of the season, and rumors abound that he'll be playing more there in the future—if he's still with the White Sox.

WHAT TO EXPECT IN '96

There was talk all season, once the Sox were clearly out of the playoff picture, that Ventura would be traded, perhaps to Los Angeles for young outfielders or pitchers. If the White Sox management makes this trade, they will have once again underestimated a player's value to the club and, not incidentally, to their fans. Ventura is a productive and popular player who is worth far more than a couple of prospects who might become good some day. He's very good right now and can play third base well for several more seasons before it might become necessary to move him to first base.

ROBIN VENTURA

Positions: 3B/1B//DH
Bats: L **Throws:** R
Ht: 6'1" **Wt:** 185
Opening Day Age: 28
Born: 7/14/1967
Drafted: CHA88 1/10
ML Seasons: 7

Overall Statistics

	G	AB	R	H	2B	3B	HR	RBI	SB	CS	BB	SO	BA	OBA
95 CHA	135	492	79	145	22	0	26	93	4	3	75	98	.295	.384
Career	881	3183	451	873	147	5	110	519	13	22	477	446	.274	.367

1995 Situational Statistics

	AB	HR	RBI	BA	OBA	SLG		AB	HR	RBI	BA	OBA	SLG
Home	222	8	36	.284	.371	.428	LHP	132	5	31	.265	.335	.409
Road	270	18	57	.304	.394	.556	RHP	360	21	62	.306	.401	.531
Apr-Jun	213	13	43	.305	.383	.540	ScPos	166	7	71	.265	.384	.440
Jul-Oct	279	13	50	.287	.384	.466	Clutch	82	2	15	.341	.412	.488

How He Compares to Other Batters

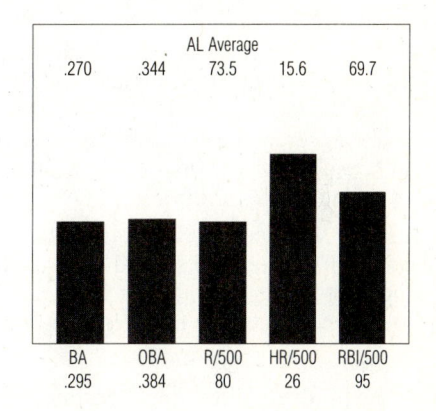

AL Average
.270 .344 73.5 15.6 69.7

BA   OBA R/500 HR/500 RBI/500
.295 .384 80   26   95

Where He Hits the Ball

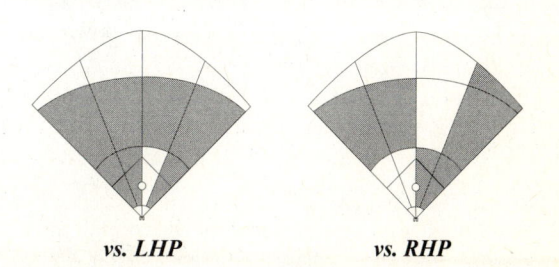

vs. LHP   vs. RHP

THE SCOUTING REPORT: 1996

CHICAGO WHITE SOX

CRAIG GREBECK

Positions: SS/3B//2B
Bats: R **Throws:** R
Ht: 5'8" **Wt:** 160
Opening Day Age: 31
Born: 12/29/1964
Drafted: CHA 8/13/86
ML Seasons: 6

Overall Statistics

	G	AB	R	H	2B	3B	HR	RBI	SB	CS	BB	SO	BA	OBA
95 CHA	53	154	19	40	12	0	1	18	0	0	21	23	.260	.360
Career	414	1071	129	273	62	6	12	110	2	8	135	152	.255	.342

1995 Situational Statistics

	AB	HR	RBI	BA	OBA	SLG		AB	HR	RBI	BA	OBA	SLG
Home	73	0	7	.342	.442	.438	LHP	87	1	4	.241	.320	.356
Road	81	1	11	.185	.283	.284	RHP	67	0	14	.284	.407	.358
Apr-Jun	68	1	10	.309	.420	.471	ScPos	39	0	17	.282	.417	.333
Jul-Oct	86	0	8	.221	.309	.267	Clutch	21	0	2	.190	.292	.286

SCOUTING REPORT

Grebeck can hit. His open stance and high-held bat allow him to make contact on high fastballs with some power. He has fine plate discipline. Craig doesn't make baserunning mistakes but has little speed and doesn't steal. He doesn't bunt often, but is adept at laying down sacrifices.

Craig is strong at three infield spots, turning the double play well at short and second with an accurate, though not strong, arm. While his range and hands are average, Grebeck's first step is good.

HOW HE PERFORMED IN '95

Grebeck again did utility duty despite Ozzie Guillen's struggles and rookie Ray Durham's streakiness. Craig committed five errors in his first 15 games, but wasn't the only Sox infielder to play Butterfinger Ball. He eventually settled down, finishing with just seven miscues.

"The Little Hurt" didn't show great pop last year, but has some sock and again reached base often in 1995.

WHAT TO EXPECT IN '96

Terry Bevington says Grebeck needs to play more, but gave him just 14 plate appearances after August 31. Craig seems locked into the reserve role.

MATT KARCHNER

Position: RP
Bats: R **Throws:** R
Ht: 6'4" **Wt:** 245
Opening Day Age: 28
Born: 6/28/1967
Drafted: KC89 9/205
ML Seasons: 1

Overall Statistics

	G	GS	GF	SV	W	L	ERA	IP	H	R	ER	HR	BB	SO
95 CHA	31	0	10	0	4	2	1.69	32.0	33	8	6	2	12	24
Career	31	0	10	0	4	2	1.69	32.0	33	8	6	2	12	24

1995 Situational Statistics

	W	L	ERA	SV	IP	BB	SO		AB	HR	RBI	BA	OBA	SLG
Home	2	2	2.75	0	19.2	3	13	LHB	54	0	4	.296	.339	.315
Road	2	0	0.00	0	12.1	9	11	RHB	66	2	12	.258	.333	.409
Apr-Jun	0	0	0.00	0	0.0	0	0	ScPos	39	0	14	.256	.389	.308
Jul-Oct	4	2	1.69	0	32.0	12	24	Clutch	77	2	11	.286	.345	.403

SCOUTING REPORT

The tall, thin Karchner uses a three-quarter delivery to bring an average-plus fastball, which has above-average velocity but tends to be straight. Matt's slider has a hard, sharp break, but the pitch sometimes loses velocity and is difficult to control. He lacks a strong off-speed pitch and is only fair at holding runners. Two runners stole against in four attempts last year.

HOW HE PERFORMED IN '95

A middle reliever for most of his seven-year career, former Royals' farmhand Karchner finally got the call in 1995. He impressed the White Sox immediately, beginning his stay in the major leagues with 15 scoreless innings. Matt generally kept the ball down and away, but struggled against lefthanders.

WHAT TO EXPECT IN '96

Unless his ears are pinned back this spring, Karchner will come north and work as a middle inning/setup pitcher. He's not going to be a closer except in an extreme emergency and still needs to prove he can get lefties out, but a middle relief pitcher who doesn't allow walks or homers is valuable enough.

CHICAGO WHITE SOX

BRIAN KEYSER

Position: RP/SP
Bats: R **Throws:** R
Ht: 6'1" **Wt:** 180
Opening Day Age: 29
Born: 10/31/1966
Drafted: CHA89 19/485
ML Seasons: 1

Overall Statistics

	G	GS	GF	SV	W	L	ERA	IP	H	R	ER	HR	BB	SO
95 CHA	23	10	0	0	5	6	4.97	92.1	114	53	51	10	27	48
Career	23	10	0	0	5	6	4.97	92.1	114	53	51	10	27	48

1995 Situational Statistics

	W	L	ERA	SV	IP	BB	SO		AB	HR	RBI	BA	OBA	SLG
Home	2	3	4.39	0	53.1	14	28	LHB	203	3	26	.345	.378	.502
Road	3	3	5.77	0	39.0	13	20	RHB	170	7	28	.259	.326	.453
Apr-Jun	1	2	5.54	0	26.0	7	12	ScPos	102	4	44	.275	.356	.480
Jul-Oct	4	4	4.75	0	66.1	20	36	Clutch	16	1	1	.125	.263	.375

SCOUTING REPORT
Keyser throws overhand, which makes his average-minus fastball easier to pick up. To compensate, Brian often sinks or turns over the heater. His change-up and curve are also slightly below average. Keyser's best pitch is an average slider that has a good break. He does not throw any of his pitches with above-average velocity.

HOW HE PERFORMED IN '95
The six-year vet was brought up from Triple-A because he, unlike most Sox pitchers, hadn't walked everyone in sight. Keyser was 2-4 at Nashville, but had allowed just nine free passes in 40 innings.

After a few starts, Brian moved into long relief. Although he has a bulldog attitude, his stuff is below average and his control wasn't quite as good as advertised. By season's end, he was mostly pitching in blowouts. Three baserunners stole successfully against him in six tries.

WHAT TO EXPECT IN '96
Keyser is a fringe pitcher who could be a long reliever this year, but he has little upside potential and probably won't have much of a big-league career.

MIKE LAVALLIERE

Position: C
Bats: L **Throws:** R
Ht: 5'9" **Wt:** 190
Opening Day Age: 35
Born: 8/18/1960
Drafted: PHI 7/12/81
ML Seasons: 12

Overall Statistics

	G	AB	R	H	2B	3B	HR	RBI	SB	CS	BB	SO	BA	OBA
95 CHA	46	98	7	24	6	0	1	19	0	0	9	15	.245	.303
Career	879	2473	185	663	109	5	18	294	5	15	321	244	.268	.351

1995 Situational Statistics

	AB	HR	RBI	BA	OBA	SLG		AB	HR	RBI	BA	OBA	SLG
Home	53	0	9	.189	.262	.245	LHP	15	1	4	.200	.263	.400
Road	45	1	10	.311	.354	.444	RHP	83	0	15	.253	.311	.325
Apr-Jun	51	0	7	.196	.263	.235	ScPos	31	0	17	.290	.333	.387
Jul-Oct	47	1	12	.298	.346	.447	Clutch	16	1	4	.313	.389	.563

SCOUTING REPORT
Mike still has very good throwing mechanics. He's not especially agile, but knows hitters well. At bat, he makes good contact but is fully a singles hitter. LaValliere is very slow.

HOW HE PERFORMED IN '95
LaValliere didn't play that often in 1995, twice going on the disabled list. However, Spanky did have a couple of extra-inning game-winning hits and provided a moment of high drama—or was that comedy?—by scoring from first base on a bases-loaded single against the Tigers in August, an event that inspired a satirical "Air Spanky" running-shoe video.

LaValliere doesn't hit for power, but will take a walk and still laces line drives. He threw out an outstanding total of 14 of 30 baserunners trying to steal against him in 1995.

WHAT TO EXPECT IN '96
The White Sox dumped LaValliere in October, but might try to re-sign him this spring. There is little catching help in the system, and Spanky is far from the worst backup receiver available.

CHICAGO WHITE SOX

BARRY LYONS

Positions: C//DH/1B
Bats: R **Throws:** R
Ht: 6'1" **Wt:** 205
Opening Day Age: 35
Born: 6/3/1960
Drafted: NYN82 15/371
ML Seasons: 7

Overall Statistics

	G	AB	R	H	2B	3B	HR	RBI	SB	CS	BB	SO	BA	OBA
95 CHA	27	64	8	17	2	0	5	16	0	0	4	14	.266	.304
Career	253	628	53	150	26	2	15	89	0	1	29	92	.239	.275

1995 Situational Statistics

	AB	HR	RBI	BA	OBA	SLG		AB	HR	RBI	BA	OBA	SLG
Home	28	3	9	.250	.276	.607	LHP	22	2	6	.273	.346	.636
Road	36	2	7	.278	.325	.472	RHP	42	3	10	.262	.279	.476
Apr-Jun	0	0	0	.000	1.000	.000	ScPos	15	3	14	.400	.375	1.000
Jul-Oct	64	5	16	.266	.294	.531	Clutch	12	0	1	.083	.077	.083

SCOUTING REPORT

The veteran catcher is a dead fastball hitter and can't do much with any other pitch. His defense is average all around. Like most veteran backstops, Barry is very slow on the basepaths.

HOW HE PERFORMED IN '95

Lyons refused to play in replacement games but still opened the season on the Sox roster. He was sent down and recalled twice more during the season, getting substantial playing time behind the plate and at DH in September. Lyons hit well, and as a consequence was placed on the Sox' 40-player winter roster.

Barry hit for more power than anyone could have guessed with the White Sox: apparently word hadn't traveled far enough that he could pound fastballs. He didn't show great throwing skills behind the plate (13 of 19 basestealers were successful), but was agile and calls a good game.

WHAT TO EXPECT IN '96

Lyons is a pretty good backup catcher who took advantage of his playing time last season. He's not a legitimate home-run threat, but might help out again if he makes the team.

NORBERTO MARTIN

Positions: 2B/OF/DH//3B/SS
Bats: R **Throws:** R
Ht: 5'10" **Wt:** 175
Opening Day Age: 29
Born: 12/10/1966
Drafted: CHA 3/27/84
ML Seasons: 3

Overall Statistics

	G	AB	R	H	2B	3B	HR	RBI	SB	CS	BB	SO	BA	OBA
95 CHA	72	160	17	43	7	4	2	17	5	0	3	25	.269	.281
Career	125	305	39	84	14	5	3	35	9	2	13	42	.275	.302

1995 Situational Statistics

	AB	HR	RBI	BA	OBA	SLG		AB	HR	RBI	BA	OBA	SLG
Home	73	1	10	.342	.359	.493	LHP	85	1	5	.247	.273	.353
Road	87	1	7	.207	.213	.322	RHP	75	1	12	.293	.291	.453
Apr-Jun	50	0	2	.160	.218	.160	ScPos	39	0	15	.231	.233	.385
Jul-Oct	110	2	15	.318	.313	.509	Clutch	26	0	2	.269	.321	.385

SCOUTING REPORT

Martin is a fastball hitter, but he has a slow bat and no power and often takes the ball to right field. He does not bunt often or effectively.

At second base, he is an average-plus defender with decent range and hands. His arm is average in strength but has plus accuracy.

HOW HE PERFORMED IN '95

Martin started slowly in 1995, but kicked it up as the year went on and finished with respectable numbers. However, Norberto still has serious problems with the strike zone. Martin's strikeout rate rose dramatically in 1995, and he literally never walks. His occasional doubles power doesn't compensate for a complete inability to get on base.

"Paco" played five positions in 1995 as well as seeing some action at DH. Martin can be too aggressive on the bases and has just average speed, but he is a good base stealer.

WHAT TO EXPECT IN '96

Last winter, Martin underwent elbow surgery to replace a screw inserted in 1992. He's expected back at 100% for 1996, but is on the bubble because the Sox are very high on young infielder Chris Snopek.

CHICAGO WHITE SOX

KIRK McCASKILL

Position: RP
Bats: R **Throws:** R
Ht: 6'1" **Wt:** 200
Opening Day Age: 34
Born: 4/9/1961
Drafted: CAL82 4/88
ML Seasons: 11

Overall Statistics

	G	GS	GF	SV	W	L	ERA	IP	H	R	ER	HR	BB	SO
95 CHA	55	1	17	2	6	4	4.89	81.0	97	50	44	10	33	50
Career	351	238	42	7	101	103	4.03	1677.1	1676	835	751	148	634	975

1995 Situational Statistics

	W	L	ERA	SV	IP	BB	SO		AB	HR	RBI	BA	OBA	SLG
Home	5	4	4.44	1	46.2	16	26	LHB	141	5	24	.319	.409	.461
Road	1	0	5.50	1	34.1	17	24	RHB	180	5	26	.289	.343	.411
Apr-Jun	4	2	4.81	0	33.2	17	18	ScPos	108	3	43	.296	.358	.417
Jul-Oct	2	2	4.94	2	47.1	16	32	Clutch	121	4	19	.273	.350	.388

SCOUTING REPORT
McCaskill throws from three-quarters. None of his five pitches are anything special, despite his average-plus velocity and control. Kirk tends to sink or turn over his average-minus fastball. His slider has a hard but early break and can be hit. He has an average-plus move to first base and is a slightly above-average fielder. Of six runners who tried to steal against him last year, three were caught.

HOW HE PERFORMED IN '95
Kirk finished second on the team in appearances, getting plenty of opportunities because of poor performances by the rotation. However, he rarely worked in a key role, getting just five save opportunities and blowing three. Lefthanders hit nearly 100 points higher against him than they had the year before. While McCaskill still has decent stuff and doesn't allow many walks, he seems to lack confidence in his fastball. Strike one is the hardest pitch for him to throw. Constant nibbling led to 10 wild pitches, 10 home runs, and 12 doubles allowed in 1995.

WHAT TO EXPECT IN '96
Kirk is under contract, so he'll pitch in the middle again. If he performs as he did last year, he won't be back in 1997.

SCOTT RADINSKY

Position: RP
Bats: L **Throws:** L
Ht: 6'3" **Wt:** 190
Opening Day Age: 28
Born: 3/3/1968
Drafted: CHA86 3/75
ML Seasons: 5

Overall Statistics

	G	GS	GF	SV	W	L	ERA	IP	H	R	ER	HR	BB	SO
95 CHA	46	0	10	1	2	1	5.45	38.0	46	23	23	7	17	14
Career	316	0	104	32	24	16	3.62	275.2	261	124	111	18	129	201

1995 Situational Statistics

	W	L	ERA	SV	IP	BB	SO		AB	HR	RBI	BA	OBA	SLG
Home	1	1	6.86	1	21.0	9	5	LHB	58	2	10	.328	.371	.569
Road	1	0	3.71	0	17.0	8	9	RHB	91	5	14	.297	.370	.495
Apr-Jun	2	0	5.89	1	18.1	12	5	ScPos	47	1	16	.213	.305	.340
Jul-Oct	0	1	5.03	0	19.2	5	9	Clutch	45	2	6	.378	.451	.600

SCOUTING REPORT
While Radinsky once had a very hard fastball, he now throws an average-plus "sneaky fast" pitch from a low three-quarter to sidearm angle. His average curve is soft and breaks laterally. Scott's control is below-average; he is average at holding runners and fielding. Two of three runners who tried to steal against him were caught in 1995.

HOW HE PERFORMED IN '95
Radinsky missed all of 1994 after undergoing treatment for Hodgkins' Disease. Returning in 1995, he had fan support but looked nothing like his former self, showing plenty of effect from the year-long layoff. Lefthanders beat the tar out of Radinsky, who had neither his old velocity nor a semblance of control. He ended up feuding with manager Terry Bevington and never got untracked.

WHAT TO EXPECT IN '96
Scott's comeback was inspiring, but he pitched about as badly as possible in 1995. Although he'd probably hate the idea, Radinsky could use some time back in the minors to get some action and regain his command. He's not going to return to his old form pitching 40 innings a season.

CHICAGO WHITE SOX

DAVE RIGHETTI

Position: SP
Bats: L **Throws:** L
Ht: 6'3" **Wt:** 198
Opening Day Age: 37
Born: 11/28/1958
Drafted: TEX77* 1/9
ML Seasons: 16

Overall Statistics

	G	GS	GF	SV	W	L	ERA	IP	H	R	ER	HR	BB	SO
95 CHA	10	9	1	0	3	2	4.20	49.1	65	24	23	6	18	29
Career	718	89	474	252	82	79	3.46	1403.2	1287	602	540	95	591	1112

1995 Situational Statistics

	W	L	ERA	SV	IP	BB	SO		AB	HR	RBI	BA	OBA	SLG
Home	1	1	3.00	0	24.0	10	12	LHB	29	1	3	.276	.344	.414
Road	2	1	5.33	0	25.1	8	17	RHB	171	5	20	.333	.383	.485
Apr-Jun	0	0	0.00	0	0.0	0	0	ScPos	39	1	14	.256	.326	.359
Jul-Oct	3	2	4.20	0	49.1	18	29	Clutch	14	0	0	.143	.200	.143

SCOUTING REPORT

Dave's average-plus slider has a short, hard, late break. It is his only quality pitch. His other four offerings are average-minus, including a fastball that he usually turns over. Righetti's control is just average. He has a plus move to first, and half of the six men who tried to steal against him last year were nailed.

HOW HE PERFORMED IN '95

Turning over a rotation spot to a 36-year-old minor-league refugee who had made only four starts in the last 11 years is a desperation move. Righetti was thoroughly mediocre and pitched just once after September 1 due to a tight shoulder.

Dave gave up 18 extra-base hits as well as plenty of singles. He was most effective pitching inside, but has neither the command nor the stuff to do that consistently.

WHAT TO EXPECT IN '96

It's hard to see Righetti being part of Chicago's plans this season, but it was inconceivable a year ago that he would make nine major-league starts. The White Sox got a lot of mileage out of Righetti after he had been discarded by numerous teams; it's not likely to happen again.

JEFF SHAW

Position: RP
Bats: R **Throws:** R
Ht: 6'2" **Wt:** 185
Opening Day Age: 29
Born: 7/7/1966
Drafted: CLE86* 1/1
ML Seasons: 6

Overall Statistics

	G	GS	GF	SV	W	L	ERA	IP	H	R	ER	HR	BB	SO
95 MO/CH	59	0	18	3	1	6	4.88	72.0	70	42	39	6	27	51
Career	203	19	56	5	11	25	4.50	363.2	380	200	182	45	125	207

1995 Situational Statistics

	W	L	ERA	SV	IP	BB	SO		AB	HR	RBI	BA	OBA	SLG
Home	1	4	5.66	2	35.0	14	25	LHB	119	2	14	.294	.361	.395
Road	0	2	4.14	1	37.0	13	26	RHB	151	4	12	.232	.314	.417
Apr-Jun	1	4	4.95	2	36.1	16	27	ScPos	79	0	17	.177	.290	.253
Jul-Oct	0	2	4.79	1	35.2	11	24	Clutch	56	0	8	.268	.431	.429

SCOUTING REPORT

Shaw uses a high three-quarter delivery to throw three average pitches: a sinking fastball (also occasionally throw a four-seamer up in the zone), a slider, and a splitter. He has no reliable off-speed pitch. Although Jeff does keep the ball low, his pitches often kick up dirt around the plate.

HOW HE PERFORMED IN '95

Shaw had pitched surprisingly well for Montreal in 1993–94, but didn't do the job in '95, earning a trade to Chicago (for Jose DeLeon) on August 28. He did strand 23 of 25 inherited runners with the Expos, but showed little with the White Sox.

Jeff cuts down the running game reasonably well (five of eight potential basestealers were thrown out in 1995) and doesn't leave ball high in the strike zone very often, but walks too many and struggles against lefthanders. He was healthy all year, but the Expos ask much for him and sure didn't get much for him.

WHAT TO EXPECT IN '96

If Shaw makes the White Sox staff in '96, it will be because several younger, more talented pitchers aren't quite ready for the majors yet.

CHICAGO WHITE SOX: TOP PROSPECTS

JEFF ABBOTT
Bats: R Throws: L Opening Day Age: 24
Ht: 6-2 Wt: 190 Born: 8/17/1972
Position: OF Drafted: 1994 #6 CHA

YR TEAM	LG/CLASS	G	AB	R	H	2B	3B	HR	RBI	SB	BA	OBA
94 White Sox	GULF/R	4	15	4	7	1	0	1	3	2	.467	.579
94 Hickory	SAL/A	63	224	47	88	16	6	6	48	2	.393	.481
95 Birmingham	SOU/AA	55	197	25	63	11	1	3	28	1	.320	.382
Pr William	CARO/A	70	264	41	92	16	4	4	47	7.348	.404

The former All-American from Kentucky was leading the Carolina League in batting when promoted to Birmingham in late June. Abbott is considered a "pure" hitter who uses the whole field and can adjust his approach to any count. The 23-year-old needs work in the outfield, however, as he doesn't get a good jump on fly balls.

LUIS ANDUJAR
Bats: R Throws: R Opening Day Age: 23
Ht: 6-2 Wt: 175 Born: 11/22/1972
Position: P Drafted: NDFA 1-25-90 by CHA

YR TEAM	LG/CLASS	G	GS	GF	SV	W	L	ERA	IP	H	HR	BB	SO	O/BA
93 Sarasota	FSL/A	18	11	4	1	6	6	1.99	86.0	67	2	28	76	.218
93 Birmingham	SOU/AA	6	6	0	0	5	0	1.82	39.2	31	3	18	48	.220
94 Birmingham	SOU/AA	15	15	0	0	3	7	5.05	76.2	90	5	25	64	.292
94 White Sox	GULF/R	2	0	0	0	1	0	0.00	6.0	3	0	1	6	.150
95 Birmingham	SOU/AA	27	27	0	0	14	8	2.85	167	147	10	44	146	.233
Chicago	AL/MAJ	5	5	0	0	2	1	3.26	30	26	4	14	9	.232

At 20, Andujar posted the minors' third best ERA (1.93) in 1993 and went 5-0, 1.82 ERA in six Double-A starts. In 1994, he tried to pitch through elbow pain but eventually succumbed to surgery, which forced him to come back slowly last season. After an opening night win, Andujar lost his next six decisions before winning 12 straight games, one of which was a no-hitter. The Southern League's Most Outstanding Pitcher used a 91-mph fastball, a slurve, an outstanding changeup and great location to earn a September promotion to Chicago.

MIKE BERTOTTI
Bats: L Throws: L Opening Day Age: 26
Ht: 6-1 Wt: 185 Born: 1/18/1970
Position: P Drafted: 1991 #31 CHA

YR TEAM	LG/CLASS	G	GS	GF	SV	W	L	ERA	IP	H	HR	BB	SO	O/BA
93 Hickory	SAL/A	9	9	0	0	3	3	2.11	59.2	42	2	29	77	.196
93 South Bend	MID/A	17	16	0	0	5	7	3.49	111.0	93	5	44	108	.230
94 Pr William	CARO/A	16	15	0	0	7	6	3.53	104.2	90	13	43	103	.233
94 Birmingham	SOU/AA	10	10	0	0	4	3	2.90	68.1	55	1	21	44	.223
95 Nashville	AMAS/AAA	7	6	1	0	2	3	8.72	32	41	8	17	35	.308
Birmingham	SOU/AA	12	12	0	0	2	7	5.00	63	60	4	36	53	.253
Chicago	AL/MAJ	4	4	0	0	1	1	12.56	14	23	6	11	15	.377

Bertotti throws harder than most lefthanders and was impressive in 1994, but struggled last year due to poor location and an inconsistent slider. Affected by the major league strike, the 25-year-old did not post his first victory until late May and lasted seven innings just twice all season.

MIKE CAMERON
Bats: R Throws: R Opening Day Age: 23
Ht: 6-1 Wt: 170 Born: 1/8/1973
Position: CF Drafted: 1991 #18 CHA

YR TEAM	LG/CLASS	G	AB	R	H	2B	3B	HR	RBI	SB	BA	OBA
93 South Bend	MID/A	122	411	52	98	14	5	0	30	19	.238	.292
94 Pr William	CARO/A	131	468	86	116	15	17	6	48	22	.248	.343
95 Birmingham	SOU/AA	107	350	64	87	20	5	11	60	21	.249	.355
Chicago	AL/MAJ	28	38	4	7	2	0	1	2	0	.184	.244

Known for his great speed, instincts and ability to play center field, Cameron is a hard worker who got called up to Chicago from Double-A despite a .249 average. Only 22, he will take a walk, has a little power, and can steal a base, but strikes out too often and has batted just .243 over his career.

TOM FORDHAM
Bats: L Throws: L Opening Day Age: 22
Ht: 6-2 Wt: 210 Born: 2/20/1974
Position: P Drafted: 1993 #11 CHA

YR TEAM	LG/CLASS	G	GS	GF	SV	W	L	ERA	IP	H	HR	BB	SO	O/BA
93 White Sox	GULF/R	3	0	1	0	1	1	1.80	10.0	9	0	3	12	.237
93 Sarasota	FSL/A	2	0	1	0	0	0	0.00	5.0	3	0	3	5	.167
93 Hickory	SAL/A	8	8	0	0	4	3	3.88	48.2	36	3	21	27	.217
94 Hickory	SAL/A	17	17	0	0	10	5	3.14	109.0	101	10	30	121	.242
94 South Bend	MID/A	11	11	0	0	4	4	4.34	74.2	82	4	14	48	.279
95 Birmingham	SOU/AA	14	14	0	0	6	3	3.38	82	79	9	28	61	.250
Pr William	CARO/A	13	13	0	0	9	0	2.04	84	66	7	35	78	.220

Only 20 years old, Fordham has won 29 games the last two seasons despite an unimpressive fastball. Spotting his "heater" with an effective change and breaking ball, Fordham led the organization in wins in 1995 and ranked second in ERA and fifth in strikeouts. He didn't lose his first game until July 3 and held Carolina League clubs to one run or less in nine of his 13 starts.

JIMMY HURST
Bats: R Throws: R Opening Day Age: 24
Ht: 6-6 Wt: 225 Born: 3/1/1972
Position: OF Drafted: 1990 #13 CHA

YR TEAM	LG/CLASS	G	AB	R	H	2B	3B	HR	RBI	SB	BA	OBA
93 South Bend	MID/A	123	464	79	113	26	0	20	79	15	.244	.307
94 Pr William	CARO/A	127	455	90	126	31	6	25	91	15	.277	.377
95 Birmingham	SOU/AA	91	301	47	57	11	0	12	34	12	.189	.270

The 1994 Carolina League All-Star broke his wrist over the winter, got off to a slow start in 1995, pressed, and never got untracked. A talented JC hoop player, Hurst is still learning baseball. He is beginning to make adjustments as a hitter, especially with two strikes, and his outfield play is improving. He still does not get a good jump on the ball, but Hurst runs well for a big man and has a decent right field arm.

THE SCOUTING REPORT: 1996

CHICAGO WHITE SOX: TOP PROSPECTS

ANDY LORRAINE
Bats: L Throws: L Opening Day Age: 24
Ht: 6-3 Wt: 195 Born: 8/11/1972
Position: P Drafted: 1993 #4 CAL

YR TEAM	LG/CLASS	G	GS	GF	SV	W	L	ERA	IP	H	HR	BB	SO	O/BA
93 Boise	NWST/A	6	6	0	0	4	1	1.29	42.0	33	3	6	39	.219
94 Vancouver	PCL/AAA	22	22	0	0	12	4	3.42	142.0	156	13	34	90	.285
94 California	AL/MAJ	4	3	0	0	0	2	10.61	18.2	30	7	11	10	.366
95 Nashville	AMAS/AAA	7	7	0	0	4	1	6.00	39	51	4	12	26	.305
Vancouver	PCL/AAA	18	18	0	0	6	6	3.96	97	105	7	30	51	.276
Chicago	AL/MAJ	5	0	2	0	0	0	3.38	8	3	0	2	5	.111

Lorraine, the Angels' first pick in 1994 was acquired in the Jim Abbott deal. A typical Stanford pitcher, the 23-year-old has a great feel, an average fastball and good breaking ball. However, his numbers were not impressive at pitcher-friendly Vancouver, and he was not particularly effective in Nashville or Chicago.

GREG NORTON
Bats: S Throws: R Opening Day Age: 24
Ht: 6-1 Wt: 182 Born: 7/6/1972
Position: 3B Drafted: 1993 #2 CHA

YR TEAM	LG/CLASS	G	AB	R	H	2B	3B	HR	RBI	SB	BA	OBA
93 White Sox	GULF/R	3	9	1	2	0	0	0	2	0	.222	.300
93 Hickory	SAL/A	71	254	36	62	12	2	4	36	0	.244	.347
94 South Bend	MID/A	127	477	73	137	22	2	6	64	5	.287	.369
95 Birmingham	SOU/AA	133	469	65	117	23	2	6	60	19	.249	.339

Norton put on plenty of fielding clinics in the Southern League last season, showing great range, reflexes and an arm capable of throwing runners out from deep third base. Offensively, the switch-hitter's numbers are not overly impressive. However, factor in pitcher-friendly Hoover Stadium in Birmingham—Norton hit .266 with all six homers on the road—and the 23-year-old's near-.300 average in the second half, and his season looks better. The Oklahoma product switch-hits, has a pretty good idea of the strike zone, and runs well.

CHARLES POE
Bats: R Throws: R Opening Day Age: 24
Ht: 6-0 Wt: 185 Born: 11/9/1971
Position: OF Drafted: 1990 #7 CHA

YR TEAM	LG/CLASS	G	AB	R	H	2B	3B	HR	RBI	SB	BA	OBA
93 Sarasota	FSL/A	95	313	45	78	16	6	11	47	5	.249	.329
93 White Sox	GULF/R	3	13	2	4	3	0	1	2	0	.308	.357
94 Pr William	CARO/A	130	469	72	126	21	3	14	83	14	.269	.345
95 Birmingham	SOU/AA	120	427	75	121	28	2	13	60	19	.283	.369

After three seasons of sub-average production, the 23-year-old Poe began to develop in 1994. He continued to improve last season, and was selected to the Southern League All-Star team. Poe put up solid power numbers at pitcher-friendly Hoover Stadium, played a pretty good left field, and showed decent speed and an adequate arm.

OLMEDO SAENZ
Bats: R Throws: R Opening Day Age: 25
Ht: 6-2 Wt: 185 Born: 10/8/1970
Position: 3B Drafted: NDFA 5-11-90 by CHA

YR TEAM	LG/CLASS	G	AB	R	H	2B	3B	HR	RBI	SB	BA	OBA
93 Sarasota	FSL/A	33	121	13	31	9	4	0	27	3	.256	.316
93 South Bend	MID/A	13	50	3	18	4	1	0	7	1	.360	.439
93 Birmingham	SOU/AA	49	173	30	60	17	2	6	29	2	.347	.427
94 Nashville	AMAS/AAA	107	383	48	100	27	2	12	59	3	.261	.326
94 Chicago	AL/MAJ	5	14	2	2	0	1	0	0	0	.143	.143
95 Nashville	AMAS/AAA	111	415	60	126	26	1	13	74	0	.304	.385

Saenz is a solid all-around player. After a slow start last season, he was the league's top hitter in June (.393) and finished among the American Association leaders in batting and RBI. In addition, he has posted a .300 average with runners in scoring position the last two seasons. However, he is stuck behind Chris Snopek in the organization and does not play any other defensive position.

MIKE SIROTKA
Bats: L Throws: L Opening Day Age: 25
Ht: 6-1 Wt: 190 Born: 5/13/1971
Position: P Drafted: 1993 #15 CHA

YR TEAM	LG/CLASS	G	GS	GF	SV	W	L	ERA	IP	H	HR	BB	SO	O/BA
93 White Sox	GULF/R	3	0	1	0	0	0	0.00	5.0	4	0	2	8	.211
93 South Bend	MID/A	7	1	3	0	0	1	6.10	10.1	12	3	6	12	.273
94 South Bend	MID/A	27	27	0	0	12	9	3.07	196.2	183	11	58	173	.245
95 Nashville	AMAS/AAA	8	8	0	0	1	5	2.83	54	51	4	13	34	.258
Birmingham	SOU/AA	16	16	0	0	7	6	3.20	101	95	11	22	79	.249
Chicago	AL/MAJ	6	6	0	0	1	2	4.19	34	39	2	17	19	.302

The LSU product has been a quick study since being drafted in 1993, arriving in the major leagues within two years. Sirotka knows how to pitch, using a mid-80's fastball with movement, a curve, a slider, and an exceptional changeup. The 24-year-old keeps the ball down, has fine location, and is not afraid to throw any pitch at any time. He led the organization in strikeouts in 1994.

CHRIS SNOPEK
Bats: R Throws: R Opening Day Age: 26
Ht: 6-1 Wt: 185 Born: 9/20/1970
Position: 3B-SS Drafted: 1992 #6 CHA

YR TEAM	LG/CLASS	G	AB	R	H	2B	3B	HR	RBI	SB	BA	OBA
93 South Bend	MID/A	22	72	20	28	8	1	5	18	1	.389	.500
93 Sarasota	FSL/A	107	371	61	91	21	4	10	50	3	.245	.354
94 Birmingham	SOU/AA	106	365	58	96	25	3	6	54	9	.263	.367
95 Nashville	AMAS/AAA	113	393	56	127	23	4	12	55	2	.323	.402
Chicago	AL/MAJ	22	68	12	22	4	0	1	7	1	.324	.403

Snopek's bat speed, plate discipline, quick hands, and strong arm are the tools that could move Robin Ventura to first base (or another organization). Snopek rebounded from a slow start—he did not hit his first homer until June—and finished second in the American Association batting race, losing the title in the last week of the season. A third baseman by trade, Snopek played every day at shortstop in 1995, but is blocked on the major league level by Ozzie Guillen, who is signed through 1997.

CHICAGO WHITE SOX: OTHERS TO WATCH

JAMES BALDWIN   Bats: R   Throws: R   Ht: 6-4   Wt: 210
Born: 7/15/1971   Drafted: 1990 #5 CHA   Pos: P

YR TEAM	LG/CLASS	G	GS	GF	SV	W	L	ERA	IP	H	HR	BB	SO	O/BA
95 Chicago	AL/MAJ	6	4	0	0	0	1	12.89	14.2	32	6	9	10	.444
95 Nashville	AMAS/AAA	18	18	0	0	5	9	5.85	95.1	120	27	44	89	.302

Baldwin has a great arm and outstanding stuff, but showed no command in 1995 and was one of the biggest disappointments in the game.

ESSEX BURTON   Bats: R   Throws: R   Ht: 5-9   Wt: 155
Born: 5/16/1969   Drafted: 1991 #26 CHA   Pos: 2B

YR TEAM	LG/CLASS	G	AB	R	H	2B	3B	HR	RBI	SB	BA	OBA
95 Birmingham	SOU/AA	142	554	95	141	15	2	1	43	60	.255	.353

The minors' top base thief the past three years is a liability on defense and hasn't developed enough with the bat.

CARMINE CAPPUCCIO   Bats: L   Throws: R   Ht: 6-3   Wt: 185
Born: 2/1/1970   Drafted: 1992 #9 CHA   Pos: OF

YR TEAM	LG/CLASS	G	AB	R	H	2B	3B	HR	RBI	SB	BA	OBA
95 Nashville	AMAS/AAA	66	216	30	59	14	0	5	24	0	.273	.360
95 Birmingham	SOU/AA	65	248	34	69	13	3	4	38	2	.278	.339

"Pooch" is a solid hitter with gap power, a good idea of the strike zone and a good arm.

ROBERT ELLIS   Bats: R   Throws: R   Ht: 6-5   Wt: 220
Born: 12/15/1970   Drafted: 1990 #4 CHA   Pos: P

YR TEAM	LG/CLASS	G	GS	GF	SV	W	L	ERA	IP	H	HR	BB	SO	O/BA
95 Nashville	AMAS/AAA	4	4	0	0	1	2	2.18	20.2	16	2	10	9	.219

Ellis is talented but has had elbow problems the last two years.

KEITH HEBERLING   Bats: L   Throws: L   Ht: 6-3   Wt: 200
Born: 9/21/1972   Drafted: 1992 #44 NYA   Pos: P

Heberling missed the entire 1995 season with shoulder problems after being acquired from Yanks in Jack McDowell deal.

ANDRE KING   Bats: R   Throws: R   Ht: 6-1   Wt: 190
Born: 11/26/1973   Drafted: 1993 #1 ATL   Pos: CF

YR TEAM	LG/CLASS	G	AB	R	H	2B	3B	HR	RBI	SB	BA	OBA
95 Durham	CARO/A	111	421	59	106	22	3	9	33	15	.252	.327
95 Prince William	CARO/A	9	32	4	5	1	1	0	3	1	.156	.289

Acquired for Mike Devereaux, King is a talented athlete with multiple tools who did not commit an error in '95, but is still learning the game—especially the strike zone.

EDDIE PEARSON   Bats: L   Throws: R   Ht: 6-3   Wt: 225
Born: 1/31/1974   Drafted: 1992 #1 CHA   Pos: 1B

YR TEAM	LG/CLASS	G	AB	R	H	2B	3B	HR	RBI	SB	BA	OBA
95 Birmingham	SOU/AA	50	201	20	45	13	0	2	25	1	.224	.251
95 White Sox	GULF/R	6	20	7	6	2	0	1	6	0	.300	.391

Lightning-quick hands make him a top batting prospect, but breaking balls, a wrist injury and poor range at first base have stalled his progress.

MIKE ROBERTSON   Bats: L   Throws: L   Ht: 6-0   Wt: 180
Born: 10/9/1970   Drafted: 1991 #3 CHA   Pos: 1B

YR TEAM	LG/CLASS	G	AB	R	H	2B	3B	HR	RBI	SB	BA	OBA
95 Nashville	AMAS/AAA	139	499	55	124	17	4	19	52	2	.248	.329

Robertson, an extremely hard worker and excellent fielder, has not hit for enough average or power.

SCOTT RUFFCORN   Bats: R   Throws: R   Ht: 6-4   Wt: 215
Born: 12/29/1969   Drafted: 1991 #1 CHA   Pos: P

YR TEAM	LG/CLASS	G	GS	GF	SV	W	L	ERA	IP	H	HR	BB	SO	O/BA
95 Nashville	AMAS/AAA	2	2	0	0	0	0	108.00	0.1	3	0	3	0	.750
95 Birmingham	SOU/AA	3	3	0	0	2	0	5.63	16.0	17	0	10	13	.279
95 White Sox	GULF/R	3	3	0	0	0	0	0.90	10.0	7	0	5	7	.175
95 Chicago	AL/MAJ	4	0	0	0	0	0	7.88	8.0	10	0	13	5	.294

Nearly as highly regarded as Baldwin, Ruffcorn struggled in the majors in early 1995, then injured his shoulder and missed most of the season.

BILL SIMAS   Bats: L   Throws: R   Ht: 6-3   Wt: 220
Born: 11/28/1971   Drafted: 1992 #9 CAL   Pos: P

YR TEAM	LG/CLASS	G	GS	GF	SV	W	L	ERA	IP	H	HR	BB	SO	O/BA
95 Nashville	AMAS/AAA	7	0	3	0	1	1	3.86	11.2	12	0	3	12	.261
95 Vancouver	PCL/AAA	30	0	24	6	6	3	3.55	38.0	44	1	14	44	.284
95 Chicago	AL/MAJ	14	0	4	0	1	1	2.57	14.0	15	1	10	16	.263

Acquired from California in the Abbott deal, Simas has closer-type stuff and good numbers since becoming a full-time reliever.

JUAN THOMAS   Bats: R   Throws: R   Ht: 6-5   Wt: 240
Born: 4/17/1972   Drafted: 1991 #10 CHA   Pos: 1B

YR TEAM	LG/CLASS	G	AB	R	H	2B	3B	HR	RBI	SB	BA	OBA
95 Pr William	CARO/A	132	464	64	109	20	4	26	69	4	.235	.305

Built like Frank Thomas, "Little Hurt" wears the same number and hits monster homers, but has a long swing that can't touch good heat.

LARRY THOMAS   Bats: R   Throws: L   Ht: 6-1   Wt: 190
Born: 10/25/1969   Drafted: 1991 #2 CHA   Pos: P

YR TEAM	LG/CLASS	G	GS	GF	SV	W	L	ERA	IP	H	HR	BB	SO	O/BA
95 Birmingham	SOU/AA	35	0	9	2	4	1	1.34	40.1	24	0	15	47	.178
95 Chicago	AL/MAJ	17	0	5	0	0	0	1.32	13.2	8	1	6	12	.163

Thomas surprised everyone last season after two poor years, showing a slider that held lefthanders to a .077 average.

KERRY VALRIE   Bats: R   Throws: R   Ht: 5-10   Wt: 195
Born: 10/31/1968   Drafted: 1990 #20 CHA   Pos: OF

YR TEAM	LG/CLASS	G	AB	R	H	2B	3B	HR	RBI	SB	BA	OBA
95 Nashville	AMAS/AAA	138	544	75	136	30	3	7	55	22	.250	.303

The former college football player has strong build and good speed, but hitting is a big question mark.

CRAIG WILSON   Bats: R   Throws: R   Ht: 6-1   Wt: 190
Born: 9/3/1970   Drafted: 1992 #13 CHA   Pos: SS

YR TEAM	LG/CLASS	G	AB	R	H	2B	3B	HR	RBI	SB	BA	OBA
95 Birmingham	SOU/AA	132	471	56	136	19	1	4	46	2	.289	.353

Wilson uses the whole field at the plate and has extremely quick hands that help make up for questionable range.

THE SCOUTING REPORT: 1996

CLEVELAND INDIANS

SANDY ALOMAR

Position: C
Bats: R **Throws:** R
Ht: 6'5" **Wt:** 200
Opening Day Age: 29
Born: 6/18/1966
Drafted: SD 10/21/83
ML Seasons: 8

SCOUTING REPORT

Sandy is normally a line-drive hitter who sprays the ball to center and right but will pull for power when he can get something down and in. However, his aggressiveness at the plate means he gets less good fastballs to drive and more breaking pitches.

Alomar is fearless at blocking pitches in the dirt and has above-average hands and mobility despite knee and back problems. Sandy has a plus arm and his throws are almost always on the mark. However, he hasn't played often enough in the last few years to establish a rhythm with his pitchers.

While Alomar is a slow runner, he usually picks his spots to steal pretty well. He is also an effective sacrifice bunter.

HOW HE PERFORMED IN '95

Once again, Alomar played well; once again, his season was gutted by injury. He didn't play until June 29 due to knee surgery and appeared in only 66 games. After returning from surgery, Alomar wore a special pad on his left calf. When he went into his catcher's crouch, the pad put space between his calf and thigh, therefore decreasing pressure on his knee.

Sandy has become a good hitter for average, but he's never been patient and his '95 walk total was particularly ugly. Over the last five years, he has hit .303 batting ninth, the best average in the majors. While Alomar had struggled against lefthanders in '94, last year he hit them with a vengeance.

Cleveland pitchers had a 4.34 ERA with Sandy on the receiving end compared to a 3.38 mark when Tony Pena was catching. All in all, Alomar is still a mix of good and bad on defense as he threw out just 26.5% of basestealers in '95. However, that lack of success is best attributed to a pitching staff easy to run on. His mobility was excellent, considering his injuries.

WHAT TO EXPECT IN '96

Indians fans hope Sandy can stay well and show them a full season's performance; many wonder why the club allows the injury-prone Alomar to play winter ball. Sandy is signed through 1997 with a club option for 1998. Will that deal conclude before he plays a full season? Alomar needs an injury-free '96 to truly become the #1 catcher the Indians want him to be. If not, the club may try to deal their talented but unlucky receiver.

Overall Statistics

	G	AB	R	H	2B	3B	HR	RBI	SB	CS	BB	SO	BA	OBA
95 CLE	66	203	32	61	6	0	10	35	3	1	7	26	.300	.332
Career	490	1658	193	451	80	4	42	215	21	14	92	191	.272	.317

1995 Situational Statistics

	AB	HR	RBI	BA	OBA	SLG		AB	HR	RBI	BA	OBA	SLG
Home	104	4	17	.327	.360	.481	LHP	44	4	12	.364	.378	.682
Road	99	6	18	.273	.301	.475	RHP	159	6	23	.283	.320	.421
Apr-Jun	3	0	0	.333	.500	.333	ScPos	55	3	25	.291	.310	.473
Jul-Oct	200	10	35	.300	.329	.480	Clutch	37	3	9	.270	.270	.568

How He Compares to Other Batters

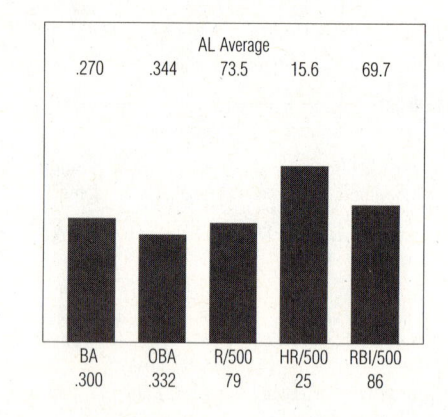

AL Average
.270   .344   73.5   15.6   69.7

BA	OBA	R/500	HR/500	RBI/500
.300	.332	79	25	86

Where He Hits the Ball

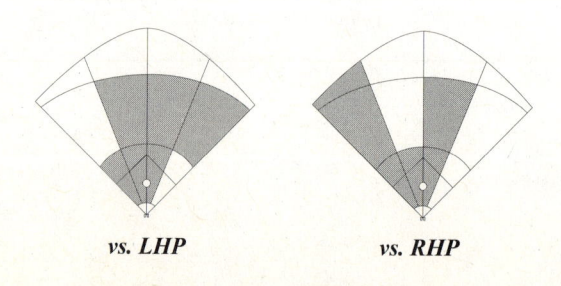

vs. LHP   vs. RHP

CLEVELAND INDIANS

CARLOS BAERGA

Positions: 2B//DH
Bats: B **Throws:** R
Ht: 5'11" **Wt:** 165
Opening Day Age: 27
Born: 11/4/1968
Drafted: SD 11/4/85
ML Seasons: 6

SCOUTING REPORT

A switch-hitting contact hitter, Baerga is very successful with the hit-and-run, bunts effectively when flashed the sac sign, and can also hit for power. Carlos is a high-ball pull hitter from the right side and uses the whole field from the left side, punching low pitches. He is very aggressive at the plate.

All of Baerga's defensive tools rate average. He has a good throwing release and turns the double play effectively, but has problems with glovework and mobility. Originally a third baseman, Carlos may end up back there or at first base in a year or two.

Baerga has just average speed on the bases but runs them well. He is an outstanding base stealer, successful in 47 of 59 career attempts.

HOW HE PERFORMED IN '95

Carlos loves to swing the bat and is good at it—1995 was the fourth straight year Baerga batted over .310 and the hits he sliced all over AL ballparks cleared a path for Cleveland to reach the World Series.

Carlos ranked fifth in the AL in hits. He improved 70 points against lefthanders and didn't strike out until his 98th at-bat, ranking second in the AL in difficulty to whiff. Baerga's .332 average with two strikes led the league by an astounding 45 points!

However, Carlos lacks patience and rarely walks. He sees his job as driving in runs, and he hit .361 with runners in scoring position. Eleven of his 15 home runs came before the All-Star game, in which Carlos started at second base for the AL. Defensively, Baerga fielded .973, making 19 errors (second-most among major-league second basemen).

WHAT TO EXPECT IN '96

Hampered late in the year by a sore wrist and hobbled during the entire post-season with a stress fracture in his left foot, Baerga is expected to be healthy for '96. Although he hustles at second and showed improved range to his left, Carlos' errors led the Indians to spend some the off-season evaluating available free-agent second basemen in search of improved defense.

Rumors swirled in the off-season about the Indians' infield, and a move to first—or even designated hitter—for Baerga is a real possibility. He should continue to hit no matter where he plays.

Overall Statistics

	G	AB	R	H	2B	3B	HR	RBI	SB	CS	BB	SO	BA	OBA
95 CLE	135	557	87	175	28	2	15	90	11	2	35	31	.314	.355
Career	819	3185	491	971	165	15	93	505	47	14	178	351	.305	.345

1995 Situational Statistics

	AB	HR	RBI	BA	OBA	SLG		AB	HR	RBI	BA	OBA	SLG
Home	265	7	48	.336	.373	.468	LHP	160	4	29	.331	.389	.494
Road	292	8	42	.295	.339	.438	RHP	397	11	61	.307	.340	.436
Apr-Jun	245	10	41	.347	.385	.547	ScPos	144	4	70	.361	.429	.500
Jul-Oct	312	5	49	.288	.331	.378	Clutch	80	0	13	.375	.422	.438

How He Compares to Other Batters

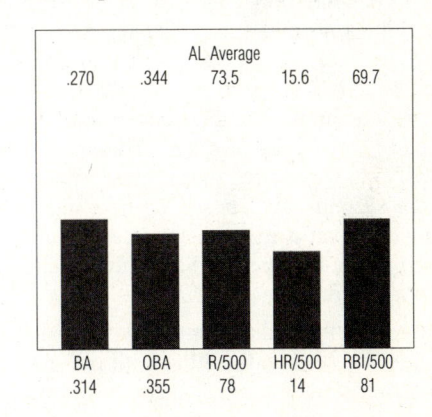

AL Average
.270 .344 73.5 15.6 69.7

BA   OBA   R/500 HR/500 RBI/500
.314   .355   78   14   81

Where He Hits the Ball

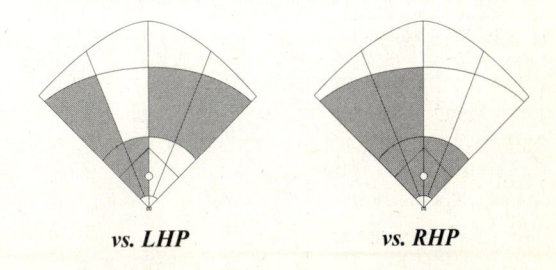

vs. LHP   vs. RHP

THE SCOUTING REPORT: 1996

CLEVELAND INDIANS

ALBERT BELLE

Positions: OF//DH
Bats: R **Throws:** R
Ht: 6'1" **Wt:** 190
Opening Day Age: 29
Born: 8/25/1966
Drafted: CLE87 1/47
ML Seasons: 7

SCOUTING REPORT

The awesomely strong Belle is an intelligent hitter with outstanding bat speed and power. He can hit with power to all fields, including the deepest portions of center field. Albert likes the fastball low and over the plate, but will also crush a hanging curve or slider which has the misfortune to visit his neighborhood. He has gotten more patient as he has earned more respect as a hitter, resulting in a high walk rate. In addition, he stays on the ball well and makes good contact for a power hitter.

Albert once had a strong arm, but it now rates as minus both in strength and throwing accuracy. His cutoff throws are particularly poor. His range and hands are just but he gets a poor jump on fly balls. Overall, his defense is questionable and he suffers from lapses in judgment.

Belle has average speed as a runner. He stole 23 bases in '93 but was caught often. Pitchers have woken up and no longer allow him to take a big lead.

HOW HE PERFORMED IN '95

It looked like a normal, good year for Albert until the All-Star break. Then, he decided to prove he was the best. After the mid-summer classic, Albert hit .322 with 36 home runs, 25 doubles and 75 RBI. His already outstanding first-half slugging percentage of .585 was bested by an astronomical .787 during the second half. His 31 homers in August and September set a major-league record and, by slugging 17 round-trippers in September, Belle tied Babe Ruth's mark.

He became the first Indians' hitter ever to pace the majors in home runs and just the 12th player to hit fifty. He ranked first in AL in slugging average, extra-base hits, doubles, homers, runs, RBI, hits, and total bases. Belle's 103 extra base hits were the fourth-highest total ever—in a short season!

WHAT TO EXPECT IN '96

There may be serious repercussions to Belle's late-season outbursts against the press and to his frequent temper tantrums. These problems must be addressed lest they recur. Excellent progress in this area during the last couple of years made these incidents especially troublesome.

Belle and the Indians are looking to return to the Series in '96 and they're both good enough to get there. It's hard to imagine Albert having a better year than in '95, but that's plenty good enough.

Overall Statistics

	G	AB	R	H	2B	3B	HR	RBI	SB	CS	BB	SO	BA	OBA
95 CLE	143	546	121	173	52	1	50	126	5	2	73	80	.317	.401
Career	755	2839	468	827	185	13	194	603	50	25	297	535	.291	.360

1995 Situational Statistics

	AB	HR	RBI	BA	OBA	SLG		AB	HR	RBI	BA	OBA	SLG
Home	268	25	53	.328	.415	.720	LHP	133	8	25	.293	.399	.571
Road	278	25	73	.306	.387	.662	RHP	413	42	101	.324	.401	.729
Apr-Jun	227	12	43	.308	.379	.581	ScPos	148	13	76	.270	.388	.615
Jul-Oct	319	38	83	.323	.416	.768	Clutch	85	7	18	.282	.354	.647

How He Compares to Other Batters

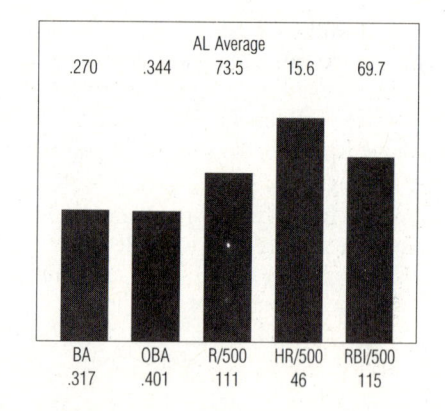

AL Average: .270 .344 73.5 15.6 69.7

	BA	OBA	R/500	HR/500	RBI/500
	.317	.401	111	46	115

Where He Hits the Ball

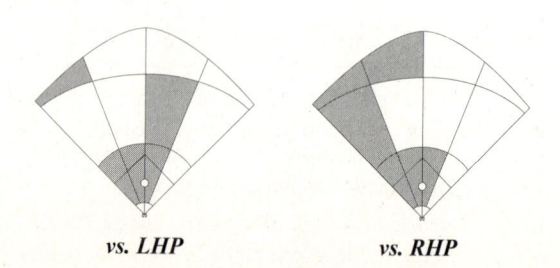

vs. LHP   vs. RHP

CLEVELAND INDIANS

MARK CLARK

Position: SP
Bats: R **Throws:** R
Ht: 6'5" **Wt:** 225
Opening Day Age: 27
Born: 5/12/1968
Drafted: SL88 11/236
ML Seasons: 5

SCOUTING REPORT
Cardinals' castoff Clark must keep his pitches down in the strike zone in order to be successful. He throws from a three-quarters, bringing home four pitches. His average fastball is always thrown to sink; a plus hard slider is Mark's best pitch.

He also has an average splitter and a change-up which he likes to use but is a minus pitch. In general, Clark's control is average, but it has to be good for him to win consistently. He led the Indians last year by flinging eight wild pitches.

An average fielder, Clark is poor at holding the runner: 19 runners stole against him in 26 tries, the highest numbers on the club.

HOW HE PERFORMED IN '95
Clark began the season as the Tribe's #2 starter but soon pitched himself out of a job and into an uncertain future. Mark was 2-2 with a 10.65 ERA in his first six starts with batters hitting .361 against him. Sent to Buffalo in late May, he returned on June 27 to replace an injured Orel Hershiser, and he gradually improved. He was far more effective during the second half.

However, Clark could never get in a comfortable groove and ended up the odd man out when Ken Hill was acquired from St. Louis. As in '94, Mark was most successful with Sandy Alomar behind the dish; other Indians' pitchers were much more effective when Tony Pena was catching.

Clark's pattern against lefties and righties last season was in direct opposition to that of the year before. This is just part of Clark's usual *modus operandi*—he doesn't pitch that differently when he's winning or losing. He simply puts the ball in play and lets things happen. Mark's hit, walk, strikeout, wild pitch, and home run totals have been remarkably similar in each of his four full big-league seasons, with the only major differences being his ERAs and won-lost records.

WHAT TO EXPECT IN '96
Clark had a disappointing year, struggling early and failing to make the playoff roster. The Indians declined to exercise his contract option for '96. Unless he negotiates a contract for less money with Cleveland, Mark will have to move on, because the Tribe no longer needs a pitcher who hasn't shown much consistency or dependability.

Overall Statistics

	G	GS	GF	SV	W	L	ERA	IP	H	R	ER	HR	BB	SO
95 CLE	22	21	0	0	9	7	5.27	124.2	143	77	73	13	42	68
Career	95	78	2	0	31	26	4.44	497.0	529	262	245	60	154	242

1995 Situational Statistics

	W	L	ERA	SV	IP	BB	SO		AB	HR	RBI	BA	OBA	SLG
Home	5	2	5.01	0	59.1	15	28	LHB	284	10	48	.317	.361	.521
Road	4	5	5.51	0	65.1	27	40	RHB	213	3	22	.249	.322	.362
Apr-Jun	3	2	8.24	0	31.2	13	15	ScPos	137	5	55	.270	.354	.445
Jul-Oct	6	5	4.26	0	93.0	29	53	Clutch	22	0	0	.136	.174	.136

How He Compares to Other Pitchers

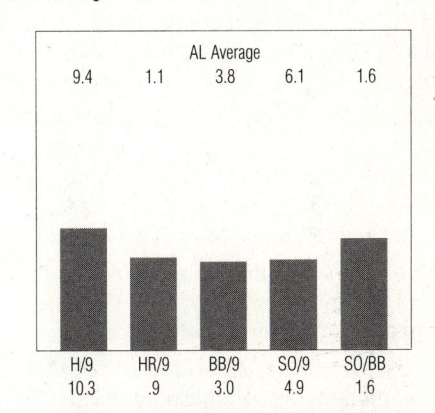

	H/9	HR/9	BB/9	SO/9	SO/BB
AL Average	9.4	1.1	3.8	6.1	1.6
	10.3	.9	3.0	4.9	1.6

How He Compares to Other Starting Pitchers

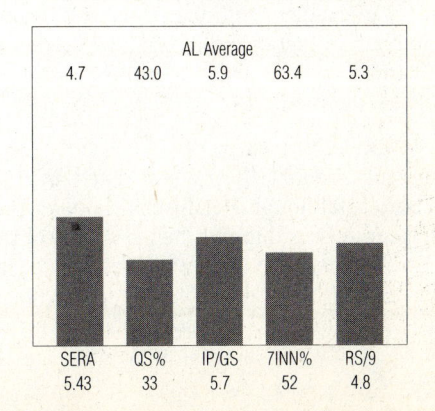

	SERA	QS%	IP/GS	7INN%	RS/9
AL Average	4.7	43.0	5.9	63.4	5.3
	5.43	33	5.7	52	4.8

CLEVELAND INDIANS

OREL HERSHISER

Position: SP
Bats: R **Throws:** R
Ht: 6'3" **Wt:** 192
Opening Day Age: 37
Born: 9/16/1958
Drafted: LA79 18/440
ML Seasons: 13

SCOUTING REPORT
Veteran righthander Hershiser throws straight over-the-top, just as he did in his 1980s power-pitcher days. By the end of the season, he had regained much of the power behind his pitches, with his fastball now average or better in velocity. The two-seamer sinks effectively and tails into righthanded batters. Orel also throws an average curve, dropping down with it against righthanders to increase the lateral break. He also has a slightly above-average slider and an average change-up that he mixed in well this season. Keeping the fastball off the plate to set up the curve, Hershiser is a master at mixing pitches and throwing off hitters' timing with his fine control.

Hershiser is a slightly above-average fielder and has worked on his pickoff move, which now rates as a plus. Last year only nine runners tried to steal against him, and four were thrown out.

HOW HE PERFORMED IN '95
Last spring, the Indians felt they needed one more quality pitcher to round out their staff and were thrilled when Orel became available. He fit his reputation as a proven winner and used his experience to help guide the Indians into the World Series.

Hershiser started 5-1 but hit a snag due to a sore back. After an 0-3, 6.55 stretch, he hit the disabled list, returning with a vengeance to go 11-2 with a 3.67 ERA to finish the year. He added some frosting by winning the ALCS MVP Award.

Hershiser went six or more innings in 21 of his 26 starts, but Mike Hargrove, wary of Orel's age and injury history, only let him throw one complete game.

However, his previous shoulder problems did not return, and eventually Orel's velocity was close to that of his glory days with the Dodgers. Hershiser loved to pitch in Jacobs Field. His 2.67 home ERA ranked third in the league, but he struggled mightily on the road.

WHAT TO EXPECT IN '96
The Indians brought the veteran back after the World Series. Although Hershiser's shoulder problems appear to be a thing of the past, he is always, in his own words, "playing with a loaded gun," and the Indians will be wise to continue to use him judiciously. If he makes 28-30 starts per season, Orel should be effective for several more years.

Overall Statistics

	G	GS	GF	SV	W	L	ERA	IP	H	R	ER	HR	BB	SO
95 CLE	26	26	0	0	16	6	3.87	167.1	151	76	72	21	51	111
Career	369	329	18	5	150	108	3.06	2323.1	2085	913	791	147	704	1554

1995 Situational Statistics

	W	L	ERA	SV	IP	BB	SO		AB	HR	RBI	BA	OBA	SLG
Home	9	2	2.67	0	81.0	24	58	LHB	349	12	46	.281	.336	.461
Road	7	4	5.00	0	86.1	27	53	RHB	271	9	27	.196	.264	.343
Apr-Jun	5	3	3.77	0	71.2	18	47	ScPos	127	7	57	.283	.349	.543
Jul-Oct	11	3	3.95	0	95.2	33	64	Clutch	25	0	3	.320	.393	.480

How He Compares to Other Pitchers

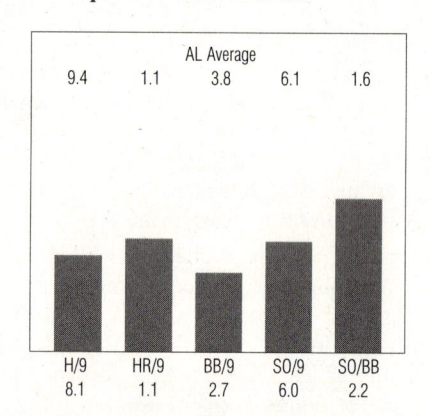

AL Average: 9.4 / 1.1 / 3.8 / 6.1 / 1.6

H/9	HR/9	BB/9	SO/9	SO/BB
8.1	1.1	2.7	6.0	2.2

How He Compares to Other Starting Pitchers

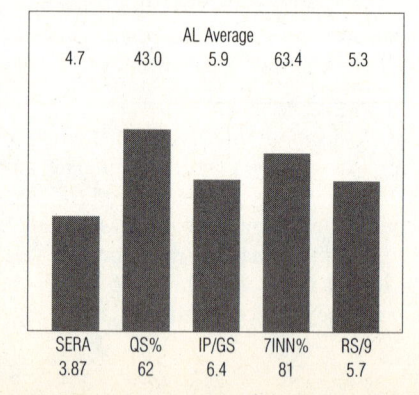

AL Average: 4.7 / 43.0 / 5.9 / 63.4 / 5.3

SERA	QS%	IP/GS	7INN%	RS/9
3.87	62	6.4	81	5.7

CLEVELAND INDIANS

KEN HILL

Position: SP
Bats: R **Throws:** R
Ht: 6'2" **Wt:** 175
Opening Day Age: 30
Born: 12/14/1965
Drafted: DET 2/14/85
ML Seasons: 8

SCOUTING REPORT

Former Expos', Cardinals', and Indians' starter Hill throws with an overhand short-armed delivery. When healthy, Ken throws a plus, hard fastball that has good sinking movement. He wasn't throwing that hard for much of last season but appeared to have regained most of his heat by the post-season.

Hill also delivers a plus hard slider, an average changeup, and an above-average split-finger fastball that breaks down and away from right-handed hitters. The splitter is his out pitch. Hill is an average fielder and an excellent bunter and hit .148 in his NL days.

His pickoff move is just average. While with St. Louis, 20 potential basestealers were successful in 23 tries. After the trade, nine men attempted to steal against Hill, six successfully.

HOW HE PERFORMED IN '95

Hill was acquired from St. Louis July 27 for three prospects. He had been 6-7 with a 5.06 ERA in 18 appearances with the Redbirds despite receiving the best run support on the staff. Seen as a proven winner who could bring power to the Indians' largely finesse-oriented rotation, he came to Cleveland amidst reports of a tired arm and dangerously reduced velocity.

In his first five starts for the Tribe, Ken had a 5.10 ERA as the coaching staff worked on correcting a flaw in his delivery. He was outstanding in September and improved his Cleveland ERA to 3.98. His run support of 6.91 per game was, again, the highest on the staff. The Indians were 9-2 in Hill's 11 starts and Ken worked into at least the sixth inning in all of them. The Indians were counting on Hill for the postseason, and he did not disappoint. Ken was 2-0 in the playoffs and, although he lost his only World Series start, he was more a victim of poor offense than his own pitching.

WHAT TO EXPECT IN '96

The Indians wanted Ken to return for '96, but weren't about to offer four million dollars a year for the privilege. However, Texas did. In December, Hill signed a two-year, $8 million pact with the Rangers, who have little in their farm system. Ken is expected to be the club's #1 starter in '96. However, there are questions about Ken's velocity and durability that can only be answered by 30 starts and 200 innings of quality pitching.

Overall Statistics

	G	GS	GF	SV	W	L	ERA	IP	H	R	ER	HR	BB	SO
95 SL/CLE	30	29	0	0	10	8	4.62	185.0	202	107	95	21	77	98
Career	198	191	1	0	74	61	3.67	1212.0	1125	554	494	84	475	720

1995 Situational Statistics

	W	L	ERA	SV	IP	BB	SO		AB	HR	RBI	BA	OBA	SLG
Home	5	6	4.53	0	105.1	41	48	LHB	368	11	49	.277	.354	.446
Road	5	2	4.74	0	79.2	36	50	RHB	356	10	47	.281	.342	.441
Apr-Jun	5	4	4.21	0	87.2	33	32	ScPos	203	3	69	.261	.338	.429
Jul-Oct	5	4	4.99	0	97.1	44	66	Clutch	50	2	8	.360	.418	.560

How He Compares to Other Pitchers

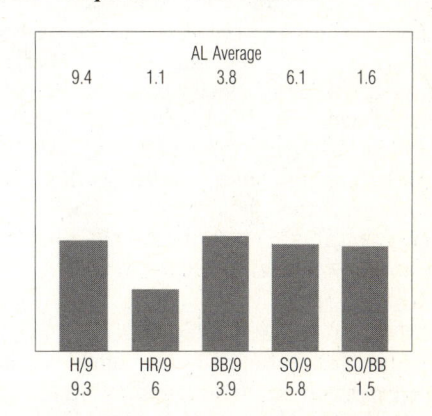

AL Average
9.4 1.1 3.8 6.1 1.6

H/9 HR/9 BB/9 SO/9 SO/BB
9.3 6 3.9 5.8 1.5

How He Compares to Other Starting Pitchers

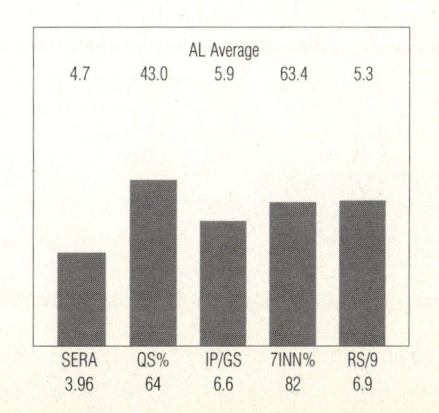

AL Average
4.7 43.0 5.9 63.4 5.3

SERA QS% IP/GS 7INN% RS/9
3.96 64 6.6 82 6.9

CLEVELAND INDIANS

KENNY LOFTON

Positions: OF//DH
Bats: L **Throws:** L
Ht: 6'0" **Wt:** 180
Opening Day Age: 28
Born: 5/31/1967
Drafted: HOU88 18/428
ML Seasons: 5

SCOUTING REPORT

Well above-average speed has always been Kenny Lofton's best attribute. He is the best drag bunter in baseball, steals bases almost at will, and is an intelligent runner who takes the extra base well.

Quick in the outfield as well, Kenny is credited by scouts with outstanding range and hands along with good leaping ability. He'll make the spectacular play and, just as often, will make the spectacular look easy. He has a poor arm with below-average accuracy, but Lofton charges balls aggressively.

He's not a bad hitter, either. Kenny likes pitches high and over the plate and has hit for power in the past. However, it appeared last season that Lofton stopped emphasizing just getting on base, which is critical for him, and was concentrating instead on trying to drive everything. It didn't work.

HOW HE PERFORMED IN '95

It was an up-and-down season for Lofton both offensively and in the field. Bothered with nagging injuries to his back, rib cage and leg, Kenny never really seemed healthy until the last few weeks of the season. He played well, but not up to his earlier standards. His walks dropped from 52 to 40 and his on-base percentage dipped fifty full points, a warning sign for any leadoff hitter. He also slumped against lefthanders and too often swung for the fences. Kenny did hit .376 in June and .336 in August, and his .386 average with runners in scoring position ranked second in the AL.

Although injuries hampered his baserunning, Lofton again won the stolen base title, stealing four times in the season's last game. He can still change the course of a game with his legs alone, and his superior speed also helped him lead the AL in triples for the first time.

Kenny had a mixed campaign in center field. His 11 assists tied for the league lead for the second straight year. Unfortunately, he also committed eight errors and showed greatly diminished range.

WHAT TO EXPECT IN '96

Lofton is the heart and soul of the Indians' offense. When Kenny is hot, he ignites the whole machine. However, his '95 season only looks impressive if it isn't compared to those of the other big guns on the club. Lofton must reach base more and regain his step in the outfield to be truly outstanding.

Overall Statistics

	G	AB	R	H	2B	3B	HR	RBI	SB	CS	BB	SO	BA	OBA
95 CLE	118	481	93	149	22	13	7	53	54	15	40	49	.310	.362
Career	546	2159	419	673	98	38	25	194	252	54	246	261	.312	.381

1995 Situational Statistics

	AB	HR	RBI	BA	OBA	SLG		AB	HR	RBI	BA	OBA	SLG
Home	273	5	26	.319	.365	.469	LHP	146	0	12	.274	.342	.342
Road	208	2	27	.298	.358	.433	RHP	335	7	41	.325	.371	.501
Apr-Jun	220	5	25	.327	.366	.491	ScPos	88	1	41	.375	.442	.568
Jul-Oct	261	2	28	.295	.359	.421	Clutch	68	0	5	.294	.351	.426

How He Compares to Other Batters

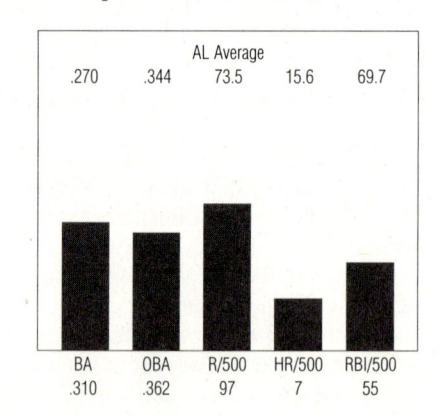

AL Average: .270 .344 73.5 15.6 69.7

BA	OBA	R/500	HR/500	RBI/500
.310	.362	97	7	55

Where He Hits the Ball

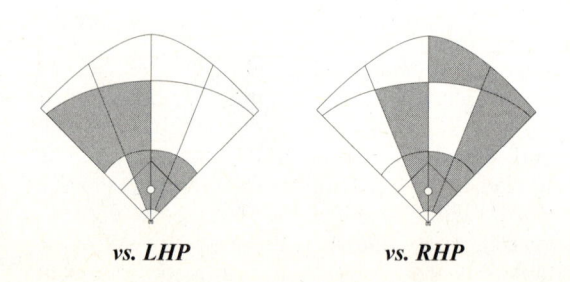

vs. LHP   vs. RHP

CLEVELAND INDIANS

SCOUTING REPORT

Martinez, a veteran finesse pitcher, has a high three-quarter motion but will drop down to low three-quarter or even sidearm against righthanders at times. He will vary his arm angle depending on the pitch and the hitter, trying to squeeze every possible edge out of his aging right arm. His pitches include two above-average curveballs: a regular curve and a change-up bender. Dennis also throws an average sinking fastball that moves in on righties and a plus straight change that he mixes in effectively. An average hard slider completes the menu. His control varies depending on his health and the umpires. During the postseason, he was getting the corners consistently from umpires.

A plus fielder with quick reactions, Martinez is quick to home and has had a good move to first in the past. However, 14 of 20 runners trying to steal last season against Dennis were successful.

HOW HE PERFORMED IN '95

Dennis has more victories than any other active pitcher in baseball. In '95, he helped elevate the Indians into the World Series and earned some well-deserved acclaim.

Martinez started the season 9-0 with a 2.35 ERA and was an easy All-Star selection. However, it then took Dennis nine more games to win his 10th. He began to get hit hard, developing control problems due to nagging knee and elbow injuries.

Dennis completed the regular season leading the staff in innings pitched, complete games, shutouts, and fewest walks per game. He had 21 quality starts and pitched six or more innings in all but two of his appearances. Martinez was third in the AL in ERA and in batting average with runners in scoring position (.183).

WHAT TO EXPECT IN '96

The Indians picked up Dennis' $4 million-plus option for '96 despite concerns over his physical status. Martinez underwent knee surgery last October, but said he will be back healthy this spring. While he has enjoyed an outstanding run over the last nine years, Dennis can't go on forever, and every serious injury has a chance of spelling the end of his effectiveness. He's not going to fall off the end of the earth unless he sustains an unexpected injury, but asking him to be a staff ace for much longer is asking too much.

DENNIS MARTINEZ

Position: SP
Bats: R **Throws:** R
Ht: 6'1" **Wt:** 185
Opening Day Age: 40
Born: 5/14/1955
Drafted: BAL 12/10/73
ML Seasons: 20

Overall Statistics

	G	GS	GF	SV	W	L	ERA	IP	H	R	ER	HR	BB	SO
95 CLE	28	28	0	0	12	5	3.08	187.0	174	71	64	17	46	99
Career	610	528	40	6	231	176	3.60	3747.2	3601	1673	1500	344	1080	2022

1995 Situational Statistics

	W	L	ERA	SV	IP	BB	SO		AB	HR	RBI	BA	OBA	SLG
Home	4	3	3.49	0	90.1	19	37	LHB	424	11	38	.229	.274	.337
Road	8	2	2.70	0	96.2	27	62	RHB	281	6	23	.274	.344	.413
Apr-Jun	7	0	2.53	0	89.0	16	46	ScPos	169	3	44	.183	.268	.260
Jul-Oct	5	5	3.58	0	98.0	30	53	Clutch	41	1	2	.244	.311	.341

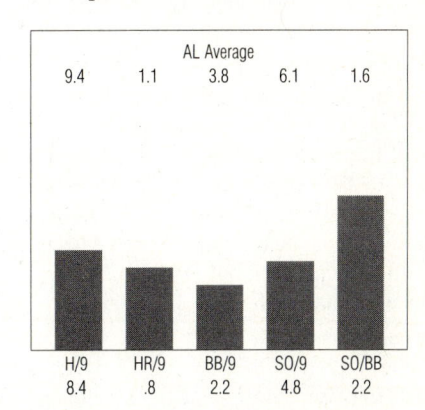

How He Compares to Other Pitchers

AL Average: 9.4 | 1.1 | 3.8 | 6.1 | 1.6

H/9: 8.4 | HR/9: .8 | BB/9: 2.2 | SO/9: 4.8 | SO/BB: 2.2

How He Compares to Other Starting Pitchers

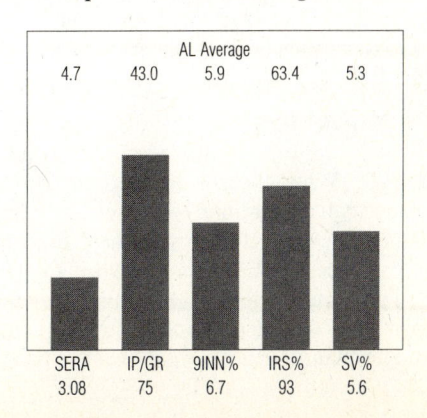

AL Average: 4.7 | 43.0 | 5.9 | 63.4 | 5.3

SERA: 3.08 | IP/GR: 75 | 9INN%: 6.7 | IRS%: 93 | SV%: 5.6

THE SCOUTING REPORT: 1996

CLEVELAND INDIANS

JOSE MESA

Position: RP
Bats: R **Throws:** R
Ht: 6'3" **Wt:** 220
Opening Day Age: 29
Born: 5/22/1966
Drafted: TOR 10/31/81
ML Seasons: 7

SCOUTING REPORT

Jose used to be extremely wild but has improved greatly and now possesses good control. He has a quick release to the plate from a standard three-quarter delivery.

Until last year, Mesa's trademark was a four-seam fastball with excellent velocity that had little movement. It was consistently one of the league's top heaters, but that and his plus hard slider were all Jose threw. In '94, then-Indians pitching coach Phil Regan had Mesa add a two-seam sinker in order to get double plays and groundouts. Jose also cuts the fastball more effectively now. He doesn't have an off-speed pitch but, like most closers, Mesa can survive on the fastball-slider power arsenal quite nicely.

Jose has a good move to first and holds runners well: only four tried to run against him in '95, three successfully. However, he is a minus fielder.

HOW HE PERFORMED IN '95

Mesa had only two saves in his whole career prior to '95. During the Indians' first trip to the postseason in 41 years, though, Mesa was baseball's dominant reliever.

He led both leagues with 46 saves in 48 chances and by himself recorded more saves than any other team in either league. Mesa set a new major-league record with 38 consecutive saves converted between May 5 and August 23. Jose had nine saves in July, allowing no runs in ten innings. Mesa's struggled a little bit early on, but his ERA for the second half was a minuscule 0.52.

He worked often, with 16 of his 46 saves coming on zero days' rest. In those games, he had an ERA of 0.51. However, Mesa, like most closers, averages only an inning per appearance and got a whopping 20 of his saves with three or four-run leads. He wasn't tested very often last year, something that could be said of his club in general.

WHAT TO EXPECT IN '96

Mesa is under contract for this year with a club option for 1997. While there is no doubt that Jose has the pure fastball to continue to succeed as a closer, he shouldn't be expected to duplicate his superb '95 performance again. Unless something goes unexpectedly wrong, he'll be good enough to serve as a key part of the puzzle for a championship-caliber team in Cleveland.

Overall Statistics

	G	GS	GF	SV	W	L	ERA	IP	H	R	ER	HR	BB	SO
95 CLE	62	0	57	46	3	0	1.13	64.0	49	9	8	3	17	58
Career	211	95	80	48	37	45	4.55	708.0	747	379	358	61	279	406

1995 Situational Statistics

	W	L	ERA	SV	IP	BB	SO		AB	HR	RBI	BA	OBA	SLG
Home	1	0	0.28	21	31.2	8	28	LHB	126	0	4	.230	.290	.246
Road	2	0	1.95	25	32.1	9	30	RHB	101	3	8	.198	.241	.307
Apr-Jun	1	0	1.91	20	28.1	8	23	ScPos	48	1	10	.125	.228	.208
Jul-Oct	2	0	0.50	26	35.2	9	35	Clutch	172	3	10	.227	.274	.297

How He Compares to Other Pitchers

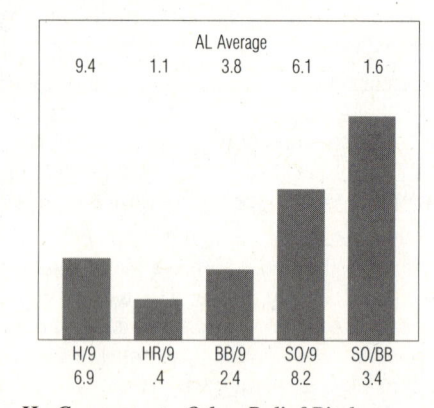

	H/9	HR/9	BB/9	SO/9	SO/BB
AL Average	9.4	1.1	3.8	6.1	1.6
	6.9	.4	2.4	8.2	3.4

How He Compares to Other Relief Pitchers

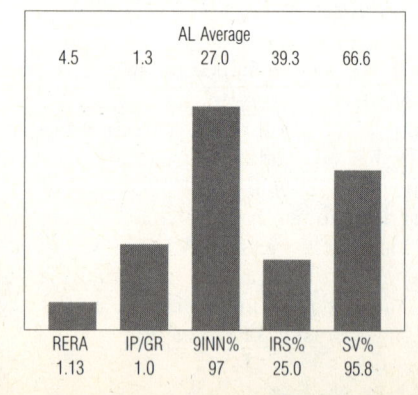

	RERA	IP/GR	9INN%	IRS%	SV%
AL Average	4.5	1.3	27.0	39.3	66.6
	1.13	1.0	97	25.0	95.8

CLEVELAND INDIANS

EDDIE MURRAY

Positions: DH/1B
Bats: B **Throws:** R
Ht: 6'2" **Wt:** 200
Opening Day Age: 40
Born: 2/24/1956
Drafted: BAL73 3/63
ML Seasons: 19

SCOUTING REPORT

Murray is rightly considered one of the best switch-hitters of all time. Even in his baseball dotage, he generates good power to all fields. A low-ball, straightaway hitter while batting lefthanded, Eddie pulls high pitches while batting from the right side. He still has good bat speed but has stopped taking the base on balls in recent seasons.

Although Murray now has well below-average speed, he is a smart runner. He is a 71% career basestealer with a surprising 105 career swipes.

In 1982-84, he was the AL's Gold Glove first baseman. Rarely used in the field any longer, Eddie shows a minus arm with average accuracy, minus range, and average hands when he does strap on a glove.

HOW HE PERFORMED IN '95

Murray spent the first two months of the season chasing his 3,000th hit. After getting it June 30th against Mike Trombley of the Twins, he broke two ribs a week later trying to steal a base and went on the disabled list. Eddie soon returned to solidify baseball's best lineup.

As it turned out, Murray's batting average was the second-best of his storied career. He was extremely consistent, batting at least .294 in every month and smacking between four and six homers in each full month except July, when he had only six at-bats.

The '95 season was Murray's nineteenth straight year with 75 or more RBI, which ties Hank Aaron's record. Eddie looks to become only the third player in major-league history with 3,000 hits and 500 home runs; he's likely to hit that magic four-bagger sometime early in '97. His .340 mark against righthanded pitching was second best in the AL, and Eddie hit .351 and slugged .561 with runners in scoring position.

Murray spent most of 1995 as a DH. He committed three errors in his 18 games at first base, although he showed better range than usual and is still fairly adept at scooping throws in the dirt.

WHAT TO EXPECT IN '96

The Indians have re-signed Murray for 1996. He has professed a love for Cleveland and, though many believe Eddie's heart is still in Baltimore, he resisted a return to the Orioles. His '95 performance—by far his best since '90 in L.A.—indicates he has more life left in his bat.

Overall Statistics

	G	AB	R	H	2B	3B	HR	RBI	SB	CS	BB	SO	BA	OBA
95 CLE	113	436	68	141	21	0	21	82	5	1	39	65	.323	.375
Career	2819	10603	1545	3071	532	34	479	1820	105	43	1257	1403	.290	.362

1995 Situational Statistics

	AB	HR	RBI	BA	OBA	SLG		AB	HR	RBI	BA	OBA	SLG
Home	210	11	47	.348	.404	.552	LHP	104	3	16	.269	.304	.404
Road	226	10	35	.301	.347	.482	RHP	332	18	66	.340	.397	.551
Apr-Jun	226	11	43	.310	.360	.496	ScPos	114	6	60	.351	.423	.561
Jul-Oct	210	10	39	.338	.391	.538	Clutch	63	5	7	.222	.329	.476

How He Compares to Other Batters

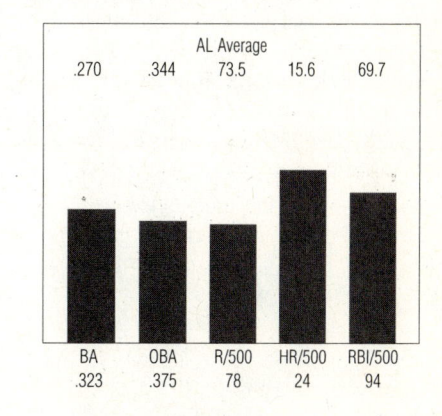

AL Average: .270 .344 73.5 15.6 69.7

BA	OBA	R/500	HR/500	RBI/500
.323	.375	78	24	94

Where He Hits the Ball

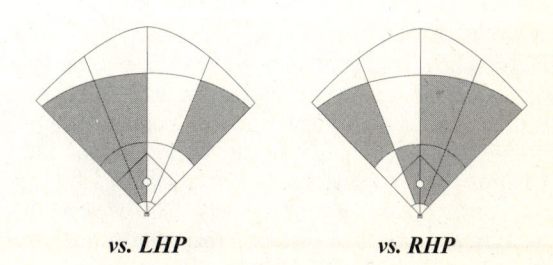

vs. LHP   vs. RHP

THE SCOUTING REPORT: 1996

CLEVELAND INDIANS

CHARLES NAGY

Position: SP
Bats: L **Throws:** R
Ht: 6'3" **Wt:** 200
Opening Day Age: 28
Born: 5/5/1967
Drafted: CLE88 2/17
ML Seasons: 6

SCOUTING REPORT
Charles throws a plus curve with a sharp downward break, an average-minus splitfinger fastball that sinks and bores in on righthanders, and an average circle change-up. The change looks like a forkball, and is thrown almost exclusively to lefthanders.

Against Nagy's three-quarter delivery, batters pound all three pitches into the dirt. He is annually one of the league's most extreme ground ball pitchers and usually leads in double plays induced. He is a plus fielder with a good move and quick delivery, but he allowed 18 stolen bases in 21 attempts in '95.

HOW HE PERFORMED IN '95
Nagy was very successful in '95, leading the team in wins and strikeouts. Perhaps his biggest accomplishment, however, was staying healthy enough to benefit from his teammates' fine play.

Nagy struggled against lefthanded batters, causing his ERA to rise more than a run from '94 and also led the staff in walks. Despite this, Nagy's shoulder didn't break down and, as a result, Charlie had a big year. He won his last six of seven starts, but his ERA ballooned to 5.46 for the second half. Despite a good record, a closer look shows a very mediocre performance. Were it not for his power-hitting teammates, this would have been a very average year for him.

The biggest reason for his success was run support: the Tribe scored nearly seven runs a game for him, bailing him out often. Nagy had only 14 quality starts, but his 16 wins were his highest total since '92.

Nagy hates to pitch on the road, where his ERA swelled nearly three runs in '95. He also has a phobia about domes and is 0-5 with a 6.82 ERA in Seattle in his career. Distaste or not, Charles has to win somewhere besides Cleveland.

WHAT TO EXPECT IN '96
Nagy was a free agent after the season, but the Indians and his agent were talking about a three-year deal. Such an agreement would, it seems, benefit both parties: his club needs the innings, and Charles wouldn't have been nearly as successful on any other team. However, Nagy has been both healthy and effective just two years out of a five-plus season career. If Charles can't repeat in '96, look for Julian Tavarez, Chad Ogea, or Albie Lopez to step into the rotation.

Overall Statistics

	G	GS	GF	SV	W	L	ERA	IP	H	R	ER	HR	BB	SO
95 CLE	29	29	0	0	16	6	4.55	178.0	194	95	90	20	61	139
Career	136	135	1	0	57	49	3.97	905.0	966	434	399	74	266	581

1995 Situational Statistics

	W	L	ERA	SV	IP	BB	SO		AB	HR	RBI	BA	OBA	SLG
Home	10	3	3.48	0	108.2	30	88	LHB	377	6	42	.313	.375	.435
Road	6	3	6.23	0	69.1	31	51	RHB	320	14	45	.237	.296	.431
Apr-Jun	5	4	4.04	0	71.1	22	53	ScPos	180	5	65	.267	.338	.417
Jul-Oct	11	2	4.89	0	106.2	39	86	Clutch	31	1	2	.258	.281	.355

How He Compares to Other Pitchers

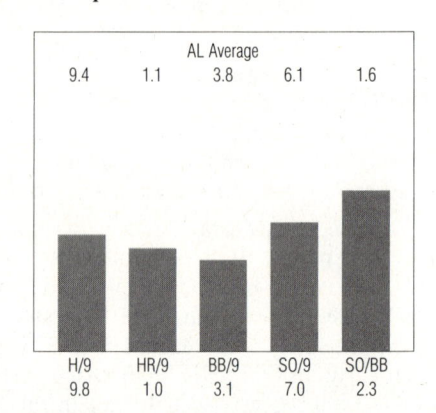

AL Average: 9.4 / 1.1 / 3.8 / 6.1 / 1.6

H/9	HR/9	BB/9	SO/9	SO/BB
9.8	1.0	3.1	7.0	2.3

How He Compares to Other Starting Pitchers

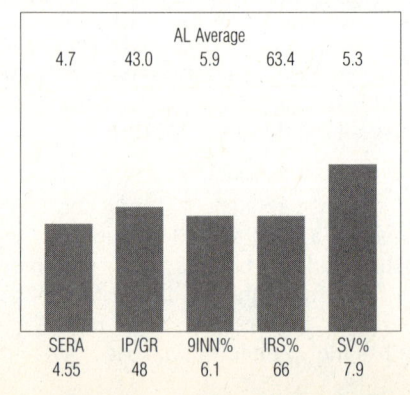

AL Average: 4.7 / 43.0 / 5.9 / 63.4 / 5.3

SERA	IP/GR	9INN%	IRS%	SV%
4.55	48	6.1	66	7.9

CLEVELAND INDIANS

MANNY RAMIREZ

Positions: OF//DH
Bats: R **Throws:** R
Ht: 6'0" **Wt:** 190
Opening Day Age: 23
Born: 5/30/1972
Drafted: CLE91 1/13
ML Seasons: 3

SCOUTING REPORT
Ramirez has excellent bat speed, plus power, and can hit the ball hard to all fields. He likes pitches down and in, which he can pull. However, Manny occasionally gets into bad habits at the dish and lacks good command of the strike zone.

Ramirez has average-plus tools in right field (range, hands, arm strength, and arm accuracy) but lacks polish. Although he has decent speed, Ramirez is a poor baserunner who often loses his concentration, forgetting the count or the number of outs.

HOW HE PERFORMED IN '95
Manny had another banner year offensively and, in only his second year, was named to the AL All-Star team. It is an indication of Cleveland's strength that he batted sixth or seventh all year despite ranking second in the league in batting against lefthanded pitching. Ramirez was a major factor in many of the Indians' come-from-behind wins and hit .341 with runners in scoring position. He carried Cleveland many times last year on his strong bat, having incredible hot streaks—including a .394 May with 11 home runs and a 10-homer July.

However, Manny still has a lot to learn. He swings too many bad pitches, although his power commands respect and he draws plenty of walks. As he did in his rookie season, Ramirez had big slumps. After that spectacular performance in May, he then batted .233 with just two homers in June. He hit a flimsy .247 with one homer after August 31.

The other parts of his game are raw as well. While Manny is potentially a good outfielder, his assists fell last year from seven to three, his errors rose from one to five, and he showed mediocre range. Ramirez is probably not going to be an efficient or proficient basestealer and can't afford to run into outs.

WHAT TO EXPECT IN '96
Despite his occasional problems, Manny is a superstar in the making who needs only to refine the rough points of his game. In order to fulfill his promise, he must concentrate harder in the field, at bat, and on the bases. If he does, he could become one of the game's best power hitters and a legitimately great player. Batting in the powerful Indians' lineup, he'll get that chance without having the pressure of being the #1 hitter on the team.

Overall Statistics

	G	AB	R	H	2B	3B	HR	RBI	SB	CS	BB	SO	BA	OBA
95 CLE	137	484	85	149	26	1	31	107	6	6	75	112	.308	.402
Career	250	827	141	236	49	1	50	172	10	8	119	192	.285	.375

1995 Situational Statistics

	AB	HR	RBI	BA	OBA	SLG		AB	HR	RBI	BA	OBA	SLG
Home	225	12	46	.289	.408	.511	LHP	123	7	28	.407	.507	.659
Road	259	19	61	.324	.397	.598	RHP	361	24	79	.274	.365	.524
Apr-Jun	200	14	41	.325	.411	.600	ScPos	129	7	74	.341	.444	.558
Jul-Oct	284	17	66	.296	.396	.528	Clutch	64	3	13	.297	.446	.484

How He Compares to Other Batters

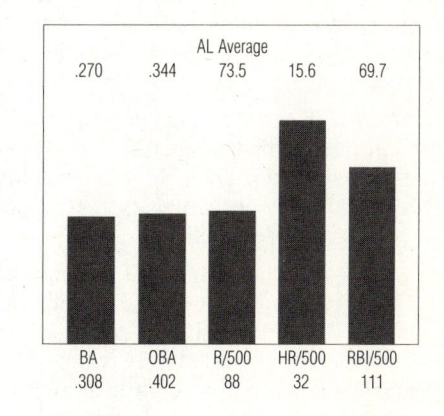

AL Average: .270 .344 73.5 15.6 69.7

BA	OBA	R/500	HR/500	RBI/500
.308	.402	88	32	111

Where He Hits the Ball

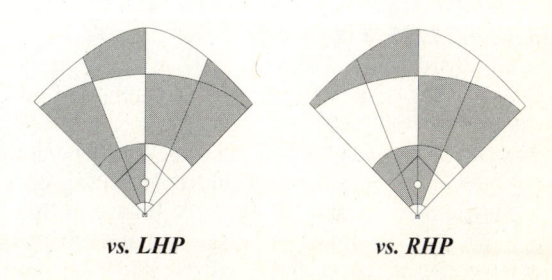

vs. LHP   vs. RHP

THE SCOUTING REPORT: 1996

CLEVELAND INDIANS

PAUL SORRENTO

Positions: 1B/DH
Bats: L **Throws:** R
Ht: 6'2" **Wt:** 195
Opening Day Age: 30
Born: 11/17/1965
Drafted: CAL86 8/108
ML Seasons: 7

SCOUTING REPORT

A strong lefthanded hitter with above-average power, Paul can pull some pitches up and over the plate, but he lacks outstanding bat speed and ends up launching a lot of drives to left and center fields. He will also hook low and inside pitches towards right. Paul will take the walk but is rarely asked to sacrifice.

He is a minus runner with minus speed and has one stolen base in the last two years. Due to a surfeit of baserunners and his own slow legs, Paul frequently grounds into double plays.

Sorrento has slightly above-average hands and executes the 3-6-3 double play very well. His arm strength and accuracy are average; he has a picture-perfect stretch and scoops throws fairly well. However, Paul has below-average range and will probably be exclusively a DH in a year or two.

HOW HE PERFORMED IN '95

The veteran first baseman had a mixed season, hitting for good power but lacking distinction in other aspects of the game. He topped his previous high in home runs by seven despite a fairly low number of at-bats, but Paul's batting average dropped 55 points and he made seven errors.

Despite hitting .270 against lefthanders in '94, Sorrento was strictly a platoon player last season, facing lefties only when Eddie Murray was hurt. He reverted to his previous struggles against portsiders but hit righthanders well.

Paul enjoyed a respectable first half, batting .258 with 13 home runs. In May, he hit .311 with eight homers and 22 RBI, giving him ten round-trippers by June 1. However, he scuffled from that point on, having trouble catching up to high heat and, surprisingly, struggling with the inside breaking ball. Sorrento hit only .167 in September and was no factor in the postseason.

WHAT TO EXPECT IN '96

A mildly disappointing year at bat, the current salary structure, and the success of young and inexpensive Herb Perry may combine to make '95 Sorrento's swan song with Cleveland. The Tribe did not pick up his option for '96 and, unless he agrees to play less often for less money, he'll have to find a new home. His power will make him attractive to many clubs, but Cleveland should be able to absorb his loss without any problem.

Overall Statistics

	G	AB	R	H	2B	3B	HR	RBI	SB	CS	BB	SO	BA	OBA
95 CLE	104	323	50	76	14	0	25	79	1	1	51	71	.235	.336
Career	568	1755	239	450	84	3	84	293	5	7	215	395	.256	.336

1995 Situational Statistics

	AB	HR	RBI	BA	OBA	SLG		AB	HR	RBI	BA	OBA	SLG
Home	161	12	38	.230	.342	.503	LHP	43	2	14	.163	.269	.326
Road	162	13	41	.241	.330	.519	RHP	280	23	65	.246	.347	.539
Apr-Jun	140	13	37	.264	.356	.593	ScPos	100	6	51	.260	.366	.510
Jul-Oct	183	12	42	.213	.321	.448	Clutch	47	3	12	.255	.333	.489

How He Compares to Other Batters

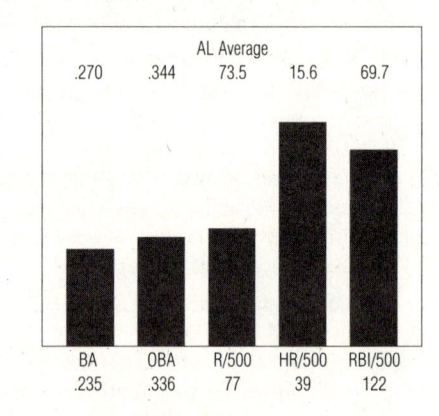

AL Average: BA .270, OBA .344, R/500 73.5, HR/500 15.6, RBI/500 69.7

Sorrento: BA .235, OBA .336, R/500 77, HR/500 39, RBI/500 122

Where He Hits the Ball

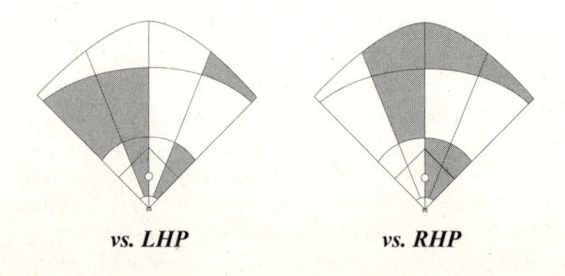

vs. LHP   vs. RHP

CLEVELAND INDIANS

JIM THOME

Positions: 3B//DH
Bats: L **Throws:** R
Ht: 6'3" **Wt:** 190
Opening Day Age: 25
Born: 8/27/1970
Drafted: CLE89 12/333
ML Seasons: 5

SCOUTING REPORT

Thome is a hard-swinging hitter with plus power. He likes the ball low and inside, and can pull with tremendous punch. Although Jim strikes out often, it's not due to lack of patience at the plate. He sees plenty of pitches and will gladly accept the walk. However, Thome has some problems with change-ups and can't always get around on high outside pitches. He does not bunt.

Despite a poor defensive reputation, Jim is a respectable fielder with slightly above-average hands and range. Although he has a strong arm, his throws tend toward wildness. He runs hard, but his heavy legs lead to average speed. Thome rarely attempts to steal and isn't often successful when he does.

HOW HE PERFORMED IN '95

Thome rolls average, power, and frequent walks into an outstanding package that has made him one of baseball's better third basemen very early in his career. After a promising '94 campaign, Jim really blew the lid off last year. Most of his homers were monster blasts that were sights to behold. He led the Tribe in walks, leaving himself on base for others while cleaning up the basepaths with a passel of extra-base hits.

Jim is still a bit raw. At times, he's too patient and might benefit by cutting at good pitches earlier in the count. His power inspired pitchers to change their approach mid-season, and as a result Thome slugged 21 homers in his first 285 at-bats before going 101 at-bats until his next one. He hit just one homer in August, but batted .307 and drew 33 walks. Thome was much more relaxed at third base this year. Although his defense improved, he was still replaced for defensive purposes late in close games. His throwing ran hot and cold as he committed 16 errors. It's certainly possible that he could end up at first base in a year or two.

WHAT TO EXPECT IN '96

Thome has a long-term contract and is viewed justifiably as a cornerstone of the Indians' plans. Wherever he plays, Jim's bat makes his future rosy. Cleveland has him signed this year with an option for '97. An intelligent young hitter with one of the key assets that many young sluggers lack—good plate discipline—he should be able to adjust well as pitchers try to find a way to get him out.

Overall Statistics

	G	AB	R	H	2B	3B	HR	RBI	SB	CS	BB	SO	BA	OBA
95 CLE	137	452	92	142	29	3	25	73	4	3	97	113	.314	.438
Career	349	1142	193	318	67	7	55	168	12	8	187	283	.278	.382

1995 Situational Statistics

	AB	HR	RBI	BA	OBA	SLG		AB	HR	RBI	BA	OBA	SLG
Home	226	13	37	.305	.431	.566	LHP	109	3	13	.275	.380	.422
Road	226	12	36	.323	.445	.549	RHP	343	22	60	.327	.456	.601
Apr-Jun	185	16	35	.324	.439	.638	ScPos	124	8	51	.242	.370	.492
Jul-Oct	267	9	38	.307	.437	.502	Clutch	72	6	16	.361	.472	.667

How He Compares to Other Batters

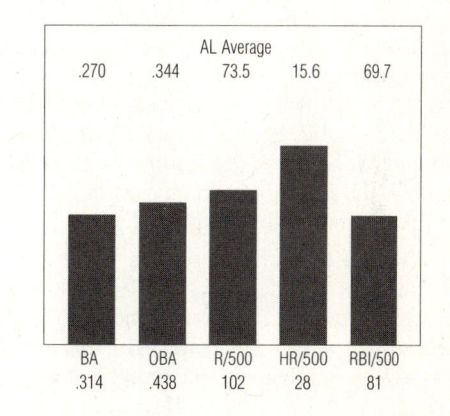

AL Average: .270 / .344 / 73.5 / 15.6 / 69.7

BA	OBA	R/500	HR/500	RBI/500
.314	.438	102	28	81

Where He Hits the Ball

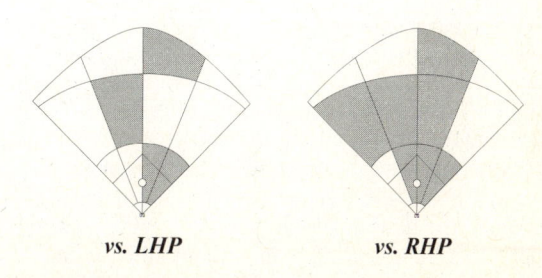

vs. LHP vs. RHP

THE SCOUTING REPORT: 1996

CLEVELAND INDIANS

OMAR VIZQUEL

Position: SS
Bats: B **Throws:** R
Ht: 5'9" **Wt:** 155
Opening Day Age: 28
Born: 4/24/1967
Drafted: SEA 4/1/84
ML Seasons: 7

SCOUTING REPORT
A Gold Glover at shortstop for the third year in a row in '95, Omar has soft hands, above-average throwing accuracy, and an extremely quick release that makes up for his average arm strength. He has above-average mobility and positions himself well.

He's not a shabby player on offense, either. Vizquel has plus speed, a little power, does a decent job in the hit-and-run category, and is probably the second-best bunter Cleveland has behind Kenny Lofton. Omar likes pitches up and over the plate to spray against lefties, preferring up and in deliveries to pull against righthanders. With Seattle, Vizquel was a very poor basestealer. However, he has improved dramatically with the Indians and is fast enough out of the box to beat out hits.

HOW HE PERFORMED IN '95
Normally accustomed to batting low in the order, Vizquel hit second for the Indians. While he displayed his typically strong defense, Omar also had his best year ever at the plate. He totaled career highs in homers, stolen bases, and RBI. He did the "little things" asked of him, ranking fifth in the AL in sacrifice flies and sacrifice bunts. Omar hit .350 with two outs and runners in scoring position and seemed at his best when the Indians needed a hit. He was comfortable batting on artificial turf and, despite a tendency towards hitting ground balls, Vizquel was the second-hardest player in the AL to double up, grounding into just four DPs all season.

In winning his second consecutive Gold Glove, Vizquel made just nine errors in 136 games and showed well above-average range. Included in this terrific season was a 47-game errorless streak. Omar could have filled the '95 Indians' defensive highlight film all by himself. He is arguably the best defensive shortstop in baseball and beautiful to watch.

WHAT TO EXPECT IN '96
Cleveland management bit the bullet this off-season, extending the contract of Vizquel through 2002. At the end of the deal, the shortstop will be 35. Though Omar had a successful year offensively, the Indians have brought Julio Franco back from Japan to hit in the #2 spot. Watch for Vizquel to migrate to the bottom spot in the order, where he will act as a second leadoff man without being asked to carry a significant portion of the load on offense.

Overall Statistics

	G	AB	R	H	2B	3B	HR	RBI	SB	CS	BB	SO	BA	OBA
95 CLE	136	542	87	144	28	0	6	56	29	11	59	59	.266	.333
Career	865	2939	349	753	98	16	13	220	81	49	255	290	.256	.315

1995 Situational Statistics

	AB	HR	RBI	BA	OBA	SLG		AB	HR	RBI	BA	OBA	SLG
Home	258	3	28	.267	.336	.345	LHP	168	2	19	.262	.330	.375
Road	284	3	28	.264	.331	.356	RHP	374	4	37	.267	.335	.340
Apr-Jun	237	4	24	.257	.322	.333	ScPos	140	1	51	.293	.327	.386
Jul-Oct	305	2	32	.272	.342	.364	Clutch	74	1	6	.257	.333	.338

How He Compares to Other Batters

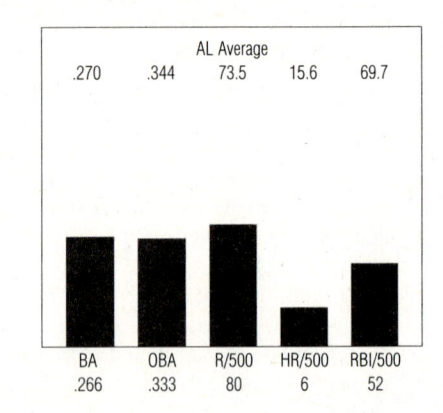

	BA	OBA	R/500	HR/500	RBI/500
AL Average	.270	.344	73.5	15.6	69.7
	.266	.333	80	6	52

Where He Hits the Ball

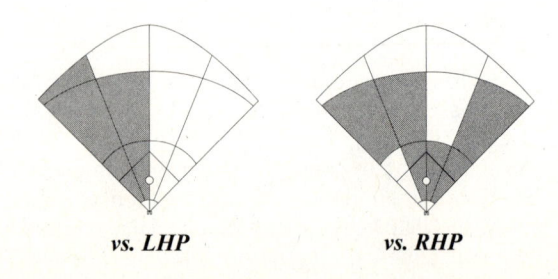

vs. LHP   vs. RHP

CLEVELAND INDIANS

PAUL ASSENMACHER

Position: RP
Bats: L **Throws:** L
Ht: 6'3" **Wt:** 195
Opening Day Age: 35
Born: 12/10/1960
Drafted: ATL 7/10/83
ML Seasons: 10

Overall Statistics

	G	GS	GF	SV	W	L	ERA	IP	H	R	ER	HR	BB	SO
95 CLE	47	0	12	0	6	2	2.82	38.1	32	13	12	3	12	40
Career	622	1	205	48	48	36	3.40	680.0	624	282	257	56	250	638

1995 Situational Statistics

	W	L	ERA	SV	IP	BB	SO		AB	HR	RBI	BA	OBA	SLG
Home	3	1	3.48	0	20.2	5	21	LHB	62	1	4	.177	.227	.226
Road	3	1	2.04	0	17.2	7	19	RHB	80	2	7	.262	.344	.400
Apr-Jun	2	1	0.79	0	11.1	5	11	ScPos	36	0	8	.167	.256	.167
Jul-Oct	4	1	3.67	0	27.0	7	29	Clutch	57	1	5	.211	.324	.298

SCOUTING REPORT

Lefthander Assenmacher's best pitch is an above-average sweeping curveball delivered from a confusing three-quarter delivery. He also has a slightly below-average sinking fastball, but it's throwing the big bender to lefthanded hitters which earns him his keep.

He changes speeds very well, especially against righthanders. Paul is an average fielder but has trouble holding runners: five tried to steal against him in '95, all successfully.

HOW HE PERFORMED IN '95

Cleveland acquired Assenmacher with lefthanded hitters in mind. Paul has led the majors with 382 appearances over the last five years and, in that time lefties have hit only .203 against him, fourth-lowest in the majors.

There was little he didn't do right in '95. Paul averaged over a strikeout per inning, something he has not accomplished since 1991 and allowed only three of 28 inherited runners to score.

WHAT TO EXPECT IN '96

Paul was a free agent last winter, but it was unlikely the Indians would let him get away. Assenmacher is still one of the best lefthanded setup pitchers in baseball.

ALVARO ESPINOZA

Positions: 2B/3B/SS//DH/1B
Bats: R **Throws:** R
Ht: 6'0" **Wt:** 170
Opening Day Age: 34
Born: 2/19/1962
Drafted: HOU 10/30/78
ML Seasons: 10

Overall Statistics

	G	AB	R	H	2B	3B	HR	RBI	SB	CS	BB	SO	BA	OBA
95 CLE	66	143	15	36	4	0	2	17	0	2	2	16	.252	.264
Career	802	2160	218	551	93	5	14	167	11	15	64	275	.255	.279

1995 Situational Statistics

	AB	HR	RBI	BA	OBA	SLG		AB	HR	RBI	BA	OBA	SLG
Home	80	0	8	.175	.193	.188	LHP	55	1	6	.218	.237	.291
Road	63	2	9	.349	.354	.492	RHP	88	1	11	.273	.281	.341
Apr-Jun	28	0	5	.250	.290	.286	ScPos	36	0	14	.278	.282	.333
Jul-Oct	115	2	12	.252	.256	.330	Clutch	19	0	1	.158	.158	.158

SCOUTING REPORT

Alvaro, a three-year regular shortstop for the Yankees from 1989-91, now works the utility role in the infield. He has average range at three infield posts, average-plus hands, and an accurate arm of average strength.

A straight-away hitter who likes fastballs over the plate, "Espy" hits with almost no power and has very little foot speed. The veteran is a very effective sacrifice bunter. Unfortunately, he walks about once for every appearance of Halley's Comet.

HOW HE PERFORMED IN '95

Espinoza split his time evenly between second base, shortstop, and third base in '95 and often served as a late-inning defensive replacement. He played especially well at short.

Alvaro hit very well early in the year but faded in the second half. Although he has historically hit lefties better than righties, '95 was an exception.

WHAT TO EXPECT IN '96

Espinoza has played well since resurrecting his career with the Tribe in '93. He was a free agent in the off-season and, while he is expected to return this spring, look for someone with more punch in his bat to push Alvaro hard for the utility job.

THE SCOUTING REPORT: 1996

CLEVELAND INDIANS

WAYNE KIRBY

Positions: OF//DH
Bats: L **Throws:** R
Ht: 5'10" **Wt:** 185
Opening Day Age: 32
Born: 1/22/1964
Drafted: LA83* 13/291
ML Seasons: 5

Overall Statistics

	G	AB	R	H	2B	3B	HR	RBI	SB	CS	BB	SO	BA	OBA
95 CLE	101	188	29	39	10	2	1	14	10	3	13	32	.207	.260
Career	352	898	146	230	38	7	13	103	39	17	68	128	.256	.309

1995 Situational Statistics

	AB	HR	RBI	BA	OBA	SLG		AB	HR	RBI	BA	OBA	SLG
Home	67	0	6	.284	.342	.373	LHP	30	0	3	.267	.324	.333
Road	121	1	8	.165	.214	.256	RHP	158	1	11	.196	.247	.291
Apr-Jun	65	1	8	.215	.278	.338	ScPos	44	0	10	.159	.235	.159
Jul-Oct	123	0	6	.203	.250	.276	Clutch	39	1	6	.231	.286	.333

SCOUTING REPORT
An eight-year Dodgers' farmhand before coming to the Indians in 1991, Wayne Kirby does lots of little things well. He is an excellent bunter, plays hit-and-run effectively, and hits to all fields. However, he rarely walks, strikes out often and has little power. Wayne likes low, inside fastballs best. Kirby can play all outfield positions, throws well, and is the second-best baserunner on the team (behind Kenny Lofton) with plus speed.

HOW HE PERFORMED IN '95
Backing up Belle, Lofton, and Ramirez doesn't offer much hope for playing time, but Kirby fills in capably offensively and defensively when asked. Wayne had more success against lefties last year but appeared mostly against righthanders. Although his performance in '95 was disappointing, Kirby hit much better in 1993–94. He committed just one error last season but threw out only two runners amid talk that his formerly-strong arm had weakened.

WHAT TO EXPECT IN '96
Kirby is signed through 1996 with club options through 1998, but prospects Jeromy Burnitz and Brian Giles are expected to get long looks this spring. Wayne can't afford to hit .207 again if he expects to play in Cleveland.

CHAD OGEA

Position: SP/RP
Bats: R **Throws:** R
Ht: 6'2" **Wt:** 200
Opening Day Age: 25
Born: 11/9/1970
Drafted: CLE91 3/86
ML Seasons: 2

Overall Statistics

	G	GS	GF	SV	W	L	ERA	IP	H	R	ER	HR	BB	SO
95 CLE	20	14	3	0	8	3	3.05	106.1	95	38	36	11	29	57
Career	24	15	3	0	8	4	3.45	122.2	116	49	47	13	39	68

1995 Situational Statistics

	W	L	ERA	SV	IP	BB	SO		AB	HR	RBI	BA	OBA	SLG
Home	5	1	2.23	0	64.2	15	36	LHB	237	6	22	.224	.270	.342
Road	3	2	4.32	0	41.2	14	21	RHB	169	5	14	.249	.302	.391
Apr-Jun	4	0	1.58	0	40.0	6	21	ScPos	87	3	24	.161	.179	.299
Jul-Oct	4	3	3.93	0	66.1	23	36	Clutch	14	0	1	.214	.313	.286

SCOUTING REPORT
Chad has a high three-quarter delivery which he uses to deliver an average fastball that bores in on the fists of righthanded batters. He also has an average curve, but Ogea's best pitch is a plus change-up. He has above-average control, is aggressive, and likes to pitch inside.

Although he has a plus move to first, Chad is easy to run on: 14 runners stole bases against him in 16 attempts during '95. He is an average fielder.

HOW HE PERFORMED IN '95
Successful in his dual role as a spot starter and long reliever, Ogea had a 3.51 ERA when starting and a 1.24 ERA out of the pen. He held lefty hitters well in check. With runners in scoring position, Ogea held batters to an excellent .169 average. On August 15, his 7.1 innings against New York was the league's longest relief stint of the year.

WHAT TO EXPECT IN '96
Ogea, just 25, is a candidate to break into the Indians' starting rotation. While not a great prospect and while he's never had the full confidence of the front office, he would likely prosper if given a sustained audition in the rotation.

CLEVELAND INDIANS

TONY PENA

Position: C
Bats: R **Throws:** R
Ht: 6'0" **Wt:** 181
Opening Day Age: 38
Born: 6/4/1957
Drafted: PIT 7/22/75
ML Seasons: 16

Overall Statistics

	G	AB	R	H	2B	3B	HR	RBI	SB	CS	BB	SO	BA	OBA
95 CLE	91	263	25	69	15	0	5	28	1	0	14	44	.262	.302
Career	1881	6229	647	1638	290	27	106	671	80	62	430	805	.263	.311

1995 Situational Statistics

	AB	HR	RBI	BA	OBA	SLG		AB	HR	RBI	BA	OBA	SLG
Home	123	1	12	.236	.271	.358	LHP	84	1	5	.298	.322	.381
Road	140	4	16	.286	.329	.393	RHP	179	4	23	.246	.293	.374
Apr-Jun	149	3	11	.215	.269	.322	ScPos	77	1	21	.221	.277	.325
Jul-Oct	114	2	17	.325	.347	.447	Clutch	25	0	1	.200	.286	.240

SCOUTING REPORT

Veteran receiver Tony Pena calls an excellent game. He now has an average-minus arm with average accuracy and slightly above-average hands and range.

Pena has good success against the curve but has problems with hard stuff. Tony likes to hit 'em high and over the plate but habitually swings at pitches almost anywhere in the zone. He is an effective sacrifice bunter. He is very slow and is a poor percentage basestealer.

HOW HE PERFORMED IN '95

In the last two years, Pena performed better as Sandy Alomar's backup catcher than anyone could have asked. While hitting respectably, he handled the pitching staff well and Tony served as Dennis Martinez' personal catcher most of the season.

Pena, always an aggressive hitter, adds only some singles and the occasional double to the offense.

Tony is still mobile and blocks pitches as well as anyone. However, he threw out only 15 of 83 potential basestealers (18%), a sharp drop from his '94 numbers. Tony also committed seven errors.

WHAT TO EXPECT IN '96

With Alomar's health still in question, Cleveland added their insurance policy by re-signing Pena for another year. In that role, he has aged well.

HERB PERRY

Positions: 1B//DH/3B
Bats: R **Throws:** R
Ht: 6'2" **Wt:** 210
Opening Day Age: 26
Born: 9/15/1969
Drafted: CLE91 2/57
ML Seasons: 2

Overall Statistics

	G	AB	R	H	2B	3B	HR	RBI	SB	CS	BB	SO	BA	OBA
95 CLE	52	162	23	51	13	1	3	23	1	3	13	28	.315	.376
Career	56	171	24	52	13	1	3	24	1	3	16	29	.304	.374

1995 Situational Statistics

	AB	HR	RBI	BA	OBA	SLG		AB	HR	RBI	BA	OBA	SLG
Home	73	3	9	.356	.385	.589	LHP	64	3	10	.344	.403	.594
Road	89	0	14	.281	.369	.360	RHP	98	0	13	.296	.358	.378
Apr-Jun	18	2	3	.389	.389	.722	ScPos	43	0	17	.326	.380	.442
Jul-Oct	144	1	20	.306	.374	.431	Clutch	22	0	1	.227	.320	.318

SCOUTING REPORT

First baseman Perry showed fine defensive skills in '95, with a slightly above-average arm with average accuracy, quick reflexes, and average range and hands. He can also play third base. A line drive hitter to all fields, Perry looks for the fastball down and in to pull. He does not look like a classic power hitter but makes good contact and sacrificed effectively last year. Although not especially fast, Perry was a good percentage basestealer in the minors.

HOW HE PERFORMED IN '95

The rookie was recalled from Buffalo on June 12th to replace an injured Dave Winfield and stayed with the Tribe for the remainder of the season—an impressive season, at that.

Herbert hit .322 in 40 starts at first base. He did not commit a single error in 45 games at the position and was surprisingly mobile. He hit lefthanded pitching well and batted .326 with men in scoring position.

WHAT TO EXPECT IN '96

Perry can play defense, as he showed in the World Series. He is likely to see more action in '96, especially against lefties. His lack of power will hurt his chances to become an everyday first sacker, however.

THE SCOUTING REPORT: 1996

CLEVELAND INDIANS

ERIC PLUNK

Position: RP
Bats: R **Throws:** R
Ht: 6'5" **Wt:** 210
Opening Day Age: 32
Born: 9/3/1963
Drafted: NYA81 4/103
ML Seasons: 10

Overall Statistics

	G	GS	GF	SV	W	L	ERA	IP	H	R	ER	HR	BB	SO
95 CLE	56	0	22	2	6	2	2.67	64.0	48	19	19	5	27	71
Career	472	41	174	32	57	44	3.73	859.2	743	398	356	80	504	793

1995 Situational Statistics

	W	L	ERA	SV	IP	BB	SO		AB	HR	RBI	BA	OBA	SLG
Home	4	0	2.67	2	30.1	9	31	LHB	109	0	13	.229	.317	.312
Road	2	2	2.67	0	33.2	18	40	RHB	119	5	9	.193	.289	.336
Apr-Jun	4	1	2.12	1	29.2	13	32	ScPos	48	1	18	.229	.328	.396
Jul-Oct	2	1	3.15	1	34.1	14	39	Clutch	138	5	19	.246	.331	.413

SCOUTING REPORT
Eric throws overhand and challenges batters with three plus pitches. His four-seam fastball rides and has good life when up, his slider has a hard break, and his curve has improved.

An average fielder, Plunk is quick to home but has a below-average move to first. Nine of 12 men trying to steal against him were successful in '95.

HOW HE PERFORMED IN '95
Plunk had made 222 appearances since April 1992 without being hurt, but his luck ran out last September as he missed three weeks due to shoulder tendinitis. Even so, Eric had another good year, serving as Jose Mesa's setup man. Plunk allowed runs in only 11 of his 56 appearances while holding both righthanded and lefthanded batters well in check. He has registered over a strikeout per inning for the last three years, and continues to belie his early reputation as a pitcher who threw hard enough but who could not master his control.

WHAT TO EXPECT IN '96
Eric will return in the same setup role in '96. He's unlikely to ever become a full-time closer except in case of emergency, but is a nice option to call on if Mesa were to be injured.

JIM POOLE

Position: RP
Bats: L **Throws:** L
Ht: 6'2" **Wt:** 190
Opening Day Age: 29
Born: 4/28/1966
Drafted: LA88 8/218
ML Seasons: 6

Overall Statistics

	G	GS	GF	SV	W	L	ERA	IP	H	R	ER	HR	BB	SO
95 CLE	42	0	9	0	3	3	3.75	50.1	40	22	21	7	17	41
Career	186	0	40	3	9	6	3.25	177.0	141	77	64	17	70	135

1995 Situational Statistics

	W	L	ERA	SV	IP	BB	SO		AB	HR	RBI	BA	OBA	SLG
Home	1	1	1.65	0	27.1	8	29	LHB	76	1	5	.211	.277	.329
Road	2	2	6.26	0	23.0	9	12	RHB	108	6	16	.222	.295	.417
Apr-Jun	1	3	3.86	0	23.1	9	16	ScPos	45	1	12	.156	.216	.222
Jul-Oct	2	0	3.67	0	27.0	8	25	Clutch	53	3	3	.113	.190	.283

SCOUTING REPORT
Lefty situational reliever Poole throws from three-quarters with a minus fastball that tails into left-handers and a slightly above-average, slow, rolling curve that he uses against lefties with great success. His forkball is a below-average pitch. Jim holds runners well and is an average fielder. Last year, four of six runners were thrown out stealing against Poole.

HOW HE PERFORMED IN '95
Poole, a union rep, benefitted from arrangements made after the end of the strike. After a miserable '94 with Baltimore, he was struggling to get a job, only hanging on with Cleveland because of the expanded roster. He took full advantage of this situation and restarted his career. AL hitters managed to hit only .156 with runners in scoring position against Poole, who allowed only four of 27 inherited runners to score. On occasion, his curves hung, as his seven home runs attest. Like most Indians' pitchers, Jim did not like working away from Jacobs Field.

WHAT TO EXPECT IN '96
All of Hargrove's lefties performed well in '95. Poole will work in the middle and later innings again, and should be successful if he keeps the ball low consistently and gets his curve over the plate.

CLEVELAND INDIANS

JULIAN TAVAREZ

Position: RP
Bats: R **Throws:** R
Ht: 6'2" **Wt:** 165
Opening Day Age: 22
Born: 5/22/1973
Drafted: CLE 2/22/90
ML Seasons: 3

Overall Statistics

	G	GS	GF	SV	W	L	ERA	IP	H	R	ER	HR	BB	SO
95 CLE	57	0	15	0	10	2	2.44	85.0	76	36	23	7	21	68
Career	66	8	15	0	12	5	3.93	123.2	135	73	54	15	35	87

1995 Situational Statistics

	W	L	ERA	SV	IP	BB	SO		AB	HR	RBI	BA	OBA	SLG
Home	6	1	1.72	0	47.0	8	40	LHB	154	5	15	.266	.319	.422
Road	4	1	3.32	0	38.0	13	28	RHB	170	2	16	.206	.255	.259
Apr-Jun	5	0	1.17	0	38.1	7	30	ScPos	76	0	20	.211	.262	.237
Jul-Oct	5	2	3.47	0	46.2	14	38	Clutch	169	4	16	.195	.266	.296

SCOUTING REPORT

Reed-thin Tavarez delivers from a high three-quarters to three-quarters with average control. He has an above-average fastball that sinks and bores in on righthanders. Julian also throws a plus hard slider that occasionally flattens out as well as an average splitter. He is quick to home, giving him plus ability to hold runners. Just five men tried to steal against Tavarez in '95, and three were nailed. Although scouts rate him an average fielder, Tavarez committed two errors in only 20 chances during '95.

HOW HE PERFORMED IN '95

Julian, the first player to come out of Indians' Dominican summer program, spent his rookie season serving as one of the AL's best middle relievers. Originally tabbed as a backup starter, Tavarez switched to the bullpen and paced the league in relief wins. He started the season 6-0 but struggled in the second half; a poor September raised Julian's ERA over 3.00. He blew all three of his save opportunities.

WHAT TO EXPECT IN '96

The Indians could use Tavarez in either starting or relief depending on which pitchers return to the wigwam. The '96 season should be an interesting one for the young righty with lots of promise.

DAVE WINFIELD

Position: DH
Bats: R **Throws:** R
Ht: 6'6" **Wt:** 220
Opening Day Age: 44
Born: 10/3/1951
Drafted: SD73 1/4
ML Seasons: 22

Overall Statistics

	G	AB	R	H	2B	3B	HR	RBI	SB	CS	BB	SO	BA	OBA
95 CLE	46	115	11	22	5	0	2	4	1	0	14	26	.191	.285
Career	2973	11003	1669	3110	540	88	465	1833	223	96	1216	1686	.283	.353

1995 Situational Statistics

	AB	HR	RBI	BA	OBA	SLG		AB	HR	RBI	BA	OBA	SLG
Home	39	1	3	.077	.217	.179	LHP	65	1	3	.154	.257	.246
Road	76	1	1	.250	.321	.342	RHP	50	1	1	.240	.321	.340
Apr-Jun	53	1	3	.189	.283	.302	ScPos	30	1	3	.100	.250	.200
Jul-Oct	62	1	1	.194	.286	.274	Clutch	15	0	0	.200	.333	.267

SCOUTING REPORT

While Winfield can still hit lefties, his bat speed has declined significantly. He still likes to extend his arms against low fastballs.

Winfield is slow out of the gate and has minus speed but runs the bases intelligently. He no longer is asked to play defense.

HOW HE PERFORMED IN '95

Dave was the oldest player in the majors last year and his age appears to have finally caught up with him. Winfield tore his rotator cuff last June 10 attempting to steal second base and never recovered.

The Indians needed him to provide some punch against lefties, which he usually does well. Unfortunately, he didn't help much in '95. After being reactivated, Winfield could barely hit the ball out of the infield. However, Dave was important to the team's chemistry and many were surprised when he was left off the playoff roster.

WHAT TO EXPECT IN '96

Bringing in the veteran DH was the only acquisition John Hart made in '95 that did not work out. If Dave is around this year, he will likely be with another team. If Winfield's career is over, it was one hell of a ride.

CLEVELAND INDIANS: TOP PROSPECTS

BART COLON
Bats: R Throws: R Opening Day Age: 21
Ht: 6-0 Wt: 185 Born: 5/24/1975
Position: P Drafted: NDFA 6-26-93 CLE

YR TEAM	LG/CLASS	G	GS	GF	SV	W	L	ERA	IP	H	HR	BB	SO	O/BA
94 Burlington	APPY/R	12	12	0	0	7	4	3.14	66.0	46	3	44	84	.192
95 Kinston	CARO/A	21	21	0	0	13	3	1.96	128	91	8	39	152	.202

After dominating the Appalachian League in 1994, Colon blossomed into the best young pitching prospect in the game last season. Showing outstanding control of a mid-90's fastball, Howe Sportsdata's 1995 Teenage Pitcher of the Year was on his way to a mound triple crown (wins, ERA, strikeouts) in the Carolina League until an elbow bruise ended his season in late July. He won ten of his last 11 decisions and allowed more than two runs just four times all season. His SO/9 IP ratio (10.63) was the second highest among minor league starting pitchers. Colon still needs work on his breaking ball and changeup.

ALAN EMBREE
Bats: L Throws: L Opening Day Age: 26
Ht: 6-2 Wt: 190 Born: 1/23/1970
Position: P Drafted: 1989 #4 CLE

YR TEAM	LG/CLASS	G	GS	GF	SV	W	L	ERA	IP	H	HR	BB	SO	O/BA
93 Canton-Akn	EAST/AA	1	1	0	0	0	0	3.38	5.1	3	0	3	4	.176
94 Canton-Akn	EAST/AA	30	27	1	0	9	16	5.50	157.0	183	15	64	81	.294
95 Buffalo	AMAS/AAA	30	0	19	5	3	4	0.89	40	31	0	19	56	.211
Cleveland	AL/MAJ	23	0	8	1	3	2	5.11	24	23	2	16	23	.237

Once regarded as the top pitcher in the organization, Embree missed virtually the entire 1993 season because of an elbow injury and was hit hard upon his return the following season. Last year, the 25-year-old moved to the bullpen, regained his consistent 90+ mph fastball and slider, and went 21.1 innings without allowing a run in one stretch at Buffalo last season. He paced American Association relievers with 12.39 SO/9 IP. Although his command does need some fine tuning, Embree was devastating against lefthanders, fanning 17 of the 39 he faced.

BRIAN GILES
Bats: L Throws: L Opening Day Age: 25
Ht: 5-11 Wt: 195 Born: 1/20/1971
Position: OF Drafted: 1989 #16 CLE

YR TEAM	LG/CLASS	G	AB	R	H	2B	3B	HR	RBI	SB	BA	OBA
93 Canton-Akn	EAST/AA	123	425	64	139	17	6	8	64	18	.327	.409
94 Charlotte	INT/AAA	128	434	74	136	18	3	16	58	8	.313	.390
95 Buffalo	AMAS/AAA	123	413	67	128	18	8	15	67	7	.310	.395
Cleveland	AL/MAJ	6	9	6	5	0	0	1	3	0	.556	.556

Giles may be a victim of Cleveland's great young outfield. He can't find a job with the Tribe, but has done everything possible at the minor league level. In his two years of Triple-A, the lefthanded swinger has hit .350 with runners in scoring position, .300 against both right and lefthanded pitching and has rarely struck out. He has shown power, especially last season where he hit 15 homers despite playing half his games at Pilot Field in Buffalo, probably the best pitchers' park in the American Association. Giles batted .325 with 13 homers in the second half and played a fine corner outfield spot showing decent speed. He finished among the top five in the league in batting, on-base percentage and slugging (.501).

DANNY GRAVES
Bats: R Throws: R Opening Day Age: 23
Ht: 5-11 Wt: 200 Born: 8/7/1973
Position: P Drafted: 1994 #3 CLE

YR TEAM	LG/CLASS	G	GS	GF	SV	W	L	ERA	IP	H	HR	BB	SO	O/BA
95 Buffalo	AMAS/AAA	3	0	3	0	0	0	3.00	3	5	0	1	2	.333
Canton-Akn	EAST/AA	17	0	17	10	1	0	0.00	23	10	0	2	11	.133
Kinston	CARO/A	38	0	37	21	3	1	0.82	44	30	0	12	46	.183

Graves was simply automatic in 1995, allowing earned runs in just five of his 56 appearances. The first-year pro did not debut in '94 due to a knee injury. He may not have the heat associated with a closer, but the 21-year-old has super makeup, a 90 mph sinking fastball, and a curveball that drops off the table. Graves also had a groundball/flyball ratio of nearly 6:1 at Canton, a ratio unheard of in pro ball.

DAMIAN JACKSON
Bats: R Throws: R Opening Day Age: 23
Ht: 5-10 Wt: 160 Born: 8/16/1973
Position: SS Drafted: 1991 #44 CLE

YR TEAM	LG/CLASS	G	AB	R	H	2B	3B	HR	RBI	SB	BA	OBA
93 Columbus	SAL/A	108	350	70	94	19	3	6	45	26	.269	.353
94 Canton-Akn	EAST/AA	138	531	85	143	29	5	5	46	37	.269	.346
95 Canton-Akn	EAST/AA	131	484	67	120	20	2	3	34	40	.248	.348

Midway through 1994 Jackson had emerged as the top position prospect in the organization, exhibiting outstanding range, a strong arm, tremendous speed, and good pop. However, ever since, the 22-year-old has struggled with the bat, having a tough time in the Arizona Fall League and in a repeat performance in the Eastern League last season. Jackson returned to Double-A in 1995 to improve his fielding and did cut his errors from 54 to 36 while surpassing his own club record for stolen bases. However, Jackson was inconsistent from month-to-month and got away from his normal game (bunting and base hits) and focused too much on trying to hit for power.

DARON KIRKREIT
Bats: R Throws: R Opening Day Age: 24
Ht: 6-6 Wt: 225 Born: 8/7/1972
Position: P Drafted: 1993 #1 CLE

YR TEAM	LG/CLASS	G	GS	GF	SV	W	L	ERA	IP	H	HR	BB	SO	O/BA
93 Watertown	NYP/A	7	7	0	0	4	1	2.23	36.1	33	1	11	44	.229
94 Kinston	CARO/A	20	19	1	0	8	7	2.68	127.2	92	9	40	116	.200
94 Canton-Akn	EAST/AA	9	9	0	0	3	5	6.22	46.1	53	5	25	54	.280
95 Canton-Akn	EAST/AA	14	14	0	0	2	9	5.69	80	74	13	46	67	.249
Kinston	CARO/A	3	3	0	0	1	5.93	13	14	1	6	14	.264

After pitching through shoulder pain that caused a loss in velocity, Kirkreit finally succumbed in mid-July and sat out the rest of the 1995 season. The 1993 first-rounder throws in the 90's when healthy, but he had trouble all season controlling his fastball and curve, his best pitches. Kirkreit is expected back at 100% this season.

CLEVELAND INDIANS: TOP PROSPECTS

STEVE KLINE
Bats: S Throws: L Opening Day Age: 24
Ht: 6-2 Wt: 200 Born: 8/22/1972
Position: P Drafted: 1993 #8 CLE

YR TEAM	LG/CLASS	G	GS	GF	SV	W	L	ERA	IP	H	HR	BB	SO	O/BA
93 Burlington	APPY/R	2	1	0	0	1	1	4.91	7.1	11	0	2	4	.355
93 Watertown	NYP/A	13	13	0	0	5	4	3.19	79.0	77	3	12	45	.248
94 Columbus	SAL/A	28	28	0	0	18	5	3.01	185.2	175	14	36	174	.251
95 Canton-Akn	EAST/AA	14	14	0	0	2	3	2.42	89	86	6	30	45	.252

After tying for the minor league lead with 18 wins and leading the South Atlantic League in strikeouts in 1994, Kline jumped past Kinston and pitched at Double-A in 1995. His win total dropped to just two as he missed ten weeks with an elbow problem. When healthy, the 23-year-old has a decent fastball, but relies mainly on locating his four-pitch assortment with pinpoint control.

JOE ROA
Bats: R Throws: R Opening Day Age: 24
Ht: 6-1 Wt: 194 Born: 10/11/1971
Position: P Drafted: 1989 #19 ATL

YR TEAM	LG/CLASS	G	GS	GF	SV	W	L	ERA	IP	H	HR	BB	SO	O/BA
93 Binghamton	EAST/AA	32	23	0	0	12	7	3.87	167.1	190	9	24	73	.291
94 Binghamton	EAST/AA	3	3	0	0	2	1	1.80	20.0	18	0	1	11	.240
94 Norfolk	INT/AAA	25	25	0	0	8	8	3.49	167.2	184	16	34	74	.283
95 Buffalo	AMAS/AAA	25	24	1	0	17	3	3.50	164	168	9	28	93	.264
Cleveland	AL/MAJ	1	1	0	0	0	1	6.00	5	9	1	2	0	.360

Considered a throw-in from the Mets in the Jeromy Burnitz trade, Roa may have had the best season among all the players the Indians received. He led the American Association in wins, totaling the second most in the minor leagues (and a Buffalo-franchise record). Roa also ended fourth in ERA and fifth in strikeouts despite allowing more hits than innings pitched. Twice during the season he won six straight starts. Roa has averaged fewer than two walks per game over his career, winning 67 times against only 33 losses. However, he barely hits 85 on the radar gun, which means despite his career success he will never be viewed as more than a marginal prospect.

RICHIE SEXSON
Bats: R Throws: R Opening Day Age: 21
Ht: 6-6 Wt: 206 Born: 12/29/1974
Position: 1B Drafted: 1993 #24 CLE

YR TEAM	LG/CLASS	G	AB	R	H	2B	3B	HR	RBI	SB	BA	OBA
93 Burlington	APPY/R	40	97	11	18	3	0	1	5	1	.186	.316
94 Columbus	SAL/A	130	488	88	133	25	2	14	77	2	.273	.336
95 Kinston	CARO/A	131	494	80	151	34	0	22	85	4	.306	.368

Sexson emerged as one of the bright young hitting prospects in the minor leagues in 1995. Playing against much older competition, the 20-year-old pursued a triple crown until the final week of the season. He showed a powerful bat, leading the Carolina League in RBI, hits, doubles and extra-base hits (56) while finishing second in batting and slugging (.508). Only a 24th-round draft pick, the 6-6, 210-pound slugger is smooth in the field, having converted from his high school position of shortstop, and is mature for his age. He batted .351 the first two months of the season with 16 doubles, 11 homers and 42 RBI in 53 games.

PAUL SHUEY
Bats: R Throws: R Opening Day Age: 26
Ht: 6-3 Wt: 215 Born: 9/16/1970
Position: P Drafted: 1992 #1 CLE

YR TEAM	LG/CLASS	G	GS	GF	SV	W	L	ERA	IP	H	HR	BB	SO	O/BA
93 Canton-Akn	EAST/AA	27	7	10	0	4	8	7.30	61.2	76	13	36	41	.308
93 Kinston	CARO/A	15	0	7	0	1	0	4.84	22.1	29	1	8	27	.326
94 Kinston	CARO/A	13	0	12	8	1	0	3.75	12.0	10	1	3	16	.227
94 Cleveland	AL/MAJ	14	0	11	5	0	1	8.49	11.2	14	1	12	16	.280
94 Charlotte	INT/AAA	20	0	18	10	2	1	1.93	23.1	15	1	10	25	.181
95 Buffalo	AMAS/AAA	25	0	19	11	1	2	2.63	27	21	2	7	27	.214
Cleveland	AL/MAJ	7	0	3	0	0	2	4.26	6	5	0	5	5	.208

The second overall pick in the 1992 draft began last season in Cleveland, went on the disabled list with a hamstring pull, was sent to Buffalo in late May to rehab, and promptly hurt his shoulder in his first appearance. Shuey returned in July and showed better command of his mid-90's fastball and big bender. After averaging better than five walks per nine innings in the past, Shuey actually pitched over 15 innings for the Bisons before walking a batter. Until Jose Mesa developed, Shuey was being counted on as the closer of the future for the Tribe.

CASEY WHITTEN
Bats: L Throws: L Opening Day Age: 24
Ht: 6-0 Wt: 175 Born: 5/23/1972
Position: P Drafted: 1993 #2 CLE

YR TEAM	LG/CLASS	G	GS	GF	SV	W	L	ERA	IP	H	HR	BB	SO	O/BA
93 Watertown	NYP/A	14	14	0	0	6	3	2.42	81.2	75	8	18	81	.245
94 Kinston	CARO/A	27	27	0	0	9	10	4.28	153.1	127	21	64	148	.228
95 Canton-Akn	EAST/AA	20	20	0	0	9	8	3.31	114	100	10	38	91	.235

Overshadowed by more high-profiled pitchers at Canton last season, Whitten emerged as a staff ace before going down with a mild shoulder strain in mid-July. He made just two starts the rest of the way. Whitten displayed an outstanding breaking ball, a decent fastball and an ability to change speeds.

ENRIQUE WILSON
Bats: S Throws: R Opening Day Age: 21
Ht: 5-11 Wt: 160 Born: 7/27/1975
Position: SS Drafted: NDFA 4-15-92 MIN

YR TEAM	LG/CLASS	G	AB	R	H	2B	3B	HR	RBI	SB	BA	OBA
93 Elizabethtn	APPY/R	58	197	42	57	8	4	13	50	5	.289	.352
94 Columbus	SAL/A	133	512	82	143	28	12	10	72	21	.279	.341
95 Kinston	CARO/A	117	464	55	124	24	7	6	52	18	.267	.301

The 20-year-old shortstop can go deep in the hole, has a great throwing arm, and only committed 21 errors last year (ten came in the month of June). Offensively, Wilson hits well from both sides of the plate, has power potential and good speed and, in 1995, was the toughest batter in his league to strike out for the second straight year. Cleveland stole him from the Twins prior to 1994 for journeyman pitcher Shawn Bryant.

THE SCOUTING REPORT: 1996

CLEVELAND INDIANS: OTHERS TO WATCH

BRUCE AVEN Bats: R Throws: R Ht: 5-9 Wt: 180
Born: 3/4/1972 Drafted: 1994 #29 CLE Position: OF

YR TEAM	LG/CLASS	G	AB	R	H	2B	3B	HR	RBI	SB	BA	OBA
95 Kinston	CARO/A	130	479	70	125	23	5	23	69	15	.261	.335

The second-year pro showed good power and speed, but needs to make better contact.

JIM BETZSOLD Bats: R Throws: R Ht: 6-3 Wt: 210
Born: 8/7/1972 Drafted: 1994 #19 CLE Position: OF

YR TEAM	LG/CLASS	G	AB	R	H	2B	3B	HR	RBI	SB	BA	OBA
95 Kinston	CARO/A	126	455	77	122	22	2	25	71	3	.268	.357

The late-round pick shows good power and has impressed at two levels in his two-year career despite a tendency to strike out.

PAT BRYANT Bats: R Throws: R Ht: 5-11 Wt: 182
Born: 10/27/1972 Drafted: 1990 #4 CLE Position: CF

YR TEAM	LG/CLASS	G	AB	R	H	2B	3B	HR	RBI	SB	BA	OBA
95 Cnton-Akn	EAST/AA	127	421	60	109	22	3	17	59	16	.259	.344

The Tribe loves his speed, centerfield play, and power potential, but he hasn't hit for average and strikes out too often.

JEROMY BURNITZ Bats: L Throws: R Ht: 6-0 Wt: 190
Born: 4/14/1969 Drafted: 1990 #1 NYN Position: OF

YR TEAM	LG/CLASS	G	AB	R	H	2B	3B	HR	RBI	SB	BA	OBA
95 Buffalo	AMAS/AAA	128	443	72	126	26	7	19	85	13	.284	.359
95 Cleveland	AL/MAJ	9	7	4	4	1	0	0	0	0	.571	.571

The Mets' former first-rounder is another potentially good all-around outfielder who may never get a shot in Cleveland.

TIM COSTO Bats: R Throws: R Ht: 6-5 Wt: 230
Born: 2/16/1969 Drafted: 1990 #1 CLE Position: 1B-OF

YR TEAM	LG/CLASS	G	AB	R	H	2B	3B	HR	RBI	SB	BA	OBA
95 Buffalo	AMAS/AAA	105	324	41	80	11	2	11	60	2	.247	.314

A former first-rounder who was traded away and reacquired, Costo has not shown consistent hitting or solidified a position.

CARLOS CRAWFORD Bats: R Throws: R Ht: 6-1 Wt: 185
Born: 10/4/1971 Drafted: 1990 #52 CLE Position: P

YR TEAM	LG/CLASS	G	GS	GF	SV	W	L	ERA	IP	H	HR	BB	SO	O/BA
95 Buffalo	AMAS/AAA	13	3	3	1	0	1	5.64	30.1	36	2	12	15	.293
95 Cnton-Akn	EAST/AA	8	8	0	0	2	2	2.61	51.2	47	1	15	36	.241

Crawford, a "spotter" who started out '94 with eight straight wins, bounced between two levels last season.

EINAR DIAZ Bats: R Throws: R Ht: 5-10 Wt: 165
Born: 12/28/1972 Drafted: NDFA 10-5-90 CLE Position: C

YR TEAM	LG/CLASS	G	AB	R	H	2B	3B	HR	RBI	SB	BA	OBA
95 Kinston	CARO/A	104	373	46	98	21	0	6	43	3	.263	.297

Diaz is an outstanding defensive catcher who rarely walks or strikes out.

RICKY GUTIERREZ Bats: R Throws: R Ht: 6-0 Wt: 170
Born: 3/23/1970 Drafted: 1994 #27 CLE Position: 2B

YR TEAM	LG/CLASS	G	AB	R	H	2B	3B	HR	RBI	SB	BA	OBA
95 Kinston	CARO/A	117	439	63	115	21	7	4	46	63	.262	.362

The Carolina League stolen base leader is excellent in the field, but his bat is a question mark.

PEP HARRIS Bats: R Throws: R Ht: 6-2 Wt: 185
Born: 9/23/1972 Drafted: 1991 #7 CLE Position: P

YR TEAM	LG/CLASS	G	GS	GF	SV	W	L	ERA	IP	H	HR	BB	SO	O/BA
95 Buffalo	AMAS/AAA	14	0	3	0	2	1	2.48	32.2	32	2	15	18	.254
95 Cnton-Akn	EAST/AA	32	7	20	10	6	3	2.39	83.0	78	4	23	40	.254

Harris throws heat and has succeeded as a closer, middle man and setup man the last two years.

JIM LEWIS Bats: R Throws: R Ht: 6-4 Wt: 190
Born: 1/31/1970 Drafted: 1991 #6 HOU Position: P

YR TEAM	LG/CLASS	G	GS	GF	SV	W	L	ERA	IP	H	HR	BB	SO	O/BA
95 Buffalo	AMAS/AAA	18	16	2	1	6	4	3.64	94.0	101	7	25	50	.276
95 Cleveland	AL/MAJ	0	0	0	0	0	0	0.00	0.0	0	0	0	0	.000

Lewis, a Rule V draftee from Houston, has good stuff but a history of arm problems.

ALBIE LOPEZ Bats: R Throws: R Ht: 6-2 Wt: 205
Born: 8/18/1971 Drafted: 1991 #20 CLE Position: P

YR TEAM	LG/CLASS	G	GS	GF	SV	W	L	ERA	IP	H	HR	BB	SO	O/BA
95 Buffalo	AMAS/AAA	18	18	0	0	5	10	4.44	101.1	101	10	51	82	.259
95 Cleveland	AL/MAJ	6	2	0	0	0	3	3.13	23.0	17	4	7	22	.205

Once regarded as highly as Julian Tavarez, Chad Ogea and Alan Embree, Lopez has been passed over, but still has good stuff and might just need to move on in order to excel.

ROD McCALL Bats: L Throws: R Ht: 6-7 Wt: 235
Born: 11/4/1971 Drafted: 1990 #11 CLE Position: 1B

YR TEAM	LG/CLASS	G	AB	R	H	2B	3B	HR	RBI	SB	BA	OBA
95 Cnton-Akn	EAST/AA	26	95	16	26	5	0	9	18	1	.274	.361
95 Bakersfield	CAL/A	96	345	61	114	19	1	20	70	2	.330	.408

A non-prospect prior to '95, the 23-year-old was loaned out for part of '95 and turned heads with a .318 average and 29 homers.

WIL MONTOYA Bats: R Throws: R Ht: 5-10 Wt: 165
Born: 3/15/1974 Drafted: NDFA 9-17-92 CLE Position: P

YR TEAM	LG/CLASS	G	GS	GF	SV	W	L	ERA	IP	H	HR	BB	SO	O/BA
95 Columbus	SAL/A	51	0	41	31	3	3	3.12	80.2	65	4	36	91	.219
95 Kinston	CARO/A	1	0	0	0	1	0	5.40	3.1	4	0	1	2	.308

The first-year closer finished second in the South Atlantic League in saves using a 90-mph fastball and good curve.

JEFF SEXTON Bats: R Throws: R Ht: 6-2 Wt: 190
Born: 10/4/1971 Drafted: NDFA 7-7-93 CLE Position: P

YR TEAM	LG/CLASS	G	GS	GF	SV	W	L	ERA	IP	H	HR	BB	SO	O/BA
95 Columbus	SAL/A	14	13	0	0	6	2	2.19	82.1	66	2	16	71	.222
95 Kinston	CARO/A	8	8	0	0	5	1	2.53	57.0	52	3	7	41	.240

A pleasant surprise: Sexton, not a hard thrower, was the Carolina League champion's best pitcher down the stretch.

JARET WRIGHT Bats: R Throws: R Ht: 6-2 Wt: 220
Born: 12/29/1975 Drafted: 1994 #1 CLE Position: P

YR TEAM	LG/CLASS	G	GS	GF	SV	W	L	ERA	IP	H	HR	BB	SO	O/BA
95 Columbus	SAL/A	24	24	0	0	5	6	3.00	129.0	93	9	79	113	.205

The son of Clyde Wright has the best arm in the organization and a sharp breaking curve, but is very raw.

DETROIT TIGERS

DANNY BAUTISTA

Positions: OF//DH
Bats: R **Throws:** R
Ht: 5'11" **Wt:** 170
Opening Day Age: 23
Born: 5/24/1972
Drafted: DET 6/24/89
ML Seasons: 3

SCOUTING REPORT
Bautista is a fastball hitter who likes the ball on the inside portion of the plate. Like most hitters, he is weak on breaking balls low and away—the problem is, he doesn't always have the good sense to lay off them. Danny experimented with many different batting stances during the season and seemed to have some success with an open stance.

Bautista has plus speed on the basepaths. He is one of the Tigers' best defensive outfielders since he combines an above-average arm with above-average range. The accuracy of his throws is average and he has average hands.

HOW HE PERFORMED IN '95
Bautista was a severe disappointment for the Tigers in '95. After showing offensive and defensive promise in '94, hitting .311 in 17 games in his big-league debut, Bautista was expected to become the everyday right fielder last season. He was mercifully optioned to Toledo on August 8 while in the midst of an 0-for-36 slump. He was recalled on September 1 and hit a respectable .280 during the final month with three home runs.

Bautista's biggest problem is his inability to put the ball in play. Until he learns more discipline at the plate and gets ahead in the count, he won't get a chance to drive many fat pitches.

WHAT TO EXPECT IN '96
One major factor working in Bautista's favor is his age: he is only 24 and has time to learn and improve. The Tigers like Bautista's arm and defensive ability, but they would also like him to learn to hit the ball more on the ground and utilize his speed to increase his batting average. Danny stole 46 bases while only getting caught nine times in 1992–93 while splitting time between Single-A Fayetteville and Double-A London.

With the emergence of Bobby Higginson in right field and the possibility of Phil Nevin learning to handle a new position in left field, Bautista's chances to play every day in Detroit in '96 might be slim. On the other hand, Nevin didn't show much after he came to Detroit and his defense in the outfield will certainly be a lot worse than Bautista's, so Danny could get another chance to prove himself if Nevin flops.

Overall Statistics

	G	AB	R	H	2B	3B	HR	RBI	SB	CS	BB	SO	BA	OBA
95 DET	89	271	28	55	9	0	7	27	4	1	12	68	.203	.237
Career	137	431	46	97	16	1	12	51	8	4	16	96	.225	.252

1995 Situational Statistics

	AB	HR	RBI	BA	OBA	SLG		AB	HR	RBI	BA	OBA	SLG
Home	136	3	9	.169	.204	.265	LHP	95	4	9	.189	.198	.326
Road	135	4	18	.237	.270	.363	RHP	176	3	18	.210	.257	.307
Apr-Jun	138	1	13	.217	.255	.275	ScPos	83	1	18	.181	.209	.265
Jul-Oct	133	6	14	.188	.217	.353	Clutch	35	0	2	.143	.211	.143

How He Compares to Other Batters

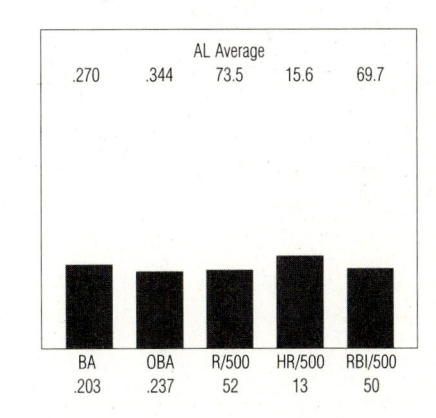

	BA	OBA	R/500	HR/500	RBI/500
AL Average	.270	.344	73.5	15.6	69.7
	.203	.237	52	13	50

Where He Hits the Ball

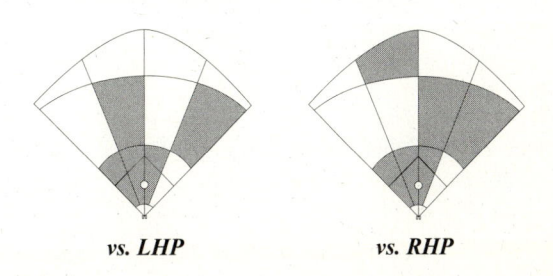

vs. LHP   vs. RHP

THE SCOUTING REPORT: 1996

DETROIT TIGERS

SEAN BERGMAN

Position: SP
Bats: R **Throws:** R
Ht: 6'4" **Wt:** 205
Opening Day Age: 25
Born: 4/11/1970
Drafted: DET91 6/114
ML Seasons: 3

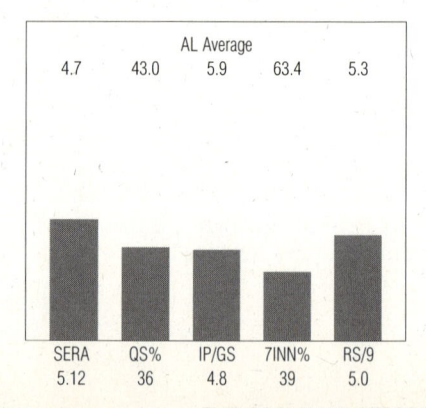

SCOUTING REPORT
Bergman delivers from a three-quarter angle, throwing across his body. He has an above-average fastball that has good sinking and tailing action. He also possesses a plus slider. Bergman's mains problems are that he does not have a quality off-speed pitch and that he does not have good enough control: his curveball is average and his change-up is slightly on the minus side. The Tigers are counting on having his control improve with experience in the major leagues. He needs to keep his pitches down and set up hitters if he is to be successful.

Sean has a minus move and clearly has trouble with runners, as 28 took off with him pitching in '95. Even worse, 25 made it safely. He made three errors to boot last year.

HOW HE PERFORMED IN '95
The '95 season was Bergman's first full season in the major leagues; he led the Tigers' shell-shocked staff with 28 starts. The highlight of Bergman's season came on August 2 when he fired a four-hit, 5-0 shut out over Boston.

However, there were plenty of negatives in Bergman's season as well. Opponents hit a robust .307 against him, with port-side swingers doing most of the damage. Bergman also allowed an astounding 240 baserunners (169 hits, four hit batsmen and 67 walks) in 135 innings, his strikeout-to-walk ratio was quite unacceptable, and he placed second in the AL with 13 wild pitches.

WHAT TO EXPECT IN '96
Because the Tigers are going completely with their youth movement, Bergman is definitely penciled in as one of the Tigers' starters next season despite his '95 performance. He will be 26 in April. Bergman needs to give the Tigers more innings (28 starts and one complete game won't do it).

Bergman will never be the anchor of a good major-league pitching staff but he should mature into a capable third or fourth starter. Unfortunately for him and the Tigers, he is shaping up as the ace of the Bengals' staff for '96—and that kind of pressure could hinder his development. He is the type of groundball pitcher who can thrive in Tiger Stadium with good command of his sinker and slider.

Overall Statistics

	G	GS	GF	SV	W	L	ERA	IP	H	R	ER	HR	BB	SO
95 DET	28	28	0	0	7	10	5.12	135.1	169	95	77	19	67	86
Career	40	37	1	0	10	15	5.28	192.2	238	135	113	27	97	117

1995 Situational Statistics

	W	L	ERA	SV	IP	BB	SO		AB	HR	RBI	BA	OBA	SLG
Home	3	4	4.74	0	62.2	31	40	LHB	337	15	65	.320	.396	.516
Road	4	6	5.45	0	72.2	36	46	RHB	214	4	21	.285	.365	.397
Apr-Jun	3	5	4.88	0	62.2	29	37	ScPos	157	5	64	.287	.392	.439
Jul-Oct	4	5	5.33	0	72.2	38	49	Clutch	13	0	0	.231	.333	.385

How He Compares to Other Pitchers

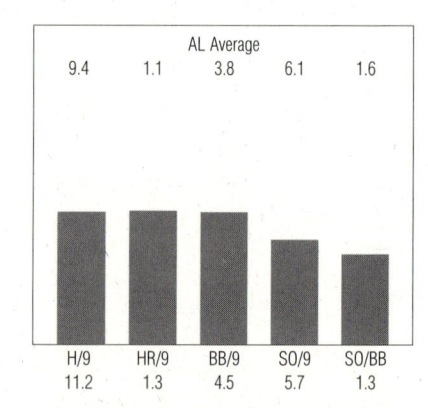

AL Average: H/9 9.4, HR/9 1.1, BB/9 3.8, SO/9 6.1, SO/BB 1.6
Bergman: H/9 11.2, HR/9 1.3, BB/9 4.5, SO/9 5.7, SO/BB 1.3

How He Compares to Other Starting Pitchers

AL Average: SERA 4.7, QS% 43.0, IP/GS 5.9, 7INN% 63.4, RS/9 5.3
Bergman: SERA 5.12, QS% 36, IP/GS 4.8, 7INN% 39, RS/9 5.0

DETROIT TIGERS

CHAD CURTIS

Position: OF
Bats: R **Throws:** R
Ht: 5'10" **Wt:** 175
Opening Day Age: 27
Born: 11/6/1968
Drafted: CAL89 45/1157
ML Seasons: 4

SCOUTING REPORT
Chad developed into a power hitter last season but would be more effective overall if he was more disciplined at the plate and not so eager to hit home runs. A fastball hitter, Curtis will take the ball straightaway and to the opposite field.

Despite average speed, Chad tries to steal bases frequently and gets thrown out far too often. He takes a lot of pitches, walks often and plays hard, but doesn't bunt.

Curtis has well above-average hands and range. He was a good fit for the cavernous dimensions of Tiger Stadium, where he patrolled the deepest center field in the majors. This is especially important to Detroit pitchers—especially finesse pitchers—and it wasn't a coincidence that the last time the Tigers were champions they had one of the best center fielders in baseball in Chet Lemon. However, like many centerfielders, Chad has a below-average arm that has just average accuracy.

HOW HE PERFORMED IN '95
Acquired from the Angels for Tony Phillips during the spring, Curtis took over as Detroit's leadoff hitter and center fielder. He enjoyed his best season in '95, posting career highs in several categories and becoming the first Tigers' player since 1987 to hit 20 homers and steal 20 bases.

Once a fine hitter against both lefties and righties, Curtis has sagged significantly against righties of late while improving against portsiders. The 104-point difference in his performance during '95 was the most pronounced of his career.

He and Travis Fryman were the only Tigers to start every game, and Chad's hard-nosed attitude endeared him to his manager and the Detroit fans. After a poor season in '94, Curtis drew far more walks and doubled his homers, but continued to struggle on the basepaths.

WHAT TO EXPECT IN '96
The Phillips-Curtis trade was an excellent deal for the Tigers, even though it was partly motivated by salary concerns. While Tony had a great year in California, Chad is only 27 years old, improving, and should have many years left as a regular. His age and defense make him much more important to the Tigers than the 37-year-old Phillips, for the Tigers are building for the future and are not a contender now.

Overall Statistics

	G	AB	R	H	2B	3B	HR	RBI	SB	CS	BB	SO	BA	OBA
95 DET	144	586	96	157	29	3	21	67	27	15	70	93	.268	.349
Career	549	2063	316	553	93	12	48	222	143	68	228	322	.268	.344

1995 Situational Statistics

	AB	HR	RBI	BA	OBA	SLG		AB	HR	RBI	BA	OBA	SLG
Home	281	11	38	.278	.372	.448	LHP	135	5	16	.348	.419	.556
Road	305	10	29	.259	.327	.423	RHP	451	16	51	.244	.328	.399
Apr-Jun	251	10	38	.283	.358	.462	ScPos	105	0	40	.257	.341	.314
Jul-Oct	335	11	29	.257	.343	.415	Clutch	76	2	3	.276	.364	.434

How He Compares to Other Batters

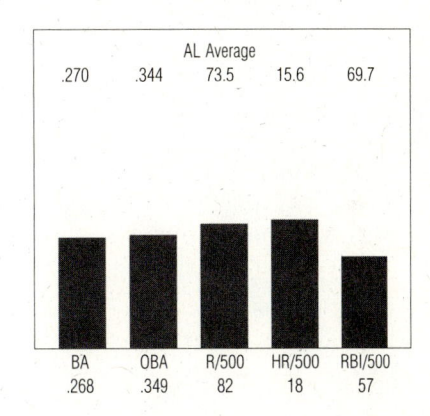

AL Average: .270 / .344 / 73.5 / 15.6 / 69.7

BA	OBA	R/500	HR/500	RBI/500
.268	.349	82	18	57

Where He Hits the Ball

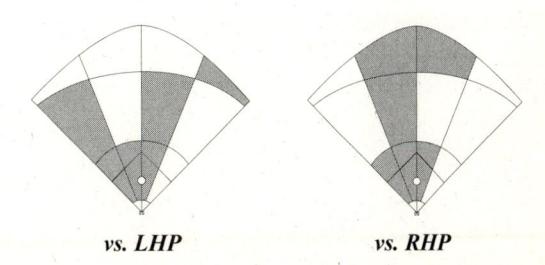

vs. LHP   vs. RHP

DETROIT TIGERS

CECIL FIELDER

Positions: 1B/DH
Bats: R **Throws:** R
Ht: 6'3" **Wt:** 230
Opening Day Age: 32
Born: 9/21/1963
Drafted: KC82 S4/67
ML Seasons: 10

SCOUTING REPORT
Fielder has the best raw power in the big leagues. He is a good, disciplined hitter who likes the ball low and out over the plate where he can extend his strong arms and drive the ball to any and all fields with good power. Defensively, Cecil belies his surname. He has well below-average range at first base, although he does have average hands and an average arm for the position.

As everyone knows who follows baseball knows, Fielder's speed on the basepaths is very poor—as one scout put it, "Fielder doesn't run, he rolls." For those who are counting, he has now played an astounding 1,095 major-league games without a single stolen base. His last successful swipe came back in 1984 at Kinston, a rookie-league affiliate of Toronto.

HOW HE PERFORMED IN '95
Fielder had another typical season in '95. He led the Tigers with 31 home runs and extended his Tigers' record of at least 25 home runs to six straight seasons: no other Tigers' hitter has done it more than four times in a row.

Cecil only hit .231 in Tiger Stadium in '95, a reversal of his usual pattern, although he did hit slightly more than half his homers at the corner of Michigan and Trumbull. Another reversal from previous form was his seriously diminished popularity with fans in Detroit—a very popular player there for years, his strong and outspoken pro-union stance during the strike rankled many in Motown.

WHAT TO EXPECT IN '96
The Tigers would welcome the opportunity to trade Fielder. While he has real value as a power hitter, he won't be around when the team's young talent develops and won't lead them to the top in the meantime. However, with two years remaining on his very hefty contract, there aren't going to be many lookers, never mind many takers.

The Tigers are intent on playing power-hitting prospect Tony Clark next season at first base, meaning that Fielder will have to settle for being the full-time designated hitter. He might be helped if the Tigers could find somebody to hit behind Fielder as pitchers constantly worked around him. The fact remains, though, that he hasn't been a top-flight hitter since his monster 1990–91 seasons.

Overall Statistics

	G	AB	R	H	2B	3B	HR	RBI	SB	CS	BB	SO	BA	OBA
95 DET	136	494	70	120	18	1	31	82	0	1	75	116	.243	.346
Career	1095	3789	570	973	148	6	250	762	0	5	502	979	.257	.345

1995 Situational Statistics

	AB	HR	RBI	BA	OBA	SLG		AB	HR	RBI	BA	OBA	SLG
Home	247	16	46	.231	.354	.445	LHP	102	6	18	.265	.330	.471
Road	247	15	36	.255	.338	.498	RHP	392	25	64	.237	.350	.472
Apr-Jun	214	17	39	.257	.374	.533	ScPos	122	6	43	.221	.377	.385
Jul-Oct	280	14	43	.232	.324	.425	Clutch	68	2	6	.206	.329	.353

How He Compares to Other Batters

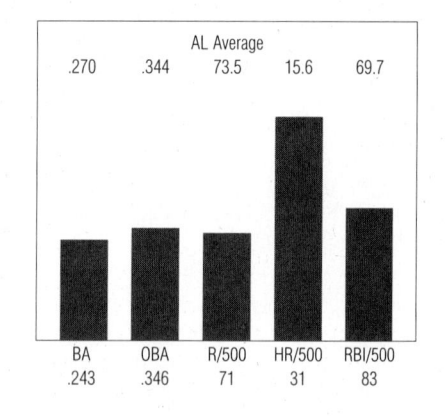

	BA	OBA	R/500	HR/500	RBI/500
AL Average	.270	.344	73.5	15.6	69.7
	.243	.346	71	31	83

Where He Hits the Ball

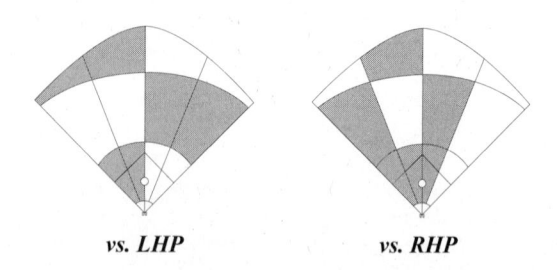

vs. LHP   vs. RHP

DETROIT TIGERS

JOHN FLAHERTY

Position: C
Bats: R **Throws:** R
Ht: 6'1" **Wt:** 195
Opening Day Age: 28
Born: 10/21/1967
Drafted: BOS88 25/641
ML Seasons: 4

SCOUTING REPORT
Flaherty has average power and likes fastballs out over the plate. A career .168 hitter in limited duty in the majors prior to '95, he showed some surprising punch early in the year, especially against righthanded pitching. Like most catchers, Flaherty has minus speed on the basepaths.

Defensively, John has average hands behind the plate with plus range. His arm and accuracy are both rated average. He became a starting catcher in '95 because of his defensive reputation (and the Tigers' drive to reduce their bloated payroll), but he had an abysmal percentage throwing out baserunners in '95.

HOW HE PERFORMED IN '95
John had two completely different seasons rolled into one in '95, which was his first full major-league season. He started off hot, hitting .339 in May and slugging nine homers by the All-Star break. The highlight of '95 for Flaherty was when he banged out six home runs in a nine-game span from June 11-23. However, he slumped terribly in the second half, hitting a meager .164 with one homer after the end of July—about what his career average would lead one to expect from him.

Another big problem was his throwing. Flaherty threw out just 18 of 96 basestealers, well below his minor-league performance. John also made 11 errors, leading both leagues in this negative category. And the Tigers as a team were next to worst in the AL in wild pitches, partly Flaherty's fault and partly due to the number of innings hurled by the many inexperienced members of the Bengals' mound corps.

WHAT TO EXPECT IN '96
The Tigers need to find a new starting catcher for '96. Flaherty is a solid backup but is a clear liability as an everyday player and there are no minor-league catchers ready to bring up from the farm system. At age 28, John could conceivably capitalize on his first extensive taste of big-league action, improving enough to stick around. Nevertheless, it could well be a disaster for the Tigers to bring Flaherty back as their #1 catcher. Unless he can make big adjustments to his batting style, he won't be able to hit a lick and his lack of extensive big-league experience won't be an asset with the Tigers' young starting pitchers.

Overall Statistics

	G	AB	R	H	2B	3B	HR	RBI	SB	CS	BB	SO	BA	OBA
95 DET	112	354	39	86	22	1	11	40	0	0	18	47	.243	.284
Career	194	485	47	108	27	1	11	48	0	1	24	71	.223	.263

1995 Situational Statistics

	AB	HR	RBI	BA	OBA	SLG		AB	HR	RBI	BA	OBA	SLG
Home	171	6	21	.269	.330	.474	LHP	86	0	8	.209	.261	.291
Road	183	5	19	.219	.238	.339	RHP	268	11	32	.254	.291	.440
Apr-Jun	144	8	22	.292	.335	.528	ScPos	74	0	25	.243	.275	.338
Jul-Oct	210	3	18	.210	.248	.319	Clutch	44	2	7	.205	.222	.341

How He Compares to Other Batters

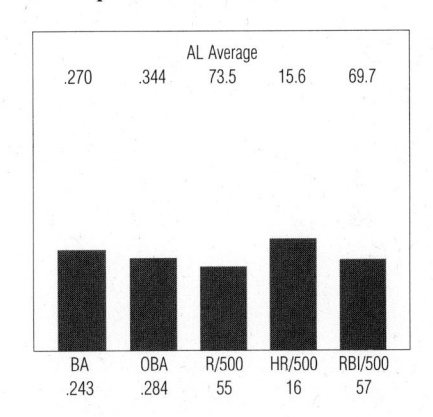

AL Average: .270 .344 73.5 15.6 69.7

BA	OBA	R/500	HR/500	RBI/500
.243	.284	55	16	57

Where He Hits the Ball

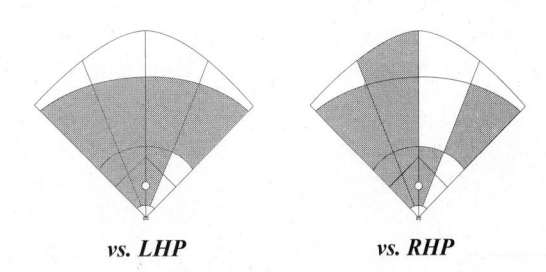

vs. LHP *vs. RHP*

THE SCOUTING REPORT: 1996

DETROIT TIGERS

TRAVIS FRYMAN

Position: 3B
Bats: R **Throws:** R
Ht: 6'1" **Wt:** 180
Opening Day Age: 27
Born: 3/25/1969
Drafted: DET87 3/30
ML Seasons: 6

SCOUTING REPORT
Fryman has plus power and likes to drive fastballs down and out over the plate. He is mostly a pull hitter, showing good bat speed with improved plate discipline, as he cut his strikeouts down dramatically in '95. Like most power hitters, he doesn't bunt.

Defensively, Travis has average range and hands at third base, but his arm is above-average in strength with average accuracy. He has a bit below-average baserunning speed. After stealing 29 bases in his first three full seasons in the majors, he has now swiped only six in the past two years.

HOW HE PERFORMED IN '95
After starting out slowly, Fryman ended up being the Tigers' most consistent player in '95. From July 23 to the end of the season, he committed just three errors, with two coming in one game. After leading the league in 1994 with 128 strikeouts in only 114 games, he cut his whiff total to 100 in '95—the lowest total of all his full seasons in the major leagues. From July 19 to the end of the season, he fanned just 28 times.

Inexplicably, Fryman hit only .211 versus left-handed pitching but .294 against righthanders last year after hitting southpaws better his whole career. Worse yet, the 15 home runs he logged were his lowest total in the majors since his rookie year of 1990 when he hit nine in 66 games after his callup on July 7.

WHAT TO EXPECT IN '96
Fryman is one of the veterans on the Tigers now. The '96 season will be his seventh major-league campaign, yet he will be just 27 years old. The Tigers might be tempted to bat him behind Cecil Fielder in '96 if they can't acquire anyone else to fill that lineup slot.

There was talk when the Tigers acquired Phil Nevin from Houston late in '95 that Nevin would play third base in '96 with Fryman moving back to his old position at shortstop. Fryman nixed that idea by saying he wasn't in favor of it. That might seem selfish, but it's both good for Fryman and for the team that he stay put at third. Moving back to short in mid-career wouldn't be smart, for Travis' role is to hit with power. While his '95 was disappointing offensively, he could easily break loose and have a very big season in '96 or '97.

Overall Statistics

	G	AB	R	H	2B	3B	HR	RBI	SB	CS	BB	SO	BA	OBA
95 DET	144	567	79	156	21	5	15	81	4	2	63	100	.275	.347
Career	785	3086	427	848	170	23	105	477	38	20	287	700	.275	.337

1995 Situational Statistics

	AB	HR	RBI	BA	OBA	SLG		AB	HR	RBI	BA	OBA	SLG
Home	267	9	41	.292	.394	.419	LHP	128	1	16	.211	.275	.281
Road	300	6	40	.260	.302	.400	RHP	439	14	65	.294	.367	.446
Apr-Jun	234	4	28	.252	.341	.333	ScPos	137	4	68	.292	.366	.423
Jul-Oct	333	11	53	.291	.351	.462	Clutch	71	3	14	.268	.369	.423

How He Compares to Other Batters

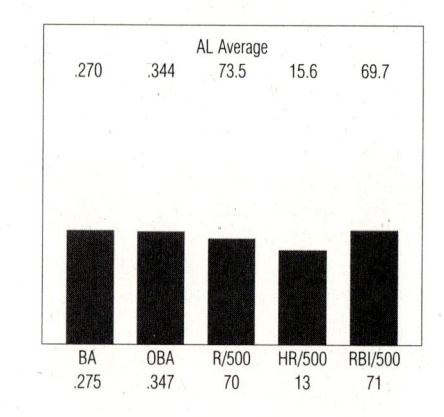

AL Average
.270   .344   73.5   15.6   69.7

BA   OBA   R/500   HR/500   RBI/500
.275 .347   70   13   71

Where He Hits the Ball

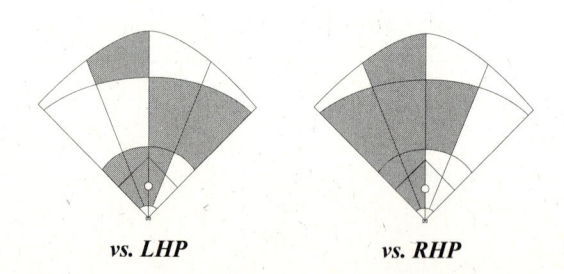

vs. LHP   vs. RHP

DETROIT TIGERS

CHRIS GOMEZ

Positions: SS/2B//DH
Bats: R **Throws:** R
Ht: 6'1" **Wt:** 183
Opening Day Age: 24
Born: 6/16/1971
Drafted: DET92 3/84
ML Seasons: 3

SCOUTING REPORT
Gomez has some power and likes fastballs up and out over the plate. However, he has problems making contact, and his impatience limits the number of good pitches he sees. Gomez sacrifices effectively when asked to do so.

Although Chris is an average-minus runner who doesn't steal often, he has good mobility in the field. He can play both shortstop and second, with plus range, and also has an above-average arm, even from shortstop. While Gomez has only average hands, he is especially strong to his glove side. His accuracy is average.

HOW HE PERFORMED IN '95
The '95 season was both disappointing and impressive for Chris. On the upside, he belted a career high 11 homers and kicked in a few walks and doubles. In addition, he was fairly solid on defense, especially considering that he split time between two positions. On the down side were 15 errors, mediocre mobility, and a drop in most offensive categories. Gomez' batting average plunged 34 points, leading to concurrent drops in on-base percentage and slugging percentage.

Trouble with righthanders is the big flashing red light for Gomez. He has to hit better than .201 in order to avoid platoon duty in the future, as his glove isn't good enough to keep him in the lineup everyday if he doesn't hit. The Tigers are trying to teach him the art of simply making contact and putting the ball in play. A lot of fundamentals need to be stressed: Chris had just 131 games of experience in the minors before coming to Detroit and obviously has plenty left to learn.

WHAT TO EXPECT IN '96
With the possible retirements of Alan Trammell and Lou Whitaker, Gomez could be the everyday shortstop in '96 or he could become the regular second baseman. Detroit acquired former shortstop Mark Lewis from Cincinnati after the season as the player to be named later in David Wells deal, and Lewis could push Gomez to the keystone position if he shows he can handle short defensively. Given the limited competition at second in Detroit, this is the most likely scenario for '96.

While he is never going to be a .300 hitter, Chris has to contribute more offensively than he did in '95 to justify an everyday spot in the lineup.

Overall Statistics

	G	AB	R	H	2B	3B	HR	RBI	SB	CS	BB	SO	BA	OBA
95 DET	123	431	49	96	20	2	11	50	4	1	41	96	.223	.292
Career	253	855	92	204	46	3	19	114	11	6	83	177	.239	.309

1995 Situational Statistics

	AB	HR	RBI	BA	OBA	SLG		AB	HR	RBI	BA	OBA	SLG
Home	221	5	29	.235	.293	.371	LHP	113	3	21	.283	.374	.451
Road	210	6	21	.210	.291	.338	RHP	318	8	29	.201	.261	.321
Apr-Jun	147	6	22	.224	.322	.395	ScPos	110	0	33	.236	.273	.282
Jul-Oct	284	5	28	.222	.276	.335	Clutch	55	0	5	.145	.213	.145

How He Compares to Other Batters

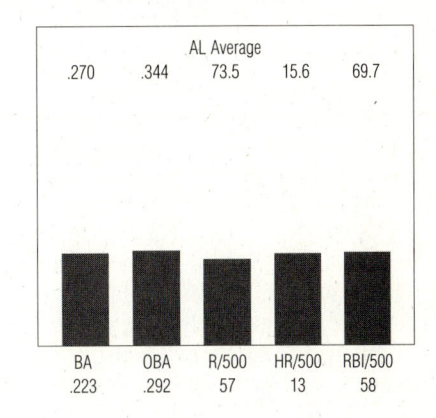

AL Average
.270   .344   73.5   15.6   69.7

BA   OBA   R/500 HR/500 RBI/500
.223 .292   57   13   58

Where He Hits the Ball

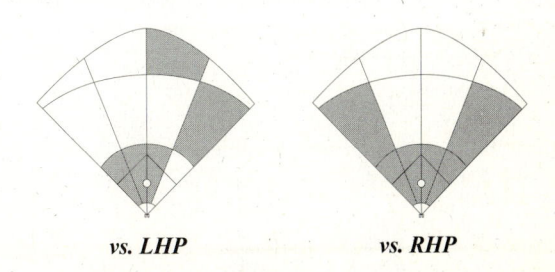

vs. LHP   *vs. RHP*

THE SCOUTING REPORT: 1996

DETROIT TIGERS

BOBBY HIGGINSON

Positions: OF//DH
Bats: L **Throws:** R
Ht: 5'11" **Wt:** 180
Opening Day Age: 25
Born: 8/18/1970
Drafted: DET92 12/336
ML Seasons: 1

SCOUTING REPORT

Higginson is a blue-collar type of ballplayer—an unheralded prospect with average tools in most respects who has worked hard to get where he is. At bat, he has average power and likes low fastballs over the plate, but he needs to work on the big uppercut in his swing. Higginson has just average speed but should steal 10-15 bases per season if he gets on base more often.

The plus tool Bobby possesses is his strong arm, which will keep him playing right field if he can hit enough to stay off the bench. Otherwise, the accuracy of his throws is average as are his range and hands.

HOW HE PERFORMED IN '95

Higginson showed he belongs in the majors in '95—with his glove. However, with his bat, he showed he needs more time in the minors. Higginson led AL outfielders with 13 outfield assists, switching between right field and left field, and also made many fine diving and running catches. He displayed above-average range in left but below par range in right, but will likely improve as he learns to play the hitters better.

At the plate, though, it was different story. Bobby hit ten home runs in the first half of the season but just four in the second half, a common plight for rookies as major-league pitchers start to pitch them differently. Worse yet, his low .224 batting average and very high 107 strikeouts in just 410 at-bats is nowhere near acceptable for a corner outfielder with medium power. Bobby hit 10 of his 14 homers at Tiger Stadium and really struggled against lefties, hitting just .212 with two homers.

WHAT TO EXPECT IN '96

Higginson is just 25 years old and '95 was his first year in the majors. The right field job in Detroit is his to lose in spring training this year but, if he struggles early on, look for him to be platooned with Danny Bautista.

There is reason to believe he can improve: he hit 23 home runs in 137 games in '94 at Triple-A Toledo and has the kind of attitude that should allow him to learn from his rookie experience. The Tigers might consider batting him fifth behind Fielder in '96, but only if he improves his average and cuts down on the whiffs. Bet that he will.

Overall Statistics

	G	AB	R	H	2B	3B	HR	RBI	SB	CS	BB	SO	BA	OBA
95 DET	131	410	61	92	17	5	14	43	6	4	62	107	.224	.329
Career	131	410	61	92	17	5	14	43	6	4	62	107	.224	.329

1995 Situational Statistics

	AB	HR	RBI	BA	OBA	SLG		AB	HR	RBI	BA	OBA	SLG
Home	206	10	24	.214	.318	.432	LHP	66	2	5	.212	.307	.333
Road	204	4	19	.235	.339	.353	RHP	344	12	38	.227	.333	.404
Apr-Jun	178	9	24	.253	.355	.472	ScPos	88	2	28	.205	.358	.295
Jul-Oct	232	5	19	.203	.308	.332	Clutch	60	1	3	.233	.352	.383

How He Compares to Other Batters

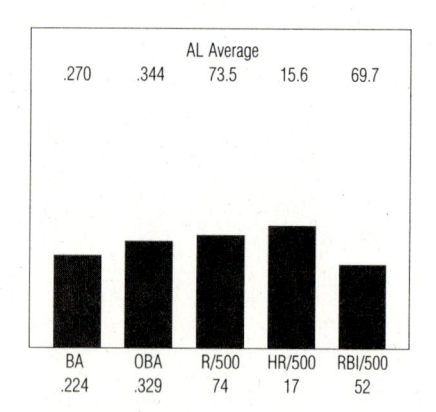

AL Average: .270 .344 73.5 15.6 69.7

BA .224 | OBA .329 | R/500 74 | HR/500 17 | RBI/500 52

Where He Hits the Ball

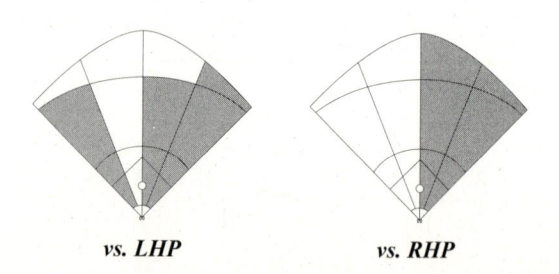

vs. LHP   vs. RHP

DETROIT TIGERS

JOSE LIMA

Position: SP
Bats: R **Throws:** R
Ht: 6'2" **Wt:** 170
Opening Day Age: 23
Born: 9/30/1972
Drafted: DET 7/5/89
ML Seasons: 2

SCOUTING REPORT

Dominican righthander Lima delivers the ball with a three-quarter motion. He has good sinking action on his fastball with somewhat above-par velocity; he also throws an average slider. Lima's best current offering is a plus circle change-up which he throws with deceptive arm action, leading batters to hack early at what they think is a fastball. He will also show a splitter.

Only four runners tried to steal on him last season, all successfully. He is a decent fielder who is very good at cutting off the running game for a young, inexperienced hurler: only four runners tried to steal off him in 74 innings in '95.

HOW HE PERFORMED IN '95

After beginning the season at Toledo and making a brief stop back in Class A, Lima was recalled on July 13 with an 8-4 record. He was thrown right into the fire, starting for a team desperate for any live pitching bodies with potential, and he had some success and quite a lot of failure in his trial by fire. Even though his final numbers were hideous, Jose improved significantly late in the season, allowing just seven earned runs in his last five starts, covering 28 innings.

Lima did have a solid two-to-one strikeout-to-walk ratio. At times, he displayed a bit of hot dog when he would pump his fist after registering a strikeout. This tactic especially rubbed Phil Garner and the Brewers the wrong way.

WHAT TO EXPECT IN '96

The talented but still-developing Lima, just 23, will be a part of the Tigers' starting rotation in the coming years. Detroit fans are hoping that the final five starts of '95 are an indication of what's in store for them the future.

However, Lima is clearly still learning. He never posted a winning record in his minor-league career, going a combined 24-45. On the positive side is the fact that Lima has never had a professional season in which his strikeout to walk ratio was worse than two-to-one. As he matures, he should add a couple of MPH to his fastball and learn to set up hitters better. This should translate into much increased success—he's very young and has lots of potential.

Overall Statistics

	G	GS	GF	SV	W	L	ERA	IP	H	R	ER	HR	BB	SO
95 DET	15	15	0	0	3	9	6.11	73.2	85	52	50	10	18	37
Career	18	16	1	0	3	10	6.72	80.1	96	62	60	12	21	44

1995 Situational Statistics

	W	L	ERA	SV	IP	BB	SO		AB	HR	RBI	BA	OBA	SLG
Home	1	5	5.45	0	38.0	5	23	LHB	177	6	23	.305	.344	.452
Road	2	4	6.81	0	35.2	13	14	RHB	118	4	16	.263	.326	.466
Apr-Jun	0	0	0.00	0	0.0	0	0	ScPos	63	4	31	.365	.431	.619
Jul-Oct	3	9	6.11	0	73.2	18	37	Clutch	6	0	1	.500	.571	.833

How He Compares to Other Pitchers

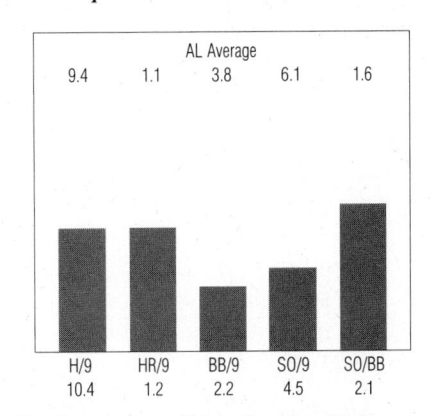

AL Average: 9.4 / 1.1 / 3.8 / 6.1 / 1.6

H/9 10.4 | HR/9 1.2 | BB/9 2.2 | SO/9 4.5 | SO/BB 2.1

How He Compares to Other Starting Pitchers

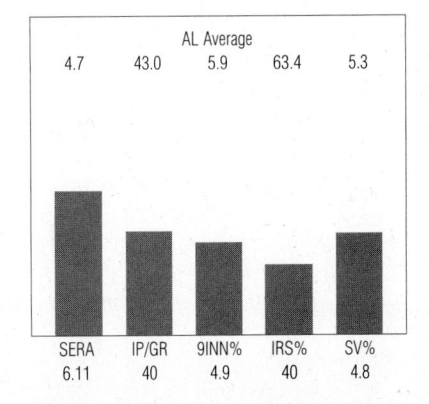

AL Average: 4.7 / 43.0 / 5.9 / 63.4 / 5.3

SERA 6.11 | IP/GR 40 | 9INN% 4.9 | IRS% 40 | SV% 4.8

THE SCOUTING REPORT: 1996

DETROIT TIGERS

FELIPE LIRA

Position: SP/RP
Bats: R **Throws:** R
Ht: 6'0" **Wt:** 170
Opening Day Age: 23
Born: 4/26/1972
Drafted: DET 3/7/90
ML Seasons: 1

SCOUTING REPORT

Lira is a 24-year-old pitcher who pitches with the moxie of a veteran. A slightly-built righthander, he delivers his pitches from three-quarters and gives them different looks to compensate for his lack of very hard stuff. He will pitch inside, which enhances his effectiveness; he hit eight batters in '95, fifth most in the league. His most effective pitch was his splitfinger fastball, which he used regardless of the count.

Even though his fastball is slightly below-average in velocity, it does have good movement and sink; Lira will turn it over at times to give it screwball action. He does have two plus pitches: a slider and a splitter. Overall, his control is average as is his fielding, but he is above-average at holding runners on: more than half of the 13 runners who tried to steal on him in '95 were nailed, even though Detroit's starting catcher had a miserable season throwing out runners otherwise. Shutting off the running game is important to pitchers like Lira who don't strike out lots of batters.

HOW HE PERFORMED IN '95

Felipe spent his entire rookie season with the Tigers, pitching both as a starter and middle reliever. He made eight relief appearances before getting his first start on May 27. The highlight of '95 was his June 21st start, in which he shut out the Rangers on six hits through 8.1 innings in his longest outing of the season. The Tigers won the game, 1-0.

Over the season, he fared much better at hitter-friendly Tiger Stadium than on the road, which could be a fluke or could represent the start of a long-term pattern. Many veteran pitchers have thrived in Tigertown in recent years—if they can keep power hitters from pulling the ball. With the slow grass field and the huge center field, Tiger Stadium hurts most types of hitters—except for pull hitters who find it to be homer-heaven.

WHAT TO EXPECT IN '96

Sparky Anderson was of the opinion that Lira was better off pitching out of the bullpen. However, since Sparky is no longer managing the Tigers, Lira will almost certainly pitch from the rotation unless he gets hammered. Lira is not ever going to dominate hitters in the majors, but he has the attitude and the skills to be effective once he gains the requisite experience.

Overall Statistics

	G	GS	GF	SV	W	L	ERA	IP	H	R	ER	HR	BB	SO
95 DET	37	22	7	1	9	13	4.31	146.1	151	74	70	17	56	89
Career	37	22	7	1	9	13	4.31	146.1	151	74	70	17	56	89

1995 Situational Statistics

	W	L	ERA	SV	IP	BB	SO		AB	HR	RBI	BA	OBA	SLG
Home	6	5	3.66	0	78.2	26	45	LHB	334	8	36	.263	.337	.404
Road	3	8	5.05	1	67.2	30	44	RHB	224	9	33	.281	.346	.487
Apr-Jun	4	4	3.10	0	58.0	21	40	ScPos	123	4	48	.220	.318	.358
Jul-Oct	5	9	5.09	1	88.1	35	49	Clutch	54	3	11	.370	.407	.648

How He Compares to Other Pitchers

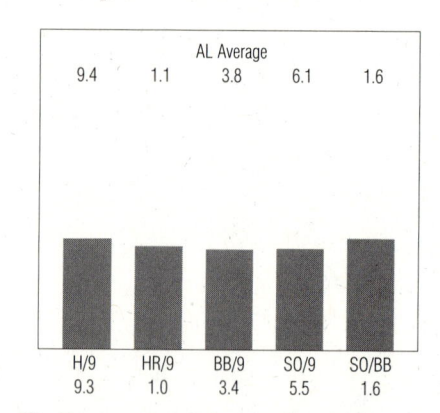

AL Average: 9.4 | 1.1 | 3.8 | 6.1 | 1.6

H/9	HR/9	BB/9	SO/9	SO/BB
9.3	1.0	3.4	5.5	1.6

How He Compares to Other Starting Pitchers

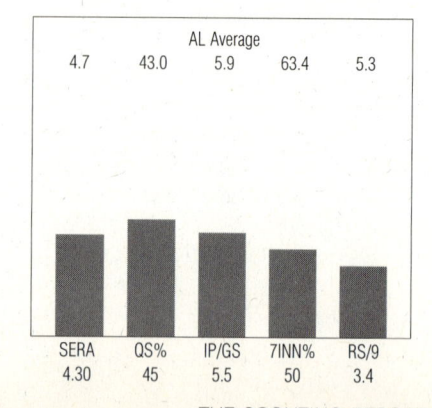

AL Average: 4.7 | 43.0 | 5.9 | 63.4 | 5.3

SERA	QS%	IP/GS	7INN%	RS/9
4.30	45	5.5	50	3.4

DETROIT TIGERS

ALAN TRAMMELL

Positions: SS//DH
Bats: R **Throws:** R
Ht: 6'0" **Wt:** 175
Opening Day Age: 38
Born: 2/21/1958
Drafted: DET76 2/26
ML Seasons: 19

SCOUTING REPORT

Trammell is a good contact hitter who still has some pop left in his bat at 37. However, he hits with far less power than in his glory days due to a slowing bat. An aggressive, dead-fastball hitter, Alan does not bunt.

Trammell still has good, soft hands, average range, and average arm accuracy at shortstop. His arm strength, however, has long been below-average. Good positioning and a quick release have allowed Alan to compensate for this weakness over the years. Trammell has just average speed on the basepaths and runs intelligently, if not often.

HOW HE PERFORMED IN '95

Alan completed his 19th major-league season, all played with the Tigers, in '95. He and second baseman Lou Whitaker set an AL record of 1,918 appearances in the lineup together last year and, of course, also hold the record for the longest-running keystone combination in major-league history.

Regrettably, what might have been their farewell campaign was played in front of sparse crowds at Tiger Stadium watching a miserable team, and the season-long Sparky Anderson psychodrama overshadowed the very appealing story of Tram and Lou potentially playing their last games in Motown.

On the field, Trammell had his share of frustrations, playing in just 74 games. Other than 1977 (his debut season) and 1992 (when he missed virtually the entire season with a fractured ankle), Trammell has never played as little as he did in '95. Alan's second and last home run of the year tied him for 12th on the all-time Tigers' homer list with Hall of Famer Charlie Gehringer.

WHAT TO EXPECT IN '96

As of mid-November, Trammell had not decided whether to return for a 20th season in '96. Those close to the Tigers and Trammell felt he would retire rather than endure another season of sitting on the bench, and he had already made it clear that he would not play with another team. Alan would like to stay in the organization as a coach after his playing days, and some feel he will be the Tigers' manager within five years. Right now, though, he can still play well enough to help the Tigers.

Overall Statistics

	G	AB	R	H	2B	3B	HR	RBI	SB	CS	BB	SO	BA	OBA
95 DET	74	223	28	60	12	0	2	23	3	1	27	19	.269	.345
Career	2227	8095	1215	2320	410	55	184	987	230	109	840	847	.287	.353

1995 Situational Statistics

	AB	HR	RBI	BA	OBA	SLG		AB	HR	RBI	BA	OBA	SLG
Home	121	1	15	.281	.348	.347	LHP	90	1	11	.311	.386	.433
Road	102	1	8	.255	.342	.353	RHP	133	1	12	.241	.318	.293
Apr-Jun	116	2	13	.302	.400	.422	ScPos	50	1	22	.340	.407	.480
Jul-Oct	107	0	10	.234	.282	.271	Clutch	46	1	9	.239	.333	.370

How He Compares to Other Batters

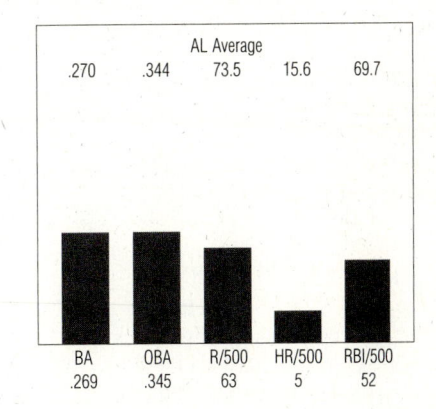

AL Average: .270 | .344 | 73.5 | 15.6 | 69.7

BA .269 | OBA .345 | R/500 63 | HR/500 5 | RBI/500 52

Where He Hits the Ball

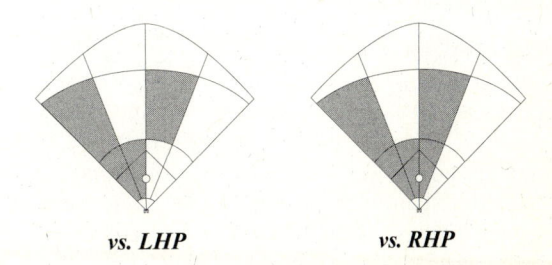

vs. LHP   vs. RHP

THE SCOUTING REPORT: 1996

DETROIT TIGERS

LOU WHITAKER

Positions: 2B//DH
Bats: L **Throws:** R
Ht: 5'11" **Wt:** 160
Opening Day Age: 38
Born: 5/12/1957
Drafted: DET75 5/99
ML Seasons: 19

SCOUTING REPORT

Despite his build, Whitaker has the swing of a left-handed slugger, loving to pull and lift fastballs down and in. He has excellent plate discipline and patiently waits for pitches he can drive.

Lou is still a solid second baseman with slightly above-average hands and a now-average arm, showing average range in '95 in limited usage. He baserunning speed has declined to average, but he was never a basestealer even when he was faster.

HOW HE PERFORMED IN '95

Like partner Alan Trammell, Lou Whitaker completed his 19th big-league season in '95—all in Detroit. He was platooned with Chris Gomez, Scott Fletcher, and Steve Rodriguez; only 26 of his at-bats were against lefthanders. This was only the first full season the durable Whitaker played in less than 100 games in his long career (he played in 92 games in the strike-shortened 1994 season and 11 games when called up in September, 1977).

Only Hall of Famers Al Kaline and Ty Cobb have played more games for the Tigers than Whitaker's 2,390, and Whitaker and Hall of Famer Joe Morgan are the only second basemen in history with 2,000 games, 2,000 hits and 200 home runs. Lou is also fifth on the Tigers' career home run list with 243.

WHAT TO EXPECT IN '96

Whitaker has quite possibly played his last game. In spring training he stated that 1995 would definitely be his last year; as the season progressed, however, he backed off, saying he would decide during the off-season about returning. With continuing back problems hampering him in the field, he wanted to play mostly at DH if he returned, but that scenario is blocked by Cecil Fielder and the acquisition of Phil Plantier.

Even though the Tigers are committing to younger players, they might make room for Whitaker because they have no sure-fire prospects at second base. Off-season acquisition Mark Lewis will probably push Chris Gomez to second base full-time. However, it's far from certain that Lewis can hold down the shortstop job everyday and, if Gomez hits like he did last year, he won't become a fixture at second base. The success or failure of these moves won't be known before the season starts, though. If the Tigers bring him back, it will be as an insurance policy—and because he's a damn good ballplayer who can still pound righthanded pitching.

Overall Statistics

	G	AB	R	H	2B	3B	HR	RBI	SB	CS	BB	SO	BA	OBA
95 DET	84	249	36	73	14	0	14	44	4	0	31	41	.293	.372
Career	2390	8570	1386	2369	420	65	244	1084	143	75	1197	1099	.276	.363

1995 Situational Statistics

	AB	HR	RBI	BA	OBA	SLG		AB	HR	RBI	BA	OBA	SLG
Home	123	11	26	.276	.377	.585	LHP	26	1	5	.308	.357	.538
Road	126	3	18	.310	.367	.452	RHP	223	13	39	.291	.374	.516
Apr-Jun	119	5	18	.319	.390	.521	ScPos	61	5	33	.295	.370	.590
Jul-Oct	130	9	26	.269	.356	.515	Clutch	54	3	14	.222	.276	.444

How He Compares to Other Batters

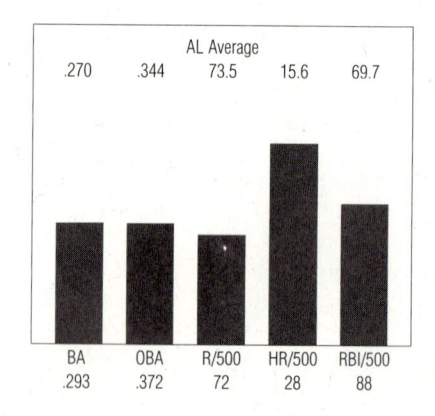

	BA	OBA	R/500	HR/500	RBI/500
AL Average	.270	.344	73.5	15.6	69.7
	.293	.372	72	28	88

Where He Hits the Ball

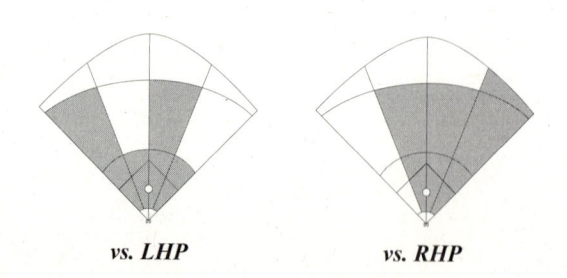

vs. LHP   vs. RHP

DETROIT TIGERS

JOE BOEVER

Position: RP
Bats: R **Throws:** R
Ht: 6'1" **Wt:** 200
Opening Day Age: 35
Born: 10/4/1960
Drafted: SL 6/25/82
ML Seasons: 11

Overall Statistics

	G	GS	GF	SV	W	L	ERA	IP	H	R	ER	HR	BB	SO
95 DET	60	0	27	3	5	7	6.39	98.2	128	74	70	17	44	71
Career	503	0	248	47	34	43	3.90	739.1	734	351	320	73	337	535

1995 Situational Statistics

	W	L	ERA	SV	IP	BB	SO		AB	HR	RBI	BA	OBA	SLG
Home	3	4	6.28	2	53.0	22	39	LHB	221	10	52	.299	.368	.489
Road	2	3	6.50	1	45.2	22	32	RHB	180	7	36	.344	.404	.561
Apr-Jun	4	3	4.17	3	45.1	13	35	ScPos	130	9	78	.354	.442	.638
Jul-Oct	1	4	8.27	0	53.1	31	36	Clutch	135	2	14	.267	.355	.400

SCOUTING REPORT
Boever uses an overhand delivery to throw his main pitch, a plus palmball. His fastball has just average movement and his slider is thrown just for show. Boever's control and fielding are just average but he is reasonably good at holding runners on: Eight of 11 basestealers made it safely with Joe on the hill in '95.

HOW HE PERFORMED IN '95
For the second consecutive season, Boever led the Tigers in appearances. For Tigers' fans, that was unfortunate. Boever was horrid in '95, getting lit up virtually every time out in the second half of the season. His ERA of 6.39 was the highest of Boever's career for a full season. The high points of the season came between June 11–24 when he picked up all three of his saves in a span of five appearances. However well or poorly he's pitching, Joe always takes the ball.

WHAT TO EXPECT IN '96
Boever signed a two year deal in April of '95 which means the Tigers will bring him back for '96. His role will continue as long reliever/setup pitcher. At 35, he may be finished, but a comeback to his decent pre-1995 performance is certainly possible.

BRIAN BOHANON

Position: RP/SP
Bats: L **Throws:** L
Ht: 6'2" **Wt:** 210
Opening Day Age: 27
Born: 8/1/1968
Drafted: TEX87 1/19
ML Seasons: 6

Overall Statistics

	G	GS	GF	SV	W	L	ERA	IP	H	R	ER	HR	BB	SO
95 DET	52	10	7	1	1	1	5.54	105.2	121	68	65	10	41	63
Career	139	47	16	1	12	14	5.59	376.2	442	256	234	42	161	212

1995 Situational Statistics

	W	L	ERA	SV	IP	BB	SO		AB	HR	RBI	BA	OBA	SLG
Home	1	0	6.60	0	43.2	21	30	LHB	128	3	16	.250	.310	.359
Road	0	1	4.79	1	62.0	20	33	RHB	296	7	51	.301	.367	.480
Apr-Jun	0	1	5.82	0	43.1	23	22	ScPos	137	3	57	.277	.338	.445
Jul-Oct	1	0	5.34	1	62.1	18	41	Clutch	53	0	10	.340	.390	.472

SCOUTING REPORT
Bohanon throws from three-quarters; his fastball is average-minus and his slider is minus. No part of Bohanon's game is overpowering, since he has just average control and is average at holding runners and fielding his position. Six of eight trying to steal against Brian last year were successful.

HOW HE PERFORMED IN '95
Bohanon spent the entire '95 season with the Tigers, splitting his time between the bullpen and starting rotation. His main function out of the bullpen was to come in late innings and get one or two key lefthanded batters out.

For the most part, he was ineffective. Even though lefties only hit .250, most of those hits came in critical situations. He and Joe Boever came to be known as the "Killer B's" to Detroit fans and media for obvious reasons. Brian's only good month was September, when he notched a 2.89 ERA and pitched in 15 games.

WHAT TO EXPECT IN '96
Brian will not be back with Detroit in '96 and may land in Triple-A. He was not offered arbitration by the Tigers, who were looking for another inexpensive veteran lefty to do what was Bohanon's job.

DETROIT TIGERS

MIKE CHRISTOPHER

Position: RP
Bats: R **Throws:** R
Ht: 6'5" **Wt:** 205
Opening Day Age: 32
Born: 11/3/1963
Drafted: NYA85 7/181
ML Seasons: 4

Overall Statistics

	G	GS	GF	SV	W	L	ERA	IP	H	R	ER	HR	BB	SO
95 DET	36	0	11	1	4	0	3.82	61.1	71	28	26	8	14	34
Career	58	0	20	1	4	0	3.51	95.0	104	42	37	13	29	57

1995 Situational Statistics

	W	L	ERA	SV	IP	BB	SO		AB	HR	RBI	BA	OBA	SLG
Home	2	0	4.00	0	27.0	7	16	LHB	120	7	20	.325	.364	.583
Road	2	0	3.67	1	34.1	7	18	RHB	123	1	9	.260	.303	.358
Apr-Jun	0	0	0.00	0	0.0	0	0	ScPos	78	3	23	.256	.294	.462
Jul-Oct	4	0	3.82	1	61.1	14	34	Clutch	92	3	7	.217	.291	.359

SCOUTING REPORT

Christopher uses a three-quarters pitching motion and has average control. His fastball is well below-average in velocity with average movement. His most effective pitch is a plus splitfinger, but he also has an average slider. Mike is below average at holding runners on and fielding his position.

HOW HE PERFORMED IN '95

Christopher was probably the most consistent Tigers' reliever after his purchase from Toledo on July 3. He won back-to-back games in his first two appearances versus Seattle on July 4-5. He was not a big favorite of the Tigers' players, especially Cecil Fielder (who was very active in the union during the strike and who was very outspoken), because of his replacement player status in the spring. Eventually, he was accepted by his teammates as the season went along.

WHAT TO EXPECT IN '96

After ten years bouncing around the minors with only 22 major-league games under his belt prior to '95, Christopher has become a definite part of the Tigers' bullpen for '96. He either will be the prime righthanded setup pitcher and perhaps even get a chance to close games if no other veteran is signed.

MILT CUYLER

Positions: OF//DH
Bats: B **Throws:** R
Ht: 5'10" **Wt:** 175
Opening Day Age: 27
Born: 10/7/1968
Drafted: DET86 2/46
ML Seasons: 6

Overall Statistics

	G	AB	R	H	2B	3B	HR	RBI	SB	CS	BB	SO	BA	OBA
95 DET	41	88	15	18	1	4	0	5	2	1	8	16	.205	.271
Career	433	1270	205	304	44	21	7	104	70	23	107	254	.239	.304

1995 Situational Statistics

	AB	HR	RBI	BA	OBA	SLG		AB	HR	RBI	BA	OBA	SLG
Home	42	0	4	.286	.348	.381	LHP	30	0	0	.167	.194	.200
Road	46	0	1	.130	.200	.239	RHP	58	0	5	.224	.308	.362
Apr-Jun	7	0	0	.000	.000	.000	ScPos	21	0	4	.190	.227	.381
Jul-Oct	81	0	5	.222	.292	.333	Clutch	15	0	0	.200	.250	.200

SCOUTING REPORT

Milt has serious problems at the plate, including a slow bat, no power, and trouble making contact. However, he will bunt effectively, take the occasional walk, and has above-average speed and basestealing ability.

In the pasture, Milt now has adequate range, good instincts, and decent hands, but he does not throw accurately. Injuries have taken some of his mobility, but he can still play all three outfield spots.

HOW HE PERFORMED IN '95

Cuyler was sent to Toledo in early May and didn't come back to Detroit until August 14. He split time in left field with Phil Nevin and was hot for two weeks, but hit progressively worse as August went on and batted only six times in the last month. Formerly a center fielder, Cuyler played there just once in '95, making 22 starts in left.

WHAT TO EXPECT IN '96

He is never going to be a starter in the majors, and a weak bat will keep Phil struggling on somebody's bench. The Red Sox might give him another chance in '96, but he could just as easily spend his summer in Pawtucket.

DETROIT TIGERS

JOHN DOHERTY

Position: RP
Bats: R **Throws:** R
Ht: 6'4" **Wt:** 200
Opening Day Age: 28
Born: 6/11/1967
Drafted: DET89 19/499
ML Seasons: 4

Overall Statistics

	G	GS	GF	SV	W	L	ERA	IP	H	R	ER	HR	BB	SO
95 DET	48	2	18	6	5	9	5.10	113.0	130	66	64	10	37	46
Career	145	61	29	9	32	31	4.86	515.0	605	306	278	46	136	174

1995 Situational Statistics

	W	L	ERA	SV	IP	BB	SO		AB	HR	RBI	BA	OBA	SLG
Home	2	3	4.48	3	64.1	19	22	LHB	235	7	30	.323	.388	.494
Road	3	6	5.92	3	48.2	18	24	RHB	216	3	30	.250	.305	.333
Apr-Jun	3	3	5.86	0	50.2	22	20	ScPos	117	1	48	.325	.434	.427
Jul-Oct	2	6	4.48	6	62.1	15	26	Clutch	132	6	14	.273	.333	.447

SCOUTING REPORT
Doherty uses an overhand delivery. While his fastball is average in velocity, it does have above-average movement and is a heavy sinker. His slider is slightly below par and he has poor command of his change-up. Above-average at holding runners (only ten ran on him in '95, eight successfully), he is an average fielder. He needs to use his breaking ball and change-up more often to be successful in the majors.

HOW HE PERFORMED IN '95
After two starts and two losses in the rotation, John was moved to the bullpen and eventually made 46 relief appearances. Before coming to the Tigers in '92, he had only made one start in the minors in 116 appearances, but 40 of his 50 appearances were starts in 1993–94. He looked more comfortable in relief, and Detroit tried him as the closer after Mike Henneman was traded. He finished by converting six of seven save situations.

WHAT TO EXPECT IN '96
Because he only throws two pitches, John's effectiveness as a starter is limited. He doesn't appear to have the personality to handle the closer's role, though, and thus is destined to middle relief in the majors.

SCOTT FLETCHER

Positions: 2B//SS/1B/DH
Bats: R **Throws:** R
Ht: 5'11" **Wt:** 173
Opening Day Age: 37
Born: 7/30/1958
Drafted: CHN79 S1/6
ML Seasons: 15

Overall Statistics

	G	AB	R	H	2B	3B	HR	RBI	SB	CS	BB	SO	BA	OBA
95 DET	67	182	19	42	10	1	1	17	1	0	19	27	.231	.312
Career	1612	5258	688	1376	243	38	34	510	99	58	514	541	.262	.332

1995 Situational Statistics

	AB	HR	RBI	BA	OBA	SLG		AB	HR	RBI	BA	OBA	SLG
Home	79	1	5	.253	.359	.329	LHP	56	1	5	.161	.226	.268
Road	103	0	12	.214	.274	.301	RHP	126	0	12	.262	.350	.333
Apr-Jun	60	0	3	.217	.304	.283	ScPos	47	1	15	.255	.333	.383
Jul-Oct	122	1	14	.238	.316	.328	Clutch	19	0	2	.158	.238	.211

SCOUTING REPORT
The diminutive veteran is a good contact hitter with a knack for bat control. Fletcher has no power but is scrappy and will take the walk. He is a good bunter.

Scott has average range, hands, throwing strength and accuracy at second base. His critical defensive tool is an ability to make the pivot on the double play. He has just average speed and rarely steals bases anymore, but does so effectively.

HOW HE PERFORMED IN '95
Fletcher was a valuable backup-up for the Tigers in '95, appearing in 67 games, primarily at second base. He did not commit an error and is now is second in career fielding percentage at second base (minimum 500 games).

Scott also received an occasional start against a left-handed pitcher. In a string of eight games in September, he knocked in six runs. However, he's just not enough of an offensive player to see any more than spot duty.

WHAT TO EXPECT IN '96
Fletcher was not offered arbitration by the Tigers, so he became a free agent. Detroit might try to re-sign him at a low cost, as he performs his limited role well. If not Motown, he'll play in some other town.

DETROIT TIGERS

BRIAN MAXCY

Position: RP
Bats: R **Throws:** R
Ht: 6'1" **Wt:** 170
Opening Day Age: 24
Born: 5/4/1971
Drafted: DET92 20/560
ML Seasons: 1

Overall Statistics

	G	GS	GF	SV	W	L	ERA	IP	H	R	ER	HR	BB	SO
95 DET	41	0	14	0	4	5	6.88	52.1	61	48	40	6	31	20
Career	41	0	14	0	4	5	6.88	52.1	61	48	40	6	31	20

1995 Situational Statistics

	W	L	ERA	SV	IP	BB	SO		AB	HR	RBI	BA	OBA	SLG
Home	3	1	7.24	0	27.1	13	10	LHB	101	4	23	.297	.398	.475
Road	1	4	6.48	0	25.0	18	10	RHB	107	2	19	.290	.373	.402
Apr-Jun	4	1	3.86	0	14.0	11	5	ScPos	74	0	33	.270	.380	.365
Jul-Oct	0	4	7.98	0	38.1	20	15	Clutch	42	3	15	.452	.554	.738

SCOUTING REPORT

Maxcy has good movement on a fastball that is slightly below-average in velocity, delivered from three-quarters. Brian also throws a slider and forkball, both of which are just average. He is average defensively off the mound, but once runners reach base, he is very good at keeping them from running: only four tried in 52 innings, three successfully.

HOW HE PERFORMED IN '95

Brian had two different seasons in '95. He was called up May 26, running his record to 4-1 by June 25 before running into problems. A month later, he was sent back to Toledo, then recalled again on August 10. His ERA reached the outer limits at 7.71 in September, although he eventually shaved it to a not-so-svelte 6.88.

The biggest problem Maxcy had was control. During his three seasons in the minors, he had more than twice as many strikeouts as walks, but his ratio in the majors was terrible.

WHAT TO EXPECT IN '96

Maxcy could return in middle relief in '96. He is young, '95 was his first in the bigs, and the Tigers aren't exactly stocked with pitching. There's lots of room for improvement, and he could improve with experience.

C. J. NITKOWSKI

Position: SP
Bats: L **Throws:** L
Ht: 6'2" **Wt:** 185
Opening Day Age: 23
Born: 3/9/1973
Drafted: CIN94 1/9
ML Seasons: 1

Overall Statistics

	G	GS	GF	SV	W	L	ERA	IP	H	R	ER	HR	BB	SO
95 CIN/DET	20	18	0	0	2	7	6.66	71.2	94	57	53	11	35	31
Career	20	18	0	0	2	7	6.66	71.2	94	57	53	11	35	31

1995 Situational Statistics

	W	L	ERA	SV	IP	BB	SO		AB	HR	RBI	BA	OBA	SLG
Home	0	5	8.56	0	27.1	13	10	LHB	57	0	9	.263	.290	.333
Road	2	2	5.48	0	44.1	22	21	RHB	235	11	47	.336	.423	.583
Apr-Jun	1	1	2.74	0	23.0	7	14	ScPos	83	3	46	.361	.457	.627
Jul-Oct	1	6	8.51	0	48.2	28	17	Clutch	3	0	0	.000	.250	.000

SCOUTING REPORT

Using a high leg kick and a three-quarter delivery, C.J. brings home an average fastball that tails into lefthanders. That, and a below-average curve and change-up, set up his out pitch, a plus knuckle-curve. However, Nitkowski won't win unless he has good location. He does have a good feel for pitching and is willing to throw inside.

An average fielder and average at holding runners, C.J. allowed 13 to steal in 19 tries.

HOW HE PERFORMED IN '95

The Reds' 1994 #1 pick began the year in the minors. Called up in June, he was 1-1 with a 2.74 ERA in six starts. However, he was then hammered in three July games before a return to the bushes and, then, a trade to the Tigers on July 31. In Detroit, C.J. struggled with his command and was hit hard. He was 1-4 in 11 starts for Detroit with a 7.09 ERA; AL righthanded hitters batted .346 against him.

WHAT TO EXPECT IN '96

Nitkowski needs time and innings. Luckily, the rebuilding Tigers have both to spare. He's a good prospect who should improve with experience.

DETROIT TIGERS

FRANKLIN STUBBS

Positions: 1B/OF//DH
Bats: L **Throws:** L
Ht: 6'2" **Wt:** 215
Opening Day Age: 35
Born: 10/21/1960
Drafted: LA82 1/19
ML Seasons: 10

Overall Statistics

	G	AB	R	H	2B	3B	HR	RBI	SB	CS	BB	SO	BA	OBA
95 DET	62	116	13	29	11	0	2	19	0	1	19	27	.250	.358
Career	945	2591	323	602	109	12	104	348	74	28	260	626	.232	.303

1995 Situational Statistics

	AB	HR	RBI	BA	OBA	SLG		AB	HR	RBI	BA	OBA	SLG
Home	50	1	7	.180	.333	.280	LHP	16	0	2	.250	.368	.313
Road	66	1	12	.303	.378	.485	RHP	100	2	17	.250	.356	.410
Apr-Jun	79	0	7	.215	.340	.291	ScPos	34	0	15	.324	.455	.500
Jul-Oct	37	2	12	.324	.395	.622	Clutch	27	0	8	.296	.429	.407

SCOUTING REPORT
Franklin generates most of his power off of pitchers' mistakes, especially looking for mediocre fastballs low and inside which he can pull. He is a liability in the outfield since he possesses a poor arm and poor range to go along with below-average hands. He has poor baserunning speed—which puts him just one notch ahead of Cecil Fielder.

HOW HE PERFORMED IN '95
Journeyman Stubbs was back in the majors in '95 for the first time since 1992. He split time between left field, first base, and pinch-hitting. He hit his first home run of the year in the second game of the July 16 doubleheader against California, then promptly dislocated his right shoulder trying to make a diving catch in left field the next inning. After a month on the disabled list, he spent the last month of the season strictly as a pinch-hitter.

WHAT TO EXPECT IN '96
It is hard to imagine the Tigers bringing back the 35-year-old Stubbs in the midst of their youth movement. A younger player could easily fill Stubbs' role and Sparky Anderson, well-known for his unpredictable spring roster selections, is no longer the Tigers' manager.

RON TINGLEY

Positions: C//1B
Bats: R **Throws:** R
Ht: 6'2" **Wt:** 180
Opening Day Age: 36
Born: 5/27/1959
Drafted: SD77 10/242
ML Seasons: 9

Overall Statistics

	G	AB	R	H	2B	3B	HR	RBI	SB	CS	BB	SO	BA	OBA
95 DET	54	124	14	28	8	1	4	18	0	1	15	38	.226	.307
Career	278	563	52	110	27	3	10	55	2	5	54	165	.195	.270

1995 Situational Statistics

	AB	HR	RBI	BA	OBA	SLG		AB	HR	RBI	BA	OBA	SLG
Home	56	3	12	.214	.333	.464	LHP	33	2	5	.333	.410	.576
Road	68	1	6	.235	.284	.353	RHP	91	2	13	.187	.267	.341
Apr-Jun	56	0	3	.179	.270	.232	ScPos	33	1	10	.212	.325	.364
Jul-Oct	68	4	15	.265	.338	.544	Clutch	25	1	5	.200	.231	.320

SCOUTING REPORT
Tingley has minus power as a hitter, preferring fastballs up and out over the plate. He has a plus arm behind the plate, as evidenced by his good percentage at throwing out runners attempting to steal: he threw out 13 of 37 would-be base stealers for the Tigers in '95. His mobility and accuracy defensively are average but, like most catchers, Tingley has well below-average speed.

HOW HE PERFORMED IN '95
Tingley had a solid season in '95 as a backup catcher despite entering the season with a woeful .187 career major-league batting average (224 games, 439 at-bats, 6 home runs). Fully 13 of his 28 hits went for extra bases, with all four of his home runs coming in the second half of the season. Tingley even connected for his first big-league grand slam on September 3 against Cleveland off ace closer Jose Mesa.

WHAT TO EXPECT IN '96
Tingley was not offered arbitration by Detroit after the season, so he became a free agent. He was a bargain for the Tigers considering what he contributed in '95, and he might do the same for another team in '96 if given the chance.

DETROIT TIGERS: TOP PROSPECTS

TONY CLARK
Bats: S Throws: R Opening Day Age: 24
Ht: 6-8 Wt: 240 Born: 6/15/1972
Position: 1B Drafted: 1990 #1 DET

YR TEAM	LG/CLASS	G	AB	R	H	2B	3B	HR	RBI	SB	BA	OBA
93 Lakeland	FSL/A	36	117	14	31	4	1	1	22	0	.265	.358
94 Trenton	EAST/AA	107	394	50	110	25	0	21	86	0	.279	.346
94 Toledo	INT/AAA	25	92	10	24	4	0	2	13	2	.261	.340
95 Toledo	INT/AAA	110	405	50	98	17	2	14	63	0	.242	.330
Detroit	AL/MAJ	27	101	10	24	5	1	3	11	0	.238	.294

After a breakthrough season in 1994, Clark stumbled at Triple-A last year, but nonetheless played nearly every day in September for the Tigers. Known for his awesome power from both sides of the plate, the 6-foot-8 Clark hit only four homers over the final two months, had problems with breaking balls and inside fastballs, and never got his batting average over .250 all season. Defensively, Clark is no threat for a Gold Glove, last year committing 13 errors in 62 games, but he did show some improvement around the bag.

MIKE DRUMRIGHT
Bats: L Throws: R Opening Day Age: 22
Ht: 6-4 Wt: 210 Born: 4/19/1974
Position: P Drafted: 1995 # DET

YR TEAM	LG/CLASS	G	GS	GF	SV	W	L	ERA	IP	H	HR	BB	SO	O/BA
95 Jacksonville	SOU/AA	5	5	0	0	0	1	3.69	31	30	4	15	34	.250
Lakeland	FSL/A	5	5	0	0	1	1	4.29	21	19	2	9	19	.247

Because of the lack of pitching in the organization, the 1995 first-round pick will be given every chance to move quickly. Drumright has good size, throws hard and has a very good slow curve. The Wichita State product averaged over a strikeout per inning in his debut season and held his own at the Double-A level.

JUAN ENCARNACION
Bats: R Throws: R Opening Day Age: 20
Ht: 6-2 Wt: 160 Born: 3/8/1976
Position: OF Drafted: NDFA 12-27-92 DET

YR TEAM	LG/CLASS	G	AB	R	H	2B	3B	HR	RBI	SB	BA	OBA
94 Fayetteville	SAL/A	24	83	6	16	1	1	1	4	1	.193	.272
94 Bristol	APPY/R	54	197	16	49	7	1	4	31	9	.249	.310
94 Lakeland	FSL/A	3	6	1	2	0	0	0	0	0	.333	.429
95 Fayetteville	SAL/A	124	457	62	129	31	7	16	72	5	.282	.336

The best prospect on a good Fayetteville club, Encarnacion has a quick bat which should produce more power once his young, thin frame fills out and he learns how to hit a breaking ball. The Dominican can run a little, is a pretty good outfielder and has a solid arm.

CADE GASPAR
Bats: R Throws: R Opening Day Age: 23
Ht: 6-3 Wt: 175 Born: 8/21/1973
Position: P Drafted: 1994 #1 DET

YR TEAM	LG/CLASS	G	GS	GF	SV	W	L	ERA	IP	H	HR	BB	SO	O/BA
94 Lakeland	FSL/A	8	8	0	0	1	3	5.58	30	28	6	8	25	.248
95 Lakeland	FSL/A	23	23	0	0	7	6	3.90	99	95	5	44	97	.260

The club's first pick in the 1994 draft was brought along slowly last season, pitching past the seventh inning just once all season. Gaspar, the son of former big leaguer Rod Gaspar, missed three starts with a strained elbow. The Pepperdine product is not overpowering, but has three solid pitches and averaged nearly a strikeout per inning for Lakeland.

PHIL NEVIN
Bats: R Throws: R Opening Day Age: 25
Ht: 6-2 Wt: 185 Born: 1/19/1971
Position: 3B-LF Drafted: 1992 #1 HOU

YR TEAM	LG/CLASS	G	AB	R	H	2B	3B	HR	RBI	SB	BA	OBA
93 Tucson	PCL/AAA	123	448	67	128	21	3	10	93	8	.286	.359
94 Tucson	PCL/AAA	118	445	67	117	20	1	12	79	3	.263	.343
95 Toledo	INT/AAA	7	23	3	7	2	0	1	3	0	.304	.333
Tucson	PCL/AAA	62	223	31	65	16	0	7	41	2	.291	.371
Detroit	AL/MAJ	29	96	9	21	3	1	2	12	0	.219	.318
Houston	NL/MAJ	18	60	4	7	1	0	0	1	1	.117	.221

In his days with the Houston organization, Nevin, the first player selected in the 1992 draft, was known more for his emotional outbursts than for his power-hitting outbursts, and power is one reason he was drafted. The Cal State-Fullerton product hit .276, but slugged just 29 homers in three seasons at Tucson and was 7-for-60 in a brief stint with the Astros. Although he has made progress at third base, Nevin still has problems there and may be moved to left field permanently. He spent much of September in the pasture.

STEVE RODRIGUEZ
Bats: R Throws: R Opening Day Age: 25
Ht: 5-9 Wt: 170 Born: 11/29/1970
Position: 2B Drafted: 1992 #4 BOS

YR TEAM	LG/CLASS	G	AB	R	H	2B	3B	HR	RBI	SB	BA	OBA
93 Lynchburg	CARO/A	120	493	78	135	26	3	3	42	20	.274	.320
94 New Britain	EAST/AA	38	159	25	45	5	2	0	14	8	.283	.324
94 Pawtucket	INT/AAA	62	233	28	70	11	0	1	21	11	.300	.340
95 Pawtucket	INT/AAA	82	324	39	78	16	3	1	24	12	.241	.301
Boston	AL/MAJ	6	8	1	1	0	0	0	0	0	.125	.222
Detroit	AL/MAJ	12	31	4	6	1	0	0	0	1	.194	.306

The 24-year-old Pepperdine product will be given a chance to compete for the second base position this season because of his solid glove, decent speed and bulldog mentality. A .265 hitter with 55 stolen bases in four seasons with the Sox, Rodriguez has little power and rarely walks, two factors that will weigh against him.

DETROIT TIGERS: TOP PROSPECTS

CAM SMITH
Bats: R Throws: R Opening Day Age: 23
Ht: 6-3 Wt: 190 Born: 9/20/1973
Position: P Drafted: 1993 #3 DET

YR TEAM	LG/CLASS	G	GS	GF	SV	W	L	ERA	IP	H	HR	BB	SO	O/BA
93 Bristol	APPY/R	9	7	0	0	3	1	3.58	37.2	25	5	22	33	.187
93 Niagara Fls	NYP/A	2	2	0	0	0	0	18.00	5.0	12	0	6	0	.522
94 Fayettevlle	SAL/A	26	26	0	0	5	13	6.06	133.2	133	10	86	128	.264
95 Fayetteville	SAL/A	29	29	0	0	13	8	3.81	149	110	6	87	166	.203

Smith, probably the hardest thrower in the organization and perhaps the most inconsistent, put everything together in his last two starts in '95, tossing 16 scoreless innings, including a two-hit, 13-strikeout performance in the season finale. The 21-year-old led the Tiger system in wins and strikeouts, but also led the South Atlantic League in walks. Although he held hitters to a .203 average and was overpowering in several starts, Smith failed to reach the fifth inning ten times.

CLINT SODOWSKY
Bats: L Throws: R Opening Day Age: 24
Ht: 6-3 Wt: 180 Born: 7/13/1972
Position: P Drafted: 1991 #11 DET

YR TEAM	LG/CLASS	G	GS	GF	SV	W	L	ERA	IP	H	HR	BB	SO	O/BA
93 Fayettevlle	SAL/A	27	27	0	0	14	10	5.09	155.2	177	11	51	80	.290
94 Lakeland	FSL/A	19	18	1	0	6	3	3.83	110.1	111	5	34	73	.263
95 Toledo	INT/AAA	9	9	0	0	5	1	2.85	60	47	5	30	32	.222
Jacksonville	SOU/AA	19	19	0	0	5	5	2.55	123	102	4	50	77	.233
Detroit	AL/MAJ	6	6	0	0	2	2	5.01	23	24	4	18	14	.289

The biggest surprise in the organization, Sodowsky returned in 1995 from his second knee operation, regained some velocity on his fastball, and used an outstanding changeup to make it to the major leagues by season end. He tossed three shutouts in the Southern League and finished second in ERA. The 23-year-old still needs better command, but throws close to 90 mph and succeeds by working the lower half of the plate effectively.

TODD STEVERSON
Bats: R Throws: R Opening Day Age: 24
Ht: 6-2 Wt: 185 Born: 11/15/1971
Position: OF Drafted: 1992 #2 TOR

YR TEAM	LG/CLASS	G	AB	R	H	2B	3B	HR	RBI	SB	BA	OBA
93 Dunedin	FSL/A	106	413	68	112	32	4	11	54	15	.271	.342
94 Knoxville	SOU/AA	124	415	59	109	24	5	9	38	20	.263	.371
95 Toledo	INT/AAA	9	28	6	3	0	0	1	0	.107	.242
Detroit	AL/MAJ	30	42	11	11	0	0	2	6	2	.262	.340

Steverson was chosen from Toronto in the Rule V draft a year ago after three seasons, 26 homers, 303 strikeouts, and a .254 average. The Arizona State product has the potential to be a 20–20 player at the major league level and is selective at the plate, but needs to make more consistent contact.

JUSTIN THOMPSON
Bats: L Throws: L Opening Day Age: 23
Ht: 6-3 Wt: 175 Born: 3/8/1973
Position: P Drafted: 1991 #1 DET

YR TEAM	LG/CLASS	G	GS	GF	SV	W	L	ERA	IP	H	HR	BB	SO	O/BA
93 Lakeland	FSL/A	11	11	0	0	4	4	3.56	55.2	65	1	16	46	.294
93 London	EAST/AA	14	14	0	0	3	6	4.09	83.2	96	9	37	72	.288
95 Jacksonville	SOU/AA	18	18	0	0	6	7	3.73	123	110	7	38	98	.242
Lakeland	FSL/A	6	6	0	0	2	1	4.88	24	30	1	8	20	.319

Thompson, the most coveted pitcher in the organization, sat out the 1994 season with a recurring elbow injury, then surrendered nine hits and runs in his first inning for Lakeland in '95. The 22-year-old settled down quickly, regained his arm strength, and was eventually promoted to Double-A in late May. After a few rough outings at Jacksonville, the lanky lefthander pitched very well the last two months of the season. Thompson features a 90+ mph fastball and a hard slider that were particularly effective on lefthanded hitters, who hit just .128 against him last year.

BUBBA TRAMMELL
Bats: R Throws: R Opening Day Age: 24
Ht: 6-2 Wt: 205 Born: 11/6/1971
Position: LF Drafted: 1994 #11 DET

YR TEAM	LG/CLASS	G	AB	R	H	2B	3B	HR	RBI	SB	BA	OBA
94 Jamestown	NYP/A	65	235	37	70	18	6	5	41	9	.298	.365
95 Lakeland	FSL/A	122	454	61	129	32	3	16	72	13	.284	.355

Trammell, no relation to Alan, tied for third in the Florida State League in homers and doubles and was second in extra-base hits. A year earlier, the University of Tennessee product finished second in the New York–Penn League in doubles and extra-base hits. A hard worker, Trammell is adequate in the field. He made five errors last season, but had the rare distinction of committing three of them in one inning alone.

DARYLE WARD
Bats: L Throws: L Opening Day Age: 21
Ht: 6-2 Wt: 230 Born: 6/27/1975
Position: 1B Drafted: 1994 #15 DET

YR TEAM	LG/CLASS	G	AB	R	H	2B	3B	HR	RBI	SB	BA	OBA
94 Bristol	APPY/R	48	161	17	43	6	0	5	30	4	.267	.343
95 Fayetteville	SAL/A	137	524	75	149	32	0	14	106	1	.284	.344

Ward, the son of former major leaguer Gary Ward, has a great swing and hitting knowledge beyond his years. Ward, who packs 240 pounds into a 6-foot-2 frame, led the organization in RBI and ranked second in the South Atlantic League. Despite playing in a park that greatly favored pitchers, Ward was on his way to a .300 average before slumping badly the last month of the season.

THE SCOUTING REPORT: 1996

DETROIT TIGERS: OTHERS TO WATCH

RICHARD ALMANZAR Bats: R Throws: R Ht: 5-10 Wt: 155
Born: 4/3/1976 Drafted: NDFA 1-24-93 DET Position: 2B

YR TEAM	LG/CLASS	G	AB	R	H	2B	3B	HR	RBI	SB	BA	OBA
95 Lakeland	FSL/A	42	140	29	43	9	0	1	14	11	.307	.401
95 Fayetteville	SAL/A	80	308	47	76	12	1	0	16	39	.247	.326

Led the organization in steals in '95, displayed good range, and batted over .300 the second half of the season.

GLEN BARKER Bats: R Throws: R Ht: 5-10 Wt: 180
Born: 5/10/1971 Drafted: 1993 #11 DET Position: CF

YR TEAM	LG/CLASS	G	AB	R	H	2B	3B	HR	RBI	SB	BA	OBA
95 Jacksonville	SOU/AA	133	507	74	121	26	4	10	49	39	.239	.296

A good fastball and decent breaking pitch dominated left-handers for the second straight season.

MATT BAUER Bats: L Throws: L Ht: 6-1 Wt: 195
Born: 3/25/1970 Drafted: 1991 #26 DET Position: P

YR TEAM	LG/CLASS	G	GS	GF	SV	W	L	ERA	IP	H	HR	BB	SO	O/BA
95 Toledo	INT/AAA	13	0	4	0	2	1	3.46	13.0	17	0	4	10	.321
95 Jacksonville	SOU/AA	27	0	7	0	1	1	4.12	43.2	43	8	22	30	.257

He can run and play center field, but refuses to make adjustments with the bat.

IVAN CRUZ Bats: L Throws: L Ht: 6-3 Wt: 210
Born: 5/3/1968 Drafted: 1989 #28 DET Position: 1B

YR TEAM	LG/CLASS	G	AB	R	H	2B	3B	HR	RBI	SB	BA	OBA
95 Toledo	INT/AAA	11	36	5	7	2	0	0	3	0	.194	.302
95 Jacksonville	SOU/AA	108	397	65	112	17	1	31	93	0	.282	.374

The Southern League's home run and RBI leader has not been able to handle Triple-A in any of the last three years.

ERIC DANAPILIS Bats: R Throws: R Ht: 6-2 Wt: 220
Born: 6/11/1971 Drafted: 1993 #27 DET Position: OF

YR TEAM	LG/CLASS	G	AB	R	H	2B	3B	HR	RBI	SB	BA	OBA
95 Jacksonville	SOU/AA	129	415	47	107	24	1	10	63	3	.258	.363

The former Notre Dame star has some pop, but his defense is shaky.

MIKE DARR Bats: L Throws: R Ht: 6-3 Wt: 205
Born: 3/21/1976 Drafted: 1994 #2 DET Position: OF

YR TEAM	LG/CLASS	G	AB	R	H	2B	3B	HR	RBI	SB	BA	OBA
95 Fayetteville	SAL/A	112	395	58	114	21	2	5	66	5	.289	.380

A very good all-around player with power and a strong arm.

RICK GREENE Bats: R Throws: R Ht: 6-5 Wt: 200
Born: 1/2/1971 Drafted: 1992 #1 DET Position: P

YR TEAM	LG/CLASS	G	GS	GF	SV	W	L	ERA	IP	H	HR	BB	SO	O/BA
95 Jacksonville	SOU/AA	32	0	6	0	6	2	3.49	38.2	45	3	15	29	.285

When he's on, the former first-rounder has a wicked slider, but he's very inconsistent.

JUSTIN MASHORE Bats: R Throws: R Ht: 5-9 Wt: 190
Born: 2/14/1972 Drafted: 1991 #5 DET Position: CF

YR TEAM	LG/CLASS	G	AB	R	H	2B	3B	HR	RBI	SB	BA	OBA
95 Toledo	INT/AAA	72	223	32	49	4	3	4	21	12	.220	.273
95 Jacksonville	SOU/AA	40	148	26	36	8	2	4	15	5	.243	.287

A major league-caliber center fielder, Mashore hasn't learned how to hit.

TREVER MILLER Bats: R Throws: L Ht: 6-3 Wt: 175
Born: 5/29/1973 Drafted: 1991 #2 DET Position: P

YR TEAM	LG/CLASS	G	GS	GF	SV	W	L	ERA	IP	H	HR	BB	SO	O/BA
95 Jacksonville	SOU/AA	31	16	4	0	8	2	2.72	122.1	122	5	34	77	.261

The crafty lefty has good stuff and a mature attitude.

MIKE MYERS Bats: L Throws: L Ht: 6-3 Wt: 197
Born: 6/26/1969 Drafted: 1990 #7 SF Position: P

YR TEAM	LG/CLASS	G	GS	GF	SV	W	L	ERA	IP	H	HR	BB	SO	O/BA
95 Charlotte	INT/AAA	37	0	12	0	0	5	5.65	36.2	41	6	15	24	.283
95 Toledo	INT/AAA	6	0	2	0	0	0	4.32	8.1	6	1	3	8	.194
95 Detroit	AL/MAJ	11	0	3	0	1	0	9.95	6.1	10	1	4	4	.345
95 Florida	NL/MAJ	2	0	2	0	0	0	0.00	2.0	1	0	3	0	.143

Myers, an original Marlins expansion draftee, throws hard and has a good arm but has been plagued by injuries.

RUDY PEMBERTON Bats: R Throws: R Ht: 6-1 Wt: 185
Born: 12/17/1969 Drafted: NDFA 6-7-87 DET Position: OF

YR TEAM	LG/CLASS	G	AB	R	H	2B	3B	HR	RBI	SB	BA	OBA
95 Detroit	AL/MAJ	12	30	3	9	3	1	0	3	0	.300	.344
95 Toledo	INT/AAA	67	224	31	77	15	3	7	23	8	.344	.393

Built powerfully, Pemberton is a solid hitter who uses the whole field and plays a decent outfield.

SHANNON PENN Bats: S Throws: R Ht: 5-10 Wt: 163
Born: 9/11/1969 Drafted: 1988 #58 TEX Position: 2B

YR TEAM	LG/CLASS	G	AB	R	H	2B	3B	HR	RBI	SB	BA	OBA
95 Toledo	INT/AAA	63	218	41	54	4	1	1	15	15	.248	.328
95 Detroit	AL/MAJ	3	9	0	3	0	0	0	0	0	.333	.400

Penn, a switch-hitter with speed was limited by a severe ankle sprain but got a trial with Detroit.

BRANDON REED Bats: R Throws: R Ht: 6-4 Wt: 185
Born: 12/18/1974 Drafted: 1993 #45 DET Position: P

YR TEAM	LG/CLASS	G	GS	GF	SV	W	L	ERA	IP	H	HR	BB	SO	O/BA
95 Fayetteville	SAL/A	55	0	53	41	3	0	0.97	64.2	40	1	18	78	.174

The minors' save leader is young and has a projectable body, but is not overpowering.

DAVE TUTTLE Bats: R Throws: R Ht: 6-3 Wt: 190
Born: 9/29/1969 Drafted: 1991 #6 CIN Position: P

YR TEAM	LG/CLASS	G	GS	GF	SV	W	L	ERA	IP	H	HR	BB	SO	O/BA
95 Chattanooga	SOU/AA	8	7	1	0	1	6	7.01	34.2	40	6	21	20	.286
95 Lakeland	FSL/A	6	4	1	0	1	4	2.90	31.0	31	1	12	28	.270
95 Win-Salem	CARO/A	10	10	0	0	3	3	3.18	62.1	49	5	19	54	.219

Tuttle, a live arm acquired from Reds in the David Wells deal, struggled in Double-A and may end up closing.

DERRICK WHITE Bats: R Throws: R Ht: 6-1 Wt: 215
Born: 10/12/1969 Drafted: 1991 #7 MON Position: OF-1B

YR TEAM	LG/CLASS	G	AB	R	H	2B	3B	HR	RBI	SB	BA	OBA
95 Detroit	AL/MAJ	39	48	3	9	2	0	0	2	1	.188	.188
95 Toledo	INT/AAA	87	309	50	82	15	3	14	49	6	.265	.332

A solid minor-league hitter with some pop, White's best position is first base.

KANSAS CITY ROYALS

KEVIN APPIER

Position: SP
Bats: R **Throws:** R
Ht: 6'2" **Wt:** 180
Opening Day Age: 28
Born: 12/6/1967
Drafted: KC87 1/9
ML Seasons: 7

SCOUTING REPORT

Appier, a hard thrower, relies primarily upon an above-average fastball and an average-plus slider. The first time through a batting order, Kevin throws mostly fastballs and likes to work in on the hitters' hands. Later in the game he mixes in his slider and a soft, average split-finger pitch of which he doesn't always have good command.

A high, exaggerated three-quarters delivery helps Appier generate good velocity, but this also causes him to fall off the mound towards the first base line. This tendency leaves him out of position to field grounders. Moreover (and most seriously), the delivery puts a large strain on his shoulder. Appier's poor footwork makes him seem clumsy covering first base. His move to first is just average, and nine of 13 basestealing attempts were successful in 1995.

HOW HE PERFORMED IN '95

Nearing the All-Star break, Kevin sat atop the list of AL pitchers with a 2.04 ERA and an 11-2 record. His early-season success came after he adopted a tighter windup which improved his control, and he made a slight adjustment to his grip on breaking balls, which provided sharper movement as well.

However, shoulder tendinitis forced him onto the disabled list after five subpar starts and Appier missed three weeks before returning to the rotation in mid-August. Kevin wasn't the same pitcher and finished the year on a 4-8 skid with an inflated 5.78 ERA. The 1995 season marked the second straight year in which in-season shoulder problems diminished his effectiveness.

WHAT TO EXPECT IN '96

Appier, the Royals' staff anchor, has been one of the American League's best starting pitchers for the last five years. His hard stuff and tenacity are the hallmarks of an ace. He's one of the most competitive players in the game: Kevin becomes intensely focused before each start and remains that way until the last out is recorded, even if he's no longer in the game.

Appier, now in his prime, will be a Cy Young candidate if he can avoid the shoulder difficulties that have sandbagged him each of the last two years. Regrettably, these kinds of injuries can recur all too frequently.

Overall Statistics

	G	GS	GF	SV	W	L	ERA	IP	H	R	ER	HR	BB	SO
95 KC	31	31	0	0	15	10	3.89	201.1	163	90	87	14	80	185
Career	190	178	2	0	81	54	3.22	1218.1	1068	477	436	72	419	961

1995 Situational Statistics

	W	L	ERA	SV	IP	BB	SO		AB	HR	RBI	BA	OBA	SLG
Home	7	6	4.38	0	109.0	44	84	LHB	430	11	53	.251	.335	.419
Road	8	4	3.31	0	92.1	36	101	RHB	308	3	26	.179	.256	.256
Apr-Jun	11	3	2.30	0	109.2	36	105	ScPos	156	3	59	.282	.343	.423
Jul-Oct	4	7	5.79	0	91.2	44	80	Clutch	46	2	10	.304	.418	.522

How He Compares to Other Pitchers

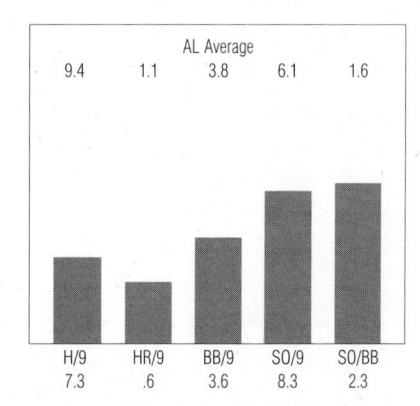

AL Average: H/9 9.4, HR/9 1.1, BB/9 3.8, SO/9 6.1, SO/BB 1.6
Appier: H/9 7.3, HR/9 .6, BB/9 3.6, SO/9 8.3, SO/BB 2.3

How He Compares to Other Starting Pitchers

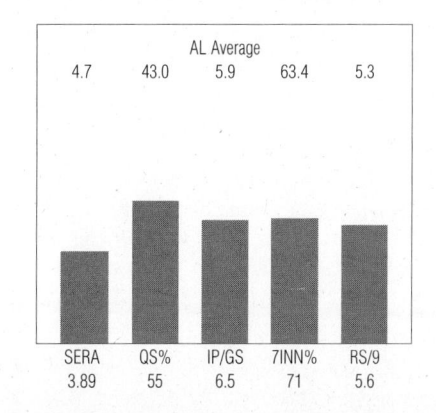

AL Average: SERA 4.7, QS% 43.0, IP/GS 5.9, 7INN% 63.4, RS/9 5.3
Appier: SERA 3.89, QS% 55, IP/GS 6.5, 7INN% 71, RS/9 5.6

THE SCOUTING REPORT: 1996

KANSAS CITY ROYALS

JOHNNY DAMON

Position: OF
Bats: L **Throws:** L
Ht: 6'0" **Wt:** 175
Opening Day Age: 20
Born: 11/5/1975
Drafted: KC92 2/35
ML Seasons: 1

SCOUTING REPORT
A superb young hitter in nearly every respect, Damon likes low fastballs. His quick reflexes allow him to adjust somewhat to breaking pitches, which he does well for a 21-year-old. Reaching the major leagues quickly didn't overwhelm Damon, who refused to be intimidated by hard throwers or lefties who pitched him inside. He is currently a slap hitter, and had mixed success bunting. Better power is expected later in his development.

Johnny has well above-average speed and can run wild on the basepaths. He played it safe when first summoned to Kansas City, then turned on the afterburners later, stealing successfully in all seven attempts. Damon's speed and plus range allow him to cover a lot of outfield territory, but a poor arm will limit him to left or center field.

HOW HE PERFORMED IN '95
With Kauffman Stadium rocking to the beat of "Johnny B. Goode" on the public address system, rookie Johnny Damon did his own kind of rocking—rocking opposition pitching, that is.

In his first season above Class A, Johnny was more than just "good," ripping Double-A pitching at a .343 clip and slugging .534 to earn a mid-August promotion to Kansas City. He maintained a torrid pace while in the majors, hitting .300 for a month before slowing as the season closed. Damon finished the year with more hits than any other professional player, combining for 198 with Wichita and Kansas City.

WHAT TO EXPECT IN '96
Damon's arrival in Kansas City is seen as a precursor to an influx of young talent from the Royals' farm system. How good or deep that well is remains to be seen, but one thing is for certain: Johnny is viewed by the organization and by many baseball professionals as the best and brightest of that talent.

He'll be the Royals leadoff hitter for 1996 before eventually moving to the third spot in the order as his power develops. At age 22, Damon is a quiet, unassuming young man brimming with talent. Watching his career unfold will be the most exciting thing about baseball in Kansas City over the next few years. He will be good, and he's got a chance to be great. You can't say that about many young players.

Overall Statistics

	G	AB	R	H	2B	3B	HR	RBI	SB	CS	BB	SO	BA	OBA
95 KC	47	188	32	53	11	5	3	23	7	0	12	22	.282	.324
Career	47	188	32	53	11	5	3	23	7	0	12	22	.282	.324

1995 Situational Statistics

	AB	HR	RBI	BA	OBA	SLG		AB	HR	RBI	BA	OBA	SLG
Home	100	1	12	.290	.330	.450	LHP	39	0	4	.231	.268	.308
Road	88	2	11	.273	.316	.432	RHP	149	3	19	.295	.337	.477
Apr-Jun	0	0	0	.000	.000	.000	ScPos	41	0	19	.293	.319	.439
Jul-Oct	188	3	23	.282	.324	.441	Clutch	26	1	2	.231	.310	.346

How He Compares to Other Batters

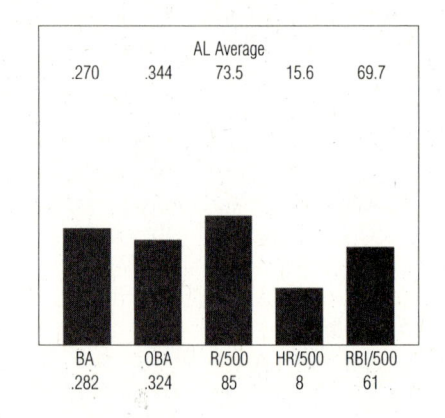

AL Average
.270   .344   73.5   15.6   69.7

BA .282 | OBA .324 | R/500 85 | HR/500 8 | RBI/500 61

Where He Hits the Ball

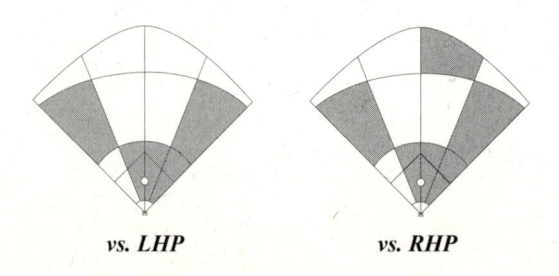

vs. LHP   vs. RHP

140 THE SCOUTING REPORT: 1996

KANSAS CITY ROYALS

GARY GAETTI

Positions: 3B/1B//DH
Bats: R **Throws:** R
Ht: 6'0" **Wt:** 184
Opening Day Age: 37
Born: 8/19/1958
Drafted: MIN79 S1/11
ML Seasons: 15

SCOUTING REPORT

Gaetti, an excellent fastball hitter, likes the ball high and inside. Hitting out of a crouch, he uses a slight uppercut in his swing to generate great power. Gaetti remains an aggressive, dead-pull hitter who rarely walks. He can be overmatched by good off-speed stuff, especially if pitchers avoid his power zone by working down and away. Later in the year Gary was counteracting this stratagem by taking outside pitches to the opposite field.

A four-time Gold Glove winner, Gaetti still flashes quick reflexes, average-plus range, and a strong, highly accurate arm. He is a very slow runner, but rarely takes risks on the basepaths. Like most power hitters, Gary is rarely asked to bunt.

HOW HE PERFORMED IN '95

In 1995, only Gaetti stood between the Royals and offensive oblivion: without his team-leading performance, they might have set new records for scoring ineptitude.

In his second full year in Kansas City, Gaetti accounted for an amazing 29% of the team's league-worst 119 homers for the year, serving as his club's only credible power threat. As it was, he still couldn't prevent Kansas City's offense from finishing dead last in runs in the American League. While setting several personal bests, Gaetti relaxed and enjoyed what could be considered his most valuable season ever.

WHAT TO EXPECT IN '96

Gaetti's career year assured him of a high salary offer as he tested the free agent waters after the season, even at the advanced age of 37. While the Royals hope that Joe Randa or Chris Stynes will be their third baseman of the future, Gaetti is clearly the team's offense of the present. He's made a remarkable comeback from his personal Death Valley in California in the early 1990s, which culminated with his outright release by the Angels in June of 1993.

The Royals' pursuit of Gaetti—or lack thereof—says a great deal about the team's penury and lack of clear vision. While Gary is unlikely to repeat his phenomenal 1995 season, he is likely to continue to produce consistent power this year while displaying a fine glove at the hot corner—wherever he plays.

Overall Statistics

	G	AB	R	H	2B	3B	HR	RBI	SB	CS	BB	SO	BA	OBA
95 KC	137	514	76	134	27	0	35	96	3	3	47	91	.261	.329
Career	1972	7203	914	1832	349	32	292	1075	86	58	499	1301	.254	.306

1995 Situational Statistics

	AB	HR	RBI	BA	OBA	SLG		AB	HR	RBI	BA	OBA	SLG
Home	257	16	43	.272	.336	.514	LHP	132	9	23	.212	.316	.432
Road	257	19	53	.249	.322	.521	RHP	382	26	73	.277	.333	.547
Apr-Jun	208	16	45	.264	.330	.538	ScPos	153	11	62	.242	.318	.503
Jul-Oct	306	19	51	.258	.328	.503	Clutch	91	11	20	.275	.333	.659

How He Compares to Other Batters

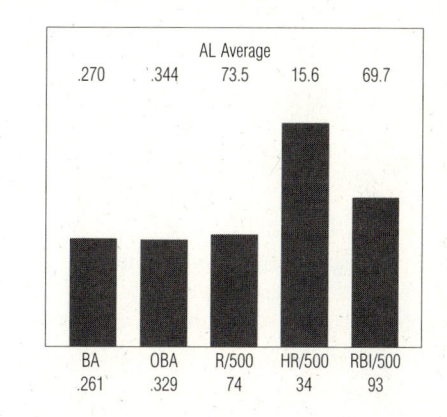

AL Average: .270 | .344 | 73.5 | 15.6 | 69.7

BA	OBA	R/500	HR/500	RBI/500
.261	.329	74	34	93

Where He Hits the Ball

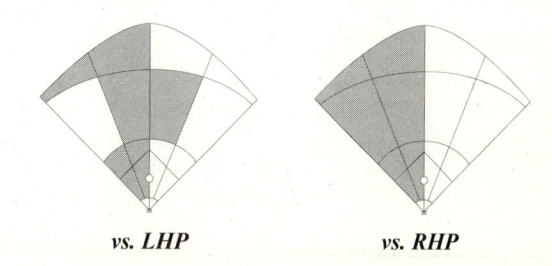

vs. LHP   vs. RHP

THE SCOUTING REPORT: 1996

KANSAS CITY ROYALS

GREG GAGNE

Positions: SS//DH
Bats: R **Throws:** R
Ht: 5'11" **Wt:** 185
Opening Day Age: 34
Born: 11/12/1961
Drafted: NYA79 5/129
ML Seasons: 13

SCOUTING REPORT

Annually considered one of the game's best fielders at the key infield defensive position, Gagne displays above-average range and hands with an accurate, deceptively strong arm. He often gets less credit than he is due because he makes many plays look easier than they really are. A pull hitter, Gagne mainly likes fastballs up in the strike zone and can be fooled by good breaking balls, particularly when behind in the count. He's vulnerable to being pitched first with inside fastballs, then with breaking balls low and away. (Of course, this pattern will get out most hitters.) Greg will also chase fastballs high and out of the strike zone. His defensive smarts don't transfer over to his baserunning. Despite plus speed, Gagne is a very poor base thief and often runs into outs which hurt his team.

HOW HE PERFORMED IN '95

Greg Gagne's three seasons in Kansas City have been nearly interchangeable. Each year, including 1995, he has produced spectacular defense peppered with streaks of fine hitting. Gagne missed a few games at mid-season last year due to a knee strain, only to return with red-hot hitting as the Royals competed for a wild-card berth.

As he has been since joining the team, Gagne was a valuable team leader and an anchor for the Royals infield. The Royals have had a pitching-and-defense approach in recent years, with Greg supplying much of that defense.

For the fourth consecutive year, he was caught stealing more often than was successful. Greg did not bunt for hits last year and, surprisingly, had little success sacrificing.

WHAT TO EXPECT IN '96

The Royals inability to re-sign free-agent Gagne bodes poorly for their immediate future. Weak-hitting David Howard will take over the position for Kansas City, while Gagne moves on to Los Angeles, where he will undoubtedly improve the Dodgers' poor defense. The National League's predominant mode of fastball pitching should be to his liking offensively, although Dodger Stadium should reduce his already marginal power. Now in his mid-30s, Gagne is aging gracefully; he should have several years left as one of baseball's better defensive shortstops.

Overall Statistics

	G	AB	R	H	2B	3B	HR	RBI	SB	CS	BB	SO	BA	OBA
95 KC	120	430	58	110	25	4	6	49	3	5	38	60	.256	.316
Career	1526	4731	615	1202	263	45	92	492	102	89	286	908	.254	.299

1995 Situational Statistics

	AB	HR	RBI	BA	OBA	SLG		AB	HR	RBI	BA	OBA	SLG
Home	202	2	25	.272	.327	.376	LHP	117	1	10	.248	.308	.350
Road	228	4	24	.241	.306	.373	RHP	313	5	39	.259	.319	.383
Apr-Jun	167	2	19	.269	.339	.407	ScPos	116	0	38	.224	.291	.319
Jul-Oct	263	4	30	.247	.301	.354	Clutch	62	1	3	.290	.362	.371

How He Compares to Other Batters

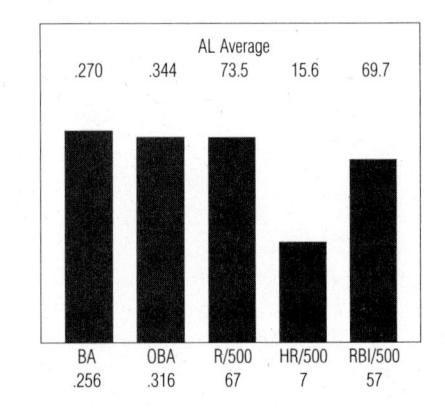

AL Average: .270 .344 73.5 15.6 69.7

BA	OBA	R/500	HR/500	RBI/500
.256	.316	67	7	57

Where He Hits the Ball

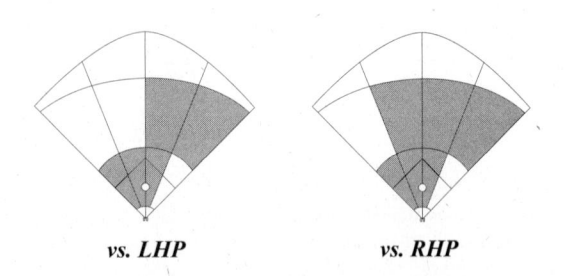

vs. LHP   vs. RHP

THE SCOUTING REPORT: 1996

KANSAS CITY ROYALS

TOM GOODWIN

Positions: OF//DH
Bats: L **Throws:** R
Ht: 6'1" **Wt:** 165
Opening Day Age: 27
Born: 7/27/1968
Drafted: LA89 2/22
ML Seasons: 5

SCOUTING REPORT

Goodwin hits from a wide-open stance and strides into low pitches, slapping them through the infield. Because he begins his upright stance almost head-on to pitchers, lefthanders can knock him off the plate, then get him to chase pitches low and away. While he hit for acceptable average verus southpaws, he had absolutely no power against them. Tom's short stroke helps him make contact, but limits his overall power; many of his 16 doubles were really stretched singles.

Goodwin led American Leaguers with fourteen sacrifices as well as bunted for hits, with drag bunts his speciality. Outstanding speed is his biggest asset. He uses it well on the bases, where he stole at will and liberally took extra bases on hits, and in the outfield, where he ran down balls deep in the gaps. Tom has average-minus hands, however, and a poor arm limits him to left or center field.

HOW HE PERFORMED IN '95

There's an old baseball adage that says you can't steal first base. It was often cited to explain why Goodwin had managed only 105 major-league at-bats in his six-year pro career.

Tom hadn't been given a chance to prove he could hit big-league pitching, but silenced the doubters by giving the Royals a quick table-setter last season. He also challenged Kenny Lofton for the league's stolen base championship. All in all, Goodwin was one of the Royals' few bright spots in 1995.

However, his lack of power, a low walk total, and a poor showing against lefties mean that platoon duty may be Tom's eventual fate.

WHAT TO EXPECT IN '96

Despite Goodwin's performance, Kansas City was slow to re-sign him after the close of the season and he became a free agent. He seems a perfect fit for this speed-and-defense franchise, but the Royals said they preferred to build upon younger, home-grown talents.

While outstanding speed gives Tom a useful weapon, he may only be able to play regularly for a weak team. He may be wondering where he will play in 1996, but no longer has to hope for a chance to prove what he can do: Goodwin's 1995 performance has already done that.

Overall Statistics

	G	AB	R	H	2B	3B	HR	RBI	SB	CS	BB	SO	BA	OBA
95 KC	133	480	72	138	16	3	4	28	50	18	38	72	.287	.346
Career	238	579	96	161	18	4	4	32	59	24	45	87	.278	.335

1995 Situational Statistics

	AB	HR	RBI	BA	OBA	SLG		AB	HR	RBI	BA	OBA	SLG
Home	239	2	12	.305	.354	.397	LHP	115	0	6	.252	.312	.296
Road	241	2	16	.270	.338	.320	RHP	365	4	22	.299	.357	.378
Apr-Jun	183	1	10	.290	.366	.339	ScPos	108	1	25	.241	.305	.333
Jul-Oct	297	3	18	.286	.333	.370	Clutch	64	1	4	.281	.333	.359

How He Compares to Other Batters

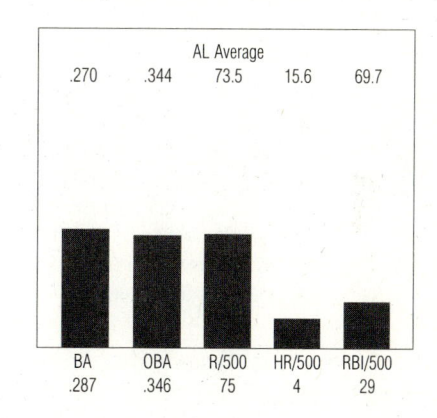

AL Average: .270 .344 73.5 15.6 69.7

BA	OBA	R/500	HR/500	RBI/500
.287	.346	75	4	29

Where He Hits the Ball

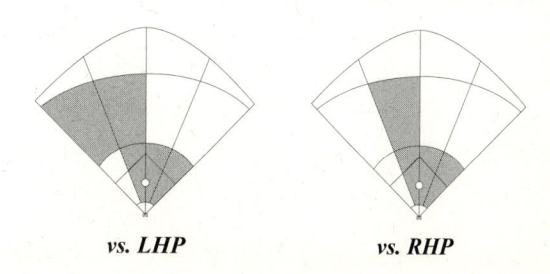

vs. LHP   vs. RHP

THE SCOUTING REPORT: 1996

KANSAS CITY ROYALS

TOM GORDON

Position: SP
Bats: R **Throws:** R
Ht: 5'9" **Wt:** 160
Opening Day Age: 28
Born: 11/18/1967
Drafted: KC86 6/157
ML Seasons: 8

SCOUTING REPORT

Tom Gordon throws three above-average pitches from a three-quarter angle: a fastball clocked in the low 90s, a hard curveball which has a late, sharp break, and a softer, bigger-breaking curveball. He also throws an average slider which often lacks sharpness and an average-minus straight change-up that he occasionally tipped off in the past.

When Gordon gets his curves over for strikes he puts hitters on the defensive, making his fastball (which he works the corners with) even more effective. When his curve isn't cooperating, Tom has to rely on a fastball that is often straight. Because he throws so many breaking balls, baserunners go wild on Gordon; he is usually near the top of the league in stolen bases allowed, although only 12 enemy baserunners stole against him in 17 tries last season.

HOW HE PERFORMED IN '95

Gordon produced another year of ups and downs, resulting in as many disappointments as highlights. He started the season winning five of his first seven decisions but struggled in the second half and worsened as the season wound to a close.

Gordon often ran deep counts and walked too many batters early in the game. What was frustrating is that it was impossible to predict what kind of stuff he would have in any given start. Tom posted a .500 record in 1995, but he needed very good run support to get it. His won-lost totals and his ERA were his worst of the last three seasons, delineating how little Gordon has progressed in his seven-year career.

He had pitched very poorly on artificial turf in the past two years, and he clearly benefitted when Kansas City installed a grass field before the start of the '95 season.

WHAT TO EXPECT IN '96

The Royals' contract offer late in 1995 was labeled an "insult" by Gordon's agent, and thus Tom became a free agent. Although he has good stuff and the ability to get a strikeout when necessary, "Flash" lacks the consistency that a staff ace must show. Whether or not he can harness his command will determine the ultimate fate of the enigmatic Gordon. It's no secret that he has lots of ability that he hasn't been able to translate into the "win" colunm.

Overall Statistics

	G	GS	GF	SV	W	L	ERA	IP	H	R	ER	HR	BB	SO
95 KC	31	31	0	0	12	12	4.43	189.0	204	110	93	12	89	119
Career	274	144	58	3	79	71	4.02	1149.2	1040	572	514	91	587	999

1995 Situational Statistics

	W	L	ERA	SV	IP	BB	SO		AB	HR	RBI	BA	OBA	SLG
Home	4	7	3.46	0	91.0	42	55	LHB	398	5	54	.314	.389	.394
Road	8	5	5.33	0	98.0	47	64	RHB	333	7	32	.237	.315	.345
Apr-Jun	5	3	4.02	0	69.1	30	49	ScPos	188	3	74	.271	.376	.351
Jul-Oct	7	9	4.66	0	119.2	59	70	Clutch	65	1	5	.215	.261	.308

How He Compares to Other Pitchers

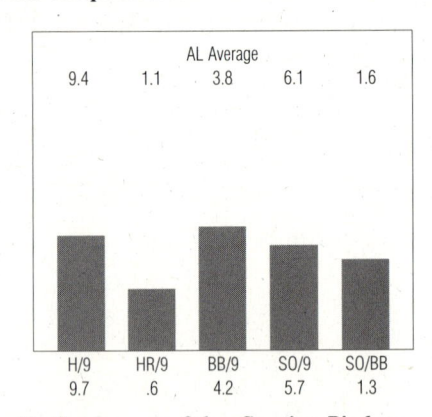

AL Average: 9.4 / 1.1 / 3.8 / 6.1 / 1.6

H/9: 9.7
HR/9: .6
BB/9: 4.2
SO/9: 5.7
SO/BB: 1.3

How He Compares to Other Starting Pitchers

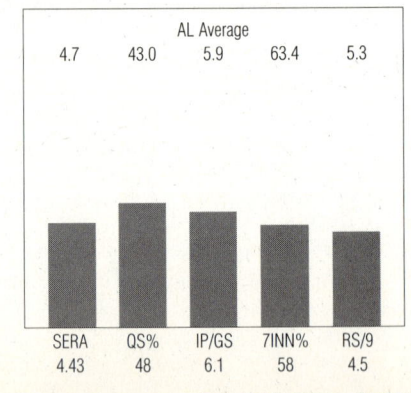

AL Average: 4.7 / 43.0 / 5.9 / 63.4 / 5.3

SERA: 4.43
QS%: 48
IP/GS: 6.1
7INN%: 58
RS/9: 4.5

KANSAS CITY ROYALS

MARK GUBICZA

Position: SP
Bats: R **Throws:** R
Ht: 6'6" **Wt:** 215
Opening Day Age: 33
Born: 8/14/1962
Drafted: KC81 2/34
ML Seasons: 12

SCOUTING REPORT
Mark Gubicza, once a fireballer, now gets by with average-plus control, guile, and experience after career-threatening injuries. He works both sides of the plate from a three-quarter angle, setting hitters up by spotting his slightly below-average fastball on both corners, then getting them to chase his late-breaking, average-plus hard slider. To keep hitters honest, he also throws an occasional change-up that has some movement but is average overall.

Gubicza throws a sinking two-seam fastball to induce grounders, and he ranked second among Royals' pitchers with 19 double-play balls in 1995. Hard work has improved Gubicza's defense, but he still looks awkward on occasion. He has shortened his delivery to better hold opposing baserunners, but ten runners still stole against Mark in 15 tries last season.

HOW HE PERFORMED IN '95
Mark lost his high-velocity fastball to serious shoulder problems five years ago. It has taken him that long to fully recover and re-emerge as a top-flight finesse pitcher. With fellow rotation members Kevin Appier and Chris Haney shelved due to injuries, Gubicza surprised many and became the Royals' most reliable starter. However, he is still limited to pitching seven innings most of the time.

He seemed to only get stronger down the stretch as the team chased a wild-card berth; his one-hit shutout in Oakland June 15 may have been his finest outing ever. Gubicza kept the Royals in almost every game he started, but he was victimized by poor run support: he received fewer than four runs in over half of his major-league-leading 33 starts.

WHAT TO EXPECT IN '96
A free agent over the winter, Gubicza was one player Kansas City hoped to bring back; he is the last active link to the 1985 world champions. Mark had informed his agent that the Royals would be his personal preference, and if he gets his wish, 1996 would be his thirteenth season with the club.

Gubicza has completed the transition from power to finesse. He is now a much more complete pitcher than he was in his hard-throwing days. A repeat of 1995 isn't guaranteed, but he should be effective again in '96.

Overall Statistics

	G	GS	GF	SV	W	L	ERA	IP	H	R	ER	HR	BB	SO
95 KC	33	33	0	0	12	14	3.75	213.1	222	97	89	21	62	81
Career	363	308	14	2	128	123	3.85	2099.1	2094	980	897	131	749	1311

1995 Situational Statistics

	W	L	ERA	SV	IP	BB	SO		AB	HR	RBI	BA	OBA	SLG
Home	6	8	3.69	0	124.1	44	55	LHB	457	9	49	.274	.323	.389
Road	6	6	3.84	0	89.0	18	26	RHB	358	12	38	.271	.330	.436
Apr-Jun	5	6	3.38	0	88.0	29	32	ScPos	173	5	61	.272	.330	.405
Jul-Oct	7	8	4.02	0	125.1	33	49	Clutch	50	0	3	.280	.339	.320

How He Compares to Other Pitchers

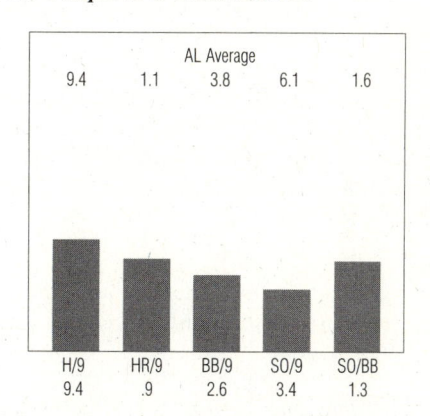

AL Average: H/9 9.4, HR/9 1.1, BB/9 3.8, SO/9 6.1, SO/BB 1.6
Gubicza: H/9 9.4, HR/9 .9, BB/9 2.6, SO/9 3.4, SO/BB 1.3

How He Compares to Other Starting Pitchers

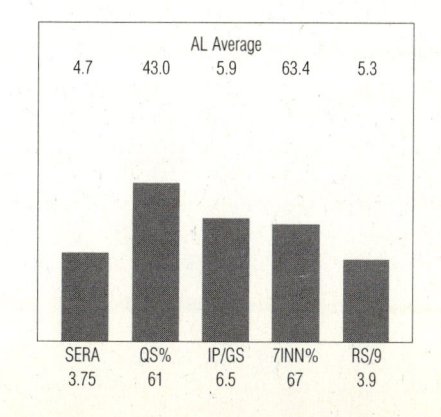

AL Average: SERA 4.7, QS% 43.0, IP/GS 5.9, 7INN% 63.4, RS/9 5.3
Gubicza: SERA 3.75, QS% 61, IP/GS 6.5, 7INN% 67, RS/9 3.9

KANSAS CITY ROYALS

JASON JACOME

Position: SP
Bats: L **Throws:** L
Ht: 6'1" **Wt:** 155
Opening Day Age: 25
Born: 11/24/1970
Drafted: NYN91 14/329
ML Seasons: 2

SCOUTING REPORT
Jacome, a lefty with a three-quarter motion, is the definitive finesse pitcher. His minus fastball is barely hard enough to break glass, but he cuts it, turns it over, sinks it, and uses his plus control to work the corners. Jacome's curve, which has a good lateral break, is his best pitch. He throws it for strikes consistently.

Jason also throws an average hard (but flat) slider and a deceptive change-up. Unfortunately, good fastball hitters can just sit on his mid-80s "heater" and adjust quite easily to the off-speed pitches.

Jacome has a good move to first and fields his position well. Eight runners stole bases against him last year in eleven tries.

HOW HE PERFORMED IN '95
Jason began the season cold. He failed to live up to the promise he displayed in a brief 1994 stint with the Mets, losing four of five starts before a demotion to Triple-A. Joining the Royals via a mid-season trade, Jacome became an overnight success, winning four straight decisions to earn recognition as the Royals' Pitcher of the Month for August.

Unfortunately, Jason ended the year as he started it—struggling. He lost his last four starts with a September ERA of 7.00, throwing a heavy supply of fat pitches right in the heart of the strike zone. He allowed one homer for each of his fifteen Royals appearances.

WHAT TO EXPECT IN '96
Once hitters catch on to what a pitcher is throwing, the pitcher must make adjustments or his career will be brief. Jacome has been able to enjoy brief spurts of success only because hitters are unfamiliar with him. Once batters learned his repertoire of off-speed deliveries, they had no troubled hitting Jason hard, first in the National League, then in the American.

For Jacome to take the next step forward as a reliable starting pitcher, he'll have to refine his pitches or have the kind of precise control which is hard for anyone to have day-in and day-out. Jacome will battle Chris Haney for the lefty spot in the Royals 1996 rotation. He's got a shot at being a 10-15 game winner in the future, but it's going to be tough with his stuff.

Overall Statistics

	G	GS	GF	SV	W	L	ERA	IP	H	R	ER	HR	BB	SO
95 NYN/KC	20	19	0	0	4	10	6.34	105.0	134	76	74	18	36	50
Career	28	27	0	0	8	13	5.09	159.0	188	93	90	21	53	80

1995 Situational Statistics

	W	L	ERA	SV	IP	BB	SO		AB	HR	RBI	BA	OBA	SLG
Home	4	3	4.56	0	51.1	14	18	LHB	72	2	10	.306	.333	.431
Road	0	7	8.05	0	53.2	22	32	RHB	357	16	63	.314	.372	.552
Apr-Jun	0	4	10.29	0	21.0	15	11	ScPos	109	5	56	.367	.425	.670
Jul-Oct	4	6	5.36	0	84.0	21	39	Clutch	17	0	1	.294	.368	.294

How He Compares to Other Pitchers

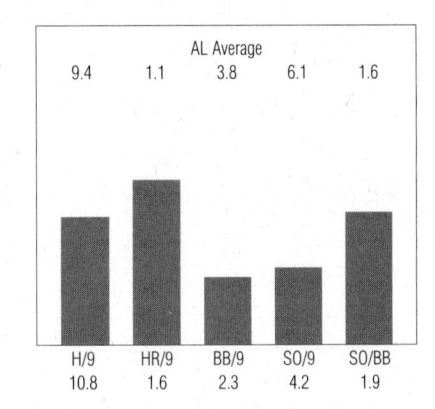

AL Average: 9.4 1.1 3.8 6.1 1.6

H/9 10.8 HR/9 1.6 BB/9 2.3 SO/9 4.2 SO/BB 1.9

How He Compares to Other Starting Pitchers

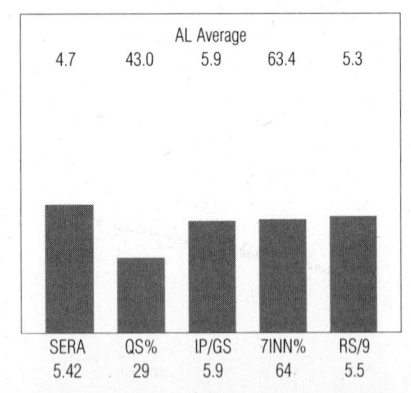

AL Average: 4.7 43.0 5.9 63.4 5.3

SERA 5.42 QS% 29 IP/GS 5.9 7INN% 64 RS/9 5.5

KANSAS CITY ROYALS

WALLY JOYNER

Positions: 1B//DH
Bats: L **Throws:** L
Ht: 6'2" **Wt:** 190
Opening Day Age: 33
Born: 6/16/1962
Drafted: CAL83 3/67
ML Seasons: 10

SCOUTING REPORT
Joyner's strength is contact hitting. Swinging out of a relaxed, upright stance, he can handle just about any pitch in any location. Wally's smooth, controlled stroke and good batting eye makes him a fine two-strike hitter, and he hits line drives to all fields and consistently walks more often than striking out. However, while Joyner makes good contact, he rarely drives the ball with authority.

Joyner has become extremely slow in recent years, and is difficult to advance more than one base at a time. His reputation for good defense is often overstated; while he throws accurately, Wally's range is slightly below-average, especially on grounders to his right.

HOW HE PERFORMED IN '95
Despite another .300 season, Joyner remained among the American League's weakest-hitting first basemen. His singles hitting and sharp batting eye would be better-used higher in the Royals batting order, but the team's shortage of power forced Wally into an inappropriate power slot.

This didn't help either Joyner or the team, and the Kansas City offense was the league's least productive. Joyner ended up second on the team in runs batted in, but he failed to produce the kind of power needed from a third-place hitter. In 146 at-bats against lefthanded pitchers, Wally collected just three extra-base hits—all doubles.

Joyner made just three errors all year, fielding .998, but again failed to win his first Gold Glove.

WHAT TO EXPECT IN '96
Because he had over 500 plate appearances in 1995, the Royals were obligated to extend Joyner's contract for an additional season—at a whopping $5 million, the residue of a overly generous contract signed four years ago. As one of the few long-time veterans on an increasingly inexperienced team, Joyner will be expected to carry a large offensive burden, again serving as an RBI man.

However, this again will be an ill fit, as Joyner is better suited to setting the table than clearing it. It is clear that 1996 will be his last season in Kansas City and, if he slumps, possibly his last as a regular anywhere. He'll never again see a contract as lucrative as the one he's now completing.

Overall Statistics

	G	AB	R	H	2B	3B	HR	RBI	SB	CS	BB	SO	BA	OBA
95 KC	131	465	69	144	28	0	12	83	3	2	69	65	.310	.394
Career	1364	5105	725	1481	290	19	158	789	50	27	560	556	.290	.359

1995 Situational Statistics

	AB	HR	RBI	BA	OBA	SLG		AB	HR	RBI	BA	OBA	SLG
Home	220	6	41	.336	.404	.473	LHP	146	0	9	.274	.327	.295
Road	245	6	42	.286	.386	.424	RHP	319	12	74	.326	.422	.517
Apr-Jun	188	4	36	.293	.405	.436	ScPos	122	3	67	.328	.452	.451
Jul-Oct	277	8	47	.321	.387	.455	Clutch	67	2	12	.313	.380	.463

How He Compares to Other Batters

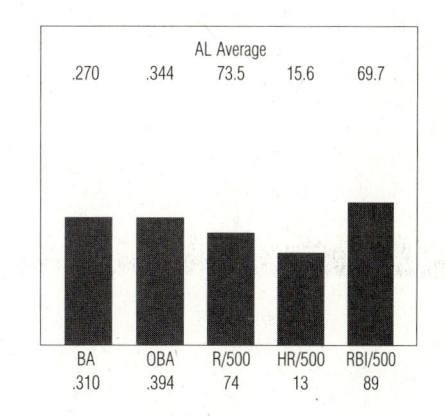

AL Average: .270 .344 73.5 15.6 69.7

BA	OBA	R/500	HR/500	RBI/500
.310	.394	74	13	89

Where He Hits the Ball

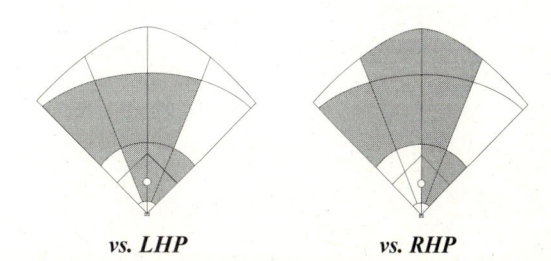

vs. LHP   vs. RHP

THE SCOUTING REPORT: 1996

KANSAS CITY ROYALS

KEITH LOCKHART

Positions: 2B/3B/DH
Bats: L **Throws:** R
Ht: 5'10" **Wt:** 170
Opening Day Age: 31
Born: 11/10/1964
Drafted: CIN86 11/280
ML Seasons: 2

SCOUTING REPORT
Primarily a low fastball hitter with some line-drive power, Lockhart attacks the first hittable pitch. He makes good contact and puts the ball in play, stroking pitches to left field or up the middle due to his mediocre bat speed. Keith does not strike out often, only occasionally takes the walk, and does not bunt. He appears typecast as a half-timer, with just 19 career major-league at-bats against left-handers. An intelligent baserunner, Lockhart has just average speed, but he picks his spots well. His defensive tools are all average, but Keith is a gritty second baseman who positions himself well and turns double plays effectively. However, Lockhart did seem out of place at third base.

HOW HE PERFORMED IN '95
Perennial Triple-A veteran Lockhart spent several years in the Reds' system, then bounced to three other organizations before landing in Kansas City for 1995, where he made the most of an opportunity. Hitting .378 at Triple-A Omaha, Keith earned a June promotion to Kansas City. He served as a reserve infielder until starting second baseman Chico Lind disappeared in June, giving Lockhart a shot at regular duty.

Keith finished the season strong, hitting .364 over the final month to lead the Royals in batting average for the year. Lockhart's emergence as a productive hitter and consistent fielder was a big surprise and a key reason that the team stayed in the pennant chase as long as it did.

He stole more bases in 1995 than he had since 1987 when he played in Class A and showed surprisingly excellent range at second base. Keith fielded a below-average .974 for the season, however.

WHAT TO EXPECT IN '96
Lockhart has now earned a shot at an everyday role, with his hold on the Royals' second base job more secure with fellow utilityman David Howard scheduled to start at shortstop. However, with manager Bob Boone's predilection for platooning, it's likely that Keith will again ultimately share playing time, possibly with young righthanded-hitting Chris Stynes.

A savvy veteran with limited skills, Lockhart is the type of player who can help the Royals in a platoon role. A reprise of 1995 as a regular would be another surprise.

Overall Statistics

	G	AB	R	H	2B	3B	HR	RBI	SB	CS	BB	SO	BA	OBA
95 KC	94	274	41	88	19	3	6	33	8	1	14	21	.321	.355
Career	121	317	45	97	19	3	8	39	9	1	18	31	.306	.345

1995 Situational Statistics

	AB	HR	RBI	BA	OBA	SLG		AB	HR	RBI	BA	OBA	SLG
Home	131	3	14	.336	.378	.473	LHP	16	0	0	.188	.188	.250
Road	143	3	19	.308	.333	.483	RHP	258	6	33	.329	.364	.492
Apr-Jun	52	1	7	.404	.459	.596	ScPos	66	2	27	.258	.309	.379
Jul-Oct	222	5	26	.302	.328	.450	Clutch	35	1	3	.229	.357	.400

How He Compares to Other Batters

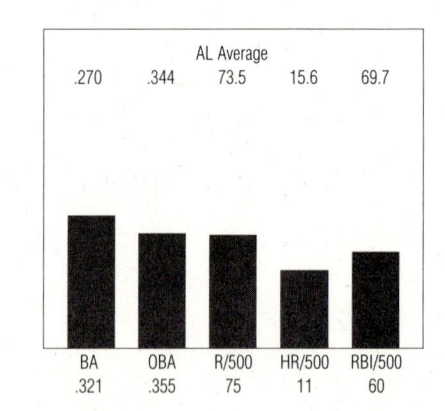

AL Average: .270 / .344 / 73.5 / 15.6 / 69.7

BA	OBA	R/500	HR/500	RBI/500
.321	.355	75	11	60

Where He Hits the Ball

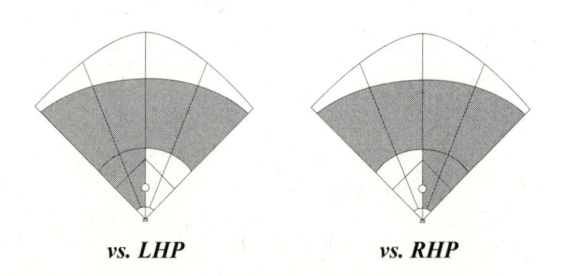

vs. LHP   vs. RHP

KANSAS CITY ROYALS

SCOUTING REPORT
Spray-hitting Brent Mayne has doubles power only, and little of that. A low fastball hitter, Brent takes the ball where it's pitched. However, he is impatient and has many holes in his swing; Mayne can be fooled by breaking balls or overmatched with good fastballs. He is a good sacrifice bunter, but is slow and overall produces little on offense.

However, his saving grace as a major-league player is that he is a fine handler of pitchers, serving as almost an on-field pitching coach. His take-charge attitude brings the most out of Royals pitchers. Brent's arm is average in strength, but he has plus accuracy. He has average-plus hands and mobility behind the plate.

HOW HE PERFORMED IN '95
Before being given the opportunity in 1995 to be Kansas City's regular catcher, Mayne claimed he could hit .300. Instead, he needed a furious September streak just to reach .250. In five seasons of semi-regular play, Mayne has batted between .251 and .257 four times with little power and few walks or stolen bases. He's been weak at the plate, but he's been consistent.

Although Mayne reached career highs in some categories last year, he played everyday for two reasons only: he is strong defensively, and previous regular Mike Macfarlane had departed for Boston as a free agent the previous winter. Thus, the Royals had no other options.

Brent made just three throwing errors all year, but on the other hand, he caught only 21% of opposing baserunners attempting to steal, one of the worst rates of regular catchers. He needs to improve on that performance to catch everyday.

WHAT TO EXPECT IN '96
Mayne's days as a regular may be over, as the Royals were actively pursuing free-agent catchers during the off-season. Because he has such a large platoon differential (he's a career .169 hitter versus lefthanders), Brent would certainly have more success sharing the catching duties. Over the last three years he has shown that he can provide strong defense and hit .250 with few offensive extras. There's no reason to expect he'll do any more or less in 1996, whether as a regular or a reserve.

BRENT MAYNE

Position: C
Bats: L **Throws:** R
Ht: 6'1" **Wt:** 195
Opening Day Age: 27
Born: 4/19/1968
Drafted: KC89 1/13
ML Seasons: 6

Overall Statistics

	G	AB	R	H	2B	3B	HR	RBI	SB	CS	BB	SO	BA	OBA
95 KC	110	307	23	77	18	1	1	27	0	1	25	41	.251	.313
Career	399	1113	104	275	50	3	8	119	6	12	94	170	.247	.306

1995 Situational Statistics

	AB	HR	RBI	BA	OBA	SLG		AB	HR	RBI	BA	OBA	SLG
Home	137	1	14	.292	.362	.409	LHP	45	0	2	.178	.229	.222
Road	170	0	13	.218	.272	.259	RHP	262	1	25	.263	.326	.344
Apr-Jun	137	1	12	.204	.253	.277	ScPos	76	0	25	.263	.321	.342
Jul-Oct	170	0	15	.288	.358	.365	Clutch	46	0	3	.217	.308	.261

How He Compares to Other Batters

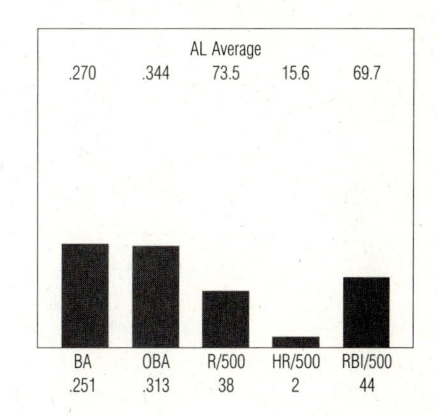

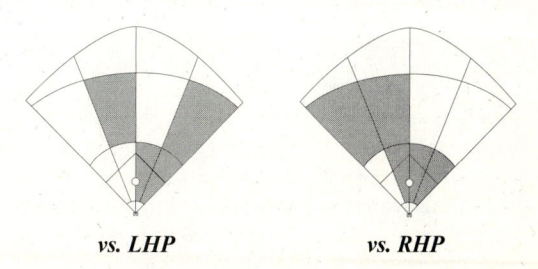

	BA	OBA	R/500	HR/500	RBI/500
AL Average	.270	.344	73.5	15.6	69.7
	.251	.313	38	2	44

Where He Hits the Ball

vs. LHP   vs. RHP

THE SCOUTING REPORT: 1996

KANSAS CITY ROYALS

JEFF MONTGOMERY

Position: RP
Bats: R **Throws:** R
Ht: 5'11" **Wt:** 180
Opening Day Age: 34
Born: 1/7/1962
Drafted: CIN83 10/212
ML Seasons: 9

SCOUTING REPORT

Once strictly a power pitcher who could fan a batter per inning, Montgomery has gradually expanded his repertoire to include a plus, hard, late-breaking slider, which he will "backdoor" as well as inside, and an average-plus change-up, a pitch that he could throw more often.

Throwing from a three-quarter to low three-quarter angle, Jeff works the count with off-speed stuff before going to his 90-mph fastball, an average pitch that is straight but thrown accurately to either corner. An above-average fielder, Montgomery has good range and holds baserunners well. Six enemy runners tried to steal against him last summer, five successfully.

HOW HE PERFORMED IN '95

Despite the lack of reliable setup help from his bullpen mates, Jeff remained one of baseball's top closers in 1995. For the fifth straight season he placed among the top ten in saves in the American League. Since 1989, only all-time saves leader Lee Smith and Oakland's Dennis Eckersley have recorded more saves than Montgomery's total of 217.

Montgomery has the classic hard stuff expected of a closer and can pitch on successive days. He was at the top of his game when the season was on the line in 1995, saving most of the Royals' victories during their pennant chase.

Jeff's normally fine control was a bit off last season, however, and lefthanded hitters slugged .419 against him. The shoulder troubles that plagued Montgomery in 1994 may have taken a little bit from his stuff. He needs more help in the future from setup pitchers to continue at the top of his game.

WHAT TO EXPECT IN '96

Montgomery has been among the American League's top closers for many years and is now commanding the kind of salary such pitchers often receive. For this reason, the frugal Royals were tempted to deal Jeff. He'll begin the 1996 season as their closer if they don't move him, but don't be surprised if Monty becomes mid-season trade bait for a contending team. Wherever he goes, Montgomery should be a reliable pitcher, combining power and control in a key bullpen role.

Overall Statistics

	G	GS	GF	SV	W	L	ERA	IP	H	R	ER	HR	BB	SO
95 KC	54	0	46	31	2	3	3.43	65.2	60	27	25	7	25	49
Career	492	1	381	218	38	33	2.72	638.2	543	217	193	43	216	559

1995 Situational Statistics

	W	L	ERA	SV	IP	BB	SO		AB	HR	RBI	BA	OBA	SLG
Home	2	0	3.09	9	32.0	9	24	LHB	138	4	20	.290	.357	.428
Road	0	3	3.74	22	33.2	16	25	RHB	100	3	14	.200	.274	.310
Apr-Jun	0	1	3.51	13	25.2	9	15	ScPos	60	1	25	.300	.365	.383
Jul-Oct	2	2	3.38	18	40.0	16	34	Clutch	157	2	24	.280	.357	.357

How He Compares to Other Pitchers

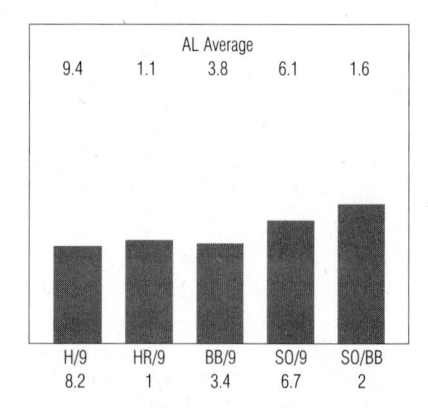

	H/9	HR/9	BB/9	SO/9	SO/BB
AL Average	9.4	1.1	3.8	6.1	1.6
	8.2	1	3.4	6.7	2

How He Compares to Other Relief Pitchers

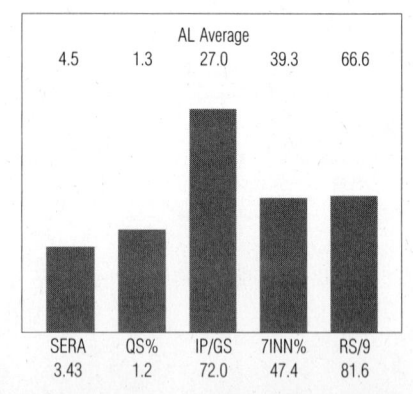

	SERA	QS%	IP/GS	7INN%	RS/9
AL Average	4.5	1.3	27.0	39.3	66.6
	3.43	1.2	72.0	47.4	81.6

KANSAS CITY ROYALS

JON NUNNALLY

Positions: OF//DH
Bats: L **Throws:** R
Ht: 5'10" **Wt:** 190
Opening Day Age: 24
Born: 11/9/1971
Drafted: CLE92 3/70
ML Seasons: 1

SCOUTING REPORT

Jon Nunnally is an extremely aggressive hitter who will chase any fastball, anywhere. He hits low fastballs very hard, but has large holes in his swing that can be easily exploited. Swinging from the heels with good bat speed, Nunnally never gets cheated. He took plenty of walks, but seldom bunted.

Jon never got cheated in the field, either, constantly giving his all to track down long flies or short bloopers. Nunnally displayed an average-plus arm with erratic accuracy. He throws well enough to play right field, but must learn to control his desire to nail every single baserunner.

HOW HE PERFORMED IN '95

Jon's star burned brightly for the Royals early in 1995. Jumping straight to the big leagues from Class A in the Cleveland system via the Rule V draft, he homered his first major-league at-bat on April 29 and had pounded fourteen homers by the All-Star break. He became a fan favorite with a flair for late-game dramatics.

However, he stumbled badly late in the season, hitting under .200 with little power in the second half. Considering Jon's slight experience, his rookie season was a huge success, although he may very well need a half-season or more of experience in the high minors in order to be able to handle big-league pitching.

Despite setting a Royals' career record with four steals of home in 1995 (all on the back end of double steals), Nunnally showed only average speed and baserunning skills. He displayed above-average range and registered five outfield assists, playing all three pasture positions.

WHAT TO EXPECT IN '96

Nunnally is a raw talent who needs the polish a full year in the high minors can yield. He succeeded early in 1995 on a steady diet of fastballs, but couldn't adjust well enough to breaking balls or refrain from chasing good heat out of the strike zone. For Nunnally to improve in 1996, he'll have to scale back his huge swing without losing too much power.

The Royals hope to start Jon in right field, but will rapidly send him back to the minors to get more experience if he can't make the necessary adjustments which are part of the constant struggle between major-league pitchers and hitters.

Overall Statistics

	G	AB	R	H	2B	3B	HR	RBI	SB	CS	BB	SO	BA	OBA
95 KC	119	303	51	74	15	6	14	42	6	4	51	86	.244	.357
Career	119	303	51	74	15	6	14	42	6	4	51	86	.244	.357

1995 Situational Statistics

	AB	HR	RBI	BA	OBA	SLG		AB	HR	RBI	BA	OBA	SLG
Home	141	6	16	.227	.343	.426	LHP	37	1	4	.162	.225	.324
Road	162	8	26	.259	.368	.512	RHP	266	13	38	.256	.373	.492
Apr-Jun	117	9	19	.274	.370	.581	ScPos	73	3	28	.247	.427	.452
Jul-Oct	186	5	23	.226	.348	.403	Clutch	48	3	6	.188	.278	.438

How He Compares to Other Batters

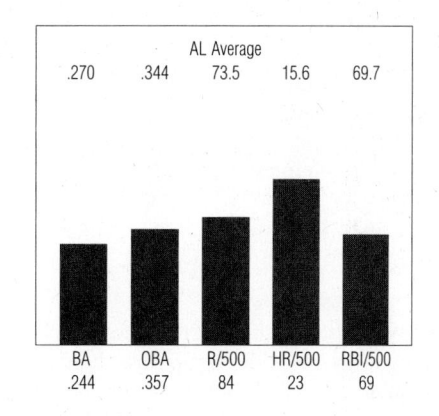

AL Average: .270   .344   73.5   15.6   69.7

	BA	OBA	R/500	HR/500	RBI/500
	.244	.357	84	23	69

Where He Hits the Ball

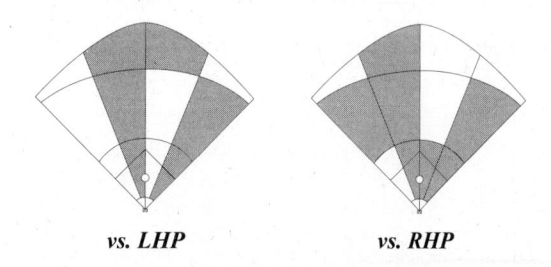

vs. LHP   vs. RHP

THE SCOUTING REPORT: 1996

KANSAS CITY ROYALS

BILLY BREWER

Position: RP
Bats: L **Throws:** L
Ht: 6'1" **Wt:** 175
Opening Day Age: 27
Born: 4/15/1968
Drafted: MON90 36/751
ML Seasons: 3

Overall Statistics

	G	GS	GF	SV	W	L	ERA	IP	H	R	ER	HR	BB	SO
95 KC	48	0	13	0	2	4	5.56	45.1	54	28	28	9	20	31
Career	144	0	44	3	8	7	3.95	123.0	113	55	54	19	56	84

1995 Situational Statistics

	W	L	ERA	SV	IP	BB	SO		AB	HR	RBI	BA	OBA	SLG
Home	2	2	4.40	0	28.2	13	13	LHB	79	5	18	.304	.375	.532
Road	0	2	7.56	0	16.2	7	18	RHB	107	4	22	.280	.358	.421
Apr-Jun	1	2	4.50	0	20.0	8	21	ScPos	65	2	31	.308	.416	.431
Jul-Oct	1	2	6.39	0	25.1	12	10	Clutch	61	3	11	.230	.299	.393

SCOUTING REPORT
Billy Brewer throws four adequate pitches from a three-quarters to high three-quarters. His fastball is hard but far too straight for comfort. His slow curve has no bite, and neither his slider nor change-up have good movement. Brewer doesn't hold baserunners very well for a lefthander. All four runners trying to steal against him last year were successful.

HOW HE PERFORMED IN '95
Billy was expected to be a lefty setup pitcher but couldn't get the ball over the plate often enough. Even when he did throw strikes, they were often hit hard; lefthanders, who he was expected to consistently retire, pounded him. Brewer earned a late-season demotion to the minors but didn't pitch any better once recalled. After the season, Kansas City took him off the 40-player roster.

WHAT TO EXPECT IN '96
Control of his live fastball remains the key for Brewer. He can become an effective situational reliever if he can keep fastballs down or develop better off-speed pitches. Billy should spend some time in the high minors refining his pitches in 1996. He's still young enough to rebound.

EDGAR CACERES

Positions: 2B//SS/1B/3B/DH
Bats: B **Throws:** R
Ht: 6'1" **Wt:** 170
Opening Day Age: 31
Born: 6/6/1964
Drafted: LA 10/19/83
ML Seasons: 1

Overall Statistics

	G	AB	R	H	2B	3B	HR	RBI	SB	CS	BB	SO	BA	OBA
95 KC	55	117	13	28	6	2	1	17	2	2	8	15	.239	.291
Career	55	117	13	28	6	2	1	17	2	2	8	15	.239	.291

1995 Situational Statistics

	AB	HR	RBI	BA	OBA	SLG		AB	HR	RBI	BA	OBA	SLG
Home	58	0	4	.155	.194	.190	LHP	50	1	8	.160	.189	.300
Road	59	1	13	.322	.385	.508	RHP	67	0	9	.299	.365	.388
Apr-Jun	49	0	9	.347	.396	.510	ScPos	40	1	17	.225	.256	.425
Jul-Oct	68	1	8	.162	.216	.235	Clutch	25	1	7	.280	.296	.600

SCOUTING REPORT
Edgar is aggressive fastball hitter who sprays the ball to all fields. He protects the plate well with two strikes, becoming less of a free-swinger. Caceres has little power and average speed; he occasionally showed poor baserunning judgment. Edgar is an average-minus fielder and his mobility and arm are no better than average.

HOW HE PERFORMED IN '95
Caceres, a replacement player, got a chance at extended major-league play due to the strike and was marginally useful. He had a fine first half, hitting over .300, but slumped to a .155 mark over the final three months. He did not show the range or consistent glovework to play regularly at second base or shortstop. However, Edgar displayed enough skill that he could easily be a bench player.

WHAT TO EXPECT IN '96
Without the strike Caceres wouldn't have reached the majors in 1995. While he proved that he deserved a chance, a player who needs nine years to get beyond Double-A is not a hot prospect. Should Caceres return to the majors in 1996, it will be strictly as a utility infielder.

KANSAS CITY ROYALS

DAVE FLEMING

Position: RP/SP
Bats: L **Throws:** L
Ht: 6'3" **Wt:** 200
Opening Day Age: 26
Born: 11/7/1969
Drafted: SEA90 3/79
ML Seasons: 5

Overall Statistics

	G	GS	GF	SV	W	L	ERA	IP	H	R	ER	HR	BB	SO
95 SEA/KC	25	12	3	0	1	6	5.96	80.0	84	61	53	19	53	40
Career	116	97	6	0	38	32	4.67	610.1	669	346	317	67	248	303

1995 Situational Statistics

	W	L	ERA	SV	IP	BB	SO		AB	HR	RBI	BA	OBA	SLG
Home	1	0	3.30	0	30.0	21	14	LHB	72	3	7	.208	.306	.347
Road	0	6	7.56	0	50.0	32	26	RHB	240	16	49	.287	.395	.554
Apr-Jun	1	5	7.06	0	43.1	29	21	ScPos	86	5	39	.267	.356	.477
Jul-Oct	0	1	4.66	0	36.2	24	19	Clutch	14	1	3	.214	.389	.429

SCOUTING REPORT
With a poor fastball, Fleming must rely on soft off-speed pitches to fool hitters. His best offering is a plus change-up curveball thrown similar to his average-minus curveball, but much slower. Dave also throws an above-average change-up that breaks late. Unfortunately, his control is poor. Too often, he falls behind in the count and his next high breaking ball is summarily deposited over the nearest outfield wall. Nine baserunners stole successfully on him in 14 tries.

HOW HE PERFORMED IN '95
Acquired in a stretch-drive deal, Dave experienced a modicum of success with the Royals as a spot starter and long reliever. Continuing control problems prompted the Mariners to give up on Fleming, who had compiled a 29-15 record in his first two big-league seasons. His strikeout rate has declined every year while his walks and homers allowed have climbed.

WHAT TO EXPECT IN '96
Fleming has never been a power pitcher, yet his control has been awful. Until he finds the plate more regularly, Fleming can't succeed in the majors. He'll fight for a long relief role in the 1996 Royals bullpen.

BOB HAMELIN

Positions: DH//1B/C
Bats: L **Throws:** L
Ht: 6'0" **Wt:** 235
Opening Day Age: 28
Born: 11/29/1967
Drafted: KC88 2/48
ML Seasons: 3

Overall Statistics

	G	AB	R	H	2B	3B	HR	RBI	SB	CS	BB	SO	BA	OBA
95 KC	72	208	20	35	7	1	7	25	0	1	26	56	.168	.278
Career	189	569	86	134	35	2	33	95	4	4	88	133	.236	.342

1995 Situational Statistics

	AB	HR	RBI	BA	OBA	SLG		AB	HR	RBI	BA	OBA	SLG
Home	98	3	11	.153	.257	.306	LHP	30	4	10	.233	.395	.667
Road	110	4	14	.182	.297	.318	RHP	178	3	15	.157	.256	.253
Apr-Jun	101	2	9	.168	.294	.257	ScPos	68	2	19	.147	.306	.279
Jul-Oct	107	5	16	.168	.262	.364	Clutch	31	4	7	.226	.333	.613

SCOUTING REPORT
A classic lefty power hitter who likes fastballs thrown low and inside, Hamelin has a relatively good batting eye. He hits righthanders especially well; they have yielded all but four of his 33 career homers. Bob's below-average defense and poor range limit him to first base. He is not quite as slow as he looks, but Hamelin isn't a basestealing threat.

HOW HE PERFORMED IN '95
The words "sophomore slump" became indelibly etched on Bob Hamelin during his Joe Charboneau-like swan dive in '95. The '94 American League Rookie of the Year started his second season poorly, swinging wildly at bad pitches while hitting with little power. Battling both Royals' hitting instructors and serious weight problems, "The Hammer" earned two separate demotions to Triple-A Omaha, with only marginally better results upon returning to Kansas City.

WHAT TO EXPECT IN '96
Despite Hamelin's summer of discontent, the Royals validated their fall proclamations about his importance to the organization by trading incumbent first baseman Wally Joyner and installing Bob in his place. For '96, the pressure is on Hamelin: he'll now be expected to meet the expectations his '94 campaign engendered.

KANSAS CITY ROYALS

CHRIS HANEY

Position: SP
Bats: L **Throws:** L
Ht: 6'3" **Wt:** 185
Opening Day Age: 27
Born: 11/16/1968
Drafted: MON90 9/51
ML Seasons: 5

Overall Statistics

	G	GS	GF	SV	W	L	ERA	IP	H	R	ER	HR	BB	SO
95 KC	16	13	0	0	3	4	3.65	81.1	78	35	33	7	33	31
Career	77	71	2	0	21	28	4.93	398.1	424	239	218	39	166	219

1995 Situational Statistics

	W	L	ERA	SV	IP	BB	SO		AB	HR	RBI	BA	OBA	SLG
Home	1	2	4.26	0	38.0	13	12	LHB	49	0	1	.184	.298	.224
Road	2	2	3.12	0	43.1	20	19	RHB	249	7	32	.277	.343	.414
Apr-Jun	3	2	2.53	0	67.2	26	27	ScPos	69	1	22	.232	.296	.319
Jul-Oct	0	2	9.22	0	13.2	7	4	Clutch	25	0	0	.160	.300	.160

SCOUTING REPORT

Lefthanded finesser Haney used his slightly below-average fastball with more confidence in '95. Chris sets up the sinker with straight fastballs, average curves, and slightly plus change-ups that break down and in.

His smooth, three-quarter delivery fools batters; Haney throws harder than it appears at first blush. Lacking a consistent move to first, Chris still holds runners well: just fourteen of 23 basestealers have succeeded against him over the last three years. He is a bit above-average fielder.

HOW HE PERFORMED IN '95

Just when Haney appeared to finally be realizing his potential, a herniated disk in his back forced a modification of his delivery. He wasn't the same pitcher and eventually finished the year on the DL. Still, Chris' 1995 results were the best he'd produced in five major-league seasons.

WHAT TO EXPECT IN '96

Haney underwent post-season back surgery and was expected to be ready for spring training. The Royals, banking heavily upon a return to health, expect Chris to be their premier lefthanded starter. Now entering his prime, Haney may be a pleasant surprise for K.C. fans this year.

DAVID HOWARD

Positions: 2B/SS/OF//1B/DH
Bats: B **Throws:** R
Ht: 6'0" **Wt:** 165
Opening Day Age: 29
Born: 2/26/1967
Drafted: KC86 25/774
ML Seasons: 5

Overall Statistics

	G	AB	R	H	2B	3B	HR	RBI	SB	CS	BB	SO	BA	OBA
95 KC	95	255	23	62	13	4	0	19	6	1	24	41	.243	.310
Career	324	817	76	189	30	7	3	69	16	9	68	157	.231	.289

1995 Situational Statistics

	AB	HR	RBI	BA	OBA	SLG		AB	HR	RBI	BA	OBA	SLG
Home	121	0	12	.298	.368	.380	LHP	111	0	5	.243	.298	.279
Road	134	0	7	.194	.255	.276	RHP	144	0	14	.243	.319	.361
Apr-Jun	45	0	1	.133	.170	.178	ScPos	65	0	16	.200	.303	.277
Jul-Oct	210	0	18	.267	.338	.357	Clutch	39	0	2	.231	.348	.308

SCOUTING REPORT

Whenever Howard is in the lineup, it's because of his glove. Howard has above-average hands and range at three infield positions, right field, and center field, with a strong and accurate arm.

At the plate, he has poor bat speed and power and is overmatched by good fastballs. He cannot hit any off-speed pitch consistently. In 1995, though, David made some adjustments and became a better situational hitter. He takes walks, is a decent bunter, and has average-plus speed.

HOW HE PERFORMED IN '95

Howard, heretofore a utility player, advanced into a platoon role at second base when Chico Lind did his mid-season disappearing act. 1995 was David's best season, as he reached career highs in most offensive categories (almost by default) while giving the Royals excellent defense. When not starting at second, Howard filled in everywhere else.

WHAT TO EXPECT IN '96

Greg Gagne's departure for Los Angeles elevated Howard to the role of regular shortstop. It's hard to believe David can be even an average offensive player after years of struggling with the bat. Still, the cost-conscious Royals have limited options, so he will play everyday.

KANSAS CITY ROYALS

MIKE MAGNANTE

Position: RP
Bats: L **Throws:** L
Ht: 6'1" **Wt:** 180
Opening Day Age: 30
Born: 6/17/1965
Drafted: KC88 11/283
ML Seasons: 5

Overall Statistics

	G	GS	GF	SV	W	L	ERA	IP	H	R	ER	HR	BB	SO
95 KC	28	0	7	0	1	1	4.23	44.2	45	23	21	6	16	28
Career	153	19	38	0	8	16	4.15	271.1	307	138	125	22	101	138

1995 Situational Statistics

	W	L	ERA	SV	IP	BB	SO		AB	HR	RBI	BA	OBA	SLG
Home	1	1	3.38	0	18.2	8	13	LHB	69	1	7	.203	.286	.275
Road	0	0	4.85	0	26.0	8	15	RHB	99	5	22	.313	.369	.495
Apr-Jun	0	0	0.00	0	0.0	0	0	ScPos	51	2	23	.235	.293	.373
Jul-Oct	1	1	4.23	0	44.2	16	28	Clutch	36	0	7	.250	.349	.333

SCOUTING REPORT

Mike Magnante's weak fastball tops out near 80 MPH, and is rarely thrown where it can be hit. Instead, he sets batters up with that "heater" and occasional sliders, throwing from a standard three-quarter angle, then fools them with a deceptive change-up that resembles a screwball. It fades away from righthanders and is clearly his best pitch. Lacking any velocity, Magnante needs precise location on all pitches. Despite having worn knee braces for many years, he's a good fielder and quick off the mound. Just four runners tried to steal against him in 1995, two successfully.

HOW HE PERFORMED IN '95

Billy Brewer's failure opened the door for Mike to emerge as a successful lefthanded setup pitcher in the Royals bullpen. Formerly used as a long reliever and spot starter, Magnante had unusually good success against lefthanded hitters in 1995, gradually earning a more important role near season's end.

WHAT TO EXPECT IN '96

Magnante has always overachieved. An unimpressive repertoire makes him seem completely replaceable. Still, he throws strikes and gets people out, so he can't be entirely ignored. In 1996 Mike will stick in the Kansas City bullpen, either in long relief or in setup duty.

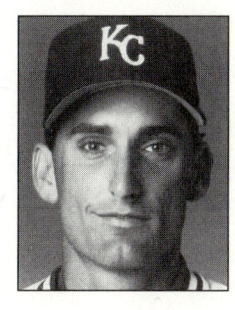

THE SCOUTING REPORT: 1996

RUSTY MEACHAM

Position: RP
Bats: R **Throws:** R
Ht: 6'2" **Wt:** 166
Opening Day Age: 28
Born: 1/27/1968
Drafted: DET87 33/858
ML Seasons: 5

Overall Statistics

	G	GS	GF	SV	W	L	ERA	IP	H	R	ER	HR	BB	SO
95 KC	49	0	26	2	4	3	4.98	59.2	72	36	33	6	19	30
Career	174	4	73	8	21	13	3.94	260.2	277	130	114	24	68	157

1995 Situational Statistics

	W	L	ERA	SV	IP	BB	SO		AB	HR	RBI	BA	OBA	SLG
Home	0	1	4.55	2	31.2	10	18	LHB	117	2	25	.291	.331	.436
Road	4	2	5.46	0	28.0	9	12	RHB	120	4	25	.317	.373	.517
Apr-Jun	2	2	4.22	0	21.1	5	11	ScPos	70	2	41	.357	.410	.557
Jul-Oct	2	1	5.40	2	38.1	14	19	Clutch	57	1	11	.368	.393	.526

SCOUTING REPORT

Using a whirling, almost sidearm delivery, stringbean Meacham throws a below-average fastball which sinks and moves in on righthanders. It's effective when thrown low and in, but he got the fastball out over the plate far too much in 1995.

Rusty also throws an average slider and a change-up that he tips off. Neither is an "out" pitch. Only two runners tried to steal while he was on the hill despite a pickoff move rated as average-minus.

HOW HE PERFORMED IN '95

Rusty's worst season was full of disappointments. His walks were up, strikeouts down, and righthanded batters hit .320 (78 points higher than in 1994) and slugged .516. Lacking overpowering velocity intensified Meacham's control problems: he'd fall behind in the count, then have to lay hittable fastballs down the middle. Meacham lost his setup role, then was demoted to the minors just as playoff rosters were being set.

WHAT TO EXPECT IN '96

The late-season demotion says a lot about Rusty's future with the Royals. If he can't be effective against righthanders, Meacham has little use. His future is with a new organization where he'll battle for a bullpen role.

KANSAS CITY ROYALS

GREGG OLSON

Position: RP
Bats: R **Throws:** R
Ht: 6'4" **Wt:** 210
Opening Day Age: 29
Born: 10/11/1966
Drafted: BAL88 1/4
ML Seasons: 8

Overall Statistics

	G	GS	GF	SV	W	L	ERA	IP	H	R	ER	HR	BB	SO
95 CLE/KC	23	0	12	3	3	3	4.09	33.0	28	15	15	4	19	21
Career	359	0	295	164	20	26	2.67	398.0	328	122	118	15	190	378

1995 Situational Statistics

	W	L	ERA	SV	IP	BB	SO		AB	HR	RBI	BA	OBA	SLG
Home	1	1	4.11	2	15.1	4	9	LHB	55	2	8	.236	.328	.400
Road	2	2	4.08	1	17.2	15	12	RHB	64	2	12	.234	.342	.391
Apr-Jun	0	0	21.60	0	1.2	1	0	ScPos	39	1	17	.308	.431	.487
Jul-Oct	3	3	3.16	3	31.1	18	21	Clutch	54	0	6	.148	.294	.167

SCOUTING REPORT

Gregg Olson works hitters from a high three-quarter angle. His mid-80s fastball is straight, and when it's thrown high, it catches too much of the plate. Gregg's sharp curveball is average-plus, but lacks its earlier consistency.

Olson's control was often absent; when he couldn't get the curve over the plate, he was hit hard. His reliance on the slow bender and a minus pickoff move led to twelve stolen bases in thirteen tries in 1995.

HOW HE PERFORMED IN '95

The former Orioles' relief ace made it back from the serious shoulder problems which had plagued him since the end of the 1993 season. Gregg began the year with Cleveland's Triple-A club, but was claimed on waivers by the Royals on July 24 and gradually moved into a setup role.

WHAT TO EXPECT IN '96

Although Olson doesn't appear to be in the Royals' immediate plans, he has proven he can again serve a useful role in the bullpen. Kansas City wanted him back, but he wanted a chance to close games so he was likely to move to another team.

HIPOLITO PICHARDO

Position: RP
Bats: R **Throws:** R
Ht: 6'1" **Wt:** 160
Opening Day Age: 26
Born: 8/22/1969
Drafted: KC 12/16/87
ML Seasons: 4

Overall Statistics

	G	GS	GF	SV	W	L	ERA	IP	H	R	ER	HR	BB	SO
95 KC	44	0	16	1	8	4	4.36	64.0	66	34	31	4	30	43
Career	150	49	37	4	29	21	4.19	440.1	479	232	205	27	156	208

1995 Situational Statistics

	W	L	ERA	SV	IP	BB	SO		AB	HR	RBI	BA	OBA	SLG
Home	6	2	3.73	1	31.1	13	24	LHB	129	3	12	.279	.350	.388
Road	2	2	4.96	0	32.2	17	19	RHB	120	1	12	.250	.355	.292
Apr-Jun	4	2	4.11	1	30.2	14	20	ScPos	66	0	19	.273	.410	.318
Jul-Oct	4	2	4.59	0	33.1	16	23	Clutch	115	1	5	.235	.343	.296

SCOUTING REPORT

Pichardo whirls and throws with a low three-quarter motion. He works primarily with two pitches: a well above-average fastball and an average split-finger pitch. He also throws a below-average slider, but it's strictly for show. Power-pitcher arsenal, right? Well, not really. Hipolito's fastball is straight and usually up in the strike zone; the splitter, his out pitch, keeps hitters honest. His splitter has good movement, but often burrows into the dirt—it's a good pitch, when controlled, and it consistently generates ground balls.

HOW HE PERFORMED IN '95

Formerly a starting pitcher, Pichardo has now spent the last two seasons in the bullpen. After starting 1995 in long relief, he gradually earned more important roles due to the failure of other righthanded relievers. Hipolito finished the year as one of the team's few reliable bullpen options.

WHAT TO EXPECT IN '96

Although he enjoyed some success in short relief, Pichardo's high walk rate is cause for concern. He seems to have the confidence of Royals' coaches, but Pichardo still needs to prove he can do the job over the long haul. He'll begin 1996 as the primary situational righthander in the bullpen.

KANSAS CITY ROYALS

JUAN SAMUEL

Positions: 1B/DH/OF//2B
Bats: R **Throws:** R
Ht: 5'11" **Wt:** 170
Opening Day Age: 35
Born: 12/9/1960
Drafted: PHI 4/29/80
ML Seasons: 13

Overall Statistics

	G	AB	R	H	2B	3B	HR	RBI	SB	CS	BB	SO	BA	OBA
95 DET/KC91	205	31	54	10	1	12	39	6	4	29	49	.263	.360
Career	1563	5748	812	1494	272	95	149	660	369	131	408	1336	.260	.314

1995 Situational Statistics

	AB	HR	RBI	BA	OBA	SLG		AB	HR	RBI	BA	OBA	SLG
Home	104	6	20	.317	.418	.577	LHP	119	8	23	.261	.362	.479
Road	101	6	19	.208	.298	.416	RHP	86	4	16	.267	.357	.523
Apr-Jun	80	8	24	.338	.442	.725	ScPos	54	2	24	.315	.431	.500
Jul-Oct	125	4	15	.216	.305	.352	Clutch	50	1	5	.260	.327	.400

SCOUTING REPORT

The same aggressive hitter he has always been, Juan Samuel looks to pull the first hittable fastball out over the plate. Pitchers who work both sides of the plate with good breaking stuff can befuddle him.

His speed has declined, and Samuel is now just a slightly above-average runner who can steal a base when necessary. Juan's defensive roles have gradually diminished; an average arm offsets his poor fielding instincts and range at second base. He can also play first and the outfield.

HOW HE PERFORMED IN '95

Often, former stars finish their careers as utility players and pinch-hitters for weak teams. Such is the case with Samuel, who filled a bench role for the Tigers in '95 before joining the Royals for their "pennant drive." Despite a decent showing in Detroit, Juan was a bust in K.C., hitting .176.

WHAT TO EXPECT IN '96

Entering his 14th season at 35, Samuel is capable of occasional power off the bench and can still serve a useful, albeit limited, role. Juan has switched teams eight times in the last seven years and will again fill out change-of-address forms in '96.

MICHAEL TUCKER

Positions: OF/DH
Bats: L **Throws:** R
Ht: 6'2" **Wt:** 185
Opening Day Age: 24
Born: 6/25/1971
Drafted: KC92 1/10
ML Seasons: 1

Overall Statistics

	G	AB	R	H	2B	3B	HR	RBI	SB	CS	BB	SO	BA	OBA
95 KC	62	177	23	46	10	0	4	17	2	3	18	51	.260	.332
Career	62	177	23	46	10	0	4	17	2	3	18	51	.260	.332

1995 Situational Statistics

	AB	HR	RBI	BA	OBA	SLG		AB	HR	RBI	BA	OBA	SLG
Home	88	1	3	.227	.320	.318	LHP	19	0	0	.211	.211	.211
Road	89	3	14	.292	.344	.449	RHP	158	4	17	.266	.345	.405
Apr-Jun	82	0	4	.207	.261	.244	ScPos	39	1	13	.256	.356	.410
Jul-Oct	95	4	13	.305	.389	.505	Clutch	22	2	4	.364	.481	.727

SCOUTING REPORT

An aggressive low-fastball hitter, Tucker fares better when he relaxes and lets his power stroke take over. Early last year, he seemed lost, over-analyzing each at-bat. Tucker has average-plus speed and can steal bases, although his baserunning judgment needs improvement. He's not yet a good defensive player, occasionally misreading fly balls and sporting an average-minus arm.

HOW HE PERFORMED IN '95

It was two different seasons for Tucker, yet another Royals' rookie outfielder. He began the year playing every day in left, struggling to hit his weight.

Demoted to Triple-A Omaha, Tucker regained the aggressive hitting demeanor which had made him a bright prospect. He returned to Kansas City in August with new focus, hitting over .300 and slugging over .500 to close the season. While his range in left field was above the league average, he threw out only three baserunners.

WHAT TO EXPECT IN '96

Tucker is a good bet to hold on to left field for a while. The last seven weeks of 1995 provided a taste of what Tucker can do: the Royals hope he can avoid prolonged slumps and really blossom in 1996.

KANSAS CITY ROYALS

JOE VITIELLO

Positions: DH//1B
Bats: R **Throws:** R
Ht: 6'2" **Wt:** 215
Opening Day Age: 25
Born: 4/11/1970
Drafted: KC91 1/7
ML Seasons: 1

Overall Statistics

	G	AB	R	H	2B	3B	HR	RBI	SB	CS	BB	SO	BA	OBA
95 KC	53	130	13	33	4	0	7	21	0	0	8	25	.254	.317
Career	53	130	13	33	4	0	7	21	0	0	8	25	.254	.317

1995 Situational Statistics

	AB	HR	RBI	BA	OBA	SLG		AB	HR	RBI	BA	OBA	SLG
Home	72	3	6	.236	.304	.389	LHP	72	6	16	.278	.358	.569
Road	58	4	15	.276	.333	.517	RHP	58	1	5	.224	.262	.293
Apr-Jun	11	0	0	.000	.154	.000	ScPos	35	2	14	.171	.237	.371
Jul-Oct	119	7	21	.277	.333	.487	Clutch	16	0	2	.125	.364	.125

SCOUTING REPORT
Vitiello is primarily a high fastball hitter, but also handles low pitches and breaking balls well, too; his swing covers the plate nicely. However, he lacks bat speed for a hitter of his size.

Reconstructive knee surgery before last season has made Joe one of the league's slowest runners, and limits him to first base and DH duty. He is a minus fielder all around.

HOW HE PERFORMED IN '95
Vitiello, the 1994 American Association batting champion, rebounded from knee problems to make a fine impression in his short major-league debut. Finishing the season as a regular, Joe put on a power display, hitting five of his seven homers in a two-week September span. Under the tutelage of hitting coach Greg Luzinski, Vitiello learned to extend his arms and use his size to drive balls deep to the outfield.

WHAT TO EXPECT IN '96
Although Wally Joyner blocks his path, Vitiello's role will expand in 1996; he will serve as a part-time DH and reserve first baseman. If he improves on his promising 1995 performance, Joe will undoubtedly be Kansas City's regular first baseman in 1997.

KANSAS CITY ROYALS: TOP PROSPECTS

JAMIE BLUMA
Bats: R Throws: R Opening Day Age: 23
Ht: 5-11 Wt: 195 Born: 5/18/1972
Position: P Drafted: 1994 #3 KC

YR TEAM	LG/CLASS	G	GS	GF	SV	W	L	ERA	IP	H	HR	BB	SO	O/BA
94 Eugene	NWST/A	26	0	23	12	2	1	0.99	36.1	19	0	6	35	.152
94 Wilmington	CARO/A	7	0	7	2	4	0	0.93	9.2	7	0	0	5	.206
95 Omaha	AMAS/AAA	18	0	10	4	0	0	3.04	23	21	1	14	12	.259
Wichita	TEX/AA	42	0	40	22	4	3	3.09	55	38	9	9	31	.190

Bluma, who led the organization in saves, has drawn as much publicity for eating bugs as he has for retiring batters. The 23-year-old, who is particularly tough on righthanders, uses a sling-shot motion to launch a high-80s fastball and a good slider. Bluma had a rough start at Triple-A after being promoted, but pitched much better at the end of the season.

SAL FASANO
Bats: R Throws: R Opening Day Age: 24
Ht: 6-2 Wt: 220 Born: 8/10/1971
Position: C Drafted: 1993 #35 KC

YR TEAM	LG/CLASS	G	AB	R	H	2B	3B	HR	RBI	SB	BA	OBA
93 Eugene	NWST/A	49	176	25	47	11	1	10	36	4	.267	.355
94 Rockford	MID/A	97	345	61	97	16	1	25	81	8	.281	.366
94 Wilmington	CARO/A	23	90	15	29	7	0	7	32	0	.322	.408
95 Wichita	TEX/AA	87	317	60	92	18	2	20	66	3	.290	.373
Wilmington	CARO/A	23	88	12	20	2	1	2	7	0	.227	.277

The 24-year-old has big-time power which he displayed in the second half of '95, belting 18 homers and 15 doubles while batting .340 in 53 games. The 1994 Midwest League MVP, who lost 30 pounds prior to that season, gained some unnecessary weight early last year and was actually shipped to extended spring training in early June for an attitude adjustment. It remains to be seen if the strong-armed Fasano, who doesn't move very well behind the plate, will make it as a catcher.

FELIX MARTINEZ
Bats: S Throws: R Opening Day Age: 21
Ht: 6-0 Wt: 168 Born: 5/18/1974
Position: SS Drafted: NDFA 2-26-93 KC

YR TEAM	LG/CLASS	G	AB	R	H	2B	3B	HR	RBI	SB	BA	OBA
93 KC	GULF/R	57	165	23	42	5	1	0	12	22	.255	.335
94 Wilmington	CARO/A	117	400	65	107	16	4	2	43	19	.268	.322
95 Wichita	TEX/AA	127	426	53	112	15	3	3	30	44	.263	.321

A flashy, switch-hitting, temperamental Dominican, Martinez led the Texas League in stolen bases, but also was fourth in the entire minor leagues with 50 errors. Scouts are unconcerned with his miscues, however, choosing to rave about his outstanding range and throwing arm. Offensively, the 21-year-old is a free swinger with little power who hits twice as many fly balls as ground balls. This tendency will have to change for him to excel at bat.

ROD MYERS
Bats: L Throws: L Opening Day Age: 23
Ht: 6-0 Wt: 190 Born: 1/14/1973
Position: OF Drafted: 1991 #13 KC

YR TEAM	LG/CLASS	G	AB	R	H	2B	3B	HR	RBI	SB	BA	OBA
93 Rockford	MID/A	129	474	69	123	24	5	9	68	49	.259	.344
94 Wilmington	CARO/A	126	457	76	120	20	4	12	65	31	.263	.363
95 Wichita	TEX/AA	131	499	71	153	22	6	7	62	29	.307	.354

Playing in the shadows of Johnny Damon the past three seasons, Myers has received little attention, but has emerged as one of the Royals' top prospects. He is a talented but raw athlete who can hit, hit for power, run and throw. The 22-year-old batted .372 in August and finished ninth in the Texas League in batting and fourth in stolen bases. The Royals were concerned by his problems with lefthanders, against whom he hit .271 but didn't homer and fanned four times more than he walked.

JIM PITTSLEY
Bats: R Throws: R Opening Day Age: 21
Ht: 6-7 Wt: 215 Born: 4/3/1974
Position: P Drafted: 1992 #2 KC

YR TEAM	LG/CLASS	G	GS	GF	SV	W	L	ERA	IP	H	HR	BB	SO	O/BA
93 Rockford	MID/A	15	15	0	0	5	5	4.26	80.1	76	3	32	87	.252
94 Wilmington	CARO/A	27	27	0	0	11	5	3.17	161.2	154	15	42	171	.250
95 Omaha	AMAS/AAA	8	8	0	0	4	1	3.21	47	38	5	16	39	.222
Kansas City	AL/MAJ	1	1	0	0	0	1	13.50	3	7	3	1	0	.438

Pittsley, the Royals' best pitching prospect, possesses a live arm and polish beyond his years, but had his 1995 season ended by an elbow injury in late May. The 21-year-old, who skipped over Double-A after an impressive '94 campaign, was pitching very well and had even made a start for Kansas City just before the injury occurred. Happily, the injury appears not as serious as initially feared. Pittsley hopes to be throwing by spring training.

KRIS RALSTON
Bats: R Throws: R Opening Day Age: 24
Ht: 6-2 Wt: 205 Born: 8/8/1971
Position: P Drafted: 1993 #19 KC

YR TEAM	LG/CLASS	G	GS	GF	SV	W	L	ERA	IP	H	HR	BB	SO	O/BA
93 Eugene	NWST/A	15	15	0	0	7	3	2.74	82.0	52	5	36	75	.184
94 Wilmington	CARO/A	20	18	0	0	10	4	2.39	109.1	84	11	38	102	.209
95 Wichita	TEX/AA	18	16	0	0	9	4	3.56	93	85	10	28	84	.244

The 24-year-old spent the first six weeks of the season rehabbing a sore shoulder and never pitched more than seven innings a start in 1995. Ralston, who features a sharp breaking ball and upper-80's heater, was the club's most effective pitcher the second half of the season. His key attributes are a bulldog mentality and knowledge of the game—Ralston carefully studies every hitter, a very unusual trait for a minor leaguer.

THE SCOUTING REPORT: 1996

KANSAS CITY ROYALS: TOP PROSPECTS

KEN RAY

Bats: R Throws: R Opening Day Age: 21
Ht: 6-2 Wt: 160 Born: 11/27/1974
Position: P Drafted: 1993 #16 KC

YR TEAM	LG/CLASS	G	GS	GF	SV	W	L	ERA	IP	H	HR	BB	SO	O/BA
93 KC	GULF/R	13	7	3	0	2	3	2.28	47.1	44	1	17	45	.240
94 Rockford	MID/A	27	18	6	3	10	4	1.82	128.2	94	5	56	128	.207
95 Wichita	TEX/AA	14	14	0	0	4	5	5.97	75	83	7	46	53	.282
Wilmington	CARO/A	13	13	0	0	6	4	2.69	77	74	3	22	63	.254

Ray is only 20, but his 6-foot-2 frame has bulked up considerably since being drafted in 1993. Considered the best long-range pitching prospect at Wichita, he was the 1995 opening night starter, but returned to Wilmington one month later after posting a 7.22 ERA. Ray came back to the Texas League after 13 appearances in Class-A and went 3-2, 5.17 ERA in his final eight starts. He throws an average fastball and a sharp breaking curve that he has trouble controlling, but Ray is still very young and far from polished.

GLENDON RUSCH

Bats: L Throws: L Opening Day Age: 21
Ht: 6-2 Wt: 170 Born: 11/7/1974
Position: P Drafted: 1993 #15 KC

YR TEAM	LG/CLASS	G	GS	GF	SV	W	L	ERA	IP	H	HR	BB	SO	O/BA
93 KC	GULF/R	11	10	0	0	4	2	1.60	62.0	43	0	11	48	.197
93 Rockford	MID/A	2	2	0	0	0	1	3.38	8.0	10	0	7	8	.313
94 Rockford	MID/A	28	17	5	1	8	5	4.66	114.0	111	5	34	122	.256
95 Wilmington	CARO/A	26	26	0	0	14	6	1.74	165	110	5	34	147	.188

The 20-year-old was the organization's biggest surprise in 1995, pacing the Carolina League in wins (14) and ERA (1.74) while finishing second in strikeouts despite not possessing an overpowering fastball. Rusch, whose 1994 highlight was a no-hitter, works quickly, and uses a very good curve and changeup to spot an average fastball. He led all minor leaguers in ERA and all starting pitchers in average against (.188), finishing the season 13-2, 1.05 ERA in his last 19 starts. Working in Rusch's favor was Frawley Stadium in Wilmington, the best pitchers' park in the league by far. There, Rusch made 16 of his 26 starts, posting a 1.33 ERA. He notched a 2.53 ERA on the road.

CHRIS STYNES

Bats: R Throws: R Opening Day Age: 23
Ht: 5-9 Wt: 170 Born: 1/19/1973
Position: 2B Drafted: 1991 #6 TOR

YR TEAM	LG/CLASS	G	AB	R	H	2B	3B	HR	RBI	SB	BA	OBA
93 Dunedin	FSL/A	123	496	72	151	28	5	7	48	59	.304	.339
94 Knoxville	SOU/AA	136	545	79	173	32	4	8	79	28	.317	.351
95 Omaha	AMAS/AAA	83	306	51	84	12	5	9	42	4	.275	.338
Kansas City	AL/MAJ	22	35	7	6	1	0	0	2	0	.171	.256

In just his second year at second base, Stynes was trying to convince the Royals that he is their second baseman of the future. A scrapper who shows gap power, can steal a base, and play steady defense, Stynes led the Southern League in hits in 1994 while finishing second in batting and rarely striking out. He hit .305 with 96 doubles and 75 steals in three seasons prior to 1995.

LARRY SUTTON

Bats: L Throws: L Opening Day Age: 25
Ht: 5-11 Wt: 175 Born: 5/14/1970
Position: 1B Drafted: 1992 #24 KC

YR TEAM	LG/CLASS	G	AB	R	H	2B	3B	HR	RBI	SB	BA	OBA
93 Rockford	MID/A	113	361	67	97	24	1	7	50	3	.269	.424
94 Wilmington	CARO/A	129	480	91	147	33	1	26	94	2	.306	.406
95 Wichita	TEX/AA	53	197	31	53	11	1	5	32	1	.269	.357

The two-time MVP missed two months of the 1995 season after fracturing his elbow while swinging a bat on the on-deck circle. When healthy, Sutton has shown a patient eye with good power and an ability to hit lefthanded pitchers very well. He is not big and doesn't run well, but is a better-than-average defensive first baseman and a class individual.

MIKE SWEENEY

Bats: R Throws: R Opening Day Age: 22
Ht: 6-1 Wt: 195 Born: 7/22/1973
Position: C Drafted: 1991 #10 KC

YR TEAM	LG/CLASS	G	AB	R	H	2B	3B	HR	RBI	SB	BA	OBA
93 Eugene	NWST/A	53	175	32	42	10	2	6	29	1	.240	.359
94 Rockford	MID/A	86	276	47	83	20	3	10	52	0	.301	.427
95 Kansas City	AL/MAJ	4	4	1	1	0	0	0	0	0	.250	.250
Wilmington	CARO/A	99	332	61	103	23	1	18	53	6	.310	.424

With Damon in the majors to stay, the Carolina League batting champ has become the Royals' top position player prospect. Sweeney hits for average and can pull the ball, has excellent strike zone judgement, works extremely hard, and has a strong, though sometimes erratic, arm. Particularly impressive was his home run total; only 31 balls left Wilmington's stadium all season long, the third lowest total of any minor league park.

DILSON TORRES

Bats: R Throws: R Opening Day Age: 25
Ht: 6-1 Wt: 215 Born: 5/31/1970
Position: P Drafted: NDFA 12-10-90 TOR

YR TEAM	LG/CLASS	G	GS	GF	SV	W	L	ERA	IP	H	HR	BB	SO	O/BA
93 St.cathrnes	NYP/A	17	0	12	3	1	4	3.13	23.0	21	3	6	23	.231
94 Wilmington	CARO/A	15	9	5	2	7	2	1.37	59.1	45	5	15	49	.215
94 Memphis	SOU/AA	10	9	0	0	6	0	1.83	59.0	47	3	10	47	.223
95 Omaha	AMAS/AAA	5	5	0	0	3	1	2.63	27	28	2	7	12	.275
Kansas City	AL/MAJ	24	2	7	0	1	2	6.09	44	56	6	17	28	.354

After a breakthrough 1994 campaign in which Torres posted the minors' second-best ERA (1.60) and allowed two runs or fewer in 17 of 18 starts, the 25-year-old began last season in the major leagues. He was inconsistent for the Royals, although he showed good control, a decent slider and an okay fastball. Sent to Omaha in late July, Torres was recalled three weeks later.

KANSAS CITY ROYALS: OTHERS TO WATCH

BRIAN BEVIL Bats: R Throws: R Ht: 6-3 Wt: 190
Born: 9/5/1971 Drafted: 1990 #28 KC Position: P

YR TEAM	LG/CLASS	G	GS	GF	SV	W	L	ERA	IP	H	HR	BB	SO	O/BA
95 Omaha	AMAS/AAA	6	6	0	0	1	3	9.41	22.0	40	7	14	10	.396
95 Wichita	TEX/AA	15	15	0	0	5	7	5.84	74.0	85	7	35	57	.290

Bevil, a member of the 40-man roster, has good stuff and has had success in the past, but never got going in '95.

MIKE BOVEE Bats: R Throws: R Ht: 5-10 Wt: 200
Born: 8/21/1973 Drafted: 1991 #6 KC Position: P

YR TEAM	LG/CLASS	G	GS	GF	SV	W	L	ERA	IP	H	HR	BB	SO	O/BA
95 Wichita	TEX/AA	20	20	0	0	8	6	4.18	114.0	118	12	43	72	.271

A curveballer with excellent control who won the 1994 Carolina League ERA title, Bovee was up and down last year and must take the game more seriously.

MEL BUNCH Bats: R Throws: R Ht: 6-1 Wt: 165
Born: 11/4/1971 Drafted: 1992 #18 KC Position: P

YR TEAM	LG/CLASS	G	GS	GF	SV	W	L	ERA	IP	H	HR	BB	SO	O/BA
95 Omaha	AMAS/AAA	12	11	0	0	1	7	4.57	65.0	63	10	20	50	.257
95 Kansas City	AL/MAJ	13	5	3	0	1	3	5.63	40.0	42	11	14	19	.271

Bunch, who features excellent control and location, surprised in 1995 by overcoming past shoulder problems to jump from Class-A to the major leagues.

TIMOTHY BYRDAK Bats: L Throws: L Ht: 5-11 Wt: 170
Born: 10/31/1973 Drafted: 1994 #5 KC Position: P

YR TEAM	LG/CLASS	G	GS	GF	SV	W	L	ERA	IP	H	HR	BB	SO	O/BA
95 Wilmington	CARO/A	27	26	0	0	11	5	2.16	166.1	118	7	45	127	.198

The crafty lefthander finished third in ERA and wins and fifth in strikeouts last season, winning seven straight starts at one point.

BART EVANS Bats: R Throws: R Ht: 6-1 Wt: 190
Born: 12/30/1970 Drafted: 1992 #12 KC Position: P

YR TEAM	LG/CLASS	G	GS	GF	SV	W	L	ERA	IP	H	HR	BB	SO	O/BA
95 Wichita	TEX/AA	7	7	0	0	0	4	10.48	22.1	22	3	45	13	.289
95 Wilmington	CARO/A	16	6	4	2	4	1	2.89	46.2	30	0	44	47	.182

The 1994 Carolina League's Most Outstanding Pitcher throws 90+, but lost all control and confidence at Double-A in 1995.

RAUL GONZALEZ Bats: R Throws: R Ht: 5-8 Wt: 175
Born: 12/27/1973 Drafted: 1990 #15 KC Position: OF

YR TEAM	LG/CLASS	G	AB	R	H	2B	3B	HR	RBI	SB	BA	OBA
95 Wichita	TEX/AA	22	79	14	23	3	2	2	11	4	.291	.356
95 Wilmington	CARO/A	86	308	36	90	19	3	11	49	6	.292	.620

Gonzalez, is a fine natural hitter, but defense and unwillingness to use the whole field have sidetracked him.

JEFF GRANGER Bats: R Throws: L Ht: 6-4 Wt: 200
Born: 12/16/1971 Drafted: 1993 #1 KC Position: P

YR TEAM	LG/CLASS	G	GS	GF	SV	W	L	ERA	IP	H	HR	BB	SO	O/BA
95 Wichita	TEX/AA	18	18	0	0	4	7	5.93	95.2	122	9	40	81	.312

The former first-rounder struggled all season, lost velocity on his fastball, and had trouble controlling his breaking ball.

PHIL GRUNDY Bats: R Throws: R Ht: 6-2 Wt: 195
Born: 9/8/1972 Drafted: 1993 #2 KC Position: P

YR TEAM	LG/CLASS	G	GS	GF	SV	W	L	ERA	IP	H	HR	BB	SO	O/BA
95 Wichita	TEX/AA	6	2	1	0	1	1	8.31	17.1	16	6	7	11	.246
95 Wilmington	CARO/A	20	16	3	1	6	6	3.31	106.0	106	7	32	90	.263

Highly regarded, and possessing a live arm, Grundy had a mediocre '95 campaign.

RICK HUISMAN Bats: R Throws: R Ht: 6-3 Wt: 200
Born: 5/17/1969 Drafted: 1990 #6 SF Position: P

YR TEAM	LG/CLASS	G	GS	GF	SV	W	L	ERA	IP	H	HR	BB	SO	O/BA
95 Omaha	AMAS/AAA	5	0	3	1	0	0	1.80	5.0	3	1	1	13	.167
95 Tucson	PCL/AAA	42	0	28	6	1	4	4.45	54.2	58	1	28	47	.271
95 Kansas City	AL/MAJ	7	0	2	0	0	0	7.45	9.2	14	2	1	12	.326
95 Houston	NL/MAJ	0	0	0	0	0	0	0.00	0.0	0	0	0	0	.000

Huisman converted 50 of 52 save chances between the Texas and Venezuelan League in '94, but was inconsistent last season.

OSCAR JIMENEZ Bats: R Throws: R Ht: 6-0 Wt: 190
Born: 12/18/1974 Drafted: NDFA 1-27-92 KC Position: RF

YR TEAM	LG/CLASS	G	AB	R	H	2B	3B	HR	RBI	SB	BA	OBA
95 Wilmington	CARO/A	121	374	42	94	18	4	1	31	11	.251	.357

Jimenez, who is still very young, has shown glimpses of his multiple skills but needs a breakout year.

MENDY LOPEZ Bats: R Throws: R Ht: 6-2 Wt: 165
Born: 10/15/1974 Drafted: NDFA 2-19-92 KC Position: 3B

YR TEAM	LG/CLASS	G	AB	R	H	2B	3B	HR	RBI	SB	BA	OBA
95 Wilmington	CARO/A	130	428	42	116	29	3	2	36	18	.271	.322

Jumped all the way to Wilmington after a great 1994 performance in the Gulf Coast League (.362, 50 RBI, 19 SB).

RODOLFO MENDEZ Bats: R Throws: R Ht: 5-11 Wt: 180
Born: 8/22/1974 Drafted: NDFA 2-4-94 KC Position: OF

YR TEAM	LG/CLASS	G	AB	R	H	2B	3B	HR	RBI	SB	BA	OBA
95 Springfield	MID/A	129	449	70	124	28	11	10	72	40	.276	.333

Mendez has shown five-tool talent his first two years in the states.

LES NORMAN Bats: R Throws: R Ht: 6-1 Wt: 185
Born: 2/25/1969 Drafted: 1991 #25 KC Position: OF

YR TEAM	LG/CLASS	G	AB	R	H	2B	3B	HR	RBI	SB	BA	OBA
95 Omaha	AMAS/AAA	83	313	46	89	19	3	9	33	5	.284	.329
95 Kansas City	AL/MAJ	24	40	6	9	0	1	0	4	0	.225	.326

A gifted hitter and defensive player, Norman has been inconsistent.

JOE RANDA Bats: R Throws: R Ht: 5-11 Wt: 190
Born: 12/18/1969 Drafted: 1991 #11 KC Position: 3B

YR TEAM	LG/CLASS	G	AB	R	H	2B	3B	HR	RBI	SB	BA	OBA
95 Omaha	AMAS/AAA	64	233	33	64	10	2	8	33	2	.275	.341
95 Kansas City	AL/MAJ	34	70	6	12	2	0	1	5	0	.171	.237

Randa, a fine glove man who has hit for average but not power, couldn't beat out Gary Gaetti for an everyday job in Kansas City and didn't hit much off the bench.

ANDY STEWART Bats: R Throws: R Ht: 5-11 Wt: 205
Born: 12/5/1970 Drafted: NDFA 9-1-89 KC Position: 1B

YR TEAM	LG/CLASS	G	AB	R	H	2B	3B	HR	RBI	SB	BA	OBA
95 Omaha	AMAS/AAA	44	156	24	47	11	0	3	21	0	.301	.381
95 Wichita	TEX/AA	60	216	28	56	18	0	3	32	1	.259	.305

The non-drafted free agent has surprised the organization with his bat and versatility, playing catcher, first base and third base.

THE SCOUTING REPORT: 1996

MILWAUKEE BREWERS

RICKY BONES

Position: SP
Bats: R **Throws:** R
Ht: 5'10" **Wt:** 175
Opening Day Age: 26
Born: 4/7/1969
Drafted: SD 5/13/86
ML Seasons: 5

SCOUTING REPORT

Ricky comes to the plate with an overhand delivery but lacks the hard stuff most overhanders boast. He does have five pitches, however. Bones' best offerings are his plus curve and change-up curve. He has an average straight change, an average slider, and a minus sinking fastball that often doesn't sink until it travels a few hundred feet. Although Bones keeps batters confused by mixing his pitches well, he is inconsistent and tries to be too fine despite having above-average control. Plus at holding baserunners, 18 runners tried to steal against him in '95, but 11 were thrown out. Bones also shows good athletic ability, especially fielding bunts and covering first.

HOW HE PERFORMED IN '95

With injuries again depleting Milwaukee's pitching staff, Bones ended up the team's #1 starting pitcher. Unfortunately, as the Brewers learned, Ricky is just not good enough to be a rotation anchor. While Bones should have had a better won-loss record (in his first 11 losses, the Brewers scored a puny 23 runs), he contributed to his own problems by allowing a club-high 26 home runs and nibbling at the corners agonizingly after getting ahead in the count. This, plus his lack of a consistent out pitch, resulted in more walks allowed than strikeouts. With a varied arsenal of pitches, Ricky has an advantage over many of his teammates. However, without an average fastball, he relies on control. When he doesn't have that ... there are months like September, when Bones racked up a 6.31 ERA in 35.2 innings, walking 22, and allowing seven home runs. His poor performance in the last month was a critical reason for the club's free-fall from playoff contention. However, despite all of his problems in '95, Bones filled a valuable role for the Brewers, taking the ball every time out and remaining healthy the entire season.

WHAT TO EXPECT IN '96

Bones will continue in the Brewers' rotation this year. A more aggressive approach and the ability to finish batters when ahead in the count could cut his rising walk total. A little luck and better run support should help, too. But if Milwaukee continues to count on Ricky as their top starter, the team will be in big trouble. Pitchers who walk as many and strike out as few as he does just cannot win consistently.

Overall Statistics

	G	GS	GF	SV	W	L	ERA	IP	H	R	ER	HR	BB	SO
95 MIL	32	31	0	0	10	12	4.63	200.1	218	108	103	26	83	77
Career	130	125	1	0	44	48	4.43	792.0	832	429	390	101	257	293

1995 Situational Statistics

	W	L	ERA	SV	IP	BB	SO		AB	HR	RBI	BA	OBA	SLG
Home	5	6	5.80	0	94.2	41	38	LHB	449	10	49	.281	.339	.405
Road	5	6	3.58	0	105.2	42	39	RHB	327	16	48	.281	.362	.511
Apr-Jun	4	6	4.15	0	84.2	35	29	ScPos	165	3	63	.224	.305	.376
Jul-Oct	6	6	4.98	0	115.2	48	48	Clutch	35	3	3	.257	.316	.514

How He Compares to Other Pitchers

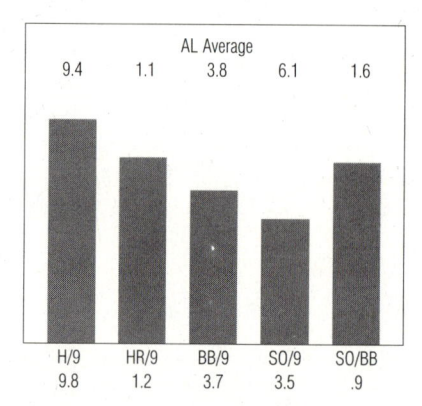

AL Average: 9.4 / 1.1 / 3.8 / 6.1 / 1.6

H/9	HR/9	BB/9	SO/9	SO/BB
9.8	1.2	3.7	3.5	.9

How He Compares to Other Starting Pitchers

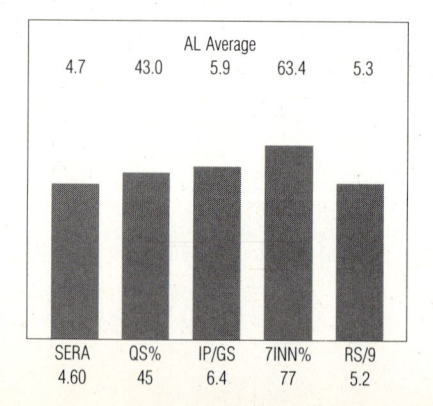

AL Average: 4.7 / 43.0 / 5.9 / 63.4 / 5.3

SERA	QS%	IP/GS	7INN%	RS/9
4.60	45	6.4	77	5.2

162   THE SCOUTING REPORT: 1996

MILWAUKEE BREWERS

JEFF CIRILLO

Positions: 3B/2B//1B/SS
Bats: R **Throws:** R
Ht: 6'2" **Wt:** 190
Opening Day Age: 26
Born: 9/23/1969
Drafted: MIL91 11/286
ML Seasons: 2

SCOUTING REPORT
Cirillo possesses one of the strongest arms of any infielder in the major leagues. As a third baseman, where he played the majority of his games in '95, Jeff showed good hands, average range, and average throwing accuracy. He can also play second base. While he's not a power machine, Cirillo occasionally pops one into the stands. He prefers fastballs down and in where he can pull, but Jeff continues to work on hitting to all fields. He has excellent strike-zone judgment, makes contact, and is quite willing to accept the walk. Milwaukee does not often ask him to sacrifice. An average baserunner, Cirillo will only steal a base on failed hit-and-run attempts or when the Brewers attempt to fool the opponent.

HOW HE PERFORMED IN '95
While never as highly rated as some of his farm system brethren, Cirillo is one of few recent Brewers to come through the minor-league system and produce in the majors. Although there is room for him to improve, Jeff is a good-looking young player. A smart hitter who finished third on the club in walks, Cirillo proved to be a tough out, especially with two strikes. Many times Jeff battled pitchers by fouling off pitch after pitch before either walking or putting the ball in play. Despite solid overall offensive numbers, however, Cirillo consistently failed to get key hits in RBI situations, batting a very poor .209 in 127 at-bats with runners on base. Cirillo spent most of the year at third base, his best position. However, manager Phil Garner experimented with Jeff briefly at second base late in the year. That switch was short-lived, however, due to Fernando Vina's encouraging defensive play. In addition, using Cirillo at second fails to adequately take advantage of his cannon arm. After batting .305 with five homers and 24 RBI in August, Jeff batted just .192 in the final month. Hampered by a sore back, he knocked in only two runs in his final 78 at-bats.

WHAT TO EXPECT IN '96
Cirillo will most likely start this season as Milwaukee's third baseman. After that, who knows? Antone Williamson, the club's top pick in the '94 draft, is being groomed as the third baseman of the future and may be ready for the '97 season. With his excellent all-around skills, however, Jeff will play somewhere everyday.

Overall Statistics

	G	AB	R	H	2B	3B	HR	RBI	SB	CS	BB	SO	BA	OBA
95 MIL	125	328	57	91	19	4	9	39	7	2	47	42	.277	.371
Career	164	454	74	121	28	4	12	51	7	3	58	58	.267	.354

1995 Situational Statistics

	AB	HR	RBI	BA	OBA	SLG		AB	HR	RBI	BA	OBA	SLG
Home	153	6	22	.320	.412	.516	LHP	119	2	15	.294	.384	.429
Road	175	3	17	.240	.333	.377	RHP	209	7	24	.268	.363	.450
Apr-Jun	98	3	5	.316	.380	.500	ScPos	80	2	32	.225	.333	.338
Jul-Oct	230	6	34	.261	.367	.417	Clutch	57	0	3	.281	.386	.404

How He Compares to Other Batters

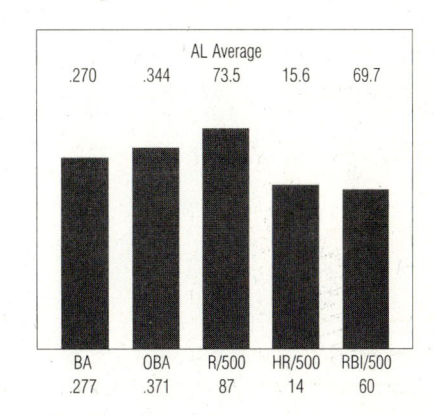

AL Average
.270 .344 73.5 15.6 69.7

BA OBA R/500 HR/500 RBI/500
.277 .371 87 14 60

Where He Hits the Ball

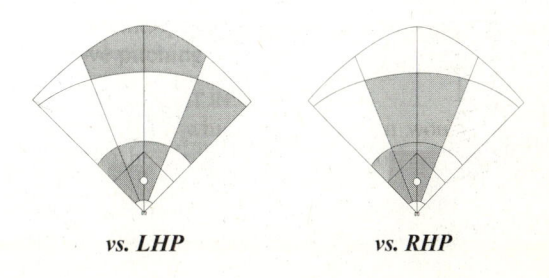

vs. LHP   vs. RHP

THE SCOUTING REPORT: 1996

MILWAUKEE BREWERS

MIKE FETTERS

Position: RP
Bats: R **Throws:** R
Ht: 6'4" **Wt:** 200
Opening Day Age: 31
Born: 12/19/1964
Drafted: CAL86 4/27
ML Seasons: 7

SCOUTING REPORT
A plus split-finger fastball is Fetters' best pitch, and he goes to it like clockwork with two strikes. He also has a slightly above-average sinking fastball that sets up the splitter. His curve is just average. Mike's overhand delivery makes his pitches especially deceptive to impatient hitters. However, Fetters has experienced difficulty with his slider and his overall control rates as poor. He walks a lot of hitters and gets into trouble often going deep in the count. Mike is generally adequate at holding runners on base and fielding his position. Last year, not a single runner tried to steal against him.

HOW HE PERFORMED IN '95
Mike Fetters may be the best unknown bullpen stopper in the major leagues. Playing in Milwaukee is an easy way to remain anonymous.

For the past three seasons, Fetters has been the only consistently effective member of the Milwaukee bullpen, first as a setup pitcher and then, in 1994–95, as the stopper. His 22 saves this year were a career high, and included a streak of 20 straight converted save opportunities dating back to '94.

He allowed his first home run of the year in August, ending a streak of nearly 90 innings without allowing a dinger. A late-season slump helped propel his ERA up from the 1.00 mark it had hovered around through most of the summer.

Even in this age of short appearances, it is unusual for a team's closer to average less than an inning per game, but Mike did just that in '95. Early-season elbow tendinitis and a lack of save opportunities due to the Brewers' losing record limited Mike's appearances for the season, much to his frustration. His pit-bull attitude—and borderline flakiness—make him the perfect personality fit for a 1990s bullpen ace.

WHAT TO EXPECT IN '96
There are two ways Fetters can get the recognition he deserves: move his game up a notch and become outstanding, or to be traded to a contending team. While Mike still fits in with the Brewers' plans, a top-flight stopper could be worth a couple of top-flight prospects, something the undernourished, low-budget Brewers could always use. If the Brewers aren't in the pennant race in the late summer (a likely situation), Fetters could be used as trade bait.

Overall Statistics

	G	GS	GF	SV	W	L	ERA	IP	H	R	ER	HR	BB	SO
95 MIL	40	0	34	22	0	3	3.37	34.2	40	16	13	3	20	33
Career	223	6	108	42	12	17	3.36	318.1	313	142	119	24	142	193

1995 Situational Statistics

	W	L	ERA	SV	IP	BB	SO		AB	HR	RBI	BA	OBA	SLG
Home	0	0	2.87	6	15.2	10	16	LHB	76	2	16	.289	.379	.434
Road	0	3	3.79	16	19.0	10	17	RHB	64	1	7	.281	.365	.406
Apr-Jun	0	0	1.46	7	12.1	3	17	ScPos	42	1	21	.357	.462	.524
Jul-Oct	0	3	4.43	15	22.1	17	16	Clutch	99	2	21	.303	.402	.455

How He Compares to Other Pitchers

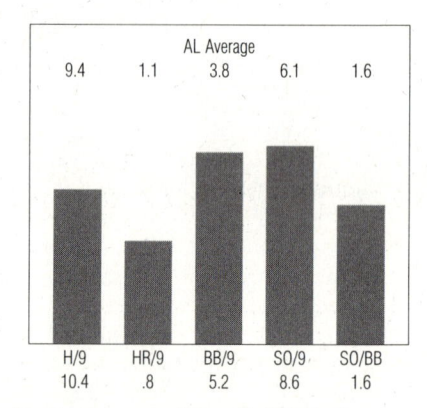

AL Average
H/9	HR/9	BB/9	SO/9	SO/BB
9.4	1.1	3.8	6.1	1.6
10.4	.8	5.2	8.6	1.6

How He Compares to Other Relief Pitchers

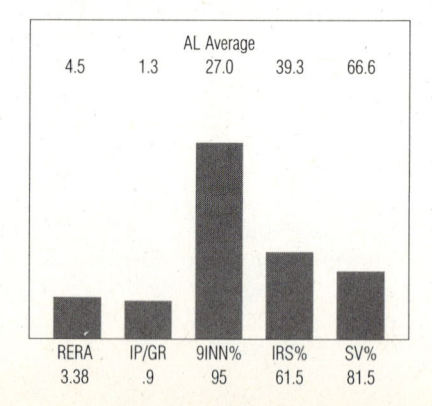

AL Average
RERA	IP/GR	9INN%	IRS%	SV%
4.5	1.3	27.0	39.3	66.6
3.38	.9	95	61.5	81.5

MILWAUKEE BREWERS

BRIAN GIVENS

Position: SP
Bats: R **Throws:** L
Ht: 6'6" **Wt:** 220
Opening Day Age: 30
Born: 11/6/1965
Drafted: NYN84* 10/234
ML Seasons: 1

SCOUTING REPORT

A physically-imposing pitcher with less-than-imposing stuff, Givens is a sinker-slider southpaw with average-minus velocity. None of his four adequate pitches rates plus. He will throw his curveball to lefties and turn over his change-up to righties, complementing both with his slider.

Brian is adequate at holding runners, with ten stealing and five caught stealing with him on the hill in '95. He doesn't impress with the leather, making two errors in only 16 chances in his first season.

HOW HE PERFORMED IN '95

Persistence finally paid off in '95 for replacement-player Givens, previously nothing more than a career minor-leaguer with a history of arm problems. After 12 years and 1,029 innings riding the buses in the bushes, Brian finally got his chance. Working in Milwaukee, which is baseball's current equivalent to a government jobs program, Brian spent much of the year in the Brewers' rotation. He sandwiched five consecutive victories in between seven mostly ugly losses.

On June 24, Givens was called up after going 7-4 at New Orleans and fanning a batter per inning. He did some things right with Milwaukee: after losing his first two, Givens was 2-0 in July with a 2.67 ERA and then won three more in August. He was especially adept at handling lefthanded hitters, who failed to homer off him in 66 at-bats.

However, Brian continued to have the control problems that have bedeviled him during his entire career. That, plus whatever bad karma pervaded Brewtown during September, led to an 0-5 record and a 5.81 ERA in September. The bad finish is a cause for concern, as big-league hitters started to catch on to Brian's strengths and began hitting him with ease down the stretch.

WHAT TO EXPECT IN '96

As is often the case with this undercapitalized team, Milwaukee has a not-too-exciting choice to make concerning their starting rotation this year: do the Brewers look at younger talent or give Givens a full-season audition? With limited help in the minors, Brewers' management may allow Brian another shot. If some prospect makes big strides within the organization, however, look for Givens to be pushed aside, as he has been for the past decade.

Overall Statistics

	G	GS	GF	SV	W	L	ERA	IP	H	R	ER	HR	BB	SO
95 MIL	19	19	0	0	5	7	4.95	107.1	116	71	59	11	54	73
Career	19	19	0	0	5	7	4.95	107.1	116	71	59	11	54	73

1995 Situational Statistics

	W	L	ERA	SV	IP	BB	SO		AB	HR	RBI	BA	OBA	SLG
Home	3	4	5.28	0	44.1	20	25	LHB	66	0	4	.212	.325	.273
Road	2	3	4.71	0	63.0	34	48	RHB	356	11	58	.287	.367	.461
Apr-Jun	0	2	12.00	0	9.0	5	9	ScPos	112	4	48	.286	.372	.473
Jul-Oct	5	5	4.30	0	98.1	49	64	Clutch	0	0	0	.000	.000	.000

How He Compares to Other Pitchers

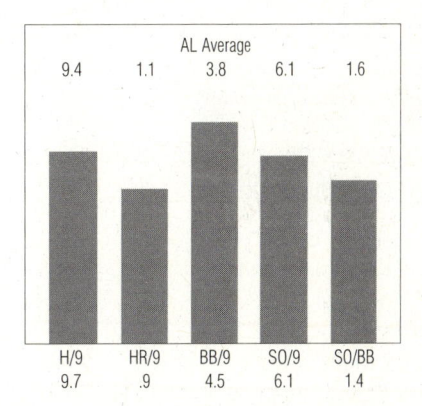

AL Average: 9.4 | 1.1 | 3.8 | 6.1 | 1.6

H/9 9.7 | HR/9 .9 | BB/9 4.5 | SO/9 6.1 | SO/BB 1.4

How He Compares to Other Starting Pitchers

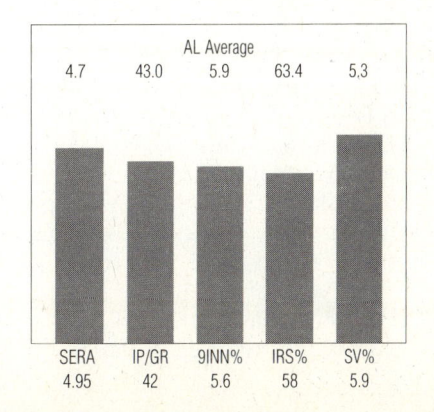

AL Average: 4.7 | 43.0 | 5.9 | 63.4 | 5.3

SERA 4.95 | IP/GR 42 | 9INN% 5.6 | IRS% 58 | SV% 5.9

THE SCOUTING REPORT: 1996

MILWAUKEE BREWERS

DARRYL HAMILTON

Positions: OF//DH
Bats: L **Throws:** R
Ht: 6'1" **Wt:** 180
Opening Day Age: 31
Born: 12/3/1964
Drafted: MIL86 11/269
ML Seasons: 7

SCOUTING REPORT

Hamilton is a line-drive hitter who cuts at fastballs up and out over the plate. He tries to hit to left field whenever possible. He bunts often, but Darryl is a more effective sacrifice specialist than a bunter for hits. Hamilton lacks much power and does not walk often. Despite numerous nagging injuries of late, Hamilton is still a solid, smart baserunner, though he won't steal as many bases as in his younger years. Defensively, Darryl has above-average range and hands which compensate for his arm, which now rates as minus. Serious elbow problems have negated his ability to throw with much strength. However, he still throws accurately and can nail the occasional runner.

HOW HE PERFORMED IN '95

Hamilton's final weeks with the Brewers had the look of an ugly divorce from a once-happy marriage. Once the Brewers' star-in-the-making outfielder, Hamilton became one of the most popular players on the team, both with teammates and fans. His approachability and quotability also made him a media favorite. However, his star began to dim in '95. He entered the season freshly recovered from reconstructive elbow surgery, but couldn't stay healthy as a series of nagging leg injuries slowed him down. Darryl ended up being listed as "day-to-day" too many times for Brewers' management to accept. His sagging batting average and struggles with runners in scoring position forced manager Phil Garner to look at other center field alternatives, much to Hamilton's consternation and, eventually, bitterness. Claiming the Brewers sat him down late in the year to prevent him from reaching incentive clauses in his contract, Darryl expressed his willingness to leave Milwaukee. The Brewers' management obliged by failing to pick up the option year of his contract. It was a sad end to a what had been, for three years, a good relationship.

WHAT TO EXPECT IN '96

A healthy Darryl Hamilton would be a valuable addition to any team. While his arm strength and speed have diminished in the past two years, he remains a versatile player still capable of the spectacular diving catch in the field and capable of advancing a base runner on the hit-and-run. Texas, a team with a grass home field and a team desperately in need of a center fielder, inked Darryl last winter and will give him plenty of at-bats.

Overall Statistics

	G	AB	R	H	2B	3B	HR	RBI	SB	CS	BB	SO	BA	OBA
95 MIL	112	398	54	108	20	6	5	44	11	1	47	35	.271	.350
Career	666	2193	323	637	94	21	23	253	109	40	206	215	.290	.351

1995 Situational Statistics

	AB	HR	RBI	BA	OBA	SLG		AB	HR	RBI	BA	OBA	SLG
Home	209	3	25	.273	.368	.383	LHP	114	0	9	.237	.346	.289
Road	189	2	19	.270	.330	.397	RHP	284	5	35	.285	.352	.430
Apr-Jun	177	2	18	.271	.348	.367	ScPos	81	1	35	.284	.413	.432
Jul-Oct	221	3	26	.271	.352	.407	Clutch	52	0	7	.250	.381	.288

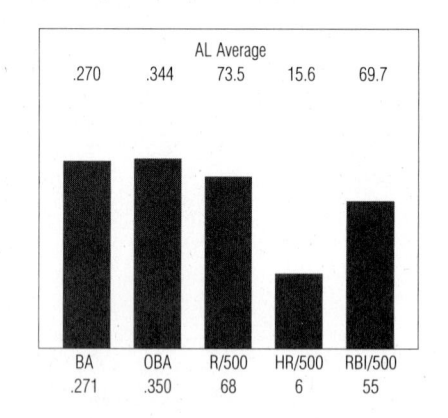

How He Compares to Other Batters

AL Average
.270 .344 73.5 15.6 69.7

BA	OBA	R/500	HR/500	RBI/500
.271	.350	68	6	55

Where He Hits the Ball

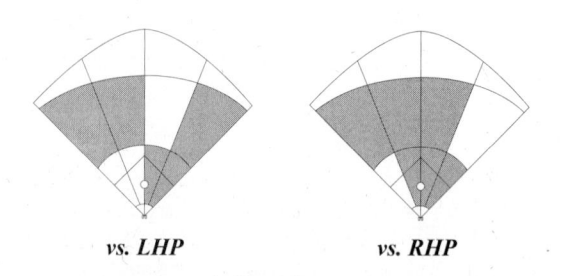

vs. LHP   vs. RHP

THE SCOUTING REPORT: 1996

MILWAUKEE BREWERS

DAVID HULSE

Position: OF
Bats: L **Throws:** L
Ht: 5'11" **Wt:** 170
Opening Day Age: 28
Born: 2/25/1968
Drafted: TEX90 13/360
ML Seasons: 4

SCOUTING REPORT
Plus speed is Hulse's key attribute. He has plus range as well as plus hands, making him valuable in center field, but has the below-average arm strength found in many players at his position. David steals bases well and is an above-average, assertive baserunner.

At the plate, he is an aggressive, line-drive pull hitter who likes his pitches down and in. This past year, Hulse tried spraying the ball more, particularly down the left field line, but continued to swing at outside pitches he couldn't do anything with and hack at high fastballs he couldn't catch up to.

HOW HE PERFORMED IN '95
Acquired by Milwaukee during spring training for minor-league pitcher Scott Taylor, David came into an ideal situation: a slow team with unhealthy players. With the Brewers savaged by injuries, Hulse got ample opportunities to play and produced career highs in games played, doubles, home runs, and runs batted in.

However, the weaknesses that had led Texas to give up on him resurfaced. An impatient hitter and mediocre bunter, Hulse refused to take advantage of his superior speed and baserunning abilities by walking or bunting for hits. He's a poor leadoff batter whose on-base percentage has dipped by at least 20 points each of the last two seasons, and it was never high to begin with.

After hitting .305 through the end last June, Hulse fell into a sinkhole the last three months, with just a .216 average in his last 208 at-bats. His on-base percentage after the All-Star break was a scarcely believable .260.

Just an average outfielder despite fine tools, Hulse also committed several bonehead defensive plays which cost the Brewers valuable runs and cost the confidence of manager Phil Garner. He threw out just two runners all year in 115 games in the field.

WHAT TO EXPECT IN '96
Given the current emphasis placed on role-players with speed, Hulse will have a roster spot on some mediocre team as long as he remains healthy. Given his limited abilities, though, David will not keep a starting outfield job for any prolonged period. In reality, he is a good Triple-A player.

Overall Statistics

	G	AB	R	H	2B	3B	HR	RBI	SB	CS	BB	SO	BA	OBA
95 MIL	119	339	46	85	11	6	3	47	15	3	18	60	.251	.285
Career	342	1148	189	310	32	20	5	97	65	15	68	188	.270	.311

1995 Situational Statistics

	AB	HR	RBI	BA	OBA	SLG		AB	HR	RBI	BA	OBA	SLG
Home	154	1	28	.299	.333	.396	LHP	76	0	11	.263	.313	.355
Road	185	2	19	.211	.242	.303	RHP	263	3	36	.247	.276	.342
Apr-Jun	131	1	25	.305	.331	.397	ScPos	101	2	44	.297	.339	.436
Jul-Oct	208	2	22	.216	.255	.313	Clutch	59	2	6	.254	.302	.407

How He Compares to Other Batters

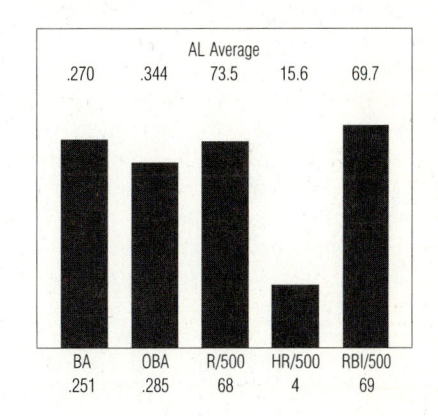

	BA	OBA	R/500	HR/500	RBI/500
AL Average	.270	.344	73.5	15.6	69.7
	.251	.285	68	4	69

Where He Hits the Ball

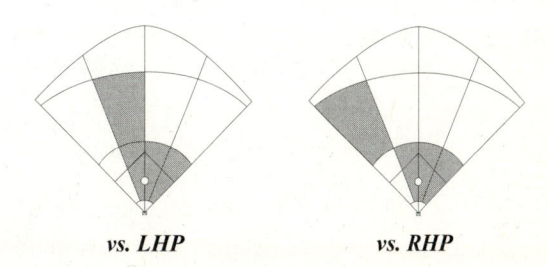

vs. LHP   vs. RHP

MILWAUKEE BREWERS

JOHN JAHA

Positions: 1B//DH
Bats: R **Throws:** R
Ht: 6'1" **Wt:** 195
Opening Day Age: 29
Born: 5/27/1966
Drafted: MIL84 14/358
ML Seasons: 4

SCOUTING REPORT
Jaha's power to right and right-center field is matched only by the league's big bombers like Cecil Fielder and Frank Thomas. He likes to drive fastballs out over the plate to the opposite field whenever possible, although he still ranks as a pull hitter. John is a team-oriented player, never afraid to get plunked by pitches or take a close pitch for a walk. He does not bunt and is not often asked to. The burly Jaha has just average range and throwing ability at first base, but he possesses surprisingly good hands. On the bases, John ranks as a minus runner and doesn't scare anyone except when steaming into second base while a second baseman tries to turn the double play.

HOW HE PERFORMED IN '95
John is baseball's version of the legendary Phoenix: every time you're about ready to count him out, he comes back strong. After several disappointing seasons checkered with streaks of promise, the Brewers had counted Jaha out of their plans until Dave Nilsson contracted Ross-River Fever and missed the beginning of the '95 season. With nowhere else to turn, the Brewers went back to Jaha, making him the team's "temporary" first baseman. Given a last chance to produce, Jaha did just that—produce—and in a big way. Setting career highs in batting average and home runs, John set a club record with three grand slam home runs. Despite a painful groin pull, he stayed in the lineup as long as possible before finally being forced to the sidelines in June. While he played well before the injury, he was truly exceptional after returning from the disabled list, batting .318 with 14 homers from August 1 through the end of the season. Even during the club's September free fall, John kept on hitting.

WHAT TO EXPECT IN '96
Despite the big numbers Jaha posted in '95, his history still raises lingering questions about durability and consistency. John's procession of nagging injuries, which have kept him out of the lineup on-and-off for years, have had a negative impact on his career. While the Brewers' brass cannot necessarily count on Jaha to be the team's regular first baseman, he did grab the club's attention with his performance at the plate last season. Jaha should contribute again in '96, most likely as a designated hitter and reserve first baseman.

Overall Statistics
	G	AB	R	H	2B	3B	HR	RBI	SB	CS	BB	SO	BA	OBA
95 MIL	88	316	59	99	20	2	20	65	2	1	36	66	.313	.389
Career	372	1255	199	335	58	3	53	184	28	13	131	280	.267	.344

1995 Situational Statistics
	AB	HR	RBI	BA	OBA	SLG		AB	HR	RBI	BA	OBA	SLG
Home	153	8	29	.281	.362	.503	LHP	71	2	13	.324	.380	.479
Road	163	12	36	.344	.415	.650	RHP	245	18	52	.310	.392	.608
Apr-Jun	105	6	21	.324	.388	.590	ScPos	81	9	47	.309	.418	.716
Jul-Oct	211	14	44	.308	.390	.573	Clutch	47	3	7	.298	.353	.489

How He Compares to Other Batters

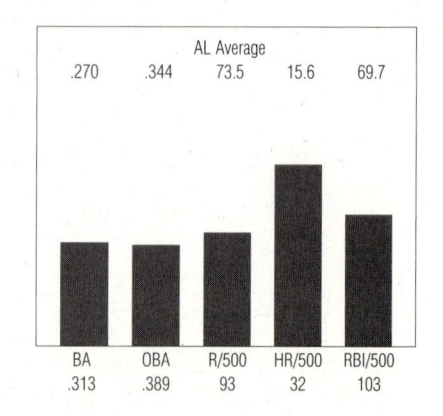

AL Average: .270 .344 73.5 15.6 69.7

BA	OBA	R/500	HR/500	RBI/500
.313	.389	93	32	103

Where He Hits the Ball

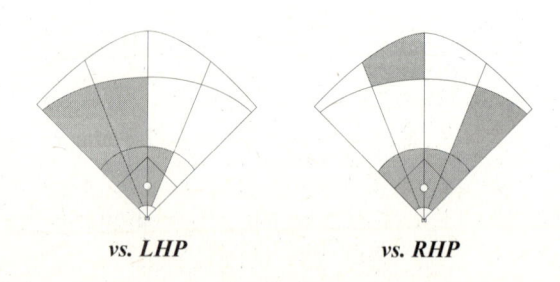

vs. LHP   vs. RHP

MILWAUKEE BREWERS

SCOTT KARL

Position: SP/RP
Bats: L **Throws:** L
Ht: 6'2" **Wt:** 195
Opening Day Age: 24
Born: 8/9/1971
Drafted: MIL92 7/164
ML Seasons: 1

SCOUTING REPORT
A young southpaw with a minus fastball which he cuts and sinks, Karl also has a plus change-up (which he palms) with good drop and an adequate curveball. Despite his age, he pitches like a veteran.

Scott has a plus move to first: only seven runners ran safely on him last year. He is an adequate fielder despite posting a shaky .897 fielding average in 29 chances.

HOW HE PERFORMED IN '95
Of all the young pitchers the Brewers shuttled in and out of town during their injury-plagued '95 campaign, Scott could have the brightest future. He enjoyed a solid rookie season, and might be able to develop into a serviceable starter.

After debuting in the bullpen in May, Karl went back to the minors on May 25, returning to the parent club on June 27 and stepping into the rotation in July. Once promoted to a starting role, he experienced some success—including wins in four straight decisions in August—and some failure—losing five in a row immediately thereafter.

Karl could be counted on by his mates to keep them in the game, going six innings or more 14 times in 18 starts and posting 12 quality starts. Like most of his fellow Brewers' pitchers, he had a wobbly last month (1-4, 4.34 ERA), which hurt his final numbers and gave what was otherwise an encouraging first-year a negative spin. However, he did end the season on a high note with a complete-game victory over Boston on the last day of the season.

Although Scott had some serious control problems with righthanders, he did settle down in the later months and was usually effective against lefties. However, Milwaukee would prefer not to make him a situational reliever, given his durability and lack of an overpowering fastball.

WHAT TO EXPECT IN '96
Karl is one of the young pitchers Brewers' management will count on to take them through the end of the decade. A starter throughout his minor-league career, Scott has a legitimate chance of being in the Milwaukee starting rotation this year. He must work on his other pitches besides the change-up in order to improve and solidify his hold on a big-league job.

Overall Statistics

	G	GS	GF	SV	W	L	ERA	IP	H	R	ER	HR	BB	SO
95 MIL	25	18	3	0	6	7	4.14	124.0	141	65	57	10	50	59
Career	25	18	3	0	6	7	4.14	124.0	141	65	57	10	50	59

1995 Situational Statistics

	W	L	ERA	SV	IP	BB	SO		AB	HR	RBI	BA	OBA	SLG
Home	4	3	3.63	0	69.1	23	38	LHB	92	4	17	.261	.317	.413
Road	2	4	4.77	0	54.2	27	21	RHB	397	6	48	.295	.365	.438
Apr-Jun	0	0	3.18	0	11.1	4	6	ScPos	134	2	53	.284	.369	.418
Jul-Oct	6	7	4.23	0	112.2	46	53	Clutch	22	0	3	.364	.440	.455

How He Compares to Other Pitchers

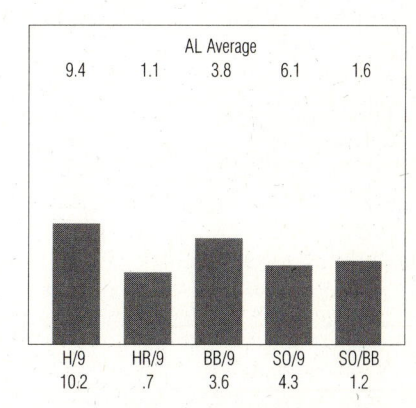

AL Average: 9.4 | 1.1 | 3.8 | 6.1 | 1.6

	H/9	HR/9	BB/9	SO/9	SO/BB
	10.2	.7	3.6	4.3	1.2

How He Compares to Other Starting Pitchers

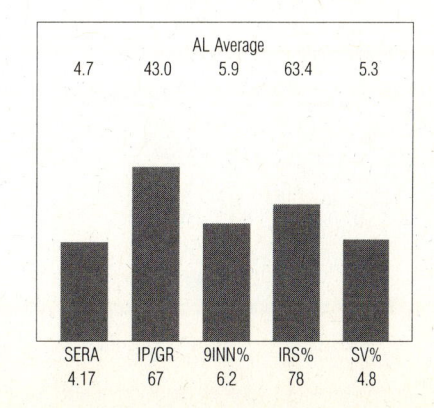

AL Average: 4.7 | 43.0 | 5.9 | 63.4 | 5.3

	SERA	IP/GR	9INN%	IRS%	SV%
	4.17	67	6.2	78	4.8

THE SCOUTING REPORT: 1996

MILWAUKEE BREWERS

DAVE NILSSON

Positions: OF/DH//1B/C
Bats: L **Throws:** R
Ht: 6'3" **Wt:** 185
Opening Day Age: 26
Born: 12/14/1969
Drafted: MIL 1/28/87
ML Seasons: 4

SCOUTING REPORT

Nilsson is very strong but has slightly below-par bat speed. He will pull off-speed pitches effectively, but sprays low fastballs to left field. Dave handles the bat well, makes good contact, and can be used to hit-and-run, but he can be blown away by good high heat. He is an average runner.

Although Nilsson has a strong arm, he flamed out at catcher because of a lack of agility and problems controlling his throws. Used mostly in the outfield now, Dave is still learning to play both left and right, and although he hustles and has decent hands, every fly ball is still an adventure.

HOW HE PERFORMED IN '95

Nilsson brought a lot of positives to Milwaukee when he was called up from the minors in '92. Something he did not bring with him was home run power—until '95. One of two Australian-born Brewers, Dave matched his career high in home runs despite missing the first two months of the season with the aftereffects of Ross-River Fever, a virus he contracted through a mosquito bite in his native Australia. The illness, which caused swollen joints, sidelined Nilsson until June 24.

Perhaps the bug brought him power too, as he began swinging a surprisingly powerful bat for a supposed doubles hitter. Even his line drives to the gaps had more zip to them last season. Penciled in as the team's likely starting first baseman prior to his illness, Dave couldn't reclaim the position when he returned due to the strong play of John Jaha. As a result, Nilsson had to learn new positions just to get into the lineup. While his outfield play was often frightening, resulting in five errors, Dave did throw out five runners and made some terrific diving catches. Nilsson slumped in the final month of the season, with talk that lingering fatigue from the viral infection could have been the cause.

WHAT TO EXPECT IN '96

Nilsson still figures to see action for the Brewers at first base. Because of his inability to throw out baserunners, he is unlikely to get extended playing time at catcher. With Phil Garner preferring versatile players, however, Dave could again toil in the outfield. If he can continue hitting home runs for an entire season, he could provide a bonus to the Brewers' attack.

Overall Statistics

	G	AB	R	H	2B	3B	HR	RBI	SB	CS	BB	SO	BA	OBA
95 MIL	81	263	41	73	12	1	12	53	2	0	24	41	.278	.337
Career	341	1120	142	296	58	6	35	187	8	8	112	156	.264	.328

1995 Situational Statistics

	AB	HR	RBI	BA	OBA	SLG		AB	HR	RBI	BA	OBA	SLG
Home	139	7	30	.317	.353	.518	LHP	55	2	9	.273	.328	.436
Road	124	5	23	.234	.319	.411	RHP	208	10	44	.279	.339	.476
Apr-Jun	22	2	7	.273	.360	.545	ScPos	80	4	41	.250	.309	.438
Jul-Oct	241	10	46	.278	.335	.461	Clutch	44	3	8	.250	.277	.500

How He Compares to Other Batters

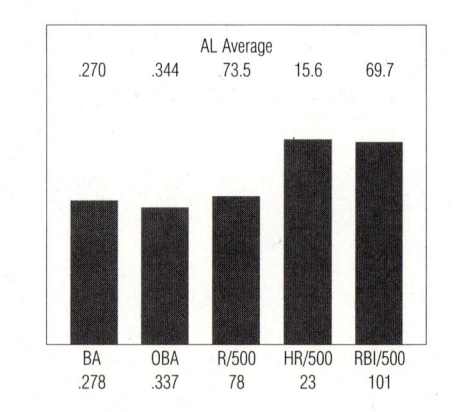

AL Average
.270 .344 73.5 15.6 69.7

BA	OBA	R/500	HR/500	RBI/500
.278	.337	78	23	101

Where He Hits the Ball

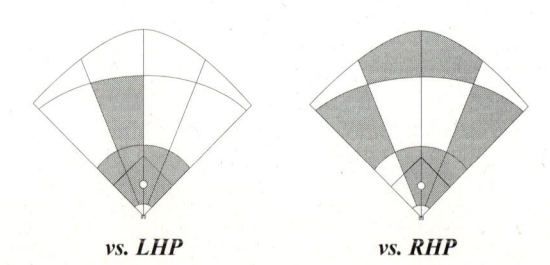

vs. LHP   vs. RHP

MILWAUKEE BREWERS

JOE OLIVER

Positions: C//DH/1B
Bats: R **Throws:** R
Ht: 6'3" **Wt:** 215
Opening Day Age: 30
Born: 7/24/1965
Drafted: CIN83 3/41
ML Seasons: 7

SCOUTING REPORT
Oliver, a pull hitter, prefers fastballs down and in. He has plus raw power but perhaps swings at too many pitches. An especially slow runner even before his 1994 leg problems, Joe tends to do more harm than good on the bases. Defensively, Oliver showcases an above-average, quite accurate throwing arm, although runners don't seem afraid to test him. His hands rate as plus. However, Joe struggles when blocking the plate and is slow to recover when pitches get past him. He handles young pitchers well.

HOW HE PERFORMED IN '95
Until baseball agrees on some sort of revenue-sharing plan, Joe Oliver is the prototypical Milwaukee Brewer of the 1990s. The script: Down and out as a former regular due to injury and nearly out of baseball, Oliver signed the Brewers for a low salary. He hit well, played solid defense, and earned respect from his new teammates. After finishing the season with solid numbers, the Brewers can't afford to keep him and he leaves for a bigger contract elsewhere with his reputation reclaimed.

The former Cincinnati Reds' regular missed most of '94 with synovitis, an odd malady that led to swelling in his ankles and knees. However, he ascended to the Brewers' starting lineup on opening day, just one month after signing a minor-league contract. Oliver skillfully handled a green pitching staff and provided needed punch to the batting order. If not for the broken bone in his right hand suffered in July, Joe's numbers could have been better.

Oliver is not quick or mobile, and having to catch knuckleballer Steve Sparks every fifth day in '95 didn't help. This combination led to Joe's total of 16 passed balls, second-worst in the AL. Despite his strong arm, 96 runners tested him last year and he threw out just 27% of them—most of the young Brewers' pitchers don't hold runners that well.

WHAT TO EXPECT IN '96
With the Brewers already tentatively planning on Mike Matheny as their 1996 opening-day starting catcher, Oliver appeared off to the land of bigger contracts and bigger markets. The only warning sign could be a recurrence of synovitis. If Joe is healthy, some team will pick up a better-than-average catcher still young enough to make a difference for several years.

Overall Statistics

	G	AB	R	H	2B	3B	HR	RBI	SB	CS	BB	SO	BA	OBA
95 MIL	97	337	43	92	20	0	12	51	2	4	27	66	.273	.332
Career	649	2107	194	525	115	1	59	304	5	8	152	391	.249	.300

1995 Situational Statistics

	AB	HR	RBI	BA	OBA	SLG		AB	HR	RBI	BA	OBA	SLG
Home	140	4	21	.286	.338	.436	LHP	77	1	8	.260	.345	.403
Road	197	8	30	.264	.329	.442	RHP	260	11	43	.277	.329	.450
Apr-Jun	189	7	29	.296	.342	.492	ScPos	88	3	38	.341	.402	.500
Jul-Oct	148	5	22	.243	.321	.372	Clutch	54	0	3	.167	.211	.204

How He Compares to Other Batters

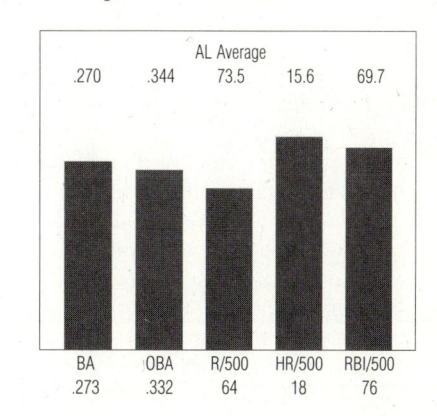

AL Average: .270 .344 73.5 15.6 69.7

BA .273   OBA .332   R/500 64   HR/500 18   RBI/500 76

Where He Hits the Ball

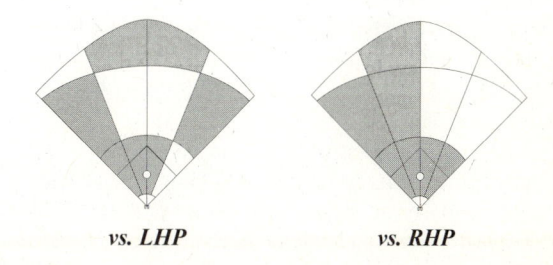

vs. LHP   vs. RHP

THE SCOUTING REPORT: 1996

MILWAUKEE BREWERS

KEVIN SEITZER

Positions: 3B/1B/DH
Bats: R **Throws:** R
Ht: 5'11" **Wt:** 180
Opening Day Age: 34
Born: 3/26/1962
Drafted: KC83 11/283
ML Seasons: 10

SCOUTING REPORT
Spraying baseballs all over the field is Kevin Seitzer's specialty. While he lacks home-run power, Kevin is apt to pull low fastballs. Given the situation, however, he puts the ball in play to any part of the diamond. He works the count effectively, but does not walk as often as before: in 1989, Seitzer drew 102 bases on balls for the Royals. A smart baserunner despite minus speed, Seitzer no longer steals often but is never afraid to go in hard trying to break up a double play. He plays hard and plays hurt. Kevin can play first and third, but spends much of his time as a designated hitter. He has plus hands and an accurate throwing arm, but his arm strength and range are average.

HOW HE PERFORMED IN '95
Both on and off the field, Seitzer had an outstanding '95. A piping-hot first half, including a .398 May, earned him a spot on the AL All-Star team. Although he batted just .238 in July, Kevin rebounded in the last two months and paced the Brewers in several offensive categories. Seitzer was the team's most reliable key-situation hitter and never went three games without collecting at least one hit. Seitzer's guts and determination didn't go unnoticed by teammates or fans. He served continually as a target for inside pitches and was seriously beaned twice. Yet he quickly bounced back, missing little action and never yielding the inside corner of the plate to the pitcher. With Milwaukee featuring several replacement players in critical roles in '95, there was potential for a clubhouse problem. Seitzer, a devout Christian, served as a calming influence in the clubhouse between the veterans and the strikebreakers. Not once did the team explode from the pressures between the two factions, and part of the credit should go to Seitzer's professional attitude and leadership.

WHAT TO EXPECT IN '96
The Brewers were able to re-sign Seitzer last winter on amicable terms, and the veteran infielder will again fill the role of utility player/DH/team leader/spiritual influence.

Kevin has considered retiring to spend more time with his wife and children, and that will probably happen in a year or two. However, considering his skills, attitude, and leadership, a future coaching or managerial position for Seitzer would seem a logical progression.

Overall Statistics

	G	AB	R	H	2B	3B	HR	RBI	SB	CS	BB	SO	BA	OBA
95 MIL	132	492	56	153	33	3	5	69	2	0	64	57	.311	.395
Career	1221	4507	627	1317	236	32	59	511	74	48	564	513	.292	.372

1995 Situational Statistics

	AB	HR	RBI	BA	OBA	SLG		AB	HR	RBI	BA	OBA	SLG
Home	237	1	23	.304	.381	.401	LHP	139	0	14	.252	.342	.317
Road	255	4	46	.318	.407	.439	RHP	353	5	55	.334	.416	.462
Apr-Jun	200	2	32	.345	.424	.485	ScPos	125	1	60	.376	.477	.488
Jul-Oct	292	3	37	.288	.375	.377	Clutch	71	1	13	.296	.383	.408

How He Compares to Other Batters

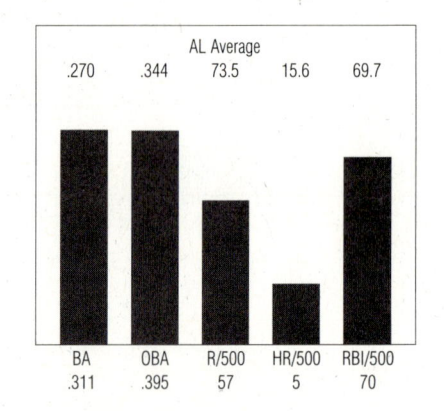

	BA	OBA	R/500	HR/500	RBI/500
AL Average	.270	.344	73.5	15.6	69.7
	.311	.395	57	5	70

Where He Hits the Ball

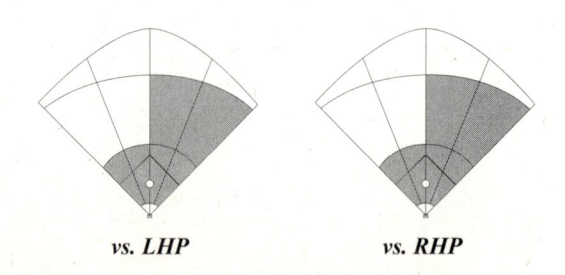

vs. LHP   vs. RHP

MILWAUKEE BREWERS

STEVE SPARKS

Position: SP/RP
Bats: R **Throws:** R
Ht: 6'0" **Wt:** 180
Opening Day Age: 30
Born: 7/2/1965
Drafted: MIL87 6/123
ML Seasons: 1

SCOUTING REPORT
Sparks is unusual all the way around. First of all, his bread and butter pitch is the knuckleball, thrown with an overhand delivery. His bread-and-butter pitch rates as average because it lacks the movement of most other knucklers. However, Steve differs from other practitioners of the pitch in that he is unafraid to use his other offerings at any time, including during tough situations. Although his curve and slider are both a bit below-average by major league standards, both look tougher and are more effective when combined with the knuckler. Sparks' poor fastball is his least effective pitch. A quick release to the plate makes Sparks difficult to steal on—if the pitch doesn't flutter away from the catcher's glove. Of the 23 runners trying to steal against Steve in '95, 16 were successful. He is a plus fielder.

HOW HE PERFORMED IN '95
The rookie and his unusual pitch didn't get as much notice as they deserved in '95, thanks to the re-emergence of Tim Wakefield. Steve showed enough potential to indicate that he will get some attention in the future. Before coming to the majors, Sparks' claim to fame was an incident during spring training '94 when, inspired by a motivational speech, Steve attempted to tear a telephone book in half. He separated his shoulder instead.

During '95, however, a healthy Sparks led the Brewers in strikeouts and innings pitched. In addition to starting, Steve worked in relief when Phil Garner needed him. A rubber arm allows Sparks to pitch effectively with fewer than four days' rest. As do all knuckleballers, Sparks spent much of the season walking the line between unhittability and uncatchability. When his knuckler was dancing, Steve was fantastic: on June 3 in Kansas City, he pitched eight innings without going to a three-ball count on a single batter. There were also times when Sparks could not have hit the strike zone with a beachball.

WHAT TO EXPECT IN '96
Despite turning 31 this July, Steve could pitch effectively for years if he maintains control of the knuckleball. He will also provide plenty of exercise for whatever catcher happens to be working that night. As Brewers' play-by-play voice Bob Uecker always says, the best way to catch the knuckler is to wait for the ball to stop rolling and then pick it up.

Overall Statistics

	G	GS	GF	SV	W	L	ERA	IP	H	R	ER	HR	BB	SO
95 MIL	33	27	2	0	9	11	4.63	202.0	210	111	104	17	86	96
Career	33	27	2	0	9	11	4.63	202.0	210	111	104	17	86	96

1995 Situational Statistics

	W	L	ERA	SV	IP	BB	SO		AB	HR	RBI	BA	OBA	SLG
Home	3	6	5.69	0	93.1	44	44	LHB	439	9	50	.280	.357	.419
Road	6	5	3.73	0	108.2	42	52	RHB	328	8	35	.265	.332	.393
Apr-Jun	3	3	3.48	0	72.1	31	37	ScPos	192	3	66	.271	.345	.401
Jul-Oct	6	8	5.28	0	129.2	55	59	Clutch	63	2	9	.333	.400	.508

How He Compares to Other Pitchers

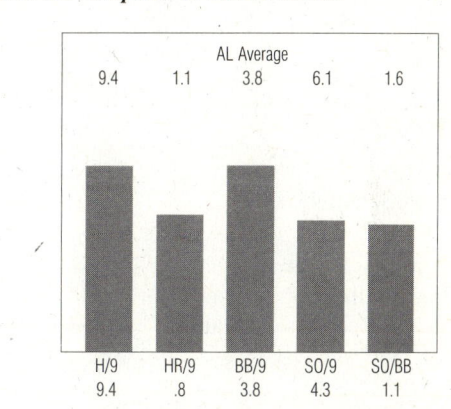

AL Average: H/9 9.4, HR/9 1.1, BB/9 3.8, SO/9 6.1, SO/BB 1.6

Sparks: H/9 9.4, HR/9 .8, BB/9 3.8, SO/9 4.3, SO/BB 1.1

How He Compares to Other Starting Pitchers

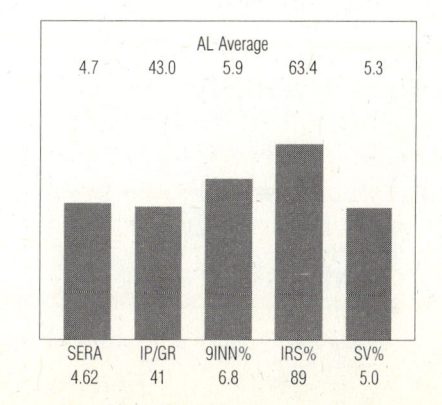

AL Average: SERA 4.7, IP/GR 43.0, 9INN% 5.9, IRS% 63.4, SV% 5.3

Sparks: SERA 4.62, IP/GR 41, 9INN% 6.8, IRS% 89, SV% 5.0

THE SCOUTING REPORT: 1996

MILWAUKEE BREWERS

B.J. SURHOFF

Positions: OF/1B/C//DH
Bats: L **Throws:** R
Ht: 6'1" **Wt:** 190
Opening Day Age: 31
Born: 8/4/1964
Drafted: MIL85 1/1
ML Seasons: 9

SCOUTING REPORT
Surhoff has always liked fastballs down and in but, before the '95 season hadn't consistently been able to drive those pitches. He makes good contact but rarely walks. B.J. made a relatively smooth transition to the outfield in '95. At first a catcher, Surhoff has also started at first and third base. In left field, he has average hands and range but minus arm strength. While B.J.'s arm was once stronger, shoulder problems have robbed him of some throwing ability. He is still a plus runner who will steal bases and bunt, both for hits and to sacrifice. However, Surhoff is just an average percentage base thief.

HOW HE PERFORMED IN '95
For years, Surhoff has suffered criticism for failing to fulfill his potential. The first player drafted in the first round in June 1985, he has fallen short of the performance of other draftees of that vintage (other 1985 first-rounders like Will Clark and Shawon Dunston, for instance). In '95, however, B.J. finally had the season the Brewers had been waiting for.

After an injury-truncated '94 that forced Surhoff to take a big pay cut to stay with the Brewers, he started last season hot. Perennially a slow starter, Surhoff batted .340 in May and .373 in June, although he didn't hit his first homer until July 4. In July and August, he combined for a .354 average, ten long balls, and 44 RBI.

However, B.J.—like his teammates—went into a free-fall during September, batting .213 with two home runs as the club slipped from playoff contention. At the season's end, Surhoff had paced Milwaukee in average, RBI, and runs, and finished sixth in the AL batting race.

Brewers' manager Phil Garner could count on B.J. at any time and at any place in '95. Surhoff played all three outfield positions, filled in at first base and strapped on the catcher's gear 18 times. While never excelling anywhere, B.J. always hustled and worked hard to improve his defensive play, even collecting eight outfield assists.

WHAT TO EXPECT IN '96
Surhoff cashed in last winter, inking a deal with the Orioles, for whom he will probably fill in all over the diamond. While B.J. had a tremendous year in '95, he had eight disappointing seasons before that, and a recent history of injury problems makes him less than a sure thing.

Overall Statistics

	G	AB	R	H	2B	3B	HR	RBI	SB	CS	BB	SO	BA	OBA
95 MIL	117	415	72	133	26	3	13	73	7	3	37	43	.320	.378
Career	1102	3884	472	1064	194	24	57	524	102	64	294	323	.274	.323

1995 Situational Statistics

	AB	HR	RBI	BA	OBA	SLG		AB	HR	RBI	BA	OBA	SLG
Home	205	7	49	.341	.409	.541	LHP	128	3	22	.367	.409	.531
Road	210	6	24	.300	.347	.443	RHP	287	10	51	.300	.365	.474
Apr-Jun	112	0	17	.348	.403	.446	ScPos	107	6	63	.383	.444	.626
Jul-Oct	303	13	56	.310	.369	.508	Clutch	60	2	6	.250	.370	.350

How He Compares to Other Batters

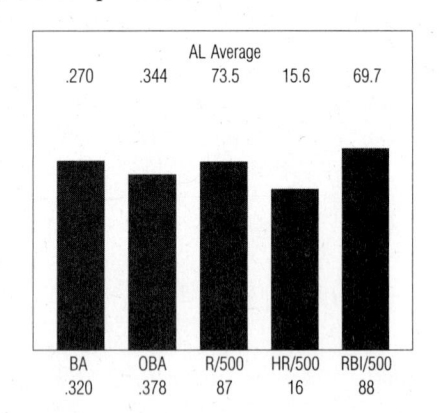

AL Average: BA .270, OBA .344, R/500 73.5, HR/500 15.6, RBI/500 69.7

B.J. Surhoff: BA .320, OBA .378, R/500 87, HR/500 16, RBI/500 88

Where He Hits the Ball

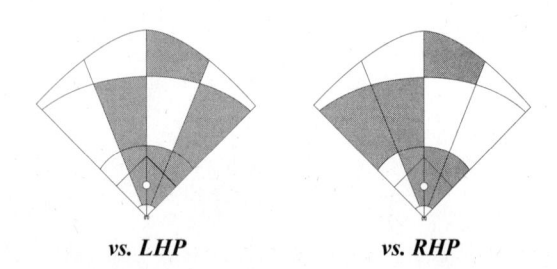

vs. LHP

vs. RHP

MILWAUKEE BREWERS

JOSE VALENTIN

Positions: SS//DH/3B
Bats: B **Throws:** R
Ht: 5'10" **Wt:** 175
Opening Day Age: 26
Born: 10/12/1969
Drafted: SD 10/12/86
ML Seasons: 4

SCOUTING REPORT
With plus range and one of the most accurate throwing arms in the game, Valentin often looks as impressive defensively as any AL shortstop. While he still has occasional problems on easy plays, Jose can make the impossible play look routine. His hands are soft and his arm strength is somewhat above-average. Valentin is a flyball hitter who likes fastballs down in the strike zone. He will take pitches and bunts often, both for hits and to sacrifice. Unfortunately, Jose struggles with breaking balls and sometimes tries too hard to hit for power. These tendencies have led to a serious strikeout problem. Although blessed with only average speed, Jose is a smart and aggressive runner who steals effectively.

HOW HE PERFORMED IN '95
Despite a less-than-healthy batting average, Valentin has a chance to become Milwaukee's next good shortstop. Although he isn't likely to fill the shoes of Robin Yount, Jose could be better than what most others at the position. Valentin started slowly, batting .188 through the end of May, but then hit .293 in June with five homers. This pattern was identical to the one Valentin showed the previous year, when he hit .287 with three home runs in June, but under .225 in every other month. After slumping during July, Jose rebounded to hit .253 in August, but a fractured finger suffered on the last day of the month limited him to eight at-bats the remainder of the season. Although Valentin set career highs in many offensive categories during '95, he is still weak offensively. Continued lack of success against lefthanders (he batted just .135 against them in '94) has led Jose to consider giving up switch-hitting and batting exclusively from the left side. Used mostly to pinch-run during September, Jose did most of his basestealing in the second half and paced the none-too-quick Brewers in that category.

WHAT TO EXPECT IN '96
Look for Valentin to be Milwaukee's starting shortstop until the team can no longer afford him. Management would like to see Jose become a better all-around offensive player, but they are willing to put up with his strikeouts in exchange for his terrific defensive play. Valentin's arrived from San Diego as part of the 1992 Gary Sheffield trade. He should continue to pay dividends for the Brewers in '96 and beyond.

Overall Statistics

	G	AB	R	H	2B	3B	HR	RBI	SB	CS	BB	SO	BA	OBA
95 MIL	112	338	62	74	23	3	11	49	16	8	37	83	.219	.293
Career	232	679	120	155	43	5	23	103	29	11	82	174	.228	.311

1995 Situational Statistics

	AB	HR	RBI	BA	OBA	SLG		AB	HR	RBI	BA	OBA	SLG
Home	172	3	23	.180	.263	.314	LHP	83	0	4	.133	.232	.157
Road	166	8	26	.259	.324	.494	RHP	255	11	45	.247	.313	.482
Apr-Jun	172	5	25	.227	.278	.419	ScPos	102	3	39	.216	.270	.441
Jul-Oct	166	6	24	.211	.307	.386	Clutch	48	1	6	.271	.397	.417

How He Compares to Other Batters

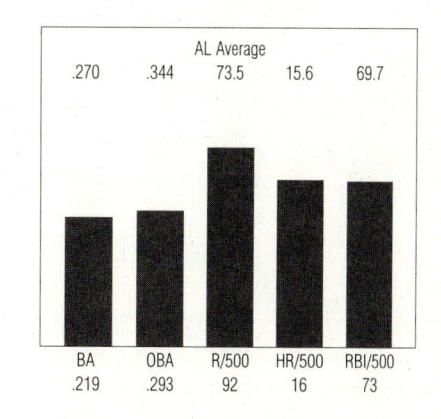

AL Average: BA .270, OBA .344, R/500 73.5, HR/500 15.6, RBI/500 69.7

Valentin: BA .219, OBA .293, R/500 92, HR/500 16, RBI/500 73

Where He Hits the Ball

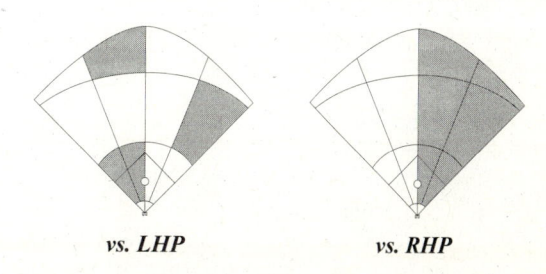

vs. LHP   vs. RHP

THE SCOUTING REPORT: 1996

MILWAUKEE BREWERS

GREG VAUGHN

Position: DH
Bats: R **Throws:** R
Ht: 6'0" **Wt:** 195
Opening Day Age: 30
Born: 7/3/1965
Drafted: MIL86 S1/4
ML Seasons: 7

SCOUTING REPORT
Vaughn is the consummate right-handed pull hitter. He tries for the left field fence on most pitches though he has experienced little success of late. He likes fastballs down and in and has good bat speed, but is susceptible to breaking pitches. When Greg hits the ball up the middle and to right field, it is clear that he is staying back on the ball and has found a good groove. The once-quick Vaughn no longer has the speed he exhibited in the minor leagues and is now a below-average baserunner. He has never been much of a basestealer and does not bunt. If he can play the field, throwing isn't likely to be a strong suit. Vaughn used to have an average arm, but now is unable to reach even that level due to rotator-cuff problems. Greg has never gone back on fly balls well, but has decent hands. He works hard.

HOW HE PERFORMED IN '95
Following his disastrous '95 season, Vaughn publicly apologized to Milwaukee baseball fans. Brewers' management probably wishes Greg's contract would have come with a money-back guarantee. For his $4 million-plus salary, Vaughn produced his worst year ever, something the small-market Brewers could hardly afford in these times. He was not able to play the outfield due to pre-season shoulder surgery, and Greg never got untracked at the plate. Poor performance in key situations led to several benchings by manager Phil Garner. Despite his woes, Vaughn kept hustling. He earned the praise of the coaching staff and other players for his relentless work ethic. Both Vaughn and erstwhile centerfielder Darryl Hamilton were nearly useless on defense over the last year due to an inability to throw, stretching the thin resources of an already undercapitalized Brewers' club—one can only have so many DHs in the lineup.

WHAT TO EXPECT IN '96
Barring a recurrence of shoulder problems, Vaughn will return to left field—in Milwaukee, it's called "Vaughn's Valley"—this year. With one year left on his megabucks contract, Greg will attempt to post big numbers akin to those from the earlier days of his career. However, if he continues to struggle offensively, or if the Brewers need to unload a big salary, look for Vaughn to be traded to a contender during the summer months. Whether Milwaukee will get anything for Greg is another matter.

Overall Statistics

	G	AB	R	H	2B	3B	HR	RBI	SB	CS	BB	SO	BA	OBA
95 MIL	108	392	67	88	19	1	17	59	10	4	55	89	.224	.317
Career	801	2869	450	694	142	13	138	471	57	38	363	662	.242	.327

1995 Situational Statistics

	AB	HR	RBI	BA	OBA	SLG		AB	HR	RBI	BA	OBA	SLG
Home	189	8	31	.265	.359	.466	LHP	118	5	18	.246	.362	.432
Road	203	9	28	.187	.277	.355	RHP	274	12	41	.215	.297	.398
Apr-Jun	201	7	29	.194	.288	.343	ScPos	112	5	42	.232	.313	.429
Jul-Oct	191	10	30	.257	.347	.476	Clutch	59	3	7	.203	.284	.407

How He Compares to Other Batters

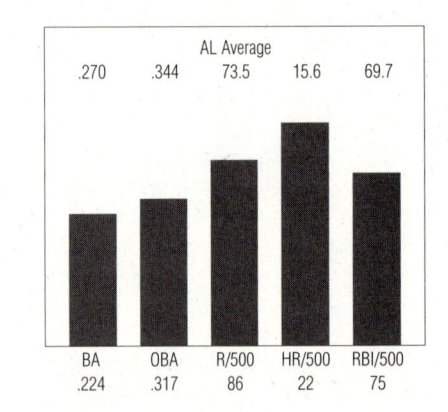

AL Average
.270 .344 73.5 15.6 69.7

BA	OBA	R/500	HR/500	RBI/500
.224	.317	86	22	75

Where He Hits the Ball

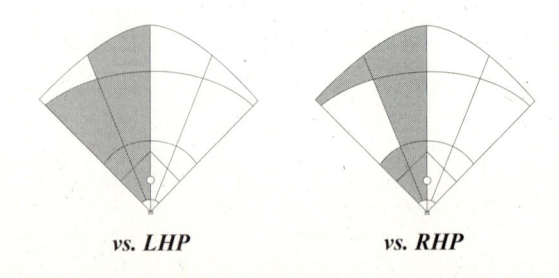

vs. LHP   vs. RHP

176

THE SCOUTING REPORT: 1996

MILWAUKEE BREWERS

MARK KIEFER

Position: RP
Bats: R **Throws:** R
Ht: 6'4" **Wt:** 175
Opening Day Age: 27
Born: 11/13/1968
Drafted: MIL87 22/539
ML Seasons: 3

Overall Statistics

	G	GS	GF	SV	W	L	ERA	IP	H	R	ER	HR	BB	SO
95 MIL	24	0	7	0	4	1	3.44	49.2	37	20	19	6	27	41
Career	37	0	12	1	5	1	3.75	69.2	55	32	29	10	40	56

1995 Situational Statistics

	W	L	ERA	SV	IP	BB	SO		AB	HR	RBI	BA	OBA	SLG
Home	2	0	4.31	0	31.1	19	20	LHB	82	4	15	.220	.347	.451
Road	2	1	1.96	0	18.1	8	21	RHB	100	2	7	.190	.270	.310
Apr-Jun	3	1	4.97	0	25.1	15	21	ScPos	37	3	16	.243	.378	.595
Jul-Oct	1	0	1.85	0	24.1	12	20	Clutch	47	1	5	.213	.315	.319

SCOUTING REPORT

With a poor fastball in the 83-85 mph range, Kiefer must rely on his plus palmball and an average curve to get hitters out. He has an overhand delivery, which makes the palmball especially effective. He is an average fielder who is adequate at holding runners on base. Five men tried to steal while Mark pitched in '95, three successfully.

HOW HE PERFORMED IN '95

Throw out the summer months and Kiefer could have enjoyed an outstanding year for the Brewers. With three victories during the first week of the season and a strong relief stint in September, Mark showed promise for a successful '96 campaign. Unfortunately, ineffectiveness in May and June led to a demotion to Triple-A New Orleans, reinforcing Kiefer's status as a borderline major-league pitching prospect. However, one has to be reasonably optimistic about a pitcher who limits opposing hitters to a .203 average.

WHAT TO EXPECT IN '96

Like so many players with strong finishes, it's an open question as to whether Mark has finally gotten his act together, or whether he just got hot during another meaningless Milwaukee September. With two elbow operations in his past, Kiefer's long-term prospects remain iffy.

PAT LISTACH

Positions: 2B/SS/OF//3B
Bats: B **Throws:** R
Ht: 5'9" **Wt:** 170
Opening Day Age: 28
Born: 9/12/1967
Drafted: MIL88 5/133
ML Seasons: 4

Overall Statistics

	G	AB	R	H	2B	3B	HR	RBI	SB	CS	BB	SO	BA	OBA
95 MIL	101	334	35	73	8	2	0	25	13	3	25	61	.219	.276
Career	364	1323	186	344	45	9	4	104	87	31	120	263	.260	.323

1995 Situational Statistics

	AB	HR	RBI	BA	OBA	SLG		AB	HR	RBI	BA	OBA	SLG
Home	159	0	12	.226	.275	.245	LHP	141	0	5	.213	.273	.270
Road	175	0	13	.211	.277	.263	RHP	193	0	20	.223	.279	.244
Apr-Jun	157	0	16	.223	.274	.248	ScPos	83	0	24	.277	.344	.313
Jul-Oct	177	0	9	.215	.278	.260	Clutch	53	0	9	.283	.309	.340

SCOUTING REPORT

While Pat still possesses plus range, various ailments have reduced his mobility. Listach has plus hands and a strong, accurate arm, which can throw out runners from the hole or up the middle. Injuries have also hurt Pat's offense. His speed, once well above-average, has declined to plus. A straightway and opposite-field hitter with little power, Listach likes fastballs out over the plate.

HOW HE PERFORMED IN '95

Back in 1992, Listach and Kenny Lofton finished one-two in the American League Rookie-of-the-Year balloting. While Lofton has turned into baseball's premier leadoff hitter, Listach spent much of the next three years collecting dust on the disabled list. Even in '95, with Listach relatively healthy, he failed to sparkle due to recurring soreness in his left knee. The biggest hit Pat registered all year was a punch to then-White Sox pitcher Rob Dibble's face during a June bench-clearing brawl.

WHAT TO EXPECT IN '96

Listach carries a sizable salary, and as a result will be in Milwaukee's plans. Second base appears to be Pat's best bet, but Fernando Vina may get the starting job. If Listach can't elude injury, he'll be just another journeyman.

THE SCOUTING REPORT: 1996

MILWAUKEE BREWERS

GRAEME LLOYD

Position: RP
Bats: L **Throws:** L
Ht: 6'7" **Wt:** 215
Opening Day Age: 28
Born: 4/9/1967
Drafted: TOR 1/26/88
ML Seasons: 3

Overall Statistics

	G	GS	GF	SV	W	L	ERA	IP	H	R	ER	HR	BB	SO
95 MIL	33	0	14	4	0	5	4.50	32.0	28	16	16	4	8	13
Career	131	0	47	7	5	12	3.97	142.2	141	68	63	13	36	75

1995 Situational Statistics

	W	L	ERA	SV	IP	BB	SO		AB	HR	RBI	BA	OBA	SLG
Home	0	2	4.32	2	16.2	1	7	LHB	47	1	2	.234	.260	.298
Road	0	3	4.11	2	15.1	7	6	RHB	67	3	14	.254	.303	.418
Apr-Jun	0	5	4.85	4	26.0	7	9	ScPos	24	0	11	.250	.290	.333
Jul-Oct	0	0	1.50	0	6.0	1	4	Clutch	60	2	9	.250	.273	.383

SCOUTING REPORT

Lloyd's three-quarter, cross-body motion was most effective in his early days with the Brewers. Unfortunately, control problems and below-average fastballs, curves, and sliders have caught up to him.

Not many baserunners test him because he's left-handed, but Graeme's slow delivery makes him easy pickings for those who do. Three out of four attempts were successful last year. Lloyd does not field his position well.

HOW HE PERFORMED IN '95

A season-ending finger injury suffered just after the All-Star break halted an inconsistent campaign for the Australian-born Lloyd. His problems pitching in County Stadium continued, making him a favorite target of the boo birds. However, a strong stretch in his final 15 games, allowing only one run in 14 innings, gave management indications that Lloyd may have straightened out.

WHAT TO EXPECT IN '96

If Graeme can stay healthy and return to his rookie form of '93, he should continue as a solid setup pitcher to Mike Fetters. He's young and lefthanded, giving him nine lives as a big-league reliever.

MIKE MATHENY

Position: C
Bats: R **Throws:** R
Ht: 6'3" **Wt:** 205
Opening Day Age: 25
Born: 9/22/1970
Drafted: MIL91 8/208
ML Seasons: 2

Overall Statistics

	G	AB	R	H	2B	3B	HR	RBI	SB	CS	BB	SO	BA	OBA
95 MIL	80	166	13	41	9	1	0	21	2	1	12	28	.247	.306
Career	108	219	16	53	12	1	1	23	2	2	15	41	.242	.303

1995 Situational Statistics

	AB	HR	RBI	BA	OBA	SLG		AB	HR	RBI	BA	OBA	SLG
Home	108	0	17	.306	.370	.380	LHP	65	0	6	.246	.269	.292
Road	58	0	4	.138	.180	.190	RHP	101	0	15	.248	.327	.327
Apr-Jun	24	0	2	.208	.240	.333	ScPos	45	0	20	.378	.429	.467
Jul-Oct	142	0	19	.254	.316	.310	Clutch	17	0	1	.353	.421	.353

SCOUTING REPORT

Matheny is a good catcher with no visible defensive weaknesses. All his tools rate solid average. An opposite-field hitter, he likes pitches out over the plate but lacks bat speed. A good fastball pitcher can blow him away. He is a minus runner.

HOW HE PERFORMED IN '95

How does a guy with a .241 career minor-league batting average go from being a borderline major-league prospect to a possible major-league starting catcher in a year where he batted only .247? Answer: Good defense and low salary. After backing up Joe Oliver for most of the '95 campaign, Matheny got his chance when Oliver suffered a hand injury. Mike's handling of the pitching staff and strong throwing arm (he threw out 33% of enemy runners) impressed the Brewers. Evidently, the small strides he made offensively were good enough.

WHAT TO EXPECT IN '96

Management would like Matheny to be their opening day catcher and appears willing to roll the dice. It helps that Mike will be making only slightly more than the major-league minimum salary. In fact, to the small-market Brewers, that might mean more than anything! He's young enough to improve into a solid backstop with some luck.

MILWAUKEE BREWERS

MATT MIESKE

Positions: OF//DH
Bats: R **Throws:** R
Ht: 6'0" **Wt:** 185
Opening Day Age: 28
Born: 2/13/1968
Drafted: SD90 17/471
ML Seasons: 3

Overall Statistics

	G	AB	R	H	2B	3B	HR	RBI	SB	CS	BB	SO	BA	OBA
95 MIL	117	267	42	67	13	1	12	48	2	4	27	45	.251	.323
Career	224	584	90	148	26	2	25	93	5	11	52	121	.253	.319

1995 Situational Statistics

	AB	HR	RBI	BA	OBA	SLG		AB	HR	RBI	BA	OBA	SLG
Home	120	3	18	.217	.317	.333	LHP	121	9	31	.306	.370	.587
Road	147	9	30	.279	.329	.531	RHP	146	3	17	.205	.285	.322
Apr-Jun	92	3	16	.272	.378	.435	ScPos	84	7	41	.250	.306	.548
Jul-Oct	175	9	32	.240	.292	.446	Clutch	53	4	11	.208	.288	.453

SCOUTING REPORT
Mieske, a pull hitter, likes fastballs down and in. Average power means he will never be a big home run threat, but he can produce some offense. Defense is Mieske's specialty. His strong throwing arm makes him a threat to nail baserunners and his range is plus in right field. Matt's hands and baserunning are average.

HOW HE PERFORMED IN '95
Mieske surely regrets how much money his inability to his right-handed pitching costs him at contract time. He has hoped for two years to earn a starting job in right field for Milwaukee. However, continuing failure against righties, strikeout problems, and an inability to produce in key spots make him just another platoon outfielder. Due to the Brewers' yearly rash of injuries, Mieske did see considerable action in '95. He set career highs in several categories and hit two pinch-homers. Matt also threw out seven runners last year from right field and showed better-than-expected range.

WHAT TO EXPECT IN '96
Same old story. If he hits righthanders, the future could look bright. Otherwise, look for Matt to remain the least productive of the three Brewers acquired for Gary Sheffield in 1992.

ANGEL MIRANDA

Position: RP/SP
Bats: L **Throws:** L
Ht: 6'1" **Wt:** 160
Opening Day Age: 26
Born: 11/9/1969
Drafted: MIL 3/4/87
ML Seasons: 3

Overall Statistics

	G	GS	GF	SV	W	L	ERA	IP	H	R	ER	HR	BB	SO
95 MIL	30	10	5	1	4	5	5.23	74.0	83	47	43	8	49	45
Career	60	35	5	1	10	15	4.28	240.0	222	128	114	28	128	157

1995 Situational Statistics

	W	L	ERA	SV	IP	BB	SO		AB	HR	RBI	BA	OBA	SLG
Home	2	3	4.78	1	32.0	21	14	LHB	53	0	3	.283	.406	.321
Road	2	2	5.57	0	42.0	28	31	RHB	232	8	37	.293	.387	.457
Apr-Jun	4	3	5.26	0	53.0	37	32	ScPos	87	0	29	.241	.364	.287
Jul-Oct	0	2	5.14	1	21.0	12	13	Clutch	29	3	7	.276	.400	.621

SCOUTING REPORT
Using an overhand delivery, Angel bends the knees of the best hitters when his plus screwball is working. He uses the scroogie as much as possible because his fastball is poor and his slider and curve are minus—as is his control. Although Angel is not that good at holding runners, four of seven attempts against him in '95 failed. Knee injuries have made him less effective than in the past when fielding his position.

HOW HE PERFORMED IN '95
Once the organization's most promising pitching prospect, Miranda's star has lost its shine due to knee problems. Mid-summer surgery, his second such operation in two years, disrupted another chance for Miranda to display his promising '93 form. He began the year in the rotation but compiled a 5.26 ERA in 15 games (10 starts) before being disabled on June 29 with torn knee cartilage. In post-injury relief work, some of his performances bordered on Mitch Williams-esque. However, he regained his command and pitched effectively in September.

WHAT TO EXPECT IN '96
Miranda will get every opportunity to pitch in '96, but he has not yet enjoyed an injury-free season in the majors and now may never fulfill his potential.

MILWAUKEE BREWERS

RON RIGHTNOWAR

Position: RP
Bats: R **Throws:** R
Ht: 6'3" **Wt:** 190
Opening Day Age: 31
Born: 9/5/1964
Drafted: DET 9/30/86
ML Seasons: 1

Overall Statistics

	G	GS	GF	SV	W	L	ERA	IP	H	R	ER	HR	BB	SO
95 MIL	34	0	13	1	2	1	5.40	36.2	35	23	22	3	18	22
Career	34	0	13	1	2	1	5.40	36.2	35	23	22	3	18	22

1995 Situational Statistics

	W	L	ERA	SV	IP	BB	SO		AB	HR	RBI	BA	OBA	SLG
Home	0	0	7.41	0	17.0	8	9	LHB	63	0	11	.270	.338	.302
Road	2	1	3.66	1	19.2	10	13	RHB	66	3	16	.273	.405	.470
Apr-Jun	1	1	8.56	1	13.2	5	9	ScPos	48	2	26	.313	.429	.542
Jul-Oct	1	0	3.52	0	23.0	13	13	Clutch	62	1	14	.242	.387	.306

SCOUTING REPORT

Rightnowar is an overhand thrower whose best pitch is an average-minus, four-seam high fastball which does not have great movement. He also relies on an average slider which has proven to be eminently hittable. A third pitch would help him.

He is quick to home plate (only one runner tried to steal on him last year) and is an average fielder.

HOW HE PERFORMED IN '95

One of the first replacement players to be activated after the lockout, Rightnowar found himself in the Milwaukee bullpen long after the other ersatz players went home. He filled roles ranging from long relief to setup.

As a career minor-leaguer of eight professional seasons, Ron did not distinguish himself as a pitcher with a long-term future in the majors. If Rightnowar had come along in the pre-expansion days of major-league baseball, he'd probably find himself nothing more than a career Double-A pitcher.

WHAT TO EXPECT IN '96

With dozens of pitchers floating around baseball with similar backgrounds and mediocre stuff, Rightnowar's major-league prospects are dim. He's not young anymore and further development isn't likely.

SID ROBERSON

Position: SP/RP
Bats: L **Throws:** L
Ht: 5'9" **Wt:** 170
Opening Day Age: 24
Born: 9/9/1971
Drafted: MIL92 30/808
ML Seasons: 1

Overall Statistics

	G	GS	GF	SV	W	L	ERA	IP	H	R	ER	HR	BB	SO
95 MIL	26	13	8	0	6	4	5.76	84.1	102	55	54	16	37	40
Career	26	13	8	0	6	4	5.76	84.1	102	55	54	16	37	40

1995 Situational Statistics

	W	L	ERA	SV	IP	BB	SO		AB	HR	RBI	BA	OBA	SLG
Home	4	3	6.97	0	51.2	25	24	LHB	66	1	6	.318	.403	.394
Road	2	1	3.86	0	32.2	12	16	RHB	266	15	49	.305	.384	.541
Apr-Jun	4	2	4.60	0	47.0	16	27	ScPos	84	7	43	.333	.414	.619
Jul-Oct	2	2	7.23	0	37.1	21	13	Clutch	10	1	3	.500	.500	.800

SCOUTING REPORT

A three-quarter, herky-jerky delivery is Roberson's trademark. He throws a plus change-up with this deceptive motion. Unfortunately, the rest of his repertoire is less imposing, including a below-average curve and a poor sinking fastball. Sid has average control, a quick release, and usually holds runners well although eight stole against him in ten tries during '95. He is adequate defensively.

HOW HE PERFORMED IN '95

The former Texas League Pitcher of the Year was impressive in his debut with the Brewers in May. The diminutive Roberson's aggressive style raised eyebrows with opponents and teammates. In his major-league debut, he was ejected by plate umpire Greg Kosc for continuing a brushback war by hitting Texas' Mark McLemore. Soon, however, Roberson began to get pounded, particularly in his second time through a batting order. After two demotions to New Orleans, Roberson returned to Milwaukee and experienced some success in relief.

WHAT TO EXPECT IN '96

Brewers' management must now determine if Roberson's significant minor-league success was the result of inferior hitters. While Sid has the right attitude, he needs good stuff as well to succeed in the bigs.

MILWAUKEE BREWERS

BOB SCANLAN

Position: SP
Bats: R **Throws:** R
Ht: 6'7" **Wt:** 215
Opening Day Age: 29
Born: 8/9/1966
Drafted: PHI84 25/636
ML Seasons: 5

Overall Statistics

	G	GS	GF	SV	W	L	ERA	IP	H	R	ER	HR	BB	SO
95 MIL	17	14	1	0	4	7	6.59	83.1	101	66	61	9	44	29
Career	226	39	80	17	20	32	4.34	460.0	487	252	222	35	170	224

1995 Situational Statistics

	W	L	ERA	SV	IP	BB	SO		AB	HR	RBI	BA	OBA	SLG
Home	3	5	7.45	0	48.1	21	16	LHB	176	5	33	.301	.386	.460
Road	1	2	5.40	0	35.0	23	13	RHB	156	4	21	.308	.396	.442
Apr-Jun	3	4	5.36	0	50.1	28	18	ScPos	93	2	42	.323	.400	.441
Jul-Oct	1	3	8.45	0	33.0	16	11	Clutch	7	0	0	.571	.571	.714

SCOUTING REPORT
Scanlan uses a high three-quarter delivery and a wrist-wrap, appearing to cup the ball before throwing it. His best pitch is a plus slider, as his average, straight fastball has lost some velocity. Scanlan's change-up and forkball are minus offerings. The tall Scanlan is slow to home and easy pickings for baserunners: 23 of 25 basestealing attempts were successful against him in '95. His fielding is awkward and subpar.

HOW HE PERFORMED IN '95
Bob Scanlan's happiest moment this year may have been October 1, the day the season finally ended. Pegged as a starter in April, Scanlan's campaign was ruined by a two-month absence due to a strained elbow. He was ineffective against both lefties and, surprisingly, righties after returning. No Brewers' pitcher was hit harder in the club's disastrous September than Scanlan, who lost six times. In a nightmarish season finale, he allowed nine runs in 1.2 innings against Boston.

WHAT TO EXPECT IN '96
One has to wonder if Scanlan can ever again be as effective as he was with the Brewers in '94. He is likely to sign somewhere as a minor-league free agent, and will have to hope for a mid-season callup.

FERNANDO VINA

Positions: 2B//SS/3B
Bats: L **Throws:** R
Ht: 5'9" **Wt:** 170
Opening Day Age: 26
Born: 4/16/1969
Drafted: NYN90 9/253
ML Seasons: 3

Overall Statistics

	G	AB	R	H	2B	3B	HR	RBI	SB	CS	BB	SO	BA	OBA
95 MIL	113	288	46	74	7	7	3	29	6	3	22	28	.257	.327
Career	216	457	71	115	15	7	3	37	15	4	38	42	.252	.340

1995 Situational Statistics

	AB	HR	RBI	BA	OBA	SLG		AB	HR	RBI	BA	OBA	SLG
Home	153	1	19	.275	.353	.340	LHP	54	0	6	.278	.400	.370
Road	135	2	10	.237	.297	.385	RHP	234	3	23	.252	.309	.359
Apr-Jun	106	2	13	.274	.355	.406	ScPos	72	1	26	.306	.381	.389
Jul-Oct	182	1	16	.247	.310	.335	Clutch	40	0	6	.375	.479	.475

SCOUTING REPORT
Fernando has above-average range and hands at second base and is simply outstanding on the pivot. He also possesses slightly above-average arm strength and accuracy. Although Vina has no power, he chases high fastballs and lifts pitches. He bunts often but badly, does not walk much, but is often hit by pitches. He is a below-average baserunner.

HOW HE PERFORMED IN '95
With extended playing time, Vina smacked his first three career homers. However, Fernando's defense and on-field toughness really set '95 apart from the rest of his previously uneventful career. He fielded .983, near the top of AL second basemen and covered a lot of ground. Fernando also filled in at shortstop and third base. Vina is fast and capable of stealing more often. However, questionable baserunning judgment, including being picked off three times in a one-week stretch, made many observers scratch their heads. Fernando must improve his bunting and hit the ball on the ground more to better utilize his speed.

WHAT TO EXPECT IN '96
Brewers' manager Phil Garner loves tough ballplayers and Vina is tough. Reasonable offensive improvement could propel Vina into a starting position at second base.

THE SCOUTING REPORT: 1996

MILWAUKEE BREWERS

BILL WEGMAN

Position: RP
Bats: R **Throws:** R
Ht: 6'5" **Wt:** 200
Opening Day Age: 33
Born: 12/19/1962
Drafted: MIL81 5/124
ML Seasons: 11

Overall Statistics

	G	GS	GF	SV	W	L	ERA	IP	H	R	ER	HR	BB	SO
95 MIL	37	4	17	2	5	7	5.35	70.2	89	45	42	14	21	50
Career	262	216	19	2	81	90	4.16	1482.2	1567	769	685	187	352	696

1995 Situational Statistics

	W	L	ERA	SV	IP	BB	SO		AB	HR	RBI	BA	OBA	SLG
Home	3	3	5.02	1	37.2	11	24	LHB	144	8	25	.326	.349	.542
Road	2	4	5.73	1	33.0	10	26	RHB	141	6	19	.298	.377	.496
Apr-Jun	1	3	6.47	0	32.0	8	17	ScPos	70	4	30	.300	.354	.543
Jul-Oct	4	4	4.42	2	38.2	13	33	Clutch	77	4	12	.312	.376	.519

SCOUTING REPORT

Wegman still throws overhand but his stuff has progressively worsened. He has an average slider and forkball, but Bill's fastball is well below par, and his curve fools nobody. He fields his position well and his pickoff move commands respect. Only five runners ran on Wegman last year, four successfully.

HOW HE PERFORMED IN '95

One incident says volumes about Wegman in '95. During a June beanball war with the White Sox, Bill tried three times to intentionally hit Ron Karkovice with a pitch—but couldn't. Finally, on the fourth pitch, Karkovice got plunked. For a once-outstanding control pitcher, this embarrassment summed up a frustrating season. Four horrible early starts (13 earned runs in 12.2 innings) banished him to the bullpen. He ended up pitching reasonably well in relief, but it became apparent that Wegman was pitching his final games in Milwaukee and, perhaps, his career.

WHAT TO EXPECT IN '96

Wegman is nowhere close to his level of the late 1980s and early 1990s when he helped anchor Milwaukee's starting rotation. Injuries have taken their toll, and Bill's baseball future looks bleak. Brewers' fans will remember the days when pinpoint control made him a true mound artist.

KEVIN WICKANDER

Position: RP
Bats: L **Throws:** L
Ht: 6'2" **Wt:** 202
Opening Day Age: 31
1 1/4/1965
Drafted: CLE86 2/30
ML Seasons: 5

Overall Statistics

	G	GS	GF	SV	W	L	ERA	IP	H	R	ER	HR	BB	SO
95 DET/MIL	29	0	9	1	0	0	1.93	23.1	19	6	5	1	12	11
Career	129	0	32	2	3	1	3.81	113.1	125	54	48	10	68	82

1995 Situational Statistics

	W	L	ERA	SV	IP	BB	SO		AB	HR	RBI	BA	OBA	SLG
Home	0	0	2.25	1	16.0	9	6	LHB	40	0	7	.250	.347	.300
Road	0	0	1.23	0	7.1	3	5	RHB	43	1	6	.209	.306	.326
Apr-Jun	0	0	3.86	0	4.2	3	0	ScPos	48	0	12	.167	.276	.188
Jul-Oct	0	0	1.45	1	18.2	9	11	Clutch	28	0	6	.143	.306	.179

SCOUTING REPORT

Wickander brings nothing special to the mound. Using a standard three-quarter delivery, he throws three minus pitches: fastball, curve, and slider. The slider tends to hang often and has caused him trouble. Poor control is also a serious problem.

Kevin is adequate at holding runners and fielding his position. Not one man attempted to steal a base in '95 while Wickander was pitching.

HOW HE PERFORMED IN '95

If Kevin were righthanded, he'd have pitched himself out of baseball by now. However, being an experienced lefthander, he still finds teams willing to take a chance on getting a few good innings out of him.

Detroit waived Wickander late in the summer, and Milwaukee then became the fourth big-league club to rent him a locker. While Kevin's pitched well for the Brewers in very limited usage, he could go either way in '96.

WHAT TO EXPECT IN '96

The Brewers will look to Wickander to take over as a lefty middle reliever this season. Given the lack of pitching depth in the Milwaukee organization, this could be the chance Kevin has been waiting for.

MILWAUKEE BREWERS: TOP PROSPECTS

BRIAN BANKS

Bats: S Throws: R Opening Day Age: 26
Ht: 6-3 Wt: 200 Born: 9/28/1970
Position: OF Drafted: 1993 #5 MIL

YR TEAM	LG/CLASS	G	AB	R	H	2B	3B	HR	RBI	SB	BA	OBA
93 Helena	PIO/R	12	48	8	19	1	1	2	8	1	.396	.500
93 Beloit	MID/A	38	147	21	36	5	1	4	19	1	.245	.284
94 Beloit	MID/A	65	237	41	71	13	1	9	47	11	.300	.375
94 Stockton	CAL/A	67	246	29	58	9	1	4	28	3	.236	.340
95 El Paso	TEX/AA	127	441	81	136	39	10	12	78	9	.308	.413

Banks, aided greatly by an outstanding hitters' park in El Paso (.329, 23 2B), was probably the biggest surprise in the organization. He was Howe Sportsdata's Minor League Player of the Month for June (.420, 12 2B, 5 HR, 24 RBI, 20 BB, 5 SB), was selected to the Texas League All-Star team and finished among the league leaders in six categories, including top figures in doubles and extra-base hits (51). The switch-hitter did well from both sides of the plate, hit .346 with runners in scoring position, and showed plate discipline. He is a decent outfielder, better suited for a corner position, but is not considered a "tools" player.

BYRON BROWNE

Bats: R Throws: R Opening Day Age: 26
Ht: 6-7 Wt: 200 Born: 8/8/1970
Position: P Drafted: 1991 #13 MIL

YR TEAM	LG/CLASS	G	GS	GF	SV	W	L	ERA	IP	H	HR	BB	SO	O/BA
93 Stockton	CAL/A	27	27	0	0	10	5	4.07	143.2	117	9	117	110	.225
94 Stockton	CAL/A	11	11	0	0	2	6	2.76	62.0	46	4	30	67	.207
94 El Paso	TEX/AA	5	5	0	0	2	1	2.48	29.0	26	3	13	33	.236
95 El Paso	TEX/AA	25	20	3	0	10	4	3.43	126	106	7	78	110	.239

Browne's stuff is major league, but he lacks command and consistency, averaging nearly seven walks per nine innings in his career. Despite a late start due to the strike, the 6-foot-7 fastball/slider pitcher equaled a career high with ten wins, finished fourth in the Texas League in strikeouts, and was more effective away from hitter-friendly El Paso (2.94 ERA, 64 IP, 49 H).

CHRIS BURT

Bats: R Throws: R Opening Day Age: 23
Ht: 6-3 Wt: 200 Born: 1/11/1973
Position: P Drafted: 1994 #7 MIL

YR TEAM	LG/CLASS	G	GS	GF	SV	W	L	ERA	IP	H	HR	BB	SO	O/BA
94 Helena	PIO/R	18	5	9	3	2	4	4.91	44.0	43	3	13	42	.259
95 Beloit	MID/A	36	0	32	27	1	3	3.80	42	34	2	17	42	.225

A football recruit at Northern Illinois, Burt, the first Beloit native to play for the hometown team, used a 90-mph fastball, an outstanding slider, and a fine changeup to record 27 saves in 29 chances. He was tied for the minor league lead in saves at the end of May—saving 12 games in as many appearances at one point—but was forced to the sidelines in mid-June for four weeks because of shoulder tendinitis.

JEFFREY D'AMICO

Bats: R Throws: R Opening Day Age: 20
Ht: 6-7 Wt: 250 Born: 12/27/1975
Position: P Drafted: 1993 #1 MIL

YR TEAM	LG/CLASS	G	GS	GF	SV	W	L	ERA	IP	H	HR	BB	SO	O/BA
95 Beloit	MID/A	21	20	0	0	13	3	2.39	132	102	7	31	119	.211

Howe Sportsdata's Comeback Player of the Year did not pitch his first two years of professional ball due to shoulder and elbow problems. However, D'Amico quickly established himself as the top pitching prospect in the organization in 1995, leading the Midwest League in ERA, pitching 5+ innings in every start, allowing two runs or fewer 13 times, and winning eight straight decisions at one point. He was selected a starting pitcher in the All-Star game. Polished for a 19-year-old, D'Amico mixes his 90-mph fastball, curve, slider and changeup well and walked more than two batters in a game just four times.

GEOFF JENKINS

Bats: L Throws: L Opening Day Age: 22
Ht: 6-1 Wt: 195 Born: 7/21/1974
Position: OF Drafted: 1995 #1 MIL

YR TEAM	LG/CLASS	G	AB	R	H	2B	3B	HR	RBI	SB	BA	OBA
95 El Paso	TEX/AA	21	79	12	22	4	2	1	13	3	.278	.341
Stockton	CAL/A	13	47	13	12	2	0	3	12	2	.255	.373
Helena	PIO/R	7	28	2	9	0	1	0	9	0	.321	.375

The Brewers hope Jenkins, their first pick in the '95 draft, will move swiftly and add some much needed punch to the lineup. The USC product, co-Player-of-the-Year in the Pac 10 last spring (.399, 23 HR, 78 RBI), led all participants in the College World Series with four homers and nine RBI. A free swinger with a very quick bat, the 21-year-old needs alot of work in the outfield, committing eight errors in 39 games.

DANNY KLASSEN

Bats: R Throws: R Opening Day Age: 21
Ht: 6-0 Wt: 175 Born: 9/22/1975
Position: SS Drafted: 1993 #6 MIL

YR TEAM	LG/CLASS	G	AB	R	H	2B	3B	HR	RBI	SB	BA	OBA
93 Brewers	ARIZ/R	38	117	26	26	5	0	2	20	14	.222	.379
93 Helena	PIO/R	18	45	8	9	1	0	0	3	2	.200	.333
94 Beloit	MID/A	133	458	61	119	20	3	6	54	28	.260	.356
95 Beloit	MID/A	59	218	27	60	15	2	2	25	12	.275	.332

A suspect hitter who missed the first half of '95 after undergoing knee surgery, Klassen is a smooth glove man with good hands, range, a superb arm and excellent makeup. Offensively, the just-turned-20-year-old can steal a base and has made strides in limiting his strikeouts—very important for a top-of-the-order hitter.

MILWAUKEE BREWERS: TOP PROSPECTS

TODD LANDRY
Bats: R Throws: L Opening Day Age: 24
Ht: 6-4 Wt: 215 Born: 8/21/1972
Position: 1B Drafted: 1993 #35 MIL

YR TEAM	LG/CLASS	G	AB	R	H	2B	3B	HR	RBI	SB	BA	OBA
93 Helena	PIO/R	29	124	27	39	10	1	5	24	4	.315	.363
93 Beloit	MID/A	38	149	26	45	6	0	4	24	4	.302	.316
94 Stockton	CAL/A	105	356	55	95	12	6	8	49	4	.267	.326
95 El Paso	TEX/AA	132	511	76	149	33	4	16	79	9	.292	.341

Another hitter aided greatly by hitter-friendly Cohen Field in El Paso (.303, 19 2B), Landry is a solid defender with a strong throwing arm. The Texas League All-Star finished second in hits and doubles and featured a five-hit game and a seven-RBI game during the season. However, the University of Arizona product is not a legitimate power hitter and could show a little better plate discipline.

MARK LORETTA
Bats: R Throws: R Opening Day Age: 25
Ht: 6-0 Wt: 175 Born: 8/14/1971
Position: SS Drafted: 1993 #11 MIL

YR TEAM	LG/CLASS	G	AB	R	H	2B	3B	HR	RBI	SB	BA	OBA
93 Helena	PIO/R	6	28	5	9	1	0	1	8	0	.321	.367
93 Stockton	CAL/A	53	201	36	73	4	1	4	31	8	.363	.427
94 El Paso	TEX/AA	77	302	50	95	13	6	0	38	8	.315	.369
94 New Orleans	AMAS/AAA	43	138	16	29	7	0	1	14	2	.210	.282
95 New Orleans	AMAS/AAA	127	479	48	137	22	5	7	79	8	.286	.340
Milwaukee	AL/MAJ	19	50	13	13	3	0	1	3	1	.260	.327

Despite exhibiting limited power, Loretta led the American Association with 28 RBI in July and finished second for the season. Although hitting is the biggest concern regarding Loretta, he has batted nearly .350 the last two years with runners in scoring position, sports a career .299 average, and finished with a flurry in Milwaukee last September. The former Northwestern star and Big Ten Player of the Year is solid defensively with good range and has the flexibility to play second or third base.

DUANE SINGLETON
Bats: L Throws: R Opening Day Age: 24
Ht: 6-1 Wt: 170 Born: 8/6/1972
Position: OF Drafted: 1990 #4 MIL

YR TEAM	LG/CLASS	G	AB	R	H	2B	3B	HR	RBI	SB	BA	OBA
93 El Paso	TEX/AA	125	456	52	105	21	6	2	61	23	.230	.285
94 El Paso	TEX/AA	39	139	25	40	11	3	2	24	10	.288	.381
94 Stockton	CAL/A	38	134	31	39	6	0	4	13	15	.291	.375
94 New Orleans	AMAS/AAA	41	133	26	37	4	5	0	14	6	.278	.362
95 New Orleans	AMAS/AAA	106	355	48	95	10	4	4	29	31	.268	.344
Milwaukee	AL/MAJ	13	31	0	2	0	0	0	1	0	.065	.094

The time has come for Singleton, possibly the most talented player in the organization, to prove he is a major leaguer. Blessed with outstanding speed and the organization's finest arm, the 23-year-old has every tool except power, but continued attitude problems, an inability to hit the ball on the ground, and trouble with lefthanded pitchers have stalled his progress.

DOUG WEBB
Bats: R Throws: R Opening Day Age: 23
Ht: 6-3 Wt: 195 Born: 8/25/1973
Position: P Drafted: 1994 #2 MIL

YR TEAM	LG/CLASS	G	GS	GF	SV	W	L	ERA	IP	H	HR	BB	SO	O/BA
94 Brewers	ARIZ/R	1	0	1	0	0	0	0.00	1.0	0	0	0	1	.000
94 Stockton	CAL/A	29	0	12	0	0	2	5.40	35.0	38	2	27	34	.262
95 El Paso	TEX/AA	18	0	16	8	2	1	4.42	18	11	3	13	11	.177
Stockton	CAL/A	32	0	31	22	0	0	1.70	37	17	3	8	34	.131

After struggling in his pro debut at Stockton in '94, Webb improved his slider and used his upper-80's fastball to go 22 for 23 in save chances last season. He picked up a save in the California League All-Star game and held hitters to a .145 average for the season, second best among minor league relievers. The 22-year-old was leading the league in saves and had been scored on in just five of 32 appearances when promoted to El Paso in late July. Webb had some trouble there, but still managed a win and six saves in as many appearances shortly after arriving.

WES WEGER
Bats: R Throws: R Opening Day Age: 26
Ht: 6-0 Wt: 170 Born: 10/3/1970
Position: 2B-SS Drafted: 1992 #10 MIL

YR TEAM	LG/CLASS	G	AB	R	H	2B	3B	HR	RBI	SB	BA	OBA
93 El Paso	TEX/AA	123	471	69	137	24	5	5	53	9	.291	.339
95 New Orleans	AMAS/AAA	64	234	28	67	16	0	2	24	0	.286	.317
El Paso	TEX/AA	45	160	22	41	9	2	0	19	1	.256	.298

Another talented Brewer middle infield prospect, Weger missed the entire 1994 season because of a broken ankle. He was a Texas League All-Star the previous year, showing a steady, if unspectacular glove, a solid bat and an ability to make contact. He returned to El Paso in 1995 and played shortstop until being promoted to New Orleans in mid-season, where he moved over to second base to play alongside Loretta.

ANTONE WILLIAMSON
Bats: L Throws: R Opening Day Age: 23
Ht: 6-1 Wt: 195 Born: 7/18/1973
Position: 3B Drafted: 1994 #1 MIL

YR TEAM	LG/CLASS	G	AB	R	H	2B	3B	HR	RBI	SB	BA	OBA
94 Helena	PIO/R	6	26	5	11	2	1	0	4	0	.423	.464
94 Stockton	CAL/A	23	85	6	19	4	0	3	13	0	.224	.274
94 El Paso	TEX/AA	14	48	8	12	3	0	1	9	0	.250	.339
95 El Paso	TEX/AA	104	392	62	121	30	6	7	90	3	.309	.383

The Brewers' first pick in 1994 got off to a great start, putting together a 22-game hit streak in April. He was then sidelined two weeks with an ankle problem, but put together another big stretch in July (18 RBI in 12 games) before spending much of August on the bench with shoulder tendinitis. A pure hitter with 10–15 home run potential, Williamson batted .366 against left-handers and finished second in the Texas League in RBI and sixth in batting. Defensively, the Arizona State product is far from a finished product, committing 28 errors and fielding .866, although the tendinitis contributed to many errors down the stretch.

MILWAUKEE BREWERS: OTHERS TO WATCH

RONNIE BELLIARD Bats: R Throws: R Ht: 5-9 Wt: 176
Born: 4/7/1975 Drafted: 1994 #8 MIL Pos: 2B

YR TEAM	LG/CLASS	G	AB	R	H	2B	3B	HR	RBI	SB	BA	OBA
95 Beloit	MID/A	130	461	76	137	28	5	13	76	16	.297	.356

The 20-year-old cousin of Rafael Belliard showed outstanding defense and pop, winning nine games in his last at-bat.

MARSHALL BOZE Bats: R Throws: R Ht: 6-1 Wt: 212
Born: 5/23/1971 Drafted: 1990 #11 MIL Pos: P

YR TEAM	LG/CLASS	G	GS	GF	SV	L	ERA	IP	H	HR	BB	SO	O/BA
95 New Orleans	AMAS/AAA	23	19	1	1	3	9	4.27	111.2	134	10	45	47	.302

After winning 30 games in 1992–93, the 24-year-old's average stuff has produced just nine wins the last two years.

TODD DUNN Bats: R Throws: R Ht: 6-5 Wt: 220
Born: 7/29/1970 Drafted: 1993 #3 MIL Pos: OF

YR TEAM	LG/CLASS	G	AB	R	H	2B	3B	HR	RBI	SB	BA	OBA
95 Stockton	CAL/A	67	249	44	73	20	2	7	40	14	.293	.347

Dunn started to show his power, range, arm and speed on a consistent basis last season, but his 1995 was cut short in early July by a broken finger.

KEN FELDER Bats: R Throws: R Ht: 6-3 Wt: 235
Born: 2/9/1971 Drafted: 1992 #1 MIL Pos: OF

YR TEAM	LG/CLASS	G	AB	R	H	2B	3B	HR	RBI	SB	BA	OBA
95 El Paso	TEX/AA	114	367	51	100	24	4	12	55	2	.272	.362

The former college quarterback's best tool is his bat, which still needs to produce more.

BOBBY HUGHES Bats: R Throws: R Ht: 6-4 Wt: 220
Born: 3/10/1971 Drafted: 1992 #3 MIL Pos: C

YR TEAM	LG/CLASS	G	AB	R	H	2B	3B	HR	RBI	SB	BA	OBA
95 El Paso	TEX/AA	51	173	11	46	12	0	7	27	0	.266	.317
95 Stockton	CAL/A	52	179	22	42	9	2	8	31	2	.235	.300

A power-hitting prospect, he has been scolded for defensive lapses in the past.

GABBY MARTINEZ Bats: R Throws: R Ht: 6-2 Wt: 170
Born: 1/7/1974 Drafted: 1992 #2 MIL Pos: SS

YR TEAM	LG/CLASS	G	AB	R	H	2B	3B	HR	RBI	SB	BA	OBA
95 El Paso	TEX/AA	44	133	13	37	3	2	0	11	5	.278	.297
95 Stockton	CAL/A	64	213	25	55	13	3	1	20	13	.258	.294

The first Puerto Rican player ever drafted as early as the second round, the 21-year-old is considered a solid defender with a questionable bat.

GREG MARTINEZ Bats: S Throws: R Ht: 5-10 Wt: 168
Born: 1/27/1972 Drafted: 1993 #28 MIL Pos: CF

YR TEAM	LG/CLASS	G	AB	R	H	2B	3B	HR	RBI	SB	BA	OBA
95 Stockton	CAL/A	114	410	80	113	8	2	0	43	55	.276	.382

A non-prospect prior to '95, Martinez has great range in center field, uses the whole field when batting, and led the organization in stolen bases.

DANNY PEREZ Bats: R Throws: R Ht: 5-10 Wt: 188
Born: 2/26/1971 Drafted: 1992 #22 MIL Pos: OF

YR TEAM	LG/CLASS	G	AB	R	H	2B	3B	HR	RBI	SB	BA	OBA
95 New Orleans	AMAS/AAA	12	34	5	10	1	0	0	0	.294	.385
95 El Paso	TEX/AA	22	76	16	21	1	1	0	7	1	.276	.317

Perez is a good athlete with a good bat, but shoulder and attitude problems have kept him from reaching his potential.

FRANK RODRIGUEZ Bats: R Throws: R Ht: 5-9 Wt: 170
Born: 1/6/1973 Drafted: NDFA 6-25-92 MIL Pos: P

YR TEAM	LG/CLASS	G	GS	GF	SV	W	L	ERA	IP	H	HR	BB	SO	O/BA
95 El Paso	TEX/AA	28	27	1	0	9	8	4.98	142.2	157	9	80	129	.288

Just 22, Rodriguez owns a live arm and has had success, but command and his 5-foot-9 stature are concerns.

MIKE STEFANSKI Bats: R Throws: R Ht: 6-2 Wt: 190
Born: 9/12/1969 Drafted: 1991 #40 MIL Pos: C

YR TEAM	LG/CLASS	G	AB	R	H	2B	3B	HR	RBI	SB	BA	OBA
95 New Orleans	AMAS/AAA	78	228	30	56	10	2	2	24	2	.246	.286
95 El Paso	TEX/AA	6	27	5	11	3	0	1	6	1	.407	.407

Stefanski, a .293 career hitter with 25 homers in five years, is nothing special behind the plate.

SCOTT TALANOA Bats: R Throws: R Ht: 6-5 Wt: 240
Born: 11/12/1969 Drafted: 1991 #15 MIL Pos: 1B

YR TEAM	LG/CLASS	G	AB	R	H	2B	3B	HR	RBI	SB	BA	OBA
95 New Orleans	AMAS/AAA	31	98	9	14	4	0	1	3	0	.143	.206
95 El Paso	TEX/AA	2	9	0	2	2	0	0	1	0	.222	.300

After blasting 53 homers in his previous two seasons, Talanoa couldn't handle Triple-A, then was sidelined by season-ending knee surgery.

BRIAN TOLLBERG Bats: R Throws: R Ht: 6-3 Wt: 195
Born: 9/16/1972 Purchased Northern League 12/94 Pos: P

YR TEAM	LG/CLASS	G	GS	GF	SV	L	ERA	IP	H	HR	BB	SO	O/BA
95 Beloit	MID/A MID/A	22	22	0	0	13	4	3.41	132.0	119	10	27	110	.243

Rescued from independent ball, Tollberg knows how to pitch, spotting an average fastball with a great changeup.

TIM UNROE Bats: R Throws: R Ht: 6-3 Wt: 200
Born: 10/7/1970 Drafted: 1992 #29 MIL Pos: 3B

YR TEAM	LG/CLASS	G	AB	R	H	2B	3B	HR	RBI	SB	BA	OBA
95 New Orleans	AMAS/AAA	102	371	43	97	21	2	6	45	4	.261	.304
95 Milwaukee	AL/MAJ	2	4	0	1	0	0	0	0	0	.250	.250

The 1994 Texas League MVP (.310, 36 2B, 15 HR, 103 RBI) was aided greatly by Cohen Field in El Paso; he leveled off last season, spending time between first and third base.

DEREK WACHTER Bats: R Throws: R Ht: 6-2 Wt: 195
Born: 8/28/1970 Drafted: 1991 #7 MIL Pos: OF

YR TEAM	LG/CLASS	G	AB	R	H	2B	3B	HR	RBI	SB	BA	OBA
95 New Orleans	AMAS/AAA	112	382	44	98	23	1	8	45	2	.257	.331

Wachter emerged in '93 at Stockton when he hit 22 homers, nine more than he has hit the last two seasons combined.

JOE WAGNER Bats: R Throws: R Ht: 6-1 Wt: 195
Born: 12/8/1971 Drafted: 1993 #4 MIL Pos: P

YR TEAM	LG/CLASS	G	GS	GF	SV	W	L	ERA	IP	H	HR	BB	SO	O/BA
95 El Paso	TEX/AA	5	5	0	0	0	4	9.95	19.0	32	7	22	8	.376
95 Stockton	CAL/A	20	18	1	0	7	6	4.35	107.2	124	8	53	76	.291

Wagner has a live arm but lacks command, as evidenced by his early numbers at El Paso.

THE SCOUTING REPORT: 1996

MINNESOTA TWINS

RICH BECKER

Position: OF
Bats: B **Throws:** R
Ht: 5'10" **Wt:** 180
Opening Day Age: 24
Born: 2/1/1972
Drafted: MIN90 6/85
ML Seasons: 3

SCOUTING REPORT

Rich is a straightaway hitter with a slow bat and little power who likes fastballs over the plate. Although he takes a lot of pitches and tries to get on base any way he can, Rich still has a lot to learn about major-league pitching—he takes too many third strikes and waves wildly at off-speed pitches.

In the field, Becker displays above-average range, but with a minus arm with average accuracy. He has average hands.

Despite knee injuries over the 1993–94 campaigns, Becker still has average-plus speed and has a quick first step when stealing or chasing balls in the field. His stolen base figures for '95 were very disappointing considering what he had done as a minor-leaguer.

HOW HE PERFORMED IN '95

Opportunity knocked for young Becker last May when Alex Cole broke his leg. Rich was hitting .309 with six home runs at Triple-A when recalled and became the Twins' everyday center fielder.

Becker, often compared to Lenny Dykstra, had a far from impressive rookie season. He showed little of his minor-league line-drive power, struck out often, didn't walk much, and hit between .200 and .240 all season. Particularly troubling were his problems with lefthanded pitching, which led Becker to give up switch-hitting in September.

His 12 outfield assists in '95 can be attributed more to fortune than sensation, as runners generally advanced fearlessly on Becker. He had his share of lost fly balls in the Metrodome roof over the course of his first full big-league season, but Rich also made some outstanding plays.

Rich did not show his advertised speed, which appears to have declined after the two knee operations. However, he ran well with the Twins in '94 and, even after surgery, had piled up good stolen base numbers, taking 42 bases in 51 tries over three seasons in the bushes.

WHAT TO EXPECT IN '96

It is too early to give up on Becker. Even with his poor play in '95, he is still young and has accomplished much for his age. Time should help cure Rich's knee ailments and experience should give him better on-field judgment. The Twins are committed to giving every opportunity to do in the majors what he has done in the minors.

Overall Statistics

	G	AB	R	H	2B	3B	HR	RBI	SB	CS	BB	SO	BA	OBA
95 MIN	106	392	45	93	15	1	2	33	8	9	34	95	.237	.303
Career	137	497	60	121	20	1	3	41	15	11	52	124	.243	.319

1995 Situational Statistics

	AB	HR	RBI	BA	OBA	SLG		AB	HR	RBI	BA	OBA	SLG
Home	180	1	14	.217	.289	.267	LHP	87	0	2	.149	.237	.161
Road	212	1	19	.255	.316	.321	RHP	305	2	31	.262	.322	.334
Apr-Jun	104	1	6	.221	.293	.269	ScPos	94	1	32	.213	.283	.330
Jul-Oct	288	1	27	.243	.307	.306	Clutch	60	1	8	.200	.294	.283

How He Compares to Other Batters

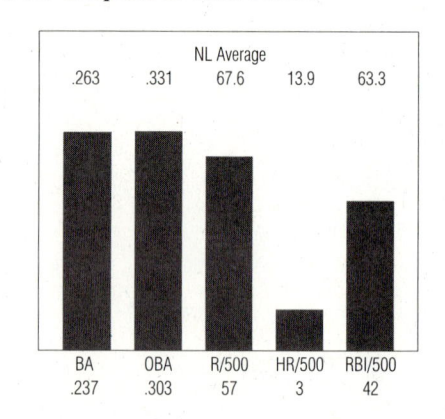

NL Average: .263 / .331 / 67.6 / 13.9 / 63.3

BA	OBA	R/500	HR/500	RBI/500
.237	.303	57	3	42

Where He Hits the Ball

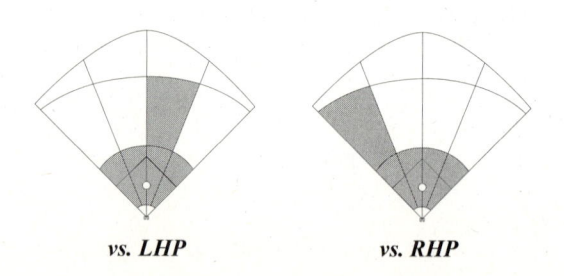

vs. LHP   vs. RHP

MINNESOTA TWINS

MARTY CORDOVA

Position: OF
Bats: R **Throws:** R
Ht: 6'0" **Wt:** 200
Opening Day Age: 26
Born: 7/10/1969
Drafted: MIN89 10/269
ML Seasons: 1

SCOUTING REPORT

Cordova is a straightaway hitter with plus power who likes fastballs down in the zone. His performance was consistent throughout 1995 and big-league pitchers were unable to exploit any apparent weakness in his debut season.

In the field, Marty has plus range and hands combined with an average arm with average accuracy. Though he played some games in center field, the decision was made early not to move him around the outfield and to keep him playing regularly in left. He is a plus baserunner who stole 20 bases, 16 of them after the All-Star break.

HOW HE PERFORMED IN '95

When Shane Mack went to Japan during the dark days of the strike, it became apparent that Marty Cordova would get his chance with the Twins in '95. Cordova did not disappoint, winning AL Rookie of the Year honors. He hit with good power, tying a Twins' record by homering in five straight games along the way. He pounded lefties, hit decently against righthanders, and ran well enough to become the Twins' third-ever "20-20" man.

Marty, quick to criticize his own performance, professed unhappiness with his strikeouts and situational hitting. Although Cordova struggled in late-and-close situations, he was extremely consistent throughout the season. Most importantly, did not slump when the league's pitchers saw him the second time around.

Marty threw out 12 runners in '95. He showed above-average range in left field, though he wasn't great in center and needs to work on timing fly balls. Cordova could be making great catches in the gaps and climbing the walls to steal homers as early as this year.

WHAT TO EXPECT IN '96

If cutting down on strikeouts and hitting better in the clutch are Cordova's primary areas for improvement, then he has a strong foundation to build on. The Twins' new ad campaign features former Twins' stars like Harmon Killebrew, Tony Oliva, Rod Carew, and Kent Hrbek, plus current idol Kirby Puckett, and ends with Cordova. While he isn't especially young and his minor-league record isn't outstanding, he has the tools and the work ethic to make the most of his talent. Barring some unforeseen disaster, he should be a popular fixture in the Twin Cities for years to come.

Overall Statistics

	G	AB	R	H	2B	3B	HR	RBI	SB	CS	BB	SO	BA	OBA
95 MIN	137	512	81	142	27	4	24	84	20	7	52	111	.277	.352
Career	137	512	81	142	27	4	24	84	20	7	52	111	.277	.352

1995 Situational Statistics

	AB	HR	RBI	BA	OBA	SLG		AB	HR	RBI	BA	OBA	SLG
Home	241	16	48	.282	.371	.535	LHP	124	3	20	.323	.386	.508
Road	271	8	36	.273	.334	.443	RHP	388	21	64	.263	.342	.479
Apr-Jun	204	10	32	.265	.338	.485	ScPos	142	6	55	.261	.345	.486
Jul-Oct	308	14	52	.286	.362	.487	Clutch	73	4	11	.205	.289	.384

How He Compares to Other Batters

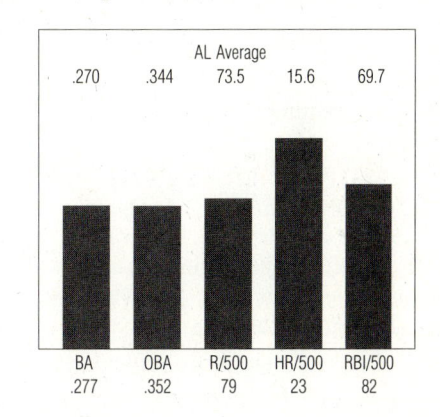

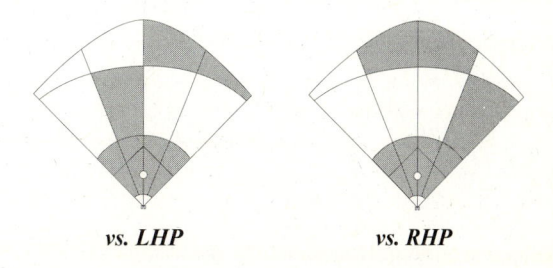

AL Average: .270 / .344 / 73.5 / 15.6 / 69.7

BA	OBA	R/500	HR/500	RBI/500
.277	.352	79	23	82

Where He Hits the Ball

vs. LHP   vs. RHP

THE SCOUTING REPORT: 1996

MINNESOTA TWINS

CHUCK KNOBLAUCH

Positions: 2B//SS
Bats: R **Throws:** R
Ht: 5'9" **Wt:** 175
Opening Day Age: 27
Born: 7/7/1968
Drafted: MIN89 1/25
ML Seasons: 5

SCOUTING REPORT
Although still an opposite field hitter, Knoblauch does not drive the ball to right quite as often as he did a couple years ago. He has adapted very well to the leadoff role, taking plenty of pitches and occasionally diving into them as well. Although Chuck has minus power, he has improved his stroke. He likes fastballs up, but will fight off inside pitches and inside-out them. He has never been much of a sacrifice expert and seldom bunts for hits.

All of Knoblauch's defensive tools are plus, including his often-remarkable range, soft hands, and strong, accurate arm. He makes the play to his right with remarkable grace and ease. Chuck is also a plus baserunner, and is stealing more often now.

HOW HE PERFORMED IN '95
Knoblauch followed up his fine '94 season with an even stronger one in '95, ranking second in batting average only to Edgar Martinez. He drew plenty of walks, ranking sixth in the AL in on-base average. Chuck also hit with more power but his strikeouts rose as well, especially early in the year. However, he batted .351, slugged .565, and hit ten of his homers from the All-Star break through the end of the season. By the end of '95, Knoblauch had set career highs in batting average, slugging average, and on-base average.

An off-season, low-fat diet created a lighter, more agile Knoblauch. He ran more and stole more but was also caught stealing a few times more. Chuck was again outstanding in the field, making both the marvelous and the mundane plays and showing toughness around the bag.

Off the field, things were more difficult. A run-in with a teenage autograph hound dampened Knoblauch's affection for his fans. He cancelled a regular radio spot and declined to sign autographs outside structured settings. Chuck also spoke out against the club's mid-season trades.

WHAT TO EXPECT IN '96
While Knoblauch didn't make the All-Star team and didn't win the Gold Glove, his '95 performance was terrific. The Twins now must open their wallets wider than they would like in order to re-sign him. After last summer's purge, most Twins' fans want the team to invest heavily in Knoblauch. There is no reason to expect a dropoff in '96, and he could even move one more step up to full-fledged stardom.

Overall Statistics

	G	AB	R	H	2B	3B	HR	RBI	SB	CS	BB	SO	BA	OBA
95 MIN	136	538	107	179	34	8	11	63	46	18	78	95	.333	.424
Career	704	2750	456	822	149	27	21	261	169	53	331	295	.299	.378

1995 Situational Statistics

	AB	HR	RBI	BA	OBA	SLG		AB	HR	RBI	BA	OBA	SLG
Home	282	4	34	.330	.413	.465	LHP	141	4	30	.355	.397	.553
Road	256	7	29	.336	.437	.512	RHP	397	7	33	.325	.433	.463
Apr-Jun	216	1	15	.315	.402	.398	ScPos	114	1	48	.360	.453	.518
Jul-Oct	322	10	48	.345	.439	.547	Clutch	76	2	10	.329	.420	.500

How He Compares to Other Batters

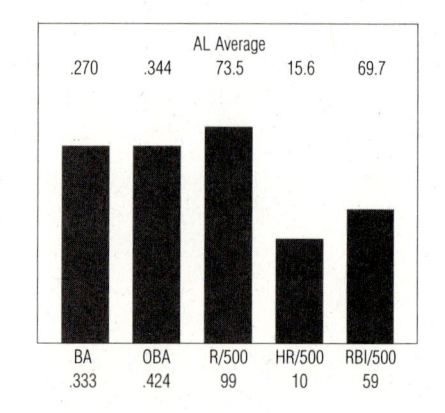

AL Average: .270 | .344 | 73.5 | 15.6 | 69.7

BA .333 | OBA .424 | R/500 99 | HR/500 10 | RBI/500 59

Where He Hits the Ball

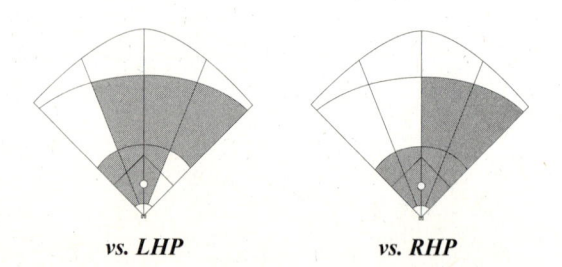

vs. LHP   vs. RHP

MINNESOTA TWINS

SCOTT LEIUS

Positions: 3B//SS/DH
Bats: R **Throws:** R
Ht: 6'3" **Wt:** 180
Opening Day Age: 30
Born: 9/24/1965
Drafted: MIN86 13/325
ML Seasons: 6

SCOUTING REPORT
Leius failed to produce in '95. Although he does possess some power, he showed little pop in his bat. He likes fastballs down and in, makes good contact, and will take plenty of walks. He does not bunt, either for hits or to sacrifice.

In the field, Scott is fairly solid, showing average range with good hands. He has a minus arm with minus accuracy, a problem that has nagged him since suffering a rotator cuff injury in 1993. With average running speed, Leius seldom steals and grounds into many double plays.

HOW HE PERFORMED IN '95
Between a quick start and a strong finish, Leius had the most dismal of his four full big-league seasons. From May 1 to August 31 he hit just .227 with only two homers—this coming off '94, his most productive homer year. Scott once again hit poorly against righthanders.

Leius was even worse with runners on base (.223) and in late-and- close situations (.163). Ron Coomer, another righthanded-hitting third sacker, was getting most of Leius' playing time by year's end. However, due to a jacked-up walk total, Scott did register his highest on-base percentage in four years.

It might have been unwise to expect Scott to continue to hit for power last season. Prior to '94, he had never hit more than eight homers in any professional season in a career spanning back to 1986. The Twins' cornermen didn't provide much power all year in '95, and Scott was perhaps the biggest disappointment.

Scott's career had looked bright as 1993 opened. He had been given the shortstop position, paired with his buddy Chuck Knoblauch at second. However, the shoulder injury that halted Leius' season after just 10 games brought his career as an everyday shortstop to an abrupt end.

WHAT TO EXPECT IN '96
The Twins wanted to re-sign Leius at a lower cost for '96. Assuming he inks with the Twins, he will fight Coomer and prospect Todd Walker for the third base job. While Walker is clearly the player of the future, the Twins like Leius' work ethic and will likely keep him at least as a utilityman. He might be much more effective, though, if he gets a chance to play in another ballpark.

Overall Statistics

	G	AB	R	H	2B	3B	HR	RBI	SB	CS	BB	SO	BA	OBA
95 MIN	117	372	51	92	16	5	4	45	2	1	49	54	.247	.335
Career	476	1373	201	346	58	10	26	155	15	15	154	214	.252	.327

1995 Situational Statistics

	AB	HR	RBI	BA	OBA	SLG		AB	HR	RBI	BA	OBA	SLG
Home	179	2	22	.223	.316	.335	LHP	117	1	13	.274	.372	.376
Road	193	2	23	.269	.353	.363	RHP	255	3	32	.235	.317	.337
Apr-Jun	173	3	27	.225	.332	.358	ScPos	103	2	41	.233	.341	.359
Jul-Oct	199	1	18	.266	.338	.342	Clutch	49	1	5	.163	.271	.245

How He Compares to Other Batters

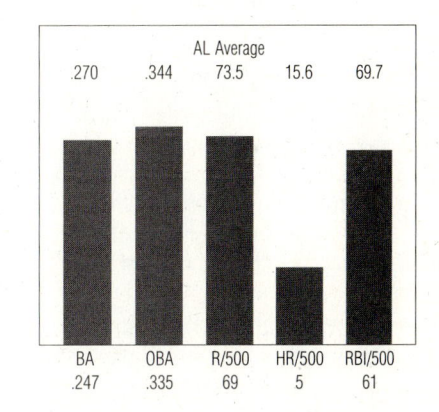

AL Average: .270 .344 73.5 15.6 69.7

BA .247 | OBA .335 | R/500 69 | HR/500 5 | RBI/500 61

Where He Hits the Ball

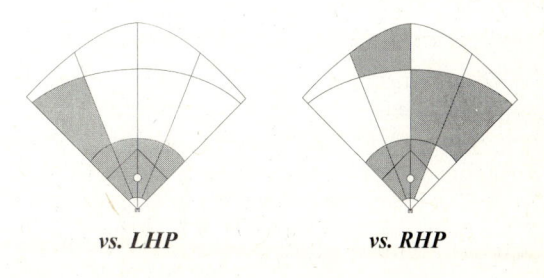

vs. LHP   vs. RHP

THE SCOUTING REPORT: 1996

MINNESOTA TWINS

PAT MEARES

Positions: SS//OF
Bats: R **Throws:** R
Ht: 6'0" **Wt:** 185
Opening Day Age: 27
Born: 9/6/1968
Drafted: MIN90 15/329
ML Seasons: 3

SCOUTING REPORT

As he showed in a surprising '95 display, Meares has some power even though he often hits to the opposite field. He likes fastballs down in the strike zone but is very aggressive and will chase a lot of pitches. He has been a streaky hitter in the past, although Pat was more consistent last year. As a shortstop, Meares has above-average range and above-average hands. His arm strength and accuracy are just average, and Pat's throwing is occasionally erratic. He has only average speed but has become increasingly bold on the bases.

HOW HE PERFORMED IN '95

Tom Kelly was pressed for time last spring in making roster decisions and as a result gave Meares, the incumbent, another shot at the shortstop job despite an inconsistent '94 performance. Pat did well in Florida and started off strong, hitting .299 in April-May. For the majority of the season, Meares hit consistently for decent average and impressive power, nearly doubling his previous professional home run total.

When brought to the majors in '93, Meares had played just 99 games above Class A. Most of his development has been at the major-league level.

His most consistent problem, poor strike-zone judgment, improved slightly in '95 as his on-base percentage topped .300 for the first time—thanks to being hit by 11 pitches—but he still fans often and rarely walks. Despite his offensive improvement, Meares rarely bats in close games when facing a tough righthanded, late-inning reliever.

Pat slumped badly in July, batting just .174, but hit at least .274 in every other full month and also stole more bases than he had in the previous two seasons combined. His baserunning has matured and last year he ran more aggressively and successfully than before. Despite leading AL shortstops with 18 errors, Meares got to plenty of ground balls, especially those hit up the middle. Pat's strong arm led to some late-season duty in center field.

WHAT TO EXPECT IN '96

The regular shortstop job is Meares to lose. The Twins like his speed and developing extra-base power and feel that his glovework and command of the strike zone will improve. He arrived in '93 with little professional experience but enough potential to be protected in the expansion draft, and Minnesota still believes in him.

Overall Statistics

	G	AB	R	H	2B	3B	HR	RBI	SB	CS	BB	SO	BA	OBA
95 MIN	116	390	57	105	19	4	12	49	10	4	15	68	.269	.311
Career	307	965	119	253	45	8	14	106	19	10	36	170	.262	.295

1995 Situational Statistics

	AB	HR	RBI	BA	OBA	SLG		AB	HR	RBI	BA	OBA	SLG
Home	194	3	20	.268	.310	.397	LHP	121	5	11	.231	.254	.413
Road	196	9	29	.270	.313	.464	RHP	269	7	38	.286	.336	.439
Apr-Jun	163	7	19	.294	.318	.497	ScPos	108	2	37	.231	.273	.361
Jul-Oct	227	5	30	.251	.307	.383	Clutch	49	2	7	.265	.321	.449

How He Compares to Other Batters

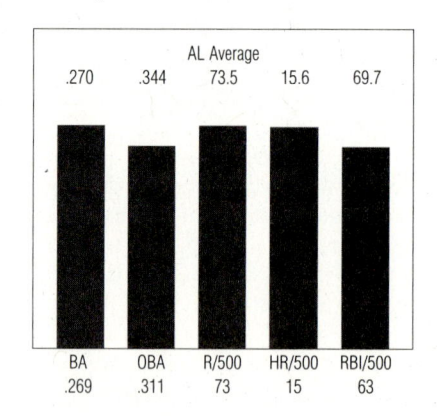

AL Average: BA .270, OBA .344, R/500 73.5, HR/500 15.6, RBI/500 69.7

Pat Meares: BA .269, OBA .311, R/500 73, HR/500 15, RBI/500 63

Where He Hits the Ball

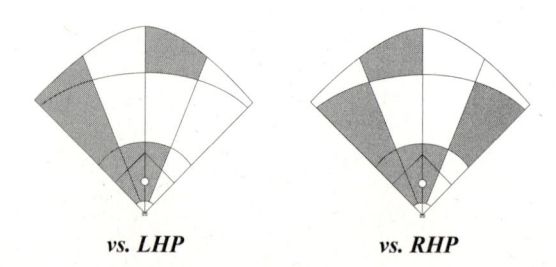

vs. LHP   vs. RHP

MINNESOTA TWINS

PEDRO MUNOZ

Positions: DH/OF//1B
Bats: R **Throws:** R
Ht: 5'11" **Wt:** 170
Opening Day Age: 27
Born: 9/19/1968
Drafted: TOR 5/31/85
ML Seasons: 6

SCOUTING REPORT
Pedro is a strict pull hitter who likes his fastballs inside. He has plus power but Munoz rarely walks and chips in more than his fair share of strikeouts.

With minus range and average fielding skills, Munoz has played his way out of the Minnesota outfield, often circling fly balls. He has below-average speed, which hurts his mobility.

Pedro has an average arm with average accuracy but lacks consistency. While he has the ability to throw out a baserunner by uncorking a cannon throw, he can on the next play let loose a screamer that soars ten feet over a waiting fielder's head.

The slow-footed Munoz hasn't stolen a base since '93 and regularly rolls into double plays. He hasn't laid down a successful sacrifice since mid-term of the Bush administration.

HOW HE PERFORMED IN '95
Munoz, acquired in 1990 for John Candelaria, was yet another of the Blue Jays' hot outfield prospects. The Twins thought he was superstar material. Six years later, he showed good power, and hit .300 for the first time. It was Pedro's most productive season yet, but again fell short of expectations.

Munoz still did not play every day, sitting against certain hard-throwing righthanders. Perhaps the worst part of his game is terrible strike zone judgment, which leads to low on-base percentages.

With much better defensive players available for Minnesota's outfield, Pedro had to find somewhere else to go. A conversion to first base was considered, but he didn't really want to move there. Once manager Tom Kelly saw Pedro play first, he had no enthusiasm for the idea either, and the experiment was dropped after three games. Designated hitting is the only alternative.

WHAT TO EXPECT IN '96
After six years in the organization, it is hard to remember that Pedro is still relatively young, although he is running out of time to mature into a good player. Minnesota fans hoped he would be a do-it-all guy, but reality has set in. As a DH, Munoz must carry a huge load with the bat, but there is concern that '95 is the best the Twins will see from him. At the least, Pedro improve his plate discipline in order to be a truly productive power hitter.

Overall Statistics

	G	AB	R	H	2B	3B	HR	RBI	SB	CS	BB	SO	BA	OBA
95 MIN	104	376	45	113	17	0	18	58	0	3	19	86	.301	.338
Career	483	1587	186	436	70	8	61	234	11	10	91	387	.275	.316

1995 Situational Statistics

	AB	HR	RBI	BA	OBA	SLG		AB	HR	RBI	BA	OBA	SLG
Home	177	10	34	.328	.368	.548	LHP	126	7	23	.310	.367	.532
Road	199	8	24	.276	.310	.437	RHP	250	11	35	.296	.322	.468
Apr-Jun	160	9	22	.275	.318	.494	ScPos	126	4	39	.270	.293	.397
Jul-Oct	216	9	36	.319	.352	.486	Clutch	47	2	5	.340	.347	.553

How He Compares to Other Batters

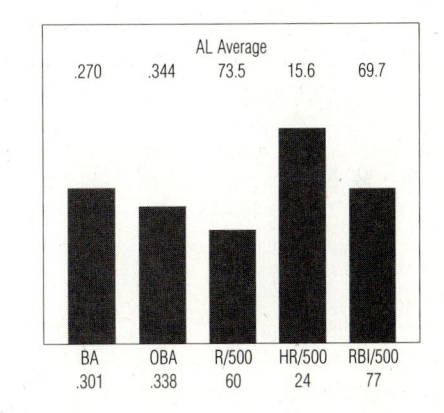

AL Average: BA .270, OBA .344, R/500 73.5, HR/500 15.6, RBI/500 69.7

BA .301, OBA .338, R/500 60, HR/500 24, RBI/500 77

Where He Hits the Ball

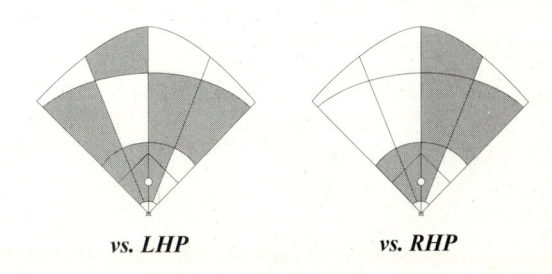

vs. LHP   vs. RHP

THE SCOUTING REPORT: 1996

MINNESOTA TWINS

KIRBY PUCKETT

Positions: OF/DH//2B/3B/SS
Bats: R **Throws:** R
Ht: 5'8" **Wt:** 210
Opening Day Age: 35
Born: 3/14/1961
Drafted: MIN82 1/3
ML Seasons: 12

SCOUTING REPORT

Kirby Puckett has been said to be difficult to pitch to because he will swing at anything—and can hit anything. He especially prefers pitches down and over the plate, and Kirby will not hesitate to look for low offerings on the first pitch. He can pull the ball, but also has no problem driving a pitch to the opposite field. He is one of the few Twins' hitters with plus power.

While no longer the Gold Glove centerfielder he was four years ago, Puckett has plus range in right field and average hands. Despite his usual high assist total, Kirby's arm is now rated by scouts as minus in strength with average accuracy.

Always speedy despite his stocky body style, Puckett is still considered an average runner, though he will rarely steal a base at this point.

HOW HE PERFORMED IN '95

Kirby batted only .229 in his first 21 games. From that point on, though, he hit very well and would have had 100 RBI had he not been beaned by Dennis Martinez in late September. The errant delivery broke Kirby's jaw and loosened some teeth, forcing him to miss the last three games of the year.

At age 35, Puckett's speed is waning but he still runs the bases as aggressively as ever. He finally seems at home in right field and, despite declining arm strength, he charges balls well and led AL right fielders in '95 with nine assists.

Kirby was uncharacteristically unhappy in reacting to the midsummer trade of Rick Aguilera; in fact, a negative sound bite of Puckett made the national sports shows. However, Kirby also joked with Frank Rodriguez on the night of the deal, pointing to Frankie in the Boston bullpen and intimating that he would soon be a Twin.

WHAT TO EXPECT IN '96

There is speculation Kirby might not be as aggressive a hitter after his late-season beaning. Knowing his character, however, it's unlikely Puckett will give anything away at bat.

Kirby was eligible to become a free agent at the '95 season's end. He certainly could get plenty of money to play elsewhere, but few expect him to do so. Puckett is still quite productive and one of the most popular players in baseball. In fact, to many fans, he is the epitome of the game at its best.

Overall Statistics

	G	AB	R	H	2B	3B	HR	RBI	SB	CS	BB	SO	BA	OBA
95 MIN	137	538	83	169	39	0	23	99	3	2	56	89	.314	.379
Career	1783	7244	1071	2304	414	57	207	1085	134	76	450	965	.318	.360

1995 Situational Statistics

	AB	HR	RBI	BA	OBA	SLG		AB	HR	RBI	BA	OBA	SLG
Home	277	13	52	.303	.373	.520	LHP	128	6	23	.320	.404	.523
Road	261	10	47	.326	.385	.510	RHP	410	17	76	.312	.371	.512
Apr-Jun	227	10	39	.282	.348	.454	ScPos	154	10	79	.312	.431	.584
Jul-Oct	311	13	60	.338	.401	.559	Clutch	85	4	15	.294	.375	.494

How He Compares to Other Batters

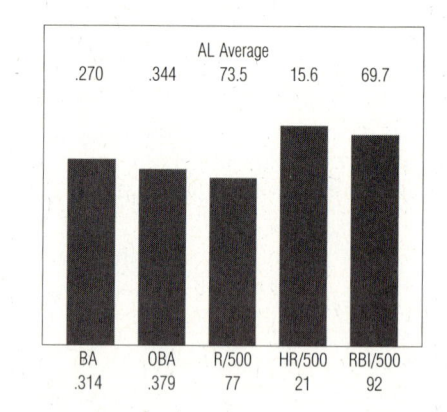

AL Average
.270 .344 73.5 15.6 69.7

BA OBA R/500 HR/500 RBI/500
.314 .379 77 21 92

Where He Hits the Ball

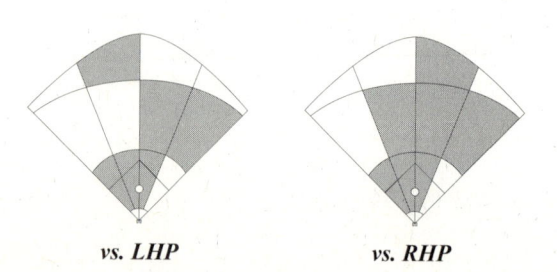

vs. LHP   *vs. RHP*

MINNESOTA TWINS

BRAD RADKE

Position: SP
Bats: R **Throws:** R
Ht: 6'2" **Wt:** 180
Opening Day Age: 23
Born: 10/27/1972
Drafted: MIN91 9/206
ML Seasons: 1

SCOUTING REPORT

Radke, a classic sinker-slider pitcher, throws with an overhand delivery utilizing a high leg kick. Although his fastball is slightly below-average in velocity, it sinks and tails into righthanded batters. However, his heater is still not overly effective with righties, with 18 of his 32 homers allowed off them. His slider is only average but his change-up—which is his out pitch—is rated as plus.

Radke is an average-minus at holding runners due to his high leg kick which slows his delivery. However, runners did not steal often or well on him in '95, making only eleven attempts, seven successful. Brad is an average fielder despite his tendency to fall off the mound to one side after delivering the ball. He fielded his position errorlessly over the course of his rookie season.

HOW HE PERFORMED IN '95

Despite performance that pales in comparison to an average American League pitcher, Brad's line shines in comparison to those of his teammates. The rookie led the team in wins, innings pitched and shutouts at age 22, doing this without the benefit of any Triple-A experience.

Poise is a word often used to describe the young Radke's demeanor on the mound. Brad did not generally walk a lot of hitters, and his habit of going right after batters in clutch situations certainly endeared him to his no-nonsense manager.

However, Radke depends almost entirely on good pitch placement, and he failed to pitch to spots as much as he might have liked. Brad allowed home runs in all but six of his appearances last year, ending up with a league-leading gopher ball total.

The four-bag barrage came partially because of his mediocre stuff and partially because he needs to learn how to pitch to batters in certain situations. Experience should help him iron the second problem out, but the first isn't likely to change.

WHAT TO EXPECT IN '96

Radke has already found some success in changing speeds and controlling his breaking pitches. Last season was his first protracted experience with failure as a professional. If can rebound, keep his head about him, and learn to set up big-league hitters better, he should be ready to take on a greater role in '96.

Overall Statistics

	G	GS	GF	SV	W	L	ERA	IP	H	R	ER	HR	BB	SO
95 MIN	29	28	0	0	11	14	5.32	181.0	195	112	107	32	47	75
Career	29	28	0	0	11	14	5.32	181.0	195	112	107	32	47	75

1995 Situational Statistics

	W	L	ERA	SV	IP	BB	SO		AB	HR	RBI	BA	OBA	SLG
Home	6	8	4.64	0	104.2	24	47	LHB	400	14	47	.268	.313	.450
Road	5	6	6.25	0	76.1	23	28	RHB	309	18	58	.285	.329	.534
Apr-Jun	3	7	5.91	0	67.0	17	31	ScPos	149	5	66	.268	.298	.443
Jul-Oct	8	7	4.97	0	114.0	30	44	Clutch	37	1	2	.216	.231	.324

How He Compares to Other Pitchers

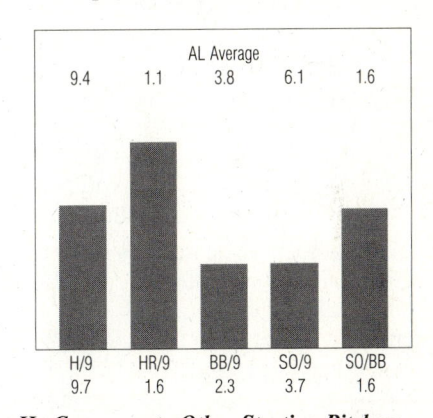

AL Average: 9.4 / 1.1 / 3.8 / 6.1 / 1.6

H/9	HR/9	BB/9	SO/9	SO/BB
9.7	1.6	2.3	3.7	1.6

How He Compares to Other Starting Pitchers

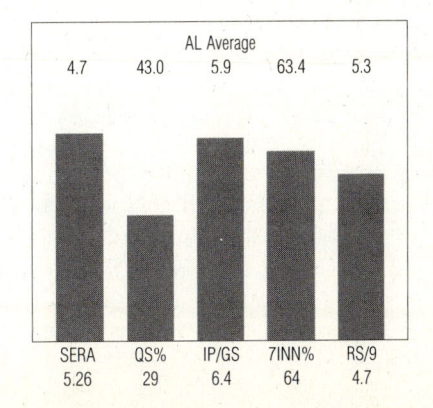

AL Average: 4.7 / 43.0 / 5.9 / 63.4 / 5.3

SERA	QS%	IP/GS	7INN%	RS/9
5.26	29	6.4	64	4.7

MINNESOTA TWINS

FRANK RODRIGUEZ

Position: SP/RP
Bats: R **Throws:** R
Ht: 6'0" **Wt:** 190
Opening Day Age: 23
Born: 12/11/1972
Drafted: BOS90 1/41
ML Seasons: 1

SCOUTING REPORT

Rodriguez comes at hitters with a straight overhand release, featuring three pitches. His best delivery is an average-plus fastball that Frankie sinks and tails into righty batters. To that, he adds an average slider and an average change-up. At times, the young hurler came in fully sidearm to some righthanders.

The still-inexperienced Rodriguez has bouts of terrible control, sometimes entering periods where he can't find the strike zone at all. Overall, his control is well below-average.

Rodriguez is above-average when holding runners on, primarily to his quick delivery. Only seven stealing attempts were made with him on the hill during the season, with just four of those being successful. Rodriguez, a former shortstop, looks very much at home when fielding his position.

HOW HE PERFORMED IN '95

Despite an ugly stat line, Rodriguez showed much promise in his rookie year. Many who mourned the trade of All-Star closer Rick Aguilera for the unknown (in Minnesota, at least) prospect were marvelling at Rodriguez by the '95 season's end.

Frank started his career playing infield in the Boston system, and he still looks like a shortstop filling in on the mound sometimes. He has very good stuff, and punched out men with his hard, moving fastball, but is raw and has much to learn.

The rap on Rodriguez is that he loses concentration easily, which leads to bouts of poor control. Unlike most Twins' pitchers, however, Rodriguez was not often victimized by the long ball; even when he's behind in the count, he can blow his fastball by most hitters. While Frank worked his stamina up to the seven-inning range by mid-season, he tailed off late in the year.

WHAT TO EXPECT IN '96

Though he does not show the most poise among the Twins' starting corps, Rodriguez has the most raw ability. At times last summer he was overpowering. It was exciting to watch him improve, and his makeup seems to be good. It appears Frank only needs experience and maturity to get better.

He is penned, with permanent marker, into the Twins' rotation for the foreseeable future. Barring injury, bigger and better things can be expected from Rodriguez in 1996.

Overall Statistics

	G	GS	GF	SV	W	L	ERA	IP	H	R	ER	HR	BB	SO
95 BOS/MIN	25	18	1	0	5	8	6.13	105.2	114	83	72	11	57	59
Career	25	18	1	0	5	8	6.13	105.2	114	83	72	11	57	59

1995 Situational Statistics

	W	L	ERA	SV	IP	BB	SO		AB	HR	RBI	BA	OBA	SLG
Home	3	4	5.45	0	67.2	38	38	LHB	219	3	30	.269	.364	.352
Road	2	4	7.34	0	38.0	19	21	RHB	192	8	34	.286	.374	.495
Apr-Jun	0	1	9.45	0	13.1	6	14	ScPos	104	3	53	.317	.400	.519
Jul-Oct	5	7	5.65	0	92.1	51	45	Clutch	11	0	1	.273	.500	.364

How He Compares to Other Pitchers

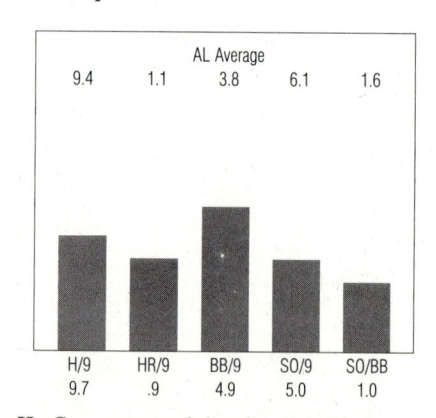

AL Average: 9.4 | 1.1 | 3.8 | 6.1 | 1.6

H/9 9.7 | HR/9 .9 | BB/9 4.9 | SO/9 5.0 | SO/BB 1.0

How He Compares to Other Starting Pitchers

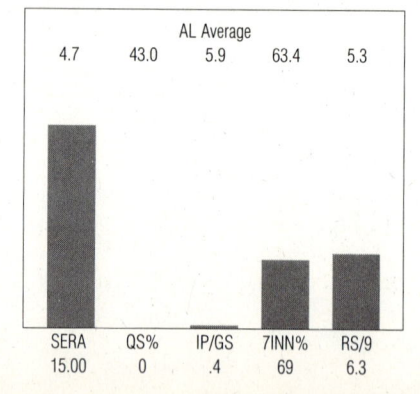

AL Average: 4.7 | 43.0 | 5.9 | 63.4 | 5.3

SERA 15.00 | QS% 0 | IP/GS .4 | 7INN% 69 | RS/9 6.3

MINNESOTA TWINS

DAVE STEVENS

Position: RP
Bats: R **Throws:** R
Ht: 6'3" **Wt:** 210
Opening Day Age: 26
Born: 3/4/1970
Drafted: CHN89 20/512
ML Seasons: 2

SCOUTING REPORT

Stevens has three hard pitches that he brings home with an overhand, power-pitcher-type delivery. His fastball is above-average with good movement. When the heater is on, it can sink and bore in on hitters effectively. His slider is just average, but Dave fools a lot of hitters by throwing a plus splitter with good sink.

Overall, Stevens' control is well above-average and he is considered mature for his age. However, this command and maturity came and went last year, along with his confidence and self-control.

Stevens is plus at holding runners due to his quick delivery. Six runners stole bases off him in seven tries in '95, not an unusual record for a righthanded power pitcher who enters games with runners on base. He is an average fielder.

HOW HE PERFORMED IN '95

Since being acquired from the Cubs in 1993, Dave has been the Twins' "closer of the future." Last July 6, the future arrived. In mid-game, Minnesota closer Rick Aguilera was removed from the bullpen due to his imminent trade to the Red Sox. Stevens then collected his first save of the year on five pitches.

Manager Tom Kelly downplayed the fact that Stevens' role was changing, saying he would be one of several pitchers to close games. However, Dave saved seven before blowing his first save of the year August 9, and finished with just two blown saves. His '95 success in the role was encouraging, and the Twins feel he has the necessary makeup for a closer.

How could a pitcher save 11 of 13 and still finish with such a high ERA or allow so many home runs? Some games in which Stevens entered to keep the team close or to mop up became disasters where fans wondered how he had ever gotten anybody out. Concentration and consistency are the major problems for him.

WHAT TO EXPECT IN '96

An angry Stevens referred to the Aguilera trade, and the other Twins mid-season payroll-slashing deals, as "jokes." This intemperate reaction might indicate that he felt unprepared to close games in the majors. If he is not ready, others might get a chance. But one thing is for sure: it's Stevens' job to lose in '96.

Overall Statistics

	G	GS	GF	SV	W	L	ERA	IP	H	R	ER	HR	BB	SO
95 MIN	56	0	34	10	5	4	5.07	65.2	74	40	37	14	32	47
Career	80	0	40	10	10	6	5.77	110.2	129	75	71	20	55	71

1995 Situational Statistics

	W	L	ERA	SV	IP	BB	SO		AB	HR	RBI	BA	OBA	SLG
Home	2	2	6.64	6	39.1	20	29	LHB	130	3	21	.315	.377	.462
Road	3	2	2.73	4	26.1	12	18	RHB	130	11	29	.254	.342	.562
Apr-Jun	3	0	5.85	0	32.1	13	20	ScPos	91	3	34	.242	.327	.440
Jul-Oct	2	4	4.32	10	33.1	19	27	Clutch	114	3	25	.281	.359	.439

How He Compares to Other Pitchers

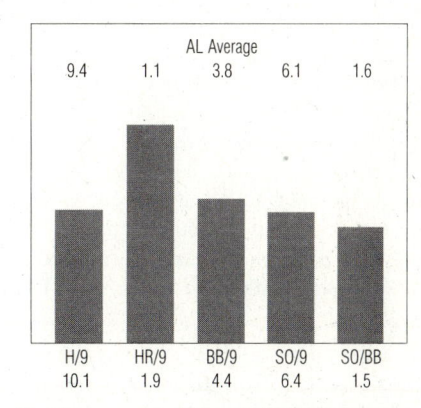

AL Average: 9.4 | 1.1 | 3.8 | 6.1 | 1.6

H/9	HR/9	BB/9	SO/9	SO/BB
10.1	1.9	4.4	6.4	1.5

How He Compares to Other Relief Pitchers

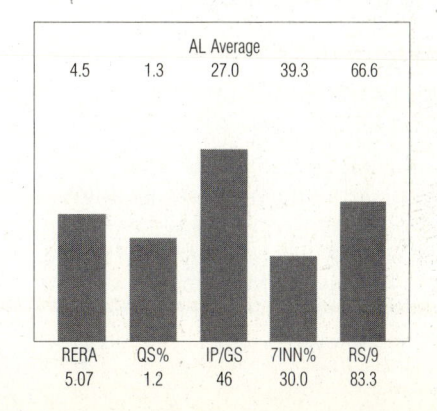

AL Average: 4.5 | 1.3 | 27.0 | 39.3 | 66.6

RERA	QS%	IP/GS	7INN%	RS/9
5.07	1.2	46	30.0	83.3

MINNESOTA TWINS

MIKE TROMBLEY

Position: SP
Bats: R **Throws:** R
Ht: 6'2" **Wt:** 200
Opening Day Age: 28
Born: 4/14/1967
Drafted: MIN89 14/373
ML Seasons: 4

SCOUTING REPORT

From a high three-quarter angle, Mike delivers four pitches. Plus control makes all of them more effective. His best pitch is a big curve that rates slightly above-average. Trombley's average fastball is thrown to sink; he also has a below-par slider. Last year, he began to renovate his formerly inadequate change-up, but the pitch still needs more time to become a good offering.

An plus fielder, Mike is has an average move to first. However, nine of ten basestealing attempts against Trombley were successful in '95.

HOW HE PERFORMED IN '95

Mike has gotten several shots at establishing residency in the Twins' rotation, and in '95 he did well in what might have been a final chance. Trombley began at Triple-A, but after going 4-0 in May, he joined the Twins June 8. Mike then spent most of the remainder of the year in the rotation. Every time he neared a demotion to the bullpen, Trombley came through, and so he kept pitching every fourth day.

After the mid-season trades, Trombley became the elder statesman amongst the starters. He spent a good deal of the season working on the change-up, development of which would help him complement his other pitches. However, even with the off-speed delivery, many feel Mike needs another plus pitch in order to allow him to set up his curve more effectively. This tinkering caused Trombley some unexpected control problems and contributed to his suffering from a common malady on the Twins—gopher ball-itis.

He has been more effective at home than on the road in his career. Mike pitches with much better command at the Metrodome, but can't find the plate while wearing a gray uniform. While Trombley holds righties to a decent average, he has allowed them to hit for more power than left-handers over his career.

WHAT TO EXPECT IN '96

Since his encouraging '92 rookie season, Trombley has contributed little to the Twins. Mike was outrighted over the winter, but will probably come to spring training with hopes of making the club's thin rotation. However, there is plenty of competition and, if Trombley hopes to prosper, he will have to expand or improve his repertoire soon.

Overall Statistics

	G	GS	GF	SV	W	L	ERA	IP	H	R	ER	HR	BB	SO
95 MIN	20	18	0	0	4	8	5.62	97.2	107	68	61	18	42	68
Career	98	35	16	2	15	16	5.11	306.2	337	196	174	48	118	223

1995 Situational Statistics

	W	L	ERA	SV	IP	BB	SO		AB	HR	RBI	BA	OBA	SLG
Home	3	3	5.16	0	45.1	17	35	LHB	219	8	27	.297	.380	.511
Road	1	5	6.02	0	52.1	25	33	RHB	173	10	31	.243	.302	.474
Apr-Jun	0	3	5.50	0	18.0	6	13	ScPos	108	5	41	.231	.303	.398
Jul-Oct	4	5	5.65	0	79.2	36	55	Clutch	20	2	2	.350	.381	.650

How He Compares to Other Pitchers

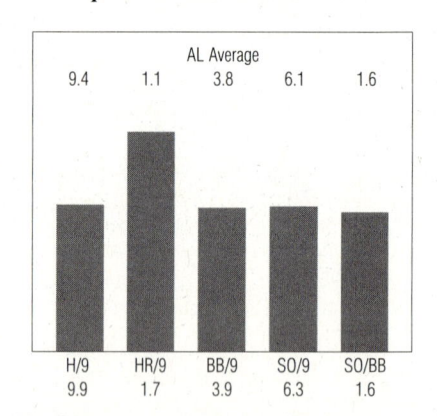

AL Average: 9.4 | 1.1 | 3.8 | 6.1 | 1.6

H/9: 9.9 | HR/9: 1.7 | BB/9: 3.9 | SO/9: 6.3 | SO/BB: 1.6

How He Compares to Other Starting Pitchers

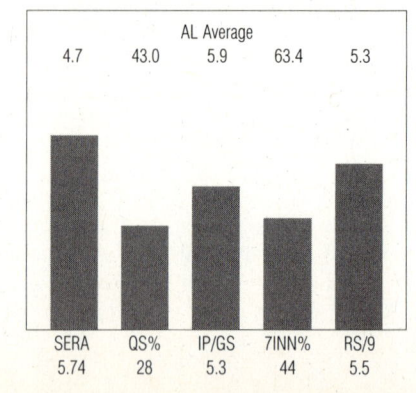

AL Average: 4.7 | 43.0 | 5.9 | 63.4 | 5.3

SERA: 5.74 | QS%: 28 | IP/GS: 5.3 | 7INN%: 44 | RS/9: 5.5

MINNESOTA TWINS

MATT WALBECK

Position: C
Bats: B **Throws:** R
Ht: 5'11" **Wt:** 195
Opening Day Age: 26
Born: 10/2/1969
Drafted: CHN87 7/192
ML Seasons: 3

SCOUTING REPORT
The slash-hitting Walbeck has minus power. He likes low pitches both as a righthander and a lefthander and hits the ball straightaway. As well as having little power, Matt rarely walks. Though he has a decided advantage as a righthanded batter, it's not enough that he will give up switch-hitting, which still gives him an edge as an everyday player. The Twins acquired Walbeck primarily to shore up what was perceived as their weakest defensive position (Minnesota's catcher for years had been Brian Harper, a fine hitter but weak behind the mask.) However, two years into his career, scouts rate Walbeck as only an average major-league receiver across the board. Like most catchers, he has minus speed, but Matt is an intelligent baserunner.

HOW HE PERFORMED IN '95
The Twins were hoping for some improvement with the bat in '95. Walbeck had hit dismally against righties the year before and this was not much help since his catching counterpart, Derek Parks, platooned against lefthanders.

Matt began the '95 season hitting much better against righthanders. On the year, he raised his batting average 53 points from his '94 mark, but any power Walbeck had exhibited in his rookie season was missing and his strikeouts rose dangerously. He hit in streaks, alternating good months with bad, but Matt was literally useless at bat for long stretches during June and August.

As has been noted, however, the Twins did not acquire him for his bat. He handles their young mound staff well but only threw out 19 of 75 baserunners (25%), largely due to an inexperienced staff that couldn't hold runners. Matt was discouraged by his poor caught stealing rate and the club's poor pitching, but manager Tom Kelly generously absolved Walbeck of blame.

WHAT TO EXPECT IN '96
If Walbeck continues to improve at bat and provides consistent play behind the plate, the Twins will be satisfied with him as their catcher. There is no competition in the farm system, so the Twins have little choice. If he brings his batting average up somewhat, hits with a little more power, and improves against righties, Matt will have given the Twins more than they bargained for when they obtained him. There's no guarantee that he can do that, but it's certainly possible.

Overall Statistics

	G	AB	R	H	2B	3B	HR	RBI	SB	CS	BB	SO	BA	OBA
95 MIN	115	393	40	101	18	1	1	44	3	1	25	71	.257	.302
Career	223	761	73	176	32	1	7	85	4	2	43	114	.231	.274

1995 Situational Statistics

	AB	HR	RBI	BA	OBA	SLG		AB	HR	RBI	BA	OBA	SLG
Home	190	1	23	.289	.332	.353	LHP	117	0	15	.308	.354	.368
Road	203	0	21	.227	.274	.281	RHP	276	1	29	.236	.279	.293
Apr-Jun	150	1	16	.233	.278	.293	ScPos	101	0	42	.307	.351	.396
Jul-Oct	243	0	28	.272	.317	.329	Clutch	69	0	11	.261	.293	.304

How He Compares to Other Batters

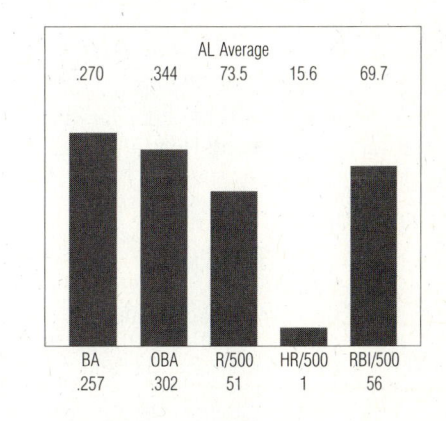

AL Average: .270 / .344 / 73.5 / 15.6 / 69.7

BA .257 | OBA .302 | R/500 51 | HR/500 1 | RBI/500 56

Where He Hits the Ball

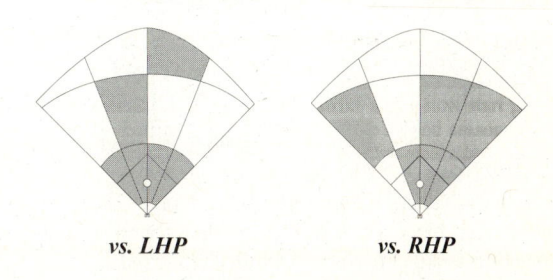

vs. LHP | vs. RHP

THE SCOUTING REPORT: 1996

MINNESOTA TWINS

JERALD CLARK

Positions: OF/1B//DH
Bats: R **Throws:** R
Ht: 6'4" **Wt:** 189
Opening Day Age: 32
Born: 8/10/1963
Drafted: SD85 12/310
ML Seasons: 7

Overall Statistics

	G	AB	R	H	2B	3B	HR	RBI	SB	CS	BB	SO	BA	OBA
95 MIN	36	109	17	37	8	3	3	15	3	0	2	11	.339	.354
Career	516	1609	170	414	79	16	44	208	17	8	83	295	.257	.301

1995 Situational Statistics

	AB	HR	RBI	BA	OBA	SLG		AB	HR	RBI	BA	OBA	SLG
Home	62	1	9	.371	.391	.581	LHP	55	2	7	.291	.310	.509
Road	47	2	6	.298	.306	.511	RHP	54	1	8	.389	.400	.593
Apr-Jun	108	3	15	.343	.357	.556	ScPos	31	0	11	.226	.219	.258
Jul-Oct	1	0	0	.000	.000	.000	Clutch	12	1	3	.333	.333	.583

SCOUTING REPORT

Jerald is strong and has some power, liking fastballs down and in but swinging at anything.

Both at first base and in the outfield, Clark is an average fielder across the board. He is also an average runner in all aspects.

HOW HE PERFORMED IN '95

Clark signed with Minnesota after a successful year in Japan. He hit .407 in spring training, then .350 as a platoon player in April-May. Because of his hot start, Clark began to play more against righthanders, seeing action at first and even in center field.

On June 16, Jerald sprained his right knee. He returned July 17 but reinjured the knee one at-bat into the game and missed the rest of the season.

From mid-August on, the word was that Clark would "soon" be activated. Manager Tom Kelly felt Jerald didn't want to play, while Clark said he wanted to play but feared a serious injury.

WHAT TO EXPECT IN '96

The Twins were disappointed that Clark did not return from his knee injury late in the season. Despite his fine early showing, it would be surprising if he returned to Minnesota, but another team should give him a chance off the bench in '96.

ALEX COLE

Positions: OF//DH
Bats: L **Throws:** L
Ht: 6'2" **Wt:** 170
Opening Day Age: 30
Born: 8/17/1965
Drafted: SL85* 2/43
ML Seasons: 6

Overall Statistics

	G	AB	R	H	2B	3B	HR	RBI	SB	CS	BB	SO	BA	OBA
95 MIN	28	79	10	27	3	2	1	14	1	3	8	15	.342	.409
Career	549	1688	273	477	53	25	5	110	143	56	209	285	.283	.362

1995 Situational Statistics

	AB	HR	RBI	BA	OBA	SLG		AB	HR	RBI	BA	OBA	SLG
Home	46	0	6	.370	.420	.500	LHP	5	0	0	.000	.286	.000
Road	33	1	8	.303	.395	.424	RHP	74	1	14	.365	.420	.500
Apr-Jun	75	1	14	.360	.422	.493	ScPos	21	1	14	.476	.522	.810
Jul-Oct	4	0	0	.000	.200	.000	Clutch	14	0	2	.286	.333	.357

SCOUTING REPORT

Cole is an opposite field, slap hitter who likes fastballs out over the plate. He has no power despite hitting the first five homers of his career in 1994-95. He is a good bunter.

Cole has plus range but a weak arm with minus accuracy. He prefers center rather than the outfield corners, feeling that he tracks the ball better from that position. Alex has average-plus speed; whether he will retain this depends on how he recovers from his injury.

HOW HE PERFORMED IN '95

Hitting .360 on May 31, Alex caught his spikes in the turf at County Stadium, breaking his right leg. He was thought to be done for '95 but worked hard to rehabilitate himself and returned September 19. As in '94, Tom Kelly was using him as a platoon player.

WHAT TO EXPECT IN '96

Cole is a valuable reserve and not an embarrassment if he has to play regularly. He's been underrated his whole career and ranks among the class acts of baseball. He made an extraordinary effort to return last season and publicly thanked the fans who sent him get-well cards after his injury.

MINNESOTA TWINS

RON COOMER

Positions: 1B/3B//DH/OF
Bats: R **Throws:** R
Ht: 5'11" **Wt:** 195
Opening Day Age: 29
Born: 11/18/1966
Drafted: OAK87 13/355
ML Seasons: 1

Overall Statistics

	G	AB	R	H	2B	3B	HR	RBI	SB	CS	BB	SO	BA	OBA
95 MIN	37	101	15	26	3	1	5	19	0	1	9	11	.257	.324
Career	37	101	15	26	3	1	5	19	0	1	9	11	.257	.324

1995 Situational Statistics

	AB	HR	RBI	BA	OBA	SLG		AB	HR	RBI	BA	OBA	SLG
Home	44	2	9	.250	.353	.455	LHP	47	3	12	.319	.407	.553
Road	57	3	10	.263	.300	.456	RHP	54	2	7	.204	.246	.370
Apr-Jun	0	0	0	.000	.000	.000	ScPos	34	2	15	.324	.361	.618
Jul-Oct	101	5	19	.257	.324	.455	Clutch	16	0	0	.063	.063	.063

SCOUTING REPORT
A chunky player with line-drive power and some bat speed, Coomer has hit better than .300 each of the past three years in the minors. He has little speed.

Ron plays third base well, displaying plus range and an adequate arm. He appears awkward at first sight, however. He can also handle the chores at first base well enough, making more starts there for the Twins than at third.

HOW HE PERFORMED IN '95
Coomer arrived from L.A. July 31 as part of the Kevin Tapani-Mark Guthrie deal. The Dodgers claimed that only Tim Wallach's presence kept Coomer, a six-year minor-leaguer, from the bigs. With the Twins, Coomer (who runs a hitting school) bashed three homers in his first 40 at-bats and hammered southpaws in limited duty.

WHAT TO EXPECT IN '96
Coomer's late start in the majors was not entirely due to lack of opportunity. He rarely walks and may not hit righthanders well enough to play regularly. However, third base prospect Todd Walker is rising quickly, and Ron may need to polish his defense at first to stay in Minneapolis in the future.

EDDIE GUARDADO

Position: RP/SP
Bats: R **Throws:** L
Ht: 6'0" **Wt:** 190
Opening Day Age: 25
Born: 10/2/1970
Drafted: MIN90 24/570
ML Seasons: 3

Overall Statistics

	G	GS	GF	SV	W	L	ERA	IP	H	R	ER	HR	BB	SO
95 MIN	51	5	10	2	4	9	5.12	91.1	99	54	52	13	45	71
Career	74	25	12	2	7	19	5.90	203.0	248	138	133	29	85	125

1995 Situational Statistics

	W	L	ERA	SV	IP	BB	SO		AB	HR	RBI	BA	OBA	SLG
Home	3	4	3.60	2	40.0	16	32	LHB	121	2	15	.223	.254	.298
Road	1	5	6.31	0	51.1	29	39	RHB	233	11	42	.309	.405	.511
Apr-Jun	0	6	6.44	0	43.1	21	28	ScPos	87	4	44	.287	.356	.483
Jul-Oct	4	3	3.94	2	48.0	24	43	Clutch	71	1	5	.211	.291	.268

SCOUTING REPORT
The hard-working Guardado comes in at three-quarters, dropping down sidearm against some lefthanders. His sinking fastball and slider rate average, and Eddie augments the basic stuff with an average curve and change-up.

Guardado has a quick delivery to the plate and is plus at holding runners; just six of 11 potential basestealers were successful against Eddie in '95. He is an average fielder.

HOW HE PERFORMED IN '95
Guardado began the year as a swingman, relieving in his first six games, then starting five of his next six appearances. From that point on, he saw action only from the bullpen. As a starter, Eddie allowed a .378 average and racked up a 9.28 ERA. In relief, opponents hit just .246, leading to a fine 3.86 ERA.

Although considered a control pitcher when he first arrived in 1993, Guardado still has frequent problems with his command and control.

WHAT TO EXPECT IN '96
Guardado must improve against righthanders and maintain his late-season success entering games with runners on base. However, considering that '95 was his first extended bullpen tour, Eddie showed great promise in relief.

MINNESOTA TWINS

CHIP HALE

Positions: DH//2B/3B/1B
Bats: L **Throws:** R
Ht: 5'11" **Wt:** 180
Opening Day Age: 31
Born: 12/2/1964
Drafted: MIN87 17/425
ML Seasons: 5

Overall Statistics

	G	AB	R	H	2B	3B	HR	RBI	SB	CS	BB	SO	BA	OBA
95 MIN	69	103	10	27	4	0	2	18	0	0	11	20	.262	.333
Career	234	476	54	134	22	1	6	62	2	3	46	58	.282	.349

1995 Situational Statistics

	AB	HR	RBI	BA	OBA	SLG		AB	HR	RBI	BA	OBA	SLG
Home	50	0	6	.300	.314	.340	LHP	4	0	0	.250	.400	.250
Road	53	2	12	.226	.349	.377	RHP	99	2	18	.263	.330	.364
Apr-Jun	25	1	8	.280	.357	.480	ScPos	30	0	16	.400	.486	.433
Jul-Oct	78	1	10	.256	.326	.321	Clutch	39	1	12	.308	.372	.410

SCOUTING REPORT

Chip Hale is a contact hitter who likes fastballs up and over the plate. He has shown little power throughout his career but will take a walk.

A liability in the field, Hale shows minus range and hands and has below-average arm strength and accuracy. Chip is a below-average runner and does not take off except in a rare hit-and-run play.

HOW HE PERFORMED IN '95

Strong performance off the pines is Hale's forte; he has averaged .337 as a pinch-hitter over the last three years. In '95, he batted .297 with 15 RBI in just 47 pinch-hit at-bats.

Chip spent time at Salt Lake City in May but came back strong, hitting .500 in June and .310 in July. Besides late-inning singles, Hale makes limited contributions, seeing little action in the field and stealing just two bases since '92.

WHAT TO EXPECT IN '96

As a pinch-hitter, more power would be nice from Hale, but a clutch single is often worth plenty. The fact that he hits lefthanded is also an advantage. Like former Twins' reserve Randy Bush, he will find that when the good pinch-hitting stops, his career will as well.

SCOTT KLINGENBECK

Position: RP/SP
Bats: R **Throws:** R
Ht: 6'2" **Wt:** 205
Opening Day Age: 25
Born: 2/3/1971
Drafted: BAL92 5/128
ML Seasons: 2

Overall Statistics

	G	GS	GF	SV	W	L	ERA	IP	H	R	ER	HR	BB	SO
95 BAL/MIN	24	9	4	0	2	4	7.12	79.2	101	65	63	22	42	42
Career	25	10	4	0	3	4	6.85	86.2	107	69	66	23	46	47

1995 Situational Statistics

	W	L	ERA	SV	IP	BB	SO		AB	HR	RBI	BA	OBA	SLG
Home	2	2	6.00	0	45.0	18	23	LHB	183	9	34	.311	.379	.546
Road	0	2	8.57	0	34.2	24	19	RHB	139	13	30	.317	.422	.662
Apr-Jun	2	1	4.97	0	25.1	15	13	ScPos	81	6	40	.296	.402	.617
Jul-Oct	0	3	8.12	0	54.1	27	29	Clutch	0	0	0	.000	.000	.000

SCOUTING REPORT

From a three-quarter angle, Klingenbeck shows three pitches. His best offerings are his average-plus curve and change-up. The curve has a hard, sharp, lateral break and the change has consistent movement despite only fair arm action. Scott also throws an average-minus fastball with some tail and sink and he changes arm speeds to increase its effectiveness. His control is erratic. He is average at holding runners. Of five men trying to steal against him last year, three were caught. Scott is as an average fielder.

HOW HE PERFORMED IN '95

The first hitter Klingenbeck faced with the Twins was Boston's Juan Bell, who took him deep on the first pitch. Scott slumped after coming over from the Orioles in July. He had a 4.88 ERA with Baltimore, but was 8.57 for Minnesota. With just seven games of Triple-A experience, Klingenbeck seemed overmatched. He allowed at least five runs and came out before the sixth inning in each of his four Minnesota starts. Scott finished the year mopping up.

WHAT TO EXPECT IN '96

Klingenbeck may start '96 in Salt Lake City. He could surface again with the Twins if he pitches well, but he needs more time to develop.

MINNESOTA TWINS

PAT MAHOMES

Position: RP/SP
Bats: R **Throws:** R
Ht: 6'1" **Wt:** 175
Opening Day Age: 25
Born: 8/9/1970
Drafted: MIN88 6/155
ML Seasons: 4

Overall Statistics

	G	GS	GF	SV	W	L	ERA	IP	H	R	ER	HR	BB	SO
95 MIN	47	7	16	3	4	10	6.37	94.2	100	74	67	22	47	67
Career	94	46	21	3	17	24	5.62	321.2	341	217	201	57	162	187

1995 Situational Statistics

	W	L	ERA	SV	IP	BB	SO		AB	HR	RBI	BA	OBA	SLG
Home	1	5	9.20	0	46.0	29	38	LHB	202	12	31	.312	.372	.550
Road	3	5	3.70	3	48.2	18	29	RHB	167	10	40	.222	.335	.455
Apr-Jun	0	4	7.99	0	41.2	24	29	ScPos	91	8	52	.330	.447	.626
Jul-Oct	4	6	5.09	3	53.0	23	38	Clutch	107	5	16	.243	.331	.411

SCOUTING REPORT

Pat throws overhand across his body with an above-average four-seam fastball. Mahomes has an average curve and slider; a deceptive plus change-up is his out pitch. Though Mahomes has good stuff, he doesn't know how to pitch, lacking control and confidence. Pat delivers quickly but awkwardly, rating average-plus at holding runners. However, concentration problems meant that 11 of 12 bases-tealing attempts succeeded. Although an average fielder, Pat is athletic and can pinch-run.

HOW HE PERFORMED IN '95

The first week after the '94 strike brought an auto accident and a DWI charge for Mahomes. He carried that lack of control through last season and didn't pitch out of the second inning in four of his first five starts. Demoted to relief, he pitched well enough to return to the rotation, but overslept, missed a team practice, and was demoted again for the rest of the season. However, by pitching fewer innings, Pat threw much harder. He fanned 49 in 66.2 relief frames but blew five save chances.

WHAT TO EXPECT IN '96

Mahomes wants to start again but is likely to remain a reliever for the immediate future. He's far too young to give up on.

DAN MASTELLER

Positions: 1B/OF//DH
Bats: L **Throws:** L
Ht: 6'0" **Wt:** 185
Opening Day Age: 28
Born: 3/17/1968
Drafted: MIN89 11/295
ML Seasons: 1

Overall Statistics

	G	AB	R	H	2B	3B	HR	RBI	SB	CS	BB	SO	BA	OBA
95 MIN	71	198	21	47	12	0	3	21	1	2	18	19	.237	.303
Career	71	198	21	47	12	0	3	21	1	2	18	19	.237	.303

1995 Situational Statistics

	AB	HR	RBI	BA	OBA	SLG		AB	HR	RBI	BA	OBA	SLG
Home	89	1	9	.225	.317	.292	LHP	14	0	2	.143	.235	.143
Road	109	2	12	.248	.291	.385	RHP	184	3	19	.245	.308	.359
Apr-Jun	12	0	0	.083	.267	.083	ScPos	57	0	17	.158	.222	.175
Jul-Oct	186	3	21	.247	.305	.360	Clutch	28	2	8	.321	.441	.607

SCOUTING REPORT

Masteller is not a strong hitter. While he likes the fastball up and over the plate, he has minus power.

In the field, where Masteller split time between the outfield and first base, he is average in range, hands, arm strength and throwing accuracy. Dan has average speed and takes few risks on the basepaths without paying for them.

HOW HE PERFORMED IN '95

Masteller's rookie year had its moments. In late July, his first big-league homer off Jack McDowell gave Minnesota its first bottom-of-the-ninth win of the season. Overall, however, he was just another of the Twins' weak lefthanded bats.

A fringe prospect, Dan played in spring replacement games. Masteller started 1-for-14 but, from there, his average increased each month until he hit .297 in September. Defensively, Dan was adequate at first but looked uncomfortable in the outfield.

WHAT TO EXPECT IN '96

Masteller's previous .300 averages in the PCL should translate to about .250-.260 in the majors. The Twins need impact hitters, however, but Dan lacks power and speed, so look for him to have a reserved seat on the Salt Lake City shuttle this season.

THE SCOUTING REPORT: 1996

MINNESOTA TWINS

MATT MERULLO

Positions: C/DH//1B
Bats: L **Throws:** R
Ht: 6'2" **Wt:** 200
Opening Day Age: 30
Born: 8/4/1965
Drafted: CHA86 7/179
ML Seasons: 6

Overall Statistics

	G	AB	R	H	2B	3B	HR	RBI	SB	CS	BB	SO	BA	OBA
95 MIN	76	195	19	55	14	1	1	27	0	1	14	27	.282	.335
Career	223	496	37	116	17	2	7	59	0	2	32	69	.234	.281

1995 Situational Statistics

	AB	HR	RBI	BA	OBA	SLG		AB	HR	RBI	BA	OBA	SLG
Home	103	1	19	.301	.351	.417	LHP	32	1	10	.438	.486	.594
Road	92	0	8	.261	.317	.337	RHP	163	0	17	.252	.306	.337
Apr-Jun	100	0	8	.290	.345	.370	ScPos	61	1	23	.197	.224	.311
Jul-Oct	95	1	19	.274	.324	.389	Clutch	40	0	2	.175	.195	.225

SCOUTING REPORT

A line-drive pull hitter with no power, Merullo likes fastballs down and in that he can lash to right field.

Matt does not counteract his lack of offensive impact with strong defensive skills. He has average range and average hands but has minus arm strength and only average accuracy. Merullo runs with well below-average speed and only moves station-to-station on the basepaths.

HOW HE PERFORMED IN '95

Merullo spent most of '94 in Triple-A but made the Twins last spring training. He added the ability to play first base as well as catch. In a measure of the team's lack of lefthanded hitting, the punchless Merullo batted anywhere in the lineup from #4 to #9. To make things worse, Matt proved a liability on defense, throwing out only 12% of runners attempting to steal (5 of 41). In addition, he only played twice at first since the club carried only two catchers all season.

WHAT TO EXPECT IN '96

Matt was waived in October but may find himself back in Minnesota. The Twins have little catching help in the system, and there is a chance that Merullo might be a better hitter this season with the added experience.

JOSE PARRA

Position: SP/RP
Bats: R **Throws:** R
Ht: 5'11" **Wt:** 160
Opening Day Age: 23
Born: 11/28/1972
Drafted: LA 12/7/89
ML Seasons: 1

Overall Statistics

	G	GS	GF	SV	W	L	ERA	IP	H	R	ER	HR	BB	SO
95 LA/MIN	20	12	0	0	1	5	7.13	72.0	93	67	57	13	28	36
Career	20	12	0	0	1	5	7.13	72.0	93	67	57	13	28	36

1995 Situational Statistics

	W	L	ERA	SV	IP	BB	SO		AB	HR	RBI	BA	OBA	SLG
Home	1	1	6.75	0	30.2	12	13	LHB	165	5	28	.285	.346	.473
Road	0	4	7.40	0	41.1	16	23	RHB	139	8	25	.331	.390	.568
Apr-Jun	0	0	0.00	0	2.0	3	2	ScPos	83	1	36	.301	.398	.386
Jul-Oct	1	5	7.33	0	70.0	25	34	Clutch	10	1	6	.600	.692	1.100

SCOUTING REPORT

Parra has above-average control and will pitch inside consistently. He delivers three pitches from three quarters: a plus fastball with good movement, an average curve, and a slightly below-par change-up.

Six runners stole against Jose in seven tries in '95. He made two errors in limited action on the mound.

HOW HE PERFORMED IN '95

Parra debuted in the Dodgers' bullpen but moved to the rotation when the Twins acquired him in July. He registered five quality starts out of twelve total, but still had an astronomical ERA. Jose had led all professional pitchers with fewer than one walk per game in '93, but he struggled with location in the majors. Like all Twins' pitchers, he gave up his share of gopher balls.

WHAT TO EXPECT IN '96

The Twins consider Parra the key to the Tapani/Guthrie deal. He had some fine starts for Minnesota, showing enough to impress management. Last year was Jose's seventh professional season; he pitched his first pro game at age 16. Keeping this in mind, it's clear Parra has the tools to succeed in the majors.

MINNESOTA TWINS

JEFF REBOULET

Positions: SS/3B/1B/2B//C
Bats: R **Throws:** R
Ht: 6'0" **Wt:** 167
Opening Day Age: 31
Born: 4/30/1964
Drafted: MIN86 10/247
ML Seasons: 4

Overall Statistics

	G	AB	R	H	2B	3B	HR	RBI	SB	CS	BB	SO	BA	OBA
95 MIN	87	216	39	63	11	0	4	23	1	2	27	34	.292	.373
Career	343	782	115	200	37	2	9	77	9	9	103	120	.256	.346

1995 Situational Statistics

	AB	HR	RBI	BA	OBA	SLG		AB	HR	RBI	BA	OBA	SLG
Home	92	1	11	.337	.419	.424	LHP	89	4	12	.281	.390	.472
Road	124	3	12	.258	.338	.379	RHP	127	0	11	.299	.360	.346
Apr-Jun	95	3	11	.263	.320	.389	ScPos	54	0	19	.315	.431	.370
Jul-Oct	121	1	12	.314	.411	.405	Clutch	27	1	3	.296	.345	.407

SCOUTING REPORT

Once an offensive liability, Reboulet has improved. A pull hitter, Jeff has below-average power, parking a few dingers down the left field line. He likes fastballs up and in.

Reboulet has plus range, plus hands, and an average arm — the Twins lose nothing in the infield wherever he plays. He has average speed in the Twins' station-to-station offense.

HOW HE PERFORMED IN '95

A media joke when he appeared on the scene in 1992 (dubbed "the Inspector"—as in Clouseau—by WGN announcers, although the nickname never caught on in Minnesota), Reboulet is laughing now, topping his career average by 50 points in '95. Jeff attributes his success to his pitch selection: he just doesn't swing at any bad ones, producing a fine strikeout-to-walk ratio and on-base percentage.

Along with filling in at all infield spots, he has played outfield in late-inning emergencies. Jeff even saw action behind the plate in one game.

WHAT TO EXPECT IN '96

Reboulet, the Twins' union rep, will see plenty of action although he will never be a regular. The Twins liked him even when he didn't hit, so everything he does at the dish is a bonus.

RICH ROBERTSON

Position: RP
Bats: L **Throws:** L
Ht: 6'4" **Wt:** 175
Opening Day Age: 27
Born: 9/15/1968
Drafted: PIT90 9/241
ML Seasons: 3

Overall Statistics

	G	GS	GF	SV	W	L	ERA	IP	H	R	ER	HR	BB	SO
95 MIN	25	4	8	0	2	0	3.83	51.2	48	28	22	4	31	38
Career	42	4	11	0	2	1	4.72	76.1	83	46	40	6	45	51

1995 Situational Statistics

	W	L	ERA	SV	IP	BB	SO		AB	HR	RBI	BA	OBA	SLG
Home	1	0	4.97	0	25.1	16	20	LHB	56	0	6	.268	.406	.321
Road	1	0	2.73	0	26.1	15	18	RHB	134	4	17	.246	.331	.373
Apr-Jun	0	0	5.68	0	25.1	20	20	ScPos	57	0	15	.228	.378	.246
Jul-Oct	2	0	2.05	0	26.1	11	18	Clutch	19	2	4	.316	.409	.632

SCOUTING REPORT

Robertson throws three-quarters with a funky, herky-jerky motion, adding deception to a below-average fastball and below-average curve. His best pitch is an average change-up. The lanky Robertson is quick to the plate, ranking average-plus at holding runners. Eight runners attempted to steal off him in '95, but only four were successful. He is an average fielder.

HOW HE PERFORMED IN '95

Robertson began the season doing mopup work. In the 22 games he appeared in before being optioned back to Triple-A in July, Rich did not appear in a game in which the Twins won. At Salt Lake City, Robertson went 5-0 with a 2.44 ERA before returning to the Twins. He made three impressive September starts for Minnesota, averaging eight innings a start, posting a 1.50 ERA, and allowing just 13 hits in 24 innings. Rich's control was better after moving into the rotation, walking nearly a hitter an inning in relief but only one every three innings when starting.

WHAT TO EXPECT IN '96

All indications are that Robertson should be a starter. There is no reason why he shouldn't join a Twins' rotation which is dying for warm bodies for '96.

THE SCOUTING REPORT: 1996

MINNESOTA TWINS

ERIK SCHULLSTROM

Position: RP
Bats: R **Throws:** R
Ht: 6'5" **Wt:** 220
Opening Day Age: 27
Born: 3/25/1969
Drafted: BAL90 2/60
ML Seasons: 2

Overall Statistics

	G	GS	GF	SV	W	L	ERA	IP	H	R	ER	HR	BB	SO
95 MIN	37	0	16	0	0	0	6.89	47.0	66	36	36	8	22	21
Career	46	0	21	1	0	0	6.00	60.0	79	43	40	8	27	34

1995 Situational Statistics

	W	L	ERA	SV	IP	BB	SO		AB	HR	RBI	BA	OBA	SLG
Home	0	0	5.81	0	26.1	9	11	LHB	86	4	23	.337	.431	.570
Road	0	0	8.27	0	20.2	13	10	RHB	113	4	19	.327	.372	.513
Apr-Jun	0	0	9.20	0	14.2	9	4	ScPos	75	1	33	.293	.407	.413
Jul-Oct	0	0	5.85	0	32.1	13	17	Clutch	22	2	4	.409	.519	.727

SCOUTING REPORT
Schullstrom throws three pitches with an overhand delivery. His best is an average-plus fastball that sinks and bores in on righties. Erik has a minus change-up, which needs a better delivery, and a minus curve.

The burly Schullstrom is slow to home but no one attempted to steal off Erik during '95. He is below-average fielding his position from the mound.

HOW HE PERFORMED IN '95
After an impressive debut in late '94, Schullstrom showed little in '95. He came to spring training overweight and out of shape, started the year in Triple-A, and was only promoted because the Twins were desperate. He threw a lot of batting practice, especially to the first batters he faced, who hit .515 and slugged a whopping .909 in 33 at-bats. He did settle down during the middle of the season, possibly due to his new contact lenses, but allowed 13 earned runs in his last 8.1 innings.

WHAT TO EXPECT IN '96
Schullstrom could land a bullpen job in Minnesota. His '94 performance was impressive, as he moved successfully from Double-A to the majors, and he may be able to capitalize on his '95 experience and pitch better this year.

SCOTT STAHOVIAK

Positions: 1B/3B//DH
Bats: L **Throws:** R
Ht: 6'5" **Wt:** 210
Opening Day Age: 26
Born: 3/6/1970
Drafted: MIN91 2/27
ML Seasons: 2

Overall Statistics

	G	AB	R	H	2B	3B	HR	RBI	SB	CS	BB	SO	BA	OBA
95 MIN	94	263	28	70	19	0	3	23	5	1	30	61	.266	.341
Career	114	320	29	81	23	0	3	24	5	3	33	83	.253	.323

1995 Situational Statistics

	AB	HR	RBI	BA	OBA	SLG		AB	HR	RBI	BA	OBA	SLG
Home	134	1	10	.261	.340	.343	LHP	13	0	0	.077	.143	.077
Road	129	2	13	.271	.343	.403	RHP	250	3	23	.276	.351	.388
Apr-Jun	127	2	9	.276	.340	.378	ScPos	70	1	21	.257	.349	.386
Jul-Oct	136	1	14	.257	.342	.368	Clutch	37	1	2	.243	.333	.351

SCOUTING REPORT
While Stahoviak is strong and has decent bat speed, he hits with little power. Fastballs down and in are his specialty; however, since Scott cannot hit breaking or off-speed pitches, he rarely sees fastballs. In the field, Stahoviak has average tools and can play both third base and first base. However, he looked better at first than third and probably won't play the hot corner much in the future. Scott has average speed as a runner and may have overachieved by stealing five bases in '95. However, he was quite a basestealer in his low level minor-league days.

HOW HE PERFORMED IN '95
Stahoviak started the season at Salt Lake City, but was called up in May. He soon established himself as a contender to replace Kent Hrbek at first, hitting for average and playing surprisingly solid defense. However, he didn't show much pop and missed most of September with an elbow injury that required surgery.

WHAT TO EXPECT IN '96
Stahoviak's defense at first was a pleasant surprise, but his bat wasn't. The Twins cannot afford to sacrifice power positions to singles hitters. Although Scott has an opportunity to win a job, it's a limited-time offer.

MINNESOTA TWINS: TOP PROSPECTS

MARC BARCELO
Bats: R Throws: R Opening Day Age: 24
Ht: 6-3 Wt: 210 Born: 1/10/1972
Position: P Drafted: 1993 #3 MIN

YR TEAM	LG/CLASS	G	GS	GF	SV	W	L	ERA	IP	H	HR	BB	SO	O/BA
93 Ft. Myers	FSL/A	7	3	3	0	1	1	2.74	23.0	18	1	4	24	.217
93 Nashville	SOU/AA	2	2	0	0	1	0	3.86	9.1	9	2	5	5	.265
94 Nashville	SOU/AA	29	28	0	0	11	6	2.65	183.1	167	11	45	153	.239
95 Salt Lake	PCL/AAA	28	28	0	0	8	13	7.05	143	214	19	59	63	.351

Coming off an outstanding '94 season, Barcelo was considered one of the top prospects in the organization. The former first round pick is a power pitcher with a good sinking fastball and hard slider, but he suffered through a miserable season last year. The 23-year-old struggled early and lost his confidence, finishing with the highest ERA in the minor leagues. Tougher on lefthanders the past two years, Barcelo allowed 60 extra-base hits and a .385 average to righthanders in 1995.

KIMERA BARTEE
Bats: S Throws: R Opening Day Age: 23
Ht: 6-0 Wt: 180 Born: 7/21/1972
Position: CF Drafted: 1993 #14 BAL

YR TEAM	LG/CLASS	G	AB	R	H	2B	3B	HR	RBI	SB	BA	OBA
93 Bluefield	APPY/R	66	264	59	65	15	2	4	37	27	.246	.358
94 Frederick	CARO/A	130	514	97	150	22	4	10	57	44	.292	.366
95 Rochester	INT/AAA	15	52	5	8	2	1	0	3	0	.154	.151
Bowie	EAST/AA	53	218	45	62	9	1	3	19	22	.284	.352
Orioles	GULF/R	5	21	5	5	0	0	1	3	1	.238	.333

Bartee, acquired from the Orioles in the Scott Erickson deal, struggled in his jump from Class-A to Triple-A last year and landed in Bowie. The Creighton product missed time with a fractured hand, but returned by the end of the season. Bartee has the outstanding speed needed to be a good base-stealer and has great range in center field, though a weak arm could force a move to left.

GUS GANDARILLAS
Bats: R Throws: R Opening Day Age: 24
Ht: 6-0 Wt: 180 Born: 7/19/1971
Position: P Drafted: 1992 #4 MIN

YR TEAM	LG/CLASS	G	GS	GF	SV	W	L	ERA	IP	H	HR	BB	SO	O/BA
93 Ft. Wayne	MID/A	52	0	48	25	5	5	3.26	66.1	66	8	22	59	.252
94 Ft. Myers	FSL/A	37	0	34	20	4	1	0.77	46.2	37	0	13	39	.218
94 Nashville	SOU/AA	28	0	20	8	2	2	3.16	37.0	34	1	10	29	.245
95 Salt Lake	PCL/AAA	22	0	13	2	2	3	6.44	29	34	5	19	17	.306
New Britain	EAST/AA	25	0	18	7	2	4	6.12	32	38	1	16	25	.290

Gandarillas entered 1995 with a 12-10 record, 66 saves and a 2.56 ERA in two and a half seasons of pro ball. The Miami product (and brother-in-law of White Sox pitcher Alex Fernandez) has good stuff with a decent fastball and tough slider, but struggled with his control last year. After a poor start at Salt Lake, he was demoted to Hardware City where his troubles continued.

LATROY HAWKINS
Bats: R Throws: R Opening Day Age: 23
Ht: 6-5 Wt: 195 Born: 12/21/1972
Position: P Drafted: 1991 #8 MIN

YR TEAM	LG/CLASS	G	GS	GF	SV	W	L	ERA	IP	H	HR	BB	SO	O/BA
93 Ft. Wayne	MID/A	26	23	1	0	15	5	2.06	157.1	110	5	41	179	.195
94 Ft. Myers	FSL/A	6	6	0	0	4	0	2.33	38.2	32	1	6	36	.224
94 Nashville	SOU/AA	11	11	0	0	9	2	2.33	73.1	50	2	28	53	.191
94 Salt Lake	PCL/AAA	12	12	0	0	5	4	4.08	81.2	92	8	33	37	.296
95 Minnesota	AL/MAJ	6	6	0	0	2	3	8.67	27	39	3	12	9	.339
Salt Lake	PCL/AAA	22	22	0	0	9	7	3.55	144	150	7	40	74	.271

After rocketing through the Twins' farm system in 1994, Hawkins opened last season in the Minnesota rotation. After just three starts (0-3, 13.50 ERA), the 22-year-old was sent back to Triple-A. He regained his confidence and was 8-3, 3.06 ERA in his last 15 starts with four complete games earning a September recall. The tall righthander has an excellent fastball with movement and good breaking pitches.

DENNY HOCKING
Bats: S Throws: R Opening Day Age: 25
Ht: 5-10 Wt: 180 Born: 4/2/1970
Position: SS Drafted: 1989 #52 MIN

YR TEAM	LG/CLASS	G	AB	R	H	2B	3B	HR	RBI	SB	BA	OBA
93 Nashville	SOU/AA	107	409	54	109	9	4	8	50	15	.267	.327
93 Minnesota	AL/MAJ	15	36	7	5	1	0	0	0	1	.139	.262
94 Salt Lake	PCL/AAA	112	394	61	110	14	6	5	57	13	.279	.327
94 Minnesota	AL/MAJ	11	31	3	10	3	0	0	2	2	.323	.323
95 Minnesota	AL/MAJ	9	25	4	5	0	2	0	3	1	.200	.259
Salt Lake	PCL/AAA	117	397	51	112	24	2	8	75	12	.282	.324

Many considered Hocking the best defensive shortstop in the Pacific Coast League last year. He has a rifle arm and good range at short and can play second base if needed. Offensively, the switch-hitter belts line drives into the gaps and has some speed on the basepaths, and batted over .340 the second half of the season.

MATT LAWTON
Bats: L Throws: R Opening Day Age: 24
Ht: 5-9 Wt: 180 Born: 11/3/1971
Position: OF Drafted: 1991 #14 MIN

YR TEAM	LG/CLASS	G	AB	R	H	2B	3B	HR	RBI	SB	BA	OBA
93 Ft. Wayne	MID/A	111	340	50	97	21	3	9	38	23	.285	.410
94 Ft. Myers	FSL/A	122	446	79	134	30	1	7	51	42	.300	.407
95 Minnesota	AL/MAJ	21	60	11	19	4	1	1	12	1	.317	.414
New Britain	EAST/AA	114	412	75	111	19	5	13	54	26	.269	.371

Lawton made the most of a September promotion to Minnesota, showing that he could hit, hit with some extra-base potential, and take walks. The 23-year-old also has good speed and tied for fourth in the Twins' farm system in stolen bases. Originally a second baseman, he switched to the outfield in 1993 but is a defensive liability with a poor arm.

MINNESOTA TWINS: TOP PROSPECTS

TRAVIS MILLER

Bats: R Throws: L Opening Day Age: 23
Ht: 6-3 Wt: 205 Born: 11/2/1972
Position: P Drafted: 1994 #2 MIN

YR	TEAM	LG/CLASS	G	GS	GF	SV	W	L	ERA	IP	H	HR	BB	SO	O/BA
94	Ft. Wayne	MID/A	11	9	0	0	4	1	2.60	55.1	52	2	12	50	.254
94	Nashville	SOU/AA	1	1	0	0	0	2	2.84	6.1	3	0	2	4	.143
95	New Britain	EAST/AA	28	27	1	0	7	9	4.37	162	172	17	65	151	.267

Miller was a supplemental first round pick in '94 after a standout college career at Kent University. The 22-year-old lefty spent the '95 campaign at Hardware City where he ranked second in the Eastern League and number one in the Twins' farm system in strikeouts. Miller started off well last season, posting a 2.91 ERA and pitching six or more innings in 12 of his first 16 starts. The 6-foot-3 southpaw keeps the ball down and was very tough on lefthanders last season. He has good control, excellent mechanics, an upper-80's fastball, and a slider that serves as his "out" pitch.

OSCAR MUNOZ

Bats: R Throws: R Opening Day Age: 26
Ht: 6-2 Wt: 205 Born: 9/25/1969
Position: P Drafted: 1990 #7 CLE

YR	TEAM	LG/CLASS	G	GS	GF	SV	W	L	ERA	IP	H	HR	BB	SO	O/BA
93	Nashville	SOU/AA	20	20	0	0	11	4	3.08	131.2	123	10	50	139	.243
93	Portland	PCL/AAA	5	5	0	0	2	2	4.31	31.1	29	2	17	29	.246
94	Salt Lake	PCL/AAA	26	26	0	0	9	8	5.88	139.1	180	20	68	100	.310
94	Nashville	SOU/AA	3	3	0	0	3	0	0.41	22.0	16	0	5	21	.200
95	Minnesota	AL/MAJ	10	3	4	0	2	1	5.60	35	40	6	17	25	.276
	Salt Lake	PCL/AAA	19	19	0	0	8	6	4.95	112	121	9	35	74	.274

Munoz came to the Twins as part of the 1992 deal that sent Paul Sorrento to the Indians, and was considered a top prospect after a terrific '93 season. The Miami product has experienced control problems since, but regained control of his best pitch, a splitter, and led the Pacific Coast League in wins and strikeouts in June (5-1, 2.86 ERA, 44 IP, 30 H, 13 BB, 35 SO). Munoz, who was promoted to Minnesota in August, also throws an upper-80's fastball, curve and changeup.

DAN SERAFINI

Bats: S Throws: L Opening Day Age: 22
Ht: 6-1 Wt: 185 Born: 1/25/1974
Position: P Drafted: 1992 #1 MIN

YR	TEAM	LG/CLASS	G	GS	GF	SV	W	L	ERA	IP	H	HR	BB	SO	O/BA
93	Ft. Wayne	MID/A	27	27	0	0	10	8	3.65	140.2	117	5	83	147	.228
94	Ft. Myers	FSL/A	23	23	0	0	9	4	4.61	136.2	149	11	57	130	.284
95	Salt Lake	PCL/AAA	1	0	1	0	0	0	6.75	4	4	2	1	4	.250
	New Britain	EAST/AA	27	27	0	0	12	9	3.38	162	155	7	72	123	.258

Serafini, a former first-round pick, has made steady progress each year and had another fine season in '95 at New Britain, ranking third in the Eastern League in wins and earning an All-Star berth. The lefthander has a major league-caliber fastball and good curve, also throws a slider, and has worked hard to develop a changeup. Serafini is quick to home plate and holds runners well, allowing just 13 steals in 24 attempts last year.

JOSE VALENTIN

Bats: S Throws: R Opening Day Age: 20
Ht: 5-10 Wt: 185 Born: 9/19/1975
Position: C Drafted: 1993 #7 MIN

YR	TEAM	LG/CLASS	G	AB	R	H	2B	3B	HR	RBI	SB	BA	OBA
93	Twins	GULF/R	32	103	18	27	6	1	1	19	0	.262	.344
93	Elizabethtn	APPY/R	9	24	3	5	1	0	0	3	0	.208	.345
94	Elizabethtn	APPY/R	54	210	23	44	5	0	9	27	0	.210	.263
95	Ft. Wayne	MID/A	112	383	59	123	26	5	19	65	0	.321	.398

As a 19-year-old, Valentin was named the Midwest League's Prospect of the Year. The brother of the Brewers' Jose Valentin ranked fifth in the league in batting, fourth in homers and second in slugging (.564). He is an aggressive hitter with great power from both sides of the plate and hit better as the year wore on, batting .374 (64-for-171) with 11 homers and 38 RBI from July 1 on. Valentin has a rifle arm and a quick release and threw out a league-best 42.5% of opposing base-stealers. While he needs to learn how to block balls in the dirt better and how to call a game, the still-young Valentin is a hard-worker with excellent instincts.

TODD WALKER

Bats: L Throws: R Opening Day Age: 22
Ht: 6-0 Wt: 180 Born: 5/25/1973
Position: 2B/3B Drafted: 1994 #1 MIN

YR	TEAM	LG/CLASS	G	AB	R	H	2B	3B	HR	RBI	SB	BA	OBA
94	Ft. Myers	FSL/A	46	171	29	52	5	2	10	34	6	.304	.406
95	New Britain	EAST/AA	137	513	83	149	27	3	21	85	23	.290	.365

A three-time All-American and SEC Player-of-the-Year at LSU, Walker was the eighth pick overall in 1994. In his first full pro season, he placed tenth in the Eastern League in batting, second in hits and total bases and tied for third in homers while leading the Twins' system in homers en route to winning organization Player of the Year honors. Walker is a pure hitter with great power and good speed who set a franchise record by smashing 14 home runs at pitcher-friendly Beehive Field. The lefthanded swinger hit only one of his home runs against lefty pitchers in 140 at-bats, however. Defensively, Walker is just adequate and, with Chuck Knoblauch ahead of him, may be moved to third base to try to solve the Twins' hot corner problems.

SCOTT WATKINS

Bats: L Throws: L Opening Day Age: 25
Ht: 6-3 Wt: 180 Born: 5/15/1970
Position: P Drafted: 1992 #24 MIN

YR	TEAM	LG/CLASS	G	GS	GF	SV	W	L	ERA	IP	H	HR	BB	SO	O/BA
93	Ft. Wayne	MID/A	15	0	8	1	2	0	3.26	30.1	26	0	9	31	.234
93	Ft. Myers	FSL/A	20	0	10	3	2	2	2.93	27.2	27	0	12	41	.243
93	Nashville	SOU/AA	13	0	3	0	0	1	5.94	16.2	19	2	7	17	.288
94	Nashville	SOU/AA	11	0	8	3	1	0	4.61	13.2	13	1	4	11	.245
94	Salt Lake	PCL/AAA	46	0	26	3	2	6	6.75	73	10	28	47	.316
95	Minnesota	AL/MAJ	27	0	7	0	0	0	5.40	21	22	2	11	11	.278
	Salt Lake	PCL/AAA	45	0	33	20	4	2	2.80	54	45	4	13	57	.226

Watkins had a breakthrough year last season, leading the Pacific Coast League in saves before joining the Twins in August. The Oklahoma State product had back-to-back tough outings against the Brewers August 26-27, but compiled an ERA under 3.00 in his other 25 outings for Minnesota. Watkins has a great slider and a low 90's fastball and is not afraid to pitch inside.

MINNESOTA TWINS: OTHERS TO WATCH

JOHN COURTRIGHT Bats: L Throws: L Ht: 6-2 Wt: 185
Born: 5/30/1970 Drafted: 1991 #8 CIN Position: P

YR TEAM	LG/CLASS	G	GS	GF	SV	W	L	ERA	IP	H	HR	BB	SO	O/BA
95 Cincinnati	NL/MAJ	1	0	0	0	0	0	9.00	1.0	2	0	0	0	.500
95 Indianapolis	AMAS/AAA	13	2	1	0	2	1	4.28	33.2	29	2	15	13	.228
95 Salt Lake	PCL/AAA	18	17	0	0	3	7	6.80	84.2	108	6	36	42	.321

The Duke product, a groundball pitcher, came from the Reds for former first-round pick Dave McCarty.

STEVE DUNN Bats: L Throws: L Ht: 6-4 Wt: 220
Born: 4/18/1970 Drafted: 1988 #4 MIN Position: 1B

YR TEAM	LG/CLASS	G	AB	R	H	2B	3B	HR	RBI	SB	BA	OBA
95 Minnesota	AL/MAJ	5	6	0	0	0	0	0	0	0	.000	.143
95 Salt Lake	PCL/AAA	109	402	57	127	31	1	12	83	3	.316	.360

This big lefthanded-hitting first baseman needs to hit with more power if hopes to make it to Minnesota.

MIKE DURANT Bats: R Throws: R Ht: 6-2 Wt: 198
Born: 9/14/1969 Drafted: 1991 #3 MIN Position: C

YR TEAM	LG/CLASS	G	AB	R	H	2B	3B	HR	RBI	SB	BA	OBA
95 Salt Lake	PCL/AAA	85	295	40	74	15	3	2	23	11	.251	.301

A sound defensive catcher out of Ohio State, Durant has a career .260 average with little power.

AARON FULTZ Bats: L Throws: L Ht: 5-11 Wt: 183
Born: 9/4/1973 Drafted: 1992 #6 SFN Position: P

YR TEAM	LG/CLASS	G	GS	GF	SV	W	L	ERA	IP	H	HR	BB	SO	O/BA
95 New Britain	EAST/AA	3	3	0	0	0	2	6.60	15.0	11	1	9	12	.208
95 Fort Myers	FSL/A	21	21	0	0	3	6	3.25	122.0	115	10	41	127	.250

Fultz is a strikeout pitcher (8.40 strikeouts per nine innings over his career) who came from the Giants as part of the Jim Deshaies trade in 1993.

GREG HANSELL Bats: R Throws: R Ht: 6-5 Wt: 215
Born: 3/12/1971 Drafted: 1989 #12 BOS Position: P

YR TEAM	LG/CLASS	G	GS	GF	SV	W	L	ERA	IP	H	HR	BB	SO	O/BA
95 Los Angeles	NL/MAJ	20	0	7	0	0	1	7.45	19.1	29	5	6	13	.349
95 Albuquerque	PCL/AAA	8	1	3	1	1	8.44	16.0	25	2	6	15	.362
95 Salt Lake	PCL/AAA	7	5	0	0	3	1	5.01	32.1	39	3	4	17	.291

Hansell was traded for the third time in his career in the Kevin Tapani deal and features a high-80's fastball with good sinking action.

STEVE HAZLETT Bats: R Throws: R Ht: 5-11 Wt: 170
Born: 3/30/1970 Drafted: 1991 #21 MIN Position: OF

YR TEAM	LG/CLASS	G	AB	R	H	2B	3B	HR	RBI	SB	BA	OBA
95 Salt Lake	PCL/AAA	127	427	71	128	25	6	4	49	8	.300	.364

The Wyoming product has hit .301 over the last three seasons and could be a useful bench player and pinch-hitter.

TORII HUNTER Bats: R Throws: R Ht: 6-2 Wt: 205
Born: 7/18/1975 Drafted: 1993 #1 MIN Position: OF

YR TEAM	LG/CLASS	G	AB	R	H	2B	3B	HR	RBI	SB	BA	OBA
95 Fort Myers	FSL/A	113	391	64	96	15	2	7	36	7	.246	.330

Hunter has outstanding tools and is an excellent defensive outfielder with a great arm, but is still learning how to hit.

RICCARDO INGRAM Bats: R Throws: R Ht: 6-0 Wt: 198
Born: 9/10/1966 Drafted: 1987 #6 DET Position: OF

YR TEAM	LG/CLASS	G	AB	R	H	2B	3B	HR	RBI	SB	BA	OBA
95 Minnesota	AL/MAJ	4	8	0	1	0	0	0	1	0	.125	.300
95 Salt Lake	PCL/AAA	122	477	80	166	43	2	12	85	4	.348	.399

A journeyman outfielder out of Georgia Tech, the 29-year-old had a career year in '95, leading the Pacific Coast League in batting and hits.

J.J. JOHNSON Bats: R Throws: R Ht: 6-0 Wt: 195
Born: 8/31/1973 Drafted: 1991 #2 BOS Position: OF

YR TEAM	LG/CLASS	G	AB	R	H	2B	3B	HR	RBI	SB	BA	OBA
95 Trenton	EAST/AA	2	6	1	3	0	0	0	1	0	.500	.500
95 Sarasota	FSL/A	107	391	49	108	16	4	10	43	7	.276	.329

The player-to-be-named-later in the Rick Aguilera trade has finally started to make the transition from great athlete to ballplayer.

DAMIAN MILLER Bats: R Throws: R Ht: 6-2 Wt: 190
Born: 10/13/1969 Drafted: 1990 #23 MIN Position: C

YR TEAM	LG/CLASS	G	AB	R	H	2B	3B	HR	RBI	SB	BA	OBA
95 Salt Lake	PCL/AAA	83	295	39	84	23	1	3	41	2	.285	.324

A decent defensive catcher, Miller has a good arm and a little extra-base pop in his bat.

BRIAN RAABE Bats: R Throws: R Ht: 5-9 Wt: 170
Born: 11/5/1967 Drafted: 1990 #44 MIN Position: 2B

YR TEAM	LG/CLASS	G	AB	R	H	2B	3B	HR	RBI	SB	BA	OBA
95 Minnesota	AL/MAJ	6	14	4	3	0	0	0	1	0	.214	.267
95 Salt Lake	PCL/AAA	112	440	88	134	32	6	3	60	15	.305	.368

The fundamentally sound Raabe was the toughest man in the minors to strike out last season and can play second, third and short.

MARK REDMAN Bats: L Throws: L Ht: 6-5 Wt: 215
Born: 1/5/1974 Drafted: 1995 #1 MIN Position: P

YR TEAM	LG/CLASS	G	GS	GF	SV	W	L	ERA	IP	H	HR	BB	SO	O/BA
95 Fort Myers	FSL/A	8	5	0	0	2	1	2.76	32.2	28	4	13	26	.239

Redman, whose best pitch is a circle change, was the Twins' first-round pick last June after a phenomenal college career at Oklahoma.

BRETT ROBERTS Bats: R Throws: R Ht: 6-7 Wt: 225
Born: 3/24/1970 Drafted: 1991 #5 MIN Position: P

YR TEAM	LG/CLASS	G	GS	GF	SV	W	L	ERA	IP	H	HR	BB	SO	O/BA
95 New Britain	EAST/AA	28	28	0	0	11	9	3.41	174.0	162	9	50	135	.244

The former NCAA basketball scoring champion from Morehead St. had his finest pro season last year, ranking eighth in the Eastern League in ERA and fourth in strikeouts.

MITCH SIMONS Bats: R Throws: R Ht: 5-9 Wt: 170
Born: 12/13/1968 Drafted: 1991 #24 MON Position: 2B

YR TEAM	LG/CLASS	G	AB	R	H	2B	3B	HR	RBI	SB	BA	OBA
95 Salt Lake	PCL/AAA	130	480	87	156	34	4	3	46	32	.325	.395

A second baseman by trade, Simons can fill in at short, third or even the outfield and has hit .321 and stolen 62 bases the last two years.

THE SCOUTING REPORT: 1996

NEW YORK YANKEES

WADE BOGGS

Positions: 3B//1B
Bats: L **Throws:** R
Ht: 6'2" **Wt:** 197
Opening Day Age: 37
Born: 6/15/1958
Drafted: BOS76 7/166
ML Seasons: 14

SCOUTING REPORT

The 14-year veteran still has outstanding bat control and strike-zone judgment. Willing to take the ball to left field, he is able to inside-out pitches nearly anywhere on the diamond, but he will also pull a pitch if he can. Boggs doesn't have great bat speed, but stands in well against all pitchers and is not spooked by lefthanders.

A minus runner and a very poor percentage base thief, Wade is always a good double-play candidate as well. He does not bunt.

While Boggs won his second Gold Glove last season to go with his first career Gold Glove from '94, he really was a better fielder earlier in his career. He now has average range and hands at the hot corner; his arm strength rates slightly above-average and he throws accurately.

HOW HE PERFORMED IN '95

Boggs continued to produce at the top of the Yankees lineup, maintaining his streak of hitting .300 or better every year in each of his big-league seasons except 1992, his last year with the Red Sox.

The New York table-setters had a fine stretch run: Wade and Bernie Williams both went on a tear at the end of the season, with Wade hitting .340 after August 1st. Usually not at his strongest at season's end, Boggs had a .442 on-base average during September. Boggs has always taken full advantage of his home park, and again last year enjoyed hitting in Yankee Stadium after hitting a robust .359 in the Bronx in '94.

At third base, he made just five errors and his .981 fielding percentage was the best in the league.

WHAT TO EXPECT IN '96

Although Boggs is 37, he still good years left. He would dearly like to get 3,000 hits, and is now just 459 hits shy of that goal. Early off-season speculation had Wade moving to first base, and he may still wind up at the position eventually. However, the Yankees' acquisition of Tino Martinez and the trade of prospect Russ Davis indicate clearly that Boggs will be back at third base for '96. Despite decreased mobility, he remains a good defensive player.

There's no reason to believe that Wade will not hit .300 again. However, look for the Yankees to rest him on occasion this year, especially against tough lefthanders.

Overall Statistics

	G	AB	R	H	2B	3B	HR	RBI	SB	CS	BB	SO	BA	OBA
95 NYA	126	460	76	149	22	4	5	63	1	1	74	50	.324	.412
Career	1991	7599	1287	2541	489	53	103	864	19	30	1213	598	.334	.424

1995 Situational Statistics

	AB	HR	RBI	BA	OBA	SLG		AB	HR	RBI	BA	OBA	SLG
Home	253	4	35	.379	.459	.502	LHP	132	1	15	.311	.397	.364
Road	207	1	28	.256	.355	.324	RHP	328	4	48	.329	.418	.445
Apr-Jun	180	2	27	.306	.397	.389	ScPos	112	1	56	.304	.410	.384
Jul-Oct	280	3	36	.336	.422	.443	Clutch	56	2	9	.250	.397	.429

How He Compares to Other Batters

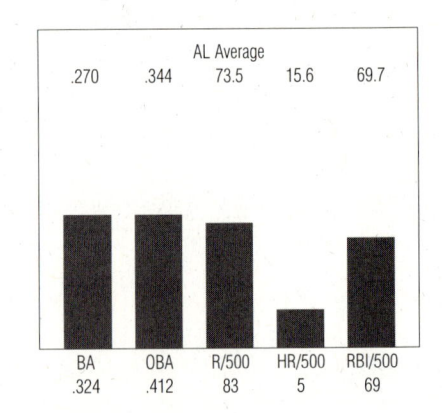

AL Average: BA .270, OBA .344, R/500 73.5, HR/500 15.6, RBI/500 69.7

Boggs: BA .324, OBA .412, R/500 83, HR/500 5, RBI/500 69

Where He Hits the Ball

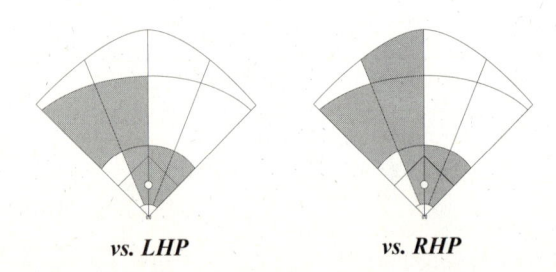

vs. LHP   vs. RHP

THE SCOUTING REPORT: 1996

NEW YORK YANKEES

DAVID CONE

Position: SP
Bats: L **Throws:** R
Ht: 6'1" **Wt:** 185
Opening Day Age: 33
Born: 1/2/1963
Drafted: KC81 4/74
ML Seasons: 10

SCOUTING REPORT

When Cone is on his game, he is in complete control—an artist at work on the mound. He has outstanding command of his breaking pitches and superb hard stuff. David throws from three quarters, with a plus fastball that moves well and can bore in hard on righthanders. He will turn over the fastball against lefties and throws a plus splitter as well.

The slider rates well above-average, as does Cone's curve, which he will throw at any time in the count. An average change-up rounds out his five-pitch arsenal, which rates with the best in the game.

David is just an average fielder, but has a plus move. However, like many of the best pitchers in the game, he concentrates on getting the hitter out instead of worrying about stolen bases. As a result 37 runners tried to steal against him last year, 28 of them successfully.

HOW HE PERFORMED IN '95

After an April 6 trade from Kansas City to Toronto, David was 9-6 team with a fine 3.38 ERA. However, with the Jays out of the race, Cone was dealt to the Yankees on July 28. Returning to the city of his greatest triumphs, Cone had an outstanding 9-2 record and 3.82 ERA in pinstripes, solidifying a shaky pitching staff devastated by the losses of Jimmy Key and Melido Perez to season-ending injuries.

David helped the Yankees' stretch drive immensely, holding the opposition to only a .223 batting average, being equally effective against lefties (.227) and righties (.217). However, Cone struggled at times with control of his hard stuff, as usual. He allowed 12 homers in 13 Yankees' games and walked 47 in his 99 innings in pinstripes. All in all, however, it was another super season for David.

WHAT TO EXPECT IN '96

The Yankees made an excellent deal in signing David to a long-term deal: he is surely happy to have shed the tag of "hired gun." Cone is critical to the Yankees' rotation, given the uncertainty of their injured pitchers and the loss of Jack McDowell to the Indians.

At 33, Cone has plenty of innings left and should anchor the Yankees' rotation for several years. David has the attitude to make it in New York and is likely to have another fine year in '96.

Overall Statistics

	G	GS	GF	SV	W	L	ERA	IP	H	R	ER	HR	BB	SO
95 TOR/NYA	30	30	0	0	18	8	3.57	229.1	195	95	91	24	88	191
Career	288	259	9	1	129	78	3.17	1922.0	1589	746	678	151	716	1741

1995 Situational Statistics

	W	L	ERA	SV	IP	BB	SO		AB	HR	RBI	BA	OBA	SLG
Home	10	3	3.27	0	104.2	40	96	LHB	500	13	52	.234	.311	.364
Road	8	5	3.83	0	124.2	48	95	RHB	355	11	35	.220	.293	.380
Apr-Jun	6	4	3.40	0	90.0	30	73	ScPos	197	5	62	.239	.332	.345
Jul-Oct	12	4	3.68	0	139.1	58	118	Clutch	97	4	10	.186	.307	.351

How He Compares to Other Pitchers

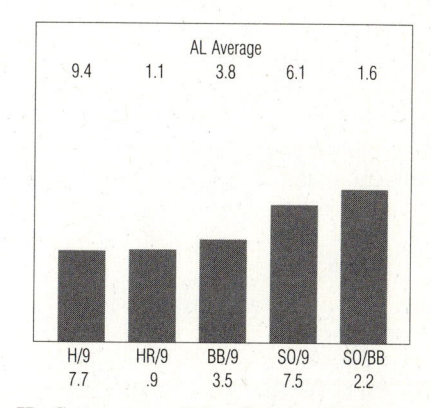

AL Average: 9.4 | 1.1 | 3.8 | 6.1 | 1.6

H/9 7.7 | HR/9 .9 | BB/9 3.5 | SO/9 7.5 | SO/BB 2.2

How He Compares to Other Starting Pitchers

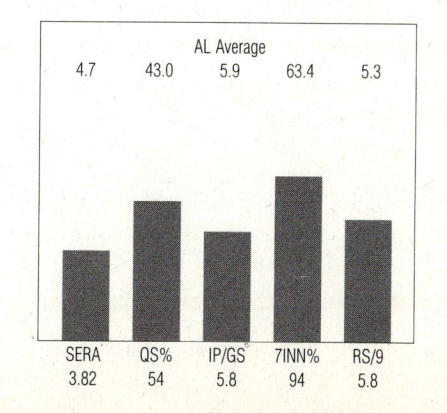

AL Average: 4.7 | 43.0 | 5.9 | 63.4 | 5.3

SERA 3.82 | QS% 54 | IP/GS 5.8 | 7INN% 94 | RS/9 5.8

THE SCOUTING REPORT: 1996

NEW YORK YANKEES

TONY FERNANDEZ

Positions: 3B//SS/2B
Bats: B **Throws:** R
Ht: 6'2" **Wt:** 175
Opening Day Age: 32
Born: 6/30/1962
Drafted: TOR 4/24/79
ML Seasons: 12

SCOUTING REPORT
A line-drive hitter with a spread-out, open stance, Fernandez will use the whole field. Not blessed with much power, Tony instead concentrates on making good contact. Like most switch-stickers, he likes the low pitch hitting lefthanded and the high pitch while batting righthanded. Though he bunts often, both for hits and to sacrifice, Fernandez is not especially effective when laying the bunt down.

He doesn't show his skills as often as his managers would like. Saddled with a reputation as a moody player, Fernandez is out of the lineup often with nagging injuries and has now played with five different clubs in the last five years.

For years one of the game's best shortstops, Tony has declined. He now has only adequate range at shortstop, although he also can play third base. His hands are plus as is his arm, and he can uncork a sidearm throw with good velocity and accuracy both from the hole and from behind second base.

At one time an excellent runner and effective basestealer, Tony has lost much of his speed and is now average.

HOW HE PERFORMED IN '95
Fernandez had a very disappointing '95 season. As a hitter, he never seemed to get untracked; as a fielder, he was surprisingly inconsistent. He didn't help himself late in the year by complaining about his lack of playing time when Randy Velarde was penciled in at shortstop.

He was up-and-down in the field, making great plays and looking awful on routine grounders. He made ten errors, fielding .976 to rank in the middle among AL shortstops, but Tony was not as mobile as he has been. He barely ran at all, and didn't hit well enough to be on base that often. Fernandez had an especially tough time against lefthanders, whom he usually hits fairly well. Nagging knee and ribcage injuries slowed him again.

WHAT TO EXPECT IN '96
The off-season buzz was that the Yanks' shortstop job belonged to young Derek Jeter. This would reduce Fernandez, who is signed through '96, to a backup role. However, given the Yankees' record in giving jobs to young players, the club may decide to work Jeter in slowly. Last year may have been just a bad year for Tony; the key will be whether he retains the drive to be a major-league shortstop.

Overall Statistics

	G	AB	R	H	2B	3B	HR	RBI	SB	CS	BB	SO	BA	OBA
94 CIN	104	366	50	102	18	6	8	50	12	7	44	40	.279	.361
Career	1574	6024	790	1714	292	87	61	593	214	108	496	565	.285	.340

1994 Situational Statistics

	AB	HR	RBI	BA	OBA	SLG		AB	HR	RBI	BA	OBA	SLG
Home	184	3	22	.245	.332	.337	LHP	100	3	16	.290	.348	.460
Road	182	5	28	.313	.391	.516	RHP	266	5	34	.274	.366	.414
Apr-Jun	234	6	33	.274	.379	.419	ScPos	88	4	45	.352	.474	.636
Jul-Oct	132	2	17	.288	.326	.439	Clutch	64	2	9	.266	.365	.375

How He Compares to Other Batters

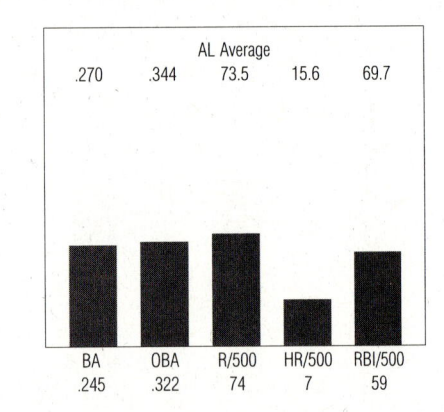

AL Average: .270 / .344 / 73.5 / 15.6 / 69.7

BA	OBA	R/500	HR/500	RBI/500
.245	.322	74	7	59

Where He Hits the Ball

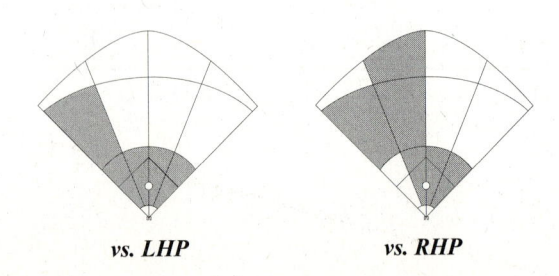

vs. LHP *vs. RHP*

THE SCOUTING REPORT: 1996

NEW YORK YANKEES

STERLING HITCHCOCK

Position: SP
Bats: L **Throws:** L
Ht: 6'1" **Wt:** 200
Opening Day Age: 24
Born: 4/29/1971
Drafted: NYA89 8/233
ML Seasons: 4

SCOUTING REPORT

Throwing with a bit of a hook, Hitchcock delivers from low three quarters. He will turn over and sink his average fastball and also has an average splitfinger fastball. Sterling's best offering is his plus curve; he tries to throw off hitters' timing with an average-minus change-up.

Most feel that struggles with control are the only thing keeping Hitchcock from assuming his place as one of baseball's best young lefthanded starters. Improved control, combined with more big-league experience, could move him upward quickly.

Just an average-minus fielder, Sterling has an average move to first base, but concentration problems—and poor throwing from Yankees' catchers—allowed 23 to steal bases against him in 27 attempts during '95.

HOW HE PERFORMED IN '95

Last season, Hitchcock surprised a lot of people. Spending his first season as a full-time starter, he did a good job, especially down the stretch. In the last month, Sterling had a 4-1 record and a 3.58 ERA. While Hitchcock did quite well against righthanders, he struggled with lefties and often couldn't throw strike one against anybody. He had serious trouble with gopher balls.

With Jimmy Key injured, Sterling became a key to the Yankees' rotation. Along with Andy Pettitte, he provided promise from the left side to go along with righthanded veterans David Cone and Jack McDowell. Hitchcock proved popular with the fans, with his battling attitude, high socks and John Wetteland-style "dirty hat."

WHAT TO EXPECT IN '96

Unfortunately for his fans in New York, Sterling was sent to the Mariners in the Tino Martinez deal. He will be in the Seattle rotation, beginning the season as the fourth or fifth starter, barring a terrible spring training. He has outstanding potential. The Yankees' handling of Hitchcock is yet another example of the their willingness to trade top young prospects and players for established—and sometimes, over-the-hill—veterans. While Tino Martinez is a good hitter, Sterling has the potential to become one of the league's best starting pitchers at a time when pitching is in short supply and when power hitting is not that hard to find. The later signing of veteran southpay Kenny Rogers to a megabucks contract just reinforces the pattern.

Overall Statistics

	G	GS	GF	SV	W	L	ERA	IP	H	R	ER	HR	BB	SO
95 NYA	27	27	0	0	11	10	4.70	168.1	155	91	88	22	68	121
Career	59	41	4	2	16	15	4.78	261.2	258	145	139	31	117	190

1995 Situational Statistics

	W	L	ERA	SV	IP	BB	SO		AB	HR	RBI	BA	OBA	SLG
Home	6	5	4.33	0	79.0	25	54	LHB	112	6	23	.304	.363	.554
Road	5	5	5.04	0	89.1	43	67	RHB	520	16	51	.233	.310	.369
Apr-Jun	3	4	5.23	0	65.1	26	56	ScPos	123	6	53	.285	.349	.512
Jul-Oct	8	6	4.37	0	103.0	42	65	Clutch	45	1	6	.267	.320	.356

How He Compares to Other Pitchers

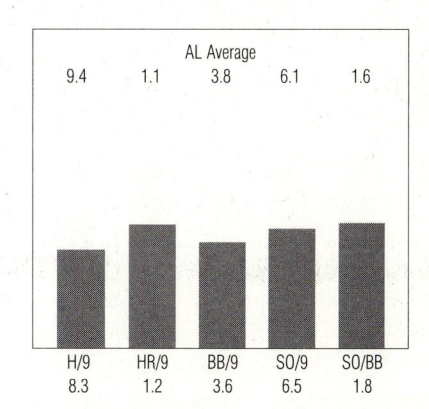

AL Average: H/9 9.4, HR/9 1.1, BB/9 3.8, SO/9 6.1, SO/BB 1.6
Hitchcock: H/9 8.3, HR/9 1.2, BB/9 3.6, SO/9 6.5, SO/BB 1.8

How He Compares to Other Starting Pitchers

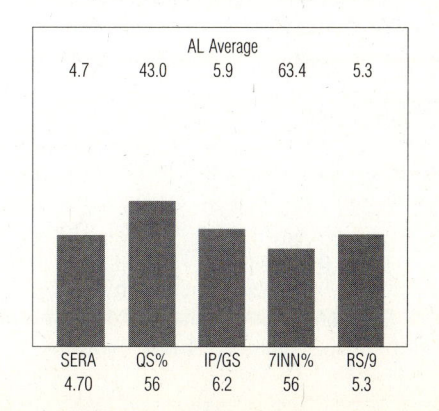

AL Average: SERA 4.7, QS% 43.0, IP/GS 5.9, 7INN% 63.4, RS/9 5.3
Hitchcock: SERA 4.70, QS% 56, IP/GS 6.2, 7INN% 56, RS/9 5.3

THE SCOUTING REPORT: 1996

NEW YORK YANKEES

DON MATTINGLY

Positions: 1B//DH
Bats: L **Throws:** L
Ht: 6'0" **Wt:** 175
Opening Day Age: 34
Born: 4/20/1961
Drafted: NYA79 19/492
ML Seasons: 14

SCOUTING REPORT
Although Mattingly is still a good line-drive hitter, back injuries and age have curtailed his power. He has outstanding bat control and continues to make fine contact at the plate, but does not walk very often and can be blown away by a good fastball. His production against lefthanded pitchers continues to be weak. Don has never had good speed and is now a minus runner who has not stolen a base since '92. He annually grounds into a high number of double plays, but he always hustles.

Defensively, Mattingly retains decent range and plus hands at first base, with an average arm and average-plus accuracy.

HOW HE PERFORMED IN '95
The '95 season was another tough one for the aging and aching Mattingly. With an eye problem that hurt his hitting in the spring, and continuing back problems all season, he still managed to hit fairly consistently for average—Don has now batted exactly .288 three times in the last five years. However, for the second straight season, he provided not all that much punch from a critical offensive position.

Generally a slow starter, Mattingly had a very poor first half. By July 1st, when Donnie had only one home run and 18 runs batted in, the New York press was clamoring for Mattingly to be platooned. He did play well during the Yankees' September stretch run, hitting .321 after August 31 to earn his first post-season berth in his illustrious 14-year career.

He continued as one of the AL's better defensive first basemen, fielding .994 with seven errors to rank in the middle of the pack, and showing above-par mobility.

WHAT TO EXPECT IN '96
Mattingly has decided to take what many see as a Ryne Sandberg-type retirement. Apparently, he will not begin the '96 season with the Yankees. With the acquisition of Tino Martinez, it is doubtful Don will ever return to the Bronx, although with his defensive and leadership, he could end up with another team, possibly in '97. However, if his back problems are as severe as some say, Donnie will probably retire permanently. There was talk that he will eventually become a coach with the expansion Arizona Diamondbacks, managed by former Yankees' skipper and his buddy Buck Showalter.

Overall Statistics

	G	AB	R	H	2B	3B	HR	RBI	SB	CS	BB	SO	BA	OBA
95 NYA	128	458	59	132	32	2	7	49	0	2	40	35	.288	.341
Career	1785	7003	1007	2153	442	20	222	1099	14	9	588	444	.307	.358

1995 Situational Statistics

	AB	HR	RBI	BA	OBA	SLG		AB	HR	RBI	BA	OBA	SLG
Home	238	5	27	.303	.337	.445	LHP	151	2	15	.265	.313	.384
Road	220	2	22	.273	.345	.377	RHP	307	5	34	.300	.355	.427
Apr-Jun	160	1	18	.269	.326	.375	ScPos	126	0	35	.230	.314	.238
Jul-Oct	298	6	31	.299	.350	.433	Clutch	62	2	7	.371	.451	.581

How He Compares to Other Batters

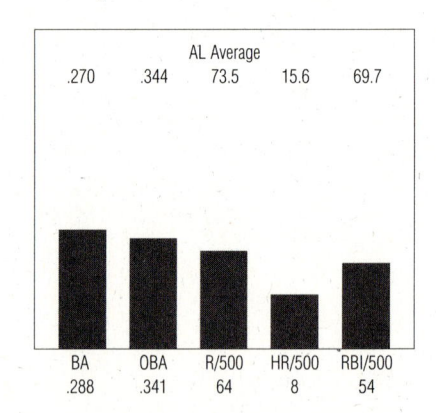

	BA	OBA	R/500	HR/500	RBI/500
AL Average	.270	.344	73.5	15.6	69.7
	.288	.341	64	8	54

Where He Hits the Ball

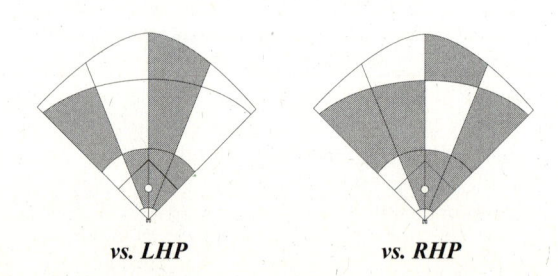

vs. LHP   vs. RHP

NEW YORK YANKEES

JACK McDOWELL

Position: SP
Bats: R **Throws:** R
Ht: 6'5" **Wt:** 180
Opening Day Age: 30
Born: 1/16/1966
Drafted: CHA87 1/5
ML Seasons: 8

SCOUTING REPORT

The gangly McDowell has what's known as an "arms and legs" windup, throwing from a three-quarter angle. His slightly above-average fastball sinks effectively when down in the zone and he can run it in on the hands of righthanders. McDowell controls the heater very well. His out pitch is a well above-average splitter, which Jack can change speeds on effectively. He sets up the splitter with an average slider and change-up and an slightly below-average curve.

Although he has a decent move to first, 25 baserunners were able to steal on him in 36 attempts last season. Of course, some of that was due to the Yankees' catchers. McDowell is a fine athlete and a slightly above-average fielder.

HOW HE PERFORMED IN '95

Jack is beginning to establish a pattern as a second-half pitcher. He came to New York in an unpopular—among White Sox' fans—trade in spring '95, but had ERAs of 4.54 in May and 5.75 in June. His early frustration was best expressed by an ugly incident in which he prominently gave fans at Yankee Stadium the middle finger after a particularly frustrating start.

Nevertheless, it was amazing how McDowell's season turned around after the "Jack the Flipper" game. Following that fateful game, he was a man with a mission: Jack's record was an impressive 11-5 after July 1st. Although he continued to have trouble with the long ball and got hit hard at times, McDowell turned out to be a good acquisition for the Yankees; as always, he gives a club quality and quantity performance and a matchless competitive fire.

WHAT TO EXPECT IN '96

Unfortunately for the Yankees, George Steinbrenner only had enough money for Tino Martinez and David Cone; as a result, McDowell will by plying his trade for the Cleveland Indians in 1996.

Jack is only 30, and should have several more good years as a quality starter left. Backed up by Albert Belle and company, he could easily be good for 20 wins in this season. With McDowell's talent and leadership, he should anchor the Cleveland staff effectively. When he ever decides to retire from baseball—the goateed, sharp-dressing Black Jack can always opt for MTV—or VH1.

Overall Statistics

	G	GS	GF	SV	W	L	ERA	IP	H	R	ER	HR	BB	SO
95 NYA	30	30	0	0	15	10	3.93	217.2	211	106	95	25	78	157
Career	221	221	0	0	106	68	3.56	1561.1	1469	668	617	130	497	1075

1995 Situational Statistics

	W	L	ERA	SV	IP	BB	SO		AB	HR	RBI	BA	OBA	SLG
Home	7	6	4.24	0	116.2	42	91	LHB	475	15	59	.255	.326	.411
Road	8	4	3.56	0	101.0	36	66	RHB	355	10	39	.254	.312	.400
Apr-Jun	4	5	4.84	0	89.1	31	65	ScPos	195	5	70	.256	.298	.405
Jul-Oct	11	5	3.30	0	128.1	47	92	Clutch	107	2	9	.168	.226	.262

How He Compares to Other Pitchers

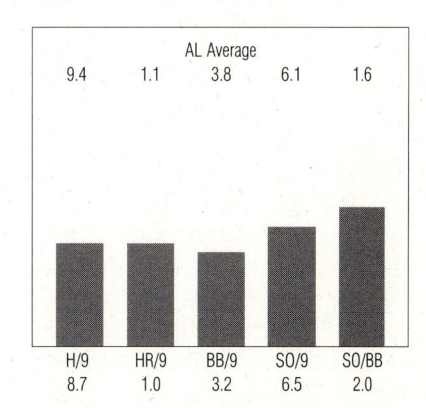

AL Average: H/9 9.4, HR/9 1.1, BB/9 3.8, SO/9 6.1, SO/BB 1.6
McDowell: H/9 8.7, HR/9 1.0, BB/9 3.2, SO/9 6.5, SO/BB 2.0

How He Compares to Other Starting Pitchers

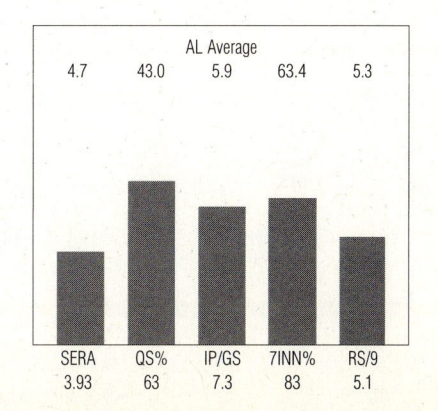

AL Average: SERA 4.7, QS% 43.0, IP/GS 5.9, 7INN% 63.4, RS/9 5.3
McDowell: SERA 3.93, QS% 63, IP/GS 7.3, 7INN% 83, RS/9 5.1

THE SCOUTING REPORT: 1996

NEW YORK YANKEES

PAUL O'NEILL

Positions: OF//DH
Bats: L **Throws:** L
Ht: 6'4" **Wt:** 205
Opening Day Age: 33
Born: 2/25/1963
Drafted: CIN81 4/93
ML Seasons: 11

SCOUTING REPORT

The productive O'Neill has outstanding bat speed and turns on the inside pitch with good power. He has improved greatly against lefthanders and now makes better contact than in the past; Paul will take the walk freely as well. However, last year he showed a tendency to jump on the first fastball he saw, which got him into trouble in some critical situations. O'Neill is most effective when he goes deep into the count, forcing the pitcher to work hard or to make a mistake.

Paul has lost his speed. Now a well below-average runner, Paul grounded into a league-leading 25 double plays last year and has stopped stealing bases.

O'Neill still has a strong arm in right field with slightly above-average accuracy. His range is slightly below par overall, mostly due to his poor speed, but Paul still has good hands.

HOW HE PERFORMED IN '95

Normally, a .300 season with 22 home runs and 76 walks for a playoff team can hardly be considered a disappointment. However, O'Neill was coming off a spectacular '94 that included the AL batting crown, and the fans and media were quick to note his 59-point drop in batting average. Another reason for the disappointment was his tepid performance down the stretch. Always a hot starter, Paul was hitting .338 on June 30, but then batted only .267 with three homers in September and October.

However, he hit for the same power he had shown in '94 and cleared the .300 mark for the third straight season. O'Neill did this despite being shuffled back and forth between left (21 starts) and right (96 starts). His hitting was markedly better when playing right field, his customary spot.

Paul threw out just three runners last season, by far his lowest total ever for a full year. Four times in the past, he had nailed more than ten.

WHAT TO EXPECT IN '96

Spending all his time in right field should help O'Neill in '96. Also, with the emergence of Bernie Williams as the Yankees' #3 hitter, Paul can bat fifth or sixth, allowing him to clear the bases without clogging them up. If he continues to improve against lefthanders, O'Neill will be productive into his mid-thirties, although he may end up as a designated hitter eventually if his defense doesn't rebound.

Overall Statistics

	G	AB	R	H	2B	3B	HR	RBI	SB	CS	BB	SO	BA	OBA
95 NYA	127	460	82	138	30	4	22	96	1	2	71	76	.300	.387
Career	1170	3944	542	1104	236	13	159	665	69	43	493	657	.280	.359

1995 Situational Statistics

	AB	HR	RBI	BA	OBA	SLG		AB	HR	RBI	BA	OBA	SLG
Home	226	12	59	.319	.419	.580	LHP	170	9	38	.259	.326	.494
Road	234	10	37	.282	.353	.474	RHP	290	13	58	.324	.419	.545
Apr-Jun	148	9	32	.338	.429	.615	ScPos	132	6	71	.288	.360	.523
Jul-Oct	312	13	64	.282	.366	.484	Clutch	53	2	10	.302	.431	.472

How He Compares to Other Batters

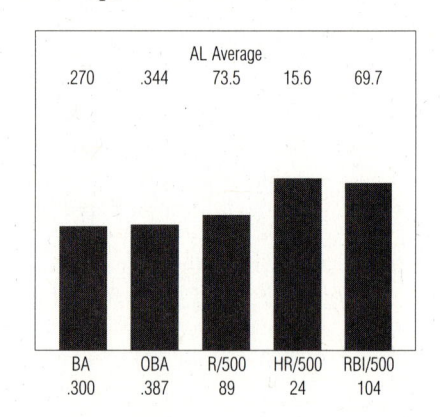

	BA	OBA	R/500	HR/500	RBI/500
AL Average	.270	.344	73.5	15.6	69.7
	.300	.387	89	24	104

Where He Hits the Ball

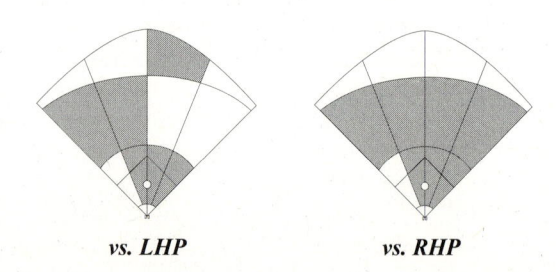

vs. LHP   vs. RHP

NEW YORK YANKEES

ANDY PETTITTE

Position: SP/RP
Bats: L **Throws:** L
Ht: 6'5" **Wt:** 235
Opening Day Age: 23
Born: 6/15/1972
Drafted: NYA90 22/594
ML Seasons: 1

SCOUTING REPORT

Andy throws from three quarters, bringing home an average-plus sinking fastball that he will cut and throw inside to batters on either side of the plate. His plus curve has good rotation, and Pettitte will throw the pitch with confidence even when behind in the count. Andy has good command of his average-plus, late-breaking slider. An average-plus splitter and average-minus change-up complete his menu.

Pettitte has good poise and maturity, especially for a young pitcher, and his willingness to throw inside and battle hitters helps augment his better-than-average stuff.

Very good at holding runners, Andy saw 17 attempt to steal against him last season, but eight of them were thrown out. He is a bit below-average in the field.

HOW HE PERFORMED IN '95

Pettitte was one of the Yankees' biggest surprises of '95. After an outstanding '94 in the Yankee farm system (14-4 in Double-A and Triple-A), Andy made the jump to the majors without breaking stride. He began the year on the big club and struggled in the bullpen. Sent down in mid-May, he returned at the end of the month. While more experienced Yankees' pitchers such as Kamieniecki and McDowell struggled early and Key and Perez went down with season-ending injuries, Pettitte entered the starting rotation May 27 and ended up like Old Man River: he just kept rolling along.

He was very effective in June and July. After some struggles in August (6.19 ERA), Andy pitched very well down the stretch, going 5-1 in September as the Yankees streaked to a wild-card berth.

While Andy was outstanding in the Bronx, he must improve in road contests. He also gets burned by poor control at times, and needs to keep the ball down more consistently against righthanders.

WHAT TO EXPECT IN '96

At 23, Pettitte has a bright future in the majors. He can only get better and, barring injuries, is likely to be a consistently strong third starter for the Yankees. Andy does not fit the pattern, however, of a rotation anchor or dominant power pitcher.

In addition, he has never experienced failure as a professional, and Pettitte will have to be ready to make adjustments after AL hitters make theirs.

Overall Statistics

	G	GS	GF	SV	W	L	ERA	IP	H	R	ER	HR	BB	SO
95 NYA	31	26	1	0	12	9	4.17	175.0	183	86	81	15	63	114
Career	31	26	1	0	12	9	4.17	175.0	183	86	81	15	63	114

1995 Situational Statistics

	W	L	ERA	SV	IP	BB	SO		AB	HR	RBI	BA	OBA	SLG
Home	8	2	2.61	0	100.0	28	64	LHB	117	1	10	.256	.307	.342
Road	4	7	6.24	0	75.0	35	50	RHB	555	14	64	.276	.339	.425
Apr-Jun	3	4	3.51	0	51.1	16	28	ScPos	151	2	55	.305	.360	.411
Jul-Oct	9	5	4.44	0	123.2	47	86	Clutch	43	1	6	.326	.356	.419

How He Compares to Other Pitchers

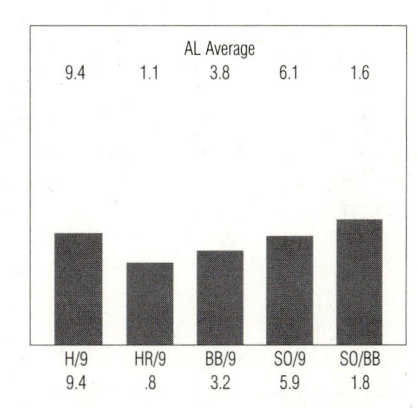

AL Average: H/9 9.4, HR/9 1.1, BB/9 3.8, SO/9 6.1, SO/BB 1.6
Pettitte: H/9 9.4, HR/9 .8, BB/9 3.2, SO/9 5.9, SO/BB 1.8

How He Compares to Other Starting Pitchers

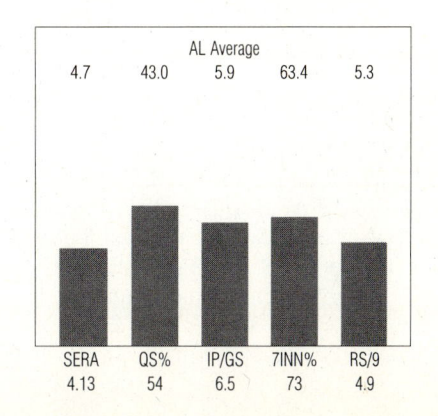

AL Average: SERA 4.7, QS% 43.0, IP/GS 5.9, 7INN% 63.4, RS/9 5.3
Pettitte: SERA 4.13, QS% 54, IP/GS 6.5, 7INN% 73, RS/9 4.9

THE SCOUTING REPORT: 1996

NEW YORK YANKEES

RUBEN SIERRA

Positions: OF/DH
Bats: B **Throws:** R
Ht: 6'1" **Wt:** 175
Opening Day Age: 30
Born: 10/6/1965
Drafted: TEX 11/21/82
ML Seasons: 10

SCOUTING REPORT
Very poor plate discipline has helped to erode the considerable talents of Sierra. He swings at pitches he cannot possibly hit: up-and-in fastballs and down-and-away breaking balls. A looping swing, especially against low pitches, creates plenty of pop-ups and short fly balls as well.

Once a strong-armed right fielder, Ruben was such a bad defensive player in Oakland that he is now considered a DH almost exclusively. He was once quite fast and stole bases effectively; now Sierra has slightly below-average speed, although he runs with a good stride. Ruben has hit one triple in the last two years, after previously smacking as many as 14 in 1989.

HOW HE PERFORMED IN '95
It would be hard to imagine two better players to be traded for each other than Danny Tartabull and Ruben Sierra. Both were unpopular, highly-paid, disappointing, defensively-poor sluggers who were on the outs with their managers—so they switched uniforms on July 26 with Ruben donning pinstripes.

Sierra wasn't long for Oakland in '95 after arguments with Sandy Alderson and Tony LaRussa—who referred to Ruben as a "village idiot"; he was batting .265 with 12 homers in 70 games when dealt. He didn't improve that much for New York, but did drive in 28 runs in August. However, Sierra's complaining about not playing every day, including a much-publicized call from his agent to Buck Showalter, did not endear him to Yankees' fans or management. His self-serving home run trots also caused some problems.

Since showing great promise in Texas between 1986-91, Ruben's career has run aground. Part of this was due to the move to the spacious Oakland Coliseum. Most of Sierra's home run production while with Texas came in home games, but his power dipped after the deal to the Athletics.

WHAT TO EXPECT IN '96
Ruben will be the Yankees' DH this year. He is certainly capable of another .275, 30 homer, 100 RBI season, but whether he will ever do that again is questionable. While Sierra is still relatively young, he has hit poorly in his prime years and is in the process of frittering away a career that, years ago, many thought could put him in the Hall of Fame.

Overall Statistics

	G	AB	R	H	2B	3B	HR	RBI	SB	CS	BB	SO	BA	OBA
95 OA/NY	126	479	73	126	32	0	19	86	5	4	46	76	.263	.323
Career	1454	5679	809	1547	306	50	220	952	126	47	419	834	.272	.318

1995 Situational Statistics

	AB	HR	RBI	BA	OBA	SLG		AB	HR	RBI	BA	OBA	SLG
Home	219	8	42	.251	.313	.416	LHP	161	5	28	.273	.326	.429
Road	260	11	44	.273	.331	.477	RHP	318	14	58	.258	.321	.459
Apr-Jun	230	12	40	.270	.327	.496	ScPos	132	6	67	.311	.365	.508
Jul-Oct	249	7	46	.257	.319	.406	Clutch	67	2	12	.224	.289	.358

How He Compares to Other Batters

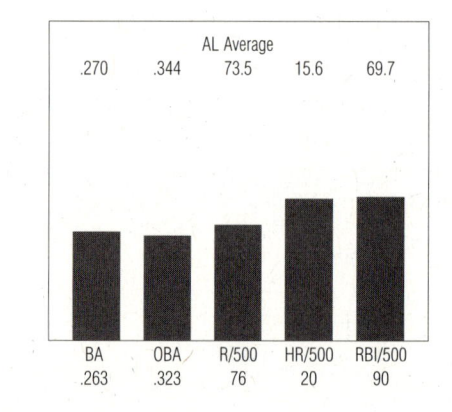

AL Average: .270 / .344 / 73.5 / 15.6 / 69.7

BA	OBA	R/500	HR/500	RBI/500
.263	.323	76	20	90

Where He Hits the Ball

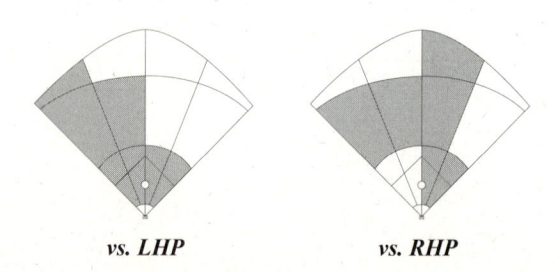

vs. LHP — vs. RHP

THE SCOUTING REPORT: 1996

NEW YORK YANKEES

MIKE STANLEY

Positions: C/DH
Bats: R **Throws:** R
Ht: 6'1" **Wt:** 185
Opening Day Age: 32
Born: 6/25/1963
Drafted: TEX85 15/395
ML Seasons: 10

SCOUTING REPORT
Mike tries to pull every pitch he sees. However, he does have outstanding bat speed which allows him to get around on most people's fastballs, resulting in excellent power—especially on anything inside. Pitchers try to work Stanley away with breaking balls and he will strike out often. However, Mike is also happy to accept a walk if offered.

Behind the plate, Stanley is a mixed bag. Yankees' hurlers loved working with Mike, who called a terrific game and had improved his throwing. His arm is average in strength but slightly below that in accuracy, and Stanley is not especially mobile and has minus hands. He is very slow on the bases and is no threat to steal.

HOW HE PERFORMED IN '95
For the third straight year, Stanley provided the Yankees with excellent offense, showing power and fine production in key situations. He hit an incredible .818 (9 for 11) with the bases loaded, smashing two grand slams and batting in 27 runs. He had his fine year despite suffering a series of nagging injuries: a foul off his left knee, a bruised left elbow, a mild concussion, and a sore thumb plagued Mike in '95.

Mike had a big August, smashing seven homers. However, he then tailed off, batting just .206 with one long ball in September and October. Overall, his average dipped 32 points from his '94 mark, and Stanley experienced an even larger disparity between his home and road performance last season. He did a good job handling the pitching staff, despite continuing to have problems throwing out runners: fully 71 of 88 larcenous runners trying to steal were successful (81%) with Mike behind the mask, a very poor ratio. He also committed 15 passed balls.

WHAT TO EXPECT IN '96
The Yankees failed to re-sign Stanley last winter, choosing instead to enter '96 by pairing NL-veteran Joe Girardi with rookie Jorge Posada. Even worse for New Yorkers, Mike inked with the hated Red Sox, for whom he will no doubt enjoy poking home runs over the Green Monster. Stanley will be a big plus for Boston; he is one of the better catchers in baseball—not only for his hitting but also for his ability to handle a pitching staff. It's a shame for Yankees' fans that he won't be doing it in pinstripes during '96.

Overall Statistics

	G	AB	R	H	2B	3B	HR	RBI	SB	CS	BB	SO	BA	OBA
95 NYA	118	399	63	107	29	1	18	83	1	1	57	106	.268	.360
Career	850	2272	325	614	116	6	85	371	8	2	333	507	.270	.364

1995 Situational Statistics

	AB	HR	RBI	BA	OBA	SLG		AB	HR	RBI	BA	OBA	SLG
Home	195	13	44	.313	.396	.590	LHP	139	8	24	.281	.380	.511
Road	204	5	39	.225	.325	.377	RHP	260	10	59	.262	.349	.465
Apr-Jun	160	6	29	.275	.364	.456	ScPos	97	4	64	.320	.400	.567
Jul-Oct	239	12	54	.264	.357	.498	Clutch	49	1	9	.367	.452	.490

How He Compares to Other Batters

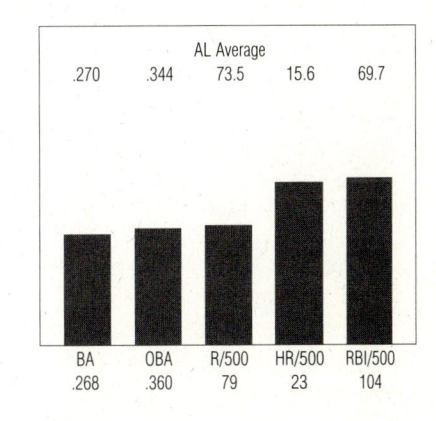

	BA	OBA	R/500	HR/500	RBI/500
AL Average	.270	.344	73.5	15.6	69.7
	.268	.360	79	23	104

Where He Hits the Ball

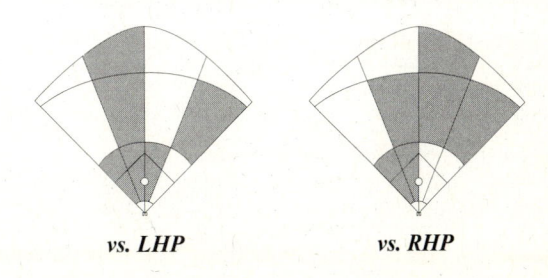

vs. LHP   vs. RHP

THE SCOUTING REPORT: 1996

NEW YORK YANKEES

RANDY VELARDE

Positions: 2B/SS/OF/3B
Bats: R **Throws:** R
Ht: 6' " **Wt:** 185
Opening Day Age: 33
Born: 11/24/1962
Drafted: CHA85 19/345
ML Seasons: 9

SCOUTING REPORT
"Bronco" is a hard-driving, aggressive player in all facets of the game. Despite slightly below-average speed, Randy is a smart runner and occasional base thief who will take the extra bag when possible. He's always been an aggressive hitter as well, but drew by far a career-high 55 walks last year. A good line-drive gap hitter, Velarde has improved against righthanders and is no longer thought of as a platoon player.

Randy can play second base, shortstop, third base, and left field, showing somewhat above-par defensive tools across the board in both the infield and the outfield.

HOW HE PERFORMED IN '95
Where would the Yankees have been without Velarde in '95? It's hard to believe that the veteran was signed at the last minute by the Yankees out of the Homestead homeless camp, and that any other team could have signed him before he had to return to the Yanks with a big salary cut. He has been an underrated—and under-appreciated—player for years in New York.

Aiding and abetting the team's wild-card chase, Randy filled in where needed at five positions, and by the end of the year had basically replaced the injured Pat Kelly as the regular second baseman. He was consistent all season. In addition to starting at four positions (second, short, third, and left), Velarde started in six different lineup spots. The skills he showed in '95 made him valuable in many roles.

WHAT TO EXPECT IN '96
In 1996, Randy will finally get his chance to be a full-time player, this time toiling for the California Angels. The Yankees will attempt to replace the talented Velarde with NL veteran Mariano Duncan—and good luck to them.

At age 33, Velarde is a old to be getting his first crack as a starting player, but the Angels are desperate for help at second base. It may take Randy a little time to adjust to a new team, after spending his entire career with the Yankees.

The motivation of becoming a regular could help Randy make the transition quickly. He should be able to give the Angels two or three good years as a starter and then close his career as he began it—as a top-flight utility player.

Overall Statistics

	G	AB	R	H	2B	3B	HR	RBI	SB	CS	BB	SO	BA	OBA
95 NYA	111	367	60	102	19	1	7	46	5	1	55	64	.278	.375
Career	658	1935	263	511	99	10	43	208	22	15	186	382	.264	.333

1995 Situational Statistics

	AB	HR	RBI	BA	OBA	SLG		AB	HR	RBI	BA	OBA	SLG
Home	162	2	24	.302	.407	.407	LHP	136	1	10	.279	.377	.375
Road	205	5	22	.259	.349	.380	RHP	231	6	36	.277	.374	.403
Apr-Jun	150	3	17	.260	.321	.367	ScPos	104	1	35	.279	.391	.356
Jul-Oct	217	4	29	.290	.409	.410	Clutch	45	1	4	.289	.385	.400

How He Compares to Other Batters

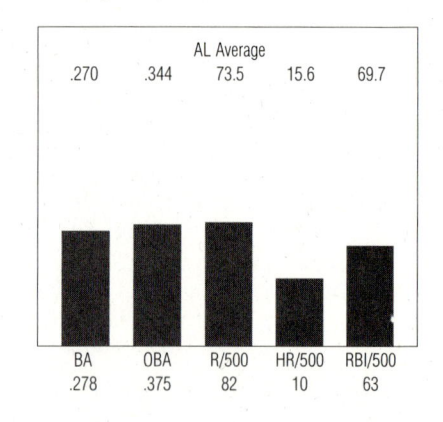

AL Average
.270   .344   73.5   15.6   69.7

BA   OBA   R/500 HR/500 RBI/500
.278 .375   82   10   63

Where He Hits the Ball

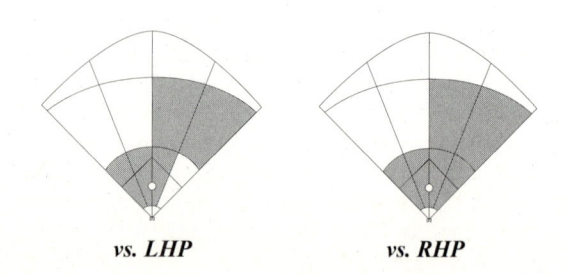

vs. LHP   vs. RHP

NEW YORK YANKEES

JOHN WETTELAND

Position: RP
Bats: R **Throws:** R
Ht: 6'2" **Wt:** 195
Opening Day Age: 29
Born: 8/21/1966
Drafted: LA85* S2/39
ML Seasons: 7

SCOUTING REPORT

Using a three-quarter delivery, John throws two very hard pitches that make him one of the game's better relievers. His plus, four-seam fastball rides in on righthanded hitters, and Wetteland will turn over the fastball against lefties. John also has a good, very hard slider that has a sharp, late break, and sometimes throws a slightly above-average curve.

John, who sports a messy, dirt-caked cap, usually doesn't bother with the preliminaries, opting instead to go right at hitters. As a result, he rarely walks anybody but will allow the occasional home run if a pitch hangs. However, his control is much improved in recent years; after tossing 16 wild pitches as a rookie in 1989, Wetteland has thrown just a single wild one in the last two seasons. He is a plus fielder but poor at holding runners: 13 of 14 runners have stolen safely on him in the past two seasons.

HOW HE PERFORMED IN '95

When he was good in '95, he threw pitches by hitters with regularity; and when he was bad, John gave up 500-foot home runs. During June, John didn't allow an earned run, and he had ERA's under 1.00 in July and September. He retired his last 22 batters of the season, collecting eight saves in September, fanning 18 and walking none in 10.2 innings.

However, for a ten-day period in May and during 18 days in August, he was awful. Most of the damage against John came during these two stretches, when he allowed 16 earned runs in just 15 innings and blew six save opportunities. Fortunately for the Yankees, he had an excellent year overall. John is still adjusting to a new league and to Yankee Stadium, but he seems to be learning very quickly.

WHAT TO EXPECT IN '96

Wetteland should be the Yankees' closer for '96 not only because he throws very hard, but also because of his dirty hat, which just makes him look like a Yankee. However, John needs to avoid those destructive stretches of ineffectiveness to reach the pinnacle of his profession. He's close to that level already, and Wetteland could easily be one of the game's premier closers for years. Although the Yankees have question marks in their starting rotation and in middle relief, they're set in the late innings.

Overall Statistics

	G	GS	GF	SV	W	L	ERA	IP	H	R	ER	HR	BB	SO
95 NYA	60	0	56	31	1	5	2.93	61.1	40	22	20	6	14	66
Career	308	17	232	137	26	30	2.93	448.1	338	164	146	34	153	487

1995 Situational Statistics

	W	L	ERA	SV	IP	BB	SO		AB	HR	RBI	BA	OBA	SLG
Home	0	4	4.06	15	31.0	10	27	LHB	113	3	18	.186	.250	.301
Road	1	1	1.78	16	30.1	4	39	RHB	103	3	9	.184	.213	.350
Apr-Jun	1	1	2.52	10	25.0	6	25	ScPos	52	2	21	.308	.345	.481
Jul-Oct	0	4	3.22	21	36.1	8	41	Clutch	131	5	21	.191	.262	.374

How He Compares to Other Pitchers

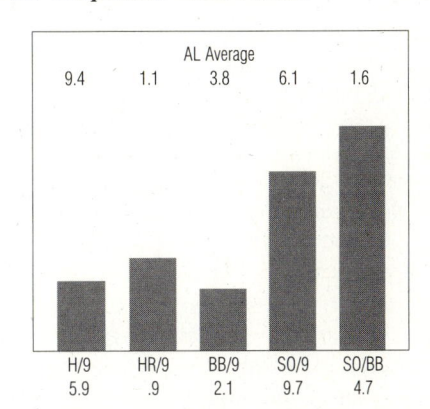

AL Average: 9.4 | 1.1 | 3.8 | 6.1 | 1.6

H/9: 5.9 | HR/9: .9 | BB/9: 2.1 | SO/9: 9.7 | SO/BB: 4.7

How He Compares to Other Starting Pitchers

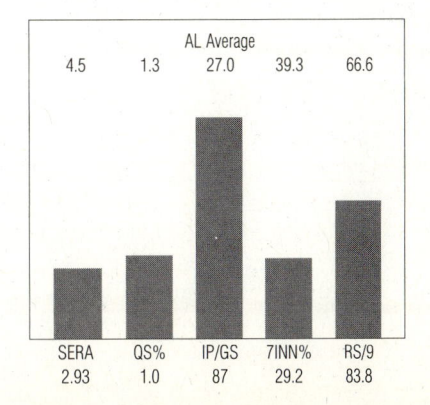

AL Average: 4.5 | 1.3 | 27.0 | 39.3 | 66.6

SERA: 2.93 | QS%: 1.0 | IP/GS: 87 | 7INN%: 29.2 | RS/9: 83.8

THE SCOUTING REPORT: 1996

NEW YORK YANKEES

BERNIE WILLIAMS

Position: OF
Bats: B **Throws:** R
Ht: 6'2" **Wt:** 180
Opening Day Age: 27
Born: 9/13/1968
Drafted: NYA 9/13/85
ML Seasons: 5

SCOUTING REPORT

The first thing that stands out about Williams is his outstanding speed. He is especially blinding on the bases, but has been a poor basestealer because he is hesitant and hasn't yet learned the art.

He hits the ball very hard and is beginning to hit with more punch. Bernie is strong and has excellent bat speed. Batting righthanded, he prefers high pitches over the plate, generating tremendous power. Williams likes low, inside pitches lefthanded. Although he still has a problem with strikeouts, Bernie is patient and will look at a lot of pitches.

A fine center fielder, Williams had a rough '95 season defensively. He has shown a strong and accurate arm in the past, but collected only one assist last year after having much better seasons. Although he has plus hands, Bernie also slumped in this category, committing eight errors. He again showed plus range and, assuming he recovers from his fielding slump in '96, he is likely to be a Gold Glove candidate.

HOW HE PERFORMED IN '95

Bernie has gotten better every year. He helped carry the Yankees the last two months of the '95 season, hitting a sizzling .359 from August 1 through onward. In fact, Williams was so hot at the end of the year that the Yankees continually delayed him from traveling home to Puerto Rico to see his newborn child because they didn't want him out of the lineup.

One of his biggest improvements was his hitting against righthanders. Williams' average against them increased 63 points last year and, for the first time, he showed outstanding power production from the left side as well.

WHAT TO EXPECT IN '96

Barring injuries, Bernie has a chance to be the Yankees' best centerfielder since Mickey Mantle. At age 27, he is entering his prime. If he could put an entire year together like he did the last two months of '95, Williams could contend for the batting title.

However, he has some steps to take before he can put a claim in on stardom. He's still a bad basestealer and must rebound defensively. If Bernie does that, '96 should be a fine season for him and the Yankees would be well-advised to think about locking him up on a long-term basis.

Overall Statistics

	G	AB	R	H	2B	3B	HR	RBI	SB	CS	BB	SO	BA	OBA
95 NYA	144	563	93	173	29	9	18	82	8	6	75	98	.307	.392
Career	538	2119	322	592	122	20	50	267	50	35	266	351	.279	.362

1995 Situational Statistics

	AB	HR	RBI	BA	OBA	SLG		AB	HR	RBI	BA	OBA	SLG
Home	280	7	39	.329	.413	.479	LHP	195	13	35	.303	.378	.590
Road	283	11	43	.286	.370	.495	RHP	368	5	47	.310	.399	.432
Apr-Jun	216	9	33	.259	.339	.458	ScPos	145	3	61	.317	.420	.469
Jul-Oct	347	9	49	.337	.424	.504	Clutch	75	1	16	.320	.384	.427

How He Compares to Other Batters

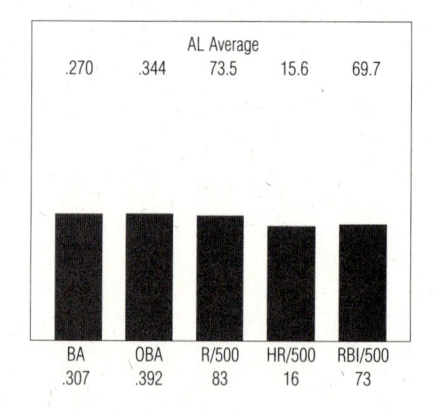

	BA	OBA	R/500	HR/500	RBI/500
AL Average	.270	.344	73.5	15.6	69.7
	.307	.392	83	16	73

Where He Hits the Ball

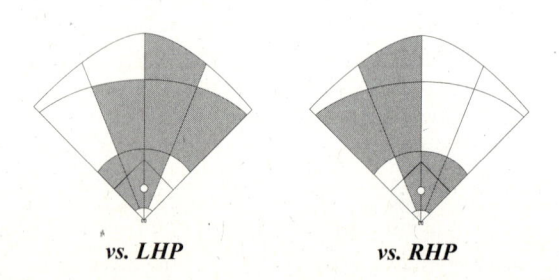

vs. LHP   vs. RHP

NEW YORK YANKEES

JOE AUSANIO

Position: RP
Bats: R **Throws:** R
Ht: 6'1" **Wt:** 205
Opening Day Age: 30
Born: 12/9/1965
Drafted: PIT88 11/278
ML Seasons: 2

Overall Statistics

	G	GS	GF	SV	W	L	ERA	IP	H	R	ER	HR	BB	SO
95 NYA	28	0	10	1	2	0	5.73	37.2	42	24	24	9	23	36
Career	41	0	15	1	4	1	5.57	53.1	58	33	33	12	29	51

1995 Situational Statistics

	W	L	ERA	SV	IP	BB	SO		AB	HR	RBI	BA	OBA	SLG
Home	1	0	2.12	1	17.0	6	17	LHB	65	3	14	.246	.315	.446
Road	1	0	8.71	0	20.2	17	19	RHB	82	6	17	.317	.424	.585
Apr-Jun	2	0	7.33	1	23.1	16	22	ScPos	56	1	19	.214	.324	.321
Jul-Oct	0	0	3.14	0	14.1	7	14	Clutch	16	2	6	.438	.500	.938

SCOUTING REPORT

Joe has a tad above-average velocity on his fastball but it's generally straight. He has a usable slider but his out pitch is a plus forkball with good tumbling action.

Ausanio is not a good fielder and does not have a good move, but he pays attention to baserunners. Only two ran on him in '95, both safely.

HOW HE PERFORMED IN '95

Ausanio bounced back and forth between the Yankees and Columbus in '95. He had a rough year in middle relief: after posting a 6.60 ERA through the end of May, Joe didn't get enough use the rest of the year to get into a groove. He was much more effective against lefthanded hitters, which is probably a fluke since it reversed his '94 numbers.

WHAT TO EXPECT IN '96

He will battle for the final spot on the Yankees' pitching staff in '96. If Ausanio can be a little more consistent, he may help the Yankees in middle relief. If he doesn't make the roster out of spring training, he will likely spend another year on the New York-Columbus shuttle.

RUSS DAVIS

Positions: 3B/DH/1B
Bats: R **Throws:** R
Ht: 6'0" **Wt:** 170
Opening Day Age: 26
Born: 9/13/1969
Drafted: NYA88 26/755
ML Seasons: 2

Overall Statistics

	G	AB	R	H	2B	3B	HR	RBI	SB	CS	BB	SO	BA	OBA
95 NYA	40	98	14	27	5	2	2	12	0	0	10	26	.276	.349
Career	44	112	14	29	5	2	2	13	0	0	10	30	.259	.325

1995 Situational Statistics

	AB	HR	RBI	BA	OBA	SLG		AB	HR	RBI	BA	OBA	SLG
Home	33	2	5	.333	.389	.576	LHP	74	2	10	.311	.378	.500
Road	65	0	7	.246	.329	.354	RHP	24	0	2	.167	.259	.208
Apr-Jun	30	1	2	.367	.441	.633	ScPos	24	1	10	.250	.379	.458
Jul-Oct	68	1	10	.235	.307	.338	Clutch	2	0	0	.000	.333	.000

SCOUTING REPORT

Davis is a strong hitter who had posted good power numbers in the high minors for three straight seasons before getting a promotion to New York. He has average major-league power now but needs more experience to fulfill his potential. Russ is slow on the basepaths and doesn't steal.

At third base, Russ has an average-plus arm with average range and hands.

HOW HE PERFORMED IN '95

Davis' first full year with the Yankees received an "incomplete" grade, playing decently in a platoon role. Russ had very disappointing power numbers overall but hit over .300 against lefties with good power. This could presage his ultimate role in the majors or could be a result of not seeing many righthanders.

WHAT TO EXPECT IN '96

Davis will finally get the chance to play full time in '96. With Tino Martinez at first and Wade Boggs at third, New York sent Russ to Seattle, where the third base job is his to lose. The Bronx Bombers can only hope Davis doesn't become another Jay Buhner—a big one that got away. At 26, it's time for him to show what he can do.

THE SCOUTING REPORT: 1996

NEW YORK YANKEES

RICK HONEYCUTT

Position: RP
Bats: L **Throws:** L
Ht: 5'11" **Wt:** 190
Opening Day Age: 43
Born: 6/29/1952
Drafted: PIT76 17/405
ML Seasons: 19

Overall Statistics

	G	GS	GF	SV	W	L	ERA	IP	H	R	ER	HR	BB	SO
95 OAK/NYA	52	0	6	2	5	1	2.96	45.2	39	16	15	6	10	21
Career	734	268	103	34	107	142	3.73	2110.2	2136	1016	875	182	649	1006

1995 Situational Statistics

	W	L	ERA	SV	IP	BB	SO		AB	HR	RBI	BA	OBA	SLG
Home	5	0	3.32	1	19.0	3	12	LHB	85	0	10	.176	.220	.200
Road	0	1	2.70	1	26.2	7	9	RHB	80	6	18	.300	.349	.538
Apr-Jun	3	1	3.79	1	19.0	3	9	ScPos	46	3	23	.413	.440	.674
Jul-Oct	2	0	2.36	1	26.2	7	12	Clutch	75	3	12	.187	.237	.320

SCOUTING REPORT

Rick depends on plus control, good command, and cutting off the running game to be effective. He delivers from three quarters with a short windup, sinking and cutting a minus fastball. He also employs a plus curve and an average change. A good fielder, Honeycutt allowed only one stolen base last year.

HOW HE PERFORMED IN '95

The veteran lefty had a fine year in his typical very short role. After a rough start, Honeycutt did not allow an earned run in 21 games during July and August. He was obtained by the Yankees in late September because Buck Showalter had lost all confidence in Steve Howe. In his brief time as with the Yanks, Rick did not impress (three earned runs in one inning).

WHAT TO EXPECT IN '96

A free agent, Rick signed with the Cardinals for '96, his fourth club in three seasons; he will re-join longtime skipper Tony LaRussa. At age 43, Honeycutt begins his 20th big-league campaign. Should he and Tony Fossas both be on the staff, St. Louis may have one of the oldest bullpens in history.

STEVE HOWE

Position: RP
Bats: L **Throws:** L
Ht: 6'1" **Wt:** 180
Opening Day Age: 38
Born: 3/10/1958
Drafted: LA79 1/16
ML Seasons: 11

Overall Statistics

	G	GS	GF	SV	W	L	ERA	IP	H	R	ER	HR	BB	SO
95 NYA	56	0	20	2	6	3	4.96	49.0	66	29	27	7	17	28
Career	472	0	253	90	47	40	2.93	589.0	567	227	192	31	133	323

1995 Situational Statistics

	W	L	ERA	SV	IP	BB	SO		AB	HR	RBI	BA	OBA	SLG
Home	5	1	6.39	1	25.1	8	12	LHB	79	1	10	.241	.268	.342
Road	1	2	3.42	1	23.2	9	16	RHB	125	6	27	.376	.448	.584
Apr-Jun	2	2	5.00	1	18.0	6	13	ScPos	72	2	31	.361	.442	.514
Jul-Oct	4	1	4.94	1	31.0	11	15	Clutch	92	3	17	.326	.388	.489

SCOUTING REPORT

Steve uses a straight-up motion to bring home three pitches from three quarters: an average sinking fastball that lost a lot of velocity in '95, a below-par curve that no longer bites, and an average slider.

Steve has a good move to first and is so hard to run on that only one runner even tried in '95. He is an average fielder.

HOW HE PERFORMED IN '95

After a very strong '94, the '95 season was a lost one for the veteran. Buck Showalter lost all confidence in Steve and, in late September, aging Rick Honeycutt was brought in to assume Howe's role.

The year began promisingly enough, with Howe being touted as a possible closer. However, with John Wetteland on board, Steve became the lefty set-up pitcher. He allowed 13 hits in 5.2 innings in May and never got straightened out. While Howe held lefties in check, he was a time bomb against righties.

WHAT TO EXPECT IN '96

If Steve gets on new Yankees' skipper Joe Torre's good side, he might get another chance in his old role. However, he's 38 and may not be able to bounce back again.

NEW YORK YANKEES

DION JAMES

Positions: OF/DH//1B
Bats: L **Throws:** L
Ht: 6'1" **Wt:** 170
Opening Day Age: 33
Born: 11/9/1962
Drafted: MIL80 1/25
ML Seasons: 10

Overall Statistics

	G	AB	R	H	2B	3B	HR	RBI	SB	CS	BB	SO	BA	OBA
95 NYA	85	209	22	60	6	1	2	26	4	1	20	16	.287	.346
Career	911	2696	361	779	142	21	32	266	42	38	317	305	.289	.364

1995 Situational Statistics

	AB	HR	RBI	BA	OBA	SLG		AB	HR	RBI	BA	OBA	SLG
Home	110	1	16	.273	.354	.355	LHP	16	0	0	.188	.235	.188
Road	99	1	10	.303	.337	.354	RHP	193	2	26	.295	.355	.368
Apr-Jun	75	1	13	.307	.369	.387	ScPos	60	1	24	.317	.394	.450
Jul-Oct	134	1	13	.276	.333	.336	Clutch	27	0	5	.333	.424	.370

SCOUTING REPORT

James is a line-drive hitter with a flat stroke without much power. His speed is now somewhat below average and he does not steal much.

In left field, Dion has a weak arm with minus accuracy, below-average range, and average-minus hands. He can also play first base if needed.

HOW HE PERFORMED IN '95

James returned to the Yankees in '95 after a year in Japan. Although he hit decently, Dion was reduced to mostly platoon designated hitting and to pinch-hitting because of the Yankees' overabundance of outfielders. He started only 23 games in the outfield in '95. A late slump saw James bat only .213 after August 31.

WHAT TO EXPECT IN '96

Dion is again a free agent. With the Yankees' outfield glut, he is likely to end up with another team. If picked up, he could again be a good fifth outfielder/pinch hitter. This will be James' role for the duration of his career and he appears ready to accept it. With no punch, defense, or speed, he's has to at least hit for a high average.

SCOTT KAMIENIECKI

Position: SP
Bats: R **Throws:** R
Ht: 6'0" **Wt:** 195
Opening Day Age: 31
Born: 4/19/1964
Drafted: NYA86 15/366
ML Seasons: 5

Overall Statistics

	G	GS	GF	SV	W	L	ERA	IP	H	R	ER	HR	BB	SO
95 NYA	17	16	1	0	7	6	4.01	89.2	83	43	40	8	49	43
Career	106	89	7	1	35	37	4.08	604.2	608	293	274	59	263	308

1995 Situational Statistics

	W	L	ERA	SV	IP	BB	SO		AB	HR	RBI	BA	OBA	SLG
Home	1	2	5.52	0	29.1	11	11	LHB	176	2	13	.244	.364	.352
Road	6	4	3.28	0	60.1	38	32	RHB	162	6	26	.247	.326	.414
Apr-Jun	0	1	8.44	0	5.1	5	3	ScPos	79	2	27	.253	.404	.392
Jul-Oct	7	5	3.74	0	84.1	44	40	Clutch	7	0	0	.000	.125	.000

SCOUTING REPORT

A blue-collar righthanded pitcher with a bulldog attitude, Scott has a plus fastball which he will use inside to righties and turn over to lefties. He also utilizes a plus curve, an average slider, and an average-minus change, delivering from high three-quarters to overhand.

Kamieniecki is an average fielder but does not have a good move: nine of 13 baserunners were successful against him in '95.

HOW HE PERFORMED IN '95

Kamieniecki saved a so-so season with some strong performances during the Yankees' stretch run. He did not pitch between May 6 and July 15 due to a strained elbow and was ineffective upon his return, walking 23 in 26 innings in August, notching a 5.13 ERA. However, Scott then turned around and went 3-1 with a 2.48 ERA in September and October.

WHAT TO EXPECT IN '96

The question is whether the 32-year-old Kamieniecki can fill the shoes of the young, talented, and now-traded Sterling Hitchcock. While Scott will be given every opportunity to make the Yankees' rotation, he hasn't made more than 20 starts since 1992 and may not be able to handle a full workload.

THE SCOUTING REPORT: 1996

NEW YORK YANKEES

PAT KELLY

Positions: 2B//DH
Bats: R **Throws:** R
Ht: 6'0" **Wt:** 180
Opening Day Age: 28
Born: 10/14/1967
Drafted: NYA88 6/235
ML Seasons: 5

Overall Statistics

	G	AB	R	H	2B	3B	HR	RBI	SB	CS	BB	SO	BA	OBA
95 NYA	89	270	32	64	12	1	4	29	8	3	23	65	.237	.307
Career	511	1578	189	399	91	10	24	171	48	25	106	308	.253	.309

1995 Situational Statistics

	AB	HR	RBI	BA	OBA	SLG		AB	HR	RBI	BA	OBA	SLG
Home	140	1	14	.236	.325	.300	LHP	92	3	13	.272	.330	.457
Road	130	3	15	.238	.286	.369	RHP	178	1	16	.219	.295	.270
Apr-Jun	73	3	7	.315	.414	.466	ScPos	69	0	22	.174	.244	.217
Jul-Oct	197	1	22	.208	.263	.284	Clutch	30	2	7	.233	.281	.467

SCOUTING REPORT

Pat is a guess hitter with a bit of line-drive power but poor bat speed. He is a good sacrifice bunter and can both drag and push the bunt for a base hit. Kelly is aggressive baserunner with average speed.

At second, Pat has plus range with an average arm and slightly below-average hands. Kelly made seven errors in '95, which was about league-average.

HOW HE PERFORMED IN '95

Last year was a tough one for Kelly, who lost the second base job to Randy Velarde at the end of the year. After hitting .311 with three homers and 11 walks in May, he missed the next five weeks June due to a torn ligament in his left wrist. After returning from the DL, Pat hit a weak .208 the rest of the way.

WHAT TO EXPECT IN '96

Fortunately for Kelly, the Yankees were unsuccessful in signing either Craig Biggio or Roberto Alomar over the winter. With Velarde going to the Angels, Pat has the inside track on regaining his job. Kelly plays hard, is still relatively young and, if he hits at all, his fielding will keep him in the lineup.

JIM LEYRITZ

Positions: C/1B/DH
Bats: R **Throws:** R
Ht: 6'0" **Wt:** 190
Opening Day Age: 32
Born: 12/27/1963
Drafted: NYA 8/24/85
ML Seasons: 6

Overall Statistics

	G	AB	R	H	2B	3B	HR	RBI	SB	CS	BB	SO	BA	OBA
95 NYA	77	264	37	71	12	0	7	37	1	1	37	73	.269	.374
Career	434	1296	180	346	60	1	50	203	3	6	163	281	.267	.362

1995 Situational Statistics

	AB	HR	RBI	BA	OBA	SLG		AB	HR	RBI	BA	OBA	SLG
Home	140	3	20	.279	.366	.400	LHP	115	5	18	.322	.435	.496
Road	124	4	17	.258	.383	.387	RHP	149	2	19	.228	.326	.315
Apr-Jun	148	4	21	.291	.393	.432	ScPos	78	1	30	.282	.380	.410
Jul-Oct	116	3	16	.241	.350	.345	Clutch	32	0	4	.313	.421	.344

SCOUTING REPORT

Jim is very aggressive at bat with good bat speed and slightly plus power. He likes pitches inside and low to pull. Leyritz has slightly below-average speed as a runner but almost never steals.

Although his primary position is behind the plate, Jim is adequate at first base and can play third base or the outfield in a pinch. At catcher, he has an average-minus arm and minus hands and mobility.

HOW HE PERFORMED IN '95

After some good years as a platoon catcher/first baseman, Leyritz slumped in '95. Part of the problem was that Yankees' manager Buck Showalter went less to his righthanded-hitting lineup down the stretch. With Mike Stanley having another good year, the need for a backup catcher was not great.

WHAT TO EXPECT IN '96

With Ruben Sierra as the Yankees' full-time designated hitter for '96, Jim will probably remain with the Yankees as a back-up catcher/first baseman and right-handed pinch hitter. He hates to sit and, although his best years are behind him at age 32, Leyritz could step in if New York's new receiver, Joe Girardi, should slump.

NEW YORK YANKEES

ROB MAC DONALD

Position: RP
Bats: L **Throws:** L
Ht: 6'3" **Wt:** 200
Opening Day Age: 30
Born: 4/27/1965
Drafted: TOR87 19/491
ML Seasons: 5

Overall Statistics

	G	GS	GF	SV	W	L	ERA	IP	H	R	ER	HR	BB	SO
95 NYA	33	0	5	0	1	1	4.86	46.1	50	25	25	7	22	41
Career	177	0	49	3	8	7	4.35	215.1	218	110	104	24	98	130

1995 Situational Statistics

	W	L	ERA	SV	IP	BB	SO		AB	HR	RBI	BA	OBA	SLG
Home	1	0	2.70	0	26.2	8	23	LHB	65	3	9	.277	.382	.477
Road	0	1	7.78	0	19.2	14	18	RHB	112	4	18	.286	.355	.446
Apr-Jun	1	1	6.98	0	19.1	10	21	ScPos	39	3	20	.359	.490	.692
Jul-Oct	0	0	3.33	0	27.0	12	20	Clutch	17	1	3	.176	.176	.353

SCOUTING REPORT
MacDonald comes from low three-quarters with a slightly above-average fastball and curve, an average slider, and slightly below-average change and splitter. He has the stuff but not the control to be successful in the majors.

Bob is an adequate fielder with an adequate move: six runners tried to steal against him in '95, three successfully.

HOW HE PERFORMED IN '95
MacDonald, who spent all of '94 in Triple-A, returned to the show in '95 and had a so-so season in middle relief. Although opponents hit .282 against him, Bob did pitch well at Yankee Stadium, which is critical for a mediocre lefty trying to retain his pinstripes. He also showed unexpected punchout ability, fanning 41 in 46 innings. However, he did not pitch effectively against lefties, making MacDonald less useful as a situational reliever.

WHAT TO EXPECT IN '96
Unless he has a good spring, Bob is likely to return to the minors. He will have to harness his pitches better to make it in middle relief, either with the Yankees or anyone else.

MELIDO PEREZ

Position: SP
Bats: R **Throws:** R
Ht: 6'4" **Wt:** 180
Opening Day Age: 30
Born: 2/15/1966
Drafted: KC 7/22/83
ML Seasons: 9

Overall Statistics

	G	GS	GF	SV	W	L	ERA	IP	H	R	ER	HR	BB	SO
95 NYA	13	12	1	0	5	5	5.58	69.1	70	46	43	10	31	44
Career	243	201	17	1	78	85	4.17	1354.2	1268	700	627	144	551	1092

1995 Situational Statistics

	W	L	ERA	SV	IP	BB	SO		AB	HR	RBI	BA	OBA	SLG
Home	3	1	3.94	0	29.2	14	17	LHB	146	6	23	.260	.341	.459
Road	2	4	6.81	0	39.2	17	27	RHB	122	4	18	.262	.331	.443
Apr-Jun	5	5	5.66	0	68.1	31	44	ScPos	67	2	30	.313	.417	.433
Jul-Oct	0	0	0.00	0	1.0	0	0	Clutch	20	2	2	.300	.364	.650

SCOUTING REPORT
When healthy, Melido has a hard sinking fastball and a sharp-breaking slider, delivered from a three-quarter angle. His best pitch is a well above-average splitter that ranks as one of the best in the game, but that is hard to control. Despite a long windup, only four runners ran on Perez last year—and three were thrown out. He is a minus fielder.

HOW HE PERFORMED IN '95
Perez' season was cut short by an inflamed right shoulder. The injury, which shelved Melido in early July, was one reason the Yankees went acquired David Cone. It's possible that he was hurt even at the start of the year, because Perez did not pitch effectively at any time. He made one relief appearance in September, but was left off the postseason roster.

WHAT TO EXPECT IN '96
Assuming Perez' shoulder is not permanently damaged and he can bounce back, he will be the Yankees' third or fourth starter. At 30, he should have several years left. If Melido stays injury-free for a whole season, he could easily give the powerful Yankees 15 wins.

NEW YORK YANKEES

MARIANO RIVERA

Position: SP/RP
Bats: R **Throws:** R
Ht: 6'4" **Wt:** 170
Opening Day Age: 26
Born: 11/29/1969
Drafted: NYA 2/17/90
ML Seasons: 1

Overall Statistics

	G	GS	GF	SV	W	L	ERA	IP	H	R	ER	HR	BB	SO
95 NYA	19	10	2	0	5	3	5.51	67.0	71	43	41	11	30	51
Career	19	10	2	0	5	3	5.51	67.0	71	43	41	11	30	51

1995 Situational Statistics

	W	L	ERA	SV	IP	BB	SO		AB	HR	RBI	BA	OBA	SLG
Home	3	2	7.11	0	31.2	14	24	LHB	142	6	22	.246	.337	.415
Road	2	1	4.08	0	35.1	16	27	RHB	125	5	17	.288	.348	.472
Apr-Jun	1	2	10.20	0	15.0	8	9	ScPos	57	5	30	.263	.333	.579
Jul-Oct	4	1	4.15	0	52.0	22	42	Clutch	14	1	3	.143	.250	.357

SCOUTING REPORT

Rivera has a plus fastball that he needs to keep down because it doesn't have lots of movement. He also has a very hard, plus slider, an average-minus change, and will show a splitter. His angle of delivery is three-quarters.

Mariano has a minus move and allowed five stole bases in seven attempts in '95. He is a plus fielder.

HOW HE PERFORMED IN '95

Rookie Rivera was called up three times in '95. He was 2-0 with a 2.54 ERA in four starts during July but worked as a reliever late in the year. He had some strong performances in September and pitched effectively in the Division Series against Seattle. Mariano's fastball was impressive and his strikeout stuff helped him get out of many jams.

WHAT TO EXPECT IN '96

With the depth of the Yankees' starting pitching (Cone, Rogers, Pettitte, Kamieniecki, Perez, and possibly Gooden or Key), Rivera's future with the Yankees may be in long relief or as a spot starter. He has a great arm, is only 26, but needs more experience—a strong performance in '96 could land him a spot in the Yankee rotation later.

DARRYL STRAWBERRY

Positions: DH/OF
Bats: L **Throws:** L
Ht: 6'6" **Wt:** 190
Opening Day Age: 34
Born: 3/12/1962
Drafted: NYN80 1/1
ML Seasons: 13

Overall Statistics

	G	AB	R	H	2B	3B	HR	RBI	SB	CS	BB	SO	BA	OBA
95 NYA	32	87	15	24	4	1	3	13	0	0	10	22	.276	.364
Career	1384	4843	808	1256	226	36	297	899	205	87	719	1182	.259	.356

1995 Situational Statistics

	AB	HR	RBI	BA	OBA	SLG		AB	HR	RBI	BA	OBA	SLG
Home	42	3	8	.286	.388	.571	LHP	12	0	0	.167	.167	.167
Road	45	0	5	.267	.340	.333	RHP	75	3	13	.293	.391	.493
Apr-Jun	0	0	0	.000	.000	.000	ScPos	23	2	10	.348	.444	.652
Jul-Oct	87	3	13	.276	.364	.448	Clutch	6	0	0	.000	.333	.000

SCOUTING REPORT

Darryl has a graceful uppercut swing that generates big power. However, he has lost bat speed as he has aged and has lost some of his rhythm due to inactivity. An average runner, he still has a strong arm with decent range.

HOW HE PERFORMED IN '95

The much-ballyhooed return of the Straw fizzled out before it really could get started. While he hit for a decent average, the prodigal New Yorker slugged only three homers, and was an adventure in the outfield in the few times he played there. He fielded just .909, but threw out two runners in 11 games.

WHAT TO EXPECT IN '96

Before the Yankees decided not to sign Darryl, the story out of the Big Apple for '96 might have read like this: Strawberry in left field and the newly-inked Doc Gooden would recast the Yankees as the 1986 Mets reborn, and the team would beat the Braves in the World Series on a ground ball through the legs of Fred McGriff.

With Darryl now a free agent, it remains to be seen if another team is willing to take a chance on him.

NEW YORK YANKEES

BOB WICKMAN

Position: RP
Bats: R **Throws:** R
Ht: 6'1" **Wt:** 207
Opening Day Age: 27
Born: 2/6/1969
Drafted: CHA90 2/44
ML Seasons: 4

Overall Statistics

	G	GS	GF	SV	W	L	ERA	IP	H	R	ER	HR	BB	SO
95 NYA	63	1	14	1	2	4	4.05	80.0	77	38	36	6	33	51
Career	165	28	42	11	27	13	4.10	340.1	338	171	155	24	149	198

1995 Situational Statistics

	W	L	ERA	SV	IP	BB	SO		AB	HR	RBI	BA	OBA	SLG
Home	1	0	3.89	0	37.0	11	22	LHB	128	3	17	.305	.369	.430
Road	1	4	4.19	1	43.0	22	29	RHB	176	3	24	.216	.312	.307
Apr-Jun	2	2	4.17	0	36.2	16	21	ScPos	107	1	34	.243	.339	.327
Jul-Oct	0	2	3.95	1	43.1	17	30	Clutch	138	2	22	.268	.340	.355

SCOUTING REPORT

Bob's primary pitch is his sinker, which has a tad above-average velocity, and is delivered from low three-quarters. He will cut the fastball, has a plus splitter with good sink, and will show a change-up. He's somewhat above-par with the glove but his problems holding runners returned in '95, as he allowed nine stolen bases in as many attempts.

HOW HE PERFORMED IN '95

Wickman spent '95 setting up for John Wetteland. For the most part, Bob had a decent year, although he did struggle with control at times. He allowed 13 runs in his first 20 innings but then straightened his season out. More effective than usual against righthanders, Wickman also had more trouble than he ordinarily does with lefties.

WHAT TO EXPECT IN '96

New Yankees' manager Joe Torre may depend on Wickman more if he can improve against left-handed batters. He has established himself as a setup pitcher although, if the Yankees get in a pinch, Bob can spot start. He is still young and has a chance to assume a greater role if he improves.

GERALD WILLIAMS

Positions: OF//DH
Bats: R **Throws:** R
Ht: 6'2" **Wt:** 190
Opening Day Age: 29
Born: 8/10/1966
Drafted: NYA87 12/367
ML Seasons: 4

Overall Statistics

	G	AB	R	H	2B	3B	HR	RBI	SB	CS	BB	SO	BA	OBA
95 NYA	100	182	33	45	18	2	6	28	4	2	22	34	.247	.327
Career	214	362	70	88	30	5	13	53	9	5	27	68	.243	.297

1995 Situational Statistics

	AB	HR	RBI	BA	OBA	SLG		AB	HR	RBI	BA	OBA	SLG
Home	95	4	16	.242	.315	.484	LHP	126	4	19	.278	.378	.508
Road	87	2	12	.253	.340	.448	RHP	56	2	9	.179	.200	.375
Apr-Jun	64	4	16	.281	.356	.609	ScPos	49	2	21	.224	.293	.408
Jul-Oct	118	2	12	.229	.311	.390	Clutch	22	0	2	.136	.231	.182

SCOUTING REPORT

Williams has some power but gets in front of pitch too much and can't hit breaking balls. He has improved his plate discipline against lefties but is ineffectual against righties.

Gerald has a bit above-average speed but doesn't steal often. His defensive tools are average except for his plus range; he is valuable because he can play center field as well as the outfield corners.

HOW HE PERFORMED IN '95

At 29, his chances of being more than a platoon player in pinstripes are just about zero, and his chances of even platooning player are slim. He started 47 games in the outfield for the Yankees in '95, hitting lefthanders very well. With the off-season acquisition of Tim Raines and with Ruben Sierra as the full-time DH, Williams will see very little live pitching.

WHAT TO EXPECT IN '96

The best thing which could happen would be for Gerald to be traded to a team who badly needs a starting outfielder. Without getting a chance to show what he can do on a regular basis, he will be typecast as a backup.

THE SCOUTING REPORT: 1996

NEW YORK YANKEES: TOP PROSPECTS

BRIAN BOEHRINGER

Bats: S Throws: R Opening Day Age: 27
Ht: 6-2 Wt: 180 Born: 1/8/1969
Position: P Drafted: 1991 #4 CHA

YR TEAM	LG/CLASS	G	GS	GF	SV	W	L	ERA	IP	H	HR	BB	SO	O/BA
93 Sarasota	FSL/A	18	17	0	0	10	4	2.80	119.0	103	2	51	92	.237
93 Birmingham	SOU/AA	7	7	0	0	2	1	3.54	40.2	41	3	14	29	.265
94 Albany	EAST/AA	27	27	0	0	10	11	3.62	171.2	165	10	57	145	.256
95 Columbus	INT/AAA	17	17	0	0	8	6	2.77	104	101	6	31	58	.254
New York	AL/MAJ	7	3	0	0	0	3	13.75	17	24	5	22	10	.338

The 26-year-old, who was acquired from the White Sox for Paul Assenmacher prior to the '94 season, has a major league arm, throwing a 90-mph fastball, slider and curve. Boehringer started the season with the Yankees, but a lack of command resulted in a trip to Triple-A in mid-May where he pitched very well in all but two starts.

NICK DELVECCHIO

Bats: L Throws: R Opening Day Age: 26
Ht: 6-5 Wt: 203 Born: 1/23/1970
Position: 1B-OF Drafted: 1992 #23 NYA

YR TEAM	LG/CLASS	G	AB	R	H	2B	3B	HR	RBI	SB	BA	OBA
93 Greensboro	SAL/A	137	485	90	131	30	3	21	80	4	.270	.397
94 Tampa	FSL/A	27	95	17	27	3	0	7	18	0	.284	.361
94 Yankees	GULF/R	4	13	1	5	0	0	0	0	0	.385	.467
95 Norwich	EAST/AA	125	430	66	112	23	4	19	74	2	.260	.390

One of the top power hitters in the organization, DelVecchio has been forced to play some left field due to a logjam at first base. He is barely adequate at either position, strikes out more than he should and struggled terribly against lefties, but has tremendous power. Only pitcher-friendly Norwich prevented DelVecchio from pounding 25 or more home runs. The Harvard grad, who missed most of '94 with a broken hand suffered when hit by a pitch, broke a 62-year-old Eastern League record with a minor league-leading 23 hit-by-pitch last season.

MATT DREWS

Bats: R Throws: R Opening Day Age: 22
Ht: 6-8 Wt: 205 Born: 8/29/1974
Position: P Drafted: 1993 #1 NYA

YR TEAM	LG/CLASS	G	GS	GF	SV	W	L	ERA	IP	H	HR	BB	SO	O/BA
94 Oneonta	NYP/A	14	14	0	0	7	6	2.10	90.0	76	1	19	69	.225
95 Tampa	FSL/A	28	28	0	0	15	7	2.27	182	142	5	58	140	.214

The most coveted pitcher in the organization, the 6-foot-8 Drews led the Florida State League in wins and innings, was second in strikeouts and ended up third in ERA, capturing allstar honors. He also led the organization in wins and ERA. The 21-year-old has a 93 mph fastball, great command considering his size and age, and a pretty decent curveball. The 1993 firstround pick, who led the New York-Penn League in ERA in '94, allowed two runs or fewer in 13 of his 28 starts last season.

MIKE FIGGA

Bats: R Throws: R Opening Day Age: 26
Ht: 6-0 Wt: 200 Born: 7/31/1970
Position: C Drafted: 1989 #43 NYA

YR TEAM	LG/CLASS	G	AB	R	H	2B	3B	HR	RBI	SB	BA	OBA
93 San Brndno	CAL/A	83	308	48	82	17	1	25	71	2	.266	.306
93 Albany	EAST/AA	6	22	3	5	0	0	0	2	1	.227	.292
94 Albany	EAST/AA	1	2	1	1	1	0	0	0	0	.500	.500
94 Tampa	FSL/A	111	420	48	116	17	5	15	75	3	.276	.312
95 Columbus	INT/AAA	8	25	2	7	1	0	1	3	0	.280	.357
Norwich	EAST/AA	109	399	59	108	22	4	13	61	1	.271	.339

A .275 hitter the past three seasons with 54 homers, Figga, just a 43rd round pick in 1989, has made a great improvement behind the plate. He threw out 32% of basestealers which led to an Eastern League All-Star berth. Still, the 25-year-old's forte is power hitting, which he would have done much more of had it not been for the park in Norwich, the toughest home run park in the Eastern League.

ANDY FOX

Bats: L Throws: R Opening Day Age: 25
Ht: 6-4 Wt: 185 Born: 1/12/1971
Position: 3B-SS Drafted: 1989 #1 NYA

YR TEAM	LG/CLASS	G	AB	R	H	2B	3B	HR	RBI	SB	BA	OBA
93 Albany	EAST/AA	65	236	44	65	16	1	3	24	12	.275	.362
94 Albany	EAST/AA	121	472	75	105	20	3	11	43	22	.222	.315
95 Columbus	INT/AAA	82	302	61	105	16	6	9	37	22	.348	.432
Norwich	EAST/AA	44	175	23	36	3	5	5	17	8	.206	.282

Fox, a third basemen by trade, had never hit until being promoted to Triple-A last June. The 24-year-old is being groomed for a utility role and played shortstop, second base, third base and the outfield last year. A talented athlete, Fox can steal a base, has the range for several positions and owns a strong arm.

DEREK JETER

Bats: R Throws: R Opening Day Age: 22
Ht: 6-3 Wt: 175 Born: 6/26/1974
Position: SS Drafted: 1992 #1 NYA

YR TEAM	LG/CLASS	G	AB	R	H	2B	3B	HR	RBI	SB	BA	OBA
93 Greensboro	SAL/A	128	515	85	152	14	11	5	71	18	.295	.376
94 Tampa	FSL/A	69	292	61	96	13	8	0	39	28	.329	.380
94 Albany	EAST/AA	34	122	17	46	7	2	2	13	12	.377	.446
94 Columbus	INT/AAA	35	126	25	44	7	1	3	16	10	.349	.439
95 Columbus	INT/AAA	123	486	96	154	27	9	2	45	20	.317	.394
New York	AL/MAJ	15	48	5	12	4	1	0	7	0	.250	.294

The 1994 Howe Sportsdata Player-of-the-Year got off to another great start in '95, putting together a 17-game hitting streak early in the season which led to a .350 average at the all-star break. Jeter, who led the organization in batting, finished among the top four in runs, hits, triples and batting in the International League, and was a league all-star. Defensively, the 21-year-old made 29 errors, but has great range and a strong arm. Jeter has also hit nearly .400 the last two seasons with runners in scoring position and his uppercut swing could result in more home runs as he physically matures.

NEW YORK YANKEES: TOP PROSPECTS

MATT LUKE

Bats: L Throws: L Opening Day Age: 25
Ht: 6-5 Wt: 225 Born: 2/26/1971
Position: OF Drafted: 1992 #6 NYA

YR TEAM	LG/CLASS	G	AB	R	H	2B	3B	HR	RBI	SB	BA	OBA
93 Greensboro	SAL/A	135	549	83	157	37	5	21	91	11	.286	.346
94 Tampa	FSL/A	57	222	52	68	11	2	16	42	4	.306	.385
94 Albany	EAST/AA	63	236	34	67	11	2	8	40	6	.284	.363
95 Columbus	INT/AAA	23	77	11	23	4	1	3	12	1	.299	.325
Norwich	EAST/AA	93	365	48	95	17	5	8	53	5	.260	.299

Like DelVechhio, Luke's best tool is his bat, one that has produced a .277 average, 91 doubles and 58 homers in four years of pro ball. The 24-year-old has a sweet power stroke and has not had a problem against lefthanders despite a long swing. However, at 6-5, 225 pounds, he does not cover a lot of ground in left field nor throw well, although he recorded 12 outfield assists in just 93 games for Norwich.

RAMIRO MENDOZA

Bats: R Throws: R Opening Day Age: 24
Ht: 6-2 Wt: 154 Born: 6/15/1972
Position: P Drafted: NDFA 11-13-91 NYA

YR TEAM	LG/CLASS	G	GS	GF	SV	W	L	ERA	IP	H	HR	BB	SO	O/BA
93 Yankees	GULF/R	15	9	3	1	4	5	2.79	67.2	59	3	7	61	.224
93 Greensboro	SAL/A	2	0	1	0	0	1	2.45	3.2	3	0	5	3	.231
94 Tampa	FSL/A	22	21	1	0	12	6	3.01	134.1	133	7	35	110	.258
95 Columbus	INT/AAA	2	2	0	0	1	0	2.57	14	10	0	2	13	.208
Norwich	EAST/AA	19	19	0	0	5	6	3.21	89	87	4	33	68	.254

The 23-year-old has a sharp curveball that he uses to complement an average fastball. On a pitch count early in the season, Mendoza didn't work seven innings until late July. He allowed only seven earned runs in his last six starts at Norwich then had two strong outings at Triple-A.

JIM MUSSELWHITE

Bats: R Throws: R Opening Day Age: 24
Ht: 6-1 Wt: 190 Born: 10/25/1971
Position: P Drafted: 1993 #5 Yankees

YR TEAM	LG/CLASS	G	GS	GF	SV	W	L	ERA	IP	H	HR	BB	SO	O/BA
93 Oneonta	NYP/A	5	4	0	0	1	1	2.25	20.0	15	0	8	18	.203
93 Greensboro	SAL/A	11	10	1	0	5	3	2.79	67.2	60	4	24	60	.236
94 Tampa	FSL/A	17	17	0	0	9	6	3.43	107.2	87	8	23	106	.218
94 Albany	EAST/AA	5	5	0	0	2	1	1.21	29.2	28	0	5	31	.257
95 Norwich	EAST/AA	24	24	0	0	5	9	4.58	131	136	11	34	96	.264

Poise, command and an effective curve and changeup have helped Musselwhite overcome an average fastball, but he struggled badly in 1995. Coming off an impressive '94 campaign, a twisted ankle and shoulder problem bothered him as he won just one game after May 17, had an ERA approaching six and lasted less than five innings in eight of his last 13.

JORGE POSADA

Bats: S Throws: R Opening Day Age: 25
Ht: 6-0 Wt: 167 Born: 8/17/1971
Position: C Drafted: 1990 #24 Yankees

YR TEAM	LG/CLASS	G	AB	R	H	2B	3B	HR	RBI	SB	BA	OBA
93 Pr William	CARO/A	118	410	71	106	27	2	17	61	17	.259	.366
93 Albany	EAST/AA	7	25	3	7	0	0	0	0	0	.280	.333
94 Columbus	INT/AAA	92	313	46	75	13	3	11	48	5	.240	.308
95 Columbus	INT/AAA	108	368	60	94	32	5	8	51	4	.255	.350
New York	AL/MAJ	1	0	0	0	0	0	0	0	0	.000	.000

Posada is a decent hitter from both sides of the plate who is better known for his strong throwing arm and above-average catching skills. The former second basemen has spent the last two seasons at Triple-A after skipping over Double-A.

RAY RICKEN

Bats: R Throws: R Opening Day Age: 23
Ht: 6-5 Wt: 225 Born: 8/11/1973
Position: P Drafted: 1994 #5 Yankees

YR TEAM	LG/CLASS	G	GS	GF	SV	W	L	ERA	IP	H	HR	BB	SO	O/BA
94 Oneonta	NYP/A	10	10	0	0	2	3	3.58	50.1	45	1	17	55	.245
94 Greensboro	SAL/A	5	5	0	0	1	2	4.68	25.0	27	1	12	19	.281
95 Norwich	EAST/AA	8	8	0	0	4	2	2.72	53	44	2	24	43	.232
Tampa	FSL/A	11	11	0	0	3	4	2.15	75	47	3	27	58	.181
Greensboro	SAL/A	10	10	0	0	3	2	2.23	64	42	2	16	77	.185

This 22-year-old was the biggest surprise in the Yankees organization last year. He was outstanding at three levels, tying for second in the minor leagues in strikeouts and finishing fourth among all minor league starters in average against (.196). The University of Michigan product is a power pitcher with a strong build, an upper-80's fastball, a slider, and an effective change. He also showed improved command and an ability to pitch deep into games, lasting at least six innings in 24 of 29 starts. He allowed two runs or less 20 times.

RUBEN RIVERA

Bats: R Throws: R Opening Day Age: 22
Ht: 6-3 Wt: 190 Born: 11/14/1973
Position: CF Drafted: NDFA 11-21-90 NYA

YR TEAM	LG/CLASS	G	AB	R	H	2B	3B	HR	RBI	SB	BA	OBA
93 Oneonta	NYP/A	55	199	45	55	7	6	13	47	12	.276	.385
94 Greensboro	SAL/A	105	400	83	115	24	3	28	81	36	.288	.372
94 Tampa	FSL/A	34	134	18	35	4	3	5	20	12	.261	.308
95 Columbus	INT/AAA	48	174	37	47	8	2	15	35	6	.270	.373
Norwich	EAST/AA	71	256	49	75	16	8	9	39	16	.293	.402
New York	AL/MAJ	5	1	0	0	0	0	0	0	0	.000	.000

Learning how to handle breaking balls is the only obstacle blocking Rivera from being an annual member of the "30–30" club at the major league level. The 21-year-old Panamanian is a true "five-tool" talent and only the strike and a slow start prevented him from reaching "30–30" for the second season in a row. Rivera had just one homer in April, didn't steal a base until May 9 and had the misfortune of spending half a season in spacious Norwich. Although he fanned 139 times, the 6-foot-3 slugger still belted 15 homers in 174 Triple-A at-bats, led Columbus and the organization in home runs and slugged .553 for the season, 12th best in the minor leagues. Rivera, selected to Howe Sportsdata's All-Minor League team, has tremendous range in center field and an arm strong enough for right field.

NEW YORK YANKEES: OTHERS TO WATCH

CHRIS ASHBY Bats: R Throws: R Ht: 6-3 Wt: 185
Born: 12/15/1974 Drafted: 1992 #26 NYA Position: C

YR TEAM	LG/CLASS	G	AB	R	H	2B	3B	HR	RBI	SB	BA	OBA
95 Greensboro	SAL/A	88	288	45	79	23	1	9	45	3	.274	.409

Good hitter with sharp eye and some pop, Ashby missed two months with a broken hand.

JAY BEVERLIN Bats: L Throws: R Ht: 6-5 Wt: 230
Born: 11/27/1973 Drafted: 1994 #4 OAK Position: P

YR TEAM	LG/CLASS	G	GS	GF	SV	W	L	ERA	IP	H	HR	BB	SO	O/BA
95 W Michigan	MID/A	22	14	1	0	3	9	4.04	89.0	76	4	40	84	.225
95 Greensboro	SAL/A	7	7	0	0	2	4	2.65	51.0	49	1	6	31	.255

Acquired from the A's in the Ruben Sierra deal, Beverlin throws 90 mph and keeps batters off balance.

BRIAN BUCHANAN Bats: R Throws: R Ht: 6-4 Wt: 220
Born: 7/21/1973 Drafted: 1994 #1 NYA Position: 1B

YR TEAM	LG/CLASS	G	AB	R	H	2B	3B	HR	RBI	SB	BA	OBA
95 Greensboro	SAL/A	23	96	19	29	3	0	3	12	7	.302	.368

Buchanan was off to a great start in '95, but a severely broken ankle ended his season early and could be career-threatening.

MIKE BUDDIE Bats: R Throws: R Ht: 6-3 Wt: 210
Born: 12/12/1970 Drafted: 1992 #2 NYA Position: P

YR TEAM	LG/CLASS	G	GS	GF	SV	W	L	ERA	IP	H	HR	BB	SO	O/BA
95 Norwich	EAST/AA	29	27	1	1	10	12	4.81	149.2	155	4	81	106	.268

Using a slider and changeup, Buddie keeps the ball on the ground, but was very inconsistent last year and lacks command.

CHRIS CORN Bats: R Throws: R Ht: 6-2 Wt: 170
Born: 10/4/1971 Drafted: 1994 #21 NYA Position: P

YR TEAM	LG/CLASS	G	GS	GF	SV	W	L	ERA	IP	H	HR	BB	SO	O/BA
95 Tampa	FSL/A	4	0	1	0	0	1	3.18	5.2	3	0	3	9	.150
95 Greensboro	SAL/A	49	0	39	24	8	7	1.76	82.0	54	3	22	101	.186

Not overpowering, Corn was among minor league leaders in average against (.183) and SO/9 IP (11.3).

ANDY CROGHAN Bats: R Throws: R Ht: 6-5 Wt: 205
Born: 10/26/1969 Drafted: 1991 #16 NYA Position: P

YR TEAM	LG/CLASS	G	GS	GF	SV	W	L	ERA	IP	H	HR	BB	SO	O/BA
95 Columbus	INT/AAA	20	0	13	4	1	1	3.60	25.0	21	1	22	22	.233

Arm injuries and lack of command stunted the growth of this hard thrower who had an excellent '94 campaign.

CMIKE DEJEAN Bats: R Throws: R Ht: 6-2 Wt: 205
Born: 9/28/1970 Drafted: 1992 #22 NYA Position: P

YR TEAM	LG/CLASS	G	GS	GF	SV	W	L	ERA	IP	H	HR	BB	SO	O/BA
95 Norwich	EAST/AA	59	0	40	20	5	5	2.99	78.1	58	5	34	57	.208

Second in the Eastern League in saves, DeJean must keep ball down to be successful.

DAN DONATO Bats: L Throws: R Ht: 6-1 Wt: 205
Born: 11/15/1972 Drafted: NDFA 4-3-95 NYA Position: 3B

YR TEAM	LG/CLASS	G	AB	R	H	2B	3B	HR	RBI	SB	BA	OBA
95 Tampa	FSL/A	3	8	1	2	0	0	1	1	0	.250	.333
95 Greensboro	SAL/A	108	387	55	123	30	1	7	69	7	.318	.381

Former Boston University star hockey player was among league leaders in batting despite a late start in his first pro season.

RICKY LEDEE Bats: L Throws: L Ht: 6-2 Wt: 160
Born: 11/22/1973 Drafted: 1990 #16 NYA Position: OF

YR TEAM	LG/CLASS	G	AB	R	H	2B	3B	HR	RBI	SB	BA	OBA
95 Tampa	FSL/A	0	0	0	0	0	0	0	0	0	.000	.000
95 Greensboro	SAL/A	89	335	65	90	16	6	14	49	10	.269	.368

A talented athlete who can hit, run and throw, LeDee started the season on the disabled list.

RAFAEL MEDINA Bats: R Throws: R Ht: 6-3 Wt: 194
Born: 2/15/1975 Drafted: NDFA 9-6-92 NYA Position: P

YR TEAM	LG/CLASS	G	GS	GF	SV	W	L	ERA	IP	H	HR	BB	SO	O/BA
95 Tampa	FSL/A	6	6	0	0	2	2	2.37	30.1	29	0	12	25	.246
95 Greensboro	SAL/A	19	19	0	0	4	4	4.01	98.2	86	8	38	108	.233

The 20-year-old has a big-league arm and is starting to show improved command.

DANNY RIOS Bats: R Throws: R Ht: 6-2 Wt: 208
Born: 11/11/1972 Drafted: NDFA 6-7-93 NYA Position: P

YR TEAM	LG/CLASS	G	GS	GF	SV	W	L	ERA	IP	H	HR	BB	SO	O/BA
95 Tampa	FSL/A	57	0	52	24	0	4	2.00	67.1	67	1	20	72	.257

The beneficiary of Resz' injury, Rios tied for the org lead in saves and fanned better than a batter per inning using a 90-mph fastball.

JASON ROBERTSON Bats: L Throws: L Ht: 6-2 Wt: 200
Born: 3/24/1971 Drafted: 1989 #2 NYA Position: OF

YR TEAM	LG/CLASS	G	AB	R	H	2B	3B	HR	RBI	SB	BA	OBA
95 Norwich	EAST/AA	117	456	60	126	29	10	6	54	19	.276	.334

The highly-regarded Robertson hit for the first time in three years of Double-A the second half of '95.

BRETT SCHLOMANN Bats: R Throws: R Ht: 6-1 Wt: 185
Born: 7/31/1974 Drafted: 1993 #40 NYA Position: P

YR TEAM	LG/CLASS	G	GS	GF	SV	W	L	ERA	IP	H	HR	BB	SO	O/BA
95 Tampa	FSL/A	2	2	0	0	2	0	1.64	11.0	10	2	0	5	.227
95 Greensboro	SAL/A	25	25	0	0	10	7	3.90	147.2	144	10	54	140	.251

Had success with a 90-mph fastball and a decent curve in 1995.

SHANE SPENCER Bats: R Throws: R Ht: 5-11 Wt: 182
Born: 2/20/1972 Drafted: 1990 #28 NYA Position: OF

YR TEAM	LG/CLASS	G	AB	R	H	2B	3B	HR	RBI	SB	BA	OBA
95 Tampa	FSL/A	134	500	87	150	31	3	16	88	14	.300	.382

Had a big power year in his repeat season with Tampa, but he's adequate at best in the outfield.

BRIEN TAYLOR Bats: L Throws: L Ht: 6-4 Wt: 215
Born: 12/26/1971 Drafted: 1991 #1 NYA Position: P

YR TEAM	LG/CLASS	G	GS	GF	SV	W	L	ERA	IP	H	HR	BB	SO	O/BA
95 Yankees	GULF/R	11	11	0	0	2	5	6.08	40.0	29	1	54	38	.218

Taylor surfaced in the Gulf Coast League and was throwing in the upper-80's, but had little control.

OAKLAND ATHLETICS

GERONIMO BERROA

Positions: DH/OF
Bats: R **Throws:** R
Ht: 6'0" **Wt:** 165
Opening Day Age: 31
Born: 3/18/1965
Drafted: TOR 9/4/83
ML Seasons: 6

SCOUTING REPORT
Geronimo has spent time as a designated hitter but isn't that bad in the outfield. A weak, though very accurate, arm, and average range and hands make him a fair defensive player, and he hustles after what comes his way. Luckily, he can hit well enough to survive. Berroa is a straightaway hitter with plus power, and a surprisingly good contact hitter who is not afraid to take a walk. He still has trouble with off-speed stuff, but he feasts on fastballs. Bunting is not in his vocabulary, although Geronimo will steal. He has average major-league speed.

HOW HE PERFORMED IN '95
Berroa's career is a beautiful illustration of the wealth of talent available at Triple-A for those who care to look for it. Now a career .279 hitter, Geronimo led the '95 Athletics in games, runs and hits, ranking second in homers only to Mark McGwire's monster season.

Despite a fine minor-league hitting pedigree, Berroa's resume looks like a failed final exam for a travel agent: Toronto, Atlanta, Seattle, Cleveland, Cincinnati, Florida, Oakland. There are Rule V drafts, outright releases, and free-agent signings on his record, and almost all of these changes have come in the last seven years!

After smacking the ball around after finally getting his shot with the desperate '94 Athletics, he even earned an everyday position last season, starting 45 of Oakland's final 57 games in right field. Although he made four errors and fielded just .971, Geronimo did tie for the team lead with five assists. By the end of the year, the hard-working Berroa looked like he belonged out there.

Fairly consistent, he hit .270 before the break and .286 after, with a career-high 17 game hitting streak. He reversed his former trend, hitting better against righties than lefties in '95.

WHAT TO EXPECT IN '96
He will be 31 on Opening Day, but doesn't look past his prime as a hitter. Geronimo should be comfortably ensconced in the middle of the Oakland batting order this season. If he, Mark McGwire and Danny Tartabull stay healthy, the homers they will hit should more than compensate for the numerous double plays they will doubtless hit into. Berroa is likely to spend the year in right field, but could move back to DH if Tartabull can't play.

Overall Statistics

	G	AB	R	H	2B	3B	HR	RBI	SB	CS	BB	SO	BA	OBA
95 OAK	141	546	87	152	22	3	22	88	7	4	63	98	.278	.351
Career	352	1075	154	300	46	5	37	162	14	8	116	201	.279	.348

1995 Situational Statistics

	AB	HR	RBI	BA	OBA	SLG		AB	HR	RBI	BA	OBA	SLG
Home	264	10	36	.288	.370	.439	LHP	152	3	17	.237	.326	.382
Road	282	12	52	.270	.332	.461	RHP	394	19	71	.294	.361	.477
Apr-Jun	221	11	40	.267	.365	.448	ScPos	139	3	53	.259	.339	.388
Jul-Oct	325	11	48	.286	.340	.452	Clutch	86	2	13	.256	.343	.360

How He Compares to Other Batters

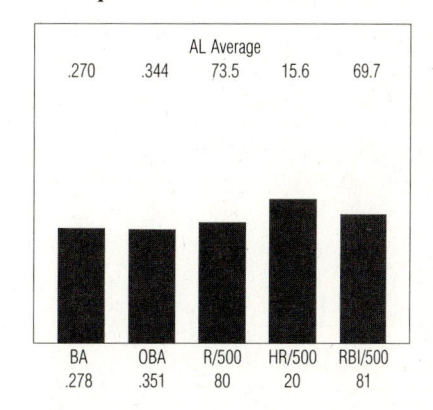

AL Average: BA .270, OBA .344, R/500 73.5, HR/500 15.6, RBI/500 69.7

BA .278   OBA .351   R/500 80   HR/500 20   RBI/500 81

Where He Hits the Ball

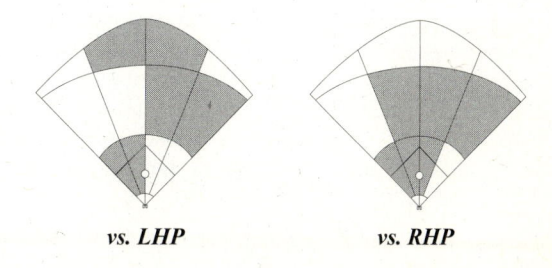

vs. LHP   vs. RHP

THE SCOUTING REPORT: 1996

OAKLAND ATHLETICS

MIKE BORDICK

Positions: SS//DH
Bats: R **Throws:** R
Ht: 5'11" **Wt:** 170
Opening Day Age: 30
Born: 7/21/1965
Drafted: OAK 7/10/86
ML Seasons: 6

SCOUTING REPORT

Mike is a good, solid contact hitter who has no power. He hates to be jammed; Bordick will step into high pitches out over the plate and take the ball the other way. He will occasionally bunt for hits and is quite effective at laying down the sacrifice. Although Mike has a bit below-average speed, he is a decent basestealer.

A very good major-league shortstop, Bordick has good hands and plus range with a very accurate arm. He is good around the bag, and Mike will dive effectively for balls in the hole and behind second.

HOW HE PERFORMED IN '95

At the plate, it was a typical year for the undrafted product of the University of Maine. He came close to his career norms in almost every offensive category—except in the power department.

Bordick hit half of his career 16 homers last year, coming on strong after the All-Star break and showing unexpected power against righthanders. Although he has been a reverse-platoon hitter, Mike was surprisingly poor against lefthanders in '95. After slumping in July (.206), he hit .286 for the remainder of the season and finished with the second highest average of his career. He made his first-ever visit to the disabled list in '95, missing 18 days in May with a sprained right ankle, but came back to start 113 of the remaining 116 games.

Mike played the entire season exclusively at shortstop, a real rarity for anyone working for Tony LaRussa's Institute for Cross-Training. Bordick was leading the league in fielding percentage until the final week, when four errors (he made ten total) dropped him to fourth in the AL with a .983 mark.

WHAT TO EXPECT IN '96

He and Brent Gates form a solid keystone combination, and both should remain productive for Oakland for several more years, presuming they don't price themselves out of Oakland's fiscally-conscious reach. Bordick will find himself to be a valuable commodity on the open market when he becomes a free agency in a year or two, and it will be hard for Oakland to keep him if money is the primary factor at that time. Maybe he'll go to St. Louis, like most of his '95 teammates.

Overall Statistics

	G	AB	R	H	2B	3B	HR	RBI	SB	CS	BB	SO	BA	OBA
95 OAK	126	428	46	113	13	0	8	44	11	3	35	48	.264	.325
Career	668	2118	227	556	76	11	16	198	43	25	188	250	.263	.329

1995 Situational Statistics

	AB	HR	RBI	BA	OBA	SLG		AB	HR	RBI	BA	OBA	SLG
Home	204	2	17	.270	.329	.324	LHP	109	2	9	.239	.298	.303
Road	224	6	27	.259	.321	.375	RHP	319	6	35	.273	.334	.367
Apr-Jun	149	2	13	.275	.349	.342	ScPos	97	1	34	.247	.309	.330
Jul-Oct	279	6	31	.258	.311	.355	Clutch	71	1	5	.282	.346	.352

How He Compares to Other Batters

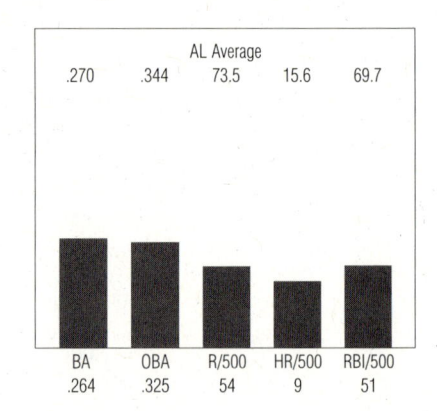

AL Average: .270 | .344 | 73.5 | 15.6 | 69.7

BA	OBA	R/500	HR/500	RBI/500
.264	.325	54	9	51

Where He Hits the Ball

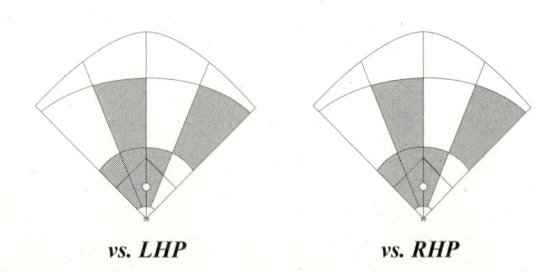

vs. LHP vs. RHP

OAKLAND ATHLETICS

SCOTT BROSIUS

Positions: 3B/OF/1B//2B/SS/DH
Bats: R **Throws:** R
Ht: 6'1" **Wt:** 185
Opening Day Age: 29
Born: 8/15/1966
Drafted: OAK87 19/511
ML Seasons: 5

SCOUTING REPORT

The versatile Brosius plays several infield and outfield positions with an average-strength but very accurate throwing arm, soft hands, and good-to-awful range, depending on where he's playing.

A fastball hitter who likes to cut at pitches low and over the plate, Scott has an uppercut swing with some power. He has tried to do too much at times, but learned in '95 how to stay within himself. He has trouble with breaking balls and off-speed stuff but has improved his plate discipline. A minus runner who rarely steals bases, Brosius will bunt, though not effectively.

HOW HE PERFORMED IN '95

At 29, Scott has spent parts of five seasons in Oakland. He became the Man Without a Position, or, rather, the Man for All Positions, in '95, starting at six different positions and playing everywhere but pitcher and catcher.

"Streaky" is an apt description of his season. Brosius hit .297 in May, but went on a 5-for-49 streak in June to fall to .218. He then had an exceptional August, batting .330 with 10 home runs and 23 RBI, before following up with an 0-for-30 to end the year. Scott is still susceptible to the breaking pitch, and gets himself out far too often. Unlike many of his mates, Brosius hit well at home in '95.

In the field, he was prone to slumps and inconsistency, as befits someone who didn't know where he'd be playing from one game to the next. At third base, he showed plus range but made 11 errors, fielding a poor .918; he showed poor range in the outfield and threw out just two runners in 49 games. It would be better for him defensively to settle down somewhere.

WHAT TO EXPECT IN '96

His .263 average of last season rated 25 points above his prior career average, and his versatility and improvement suggests Brosius should have a job in '96—the question is where. It appears that Scott is shut out at third, first, or center, so with Rickey Henderson's departure, Brosius will probably play most of the season in left field. New manager Art Howe isn't likely to ask Scott to shift around as much this year as he did last season.

Overall Statistics

	G	AB	R	H	2B	3B	HR	RBI	SB	CS	BB	SO	BA	OBA
95 OAK	123	388	69	102	19	2	17	46	4	2	41	67	.263	.342
Career	363	1080	148	267	50	4	43	137	18	9	85	185	.247	.306

1995 Situational Statistics

	AB	HR	RBI	BA	OBA	SLG		AB	HR	RBI	BA	OBA	SLG
Home	177	12	25	.271	.337	.514	LHP	124	3	8	.234	.324	.371
Road	211	5	21	.256	.347	.403	RHP	264	14	38	.277	.351	.492
Apr-Jun	177	5	14	.249	.348	.401	ScPos	97	3	29	.216	.316	.361
Jul-Oct	211	12	32	.275	.338	.498	Clutch	55	0	2	.218	.338	.255

How He Compares to Other Batters

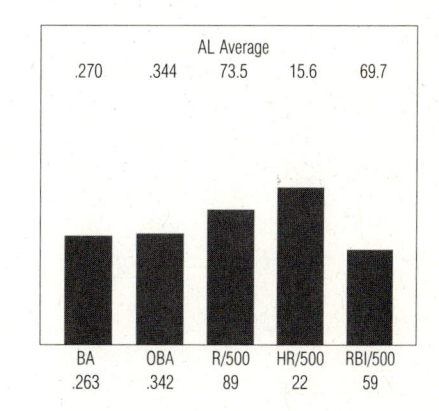

	BA	OBA	R/500	HR/500	RBI/500
AL Average	.270	.344	73.5	15.6	69.7
	.263	.342	89	22	59

Where He Hits the Ball

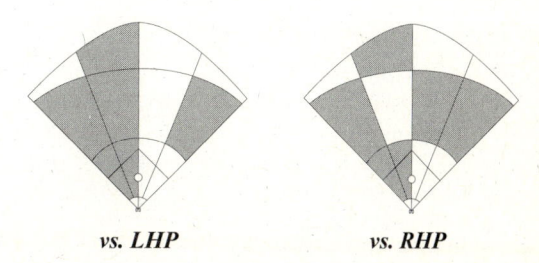

vs. LHP   vs. RHP

THE SCOUTING REPORT: 1996

OAKLAND ATHLETICS

DENNIS ECKERSLEY

Position: RP
Bats: R **Throws:** R
Ht: 6'2" **Wt:** 190
Opening Day Age: 41
Born: 10/3/1954
Drafted: CLE72 3/50
ML Seasons: 21

SCOUTING REPORT

The tall, lean veteran has a deceptive delivery, coming in low three-quarter to sidearm with a long, slender arm with whip-like action. Dennis' fastball now is a cut below average. However, he will bore it into righties and sink it down and away from lefties. A plus slider is Eckersley's best pitch, and he can spot it right on the black when he needs to—and umpires help him by stretching the plate at times.

He's never really needed a change-up; when you don't walk anyone, two good pitches are enough. Although he usually holds runners well, nine stole against Dennis in ten tries during '95. He's an outstanding fielder; Eckersley's error on May 7 was his first since April, 1987. Aggressive and intense, Eck has still has mental makeup of a "go-to" guy and hasn't lost any of his drive despite diminishing skills.

HOW HE PERFORMED IN '95

A huge and growing platoon differential was Dennis' nemesis last year, as lefties have hit .311 when facing him since 1992, while righties have batted only .180 over the past four years. This is common for righthanders with a subpar fastball and a low motion; when Eck can't place the slider precisely where he wants, lefthanders feast on his pitches.

His 4.83 ERA in '95 was a run-and-a-half above his career total and his nine blown saves led the AL in that dubious category, although only one of 19 inherited runners scored off him. His career strikeout to walk ratio of 3.19-to-1 is the third-best in major-league history. He reached career save #300 last May 24, in his 499th relief appearance—162 games sooner than Bruce Sutter had.

WHAT TO EXPECT IN '96

Dennis' "off" year had him talking retirement at the end of the season, but he is considering following Tony LaRussa to St. Louis. After pitching at a level from 1988-92 unparalleled by any other reliever in history, Eckersley has had three straight years of diminishing effectiveness. Nevertheless, he is still a valuable pitcher, and fans would surely enjoy seeing him come back at 41 for another tour of duty. Along with his manager Tony LaRussa, Eck is the pitcher who revolutionized the closer's role—long after he's gone, people will remember how special he was.

Overall Statistics

	G	GS	GF	SV	W	L	ERA	IP	H	R	ER	HR	BB	SO
95 OAK	52	0	48	29	4	6	4.83	50.1	53	29	27	5	11	40
Career	901	361	464	323	192	159	3.48	3133.0	2916	1311	1212	324	716	2285

1995 Situational Statistics

	W	L	ERA	SV	IP	BB	SO		AB	HR	RBI	BA	OBA	SLG
Home	3	3	5.68	18	25.1	7	21	LHB	122	3	21	.344	.383	.500
Road	1	3	3.96	11	25.0	4	19	RHB	75	2	7	.147	.179	.253
Apr-Jun	1	2	3.12	16	26.0	3	17	ScPos	52	2	23	.288	.350	.500
Jul-Oct	3	4	6.66	13	24.1	8	23	Clutch	121	5	24	.298	.331	.479

How He Compares to Other Pitchers

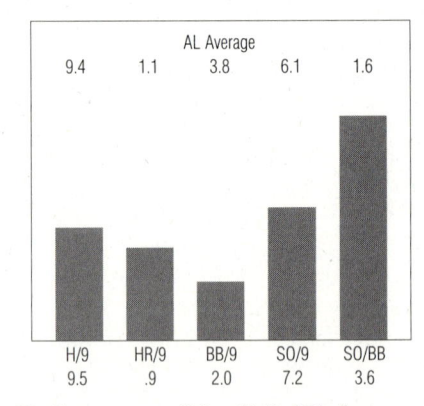

AL Average: H/9 9.4, HR/9 1.1, BB/9 3.8, SO/9 6.1, SO/BB 1.6
Eckersley: H/9 9.5, HR/9 .9, BB/9 2.0, SO/9 7.2, SO/BB 3.6

How He Compares to Other Relief Pitchers

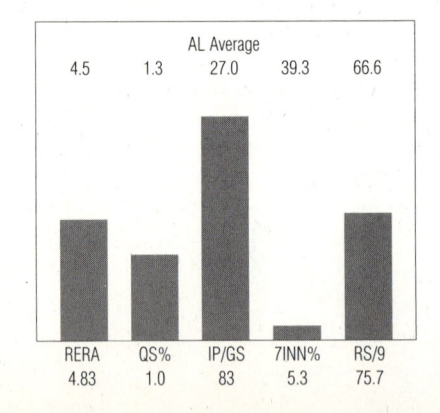

AL Average: RERA 4.5, QS% 1.3, IP/GS 27.0, 7INN% 39.3, RS/9 66.6
Eckersley: RERA 4.83, QS% 1.0, IP/GS 83, 7INN% 5.3, RS/9 75.7

OAKLAND ATHLETICS

BRENT GATES

Positions: 2B//DH/1B
Bats: B **Throws:** R
Ht: 6'1" **Wt:** 180
Opening Day Age: 26
Born: 3/14/1970
Drafted: OAK91 1/26
ML Seasons: 3

SCOUTING REPORT
An improved and now-average defender, Brent has average hands, somewhat above-average range, and an average arm with ordinary accuracy at the keystone position.

Gates is a switch-hitting, spray hitter with a slow bat and little power; he likes pitches up and out over the plate from both sides—the Athletics have too many hitters like this already. After hitting .290 in his rookie season of 1993, he has not adjusted well as pitchers learned that he can't handle good hard stuff. Never fast, his speed is now minus.

HOW HE PERFORMED IN '95
He started the year as a reserve but took over at second base when Mike Bordick went down May 8, eventually starting 128 games there. In only his third season, he is already fourth all-time on the Oakland list of games played at second base with 334—remember Dick Green? Fourth among AL second basemen with a .982 fielding average, his glove kept him in the lineup when his bat deserted him, as it did for much of the season.

Gates has clearly been a disappointment at a hitter: a career .285 hitter coming into the season, he was expected to improve to a solid .300 batsman with some line-drive power. Yet in another big offensive season around baseball, Brent slid to .254 and his .308 OBA was fourth worst among AL regular players. Even worse, he rescued his season with a late 17-game hitting streak during a 41-game stretch where he hit .337—he was hitting a lowly .226 coming into August. The mark of a player and a team adrift: Gates hit in every spot in the batting order but cleanup.

WHAT TO EXPECT IN '96
Gates, Bordick and Steinbach will keep the A's strong up the middle in '96, and Jose Herrera will likely complete that strong defensive set in center field in '96. The first-round pick in the June, 1991, draft could be a solid, occasionally All-Star-caliber second baseman for years to come if he regains his early form as a hitter. If not, his defense will keep him around for awhile, but it's not good enough to carry his bat forever. Ironically, his reputation a couple of years ago was that of a good-hitting, weak-fielding player.

Overall Statistics

	G	AB	R	H	2B	3B	HR	RBI	SB	CS	BB	SO	BA	OBA
95 OAK	136	524	60	133	24	4	5	56	3	3	46	84	.254	.308
Career	339	1292	153	354	64	7	14	149	13	6	123	191	.274	.334

1995 Situational Statistics

	AB	HR	RBI	BA	OBA	SLG		AB	HR	RBI	BA	OBA	SLG
Home	259	3	20	.278	.334	.363	LHP	134	2	13	.269	.322	.396
Road	265	2	36	.230	.282	.325	RHP	390	3	43	.249	.303	.326
Apr-Jun	200	2	21	.230	.308	.320	ScPos	119	1	50	.286	.342	.387
Jul-Oct	324	3	35	.269	.308	.358	Clutch	84	2	15	.214	.239	.321

How He Compares to Other Batters

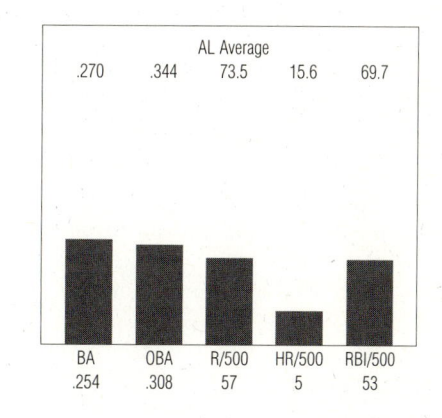

AL Average: .270 .344 73.5 15.6 69.7

	BA	OBA	R/500	HR/500	RBI/500
	.254	.308	57	5	53

Where He Hits the Ball

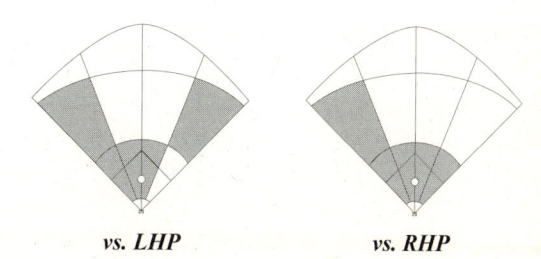

vs. LHP   vs. RHP

THE SCOUTING REPORT: 1996

OAKLAND ATHLETICS

RICKEY HENDERSON

Positions: OF/DH
Bats: R **Throws:** L
Ht: 5'10" **Wt:** 195
Opening Day Age: 37
Born: 12/25/1958
Drafted: OAK76 4/96
ML Seasons: 17

SCOUTING REPORT

Slowing down to mortal speed, he's still a good baserunner and basestealer but can't outrun the ball any more. At bat, Henderson has lost most of his mid-career over-the-fence power but lashed out plenty of doubles. He retains his excellent plate discipline and famously small strike zone—due to his deep crouch—as well as his famously argumentative demeanor toward marginal called strikes. He is a high fastball hitter to all fields who likes the ball out over the plate.

Possessing outstanding range in left field for much of his career, he's the only non-centerfielder in the top ten lifetime in chances in the AL. Rickey's arm has always been weak but accurate. His hands are average but he displayed subpar range in '95.

HOW HE PERFORMED IN '95

Rickey hit .300 for the sixth time in his career; his average was 12 points above his career mark. He was one of the top clutch hitters in baseball, leading the majors with a .419 mark with runners in scoring position. His slugging and on-base averages were right about his career norms, which is a positive at his age.

Henderson's game has not changed that much with age: he's just not as good as he used to be. He scored only 67 runs in 112 games in '95—an abnormally low rate for the best leadoff hitter in baseball history. This was partly due to the mediocre Oakland offense (eighth in the AL in runs), but it was also well below his rate of the previous season (66 runs in 87 games) and showed how he's slowed down.

WHAT TO EXPECT IN '96

Rickey turned 37 on Christmas Day as the A's let him go to free agency again. He is still a valuable contributor to a team that can deal with the periods when he is physically unable to play: his always tenuous bond with manager Tony LaRussa had totally evaporated by the end of the season, when he was actually benched even though healthy.

Hitting ahead of a good lineup, he could easily score 100 runs in '96 and help elevate the Padres into contention in the NL West. The move to San Diego was somewhat of a surprise, but the smaller, warmer park should help extend his career.

Overall Statistics

	G	AB	R	H	2B	3B	HR	RBI	SB	CS	BB	SO	BA	OBA
95 OAK	112	407	67	122	31	1	9	54	32	10	72	66	.300	.407
Career	2192	8063	1719	2338	395	57	235	858	1149	265	1550	1101	.290	.406

1995 Situational Statistics

	AB	HR	RBI	BA	OBA	SLG		AB	HR	RBI	BA	OBA	SLG
Home	208	3	25	.298	.403	.404	LHP	120	2	10	.233	.374	.325
Road	199	6	29	.302	.412	.492	RHP	287	7	44	.328	.422	.498
Apr-Jun	177	4	25	.266	.383	.401	ScPos	74	1	43	.419	.535	.541
Jul-Oct	230	5	29	.326	.426	.483	Clutch	56	2	9	.357	.479	.607

How He Compares to Other Batters

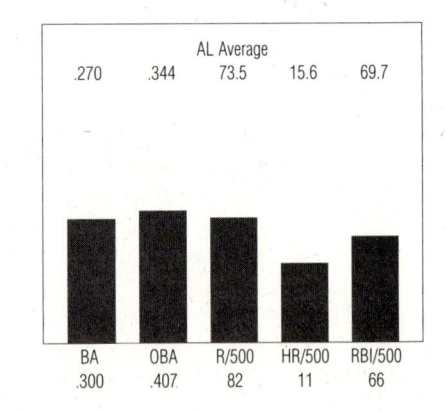

	BA	OBA	R/500	HR/500	RBI/500
AL Average	.270	.344	73.5	15.6	69.7
	.300	.407	82	11	66

Where He Hits the Ball

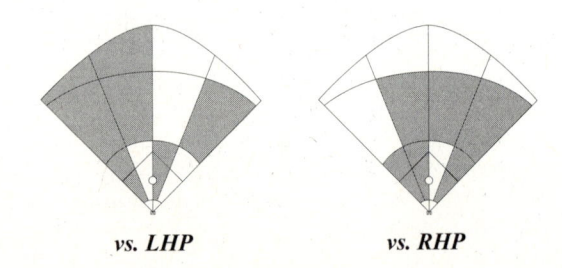

vs. LHP   vs. RHP

236   THE SCOUTING REPORT: 1996

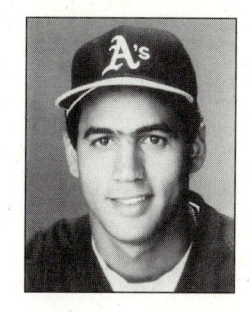

OAKLAND ATHLETICS

STAN JAVIER

Positions: OF//3B
Bats: B **Throws:** R
Ht: 6'0" **Wt:** 185
Opening Day Age: 32
Born: 1/9/1964
Drafted: SL 3/26/81
ML Seasons: 11

SCOUTING REPORT
Javier gets a good jump in center field, displaying plus range, soft hands, and a weak arm with average-plus accuracy. He plays the field a lot like Gold Glover Darren Lewis, who patrolled center for San Francisco until last July.

A good contact hitter with minus power who takes the ball to all fields, he's not patient at the plate and would be more valuable if he took more walks and got on base more often. He has trouble with off-speed stuff and, typical of most switch-hitters, is a low-ball hitter lefthanded and a high-ball hitter from the right side. While his speed is now approaching average, Stan remains an excellent basestealer.

HOW HE PERFORMED IN '95
After laboring in relative obscurity for many years as a fourth or fifth outfielder in New York, Oakland, Los Angeles, Philadelphia, and California, Javier finally won a regular job with the Athletics in 1994, setting career highs in most batting categories. He then broke most of those career marks in 1995 while posting a perfect season in the field, setting an AL record for most errorless chances by an outfielder with 335.

Javier started the season slowly but closed with a .353 burst with 35 runs batted in in his final 57 games to finish 23 points above his previous career average. His slugging average was 46 points above his previous career average. He hit better on the road than at home in 1994-95, but changing sides of the bay won't help much.

WHAT TO EXPECT IN '96
Javier suffered the same fate as many of his '95 Oakland teammates: two good years in a row made him too expensive for the cost-conscious operation new manager Art Howe will oversee. The Athletics allowed Stan to become a free agent after last season, and he only needed to make a local phone call to find work in San Francisco.

He will bring to Candlestick similar offensive skills as Deion Sanders along with the defensive skills of Darren Lewis. Only 32—he seems older because he made his major-league debut at age 20 in 1984—he should have several seasons ahead of him in the same mold as the last two.

Overall Statistics

	G	AB	R	H	2B	3B	HR	RBI	SB	CS	BB	SO	BA	OBA
95 OAK	130	442	81	123	20	2	8	56	36	5	49	63	.278	.353
Career	1089	2896	439	748	120	23	31	275	155	30	316	481	.258	.332

1995 Situational Statistics

	AB	HR	RBI	BA	OBA	SLG		AB	HR	RBI	BA	OBA	SLG
Home	202	3	25	.257	.342	.376	LHP	119	3	18	.303	.359	.471
Road	240	5	31	.296	.362	.396	RHP	323	5	38	.269	.351	.356
Apr-Jun	184	3	15	.261	.317	.332	ScPos	132	2	47	.280	.340	.356
Jul-Oct	258	5	41	.291	.377	.426	Clutch	77	2	11	.247	.298	.325

How He Compares to Other Batters

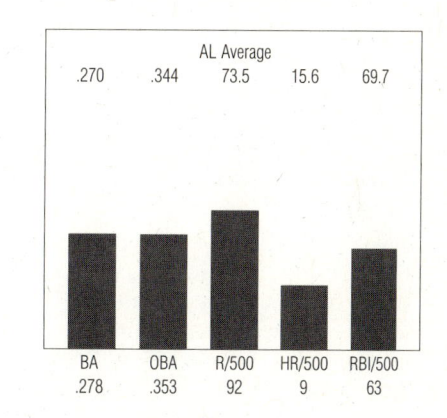

AL Average: .270 .344 73.5 15.6 69.7

BA	OBA	R/500	HR/500	RBI/500
.278	.353	92	9	63

Where He Hits the Ball

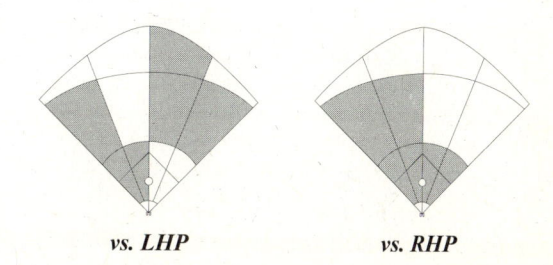

vs. LHP   vs. RHP

THE SCOUTING REPORT: 1996

OAKLAND ATHLETICS

MARK MCGWIRE

Positions: 1B/DH
Bats: R **Throws:** R
Ht: 6'5" **Wt:** 225
Opening Day Age: 32
Born: 10/1/1963
Drafted: OAK84 1/10
ML Seasons: 10

SCOUTING REPORT

McGwire hits out of a deep, uncomfortable-looking crouch with his hands close to his chest. When he decides to swing, he uncoils from the crouch, generating tremendous bat speed and power. He stands up on the plate, making him vulnerable to being drilled by pitchers without good control—and also by pitchers with good control off whom he has clobbered one of his titanic home runs. A low fastball hitter, he can also handle most breaking stuff.

Mark is a flyball hitter who hits into quite a few double plays because he's a slow righthanded batter who hits the ball extremely hard. Describing his running speed as slow is charitable, but you don't need a quick first step when you routinely hit the ball 400 feet.

Adequate hands and range with an accurate arm make him a decent defensive first sacker. He had a poor year defensively in '95: his 12 errors led AL first basemen, although he played just 91 games in the field, and his fielding average was a low .986.

HOW HE PERFORMED IN '95

Few major-league hitters have ever had a season like McGwire's '95. He played in just 111 games but hit 39 home runs in 317 at-bats: one homer per 8.1 at-bats. That is a new record, erasing Babe Ruth's mark of 54 home runs in 458 at-bats in 1920 (one per 8.5 at-bats).

His incredible power display could not chase away the injury jinx, however. Hit in the head by a David Cone pitch July 8, he missed five games. A bruised left foot put him on the DL July 18; he came back on August 2, but then promptly returned to the DL two days later with an aching back. After returning August 26, he finished the season on a tear with 11 homers in his last 18 games, passing Reggie Jackson for first place on the all-time Oakland home run list.

WHAT TO EXPECT IN '96

Only 32, it's obvious from '95 that he could still have monster seasons ahead of him. Little, if anything, else seems out of his reach—if he can just remain healthy. Oakland might have problems affording his salary but, since they have to sell tickets to somebody, they can't afford to let him go.

Overall Statistics

	G	AB	R	H	2B	3B	HR	RBI	SB	CS	BB	SO	BA	OBA
95 OAK	104	317	75	87	13	0	39	90	1	1	88	77	.274	.441
Career	1094	3659	621	921	150	5	277	747	7	8	673	833	.252	.369

1995 Situational Statistics

	AB	HR	RBI	BA	OBA	SLG		AB	HR	RBI	BA	OBA	SLG
Home	145	15	38	.248	.425	.586	LHP	79	14	28	.278	.478	.835
Road	172	24	52	.297	.454	.767	RHP	238	25	62	.273	.427	.634
Apr-Jun	191	22	55	.288	.444	.681	ScPos	69	9	45	.304	.500	.739
Jul-Oct	126	17	35	.254	.436	.690	Clutch	47	5	14	.255	.500	.596

How He Compares to Other Batters

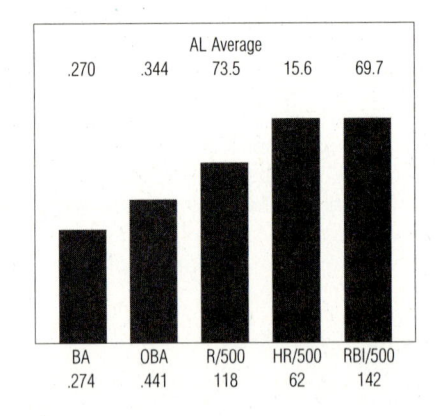

AL Average: BA .270, OBA .344, R/500 73.5, HR/500 15.6, RBI/500 69.7

McGwire: BA .274, OBA .441, R/500 118, HR/500 62, RBI/500 142

Where He Hits the Ball

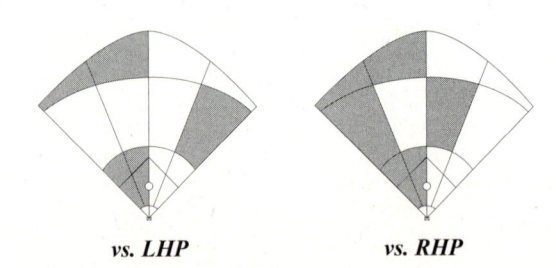

vs. LHP   vs. RHP

THE SCOUTING REPORT: 1996

OAKLAND ATHLETICS

STEVE ONTIVEROS

Position: SP
Bats: R **Throws:** R
Ht: 6'0" **Wt:** 180
Opening Day Age: 35
Born: 3/5/1961
Drafted: OAK82 1/54
ML Seasons: 9

SCOUTING REPORT
Using a compact, high three-quarter delivery, Steve has plus control and plenty of grit. Stamina and health have always been the problems for him. None of his deliveries is above-average: Ontiveros' fastball is slightly below-average, as are his overhand curve, slider, and splitter. However, Steve spots the ball and moves it around well, preying on hitters' impatience and keeping his pitches good and low.

He fields his position like a true professional despite a history of injuries. Although Ontiveros has an average move, he is hard to run on and pays attention to runners: just ten tried to steal with him on the mound in '95, and five were thrown out.

HOW HE PERFORMED IN '95
The 1994 American League ERA leader picked right up where he left off last season, racking up an 8-2 mark and 2.59 ERA through his first 11 starts, which earned him his first All-Star trip.

However, like clockwork, Steve again was felled by injury. Shortly before the All-Star break, he began to suffer from a stiff right forearm. Ultimately, the injury forced him onto the disabled list for five weeks, Ontiveros was just 1-4 with a 5.02 ERA over his final 11 starts. AL hitters clubbed him at a .330 clip after the midsummer hiatus.

The troubles Steve had with righthanders in '95 are unusually serious, but he has been a reverse-platoon performer for the last three years. Despite his injury and the resultant problems, he ranked second on the Athletics in starts and wins, and continued to be stingy with walks. Ontiveros takes full advantage of his spacious home park, as he pays for his occasional fat pitches high in the strike zone.

WHAT TO EXPECT IN '96
The successful but fragile Ontiveros has reached the end of the line in Oakland, as the Athletics allowed him to become a free agent immediately at the after the '95 season.

Injuries have severely limited a promising career, which consists of only 656 major-league innings. He is likely to take a pay cut to work in '96, which is appropriate given his injury history. Even with pitching hard to find, Ontiveros' medical report is so lengthy that it will be hard for him to get more than a one-year deal anywhere.

Overall Statistics

	G	GS	GF	SV	W	L	ERA	IP	H	R	ER	HR	BB	SO
95 OAK	22	22	0	0	9	6	4.37	129.2	144	75	63	12	38	77
Career	204	72	65	19	33	30	3.62	656.1	613	302	264	59	203	381

1995 Situational Statistics

	W	L	ERA	SV	IP	BB	SO		AB	HR	RBI	BA	OBA	SLG
Home	5	3	3.88	0	67.1	16	39	LHB	328	8	33	.262	.303	.399
Road	4	3	4.91	0	62.1	22	38	RHB	180	4	29	.322	.389	.467
Apr-Jun	8	2	2.65	0	78.0	17	49	ScPos	112	4	49	.277	.315	.464
Jul-Oct	1	4	6.97	0	51.2	21	28	Clutch	21	1	2	.286	.360	.429

How He Compares to Other Pitchers

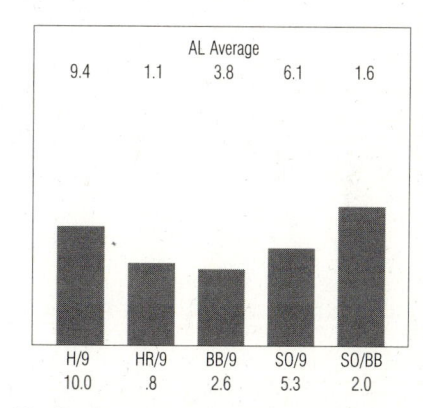

AL Average: H/9 9.4 | HR/9 1.1 | BB/9 3.8 | SO/9 6.1 | SO/BB 1.6
His values: H/9 10.0 | HR/9 .8 | BB/9 2.6 | SO/9 5.3 | SO/BB 2.0

How He Compares to Other Starting Pitchers

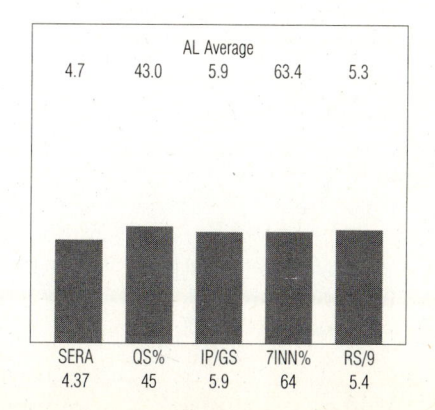

AL Average: SERA 4.7 | QS% 43.0 | IP/GS 5.9 | 7INN% 63.4 | RS/9 5.3
His values: SERA 4.37 | QS% 45 | IP/GS 5.9 | 7INN% 64 | RS/9 5.4

OAKLAND ATHLETICS

TERRY STEINBACH

Positions: C//1B
Bats: R **Throws:** R
Ht: 6'1" **Wt:** 195
Opening Day Age: 34
Born: 3/2/1962
Drafted: OAK83 9/215
ML Seasons: 10

SCOUTING REPORT
Steinbach has average power and a relatively quick bat. A first-ball hitter, he likes fastballs and will hack at them high or low out over the plate. He longer bunts as often as he once did, and he runs like a ten-year veteran catcher.

Terry has average arm strength but throws quite accurately and releases the ball quickly. He has good footwork and above-average agility behind the plate and possesses slightly above-average hands.

HOW HE PERFORMED IN '95
Although Terry quietly put together another fine season in '95, it didn't look that different from the other fine seasons in his career. He is an incredibly consistent performer at the plate who has hit between .274 and .289 each of the last five years, with steady strikeout, walk, and home run numbers—although his '95 four-bagger total was his highest since his rookie year of 1987. Usually, Oakland cuts down his power production, but for the first time, Terry showed above-average home run sock in the Coliseum.

He's not much of an on-base threat, but Steinbach makes decent contact and is a dependable situational hitter. Although he annually hits .300 against lefthanders, Terry is no slouch against righties.

The combative Steinbach is also consistently hurt at least once a year. He missed two weeks last August because of a sore lower back. Usually a poor finisher, Terry came off the DL last August 29 and hit .318 in September with his three home runs.

He started 106 games behind the plate and made only five errors, and went 67 games during '95 without committing a miscue. Steinbach threw out 33 of 93 runners, a 36% success rate that ranked third-best among AL receivers. A mobile catcher who constantly hustles, Terry allowed just three passed balls all year.

WHAT TO EXPECT IN '96
Steiny was the talk of trade rumors throughout the off-season. Possibly the most indispensable of the veteran Athletics, he is needed to help a young, inexperienced, low-cost pitching staff learn the ropes. In addition, Terry provides a steady bat that can't easily be replaced by a budget-price alternative. If the new management deals him, it will have serious repercussions for the pitching staff.

Overall Statistics

	G	AB	R	H	2B	3B	HR	RBI	SB	CS	BB	SO	BA	OBA
95 OAK	114	406	43	113	26	1	15	65	1	3	25	74	.278	.322
Career	1054	3648	419	1004	180	13	97	495	15	17	258	574	.275	.326

1995 Situational Statistics

	AB	HR	RBI	BA	OBA	SLG		AB	HR	RBI	BA	OBA	SLG
Home	189	9	36	.270	.298	.476	LHP	123	6	25	.301	.365	.504
Road	217	6	29	.286	.342	.442	RHP	283	9	40	.269	.302	.438
Apr-Jun	197	8	37	.254	.310	.452	ScPos	94	9	57	.330	.391	.660
Jul-Oct	209	7	28	.301	.333	.464	Clutch	76	5	23	.329	.342	.605

How He Compares to Other Batters

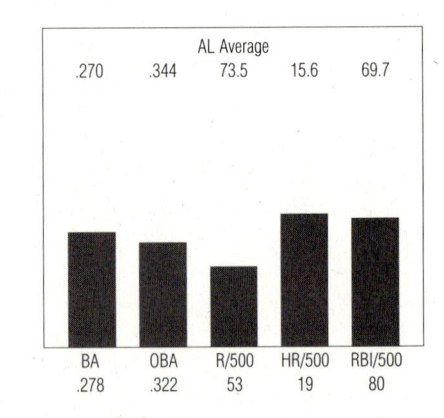

AL Average: .270 .344 73.5 15.6 69.7

BA	OBA	R/500	HR/500	RBI/500
.278	.322	53	19	80

Where He Hits the Ball

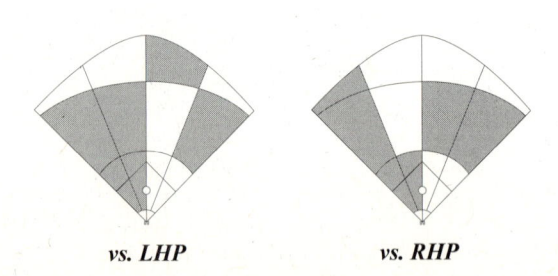

vs. LHP   vs. RHP

THE SCOUTING REPORT: 1996

OAKLAND ATHLETICS

TODD STOTTLEMYRE

Position: SP
Bats: L **Throws:** R
Ht: 6'3" **Wt:** 195
Opening Day Age: 30
Born: 5/20/1965
Drafted: TOR85 S1/3
ML Seasons: 8

SCOUTING REPORT
Throwing from a high three-quarter angle, Todd delivers an average four-seam fastball with some movement, an average curveball with a steep downward break, and a plus slider with a quick, tight little break that is his strikeout pitch. He complements this with an average change-up; he is also developing a splitfinger, which was minus in '95 but which could develop into his best pitch within a year.

Stottlemyre is excellent at holding runners (12 of 30 testing him were nailed in '95) and also at fielding his position, as you might expect of a second-generation major-league pitcher.

HOW HE PERFORMED IN '95
The fiery, highly competitive Stottlemyre became a team leader in his first season in Oakland, both on the field and off. Signed as a free agent, he had perhaps his finest season, with a career high 205 strikeouts (his previous best was 116), second only to Randy Johnson in the AL. Starting out the season 7-1, his best start was a no-decision at Kansas City on June 16 when he went ten innings, striking out 15 and surrendering only one earned run on five hits.

Although he won seven games after the All-Star break, his ERA ballooned to 5.15 and opposing batters hit him at a .309 clip, indicating that they had adjusted successfully to him. Also worrisome (if he leaves the green-and-gold) was the fact that he pitched much better in the pitcher-friendly Coliseum than on the road. He allowed 26 homers, not uncommon for a high fastball pitcher, third highest in the league. Righthanders hit him harder than lefties last season, a reversal of his career pattern.

WHAT TO EXPECT IN '96
One would think that a team with such a paucity of starting pitching would gladly hold onto Stottlemyre, but the winter rumor mill was rife with indications that arbitration-eligible Stottlemyre might follow pitching coach Dave Duncan and manager Tony LaRussa to St. Louis. It would be very hard for Oakland to replace Todd—he will surely be the 1996 Opening Day starter in either Oakland or St. Louis. However, his late-season performance and his road performance give reason to believe he might not be so successful in '96.

Overall Statistics

	G	GS	GF	SV	W	L	ERA	IP	H	R	ER	HR	BB	SO
95 OAK	31	31	0	0	14	7	4.55	209.2	228	117	106	26	80	205
Career	237	206	11	1	83	77	4.41	1348.2	1410	714	661	141	494	867

1995 Situational Statistics

	W	L	ERA	SV	IP	BB	SO		AB	HR	RBI	BA	OBA	SLG
Home	6	5	3.89	0	118.0	43	124	LHB	483	11	49	.259	.333	.385
Road	8	2	5.40	0	91.2	37	81	RHB	343	15	56	.300	.356	.481
Apr-Jun	6	1	3.95	0	82.0	33	89	ScPos	202	5	78	.287	.368	.416
Jul-Oct	8	6	4.93	0	127.2	47	116	Clutch	54	1	4	.204	.259	.315

How He Compares to Other Pitchers

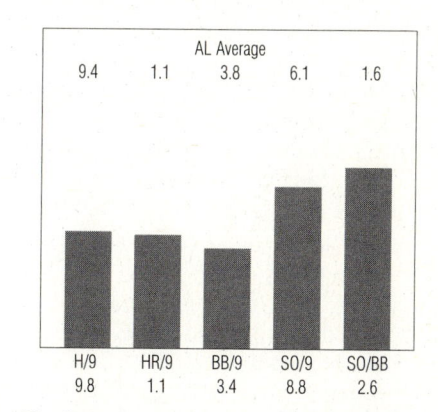

AL Average: 9.4 / 1.1 / 3.8 / 6.1 / 1.6

H/9 9.8 | HR/9 1.1 | BB/9 3.4 | SO/9 8.8 | SO/BB 2.6

How He Compares to Other Starting Pitchers

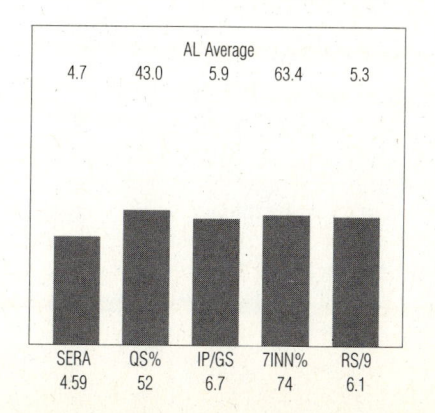

AL Average: 4.7 / 43.0 / 5.9 / 63.4 / 5.3

SERA 4.59 | QS% 52 | IP/GS 6.7 | 7INN% 74 | RS/9 6.1

OAKLAND ATHLETICS

DANNY TARTABULL

Positions: DH/OF
Bats: R **Throws:** R
Ht: 6'1" **Wt:** 205
Opening Day Age: 33
Born: 10/30/1962
Drafted: CIN80 5/71
ML Seasons: 12

SCOUTING REPORT

Tartabull has thrived his whole career by ripping pitches out of the park with his good bat speed and plus power. Unfortunately, his bat speed is declining, meaning that he can no longer get around on good hard stuff from righthanded pitchers. Therefore, although he did not have much of a platoon split in his career up till '94, he has hit southpaws hard but been relatively helpless against righties the past two years. He is a low-ball hitter.

Danny has never possessed much speed; the trio of Tartabull, McGwire and Steinbach could produce a lot of station-to-station baseball by the Bay when McGwire does not launch his gargantuan homers.

Danny played 19 games in the outfield last season and probably won't play more than that in '96. His defensive skills are minus all around.

HOW HE PERFORMED IN '95

A wholly disappointing season for Tartabull. Acquired from the Yankees on July 28 for equally disappointing Reuben Sierra—ripped as "the village idiot" by manager Tony LaRussa before his departure for the East Coast—and minor-league pitcher Jason Beverlin, the big slugger's career continued on its downward slide in '95. The trade was clearly made in the hopes that changes of scenery would help the two unhappy and unproductive players. Tartabull was hitting only .224 with six homers in 59 games in the Bronx when he was traded.

True to form, Danny made his Oakland debut July 30, went 1-for-11 in his first three games, then pulled a rib cage muscle and stayed on the DL until rosters expanded, next playing September 5. He hit .261 with two homers and seven RBI in 24 games for the Athletics.

WHAT TO EXPECT IN '96

Tartabull's skills are clearly declining, even though he's not that old. With his difficulty staying healthy enough to play, he will be a designated hitter for the remainder of his career. With his current platoon differential, he will be lucky to avoid being a half-time player in '96.

Danny's power potential is very important to the A's; without another strong bat in the middle of the lineup, Steinbach and McGwire won't be able to generate enough offense by themselves to lift the rebuilding team back toward respectability.

Overall Statistics

	G	AB	R	H	2B	3B	HR	RBI	SB	CS	BB	SO	BA	OBA
95 NYA/OAK	83	280	34	66	16	0	8	35	0	2	43	82	.236	.335
Career	1271	4532	696	1246	266	19	235	824	36	28	700	1230	.275	.371

1995 Situational Statistics

	AB	HR	RBI	BA	OBA	SLG		AB	HR	RBI	BA	OBA	SLG
Home	113	3	18	.274	.339	.425	LHP	99	6	17	.253	.392	.495
Road	167	5	17	.210	.333	.347	RHP	181	2	18	.227	.300	.315
Apr-Jun	156	4	23	.244	.348	.391	ScPos	73	1	26	.219	.307	.342
Jul-Oct	124	4	12	.226	.319	.363	Clutch	46	2	8	.283	.389	.457

How He Compares to Other Batters

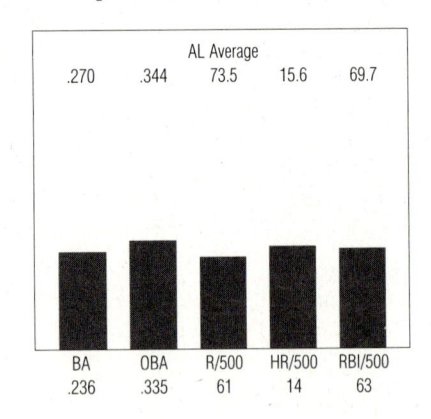

AL Average: .270 .344 73.5 15.6 69.7

BA .236 OBA .335 R/500 61 HR/500 14 RBI/500 63

Where He Hits the Ball

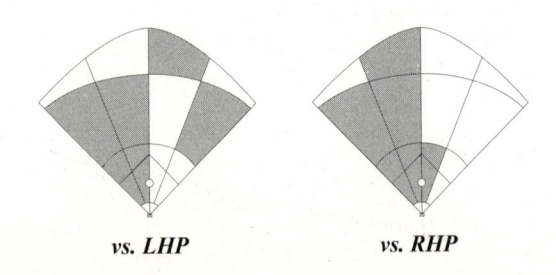

vs. LHP   vs. RHP

OAKLAND ATHLETICS

TODD VAN POPPEL

Position: RP/SP
Bats: R **Throws:** R
Ht: 6'5" **Wt:** 210
Opening Day Age: 24
Born: 12/9/1971
Drafted: OAK90 1/14
ML Seasons: 4

SCOUTING REPORT
Todd has three pitches of widely varying quality. His curveball is a plus pitch and is his out pitch. His four-seam fastball is a bit above-average in velocity but too straight—it gets hit hard when he leaves it up in the zone. His change-up is minus and almost an after-thought, although he will not become a good big-league pitcher until he can use it with confidence.

Van Poppel has developed a stylish three-quarter delivery, but he does not pay enough attention to baserunners and has a poor move to first, resulting in 12 of 17 base thieves arriving safely. He is an acceptable fielder who could still improve.

HOW HE PERFORMED IN '95
Van Poppel underwent a major role change last season. After starting every game he had pitched in in the majors (40 consecutive starts entering '95), Todd began the year in the bullpen, making 21 relief appearances (1-2, 3.21 ERA). The change went well: he allowed only one of 11 inherited runners to score and allowed opponents only a .209 average as a reliever (sixth best in the AL). He scorched hitters for a four-game stretch where he retired 23 in a row, striking out 13 of the last 16 he faced.

As a reward for his success, he then started 14 games in a row with mixed results: he recorded his first complete game on September 17, but had a 7.28 ERA in September and finished 3-6 with a 5.60 ERA in 14 starts. Overall, his control was vastly improved, dropping from his career average of 6.7 walks per nine innings to 3.6 per nine.

WHAT TO EXPECT IN '96
With Corsi and Acre established in the pen and Mohler a likely bullpen member, Van Poppel will have to work his way back into the starting rotation to hold a regular job. The good news for Todd is that there are no strong contenders for his starting spot. His improved control in '95 allowed him to achieve career highs in games (36), innings (138.1) and strikeouts (122), and he should improve on all those numbers in '96. He's still very young and the Athletics will give him plenty of time and plenty of chances to develop—they have to.

Overall Statistics

	G	GS	GF	SV	W	L	ERA	IP	H	R	ER	HR	BB	SO
95 OAK	36	14	10	0	4	8	4.88	138.1	125	77	75	16	56	122
Career	76	54	10	0	17	24	5.39	343.2	316	212	206	47	209	258

1995 Situational Statistics

	W	L	ERA	SV	IP	BB	SO		AB	HR	RBI	BA	OBA	SLG
Home	2	5	4.00	0	81.0	32	77	LHB	291	10	39	.247	.344	.426
Road	2	3	6.12	0	57.1	24	45	RHB	222	6	34	.239	.285	.378
Apr-Jun	1	1	2.55	0	35.1	13	30	ScPos	105	6	58	.371	.424	.638
Jul-Oct	3	7	5.68	0	103.0	43	92	Clutch	63	3	6	.222	.269	.397

How He Compares to Other Pitchers

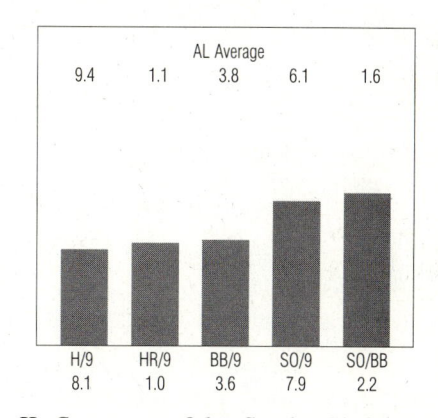

AL Average: H/9 9.4 | HR/9 1.1 | BB/9 3.8 | SO/9 6.1 | SO/BB 1.6

Van Poppel: H/9 8.1 | HR/9 1.0 | BB/9 3.6 | SO/9 7.9 | SO/BB 2.2

How He Compares to Other Starting Pitchers

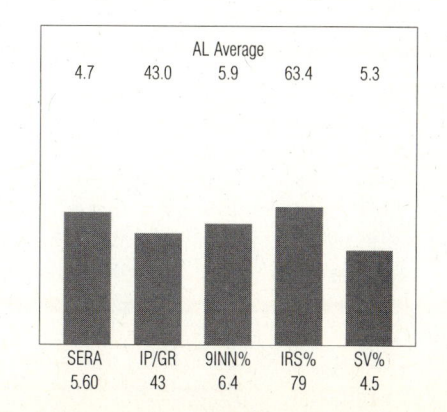

AL Average: SERA 4.7 | IP/GR 43.0 | 9INN% 5.9 | IRS% 63.4 | SV% 5.3

Van Poppel: SERA 5.60 | IP/GR 43 | 9INN% 6.4 | IRS% 79 | SV% 4.5

THE SCOUTING REPORT: 1996

OAKLAND ATHLETICS

MARK ACRE

Position: RP
Bats: R **Throws:** R
Ht: 6'8" **Wt:** 235
Opening Day Age: 27
Born: 9/16/1968
Drafted: OAK 8/5/91
ML Seasons: 2

Overall Statistics

	G	GS	GF	SV	W	L	ERA	IP	H	R	ER	HR	BB	SO
95 OAK	43	0	10	0	1	2	5.71	52.0	52	35	33	7	28	47
Career	77	0	16	0	6	3	4.80	86.1	76	48	46	11	51	68

1995 Situational Statistics

	W	L	ERA	SV	IP	BB	SO		AB	HR	RBI	BA	OBA	SLG
Home	0	0	6.00	0	18.0	6	13	LHB	93	2	15	.247	.369	.344
Road	1	2	5.56	0	34.0	22	34	RHB	110	5	26	.264	.331	.509
Apr-Jun	1	2	5.33	0	27.0	14	25	ScPos	71	3	34	.239	.341	.451
Jul-Oct	0	0	6.12	0	25.0	14	22	Clutch	52	4	17	.385	.508	.712

SCOUTING REPORT

Mark uses a protracted, high three-quarter delivery to hurl a plus four-seam fastball, an average slider, and an unimpressive change-up. Poor command renders Mark's pitches less effective.

Despite his motion, he held runners well in '95; just three tried to steal, one successfully. Acre is a minus fielder.

HOW HE PERFORMED IN '95

The huge, tall righthander spent his first full season in the big leagues. Despite a power arsenal, he had a reverse platoon effect. Mark started very slowly, sporting an ERA over 7.00 on June 1, but had a good streak that month before having some hard times later in the summer. After missing time with a pulled hamstring, Acre returned from the disabled list to surrender ten hits and five runs in his last seven innings of work.

WHAT TO EXPECT IN '96

Although Mark is not quite as tall as Randy Johnson, his legs are longer than Johnson's. Acre's control is also as poor as Johnson's was in his early seasons. Although his poor command will hinder him as closer material, Oakland sees Mark taking that job eventually, perhaps as soon as '96.

JIM CORSI

Position: RP
Bats: R **Throws:** R
Ht: 6'1" **Wt:** 210
Opening Day Age: 34
Born: 9/9/1961
Drafted: NYA82 24/642
ML Seasons: 6

Overall Statistics

	G	GS	GF	SV	W	L	ERA	IP	H	R	ER	HR	BB	SO
95 OAK	38	0	7	2	2	4	2.20	45.0	31	14	11	2	26	26
Career	165	1	65	2	7	16	2.99	246.2	225	96	82	14	93	136

1995 Situational Statistics

	W	L	ERA	SV	IP	BB	SO		AB	HR	RBI	BA	OBA	SLG
Home	1	3	1.86	1	19.1	13	11	LHB	80	0	7	.213	.333	.262
Road	1	1	2.45	1	25.2	13	15	RHB	73	2	6	.192	.314	.315
Apr-Jun	2	3	1.67	2	27.0	16	15	ScPos	46	0	11	.130	.255	.152
Jul-Aug	0	1	3.00	0	18.0	10	11	Clutch	88	1	7	.239	.356	.307

SCOUTING REPORT

The stocky Corsi's short-windup, maximum-effort, high three-quarter delivery makes him appear to explode off the mound. Jim is not afraid to throw his sinking fastball inside, but the pitch has minus velocity and runs straight. An average, old-fashioned overhand-drop curve is his out pitch. He relies on changing speeds and working the corners.

Controlling runners with his quick, jerky delivery, Jim saw only three runners try to steal on him in '95. He is an average fielder.

HOW HE PERFORMED IN '95

Oakland's top setup pitcher before a bout with shoulder tendinitis, Corsi got off to a terrific start. He did not allow a run in his first 18 innings, with opposing hitters going 0-for-35 with runners on base.

His ERA ballooned in early June and, after losing three games in five days, Jim hit the disabled list. Overall, Corsi held batters to .137 with runners on and .130 with runners in scoring position, both ranking third-best in the AL.

WHAT TO EXPECT IN '96

While Corsi was excellent at times, he was streaky, struggled with control, and was not durable. Oakland would be wise not to count on Jim too heavily.

OAKLAND ATHLETICS

MIKE GALLEGO

Positions: 2B/SS/3B
Bats: R **Throws:** R
Ht: 5'8" **Wt:** 160
Opening Day Age: 35
Born: 10/31/1960
Drafted: OAK81 2/33
ML Seasons: 11

Overall Statistics

	G	AB	R	H	2B	3B	HR	RBI	SB	CS	BB	SO	BA	OBA
95 OAK	43	120	11	28	0	0	0	8	0	1	9	24	.233	.292
Career	1033	2745	356	663	107	12	42	277	24	31	313	428	.242	.324

1995 Situational Statistics

	AB	HR	RBI	BA	OBA	SLG		AB	HR	RBI	BA	OBA	SLG
Home	53	0	4	.264	.316	.264	LHP	48	0	4	.354	.404	.354
Road	67	0	4	.209	.274	.209	RHP	72	0	4	.153	.218	.153
Apr-Jun	59	0	5	.186	.250	.186	ScPos	28	0	8	.179	.303	.179
Jul-Oct	61	0	3	.279	.333	.279	Clutch	12	0	1	.167	.333	.167

SCOUTING REPORT

Time and age have stolen his skills. Once quick, he now has poor speed, a slow bat, and little power, getting tied up by good fastballs. Mike still likes low pitches that allow him to extend his arms.

His defense is still above-average: Gallego's average arm strength and accuracy are augmented by adequate or better range (depending on the position), soft hands, and knowledge of AL hitters.

HOW HE PERFORMED IN '95

Although he was the Opening Day second baseman, Mike moved to shortstop May 8, replacing injured Mike Bordick. After starting nine games, Gallego himself went down, tearing up his left heel and missing 78 contests.

He assumed a utility infield role on his return. Hitting only .186 when disabled, he batted .279 after and again creamed lefthanders. However, he went 120 at-bats without an extra-base hit, setting an Oakland franchise record—it was the longest such AL streak since pitcher Wilbur Wood did it in 1972.

WHAT TO EXPECT IN '96

Mike is too old and too expensive for the new Oakland regime, and his disappointing production means he must take another pay cut to remain in the majors.

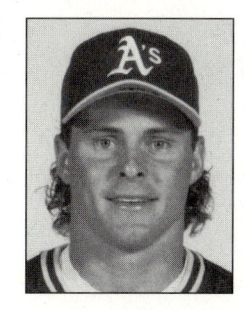

JASON GIAMBI

Positions: 3B/1B//DH
Bats: L **Throws:** R
Ht: 6'2" **Wt:** 200
Opening Day Age: 25
Born: 1/8/1971
Drafted: OAK92 2/58
ML Seasons: 1

Overall Statistics

	G	AB	R	H	2B	3B	HR	RBI	SB	CS	BB	SO	BA	OBA
95 OAK	54	176	27	45	7	0	6	25	2	1	28	31	.256	.364
Career	54	176	27	45	7	0	6	25	2	1	28	31	.256	.364

1995 Situational Statistics

	AB	HR	RBI	BA	OBA	SLG		AB	HR	RBI	BA	OBA	SLG
Home	97	3	12	.227	.333	.361	LHP	18	1	2	.222	.333	.389
Road	79	3	13	.291	.400	.443	RHP	158	5	23	.259	.367	.399
Apr-Jun	11	0	0	.182	.308	.182	ScPos	48	1	20	.313	.453	.417
Jul-Oct	165	6	25	.261	.367	.412	Clutch	28	1	4	.143	.333	.286

SCOUTING REPORT

Giambi plays the corner infield positions with average hands and range and a weak but accurate arm.

A line-drive hitter who likes fastballs, Jason likes the ball low and inside. He will see more breaking pitches in '96. He's built like a third baseman but already runs like a first baseman.

HOW HE PERFORMED IN '95

The promising rookie made his debut in '95, hitting .342 at Edmonton before a July 7 promotion. Giambi hit .290 for the Athletics in July, and homered in three straight August games. He hit quite well in clutch situations and showed terrific plate discipline for a youngster.

However, Jason suffered several nagging injuries as the season wound down, losing games to hamstring and rib ailments as well as a concussion. Although he made 20 starts at first base, Giambi is the third baseman of the present and future in Oakland. He made just three errors at the hot corner in 30 games.

WHAT TO EXPECT IN '96

While Jason's power could well increase with experience and age, he appears to be a line-drive hitter and may project as a platoon player; Giambi got little time against lefthanders in '95.

OAKLAND ATHLETICS

ERIC HELFAND

Position: C
Bats: L **Throws:** R
Ht: 6'0" **Wt:** 195
Opening Day Age: 27
Born: 3/25/1969
Drafted: OAK90 6/65
ML Seasons: 3

Overall Statistics

	G	AB	R	H	2B	3B	HR	RBI	SB	CS	BB	SO	BA	OBA
95 OAK	38	86	9	14	2	1	0	7	0	0	11	25	.163	.265
Career	53	105	11	18	2	1	0	9	0	0	11	27	.171	.256

1995 Situational Statistics

	AB	HR	RBI	BA	OBA	SLG		AB	HR	RBI	BA	OBA	SLG
Home	51	0	6	.196	.317	.255	LHP	12	0	1	.333	.385	.333
Road	35	0	1	.114	.184	.143	RHP	74	0	6	.135	.247	.189
Apr-Jun	24	0	1	.167	.231	.292	ScPos	22	0	7	.318	.423	.409
Jul-Oct	62	0	6	.161	.278	.177	Clutch	7	0	0	.000	.125	.000

SCOUTING REPORT
Helfand has a slow bat and is a weak hitter with little power. He likes the ball low and inside; it's the only place he can catch up to it.

He already runs like a veteran catcher. Though Eric has just average arm strength and accuracy, he is quick out of the crouch and covers a lot of ground on pop-ups. Average hands complete a defense-oriented backup catcher.

HOW HE PERFORMED IN '95
Helfand didn't play often but spent most of the season on Oakland's roster. Called up when Brian Harper suddenly retired May 4, Eric stayed up until July 27, then returned August 14 when Terry Steinbach was injured.

Although he provided abysmal offense, Eric didn't allow a passed ball all season and only seven wild pitches came on his beat, but he threw out just five of 26 (19%) basestealers.

WHAT TO EXPECT IN '96
Eric is young, hits lefthanded, and is a catcher. Those three attributes indicate that Helfand should back up any number of starting catchers for several years if he can show even marginal improvement at the dish.

DOUG JOHNS

Position: SP
Bats: R **Throws:** L
Ht: 6'2" **Wt:** 185
Opening Day Age: 28
Born: 12/19/1967
Drafted: OAK90 21/451
ML Seasons: 1

Overall Statistics

	G	GS	GF	SV	W	L	ERA	IP	H	R	ER	HR	BB	SO
95 OAK	11	9	1	0	5	3	4.61	54.2	44	32	28	5	26	25
Career	11	9	1	0	5	3	4.61	54.2	44	32	28	5	26	25

1995 Situational Statistics

	W	L	ERA	SV	IP	BB	SO		AB	HR	RBI	BA	OBA	SLG
Home	4	0	3.31	0	35.1	17	14	LHB	54	1	5	.241	.300	.333
Road	1	3	6.98	0	19.1	9	11	RHB	141	4	22	.220	.341	.362
Apr-Jun	0	0	0.00	0	0.0	0	0	ScPos	42	1	22	.286	.426	.429
Jul-Oct	5	3	4.61	0	54.2	26	25	Clutch	12	0	0	.167	.231	.167

SCOUTING REPORT
Doug delivers from a three-quarter angle, using an average curve and change-up as his out pitches. He sets up hitters with a minus-velocity fastball, which sinks and tails in on lefthanders, and a slightly subpar slider.

Johns has average control but is savvy and changes speeds well. He throws enough pitches with enough intelligence to become a decent fourth starter, but he must keep the ball down. A plus fielder, he holds runners well. Just six tried to steal against him in '95, two successfully.

HOW HE PERFORMED IN '95
One of eight pitchers making major-league debuts with the Athletics in '95, Doug was called up four times after July 8. After appearing just three times during his first three call-ups, Johns came up for good August 20. He won three straight starts (0.96 ERA), but struggled in September despite putting a nail in the Angels' coffin with a two-hit shutout on the 18th.

WHAT TO EXPECT IN '96
Doug fits in well with an Oakland staff painfully short on stuff. However, he has been impressive in the minors and could easily get 30 starts this season.

OAKLAND ATHLETICS

MIKE MOHLER

Position: RP
Bats: R **Throws:** L
Ht: 6'2" **Wt:** 195
Opening Day Age: 27
Born: 7/26/1968
Drafted: OAK89 41/1101
ML Seasons: 3

Overall Statistics

	G	GS	GF	SV	W	L	ERA	IP	H	R	ER	HR	BB	SO
95 OAK	28	0	6	1	1	1	3.04	23.2	16	8	8	0	18	15
Career	71	10	10	1	2	8	4.98	90.1	75	56	50	11	64	61

1995 Situational Statistics

	W	L	ERA	SV	IP	BB	SO		AB	HR	RBI	BA	OBA	SLG
Home	0	0	1.64	0	11.0	4	6	LHB	39	0	5	.256	.341	.282
Road	1	1	4.26	1	12.2	14	9	RHB	42	0	4	.143	.345	.167
Apr-Jun	0	0	0.00	0	0.0	0	0	ScPos	28	0	9	.179	.324	.214
Jul-Oct	1	1	3.04	1	23.2	18	15	Clutch	30	0	5	.267	.333	.333

SCOUTING REPORT
Mohler's three pitches (fastball, curve, and slider) are all rated minus. A high three-quarter delivery does not seem to enhance his relatively poor control. Mike owes his employment to the annual need for lefthanded spot relievers.

Average at holding runners, Mohler fields his position adequately. Nobody tried to steal on him in '95.

HOW HE PERFORMED IN '95
Mike was called up from Edmonton in late July when Dave Stewart's retirement left a vacancy. After a rough start, Mohler pitched well in August and September, and did not allow a homer all season in either the majors or Triple-A—he had given up 10 long balls in 64 innings with Oakland in '93. His good '95 stat line was probably a freak occurrence, but Mike will take it anyway—big-league pitchers who walk more hitters than they fan aren't noted for their longevity.

WHAT TO EXPECT IN '96
Although he had ten starts in his first 43 big-league appearances, Mohler is now strictly a spot reliever. At 27, he can only hope for a future as a lefthanded long or middle relief role.

CRAIG PAQUETTE

Positions: 3B/OF//SS/1B
Bats: R **Throws:** R
Ht: 6'0" **Wt:** 190
Opening Day Age: 27
Born: 3/28/1969
Drafted: OAK89 7/218
ML Seasons: 3

Overall Statistics

	G	AB	R	H	2B	3B	HR	RBI	SB	CS	BB	SO	BA	OBA
95 OAK	105	283	42	64	13	1	13	49	5	2	12	88	.226	.256
Career	224	725	77	157	35	5	25	95	10	4	26	210	.217	.243

1995 Situational Statistics

	AB	HR	RBI	BA	OBA	SLG		AB	HR	RBI	BA	OBA	SLG
Home	154	8	22	.240	.255	.455	LHP	108	6	16	.213	.254	.407
Road	129	5	27	.209	.257	.372	RHP	175	7	33	.234	.257	.423
Apr-Jun	95	7	21	.284	.313	.568	ScPos	78	4	38	.269	.271	.538
Jul-Oct	188	6	28	.197	.228	.340	Clutch	34	1	5	.235	.270	.353

SCOUTING REPORT
A high-fastball devotee who likes the ball out over the plate, Paquette tries to pull incessantly and will swing at anything; with an uppercut swing and average power, he pops up and strikes out recurrently. Paquette is a below-average runner, but will steal and sacrifice.

He plays adequate defense at third. His average arm is very accurate, and Craig's below-par range is similarly improved by soft, sure hands.

HOW HE PERFORMED IN '95
Paquette spent the entire season with Oakland, enjoying good times and bad. He began cold, but hit .346 in June with six homers and 15 RBI. He then batted .077 (4-for-52) in July, including an 0-for-30 string. Next, Craig ripped off a 15-game hit streak in a hot August and closed out the year in a 1-for-35 free-fall.

Poor strike-zone judgment gets Paquette into terrible slumps; no hitter can survive whiffing seven times as often as they walk.

WHAT TO EXPECT IN '96
Craig will spend his career as a utilityman. He made 12 starts in the outfield plus one each at first base and shortstop as Jason Giambi staked his claim on third.

OAKLAND ATHLETICS

ARIEL PRIETO

Position: SP/RP
Bats: R **Throws:** R
Ht: 6'3" **Wt:** 225
Opening Day Age: 26
Born: 10/22/1969
Drafted: OAK95 1/5
ML Seasons: 1

Overall Statistics

	G	GS	GF	SV	W	L	ERA	IP	H	R	ER	HR	BB	SO
95 OAK	14	9	1	0	2	6	4.97	58.0	57	35	32	4	32	37
Career	14	9	1	0	2	6	4.97	58.0	57	35	32	4	32	37

1995 Situational Statistics

	W	L	ERA	SV	IP	BB	SO		AB	HR	RBI	BA	OBA	SLG
Home	2	3	3.94	0	32.0	19	23	LHB	112	1	12	.241	.368	.304
Road	0	3	6.23	0	26.0	13	14	RHB	104	3	17	.288	.370	.404
Apr-Jun	0	0	0.00	0	0.0	0	0	ScPos	61	2	24	.262	.373	.377
Jul-Oct	2	6	4.97	0	58.0	32	37	Clutch	16	0	0	.188	.235	.188

SCOUTING REPORT

Prieto looks every bit the polished performer, throwing from high three-quarters with good savvy. His average fastball is usually a four-seamer, but occasionally is turned over against plate-crowding righthanders.

Ariel's bread and butter are his above-average slider and change-up. His curve needs improvement. Average at holding runners, six tried to run on him last year, five successfully. Prieto is a fine fielder who has shown better control in the past.

HOW HE PERFORMED IN '95

The Athletics' first pick in the June 1995 draft, Cuban refugee Prieto went straight from independent Class A to the majors. He made his big-league debut July 2, plunking the first batter he faced. From that point, Ariel pitched fairly effectively. He lost three of his first four starts despite a 2.63 ERA, then struggled in August before spending two weeks disabled with biceps tendinitis.

WHAT TO EXPECT IN '96

Although he was drafted to be a starter, Prieto needs to refine his pitches and regain his command. This may happen in the bullpen or at Triple-A in '96, but Ariel is expected to be in the Oakland rotation again soon.

CARLOS REYES

Position: RP
Bats: B 231 R
Ht: 6'1" **Wt:** 190
Opening Day Age: 26
Born: 4/4/1969
Drafted: ATL 6/21/91
ML Seasons: 2

Overall Statistics

	G	GS	GF	SV	W	L	ERA	IP	H	R	ER	HR	BB	SO
95 OAK	40	1	19	0	4	6	5.09	69.0	71	43	39	10	28	48
Career	67	10	27	1	4	9	4.59	147.0	142	81	75	20	72	105

1995 Situational Statistics

	W	L	ERA	SV	IP	BB	SO		AB	HR	RBI	BA	OBA	SLG
Home	2	0	3.86	0	32.2	15	23	LHB	145	2	14	.283	.354	.372
Road	2	6	6.19	0	36.1	13	25	RHB	124	8	25	.242	.333	.476
Apr-Jun	0	1	4.15	0	30.1	10	19	ScPos	74	4	32	.243	.364	.459
Jul-Oct	4	5	5.82	0	38.2	18	29	Clutch	89	4	13	.315	.396	.506

SCOUTING REPORT

Reyes delivers high three quarters with a deceptive release. He lacks overpowering stuff, but moves the ball around and keeps hitters guessing. His fastball is straight with minus velocity, his soft slider is minus as well. His curve is somewhat better; his out pitch is a change-up, as good as any on the A's staff.

Reyes is average at holding runners: eight of 12 potential base thieves were successful in '95. He is very quick off the mound and a fine fielder.

HOW HE PERFORMED IN '95

Carlos was used almost exclusively in relief. Short relief was his only truly effective stint, as he allowed a 2.25 ERA and one walk in 12.1 innings over 12 games in July. He was scored on in 14 of 21 outings after the break and, while fine in Oakland, Carlos is 2-8, 5.99 ERA lifetime abroad.

WHAT TO EXPECT IN '96

With the ownership change and subsequent priority on low salaries, Reyes should have a chance to prove himself in Art Howe's new regime. With several veterans expected to be jettisoned, Reyes could work either as a swing man or a starter in '96.

OAKLAND ATHLETICS: TOP PROSPECTS

WILLIE ADAMS

Bats: R Throws: R Opening Day Age: 24
Ht: 6-7 Wt: 215 Born: 10/8/1972
Position: P Drafted: 1993 #2 OAK

YR TEAM	LG/CLASS	G	GS	GF	SV	W	L	ERA	IP	H	HR	BB	SO	O/BA
93 Madison	MID/A	5	5	0	0	0	2	3.38	18.2	21	2	8	22	.284
94 Modesto	CAL/A	11	5	6	2	7	1	3.38	45.1	41	7	10	42	.243
94 Huntsville	SOU/AA	10	10	0	0	4	3	4.30	60.2	58	3	23	33	.260
95 Edmonton	PCL/AAA	11	10	1	0	2	5	4.37	68.0	73	2	15	40	.278
95 Huntsville	SOU/AA	13	13	0	0	6	5	3.01	80.2	75	8	17	72	.244

Bone chips in his pitching elbow ended the tall righthander's 1994 season that July. Following successful surgery, Adams was outstanding last year. A change in his mechanics brought his fastball up into the high-80's, enabling him to rely on it more and to pitch more aggressively. The Stanford product has good command of his pitches and also throws a slider, change, and a good curve. Adams had an excellent strikeout-to-walk ratio last season and won his last four starts for Huntsville before a July promotion to Edmonton.

TONY BATISTA

Bats: R Throws: R Opening Day Age: 22
Ht: 6-0 Wt: 180 Born: 12/9/1973
Position: SS Drafted: NDFA 6-24-92 OAK

YR TEAM	LG/CLASS	G	AB	R	H	2B	3B	HR	RBI	SB	BA	OBA
93 Athletics	ARIZ/R	24	104	21	34	6	2	2	17	6	.327	.357
93 Tacoma	PCL/AAA	4	12	1	2	1	0	0	1	0	.167	.286
94 Modesto	CAL/A	119	466	91	131	26	3	17	68	7	.281	.359
95 Huntsville	SOU/AA	120	419	55	107	23	1	16	61	7	.255	.305

The Dominican native made a name for himself in 1994, swatting 17 homers while playing good defense at shortstop for Modesto. Idled because of the strike, Batista got off to a slow start last year, but hit .267, smacked 15 homers and drove in 41 runs in the second half. The 22-year-old has excellent power for a middle infielder, but is a free swinger who must draw more walks and cut down on his strikeouts. In the field, he is quick and has a good arm, but will botch a routine play.

STEVE COX

Bats: L Throws: L Opening Day Age: 21
Ht: 6-4 Wt: 225 Born: 10/31/1974
Position: 1B Drafted: 1992 #6 OAK

YR TEAM	LG/CLASS	G	AB	R	H	2B	3B	HR	RBI	SB	BA	OBA
93 SOU Oregon	NWST/A	15	57	10	18	4	1	2	16	0	.316	.359
94 W Michigan	MID/A	99	311	37	75	19	2	6	32	2	.241	.334
95 Modesto	CAL/A	132	483	95	144	29	3	30	110	5	.298	.409

After three injury-riddled seasons in the organization, Cox surprised everyone by leading the California League in homers and RBI, placing second in walks and extra-base hits, and finishing third in runs scored last season. Named to the All-Star team, the 21-year-old slugger was also selected as the Athletics' Organization Player of the Year. Cox showed great power to all fields and good knowledge of the strike zone. His success was not only a function of health but also due to an improved swing and increased strength--both the result of a winter of hard work. A sound all-around player, Cox is also a good fielder at first base.

FAUSTO CRUZ

Bats: R Throws: R Opening Day Age: 24
Ht: 5-11 Wt: 165 Born: 1/5/1972
Position: SS Drafted: NDFA 1-15-90 OAK

YR TEAM	LG/CLASS	G	AB	R	H	2B	3B	HR	RBI	SB	BA	OBA
93 Modesto	CAL/A	43	165	39	39	3	0	1	20	6	.236	.330
93 Huntsville	SOU/AA	63	251	45	84	15	2	3	31	2	.335	.383
93 Tacoma	PCL/AAA	21	74	13	18	2	1	0	6	3	.243	.291
94 Tacoma	PCL/AAA	65	218	27	70	19	0	1	17	2	.321	.377
94 Oakland	AL/MAJ	17	28	2	3	0	0	0	0	0	.107	.219
95 Edmonton	PCL/AAA	114	448	72	126	23	2	11	67	7	.281	.334
95 Oakland	AL/MAJ	8	23	0	5	0	0	0	5	1	.217	.286

Cruz, an excellent defensive shortstop with great range and a strong arm, can also play second and third base. The Pacific Coast League All-Star also showed decent extra-base potential and the ability to handle batting in the number two spot. The 24-year-old Dominican native has struggled with the bat in brief stints with the A's over the last two seasons, but versatility and defensive prowess make him a prospect.

BEN GRIEVE

Bats: L Throws: R Opening Day Age: 20
Ht: 6-4 Wt: 200 Born: 5/4/1976
Position: OF Drafted: 1994 #1 OAK

YR TEAM	LG/CLASS	G	AB	R	H	2B	3B	HR	RBI	SB	BA	OBA
94 Sou Oregon	NWST/A	72	252	44	83	13	0	7	50	2	.329	.456
95 Modesto	CAL/A	28	107	17	28	5	0	2	14	2	.262	.347
95 W Michigan	MID/A	102	371	53	97	16	1	4	62	11	.261	.371

The son of former Ranger outfielder and General Manager Tom Grieve, Ben has great instincts and excellent offensive tools. The second overall pick in the '94 draft is a pure hitter with a natural swing, but has only adequate speed and needs some work in the outfield. While he has not put up big power numbers in his brief career, Grieve is just 19 and should hit more homers as he becomes bigger and stronger. Grieve is already a disciplined hitter who will draw a walk and rarely swing at bad pitches.

JOSE HERRERA

Bats: L Throws: L Opening Day Age: 24
Ht: 6-0 Wt: 164 Born: 8/30/1972
Position: OF Drafted: NDFA 9-23-89 TOR

YR TEAM	LG/CLASS	G	AB	R	H	2B	3B	HR	RBI	SB	BA	OBA
93 Hagerstown	SAL/A	95	388	60	123	22	5	5	42	36	.317	.367
93 Madison	MID/A	4	14	1	3	0	0	0	1	1	.214	.214
94 Modesto	CAL/A	103	370	59	106	20	3	11	56	21	.286	.363
95 Huntsville	SOU/AA	92	358	37	101	11	4	6	45	9	.282	.334
95 Oakland	AL/MAJ	33	70	9	17	1	2	0	2	1	.243	.299

Acquired from the Blue Jays in the Rickey Henderson deal in 1993, Herrera is a gifted athlete praised by scouts for his tools. He runs well, can hit for both average and power, hangs in against southpaws, has a terrific arm, and is an excellent defensive outfielder. The 23-year-old Dominican lacks only experience, reaching the big leagues after less than one full season at Double-A. Herrera is still learning to hit breaking pitches and needs to add strength to achieve his power potential, which already includes an uppercut swing.

THE SCOUTING REPORT: 1996

OAKLAND ATHLETICS: TOP PROSPECTS

BRIAN LESHER

Bats: R Throws: L Opening Day Age: 25
Ht: 6-5 Wt: 205 Born: 3/5/1971
Position: OF

YR TEAM	LG/CLASS	G	AB	R	H	2B	3B	HR	RBI	SB	BA	OBA
93 Madison	MID/A	119	394	63	108	13	5	5	47	20	.274	.358
94 Modesto	CAL/A	117	393	76	114	21	0	14	68	11	.290	.414
95 Huntsville	SOU/AA	127	471	78	123	23	2	19	71	7	.261	.351

The Delaware product had not shown the power expected of someone his size until last season, when an adjustment to his swing resulted in a career-best 19 homers and 71 RBI before shoulder tendinitis cut short his season in in August. Lesher will need to get stronger both to continue his power surge and avoid injury. Defensively, he is a solid outfielder and played both left and right field for the Stars last summer.

BRAD RIGBY

Bats: R Throws: R Opening Day Age: 23
Ht: 6-6 Wt: 203 Born: 5/14/1973
Position: P

YR TEAM	LG/CLASS	G	GS	GF	SV	W	L	ERA	IP	H	HR	BB	SO	O/BA
94 Modesto	CAL/A	11	1	3	2	2	1	3.80	23.2	20	0	10	28	.230
95 Modesto	CAL/A	31	23	4	2	11	4	3.84	154.2	135	5	48	145	.231

Rigby has great stuff. With an above average fastball, outstanding curve, a slider and a developing changeup, the former Georgia Tech star can be overpowering at times. The 22-year-old righthander also has sound mechanics and shows good poise on the hill. He led the A's farm system in strikeouts last year and was voted the league's top pitching prospect in one survey. Rigby needs only to refine his changeup and be more consistent with all his pitches.

SCOTT SPIEZIO

Bats: S Throws: R Opening Day Age: 24
Ht: 6-2 Wt: 205 Born: 9/21/1972
Position: 3B

YR TEAM	LG/CLASS	G	AB	R	H	2B	3B	HR	RBI	SB	BA	OBA
93 SOU Oregon	NWST/A	31	125	32	41	10	2	3	19	0	.328	.404
93 Modesto	CAL/A	32	110	12	28	9	1	1	13	1	.255	.388
94 Modesto	CAL/A	127	453	84	127	32	5	14	68	5	.280	.399
95 Huntsville	SOU/AA	141	528	78	149	33	8	13	86	10	.282	.359

Spiezio put together his second straight solid season last year, ranking second in the Southern League in doubles, third in hits and extra-base hits, fourth in RBI and fifth in total bases and walks, earning a berth on the league's All-Star team. The 23-year-old switch-hitter batted almost identically from both sides of the plate last season. The son of former major leaguer Ed Spiezio was a one-dimensional slugger coming out of Illinois, but has a strong arm and is working hard to become a good defensive third baseman.

JOHN WASDIN

Bats: R Throws: R Opening Day Age: 24
Ht: 6-2 Wt: 195 Born: 8/5/1972
Position: P Drafted: 1993 #1 OAK

YR TEAM	LG/CLASS	G	GS	GF	SV	W	L	ERA	IP	H	HR	BB	SO	O/BA
93 Athletics	ARIZ/R	1	1	0	0	0	0	3.00	3.0	3	0	0	1	.250
93 Madison	MID/A	9	9	0	0	2	3	1.86	48.1	32	1	9	40	.186
93 Modesto	CAL/A	3	3	0	0	0	3	3.86	16.1	17	0	4	11	.266
94 Modesto	CAL/A	6	4	2	0	3	1	1.69	26.2	17	2	5	30	.179
94 Huntsville	SOU/AA	21	21	0	0	12	3	3.43	141.2	126	13	29	108	.236
95 Edmonton	PCL/AAA	29	28	0	0	12	8	5.52	174.1	193	26	38	111	.281
95 Oakland	AL/MAJ	5	2	3	0	1	1	4.67	17.1	14	4	3	6	.215

Wasdin, out of Florida State, has good command of his pitches and solid work habits. After an outstanding '94 campaign, he finished third in the hitter-friendly Pacific Coast League last year in wins, strikeouts and innings pitched and his 12 wins ranked second in the Oakland farm system. The 23-year-old's upper-80's-fastball complements a slider and changeup and he throws all three consistently for strikes. However, Wasdin got the ball up in the strike zone a lot more last season, surrendering 74 extra-base hits and a league-high 26 home runs.

GEORGE WILLIAMS

Bats: S Throws: R Opening Day Age: 27
Ht: 5-10 Wt: 190 Born: 4/22/1969
Position: C Drafted: 1991 #26 OAK

YR TEAM	LG/CLASS	G	AB	R	H	2B	3B	HR	RBI	SB	BA	OBA
93 Huntsville	SOU/AA	124	434	80	128	26	2	14	77	6	.295	.401
94 W Michigan	MID/A	63	221	40	67	20	1	8	48	6	.303	.434
95 Edmonton	PCL/AAA	81	290	53	90	20	0	13	55	0	.310	.413
95 Oakland	AL/MAJ	29	79	13	23	5	1	3	14	0	.291	.383

A Southern League All-Star in 1993, Williams missed much of the '94 season after off-season shoulder surgery. Healthy again last year, the 26-year-old switch-hitter re-established himself as one of the organization's top power prospects and earned a spot on the Pacific Coast League All-Star team. With a career average of .291 and on-base percentage of .415, Williams has shown that he is a solid hitter with good strike zone judgement. He hits equally well from both sides of the plate. Due in part to the bad shoulder, Williams is not among the better backstops in the organization and has seen as much time in the outfield and the DH spot as behind the dish.

ERNIE YOUNG

Bats: R Throws: R Opening Day Age: 27
Ht: 6-1 Wt: 190 Born: 7/8/1969
Position: OF Drafted: 1990 #15 OAK

YR TEAM	LG/CLASS	G	AB	R	H	2B	3B	HR	RBI	SB	BA	OBA
93 Modesto	CAL/A	85	301	83	92	18	6	23	71	23	.306	.442
93 Huntsville	SOU/AA	45	120	26	25	5	0	5	15	8	.208	.345
94 Huntsville	SOU/AA	72	257	45	89	19	4	14	55	5	.346	.427
94 Oakland	AL/MAJ	11	30	2	2	1	0	0	3	0	.067	.097
94 Tacoma	PCL/AAA	29	102	19	29	4	0	6	16	0	.284	.370
95 Edmonton	PCL/AAA	95	347	70	96	21	4	15	72	2	.277	.365
95 Oakland	AL/MAJ	26	50	9	10	3	0	2	5	0	.200	.310

A tenth-round draft pick in 1990, Young has done everything at the minor league level. He has hit for average and power and showed defensive ability and a strong arm. However, in brief stints with the A's over the past two seasons, he has yet to prove himself as a major league hitter and is now 26 years old. While Young does have great raw power, scouts feel his unusual swing leaves him susceptible to major league breaking pitches.

OAKLAND ATHLETICS: OTHERS TO WATCH

BOBBY CHOUINARD Bats: R Throws: R Ht: 6-1 Wt: 188
Born: 5/1/1972   Drafted: 1990 #6 BAL   Position: P

YR TEAM	LG/CLASS	G	GS	GF	SV	W	L	ERA	IP	H	HR	BB	SO	O/BA
95 Huntsville	SOU/AA	29	29	0	0	14	8	3.62	166.2	155	10	50	106	.246

Chouinard led the Southern League in starts and ranked fifth in innings pitched while leading the A's farm system in wins.

JIM DASPIT Bats: R Throws: R Ht: 6-7 Wt: 210
Born: 8/10/1969   Drafted: 1990 #14 LA   Position: P

YR TEAM	LG/CLASS	G	GS	GF	SV	W	L	ERA	IP	H	HR	BB	SO	O/BA
95 Tucson	PCL/AAA	36	0	11	1	5	1	3.57	63.0	63	3	22	49	.261
95 Edmonton	PCL/AAA	2	0	0	0	0	1	10.80	5.0	6	2	2	5	.300

Daspit, signed as a free agent, has a deceptive delivery that adds a few feet to his fastball and was very effective out of the bullpen for Tucson last year.

RAMON FERMIN Bats: R Throws: R Ht: 6-3 Wt: 180
Born: 11/25/1972   Drafted: NDFA 12-1-89 OAK   Position: P

YR TEAM	LG/CLASS	G	GS	GF	SV	W	L	ERA	IP	H	HR	BB	SO	O/BA
95 Huntsville	SOU/AA	32	13	16	7	6	7	3.86	100.1	105	5	45	58	.279
95 Oakland	AL/MAJ	1	0	1	0	0	0	13.50	1.1	4	0	1	0	.500

The 23-year-old Dominican has a good, hard fastball with movement and a change, but needs to be more consistent and come up with a breaking pitch.

BENJI GRIGSBY Bats: R Throws: R Ht: 6-1 Wt: 200
Born: 12/2/1970   Drafted: 1992 #1 OAK   Position: P

YR TEAM	LG/CLASS	G	GS	GF	SV	W	L	ERA	IP	H	HR	BB	SO	O/BA
95 Huntsville	SOU/AA	30	6	8	3	5	4.01	76.1	66	7	20	55	.234

Grigsby is trying to work his way back from shoulder problems, but hasn't regained the velocity on his fastball.

STACY HOLLINS Bats: R Throws: R Ht: 6-3 Wt: 195
Born: 7/31/1972   Drafted: 1992 #44 OAK   Position: P

YR TEAM	LG/CLASS	G	GS	GF	SV	W	L	ERA	IP	H	HR	BB	SO	O/BA
95 Edmonton	PCL/AAA	7	7	0	0	0	7	10.31	29.2	47	4	21	25	.353
95 Huntsville	SOU/AA	15	15	0	0	8	5	3.33	82.2	80	10	42	62	.256

After winning 20 times in 1994 (combining the regular season and the Arizona Fall League), Hollins' stock skyrocketed, but he pitched poorly all of last year and lost all seven of his starts at Triple-A.

MIGUEL JIMENEZ Bats: R Throws: R Ht: 6-2 Wt: 205
Born: 8/19/1969   Drafted: 1991 #14 OAK   Position: P

YR TEAM	LG/CLASS	G	GS	GF	SV	W	L	ERA	IP	H	HR	BB	SO	O/BA
95 Edmonton	PCL/AA	6	3	2	0	0	1	12.27	7.1	12	0	10	4	.375
95 Huntsville	SOU/AA	6	6	0	0	3	2	3.60	30.0	25	3	11	28	.223
95 Modesto	CAL/A	4	4	0	0	1	2	6.00	18.0	14	5	14	11	.212

Once a top prospect, Jimenez has good stuff, but lacks command and suffered through an injury-riddled 1995 after a terrible '94 campaign.

SCOTT LYDY Bats: R Throws: R Ht: 6-5 Wt: 205
Born: 10/26/1968   Drafted: 1989 #1 OAK   Position: OF

YR TEAM	LG/CLASS	G	AB	R	H	2B	3B	HR	RBI	SB	BA	OBA
95 Edmonton	PCL/AAA	104	400	78	116	29	7	16	65	15	.290	.349

An adequate defensive outfielder, Lydy hasn't received a chance despite slugging .508 over the last two years in Triple-A and batting .347 with runners in scoring position.

DAMON MASHORE Bats: S Throws: R Ht: 5-11 Wt: 195
Born: 10/31/1969   Drafted: 1991 #11 OAK   Position: CF

YR TEAM	LG/CLASS	G	AB	R	H	2B	3B	HR	RBI	SB	BA	OBA
95 Edmonton	PCL/AAA	117	337	50	101	19	5	1	37	17	.300	.382

The Arizona product is a switch-hitter with good speed on the bases and a decent glove in the outfield.

KERWIN MOORE Bats: S Throws: R Ht: 6-1 Wt: 190
Born: 10/29/1970   Drafted: 1988 #16 KC   Position: CF

YR TEAM	LG/CLASS	G	AB	R	H	2B	3B	HR	RBI	SB	BA	OBA
95 Edmonton	PCL/AAA	72	265	53	74	14	4	2	26	10	.279	.389
95 Modesto	CAL/A	15	53	8	13	3	1	1	6	4	.245	.388

Moore, a fast leadoff hitter who will take a walk, finally reached Triple-A in his eighth season but has a .236 career average and a poor swing which lifts too many pitches and neutralizes his speed.

STEVE PHOENIX Bats: R Throws: R Ht: 6-3 Wt: 183
Born: 1/31/1968   Drafted: NDFA 6-18-90 OAK   Position: P

YR TEAM	LG/CLASS	G	GS	GF	SV	W	L	ERA	IP	H	HR	BB	SO	O/BA
95 Edmonton	PCL/AAA	40	0	25	5	4	3	4.50	64.0	66	6	28	28	.272
95 Oakland	AL/MAJ	1	0	0	0	0	0	32.40	1.2	3	1	3	3	.429

The 28-year-old jukballer has good control, changes speeds well, and has a good split-finger pitch and slider.

TODD REVENIG Bats: R Throws: R Ht: 6-1 Wt: 185
Born: 6/28/1969   Drafted: 1990 #42 OAK   Position: P

YR TEAM	LG/CLASS	G	GS	GF	SV	W	L	ERA	IP	H	HR	BB	SO	O/BA
95 Edmonton	PCL/AAA	45	0	30	10	4	5	4.31	54.1	53	5	15	28	.256

Finally healthy last season after two years of rehabbing his elbow, Revenig pitched well, but so far has not regained his 90+-mph fastball.

DEMOND SMITH Bats: S Throws: R Ht: 5-11 Wt: 170
Born: 11/6/1972   Drafted: 1990 #6 NYN   Position: CF

YR TEAM	LG/CLASS	G	AB	R	H	2B	3B	HR	RBI	SB	BA	OBA
95 L Elsinore	CAL/A	34	148	32	52	8	2	7	26	14	.351	.401
95 Cdr Rapids	MID/A	79	317	64	108	25	7	7	41	37	.341	.410
95 W Michigan	MID/A	8	32	6	10	1	1	2	3	3	.313	.371

Released by the Mets, the multi-skilled Midwest League batting champion resurrected his career with the Angels before coming to the A's for Mike Aldrete.

DON WENGERT Bats: R Throws: R Ht: 6-3 Wt: 205
Born: 11/6/1969   Drafted: 1992 #5 OAK   Position: P

YR TEAM	LG/CLASS	G	GS	GF	SV	W	L	ERA	IP	H	HR	BB	SO	O/BA
95 Edmonton	PCL/AAA	16	6	4	1	1	1	7.38	39.0	55	5	16	20	.344
95 Oakland	AL/MAJ	19	0	10	0	1	1	3.34	29.2	30	3	12	16	.263

A power pitcher with a 90-mph fastball and good slider, the Iowa State product pitched more effectively for Oakland than Edmonton last year.

TODD WILLIAMS Bats: R Throws: R Ht: 6-3 Wt: 185
Born: 2/13/1971   Drafted: 1990 #54 LA   Position: P

YR TEAM	LG/CLASS	G	GS	GF	SV	W	L	ERA	IP	H	HR	BB	SO	O/BA
95 Albuquerque	PCL/AAA	25	0	5	0	4	1	3.38	45.1	59	4	15	23	.319
95 Los Angeles	NL/MAJ	16	0	5	0	2	2	5.12	19.1	19	3	7	8	.264

Williams, a veteran Triple-A reliever who reached the majors last year, was acquired from the Dodgers in September.

THE SCOUTING REPORT: 1996

SEATTLE MARINERS

BOBBY AYALA

Position: RP
Bats: R **Throws:** R
Ht: 6'2" **Wt:** 190
Opening Day Age: 26
Born: 7/8/1969
Drafted: CIN 6/27/88
ML Seasons: 4

SCOUTING REPORT
Pitching from the stretch, Bobby turns his back to the plate during his motion and brings the ball home from a three-quarter angle. He has three pitches, the best of which is a good, hard, splitfinger fastball. His regular fastball rates plus and he augments these two pitches with an average slider. Ayala has no off-speed pitch, which has presented a problem at times.

His control has been plus in the past but was well below that in '95. He is quick off the mound and an above-average fielder, but Bobby's protracted windup allows runners to steal easily against him: a surprisingly low four runners stole against him in four chances during '95.

HOW HE PERFORMED IN '95
After a fine '94 campaign, Bobby started '95 as the Mariners' closer. Unfortunately, he ended it far from the limelight, having lost his job to Norm Charlton by late August.

Despite having troubles throwing strikes all year, Ayala pitched quite well early (eight saves by the end of May with a 1.89 ERA). However, even when used to pitch only the ninth, sometimes with big leads, Bobby had serious problems the rest of the year, posting ERAs over 5.00 in each of the final four months. He blew eight of 27 save opportunities in '95—and it seemed much worse. By September, Ayala was a forgotten man, working in middle and setup relief.

Equally effective against lefties and righties in the past, Ayala was miserable against righthanders in '95. He survives by keeping the ball low, but poor location meant Bobby allowed a homer every eight innings last season. He pitched well at home, but was just horrible, especially with his location, on the road.

WHAT TO EXPECT IN '96
There is some talk he might be converted into a starter, but it is likely he will inherit Bill Risley's old setup role, at least in April. However, given Norm Charlton's injury history and the trade of Jeff Nelson, Bobby could well end up as the closer again in '96. He's still young, has pitched outstanding baseball in past seasons, and has a terrific arm—Ayala has to get at least one more chance in late relief.

Overall Statistics

	G	GS	GF	SV	W	L	ERA	IP	H	R	ER	HR	BB	SO
95 SEA	63	0	50	19	6	5	4.44	71.0	73	42	35	9	30	77
Career	157	14	98	40	19	19	4.52	254.2	254	154	128	28	114	241

1995 Situational Statistics

	W	L	ERA	SV	IP	BB	SO		AB	HR	RBI	BA	OBA	SLG
Home	5	0	3.41	11	37.0	9	47	LHB	175	5	31	.229	.307	.383
Road	1	5	5.56	8	34.0	21	30	RHB	104	4	19	.317	.403	.529
Apr-Jun	1	1	3.07	12	29.1	8	29	ScPos	98	3	42	.306	.388	.459
Jul-Oct	5	4	5.40	7	41.2	22	48	Clutch	153	5	26	.229	.308	.399

How He Compares to Other Pitchers

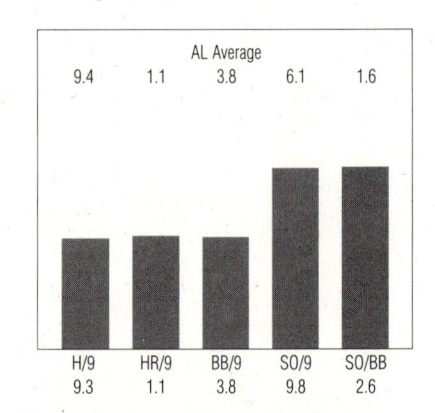

AL Average
9.4 1.1 3.8 6.1 1.6

H/9 HR/9 BB/9 SO/9 SO/BB
9.3 1.1 3.8 9.8 2.6

How He Compares to Other Relief Pitchers

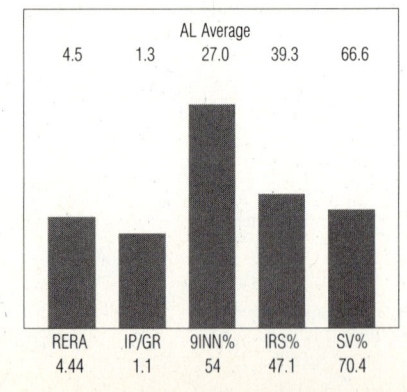

AL Average
4.5 1.3 27.0 39.3 66.6

RERA IP/GR 9INN% IRS% SV%
4.44 1.1 54 47.1 70.4

SEATTLE MARINERS

TIM BELCHER

Position: SP
Bats: R **Throws:** R
Ht: 6'3" **Wt:** 210
Opening Day Age: 34
Born: 10/19/1961
Drafted: NYA84* S1/1
ML Seasons: 9

SCOUTING REPORT

Although Tim throws five pitches, none of them is as good as they were a few seasons ago. Using an over-the-top delivery, the hard-working and ultra-competitive Belcher has a straight, slightly below-average fastball that has lost a lot of velocity. His slider also rates slightly below-par. A slightly above-average curve that breaks sharply downward is Tim's best pitch. He also throws a minus change and an average forkball. He struggles with location on all his pitches and pays dearly when he leaves any of them, especially the fastball, up in the strike zone.

Belcher pays close attention to runners: 15 tried to steal on him last year, but 11 were thrown out. He is an average defender.

HOW HE PERFORMED IN '95

Picked up off the scrap heap by the Mariners (his fourth team in three years) last spring, Belcher served as a durable and, at times, effective fourth starter. He still has trouble getting the ball over the plate and gets creamed on occasion. However, he took the ball, and at least was consistent from month to month, posting ERAs between 4.30 and 5.02 between April and September.

Tim has become much less effective against righthanders recently, largely due to a deterioration of his stuff. He has not been able to make the transition from power pitching to finesse and, while Belcher can still strike hitters out, he just gets blasted if he tries to overpower them.

Run support was the determining factor in Belcher's success. He had ten starts, mostly late in the year, in which the Mariners scored two runs or fewer, and went 1-7 in those contests. He also had 11 games in which the team scored five or more. In those starts, Belcher was 7-0—meaning he couldn't win four of the games in which his team scored at least five runs.

WHAT TO EXPECT IN '96

Tim can probably sign with some other pitching-poor club this year, but it won't be with the Mariners. Although the club wanted him back, largely to eat up innings, Belcher's asking price was too high. Seattle believed they could the same quality at a much cheaper rate and, in a market rapidly becoming depressed for midline talent, they are correct.

Overall Statistics

	G	GS	GF	SV	W	L	ERA	IP	H	R	ER	HR	BB	SO
95 SEA	28	28	0	0	10	12	4.52	179.1	188	101	90	19	88	96
Career	260	239	13	5	94	90	3.78	1583.2	1459	746	666	133	581	1089

1995 Situational Statistics

	W	L	ERA	SV	IP	BB	SO		AB	HR	RBI	BA	OBA	SLG
Home	5	7	4.36	0	99.0	48	56	LHB	425	9	45	.268	.350	.405
Road	5	5	4.71	0	80.1	40	40	RHB	275	10	39	.269	.356	.469
Apr-Jun	3	3	4.80	0	54.1	24	30	ScPos	170	6	66	.241	.359	.418
Jul-Oct	7	9	4.39	0	125.0	64	66	Clutch	50	0	2	.200	.268	.280

How He Compares to Other Pitchers

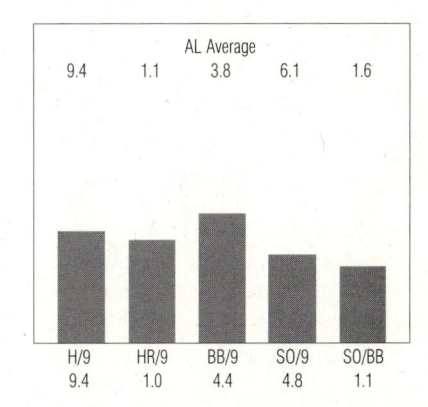

AL Average: H/9 9.4 | HR/9 1.1 | BB/9 3.8 | SO/9 6.1 | SO/BB 1.6
Belcher: H/9 9.4 | HR/9 1.0 | BB/9 4.4 | SO/9 4.8 | SO/BB 1.1

How He Compares to Other Starting Pitchers

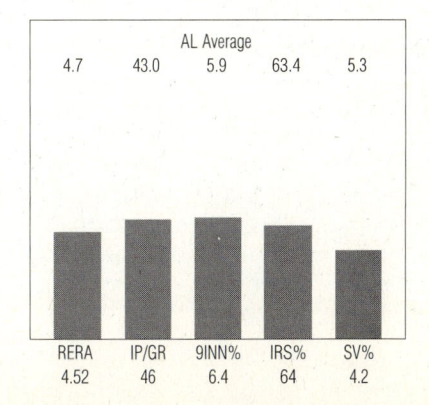

AL Average: RERA 4.7 | IP/GR 43.0 | 9INN% 5.9 | IRS% 63.4 | SV% 5.3
Belcher: RERA 4.52 | IP/GR 46 | 9INN% 6.4 | IRS% 64 | SV% 4.2

SEATTLE MARINERS

ANDY BENES

Position: SP
Bats: R **Throws:** R
Ht: 6'6" **Wt:** 235
Opening Day Age: 28
Born: 8/20/1967
Drafted: SD88 1/1
ML Seasons: 7

SCOUTING REPORT

Benes, a classic righthanded power pitcher, has a high three-quarter delivery, using a high-kick windup and three fine pitches. His slightly above-average fastball, which was surprisingly straight in Seattle, is thrown both with two seams (to sink) and four seams. Andy also has a plus, hard slider; his best pitch is a good change-up that he does not throw often enough. Scouts feel that Benes needs to change speeds more effectively and pitch inside more often.

A .150 hitter last year (6-for-40, 18 strikeouts), Andy is a .126 lifetime batter with 48 sacrifice bunts. He is an average fielder. Although his move to first isn't that good, only ten of 21 basestealing attempts against Benes were successful last year.

HOW HE PERFORMED IN '95

The talented Benes was having another rough season with the Padres before being traded to the Mariners on July 31 for prospects Ron Villone and Marc Newfield. While he did rack up a 7-2 record for the Mariners, Benes left for free agency at year's end; this trade could be a real steal for San Diego if Villone and Newfield develop into good players. Andy ranked second amongst NL pitchers in strikeouts for the Padres before the deal, but was not winning.

Although he held AL righthanded hitters to a .207 average, Benes was bedeviled by the AL tactic of stacking lineups with lefties, who ate his lunch (.329 average, .530 slugging percentage). He saw twice as many southpaws as righties while pitching for Seattle.

In Mariners' garb, Benes had a fine 5-0, 3.62 ERA streak from August 29 to September 6. The rest of his time in the Northwest, however, he was bad, being hit hard and experiencing control problems. He enjoyed excellent run support in Seattle.

WHAT TO EXPECT IN '96

The Cardinals, aching for starting pitchers able to break glass with their fastballs, inked Benes to a long-term deal this winter, so Andy will join his kid brother Alan in the St. Louis rotation. Benes the elder is strong, intelligent, and talented, and still capable of good seasons. He will almost certainly improve from his '95 performance, but how much?

Overall Statistics

	G	GS	GF	SV	W	L	ERA	IP	H	R	ER	HR	BB	SO
95 SD/SEA	31	31	0	0	11	9	4.76	181.2	193	107	96	18	78	171
Career	199	198	1	0	76	77	3.68	1298.0	1200	581	531	123	435	1081

1995 Situational Statistics

	W	L	ERA	SV	IP	BB	SO		AB	HR	RBI	BA	OBA	SLG
Home	4	6	4.35	0	99.1	44	90	LHB	381	7	50	.283	.371	.412
Road	7	3	5.25	0	82.1	34	81	RHB	332	11	45	.256	.311	.419
Apr-Jun	2	5	3.87	0	81.1	23	79	ScPos	168	3	71	.274	.384	.381
Jul-Oct	9	4	5.47	0	100.1	55	92	Clutch	40	0	0	.125	.186	.175

How He Compares to Other Pitchers

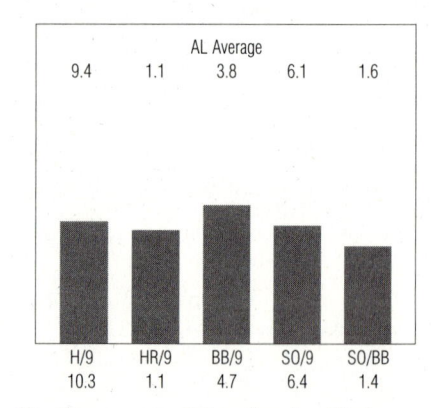

	H/9	HR/9	BB/9	SO/9	SO/BB
AL Average	9.4	1.1	3.8	6.1	1.6
	10.3	1.1	4.7	6.4	1.4

How He Compares to Other Starting Pitchers

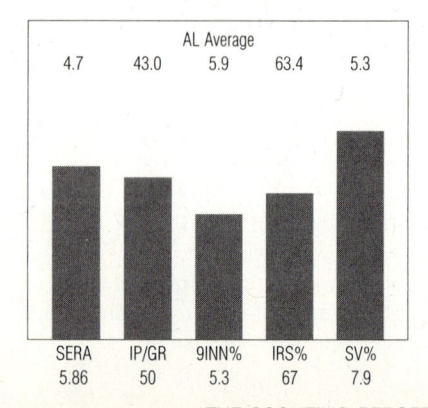

	SERA	IP/GR	9INN%	IRS%	SV%
AL Average	4.7	43.0	5.9	63.4	5.3
	5.86	50	5.3	67	7.9

SEATTLE MARINERS

MIKE BLOWERS

Positions: 3B//1B/OF
Bats: R **Throws:** R
Ht: 6'2" **Wt:** 190
Opening Day Age: 30
Born: 4/24/1965
Drafted: MON86 10/252
ML Seasons: 7

SCOUTING REPORT

Blowers has good tools at third base, including decent range and hands and a very strong and reasonably accurate arm. However, he played badly at third in '95, is very inconsistent in the field, and makes a lot of errors: Mike has simply never played as well as it seems he could.

A very streaky hitter with plus power, Blowers struggles with the strike zone. He is a good mistake hitter but can be overpowered by good fastballs. Surprisingly, Mike is a pretty effective bunter despite his problems making contact. A poor runner, Blowers is no threat to steal.

HOW HE PERFORMED IN '95

Mike had a big season for Seattle. Or rather, maybe one should say that he had a big season *in* Seattle. He did almost nothing away from the Kingdome last year. His offensive punch at home came from a newfound ability to deal with pitchers who worked him away: standing deep in the box, Blowers would step into outside pitches and drive them to right field—which meant success in the Kingdome.

Mike was known for several big games and, in fact, 43 of his runs batted in came in just eight contests. Blowers was hot after the All-Star game, but slumped after he was moved back into the seventh spot in the order following Ken Griffey's return to action.

His career average almost 100 points higher against lefthanders, and Mike is certainly capable of being a good platoon hitter. However, he is weak against righthanders, despite his power show of '95, and strikes out at a worrisome rate. Blowers' bat made up for his poor glovework. He showed well below-average range, made 14 errors, fielded a sub-average .947, and participated in just nine double plays—the lowest total of any AL regular third baseman.

WHAT TO EXPECT IN '96

Blowers cashed in this off-season, going to Los Angeles. He is expected to add power to the Dodgers' lineup and anchor the defense. However, that's a big gamble: Mike is coming off his career year, hit only .210 on grass in '95, and has fielded .951 or worse each of the last three years. If he tries to take the ball to right-center field in Dodger Stadium, the result will be a lot of warning-track outs.

Overall Statistics

	G	AB	R	H	2B	3B	HR	RBI	SB	CS	BB	SO	BA	OBA
95 SEA	134	439	59	113	24	1	23	96	2	1	53	128	.257	.335
Career	453	1378	179	355	67	4	54	229	6	8	147	372	.258	.329

1995 Situational Statistics

	AB	HR	RBI	BA	OBA	SLG		AB	HR	RBI	BA	OBA	SLG
Home	232	17	59	.297	.383	.582	LHP	129	7	34	.341	.407	.589
Road	207	6	37	.213	.279	.353	RHP	310	16	62	.223	.306	.426
Apr-Jun	158	6	29	.234	.291	.405	ScPos	135	8	74	.319	.375	.600
Jul-Oct	281	17	67	.270	.359	.512	Clutch	73	3	11	.219	.287	.370

How He Compares to Other Batters

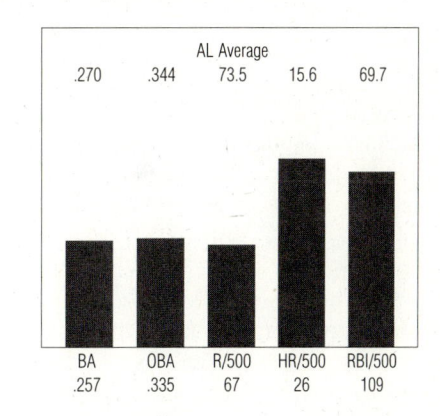

	BA	OBA	R/500	HR/500	RBI/500
AL Average	.270	.344	73.5	15.6	69.7
	.257	.335	67	26	109

Where He Hits the Ball

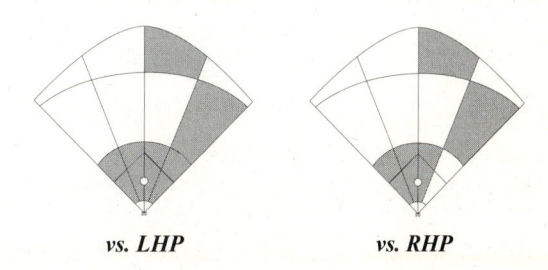

vs. LHP   vs. RHP

THE SCOUTING REPORT: 1996

SEATTLE MARINERS

CHRIS BOSIO

Position: SP
Bats: R **Throws:** R
Ht: 6'3" **Wt:** 235
Opening Day Age: 32
Born: 4/3/1963
Drafted: MIL82* S2/44
ML Seasons: 10

SCOUTING REPORT
Delivering high three-quarters to overhand, Chris shows five pitches with mediocre control. His sinking fastball, curve, and slider all rate slightly below-average at this juncture, and Bosio's forkball is a notch below that. He did not often use the change-up in '95.

Chris still works intelligently, moving the ball around and changing speeds, but hangs a lot of pitches. A minus fielder with poor mobility, Bosio has an average move to first but cut off the running game in '95; ten runners tried to steal, five successfully.

HOW HE PERFORMED IN '95
A poor overall performance in '95 raised doubts about Bosio's health and future. After an effective beginning, compiling a 4-0 record and a 2.47 ERA through June 7, Bosio struggled. He allowed at least three earned runs in 20 of his last 25 starts. Chris only went more than seven innings once all year and didn't complete a game after being something of a workhorse in the past. Basically, he won many games only because of good run support.

What happened? One problem was weight. Bosio, chunky and rendered even less mobile by knee problems, was forced to exit three games in '95 after being hit by batted balls he couldn't dodge—most observers feel he could benefit from losing 30 pounds or so.

Perhaps the most troubling part of Bosio's year was his horrible struggle with righthanders. Coming into the season he had held them to a .229 lifetime average, but Chris was chewed up and spit out by righties in '95.

WHAT TO EXPECT IN '96
This is the last year of Bosio's contract. He has to both stay healthy and pitch effectively in order to have hopes of being in anyone's rotation in '97. Seattle may use him in long relief this season until other starters flame out or until Chris pitches himself back into the rotation.

Chris had never walked as many hitters as he did last season, and his wild pitch count was uncommonly high. Bosio also continues to struggle with the home run. Much of this slippage may also be due to a bad knee, but he is also getting up in years.

Overall Statistics

	G	GS	GF	SV	W	L	ERA	IP	H	R	ER	HR	BB	SO
95 SEA	31	31	0	0	10	8	4.92	170.0	211	98	93	18	69	85
Career	291	237	28	9	90	89	3.89	1649.1	1670	791	713	154	457	1020

1995 Situational Statistics

	W	L	ERA	SV	IP	BB	SO		AB	HR	RBI	BA	OBA	SLG
Home	8	4	5.52	0	88.0	33	59	LHB	377	5	46	.313	.379	.443
Road	2	4	4.28	0	82.0	36	26	RHB	298	13	41	.312	.369	.517
Apr-Jun	6	1	4.24	0	68.0	29	36	ScPos	182	6	73	.242	.326	.418
Jul-Oct	4	7	5.38	0	102.0	40	49	Clutch	15	1	2	.400	.400	.667

How He Compares to Other Pitchers

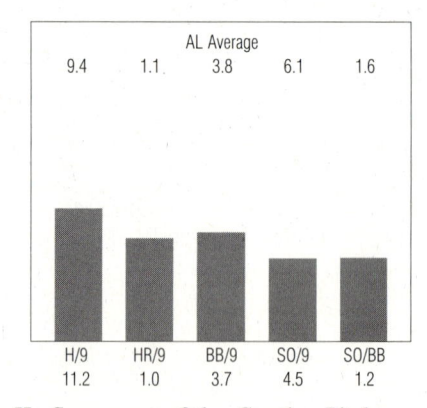

AL Average: 9.4 / 1.1 / 3.8 / 6.1 / 1.6

H/9	HR/9	BB/9	SO/9	SO/BB
11.2	1.0	3.7	4.5	1.2

How He Compares to Other Starting Pitchers

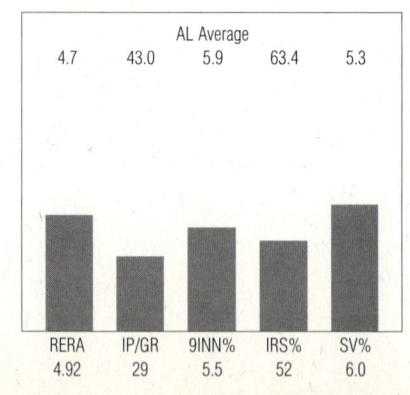

AL Average: 4.7 / 43.0 / 5.9 / 63.4 / 5.3

RERA	IP/GR	9INN%	IRS%	SV%
4.92	29	5.5	52	6.0

SEATTLE MARINERS

JAY BUHNER

Positions: OF//DH
Bats: R **Throws:** R
Ht: 6'3" **Wt:** 205
Opening Day Age: 31
Born: 8/13/1964
Drafted: PIT84* S2/36
ML Seasons: 9

SCOUTING REPORT
Although Jay tries constantly to hit home runs, he has enough bat speed and power to succeed. Using an uppercut swing and stepping into the ball, he will take the high pitch over the plate and drive it to right and can also pull inside pitches.

With well above-average hands and a strong and very accurate arm, Jay appears to be the textbook right fielder. However, he displays very poor range, which is only partially modified by an ability to play caroms off the Kingdome wall effectively.

HOW HE PERFORMED IN '95
Despite some problems, Buhner continues to do exactly what he's asked to do: drive in runs. He set career highs in homers and runs batted in in '95, and while he struggled in some important ways, Jay is a good, athletic, hard-driving player who has continued to confound expectations. He hit nine home runs in August as the Mariners made their move, then slammed 14 long balls from September 1st onward, batting in 33 runs during the club's last-month pennant chase.

One troubling aspect of Buhner's game was an increase in strikeouts. In '94, he had actually taken 66 walks and fanned just 63 times; with the power increase of '95 came a lower batting average, a 51-point decline in his on-base average, and a doubling of strikeouts.

Jay isn't that slow but is a poor runner with absolutely no basestealing ability; he is one of the worst percentage base thieves in modern major-league history. Buhner also hits into a lot of double plays.

Jay didn't have much of a '95 defensively, throwing out only five runners and showing range as poor as any right fielder in the game. He had problems picking up line drives and low fly balls, often losing balls amidst the crowd. However, he made just two errors, fielding .989.

WHAT TO EXPECT IN '96
It's hard to tell which Jay Buhner will show up in '96: the one who made good contact with some power, or the all-or-nothing swinger from '95. If Buhner doesn't hit lots of long balls, it could be a long year in the Northwest. The team depends on Buhner's run production to elevate it from mediocrity to contention.

Overall Statistics

	G	AB	R	H	2B	3B	HR	RBI	SB	CS	BB	SO	BA	OBA
95 SEA	126	470	86	123	23	0	40	121	0	1	60	120	.262	.343
Career	875	2990	463	769	146	16	169	548	6	21	415	794	.257	.350

1995 Situational Statistics

	AB	HR	RBI	BA	OBA	SLG		AB	HR	RBI	BA	OBA	SLG
Home	236	21	62	.284	.376	.597	LHP	118	8	30	.254	.341	.500
Road	234	19	59	.239	.308	.534	RHP	352	32	91	.264	.343	.588
Apr-Jun	161	9	35	.273	.318	.528	ScPos	157	15	90	.287	.376	.624
Jul-Oct	309	31	86	.256	.354	.586	Clutch	72	5	17	.292	.402	.569

How He Compares to Other Batters

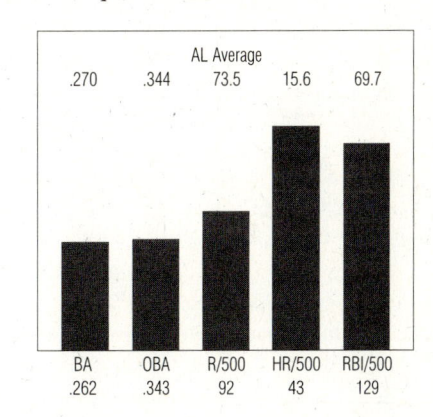

AL Average: .270 | .344 | 73.5 | 15.6 | 69.7

BA	OBA	R/500	HR/500	RBI/500
.262	.343	92	43	129

Where He Hits the Ball

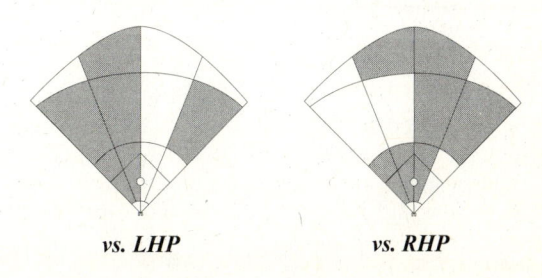

vs. LHP   vs. RHP

THE SCOUTING REPORT: 1996

SEATTLE MARINERS

VINCE COLEMAN

Positions: OF//DH
Bats: B **Throws:** R
Ht: 6'0" **Wt:** 170
Opening Day Age: 34
Born: 9/22/1961
Drafted: SL82 10/257
ML Seasons: 11

SCOUTING REPORT
In recent years, the switch-hitting Coleman has begun to struggle against lefthanded pitching. He is a fine fastball hitter but continues to chase bad pitches far too often for a leadoff man. He does not work the count and seldom walks, but Vince will bunt often for hits. In a year or two, Coleman will probably end up as a platoon player against righthanders. He has plus speed and baserunning skills.

Although Coleman has a very weak arm, he charges balls aggressively and throws with slightly above-average accuracy. His hands are just average, but Vince's range rates above-par.

HOW HE PERFORMED IN '95
The erstwhile speed demon resurrected his career in '95, contributing to the September charge that helped the Mariners reach the ALCS. He actually hit well both in Kansas City and Seattle, batting .287 before being acquired by the Mariners on August 15 and .290 for his new club.

In fact, he batted .323 in May and .329 in July for the Royals, before a late slump (8-for-40 in early August) and the play of minor-leaguer Johnny Damon precipitated Vince's departure from Kansas City. He lit a fire under the Mariners after the deal, scoring 27 runs in 40 games and filling a left field position that had been a black hole for much of the season. Although he isn't the dominant basestealer he once was, Coleman has regained a major part of his value.

One place he continues to contribute is left field. He threw out nine runners last year and played especially well in the pasture for Seattle, making only three errors in '95.

WHAT TO EXPECT IN '96
Despite contributing significantly to Seattle's season-ending charge, Vince will not return this year. Young Darren Bragg will get another shot at the job for the cost-cutting Mariners.

Coleman will be somebody's left fielder and leadoff hitter again in '96. He is a .285 hitter on artificial turf, 30 points below that on grass fields—if he plays on grass, he won't able to beat the ball into the ground and leg out hits as he has done for so long. He is better than many younger alternatives; at 34, he has a couple of years left.

Overall Statistics

	G	AB	R	H	2B	3B	HR	RBI	SB	CS	BB	SO	BA	OBA
95 KC/SEA	115	455	66	131	23	6	5	29	42	16	37	80	.288	.343
Career	1332	5308	839	1411	175	88	27	342	740	175	467	926	.266	.326

1995 Situational Statistics

	AB	HR	RBI	BA	OBA	SLG		AB	HR	RBI	BA	OBA	SLG
Home	240	3	16	.292	.339	.412	LHP	138	3	10	.254	.309	.384
Road	215	2	13	.284	.349	.381	RHP	317	2	19	.303	.358	.404
Apr-Jun	168	2	10	.286	.349	.417	ScPos	73	2	25	.274	.349	.411
Jul-Oct	287	3	19	.289	.340	.387	Clutch	70	1	5	.271	.346	.386

How He Compares to Other Batters

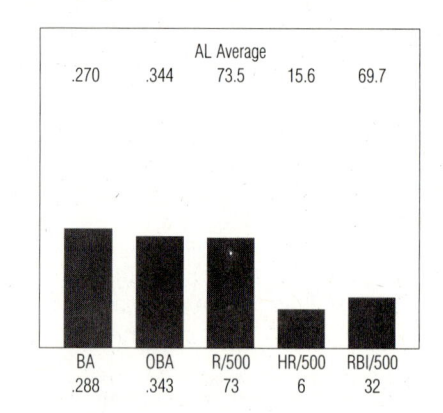

AL Average
.270 .344 73.5 15.6 69.7

BA OBA R/500 HR/500 RBI/500
.288 .343 73 6 32

Where He Hits the Ball

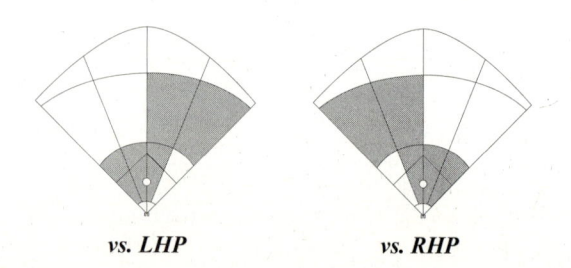

vs. LHP   vs. RHP

THE SCOUTING REPORT: 1996

SEATTLE MARINERS

JOEY CORA

Positions: 2B//SS
Bats: B **Throws:** R
Ht: 5'8" **Wt:** 150
Opening Day Age: 30
Born: 5/14/1965
Drafted: SD85 1/23
ML Seasons: 8

SCOUTING REPORT

Joey has above-average mobility at second and plus hands. However, he showed poor range last season despite a tendency to dive for anything he could. On grass fields, Cora is effective at diving for balls in the hole, skidding on the grass, and turning around to fire the ball to first from his knees. However, he is generally poor at throwing to first, and has slightly below-average arm strength. Joey will hang in when turning the double play despite his size.

Although Cora is a good bunter, both pushing and dragging, he did not bunt for hits in '95 until the post-season. He is very effective at laying down the sacrifice.

Joey stands deep in the box and swings like a power hitter, although he literally has no power. He will work the strike zone, but could take the ball the other way more often. Unlike most switch-hitters, he will swing at the high pitch from the left side.

HOW HE PERFORMED IN '95

An odd mix of strengths and weaknesses, Cora had an impressive '95 season in many ways, but might not have played well enough to keep his job. Although Cora had the highest average in his career in '95 (previous high, .276 in '94), he also walked less than he had since becoming a regular so that his on-base percentage wasn't much higher than his usual mark.

He ranked third in the AL in sacrifice bunts and rarely struck out. However, despite good speed, Joey grounds into a lot of double plays (especially for someone who often bats leadoff) and isn't a great percentage base stealer. His extra-base power was virtually nil. Cora batted .392 in August but tends to wear down late in the season.

He's a gutty little player, but not much of a second baseman. His 22 errors far and away led all big-league second sackers, and Joey didn't get to many balls to begin with.

WHAT TO EXPECT IN '96

The Mariners have a logjam of infielders and an unsettled situation at short and second for this season. Joey could be a regular again, if only because he doesn't have a platoon split, but unless he hits close to .300 again or improves his glovework, he won't be helping Seattle.

Overall Statistics

	G	AB	R	H	2B	3B	HR	RBI	SB	CS	BB	SO	BA	OBA
95 SEA	120	427	64	127	19	2	3	39	18	7	37	31	.297	.359
Career	671	2028	318	543	67	25	7	163	91	42	219	195	.268	.344

1995 Situational Statistics

	AB	HR	RBI	BA	OBA	SLG		AB	HR	RBI	BA	OBA	SLG
Home	198	1	17	.293	.370	.354	LHP	40	0	5	.325	.391	.375
Road	229	2	22	.301	.348	.389	RHP	387	3	34	.295	.355	.372
Apr-Jun	174	1	15	.276	.326	.333	ScPos	105	1	37	.333	.388	.390
Jul-Oct	253	2	24	.312	.380	.399	Clutch	74	0	9	.392	.464	.473

How He Compares to Other Batters

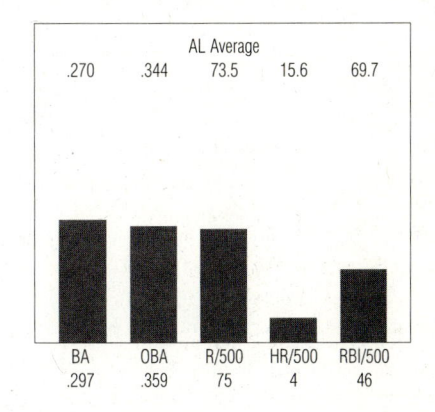

AL Average: .270 .344 73.5 15.6 69.7

BA	OBA	R/500	HR/500	RBI/500
.297	.359	75	4	46

Where He Hits the Ball

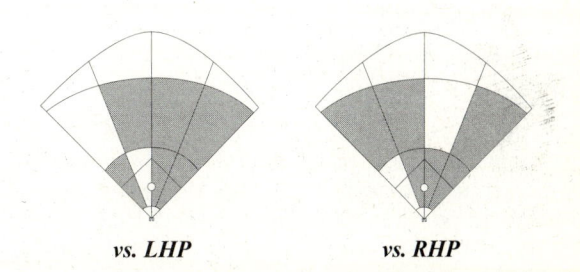

vs. LHP   vs. RHP

SEATTLE MARINERS

KEN GRIFFEY

Positions: OF//DH
Bats: L **Throws:** L
Ht: 6'3" **Wt:** 195
Opening Day Age: 26
Born: 11/21/1969
Drafted: SEA87 1/1
ML Seasons: 7

SCOUTING REPORT

Using an uppercut swing and excellent power, Ken can pull any pitch out of any park. He has gradually improved against lefthanders and is now just as productive against southpaws against righties. He prefers to pick on low pitches, either inside or out, and can be by good stuff high in the zone. But who wants to throw Ken Griffey a high fastball?

Ken has plus speed and if used differently could probably steal 30 bases in a year. He is an outstanding going from first to third on base hits and accelerates well. However, Griffey is not a great percentage base thief.

Junior got to a lot of balls in center in his abbreviated season, throwing out five runners and making only two errors. He has plus arm strength and accuracy and good hands.

HOW HE PERFORMED IN '95

After tailing off in the last part of '94, Junior began last season with a bang, hitting a three-run homer in a 3-0 Opening Day win. He struggled early and was batting just .263 with seven homers on May 26 when he fractured his left wrist crashing into the Kingdome wall after robbing Kevin Bass of a hit. The injury, which at first was thought to be season-ending, required inserting a plate in the wrist; it sidelined Ken until August 15.

On his return, Griffey reassumed his place in the lineup but needed time to get his stroke back. He hit just .217 for the rest of the month, but helped the Mariners' playoff drive in September by batting .277 with seven homers and 20 RBI. He was every inch the superstar in the Division Series victory against New York, crashing five homers in five games and batting .391.

Owner of a career average of over .300 against both righties and lefties, Junior struggled unexpectedly against righthanded pitching in '95. However, it's hard to read anything into an injury-ridden season that started late.

WHAT TO EXPECT IN '96

Following the ALCS, Griffey underwent surgery to remove the metal plate in his wrist. Given an off-season to recover, and a normal 162-game season, there is no reason Ken cannot resume his place at the top of baseball's hitters. It's hard to believe he's been a major-leaguer for seven seasons and hasn't even entered his prime yet.

Overall Statistics

	G	AB	R	H	2B	3B	HR	RBI	SB	CS	BB	SO	BA	OBA
95 SEA	72	260	52	67	7	0	17	42	4	2	52	53	.258	.379
Career	917	3440	570	1039	201	19	189	585	92	43	426	530	.302	.379

1995 Situational Statistics

	AB	HR	RBI	BA	OBA	SLG		AB	HR	RBI	BA	OBA	SLG
Home	133	13	29	.308	.419	.639	LHP	86	3	10	.279	.370	.419
Road	127	4	13	.205	.338	.315	RHP	174	14	32	.247	.383	.511
Apr-Jun	99	7	15	.263	.387	.505	ScPos	78	4	26	.244	.396	.436
Jul-Oct	161	10	27	.255	.374	.466	Clutch	33	2	8	.242	.395	.424

How He Compares to Other Batters

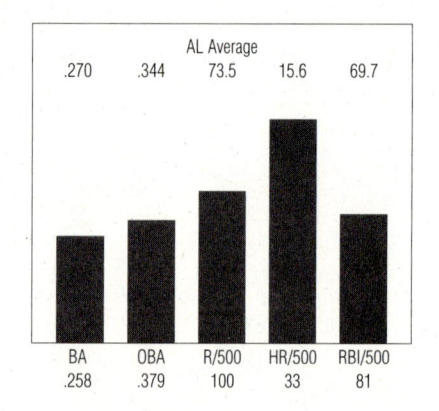

AL Average
.270 .344 73.5 15.6 69.7

BA   OBA   R/500 HR/500 RBI/500
.258 .379 100   33   81

Where He Hits the Ball

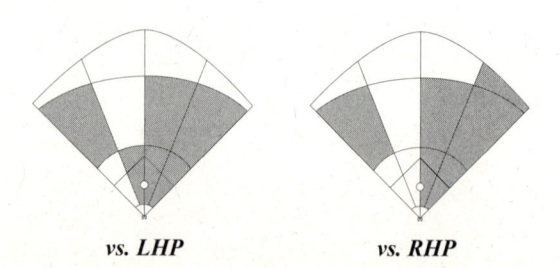

vs. LHP   vs. RHP

SEATTLE MARINERS

RANDY JOHNSON

Position: SP
Bats: R **Throws:** L
Ht: 6'10" **Wt:** 225
Opening Day Age: 32
Born: 9/10/1963
Drafted: MON85 2/36
ML Seasons: 8

SCOUTING REPORT
Johnson throws from a low three-quarter angle, bringing home an outstanding fastball that still ranks among the best pitches in baseball and can hit triple-digits on the Juggs guns. He will drop down sidearm, especially when tired, which happened often last year.

Randy complements the fastball with two well above-average pitches, a curve and a slider, that look similar coming out of his hand but break differently. The Big Unit also has an average change-up, often throwing it sidearm to confuse matters. His overall control was once poor, but now rates above-average.

Although Johnson pays enough attention to runners on first, his motion makes him relatively easy to run on: 18 of 26 stole successfully against him during '95. He is an average fielder.

HOW HE PERFORMED IN '95
The dominating lefty pitched almost inconceivably well in '95. He had his highest strikeout ratio ever, and very nearly his highest raw total ever, despite pitching in an abbreviated season. Randy has now led the AL in strikeouts four straight years, and his 10.01 strikeouts per nine innings is the best of any pitcher in major-league history.

Although he still blew away hitters almost at will, Johnson came to rely more on breaking and off-speed pitches last year. Randy has improved his location considerably, walking far fewer than he did and rarely hitting batters with pitches. Home runs aren't a problem anymore, either.

Only in June (4.06) was his monthly ERA over 2.55. He matched his usual performance against both lefties and righties, except that he went from being unhittable against southpaws to ... well, what's past unhittable?

WHAT TO EXPECT IN '96
The only warning sign for Johnson is a possible shoulder problem. He missed three starts late in the season due to shoulder inflammation and stiffness and clearly was exhausted late in the season. Randy loses some of his stuff if he is worked too hard—as he showed during the ALCS—but will always take the ball and is currently the league's dominant pitcher. If the Mariners give Johnson a normal workload for a staff ace, he should keep clear-cutting AL lineups for the next several years.

Overall Statistics

	G	GS	GF	SV	W	L	ERA	IP	H	R	ER	HR	BB	SO
95 SEA	30	30	0	0	18	2	2.48	214.1	159	65	59	12	65	294
Career	218	216	2	1	99	64	3.52	1459.2	1125	638	571	118	755	1624

1995 Situational Statistics

	W	L	ERA	SV	IP	BB	SO		AB	HR	RBI	BA	OBA	SLG
Home	11	1	2.57	0	122.1	44	175	LHB	85	0	5	.129	.196	.188
Road	7	1	2.35	0	92.0	21	119	RHB	707	12	54	.209	.275	.317
Apr-Jun	8	1	3.05	0	94.1	30	131	ScPos	183	5	48	.164	.249	.284
Jul-Oct	10	1	2.03	0	120.0	35	163	Clutch	77	1	7	.208	.256	.286

How He Compares to Other Pitchers

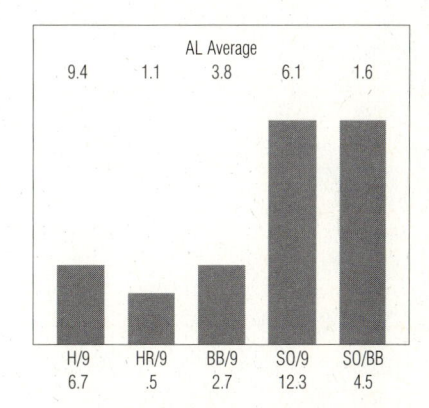

AL Average: 9.4 | 1.1 | 3.8 | 6.1 | 1.6

H/9: 6.7 | HR/9: .5 | BB/9: 2.7 | SO/9: 12.3 | SO/BB: 4.5

How He Compares to Other Starting Pitchers

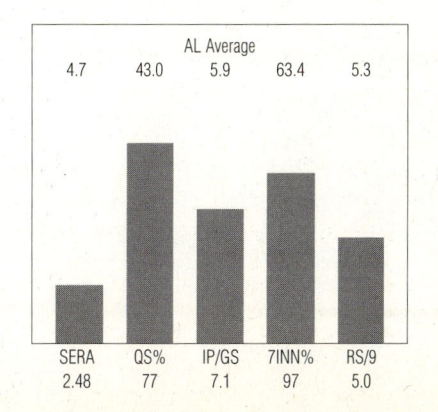

AL Average: 4.7 | 43.0 | 5.9 | 63.4 | 5.3

SERA: 2.48 | QS%: 77 | IP/GS: 7.1 | 7INN%: 97 | RS/9: 5.0

THE SCOUTING REPORT: 1996

SEATTLE MARINERS

EDGAR MARTINEZ

Positions: DH//3B/1B
Bats: R **Throws:** R
Ht: 6' " **Wt:** 175
Opening Day Age: 33
Born: 1/2/1963
Drafted: SEA 12/19/82
ML Seasons: 9

SCOUTING REPORT

Holding his bat behind his head and whipping it through the strike zone with tremendous speed, Martinez is hard to defense. He has plus power and will pull inside pitches down the left field line, but also is effective at inside-outing pitches to right field. Another reason Edgar is hard to defense is that he can clear the fences off anybody's high fastball. In addition, Edgar has outstanding strike-zone judgment and walks as much as anyone—he truly is the total hitting package. Although Martinez has poor speed, he is a smart runner and a decent percentage basestealer.

Although Edgar used to play third base regularly, his throwing strength never came back after 1992 shoulder surgery. He still has above-average hands and average range.

HOW HE PERFORMED IN '95

In 1992, a healthy Martinez won the AL batting championship. After losing most of 1993-94 to injuries, he was healthy again in '95 and won another batting championship. It was a great year—so good, in fact, that it is out of character even for a fine hitter like Martinez. Who hits .433 against left-handers?

He hit .402 in June with eight homers and then .398 during August, adding nine homers and 33 RBI. He is a consistently good hitter who rarely has slumps, which is why his poor performance in the ALCS was particularly disappointing. One good thing is that Martinez will at least take walks if he's not hitting. He looks at plenty of pitches and knows what's a strike and what isn't.

Edgar spent most of '95 as a DH, which theoretically decreases his chance of injury. However, Martinez' painful hamstring injury of '93 came while on the bases, and his broken wrist in '94 came when hit by a pitch. The Mariners gave him only four starts at third base and three at first.

WHAT TO EXPECT IN '96

If they can't sign or trade for a first baseman, Seattle may move Edgar to first base full-time to replace the traded Tino, but their preference is to let Edgar play designated hitter every day. Edgar probably isn't going to do in '96 what he did last season, but he's always dangerous with a bat and has several more years of excellent performance left in him.

Overall Statistics

	G	AB	R	H	2B	3B	HR	RBI	SB	CS	BB	SO	BA	OBA
95 SEA	145	511	121	182	52	0	29	113	4	3	116	87	.356	.479
Career	797	2777	483	868	204	9	91	381	27	17	432	381	.313	.408

1995 Situational Statistics

	AB	HR	RBI	BA	OBA	SLG		AB	HR	RBI	BA	OBA	SLG
Home	252	16	59	.377	.498	.694	LHP	127	8	32	.433	.562	.709
Road	259	13	54	.336	.460	.564	RHP	384	21	81	.331	.449	.602
Apr-Jun	209	13	52	.373	.480	.665	ScPos	138	9	85	.384	.532	.674
Jul-Oct	302	16	61	.344	.478	.603	Clutch	73	4	27	.397	.554	.644

How He Compares to Other Batters

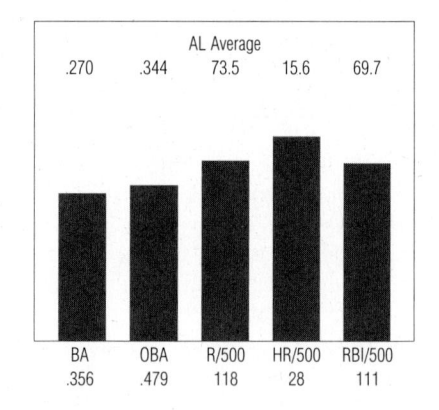

AL Average
.270 .344 73.5 15.6 69.7

BA	OBA	R/500	HR/500	RBI/500
.356	.479	118	28	111

Where He Hits the Ball

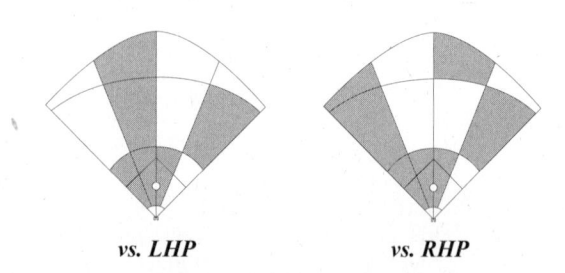

vs. LHP   vs. RHP

SEATTLE MARINERS

TINO MARTINEZ

Positions: 1B//DH
Bats: L **Throws:** R
Ht: 6'2" **Wt:** 205
Opening Day Age: 28
Born: 12/7/1967
Drafted: SEA88 1/14
ML Seasons: 6

SCOUTING REPORT

Martinez has plus power and good bat speed, though his swing starts a little slowly. He is a dead-pull hitter who likes low pitches and who still has trouble with breaking pitches. Occasionally, he will lay down a sacrifice. A poor runner, Martinez does not steal but showed slightly improved speed last year as he continued his recovery from 1993 left knee surgery.

He has average range and hands at first base but scoops throws very well. Tino's arm is quite accurate, but his throws are weak. His mobility was slightly improved in the field in '95. He made eight errors and fielded an average .993.

HOW HE PERFORMED IN '95

Martinez was a disappointment in his first two full years in the majors (1992-93) but improved substantially in 1994. Then, last season, he finally had the big year. Establishing career highs in every major offensive category, Tino justified the Mariners' faith and earned himself a big contract and a ticket to the Big Apple.

Key to Martinez' improvement in '95 was a career-best performance against lefthanders, who in the past he hadn't done much with (.250 average, 13 homers in 360 at-bats coming into last year). Consistent all season long in terms of power and average, Martinez—unlike other Mariners' hitters—was much more effective in road games.

Tino played in his first All-Star game and had a terrific Division Series against the Yankees (.409, one home run, four runs, five RBIs), obviously impressing his then-unknown future employers. One extra bit of good news for the Yankees is that Martinez has been a better hitter in his career on grass fields.

WHAT TO EXPECT IN '96

Although he should do well in pinstripes, hooking homers around the right field foul pole at Yankee Stadium, '95 was Martinez' first outstanding season. Many players have their best years at age 27, and Tino has to prove that he can sustain that level of production and justify the multi-millions George Steinbrenner is paying him. He will now be playing in front of an very critical audience that will be judging him not only on his performance, but also on how he compares to his predecessor. Can Martinez play enough?

Overall Statistics

	G	AB	R	H	2B	3B	HR	RBI	SB	CS	BB	SO	BA	OBA
95 SEA	141	519	92	152	35	3	31	111	0	0	62	91	.293	.369
Career	543	1896	250	502	106	6	88	312	3	6	198	309	.265	.334

1995 Situational Statistics

	AB	HR	RBI	BA	OBA	SLG		AB	HR	RBI	BA	OBA	SLG
Home	256	14	56	.273	.371	.508	LHP	152	10	46	.322	.389	.605
Road	263	17	55	.312	.366	.593	RHP	367	21	65	.281	.361	.529
Apr-Jun	205	13	46	.288	.371	.561	ScPos	150	11	86	.307	.415	.633
Jul-Oct	314	18	65	.296	.367	.545	Clutch	93	5	22	.290	.368	.527

How He Compares to Other Batters

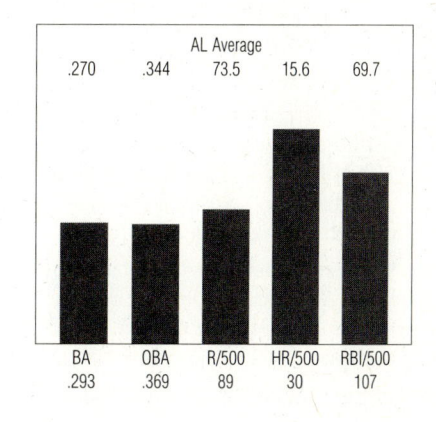

AL Average: .270 / .344 / 73.5 / 15.6 / 69.7

BA .293 | OBA .369 | R/500 89 | HR/500 30 | RBI/500 107

Where He Hits the Ball

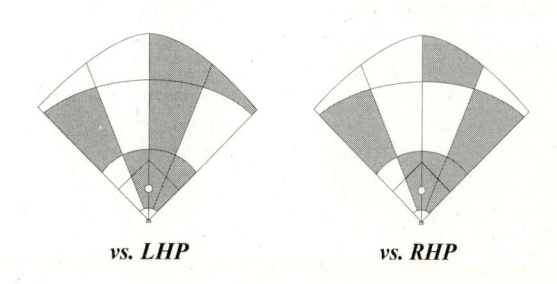

vs. LHP   vs. RHP

THE SCOUTING REPORT: 1996

SEATTLE MARINERS

LUIS SOJO

Positions: SS/2B//OF
Bats: R **Throws:** R
Ht: 5'11" **Wt:** 170
Opening Day Age: 30
Born: 1/3/1966
Drafted: TOR 1/3/86
ML Seasons: 6

SCOUTING REPORT

Luis is the good high fastball hitter: if it's up and over the plate, he's swinging but, since Sojo has little power, he ends up taking most pitches to right field. However, Luis is strong and can pull a mistake pitch. A very aggressive hitter who rarely walks but makes good contact, he lays down sacrifice bunts effectively. Due to his poor speed, Sojo does not often try to steal bases and isn't successful when he does. He does not bunt for hits.

Part of what may have been the worst defensive infield in baseball, Sojo (nicknamed both "So Slow" and "Slowjo" in Seattle) is steady but not flashy. He has slightly below-average range but plus hands and a weak, but very accurate, arm. Luis' range is better at second base, but his glove was far more reliable at shortstop last season. He has also been used at third in the past.

HOW HE PERFORMED IN '95

Sometimes, the answer is right in front of you. When veteran shortstop Felix Fermin went down with a knee injury last year, and prospect Alex Rodriguez wasn't up to hitting major-league pitching, Sojo stepped in and provided his usual level of production while holding the fort at short for Seattle.

Luis had another decent year at the plate, hitting especially well during the second half of the season. Sojo also sliced his strikeouts, increased his walks threefold, and thumped southpaws for a surprising .360 average and .477 slugging average.

He made five errors each at second base and shortstop in '95, playing much more often at short. Nobody was nominating him for a Gold Glove, but he did what was needed when he was asked.

WHAT TO EXPECT IN '96

While the Mariners hope that super prospect Alex Rodriguez is ready to take over the everyday shortstop role this season, it's likely that Sojo will continue to find playing time somewhere, at least in a platoon role. He was on the trading block over the winter. While both California and Toronto search for answers at second base, Luis—discarded by both clubs—has established himself as a major-league hitter and a decent, though uninspiring, defensive player. One could do worse.

Overall Statistics

	G	AB	R	H	2B	3B	HR	RBI	SB	CS	BB	SO	BA	OBA
95 SEA	102	339	50	98	18	2	7	39	4	2	23	19	.289	.335
Career	436	1411	176	377	58	8	24	139	18	17	68	101	.267	.304

1995 Situational Statistics

	AB	HR	RBI	BA	OBA	SLG		AB	HR	RBI	BA	OBA	SLG
Home	189	4	28	.259	.303	.386	LHP	111	5	19	.360	.418	.577
Road	150	3	11	.327	.374	.453	RHP	228	2	20	.254	.293	.338
Apr-Jun	116	2	11	.267	.301	.379	ScPos	70	1	28	.286	.329	.457
Jul-Oct	223	5	28	.300	.353	.435	Clutch	42	1	9	.190	.261	.381

How He Compares to Other Batters

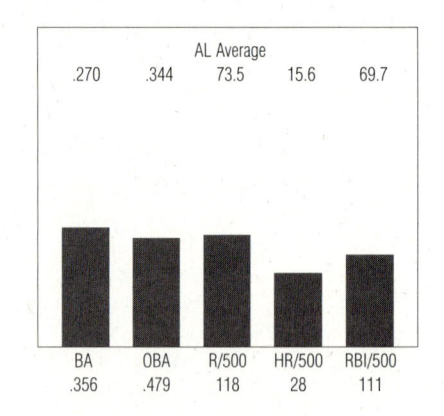

	BA	OBA	R/500	HR/500	RBI/500
AL Average	.270	.344	73.5	15.6	69.7
	.356	.479	118	28	111

Where He Hits the Ball

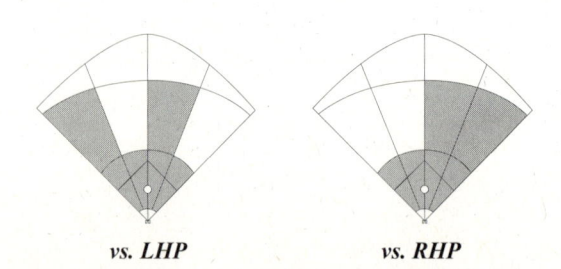

vs. LHP   vs. RHP

SEATTLE MARINERS

DAN WILSON

Position: C
Bats: R **Throws:** R
Ht: 6'3" **Wt:** 190
Opening Day Age: 27
Born: 3/25/1969
Drafted: CIN90 1/7
ML Seasons: 4

SCOUTING REPORT

Dan Wilson has a slow bat, but a rigorous weight-training program before last season resulted in a gain in weight and strength that increased his power production. He likes high pitches out and over the plate and uses a slight uppercut swing. Dan became more patient at bat in '95. An effective sacrifice bunter, Wilson has well poor speed and is no threat to steal bases.

Most of Dan's skill behind the plate involves calling pitches. He has average range and hands and, although his arm strength is average, he rushes his throws, which results in below-average accuracy.

HOW HE PERFORMED IN '95

Looking like a completely different player than he had in '94, Wilson had a surprisingly effective year at bat, hitting for unexpected power. A first-round pick of the Reds in 1990, Dan was always more potential than production, even in the low minors. However, handed a job by Lou Piniella, Wilson has justified Seattle's faith.

Dan cut his strikeout rate last year and more than tripled his walks. Increased patience and knowledge of the strike zone gave him more productive at-bats, which was reflected by increased extra-base production. Wilson hit especially well against righthanders, after coming into '95 with just one career homer against them in 282 at-bats. He's been very consistent against lefties. He had never hit this well in a full season at any level, and whether Dan can keep it up will be an interesting question in '96.

He threw out 30 of 89 runners trying to steal last year (34%), slightly above his previous career average. Wilson led league catchers in putouts (thank you, Randy Johnson) and allowed fewer wild pitches and passed balls than the league average. Perhaps most importantly, Dan was praised by the Mariners' pitchers and coaching staff for his game-calling skills.

WHAT TO EXPECT IN '96

Worn out by September and completely overmatched in the playoffs, Wilson will benefit if Chris Widger can get some playing time this season. The lack of a decent backup for much of '95 meant Wilson had to carry a very heavy load. Probably the most improved player on the team last year, Dan would be one of the hardest Mariners to replace.

Overall Statistics

	G	AB	R	H	2B	3B	HR	RBI	SB	CS	BB	SO	BA	OBA
95 SEA	119	399	40	111	22	3	9	51	2	1	33	63	.278	.336
Career	258	782	72	198	40	5	12	89	3	3	55	144	.253	.303

1995 Situational Statistics

	AB	HR	RBI	BA	OBA	SLG		AB	HR	RBI	BA	OBA	SLG
Home	193	5	29	.285	.361	.461	LHP	102	3	16	.235	.304	.353
Road	206	4	22	.272	.311	.374	RHP	297	6	35	.293	.347	.438
Apr-Jun	146	2	15	.260	.325	.363	ScPos	97	1	41	.320	.407	.433
Jul-Oct	253	7	36	.289	.342	.447	Clutch	50	2	5	.360	.429	.520

How He Compares to Other Batters

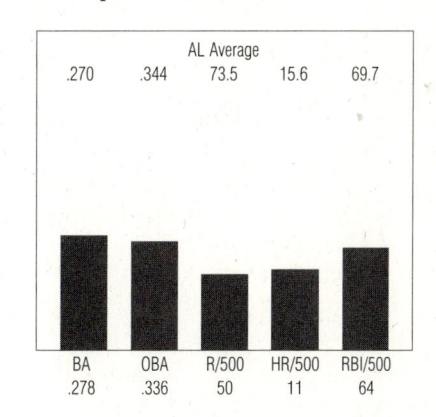

AL Average: .270 .344 73.5 15.6 69.7

BA .278 | OBA .336 | R/500 50 | HR/500 11 | RBI/500 64

Where He Hits the Ball

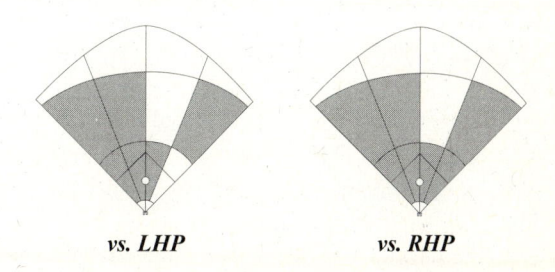

vs. LHP | vs. RHP

THE SCOUTING REPORT: 1996

SEATTLE MARINERS

RICH AMARAL

Positions: OF//DH
Bats: R **Throws:** R
Ht: 6'0" **Wt:** 175
Opening Day Age: 33
Born: 4/1/1962
Drafted: CHN83 2/34
ML Seasons: 5

Overall Statistics

	G	AB	R	H	2B	3B	HR	RBI	SB	CS	BB	SO	BA	OBA
95 SEA	90	238	45	67	14	2	2	19	21	2	21	33	.282	.342
Career	326	955	146	260	51	5	8	88	49	16	84	136	.272	.333

1995 Situational Statistics

	AB	HR	RBI	BA	OBA	SLG		AB	HR	RBI	BA	OBA	SLG
Home	121	1	8	.298	.351	.430	LHP	128	1	8	.273	.326	.359
Road	117	1	11	.265	.333	.333	RHP	110	1	11	.291	.361	.409
Apr-Jun	115	1	8	.296	.352	.426	ScPos	52	1	18	.269	.309	.404
Jul-Oct	123	1	11	.268	.333	.341	Clutch	38	1	3	.237	.275	.368

SCOUTING REPORT

A utility infielder, Amaral was converted to left field last season. He has a weak arm but average defensive tools in other ways in the outfield.

A fine fastball hitter when the ball is over the plate, he has gap power and decent strike-zone judgment. Rich has lost some of his speed and now rates average in that category, but he is a smart runner. Amaral will bunt occasionally.

HOW HE PERFORMED IN '95

Filling in at all three outfield spots, Rich was valuable when other players were hurt or flamed out. He slumped a bit against lefthanders, whom he usually hammers, but improved against righthanders and was outstanding on the bases. However, when Ken Griffey returned from the DL and Vince Coleman was acquired to leadoff, Amaral's playing time evaporated: he only had 12 at-bats after August 31.

In the outfield, Rich threw out six runners and committed just one error as runners tested the throwing ability of the new outfielder.

WHAT TO EXPECT IN '96

The Mariners are expected to bring Amaral back for '96, and he will fill in wherever needed as a valuable reserve who can contribute with the bat.

DARREN BRAGG

Positions: OF//DH
Bats: L **Throws:** R
Ht: 5'9" **Wt:** 180
Opening Day Age: 26
Born: 9/7/1969
Drafted: SEA91 22/578
ML Seasons: 2

Overall Statistics

	G	AB	R	H	2B	3B	HR	RBI	SB	CS	BB	SO	BA	OBA
95 SEA	52	145	20	34	5	1	3	12	9	0	18	37	.234	.331
Career	60	164	24	37	6	1	3	14	9	0	20	42	.226	.321

1995 Situational Statistics

	AB	HR	RBI	BA	OBA	SLG		AB	HR	RBI	BA	OBA	SLG
Home	56	1	6	.250	.313	.357	LHP	13	0	2	.308	.474	.385
Road	89	2	6	.225	.343	.337	RHP	132	3	10	.227	.313	.341
Apr-Jun	113	2	10	.212	.331	.292	ScPos	41	0	8	.146	.275	.195
Jul-Oct	32	1	2	.313	.333	.531	Clutch	19	0	1	.211	.375	.263

SCOUTING REPORT

A small player with some bat speed and power, Darren is an overachiever who displayed good range and a strong arm in left field in Seattle. He can also play right and center if needed. He is a good baserunner who stole nine bases in as many attempts with the M's.

HOW HE PERFORMED IN '95

Bragg began '95 as the Mariners' left fielder after a terrific '94 campaign at Triple-A. However, he didn't hit a thing and was sent out to Tacoma in July, returning for only two at-bats in September. Despite struggling at the plate, Darren showed fine defensive skills. He threw out seven runners in 47 games and also made just one error.

WHAT TO EXPECT IN '96

A young player with speed and defense would seem to rate a chance to fail for a full season. However, the Mariners felt they couldn't afford to give Bragg the time to hit his way out of his slump in '95. He should get his chance in '96, platooning with Rich Amaral in left or possibly winning the job outright. At his age, he might not get another chance.

SEATTLE MARINERS

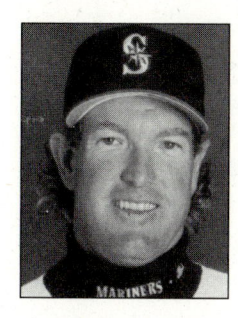

NORM CHARLTON

Position: RP
Bats: B **Throws:** L
Ht: 6'3" **Wt:** 195
Opening Day Age: 33
Born: 1/6/1963
Drafted: MON84 2/28
ML Seasons: 7

Overall Statistics

	G	GS	GF	SV	W	L	ERA	IP	H	R	ER	HR	BB	SO
95 PHI/SEA	55	0	27	14	4	6	3.36	69.2	46	31	26	4	31	70
Career	327	37	152	61	36	33	3.00	605.0	497	237	202	42	238	539

1995 Situational Statistics

	W	L	ERA	SV	IP	BB	SO		AB	HR	RBI	BA	OBA	SLG
Home	4	1	3.19	5	36.2	17	35	LHB	77	1	7	.195	.308	.247
Road	0	5	3.55	9	33.0	14	35	RHB	166	3	18	.187	.280	.271
Apr-Jun	2	4	6.75	0	18.2	12	11	ScPos	68	0	19	.221	.337	.279
Jul-Oct	2	2	2.12	14	51.0	19	59	Clutch	139	2	14	.173	.275	.245

SCOUTING REPORT

Charlton finally made it all the way back after blowing out his elbow in '93. His fastball had plus velocity all year, but he couldn't control it in the NL. His out pitch is a good splitfinger fastball; he will also throw a slider.

Like many dominating power pitchers, Norm isn't an especially good fielder and doesn't pay much attention to runners: eight of nine thieves were successful in '95.

HOW HE PERFORMED IN '95

While the Phillies exhibited lots of patience with Charlton, it eventually ran out. He started '95 as the closer but lost his job within a week, pitching so badly (2-5, 7.36) that the pitching-hungry Phils cut him loose on July 10.

Norm was reborn in Seattle. He immediately ran off an 11-inning scoreless string and began closing games in late August, supplanting struggling Bobby Ayala. Charlton was awesomely dominating, fanning 58 and walking 16 in 47.2 innings—it's fair to say that Seattle couldn't have won the division without him.

WHAT TO EXPECT IN '96

His injury history is a red flag, but the Mariners have other options if Norm's elbow can't handle the strain. Judicious use of Charlton remains advisable.

ALEX DIAZ

Position: OF
Bats: B **Throws:** R
Ht: 5'11" **Wt:** 175
Opening Day Age: 27
Born: 10/5/1968
Drafted: NYN 8/24/86
ML Seasons: 4

Overall Statistics

	G	AB	R	H	2B	3B	HR	RBI	SB	CS	BB	SO	BA	OBA
95 SEA	103	270	44	67	14	0	3	27	18	8	13	27	.248	.286
Career	236	535	75	137	21	7	4	46	31	18	23	58	.256	.287

1995 Situational Statistics

	AB	HR	RBI	BA	OBA	SLG		AB	HR	RBI	BA	OBA	SLG
Home	147	3	14	.259	.295	.354	LHP	46	1	8	.304	.304	.478
Road	123	0	13	.236	.275	.309	RHP	224	2	19	.237	.282	.304
Apr-Jun	136	2	14	.243	.286	.331	ScPos	67	2	26	.239	.264	.373
Jul-Oct	134	1	13	.254	.286	.336	Clutch	50	1	4	.220	.316	.320

SCOUTING REPORT

Although Diaz has a good stroke, he lacks power and strike-zone judgment. He likes pitches out over the plate but will chase too many bad pitches. An above-average runner, will bunt successfully for the hit and to sacrifice and is an effective base thief.

Alex's calling card is fine defense in center field and his ability to play the outfield corners. He sports well above-average range, hands, and arm accuracy, despite weak arm strength.

HOW HE PERFORMED IN '95

Seeing unexpected playing time due to Ken Griffey's injury, Alex hit well off the bench but poorly as a regular. In June and July, with Junior out, Diaz batted only .220 in 168 at-bats. After recovering a bit in August, Alex was sent to Triple-A because the Mariners needed to make a roster spot for pitcher Bob Wolcott. However, Diaz returned in September and hit a game-winning pinch-homer on the 22nd, capping a big Mariners' comeback.

WHAT TO EXPECT IN '96

He's an effective reserve and plays good defense, but Alex has holes in his swing and in his plate discipline that will keep him from expanding his role.

THE SCOUTING REPORT: 1996

SEATTLE MARINERS

FELIX FERMIN

Positions: SS/2B
Bats: R **Throws:** R
Ht: 5'11" **Wt:** 179
Opening Day Age: 32
Born: 10/9/1963
Drafted: PIT 6/11/83
ML Seasons: 9

Overall Statistics

	G	AB	R	H	2B	3B	HR	RBI	SB	CS	BB	SO	BA	OBA
95 SEA	73	200	21	39	6	0	0	15	2	0	6	6	.195	.232
Career	892	2751	290	716	85	11	4	206	27	21	164	147	.260	.306

1995 Situational Statistics

	AB	HR	RBI	BA	OBA	SLG		AB	HR	RBI	BA	OBA	SLG
Home	101	0	6	.198	.229	.238	LHP	89	0	5	.169	.202	.213
Road	99	0	9	.192	.236	.212	RHP	111	0	10	.216	.256	.234
Apr-Jun	94	0	7	.181	.222	.213	ScPos	55	0	14	.109	.180	.127
Jul-Oct	106	0	8	.208	.241	.236	Clutch	25	0	2	.240	.345	.280

SCOUTING REPORT

While Fermin can hit .300 and make contact as well as anyone, he has absolutely no power and never walks. He can lay his slow bat on most pitches, slapping hits on "seeing-eye" grounders and bloopers, so pitchers try to move the ball around on him. A minus runner, he is an outstanding bunter.

At both shortstop and second base, The Cat shows well above-average mobility and soft hands. His throwing arm is average in strength but very accurate.

HOW HE PERFORMED IN '95

One of the world's least productive career .260 hitters, Fermin saw his batting average dip 122 points in '95 due to injuries and the fact that he's simply not that good. Lefthanders, who Felix usually hits, were especially tough on him. Calf and knee injuries hampered him, but the hitting of Luis Sojo and Joey Cora were the main reasons Fermin was out of the lineup late in the season.

WHAT TO EXPECT IN '96

The Mariners are trying to trade one of their veteran infielders. Fermin is likely to hang around a few more seasons as a utility middle infielder due to his fine defense, his bunting, and his ability to make contact.

JEFF NELSON

Position: RP
Bats: R **Throws:** R
Ht: 6'8" **Wt:** 225
Opening Day Age: 29
Born: 11/17/1966
Drafted: LA84 22/569
ML Seasons: 4

Overall Statistics

	G	GS	GF	SV	W	L	ERA	IP	H	R	ER	HR	BB	SO
95 SEA	62	0	24	2	7	3	2.17	78.2	58	21	19	4	27	96
Career	227	0	71	9	13	13	3.16	262.0	221	103	92	19	125	247

1995 Situational Statistics

	W	L	ERA	SV	IP	BB	SO		AB	HR	RBI	BA	OBA	SLG
Home	5	2	1.24	1	43.2	10	65	LHB	120	2	11	.233	.343	.317
Road	2	1	3.34	1	35.0	17	31	RHB	157	2	15	.191	.249	.280
Apr-Jun	3	1	1.60	1	33.2	17	34	ScPos	99	0	21	.182	.288	.232
Jul-Oct	4	2	2.60	1	45.0	10	62	Clutch	94	2	10	.245	.342	.351

SCOUTING REPORT

Working from the stretch, Nelson uses an unorthodox delivery, turning his back and throwing cross-fire from a low three-quarter angle. The odd motion helps make his pitches much harder to pick up, making his stuff more effective. Jeff's fastball is slightly above-average in velocity with good sink, and he complements it effectively with an average curve and change-up. A not-very-hard slider completes the picture.

The involved pitching motion means that runners can take off against Nelson easily: 14 tried to steal against him in '95, 12 successfully. He is an average fielder.

HOW HE PERFORMED IN '95

In the 62 games in which he appeared in '95, Jeff was scored on in just 12 of them. He has shown durability and surprising strikeout ability with the Mariners and keeps getting better against righthanders. Last season he shut down lefties, too, and hitters took him deep only four times.

WHAT TO EXPECT IN '96

Sent to New York in the Tino Martinez deal, Nelson might wrest setup duties from Bob Wickman if the latter slumps. However, he does not fit the pattern of a closer, and still has occasional bouts of poor control.

SEATTLE MARINERS

WARREN NEWSON

Positions: OF//DH
Bats: L **Throws:** L
Ht: 5'7" **Wt:** 190
Opening Day Age: 31
Born: 7/3/1964
Drafted: SD86* 4/90
ML Seasons: 5

Overall Statistics

	G	AB	R	H	2B	3B	HR	RBI	SB	CS	BB	SO	BA	OBA
95 CHA/SEA	84	157	34	41	2	2	5	15	2	1	39	45	.261	.411
Career	307	567	98	148	15	2	14	64	8	3	127	152	.261	.397

1995 Situational Statistics

	AB	HR	RBI	BA	OBA	SLG		AB	HR	RBI	BA	OBA	SLG
Home	77	4	12	.286	.439	.506	LHP	5	0	1	.200	.636	.200
Road	80	1	3	.237	.384	.287	RHP	152	5	14	.263	.398	.401
Apr-Jun	75	3	9	.267	.444	.440	ScPos	40	0	10	.175	.389	.250
Jul-Oct	82	2	6	.256	.378	.354	Clutch	39	0	3	.308	.357	.333

SCOUTING REPORT
Newson, a mistake hitter with average power, likes low fastballs and will take them to the opposite field. He knows the strike zone well and walks frequently, and is an above-average runner although he does not steal often.

In left field, Warren has average range, but below-average hands and throwing skills. He can also play right, but he's really a DH.

HOW HE PERFORMED IN '95
"The Deacon" was hitting just .235 in a reserve role for the White Sox when he was traded to Seattle on July 18, for a player to be named who turned out to be pitcher Jeff Darwin.

A popular and productive hitter in his five seasons with Chicago, Newson made 26 starts for Seattle, batting .292 with a .420 on-base percentage in 33 games. However, he was left off the Mariners' postseason roster, another instance of a general lack of respect this fine offensive player annually receives.

WHAT TO EXPECT IN '96
Signed this winter by Texas, Warren will fill his usual role, coming off the bench against righthanders but rarely getting a chance to play against lefties.

BILL RISLEY

Position: RP
Bats: R **Throws:** R
Ht: 6'2" **Wt:** 215
Opening Day Age: 28
Born: 5/29/1967
Drafted: CIN87 14/362
ML Seasons: 4

Overall Statistics

	G	GS	GF	SV	W	L	ERA	IP	H	R	ER	HR	BB	SO
95 SEA	45	0	5	1	2	1	3.13	60.1	55	21	21	7	18	65
Career	85	1	13	1	12	7	3.28	120.2	92	45	44	15	40	130

1995 Situational Statistics

	W	L	ERA	SV	IP	BB	SO		AB	HR	RBI	BA	OBA	SLG
Home	1	0	2.73	1	33.0	9	41	LHB	128	3	18	.234	.281	.352
Road	1	1	3.62	0	27.1	9	24	RHB	97	4	17	.258	.324	.423
Apr-Jun	1	1	1.40	1	25.2	7	35	ScPos	66	3	29	.303	.372	.500
Jul-Oct	1	0	4.41	0	34.2	11	30	Clutch	105	3	20	.267	.331	.400

SCOUTING REPORT
Throwing from three quarters with what scouts call a "maximum effort" delivery, Risley has two above-average pitches (fastball and slider) and has improved his formerly awful control. He throws the two premium pitches almost exclusively, only rarely using his curve. Although either of the two hard pitches can get Bill strikeouts, he could be truly dangerous with a good off-speed or breaking pitch.

Bill was much more agile off the mound in '95. Despite a poor move to first base, only five runners tried to steal against him, three successfully.

HOW HE PERFORMED IN '95
Risley started the season hot, allowing two earned runs in his first 18 innings. He missed two weeks in June with a strained rib cage, but the injury didn't seem to affect him. Unfortunately, Risley was awful in August and September when the M's were driving for the division lead, lowering his future stock with the team.

WHAT TO EXPECT IN '96
At the advanced age of 29, Risley still hasn't pitched many innings in the majors, but one thing is clear—he can pitch. Improved control could make him a very good setup pitcher or even the closer in Toronto in '96.

SEATTLE MARINERS

ALEX RODRIGUEZ

Position: SS
Bats: R **Throws:** R
Ht: 6'3" **Wt:** 190
Opening Day Age: 20
Born: 7/27/1975
Drafted: SEA93 1/1
ML Seasons: 2

Overall Statistics

	G	AB	R	H	2B	3B	HR	RBI	SB	CS	BB	SO	BA	OBA
95 SEA	48	142	15	33	6	2	5	19	4	2	6	42	.232	.264
Career	65	196	19	44	6	2	5	21	7	2	9	62	.224	.257

1995 Situational Statistics

	AB	HR	RBI	BA	OBA	SLG		AB	HR	RBI	BA	OBA	SLG
Home	57	1	8	.298	.333	.456	LHP	53	2	7	.245	.298	.491
Road	85	4	11	.188	.216	.376	RHP	89	3	12	.225	.242	.360
Apr-Jun	74	2	9	.257	.267	.378	ScPos	39	0	12	.256	.275	.308
Jul-Oct	68	3	10	.206	.260	.441	Clutch	24	0	1	.208	.208	.208

SCOUTING REPORT

One of the most highly-touted prospects in recent years, Alex is a five-tool player who needs time and experience to reach his outstanding potential. He has plus range and a strong arm in the field, plus power with good bat speed at the plate, and decent speed on the basepaths.

HOW HE PERFORMED IN '95

Rodriguez spent much of the season seeing spot duty at shortstop for the Mariners. He was recalled four times from Tacoma hitting a lusty .360 while at Triple-A.

Alex has not been a patient hitter in the minors, and that trait was exploited by experienced major-league pitchers. However, he did show good power and made plenty of spectacular plays at shortstop. He had occasional lapses in the field, fielding just .953, but is going to be a terrific defensive player.

WHAT TO EXPECT IN '96

Alex may need more time in the bushes to eliminate the holes in his swing, but he's got a good attitude and the Mariners are already running out of options on him. He should be a big star in a very few years and could play regularly in '96.

DOUG STRANGE

Positions: 3B//2B/OF/DH
Bats: B **Throws:** R
Ht: 6'2" **Wt:** 170
Opening Day Age: 31
Born: 4/13/1964
Drafted: DET85 7/184
ML Seasons: 6

Overall Statistics

	G	AB	R	H	2B	3B	HR	RBI	SB	CS	BB	SO	BA	OBA
95 SEA	74	155	19	42	9	2	2	21	0	3	10	25	.271	.323
Career	411	1164	126	275	56	4	16	127	12	13	95	184	.236	.298

1995 Situational Statistics

	AB	HR	RBI	BA	OBA	SLG		AB	HR	RBI	BA	OBA	SLG
Home	53	1	7	.264	.350	.358	LHP	9	0	1	.222	.222	.333
Road	102	1	14	.275	.308	.412	RHP	146	2	20	.274	.329	.397
Apr-Jun	79	1	11	.291	.349	.405	ScPos	39	1	18	.256	.341	.436
Jul-Oct	76	1	10	.250	.296	.382	Clutch	37	1	8	.270	.325	.405

SCOUTING REPORT

Like most switch-hitters, Doug hits low balls from the left side and high pitches righthanded. He does not have power or speed and rarely walks, but Strange makes contact and can lay down the sacrifice.

Able to fill in at several infield positions, he is steady but far from spectacular. Doug has plus hands and throwing accuracy, but just average range and arm strength in the infield.

HOW HE PERFORMED IN '95

Rebounding from a poor, injury-filled '94 season with Texas, Strange established a career high in batting average, largely because of .300 performances in May and June. He saw most of his action at third base, but made token appearances at second base and left field.

Despite being a switch-hitter, Doug is habitually awful against lefties. He saw almost no action against southpaws in '95 and may be permanently cast as a platoon player.

WHAT TO EXPECT IN '96

He is likely to return to the Mariners this year and fill a utility role. Strange is not going to be a starter again but can contribute in a minor role.

SEATTLE MARINERS

SALOMON TORRES

Position: SP/RP
Bats: R **Throws:** R
Ht: 5'11" **Wt:** 150
Opening Day Age: 24
Born: 3/11/1972
Drafted: SF 9/15/89
ML Seasons: 3

Overall Statistics

	G	GS	GF	SV	W	L	ERA	IP	H	R	ER	HR	BB	SO
95 SF/SEA	20	14	4	0	3	9	6.30	80.0	100	61	56	16	49	47
Career	44	36	6	0	8	22	5.47	209.0	232	137	127	31	110	112

1995 Situational Statistics

	W	L	ERA	SV	IP	BB	SO		AB	HR	RBI	BA	OBA	SLG
Home	1	5	6.46	0	39.0	23	24	LHB	200	5	26	.340	.433	.485
Road	2	4	6.15	0	41.0	26	23	RHB	132	11	32	.242	.333	.530
Apr-Jun	2	5	5.70	0	42.2	32	26	ScPos	107	4	40	.252	.344	.402
Jul-Oct	1	4	6.99	0	37.1	17	21	Clutch	17	0	2	.294	.400	.353

SCOUTING REPORT

Throwing with a loose-armed, three-quarter delivery, Salomon has two classic power pitches (fastball and curve, both plus) and an average slider that hangs often. He has no off-speed pitch. Worst of all, Torres' command of all his pitches is incredibly erratic. He puts runners on with walks and his get-me-over offerings are blasted out of the park.

Just average at holding runners, Salomon loses concentration at times. Eight runners stole against him in 11 tries last year. He is a fine athlete and a plus fielder.

HOW HE PERFORMED IN '95

Torres' once-bright star is burning out quickly due to poor control. The Giants, exasperated with his inconsistency and doubtful of his commitment to pitching (Torres is a devout Jehovah's Witness), sent the promising righty to Seattle's Tacoma affiliate May 21. Called up June 1, Torres spent two months with the Mariners without establishing consistency. After three horrid August outings, he pitched only once in September and was left off the postseason roster.

WHAT TO EXPECT IN '96

It's impossible to know what to expect from Salomon, who has a world of talent but has not to date found the discipline to utilize it.

THE SCOUTING REPORT: 1996

BOB WELLS

Position: RP
Bats: R **Throws:** R
Ht: 6'0" **Wt:** 180
Opening Day Age: 29
Born: 11/1/1966
Drafted: PHI 8/18/88
ML Seasons: 2

Overall Statistics

	G	GS	GF	SV	W	L	ERA	IP	H	R	ER	HR	BB	SO
95 SEA	30	4	3	0	4	3	5.75	76.2	88	51	49	11	39	38
Career	37	4	5	0	6	3	5.36	85.2	96	53	51	11	43	44

1995 Situational Statistics

	W	L	ERA	SV	IP	BB	SO		AB	HR	RBI	BA	OBA	SLG
Home	1	2	6.35	0	34.0	17	19	LHB	139	5	22	.295	.379	.525
Road	3	1	5.27	0	42.2	22	19	RHB	171	6	22	.275	.352	.456
Apr-Jun	2	3	7.53	0	34.2	14	19	ScPos	82	2	28	.244	.356	.402
Jul-Oct	2	0	4.29	0	42.0	25	19	Clutch	29	2	6	.379	.471	.621

SCOUTING REPORT

Throwing from high three quarters, Wells brings home three pitches with well above-average control. His fastball and change-up are just average, and his slider rates a little below that. Bob survives by moving the ball around the strike zone, but he had uncharacteristic location problems in '95.

He augments his mediocre stuff with above-average skills when fielding and holding runners. Only six runners tried to run on him in '95, five successfully.

HOW HE PERFORMED IN '95

Wells began the season in the Mariners' rotation, but was exiled to the bullpen after four starts in which he had allowed 14 runs in 14.2 innings. Although Bob wasn't much better as a garbage-time reliever (5.09 ERA), he did pitch quite well at times, and stayed healthy for the first time in five years. He even appeared in the ALCS, eating up innings—as he had done all season.

WHAT TO EXPECT IN '96

At age 29, with an undistinguished major-league record, Wells will have to struggle to make a staff as a tenth or eleventh pitcher.

SEATTLE MARINERS: TOP PROSPECTS

JAMES BONNICI
Bats: R Throws: R Opening Day Age: 24
Ht: 6-4 Wt: 230 Born: 1/21/1972
Position: 1B Drafted: 1990 #58 SEA

YR TEAM	LG/CLASS	G	AB	R	H	2B	3B	HR	RBI	SB	BA	OBA
93 Riverside	CAL/A	104	375	69	115	21	1	9	58	0	.307	.411
94 Riverside	CAL/A	113	397	71	111	23	3	10	71	1	.280	.393
95 Port City	SOU/AA	138	508	75	144	36	3	20	91	2	.283	.384

Bonnici, previously a poor defensive catcher, became a full-time first baseman last season and came alive offensively as a result. The Southern League All-Star led the league in total bases (246), extra-base hits (59) and doubles, was third in RBI, walks, and homers, and ranked fifth in hits. The big cleanup hitter has good power potential, worked hard on his defense at first base, and improved steadily as the season wore on.

RAFAEL CARMONA
Bats: L Throws: R Opening Day Age: 23
Ht: 6-2 Wt: 185 Born: 10/2/1972
Position: P Drafted: 1993 #12 SEA

YR TEAM	LG/CLASS	G	GS	GF	SV	W	L	ERA	IP	H	HR	BB	SO	O/BA
93 Bellingham	NWST/A	23	0	9	2	2	3	3.79	35.2	33	1	14	30	.239
94 Riverside	CAL/A	50	0	48	21	8	2	2.81	67.1	48	3	19	63	.200
95 Tacoma		8	8	0	0	4	3	5.06	48.0	52	6	19	37	.278
95 Port City		15	0	15	4	0	1	1.80	15.0	11	0	3	17	.212
95 Seattle		15	3	6	1	2	4	5.66	47.2	55	9	34	28	.293

The Puerto Rican native was considered one of the Mariners' top closer prospects after a strong '94 season. Featuring a solid fastball, slider and control, he got off to a great start last year at Port City and was promoted to Seattle. He was sent to Tacoma in July, moved into the starting rotation, and put together a streak of 17.1 scoreless innings in August, including a four-hit, 10-strikeout shutout of Phoenix.

JOSE CRUZ, JR.
Bats: S Throws: R Opening Day Age: 21
Ht: 6-0 Wt: 190 Born: 4/19/1974
Position: OF Drafted: 1995 #1 SEA

YR TEAM	LG/CLASS	G	AB	R	H	2B	3B	HR	RBI	SB	BA	OBA
95 Riverside	CAL/A	35	144	34	37	7	1	7	29	3	.257	.359
95 Everett	NWST/A	3	11	6	5	0	0	0	2	1	.455	.571

During three seasons at Rice, Cruz set school records in batting (.375), homers (43), and RBI (203), and earned First Team All-America honors twice. The Mariners selected the son of Jose and nephew of Hector Cruz with the third overall pick last June. The switch-hitting outfielder has all the tools and was considered the best college power hitter in the draft. Cruz has great instincts and knows the strike zone and did well in his pro debut. Defensively, he can play all three outfield positions, but his arm may make him a left-fielder.

SCOTT DAVISON
Bats: R Throws: R Opening Day Age: 25
Ht: 6-0 Wt: 190 Born: 10/16/1970
Position: P Drafted: 1988 #5 MON

YR TEAM	LG/CLASS	G	GS	GF	SV	W	L	ERA	IP	H	HR	BB	SO	O/BA
94 Bellingham	NWST/A	13	0	11	7	0	1	1.80	15.0	11	0	6	21	.190
94 Appleton	MID/A	4	0	2	0	0	1	3.68	7.1	7	0	2	7	.269
94 Calgary	PCL/AAA	11	0	3	0	0	1	6.14	14.2	20	1	6	17	.333
95 Tacoma		8	3	2	0	1	1	5.32	22.0	21	1	4	12	.247
95 Port City		34	0	28	10	2	0	0.89	40.2	22	1	16	50	.168
95 Seattle		3	0	3	0	0	0	6.23	4.1	7	1	1	3	.350

Shortly before spring training in 1992, the Expos released a light-hitting shortstop named Scott Davison after four lackluster seasons in which he never got out of Class-A. After two years as a high school coach, Davison re-emerged as a flame-throwing reliever in the Mariners' system. The 25-year-old righty dominated Southern League hitters last year, ranking second among the league's relievers in opponents' batting average (.168) and fifth in SO/9 IP (11.07) before climbing all the way to the big leagues. Davison is regarded as a top closer prospect and has the mid-90's fastball and tough slider the job requires.

RAUL IBANEZ
Bats: L Throws: R Opening Day Age: 23
Ht: 6-2 Wt: 210 Born: 6/2/1972
Position: C Drafted: 1992 #36 SEA

YR TEAM	LG/CLASS	G	AB	R	H	2B	3B	HR	RBI	SB	BA	OBA
93 Appleton	MID/A	52	157	26	43	9	0	5	21	0	.274	.370
93 Bellingham	NWST/A	43	134	16	38	5	2	0	15	0	.284	.378
94 Appleton	MID/A	91	327	55	102	30	3	7	59	10	.312	.375
95 Riverside	CAL/A	95	361	59	120	23	9	20	108	4	.332	.395

Despite missing the first six weeks of the season with a broken wrist, Ibanez was named the Mariners' Organization Player of the Year after leading the system in batting and RBI and tying for the home run lead. He made the California League All-Star team, leading the loop in slugging (.564), finishing second in triples and RBI, and ending third in the batting race. The 23-year-old, originally an outfielder, needs more experience behind the plate and had trouble throwing out basestealers, but by the end of last season was one of the most improved players in the league. Offensively, Ibanez is an excellent hitter with great left-handed power for a catcher.

JIM MECIR
Bats: S Throws: R Opening Day Age: 25
Ht: 6-1 Wt: 195 Born: 5/16/1970
Position: P Drafted: 1991 #3 SEA

YR TEAM	LG/CLASS	G	GS	GF	SV	W	L	ERA	IP	H	HR	BB	SO	O/BA
93 Riverside	CAL/A	26	26	0	0	9	11	4.33	145.1	160	3	58	85	.281
94 Jacksonville	SOU/AA	46	0	34	13	6	5	2.69	80.1	73	5	35	53	.245
95 Tacoma		40	0	22	8	1	4	3.10	69.2	63	3	28	46	.238
95 Seattle		2	0	1	0	0	0	0.00	4.2	5	0	2	3	.263

The 25-year-old righthander is one of the rare pitchers who throws a screwball and also features a fastball in the low 90's, a slider, and a change. His fastball has good sinking action and Mecir induces ground ball after ground ball. He is not highly touted, but Mecir has been very effective since moving to the bullpen at the start of the '94 season and pitched well in two appearances with Seattle last September.

SEATTLE MARINERS: TOP PROSPECTS

TREY MOORE

Bats: L Throws: L Opening Day Age: 23
Ht: 6-1 Wt: 200   Born: 10/2/1972
Position: P   Drafted: 1994 #2 SEA

YR TEAM	LG/CLASS	G	GS	GF	SV	W	L	ERA	IP	H	HR	BB	SO	O/BA
94 Bellingham	NWST/A	11	10	0	0	5	2	2.63	61.2	48	4	24	73	.219
95 Riverside		24	24	0	0	14	6	3.09	148.1	122	6	58	134	.228

After going 12-0 with a 2.77 ERA in his sophomore season at Texas A&M, the Third Team All-American was projected as a first-round pick, but he slumped to 5-5, 3.59 ERA in his junior year and lasted until the middle of the draft's second round. However, Moore pitched well after signing and proved that he had returned to form last summer, leading the Mariners' system in wins and ERA and posting the lowest opponents' batting average in the California League. While Moore is not a hard thrower, he is poised, knows how to pitch, and has an average fastball and good slider.

ARQUIMEDEZ POZO

Bats: R Throws: R Opening Day Age: 22
Ht: 5-10 Wt: 160   Born: 8/24/1973
Position: 2B/3B   Drafted: NDFA 8-26-90 SEA

YR TEAM	LG/CLASS	G	AB	R	H	2B	3B	HR	RBI	SB	BA	OBA
93 Riverside	CAL/A	127	515	98	176	44	6	13	83	10	.342	.405
94 Jacksonville	SOU/AA	119	447	70	129	31	1	14	54	11	.289	.341
95 Tacoma	PCL/AAA	122	450	57	135	19	6	10	62	3	.300	.340
95 Seattle	AL/MAJ	1	1	0	0	0	0	0	0	0	.000	.000

With a career average of .307 and slugging percentage of .471, the Dominican native has shown that he can hit and produce good extra-base power. Strong and stout, he is an aggressive hitter with a beautiful swing that produces sharp line drives. He does not swing and miss often, and 1995 marked the third straight year he ranked among league leaders in strikeouts per plate appearance. The knock on Pozo has been that his defense will never be major league-caliber, but he has made great strides with the glove and may hit well enough to negate his defensive flaws. A glut of middle infielders in the organization, resulted in Pozo being shifted to third base late last summer.

DESI RELAFORD

Bats: S Throws: R Opening Day Age: 22
Ht: 5-8 Wt: 155   Born: 9/16/1973
Position: 2B/SS   Drafted: 1991 #4 SEA

YR TEAM	LG/CLASS	G	AB	R	H	2B	3B	HR	RBI	SB	BA	OBA
93 Jacksonville	SOU/AA	133	472	49	115	16	4	8	47	16	.244	.323
94 Jacksonville	SOU/AA	37	143	24	29	7	3	3	11	10	.203	.305
94 Riverside	CAL/A	99	374	95	116	27	5	5	59	27	.310	.429
95 Tacoma	PCL/AAA	30	113	20	27	5	1	2	7	6	.239	.313
95 Port City	SOU/AA	90	352	51	101	11	2	7	27	25	.287	.365

Although Relaford is inconsistent, he is an outstanding defensive shortstop with terrific range, good hands and a strong arm with a quick release. With phenom Alex Rodriguez blocking his path at short, the 22-year-old switch-hitter was shifted to second base late in 1995. Offensively, Relaford is fast and the potential to hit for a good average, though he doesn't have much power and needs to hit the ball on the ground more to take better advantage of his speed.

JASON VARITEK

Bats: S Throws: R Opening Day Age: 23
Ht: 6-2 Wt: 210   Born: 4/11/1972
Position: C   Drafted: 1994 #1 SEA

YR TEAM	LG/CLASS	G	AB	R	H	2B	3B	HR	RBI	SB	BA	OBA
95 Port City	SOU/AA	104	352	42	79	14	2	10	44	0	.224	.340

Varitek was one of the most highly touted (and difficult to sign) players to come out of college. He was a First Team All-American three times and won the Golden Spikes Award. Twice a first-round pick, he spurned the Twins' offer and returned to Georgia Tech for his senior season before being drafted by the Mariners. He signed a pro contract last April and reported to Port City. Considered solid defensively with big-time power potential, the switch-hitting former Yellow Jacket backstop struggled with all aspects of his game last year. Varitek has a great work ethic and calls a good game, but runners stole almost at will against him. At the plate, trouble with breaking pitches led to strikeouts better than once every three at-bats.

CHRIS WIDGER

Bats: R Throws: R Opening Day Age: 24
Ht: 6-3 Wt: 195   Born: 5/21/1971
Position: C   Drafted: 1992 #3 SEA

YR TEAM	LG/CLASS	G	AB	R	H	2B	3B	HR	RBI	SB	BA	OBA
93 Riverside	CAL/A	97	360	44	95	28	2	9	58	5	.264	.303
94 Jacksonville	SOU/AA	116	388	58	101	15	3	16	59	8	.260	.334
95 Tacoma	PCL/AAA	50	174	29	48	11	1	9	21	0	.276	.311
95 Seattle	AL/MAJ	23	45	2	9	0	0	1	2	0	.200	.245

The George Mason product has emerged as the Mariners' top catching prospect. A solid hitter with some power, he was drafted for his offensive potential. He has become a defensive whiz behind the plate with a strong and accurate arm and has worked hard at blocking pitches in the dirt. A SL All-Star in '94, Widger started 1995 at Tacoma, but was summoned to the big leagues at the end of June and eventually beat out Chad Kreuter to become the number two catcher behind Dan Wilson.

BOB WOLCOTT

Bats: R Throws: R Opening Day Age: 22
Ht: 6-0 Wt: 190   Born: 9/8/1973
Position: P   Drafted: 1992 #2 SEA

YR TEAM	LG/CLASS	G	GS	GF	SV	W	L	ERA	IP	H	HR	BB	SO	O/BA
93 Bellingham	NWST/A	15	15	0	0	8	4	2.64	95.1	70	7	26	79	.199
94 Riverside	CAL/A	26	26	0	0	14	8	2.84	180.2	173	11	50	142	.248
94 Calgary	PCL/AAA	1	1	0	0	1	0	3.00	6.0	6	1	3	5	.273
95 Tacoma		13	13	0	0	6	3	4.08	79.1	94	10	16	43	.293
95 Port City		12	12	0	0	7	3	2.20	86.0	60	6	13	53	.200
95 Seattle		7	6	0	0	3	2	4.42	36.2	43	6	14	19	.297

The Mariners' Minor League Pitcher of the Year showed in the American League Championship Series why he's the organization's top mound prospect. Added to the post-season roster to help save a tired pitching staff, Wolcott struck out Albert Belle with the bases loaded in the first inning and shut down the high-powered Cleveland offense to pick up the win in Game One. The 22-year-old won 13 games for Port City and Tacoma last year before an August promotion to Seattle where he pitched well. Wolcott knows how to pitch and has a solid fastball and good slider to go along with a curve and change. He is at his best when he challenges hitters and mixes his pitches well.

SEATTLE MARINERS: OTHERS TO WATCH

MATT APANA   Bats: R Throws: R   Ht: 6-0 Wt: 195
Born: 1/16/1971   Drafted: 1993 #21 SEA   Position: P

YR TEAM	LG/CLASS	G	GS	GF	SV	W	L	ERA	IP	H	HR	BB	SO	O/BA
95 Tacoma	PCL/AAA	21	20	0	0	8	8	4.95	103.2	121	9	61	58	.298
95 Port City	SOU/AA	6	6	0	0	1	3	4.32	33.1	34	4	24	28	.268

The Hawaii product has good stuff and poise, but struggled with his command after a great start in 1995.

EDDY DIAZ   Bats: R Throws: R   Ht: 5-10 Wt: 160
Born: 9/29/1971   Drafted: NDFA 2-15-90 SEA   Position: SS/2B

YR TEAM	LG/CLASS	G	AB	R	H	2B	3B	HR	RBI	SB	BA	OBA
95 Tacoma	PCL/AAA	11	36	5	12	2	0	0	5	0	.333	.400
95 Port City	SOU/AA	110	421	66	110	22	0	16	47	9	.261	.334

The 24-year-old infielder showed surprising power last year and doesn't strike out, but has trouble hitting lefthanders.

OSVALDO FERNANDEZ   Bats: L Throws: L   Ht: 6-2 Wt: 193
Born: 4/15/1970   Drafted: 1994 #22 SEA   Position: P

YR TEAM	LG/CLASS	G	GS	GF	SV	W	L	ERA	IP	H	HR	BB	SO	O/BA
95 Port City	SOU/AA	27	26	0	0	12	7	3.57	156.1	139	6	60	160	.238

The Cuban lefty does not throw hard, but led the SL in strikeouts and has five pitches, including a screwball and two curves.

GEORGE GLINATSIS   Bats: R Throws: R   Ht: 6-4 Wt: 195
Born: 6/29/1969   Drafted: 1991 #32 SEA   Position: P

YR TEAM	LG/CLASS	G	GS	GF	SV	W	L	ERA	IP	H	HR	BB	SO	O/BA
95 Tacoma	PCL/AAA	8	8	0	0	1	2	7.34	30.2	39	4	13	13	.320
95 Port City	SOU/AA	18	18	0	0	6	7	5.30	93.1	104	6	44	68	.286

A righthander out of Cincinnati, Glinatsis went from Class-A to the majors in '94, but scuffled at two minor league stops in '95.

TIM HARIKKALA   Bats: R Throws: R   Ht: 6-2 Wt: 185
Born: 7/15/1971   Drafted: 1992 #34 SEA   Position: P

YR TEAM	LG/CLASS	G	GS	GF	SV	W	L	ERA	IP	H	HR	BB	SO	O/BA
95 Tacoma	PCL/AAA	25	24	0	0	5	12	4.24	146.1	151	13	55	73	.263
95 Seattle	AL/MAJ	1	0	1	0	0	0	16.20	3.1	7	1	1	1	.412

After going 16-4, 2.34 ERA in '94 to win the organization's Pitcher of the Year award, Harikkala fell to 5-12 at Tacoma.

RANDY JORGENSEN   Bats: L Throws: L   Ht: 6-2 Wt: 200
Born: 4/3/1972   Drafted: 1993 #11 SEA   Position: 1B

YR TEAM	LG/CLASS	G	AB	R	H	2B	3B	HR	RBI	SB	BA	OBA
95 Riverside	CAL/A	133	495	78	148	32	2	12	97	4	.299	.371

An excellent defensive first baseman, Jorgensen's bat came alive as he finished fourth in the CL in RBI and fifth in hits.

GREG KEAGLE   Bats: R Throws: R   Ht: 6-2 Wt: 185
Born: 6/28/1971   Drafted: 1993 #6 SD   Position: P

YR TEAM	LG/CLASS	G	GS	GF	SV	W	L	ERA	IP	H	HR	BB	SO	O/BA
95 Las Vegas	PCL/AAA	14	13	1	0	7	6	4.28	75.2	76	3	42	69	.260
95 Memphis	SOU/AA	15	15	0	0	4	9	5.11	81.0	82	11	41	82	.261
95 R C-monga	CAL/A	2	2	0	0	0	4	4.50	14.0	14	1	2	11	.259

A hard thrower with little command and a weak curveball, Keagle arrived as a player-to-be-named later in the Benes deal.

RICK LADJEVICH   Bats: R Throws: R   Ht: 6-3 Wt: 220
Born: 2/17/1972   Drafted: 1994 #26 SEA   Position: 3B

YR TEAM	LG/CLASS	G	AB	R	H	2B	3B	HR	RBI	SB	BA	OBA
95 Riverside	CAL/A	122	470	74	145	26	0	7	71	3	.309	.370

Ladjevich was named to the CL All-Star team in his first full season, but didn't show the power needed for the hot corner.

GREG PIRKL   Bats: R Throws: R   Ht: 6-5 Wt: 225
Born: 8/7/1970   Drafted: 1988 #2 SEA   Position: 1B

YR TEAM	LG/CLASS	G	AB	R	H	2B	3B	HR	RBI	SB	BA	OBA
95 Tacoma	PCL/AAA	47	174	29	51	8	2	15	44	1	.293	.347
95 Seattle	AL/MAJ	10	17	2	4	0	0	0	0	0	.235	.278

Pirkl, who has shuttled between Triple-A and the majors the last three years, has 64 career Triple-A homers and seven in 93 at-bats.

MARINO SANTANA   Bats: R Throws: R   Ht: 6-1 Wt: 188
Born: 5/10/1972   Drafted: NDFA 4-28-90 SEA   Position: P

YR TEAM	LG/CLASS	G	GS	GF	SV	W	L	ERA	IP	H	HR	BB	SO	O/BA
95 Riverside	CAL/A	9	9	0	0	3	5	6.19	48.0	44	10	25	57	.244
95 Wisconsin	MID/A	15	15	0	0	8	3	1.77	96.2	57	5	25	110	.169

The 23-year-old Dominican has great movement on his slider and a good change and led the farm system in strikeouts last year.

ANDY SHEETS   Bats: R Throws: R   Ht: 6-2 Wt: 180
Born: 11/19/1971   Drafted: 1992 #4 SEA   Position: SS

YR TEAM	LG/CLASS	G	AB	R	H	2B	3B	HR	RBI	SB	BA	OBA
95 Tacoma	PCL/AAA	132	437	57	128	29	9	2	47	8	.293	.338

Primarily a shortstop, is a great defensive player who can play second and third and could become a valuable utility player.

MAC SUZUKI   Bats: R Throws: R   Ht: 6-4 Wt: 195
Born: 5/31/1975   Purchased: JAPAN 10-93   Position: P

YR TEAM	LG/CLASS	G	GS	GF	SV	W	L	ERA	IP	H	HR	BB	SO	O/BA
95 Riverside	CAL/A	6	0	1	0	0	1	4.70	7.2	10	0	6	6	.313
95 Mariners	ARIZ/R	4	3	0	0	1	0	6.75	4.0	5	1	0	3	.278

A closer prospect from Japan, Suzuki has pitched just 24.1 innings the last two seasons due to a variety of arm problems.

SAL URSO   Bats: R Throws: L   Ht: 5-11 Wt: 195
Born: 1/19/1972   Drafted: 1990 #36 SEA   Position: P

YR TEAM	LG/CLASS	G	GS	GF	SV	W	L	ERA	IP	H	HR	BB	SO	O/BA
95 Port City	SOU/AA	51	0	8	1	2	0	2.17	45.2	41	0	21	44	.250

Urso, a workhorse out of the pen for Port City last year, has a biting slider to go along with a mid-80's fastball and good control.

MATT WAGNER   Bats: R Throws: R   Ht: 6-5 Wt: 215
Born: 4/4/1972   Drafted: 1994 #3 SEA   Position: P

YR TEAM	LG/CLASS	G	GS	GF	SV	W	L	ERA	IP	H	HR	BB	SO	O/BA
95 Tacoma	PCL/AAA	6	6	0	0	1	5	6.27	33.0	43	3	17	33	.312
95 Port City	SOU/AA	23	23	0	0	5	8	2.82	137.0	121	9	33	111	.232

Wagner has a history of shoulder problems, but the righthander has a low-90's fastball, a tough slider and two changeups.

TREY WITTE   Bats: R Throws: R   Ht: 6-1 Wt: 190
Born: 1/15/1970   Drafted: 1991 #9 SEA   Position: P

YR TEAM	LG/CLASS	G	GS	GF	SV	W	L	ERA	IP	H	HR	BB	SO	O/BA
95 Port City	SOU/AA	48	0	34	11	3	2	1.73	62.1	48	0	14	39	.216

A fastball/slider pitcher who needs to work on his changeup, Witte put together a streak of 28 innings without allowing an earned run last season.

TEXAS RANGERS

WILL CLARK

Positions: 1B//DH
Bats: L **Throws:** L
Ht: 6'2" **Wt:** 190
Opening Day Age: 32
Born: 3/13/1964
Drafted: SF85 1/2
ML Seasons: 10

SCOUTING REPORT
Will is one of baseball's best "guess" hitters. He is smart, studies pitchers and has a good idea of how they pitch to him. He has a good idea of the strike zone and does not swing at pitches he is not looking for, unless he is fooled. However, Clark struggles with pitchers who outsmart him by mixing their pitches effectively. Low and inside pitches are his favorite, and he can pull them, but Will's power has decreased. Bunting is no longer in his vocabulary; he has just one sacrifice in the last eight years.

Never fast, he now has average-minus speed and is not a very good baserunner. Defensively, Clark has a poor throwing arm with average accuracy and only average range, but he has quick hands and does an effective job of picking less than perfect throws from other infielders.

HOW HE PERFORMED IN '95
"The Thrill" started '95 behind the local fans' 8-ball when his tough union stance towards replacement players was not received well. The fans' reaction distressed Clark, who plays hard and often plays through injuries. Will still did his best at the plate, hitting at least .273 in each month. He hit five homers in both June and August, and a late-season rush pushed his average over .300. Clark's .302 lifetime mark now ranks eighth among active major-leaguers. He registered his highest RBI total since 1991 despite missing 21 games with nagging injuries. An elbow problem, in particular, curtailed his swing and robbed him of some power.

He did, however, field his position better than he had in '94, with his fielding percentage ranking fifth and double play total ranking second among AL first basemen.

WHAT TO EXPECT IN '96
The five-year, $25 million-plus contract Clark received in '93 was the most lucrative contract in Rangers' history. It looked like a coup for Texas at the time, but his salary is now an albatross around the club's neck. Will would be dealt if the Rangers could find a taker, but it doesn't look that this will happen soon. Clark is not the player the Rangers expected and it's doubtful he ever will be. He is often hurt and carries at least ten more pounds than he did during his glory days in San Francisco. It should not be a surprise if nagging injuries cause further deterioration of his play in '96.

Overall Statistics

	G	AB	R	H	2B	3B	HR	RBI	SB	CS	BB	SO	BA	OBA
95 TEX	123	454	85	137	27	3	16	92	0	1	68	50	.302	.389
Career	1393	5112	845	1543	300	42	205	881	57	43	645	853	.302	.379

1995 Situational Statistics

	AB	HR	RBI	BA	OBA	SLG		AB	HR	RBI	BA	OBA	SLG
Home	218	10	42	.303	.409	.518	LHP	148	4	32	.291	.384	.453
Road	236	6	50	.301	.370	.445	RHP	306	12	60	.307	.392	.493
Apr-Jun	186	8	36	.290	.389	.478	ScPos	129	3	72	.341	.418	.473
Jul-Oct	268	8	56	.310	.389	.481	Clutch	56	1	12	.339	.448	.464

How He Compares to Other Batters

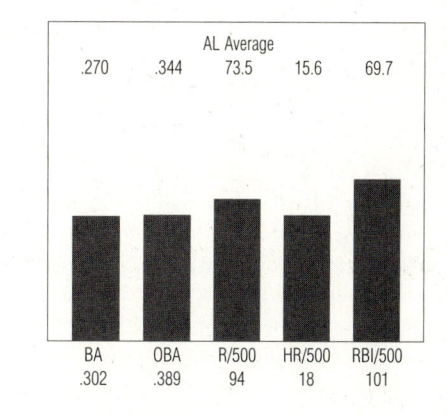

AL Average: .270 / .344 / 73.5 / 15.6 / 69.7

BA	OBA	R/500	HR/500	RBI/500
.302	.389	94	18	101

Where He Hits the Ball

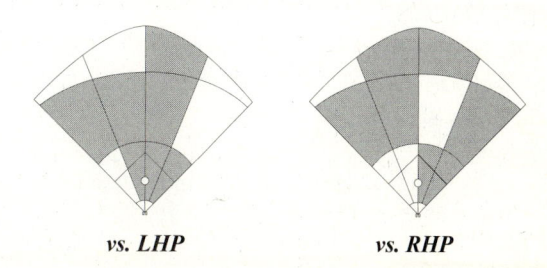

vs. LHP   vs. RHP

THE SCOUTING REPORT: 1996

TEXAS RANGERS

BENJI GIL

Position: SS
Bats: R **Throws:** R
Ht: 6'2" **Wt:** 180
Opening Day Age: 23
Born: 10/6/1972
Drafted: TEX91 1/19
ML Seasons: 2

SCOUTING REPORT

Defense is Gil's calling card. His range is slightly above-average and is expected to improve with experience. While Gil's hands are just average now, scouts predict they will eventually be plus, and he throws with average-plus strength and plus accuracy. As last season went on, Benji's arm appeared to get stronger.

He currently handles fastballs well and should improve, but has serious problems with breaking balls and off-speed pitches. This will cut down the number of heaters Gil sees until he cuts down on his aggressive swinging—Benji chases pitches up in the strike zone with regularity. Power is expected to develop, but he may never be more than an average runner.

HOW HE PERFORMED IN '95

Early in his tenure, Johnny Oates decided rookie Benji Gil would be the Rangers' shortstop. Gil's '93 flop with the Rangers and his .248 performance at Oklahoma City in '94 didn't serve as much of a rack for him to hang future major-league success on, and some in the local media predicted Benji would be gone by June 1.

However, "The Kid" immediately showed himself one of the AL's top defensive shortstops and hit well during the first two months. By season's end, Gil had a lock on the shortstop job.

He's still got plenty of work to do. Benji batted .187 in his final 81 games, homering just twice in final 71 contests, and barely cleared the "Mendoza Line" while ending up second in the AL in strikeouts. Oddly for a righthanded batter, Gil was utterly helpless against lefthanders. He did lead the Rangers with 10 sacrifice bunts.

In the field, he was outstanding, ranking second among AL shortstops in total chances, assists, and double plays. While Gil isn't perfect with the glove, he showed clear improvement: after making 37 errors in Triple-A during '94, he cut that total to 17 while making the jump to the majors last year.

WHAT TO EXPECT IN '96

Gil will be the Ranger shortstop in '96 and is expected to hold the job for a long time. He couldn't be much better in the field, but should be—and has to be—a whole lot better offensively. It's likely that he will continue to bat very low in the order until he figures out how pitchers work the strike zone.

Overall Statistics

	G	AB	R	H	2B	3B	HR	RBI	SB	CS	BB	SO	BA	OBA
95 TEX	130	415	36	91	20	3	9	46	2	4	26	147	.219	.266
Career	152	472	39	98	20	3	9	48	3	6	31	169	.208	.257

1995 Situational Statistics

	AB	HR	RBI	BA	OBA	SLG		AB	HR	RBI	BA	OBA	SLG
Home	203	5	22	.251	.295	.404	LHP	102	0	8	.108	.225	.157
Road	212	4	24	.189	.238	.292	RHP	313	9	38	.256	.281	.409
Apr-Jun	200	7	29	.255	.301	.415	ScPos	108	2	37	.278	.328	.426
Jul-Oct	215	2	17	.186	.232	.284	Clutch	49	1	4	.102	.185	.184

How He Compares to Other Batters

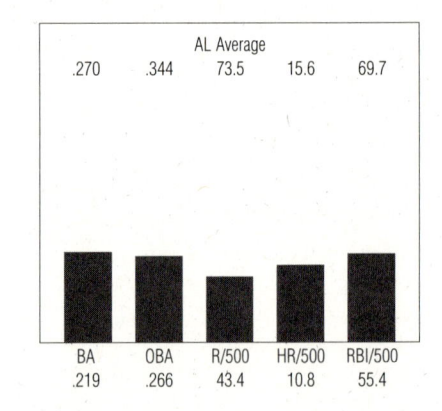

AL Average: .270 .344 73.5 15.6 69.7

BA	OBA	R/500	HR/500	RBI/500
.219	.266	43.4	10.8	55.4

Where He Hits the Ball

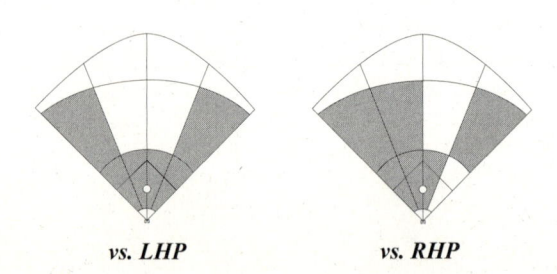

vs. LHP   vs. RHP

TEXAS RANGERS

JUAN GONZALEZ

Positions: DH//OF
Bats: R **Throws:** R
Ht: 6'3" **Wt:** 175
Opening Day Age: 26
Born: 10/20/1969
Drafted: TEX 5/30/86
ML Seasons: 7

SCOUTING REPORT

The extremely strong but injury-prone Gonzalez is a pure fastball hitter who likes low heat out over the plate. He has tremendous power. Unfortunately, Juan tries to pull everything; he swings early and consequently gets fooled by outside breaking balls although he can hit the breaking pitch inside. He is not patient and many pitchers get him out without having to throw strikes.

Gonzalez is rated as an average-minus baserunner, and is no threat to steal at any time.

Injuries relegated Juan to DH duties in '95. When he can play the field, it's strictly as a left fielder and is, at best, adequate. His arm is reasonably strong but somewhat erratic. It's hard to believe that just a few years ago, Juan was playing center field.

HOW HE PERFORMED IN '95

Gonzalez led the AL in home runs in both 1992 and 1993, and at the age of 26 is already the Rangers' all-time home run leader and is signed to a $40 million-plus contract. He should have been on top of the world, but Juan had a miserable '95 season. Back troubles placed him on the DL twice, forcing him out of left field and into designated hitting.

Although his performance declined, he still did some things very well. Gonzalez drove in almost one run per game and homered once every 13 at-bats, showing that he still has his awesome power.

However, he still tends to get himself out at the plate, and needs to take the base on balls more often. In both June and August, he walked just once, but in September, where he batted .339 with eight homers, Gonzalez drew 10 walks.

Juan was named AL "Player of the Week"—his first such award—for the week of September 4-11. This is noteworthy because an unknown Orioles' shortstop eclipsed an old record that week.

WHAT TO EXPECT IN '96

Gonzalez missed 54 games, almost 40% of the '95 season, and could not play the field. For a $7 million annual salary, the Rangers expected a more.

Juan vowed to come back in '96 healthy enough to play the outfield. However, even at his best, Gonzalez' annual price tag is nearly a quarter of the Rangers targeted payroll and robs the club of flexibility in building their team. Whether he will ever again be the player he once was is anybody's guess.

Overall Statistics

	G	AB	R	H	2B	3B	HR	RBI	SB	CS	BB	SO	BA	OBA
95 TEX	90	352	57	104	20	2	27	82	0	0	17	66	.295	.324
Career	683	2589	391	717	139	11	167	515	14	11	169	527	.277	.326

1995 Situational Statistics

	AB	HR	RBI	BA	OBA	SLG		AB	HR	RBI	BA	OBA	SLG
Home	161	15	44	.317	.349	.689	LHP	101	9	26	.327	.352	.653
Road	191	12	38	.277	.302	.513	RHP	251	18	56	.283	.312	.570
Apr-Jun	98	8	25	.296	.294	.633	ScPos	94	8	53	.287	.333	.628
Jul-Oct	254	19	57	.295	.335	.579	Clutch	49	2	9	.224	.255	.408

How He Compares to Other Batters

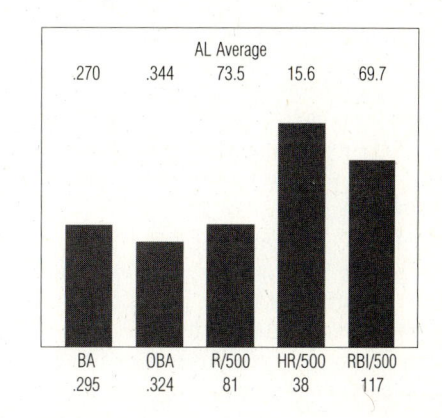

	BA	OBA	R/500	HR/500	RBI/500
AL Average	.270	.344	73.5	15.6	69.7
	.295	.324	81	38	117

Where He Hits the Ball

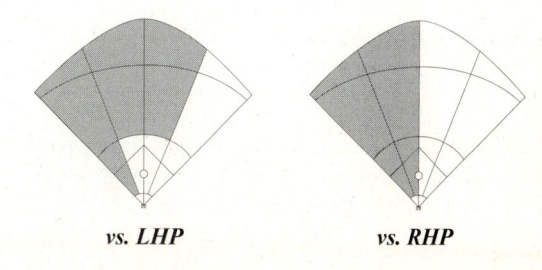

vs. LHP   vs. RHP

TEXAS RANGERS

RUSTY GREER

Positions: OF//1B
Bats: L **Throws:** L
Ht: 6'0" **Wt:** 190
Opening Day Age: 27
Born: 1/21/1969
Drafted: TEX90 10/279
ML Seasons: 2

SCOUTING REPORT
A good but not excellent fastball hitter, Greer has some power and bat speed. He's more of a line-drive guy and thrives on pitchers' mistakes. Rusty hangs in decently on breaking balls and is both willing and capable of working the count effectively. He'll take the walk when it's offered.

The little game is not Greer's specialty. He does not bunt and has minus speed.

The Rangers have used Rusty at all three outfield positions; in fact, his diving catch in center field saved Kenny Rogers' perfect game in '94. However, he is best suited to right. His arm is average-plus and has above-average accuracy. His range is slightly below par but his hands are sure. Greer gets a good jump and is a better defensive player overall than his skills might indicate.

HOW HE PERFORMED IN '95
There was no sophomore slump for the Rangers' top 1994 rookie. Although Greer isn't star material, he can play well and contribute. Injuries to several Texas regulars and a lack of other good players meant he played almost every game in '95. Rusty made 107 starts and, surprisingly for a young player, showed prowess as a pinch hitter (.429 in 14 at-bats with two home runs). Four times he won games by driving in runs during the last at bat of the game, including hitting a grand slam against Milwaukee on May 18.

Rusty switched between right and left field, occasionally spelling the Rangers' regulars at first base and center. He hustled every day and never complained about his irregular usage. Texas was never short with him in the field; his nine outfield assists placed Greer sixth among AL outfielders.

He both started and ended the season hot, only slumping in July (.181). Greer isn't much of a hitter in The Ballpark in Arlington, and unfortunately, it doesn't look like Rusty is going to do much with lefthanded pitchers.

WHAT TO EXPECT IN '96
If Juan Gonzalez returns healthy enough to play left field, Greer could platoon in right field against righthanders. Although the Rangers need an offensive force in right, the club will probably run out of money before they address this need, so Rusty has a good shot at 400 at-bats again. For Texas to win, Greer needs to provide more sock if he gets that opportunity.

Overall Statistics

	G	AB	R	H	2B	3B	HR	RBI	SB	CS	BB	SO	BA	OBA
95 TEX	131	417	58	113	21	2	13	61	3	1	55	66	.271	.355
Career	211	694	94	200	37	3	23	107	3	1	101	112	.288	.378

1995 Situational Statistics

	AB	HR	RBI	BA	OBA	SLG		AB	HR	RBI	BA	OBA	SLG
Home	190	7	30	.232	.332	.379	LHP	78	2	9	.244	.314	.346
Road	227	6	31	.304	.375	.463	RHP	339	11	52	.277	.364	.442
Apr-Jun	176	6	32	.273	.377	.432	ScPos	121	6	52	.273	.397	.463
Jul-Oct	241	7	29	.270	.338	.419	Clutch	65	4	12	.231	.320	.415

How He Compares to Other Batters

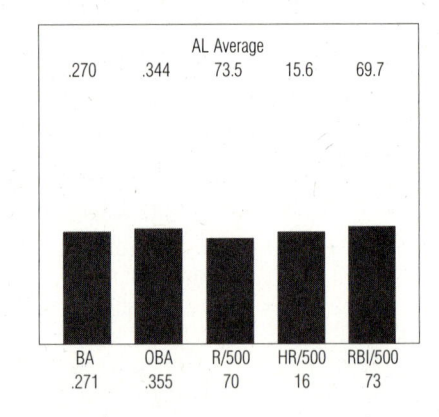

AL Average: .270 / .344 / 73.5 / 15.6 / 69.7

BA .271 | OBA .355 | R/500 70 | HR/500 16 | RBI/500 73

Where He Hits the Ball

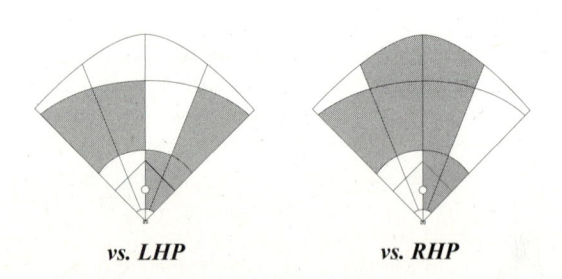

vs. LHP | vs. RHP

TEXAS RANGERS

SCOUTING REPORT
Veteran righthander Kevin Gross has a three-quarter to high three-quarter motion. His fastball, once an effective pitch, is now minus in velocity. Kevin usually turns over and sinks the fastball and the pitch has early movement. His two curves are rated average-plus. He has one bender with a sharp downward break and another with a sharp lateral break. The slider is an average-minus offering for Gross, and his control is now rated minus. If Kevin is to be successful, he needs good location and needs to get ahead in the count.

Gross uses the slide step to hold runners on first, giving him an average-plus move. Of the 21 runners who tried to steal while he was pitching in '95, 13 were successful. His fielding is slightly above-average.

HOW HE PERFORMED IN '95
Gross allowed nine runs in two innings at the Rangers' home opener and his season never got much better. Kevin ended up with the highest ERA in the majors among pitchers qualifying for the ERA title and led the AL in losses. By June, he was talking retirement. He stayed in the rotation only because Texas had no options. In a five-start string in August, he went 3-2 with a 2.68 ERA. It was a small piece of heaven in an otherwise ugly year.

Gross does not have the velocity or command of pitches he once had. He is constantly nibbling at the corners of the plate, leading to high pitch counts, too many walks (nearly two more per game in '95 than a year earlier), and big hits from batters ahead in the count.

WHAT TO EXPECT IN '96
The two-year deal, $6 million deal Gross signed with the Rangers in late 1994 is easily GM Doug Melvin's worst player move to date. Had Kevin signed after the strike ended last spring, he would have been fortunate to receive a one-year deal at half the salary. The penny-pinching Rangers will commit a '96 rotation spot to Gross, perhaps baseball's only pitcher with a last name that describes his 1995 performance. His late-season "resurgence" gives some hope he can improve. However, facts are facts. In 13 major-league seasons, Gross has posted exactly two winning records. One could understand a lefthander getting big money for being durable and hanging close to .500, but a righthander?

KEVIN GROSS

Position: SP
Bats: R **Throws:** R
Ht: 6'5" **Wt:** 215
Opening Day Age: 34
Born: 6/8/1961
Drafted: PHI81* S1/11
ML Seasons: 13

Overall Statistics

	G	GS	GF	SV	W	L	ERA	IP	H	R	ER	HR	BB	SO
95 TEX	31	30	0	0	9	15	5.54	183.2	200	124	113	27	89	106
Career	434	346	32	5	129	149	4.02	2333.0	2338	1147	1043	207	916	1629

1995 Situational Statistics

	W	L	ERA	SV	IP	BB	SO		AB	HR	RBI	BA	OBA	SLG
Home	4	7	6.35	0	79.1	39	49	LHB	378	11	52	.280	.347	.439
Road	5	8	4.92	0	104.1	50	57	RHB	337	16	49	.279	.379	.472
Apr-Jun	3	7	8.11	0	64.1	43	39	ScPos	154	4	72	.286	.400	.409
Jul-Oct	6	8	4.15	0	119.1	46	67	Clutch	26	0	1	.192	.417	.269

How He Compares to Other Pitchers

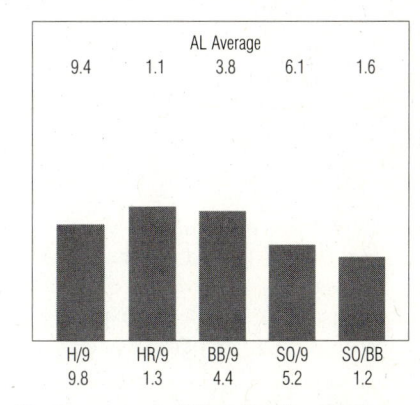

AL Average: 9.4 / 1.1 / 3.8 / 6.1 / 1.6

H/9	HR/9	BB/9	SO/9	SO/BB
9.8	1.3	4.4	5.2	1.2

How He Compares to Other Starting Pitchers

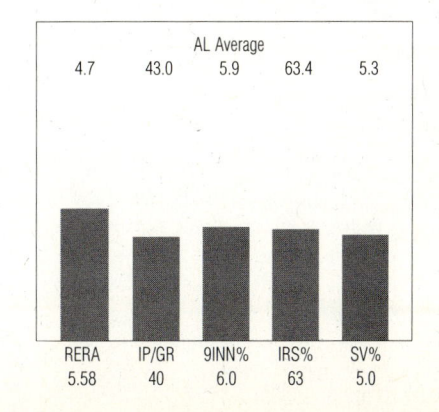

AL Average: 4.7 / 43.0 / 5.9 / 63.4 / 5.3

RERA	IP/GR	9INN%	IRS%	SV%
5.58	40	6.0	63	5.0

TEXAS RANGERS

MARK MCLEMORE

Positions: OF/2B//DH
Bats: B **Throws:** R
Ht: 5'11" **Wt:** 195
Opening Day Age: 31
Born: 10/4/1964
Drafted: CAL82 8/218
ML Seasons: 10

SCOUTING REPORT

McLemore has average-plus speed and baserunning ability. He is a good bunter, both for sacrifices and base hits. A lefthander, he can handle low fastballs. He can't hit the low heat batting righthanded, instead preferring the ball high, and all breaking pitches and off-speed stuff give him trouble. Mark walks fairly often but has minuscule power.

At second base, his original position, he has a minus arm with average-plus accuracy. McLemore's range is slightly above-average but he is only adequate turning the double play. However, he is slightly above-average as a left fielder, catching everything he should and a little more and throwing reasonably well.

HOW HE PERFORMED IN '95

McLemore was the Rangers' surprise MVP for the first half of '95. When his bat was going well early in the year, he keyed the Rangers' attack from the #2 spot. Unfortunately, when his bat vanished in the second half, the Rangers quit scoring runs. He spent most of the first half as Juan Gonzalez's replacement in left field. Through June 11 Mark was batting .340, but he hit only .224 the rest of the season, and 15 of his 20 stolen bases came in his first 49 games. Nagging injuries and an inability to reach base slowed his baserunning, but it's hard to explain his sagging bat—Mark has usually done his best hitting in the summer months.

At the All-Star break the Rangers were 10 games over .500 and led the AL West. For the rest of the year, the club was six games under .500, and there was some correlation between the team's results and McLemore's fall off in performance.

The Rangers' starting second baseman most of the second half, McLemore fielded well. He fashioned a 32-game errorless streak at second and made just two miscues in almost 300 chances. However, he did not throw out a single runner from the outfield, despite making 62 starts in the pasture.

WHAT TO EXPECT IN '96

McLemore's lack of power means he has little future as a regular corner outfielder. He will be the Rangers' everyday second baseman in '96 if an alternative cannot be found. A fringe player until he teamed up with Johnny Oates in Baltimore, Mark has become a valuable player coming off the bench—combining speed, versatility, and experience. However, he's a mediocre everyday player.

Overall Statistics

	G	AB	R	H	2B	3B	HR	RBI	SB	CS	BB	SO	BA	OBA
95 TEX	129	467	73	122	20	5	5	41	21	11	59	71	.261	.346
Career	783	2513	361	632	95	19	17	244	118	54	286	388	.251	.327

1995 Situational Statistics

	AB	HR	RBI	BA	OBA	SLG		AB	HR	RBI	BA	OBA	SLG
Home	240	3	25	.292	.375	.400	LHP	131	1	6	.267	.358	.359
Road	227	2	16	.229	.315	.313	RHP	336	4	35	.259	.341	.357
Apr-Jun	206	3	26	.296	.395	.388	ScPos	105	4	39	.286	.395	.467
Jul-Oct	261	2	15	.234	.304	.333	Clutch	62	1	9	.274	.392	.403

How He Compares to Other Batters

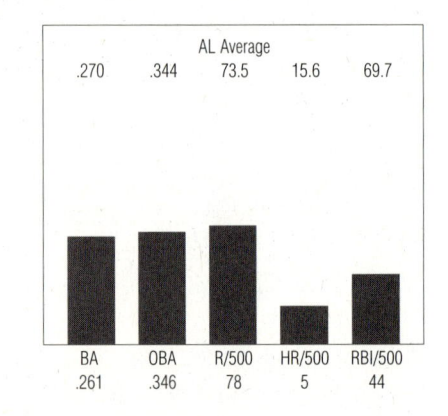

AL Average: .270 .344 73.5 15.6 69.7

BA .261 | OBA .346 | R/500 78 | HR/500 5 | RBI/500 44

Where He Hits the Ball

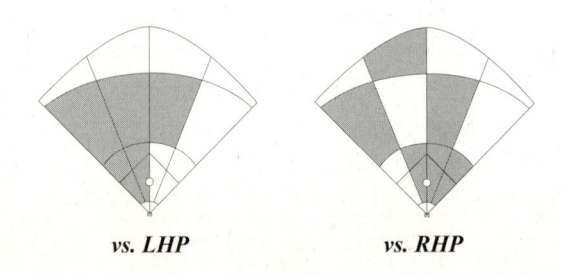

vs. LHP   vs. RHP

TEXAS RANGERS

SCOUTING REPORT
Nixon is an outstanding runner. His speed extends into, and improves, every area of his game. The veteran's baserunning is excellent, and his basestealing still above-average, although Nixon is not the superb thief he once was.

Otis is an excellent bunter and bunts often, mostly for hits. A slap hitter, he hangs over the plate, taking fastballs anywhere they're pitched. He hits better righthanded than as a lefty, but doesn't get to hit righty all that often. Breaking pitches give him some trouble.

Otis' fielding and range are both well above-average. Despite minus arm strength, he throws accurately.

HOW HE PERFORMED IN '95
Trading for Nixon was one of Rangers' GM Doug Melvin's better gambits, saving $1.5 million in salary by swapping Jose Canseco's contract for Nixon's and receiving an everyday center fielder whose defense improved the pitching staff.

He also got a lead-off man who stole 50 bases and batted a career-high .295. Nixon never went more than three consecutive games without a hit. Otis was also a welcome addition to the clubhouse, a point emphasized by both Melvin and manager Johnny Oates.

Otis set career highs in almost every offensive category last year, except batting average, walks, and stolen bases. There were long stretches where Nixon didn't walk at all, but he batted over .270 in each month and hit well against both lefties and righties and in most situations.

So far, so good, but Nixon was 36 last year and his age has begun to show. His 21 times caught stealing led the AL, and his low walk total gave him an undistinguished on-base percentage. Otis also fanned 85 times and had his worst strikeout-to-walk ratio in several years.

WHAT TO EXPECT IN '96
The Rangers chose not to exercise the $2.6 million '96 option on Otis' contract, opting instead to renegotiate for a lower salary. An incensed Nixon then filed for free agency and signed with Toronto for two years. Although he may be fading, the lights are not out yet on the speedy flychaser, who now joins his third club in the last three seasons.

OTIS NIXON

Position: OF
Bats: B **Throws:** R
Ht: 6'2" **Wt:** 180
Opening Day Age: 37
Born: 1/9/1959
Drafted: NYA79 S1/3
ML Seasons: 13

Overall Statistics

	G	AB	R	H	2B	3B	HR	RBI	SB	CS	BB	SO	BA	OBA
95 TEX	139	589	87	174	21	2	0	45	50	21	58	85	.295	.357
Career	1245	3444	605	920	101	16	7	217	444	147	382	477	.267	.339

1995 Situational Statistics

	AB	HR	RBI	BA	OBA	SLG		AB	HR	RBI	BA	OBA	SLG
Home	299	0	29	.274	.338	.314	LHP	177	0	13	.333	.376	.379
Road	290	0	16	.317	.376	.362	RHP	412	0	32	.279	.349	.320
Apr-Jun	251	0	22	.287	.337	.311	ScPos	138	0	43	.290	.331	.341
Jul-Oct	338	0	23	.302	.371	.358	Clutch	79	0	11	.278	.352	.291

How He Compares to Other Batters

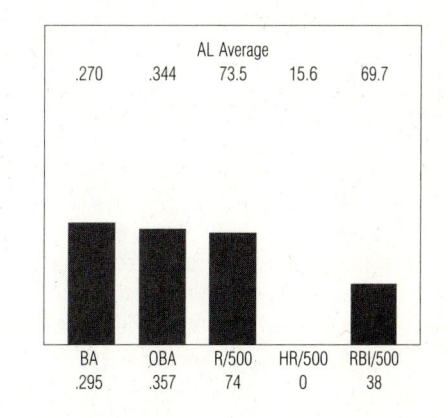

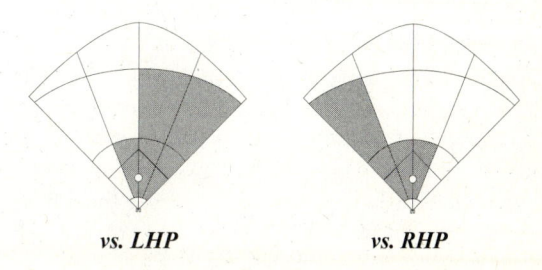

	BA	OBA	R/500	HR/500	RBI/500
AL Average	.270	.344	73.5	15.6	69.7
	.295	.357	74	0	38

Where He Hits the Ball

vs. LHP   vs. RHP

THE SCOUTING REPORT: 1996

TEXAS RANGERS

DEAN PALMER

Position: 3B
Bats: R **Throws:** R
Ht: 6'1" **Wt:** 175
Opening Day Age: 27
Born: 12/27/1968
Drafted: TEX86 3/59
ML Seasons: 6

SCOUTING REPORT
When he's healthy, Palmer is a strong fastball hitter, but he has had trouble with breaking and off-speed pitches in the past. He showed marked improvement in this area in '95. Dean has surprisingly good power, especially for his size, and would be more successful if he could make contact more consistently. He is quite slow, and is a very poor percentage basestealer. Dean doesn't bunt.

Scouts rate Palmer with plus arm strength and plus accuracy. While his throwing has been erratic over the years, part of this is due to his average-minus range and hands, which cause him at times to rush his throws. At times, Dean can both routine grounders, though he does makes some difficult plays.

HOW HE PERFORMED IN '95
Palmer put himself out of action last June 3, to the relief of AL pitchers but the unhappiness of the Rangers. During a typically big, violent swing, Palmer's left biceps tendon literally became detached at the elbow. Dean looked down to see the biceps muscle rolling up towards his shoulder. The injury ruined what looked to be a breakthrough year. Palmer has always had 30-homer power but was inconsistent; outstanding hot streaks were quickly followed by prolonged droughts. Prior to '95, he was a career .229 hitter. At the time of his injury, Palmer ranked in the AL's top ten in batting average, home runs, runs, and on-base percentage.

Dean's old minor-league hitting coach, Rudy Jaramillo, joined Texas in '95. Jaramillo shortened and quickened Palmer's batting stroke and, consequently, Dean waited on pitches better and hit more balls to the opposite field without a loss in power from the alteration to his swing. While he wouldn't have hit .336 over a full season, it's clear that Palmer would have exceeded his usual performance if not for the injury.

WHAT TO EXPECT IN '96
The Rangers plan on Palmer being their regular third baseman. This is based on two perilous assumptions: that Palmer will be healthy enough to play and that his salary requirements can be met by the Rangers. If he does return strong, he should continue this year where he left off last June. He would easily move into the top level of AL third basemen with a full campaign that is anything like his pre-injury performance last season.

Overall Statistics

	G	AB	R	H	2B	3B	HR	RBI	SB	CS	BB	SO	BA	OBA
95 TEX	36	119	30	40	6	0	9	24	1	1	21	21	.336	.448
Career	526	1808	280	427	87	6	102	289	25	21	194	528	.236	.315

1995 Situational Statistics

	AB	HR	RBI	BA	OBA	SLG		AB	HR	RBI	BA	OBA	SLG
Home	71	5	17	.338	.448	.592	LHP	37	3	10	.432	.500	.757
Road	48	4	7	.333	.448	.646	RHP	82	6	14	.293	.427	.549
Apr-Jun	115	9	24	.330	.447	.617	ScPos	27	1	13	.259	.447	.407
Jul-Oct	4	0	0	.500	.500	.500	Clutch	13	3	4	.308	.500	1.000

How He Compares to Other Batters

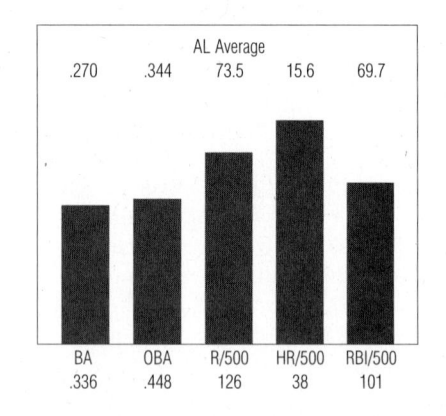

AL Average: .270 / .344 / 73.5 / 15.6 / 69.7

BA	OBA	R/500	HR/500	RBI/500
.336	.448	126	38	101

Where He Hits the Ball

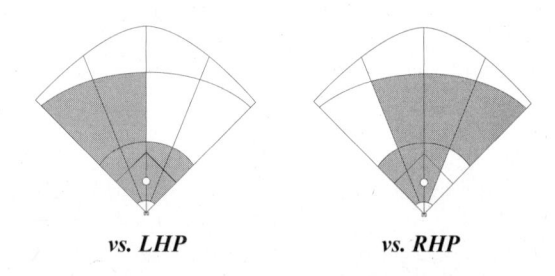

vs. LHP   vs. RHP

TEXAS RANGERS

ROGER PAVLIK

Position: SP
Bats: B **Throws:** R
Ht: 6'3" **Wt:** 220
Opening Day Age: 28
Born: 10/4/1967
Drafted: TEX86 2/32
ML Seasons: 4

SCOUTING REPORT

Pavlik throws four pitches, but none of them rates even as of average major-league quality. His average-minus velocity fastball is too straight, so Roger will turn it over in order to move it down and away from lefthanded hitters.

His hard slider is also an average-minus pitch. His splitfinger fastball is inconsistent—when Pavlik's arm action is good, hitters think the pitch is a straight fastball and can't pick up the splitter's early break. A seldom-used curve is a minus choice.

Pavlik's control is inconsistent as well. However, his fielding is a bit above-average and he holds runners on base well. Although he has a long, sweeping three-quarter motion and what scouts call a "funny body," Roger releases the ball quickly. Of 17 potential base thieves who took off last year, eight were gunned down.

HOW HE PERFORMED IN '95

Pavlik has terrible pitching mechanics. When he pitches with his natural motion, he's effective but gets hurt. When pitching coaches clean up his mechanics, Roger stays healthy, but can't get anyone out. He has had serious shoulder and elbow problems in the past and was disabled three times in '94, but Pavlik managed to stay healthy in '95 and pitched encouragingly well.

Roger has always been a starter, but he has a history of first inning woes. And as the '95 season progressed, he had woes in other innings too. Control is Roger's big problem: he walks plenty of batters and last year loosed 10 wild pitches. However, because other pitchers were hurt, Pavlik never skipped a turn in the rotation, and he finished the year on a high note (4-1, 1.90 ERA in September). Even with the shortened season, Roger notched career highs in innings pitched, starts and shutouts. Four times, he left games with leads and received no decision.

WHAT TO EXPECT IN '96

Pavlik now figures to be a fixture in the '96 rotation. He is still only 28, so there is some room for improvement. With a fast finish and no injuries in '95, the Rangers harbor hopes Pavlik will continue his recovery, improve his velocity, and break through to become a 15-game winner—as long as he can stay off the disabled list. It's not a great bet, but one Texas will take.

Overall Statistics

	G	GS	GF	SV	W	L	ERA	IP	H	R	ER	HR	BB	SO
95 TEX	31	31	0	0	10	10	4.37	191.2	174	96	93	19	90	149
Career	81	80	0	0	28	25	4.36	470.1	452	240	228	48	234	356

1995 Situational Statistics

	W	L	ERA	SV	IP	BB	SO		AB	HR	RBI	BA	OBA	SLG
Home	6	6	5.29	0	100.1	40	69	LHB	410	10	43	.234	.315	.368
Road	4	4	3.35	0	91.1	50	80	RHB	306	9	37	.255	.348	.408
Apr-Jun	4	3	6.42	0	68.2	33	48	ScPos	169	5	61	.260	.366	.396
Jul-Oct	6	7	3.22	0	123.0	57	101	Clutch	79	2	8	.278	.380	.430

How He Compares to Other Pitchers

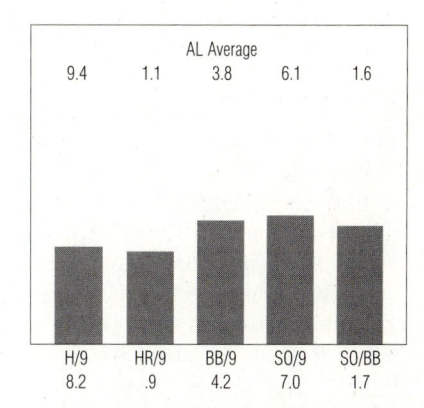

AL Average: 9.4 / 1.1 / 3.8 / 6.1 / 1.6

H/9	HR/9	BB/9	SO/9	SO/BB
8.2	.9	4.2	7.0	1.7

How He Compares to Other Starting Pitchers

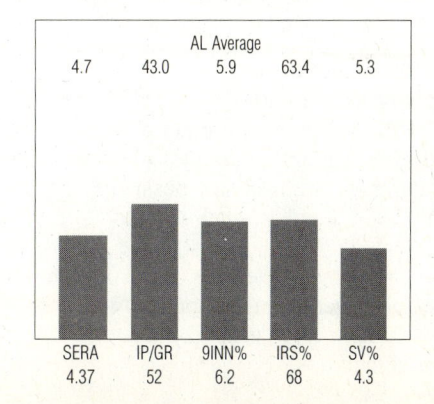

AL Average: 4.7 / 43.0 / 5.9 / 63.4 / 5.3

SERA	IP/GR	9INN%	IRS%	SV%
4.37	52	6.2	68	4.3

TEXAS RANGERS

IVAN RODRIGUEZ

Positions: C//DH
Bats: R **Throws:** R
Ht: 5'9" **Wt:** 165
Opening Day Age: 24
Born: 11/27/1971
Drafted: TEX 7/27/88
ML Seasons: 5

SCOUTING REPORT

Ivan is the most gifted catcher in the world. His outstanding arm strength ranks tops at his position and he throws with well above-average accuracy. His release is very quick and his hands and range are both rated plus.

He's no slouch at the plate, either. Rodriguez has improved greatly since his early days and is now a good hitter. With fine bat speed, he can hit anybody's fastball, and he has matured towards the breaking ball. He also goes to right field more and can do so with some power. There's no reason he can't improve, but it will only come with a better working knowledge of the strike zone. Ivan has poor speed. He has cut down on his basestealing, which was hurting his team. Rodriguez grounds into a lot of double plays because he is slow and hits the ball hard.

HOW HE PERFORMED IN '95

The outstanding young catcher had another fine year in '95. His throwing arm was lethal, and his defense improved. Offensively, he set career highs in several categories. To top it off, he made his fourth consecutive All-Star appearance and won his fourth Gold Glove. Ivan's 43.7% caught stealing percentage led the majors, and he paced the AL in assists and was second in putouts and chances. He's clearly the best defensive catcher in baseball.

Working with new Rangers' hitting coach Rudy Jaramillo, who had tutored "Pudge" in the 1980s, Ivan tightened and quickened his swing, allowing him to make better contact, resulting in Rodriguez' first .300 season. However, Rodriguez's walks dipped by half despite over 100 more at-bats, and as a result his on-base percentage was unacceptably low. His slugging average also fell by 40 points. While Ivan hit more singles and doubles, he did so at the expense of walks and homers.

WHAT TO EXPECT IN '96

Amazingly, Rodriguez is just 24 as the season opens. He is the most important position player on the Rangers and has enough talent that further offensive improvement is still possible. Injuries are the only impediment to an already good career. Unfortunately, he has the most trade value of any Rangers' player, and the right offer could move Rodriguez elsewhere. This unappealing possibility is not as unlikely as it seems because of the club's payroll logjam.

Overall Statistics

	G	AB	R	H	2B	3B	HR	RBI	SB	CS	BB	SO	BA	OBA
95 TEX	130	492	56	149	32	2	12	67	0	2	16	48	.303	.327
Career	577	2028	231	569	111	8	49	254	14	13	105	275	.281	.318

1995 Situational Statistics

	AB	HR	RBI	BA	OBA	SLG		AB	HR	RBI	BA	OBA	SLG
Home	232	5	31	.297	.333	.431	LHP	146	4	16	.301	.340	.452
Road	260	7	36	.308	.321	.465	RHP	346	8	51	.303	.321	.448
Apr-Jun	177	4	27	.311	.340	.475	ScPos	140	1	50	.271	.305	.371
Jul-Oct	315	8	40	.298	.319	.435	Clutch	69	1	13	.319	.377	.449

How He Compares to Other Batters

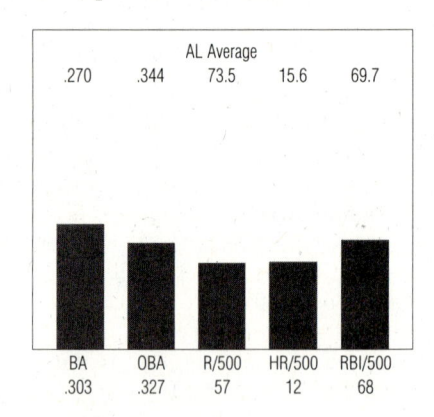

	BA	OBA	R/500	HR/500	RBI/500
AL Average	.270	.344	73.5	15.6	69.7
	.303	.327	57	12	68

Where He Hits the Ball

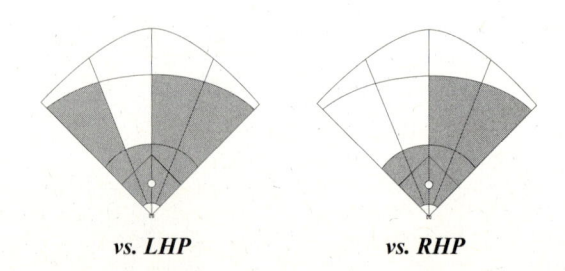

vs. LHP   vs. RHP

TEXAS RANGERS

KENNY ROGERS

Position: SP
Bats: L **Throws:** L
Ht: 6'1" **Wt:** 200
Opening Day Age: 31
Born: 11/10/1964
Drafted: TEX82 38/816
ML Seasons: 7

SCOUTING REPORT
Although his stuff is not overwhelming like that of Randy Johnson, Kenny is a very effective and durable starting pitcher. Rogers has an average-minus fastball but does interesting things with it. He can turn it over and sink it effectively and will also vary the velocity; this makes the fastball look a little like his change-up, but they are two different pitches.

His straight change is a plus offering, with very good arm action that fools hitters and with some movement. Kenny will use the change to both sides of the plate. While his curve is just average, Rogers can register called strikes on "back door" benders.

He holds runners on base well. Just ten runners tried to steal with Kenny pitching in '95, and five were thrown out. His fielding is average.

HOW HE PERFORMED IN '95
Kenny was converted to starting by former Rangers' manager Kevin Kennedy in '93. The left-hander had spent his first four major-league seasons as an oft-used middle and late reliever, and the move into the rotation was a daring one.

It has turned out well. Rogers has now led the Rangers in wins for three consecutive years. His 17 wins during '95 ranked fourth in the AL, his ERA was fifth-best, and he was selected to the All-Star team. All in all, it was Kenny's best season.

After losing his first two starts, Rogers won his next seven and was AL Pitcher of the Month for May. He also set a team record by tossing 39 consecutive scoreless innings during May and June. Although he swooned in mid-season (2-3 record and 5.43 ERA in nine starts after the scoreless streak), he finished strong (5-0 in September).

He was especially tough at home and held left-handed batters well in check, allowing them but two home runs. Rogers was strong, leading the Rangers' staff in innings and he was reliable, going at least seven innings 20 times.

WHAT TO EXPECT IN '96
Kenny, a free agent, had two things going for him that would get him a lucrative contract: he has the bearing and statistics of a rotation anchor, and he is lefthanded. The Rangers want him back, but may have difficulty finding the financial wherewithal to make the right deal, even though Rogers wanted to return.

Overall Statistics

	G	GS	GF	SV	W	L	ERA	IP	H	R	ER	HR	BB	SO
95 TEX	31	31	0	0	17	7	3.38	208.0	192	87	78	26	76	140
Career	376	100	128	28	70	51	3.88	943.1	925	468	407	97	370	680

1995 Situational Statistics

	W	L	ERA	SV	IP	BB	SO		AB	HR	RBI	BA	OBA	SLG
Home	9	1	2.96	0	109.1	39	69	LHB	115	2	9	.157	.248	.226
Road	8	6	3.83	0	98.2	37	71	RHB	676	24	68	.257	.319	.408
Apr-Jun	8	3	2.59	0	83.1	30	57	ScPos	134	3	47	.246	.321	.343
Jul-Oct	9	4	3.90	0	124.2	46	83	Clutch	74	2	5	.324	.363	.459

How He Compares to Other Pitchers

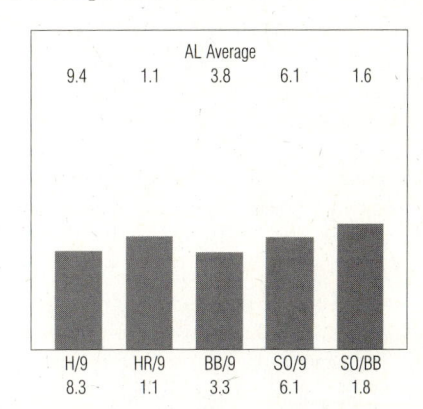

AL Average: 9.4 / 1.1 / 3.8 / 6.1 / 1.6

H/9	HR/9	BB/9	SO/9	SO/BB
8.3	1.1	3.3	6.1	1.8

How He Compares to Other Starting Pitchers

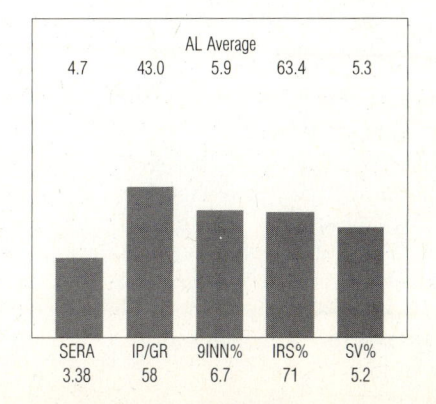

AL Average: 4.7 / 43.0 / 5.9 / 63.4 / 5.3

SERA	IP/GR	9INN%	IRS%	SV%
3.38	58	6.7	71	5.2

TEXAS RANGERS

MICKEY TETTLETON

Positions: OF/DH//1B/C
Bats: B **Throws:** R
Ht: 6'2" **Wt:** 200
Opening Day Age: 35
Born: 9/16/1960
Drafted: OAK81 5/118
ML Seasons: 12

SCOUTING REPORT

Although Tettleton has an extremely quick bat, he has an odd stance in which he holds the bat straight up next to his head. This tends to force him to commit early, leading to trouble with off-speed pitches and breaking balls. However, Mickey's outstanding knowledge of the strike zone forces opposing pitchers to work hard to get him out.

Tettleton does not conform to the standard switch-hitting pattern. While batting lefthanded, he prefers low fastballs inside, but as a righthander, he eschews the high pitches most switch-hitters prefer in favor of low fastballs anywhere in the zone.

At one time a catcher, Tettleton now serves as an outfielder, fill-in first baseman, and DH. He has minus speed and doesn't ever steal, slightly below-average range, and average hands. His arm is average-plus, both in strength and accuracy.

HOW HE PERFORMED IN '95

The Rangers signed Tettleton less than a week before the season, in new GM Doug Melvin's best player move to date. Both parties were satisfied in '95, as Mickey had another fine season, leading the Rangers in home runs. Many look askance at Tettleton's low batting average and considerable strikeout total. However, he contributes a lot to an offense, with his excellent knowledge of the strike zone leading to an annually high finish among the league leaders in walks. He always has a fine on-base percentage in addition to his tremendous power.

He was signed to fill the designated hitter role in '95, but injuries to other players forced him to the outfield. A severe knee injury suffered in Kansas City over Labor Day weekend necessitated immediate surgery. However, with the Rangers in the playoff race, Tettleton not only returned quickly, but excelled. He was named AL Player of the Week for the last week of the season when he hit .556 with five home runs.

WHAT TO EXPECT IN '96

Texas needs Mickey's big bat in the middle of its lineup, and decided to re-sign him for two more years over the winter. Tettleton reportedly took $1 million less to stay with Texas than he would have made had he accepted an offer to play with the Yankees. Playing for the Rangers suits Tettleton's lifestyle as he owns a ranch two hours' driving time from Arlington.

Overall Statistics

	G	AB	R	H	2B	3B	HR	RBI	SB	CS	BB	SO	BA	OBA
95 TEX	134	429	76	102	19	1	32	78	0	0	107	110	.238	.396
Career	1325	4163	628	1007	183	15	218	645	21	28	851	1158	.242	.371

1995 Situational Statistics

	AB	HR	RBI	BA	OBA	SLG		AB	HR	RBI	BA	OBA	SLG
Home	228	22	54	.263	.414	.610	LHP	142	8	21	.225	.358	.444
Road	201	10	24	.209	.374	.398	RHP	287	24	57	.244	.413	.544
Apr-Jun	199	12	32	.216	.363	.427	ScPos	104	9	49	.231	.435	.519
Jul-Oct	230	20	46	.257	.423	.583	Clutch	52	5	12	.365	.528	.692

How He Compares to Other Batters

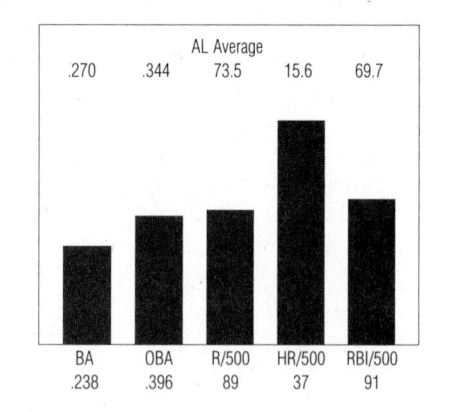

AL Average
.270 .344 73.5 15.6 69.7

BA   OBA   R/500   HR/500   RBI/500
.238 .396   89   37   91

Where He Hits the Ball

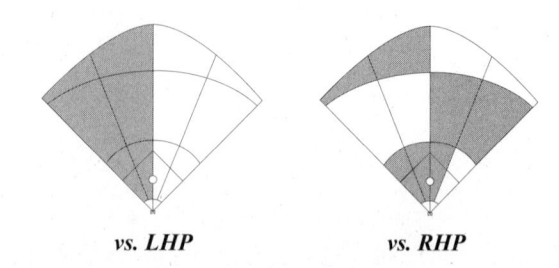

vs. LHP   vs. RHP

TEXAS RANGERS

BOB TEWKSBURY

Position: SP
Bats: R **Throws:** R
Ht: 6'4" **Wt:** 200
Opening Day Age: 35
Born: 11/30/1960
Drafted: NYA81 19/493
ML Seasons: 10

SCOUTING REPORT
The soft-tossing Tewksbury has poor velocity, but that hasn't stopped him from putting together a good career. Working from three-quarters, he will cut his fastball against righthanders and turn it over against lefthanders, getting some early movement in both cases. He will occasionally back door his average curve and also throws an average change-up, which doesn't look too different from his fastball. A slightly below-average soft slider with a long, late break completes his arsenal.

Of course, the pitches don't make Tewksbury a major-league pitcher—well above-average control does. He can throw any of his pitches exactly where he wants them at a variety of speeds. If he doesn't have location, of course, Bob will get hammered. He reminds some people of a slow-pitch softball chucker, only Tewk doesn't throw as hard.

Bob holds runners well. Just six runners tried stealing bases with him on the mound in '95, and three were retired. He is an average-plus fielder.

HOW HE PERFORMED IN '95
Tewksbury joined the Rangers in the flurry of player signings following the end of the work stoppage. He proved to be something of a find, serving as Texas' number two starter until being felled by injuries. His strength is his command and location. While his slow-arriving pitches are painful for some hitters to deal with, Bob is a fan's delight, working quickly and efficiently.

Tewk registered few strikeouts (less than four per game) and even fewer walks (1.4 per game) in '95; this is his usual *modus operandi*, although his control has been better in the past. Opposing batters put the ball in play often against Bob, a tendency that usually works for him. Sometimes, however, he falls behind in the count with runners on base and gets hit hard.

Injuries ruined his '95 season after the All-Star break. Tewksbury won just once after July 28. His win total failed to reach double digits for the first time in the 1990s.

WHAT TO EXPECT IN '96
Tewksbury only signed a one-year deal with the Rangers. He moved to the Padres last winter, signing for two seasons, and will be work as the team's fourth starter.

Overall Statistics

	G	GS	GF	SV	W	L	ERA	IP	H	R	ER	HR	BB	SO
95 TEX	21	21	0	0	8	7	4.58	129.2	169	75	66	8	20	53
Career	214	193	8	1	85	66	3.72	1283.1	1445	603	530	94	198	534

1995 Situational Statistics

	W	L	ERA	SV	IP	BB	SO		AB	HR	RBI	BA	OBA	SLG
Home	3	3	3.72	0	65.1	7	26	LHB	327	5	40	.300	.331	.434
Road	5	4	5.46	0	64.1	13	27	RHB	202	3	24	.351	.370	.465
Apr-Jun	6	3	3.70	0	75.1	11	27	ScPos	126	3	57	.341	.386	.508
Jul-Oct	2	4	5.80	0	54.1	9	26	Clutch	0	0	0	.000	.000	.000

How He Compares to Other Pitchers

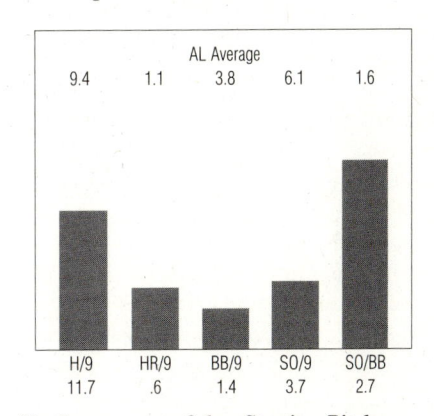

AL Average: 9.4 / 1.1 / 3.8 / 6.1 / 1.6

H/9	HR/9	BB/9	SO/9	SO/BB
11.7	.6	1.4	3.7	2.7

How He Compares to Other Starting Pitchers

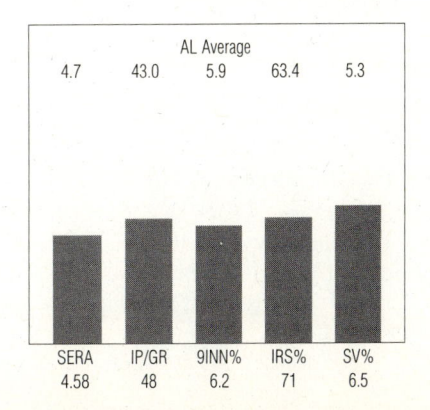

AL Average: 4.7 / 43.0 / 5.9 / 63.4 / 5.3

SERA	IP/GR	9INN%	IRS%	SV%
4.58	48	6.2	71	6.5

TEXAS RANGERS

BOBBY WITT

Position: SP
Bats: R **Throws:** R
Ht: 6'2" **Wt:** 205
Opening Day Age: 31
Born: 5/11/1964
Drafted: TEX85 1/3
ML Seasons: 10

SCOUTING REPORT

Witt once had a very good fastball with very little command. He still throws from high three-quarters to overhand, but Bobby's fastball is now rated as only average. However, control of all his pitches has improved—to somewhat below-average

His four-seam fastball tends to be straight. Although the two-seam fastball doesn't sink, it does run in on right-handed batters. His other two pitches (a slider with a late, short break and a change-up that moves well but is tipped off) are also just average. He is still inconsistent, alternating between good days when he appears in command and bad days, when one wonders why Bobby is in the major leagues.

He is a plus fielder and rates slightly above-average at holding runners: 13 of 22 runners trying to steal against Bobby were successful in '95.

HOW HE PERFORMED IN '95

Witt, the Rangers' top pick in the 1985 draft, spent five and a half years with Texas before going to Oakland in the '92 Jose Canseco trade. After some up-and-down times by the Bay, Bobby signed with Florida for '95, but didn't make much of an impression in Miami. Needing pitching help, the Rangers easily struck a deal in July when Witt cleared waivers.

He was a different pitcher than Texas fans had seen previously. Gone was the wild thrower of the old days. The influence of Oakland pitching coach Dave Duncan was evident, as the new Bobby Witt both struck out and walked fewer batters.

However, Bobby still lacks consistency. His ERA was 2.94 in his first five Rangers' starts and 6.51 in the last five. Even so, his 5-11 overall record was deceiving, as the Rangers and Marlins scored only 38 runs in his 24 losses or no-decisions.

WHAT TO EXPECT IN '96

Witt maintains his permanent residence in the Dallas area. He was thrilled to return last August, as the trade got him home in time to see his six year-old daughter leave for her first day of school.

Bobby filed for free agency in the off-season but wanted to return, and the Rangers wanted him back. Witt is still just 30 years old, so hope remains that some good seasons are in his future. Of course, that future is now; Bobby is no longer young and no longer throws nearly as hard as he once did.

Overall Statistics

	G	GS	GF	SV	W	L	ERA	IP	H	R	ER	HR	BB	SO
95 FLO/TEX	29	29	0	0	5	11	4.13	172.0	185	87	79	12	68	141
Career	279	274	1	0	96	107	4.52	1700.2	1586	942	854	137	1025	1459

1995 Situational Statistics

	W	L	ERA	SV	IP	BB	SO		AB	HR	RBI	BA	OBA	SLG
Home	4	4	3.74	0	86.2	37	65	LHB	348	8	40	.307	.382	.451
Road	1	7	4.54	0	85.1	31	76	RHB	317	4	35	.246	.305	.356
Apr-Jun	1	5	4.35	0	62.0	30	47	ScPos	179	5	61	.235	.294	.397
Jul-Oct	4	6	4.01	0	110.0	38	94	Clutch	40	0	3	.350	.395	.475

How He Compares to Other Pitchers

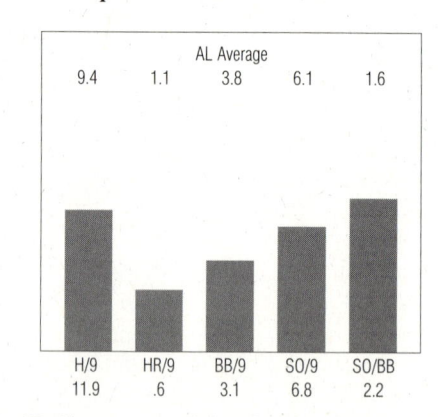

AL Average: 9.4 1.1 3.8 6.1 1.6

H/9: 11.9
HR/9: .6
BB/9: 3.1
SO/9: 6.8
SO/BB: 2.2

How He Compares to Other Starting Pitchers

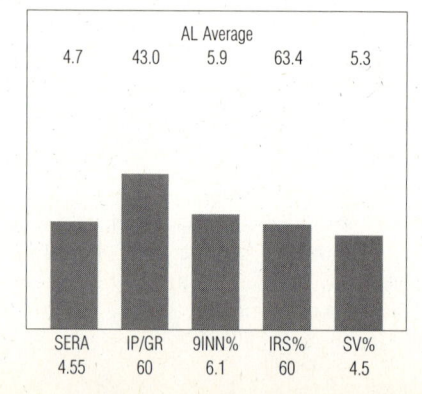

AL Average: 4.7 43.0 5.9 63.4 5.3

SERA: 4.55
IP/GR: 60
9INN%: 6.1
IRS%: 60
SV%: 4.5

TEXAS RANGERS

ESTEBAN BELTRE

Positions: SS/2B//3B
Bats: R **Throws:** R
Ht: 5'10" **Wt:** 155
Opening Day Age: 28
Born: 12/26/1967
Drafted: MON 5/9/84
ML Seasons: 4

Overall Statistics

	G	AB	R	H	2B	3B	HR	RBI	SB	CS	BB	SO	BA	OBA
95 TEX	54	92	7	20	8	0	0	7	0	0	4	15	.217	.250
Career	159	339	40	79	15	0	1	29	4	5	24	59	.233	.282

1995 Situational Statistics

	AB	HR	RBI	BA	OBA	SLG		AB	HR	RBI	BA	OBA	SLG
Home	48	0	6	.250	.294	.333	LHP	27	0	3	.222	.300	.333
Road	44	0	1	.182	.200	.273	RHP	65	0	4	.215	.227	.292
Apr-Jun	28	0	3	.214	.241	.286	ScPos	18	0	5	.167	.250	.278
Jul-Oct	64	0	4	.219	.254	.313	Clutch	15	0	3	.400	.400	.533

SCOUTING REPORT

Defense is Beltre's strong suit. While his range, accuracy, and hands are just average, he does have an above-average throwing arm. In general, Esteban is a reliable infielder and can play three positions.

He is not a very good hitter, but does well with fastballs, and is an average base runner. Although Beltre can hit for average if he gets into a groove, he lacks power. A decent sacrifice bunter, Esteban is not a much of a pinch-hitter.

HOW HE PERFORMED IN '95

Beltre, a shortstop by trade, has developed into a good utility infielder. He saw time at third in '95 and played second base for the first time last season. Why he doesn't play more is a mystery. Esteban regularly shows off a rifle arm, and when given consistent playing time, hits decently. The mystery grew in the second half of the season as shortstop Benji Gil struggled offensively. Beltre's career-high 54 appearances came courtesy of injuries affecting other Texas infielders.

WHAT TO EXPECT IN '96

Justified or not, Beltre has earned the "utility" label. That will be his role whether he's back in Texas or if he goes anywhere else.

DENNIS COOK

Position: RP
Bats: L **Throws:** L
Ht: 6'3" **Wt:** 185
Opening Day Age: 33
Born: 10/4/1962
Drafted: SF85 18/446
ML Seasons: 8

Overall Statistics

	G	GS	GF	SV	W	L	ERA	IP	H	R	ER	HR	BB	SO
95 CLE/TEX	46	1	10	2	0	2	4.53	57.2	63	32	29	9	26	53
Career	235	71	31	3	32	28	3.91	619.1	596	308	269	90	218	361

1995 Situational Statistics

	W	L	ERA	SV	IP	BB	SO		AB	HR	RBI	BA	OBA	SLG
Home	0	1	4.72	1	26.2	13	20	LHB	88	3	21	.284	.353	.443
Road	0	1	4.35	1	31.0	13	33	RHB	130	6	23	.292	.369	.531
Apr-Jun	0	0	5.23	1	20.2	13	19	ScPos	73	2	33	.247	.326	.452
Jul-Oct	0	2	4.14	1	37.0	13	34	Clutch	33	2	9	.242	.333	.515

SCOUTING REPORT

Southpaw Cook has a high three-quarter delivery. His too-straight fastball is rated average-minus; his soft slider and none-too-sharp curve are also average-minus. Dennis' change-up is average and does have some movement. The rest of Cook's package (control, fielding, holding runners) is also rated average, but just two of six potential basestealers were successful running against Cook in '95.

HOW HE PERFORMED IN '95

Cook started the season with pitching-rich Cleveland and became the odd man out in June. Even though his ERA was north of 6.00, at least four teams were interested when he was designated for assignment. The Rangers made the winning bid. Dennis was used in middle relief and against left-handed batters late in games, though he did make one start due to injuries to other pitchers. Overall, his '95 performance was streaky, but not altogether horrible, but he limped home with a 6.14 September ERA.

WHAT TO EXPECT IN '96

His '95 performance was a drastic dropoff from his fine '94 showing in Chicago, but lefthanded relievers are the felines of baseball. Cook hasn't used up his nine lives yet.

TEXAS RANGERS

DANNY DARWIN

Position: SP/RP
Bats: R **Throws:** R
Ht: 6'3" **Wt:** 190
Opening Day Age: 40
Born: 10/25/1955
Drafted: TEX 5/10/76
ML Seasons: 18

Overall Statistics

	G	GS	GF	SV	W	L	ERA	IP	H	R	ER	HR	BB	SO
95 TOR/TEX	2015	0	0	3	10	7.45	99.0	131	87	82	25	31	58
Career	618	297	168	32	148	150	3.71	2546.0	2434	1169	1050	256	753	1673

1995 Situational Statistics

	W	L	ERA	SV	IP	BB	SO		AB	HR	RBI	BA	OBA	SLG
Home	2	5	7.11	0	50.2	14	29	LHB	253	11	36	.344	.399	.561
Road	1	5	7.82	0	48.1	17	29	RHB	152	14	38	.289	.329	.625
Apr-Jun	1	8	7.44	0	61.2	21	34	ScPos	83	5	49	.373	.424	.614
Jul-Oct	2	2	7.47	0	37.1	10	24	Clutch	4	0	1	.750	.800	1.500

SCOUTING REPORT

Veteran righty Darwin comes home with a three-quarter motion. He has average-minus velocity on his fastball, but will turn it over and sink it to make up for the lack of speed. He throws an average-minus slow, rolling curve, an average hard slider, and an average change-up that moves effectively.

He still has his control and an effective move to first base. Five of eight runners stole successfully against Danny last season. He is an average fielder.

HOW HE PERFORMED IN '95

Darwin was plain awful with Toronto (1-7, 7.62 ERA) last season and got his release. He joined the Rangers August 10 only because Texas was desperate for starting pitching. He was slightly better than the "Undecided" option as a starter, winning two of four appearances before being shuffled to the bullpen. Danny made three September relief appearances, working at least four innings each time. He allowed at least one home run in each of his seven Texas appearances, and twelve dingers altogether with the Rangers.

WHAT TO EXPECT IN '96

Darwin is 40 years old. If he returns to the majors in 1996, it will be a clear sign of how desperate teams are for pitching.

LOU FRAZIER

Positions: OF//DH/2B
Bats: B **Throws:** R
Ht: 6'2" **Wt:** 175
Opening Day Age: 31
Born: 1/26/1965
Drafted: HOU86 S1/
ML Seasons: 3

Overall Statistics

	G	AB	R	H	2B	3B	HR	RBI	SB	CS	BB	SO	BA	OBA
95 MON/TEX	84	162	25	33	4	0	0	11	13	1	15	32	.204	.286
Career	272	491	77	125	14	2	1	41	50	7	49	79	.255	.327

1995 Situational Statistics

	AB	HR	RBI	BA	OBA	SLG		AB	HR	RBI	BA	OBA	SLG
Home	62	0	9	.194	.282	.210	LHP	51	0	7	.216	.298	.235
Road	100	0	2	.210	.288	.240	RHP	111	0	4	.198	.280	.225
Apr-Jun	63	0	3	.190	.297	.222	ScPos	37	0	10	.216	.318	.216
Jul-Oct	99	0	8	.212	.278	.232	Clutch	31	0	2	.226	.314	.226

SCOUTING REPORT

Frazier's plus speed gives him better-than-average range and allows him to steal bases and run effectively. He also is a smart player with good baseball sense. Taking advantage of his speed and intelligence, Lou is an effective and frequent bunter, both for hits and when sacrificing. His arm strength and throwing accuracy are only average. Although he lacks power, Lou likes fastballs, and fits the pattern of choosing high pitches righthanded and low deliveries lefthanded. Breaking pitches frequently fool him.

HOW HE PERFORMED IN '95

Frazier started the season with Montreal, but hit .190 in 35 games before being optioned to Ottawa. The Rangers traded for the fleet, switch-hitting Frazier July 30. He played in 49 of the Rangers' final 57 games, starting 23 times. Lou's trademark speed, which he showed in abundance again last season, has led to 50 successful steals in 57 major-league attempts. The problem has always been getting on base in the first place.

WHAT TO EXPECT IN '96

With his speed and defensive prowess, Frazier should have a role somewhere on the Rangers in '96. He's never going to be a regular but could stick around for awhile as a valuable bench player.

TEXAS RANGERS

JEFF FRYE

Position: 2B
Bats: R **Throws:** R
Ht: 5'9" **Wt:** 180
Opening Day Age: 29
Born: 8/31/1966
Drafted: TEX88 30/765
ML Seasons: 3

Overall Statistics

	G	AB	R	H	2B	3B	HR	RBI	SB	CS	BB	SO	BA	OBA
95 TEX	90	313	38	87	15	2	4	29	3	3	24	45	.278	.335
Career	214	717	99	205	44	6	5	59	10	7	69	95	.286	.352

1995 Situational Statistics

	AB	HR	RBI	BA	OBA	SLG		AB	HR	RBI	BA	OBA	SLG
Home	154	2	16	.299	.382	.422	LHP	92	3	12	.272	.333	.424
Road	159	2	13	.258	.286	.333	RHP	221	1	17	.281	.336	.357
Apr-Jun	149	0	11	.315	.372	.369	ScPos	74	2	27	.297	.325	.473
Jul-Oct	164	4	18	.244	.302	.384	Clutch	49	1	2	.224	.333	.286

SCOUTING REPORT
The scrappy Frye swings at low pitches and especially likes first-pitch fastballs. He lacks power but has some idea of the strike zone. So far in his career, he has hit effectively against both righthanders and lefties. Jeff is a very good sacrifice bunter, but is now just an average runner due to '93 knee surgery. His throwing arm is slightly below-average with average accuracy. Nothing special turning the double play, Frye's hands are minus and his range is now average-minus.

HOW HE PERFORMED IN '95
Frye hit .310 while starting 34 of the Rangers' first 35 games at second base but missed most of the next month with a pulled hamstring. After returning, Jeff batted just .244 and lost his job to Mark McLemore. Late in the season, Frye complained publicly about his lack of playing time, and received a sharp reprimand from Texas management.

WHAT TO EXPECT IN '96
Frye is a marginal major-league player with a history of injuries. Although he wants to start, and wants out of Texas to get that chance, he will probably have a limited role on whatever big league team he plays for in '96.

CANDY MALDONADO

Positions: OF//DH
Bats: R **Throws:** R
Ht: 6'0" **Wt:** 190
Opening Day Age: 35
Born: 9/5/1960
Drafted: LA 6/6/78
ML Seasons: 15

Overall Statistics

	G	AB	R	H	2B	3B	HR	RBI	SB	CS	BB	SO	BA	OBA
95 TOR/TEX	74	190	28	50	16	0	9	30	1	2	32	50	.263	.370
Career	1410	4106	498	1042	227	17	146	618	34	33	391	864	.254	.322

1995 Situational Statistics

	AB	HR	RBI	BA	OBA	SLG		AB	HR	RBI	BA	OBA	SLG
Home	96	7	20	.250	.364	.552	LHP	103	5	14	.262	.367	.485
Road	94	2	10	.277	.376	.426	RHP	87	4	16	.264	.374	.494
Apr-Jun	90	5	18	.311	.409	.567	ScPos	47	3	21	.234	.350	.511
Jul-Oct	100	4	12	.220	.333	.420	Clutch	39	3	7	.256	.318	.564

SCOUTING REPORT
A better fastball than breaking-ball hitter, Maldonado has gotten smarter at the plate and will now take breaking balls to right field. He still has some power left. He is a poor runner, and is just a 51% career base-stealer in 67 tries. But for some reason, Candy still occasionally tries to steal. Defensively, he is below par in range and arm strength. However, he has average accuracy and hands.

HOW HE PERFORMED IN '95
Maldonado came to the Rangers in an August 31 trade with Toronto. Texas, contending for the playoffs, sought an experienced righthanded bat to come off the bench. Candy promptly won a game with a home run in his first appearance for his new club.

Coming off a poor '94 showing, it took hard work for Maldonado to even make a big-league club. He was popular with his Blue Jays' teammates and with Cito Gaston, but it's questionable whether Candy should have gotten 40 starts in Toronto.

WHAT TO EXPECT IN '96
Maldonado did not figure in the Rangers plans. However, he played well in '95 and should get an opportunity somewhere else in '96.

TEXAS RANGERS

ROGER McDOWELL

Position: RP
Bats: R **Throws:** R
Ht: 6'1" **Wt:** 175
Opening Day Age: 35
Born: 12/21/1960
Drafted: NYN82 3/59
ML Seasons: 11

Overall Statistics

	G	GS	GF	SV	W	L	ERA	IP	H	R	ER	HR	BB	SO
95 TEX	64	0	26	4	7	4	4.02	85.0	86	39	38	5	34	49
Career	682	2	419	155	69	69	3.24	990.2	976	422	357	43	387	504

1995 Situational Statistics

	W	L	ERA	SV	IP	BB	SO		AB	HR	RBI	BA	OBA	SLG
Home	4	1	3.43	1	42.0	18	24	LHB	134	2	15	.269	.367	.373
Road	3	3	4.60	3	43.0	16	25	RHB	177	3	26	.282	.343	.373
Apr-Jun	3	0	3.62	1	37.1	14	22	ScPos	90	1	32	.233	.357	.333
Jul-Oct	4	4	4.34	3	47.2	20	27	Clutch	141	1	13	.213	.301	.270

SCOUTING REPORT

McDowell's best pitch is a two-seam sinking fastball that sinks and runs a little, but no longer has a big drop. His four-seam fastball is straight. His soft slider has a good break but only average velocity. His control is average.

Only four runners tried to steal against Roger in '95. Like many sinkerballers, his fielding is plus—a matter of survival if a pitcher gets a lot of ground balls hit to him.

HOW HE PERFORMED IN '95

McDowell needs constant work for his sinker to be effective. With too much rest, Roger's arm gets too strong and his ball won't sink. He didn't have to worry about cobwebs in '95, ranking second in the league in appearances. Roger recorded both his first win and save since '93 with Texas last season but went just four for eight in save opportunities.

WHAT TO EXPECT IN '96

McDowell can pitch in any relief role, from middle to closing. His sinker gets ground balls, which makes him effective with runners on base. His best major-league years are in the past, but after his fine work in '95, Baltimore was eager to snap him up for '96.

DARREN OLIVER

Position: RP/SP
Bats: R **Throws:** L
Ht: 6'0" **Wt:** 170
Opening Day Age: 25
Born: 10/6/1970
Drafted: TEX88 3/63
ML Seasons: 3

Overall Statistics

	G	GS	GF	SV	W	L	ERA	IP	H	R	ER	HR	BB	SO
95 TEX	17	7	2	0	4	2	4.22	49.0	47	25	23	3	32	39
Career	62	7	12	2	8	2	3.78	102.1	89	50	43	8	68	93

1995 Situational Statistics

	W	L	ERA	SV	IP	BB	SO		AB	HR	RBI	BA	OBA	SLG
Home	2	1	4.32	0	25.0	13	23	LHB	40	1	4	.350	.469	.500
Road	2	1	4.13	0	24.0	19	16	RHB	143	2	19	.231	.339	.329
Apr-Jun	4	2	4.22	0	49.0	32	39	ScPos	54	1	20	.278	.403	.370
Jul-Oct	0	0	0.00	0	0.0	0	0	Clutch	17	0	4	.294	.455	.412

SCOUTING REPORT

Darren has a relaxed three-quarter delivery with an average, straight, sneaky-fast fastball, a sharp average-plus curve that has lateral break, and an average-plus change-up curve. A minus, seldom used straight change completes Oliver's arsenal. Unfortunately, his control is below-average and he is just average as a fielder and in holding baserunners. Ten runners tried to steal against him last year, seven successfully.

HOW HE PERFORMED IN '95

Darren, the son of former big-league first baseman Bob Oliver, has a history of arm problems and a bad wing felled him again in '95. He started the year in middle relief then went into the rotation May 30. In seven starts, he was 3-2 with a 2.83 ERA. Oliver's last start was June 26, when he left after one inning with a partially torn left rotator cuff, spending the balance of the season on the DL and undergoing surgery in August.

WHAT TO EXPECT IN '96

Assuming Oliver is physically able when spring training begins, he will vie for a spot in the rotation. He has a great arm and could surprise, but it often takes a long time for pitchers to recover from such arm problems.

TEXAS RANGERS

LUIS ORTIZ

Positions: 3B//DH
Bats: R **Throws:** R
Ht: 6'0" **Wt:** 190
Opening Day Age: 25
Born: 5/25/1970
Drafted: BOS91 11/226
ML Seasons: 3

Overall Statistics

	G	AB	R	H	2B	3B	HR	RBI	SB	CS	BB	SO	BA	OBA
95 TEX	41	108	10	25	5	2	1	18	0	1	6	18	.231	.270
Career	57	138	13	31	7	2	1	25	0	1	7	25	.225	.255

1995 Situational Statistics

	AB	HR	RBI	BA	OBA	SLG		AB	HR	RBI	BA	OBA	SLG
Home	51	1	12	.333	.352	.510	LHP	62	1	10	.242	.262	.371
Road	57	0	6	.140	.197	.193	RHP	46	0	8	.217	.280	.304
Apr-Jun	25	1	4	.280	.308	.560	ScPos	25	0	16	.440	.464	.680
Jul-Oct	83	0	14	.217	.258	.277	Clutch	18	0	3	.222	.263	.389

SCOUTING REPORT

Luis is a good fastball hitter and especially likes the fastball up. Unfortunately, he likes it up so much that he often chases fastballs way out of the strike zone. Ortiz is a decent breaking-ball hitter as well and can drive the ball. He will not walk much, though, and does not bunt.

Defensively, he has an average throwing arm, in strength and accuracy. His hands and range at third base are slightly below par.

HOW HE PERFORMED IN '95

Ortiz came from Boston in the Otis Nixon-Jose Canseco deal. He would have spent most of '95 at Triple-A if not for Dean Palmer's injury. He was shuffled between Oklahoma City and Texas three times after Palmer went down.

At third base, Ortiz performed poorly, committing eight errors in just 60 chances, which bothered defensive-minded manager Johnny Oates, to say the least. While he showed some power, very poor plate discipline kept Ortiz hamstrung.

WHAT TO EXPECT IN '96

If Palmer returns healthy, Ortiz figures to play at Triple-A this year. Luis needs seasoning, but is a good athlete and good prospect who could be included in a deal.

MIKE PAGLIARULO

Positions: 3B/1B
Bats: L **Throws:** R
Ht: 6'1" **Wt:** 205
Opening Day Age: 36
Born: 3/15/1960
Drafted: NYA81 6/155
ML Seasons: 11

Overall Statistics

	G	AB	R	H	2B	3B	HR	RBI	SB	CS	BB	SO	BA	OBA
95 TEX	86	241	27	56	16	0	4	27	0	0	15	49	.232	.277
Career	1246	3901	462	942	206	18	134	505	18	16	343	785	.241	.306

1995 Situational Statistics

	AB	HR	RBI	BA	OBA	SLG		AB	HR	RBI	BA	OBA	SLG
Home	114	1	8	.219	.252	.272	LHP	18	0	5	.222	.364	.333
Road	127	3	19	.244	.298	.417	RHP	223	4	22	.233	.269	.350
Apr-Jun	104	0	12	.260	.304	.327	ScPos	54	0	18	.185	.266	.222
Jul-Oct	137	4	15	.212	.257	.365	Clutch	40	0	1	.200	.200	.225

SCOUTING REPORT

Once a fearsome long-ball threat, Mike is a dead fastball hitter but now can be overmatched. He has well below-average speed and does not bunt. The veteran third sacker has lost range in the field but still performed well in Texas. His hands are average and his arm is average-plus in strength and average in accuracy.

HOW HE PERFORMED IN '95

Pagliarulo made the Rangers as a non-roster invitee after a year in Japan. Projected as a pinch-hitter and reserve cornerman, Mike took over at third base against righthanders when regular Dean Palmer went down. After a good start, Mike hit .158 over 36-game span beginning on July 5, a span that mirrored the Rangers' fall from first place. Texas never found a bat to replace Palmer's, and Pagliarulo failed to recapture his old magic. While in Texas, he made all the routine plays and was highly regarded defensively.

WHAT TO EXPECT IN '96

Pagliarulo's glove made him a Johnny Oates favorite. He is not nearly the hitter he once was, but his '95 season has rejuvenated his career. He's not good enough to play regularly, but should stick in '96 as a reserve or platoon player.

TEXAS RANGERS

JEFF RUSSELL

Position: RP
Bats: R **Throws:** R
Ht: 6'3" **Wt:** 210
Opening Day Age: 34
Born: 9/2/1961
Drafted: CIN79 8/126
ML Seasons: 13

Overall Statistics

	G	GS	GF	SV	W	L	ERA	IP	H	R	ER	HR	BB	SO
95 TEX	37	0	32	20	1	0	3.03	32.2	36	12	11	3	9	21
Career	534	79	329	183	53	70	3.77	1043.2	1007	503	437	95	393	670

1995 Situational Statistics

	W	L	ERA	SV	IP	BB	SO		AB	HR	RBI	BA	OBA	SLG
Home	0	0	4.40	8	14.1	6	9	LHB	73	2	6	.274	.312	.356
Road	1	0	1.96	12	18.1	3	12	RHB	57	1	11	.281	.339	.368
Apr-Jun	1	0	3.06	12	17.2	4	11	ScPos	42	2	16	.357	.413	.524
Jul-Oct	0	0	3.00	8	15.0	5	10	Clutch	85	2	12	.294	.355	.376

SCOUTING REPORT

While Russell lacks his old stuff, he can still be effective if used selectively. From three-quarters, he has an average, straight four-seam fastball and a two-seamer that has some movement. His now average hard slider has a sharp break.

While his control is average-plus, Jeff has some trouble keeping pitches down in the strike zone. Often, he will throw strikes, but not exactly where he wants them. Russell is average with the glove and with holding runners. Just three runners tried to steal bases in '95, with two being retired.

HOW HE PERFORMED IN '95

Russell, the all-time Rangers' leader in saves, was the closest the Rangers had to a closer in '95. Jeff spent two stints on the DL due to back injuries but, when healthy, he converted 20 of 24 save opportunities and allowed runs in only eight of 37 appearances.

WHAT TO EXPECT IN '96

While Russell had planned to retire after '95, there was a good possibility that he would return as a setup pitcher. If the Rangers are to contend, they will need to upgrade in late relief, but Jeff could be a helpful in the setup role.

DAVE VALLE

Positions: C//1B
Bats: R **Throws:** R
Ht: 6'2" **Wt:** 200
Opening Day Age: 35
Born: 10/30/1960
Drafted: SEA78 2/32
ML Seasons: 12

Overall Statistics

	G	AB	R	H	2B	3B	HR	RBI	SB	CS	BB	SO	BA	OBA
95 TEX	36	75	7	18	3	0	0	5	1	0	6	18	.240	.305
Career	928	2689	300	632	115	11	74	333	5	7	249	396	.235	.313

1995 Situational Statistics

	AB	HR	RBI	BA	OBA	SLG		AB	HR	RBI	BA	OBA	SLG
Home	44	0	1	.250	.298	.318	LHP	16	0	0	.188	.188	.188
Road	31	0	4	.226	.314	.226	RHP	59	0	5	.254	.333	.305
Apr-Jun	51	0	3	.216	.310	.255	ScPos	23	0	5	.261	.292	.261
Jul-Oct	24	0	2	.292	.292	.333	Clutch	9	0	1	.333	.333	.333

SCOUTING REPORT

Perhaps Dave's most distinguished trait is his well below-average running speed. He is not much of a hitter, liking high fastballs but having no luck at all with any breaking pitch.

Valle is rated an average defensive catcher, though his throwing arm isn't particularly good. With Seattle, he showed a guts but was injury-prone due to frequent collisions at home plate and his generally all-out playing style.

HOW HE PERFORMED IN '95

Valle's role was limited in '95 due to injuries and Ivan Rodriguez' high-quality play. Dave's season ended September 9, when he separated his shoulder in batting practice. He had never seen this little action since coming to the majors nine years ago.

He calls a good game and the Rangers were 14-8 in the games he started, but Dave threw out only three of 15 potential basestealers. He also spent some time at first base in '95.

WHAT TO EXPECT IN '96

Contracts like the two-year, $500,000-plus per season deal Valle signed in late '94 no longer exist for backup catchers. Assuming Ivan Rodriguez is back, Valle will play the same role he did in '95.

TEXAS RANGERS

ED VOSBERG

Position: RP
Bats: L **Throws:** L
Ht: 6'1" **Wt:** 190
Opening Day Age: 34
Born: 9/28/1961
Drafted: SD83 3/64
ML Seasons: 4

Overall Statistics

	G	GS	GF	SV	W	L	ERA	IP	H	R	ER	HR	BB	SO
95 TEX	44	0	20	4	5	5	3.00	36.0	32	15	12	3	16	36
Career	83	3	27	4	6	9	4.41	87.2	86	49	43	9	42	68

1995 Situational Statistics

	W	L	ERA	SV	IP	BB	SO		AB	HR	RBI	BA	OBA	SLG
Home	3	4	1.17	2	23.0	5	21	LHB	52	2	6	.250	.344	.423
Road	2	1	6.23	2	13.0	11	15	RHB	81	1	15	.235	.297	.284
Apr-Jun	2	2	3.60	1	15.0	6	15	ScPos	53	2	20	.302	.394	.434
Jul-Oct	3	3	2.57	3	21.0	10	21	Clutch	73	1	10	.288	.384	.370

SCOUTING REPORT
Ed comes home with a three-quarter to high three-quarter delivery, bringing an average, straight fastball, although he does spot the fastball effectively. His out pitch is an average-plus hard slider with late break and good location. An underused, slightly below-average curve rounds out the menu.

Ed is an average fielder and average at holding runners on base. Three runners tried to steal against him last year, two successfully.

HOW HE PERFORMED IN '95
Ed rekindled his waning career in '95. The Rangers used him predominantly late in games against left-handed batters for short stints (he pitched less than one inning 27 times). His win May 20 was his first in the majors since 1990, and his strikeout rate per inning was the best on the club.

WHAT TO EXPECT IN '96
It is amazing how many opportunities lefthanded pitchers get over comparable righthanders. Vosberg, one of the beneficiaries of this preference, is better than most fringe southpaws, as he is effective at holding runners and slowing the opponent's running game. He will be back in the majors in '96, probably in Texas because manager Johnny Oates likes to have at least three lefty relievers.

MATT WHITESIDE

Position: RP
Bats: R **Throws:** R
Ht: 6'0" **Wt:** 185
Opening Day Age: 28
Born: 8/8/1967
Drafted: TEX90 25/678
ML Seasons: 4

Overall Statistics

	G	GS	GF	SV	W	L	ERA	IP	H	R	ER	HR	BB	SO
95 TEX	40	0	18	3	5	4	4.08	53.0	48	24	24	5	19	46
Career	167	0	52	9	10	8	4.14	215.0	220	109	99	19	81	135

1995 Situational Statistics

	W	L	ERA	SV	IP	BB	SO		AB	HR	RBI	BA	OBA	SLG
Home	4	1	3.00	2	27.0	7	24	LHB	77	2	8	.247	.341	.351
Road	1	3	5.19	1	26.0	12	22	RHB	121	3	13	.240	.286	.331
Apr-Jun	2	1	3.28	0	24.2	10	24	ScPos	62	1	16	.161	.247	.210
Jul-Oct	3	3	4.76	3	28.1	9	22	Clutch	116	4	17	.267	.320	.397

SCOUTING REPORT
Whiteside, a short-armer, has a high three-quarter motion and the classic two-pitch closer repertoire, although he may not have the velocity to excel in the role. Matt's average-plus fastball tends to be straight, but he is working on a cutter that he can use back door and off the plate. His slider has average velocity with a hard, short break. While Whiteside's control is just average, he is an average-plus fielder. His move to first is average, but only one runner stole against Matt in '95.

HOW HE PERFORMED IN '95
Originally slated for occasional closing duties, Whiteside was used instead in middle relief and setup roles. He never seemed to gain Johnny Oates' confidence and only received four save opportunities. Matt pitched even fewer innings in '95 than a year earlier when the season was shorter. He allowed just seven of 36 inherited base runners to score, the seventh-best ratio in the AL.

WHAT TO EXPECT IN '96
This will be Whiteside's fourth major-league season. Unless the Rangers procure a proven bullpen stopper, he will get a shot at the job. He was a closer in the minors and recorded 61 minor-league saves.

TEXAS RANGERS: TOP PROSPECTS

MIKE BELL

Bats: R Throws: R Opening Day Age: 21
Ht: 6-2 Wt: 185 Born: 12/7/1974
Position: 3B Drafted: 1993 #1 TEX

YR TEAM	LG/CLASS	G	AB	R	H	2B	3B	HR	RBI	SB	BA	OBA
93 Rangers	GULF/R	60	230	48	73	13	6	3	34	9	.317	.395
94 Charlstn-SC	SAL/A	120	475	58	125	22	6	6	58	16	.263	.330
95 Charlotte	FSL/A	129	470	49	122	20	1	5	52	9	.260	.327

The son of Buddy, grandson of Gus and brother of David Bell was a supplemental first-round pick in the 1993 draft. He is a line drive hitter with a good approach at the plate; the line drives could turn into home runs as his frame fills out and he gets stronger. The 21-year-old has some speed and is a good baserunner. In the field, Bell has a strong arm and good hands, but led his league in errors each of the last two seasons. His throwing has been a problem and he needs to get his body in front of the ball more.

MARK BRANDENBURG

Bats: R Throws: R Opening Day Age: 26
Ht: 6-0 Wt: 170 Born: 7/14/1970
Position: P Drafted: 1992 #26 TEX

YR TEAM	LG/CLASS	G	GS	GF	SV	W	L	ERA	IP	H	HR	BB	SO	O/BA
93 Chston-SC	SAL/A	44	0	18	4	6	3	1.46	80.0	62	2	22	67	.215
94 Charlotte	FSL/A	25	0	15	5	0	2	0.87	41.1	23	1	15	44	.165
94 Tulsa	TEX/AA	37	0	26	8	5	4	1.74	62.0	50	2	12	63	.216
95 Okla City	AMAS/AAA	35	0	15	2	0	5	2.02	58.0	52	2	15	51	.243
95 Texas	AL/MAJ	11	0	5	0	0	1	5.93	27.1	36	5	7	21	.316

Brandenburg's fastball will never impress a scout holding a radar gun, but it has been very effective for him. The Texas Tech product tops out at about 80 mph, but has a very deceptive sidearm delivery. He has excellent control, keeps the ball down, and does not give up many home runs. Brandenburg struggled in middle relief in a brief stint with the Rangers last season and is basically a "once through the order" pitcher.

KEVIN BROWN

Bats: R Throws: R Opening Day Age: 23
Ht: 6-2 Wt: 200 Born: 4/21/1973
Position: C Drafted: 1994 #1 TEX

YR TEAM	LG/CLASS	G	AB	R	H	2B	3B	HR	RBI	SB	BA	OBA
94 Hudson Val	NYP/A	68	232	33	57	19	1	6	32	0	.246	.317
95 Okla City	AMAS/AAA	3	10	1	4	1	0	0	0	0	.400	.500
95 Charlotte	FSL/A	107	355	48	94	25	1	11	57	2	.265	.366

After a successful small-college career at Southern Indiana, Brown was a second-round pick in the '94 draft. The Rangers sent him to Charlotte last season to work with manager (and former catcher) Butch Wynegar. Brown has an ideal catchers' build and a strong arm and he moves well behind the plate. Despite his good arm, the 22-year-old threw out just 28.6% of opposing base-stealers last year because he struggled with his release point. Offensively, Brown is a good pull hitter with power potential, but has been handcuffed by quality breaking pitches.

JEFF DAVIS

Bats: R Throws: R Opening Day Age: 24
Ht: 6-0 Wt: 170 Born: 9/20/1972
Position: P Drafted: 1993 #28 TEX

YR TEAM	LG/CLASS	G	GS	GF	SV	W	L	ERA	IP	H	HR	BB	SO	O/BA
93 Erie	NYP/A	27	0	24	13	0	5	3.65	37.0	32	3	10	41	.234
94 Charlstn-SC	SAL/A	45	0	43	19	2	3	3.99	49.2	53	3	11	72	.265
95 Charlotte	FSL/A	26	26	0	0	12	7	2.89	165.1	159	10	37	105	.250
95 Tulsa	TEX/AA	1	1	0	0	1	0	0.00	7.0	2	0	1	4	.087

A closer in his first two pro seasons, Davis led the Rangers' farm system in saves in 1994. As a starter in '95, he led the organization in wins and ranked third in ERA. The 23-year-old also tied for third in the Florida State League in wins and was fourth in innings pitched. He is not overpowering, but has outstanding control and command of his pitches. An improved changeup has given him three solid deliveries that he can throw for strikes. Davis uses both sides of the plate and keeps hitters off balance. He pitched well in one start for Double-A Tulsa.

EDWIN DIAZ

Bats: R Throws: R Opening Day Age: 21
Ht: 5-11 Wt: 170 Born: 1/15/1975
Position: 2B Drafted: 1993 #2 TEX

YR TEAM	LG/CLASS	G	AB	R	H	2B	3B	HR	RBI	SB	BA	OBA
93 Rangers	GULF/R	43	154	27	47	10	5	1	23	12	.305	.391
94 Charlstn-SC	SAL/A	122	413	52	109	22	7	11	60	11	.264	.308
95 Charlotte	FSL/A	115	450	48	128	26	5	8	56	8	.284	.341

Diaz is one of the Rangers few legitimate blue-chip prospects and has the potential to become an outstanding offensive second baseman. The 21-year-old has excellent bat speed, strong wrists and good upper-body strength, translating into suprising extra-base power for someone his size. A free swinger, the Puerto Rican native needs to cut down on his strikeouts and draw more walks. Defensively, the converted shortstop is solid with a good glove and quick feet around the bag. Diaz also has good speed, but is careless on the basepaths and has been successful on less 50% of his stolen base attempts over his career.

JON JOHNSON

Bats: R Throws: R Opening Day Age: 22
Ht: 6-0 Wt: 180 Born: 7/16/1974
Position: P Drafted: 1995 #1 TEX

YR TEAM	LG/CLASS	G	GS	GF	SV	W	L	ERA	IP	H	HR	BB	SO	O/BA
95 Charlotte	FSL/A	8	7	1	0	1	5	2.70	43.1	34	2	16	25	.214

Johnson, formerly of Team USA, was selected by the Rangers with the seventh overall pick in last June's draft. The Florida State righthander went 33-5 with a 2.64 ERA in three seasons for the Seminoles and was a First Team All-American last year. He pitched well for Charlotte last summer, throwing at least five innings in each of his seven starts and never allowing more than three runs in a game. Johnson is a power pitcher with a great arm and a bulldog approach. He has good command, a feel for pitching, and is poised on the hill. Johnson was considered one of the most polished pitchers in last year's draft. His best pitch is a curve he can throw for strikes at any time in the count.

TEXAS RANGERS: TOP PROSPECTS

KERRY LACY

Bats: R Throws: R Opening Day Age: 24
Ht: 6-2 Wt: 195 Born: 8/7/1972
Position: P Drafted: 1991 #15 TEX

YR TEAM	LG/CLASS	G	GS	GF	SV	W	L	ERA	IP	H	HR	BB	SO	O/BA
93 Chston-SC	SAL/A	58	0	57	36	0	6	3.15	60.0	49	1	32	54	.221
93 Charlotte	FSL/A	4	0	3	2	0	0	1.93	4.2	2	0	3	3	.118
94 Tulsa	TEX/AA	41	0	35	12	2	6	3.68	63.2	49	4	37	46	.218
95 Okla City	AMAS/AAA	1	0	1	1	0	0	0.00	2.1	0	0	0	1	.000
95 Tulsa	TEX/AA	28	7	16	9	2	7	4.28	82.0	94	5	39	49	.298

Lacy ranked second in the South Atlantic League in saves in 1993, then skipped a level in '94 and was effective in relief for Tulsa before undergoing off-season surgery to remove bone chips from his elbow. Healthy in '95, the Rangers tried him as a starter to get him more innings and experience, but he was shelled in seven starts and returned to the pen. The Chattanooga State product then was 2-3 with 9 saves and a 2.01 ERA in 21 relief outings. The 23-year-old is a hard thrower with a good sinking fastball and breaking pitch and is unafraid to pitch inside. Lacy is a ground ball pitcher who doesn't give up many home runs, but has had trouble with lefties.

TERRELL LOWERY

Bats: R Throws: R Opening Day Age: 26
Ht: 6-3 Wt: 175 Born: 10/25/1970
Position: CF Drafted: 1991 #2 TEX

YR TEAM	LG/CLASS	G	AB	R	H	2B	3B	HR	RBI	SB	BA	OBA
93 Charlotte	FSL/A	65	257	46	77	7	9	3	36	14	.300	.408
93 Tulsa	TEX/AA	66	258	29	62	5	1	3	14	10	.240	.316
94 Tulsa	TEX/AA	129	496	89	142	34	8	8	54	33	.286	.365
95 Charlotte	FSL/A	11	35	4	9	2	2	0	4	1	.257	.381
95 Rangers	GULF/R	10	34	10	9	3	1	3	7	1	.265	.375

1995 was a lost season for Lowery, the only basketball player in NCAA history to place in the top ten in scoring and assists in the same year. The former Loyola-Marymount point guard sat out until August with an Achilles tendon injury. Lowery appeared to be coming into his own in the second half of '94, hitting for a higher average with more power and stealing more bases more successfully than at any time in his career. The 25-year-old could become the Rangers' leadoff hitter if he continues to improve his hitting and basestealing. His terrific speed helps him cover ground in centerfield, and Lowery is very intelligent with good baseball instincts. His baseball experience is limited due to his earlier focus on basketball and Lowery lost valuable time last year.

JULIO SANTANA

Bats: R Throws: R Opening Day Age: 23
Ht: 6-0 Wt: 175 Born: 1/20/1973
Position: P Drafted: NDFA 2-18-90 TEX

YR TEAM	LG/CLASS	G	GS	GF	SV	W	L	ERA	IP	H	HR	BB	SO	O/BA
93 Rangers	GULF/R	26	0	12	7	4	1	1.38	39.0	31	0	7	50	.214
94 Charlstn-SC	SAL/A	16	16	0	0	6	7	2.46	91.1	65	3	44	103	.198
94 Tulsa	TEX/AA	11	11	0	0	7	2	2.90	71.1	50	1	41	45	.205
95 Okla City	AMAS/AAA	2	2	0	0	0	2	39.00	3.0	9	3	7	6	.500
95 Charlotte	FSL/A	5	5	0	0	0	3	3.73	31.1	32	1	16	27	.271
95 Tulsa	TEX/AA	15	15	0	0	6	4	3.15	103.0	91	8	52	71	.239

Santana, the Rangers' top pitching prospect, has the potential to develop into a dominating number one starter. The 23-year-old has a 90-mph fastball, a slider that could become a plus pitch, and a developing changeup. The Dominican native, a converted shortstop, has limited pitching experience and needs to improve his control and command, learn to mix his pitches, and change speeds more effectively. He got off to a slow start at Oklahoma City last year due to the shortened spring training, but was throwing well by the end of the season at Tulsa.

MIKE SMITH

Bats: R Throws: R Opening Day Age: 26
Ht: 6-0 Wt: 180 Born: 12/1/1969
Position: 2B Drafted: 1992 #5 TEX

YR TEAM	LG/CLASS	G	AB	R	H	2B	3B	HR	RBI	SB	BA	OBA
93 Charlotte	FSL/A	86	327	33	77	16	4	3	43	3	.235	.316
94 High Desert	CAL/A	132	512	96	149	23	6	21	94	28	.291	.382
95 Tulsa	TEX/AA	132	499	65	128	22	3	16	64	11	.257	.336

The NCAA Division One Triple Crown winner in 1992 for Indiana, Smith's pro career seemed to be going nowhere at the start of the '94 season when he was assigned to High Desert, a co-op club. He responded with a career year for the Mavericks, showing that he could hit, hit for power, and swipe a few bases. At Tulsa, the 26-year-old led the Rangers' farm system in home runs.

ANDREW VESSEL

Bats: R Throws: R Opening Day Age: 21
Ht: 6-3 Wt: 205 Born: 3/11/1975
Position: LF Drafted: 1993 #3 TEX

YR TEAM	LG/CLASS	G	AB	R	H	2B	3B	HR	RBI	SB	BA	OBA
93 Rangers	GULF/R	51	192	23	42	10	2	1	31	6	.219	.246
94 Charlstn-SC	SAL/A	114	411	40	99	23	2	8	55	7	.241	.304
95 Charlotte	FSL/A	129	498	67	132	26	2	9	78	3	.265	.324

Vessel, an outstanding athlete, turned down a football scholarship to Washington State and signed with the Rangers. He began to blossom as a player last year, finishing second in the farm system in RBI. The 21-year-old has tremendous raw talent and the tools to become a middle of the order run-producer. He has a quick bat and hits to all fields, but will also turn on pitches and pull them with power. An aggressive hitter, he has had trouble with breaking pitches, but is learning to judge the curve. In the outfield, Vessel has worked hard and is now a good leftfielder despite an average arm.

TEXAS RANGERS: OTHERS TO WATCH

JOSE ALBERRO   Bats: R   Throws: R   Ht: 6-2   Wt: 190
Born: 6/29/1969   Drafted: NDFA 6-11-91 TEX   Position: P

YR TEAM	LG/CLASS	G	GS	GF	SV	W	L	ERA	IP	H	HR	BB	SO	O/BA
95 Okla City	AMAS/AAA	20	10	7	0	4	2	3.36	77.2	73	4	27	55	.247
95 Texas	AL/MAJ	12	0	7	0	0	0	7.40	20.2	26	2	12	10	.413

Alberro, a forkball pitcher with good control, opened last season with Texas due to the expanded rosters before joining Oklahoma City.

JIM BROWER   Bats: R   Throws: R   Ht: 6-2   Wt: 205
Born: 12/29/1972   Drafted: 1994 #5 TEX   Position: P

YR TEAM	LG/CLASS	G	GS	GF	SV	W	L	ERA	IP	H	HR	BB	SO	O/BA
95 Charlotte	FSL/A	27	27	0	0	7	10	3.89	173.2	170	16	62	110	.256

The Minnesota product has good control, a high-80's fastball, a good breaking pitch, and a decent change.

CLIFF BRUMBAUGH   Bats: R   Throws: R   Ht: 6-2   Wt: 205
Born: 4/21/1974   Drafted: 1995 #13 TEX   Position: 3B

YR TEAM	LG/CLASS	G	AB	R	H	2B	3B	HR	RBI	SB	BA	OBA
95 Hudson Vly	NYP/A	74	282	44	101	19	4	2	45	15	.358	.437

The New York-Penn Player of the Year plays good defense at third and is a line drive hitter who should develop power.

STEVE DREYER   Bats: R   Throws: R   Ht: 6-3   Wt: 180
Born: 11/19/1969   Drafted: 1990 #8 TEX   Position: P

YR TEAM	LG/CLASS	G	GS	GF	SV	W	L	ERA	IP	H	HR	BB	SO	O/BA
95 Rangers	GULF/R	2	2	0	0	0	1	1.00	9.0	6	0	2	7	.194
95 Tulsa	TEX/AA	10	10	0	0	2	4	2.89	62.1	56	6	19	48	.246

Dreyer got a late start last year after off season shoulder surgery, but seemed to be back at full strength by the end of the summer.

DAVE GEEVE   Bats: R   Throws: R   Ht: 6-3   Wt: 190
Born: 10/19/1969   Drafted: 1991 #10 TEX   Position: P

YR TEAM	LG/CLASS	G	GS	GF	SV	W	L	ERA	IP	H	HR	BB	SO	O/BA
95 Okla City	AMAS/AAA	10	10	0	0	2	5	5.66	55.2	72	7	13	30	.321
95 Tulsa	TEX/AA	15	14	0	0	3	8	5.17	94.0	108	16	20	38	.288

A control pitcher returning from elbow problems, Geeve struggled with his control but averaged over seven innings per start for Oklahoma City.

RICK HELLING   Bats: R   Throws: R   Ht: 6-3   Wt: 215
Born: 12/15/1970   Drafted: 1992 #1 TEX   Position: P

YR TEAM	LG/CLASS	G	GS	GF	SV	W	L	ERA	IP	H	HR	BB	SO	O/BA
95 Okla City	AMAS/AAA	20	20	0	0	4	8	5.33	109.2	132	13	41	80	.304
95 Texas	AL/MAJ	3	3	0	0	0	2	6.57	12.1	17	2	8	5	.340

The former first-rounder has had to rely on a very hittable fastball and has been a bust since winning his first three major league decisions in 1994.

LELAND MACON   Bats: R   Throws: R   Ht: 6-2   Wt: 205
Born: 5/4/1973   Drafted: 1993 #21 TEX   Position: RF

YR TEAM	LG/CLASS	G	AB	R	H	2B	3B	HR	RBI	SB	BA	OBA
95 Charlotte	FSL/A	119	405	52	105	15	3	2	38	14	.259	.354

A solid outfielder with a strong arm and some speed, Macon has little power and will need to make better contact to use his speed more.

ERIC MOODY   Bats: R   Throws: R   Ht: 6-6   Wt: 185
Born: 1/6/1971   Drafted: 1993 #24 TEX   Position: P

YR TEAM	LG/CLASS	G	GS	GF	SV	W	L	ERA	IP	H	HR	BB	SO	O/BA
95 Charlotte	FSL/A	13	13	0	0	5	5	2.75	88.1	84	2	13	57	.254

A shortstop in college, Moody has great control and tossed a no-hitter last April 20, blanking Sarasota 11-0.

JOHN POWELL   Bats: R   Throws: R   Ht: 5-10   Wt: 180
Born: 4/7/1971   Drafted: 1994 #8 TEX   Position: P

YR TEAM	LG/CLASS	G	GS	GF	SV	W	L	ERA	IP	H	HR	BB	SO	O/BA
95 Charlotte	FSL/A	19	2	9	2	4	1	3.00	48.0	44	2	13	47	.243
95 Tulsa	TEX/AA	7	7	0	0	1	4	3.89	39.1	45	9	16	27	.290

Powell is a control-type reliever with a good split-finger pitch who left Auburn with the NCAA record for career strikeouts.

MARC SAGMOEN   Bats: L   Throws: L   Ht: 5-11   Wt: 180
Born: 4/6/1971   Drafted: 1993 #13 TEX   Position: RF

YR TEAM	LG/CLASS	G	AB	R	H	2B	3B	HR	RBI	SB	BA	OBA
95 Okla City	AMAS/AAA	56	188	20	42	11	3	3	25	5	.223	.286
95 Tulsa	TEX/AA	63	242	36	56	8	5	6	22	5	.231	.306

Sagmoen, a former Big Eight Player of the Year at Nebraska, lacks great tools but is an overachiever with a great work ethic.

LANCE SCHUERMANN   Bats: L   Throws: L   Ht: 6-2   Wt: 200
Born: 2/7/1970   Drafted: 1991 #11 TEX   Position: P

YR TEAM	LG/CLASS	G	GS	GF	SV	W	L	ERA	IP	H	HR	BB	SO	O/BA
95 Okla City	AMAS/AAA	33	13	6	0	4	7	4.67	88.2	101	12	40	44	.288

The 26-year-old lefthander out of Nevada-Las Vegas was used as a spot starter/long reliever last year at Oklahoma City.

JON SHAVE   Bats: R   Throws: R   Ht: 6-0   Wt: 180
Born: 11/4/1967   Drafted: 1990 #5 TEX   Position: 2B

YR TEAM	LG/CLASS	G	AB	R	H	2B	3B	HR	RBI	SB	BA	OBA
95 Oklahoma City	AMAS/AAA	32	83	10	17	1	0	0	5	1	.205	.275

Shave is a solid hitter with a good glove at second who has been derailed by injuries since reaching the majors briefly in 1993.

DAN SMITH   Bats: L   Throws: L   Ht: 6-5   Wt: 190
Born: 8/20/1969   Drafted: 1990 #1 TEX   Position: P

The former Creighton lefty has battled injuries for years and missed all last season, but has been effective when healthy.

FERNANDO TATIS   Bats: S   Throws: R   Ht: 6-1   Wt: 175
Born: 1/1/1975   Drafted: NDFA 8-25-92 TEX   Position: 3B

YR TEAM	LG/CLASS	G	AB	R	H	2B	3B	HR	RBI	SB	BA	OBA
95 Chrlston-SC	SAL/A	131	499	74	151	43	4	15	84	22	.303	.366

The Rangers' Organization Player of the Year led the chain in RBI, tied for the South Atlantic League lead in hits, and was second in extra-base hits.

SCOTT TAYLOR   Bats: R   Throws: R   Ht: 6-3   Wt: 200
Born: 10/3/1966   Drafted: 1988 #15 FLO   Position: P

YR TEAM	LG/CLASS	G	GS	GF	SV	W	L	ERA	IP	H	HR	BB	SO	O/BA
95 N Orleans	AMAS/AAA	2	2	0	0	1	0	2.38	11.1	10	0	3	9	.233
95 Okla City	AMAS/AAA	22	19	0	0	7	8	3.66	118.0	122	12	38	65	.265
95 Texas	AL/MAJ	3	3	0	0	1	2	9.39	15.1	25	6	5	10	.379

Taylor, acquired from the Brewers for David Hulse last April, is a veteran righthander with a sinker/slider repertoire.

TORONTO BLUE JAYS

ROBERTO ALOMAR

Position: 2B
Bats: B **Throws:** R
Ht: 6'0" **Wt:** 184
Opening Day Age: 28
Born: 2/5/1968
Drafted: SD 2/16/85
ML Seasons: 8

SCOUTING REPORT

Alomar is considered by most in baseball to be a "complete" player: a term which isn't used much anymore. He has all the tools and can make all the plays, although he hasn't taken advantage of the league-wide offensive boom of the past two years. Roberto has good bat speed, especially from the left side. He is less disciplined from the right side and lefthanded pitchers try to fool him. However, Alomar is an excellent contact hitter from both sides with bat control who can execute the hit-and-run. Roberto hits line drives to both power alleys. In the field, he has average to above-average range. He turns the double play well and has soft hands and a strong, accurate arm. He has plus speed and is an above-average baserunner, who can and does both sacrifice bunt and bunt for base hits from each side of the dish.

HOW HE PERFORMED IN '95

Roberto should have known 1995 would be weird when he opened the campaign batting sixth in Cito Gaston's misguided attempt to "protect" John Olerud. Seemingly unaffected, Alomar hit .340 and slugged .631 in May and, early in the season, set an AL record for consecutive errorless games.

Things quickly got worse. The misery began with the capture of a wayward woman wandering through the Skydome Hotel packing a pistol intended for Roberto. This, combined with the demise of the once-powerful Jays, the trade of David Cone, and Toronto's decision to let Alomar play out his option induced a season-long funk that manifested itself in his mediocre play.

Roberto had huge platoon splits for the third consecutive season. He has hit at least 73 points higher against righthanders than lefties for three straight years. His baserunning improved last year as he curbed a growing recklessness, resulting in his outstanding stolen base percentage.

Defensively, Alomar won his fifth consecutive Gold Glove on the strength of his usual assortment of highlight-reel plays. He is good on the double play and doesn't make many errors.

WHAT TO EXPECT IN '96

It seemed relatively certain after the season that Roberto wouldn't be back in Toronto. Wherever he goes, however, expect a big season. Free of the distractions of the '95 season, a return to the form that makes him a legitimate MVP threat is highly likely.

Overall Statistics

	G	AB	R	H	2B	3B	HR	RBI	SB	CS	BB	SO	BA	OBA
95 TOR	130	517	71	155	24	7	13	66	30	3	47	45	.300	.354
Career	1151	4460	697	1329	230	48	77	499	296	76	470	522	.298	.365

1995 Situational Statistics

	AB	HR	RBI	BA	OBA	SLG		AB	HR	RBI	BA	OBA	SLG
Home	247	7	38	.296	.347	.429	LHP	130	2	9	.231	.289	.308
Road	270	6	28	.304	.360	.467	RHP	387	11	57	.323	.375	.496
Apr-Jun	221	8	33	.317	.370	.529	ScPos	116	2	51	.302	.380	.474
Jul-Oct	296	5	33	.287	.341	.389	Clutch	72	2	5	.389	.464	.514

How He Compares to Other Batters

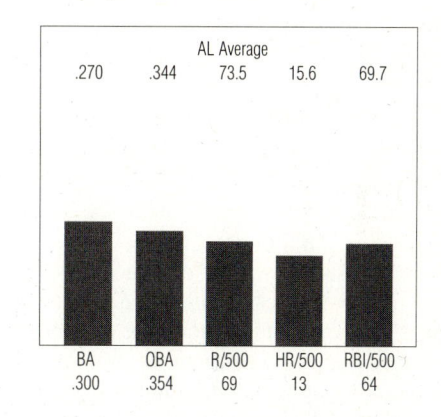

	BA	OBA	R/500	HR/500	RBI/500
AL Average	.270	.344	73.5	15.6	69.7
	.300	.354	69	13	64

Where He Hits the Ball

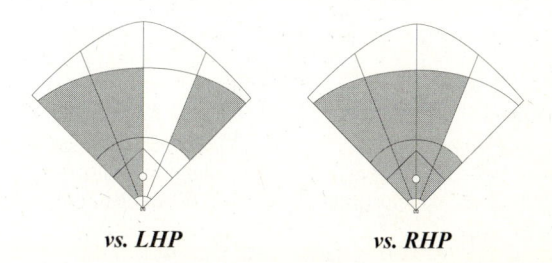

vs. LHP   vs. RHP

THE SCOUTING REPORT: 1996

TORONTO BLUE JAYS

JOE CARTER

Positions: OF//1B/DH
Bats: R **Throws:** R
Ht: 6'3" **Wt:** 215
Opening Day Age: 36
Born: 3/7/1960
Drafted: CHN81 1/2
ML Seasons: 13

SCOUTING REPORT

Joe Carter generates most of his considerable power from his big, strong arms. He has quick, strong wrists, but his long swing forces him to commit to pitches early. Like most power hitters, he loves to hack at fastballs, and especially goes for low and inside pitches. His trouble zones are high and inside and low and away where he can't pull any pitches.

Carter continues to carry a reputation as a guy who "comes to play," giving 100% effort despite nagging injuries and encroaching age. He still has an above-average jump on the ball and has plus range in both left and right field, although his hands are not good. An above-average baserunner, Joe maintains has above-average speed.

HOW HE PERFORMED IN '95

Carter got off to a good start in the 1995 season, hitting .330 through the end of May. Unfortunately, he hit just .233 the rest of the way. This is becoming a trend for Joe; he had also gotten off to a blistering start in 1994 before tailing off. Carter did still manage to show good power in 1995, homering at a rate close to his career pace.

Joe's recent fine performance on the basepaths continued in 1995. He has now swiped 31 bases in 35 attempts over the past three seasons, a remarkable achievement for a player of his age and stature.

Carter saw a fair bit of action in center field last year while filling in for an injured Devon White. At his regular position in left field, he got to plenty of balls, but didn't field especially well. His frequent misadventures evoked not-so-fond memories of George Bell's past performances for long-time Blue Jays fans. Joe registered nine outfield assists last season, but his arm is losing some pop.

WHAT TO EXPECT IN '96

Carter's status in Toronto was unclear after the season. Ideally, the Blue Jays would deal him and his high salary to make room for Carlos Delgado in the lineup. Unfortunately, Carter's $6 million paycheck, his advancing age, and his diminishing productivity will make a trade difficult. He still retains a "good RBI man" reputation that in some ways masks his declining skills and production as he ages.

Overall Statistics

	G	AB	R	H	2B	3B	HR	RBI	SB	CS	BB	SO	BA	OBA
95 TOR	139	558	70	141	23	0	25	76	12	1	37	87	.253	.300
Career	1749	6797	959	1782	345	41	327	1173	212	57	419	1115	.262	.308

1995 Situational Statistics

	AB	HR	RBI	BA	OBA	SLG		AB	HR	RBI	BA	OBA	SLG
Home	275	13	34	.258	.307	.455	LHP	136	8	20	.294	.331	.529
Road	283	12	42	.247	.293	.403	RHP	422	17	56	.239	.290	.396
Apr-Jun	218	10	31	.284	.328	.463	ScPos	157	5	50	.229	.304	.344
Jul-Oct	340	15	45	.232	.283	.406	Clutch	88	4	11	.273	.330	.455

How He Compares to Other Batters

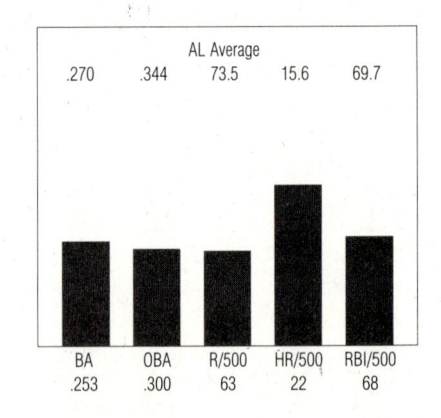

AL Average
.270 .344 73.5 15.6 69.7

BA .253 OBA .300 R/500 63 HR/500 22 RBI/500 68

Where He Hits the Ball

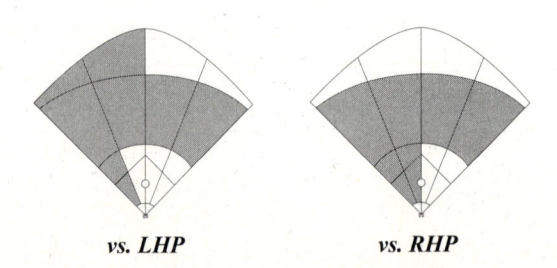

vs. LHP   vs. RHP

THE SCOUTING REPORT: 1996

TORONTO BLUE JAYS

TONY CASTILLO

Position: RP
Bats: L **Throws:** L
Ht: 5'10" **Wt:** 177
Opening Day Age: 33
Born: 3/1/1963
Drafted: TOR 2/16/83
ML Seasons: 7

SCOUTING REPORT
Lefthander Tony Castillo comes home with a high three-quarter delivery. He is a "nibbler" who lacks any outstanding pitch and must work to spots to be effective. His fastball has average velocity, and Tony will try and sink it in order to set up his sharp-breaking curve, which is also just average but serves as his out pitch. He also throws a turned-over changeup, which is mediocre. Castillo's control is average, but he has thrown only one wild pitch in his last four seasons, totalling 164 games!

Tony has an above-average move to first base with average time coming home. Nine enemy runners attempted to steal while Castillo was pitching in 1995, and six were successful—an average rate.

HOW HE PERFORMED IN '95
A rash of injuries to the Toronto bullpen last June resulted in Tony, a middle reliever for most of his career, being thrust into the unlikely role of closer for the defending World Series champions. Castillo really doesn't have the stuff to close, but he went six for six in save opportunities in July, posting a 1.20 ERA. Then came August, and he went five for nine with a 4.38 ERA, clearly showing his limitations in that role.

Castillo struggled early in the season, posting a 3.57 ERA but allowing a lofty 12 of his first 17 inherited runners to score through the end of May. Fortunately he soon corrected that, allowing just 14 of his remaining 38 inherited runners to cross the plate.

Despite his slump in August, there is no reason to criticize Castillo. By his normal standards and those of most other lefthanded middle relievers, he had a fine season. Tony held opposition hitters to a .308 on-base percentage and his ERA, though "deceptively" good, was still good by those standards.

WHAT TO EXPECT IN '96
There's no reason to think Castillo won't continue to contribute as a lefty middleman in the future. He's shown over the past three years to be reliable in his established role and, occasionally, in a more demanding job. However, he's not capable of serving as a closer for too long a period of time.

Overall Statistics

	G	GS	GF	SV	W	L	ERA	IP	H	R	ER	HR	BB	SO
95 TOR	55	0	31	13	1	5	3.22	72.2	64	27	26	7	24	38
Career	259	6	77	16	18	13	3.52	342.1	348	149	134	29	121	220

1995 Situational Statistics

	W	L	ERA	SV	IP	BB	SO		AB	HR	RBI	BA	OBA	SLG
Home	1	2	1.80	4	30.0	12	15	LHB	80	1	21	.262	.344	.363
Road	0	3	4.22	9	42.2	12	23	RHB	183	6	29	.235	.293	.388
Apr-Jun	0	2	2.97	1	36.1	10	19	ScPos	83	1	41	.313	.392	.410
Jul-Oct	1	3	3.47	12	36.1	14	19	Clutch	147	5	31	.245	.307	.415

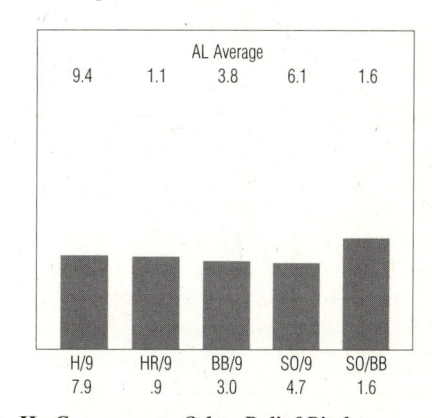

How He Compares to Other Pitchers

AL Average: 9.4 | 1.1 | 3.8 | 6.1 | 1.6

H/9	HR/9	BB/9	SO/9	SO/BB
7.9	.9	3.0	4.7	1.6

How He Compares to Other Relief Pitchers

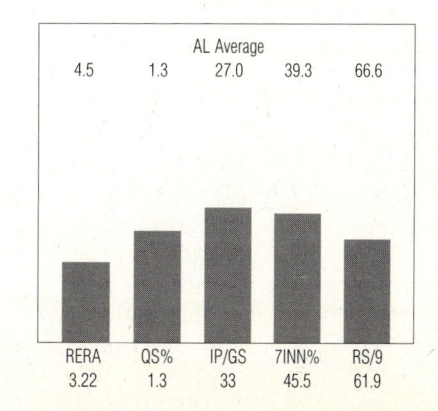

AL Average: 4.5 | 1.3 | 27.0 | 39.3 | 66.6

RERA	QS%	IP/GS	7INN%	RS/9
3.22	1.3	33	45.5	61.9

THE SCOUTING REPORT: 1996

TORONTO BLUE JAYS

ALEX GONZALEZ

Positions: SS//3B/DH
Bats: R **Throws:** R
Ht: 6'0" **Wt:** 180
Opening Day Age: 22
Born: 4/8/1973
Drafted: TOR91 16/380
ML Seasons: 2

SCOUTING REPORT

The highly-touted Gonzalez showed terrific skills but had some trouble in his first regular season. He has plus hands and average mobility, although his range was not good—something which will likely improve with experience. His arm is strong with average accuracy. The biggest problem Alex had at shorstop involved reading ground balls. He needs to charge the ball more often rather than let the balls play him.

Hitting is a strength for the young shortstop and will improve. He has some power and hits the ball hard. An up-and-in fastball hitter, Gonzalez tries to pull outside pitches too often and would make more consistent contact by cutting down on his big swing.

Alex has average speed but is a good baserunner. He can lay down a sacrifice and bunt for hits as well.

HOW HE PERFORMED IN '95

By any standard, the Toronto shortstop enjoyed a fine rookie season, both defensively and with the bat. He opened the season batting second, but shortly thereafter was shifted to the nine-hole, which seemed a better place for him at this point in his career. Alex's biggest offensive problem is making contact. Despite the whiffs, he does have pretty good strike-zone judgment as evidenced by walking once every nine plate appearances. He also showed good power, especially against southpaws. Defensively, Alex had a few erratic moments but his raw tools are excellent and he throws very well.

The Blue Jays handled their top prospect rather erratically. After he hit just .202 in July, Alex's playing time was reduced at the expense of utilityman Domingo Cedeno. Gonzalez then found himself on the bench in September so the Blue Jays could play Rule V draftee Tomas Perez. Alex never complained, though many hot prospects in his position might have.

WHAT TO EXPECT IN '96

The Blue Jays may deal third baseman Ed Sprague in the off–season and move Alex to third base. There are two reasons this would be a mistake: he has excellent tools at shortstop and his bat is a much greater asset at shortstop than at the hot corner. Nevertheless, the Blue Jays' handling of Alex in 1995 indicates that his status as shortstop–of–the–future is not certain.

Overall Statistics

	G	AB	R	H	2B	3B	HR	RBI	SB	CS	BB	SO	BA	OBA
95 TOR	111	367	51	89	19	4	10	42	4	4	44	114	.243	.322
Career	126	420	58	97	22	5	10	43	7	4	48	131	.231	.310

1995 Situational Statistics

	AB	HR	RBI	BA	OBA	SLG		AB	HR	RBI	BA	OBA	SLG
Home	206	8	32	.262	.343	.471	LHP	110	3	10	.273	.372	.445
Road	161	2	10	.217	.295	.304	RHP	257	7	32	.230	.300	.377
Apr-Jun	168	5	28	.262	.347	.411	ScPos	87	2	30	.276	.374	.402
Jul-Oct	199	5	14	.226	.300	.387	Clutch	49	0	4	.245	.362	.408

How He Compares to Other Batters

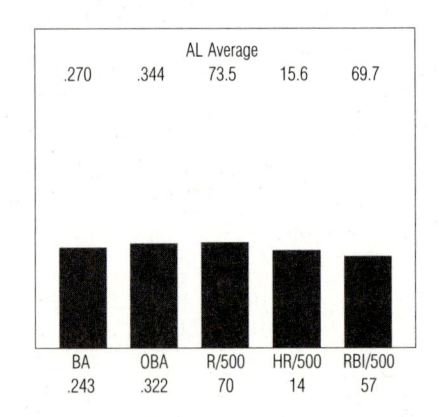

AL Average
.270 .344 73.5 15.6 69.7

BA .243 OBA .322 R/500 70 HR/500 14 RBI/500 57

Where He Hits the Ball

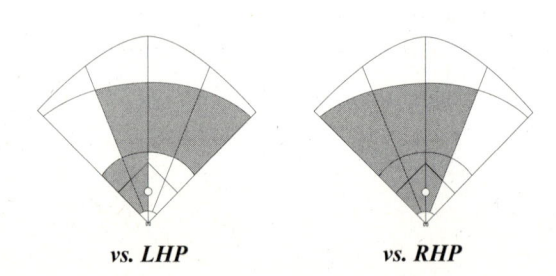

vs. LHP   vs. RHP

TORONTO BLUE JAYS

SHAWN GREEN

Position: OF
Bats: L **Throws:** L
Ht: 6'4" **Wt:** 190
Opening Day Age: 23
Born: 11/10/1972
Drafted: TOR91 1/16
ML Seasons: 3

SCOUTING REPORT

Shawn Green has a picture-book, fluid swing that baseball professionals love. He has line-drive sock and is expected to develop more power as he goes along. He doesn't walk very often yet, but he isn't a completely undisciplined hitter; Shawn goes with the pitch and has the aptitude to improve dramatically against lefthanded pitchers.

Shawn played well in right field in his first full big-league season. He has average hands and average-minus range, displaying some problems going back on balls. Green's arm is slightly better than average with average accuracy, and he threw out eight enemy runners in 1995.

He is lanky and loose, running with a long stride but just average speed.

HOW HE PERFORMED IN '95

Shawn had a very good rookie season, getting stronger as the season went along. Indeed, a late-season charge allowed him to at least merit consideration on Rookie of the Year ballots.

He began the season platooning with Candy Maldonado as Jays' Manager Cito Gaston again demonstrated his preference for veterans at the expense of rookies. Despite his somewhat limited playing time, Green was second on the team in doubles, tied for third in triples, and finished third in home runs while being the only Blue Jays' hitter to slug over .500. But for a bad month of June (a weak .207 batting average with only one home run and six runs batted in), Shawn would have had an even more impressive rookie season.

On the down side: Green's poor (though infrequent) performance against lefties, his poor on-base percentage, and his problems with fly balls. All three of these flaws should dissipate with time and experience.

WHAT TO EXPECT IN '96

Shawn's future is very bright. The late-season trade of Maldonado should sensibly ensure that his platooning days are over. Count on Shawn playing right field every day for the foreseeable future, as he slowly but surely moves up in the batting order. Until his plate discipline improves substantially, however, it would be wise to keep him from the top three lineup slots. If he does become more patient, pitchers will give him better pitches to hit and his production will be even better.

Overall Statistics

	G	AB	R	H	2B	3B	HR	RBI	SB	CS	BB	SO	BA	OBA
95 TOR	121	379	52	109	31	4	15	54	1	2	20	68	.288	.326
Career	138	418	53	112	32	4	15	55	2	2	21	77	.268	.306

1995 Situational Statistics

	AB	HR	RBI	BA	OBA	SLG		AB	HR	RBI	BA	OBA	SLG
Home	182	5	26	.247	.292	.418	LHP	45	0	4	.222	.234	.333
Road	197	10	28	.325	.357	.594	RHP	334	15	50	.296	.338	.533
Apr-Jun	139	6	20	.252	.318	.482	ScPos	110	3	38	.300	.350	.482
Jul-Oct	240	9	34	.308	.331	.525	Clutch	56	5	7	.268	.293	.571

How He Compares to Other Batters

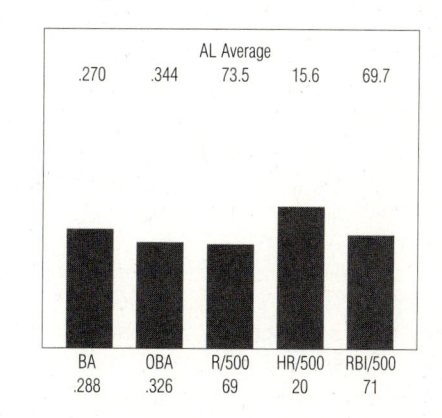

AL Average: .270 .344 73.5 15.6 69.7

BA	OBA	R/500	HR/500	RBI/500
.288	.326	69	20	71

Where He Hits the Ball

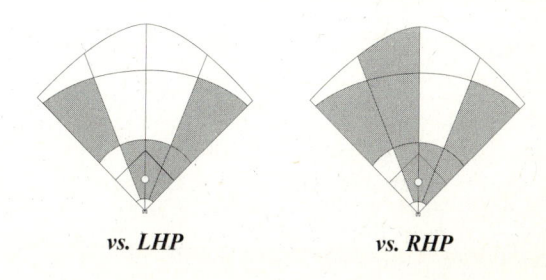

vs. LHP

vs. RHP

TORONTO BLUE JAYS

JUAN GUZMAN

Position: SP
Bats: R **Throws:** R
Ht: 5'11" **Wt:** 190
Opening Day Age: 29
Born: 10/28/1966
Drafted: LA 3/16/85
ML Seasons: 5

SCOUTING REPORT
Hard-throwing Juan Guzman comes at hitters from a high three-quarter to overhand delivery. His fastball no longer has consistently good velocity and now ranks as average-plus. Juan tries to cut the fastball on occasion. His out pitch is an average slider that breaks straight down. He also has a plus changeup.

Guzman's fielding is slightly below average. He has an average-minus move to first, which last year resulted in 15 of 20 men stealing successfully as he pitched. This has consistently been a problem for Juan in the past, although when he was pitching well, he could afford to ignore runners.

He is a slow worker who is plagued by inconsistent control and location, especially with his slider. Injuries have greatly reduced Guzman's velocity in the past two years.

HOW HE PERFORMED IN '95
This was the second consecutive horrific season for Guzman, whose ERA soared substantially over 1994's lofty 5.68 mark. He was at or over 5.00 in every home/road, grass/turf, day/night split and he had only one month, June, in which he pitched over 15 innings and kept his ERA under 5.30.

Guzman has had serious physical trouble in each of the past two seasons. There was much speculation about arm trouble in 1994, which was later confirmed in an almost clandestine manner. In 1995, he made two trips to the DL. In mid-May he sat with a "muscle imbalance" in his throwing shoulder and revisited the disabled list in mid-August with swelling beneath his right armpit.

It should be noted that there appears to be a genuine problem with miscommunication between Juan and the Blue Jays' management. While no malevolent feelings exist on either side, this manifests itself in conflicting accounts of Juan's physical health, depending on who is speaking.

WHAT TO EXPECT IN '96
Who can know for certain what the immediate future holds for Juan? Pitchers are an unpredictable breed in the best of times. Throw in the even higher number of variables attendant to Guzman, and a prediction of future performance is dicey at best. His age argues that he can regain effectiveness, but he is not a physically big pitcher and may never regain his full health or effectiveness.

Overall Statistics

	G	GS	GF	SV	W	L	ERA	IP	H	R	ER	HR	BB	SO
95 TOR	24	24	0	0	4	14	6.32	135.1	151	101	95	13	73	94
Career	133	133	0	0	56	36	4.21	823.0	760	419	385	62	397	700

1995 Situational Statistics

	W	L	ERA	SV	IP	BB	SO		AB	HR	RBI	BA	OBA	SLG
Home	2	5	5.36	0	82.1	31	59	LHB	298	5	48	.299	.390	.413
Road	2	9	7.81	0	53.0	42	35	RHB	240	8	36	.258	.342	.433
Apr-Jun	2	3	6.57	0	49.1	31	26	ScPos	155	2	67	.258	.364	.406
Jul-Oct	2	11	6.17	0	86.0	42	68	Clutch	35	1	9	.457	.548	.629

How He Compares to Other Pitchers

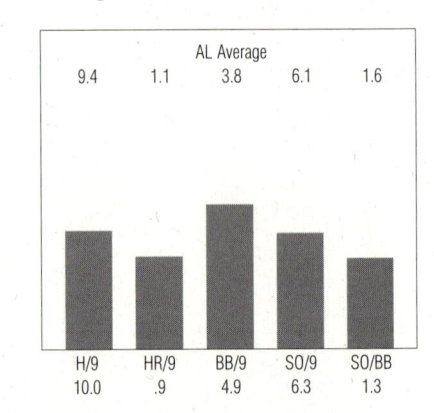

AL Average: 9.4 / 1.1 / 3.8 / 6.1 / 1.6

H/9: 10.0
HR/9: .9
BB/9: 4.9
SO/9: 6.3
SO/BB: 1.3

How He Compares to Other Starting Pitchers

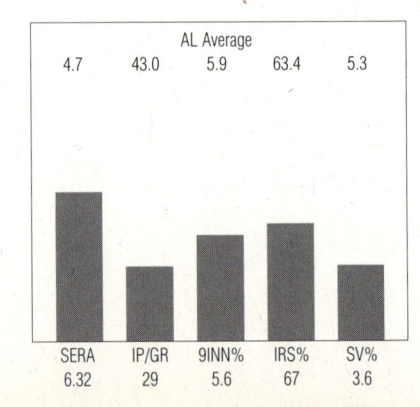

AL Average: 4.7 / 43.0 / 5.9 / 63.4 / 5.3

SERA: 6.32
IP/GR: 29
9INN%: 5.6
IRS%: 67
SV%: 3.6

TORONTO BLUE JAYS

PAT HENTGEN

Position: SP
Bats: R **Throws:** R
Ht: 6'2" **Wt:** 200
Opening Day Age: 27
Born: 11/13/1968
Drafted: TOR86 5/133
ML Seasons: 5

SCOUTING REPORT
While Pat hasn't been consistent as a pitcher, he is strong and athletic and has three above-average pitches. He has a live arm and uses a high three-quarters delivery to deliver a plus four-seam fastball that rises. Hentgen also cuts the fastball on occasion. His changeup is also a plus pitch. His best offering however, is a well above-average curve that has a sharp break but sometimes is wild. In general, Pat's control is average and tends to disappear at inopportune times.

Although Pat's move to first is just average, it's better than it was. Only 16 runners tried to steal against him in '95 and seven of them were thrown out. Hentgen has improved in this category two straight seasons. He is a plus fielder.

HOW HE PERFORMED IN '95
Hentgen continues to defy expectations. After emerging from the minor leagues with a very mediocre history and living down to the resultant low expectations in 1992, he surprised all by stepping into the rotation and posting two very good seasons in 1993 and 1994 (32 wins with a composite 3.66 ERA). Having thus established high expectations, Pat crashed and burned in 1995. His hits and walks allowed skyrocketed and his strikeouts fell—a basic recipe for disaster.

Hentgen's problems stemmed directly from poor control. He still threw well, but he frequently got behind hitters or, worse, put them on base due to walks. As a result Pat tried to compensate by getting fastballs over. His stuff is good, but not good enough that he can groove pitches and survive.

WHAT TO EXPECT IN '96
Hentgen's best news for 1996 is the way in which he closed last season. Over his final six starts he struck out 36 and walked 15 while posting a 3.14 ERA.

The one constant in Pat's career has been his ability to defy prognostications. With three full years in the rotation he enters the 1996 season with no expectations. That said, expect an improvement over his 1995 performance. There's nothing wrong with Hentgen's stuff, he has no history of arm problems, and the strong finish augurs well for a comeback.

Overall Statistics

	G	GS	GF	SV	W	L	ERA	IP	H	R	ER	HR	BB	SO
95 TOR	30	30	0	0	10	14	5.11	200.2	236	129	114	24	90	135
Career	119	89	11	0	47	33	4.23	649.1	663	338	305	80	258	446

1995 Situational Statistics

	W	L	ERA	SV	IP	BB	SO		AB	HR	RBI	BA	OBA	SLG
Home	4	8	5.69	0	112.1	44	79	LHB	453	11	71	.298	.379	.442
Road	6	6	4.38	0	88.1	46	56	RHB	362	13	45	.279	.343	.448
Apr-Jun	4	6	6.22	0	76.2	37	46	ScPos	235	5	87	.264	.358	.404
Jul-Oct	6	8	4.43	0	124.0	53	89	Clutch	69	3	7	.203	.267	.362

How He Compares to Other Pitchers

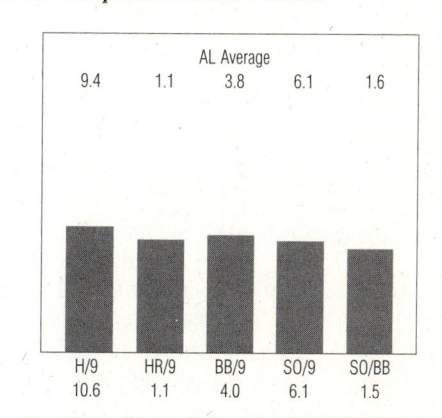

AL Average: 9.4 | 1.1 | 3.8 | 6.1 | 1.6
H/9: 10.6 | HR/9: 1.1 | BB/9: 4.0 | SO/9: 6.1 | SO/BB: 1.5

How He Compares to Other Starting Pitchers

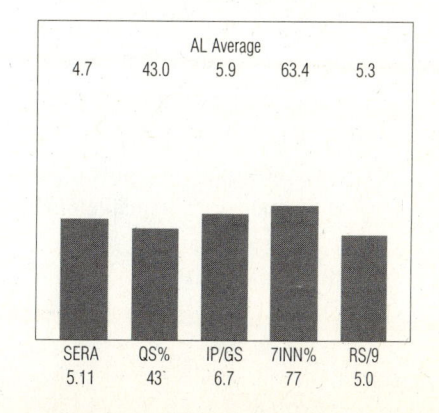

AL Average: 4.7 | 43.0 | 5.9 | 63.4 | 5.3
SERA: 5.11 | QS%: 43 | IP/GS: 6.7 | 7INN%: 77 | RS/9: 5.0

THE SCOUTING REPORT: 1996

TORONTO BLUE JAYS

AL LEITER

Position: SP
Bats: L **Throws:** L
Ht: 6'3" **Wt:** 210
Opening Day Age: 30
Born: 10/23/1965
Drafted: NYA84 2/50
ML Seasons: 9

SCOUTING REPORT

While Leiter has good stuff, inconsistent mechanics cause him control problems. His poor location on pitches and his herky-jerky, three-quarters motion keep a lot of lefthanded hitters from digging in.

Al has a better fastball than most lefthanders. It's a plus pitch that has plenty of life. He needs to keep it low, however, because it's straight and hittable when high. His out pitch is a well above-average curve that has a sharp, late break. The former Yankees hurler also has a below-average curve and a slider that he only uses for show.

Leiter's move to first base is above-average and intimidates runners: 19 runners tried to steal while Leiter was on the mound last year, and nine of them were thrown out. He has now allowed just 20 stolen bases in 38 attempts in 400 innings pitched over the past three years. His fielding is just average.

HOW HE PERFORMED IN '95

Last season was, in many ways, a breakthrough season for Al Leiter. Injury-free for the first time in his career, he posted a personal-best 3.64 ERA in 28 starts and was, due to the mid-season trade of David Cone, the only Toronto starter to keep his ERA below 5.00.

However, there were complications. Despite cutting one-and-a-half runs off his 1994 ERA, he continued to allow a dangerous amount of walks, his strikeout rate dipped slightly and his home-runs-allowed rate rose slightly. The key to his good ERA was a dramatic decline in hits allowed (from ten per game in 1994 to eight last year) as he held opposing hitters to a .238 batting average and .363 slugging percentage.

WHAT TO EXPECT IN '96

Al was a free agent at the end of the '95 season. He has expressed a desire to return to Toronto, and the Blue Jays would like to have him back. Given the state of their projected rotation, he'll be an asset regardless of whether or not he can harness his control. If he could do that, however, he'd be an asset to any organization and a very valuable pitcher.

Overall Statistics

	G	GS	GF	SV	W	L	ERA	IP	H	R	ER	HR	BB	SO
95 TOR	28	28	0	0	11	11	3.64	183.0	162	80	74	15	108	153
Career	113	83	7	2	33	32	4.36	522.0	490	272	253	40	309	439

1995 Situational Statistics

	W	L	ERA	SV	IP	BB	SO		AB	HR	RBI	BA	OBA	SLG
Home	6	4	3.05	0	97.1	49	89	LHB	126	4	16	.254	.319	.421
Road	5	7	4.31	0	85.2	59	64	RHB	555	11	53	.234	.351	.350
Apr-Jun	5	2	2.97	0	66.2	49	53	ScPos	168	2	50	.220	.357	.310
Jul-Oct	6	9	4.02	0	116.1	59	100	Clutch	36	0	2	.194	.326	.222

How He Compares to Other Pitchers

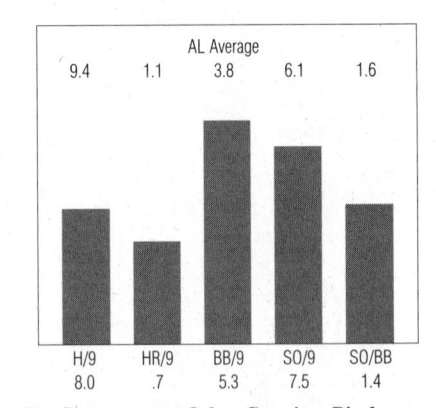

AL Average: H/9 9.4, HR/9 1.1, BB/9 3.8, SO/9 6.1, SO/BB 1.6
Leiter: H/9 8.0, HR/9 .7, BB/9 5.3, SO/9 7.5, SO/BB 1.4

How He Compares to Other Starting Pitchers

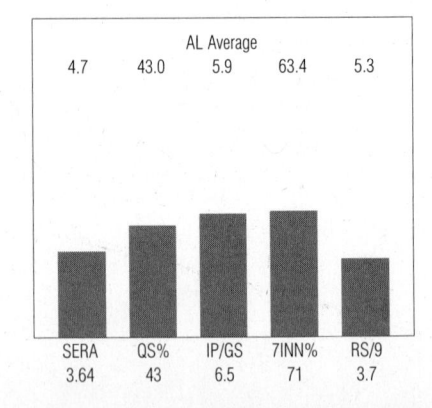

AL Average: SERA 4.7, QS% 43.0, IP/GS 5.9, 7INN% 63.4, RS/9 5.3
Leiter: SERA 3.64, QS% 43, IP/GS 6.5, 7INN% 71, RS/9 3.7

TORONTO BLUE JAYS

ANGEL MARTINEZ

Position: C
Bats: L **Throws:** R
Ht: 6'2" **Wt:** 200
Opening Day Age: 23
Born: 10/3/1972
Drafted: TOR 1/10/90
ML Seasons: 1

SCOUTING REPORT

Defensively, Martinez is already at his level. He has an arm ranked by scouts as one of the best in the league, with well above-average strength and plus accuracy. His throwing mechanics are also quite good. Sandy is agile behind the plate and has average hands.

However, he still needs work on catching breaking pitches and, like most young receivers, he has a lot to learn about calling games. He will almost certainly improve in these areas as he gains experience in the big leagues. In Toronto, he was working with a lot of pitchers as inexperienced as he was during his rookie season.

At bat, he is far less accomplished. Currently he has trouble with lefthanders. Martinez needs to make better contact: he has some power and likes fastballs, but needs to work on better gauging breaking balls and off-speed pitches.

HOW HE PERFORMED IN '95

Entering the 1995 season, Martinez had a career average of .249 over three years of pro ball, all spent at the Rookie and Class A levels. He opened the '95 season at Double-A Knoxville, and after hitting .229 with two home runs in 144 at-bats, the Blue Jays called him up and gave him the lion's share of the catching duties over the rest of the season.

Given his previous showings, Sandy's poor offensive production in Toronto should have been expected. His .321 average in 53 at-bats with runners in scoring position is as likely due to chance as anything else.

Fortunately, Sandy wasn't brought to Toronto on the strength of his bat. He has a great throwing arm, nailing 40% of opposition basestealers. However, he is still very raw behind the plate.

WHAT TO EXPECT IN '96

Barring an off-season signing, bet on Martinez to see a lot of playing time in 1996. The Blue Jays appear to have no confidence in Randy Knorr, so no matter if Sandy's batting average sinks, he will play. The Blue Jays are excited about his defense, particularly his cannon arm, but he is far from ready for major-league pitching at this point. Given that fact, a return to Triple-A for more seasoning isn't unlikely.

Overall Statistics

	G	AB	R	H	2B	3B	HR	RBI	SB	CS	BB	SO	BA	OBA
95 TOR	62	191	12	46	12	0	2	25	0	0	7	45	.241	.270
Career	62	191	12	46	12	0	2	25	0	0	7	45	.241	.270

1995 Situational Statistics

	AB	HR	RBI	BA	OBA	SLG		AB	HR	RBI	BA	OBA	SLG
Home	80	1	7	.225	.253	.363	LHP	17	0	1	.118	.211	.118
Road	111	1	18	.252	.282	.315	RHP	174	2	24	.253	.276	.356
Apr-Jun	7	1	3	.429	.429	1.000	ScPos	53	2	24	.321	.351	.491
Jul-Oct	184	1	22	.234	.264	.310	Clutch	25	1	7	.280	.333	.480

How He Compares to Other Batters

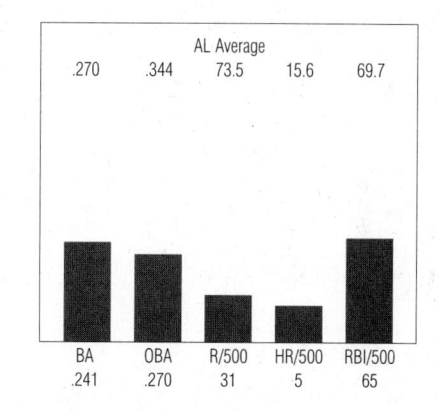

AL Average
.270   .344   73.5   15.6   69.7

BA	OBA	R/500	HR/500	RBI/500
.241	.270	31	5	65

Where He Hits the Ball

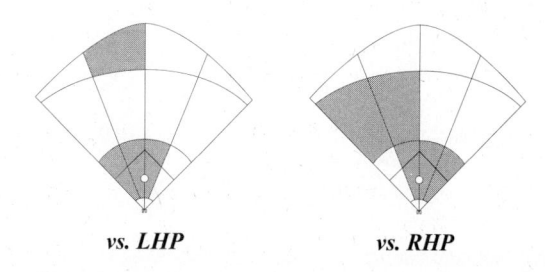

vs. LHP   vs. RHP

THE SCOUTING REPORT: 1996

TORONTO BLUE JAYS

PAUL MOLITOR

Position: DH
Bats: R **Throws:** R
Ht: 6'0" **Wt:** 185
Opening Day Age: 39
Born: 8/22/1956
Drafted: MIL77 1/3
ML Seasons: 18

SCOUTING REPORT
Paul stands high in the batters' box and remains still until he unleashes a strong bat with quick wrists. He's a smart, patient hitter who can still pick on a first-pitch fastball high in the strike zone and lash it with authority to any field. Off-speed and breaking pitches give him occasional problems.

Earlier in his career, Molitor was an above-average defender at several different positions. He did not play an inning of defense in 1995, but can still fill in at first base if needed.

He doesn't have above-average speed anymore, but Molitor is a smart runner who knows what he can and cannot do. Paul still bunts, but was not particularly effective at it last season.

HOW HE PERFORMED IN '95
Paul struggled mightily in 1995 as the combination of an active role in the labor negotiations and a string of injuries took their toll. Early in the year, both shoulders were sore, which led to a slump. He hit just .233 through June. At other times, a sore rib cage and hamstring pulls bothered him.

He started poorly before a late-season surge made his final numbers respectable. Over the final two months of the season he hit .308 and slugged .500. However, for the first time in three years, Paul didn't hit better at home than on the road.

Despite his physical ailments, Molitor remains a terrific baserunner. For the second consecutive year he was perfect in stolen bases, and is now an astonishing 54 for 58 in his three years with the Blue Jays.

WHAT TO EXPECT IN '96
Molitor is one of the most popular players in town: management, the media and the fans adore him. The Blue Jays' decision to buy out his option for 1996 was a purely financial move, and Toronto wanted him back despite having no position in the lineup open for him. There's still tread on the tires at 39, and when Paul's 1995 season is put in context, it's clear that he can contribute in 1996.

Minnesota signed him to a one-year contract last winter, bringing him back to his hometown so he can pursue his goal of getting 3,000 hits.

Overall Statistics

	G	AB	R	H	2B	3B	HR	RBI	SB	CS	BB	SO	BA	OBA
95 TOR	130	525	63	142	31	2	15	60	12	0	61	57	.270	.350
Career	2261	9135	1545	2789	503	97	211	1036	466	119	948	1058	.305	.370

1995 Situational Statistics

	AB	HR	RBI	BA	OBA	SLG		AB	HR	RBI	BA	OBA	SLG
Home	252	6	24	.270	.361	.417	LHP	111	4	18	.279	.371	.468
Road	273	9	36	.271	.339	.429	RHP	414	11	42	.268	.343	.411
Apr-Jun	189	4	24	.233	.327	.339	ScPos	115	1	38	.304	.391	.357
Jul-Oct	336	11	36	.292	.362	.470	Clutch	86	2	12	.221	.292	.314

How He Compares to Other Batters

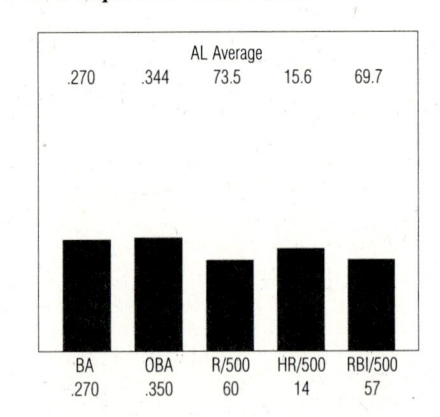

AL Average: .270 .344 73.5 15.6 69.7

BA .270 | OBA .350 | R/500 60 | HR/500 14 | RBI/500 57

Where He Hits the Ball

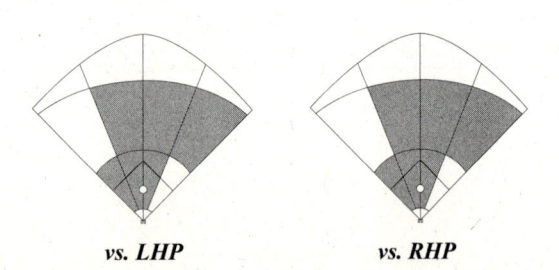

vs. LHP   vs. RHP

TORONTO BLUE JAYS

JOHN OLERUD

Position: 1B
Bats: L **Throws:** L
Ht: 6'5" **Wt:** 205
Opening Day Age: 27
Born: 8/5/1968
Drafted: TOR89 4/79
ML Seasons: 7

SCOUTING REPORT

John has the kind of compact, smooth swing prized by baseball people. His stroke generates good power and plenteous line drives. He generally doesn't swing at what he doesn't think he can hit, thus leading to a lot of deep counts and walks. However, he can be pitched inside effectively with good fastballs, and Olerud doesn't yet pull the ball as often as he might.

John is slow. He doesn't try to steal bases, and his combination of batting in the middle of the order, his poor speed and lots of hard-hit balls means he grounds into a lot of double plays (17 last year).

He is a steady fielder with average range, slightly above-average hands, and an average arm. He made just four errors in 1995.

HOW HE PERFORMED IN '95

Olerud has declined dramatically at the plate since 1993. From that season's .599 slugging percentage, he slid to .477 the next year and .404 in 1995. The latter two figures are all the more troubling considering the league-wide explosion in offense. John hit 24 homers in '93, 12 in 1994, and sank to a paltry eight in '95.

The good news for Olerud remains his on-base percentage. Due to his extreme patience at the plate, he matched his career mark of .397. But that patience may have actually worked against John. At times in '95, he looked paralyzed at the plate, as though he wanted to pull the trigger on a good pitch but couldn't. John has the ability to pull and drive pitches, but as yet has not done it consistently.

However, he improved in the second half of last season, driving the ball to right field more often. The numbers reflect this: from July 1 through the end of the year, he hit .330 with 21 doubles.

WHAT TO EXPECT IN '96

There was talk after the season in Toronto that the Blue Jays should deal Olerud, but that doesn't make much sense. His high price tag makes his trade value low, as does the fact that he's coming off a very poor season. Furthermore, intelligent, patient hitters with swings like John's are a rare commodity. Why give up on such a player when he's not yet 28? Another big year isn't unlikely.

Overall Statistics

	G	AB	R	H	2B	3B	HR	RBI	SB	CS	BB	SO	BA	OBA
95 TOR	135	492	72	143	32	0	8	54	0	0	84	54	.291	.398
Career	795	2705	405	801	188	6	91	410	2	8	454	393	.296	.397

1995 Situational Statistics

	AB	HR	RBI	BA	OBA	SLG		AB	HR	RBI	BA	OBA	SLG
Home	237	1	18	.270	.384	.359	LHP	143	1	17	.259	.333	.350
Road	255	7	36	.310	.410	.447	RHP	349	7	37	.304	.422	.427
Apr-Jun	210	3	20	.238	.331	.333	ScPos	142	1	45	.246	.410	.310
Jul-Oct	282	5	34	.330	.444	.457	Clutch	74	0	7	.270	.372	.324

How He Compares to Other Batters

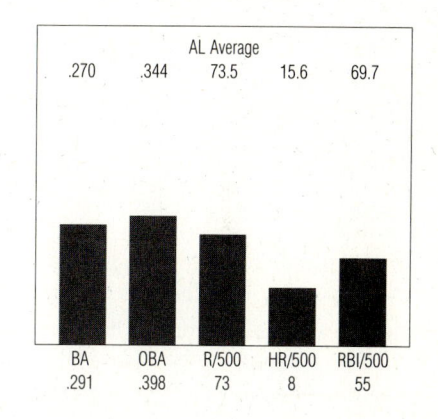

AL Average: .270 .344 73.5 15.6 69.7

BA .291 OBA .398 R/500 73 HR/500 8 RBI/500 55

Where He Hits the Ball

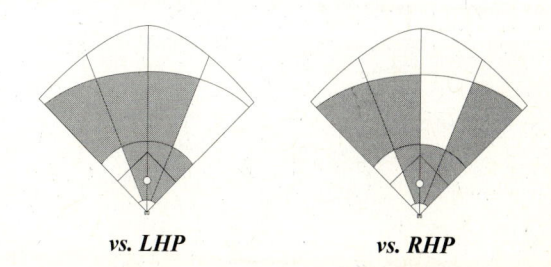

vs. LHP   vs. RHP

THE SCOUTING REPORT: 1996

TORONTO BLUE JAYS

ED SPRAGUE

Positions: 3B//1B/DH
Bats: R **Throws:** R
Ht: 6'2" **Wt:** 215
Opening Day Age: 28
Born: 7/25/1967
Drafted: TOR88 1/25
ML Seasons: 5

SCOUTING REPORT

Ed displayed improved power last season, and he can drive the ball to both alleys if he is disciplined. Unfortunately for his overall production, he still swings at too many bad pitches. He is a good fastball hitter, but he frequently lunges after curves in the dirt. Sprague is very slow, and as a result, doesn't steal bases. Another consequence of his lact of speed was that he grounded into 19 double plays last season, which ranked third highest in the AL.

Third base is where Sprague wound up, but he could also play first base and catch on more than an emergency basis. A plus arm helps him at any position, but his range and arm are both average-minus-which makes a move from third a possibility.

HOW HE PERFORMED IN '95

Sprague broke from the gate quickly, clubbing a grand slam and driving in seven runs in Toronto's first two games. He sandwiched a June .382 on-base percentage with high slugging percentages in May and July (.510 and .480 respectively) before driving off a cliff. Over the final two months of the season he batted .206 and slugged .317. This was atypical, for though 1995 was the first year in which Ed played every game, he's had a heavy workload in the past with no late-season collapses.

The single best sign of growth for Sprague last year was his improved strike zone judgment. He walked much more than ever before, adding 90 points to his on-base percentage with these free passes.

Sprague deserves credit for working hard on his defense, but he's never going to be a Gold Glove candidate at third. His range has become adequate but he still struggles too often with pop flies.

WHAT TO EXPECT IN '96

Several teams were interested in acquiring Sprague in the off–season. It's very likely that 1995 was Ed's career year, but it just wasn't that good. His ability to move around the diamond at other spots would make Sprague a useful utility player, but he is a below-average everyday third baseman in a power–based league in a high-offense era.

Overall Statistics

	G	AB	R	H	2B	3B	HR	RBI	SB	CS	BB	SO	BA	OBA
95 TOR	144	521	77	127	27	2	18	74	0	0	58	96	.244	.333
Career	486	1679	188	421	86	4	46	218	2	3	135	326	.251	.318

1995 Situational Statistics

	AB	HR	RBI	BA	OBA	SLG		AB	HR	RBI	BA	OBA	SLG
Home	252	12	39	.242	.355	.437	LHP	135	5	14	.222	.282	.341
Road	269	6	35	.245	.311	.379	RHP	386	13	60	.251	.350	.430
Apr-Jun	201	9	28	.284	.361	.468	ScPos	153	3	53	.203	.295	.327
Jul-Oct	320	9	46	.219	.315	.369	Clutch	80	4	11	.250	.354	.450

How He Compares to Other Batters

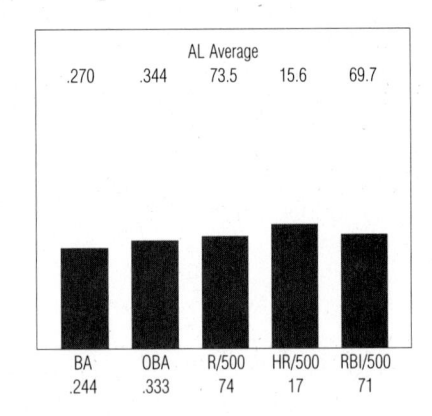

	BA	OBA	R/500	HR/500	RBI/500
	.244	.333	74	17	71
AL Average	.270	.344	73.5	15.6	69.7

Where He Hits the Ball

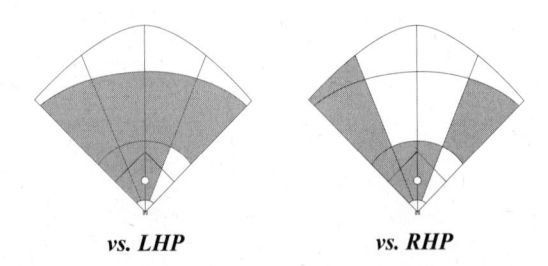

vs. LHP   *vs. RHP*

TORONTO BLUE JAYS

SCOUTING REPORT
Speed is Devon White's game. It allows him to catch up to fly balls other center fielders couldn't get, to take extra bases at bat, and even to outrun his own mistakes on the bases. He has excellent speed and is an above-average baserunner.

White is better from the left side, but cuts at anybody's fastball. He has poor plate discipline and can be pitched to, especially hitting from the right side. Devon doesn't bunt as often as he might, considering his quickness.

Defensively, he reads line drives very well in center field and has a great jump. Although Devon's arm is accurate, it lacks strength. This is not uncommon among centerfielders, and is not a big drawback.

HOW HE PERFORMED IN '95
When Devon broke his right foot by fouling a pitch off it last August 31, it capped his second straight season of diminished effectiveness because of injuries. An earlier hamstring problem caused him to miss several games and reduced his effectiveness and baserunning aggressiveness when he could play.

Despite his physical problems, White is still a good percentage base stealer. Fortunately, his ailments have not affected his defense. He is as good as ever in center field and was a deserving winner of his seventh consecutive Gold Glove. Devon nailed eight baserunners last year, posted well-above-average range, and made another handful of spectacular catches.

White retains the offensive characteristics of a good six-hole hitter, though he has declining power and a relatively low on-base percentage. Unfortunately, the Blue Jays have used him as a leadoff hitter, which doesn't emphasize his skills and magnifies his weaknesses. For the third time in the past four years he hit significantly better against right-handed pitching.

WHAT TO EXPECT IN '96
Toronto wanted Devon to return in 1996 because prospect Shannon Stewart still needs seasoning. However, White's desire to get away from playing on artificial turf and to move closer to his family meant that the Florida Marlins can expect great defense and decent offensive production from their new center fielder in 1996. The presence of Quilvio Veras might allow Rene Lachemann to use White lower in the order.

DEVON WHITE

Position: OF
Bats: B **Throws:** R
Ht: 6'2" **Wt:** 180
Opening Day Age: 33
Born: 12/29/1962
Drafted: CAL81 2/132
ML Seasons: 11

Overall Statistics

	G	AB	R	H	2B	3B	HR	RBI	SB	CS	BB	SO	BA	OBA
95 TOR	101	427	61	121	23	5	10	53	11	2	29	97	.283	.334
Career	1268	4942	789	1284	246	58	131	515	249	65	353	1047	.260	.313

1995 Situational Statistics

	AB	HR	RBI	BA	OBA	SLG		AB	HR	RBI	BA	OBA	SLG
Home	210	4	24	.300	.354	.471	LHP	100	1	13	.230	.287	.330
Road	217	6	29	.267	.315	.392	RHP	327	9	40	.300	.348	.462
Apr-Jun	197	5	28	.289	.341	.462	ScPos	82	3	42	.341	.406	.524
Jul-Oct	230	5	25	.278	.328	.404	Clutch	56	3	13	.339	.377	.571

How He Compares to Other Batters

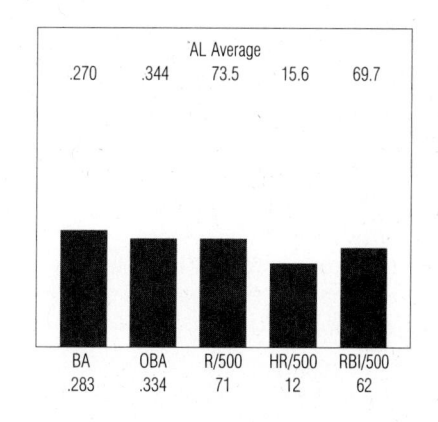

AL Average: .270   .344   73.5   15.6   69.7

BA	OBA	R/500	HR/500	RBI/500
.283	.334	71	12	62

Where He Hits the Ball

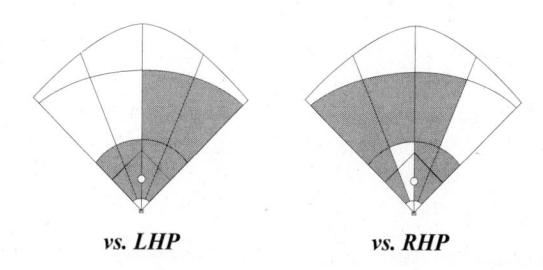

vs. LHP   vs. RHP

THE SCOUTING REPORT: 1996

TORONTO BLUE JAYS

DOMINGO CEDENO

Positions: SS/2B//3B
Bats: B **Throws:** R
Ht: 6'0" **Wt:** 170
Opening Day Age: 27
Born: 11/4/1968
Drafted: TOR 9/4/87
ML Seasons: 3

Overall Statistics

	G	AB	R	H	2B	3B	HR	RBI	SB	CS	BB	SO	BA	OBA
95 TOR	51	161	18	38	6	1	4	14	0	1	10	35	.236	.289
Career	113	304	37	65	8	4	4	31	2	3	21	76	.214	.265

1995 Situational Statistics

	AB	HR	RBI	BA	OBA	SLG		AB	HR	RBI	BA	OBA	SLG
Home	58	1	4	.155	.210	.276	LHP	39	2	7	.256	.293	.487
Road	103	3	10	.282	.333	.408	RHP	122	2	7	.230	.288	.320
Apr-Jun	53	1	2	.302	.373	.396	ScPos	41	3	13	.171	.244	.390
Jul-Oct	108	3	12	.204	.246	.343	Clutch	29	2	7	.241	.353	.483

SCOUTING REPORT

The wiry Cedeno has decent bat control but mediocre bat speed and can be blown away by good fastballs. His stance is closed, which allows him to move in the batter's box, but reduces the sock he can put in his already weak swing. Domingo bunts well and is fast but doesn't use his speed especially well.

Domingo is a strong defensive shortstop. His arm is above-average and he gets rid of the ball quickly. He is also capable of playing the outfield if needed.

HOW HE PERFORMED IN '95

Just 79 at-bats of hitting .304 early in the season apparently convinced Cito Gaston that, despite six years of evidence to the contrary, Cedeno was a good major-league hitter. Domingo therefore picked up way too much of blue-chip rookie Alex Gonzalez' playing time in August, but he proceeded to bat .171 in his final 82 at-bats.

Domingo often played shortstop in the late innings last year. He improved his concentration and made just three errors.

WHAT TO EXPECT IN '96

The Blue Jays are high on Cedeno. He may receiving extensive playing time in 1996, although it is clear that he is best used as a utility player.

DANNY COX

Position: RP
Bats: R **Throws:** R
Ht: 6'4" **Wt:** 235
Opening Day Age: 36
Born: 9/21/1959
Drafted: SL81 12/319
ML Seasons: 11

Overall Statistics

	G	GS	GF	SV	W	L	ERA	IP	H	R	ER	HR	BB	SO
95 TOR	24	0	7	0	1	3	7.40	45.0	57	40	37	4	33	38
Career	278	174	35	8	74	75	3.64	1298.0	1292	602	525	102	432	723

1995 Situational Statistics

	W	L	ERA	SV	IP	BB	SO		AB	HR	RBI	BA	OBA	SLG
Home	1	1	6.26	0	23.0	19	21	LHB	92	3	20	.293	.400	.457
Road	0	2	8.59	0	22.0	14	17	RHB	88	1	9	.341	.439	.455
Apr-Jun	1	2	6.92	0	26.0	22	25	ScPos	63	1	25	.317	.425	.476
Jul-Oct	0	1	8.05	0	19.0	11	13	Clutch	42	1	8	.381	.491	.548

SCOUTING REPORT

Danny Cox' best attribute may be his bulldog attitude, as his only above-average pitch is his plus changeup. He uses a confusing, herky-jerky motion and throws from three-quarters. He throws a sinking fastball and a slider with average command and control.

Cox has a quick move to home, but is slow to first base. Twelve men tried to steal on him, a high number considering his innings, and eight were successful. He's an average fielder.

HOW HE PERFORMED IN '95

After missing over three months in 1994 due to arm surgery, Cox pitched well in ten appearances after returning. This gave cause for optimism concerning 1995, but Danny was again bothered by injuries last season. He tried to pitch through them though, as a result, he was awful. His strikeout-to-walk ratio worsened dramatically in 1995, and opposing hitters reached base at a .419 rate.

WHAT TO EXPECT IN '96

Consecutive injury-racked years for a pitcher in his late thirties are certainly worrisome. However, Cox has been counted out before only to return and pitch well. A comeback is unlikely but, given his history, certainly not impossible.

TORONTO BLUE JAYS

TIM CRABTREE

Position: RP
Bats: R **Throws:** R
Ht: 6'4" **Wt:** 205
Opening Day Age: 26
Born: 10/13/1969
Drafted: TOR92 4/66
ML Seasons: 1

Overall Statistics

	G	GS	GF	SV	W	L	ERA	IP	H	R	ER	HR	BB	SO
95 TOR	31	0	19	0	0	2	3.09	32.0	30	16	11	1	13	21
Career	31	0	19	0	0	2	3.09	32.0	30	16	11	1	13	21

1995 Situational Statistics

	W	L	ERA	SV	IP	BB	SO		AB	HR	RBI	BA	OBA	SLG
Home	0	2	3.18	0	17.0	8	9	LHB	71	1	9	.296	.346	.408
Road	0	0	3.00	0	15.0	5	12	RHB	54	0	6	.167	.286	.185
Apr-Jun	0	0	0.00	0	1.1	1	0	ScPos	33	0	12	.273	.342	.333
Jul-Oct	0	2	3.23	0	30.2	12	21	Clutch	15	0	4	.333	.545	.400

SCOUTING REPORT
Tim Crabtree throws from a three-quarter angle with average control and command. He has two above-average pitches: a good two-seam sinking fastball and a plus, hard slider. He does not hold runners well, allowing two men to steal against him in two tries, and is an average-minus fielder at this point.

HOW HE PERFORMED IN '95
Despite a 5.40 ERA in 32 innings at Syracuse, Toronto summoned Crabtree in late June. The rookie pitched fairly well, and the Blue Jays hope he can assume a key bullpen role in the near future.

Tim was extremely tough on righthanders in '95, holding them to just one extra-base hit in 55 at-bats. A rough August (7.56 ERA, eight walks in 8.1 innings) prevented him from compiling some very impressive numbers.

WHAT TO EXPECT IN '96
The Jays' bullpen is anything but deep, so Crabtree will pitch a lot in '96. If Toronto can't obtain a big-name closer, Tim could find himself in a critical role well ahead of schedule. He has the tools to do the job, but he needs confidence and experience.

MIKE HUFF

Position: OF
Bats: R **Throws:** R
Ht: 6'1" **Wt:** 180
Opening Day Age: 32
Born: 8/11/1963
Drafted: LA85 17/510
ML Seasons: 6

Overall Statistics

	G	AB	R	H	2B	3B	HR	RBI	SB	CS	BB	SO	BA	OBA
95 TOR	61	138	14	32	9	1	1	9	1	1	22	21	.232	.337
Career	358	772	108	193	42	6	9	75	19	9	108	141	.250	.349

1995 Situational Statistics

	AB	HR	RBI	BA	OBA	SLG		AB	HR	RBI	BA	OBA	SLG
Home	83	0	3	.205	.313	.277	LHP	70	0	4	.200	.269	.271
Road	55	1	6	.273	.373	.418	RHP	68	1	5	.265	.400	.397
Apr-Jun	53	1	5	.189	.368	.302	ScPos	34	0	8	.147	.184	.176
Jul-Oct	85	0	4	.259	.316	.353	Clutch	34	0	5	.412	.463	.529

SCOUTING REPORT
Mike is a high-ball hitter who can't get around on a good fastball. However, he doesn't chase bad pitches, makes contact, and walks as often as he strikes out. Huff lacks power but can sacrifice effectively.

He is a good baserunner with a quick first step but has average-minus speed. While Huff can play left and center field due to his hands and mobility, his arm isn't strong enough for him to play right often.

HOW HE PERFORMED IN '95
1995 was a lost season for Huff. Injuries to his right quadriceps and hamstring necessitated two trips to the DL. Those injuries, and Candy Maldonado's presence, resulted in greatly reduced playing time for him. Huff's batting average dropped significantly but he retained his discerning eye at the plate.

WHAT TO EXPECT IN '96
If healthy, Huff should bounce back to the form he showed in 1994. He's a smart player who gets on base, adds good defense, and has the attitude and ability to come off the bench. Every team can use a Michael Huff, but the Jays may not ask him back.

TORONTO BLUE JAYS

EDWIN HURTADO

Position: SP
Bats: R **Throws:** R
Ht: 6'3" **Wt:** 215
Opening Day Age: 26
Born: 2/1/1970
Drafted: TOR 12/10/90
ML Seasons: 1

Overall Statistics

	G	GS	GF	SV	W	L	ERA	IP	H	R	ER	HR	BB	SO
95 TOR	14	10	0	0	5	2	5.45	77.2	81	50	47	11	40	33
Career	14	10	0	0	5	2	5.45	77.2	81	50	47	11	40	33

1995 Situational Statistics

	W	L	ERA	SV	IP	BB	SO		AB	HR	RBI	BA	OBA	SLG
Home	2	2	4.26	0	38.0	20	17	LHB	170	8	33	.294	.376	.482
Road	3	0	6.58	0	39.2	20	16	RHB	125	3	14	.248	.356	.384
Apr-Jun	0	0	0.00	0	2.0	0	3	ScPos	70	4	35	.286	.376	.557
Jul-Oct	5	2	5.59	0	75.2	40	30	Clutch	21	1	5	.476	.500	.762

SCOUTING REPORT

Hurtado throws from a high three-quarters slot, but drops down against righthanders. His average-minus fastball lacks movement and has inconsistent velocity. He cuts the fastball at times. An average splitter serves as his out pitch, and Edwin also throws a curve and slider.

Hurtado's move to first is average, but four of eight men trying to steal against him were nailed. He is an average fielder.

HOW HE PERFORMED IN '95

Hurtado's 11 starts at Double-A Knoxville last year were his first above Class A. They were enough for the Jays, who called him and his 4.45 ERA up last May. Given his utter lack of experience, the results weren't that bad. Edwin had his moments, posting a 2.83 ERA in his first 28.2 innings, but was well over his head, as evidenced by 32 walks and just 15 strikeouts over his final 49 frames.

WHAT TO EXPECT IN '96

Hurtado needs at least a full season of experience at Triple-A in order to develop. Whether he will get it is another matter: the Blue Jays do many things well, but handling young pitchers is not one of them.

RANDY KNORR

Position: C
Bats: R **Throws:** R
Ht: 6'2" **Wt:** 205
Opening Day Age: 27
Born: 11/12/1968
Drafted: TOR86 10/263
ML Seasons: 5

Overall Statistics

	G	AB	R	H	2B	3B	HR	RBI	SB	CS	BB	SO	BA	OBA
95 TOR	45	132	18	28	8	0	3	16	0	0	11	28	.212	.273
Career	135	377	50	88	13	2	15	57	0	0	32	98	.233	.294

1995 Situational Statistics

	AB	HR	RBI	BA	OBA	SLG		AB	HR	RBI	BA	OBA	SLG
Home	66	2	9	.227	.301	.364	LHP	47	3	8	.234	.294	.489
Road	66	1	7	.197	.243	.318	RHP	85	0	8	.200	.261	.259
Apr-Jun	86	3	11	.244	.301	.407	ScPos	38	0	12	.211	.268	.342
Jul-Oct	46	0	5	.152	.220	.217	Clutch	18	0	1	.222	.222	.278

SCOUTING REPORT

Randy has average hands but minus mobility behind the plate. His arm is above-average and has average accuracy. At the plate, he is aggressive with occasional power and can hit most fastballs. Knorr is one of the slower players in the league, so he isn't asked to run much.

HOW HE PERFORMED IN '95

Carlos Delgado's shoulder problems should have made Knorr a logical beneficiary of increased playing time. Then the Blue Jays signed Lance Parrish, who became the opening day catcher.

Knorr started adequately with the bat but struggled defensively, prompting GM Gord Ash to proclaim during June that "we over-estimated Randy." Knorr then fractured his right thumb and missed almost two months, closing the season in a 2-for-30 funk. Defensively, 30 of 40 basestealing attempts (75%) were successful.

WHAT TO EXPECT IN '96

For some reason, the management does not appear to be comfortable with Knorr. That's unfortunate, because he can play. He has some pop, especially against lefthanders, and will accept a walk. He'll never be a full-time receiver, but could prosper in a platoon role.

TORONTO BLUE JAYS

PAUL MENHART

Position: RP/SP
Bats: R **Throws:** R
Ht: 6'2" **Wt:** 190
Opening Day Age: 27
Born: 3/25/1969
Drafted: TOR90 9/231
ML Seasons: 1

Overall Statistics

	G	GS	GF	SV	W	L	ERA	IP	H	R	ER	HR	BB	SO
95 TOR	21	9	6	0	1	4	4.92	78.2	72	49	43	9	47	50
Career	21	9	6	0	1	4	4.92	78.2	72	49	43	9	47	50

1995 Situational Statistics

	W	L	ERA	SV	IP	BB	SO		AB	HR	RBI	BA	OBA	SLG
Home	1	2	5.52	0	44.0	26	36	LHB	170	5	19	.247	.365	.418
Road	0	2	4.15	0	34.2	21	14	RHB	120	4	25	.250	.354	.425
Apr-Jun	1	1	9.39	0	15.1	16	18	ScPos	85	3	36	.200	.339	.365
Jul-Oct	0	3	3.84	0	63.1	31	32	Clutch	29	3	8	.276	.462	.690

SCOUTING REPORT

He comes from a three-quarters delivery with average control and velocity. Menhart's sinking fastball and slider are just average. His real strengths are the curve, a plus pitch that is improving, and his average-plus changeup, which he should use more. He is above-average at holding runners, but five stole bases in seven tries last season. Mehnart is a plus fielder.

HOW HE PERFORMED IN '95

After missing a year because of shoulder surgery, Menhart returned successfully in 1995. He opened the season in Toronto due to the expanded rosters, but was sent to Triple-A in early June with a 9.40 ERA in 15.1 innings. Despite pitching poorly at Syracuse (6.31 ERA in 10 starts) he was recalled in late July and made seven starts among his 13 final appearances. He pitched well, posting a 3.27 ERA and allowing fewer than eight hits per game, though his strikeout-to-walk ratio was barely better than even.

WHAT TO EXPECT IN '96

Menhart was the only reliable Toronto starter under contract after the season, so he figures to get a chance at the rotation in '96. Injuries have hampered his development to date, but Paul is still young and talented.

LANCE PARRISH

Positions: C//DH
Bats: R **Throws:** R
Ht: 6'3" **Wt:** 220
Opening Day Age: 39
Born: 6/15/1956
Drafted: DET74 1/16
ML Seasons: 19

Overall Statistics

	G	AB	R	H	2B	3B	HR	RBI	SB	CS	BB	SO	BA	OBA
95 TOR	70	178	15	36	9	0	4	22	0	0	15	52	.202	.265
Career 1988	7067	856	1782	305	27	324	1070	28	37	612	1527	.252	.313

1995 Situational Statistics

	AB	HR	RBI	BA	OBA	SLG		AB	HR	RBI	BA	OBA	SLG
Home	100	4	16	.230	.282	.400	LHP	58	0	7	.207	.288	.276
Road	78	0	6	.167	.244	.218	RHP	120	4	15	.200	.254	.342
Apr-Jun	105	3	9	.190	.248	.314	ScPos	58	2	19	.224	.254	.379
Jul-Oct	73	1	13	.219	.289	.329	Clutch	33	1	6	.182	.250	.273

SCOUTING REPORT

Parrish's bat is still reasonably quick. He can hit high inside fastballs with power. However, he's never been a good judge of the strike zone. Surprisingly, he is effective at laying down sacrifice bunts.

Lance has very good throwing mechanics and catches the ball well. However, he has bad knees that have robbed him of strength and agility, and Parrish was slow even in his early twenties.

HOW HE PERFORMED IN '95

The Blue Jays obtained Parrish in order to use him as a backup. However, an injury to Delgado, combined with lack of confidence in Knorr, meant Parrish received more at-bats than both of them. Three home runs in May was all the justification the brass needed to give Lance more playing time than he deserved.

Lance retains some defensive skills, gunning down 42% of enemy basestealers last year, but his bat is gone. The veteran receiver wore down in the heat of the summer, hitting a combined .160 in June, July and August.

WHAT TO EXPECT IN '96

Lance figures to have a major fight on his hands if he wants to win a roster spot anywhere in 1996.

THE SCOUTING REPORT: 1996

TORONTO BLUE JAYS

TOMAS PEREZ

Positions: SS//2B/3B
Bats: R **Throws:** R
Ht: 5'11" **Wt:** 165
Opening Day Age: 22
Born: 12/29/1973
Drafted: MON 7/18/91
ML Seasons: 1

Overall Statistics

	G	AB	R	H	2B	3B	HR	RBI	SB	CS	BB	SO	BA	OBA
95 TOR	41	98	12	24	3	1	1	8	0	1	7	18	.245	.292
Career	41	98	12	24	3	1	1	8	0	1	7	18	.245	.292

1995 Situational Statistics

	AB	HR	RBI	BA	OBA	SLG		AB	HR	RBI	BA	OBA	SLG
Home	61	1	8	.213	.279	.328	LHP	21	1	4	.238	.238	.381
Road	37	0	0	.297	.316	.324	RHP	77	0	4	.247	.306	.312
Apr-Jun	8	0	1	.250	.250	.375	ScPos	30	1	7	.233	.250	.333
Jul-Oct	90	1	7	.244	.296	.322	Clutch	24	0	1	.250	.250	.250

SCOUTING REPORT

The very young and inexperienced Perez has little power and hits straightaway, hitting line drives off fastballs up and over the plate. Tomas has slightly below-average speed. He has average tools in the field all around now, but is regarded as having excellent defensive potential.

HOW HE PERFORMED IN '95

The Angels selected Perez in the Rule V draft, then traded him to Toronto. As is usually the case with such players, Tomas spent the vast majority of his time picking splinters out of his posterior, receiving just eight at-bats through the end of June. He got 33 at-bats over the next two months, then started eight consecutive games at shortstop in September. In limited playing time, Perez looked good both at bat and in the field.

WHAT TO EXPECT IN '96

Prior to '95, Tomas had never played higher than Class A ball. Therefore, at least one full season in the minors is certainly in order. Expect him back in Toronto, perhaps as soon as '97; he quickly became a favorite of Blue Jays manager Cito Gaston.

MIKE TIMLIN

Position: RP
Bats: R **Throws:** R
Ht: 6'4" **Wt:** 205
Opening Day Age: 30
Born: 3/10/1966
Drafted: TOR87 5/127
ML Seasons: 5

Overall Statistics

	G	GS	GF	SV	W	L	ERA	IP	H	R	ER	HR	BB	SO
95 TOR	31	0	19	5	4	3	2.14	42.0	38	13	10	1	17	36
Career	208	3	93	12	19	14	3.73	289.2	281	136	120	19	134	243

1995 Situational Statistics

	W	L	ERA	SV	IP	BB	SO		AB	HR	RBI	BA	OBA	SLG
Home	4	3	2.25	1	28.0	12	23	LHB	94	1	12	.298	.340	.415
Road	0	0	1.93	4	14.0	5	13	RHB	63	0	6	.159	.303	.175
Apr-Jun	3	1	3.63	3	22.1	10	19	ScPos	48	1	17	.250	.368	.396
Jul-Oct	1	2	0.46	2	19.2	7	17	Clutch	94	1	17	.255	.340	.372

SCOUTING REPORT

Mike throws two fastballs: a well above-average, nasty two-seam sinker, and a below-average four-seamer. His hard slider ranks as a plus pitch, and he has an average changeup.

Timlin throws low three-quarters to three-quarters with average control. His motion makes him tough on righties but vulnerable to lefthanders. His fielding is average. Only one runner tried to steal against him in 1995.

HOW HE PERFORMED IN '95

Mike missed two months of action after mid-season arthroscopic surgery to replace bone chips in his elbow. After the surgery, he was terrific, allowing just one earned run in his last 19.2 innings.

Lefties hit Mike as well as usual. Righthanders couldn't touch him, losing points off their poor .229 career mark. Timlin allowed them just one extra-base hit in 63 at-bats.

WHAT TO EXPECT IN '96

Good health appears to be the only thing standing between Timlin and a fine career. If he develops an out pitch for lefties, he could finally become a top-notch closer. Failing that, he'll make a very good set up man.

TORONTO BLUE JAYS

WOODY WILLIAMS

Position: RP
Bats: R **Throws:** R
Ht: 6'0" **Wt:** 180
Opening Day Age: 29
Born: 8/19/1966
Drafted: TOR88 28/732
ML Seasons: 3

Overall Statistics

	G	GS	GF	SV	W	L	ERA	IP	H	R	ER	HR	BB	SO
95 TOR	23	3	10	0	1	2	3.69	53.2	44	23	22	6	28	41
Career	91	3	33	0	5	6	3.84	150.0	128	65	64	13	83	121

1995 Situational Statistics

	W	L	ERA	SV	IP	BB	SO		AB	HR	RBI	BA	OBA	SLG
Home	0	1	3.94	0	29.2	17	24	LHB	117	4	13	.231	.323	.385
Road	1	1	3.38	0	24.0	11	17	RHB	83	2	6	.205	.320	.349
Apr-Jun	0	2	3.86	0	39.2	23	32	ScPos	46	1	12	.217	.308	.348
Jul-Oct	1	0	3.21	0	14.0	5	9	Clutch	42	2	3	.143	.294	.310

SCOUTING REPORT

Williams throws across his body with a three-quarters motion. He uses an average-minus sinking fastball, which gets plenty of ground balls. His curve and slider are slightly below-average. Either his minus changeup or minus splitter must improve, and Woody needs to throw strike one consistently, lacking the stuff to pitch behind in the count.

William's is move to first is plus. Just four men tried to steal against Woody last year, all successfully.

HOW HE PERFORMED IN '95

It was shaping up as another pretty good season for Williams before inflammation in his right shoulder shut him down for good in mid-July. Woody pitched well in his middle relief role and even acquitted himself competently in three emergency starts. For the second consecutive year, Woody was significantly better on grass than the ersatz turf.

WHAT TO EXPECT IN '96

Woody is ideally suited to the middle relief/setup/spot-starter role the Blue Jays cast him in during 1995. It took him six years to get to the majors, but Williams has worked hard to earn his paycheck.

TORONTO BLUE JAYS: TOP PROSPECTS

HOWARD BATTLE
Bats: R Throws: R Opening Day Age: 24
Ht: 6-0 Wt: 197 Born: 3/25/1972
Position: 3B Drafted: 1990 #5 TOR

YR TEAM	LG/CLASS	G	AB	R	H	2B	3B	HR	RBI	SB	BA	OBA
93 Knoxville	SOU/AA	141	521	66	145	21	5	7	70	12	.278	.342
94 Syracuse	INT/AAA	139	517	72	143	26	8	14	75	26	.277	.328
95 Toronto	AL/MAJ	9	15	3	3	0	0	0	1	.200	.368
95 Syracuse	INT/AAA	118	443	43	111	17	4	8	48	10	.251	.314

Despite his 33 errors in 1995, Battle is regarded as a fine third baseman versatile enough to fill in at shortstop. Offensively, the 23-year-old is known for his powerful bat and good speed. However, he set career lows in both slugging and on-base percentage last season and was caught stealing more times than he was successful. He had hit .272 in his previous four seasons with 107 doubles, 58 homers and 59 stolen bases.

DEREK BRANDOW
Bats: R Throws: R Opening Day Age: 26
Ht: 6-1 Wt: 200 Born: 1/25/1970
Position: P Drafted: 1992 #31 TOR

YR TEAM	LG/CLASS	G	GS	GF	SV	W	L	ERA	IP	H	HR	BB	SO	O/BA
93 Hagerstown	SAL/A	40	1	27	6	4	5	3.66	76.1	76	5	34	62	.255
94 Dunedin	FSL/A	29	21	3	1	7	6	3.21	140.1	122	6	58	123	.233
95 Knoxville	SOU/AA	25	21	1	1	5	6	4.29	107.0	95	13	50	106	.238

Brandow doesn't own a classic power pitcher's body, but he has command of an 88-92 mph fastball, a decent curve, and a changeup. He battled wrist and elbow injuries during the season but was still overpowering at times. The Oklahoma State product fanned 10 batters in four innings against Chattanooga in late-May and had 13 K's in seven innings against Greenville in June.

TILSON BRITO
Bats: R Throws: R Opening Day Age: 23
Ht: 6-0 Wt: 170 Born: 5/28/1972
Position: SS Drafted: NDFA 1-10-90 Toronto

YR TEAM	LG/CLASS	G	AB	R	H	2B	3B	HR	RBI	SB	BA	OBA
93 Dunedin	FSL/A	126	465	80	125	21	3	6	44	27	.269	.361
94 Knoxville	SOU/AA	139	476	61	127	17	7	5	57	33	.267	.323
95 Syracuse	INT/AAA	90	327	49	79	16	3	7	32	17	.242	.310

The 23-year-old Dominican Republic native suffered through a miserable year in 1995, primarily due to a flu-like virus which was later diagnosed as tonsillitis. Because the virus left him very weak, Brito hit a career-low .242, but still displayed some pop, played well in the field, and managed to steal 17 bases. Brito led the organization with 33 steals in 1994 and showed excellent range and a good arm.

CHRIS CARPENTER
Bats: R Throws: R Opening Day Age: 20
Ht: 6-6 Wt: 220 Born: 4/27/1975
Position: P Drafted: 1993 #1 TOR

YR TEAM	LG/CLASS	G	GS	GF	SV	W	L	ERA	IP	H	HR	BB	SO	O/BA
94 Med Hat	PIO/R	15	15	0	0	6	3	2.76	84.2	76	3	39	80	.243
95 Knoxville	SOU/AA	12	12	0	0	3	7	5.18	64.1	71	3	31	53	.284
95 Dunedin	FSL/A	15	15	0	0	3	5	2.17	99.1	83	3	50	56	.229

At 6-foot-6, 220 pounds, Carpenter is developing into a classic power pitcher. He throws a mid-90's fastball and a power curve. Chris is one of the best starting pitchers in the system right now, and will get even better as he gains more experience and develops an off-speed pitch. He allowed three earned runs or less in 13 of 15 outings in the Florida State League, earning him a promotion to Double-A at age 20. Carpenter struggled for Knoxville as he could no longer rely on his fastball to dominate hitters.

FELIPE CRESPO
Bats: S Throws: R Opening Day Age: 23
Ht: 5-11 Wt: 190 Born: 3/5/1973
Position: 2B Drafted: 1990 #4 TOR

YR TEAM	LG/CLASS	G	AB	R	H	2B	3B	HR	RBI	SB	BA	OBA
93 Dunedin	FSL/A	96	345	51	103	16	8	6	39	18	.299	.387
94 Knoxville	SOU/AA	129	502	74	135	30	4	8	49	20	.269	.345
95 Syracuse	INT/AAA	88	347	56	102	20	5	13	41	12	.294	.371

The 22-year-old Puerto Rico native, built in the Carlos Baerga mold, is a switch-hitter with some power and speed. In the field, he has average range and turns the double play pivot well with most of his 25 errors related to a leg contusion which put him on the bench for seven weeks. Crespo failed in a conversion to third base in 1994, but may be moved to the outfield to take advantage of his offensive skills.

CARLOS DELGADO
Bats: L Throws: R Opening Day Age: 23
Ht: 6-3 Wt: 206 Born: 6/25/1972
Position: 1B Drafted: NDFA 10-9-88 Toronto

YR TEAM	LG/CLASS	G	AB	R	H	2B	3B	HR	RBI	SB	BA	OBA
93 Knoxville	SOU/AA	140	468	91	142	28	0	25	102	10	.303	.430
93 Toronto	AL/MAJ	2	1	0	0	0	0	0	0	0	.000	.500
94 Toronto	AL/MAJ	43	130	17	28	2	0	9	24	1	.215	.352
94 Syracuse	INT/AAA	85	307	52	98	11	0	19	58	1	.319	.404
95 Toronto	AL/MAJ	37	91	7	15	3	0	3	11	0	.165	.212
95 Syracuse	INT/AAA	91	333	59	106	23	4	22	74	0	.318	.403

Delgado has been considered the top prospect in the system over the last four years, but he has had trouble sticking in the majors due to his defense and inability to hit the breaking ball. He has dominated the minor leagues in each of the last four years and has nothing left to prove there offensively. The only reason the former catcher spent most of 1995 in Triple-A was so he could learn to play first base. He played like a natural at his new position, committing only four errors there all season.

TORONTO BLUE JAYS: TOP PROSPECTS

MARTY JANZEN

Bats: R Throws: R Opening Day Age: 22
Ht: 6-3 Wt: 197 Born: 5/31/1973
Position: P Drafted: NDFA 8-8-91 NYA

YR TEAM	LG/CLASS	G	GS	GF	SV	W	L	ERA	IP	H	HR	BB	SO	O/BA
93 Yankees	GULF/R	5	5	0	0	0	1	1.21	22.1	20	0	3	19	.225
94 Greensboro	SAL/A	17	17	0	0	3	7	3.89	104.0	98	8	25	92	.243
95 Norwich	EAST/AA	3	3	0	0	1	2	4.95	20.0	17	2	7	16	.224
95 Knoxville	SOU/AA	7	7	0	0	5	1	2.63	48.0	35	2	14	44	.205
95 Tampa	FSL/A	18	18	0	0	10	3	2.61	113.2	102	4	30	104	.241

Janzen was the key player the Jays acquired from the Yankees for David Cone. He won his first five starts for Tampa, and went 10-3, 2.61 ERA before a promotion to Double-A. He struggled a little at Norwich, but finished strong with Knoxville after the trade, going 5-1, 2.63 ERA in seven appearances in the Southern League. Janzen finished the year with 164 strikeouts, surrendered only eight homers, and held foes to a .230 average. The 22-year-old Floridian may be the best pitching prospect in the Toronto system, throwing a moving low 90's-fastball, a curveball, a slider, and change with excellent command.

ROBERT PEREZ

Bats: R Throws: R Opening Day Age: 26
Ht: 6-3 Wt: 195 Born: 6/4/1969
Position: OF Drafted: NDFA 5-1-89 TOR

YR TEAM	LG/CLASS	G	AB	R	H	2B	3B	HR	RBI	SB	BA	OBA
93 Syracuse	INT/AAA	138	524	72	154	26	10	12	64	13	.294	.329
94 Syracuse	INT/AAA	128	510	63	155	28	3	10	65	4	.304	.336
94 Toronto	AL/MAJ	4	8	0	1	0	0	0	0	0	.125	.125
95 Toronto	AL/MAJ	17	48	2	9	2	0	1	3	0	.188	.188
95 Syracuse	INT/AAA	122	502	70	172	38	6	9	67	7	.343	.359

Perez has hit .296 throughout his six-year minor league career, but has batted only .179 over 21 games in two cups of coffee with Toronto. The Venezuelan had an All-Star year in 1995, winning the International League batting crown while leading the league in hits (third-best in the minors) and doubles. The 26-year-old stayed consistent all year and has feasted on lefthanded pitching, hitting .336 over the last three seasons. Despite the great year, questions remain about Perez' defense, power potential and strike zone judgment—he walked only 13 times last season.

JOSE PETT

Bats: R Throws: R Opening Day Age: 20
Ht: 6-6 Wt: 190 Born: 1/8/1976
Position: P Drafted: NDFA 7-2-92 TOR

YR TEAM	LG/CLASS	G	GS	GF	SV	W	L	ERA	IP	H	HR	BB	SO	O/BA
93 Blue Jays	GULF/R	4	4	0	0	1	1	3.60	10.0	10	0	3	7	.250
94 Dunedin	FSL/A	15	15	0	0	4	8	3.77	90.2	103	1	20	49	.289
95 Knoxville	SOU/AA	26	25	0	0	8	9	4.26	141.2	132	16	48	89	.244

The native of Brazil was signed at age 16 and was the youngest pitcher in the Southern League in 1995. He showed improvement with his command, throwing a low-90-mph fastball and a good changeup, but he was still learning to master the curveball. He posted a 4-3 record with a 3.02 ERA through June 4, but ran out of gas in the second half, as his ERA was 5.33 the rest of the way. Pett was victimized by poor defense and had a tendency to lose his poise at times.

JOSE SILVA

Bats: R Throws: R Opening Day Age: 22
Ht: 6-5 Wt: 210 Born: 12/19/1973
Position: P Drafted: 1991 #9 TOR

YR TEAM	LG/CLASS	G	AB	R	H	2B	3B	HR	RBI	SB	BA	OBA
95 Toronto	AL/MAJ	0	0	0	0	0	0	0	0	0	.000	.000
95 Knoxville	SOU/AA	3	0	0	0	0	0	0	0	0	.000	.000

After an outstanding 1993 campaign, Silva was regarded as the top pitching prospect in the organization. He then had a sub-par year in '94 playing against much older competition, and was in an automobile accident after the season that caused severe facial injuries. The 22-year-old returned in mid-August and had one pitch clocked at 100 mph, but developed elbow tendinitis and was shut down after just three appearances.

SHANNON STEWART

Bats: R Throws: R Opening Day Age: 22
Ht: 6-1 Wt: 185 Born: 2/25/1974
Position: OF Drafted: 1992 #1 TOR

YR TEAM	LG/CLASS	G	AB	R	H	2B	3B	HR	RBI	SB	BA	OBA
93 St.Cathrnes	NYP/A	75	301	53	84	15	2	3	29	25	.279	.351
94 Hagerstown	SAL/A	56	225	39	73	10	5	4	25	15	.324	.386
95 Toronto	AL/MAJ	12	38	2	8	0	0	0	1	2	.211	.318
95 Knoxville	SOU/AA	138	498	89	143	24	6	5	55	42	.287	.398

Playing a full season for the first time in his career, Stewart was promoted to Toronto in September at the tender age of 21. The 1992 first-round pick led the Southern League in walks, was third in runs and fourth in on-base percentage last year. An outstanding athlete who uses all fields, Stewart is the fastest runner in the organization, a good basestealer and center fielder, but has a below-average throwing arm.

JEFF WARE

Bats: R Throws: R Opening Day Age: 25
Ht: 6-3 Wt: 190 Born: 11/11/1970
Position: P Drafted: 1991 #2 TOR

YR TEAM	LG/CLASS	G	GS	GF	SV	W	L	ERA	IP	H	HR	BB	SO	O/BA
92 Dunedin	FSL/A	12	12	0	0	5	3	2.63	75.1	64	1	30	49	.226
94 Knoxville	SOU/AA	10	10	0	0	7	6.87	38.0	50	5	16	31	.323
95 Toronto	AL/MAJ	5	5	0	0	2	1	5.47	26.1	28	2	21	18	.277
95 Syracuse	INT/AAA	16	16	0	0	7	0	3.00	75.0	62	8	46	76	.230

In 1995, Ware stayed healthy after battling elbow problems for three years. The 24-year-old has an upper-80 mph fastball which helped him fan 76 batters in 75 innings of work. He pitched his best game in late June, holding Pawtucket to one hit and no runs over eight innings while striking out a season-high 11 batters. He was called up to the majors in September and was so-so in five starts.

THE SCOUTING REPORT: 1996

TORONTO BLUE JAYS: OTHERS TO WATCH

TRAVIS BAPTIST Bats: S Throws: L Ht: 6-0 Wt: 190
Born: 12/30/1971 Drafted: 1990 #46 TOR Position: P

YR TEAM	LG/CLASS	G	GS	GF	SV	W	L	ERA	IP	H	HR	BB	SO	O/BA
95 Syracuse	INT/AAA	15	13	0	0	3	4	4.33	79.0	83	12	32	52	.262

Baptist is coming back from an arm injury and his curve could be his ticket to the majors.

TOM EVANS Bats: R Throws: R Ht: 6-1 Wt: 180
Born: 7/9/1974 Drafted: 1992 #6 TOR Position: 3B

YR TEAM	LG/CLASS	G	AB	R	H	2B	3B	HR	RBI	SB	BA	OBA
95 Dunedin	FSL/A	130	444	63	124	29	3	9	66	7	.279	.359

Evans remained healthy all year after 1994 knee surgery, and hit .340 with eight homers after July 1.

HUCK FLENER Bats: S Throws: L Ht: 5-11 Wt: 180
Born: 2/25/1969 Drafted: 1990 #10 TOR Position: P

YR TEAM	LG/CLASS	G	GS	GF	SV	W	L	ERA	IP	H	HR	BB	SO	O/BA
95 Syracuse	INT/AAA	30	23	3	0	6	11	3.94	134.2	131	20	41	83	.253

The junkballer had a great second half and finished tenth in the International League in ERA in 1995.

MIKE GORDON Bats: L Throws: R Ht: 6-2 Wt: 195
Born: 11/30/1972 Drafted: 1992 #9 NYA Position: P

YR TEAM	LG/CLASS	G	GS	GF	SV	W	L	ERA	IP	H	HR	BB	SO	O/BA
95 Tampa	FSL/A	21	21	0	0	4	6	3.04	124.1	111	6	49	96	.239
95 Dunedin	FSL/A	7	6	0	0	1	2	5.89	36.2	44	6	24	36	.293

Acquired in the David Cone trade, Gordon rebounded from a terrible 1994 to post strong strikeout and ERA totals.

RYAN JONES Bats: R Throws: R Ht: 6-3 Wt: 220
Born: 11/5/1974 Drafted: 1993 #6 TOR Position: 1B

YR TEAM	LG/CLASS	G	AB	R	H	2B	3B	HR	RBI	SB	BA	OBA
95 Dunedin	FSL/A	127	478	65	119	28	0	18	78	1	.249	.315

Jones, who resembles a smaller version of Mark McGwire, led the system in RBI and placed second in the Florida State League in homers, but he has some work to do with the glove.

JEFF LADD Bats: R Throws: R Ht: 6-3 Wt: 200
Born: 7/10/1970 Drafted: 1992 #43 TOR Position: C

YR TEAM	LG/CLASS	G	AB	R	H	2B	3B	HR	RBI	SB	BA	OBA
95 Knoxville	SOU/AA	9	24	1	7	1	1	0	2	0	.292	.433
95 Hagerstown	SAL/A	94	311	54	95	17	3	19	58	6	.305	.454

His .454 on-base percentage led the entire minor leagues and he has a .501 career slugging percentage, but the lack of a position has impeded Ladd's progress.

JOE LIS Bats: R Throws: R Ht: 5-10 Wt: 170
Born: 11/3/1968 Drafted: 1991 #33 TOR Position: 2B

YR TEAM	LG/CLASS	G	AB	R	H	2B	3B	HR	RBI	SB	BA	OBA
95 Syracuse	INT/AAA	130	485	68	127	33	4	17	56	6	.262	.325

Lis can play several positions and showed unusual power for a middle infielder, pacing the International League with 54 extra-base hits.

JULIO MOSQUERA Bats: R Throws: R Ht: 6-0 Wt: 165
Born: 1/29/1972 Drafted: NDFA 5-16-91 TOR Position: C

YR TEAM	LG/CLASS	G	AB	R	H	2B	3B	HR	RBI	SB	BA	OBA
95 Hagerstown	SAL/A	108	406	64	118	22	5	3	46	5	.291	.353

The South Atlantic League All-Star threw out 51% of would-be basestealers in 1995, and is a career .301 hitter with excellent bat control and decent speed.

ANGEL RAMIREZ Bats: R Throws: R Ht: 5-10 Wt: 166
Born: 1/24/1973 Drafted: NDFA 5-16-91 TOR Position: OF

YR TEAM	LG/CLASS	G	AB	R	H	2B	3B	HR	RBI	SB	BA	OBA
95 Dunedin	FSL/A	131	541	78	149	19	5	8	52	17	.275	.308

Ramirez is a streaky hitter with gap power, decent speed and a great arm (17 outfield assists in 1995), but he could improve by being more selective at the plate.

LONELL ROBERTS Bats: S Throws: R Ht: 6-0 Wt: 172
Born: 6/7/1971 Drafted: 1989 #9 TOR Position: OF

YR TEAM	LG/CLASS	G	AB	R	H	2B	3B	HR	RBI	SB	BA	OBA
95 Knoxville	SOU/AA	116	454	66	107	12	3	1	29	57	.236	.281

A switch-hitter with excellent speed and a quick first step, Roberts led the organization with 57 steals, but walked only 27 times, fanned 97 times and has just a .232 career average.

KEN ROBINSON Bats: R Throws: R Ht: 5-9 Wt: 175
Born: 11/3/1969 Drafted: 1991 #13 TOR Position: P

YR TEAM	LG/CLASS	G	GS	GF	SV	W	L	ERA	IP	H	HR	BB	SO	O/BA
95 Toronto	AL/MAJ	21	0	9	0	1	2	3.69	39.0	25	7	22	31	.179
95 Syracuse	INT/AAA	38	0	12	2	5	3	3.22	50.1	37	6	12	61	.202

Although he is only 5-foot-9, Robinson throws strikes with a low-90-mph fastball and good slider.

MARK SIEVERT Bats: L Throws: R Ht: 6-4 Wt: 180
Born: 2/16/1973 Drafted: NDFA 8-24-91 TOR Position: P

YR TEAM	LG/CLASS	G	GS	GF	SV	W	L	ERA	IP	H	HR	BB	SO	O/BA
95 Hagerstown	SAL/A	27	27	0	0	12	6	2.91	160.2	126	14	46	140	.214

A non-drafted free agent, Sievert has a career 25-13 record and throws four pitches, including a low-90's fastball.

BRIAN SMITH Bats: R Throws: R Ht: 5-11 Wt: 185
Born: 7/19/1972 Drafted: 1994 #27 TOR Position: P

YR TEAM	LG/CLASS	G	GS	GF	SV	W	L	ERA	IP	H	HR	BB	SO	O/BA
95 Hagerstown	SAL/A	47	0	36	21	9	1	0.87	104.0	77	1	16	101	.205

The University of North Carolina product had a dream season as a closer, finishing the year throwing 47.1 consecutive innings without surrendering an earned run—the longest streak in the minors in '95.

PAUL SPOLJARIC Bats: R Throws: L Ht: 6-3 Wt: 205
Born: 9/24/1970 Drafted: NDFA 8-26-89 TOR Position: P

YR TEAM	LG/CLASS	G	GS	GF	SV	W	L	ERA	IP	H	HR	BB	SO	O/BA
95 Syracuse	INT/AAA	43	9	27	10	2	10	4.93	87.2	69	13	54	108	.214

After struggling as a starter, the Canadian moved to the pen in mid-season, posted a 2.18 ERA with ten saves and help opposing lefties to a .106 average.

CHRIS WEINKE Bats: L Throws: L Ht: 6-3 Wt: 205
Born: 7/31/1972 Drafted: 1990 #2 TOR Position: 1B

YR TEAM	LG/CLASS	G	AB	R	H	2B	3B	HR	RBI	SB	BA	OBA
95 Syracuse	INT/AAA	113	341	42	77	12	2	10	41	4	.226	.314

Weinke, once considered the top first base prospect in the system, didn't hit average or produce runs in 1995, and hasn't homered off a lefty in two years.

National League

ATLANTA BRAVES

STEVE AVERY

Position: SP
Bats: L **Throws:** L
Ht: 6'4" **Wt:** 180
Opening Day Age: 25
Born: 4/14/1970
Drafted: ATL88 1/3
ML Seasons: 6

SCOUTING REPORT
Many veteran baseball observers think that Steve has the best stuff of any Braves' starter. All three of his pitches are above par, with his best pitch being an outstanding change-up. His average-plus sinking fastball runs into lefthanders and Avery will cut the fastball as well. His plus curve has a quick break but often breaks out of the strike zone. Control and inconsistent velocity have been problems for Steve. He tends to nibble too much and can't win unless the ball stays down.

His most distinctive feature on the hill is a high leg kick which leads a slow, high three-quarter delivery. The kick helps Avery hide the ball from batters but makes it hard to hold runners. While Steve picked off 13 runners (including 1-3-6 caught stealings), he was victimized by a team-high 30 stolen bases in 41 attempts. He is an average fielder.

HOW HE PERFORMED IN '95
The talented lefty was just plain bad for most of the year. He won two straight games only once, in early July, and lost four straight and eight of ten from July 26 to September 12. Avery straightened things out after that, throwing his third complete game of the year September 18, then fanning 11 in his next start. Steve allowed only three runs over 21 innings in his last three starts and carried his momentum into the postseason, where he won a start in the NLCS and one more in the World Series.

Avery kept up his usual dominance against lefthanders and didn't allow a homer to them all year. However, he allowed multiple home runs to righties seven times and struggled despite decent support: Steve had four or more runs in 16 starts, including six or more runs nine times. Usually an effective pitcher in day games, Avery was winless in eight '95 starts under the sun, compiling a 6.50 ERA.

He hit his first two career home runs last year, becoming the first Braves pitcher to take two downtown in a season since Derek Lilliquist in 1990. Steve batted .208 with eight sacrifices and now has a .176 lifetime average.

WHAT TO EXPECT IN '96
Avery has had two straight seasons with an ERA above 4.00, but he's only 26. His last three regular season starts and his two fine postseason appearances should help Steve's and the Braves' confidence coming into '96.

Overall Statistics

	G	GS	GF	SV	W	L	ERA	IP	H	R	ER	HR	BB	SO
95 ATL	29	29	0	0	7	13	4.67	173.1	165	92	90	22	52	141
Career	179	178	1	0	65	52	3.75	1091.1	1034	507	455	93	331	729

1995 Situational Statistics

	W	L	ERA	SV	IP	BB	SO		AB	HR	RBI	BA	OBA	SLG
Home	4	5	4.35	0	82.2	28	70	LHB	91	0	7	.198	.288	.253
Road	3	8	4.96	0	90.2	24	71	RHB	565	22	77	.260	.314	.446
Apr-Jun	2	5	4.27	0	71.2	19	64	ScPos	139	6	58	.281	.373	.489
Jul-Oct	5	8	4.96	0	101.2	33	77	Clutch	23	0	2	.217	.379	.261

How He Compares to Other Pitchers

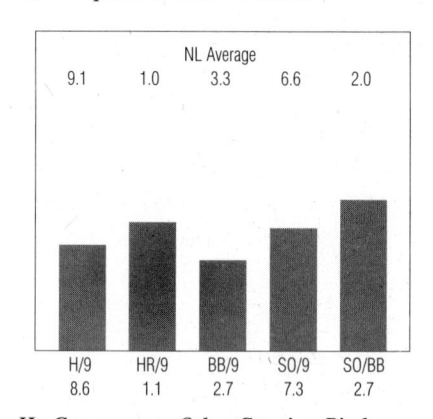

NL Average: H/9 9.1, HR/9 1.0, BB/9 3.3, SO/9 6.6, SO/BB 2.0

H/9 8.6, HR/9 1.1, BB/9 2.7, SO/9 7.3, SO/BB 2.7

How He Compares to Other Starting Pitchers

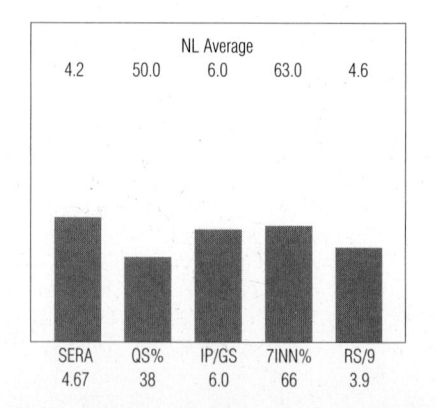

NL Average: SERA 4.2, QS% 50.0, IP/GS 6.0, 7INN% 63.0, RS/9 4.6

SERA 4.67, QS% 38, IP/GS 6.0, 7INN% 66, RS/9 3.9

ATLANTA BRAVES

JEFF BLAUSER

Position: SS
Bats: R **Throws:** R
Ht: 6'1" **Wt:** 180
Opening Day Age: 30
Born: 11/8/1965
Drafted: ATL 84 S1/5
ML Seasons: 9

SCOUTING REPORT
Blauser likes to jump on the fastball, especially if it's the first pitch he sees. He will pull high, inside pitches and has plus power. The wiry shortstop will also take full advantage of any mistake pitches that come his way. Standing close to the plate, he gets hit by plenty of pitches and takes plenty of pitches as well, walking often.

Although Jeff's range at short is just average, he more than makes up for this with above-average hands, arm strength, and throwing accuracy.

With average speed, Blauser does not often try to steal. He is also not a particularly good sacrifice bunter, which makes his use in the #2 spot non-traditional.

HOW HE PERFORMED IN '95
Blauser missed a good portion of the second half of the season with a knee injury he suffered when diving for a ball in early August. He missed 11 straight games after getting hurt, then 13 more in the first half of September. He came back after that, but was never able to play consistently the rest of the season and missed many of the postseason games because of the injury.

Overall, it was a very disappointing season for Blauser, who hit 52 points below his career average after signing a big, multi-year contract. It was the first time he failed to hit at least .258 in a full season in the majors. He did break double figures in home runs for the fourth time in the past five seasons and the fifth time in his seven big-league seasons, but he had unprecedented strikeout problems.

The knee problem affected Jeff's defense in terms of mobility, but didn't seem to hurt his consistency. He fielded exactly .970 for the third straight year, making 15 errors.

WHAT TO EXPECT IN '96
Blauser is signed through the '97 season and the Braves are committed to him at shortstop. He's only had one season where he's hit better than .270, so he may get more credit for being a good hitter than he should.

However, if you ignore 1995, his worst season, and 1993, when he had his career year, he's been between .258 and .270 with about 12 home runs per campaign—about what to expect out of Blauser if healthy. There is no plan to move Chipper Jones to shortstop anytime soon.

Overall Statistics

	G	AB	R	H	2B	3B	HR	RBI	SB	CS	BB	SO	BA	OBA
95 ATL	115	431	60	91	16	2	12	31	8	5	57	107	.211	.319
Career	950	3177	463	835	156	23	82	356	50	36	373	637	.263	.347

1995 Situational Statistics

	AB	HR	RBI	BA	OBA	SLG		AB	HR	RBI	BA	OBA	SLG
Home	203	7	19	.217	.324	.369	LHP	84	1	5	.226	.383	.286
Road	228	5	12	.206	.314	.316	RHP	347	11	26	.207	.301	.354
Apr-Jun	224	8	17	.232	.344	.393	ScPos	83	2	19	.169	.355	.277
Jul-Oct	207	4	14	.188	.292	.285	Clutch	58	3	8	.241	.392	.483

How He Compares to Other Batters

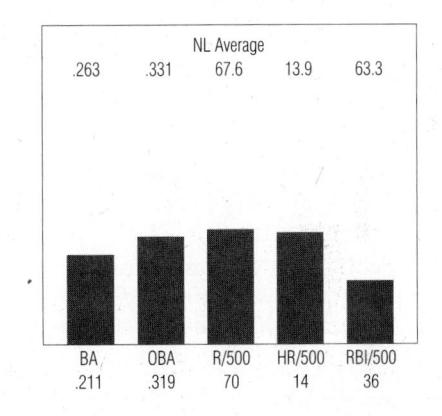

NL Average
.263   .331   67.6   13.9   63.3

BA   OBA   R/500   HR/500   RBI/500
.211 .319   70   14   36

Where He Hits the Ball

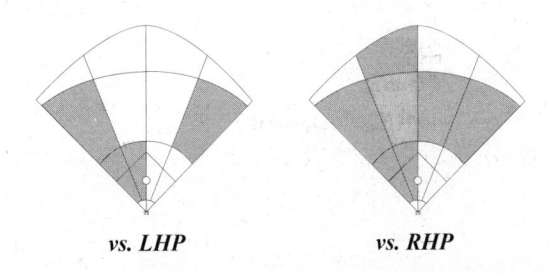

vs. LHP   vs. RHP

THE SCOUTING REPORT: 1996

ATLANTA BRAVES

TOM GLAVINE

Position: SP
Bats: L **Throws:** L
Ht: 6'1" **Wt:** 190
Opening Day Age: 30
Born: 3/25/1966
Drafted: ATL84 2/47
ML Seasons: 9

SCOUTING REPORT

Tom has a slightly below-average slider and curve and just an average fastball, but succeeds in getting opponents out because he is a master at changing speeds and setting up hitters. He does have a well above-average change-up which he turns over, and Glavine's fastball sinks effectively despite its lack of velocity. He will also throw a cut fastball and, occasionally, a four-seamer as well.

In addition to using the baffling change-up, Glavine throws hitters' timing off by hiding the ball well, delivering from a standard three-quarter motion. A hockey player in college, Tom is one of baseball's best fielding pitchers and a superior athlete.

Although he is just average at holding runners, Glavine has developed a slide-step to help keep runners closer at first. However, 15 stole in 20 attempts against Tom last year.

HOW HE PERFORMED IN '95

Glavine has won one Cy Young award but, with Greg Maddux on the same team, he has been overshadowed. However, Tom ranks second only to Maddux in wins during the 1990s (101 to 105), and his 91 wins over the last five are one higher than Greg. Last season Glavine ranked fourth in the league with 16 victories, marking the fifth straight year he has been among the top five NL winners. He sliced his walks allowed last year and did not issue a single intentional pass after giving away ten of them in '94.

Tom recorded his 1,000th career strikeout August 21 at Houston, when he fanned Doug Drabek in the third inning. However, he wins by getting ground balls, not by going deep in the count.

As was seen in the postseason, Tom is almost unbeatable when he settles into a groove. In '95, he had an ERA of 7.76 in the first inning, compared with a 2.28 ERA in the other eight innings. Tom is a good hitter, clubbing his first career homer and tying for the team lead with eight sacrifice bunts. His .222 average in 63 at-bats raised his lifetime mark to .187.

WHAT TO EXPECT IN '96

Expect more of the same from Glavine in '96. His strikeout total has been between 120 and 140 each of the last five years except in his '91 Cy Young season. While Maddux gets a lot of deserved attention, Glavine goes out every fifth day and gets the job done as well.

Overall Statistics

	G	GS	GF	SV	W	L	ERA	IP	H	R	ER	HR	BB	SO
95 ATL	29	29	0	0	16	7	3.08	198.2	182	76	68	9	66	127
Career	262	262	0	0	124	82	3.52	1721.0	1649	751	673	113	579	1031

1995 Situational Statistics

-	W	L	ERA	SV	IP	BB	SO		AB	HR	RBI	BA	OBA	SLG
Home	6	4	3.63	0	91.2	33	62	LHB	136	2	17	.316	.392	.419
Road	10	3	2.61	0	107.0	33	65	RHB	603	7	51	.231	.292	.315
Apr-Jun	6	4	3.59	0	80.1	27	56	ScPos	163	0	52	.252	.362	.301
Jul-Oct	10	3	2.74	0	118.1	39	71	Clutch	81	1	7	.235	.292	.309

How He Compares to Other Pitchers

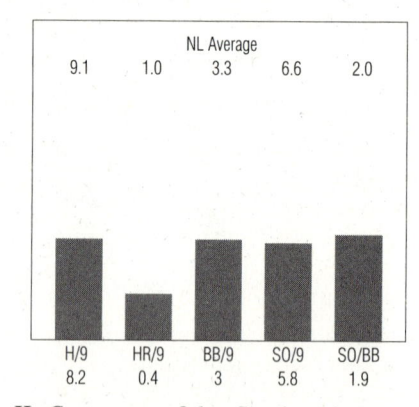

NL Average: H/9 9.1, HR/9 1.0, BB/9 3.3, SO/9 6.6, SO/BB 2.0

Glavine: H/9 8.2, HR/9 0.4, BB/9 3, SO/9 5.8, SO/BB 1.9

How He Compares to Other Starting Pitchers

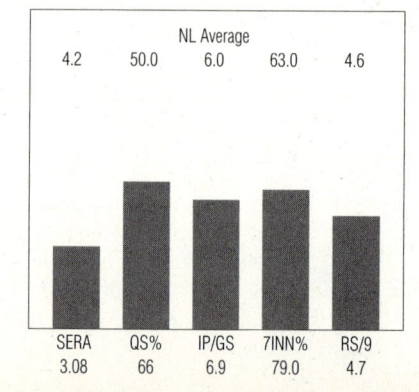

NL Average: SERA 4.2, QS% 50.0, IP/GS 6.0, 7INN% 63.0, RS/9 4.6

Glavine: SERA 3.08, QS% 66, IP/GS 6.9, 7INN% 79.0, RS/9 4.7

ATLANTA BRAVES

MARQUIS GRISSOM

Position: OF
Bats: R **Throws:** R
Ht: 5'11" **Wt:** 190
Opening Day Age: 28
Born: 4/17/1967
Drafted: MON88 4/76
ML Seasons: 7

SCOUTING REPORT
Despite a mediocre on-base percentage, Grissom leads off for the Braves because he is their fastest player. He has outstanding speed and steals bases effectively, but Marquis lacks the plate discipline to be a top-flight leadoff hitter. He has decent bat speed, but a long swing makes him most effective on breaking pitches. Good fastballs overpower him.

He has already won three straight Gold Glove awards and Marquis will be a candidate to win the award for several more seasons. Grissom's range ranks well above-average, which allows him to play shallow and go back on balls—which he does very effectively. His arm is only average in strength but has above-average accuracy. Marquis' ability to play shallow and charge base hits also improves his throwing.

HOW HE PERFORMED IN '95
Grissom had his worst season in the big leagues in '95. Much of his troubles can be blamed on an injured heel that dogged him throughout the season. The malady limited his basestealing ability (his 29 stolen bases were his lowest total in any full season in the majors) and hampered him at the plate. His batting average was far short of the .298 mark of '93 and the .288 he had registered during '94 even though he made contact more consistently than ever before.

He ran very hot and very cold all year, racking up several streaks where he would get only three or four hits in 50 at-bats, then turn around and bat .500 for a couple of weeks. Grissom's 14-game hitting streak in June was the longest any Braves' player put together in '95. Coming on strong during the stretch drive, Marquis hit .303 from September 1 on.

He's always terrific with the leather, but Grissom's defensive performance in center field was particularly outstanding during the second half of '95, as he played his last 91 games without making an error and his nine assists led NL centerfielders.

WHAT TO EXPECT IN '96
Grissom's '95 totals were the worst of his career but the Braves didn't hesitate long before signing him to a lucrative four-year contract last November. Attribute last season's dip to the foot injury and plan on a stellar '96 season in the fashion of his first four.

Overall Statistics

	G	AB	R	H	2B	3B	HR	RBI	SB	CS	BB	SO	BA	OBA
95 ATL	139	551	80	142	23	3	12	42	29	9	47	61	.258	.317
Career	837	3229	510	889	153	26	66	318	295	57	255	434	.275	.329

1995 Situational Statistics

	AB	HR	RBI	BA	OBA	SLG		AB	HR	RBI	BA	OBA	SLG
Home	257	5	14	.230	.293	.335	LHP	132	4	8	.273	.338	.432
Road	294	7	28	.282	.339	.412	RHP	419	8	34	.253	.311	.358
Apr-Jun	242	7	25	.298	.337	.438	ScPos	93	4	33	.290	.386	.473
Jul-Oct	309	5	17	.227	.303	.327	Clutch	81	3	10	.222	.284	.333

How He Compares to Other Batters

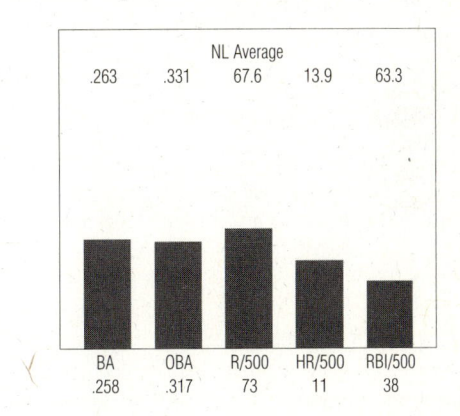

NL Average: BA .263 | OBA .331 | R/500 67.6 | HR/500 13.9 | RBI/500 63.3

BA .258 | OBA .317 | R/500 73 | HR/500 11 | RBI/500 38

Where He Hits the Ball

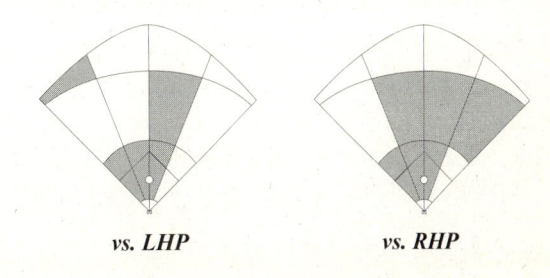

vs. LHP   vs. RHP

THE SCOUTING REPORT: 1996

ATLANTA BRAVES

CHIPPER JONES

Positions: 3B/OF
Bats: B **Throws:** R
Ht: 6'3" **Wt:** 185
Opening Day Age: 23
Born: 4/24/1972
Drafted: ATL90 1/1
ML Seasons: 2

SCOUTING REPORT

Larry Wayne Jones is a switch-hitter with better bat speed from the left side but good plate discipline batting both ways. Opposing pitchers will try and move the ball around on Chipper when he hits left-handed but simply attempt to blow Jones away when he is batting from the right side.

Once seen as a liability defensively (149 errors in 456 minor-league games, all spent at shortstop), Jones handled the conversion to third base remarkably well. His strengths are a well above-average throwing arm and well above-average hands.

The aim on his throws was a serious problem early in the season, but by September his accuracy rated plus. Many of his 25 errors were on errant tosses. Chipper's range at the hot corner is also plus, and he also filled in 20 times in the outfield without making an error.

After blowing out his left knee during spring training in 1994, Chipper's speed has declined and is now just average.

HOW HE PERFORMED IN '95

Jones easily could have been the National League Rookie of the Year, had it not been for a 27-year-old Japanese veteran. How many rookies can take over the #3 spot in the lineup for a team that ends up winning the World Series?

Maybe the most impressive thing about Chipper, the #1 overall selection in the 1990 draft, is his remarkable mastery of the strike zone. The rookie ranked up there with veterans like Fred McGriff and David Justice in that area. When his batting average dipped into the mid .250s in the middle of the season, Jones said it was because he was swinging at too many bad pitches. He decided to take more walks, which also helped boost his average when he got better pitches to hit.

Jones showed few ill effects of the serious '94 knee injury. His eight stolen bases was the lowest total since rookie ball, but with McGriff and Justice on deck, why would Bobby Cox take any chances?

WHAT TO EXPECT IN '96

Jones started at three different positions last season (121 games at third, 13 in left, and four in right) but now appears entrenched in the infield. The sky's the limit: Don't be surprised at anything this young man does at the plate or in the field during '96.

Overall Statistics

	G	AB	R	H	2B	3B	HR	RBI	SB	CS	BB	SO	BA	OBA
95 ATL	140	524	87	139	22	3	23	86	8	4	73	99	.265	.353
Career	148	527	89	141	23	3	23	86	8	4	74	100	.268	.355

1995 Situational Statistics

	AB	HR	RBI	BA	OBA	SLG		AB	HR	RBI	BA	OBA	SLG
Home	268	15	46	.272	.356	.493	LHP	127	3	13	.283	.393	.417
Road	256	8	40	.258	.349	.406	RHP	397	20	73	.259	.339	.461
Apr-Jun	231	11	42	.242	.340	.446	ScPos	121	4	57	.298	.403	.455
Jul-Oct	293	12	44	.283	.363	.454	Clutch	87	5	9	.230	.330	.471

How He Compares to Other Batters

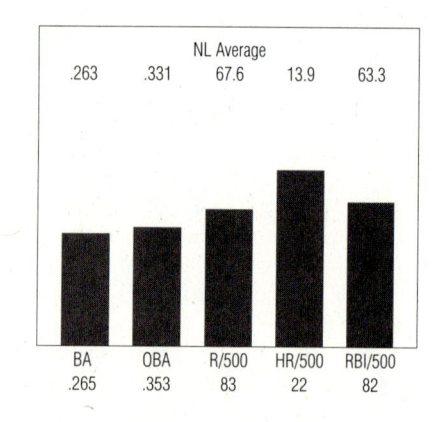

NL Average: .263 .331 67.6 13.9 63.3

BA .265 | OBA .353 | R/500 83 | HR/500 22 | RBI/500 82

Where He Hits the Ball

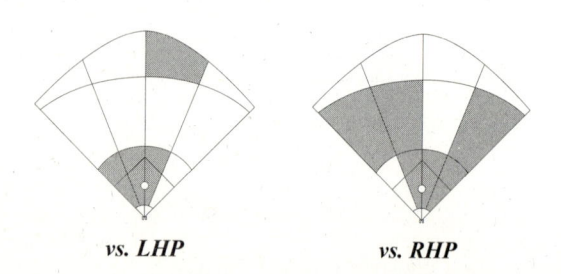

vs. LHP   vs. RHP

ATLANTA BRAVES

DAVID JUSTICE

Position: OF
Bats: L **Throws:** L
Ht: 6'3" **Wt:** 195
Opening Day Age: 29
Born: 4/14/1966
Drafted: ATL85 3/94
ML Seasons: 7

SCOUTING REPORT
Justice is a typical lefthanded slugger in that he is a dead low-inside fastball hitter with above-average pull power. He has a long swing with a fierce uppercut, judges the strike zone well, and makes contact fairly well for a slugger. David's one career sacrifice bunt came back in 1989, his first season.

A slightly below-average runner, Justice gets a slow start on the bases and is rarely asked to steal. Despite this lack of speed, however, he has average-plus range in right field and gets a good jump on the ball. David's arm has lost some strength and is now average, but his accuracy has now improved and is plus. He also has good hands.

HOW HE PERFORMED IN '95
Justice posted decent numbers in '95 despite being bothered all season with shoulder problems. He first hurt his right shoulder in early May diving for a ball in the outfield, and on June 2 went on the DL with torn ligaments in the shoulder.

Although David normally lets go of the bat with his left hand on his follow-through, the pain and weakness in the shoulder forced him to keep both hands on the bat. That caused some minor difficulties, although he was ultimately able to make the necessary adjustments. He smashed 20 of his home runs after coming off the disabled list on June 16. His 78 RBI on the year moved David to fourth on Atlanta's career list. Despite hitting the ball hard to the right side and consistently batting with runners on base, he was the eighth-hardest player in the National League to double up, rapping into a twin killing just once every 82 at-bats.

While Justice's eight assists from right field ranked in the lower half of NL right fielders, he made just four errors on the season.

WHAT TO EXPECT IN '96
Justice will be 30 but he should have several more productive seasons left. If healthy, David probably has another run at his '93 totals (40 home runs, 120 RBIs) left in him. Even if he falls short of that kind of monster year, Justice is still a very valuable player to Atlanta due to his power and production. It is only fitting that he was one of the Braves' World Series heroes.

Overall Statistics

	G	AB	R	H	2B	3B	HR	RBI	SB	CS	BB	SO	BA	OBA
95 ATL	120	411	73	104	17	2	24	78	4	2	73	68	.253	.365
Career	777	2718	452	741	118	16	154	497	32	30	431	470	.273	.372

1995 Situational Statistics

	AB	HR	RBI	BA	OBA	SLG		AB	HR	RBI	BA	OBA	SLG
Home	189	15	39	.302	.390	.614	LHP	141	7	23	.241	.366	.433
Road	222	9	39	.212	.344	.365	RHP	270	17	55	.259	.364	.504
Apr-Jun	131	7	28	.267	.405	.504	ScPos	111	5	51	.261	.400	.441
Jul-Oct	280	17	50	.246	.345	.468	Clutch	65	4	12	.323	.423	.523

How He Compares to Other Batters

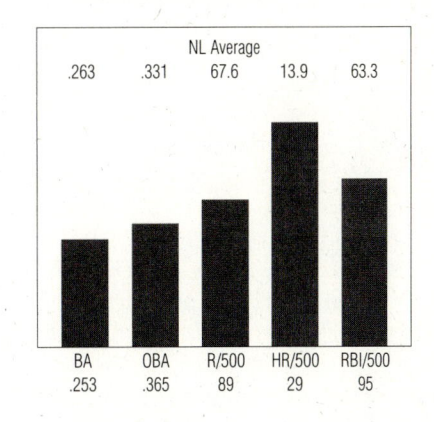

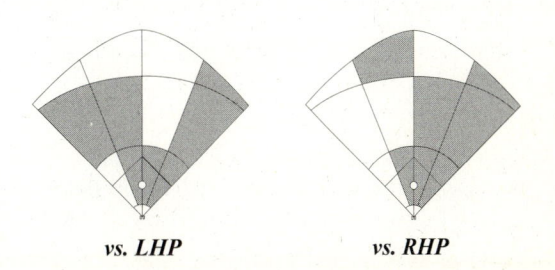

NL Average: BA .263, OBA .331, R/500 67.6, HR/500 13.9, RBI/500 63.3

David Justice: BA .253, OBA .365, R/500 89, HR/500 29, RBI/500 95

Where He Hits the Ball

vs. LHP   vs. RHP

THE SCOUTING REPORT: 1996

ATLANTA BRAVES

RYAN KLESKO

Positions: OF//1B
Bats: L **Throws:** L
Ht: 6'3" **Wt:** 220
Opening Day Age: 24
Born: 6/12/1971
Drafted: ATL89 6/116
ML Seasons: 4

SCOUTING REPORT
Like teammate David Justice, Klesko has the hack of a typical lefthanded power swinger. He still likes the low fastball but has changed his approach to hitting in the last season. Ryan altered his stance is now much more prone to using the entire field and no longer tries to pull everything. He has good judgment of the strike zone. Ryan has slightly below-average speed and accelerates very slowly.

As a left fielder, Klesko has below-average range and a minus throwing arm in both strength and accuracy. He does not get a good jump but has average hands once he gets to the ball. While he lacks good outfield instincts, Klesko has worked hard to avoid being terrible out there. Of course, there is an excellent chance he will wind up at first base eventually.

HOW HE PERFORMED IN '95
Klesko had his best season to date, despite having to fight through an early-season thumb injury. After spraining his left thumb in the first week of the season sliding into second base, Ryan was out until late May. He struggled for about a week after coming off the disabled list, but he soon caught fire and was the Braves' hottest hitter until the All-Star break.

Klesko hit anything and everything the first half of the year—and hit anything and everything a long, long way. He hit .435 with seven homers and 22 RBIs in June and slugged another five homers in July.

Bobby Cox used Klesko in a platoon situation after the injury, but began to play Ryan against lefthanders late in the year. He hit his first career homer off a lefty July 25 against Denny Neagle and eventually wound up with three homers against them. In addition, Ryan played most of Atlanta's post-season contests against lefthanded starters.

In the field, he threw out just two runners in '95 and made seven errors. Klesko's .942 fielding percentage was easily the worst of any major-league regular left fielder.

WHAT TO EXPECT IN '96
The promising Klesko will be back in left field this year as the Braves have re-signed Fred McGriff. While Ryan might still sit against some tough lefties, he should wind up playing in the majority of Atlanta's games in '96. There's no reason to believe he has peaked yet as a hitter.

Overall Statistics

	G	AB	R	H	2B	3B	HR	RBI	SB	CS	BB	SO	BA	OBA
95 ATL	107	329	48	102	25	2	23	70	5	4	47	72	.310	.396
Career	234	605	93	176	39	5	42	123	6	4	76	129	.291	.370

1995 Situational Statistics

	AB	HR	RBI	BA	OBA	SLG		AB	HR	RBI	BA	OBA	SLG
Home	172	15	41	.302	.374	.605	LHP	78	3	12	.244	.348	.449
Road	157	8	29	.318	.419	.611	RHP	251	20	58	.331	.412	.657
Apr-Jun	111	7	23	.342	.417	.622	ScPos	82	5	42	.317	.427	.610
Jul-Oct	218	16	47	.294	.386	.601	Clutch	54	2	8	.259	.369	.426

How He Compares to Other Batters

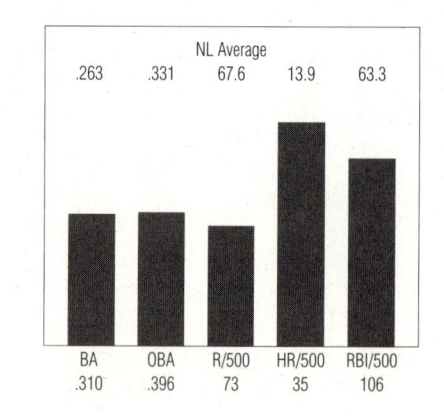

	BA	OBA	R/500	HR/500	RBI/500
NL Average	.263	.331	67.6	13.9	63.3
	.310	.396	73	35	106

Where He Hits the Ball

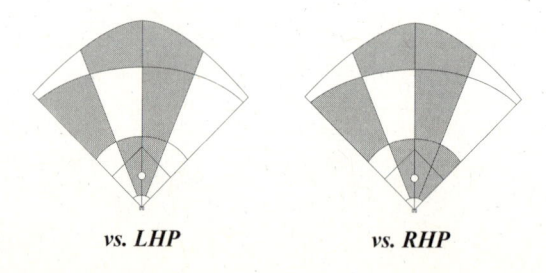

vs. LHP   *vs. RHP*

ATLANTA BRAVES

MARK LEMKE

Position: 2B
Bats: B **Throws:** R
Ht: 5'10" **Wt:** 167
Opening Day Age: 30
Born: 8/13/1965
Drafted: ATL83 27/677
ML Seasons: 8

SCOUTING REPORT

The Braves love Lemke for his defense: he is excellent at turning the double play. Mark's hands and range are well above-average and, though his arm has just average strength, it has plus accuracy.

The gritty Lemke chokes up on the bat and is a line-drive contact hitter. He likes the ball high and over the plate while hitting righthanded, but low and inside while batting from the left side. Mark is a very efficient sacrifice bunter.

A slightly below-average runner, he is slow getting out of the batter's box and is a horrid percentage base stealer. Oddly, he has never been hit by a pitch in the major leagues.

HOW HE PERFORMED IN '95

Lemke's season took off in August when he was moved into the second spot in the batting order. He hit .301 batting second, going 47-for-156.

The usually singles-hitting Lemke had one of the best power years of his career. He smacked a career-high five triples, and his 16 doubles was his second highest total ever. Mark was just two homers away from his career high in that category as well in the shortened '95 season.

Lemke's home run off Mark Portugal in April was his first as a lefthanded batter since '93, but he has now hit at least .290 in each of the last two seasons from that side after several years of sub-.230 performance. However, Mark continues to show a rally-strangling tendency to hit into twin killings. His 17 DPs in '95 tied for fifth most in the NL and gave him 49 in the past three seasons.

Braves' fans lobbied for Lemke to get a Gold Glove award for his defensive play, but the award went to Craig Biggio. Mark made only five errors on the season and had gone 78 games without making an error between May '94 and May '95.

WHAT TO EXPECT IN '96

Although Lemke has never been much of a hitter, the Braves value him because of his keystone defense and the stability he provides in the infield. Since he's walked more than he's struck out every year since 1990, he might be the ideal guy to hit behind Marquis Grissom in Atlanta's lineup if he did something else for the offense besides provide bat control.

Overall Statistics

	G	AB	R	H	2B	3B	HR	RBI	SB	CS	BB	SO	BA	OBA
95 ATL	116	399	42	101	16	5	5	38	2	2	44	40	.253	.325
Career	794	2290	242	565	87	14	25	200	4	16	256	227	.247	.320

1995 Situational Statistics

	AB	HR	RBI	BA	OBA	SLG		AB	HR	RBI	BA	OBA	SLG
Home	191	3	17	.251	.308	.361	LHP	93	2	12	.290	.362	.441
Road	208	2	21	.255	.340	.351	RHP	306	3	26	.242	.314	.330
Apr-Jun	166	2	16	.241	.326	.355	ScPos	84	1	29	.274	.379	.429
Jul-Oct	233	3	22	.262	.324	.356	Clutch	55	1	9	.218	.297	.345

How He Compares to Other Batters

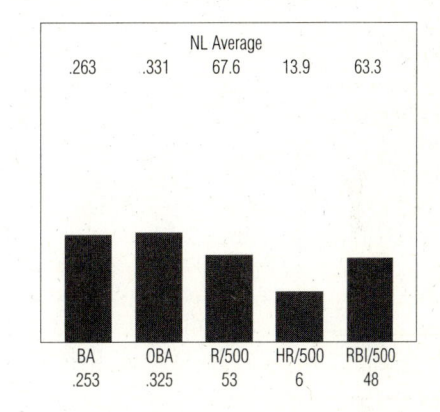

NL Average: .263 .331 67.6 13.9 63.3

BA	OBA	R/500	HR/500	RBI/500
.253	.325	53	6	48

Where He Hits the Ball

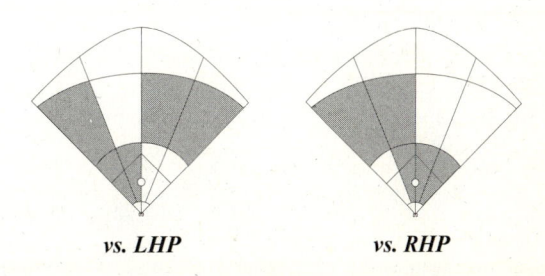

vs. LHP   vs. RHP

THE SCOUTING REPORT: 1996

ATLANTA BRAVES

JAVY LOPEZ

Position: C
Bats: R **Throws:** R
Ht: 6'3" **Wt:** 185
Opening Day Age: 25
Born: 11/5/1970
Drafted: ATL 11/6/87
ML Seasons: 4

SCOUTING REPORT
Scouts think Lopez developed defensively in '95. He has a strong, well above-average arm, and his accuracy has improved and now is only slightly below-average. While he showed in the post-season that he has the strength to pick runners off first, Javy tends to throw the ball high to second. He has plus hands and mobility behind the plate.

Lopez is an aggressive—some would say overaggressive—fastball hitter with power who likes pitches high and over the plate. He is a below-average runner and no threat to steal or bunt.

HOW HE PERFORMED IN '95
Lopez had a fine second year, providing more production in '95 than he had the season before. He put up excellent numbers for an organization not known for good-hitting catchers, becoming the first Braves' receiver to top .300 since Joe Torre in 1966. And Javy was only the second Braves' catcher since 1972 to have consecutive seasons with 10 or more homers.

Lopez did some of his best hitting in the late innings. Six of his home runs came in the seventh inning or later, and he had three hits to win games in his final at-bat.

Some of Atlanta's starting pitchers, Greg Maddux in particular, said Charlie O'Brien called a much better game than Javy, but this is certainly understandable due to Lopez' lack of experience. The staff did say that Lopez improved as the year went on, but game-calling is the main reason Javy only played three or four days a week in '95. Although he did allow eight passed balls in '95, Lopez improved at blocking pitches as the year progressed.

WHAT TO EXPECT IN '96
While Javy raised his batting average by 60 points and cut his strikeouts, his walks dropped even though he had far more plate appearances in '95. It is doubtful that he can hit .300 consistently with such poor plate discipline, and one hopes he can avoid the gradual deterioration of Benito Santiago, whose considerable offensive gifts withered due to an inability to stop swinging at bad pitches.

Lopez will get a chance to play more often now that Charlie O'Brien has moved to Toronto. Javy served as Atlanta's primary catcher in the postseason, even catching Maddux in the World Series, and this indicates how manager Bobby Cox will use Lopez in the future.

Overall Statistics

	G	AB	R	H	2B	3B	HR	RBI	SB	CS	BB	SO	BA	OBA
95 ATL	100	333	37	105	11	4	14	51	0	1	14	57	.315	.344
Career	197	642	68	185	23	5	28	90	0	3	31	121	.288	.327

1995 Situational Statistics

	AB	HR	RBI	BA	OBA	SLG		AB	HR	RBI	BA	OBA	SLG
Home	178	8	23	.326	.348	.522	LHP	86	2	8	.291	.333	.407
Road	155	6	28	.303	.339	.471	RHP	247	12	43	.324	.347	.530
Apr-Jun	159	7	24	.283	.331	.459	ScPos	78	3	37	.359	.398	.551
Jul-Oct	174	7	27	.345	.356	.534	Clutch	60	3	15	.333	.394	.550

How He Compares to Other Batters

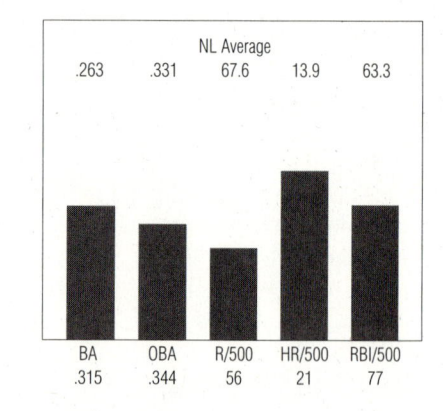

NL Average: .263 .331 67.6 13.9 63.3

BA	OBA	R/500	HR/500	RBI/500
.315	.344	56	21	77

Where He Hits the Ball

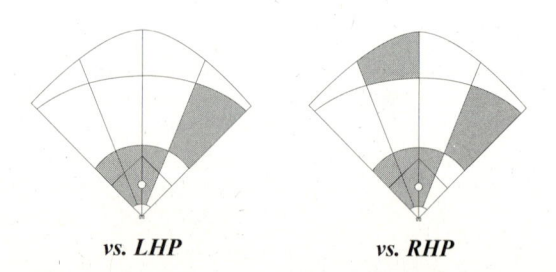

vs. LHP   vs. RHP

ATLANTA BRAVES

SCOUTING REPORT
Using a picture-perfect, textbook three-quarter windup and delivery, Maddux throws five pitches: a fastball, a cut fastball, slider, change and curve. He lacks overpowering stuff, with a fastball topping at 87 MPH, but has outstanding control.

Although Maddux usually sinks the fastball, he occasionally throws a four-seamer. Greg credits his cutter with making him a better pitcher, but his slider and curve are plus offerings. He mixes pitches and changes speeds effectively, setting up hitters better than anyone in recent memory. As a result, Maddux gets plenty of strikeouts with his outstanding change-up.

While Greg has well above-average skills at holding runners, he often ignores runners on the bases, allowing 26 to steal in 32 tries last season. However, he is an excellent fielder who didn't make an error in '95 and won his sixth consecutive Gold Glove. Maddux is usually a good hitter. He owns a .182 lifetime average, but batted just .153 last year with six sacrifice hits.

HOW HE PERFORMED IN '95
Maddux received all 28 first-place votes in winning his fourth straight Cy Young award. And why not? He became the first pitcher in 75 years to have consecutive seasons with an ERA under 1.80 (Walter Johnson was the last, in 1918-19). Greg's ERA was over 2.5 runs lower than the league average and good enough to lead the league for the third straight year. No NL pitcher had won three ERA crowns since Sandy Koufax.

He tossed four straight complete games from August 20 to September 5, which included a one-hitter against the Cardinals that took a mere one hour, 50 minutes to complete.

WHAT TO EXPECT IN '96
There must be a big, red "S" on his chest, because there's no pitcher on this planet who's even close to Greg Maddux right now. In the last four years Maddux is 75-29 with 37 complete games, 11 shutouts and a 1.98 ERA—what is truly scary is that he shows no signs of letting up. Greg has missed only one start in the last three years and hasn't had the slightest hint of arm problems. No one has been this dominating for this long in the last 20 years, and with another year or two at this pace he will have to be considered one of the best pitchers in baseball history.

GREG MADDUX

Position: SP
Bats: R **Throws:** R
Ht: 6'0" **Wt:** 150
Opening Day Age: 29
Born: 4/14/1966
Drafted: CHN84 2/31
ML Seasons: 10

Overall Statistics

	G	GS	GF	SV	W	L	ERA	IP	H	R	ER	HR	BB	SO
95 ATL	28	28	0	0	19	2	1.63	209.2	147	39	38	8	23	181
Career	301	297	3	0	150	93	2.88	2120.2	1877	783	679	108	561	1471

1995 Situational Statistics

	W	L	ERA	SV	IP	BB	SO		AB	HR	RBI	BA	OBA	SLG
Home	6	2	2.23	0	97.0	12	84	LHB	354	2	14	.195	.219	.234
Road	13	0	1.12	0	112.2	11	97	RHB	394	6	21	.198	.229	.279
Apr-Jun	7	1	1.85	0	87.1	8	69	ScPos	127	2	26	.157	.206	.228
Jul-Oct	12	1	1.47	0	122.1	15	112	Clutch	107	2	8	.187	.209	.290

How He Compares to Other Pitchers

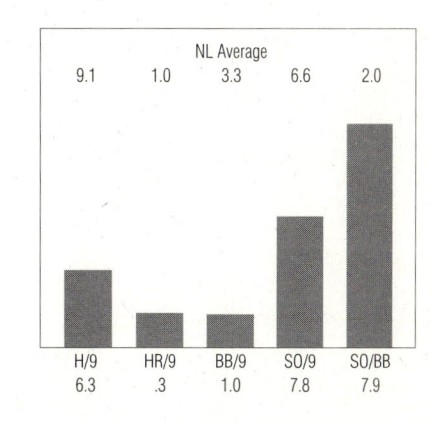

NL Average: H/9 9.1, HR/9 1.0, BB/9 3.3, SO/9 6.6, SO/BB 2.0
Maddux: H/9 6.3, HR/9 .3, BB/9 1.0, SO/9 7.8, SO/BB 7.9

How He Compares to Other Starting Pitchers

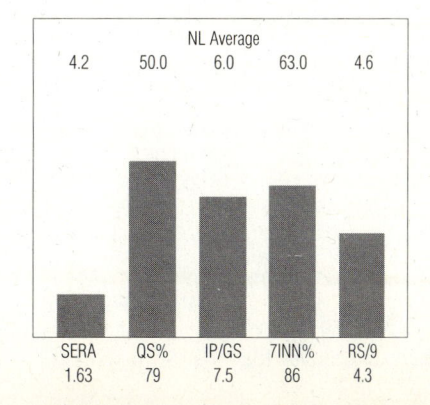

NL Average: SERA 4.2, QS% 50.0, IP/GS 6.0, 7INN% 63.0, RS/9 4.6
Maddux: SERA 1.63, QS% 79, IP/GS 7.5, 7INN% 86, RS/9 4.3

ATLANTA BRAVES

FRED MCGRIFF

Position: 1B
Bats: L **Throws:** L
Ht: 6'3" **Wt:** 215
Opening Day Age: 32
Born: 10/31/1963
Drafted: NYA81 9/233
ML Seasons: 10

SCOUTING REPORT

McGriff doesn't pull everything because he doesn't have to. He has well above-average power to all fields and lifts the ball well with his smooth swing. Fred likes low pitches over the plate and is very patient, drawing plenty of walks.

Not only does Fred save his infielders from many throwing errors with his plus hands, but McGriff also provides a good target for those infielders to throw to in the first place. He has plus range and an average arm with plus accuracy.

Fred is a poor baserunner who has been a surprisingly good basestealer throughout his career. He has not laid down a sacrifice bunt in five years. Why should he?

HOW HE PERFORMED IN '95

When his late-season charge fell short, McGriff lost his chance to extend his streak of consecutive 30-plus home run seasons to eight. The Braves wrapped up the NL East title early, and McGriff had said that getting 30 homers was a big goal for him.

Despite being a key player on a World Series Champion, it wasn't the best of years for Fred individually. He had his lowest batting average and slugging percentage since 1991 and his worst on-base percentage ever. His 19 double plays grounded into ranked among the highest in the NL.

However, it wasn't all bad. For the third straight year, McGriff was outstanding in the clutch. He hit .313 with two outs and runners in scoring position, .333 with runners on third, and .364 with the bases loaded. That helped him lead the club with 93 RBIs, his fifth straight season with at least that many.

WHAT TO EXPECT IN '96

McGriff was the best of the bunch, and a big bunch at that, of free-agent first basemen in the off-season. He was also the first to sign. Even though the Braves already had resigned Marquis Grissom, they paid $20 million over four years for the Crime Dog. It should be a good investment, even though Fred seems older than 33 because he has been around forever. With a full schedule, he's a virtual lock to hit 30 homers and drive in 100 runs. He's durable, too, having started all 144 games in '95 and has missed only one game since becoming a Brave in July 1993. He's a class act who has been an underrated player for most of his career.

Overall Statistics

	G	AB	R	H	2B	3B	HR	RBI	SB	CS	BB	SO	BA	OBA
95 ATL	144	528	85	148	27	1	27	93	3	6	65	99	.280	.361
Career	1291	4512	788	1284	229	17	289	803	48	29	744	1019	.285	.386

1995 Situational Statistics

	AB	HR	RBI	BA	OBA	SLG		AB	HR	RBI	BA	OBA	SLG
Home	261	15	45	.291	.368	.510	LHP	188	6	28	.255	.332	.410
Road	267	12	48	.270	.354	.468	RHP	340	21	65	.294	.377	.532
Apr-Jun	215	10	38	.274	.376	.484	ScPos	134	9	68	.291	.399	.552
Jul-Oct	313	17	55	.284	.350	.492	Clutch	81	2	8	.272	.398	.395

How He Compares to Other Batters

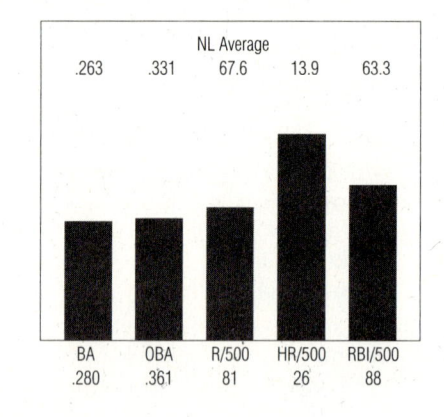

NL Average: .263 | .331 | 67.6 | 13.9 | 63.3

BA	OBA	R/500	HR/500	RBI/500
.280	.361	81	26	88

Where He Hits the Ball

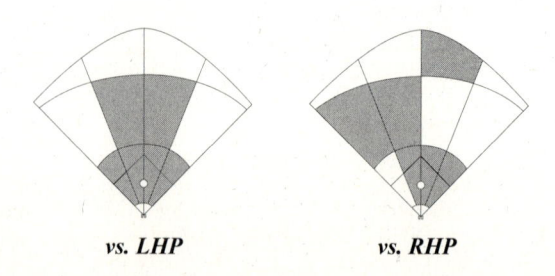

vs. LHP   vs. RHP

ATLANTA BRAVES

GREG MCMICHAEL

Position: RP
Bats: R **Throws:** R
Ht: 6'3" **Wt:** 215
Opening Day Age: 29
Born: 12/1/1966
Drafted: CLE88 9/163
ML Seasons: 3

SCOUTING REPORT

McMichael's out pitch is an outstanding circle change. He varies the break on the change-up (which some call a palmball) and he has plus control of it—as he does of all his pitches.

Greg throws from three-quarters but varies his arm angle and release point depending on the pitch and hitter. His sinking fastball has minus velocity and his curve is mostly used for show. He must keep the fastball down to be effective.

For a righthander, McMichael's move to first is well above-average and he is also quick to home. However, seven men stole in nine tries with Greg on the mound in '95. He is no threat at the plate; hitless in six trips last year, McMichael is 0-for-11 lifetime. Greg is a decent fielder but he has made four errors in 47 career chances for a poor .915 fielding percentage.

HOW HE PERFORMED IN '95

McMichael was used primarily as a setup man in '95 after totaling 40 saves in his first two seasons. However, even though he had only two saves last year, his seven wins were a career high and bettered his total from the past two campaigns combined.

After struggling in May and most of July, Greg allowed only five runs in 34.2 innings after July 22. He allowed four home runs in four outings during mid-May, but he then allowed just four more over his last 72 innings.

The late-blooming McMichael has had an ERA of less than 2.80 in two of three seasons in Atlanta; as he had been in his rookie year, Greg was more effective against lefthanders than righties. Although he is durable and can be frequently used, the Atlanta bullpen is now very short on experienced relievers, which could lead to Greg being called on even more in the future. He can't be asked shoulder the whole load himself.

WHAT TO EXPECT IN '96

After experiencing trouble as a closer in '94, McMichael became firmly rooted in his setup role last year. The explosive emergence of Mark Wohlers in the second half of '95 made the transition easy for Atlanta. Greg has pitched well for the Braves, and he will be counted on heavily in the coming season to set up for Wohlers and to close a few games if Mark is injured or inconsistent.

Overall Statistics

	G	GS	GF	SV	W	L	ERA	IP	H	R	ER	HR	BB	SO
95 ATL	67	0	16	2	7	2	2.79	80.2	64	27	25	8	32	74
Career	192	0	97	42	13	11	2.77	231.0	198	78	71	12	80	210

1995 Situational Statistics

	W	L	ERA	SV	IP	BB	SO		AB	HR	RBI	BA	OBA	SLG
Home	4	2	3.86	0	39.2	10	35	LHB	127	3	10	.197	.255	.339
Road	3	0	1.76	2	41.0	22	39	RHB	173	5	10	.225	.313	.347
Apr-Jun	4	0	2.78	1	35.2	9	33	ScPos	68	0	10	.132	.322	.147
Jul-Oct	3	2	2.80	1	45.0	23	41	Clutch	156	5	11	.237	.335	.410

How He Compares to Other Pitchers

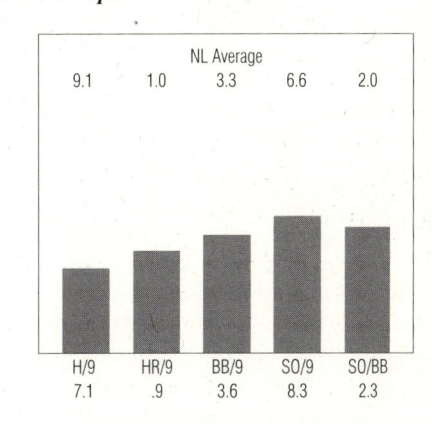

	H/9	HR/9	BB/9	SO/9	SO/BB
NL Average	9.1	1.0	3.3	6.6	2.0
	7.1	.9	3.6	8.3	2.3

How He Compares to Other Starting Pitchers

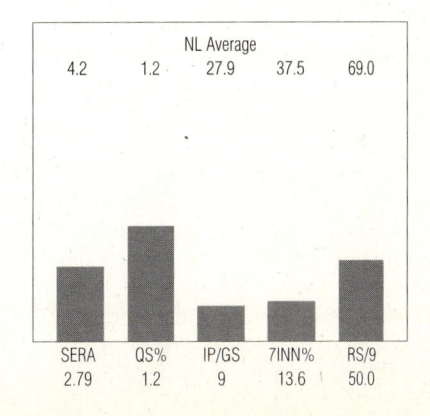

	SERA	QS%	IP/GS	7INN%	RS/9
NL Average	4.2	1.2	27.9	37.5	69.0
	2.79	1.2	9	13.6	50.0

THE SCOUTING REPORT: 1996

ATLANTA BRAVES

KENT MERCKER

Position: SP
Bats: L **Throws:** L
Ht: 6'1" **Wt:** 175
Opening Day Age: 28
Born: 2/1/1968
Drafted: ATL86 1/5
ML Seasons: 7

SCOUTING REPORT

Kent throws with a high three-quarter delivery, bringing home two strong power pitches. His slider is above-average and his fastball, which tails in on lefthanded batters, rates slightly above-average.

It's the finesse part of the game that troubles Mercker. His turned-over change-up rates average-minus, and scouts feel he must improve it in order to better set up his fastball and slider. While Kent has an average curve, he doesn't use it very much. His control is below-average and inconsistent, leading to walks and too many fat fastballs.

Mercker is an average fielder but has a minus move to first. Of the ten men trying to steal bases against Kent in '95, nine succeeded. One thing he's probably happy not to do anymore is hit. Just a .104 batter in 48 at-bats during '95, he goes to the AL sporting an .048 lifetime average with 56 strikeouts in 117 at-bats. Kent did improve his bunting, though, laying down six successful sacrifices last year.

HOW HE PERFORMED IN '95

The still-promising lefty was in the Braves' starting rotation on Opening Day and stayed there for the entire season, except for three relief appearances in September. Mercker pitched the most innings of his big-league career and the third-most of his professional career. The last time he pitched more was in 1989, when he made 27 starts for Triple-A Richmond.

Kent had a 10-strikeout game against the Dodgers on June 1, but overall his strikeout rate declined as he had fanned a batter an inning in '94. There was no talk of decreased velocity or serious arm trouble, however.

He did miss one game in September and had to leave another game early later in the month with an injured triceps muscle in his left arm. It was then that he came in a few times from the bullpen just to keep sharp.

WHAT TO EXPECT IN '96

How many teams would like a fifth starter who put up the kind of numbers Mercker did? Not the Braves, who decided that salary requirements and the emergence of prospect Jason Schmidt combined to make Kent expendable. Dealt to Baltimore, he's sure to make 30 starts for the Orioles, and is one adjustment or so away from a big season.

Overall Statistics

	G	GS	GF	SV	W	L	ERA	IP	H	R	ER	HR	BB	SO
95 ATL	29	26	1	0	7	8	4.15	143.0	140	73	66	16	61	102
Career	233	54	85	19	31	25	3.49	515.2	440	221	200	49	242	426

1995 Situational Statistics

	W	L	ERA	SV	IP	BB	SO		AB	HR	RBI	BA	OBA	SLG
Home	3	4	5.01	0	79.0	33	68	LHB	75	2	5	.213	.289	.320
Road	4	4	3.09	0	64.0	28	34	RHB	468	14	58	.265	.339	.429
Apr-Jun	4	4	4.68	0	67.1	32	56	ScPos	136	4	46	.228	.304	.382
Jul-Oct	3	4	3.69	0	75.2	29	46	Clutch	24	1	4	.292	.433	.500

How He Compares to Other Pitchers

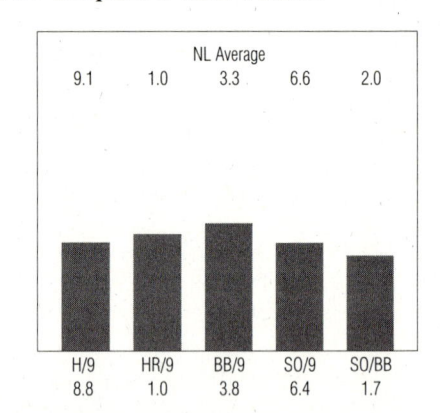

NL Average
H/9	HR/9	BB/9	SO/9	SO/BB
9.1	1.0	3.3	6.6	2.0
8.8	1.0	3.8	6.4	1.7

How He Compares to Other Starting Pitchers

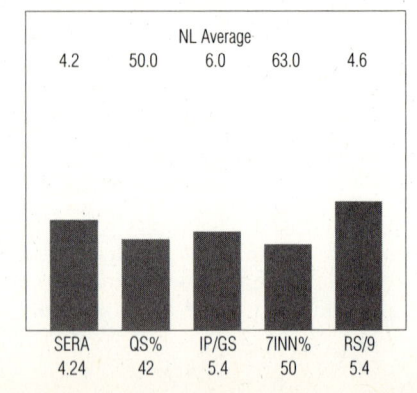

NL Average
SERA	QS%	IP/GS	7INN%	RS/9
4.2	50.0	6.0	63.0	4.6
4.24	42	5.4	50	5.4

ATLANTA BRAVES

JOHN SMOLTZ

Position: SP
Bats: R **Throws:** R
Ht: 6'3" **Wt:** 210
Opening Day Age: 28
Born: 5/15/1967
Drafted: DET85 22/574
ML Seasons: 8

SCOUTING REPORT
Smoltz has the classic high three-quarter, righthanded power pitcher's motion. He also has the classic stuff required for the role, with both a two-seam sinking fastball and a rising four-seamer that are well above-average in velocity.

John also has a plus hard slider which can get hit hard if it hangs. His curve, change-up, and splitter (which he seldom uses except with two strikes) all rank as average; his control is inconsistent.

A good athlete with quick feet, Smoltz is an outstanding fielder on a pitching staff stuffed with Gold Glove candidates. He has a quick delivery and a fine pickoff move: in '95, just 14 baserunners tried to steal against him, ten successfully.

He's not usually a poor hitter, but John batted just .107 (6-for-56) last year. His career average is .142 in 457 at-bats, though, and Smoltz has three career homers and 57 career sacrifice bunts.

HOW HE PERFORMED IN '95
Elbow surgery is seldom looked on as promising. However, the operation John had following the '94 season seemed to be the best thing that could have happened to Smoltz, as he rebounded to have a very fine season in '95.

Ranking second in the league in strikeouts, he has now finished either first or second in that category in three of the last four years. John never allowed more than four runs in any start and recorded his first shutout in two years in mid-June against the Reds. The contest was the second of two straight complete-game victories.

Most significantly, Smoltz appeared to be throwing as hard as ever despite the surgery and threw consistently well all year. He might have had his best stuff in Game Two of the NLCS against Cincinnati, when he absolutely dominated the Reds for the first four innings.

WHAT TO EXPECT IN '96
Smoltz was solid all year in '95 although he always throws a lot of pitches. If his arm holds up well, he will probably post numbers in '96 similar to his career totals. He's one of the most intimidating pitchers in the league when he's healthy and on top of his game, but control problems—and Greg Maddux—will probably keep John from having the Cy Young season that seems tantalizingly possible for him.

Overall Statistics

	G	GS	GF	SV	W	L	ERA	IP	H	R	ER	HR	BB	SO
95 ATL	29	29	0	0	12	7	3.18	192.2	166	76	68	15	72	193
Career	231	231	0	0	90	82	3.53	1550.2	1346	668	609	131	572	1252

1995 Situational Statistics

	W	L	ERA	SV	IP	BB	SO		AB	HR	RBI	BA	OBA	SLG
Home	6	4	3.59	0	102.2	43	104	LHB	345	7	35	.261	.345	.380
Road	6	3	2.70	0	90.0	29	89	RHB	369	8	33	.206	.264	.314
Apr-Jun	7	4	3.00	0	84.0	32	83	ScPos	174	5	51	.207	.292	.322
Jul-Oct	5	3	3.31	0	108.2	40	110	Clutch	69	2	12	.304	.368	.464

How He Compares to Other Pitchers

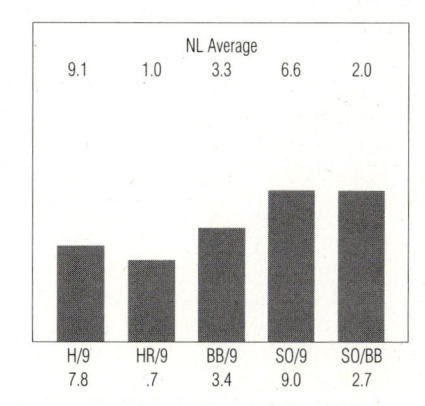

	H/9	HR/9	BB/9	SO/9	SO/BB
NL Average	9.1	1.0	3.3	6.6	2.0
	7.8	.7	3.4	9.0	2.7

How He Compares to Other Starting Pitchers

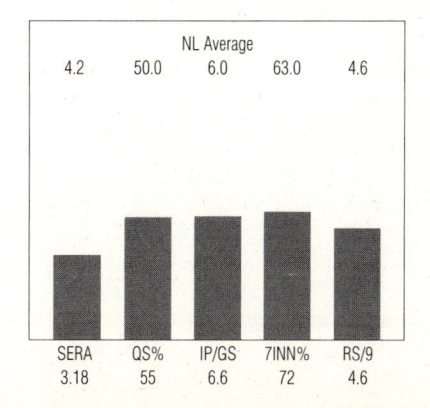

	SERA	QS%	IP/GS	7INN%	RS/9
NL Average	4.2	50.0	6.0	63.0	4.6
	3.18	55	6.6	72	4.6

ATLANTA BRAVES

MARK WOHLERS

Position: RP
Bats: R **Throws:** R
Ht: 6'4" **Wt:** 207
Opening Day Age: 26
Born: 1/23/1970
Drafted: ATL88 10/190
ML Seasons: 5

SCOUTING REPORT

Wohlers' outstanding fastball is one of the best in baseball. It regularly tops 100 MPH on the Juggs gun and its speed alone makes up for the relative straightness of the pitch. Coming in from three-quarters, Mark also has an average hard slider and an average splitter. He throws his average change-up only to keep hitters off-balance. His control has now improved to average. While Wohlers' fielding is just par, he has a plus move to first and rates plus at holding runners. Only five runners tried to steal on him in '95 in 65 innings, although all were successful.

HOW HE PERFORMED IN '95

In '95, Mark finally became the pitcher the Braves thought he would be ever since 1991. That season, he saved 32 games with an ERA of less than 1.00, splitting his time between Double-A Greenville and Triple-A Richmond.

Since that signal season, Wohlers hadn't harnessed his awesome fastball, going deep into counts and walking too many hitters for comfort. However, there was no way Atlanta was going to give up on Mark's arm, and the Braves stuck with him.

It's easy to see why Wohlers had such success in '95: his walks decreased and his strikeouts rose. He had walked a batter every two innings his first two years with Atlanta, but Mark walked just one every three last year.

Although Wohlers gave up six earned runs in the first two weeks of the season, he was unhittable after that, wresting the closer's job from Greg McMichael. Mark began a streak of saves covering 21 straight appearances on May 15, and from there to the end of the year he gave up only nine earned runs in 60 innings (1.35 ERA), collecting 84 strikeouts. He allowed only one earned run in July and August combined!

Wohlers is about as helpless at bat as most hitters are against him, fanning in all three of his '95 at-bats. Mark has now fanned six times in seven career tries. In his other at-bat, he collected a single.

WHAT TO EXPECT IN '96

For the first time, Wohlers will be the main man in the bullpen from day one. Other closers will get more saves than him, but only because other teams don't have the dominant starting pitchers Atlanta has. He's the best reliever in the NL now.

Overall Statistics

	G	GS	GF	SV	W	L	ERA	IP	H	R	ER	HR	BB	SO
95 ATL	65	0	49	25	7	3	2.09	64.2	51	16	15	2	24	90
Career	211	0	97	32	24	10	3.38	218.2	184	94	82	6	106	223

1995 Situational Statistics

	W	L	ERA	SV	IP	BB	SO		AB	HR	RBI	BA	OBA	SLG
Home	7	2	0.97	14	37.0	14	43	LHB	111	1	9	.234	.336	.297
Road	0	1	3.58	11	27.2	10	47	RHB	131	1	10	.191	.237	.244
Apr-Jun	1	2	3.38	5	24.0	16	34	ScPos	63	2	19	.254	.365	.413
Jul-Oct	6	1	1.33	20	40.2	8	56	Clutch	159	1	14	.226	.293	.277

How He Compares to Other Pitchers

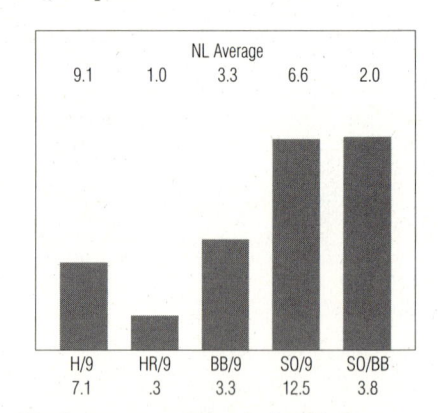

NL Average: 9.1 | 1.0 | 3.3 | 6.6 | 2.0

H/9: 7.1 | HR/9: .3 | BB/9: 3.3 | SO/9: 12.5 | SO/BB: 3.8

How He Compares to Other Relief Pitchers

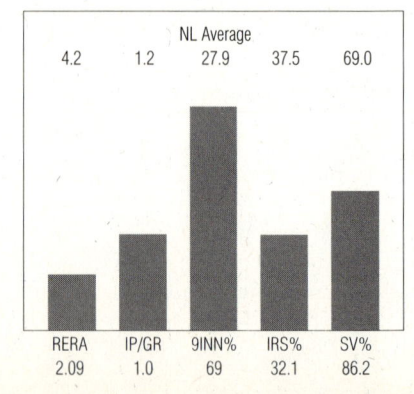

NL Average: 4.2 | 1.2 | 27.9 | 37.5 | 69.0

RERA: 2.09 | IP/GR: 1.0 | 9INN%: 69 | IRS%: 32.1 | SV%: 86.2

ATLANTA BRAVES

RAFAEL BELLIARD

Positions: SS/2B
Bats: R **Throws:** R
Ht: 5'6" **Wt:** 160
Opening Day Age: 34
Born: 10/24/1961
Drafted: PIT 7/10/80
ML Seasons: 14

Overall Statistics

	G	AB	R	H	2B	3B	HR	RBI	SB	CS	BB	SO	BA	OBA
95 ATL	75	180	12	40	2	1	0	7	2	2	6	28	.222	.255
Career	989	2068	198	464	45	14	1	135	40	15	133	344	.224	.278

1995 Situational Statistics

	AB	HR	RBI	BA	OBA	SLG		AB	HR	RBI	BA	OBA	SLG
Home	92	0	2	.207	.232	.217	LHP	43	0	2	.302	.318	.302
Road	88	0	5	.239	.280	.273	RHP	137	0	5	.197	.236	.226
Apr-Jun	39	0	1	.231	.250	.231	ScPos	39	0	7	.308	.372	.359
Jul-Oct	141	0	6	.220	.257	.248	Clutch	24	0	2	.333	.407	.375

SCOUTING REPORT

Belliard chokes up on the bat at all times, slapping pitches to right. He likes high fastballs even though he has no power. When called on to sacrifice, he can do so effectively. Rafael, a slightly below-average runner, is normally no threat to steal. His two swipes last year were his first since '91.

Defensively, Rafael has an above-average arm in strength and accuracy but a slow release. His range is average, but his sure hands rate well above-average.

HOW HE PERFORMED IN '95

Belliard played more than expected due to injuries to second baseman Mark Lemke and shortstop Jeff Blauser. Usually struggling just to get in during the late innings, Rafael wound up starting 24 games at second and 30 at short in '95.

Hanging around because of his defense, he made only one error last season and now has made just one error in each of the last three years.

WHAT TO EXPECT IN '96

The Braves are content keeping Belliard around, although it's doubtful that many other teams in the majors could afford to carry the sure-handed infielder, given his extremely weak stick.

PEDRO BORBON

Position: RP
Bats: R **Throws:** L
Ht: 6'1" **Wt:** 205
Opening Day Age: 28
Born: 11/15/1967
Drafted: CHA 6/4/88
ML Seasons: 3

Overall Statistics

	G	GS	GF	SV	W	L	ERA	IP	H	R	ER	HR	BB	SO
95 ATL	41	0	19	2	2	2	3.09	32.0	29	12	11	2	17	33
Career	46	0	21	2	2	3	4.11	35.0	34	17	16	2	21	36

1995 Situational Statistics

	W	L	ERA	SV	IP	BB	SO		AB	HR	RBI	BA	OBA	SLG
Home	2	0	2.21	2	20.1	4	22	LHB	42	1	3	.167	.205	.238
Road	0	2	4.63	0	11.2	13	11	RHB	79	1	10	.278	.396	.443
Apr-Jun	0	1	3.18	2	11.1	2	12	ScPos	34	1	11	.235	.386	.353
Jul-Oct	2	1	3.05	0	20.2	15	21	Clutch	46	1	7	.304	.400	.478

SCOUTING REPORT

Although Borbon has just average gifts, he knows how to pitch. He slings the ball with a three-quarter delivery, bringing home an average curve and a below-average fastball. His turns over his average change-up often

Pedro is an average fielder with an average move. However, eight runners tried to steal against him in '95, seven successfully. He was hitless in his only at-bat.

HOW HE PERFORMED IN '95

Rookie Borbon was used primarily to get left-handed hitters out and did that job well. However, he pitched only 13 innings in the first 13 weeks of the season. Over the season, he allowed only five of 29 inherited runners to score.

Borbon recorded his first save May 13 against the Cincinnati Reds, the team his dad starred for in the 1970s. He and his father now have the record for most saves by a father-son duo: The elder Pedro saved 80 games during his 11-year career.

WHAT TO EXPECT IN '96

Since Pedro gets lefties out and comes cheap, he'll be back in Atlanta. He won't get many save chances with Wohlers around, but could wind up being one of Atlanta's top set-up pitchers if he matures.

THE SCOUTING REPORT: 1996

ATLANTA BRAVES

BRAD CLONTZ

Position: RP
Bats: R **Throws:** R
Ht: 6'1" **Wt:** 180
Opening Day Age: 24
Born: 4/25/1971
Drafted: ATL92 10/285
ML Seasons: 1

Overall Statistics

	G	GS	GF	SV	W	L	ERA	IP	H	R	ER	HR	BB	SO
95 ATL	59	0	14	4	8	1	3.65	69.0	71	29	28	5	22	55
Career	59	0	14	4	8	1	3.65	69.0	71	29	28	5	22	55

1995 Situational Statistics

	W	L	ERA	SV	IP	BB	SO		AB	HR	RBI	BA	OBA	SLG
Home	3	1	2.93	1	40.0	13	34	LHB	92	1	19	.348	.419	.467
Road	5	0	4.66	3	29.0	9	21	RHB	172	4	14	.227	.283	.326
Apr-Jun	1	1	4.56	4	25.2	10	16	ScPos	73	0	25	.260	.371	.288
Jul-Oct	7	0	3.12	0	43.1	12	39	Clutch	93	4	14	.237	.321	.419

SCOUTING REPORT
Clontz has an underhand delivery and throws across his body. This makes him tough on righthanders, but Brad needs to figure out a way to retire lefties consistently.

His sinking fastball and slider are average and his change-up a notch below that, but he does possess above-par control. Clontz' fielding and move are average; six runners tried to steal last year against Clontz, four successfully. He was hitless in his only two at-bats.

HOW HE PERFORMED IN '95
Although Brad, a rookie, began the season as Atlanta's closer and saved four games in less than two weeks, he soon lost his job as Mark Wohlers began to dominate hitters.

The durable Clontz won eight straight games from late June to early September and had a streak of 18 2/3 scoreless innings during the middle of the season. Among the Braves, only Wohlers, Greg Maddux and John Smoltz had longer streaks.

WHAT TO EXPECT IN '96
Clontz has real potential but will have to learn to get lefties out before he can be a closer. He's only 26 and was pitching in Double-A only two years ago, so he's got plenty of time to learn.

MIKE DEVEREAUX

Position: OF
Bats: R **Throws:** R
Ht: 6' " **Wt:** 195
Opening Day Age: 32
Born: 4/10/1963
Drafted: LA85 6/116
ML Seasons: 9

Overall Statistics

	G	AB	R	H	2B	3B	HR	RBI	SB	CS	BB	SO	BA	OBA
95 CHA/ATL	121	388	55	116	24	1	11	63	8	6	27	62	.299	.342
Career	921	3332	434	856	155	31	97	438	76	53	252	570	.257	.308

1995 Situational Statistics

	AB	HR	RBI	BA	OBA	SLG		AB	HR	RBI	BA	OBA	SLG
Home	179	5	36	.279	.327	.413	LHP	130	5	26	.308	.353	.477
Road	209	6	27	.316	.356	.483	RHP	258	6	37	.295	.337	.438
Apr-Jun	171	4	24	.292	.337	.427	ScPos	130	1	46	.285	.347	.346
Jul-Oct	217	7	39	.304	.346	.470	Clutch	70	2	13	.257	.333	.443

SCOUTING REPORT
A pure high fastball hitter, Devereaux has big trouble with breaking balls and off-speed pitches. He has a slight knee raise before his stride, which junkballers exploit by throwing off Mike's timing. He has slightly below average speed and does not bunt.

Mike plays all three outfield positions with now-average range and hands. His arm is of average accuracy but has minus strength. Left field is his best position now.

HOW HE PERFORMED IN '95
Devereaux was having his best season in the major leagues when the Braves traded for him to help solidify their bench. He hit .306 in 333 at-bats for the White Sox before the August 25 trade. Mike's combined .299 average was 23 points higher than his previous career high, set in '92 with Baltimore. With the Braves, Devereaux was used mostly as a pinch-hitter and late-inning defensive replacement for left fielder Ryan Klesko, but did make starts at all three garden spots.

WHAT TO EXPECT IN '96
Wherever he goes this spring, Devereaux could compete for a starting spot. He's been a below-average hitter for his whole career, however, so his days as a regular may well be over.

ATLANTA BRAVES

MIKE KELLY

Position: OF
Bats: R **Throws:** R
Ht: 6'4" **Wt:** 195
Opening Day Age: 25
Born: 6/2/1970
Drafted: ATL91 1/2
ML Seasons: 2

Overall Statistics

	G	AB	R	H	2B	3B	HR	RBI	SB	CS	BB	SO	BA	OBA
95 ATL	97	137	26	26	6	1	3	17	7	3	11	49	.190	.258
Career	127	214	40	47	16	2	5	26	7	4	13	66	.220	.273

1995 Situational Statistics

	AB	HR	RBI	BA	OBA	SLG		AB	HR	RBI	BA	OBA	SLG
Home	50	0	3	.140	.228	.160	LHP	69	2	13	.217	.260	.391
Road	87	3	14	.218	.277	.402	RHP	68	1	4	.162	.256	.235
Apr-Jun	100	3	14	.210	.269	.350	ScPos	30	2	14	.333	.382	.633
Jul-Oct	37	0	3	.135	.233	.216	Clutch	27	0	1	.111	.194	.148

SCOUTING REPORT

Mike has good tools but hasn't developed into a good ballplayer. Kelly makes poor contact because he tries to pull everything. He chases breaking balls incessantly, and can be overmatched by an above-average fastball. He bunts well, though.

Kelly has above-average range but a below-average arm with average accuracy and hands in the outfield. Mike is a plus runner who can steal bases.

HOW HE PERFORMED IN '95

Kelly started 18 games in left, mostly when Ryan Klesko was on the disabled list. Once Klesko returned, Mike went back to pinch-hitting and late-inning defense. Kelly failed to hit lefthanders well enough to earn platoon duty; his average was 27 points lower than that of lefty-swinging Klesko. Mike was so ineffective that he sent to Triple-A on August 12 and not recalled until September 10, excluding him from the postseason roster.

WHAT TO EXPECT IN '96

The second player chosen in the 1991 draft, Kelly was a decent prospect after hitting .262 and slugging .476 at Richmond in '94. However, his poor performance may have cost him his shot with the Braves. He'll only play if Klesko absolutely can't hit lefthanded pitching.

MIKE MORDECAI

Positions: 2B//1B/3B/SS/OF
Bats: B **Throws:** R
Ht: 5'11" **Wt:** 175
Opening Day Age: 28
Born: 12/13/1967
Drafted: ATL89 7/142
ML Seasons: 2

Overall Statistics

	G	AB	R	H	2B	3B	HR	RBI	SB	CS	BB	SO	BA	OBA
95 ATL	69	75	10	21	6	0	3	11	0	0	9	16	.280	.353
Career	73	79	11	22	6	0	4	14	0	0	10	16	.278	.356

1995 Situational Statistics

	AB	HR	RBI	BA	OBA	SLG		AB	HR	RBI	BA	OBA	SLG
Home	41	1	5	.171	.261	.293	LHP	26	2	4	.385	.407	.769
Road	34	2	6	.412	.462	.706	RHP	49	1	7	.224	.328	.327
Apr-Jun	18	0	1	.278	.278	.444	ScPos	16	1	9	.438	.524	.750
Jul-Oct	57	3	10	.281	.373	.491	Clutch	27	1	6	.333	.400	.519

SCOUTING REPORT

An aging prospect who developed some home-run power in '94 at Triple-A, Mike has given up switch-hitting and now bats exclusively righthanded. A bit of evidence that he made the right move was his big lefty/righty split in limited usage in '95. He has average speed and stole a few bases in the minors.

In the field, Mike has adequate range and a strong enough arm to play the left side of the infield; his primary position is shortstop.

HOW HE PERFORMED IN '95

Mordecai was the ultimate utility man in '95. He played five different positions—all infield posts plus center—and didn't commit an error. On the Braves' roster the entire season, he didn't make his first start until July 16 and started just five games the entire year. Who can break into that lineup? Mike showed some pop in his bat when given a chance to play.

WHAT TO EXPECT IN '96

Mordecai is 28 and too old to become an everyday player. However, he should stick in the majors as a backup infielder and could be a starter for some teams if given the chance.

THE SCOUTING REPORT: 1996

ATLANTA BRAVES

CHARLIE O'BRIEN

Position: C
Bats: R **Throws:** R
Ht: 6'2" **Wt:** 195
Opening Day Age: 35
Born: 5/1/1960
Drafted: OAK82 4/132
ML Seasons: 10

Overall Statistics

	G	AB	R	H	2B	3B	HR	RBI	SB	CS	BB	SO	BA	OBA
95 ATL	67	198	18	45	7	0	9	23	0	1	29	40	.227	.343
Career	524	1427	144	312	77	3	33	166	1	7	145	189	.219	.302

1995 Situational Statistics

	AB	HR	RBI	BA	OBA	SLG		AB	HR	RBI	BA	OBA	SLG
Home	83	4	10	.229	.354	.398	LHP	35	1	3	.171	.326	.286
Road	115	5	13	.226	.336	.400	RHP	163	8	20	.239	.347	.423
Apr-Jun	67	5	10	.299	.397	.582	ScPos	64	2	14	.141	.295	.281
Jul-Oct	131	4	13	.191	.316	.305	Clutch	32	1	3	.281	.410	.406

SCOUTING REPORT

Charlie is a strong defensive catcher. His hands rate well above-average, and his arm and accuracy are both above-average. O'Brien has average mobility.

Although he has some power and can hit high pitches over the plate, he does not judge pitches particularly well. He is very, very slow, but actually bunted for a hit last season.

HOW HE PERFORMED IN '95

Everyone expected O'Brien to be just a backup but he played his way into a semi-regular spot with a good first half of the season, batting .281 in May and .324 in June.

By the All-Star break, Charlie had become the personal catcher for both Steve Avery and Greg Maddux. Both pitchers thought he called a much better game than the inexperienced Javy Lopez, and O'Brien wound up behind the plate for all but one of Avery's starts and for most of Maddux's.

WHAT TO EXPECT IN '96

The Braves didn't offer O'Brien arbitration over the winter, leaving him as a free agent. He signed with Toronto, who was desperate for someone to help young receiver Sandy Martinez learn the ropes. This should be a good fit.

ALEJANDRO PENA

Position: RP
Bats: R **Throws:** R
Ht: 6'1" **Wt:** 205
Opening Day Age: 36
Born: 6/25/1959
Drafted: LA 9/10/78
ML Seasons: 14

Overall Statistics

	G	GS	GF	SV	W	L	ERA	IP	H	R	ER	HR	BB	SO
95 BO/FL/AT	44	0	11	0	3	1	4.72	55.1	55	32	29	8	19	64
Career	499	72	229	74	56	51	3.10	1053.2	955	422	363	73	330	834

1995 Situational Statistics

	W	L	ERA	SV	IP	BB	SO		AB	HR	RBI	BA	OBA	SLG
Home	2	1	6.85	0	23.2	10	32	LHB	87	3	12	.207	.303	.356
Road	1	0	3.13	0	31.2	9	32	RHB	132	5	20	.280	.317	.485
Apr-Jun	1	1	7.40	0	24.1	12	25	ScPos	57	4	26	.281	.379	.579
Jul-Oct	2	0	2.61	0	31.0	7	39	Clutch	91	2	6	.209	.242	.330

SCOUTING REPORT

Pena throws awfully hard for a guy who's been around this long and injured so often. From three-quarters, he has an plus, live four-seam fastball. He augments it with an average slider and a below-par change-up. Alejandro is a decent fielder, but seven runners stole in nine attempts with him on the mound in '95.

HOW HE PERFORMED IN '95

Left for dead by the cellar-dwelling Pirates in June of '94, Pena surprisingly contributed to a World Series champion in '95. The Braves acquired Pena late in the season, as they had done four years earlier. However, unlike in 1991 when he saved 11 games, he was strictly a set-up pitcher last year.

Alejandro played for three teams in '95. He was awful with Boston but had a 1.50 ERA in 13 games for Florida before coming to Atlanta, where he Pena fanned 18 in 13 innings.

WHAT TO EXPECT IN '96

Pena first appeared in the majors during Ronald Reagan's first term, although it seems like it was during Reagan's days as Governor of California. Although Alejandro keeps getting his chances, he rarely pitches well enough to stick around in one place very long.

ATLANTA BRAVES

LUIS POLONIA

Position: OF
Bats: L **Throws:** L
Ht: 5'8" **Wt:** 155
Opening Day Age: 31
Born: 10/12/1964
Drafted: OAK 1/3/84
ML Seasons: 9

Overall Statistics

	G	AB	R	H	2B	3B	HR	RBI	SB	CS	BB	SO	BA	OBA
95 NYA/ATL95	291	43	76	16	3	2	17	13	4	28	38	.261	.322
Career	1095	3957	606	1159	150	56	17	327	283	122	313	456	.293	.344

1995 Situational Statistics

	AB	HR	RBI	BA	OBA	SLG		AB	HR	RBI	BA	OBA	SLG
Home	144	2	11	.257	.323	.368	LHP	29	1	2	.241	.313	.414
Road	147	0	6	.265	.321	.347	RHP	262	1	15	.263	.323	.351
Apr-Jun	155	1	12	.265	.329	.355	ScPos	64	0	14	.172	.278	.219
Jul-Oct	136	1	5	.257	.313	.360	Clutch	43	0	2	.326	.388	.419

SCOUTING REPORT

Luis is a contact hitter who likes the pitch high, sometimes in his eyes. He has little power and is most effective spraying the ball around, but Polonia will try to pull off-speed pitches. A plus runner, Luis is an erratic basestealer.

In left field, he has a weak arm with average accuracy. Polonia has slightly above-average range, but does not read fly balls well. His hands are average.

HOW HE PERFORMED IN '95

Polonia was another of Atlanta's late-season, pennant-insurance acquisitions—even though the Braves weren't in a close race in the NL East. The Braves obtained him on August 11 from the Yankees; he started just six games the rest of the year. Polonia did his best hitting in Atlanta coming off the bench, with eight hits in 18 pinch-hit at-bats (.444).

WHAT TO EXPECT IN '96

Polonia is going to be best remembered for his off-field problems from several years ago. He could hang on as a fifth outfielder in the majors, sign a minor-league contract for '96, or he could just fade away into obscurity.

DWIGHT SMITH

Position: OF
Bats: L **Throws:** R
Ht: 5'11" **Wt:** 175
Opening Day Age: 32
Born: 11/8/1963
Drafted: CHN84 S3/62
ML Seasons: 7

Overall Statistics

	G	AB	R	H	2B	3B	HR	RBI	SB	CS	BB	SO	BA	OBA
95 ATL	103	131	16	33	8	2	3	21	0	3	13	35	.252	.327
Career	712	1654	228	466	83	20	43	210	41	34	133	292	.282	.338

1995 Situational Statistics

	AB	HR	RBI	BA	OBA	SLG		AB	HR	RBI	BA	OBA	SLG
Home	73	1	12	.205	.289	.301	LHP	8	0	0	.125	.364	.125
Road	58	2	9	.310	.375	.552	RHP	123	3	21	.260	.324	.431
Apr-Jun	61	2	9	.279	.323	.475	ScPos	41	2	20	.268	.326	.488
Jul-Oct	70	1	12	.229	.329	.357	Clutch	40	2	13	.275	.375	.500

SCOUTING REPORT

Smith has a quick bat with some power. He will crush low pitches and uses the whole field, but he struggles against lefthanders. In the outfield, Dwight has minus range and a minus arm with average hands and accuracy. Smith was a fine basestealer in the minors but now has just average speed.

HOW HE PERFORMED IN '95

Smith was the dictionary definition of a pinch-hitter in '95, getting only 131 at bats in 101 games and faring quite well in the role. Dwight had 16 pinch-hits and 18 pinch-RBIs, which nearly broke the Atlanta record in both categories (20 and 23, respectively). He had two pinch-hit home runs, including a grand slam off Florida's Richie Lewis to win a game in May.

Smith started 16 games, nine in right field and seven in left, hitting .260 (13-for-50). He also sang the pre-game National Anthem again.

WHAT TO EXPECT IN '96

It didn't take the Braves long after the postseason was over to sign the popular and affable Smith to a two year-contract. It's obvious that Atlanta likes him, and equally obvious that Dwight appreciates his role and is good at what he does.

ATLANTA BRAVES: TOP PROSPECTS

JERMAINE DYE
Bats: R Throws: R Opening Day Age: 22
Ht: 6-0 Wt: 195 Born: 1/28/1974
Position: RF Drafted: 1993 #16 ATL

YR TEAM	LG/CLASS	G	AB	R	H	2B	3B	HR	RBI	SB	BA	OBA
93 Braves	GULF/R	31	124	17	43	14	0	0	27	5	.347	.393
93 Danville	APPY/R	25	94	6	26	6	1	2	12	4	.277	.327
94 Macon	SAL/A	135	506	73	151	41	1	15	98	19	.298	.346
95 Greenville	SOU/AA	104	403	50	115	26	4	15	71	4	.285	.329

An outstanding athlete who had both football and basketball scholarships, Dye turned in his third solid season while making the jump to Double-A in 1995. A line-drive specialist, he put together a 12-game hitting streak on his way to finishing ninth in the organization in batting. In the field, Dye shows good range to go along with an outstanding throwing arm. The All-Star right fielder registered 22 assists in each of the past two seasons, both league-leading totals.

ANTON FRENCH
Bats: S Throws: R Opening Day Age: 21
Ht: 5-10 Wt: 175 Born: 7/25/1975
Position: OF Drafted: 1993 #14 SL

YR TEAM	LG/CLASS	G	AB	R	H	2B	3B	HR	RBI	SB	BA	OBA
93 Cardinals	ARIZ/R	34	106	19	29	3	2	1	17	15	.274	.333
94 Cardinals	ARIZ/R	52	204	30	45	8	8	2	29	11	.221	.275
95 Durham	CARO/A	7	26	3	7	1	0	0	2	4	.269	.367
95 Peoria	MID/A	116	417	71	114	19	5	10	37	57	.273	.341

French, acquired from the Cardinals for Jose Oliva, has the ability to ignite the top of the order. The switch-hitter spent most of the year in the Midwest League where he totaled 57 of his 61 stolen bases, good for second in the league. The 20-year-old spent two years in rookie ball, including 1994, where he finished among Arizona League leaders in triples, extra-base hits and RBI. In order to be a good leadoff hitter, however, French must improve his strike zone judgment.

KEVIN GRIJAK
Bats: L Throws: R Opening Day Age: 26
Ht: 6-2 Wt: 195 Born: 8/6/1970
Position: 1B Drafted: 1991 #28 ATL

YR TEAM	LG/CLASS	G	AB	R	H	2B	3B	HR	RBI	SB	BA	OBA
93 Macon	SAL/A	120	389	50	115	26	5	7	58	9	.296	.356
94 Durham	CARO/A	22	68	18	25	3	0	11	22	1	.368	.476
94 Greenville	SOU/AA	100	348	40	94	19	1	11	58	2	.270	.315
95 Richmond	INT/AAA	106	309	35	92	16	5	12	56	1	.298	.354
95 Greenville	SOU/AA	21	74	14	32	5	0	2	11	0	.432	.482

Grijak began the 1995 season at Double-A, was leading the league in batting at .432 when promoted May 1, and continued to lead the entire minor leagues with a .399 average through the end of May. Not considered a tools player or a slugger, Grijak has hit .303 and slugged .488 in his five-year career.

DAMON HOLLINS
Bats: R Throws: L Opening Day Age: 22
Ht: 5-11 Wt: 180 Born: 6/12/1974
Position: CF Drafted: 1992 #4 ATL

YR TEAM	LG/CLASS	G	AB	R	H	2B	3B	HR	RBI	SB	BA	OBA
93 Danville	APPY/R	62	240	37	77	15	2	7	51	10	.321	.369
94 Durham	CARO/A	131	485	76	131	28	0	23	88	12	.270	.335
95 Greenville	SOU/AA	129	466	64	115	26	2	18	77	6	.247	.313

A rare combination of righty batting and lefty throwing, Hollins is a fierce competitor with above-average tools who struggled both at the plate and in the field in 1995. After posting a .321 average in 1993, Hollins has seen his average drop 74 points in two years. However, the 21-year-old has kept his power numbers up, finishing fifth in the organization in RBI. A center fielder with a strong arm, Hollins totaled 18 assists last year, but misreading fly balls has led to 28 errors in his four-year career.

ANDRUW JONES
Bats: R Throws: R Opening Day Age: 19
Ht: 6-1 Wt: 170 Born: 4/23/1977
Position: CF Drafted: NDFA 7-12-93 ATL

YR TEAM	LG/CLASS	G	AB	R	H	2B	3B	HR	RBI	SB	BA	OBA
94 Braves	GULF/R	27	95	22	21	5	1	2	10	5	.221	.345
94 Danville	APPY/R	36	143	20	48	9	2	1	16	16	.336	.385
95 Macon	SAL/A	139	537	104	149	41	5	25	100	56	.277	.372

Jones may be the most exciting player in the minors. He became the first farmhand since 1961 to register a 20-homer, 50-stolen base and 100-RBI season. He turned 18 during a fabulous April in which he hit .341 with a minor league-high nine homers. A center fielder with an arm that ranks with the organization's best, Jones has tremendous bat speed and was voted the South Atlantic League's Most Outstanding Prospect. His only weakness is hitting the breaking ball, which he was fed a steady diet of after the first month of the season.

DARRELL MAY
Bats: L Throws: L Opening Day Age: 24
Ht: 6-2 Wt: 170 Born: 6/13/1972
Position: P Drafted: 1992 #46 ATL

YR TEAM	LG/CLASS	G	GS	GF	SV	W	L	ERA	IP	H	HR	BB	SO	O/BA
93 Macon	SAL/A	17	17	0	0	10	4	2.24	104.1	81	6	22	111	.213
93 Durham	CARO/A	9	9	0	0	5	2	2.09	51.2	44	4	16	47	.232
94 Durham	CARO/A	12	12	0	0	8	2	3.01	74.2	74	6	17	73	.259
94 Greenville	SOU/AA	11	11	0	0	5	3	3.11	63.2	61	4	17	42	.251
95 Atlanta	NL/MAJ	2	0	1	0	0	0	11.25	4.0	10	0	0	1	.500
95 Richmond	INT/AAA	9	9	0	0	4	2	3.71	51.0	53	1	16	42	.270
95 Greenville	SOU/AA	15	15	0	0	2	8	3.55	91.1	81	18	20	79	.233

Despite allowing two earned runs or fewer in his first ten games, May was just 2-8 at Greenville before being promoted to Richmond. A lefthander with good control, May has posted a 38-24 record in his four-year career. The 23-year-old is tough on lefties and effectively shuts down the opponent's running game.

ATLANTA BRAVES: TOP PROSPECTS

ALDO PECORILLI

Bats: R Throws: R Opening Day Age: 26
Ht: 5-11 Wt: 185 Born: 9/12/1970
Position: 1B Drafted: NDFA 1-25-92 SL

YR TEAM	LG/CLASS	G	AB	R	H	2B	3B	HR	RBI	SB	BA	OBA
93 Savannah	SAL/A	141	515	75	157	30	7	14	93	16	.305	.400
94 St. Pete	FSL/A	135	508	76	141	26	3	18	78	13	.278	.352
95 Richmond	INT/AAA	49	127	16	33	3	0	6	17	0	.260	.365
95 Greenville	SOU/AA	70	265	51	102	17	2	7	42	2	.385	.438

Acquired from the Cardinals in an off-season deal for Ramon Caraballo, Pecorilli wields a potent bat. He started the year at Double-A with an 18-game hitting streak and was batting .385 with 7 homers when promoted in early July. The 25-year-old hits well versus righties and lefties and he led the Braves organization in average in 1995. Pecorilli has no real defensive position, as he's played both corner infield and outfield positions, as well as catcher, in his four-year career.

JASON SCHMIDT

Bats: R Throws: R Opening Day Age: 23
Ht: 6-5 Wt: 185 Born: 1/29/1973
Position: P Drafted: 1991 #7 ATL

YR TEAM	LG/CLASS	G	GS	GF	SV	W	L	ERA	IP	H	HR	BB	SO	O/BA
93 Durham	CARO/A	22	22	0	0	7	11	4.94	116.2	128	12	47	110	.286
94 Greenville	SOU/AA	24	24	0	0	8	7	3.65	140.2	135	9	54	131	.255
95 Atlanta	NL/MAJ	9	2	1	0	2	2	5.76	25.0	27	2	18	19	.287
95 Richmond	INT/AAA	19	19	0	0	8	6	2.25	116.0	97	2	48	95	.233

A power pitcher who keeps the ball down, Schmidt allowed two runs or less in 15 of his 19 starts on his way to the International League ERA title. Featuring a mid-90's fastball that is the best in the organization, he finished fourth in the league with 7.37 strikeouts per nine innings. The long and lean Schmidt helps himself by being a good fielder and by limiting the running game.

CARL SCHUTZ

Bats: L Throws: L Opening Day Age: 25
Ht: 5-11 Wt: 200 Born: 8/22/1971
Position: P Drafted: 1993 #2 ATL

YR TEAM	LG/CLASS	G	GS	GF	SV	W	L	ERA	IP	H	HR	BB	SO	O/BA
93 Danville	APPY/R	12	0	9	4	1	0	0.66	13.2	6	0	6	25	.128
93 Greenville	SOU/AA	22	0	16	3	2	1	5.06	21.1	17	3	22	19	.233
94 Durham	CARO/A	53	0	47	20	3	3	4.89	53.1	35	6	46	81	.187
95 Greenville	SOU/AA	51	0	46	26	3	7	4.94	58.1	53	4	36	56	.244

Schutz, the premier relief prospect in the organization, turned in his second straight year of 20 or more saves in 1995 to rank third in the Southern League. After registering nine saves in ten appearances in April, however, Schutz was ineffective in the middle of the year, giving up hits and runs in bunches. A lefthander with nasty stuff, Schutz' out pitch is his slider.

BOBBY SMITH

Bats: R Throws: R Opening Day Age: 22
Ht: 6-3 Wt: 190 Born: 4/10/1974
Position: 3B Drafted: 1992 #11 ATL

YR TEAM	LG/CLASS	G	AB	R	H	2B	3B	HR	RBI	SB	BA	OBA
93 Macon	SAL/A	108	384	53	94	16	7	4	38	12	.245	.296
94 Durham	CARO/A	127	478	49	127	27	2	12	71	18	.266	.329
95 Greenville	SOU/AA	127	444	75	116	27	3	14	58	12	.261	.331

Voted his league's best defensive third baseman in both 1994 and 1995, Smith also produces at the plate. Smith is an intense competitor with some sock in his bat who set career marks in homers, slugging and on-base percentage in 1995. The 21-year-old must be more consistent, as he hit .333 in June and .350 in July but under .200 in both May and August.

TERRELL WADE

Bats: L Throws: L Opening Day Age: 23
Ht: 6-3 Wt: 204 Born: 1/25/1973
Position: P Drafted: NDFA 6-17-91 ATL

YR TEAM	LG/CLASS	G	GS	GF	SV	W	L	ERA	IP	H	HR	BB	SO	O/BA
93 Macon	SAL/A	14	14	0	0	8	2	1.73	83.1	57	1	36	121	.191
93 Durham	CARO/A	5	5	0	0	2	1	3.27	33.0	26	3	18	47	.220
93 Greenville	SOU/AA	8	8	0	0	2	1	3.21	42.0	32	6	29	40	.216
94 Greenville	SOU/AA	21	21	0	0	9	3	3.83	105.2	87	7	58	105	.228
94 Richmond	INT/AAA	4	4	0	0	2	2	2.63	24.0	23	1	15	26	.264
95 Atlanta	NL/MAJ	3	0	0	0	0	1	4.50	4.0	3	1	4	3	.214
95 Richmond	INT/AAA	24	23	0	0	10	9	4.56	142.0	137	6	63	124	.259

Wade, signed as a non-drafted free agent back in 1991, continued his rise to stardom in 1995. Despite having his season delayed by the strike, the big lefthander finished second in the International League in strikeouts and ended his season by winning his last five decisions. A hard thrower with an easy delivery, Wade needs an off-speed pitch added to his fastball/slider arsenal to become a dominating major league hurler.

JUAN WILLIAMS

Bats: L Throws: R Opening Day Age: 24
Ht: 6-0 Wt: 180 Born: 10/9/1972
Position: OF Drafted: 1990 #18 ATL

YR TEAM	LG/CLASS	G	AB	R	H	2B	3B	HR	RBI	SB	BA	OBA
93 Durham	CARO/A	124	403	49	93	16	2	11	44	11	.231	.295
94 Durham	CARO/A	122	394	55	86	14	0	19	57	7	.218	.311
95 Richmond	INT/AAA	45	129	18	34	5	0	5	11	6	.264	.347
95 Greenville	SOU/AA	62	192	40	60	14	2	15	39	4	.313	.369

A pull hitter with power, Williams was leading the minors in slugging with a .657 mark through July 8th. Starting the year at Greenville, he hit .313 with 15 homers, averaging a longball every 12.8 at-bats before earning his promotion to Richmond, where he struggled. For the year, he finished fourth in the organization in homers and seventh in batting. A Braves farmhand since 1990, the lefthanded-hitting Williams cracked 19 homers in 1994 at Durham.

ATLANTA BRAVES: OTHERS TO WATCH

JAMIE ARNOLD Bats: R Throws: R Ht: 6-2 Wt: 188
Born: 3/24/1974 Drafted: 1992 #1 ATL Position: P

YR TEAM	LG/CLASS	G	GS	GF	SV	W	L	ERA	IP	H	HR	BB	SO	O/BA
95 Greenville	SOU/AA	10	10	0	0	1	5	6.35	56.2	76	8	25	19	.329
95 Durham	CARO/A	15	14	0	0	4	8	3.94	80.0	86	5	21	44	.276

The former first-round pick suffered through a tough season that included a seven-game losing streak and a three-week stint on the disabled list with an elbow injury suffered when hit by a line drive.

TONY GRAFFANINO Bats: R Throws: R Ht: 6-1 Wt: 200
Born: 6/6/1972 Drafted: 1990 #9 ATL Position: 2B

YR TEAM	LG/CLASS	G	AB	R	H	2B	3B	HR	RBI	SB	BA	OBA
95 Richmond	INT/AAA	50	179	20	34	6	0	4	17	2	.190	.254

The former top prospect was sidelined most of the year with a career-threatening lower back injury.

TOM HARRISON Bats: R Throws: R Ht: 6-2 Wt: 185
Born: 9/30/1971 Drafted: Position: P

YR TEAM	LG/CLASS	G	GS	GF	SV	W	L	ERA	IP	H	HR	BB	SO	O/BA
95 Richmond	INT/AAA	9	6	1	1	2	1	3.21	42.0	34	2	20	16	.222
95 Greenville	SOU/AA	14	14	0	0	6	4	4.38	88.1	87	9	27	57	.261
95 Durham	CARO/A	7	6	0	0	3	1	0.96	37.2	22	1	13	25	.169

The former replacement player notched 11 wins at three different levels in '95.

WES HELMS Bats: R Throws: R Ht: 6-4 Wt: 210
Born: 5/12/1976 Drafted: 1994 #12 ATL Position: 3B

YR TEAM	LG/CLASS	G	AB	R	H	2B	3B	HR	RBI	SB	BA	OBA
95 Macon	SAL/A	136	539	89	149	32	1	11	85	2	.276	.347

The South Atlantic League All-Star finished third in the organization in RBI in addition to being a good defensive third baseman with a solid arm.

TYLER HOUSTON Bats: L Throws: R Ht: 6-2 Wt: 210
Born: 1/17/1971 Drafted: 1989 #1 ATL Position: 1B

YR TEAM	LG/CLASS	G	AB	R	H	2B	3B	HR	RBI	SB	BA	OBA
95 Richmond	INT/AAA	103	349	41	89	10	3	12	42	3	.255	.298

The nation's second pick in 1989 tripled his home run production from a year ago.

RYAN JACOBS Bats: R Throws: L Ht: 6-2 Wt: 175
Born: 2/3/1974 Drafted: 1992 #33 ATL Position: P

YR TEAM	LG/CLASS	G	GS	GF	SV	W	L	ERA	IP	H	HR	BB	SO	O/BA
95 Durham	CARO/A	29	25	3	0	11	6	3.51	148.2	145	12	57	99	.255

The lefthander went 6-0 with a 1.77 ERA in his last six starts.

GUS KENNEDY Bats: R Throws: R Ht: 5-10 Wt: 195
Born: 12/26/1973 Drafted: 1994 #33 ATL Position: LF

YR TEAM	LG/CLASS	G	AB	R	H	2B	3B	HR	RBI	SB	BA	OBA
95 Macon	SAL/A	128	439	83	111	29	5	24	76	20	.253	.386

The South Atlantic League All-Star finished third in the organization in homers while making all of the plays in left field.

MARC LEWIS Bats: R Throws: R Ht: 6-2 Wt: 175
Born: 5/20/1975 Drafted: 1994 #24 BOS Position: OF

YR TEAM	LG/CLASS	G	AB	R	H	2B	3B	HR	RBI	SB	BA	OBA
95 Michigan	MID/A	36	92	14	14	2	1	1	5	10	.152	.228
95 Utica	NYP/A	69	272	47	82	15	5	5	39	24	.301	.339

Acquired from the Boston Red Sox in the Matt Murray deal, Lewis is a pure athlete with incredible speed.

WONDER MONDS Bats: R Throws: R Ht: 6-3 Wt: 190
Born: 1/11/1973 Drafted: 1993 #49 ATL Position: RF

YR TEAM	LG/CLASS	G	AB	R	H	2B	3B	HR	RBI	SB	BA	OBA
95 Durham	CARO/A	81	297	44	83	17	0	6	33	28	.279	.320
95 Braves	GULF/R	4	15	1	2	0	0	0	1	2	.133	.188

A right fielder with a strong arm, Monds' season was cut short when his hand was broken by a pitch.

DAMIAN MOSS Bats: R Throws: L Ht: 6-0 Wt: 187
Born: 11/24/1976 Drafted: NDFA 7-30-93 ATL Position: P

YR TEAM	LG/CLASS	G	GS	GF	SV	W	L	ERA	IP	H	HR	BB	SO	O/BA
95 Macon	SAL/A	27	27	0	0	9	10	3.56	149.1	134	13	70	177	.236

The 19-year-old converted outfielder had 15 games with seven or more strikeouts, including five games with 10+ on his way to leading the organization in whiffs.

RAMON NUNEZ Bats: R Throws: R Ht: 6-0 Wt: 150
Born: 9/22/1972 Drafted: NDFA 2-12-89 ATL Position: 1B

YR TEAM	LG/CLASS	G	AB	R	H	2B	3B	HR	RBI	SB	BA	OBA
95 Greenville	SOU/AA	81	241	34	63	15	2	9	34	1	.261	.309
95 Durham	CARO/A	17	54	13	20	4	0	5	15	0	.370	.444

The Dominican native hit .310 with seven homers at hitter-friendly Greenville Municipal Stadium, but just .192 with two homers away from home in 81 games at Double-A.

CAREY PAIGE Bats: R Throws: R Ht: 6-3 Wt: 175
Born: 3/2/1974 Drafted: 1992 #3 ATL Position: P

YR TEAM	LG/CLASS	G	GS	GF	SV	W	L	ERA	IP	H	HR	BB	SO	O/BA
95 Greenville	SOU/AA	7	7	0	0	1	4	5.01	41.1	45	5	11	26	.268
95 Durham	CARO/A	10	10	0	0	5	3	3.38	64.0	53	8	15	37	.229

Paige recorded five straight wins to earn a promotion to Double-A after starting the season disabled with strained knee ligaments.

PEDRO SWANN Bats: L Throws: R Ht: 6-0 Wt: 195
Born: 10/27/1970 Drafted: 1991 #26 ATL Position: OF

YR TEAM	LG/CLASS	G	AB	R	H	2B	3B	HR	RBI	SB	BA	OBA
95 Richmond	INT/AAA	15	38	2	8	1	0	0	3	0	.211	.250
95 Greenville	SOU/AA	102	339	57	110	24	2	11	64	14	.324	.405

The Southern League's top hitter in June with a .413 mark, the lefty hitter finished third in the league in on-base percentage and hung in well against southpaws.

MIKE WARNER Bats: L Throws: L Ht: 5-10 Wt: 170
Born: 5/9/1971 Drafted: 1992 #22 ATL Position: OF

YR TEAM	LG/CLASS	G	AB	R	H	2B	3B	HR	RBI	SB	BA	OBA
95 Richmond	INT/AAA	28	97	10	20	4	1	2	8	0	.206	.287
95 Greenville	SOU/AA	53	173	31	41	12	0	0	7	12	.237	.399

A line drive hitter with some pop, the lefty-hitting Warner can play all three outfield positions.

RON WRIGHT Bats: R Throws: R Ht: 6-0 Wt: 215
Born: 1/21/1976 Drafted: 1994 #9 ATL Position: 1B

YR TEAM	LG/CLASS	G	AB	R	H	2B	3B	HR	RBI	SB	BA	OBA
95 Macon	SAL/A	135	527	93	143	23	1	32	104	2	.271	.348

A consistent slugger who finished first in the organization in both homers and RBI, only once did Wright go three games without a hit.

CHICAGO CUBS

JIM BULLINGER

Position: SP
Bats: R **Throws:** R
Ht: 6'2" **Wt:** 185
Opening Day Age: 30
Born: 8/21/1965
Drafted: CHN86 9/220
ML Seasons: 4

SCOUTING REPORT
The Louisiana native uses a plus curve with good rotation and a big break as his out pitch. Bullinger throws from a three-quarters motion with average control, sinking his slightly below-average fastball also throwing a cut fastball at times. His change-up is average.

"Bully" is intelligent on the mound, working hitters well, and keeps the ball low. Unfortunately, he nibbles too much and falls behind in the count, and his low deliveries can be hard for catchers to scoop up with runners moving.

Despite an average move to first, he allowed a whopping 27 runners to steal against him in 31 tries last year. A converted shortstop, Jim is a well above-average fielder.

HOW HE PERFORMED IN '95
Bullinger pitched well in a swing role during 1994, and came to camp in 1995 ready to assume a spot in the rotation. Given the opening day assignment, he threw six shutout innings at the Reds. From this auspicious beginning, Bullinger did a tremendous job for much of the season despite missing a month with tendinitis in his right elbow.

On August 16, Jim was 10-2 with a 2.71 ERA, a mark ranking fifth in the league, and had walked just 34 men in 99.2 innings. From that point, however, Bullinger's season fell apart. He couldn't get the ball over the plate and allowed 39 earned runs in his final 50.1 innings, for a lofty 6.97 ERA.

Whether he was hurting is open to question, given the earlier elbow injury. However, Bullinger took his turn every five days and never complained. He just didn't make good pitches.

Jim hit just .128 in 47 at-bats, but smacked three doubles and laid down eight sacrifice bunts. As a former infielder, he is one of the better-hitting pitchers in the league.

WHAT TO EXPECT IN '96
The Cubs expect Bullinger to be in their rotation again this season, but he can't hang around pitching the way he did during the last six weeks of 1995. Control has always come and gone for Bullinger, but he put the ball where he wanted it early last year, giving the Cubs hope that he can solve his problems.

Overall Statistics

	G	GS	GF	SV	W	L	ERA	IP	H	R	ER	HR	BB	SO
95 CHN	24	24	0	0	12	8	4.14	150.0	152	80	69	14	65	93
Career	111	43	31	10	21	18	4.12	351.2	329	181	161	30	162	211

1995 Situational Statistics

	W	L	ERA	SV	IP	BB	SO		AB	HR	RBI	BA	OBA	SLG
Home	4	5	5.54	0	76.1	34	47	LHB	264	5	36	.273	.377	.409
Road	8	3	2.69	0	73.2	31	46	RHB	310	9	36	.258	.318	.400
Apr-Jun	4	1	3.14	0	43.0	15	22	ScPos	142	3	55	.282	.399	.437
Jul-Oct	8	7	4.54	0	107.0	50	71	Clutch	23	2	5	.348	.423	.696

How He Compares to Other Pitchers

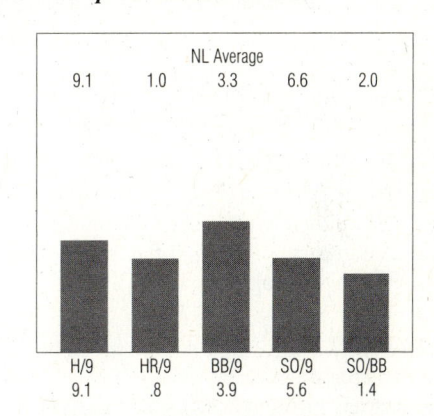

NL Average: H/9 9.1, HR/9 1.0, BB/9 3.3, SO/9 6.6, SO/BB 2.0

Bullinger: H/9 9.1, HR/9 .8, BB/9 3.9, SO/9 5.6, SO/BB 1.4

How He Compares to Other Starting Pitchers

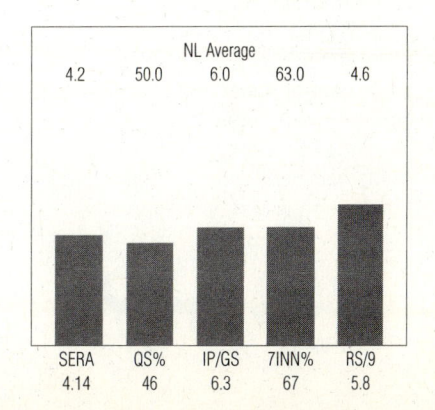

NL Average: SERA 4.2, QS% 50.0, IP/GS 6.0, 7INN% 63.0, RS/9 4.6

Bullinger: SERA 4.14, QS% 46, IP/GS 6.3, 7INN% 67, RS/9 5.8

CHICAGO CUBS

FRANK CASTILLO

Position: SP
Bats: R **Throws:** R
Ht: 6'1" **Wt:** 180
Opening Day Age: 26
Born: 4/1/1969
Drafted: CHN87 5/140
ML Seasons: 5

SCOUTING REPORT
Frank Castillo does everything right on the mound except throw hard. His power pitches (sinking fastball and slider) are below-average, but his other offerings are much better. Frank's circle change, his out pitch, is one of the best in the league. His plus curve has good bite and gets him many strikeouts. He is a good fielder and a decent athlete.

HOW HE PERFORMED IN '95
Castillo was arguably the Cubs' best starting pitcher last season after missing most of 1994 with a finger injury. His control was outstanding, as he walked fewer than two and a half men per game and rarely had to come in with fastballs when down in the count. His mix of pitches, control, and durability made the Cubs' rotation much better than anyone had expected.

The Cubs' desperate wild-card chase was punctuated by Castillo's dominating one-hitter over St. Louis on September 25, in which he fanned a career-best 13 hitters. Only Bernard Gilkey's ninth-inning, two-out triple kept Frank from the record books.

Often it seemed Castillo had to throw a shutout to win: his teammates gave him just 3.8 runs a game of support. In 16 of his starts, he allowed two or fewer earned runs, and only twice did he surrender as many as five runs in a start.

Castillo has a plus move to first, maybe the best on the staff, and gets rid of the ball in a hurry. Only 19 runners tried to steal against him last year, 12 successfully.

He has a poor .114 average and no extra-base hits in 211 career at-bats. Last season, Frank hit just .102 in 59 tries, but laid down seven sacrifices.

WHAT TO EXPECT IN '96
Frank credited getting married with centering him for 1995, and with a good year under his belt, there's no reason he can't pitch this well again in 1996. The Cubs will count heavily on Castillo, but should monitor his strength; although he pitched two shutouts last September, he also had his three shortest outings in that month.

Overall Statistics

	G	GS	GF	SV	W	L	ERA	IP	H	R	ER	HR	BB	SO
95 CHN	29	29	0	0	11	10	3.21	188.0	179	75	67	22	52	135
Career	113	109	0	0	34	37	3.86	669.1	652	318	287	69	192	446

1995 Situational Statistics

	W	L	ERA	SV	IP	BB	SO		AB	HR	RBI	BA	OBA	SLG
Home	5	6	2.78	0	90.2	24	70	LHB	309	6	23	.256	.325	.362
Road	6	4	3.61	0	97.1	28	65	RHB	414	16	46	.242	.285	.386
Apr-Jun	6	4	2.86	0	78.2	20	57	ScPos	146	1	45	.226	.333	.274
Jul-Oct	5	6	3.46	0	109.1	32	78	Clutch	79	3	8	.278	.333	.430

How He Compares to Other Starting Pitchers

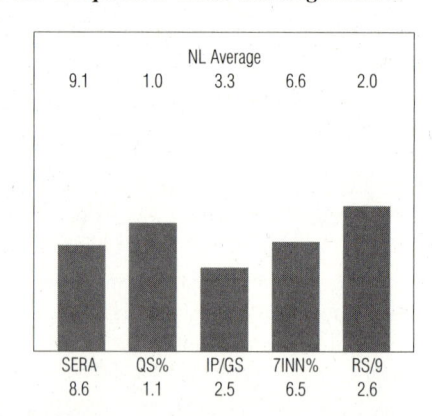

NL Average
9.1   1.0   3.3   6.6   2.0

SERA   QS%   IP/GS   7INN%   RS/9
8.6   1.1   2.5   6.5   2.6

How He Compares to Other Starting Pitchers

NL Average
4.2   50.0   6.0   63.0   4.6

SERA   IP/GR   9INN%   IRS%   SV%
3.21   66   6.5   69   4.0

346 — THE SCOUTING REPORT: 1996

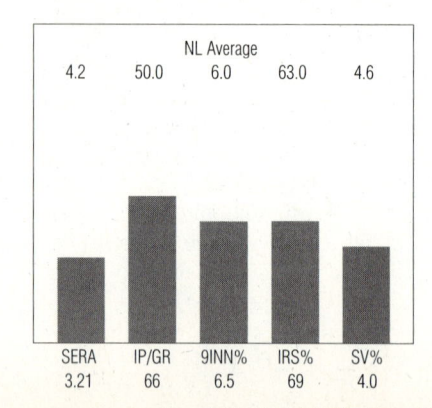

CHICAGO CUBS

SHAWON DUNSTON

Position: SS
Bats: R **Throws:** R
Ht: 6'1" **Wt:** 175
Opening Day Age: 33
Born: 3/21/1963
Drafted: CHN82 1/1
ML Seasons: 11

SCOUTING REPORT
Shawon Dunston still has a very quick bat that generates power on high and inside pitches. However, he has never mastered the strike zone and chases way too many bad pitches. He still has well above-average speed, but didn't use it much last season. Shawon is a pretty good bunter, both for base hits and sacrifices.

In the field, his arm strength remains outstanding and his accuracy has improved. In past seasons Dunston regularly overshot the first basemen, but he now has average aim. Shawon has good hands and is especially good going into the hole. His range is average-minus only because he has trouble reading some types of ground balls and tries to "circle" them instead of charging them.

HOW HE PERFORMED IN '95
For Dunston to miss nearly two years of action with back problems and return at nearly full strength in 1994 was a tremendous achievement. Shawon worked hard to come back, showed his trademark hustle, and by year's end had established that he can still play shortstop almost every day in the majors.

He still needed to rest on artificial turf and in very cold weather, but did play 125 games at shortstop and performed at levels close to his past. His batting average was the best of his career and he showed good power. Dunston is one of few players who hits well drawing few bases on balls, but his worrisome 7.5 to 1 strikeout/walk ratio of 1995 is his worst ever by far.

WHAT TO EXPECT IN '96
In late July, Dunston was hitting well over .340, second-best in the NL, but sagged badly over the last two months, batting only .232. Whether this, and his K/W numbers, indicate an imminent decline is a question the Cubs have to answer this winter.

Ryne Sandberg's decision to come back could end Shawon's career in Chicago if the Cubs move Rey Sanchez to short. Sandberg might also end up at third, allowing Chicago to re-sign their popular free-agent shortstop. At age 33, Dunston's long-term value is in question.

Overall Statistics

	G	AB	R	H	2B	3B	HR	RBI	SB	CS	BB	SO	BA	OBA
95 CHN	127	477	58	141	30	6	14	69	10	5	10	75	.296	.317
Career	1140	4151	506	1100	208	44	98	448	146	64	163	706	.265	.294

1995 Situational Statistics

	AB	HR	RBI	BA	OBA	SLG		AB	HR	RBI	BA	OBA	SLG
Home	232	8	37	.306	.321	.474	LHP	138	5	24	.348	.372	.543
Road	245	6	32	.286	.313	.469	RHP	339	9	45	.274	.293	.442
Apr-Jun	192	6	32	.333	.345	.521	ScPos	121	4	55	.339	.362	.504
Jul-Oct	285	8	37	.270	.298	.439	Clutch	84	3	10	.333	.371	.548

How He Compares to Other Batters

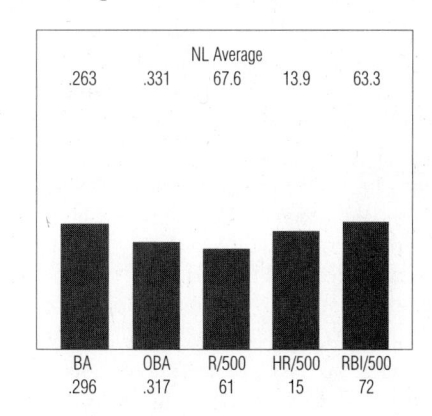

NL Average: .263 .331 67.6 13.9 63.3

BA .296 | OBA .317 | R/500 61 | HR/500 15 | RBI/500 72

Where He Hits the Ball

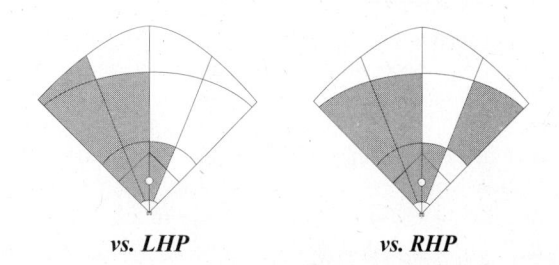

vs. LHP | vs. RHP

CHICAGO CUBS

KEVIN FOSTER

Position: SP
Bats: R **Throws:** R
Ht: 6'1" **Wt:** 160
Opening Day Age: 27
Born: 1/13/1969
Drafted: MON87 31/746
ML Seasons: 3

SCOUTING REPORT

Kevin really has only two pitches. His four-seam fastball had only average or slightly-above velocity at times last season but was "sneaky fast." However, it didn't have the velocity to be as high in the strike zone as he used it. Most of his many home runs are allowed on this pitch.

The best thing Foster has is a well above-average change with deceptive arm action. He will throw the pitch any time with confidence. The Cubs are working with Kevin on developing his curve and slider, both of which are just average and are underused at this point.

He throws across his body with a three-quarters motion. Foster's mechanics are good and his control average, and he knows how to pitch despite limited experience. Kevin is a plus fielder with a plus move to first; while 21 men tried to steal against him in 1995, ten were caught.

HOW HE PERFORMED IN '95

How does a pitcher hold righthanded batters to a .221 average, strike out nearly a man per inning, cut down the running game, and allow opponents a .315 on-base percentage—and still have a 4.51 earned run average? Foster did it by allowing an NL-high 32 home runs.

His propensity for allowing long balls at inopportune times haunted him all season, but should not overshadow the considerable talents of a relatively inexperienced youngster. Originally a shortstop, Kevin moved to pitching in 1990. Coming into 1995, he had made only 29 starts above Double-A.

Foster can hit. He came into 1995 with a 2-for-29 lifetime mark, but last year he batted .250 in 60 at-bats with 9 RBI. However, bunting is not one of his better skills.

WHAT TO EXPECT IN '96

Foster, whose acquisition for Shawn Boskie was one of former Cubs' GM Larry Himes' better deals, has considerable talent and will likely be in the Cubs' rotation again. His pitching coach, Fergie Jenkins, used to give up plenty of home runs and win plenty of games, and if Foster adds a third pitch and improves the location of his fastball, he's capable of winning 15 games a season.

Overall Statistics

	G	GS	GF	SV	W	L	ERA	IP	H	R	ER	HR	BB	SO
95 CHN	30	28	1	0	12	11	4.51	167.2	149	90	84	32	65	146
Career	45	42	1	0	15	16	4.27	255.1	232	132	121	42	107	227

1995 Situational Statistics

	W	L	ERA	SV	IP	BB	SO		AB	HR	RBI	BA	OBA	SLG
Home	7	4	4.15	0	78.0	26	64	LHB	287	12	28	.261	.324	.432
Road	5	7	4.82	0	89.2	39	82	RHB	335	20	51	.221	.307	.451
Apr-Jun	5	5	5.40	0	66.2	31	58	ScPos	114	5	47	.246	.361	.412
Jul-Oct	7	6	3.92	0	101.0	34	88	Clutch	37	4	10	.270	.349	.649

How He Compares to Other Pitchers

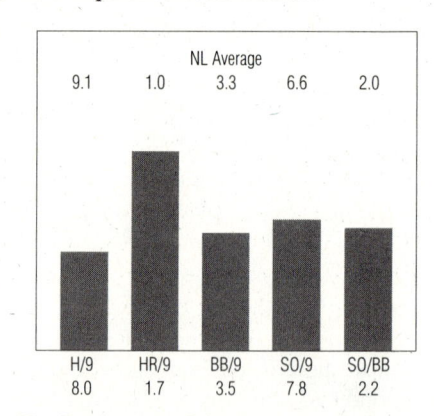

NL Average: 9.1 | 1.0 | 3.3 | 6.6 | 2.0

H/9: 8.0 | HR/9: 1.7 | BB/9: 3.5 | SO/9: 7.8 | SO/BB: 2.2

How He Compares to Other Starting Pitchers

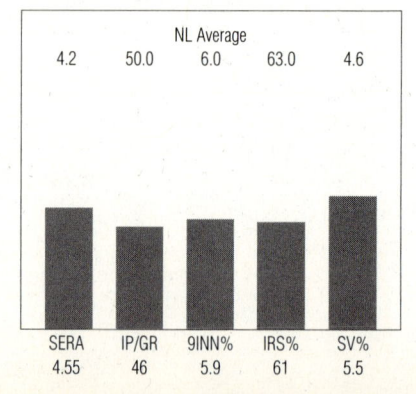

NL Average: 4.2 | 50.0 | 6.0 | 63.0 | 4.6

SERA: 4.55 | IP/GR: 46 | 9INN%: 5.9 | IRS%: 61 | SV%: 5.5

CHICAGO CUBS

LUIS GONZALEZ

Position: OF
Bats: L **Throws:** R
Ht: 6'2" **Wt:** 180
Opening Day Age: 28
Born: 9/3/1967
Drafted: HOU88 5/90
ML Seasons: 6

SCOUTING REPORT
Luis is thin and somewhat gawky-looking, but is a very graceful baseball player. He has plus speed and is an above-average baserunner, despite poor basestealing totals of late.

Gonzalez is a fine left fielder with well above-average hands. His arm has minus strength but is very accurate. He positions himself well, gets an excellent first step on fly balls, and shows excellent range every season. He gets to balls many other left fielders couldn't even approach.

At the plate, he likes breaking balls and off-speed pitches low and over the plate. Line-drive power to all fields is his game. Luis is not especially disciplined at bat, and does not hit good fastballs because of below-average bat speed. He bunted just once last year.

HOW HE PERFORMED IN '95
When Houston woke up in June with three left-handed hitting left fielders (Gonzalez, Phil Plantier, and Derrick May), it was apparent that at least one of them would soon be gone. Gonzalez was dealt to Chicago on June 30 with Scott Servais for Rick Wilkins, and most feel the Cubs got a steal.

Gonzalez, who had always hit the Cubs well, chipped in his share of big hits for Chicago. Perhaps the biggest was a game-winning tenth-inning single against his old team on September 29 that kept the Cubs in the wild-card hunt. He batted .290 with seven homers in 77 games after the trade, and showed enough on-base skill that he hit leadoff more than once. However, he had very poor basestealing numbers in 1995 after swiping 35 sacks the previous two years.

WHAT TO EXPECT IN '96
This winter, Gonzalez' status with the Cubs was uncertain. He showed plenty of interest in coming back for 1996, but Chicago had other free agents they wanted to concentrate on first. He's a good player both in the field and at bat, but needs to have a big year—somewhere—in order to avoid becoming an itinerant fill-in.

Overall Statistics

	G	AB	R	H	2B	3B	HR	RBI	SB	CS	BB	SO	BA	OBA
95 HO/CH	133	471	69	130	29	8	13	69	6	8	57	63	.276	.357
Career	670	2284	300	617	141	27	59	332	58	44	219	361	.270	.338

1995 Situational Statistics

	AB	HR	RBI	BA	OBA	SLG		AB	HR	RBI	BA	OBA	SLG
Home	230	6	33	.274	.365	.430	LHP	112	4	19	.268	.346	.500
Road	241	7	36	.278	.350	.477	RHP	359	9	50	.279	.361	.440
Apr-Jun	217	6	35	.253	.315	.419	ScPos	134	2	51	.284	.400	.418
Jul-Oct	254	7	34	.295	.391	.484	Clutch	75	3	8	.240	.329	.373

How He Compares to Other Batters

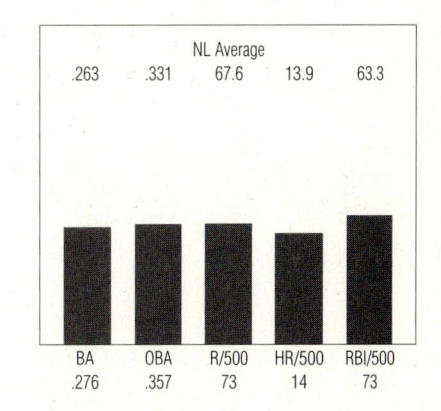

	BA	OBA	R/500	HR/500	RBI/500
NL Average	.263	.331	67.6	13.9	63.3
	.276	.357	73	14	73

Where He Hits the Ball

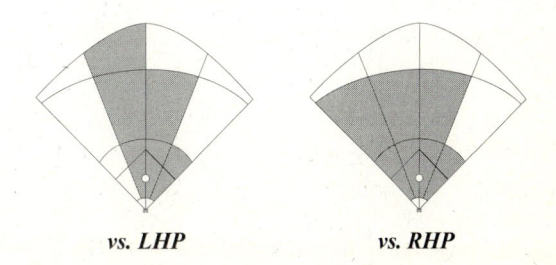

vs. LHP   vs. RHP

THE SCOUTING REPORT: 1996

CHICAGO CUBS

MARK GRACE

Position: 1B
Bats: L **Throws:** L
Ht: 6'2" **Wt:** 190
Opening Day Age: 31
Born: 6/28/1964
Drafted: CHN85 25/624
ML Seasons: 8

SCOUTING REPORT

"Amazing" Grace is a smart, disciplined hitter who will go with a pitch and drive it anywhere. He has alley power and is a very smart situational hitter. However, Mark can be jammed and is best when he can extend his arms. The two-time All Star has average-minus power and a relatively slow bat, but makes excellent contact.

Mark has minus speed but is an intelligent baserunner who knows his limitations. He runs hard.

At first base, Grace is one of the best and turned in his trademark Gold Glove-caliber defense at first base. He has a plus arm with average accuracy, well above-average hands, and plus range.

HOW HE PERFORMED IN '95

1995 was Mark Grace's best season. He finished fifth in the league in batting, eighth in on-base percentage, and tenth in slugging percentage, largely because of his league-leading 51 doubles—the highest two-bagger total by an NL hitter since 1978.

He led the Cubs in most offensive categories and kicked in a career-high 16 homers as well. He has hit at least .275 against lefthanders every year since 1989. All in all, it was a strong free-agent campaign.

Mark missed just one game despite suffering plenty of nagging injuries, including a painful hip pointer. His teammates value Grace's grit and drive in the clubhouse, and reporters love talking to him, because he's approachable, self-deprecating, and "gives good quote."

WHAT TO EXPECT IN '96

At 1995 levels, Grace is one of the best first basemen in the game. However, he's highly unlikely to repeat at this level in 1996. Mark is extremely popular in Chicago, and in the past, his fan appeal was sometimes much higher than his performance warranted. Grace doesn't show the pop associated with a corner infielder, and if he's not hitting .300, his value is substantially reduced.

However, he may end up a Cub for several more seasons. Re-signing Mark would force the Cubs to open up the outfield for power-hitting young Brooks Kieschnick, who appears to be a first baseman waiting to happen.

Overall Statistics

	G	AB	R	H	2B	3B	HR	RBI	SB	CS	BB	SO	BA	OBA
95 CHN	143	552	97	180	51	3	16	92	6	2	65	46	.326	.395
Career	1155	4356	608	1333	261	28	82	589	55	28	525	347	.306	.379

1995 Situational Statistics

	AB	HR	RBI	BA	OBA	SLG		AB	HR	RBI	BA	OBA	SLG
Home	280	4	41	.375	.421	.550	LHP	186	3	30	.290	.330	.430
Road	272	12	51	.276	.369	.482	RHP	366	13	62	.344	.425	.560
Apr-Jun	229	9	42	.336	.395	.594	ScPos	129	1	66	.310	.425	.473
Jul-Oct	323	7	50	.319	.395	.461	Clutch	89	2	7	.348	.420	.472

How He Compares to Other Batters

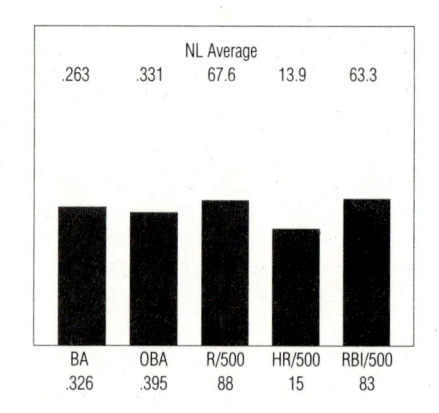

	BA	OBA	R/500	HR/500	RBI/500
NL Average	.263	.331	67.6	13.9	63.3
	.326	.395	88	15	83

Where He Hits the Ball

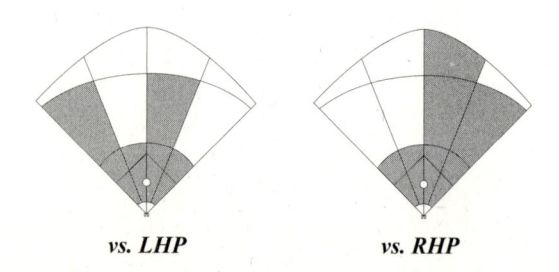

vs. LHP   vs. RHP

CHICAGO CUBS

BRIAN MCRAE

Position: OF
Bats: B **Throws:** R
Ht: 6'0" **Wt:** 175
Opening Day Age: 28
Born: 8/27/1967
Drafted: KC85 1/17
ML Seasons: 6

SCOUTING REPORT

Brian McRae fits the classic switch-hitting pattern of going after low balls as a lefty and high pitches righthanded. However, he can't handle inside fastballs on either side. McRae has some power, displays well above-average speed and steals bases. Last year, he bunted often, but surprisingly ineffectively.

Brian has well-above average hands and is a master at flashy catches. His great speed allows him to go a long way for fly balls, although his range has not been exceptional in the past, most likely due to his positioning. His arm is minus with average-minus accuracy, so McRae charges in on base hits in order to compensate.

HOW HE PERFORMED IN '95

If asked to pick a team leader, most Cubs would select Brian McRae. He gave Chicago good production at bat, provided solid defense in center field, hustled every day, and played through numerous injuries that might have shelved others. While he doesn't walk enough to be a good leadoff man, he accepted the role given to him and kicked in extra-base pop and stolen bases.

The speedy and athletic McRae dazzled Cubs fans with diving grabs, but didn't amaze anyone with his sub-average arm, collecting just four assists all season. He plays very shallow, which sometimes leads to extra-base hits over his head but cuts off popfly singles to short center. Brian made only three errors all season. There are some terrific center fielders in the NL, and McRae isn't quite up there with Steve Finley or Marquis Grissom.

WHAT TO EXPECT IN '96

Brian was a free agent after the season, but Chicago was expected to ink him to a multi-year deal. He is seen as one of the team's building blocks for future success. Despite McRae's good season at the dish, however, the Cubs still need a true leadoff hitter. Brian will do whatever Jim Riggleman asks, but a move down in the order would better fit his offensive skills.

Overall Statistics

	G	AB	R	H	2B	3B	HR	RBI	SB	CS	BB	SO	BA	OBA
95 CHN	137	580	92	167	38	7	12	48	27	8	47	92	.288	.348
Career	751	2973	411	794	147	39	42	296	120	49	213	480	.267	.320

1995 Situational Statistics

	AB	HR	RBI	BA	OBA	SLG		AB	HR	RBI	BA	OBA	SLG
Home	283	6	30	.286	.350	.428	LHP	163	2	12	.313	.333	.429
Road	297	6	18	.290	.346	.451	RHP	417	10	36	.278	.353	.444
Apr-Jun	243	5	22	.272	.331	.436	ScPos	108	1	37	.287	.371	.370
Jul-Oct	337	7	26	.300	.360	.442	Clutch	92	2	8	.261	.333	.435

How He Compares to Other Batters

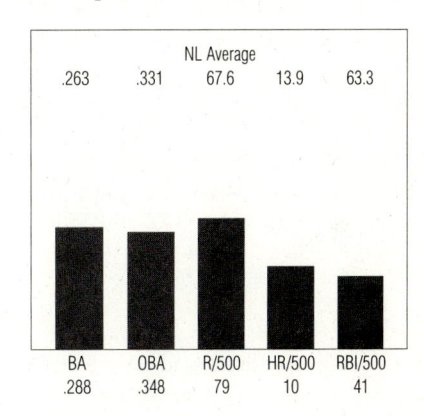

NL Average: .263 .331 67.6 13.9 63.3

BA	OBA	R/500	HR/500	RBI/500
.288	.348	79	10	41

Where He Hits the Ball

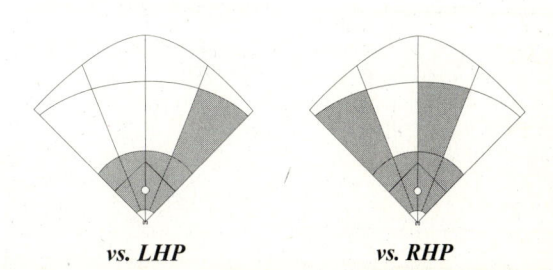

vs. LHP   vs. RHP

THE SCOUTING REPORT: 1996

CHICAGO CUBS

RANDY MYERS

Position: RP
Bats: L **Throws:** L
Ht: 6'1" **Wt:** 190
Opening Day Age: 33
Born: 9/19/1962
Drafted: NYN82 S1/9
ML Seasons: 11

SCOUTING REPORT

When he pitches inside and works aggressively, Myers is still one of the best closers in baseball. However, he has bouts of poor control and has lost a little off his fastball.

He throws with a high three-quarters to overhand delivery and still has an average-plus heater that tails in to lefthanded batters. His slider is just average, and his curve and changeup are rarely taken out of mothballs.

Myers has worked hard on his pickoff move, which was rated as minus. Only three runners tried to steal on him last season and two were thrown out. He lacks quickness off the mound and is a below-average fielder. Randy is 11 for 59 (.186) in his career—good for a relief pitcher—with his only plate appearance of 1995 resulting in a walk.

HOW HE PERFORMED IN '95

It was an eventful season for Randy Myers. He led the NL in saves for the second time in the last three seasons, completely squelched lefthanded hitters, and made the All-Star team for the third time. He also provided some non-baseball entertainment on September 28 at Wrigley Field: in one of the season's more bizarre events, Myers slugged a crazed fan who ran onto the diamond and charged the relief ace after he allowed a key home run.

He doesn't have the fastball he once did and throws more sliders than he used to, but Randy still strikes out plenty of hitters by spotting his fastball effectively and is fearless against lefties. Control was a problem at times for Myers last season, as he walked a batter every two innings. However, he avoided a prolonged slump and is still a superior closer.

WHAT TO EXPECT IN '96

The Cubs are working to bring free-agent Myers back, although young Terry Adams is viewed by management as the team's future closer. Randy won't give up the job quietly, however, and if the Cubs don't want him to return, there are plenty of clubs who will.

Overall Statistics

	G	GS	GF	SV	W	L	ERA	IP	H	R	ER	HR	BB	SO
95 CHN	57	0	47	38	1	2	3.88	55.2	49	25	24	7	28	59
Career	543	12	399	243	34	49	3.17	709.2	592	271	250	54	319	713

1995 Situational Statistics

	W	L	ERA	SV	IP	BB	SO		AB	HR	RBI	BA	OBA	SLG
Home	0	0	4.50	17	26.0	16	31	LHB	46	0	6	.130	.196	.196
Road	1	2	3.34	21	29.2	12	28	RHB	161	7	27	.267	.358	.453
Apr-Jun	0	1	2.70	16	23.1	13	26	ScPos	58	3	27	.293	.397	.534
Jul-Oct	1	1	4.73	22	32.1	15	33	Clutch	168	6	32	.256	.333	.435

How He Compares to Other Pitchers

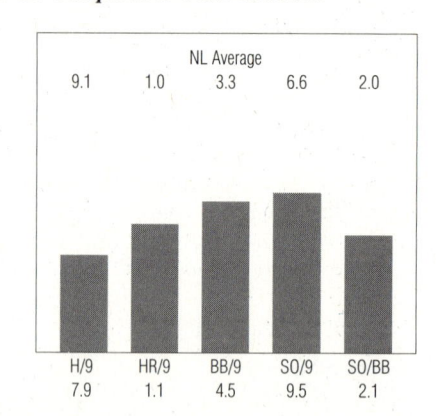

	H/9	HR/9	BB/9	SO/9	SO/BB
NL Average	9.1	1.0	3.3	6.6	2.0
	7.9	1.1	4.5	9.5	2.1

How He Compares to Other Relief Pitchers

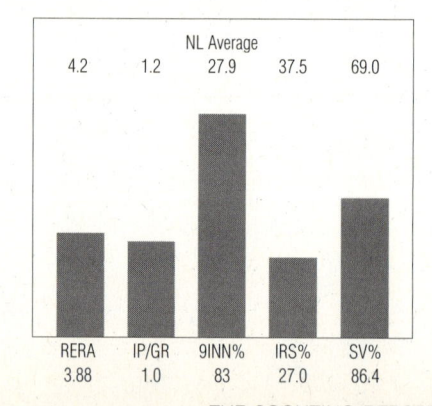

	RERA	IP/GR	9INN%	IRS%	SV%
NL Average	4.2	1.2	27.9	37.5	69.0
	3.88	1.0	83	27.0	86.4

CHICAGO CUBS

JAIME NAVARRO

Position: SP
Bats: R **Throws:** R
Ht: 6'4" **Wt:** 210
Opening Day Age: 29
Born: 3/27/1967
Drafted: MIL87 4/71
ML Seasons: 7

SCOUTING REPORT
Navarro hasn't been consistent so far, having good years and bad. When he pitches well, he uses his high three-quarters, cross-body motion to deliver two strong pitches with average control.

His average-plus fastball improved in velocity last year and has good sink, and his plus slider has a short, quick, late break. Jaime's change-up is a minus offering, largely because he tips it off by slowing down his pitching motion. It's hard for starting pitchers to succeed over the long haul with only two quality deliveries.

For an AL refugee, Navarro did quite well at bat, hitting .185 with five doubles. He's big, but runs well and is an average fielder. His pickoff move is rated as minus, and 16 of 22 basestealers were successful against Jaime in 1995.

HOW HE PERFORMED IN '95
After successful seasons in 1991–92, Navarro apparently fell into poor work habits and conditioning. He lost his command and pitched his way right out of Milwaukee, which is not easy to do. Signed by the Cubs for 1995, Jaime won his first five decisions en route to his best season in the majors, pacing the staff in innings and wins and walking just two and a half batters per game.

Navarro kept the ball down consistently, held the fort against both lefties and righties and, despite not really being a strikeout pitcher, had seven games where he fanned six or more. He was often dominating, and only three times did he allow five or more earned runs.

WHAT TO EXPECT IN '96
Navarro wants to stay in Chicago and is pursuing a long-term contract. However, whether he will sag after inking such a deal, as he did in Milwaukee, is a question Andy MacPhail has to consider. Jaime showed in 1995 that he is capable of success in a major-league rotation. The challenge now involves improving on what he's got in order to remain at that level.

Overall Statistics

	G	GS	GF	SV	W	L	ERA	IP	H	R	ER	HR	BB	SO
95 CHN	29	29	0	0	14	6	3.28	200.1	194	79	73	19	56	128
Career	212	180	10	1	76	65	4.13	1243.1	1319	630	571	99	374	652

1995 Situational Statistics

	W	L	ERA	SV	IP	BB	SO		AB	HR	RBI	BA	OBA	SLG
Home	5	4	3.24	0	97.1	30	67	LHB	336	7	29	.250	.314	.351
Road	9	2	3.32	0	103.0	26	61	RHB	437	12	40	.252	.295	.371
Apr-Jun	5	2	3.14	0	77.1	20	48	ScPos	167	2	45	.246	.321	.311
Jul-Oct	9	4	3.37	0	123.0	36	80	Clutch	68	0	3	.206	.217	.250

How He Compares to Other Pitchers

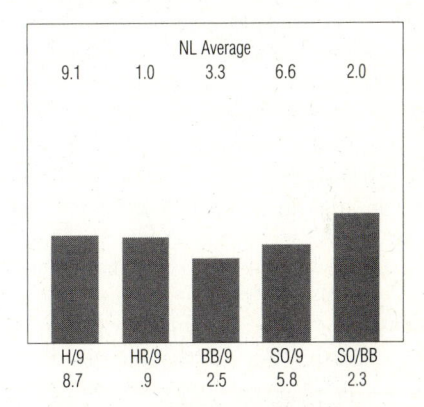

NL Average

H/9	HR/9	BB/9	SO/9	SO/BB
9.1	1.0	3.3	6.6	2.0
8.7	.9	2.5	5.8	2.3

How He Compares to Other Starting Pitchers

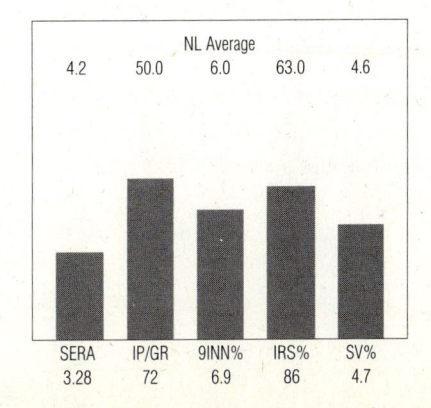

NL Average

SERA	IP/GR	9INN%	IRS%	SV%
4.2	50.0	6.0	63.0	4.6
3.28	72	6.9	86	4.7

CHICAGO CUBS

REY SANCHEZ

Positions: 2B//SS
Bats: R **Throws:** R
Ht: 5'10" **Wt:** 180
Opening Day Age: 28
Born: 10/5/1967
Drafted: TEX86 13/313
ML Seasons: 5

SCOUTING REPORT
Sanchez has good bat control and average bat speed. He hits high and over-the-plate fastballs the other way and likes to hit through the hole. However, he lacks power and doesn't know when to lay off a pitch; consequently, he isn't that much of a threat. Rey is normally a good bunter, although he had a very poor 1995 season in this category.

In the field, he combines plus range and good hands with an above-average arm with average accuracy. The former Rangers' farmhand is mobile and positions himself very well, compensating for his average speed.

HOW HE PERFORMED IN '95
Sanchez opened the year as the Cubs' regular second-sacker for the first time. As usual, he shone in the field, showing excellent range and double-play ability despite mediocre speed. He made only seven errors.

He also showed his basic offensive package. Sanchez makes contact, executes the hit-and-run, and in 1994-95 fared better against righties than lefties. However, Sanchez had problems sacrificing all season, rarely walked, and rarely took pitches while batting second. Jim Riggleman responded by temporarily dropping Sanchez to the #8 hole.

Sanchez was hitting .300 before suffering a broken bone in his left wrist (misdiagnosed as tendinitis) in July. The hand hurt enough that Sanchez missed games in August and September because he literally couldn't swing the bat. When he did play, he wasn't at full strength and his average dipped. His three home runs and 22 doubles aren't impressive but were more than he had produced before. Coming into 1995, Sanchez had just five homers in eight pro seasons.

WHAT TO EXPECT IN '96
His wrist is apparently healed, but Sanchez' role for 1996 depends on whether the Cubs re-sign Shawon Dunston and whether Ryne Sandberg can return as the regular second baseman. Sanchez is a Gold Glove candidate at second as well as a good shortstop.

A lack of punch, speed, and on-base ability indicate that Rey merits a reduced offensive role. If he can't excel at "little ball," then Sanchez has no offensive value. He's going to play because of his excellent defensive skills, however.

Overall Statistics

	G	AB	R	H	2B	3B	HR	RBI	SB	CS	BB	SO	BA	OBA
95 CHN	114	428	57	119	22	2	3	27	6	4	14	48	.278	.301
Career	402	1341	143	369	60	8	4	100	11	11	63	119	.275	.313

1995 Situational Statistics

	AB	HR	RBI	BA	OBA	SLG		AB	HR	RBI	BA	OBA	SLG
Home	197	0	9	.294	.322	.345	LHP	114	1	7	.263	.276	.360
Road	231	3	18	.264	.283	.372	RHP	314	2	20	.283	.310	.360
Apr-Jun	249	0	10	.293	.307	.361	ScPos	86	1	21	.256	.313	.360
Jul-Oct	179	3	17	.257	.293	.358	Clutch	60	2	10	.283	.290	.450

How He Compares to Other Batters

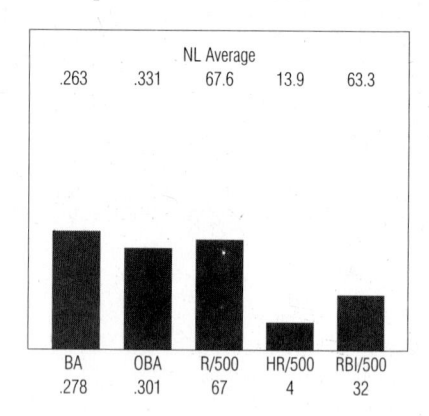

NL Average: .263 .331 67.6 13.9 63.3

BA	OBA	R/500	HR/500	RBI/500
.278	.301	67	4	32

Where He Hits the Ball

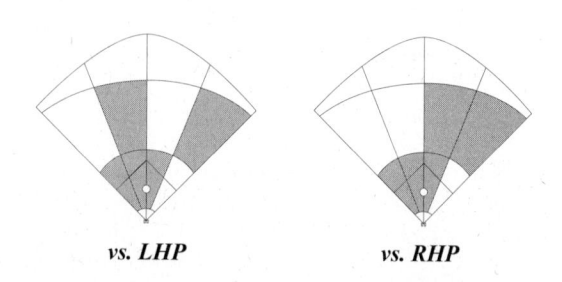

vs. LHP   vs. RHP

CHICAGO CUBS

SCOTT SERVAIS

Position: C
Bats: R **Throws:** R
Ht: 6'2" **Wt:** 195
Opening Day Age: 28
Born: 6/4/1967
Drafted: HOU88 4/64
ML Seasons: 5

SCOUTING REPORT
Scott Servais is a ballplayer of some extremes. He is extremely slow, handles pitchers extremely well, and has had an extremely poor record at throwing out baserunners despite a plus arm with average accuracy. His hands are well above-average but his range is minus.

He likes to hit high fastballs over the plate, but is extremely troubled by breaking balls. Servais' bat speed has improved, as has his strike-zone judgment, which at one time was extremely poor. Although he still whiffs fairly often, he does sport major-league power.

HOW HE PERFORMED IN '95
Servais had lost his job in Houston to Tony Eusebio early in 1995, and he was traded to Chicago on June 30 batting just .224 with one home run. However, Scott was extremely successful in pinstripes, cracking 12 home runs in 175 at-bats with the Cubs and hitting .286.

In previous years, Servais had problems making contact, but he improved substantially in 1995. He hit identically well at home and on the road after his trade to Chicago. Scott generally hits 80 to 100 points higher against lefthanders than righthanders, and certainly profits by leaving the Astrodome.

He has never been lauded for his throwing or agility, but Servais was praised by Cubs' pitchers for his pitch-calling and knowledge of hitters. He threw out just 6 of 33 runners while with Houston, but improved somewhat in Chicago, nailing 18 of 63.

On July 9, Darren Daulton's unnecessary (some said dirty) slide landed Servais on the disabled list for nearly a month with torn knee ligaments, but the injury didn't seem to have lingering effects for the extremely slow catcher when he returned.

WHAT TO EXPECT IN '96
Scott is certain to be back with the Cubs this year and should play 110-120 games, and is likely to continue to hit better playing half his games in Wrigley Field rather than in the Astrodome. Defensively, he's helpful in most areas, a fact that makes the Cubs willing to put up with his below-par throwing.

Overall Statistics

	G	AB	R	H	2B	3B	HR	RBI	SB	CS	BB	SO	BA	OBA
95 HO/CH	80	264	38	70	22	0	13	47	2	2	32	52	.265	.348
Career	336	1015	101	237	60	1	33	141	2	2	79	174	.233	.297

1995 Situational Statistics

	AB	HR	RBI	BA	OBA	SLG		AB	HR	RBI	BA	OBA	SLG
Home	129	8	25	.248	.338	.496	LHP	69	2	18	.348	.447	.594
Road	135	5	22	.281	.358	.496	RHP	195	11	29	.236	.309	.462
Apr-Jun	97	1	12	.227	.296	.361	ScPos	70	1	31	.243	.349	.414
Jul-Oct	167	12	35	.287	.376	.575	Clutch	45	2	7	.311	.385	.489

How He Compares to Other Batters

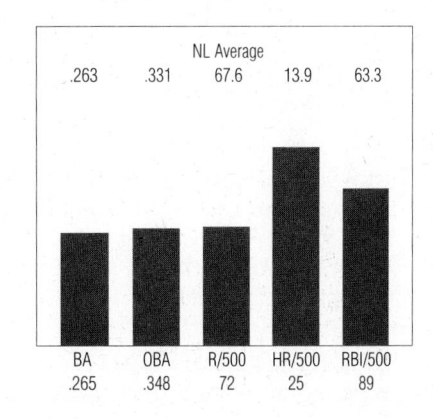

NL Average: .263 .331 67.6 13.9 63.3

BA .265 | OBA .348 | R/500 72 | HR/500 25 | RBI/500 89

Where He Hits the Ball

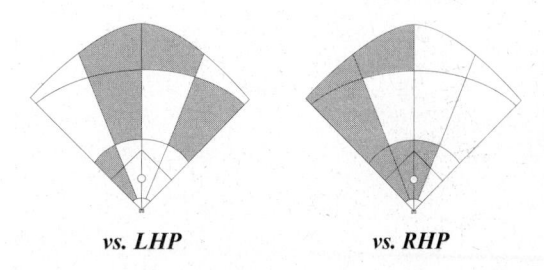

vs. LHP | vs. RHP

CHICAGO CUBS

SAMMY SOSA

Position: OF
Bats: R **Throws:** R
Ht: 6'0" **Wt:** 165
Opening Day Age: 27
Born: 11/12/1968
Drafted: TEX 7/30/85
ML Seasons: 7

SCOUTING REPORT

There is no question concerning the tools of Mr. Samuel Sosa. He has well above-average speed, a well above-average throwing arm with plus accuracy, plus range, well above-average hands, and better than average bat speed and power. In addition, he is attempting to smooth out some of the rough points of his game.

However, he is still at best an erratic talent. His range and hands are prone to slumps, and Sammy's penchant for all-or-nothing swings makes for both frustrating and exhilirating flashes at the plate. Sosa doesn't bunt well, runs the bases like a kamikaze, and still misses cutoff men way too often.

HOW HE PERFORMED IN '95

Sammy enjoyed another excellent season in 1995. The up-and-down Sosa finished second in the NL last year in homers, RBI, and strikeouts. He registered thirteen assists from right field but made made thirteen errors.

Sosa had dominating streaks: he hit ten homers between August 17 and August 30, and was twice named the NL Player of the Week. However, there were also disastrous slumps, including a punchless 15-for-71 swoon to end the season that brought his average down to a mediocre .268.

To his credit, Sosa worked hard in 1995 to cut down on his swing, often taking pitches the other way. However, for the second straight year he hit just 17 doubles; Sammy's uppercut swing creates plenty of homers, popups, and strikeouts, but few line drives.

His 58 walks are below-average for a power hitter, but they ranked second on the team and were easily a career high. Once again he joined the 30-30 club, providing critical baserunning speed on a slow team.

WHAT TO EXPECT IN '96

The Cubs want Sosa back, but the price will be high. Despite his inconsistency, Sosa provides tremendous power and speed and has improved greatly with experience. He is popular with the fans and, although he is still somewhat short of true superstar status, he would be hard to let go free-agent. The question for the Cubs is how many millions he is worth.

Overall Statistics

	G	AB	R	H	2B	3B	HR	RBI	SB	CS	BB	SO	BA	OBA
95 CHN	144	564	89	151	17	3	36	119	34	7	58	134	.268	.340
Career	802	2881	419	738	110	27	131	423	159	65	198	719	.256	.308

1995 Situational Statistics

	AB	HR	RBI	BA	OBA	SLG		AB	HR	RBI	BA	OBA	SLG
Home	276	19	62	.272	.342	.514	LHP	148	9	27	.257	.345	.493
Road	288	17	57	.264	.339	.486	RHP	416	27	92	.272	.338	.502
Apr-Jun	245	14	48	.286	.335	.502	ScPos	163	14	84	.344	.441	.656
Jul-Oct	319	22	71	.254	.344	.498	Clutch	84	3	11	.226	.330	.345

How He Compares to Other Batters

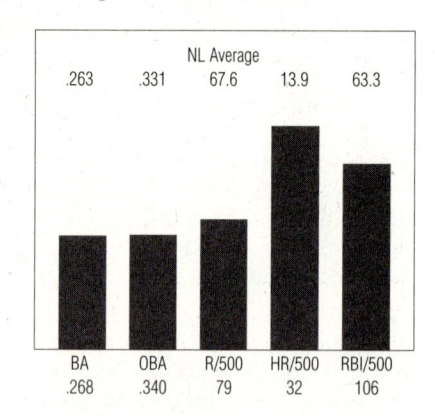

NL Average: .263 / .331 / 67.6 / 13.9 / 63.3

BA	OBA	R/500	HR/500	RBI/500
.268	.340	79	32	106

Where He Hits the Ball

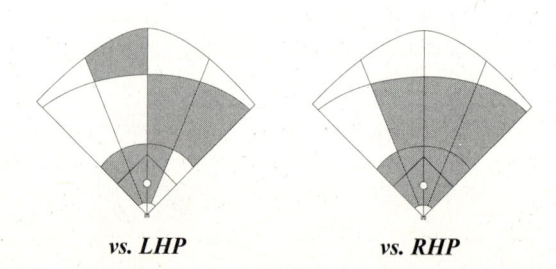

vs. LHP   vs. RHP

CHICAGO CUBS

STEVE TRACHSEL

Position: SP
Bats: R **Throws:** R
Ht: 6'3" **Wt:** 185
Opening Day Age: 25
Born: 10/31/1970
Drafted: CHN91 7/215
ML Seasons: 3

SCOUTING REPORT

Steve Trachsel doesn't look comfortable to hit against. He uses a jerky three-quarters motion to deliver an average-plus fastball that has good movement, especially in on the fists of righthanders. His curve is plus with good rotation.

However, his formerly plus splitter was just average in 1995 and his control was surprisingly poor last year as well. He must regain his command of the splitfinger pitch in order to be less vulnerable to the home run ball in the future.

Trachsel hustles, is very intelligent, and is a plus fielder with a plus move to first. However, concentration troubles led to 20 of 26 basestealing attempts being successful, the worst ratio among Cubs' starters. He batted .265 in 49 at-bats, raising his career average to an excellent .224.

HOW HE PERFORMED IN '95

Somebody pulled a fast one on the Cubs, replacing the Steve Trachsel who anchored the staff in 1994 with a fellow, also named Steve Trachsel, who didn't resemble the old pitcher at all.

This new Trachsel struggled with his control, routinely forgot about baserunners, worked slowly, and spent an inordinate amount of time nibbling around the corners—all indications of a pitcher fighting confidence problems.

Trachsel couldn't string three straight good starts together in 1995. He walked four or more hitters in 11 of his appearances and, despite not going after hitters as he had in 1994, still tied for second in the league in home runs allowed. His well-documented problems winning in Wrigley Field were mostly due to bad luck in 1994, but last season his home ERA was well over six.

While Steve did pitch poorly, he didn't blame anyone but himself and took the ball every time. His velocity was there and he looked strong, but Trachsel just didn't do what he needed to do in order to win.

WHAT TO EXPECT IN '96

He'll get another shot at the rotation this year. The physical talent is there; all he needs now is to deliver on his potential. However, if he doesn't believe in himself and have command of his pitches, Trachsel isn't going to be very successful.

Overall Statistics

	G	GS	GF	SV	W	L	ERA	IP	H	R	ER	HR	BB	SO
95 CHN	30	29	0	0	7	13	5.15	160.2	174	104	92	25	76	117
Career	55	54	0	0	16	22	4.25	326.1	323	171	154	48	133	239

1995 Situational Statistics

	W	L	ERA	SV	IP	BB	SO		AB	HR	RBI	BA	OBA	SLG
Home	2	8	6.19	0	75.2	38	63	LHB	295	13	38	.254	.343	.444
Road	5	5	4.24	0	85.0	38	54	RHB	334	12	46	.296	.360	.461
Apr-Jun	2	6	4.06	0	71.0	29	57	ScPos	142	4	55	.282	.389	.408
Jul-Oct	5	7	6.02	0	89.2	47	60	Clutch	29	0	1	.172	.368	.241

How He Compares to Other Pitchers

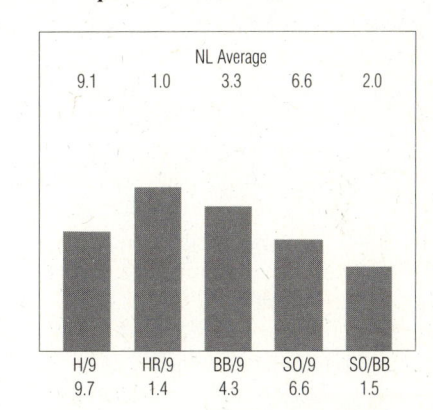

NL Average: 9.1 | 1.0 | 3.3 | 6.6 | 2.0

H/9	HR/9	BB/9	SO/9	SO/BB
9.7	1.4	4.3	6.6	1.5

How He Compares to Other Starting Pitchers

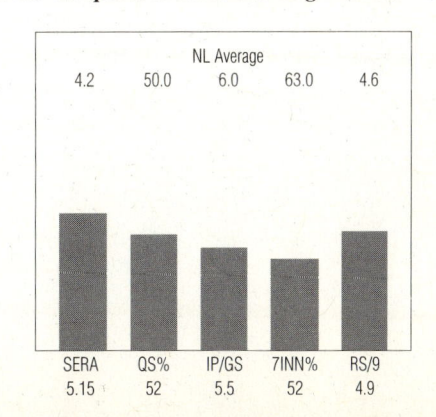

NL Average: 4.2 | 50.0 | 6.0 | 63.0 | 4.6

SERA	QS%	IP/GS	7INN%	RS/9
5.15	52	5.5	52	4.9

CHICAGO CUBS

TODD ZEILE

Positions: 3B/1B//OF
Bats: R **Throws:** R
Ht: 6'1" **Wt:** 190
Opening Day Age: 30
Born: 9/9/1965
Drafted: SL86 3/55
ML Seasons: 7

SCOUTING REPORT
Whatever it was that caused Todd's 1995 slump, he has much better ability than he showed. He has a quick bat and can lash high pitches to all fields, but lacks strong pull power and is not aggressive enough. Todd does draw his share of walks and makes pretty good contact.

Zeile, a former catcher, is a minus runner rarely called on to do anything special on the bases. He has a plus arm with plus accuracy, but below-average range. Usually, his hands are average, but Zeile slumped seriously in the field in 1995. Some still wonder the Cardinals made the right decision to move him from behind the plate.

HOW HE PERFORMED IN '95
The Cardinals shifted Zeile to first base last season and then shifted him out of town after supposedly reneging on an oral agreement to offer him to a long-term contract. The bitter Zeile was happy to start over at third base with the Cubs, but didn't play well and batted just once after September 10 due to a severe bruise on his right thumb.

Todd hit just .227 for Chicago with nine homers, a surprisingly low 16 walks, and 53 strikeouts in only 299 at-bats. Expected to provide fuel to a pennant contender, he was even worse at the plate than the departed Steve Buechele. Zeile has always been a second-half hitter, but failed to turn on the juice in September and ended the year on an 8-for-47 skid.

Defensively, Zeile showed his strong arm but displayed mediocre range and made 11 errors in limited duty at third, compiling an weak .939 fielding percentage. At first base, he's adequate but doesn't hit enough to play there regularly.

WHAT TO EXPECT IN '96
Zeile's 1995 performance was disappointing and doesn't make him an especially attractive free agent. He might be back with the Cubs, but at a greatly reduced price; if not, there are still some teams who will gamble on Zeile. He is fully capable of hitting .280 with 20 home runs and 70 walks, but has to do that to earn his keep because of his lack of defensive value.

Overall Statistics

	G	AB	R	H	2B	3B	HR	RBI	SB	CS	BB	SO	BA	OBA
95 SL/CHN	113	426	50	105	22	0	14	52	1	0	34	76	.246	.305
Career	836	2993	390	787	165	13	84	424	33	32	362	463	.263	.341

1995 Situational Statistics

	AB	HR	RBI	BA	OBA	SLG		AB	HR	RBI	BA	OBA	SLG
Home	180	8	24	.239	.284	.411	LHP	106	3	10	.170	.226	.321
Road	246	6	28	.252	.320	.386	RHP	320	11	42	.272	.331	.422
Apr-Jun	187	7	27	.289	.355	.460	ScPos	91	2	33	.275	.372	.396
Jul-Oct	239	7	25	.213	.264	.347	Clutch	62	1	8	.226	.242	.371

How He Compares to Other Batters

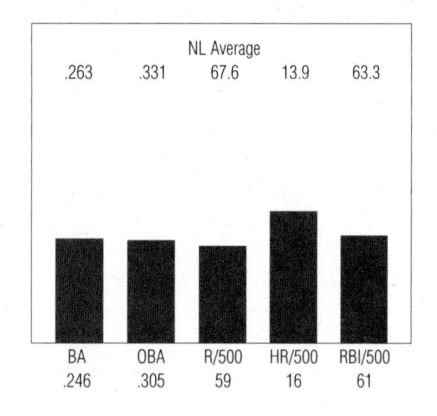

NL Average: .263 / .331 / 67.6 / 13.9 / 63.3

	BA	OBA	R/500	HR/500	RBI/500
	.246	.305	59	16	61

Where He Hits the Ball

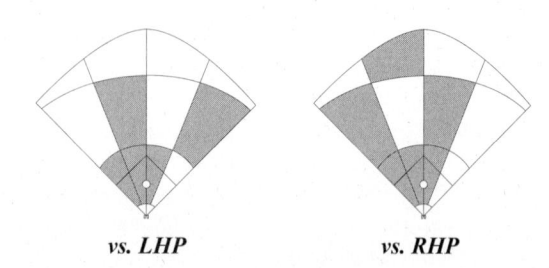

vs. LHP   vs. RHP

CHICAGO CUBS

SCOTT BULLETT

Position: OF
Bats: B **Throws:** L
Ht: 6'2" **Wt:** 200
Opening Day Age: 27
Born: 12/25/1968
Drafted: PIT 6/20/88
ML Seasons: 3

Overall Statistics

	G	AB	R	H	2B	3B	HR	RBI	SB	CS	BB	SO	BA	OBA
95 CHN	104	150	19	41	5	7	3	22	8	3	12	30	.273	.331
Career	138	209	23	52	5	9	3	26	12	6	15	48	.249	.304

1995 Situational Statistics

	AB	HR	RBI	BA	OBA	SLG		AB	HR	RBI	BA	OBA	SLG
Home	60	2	8	.267	.353	.433	LHP	12	0	6	.333	.429	.583
Road	90	1	14	.278	.316	.478	RHP	138	3	16	.268	.322	.449
Apr-Jun	96	1	9	.219	.265	.333	ScPos	42	1	16	.286	.362	.476
Jul-Oct	54	2	13	.370	.443	.685	Clutch	46	2	6	.261	.292	.500

SCOUTING REPORT

Scott Bullett can play all three outfield positions. His arm strength is plus, his accuracy average. Because of his speed, he has above-average range in the field, which could improve in the future with more big-league experience.

At bat, he is mainly submarined by problems with the strike zone. Scott does not make consistent contact. The "little game" is a strong suit for him, as Bullett will bunt for hits and has outstanding speed. However, he could bunt more often.

HOW HE PERFORMED IN '95

Bullett hit .308 with 13 homers at Triple-A Iowa in 1994, earning a shot as a fifth outfielder with the Cubs last season. He was the Cubs' most frequent and prolific pinch-hitter in 1995, going 12-for-37 in the role, and showed speed and gap power. Unfortunately, he fanned once in every five at-bats and didn't walk often.

WHAT TO EXPECT IN '96

Speed and line-drive power make Bullett a decent reserve, but he doesn't have enough home run pop or on-base ability to be an everyday player. Scott is likely to accept a bench role, however, and can help a club.

LARRY CASIAN

Position: RP
Bats: R **Throws:** L
Ht: 6'0" **Wt:** 170
Opening Day Age: 30
Born: 10/28/1965
Drafted: MIN87 6/139
ML Seasons: 6

Overall Statistics

	G	GS	GF	SV	W	L	ERA	IP	H	R	ER	HR	BB	SO
95 CHN	42	0	5	0	1	0	1.93	23.1	23	6	5	1	15	11
Career	162	3	29	2	10	9	4.54	176.1	216	99	89	20	57	81

1995 Situational Statistics

	W	L	ERA	SV	IP	BB	SO		AB	HR	RBI	BA	OBA	SLG
Home	0	0	1.69	0	10.2	7	4	LHB	52	0	7	.308	.362	.385
Road	1	0	2.13	0	12.2	8	7	RHB	37	1	5	.189	.354	.270
Apr-Jun	0	0	1.64	0	11.0	4	6	ScPos	30	0	10	.267	.400	.367
Jul-Oct	1	0	2.19	0	12.1	11	5	Clutch	30	0	5	.300	.410	.300

SCOUTING REPORT

Most of Casian's success comes from his change-up. His fastball, curve, and slider are average at best, and he almost always sinks his fastball to compensate for its lack of velocity. Larry has inconsistent control. He throws three-quarters, but drops down against lefthanders.

Larry has a plus move to first base, evidenced by the fact that only one runner tried to steal against him last year. He is an average fielder.

HOW HE PERFORMED IN '95

Casian won a job as a one-out lefty with the Cubs after coming to Arizona as a non-roster player, and compiled the requisite odd stat line. Although Larry allowed just one homer, he sagged for the second straight year against lefthanders and at one point allowed 11 hits in 19 at-bats—a disastrous streak for a late-inning man brought in specifically to get one hitter.

He went 0-for-2 at bat, the first plate appearances of his six-season major-league career.

WHAT TO EXPECT IN '96

He didn't pitch that well last season, and probably isn't any better than a dozen similar pitchers at Triple-A. However, Casian had the job in 1995, so it will probably be his to lose this season.

CHICAGO CUBS

JOSE HERNANDEZ

Positions: SS/2B/3B
Bats: R **Throws:** R
Ht: 6'1" **Wt:** 180
Opening Day Age: 26
Born: 7/14/1969
Drafted: TEX 1/13/87
ML Seasons: 4

Overall Statistics

	G	AB	R	H	2B	3B	HR	RBI	SB	CS	BB	SO	BA	OBA
95 CHN	93	245	37	60	11	4	13	40	1	0	13	69	.245	.281
Career	197	479	63	110	15	8	14	53	3	3	24	131	.230	.267

1995 Situational Statistics

	AB	HR	RBI	BA	OBA	SLG		AB	HR	RBI	BA	OBA	SLG
Home	119	6	16	.193	.224	.395	LHP	72	4	12	.264	.293	.514
Road	126	7	24	.294	.333	.563	RHP	173	9	28	.237	.276	.468
Apr-Jun	75	3	10	.253	.282	.427	ScPos	67	1	25	.269	.320	.403
Jul-Oct	170	10	30	.241	.280	.506	Clutch	44	1	3	.205	.255	.364

SCOUTING REPORT

Jose has good bat speed and is an aggressive hitter who picks on fastballs. However, he swings at a lot of bad pitches. He is an average-minus runner and an above-average sacrifice bunter.

In the field, Jose plays three infield positions well and displays a plus arm with plus accuracy. His range and hands are well above-average. Hernandez played at least 20 games at shortstop, second, and third last season. He's good at all of them, but best at shortstop.

HOW HE PERFORMED IN '95

Hernandez, a former Indians and Rangers prospect with 18 career homers coming into 1995, showed surprising pop. He proved clearly that he could hit anybody's fastball out of the park. However, Jose may never see another heater again, since he has no idea of the strike zone and doesn't judge off-speed pitches well.

WHAT TO EXPECT IN '96

The Cubs don't view Hernandez as a potential regular. There's no opening for him, and his above-average defense makes him an ideal utility player. The only thing he adds on offense is power, and he must prove this season that his 1995 punch wasn't a fluke. If he does, he could have a long career as a valuable reserve.

HOWARD JOHNSON

Positions: 3B/OF//2B/1B/SS
Bats: B **Throws:** R
Ht: 5'11" **Wt:** 178
Opening Day Age: 35
Born: 11/29/1960
Drafted: DET79* S1/12
ML Seasons: 14

Overall Statistics

	G	AB	R	H	2B	3B	HR	RBI	SB	CS	BB	SO	BA	OBA
95 CHN	87	169	26	33	4	1	7	22	1	1	34	46	.195	.330
Career	1531	4940	760	1229	247	22	228	760	231	77	692	1053	.249	.340

1995 Situational Statistics

	AB	HR	RBI	BA	OBA	SLG		AB	HR	RBI	BA	OBA	SLG
Home	108	6	18	.250	.376	.463	LHP	22	0	1	.182	.357	.182
Road	61	1	4	.098	.247	.164	RHP	147	7	21	.197	.326	.381
Apr-Jun	82	5	11	.122	.277	.317	ScPos	42	1	13	.167	.362	.262
Jul-Oct	87	2	11	.264	.381	.391	Clutch	39	1	6	.205	.360	.282

SCOUTING REPORT

HoJo used to be a dynamic blend of speed and power. He is now just an average runner and has lost much of his bat speed due to shoulder surgery and age. Howard no longer hits good high fastballs, but can jack low and inside pitches 400 feet with ease. Although he's a switch-hitter, all of his production comes from the left side.

Johnson has an average arm that is not especially accurate, but still has adequate range at third. He can be used in left field as well, but he has never had good hands.

HOW HE PERFORMED IN '95

After signing with the Cubs out of Camp Homestead, Johnson couldn't get into a groove and was batting just .124 in late July before a late-season surge. Hojo hits the ball hard and takes plenty of walks, but hasn't hit over .240 since 1991. An attempt to use him at second base proved disastrous, although his glovework at third was adequate.

WHAT TO EXPECT IN '96

Johnson is well-liked and has some power, but is just hanging by a thread at this point in his career. If he can't regain some of his former power at the plate soon, he is likely to be through.

CHICAGO CUBS

MARK PARENT

Position: C
Bats: R **Throws:** R
Ht: 6'5" **Wt:** 224
Opening Day Age: 34
Born: 9/16/1961
Drafted: SD79 5/92
ML Seasons: 10

Overall Statistics

	G	AB	R	H	2B	3B	HR	RBI	SB	CS	BB	SO	BA	OBA
95 PIT/CHN	81	265	30	62	11	0	18	38	0	0	26	69	.234	.302
Career	345	940	84	206	36	0	43	124	2	1	76	213	.219	.277

1995 Situational Statistics

	AB	HR	RBI	BA	OBA	SLG		AB	HR	RBI	BA	OBA	SLG
Home	139	7	18	.230	.301	.424	LHP	62	9	14	.274	.357	.742
Road	126	11	20	.238	.304	.540	RHP	203	9	24	.222	.285	.399
Apr-Jun	126	10	24	.286	.343	.571	ScPos	66	2	18	.167	.304	.288
Jul-Oct	139	8	14	.187	.266	.396	Clutch	63	1	7	.159	.209	.254

SCOUTING REPORT
There are truck-sized holes in Parent's swing, but he can hit high and inside pitches a long way. He is a very poor baserunner. Parent may be the slowest player in the league, but he's reasonably agile behind the plate and threw out 35 of 88 runners trying to steal last season, a nifty 39%.

Mark's arm is plus with average accuracy. He has average range and hands. With lots of experience, he is a good reserve catcher who can help out defensively and surprise occasionally offensively.

HOW HE PERFORMED IN '95
Few people in Chicago understood why the popular Parent was waived after the 1994 season. When his replacement, Todd Pratt, crash-landed last spring, Mark was missed even more. The Cubs rectified the situation by purchasing Parent from Pittsburgh on August 31, where he had slugged 15 homers. He added three more for Chicago in 32 at-bats.

WHAT TO EXPECT IN '96
Mark is a free agent and, while the Cubs want him back, his initial contract demands after the season were a bit too high for the Cubs' liking. Parent strikes out a lot, but he has power, takes the walk, throws well, is well-liked, and accepts the reserve role. He's quite valuable.

MIKE PEREZ

Position: RP
Bats: R **Throws:** R
Ht: 6'0" **Wt:** 185
Opening Day Age: 31
Born: 10/19/1964
Drafted: SL86 13/312
ML Seasons: 6

Overall Statistics

	G	GS	GF	SV	W	L	ERA	IP	H	R	ER	HR	BB	SO
95 CHN	68	0	18	2	2	6	3.66	71.1	72	30	29	8	27	49
Career	273	0	92	22	21	16	3.47	298.2	290	126	115	22	99	185

1995 Situational Statistics

	W	L	ERA	SV	IP	BB	SO		AB	HR	RBI	BA	OBA	SLG
Home	2	5	3.72	0	36.1	19	22	LHB	93	2	9	.290	.368	.366
Road	0	1	3.60	2	35.0	8	27	RHB	176	6	28	.256	.325	.403
Apr-Jun	0	4	2.97	2	30.1	11	20	ScPos	84	2	31	.226	.352	.345
Jul-Oct	2	2	4.17	0	41.0	16	29	Clutch	139	3	23	.273	.344	.388

SCOUTING REPORT
Mike Perez throws with a smooth three-quarters delivery, then immediately recoils if the hitter swings. Due to this reaction, he's a minus fielder.

His average-minus sinking fastball doesn't vex anybody, but Mike has a plus curve with a quick, sharp break that serves as his out pitch. He also throws an average splitter. Control is average on all of his deliveries.

HOW HE PERFORMED IN '95
After missing most of 1994 with a torn rotator cuff that required surgery, Perez spent last season as a setup pitcher with the Cubs. He had rocky times, but improved as the year progressed.

Perez has a minus move to first (12 runners stole bases in 16 tries) and allowed some key gopher balls. His performance was adequate, at best, in almost every category.

Mike was 0-for-4 as a batter last year and is hitless in 10 career trips.

WHAT TO EXPECT IN '96
Perez' durability in 1995 was impressive considering his injury troubles, and he could well return to the Cubs' bullpen. However, he's never going to get out of middle relief, and is not likely to ever have much job security.

CHICAGO CUBS

OZZIE TIMMONS

Position: OF
Bats: R **Throws:** R
Ht: 6'2" **Wt:** 205
Opening Day Age: 25
Born: 9/18/1970
Drafted: CHN91 4/137
ML Seasons: 1

Overall Statistics

	G	AB	R	H	2B	3B	HR	RBI	SB	CS	BB	SO	BA	OBA
95 CHN	77	171	30	45	10	1	8	28	3	0	13	32	.263	.314
Career	77	171	30	45	10	1	8	28	3	0	13	32	.263	.314

1995 Situational Statistics

	AB	HR	RBI	BA	OBA	SLG		AB	HR	RBI	BA	OBA	SLG
Home	90	5	10	.256	.302	.456	LHP	92	3	14	.315	.351	.489
Road	81	3	18	.272	.326	.494	RHP	79	5	14	.203	.273	.456
Apr-Jun	87	4	15	.276	.319	.471	ScPos	44	0	16	.318	.392	.409
Jul-Oct	84	4	13	.250	.308	.476	Clutch	40	0	5	.125	.146	.150

SCOUTING REPORT

Ozzie Timmons has plus bat speed and promising power. He has fine plate discipline and can turn on high and inside pitches. If he improves against off-speed stuff, Ozzie could develop into a good big-league hitter. He also has plus speed but is not a good baserunner.

Timmons didn't look good in the outfield and has below-average range, but has a plus arm with average accuracy and well above-average hands.

HOW HE PERFORMED IN '95

Timmons began his rookie season as the Cubs' left fielder against lefthanders, but Luis Gonzalez' acquisition pushed Ozzie to the bench. He didn't make a fuss, continuing to play well when called on.

Although Timmons has fine power and will take a walk, strikeouts are a concern. Since the youngster is nothing special on the bases or in the outfield, he must hit his way into the lineup.

WHAT TO EXPECT IN '96

The Cubs' outfield picture is scrambled for 1996, and Ozzie may continue in a reserve role. This might not be the best thing for him; Timmons could use another season at Triple-A to cut down on his swing and get more experience.

MIKE WALKER

Position: RP
Bats: R **Throws:** R
Ht: 6'2" **Wt:** 195
Opening Day Age: 29
Born: 10/4/1966
Drafted: CLE86* 2/27
ML Seasons: 4

Overall Statistics

	G	GS	GF	SV	W	L	ERA	IP	H	R	ER	HR	BB	SO
95 CHN	42	0	12	1	1	3	3.22	44.2	45	22	16	2	24	20
Career	68	12	17	1	3	11	4.39	133.1	141	79	65	8	78	63

1995 Situational Statistics

	W	L	ERA	SV	IP	BB	SO		AB	HR	RBI	BA	OBA	SLG
Home	0	2	3.76	0	26.1	17	13	LHB	54	1	10	.278	.355	.463
Road	1	1	2.45	1	18.1	7	7	RHB	120	1	17	.250	.336	.317
Apr-Jun	1	2	2.43	0	33.1	15	13	ScPos	65	1	24	.215	.295	.323
Jul-Oct	0	1	5.56	1	11.1	9	7	Clutch	60	1	10	.333	.406	.483

SCOUTING REPORT

Nothing about Walker is above-average. He throws from a standard three-quarters delivery and has average control.

His fastball, which is always thrown to sink, is an average-minus pitch. His slider and splitter are both mediocre. Mike is average at fielding and holding runners.

HOW HE PERFORMED IN '95

Walker, a journeyman righthander, hadn't been in the majors since 1991. However, he spent much of the year as the low man in the Cubs' bullpen. Jim Riggleman showed little confidence in him, and despite a fairly low ERA, Mike never broke out of his garbage-time role. Control was a problem for him all season and he rarely pitched in a key situation.

Six runners tried to steal against Walker in 1995, four successfully. He was hitless in three at-bats, his first big-league plate action.

WHAT TO EXPECT IN '96

He's a good candidate not to be back in Chicago this year and is very replaceable. However, his numbers were good enough that Walker might get a chance to hook on as somebody else's 10th or 11th pitcher. More likely, he'll be back in Triple-A.

CHICAGO CUBS

TURK WENDELL

Position: RP
Bats: B **Throws:** R
Ht: 6'2" **Wt:** 180
Opening Day Age: 28
Born: 5/19/1967
Drafted: ATL88 7/112
ML Seasons: 3

Overall Statistics

	G	GS	GF	SV	W	L	ERA	IP	H	R	ER	HR	BB	SO
95 CHN	43	0	17	0	3	1	4.92	60.1	71	35	33	11	24	50
Career	56	6	19	0	4	4	5.83	97.1	117	68	63	14	42	74

1995 Situational Statistics

	W	L	ERA	SV	IP	BB	SO		AB	HR	RBI	BA	OBA	SLG
Home	2	0	4.87	0	40.2	15	41	LHB	96	4	16	.333	.398	.490
Road	1	1	5.03	0	19.2	9	9	RHB	142	7	26	.275	.340	.486
Apr-Jun	1	0	4.82	0	18.2	5	9	ScPos	74	4	32	.338	.422	.514
Jul-Oct	2	1	4.97	0	41.2	19	41	Clutch	35	1	4	.314	.400	.486

SCOUTING REPORT

Wendell delivers at a three-quarter angle. He has an average fastball with good sink, which he often cuts effectively. Turk has an average forkball and a slightly below-par slider and curve. Control and consistency are problematic for the animated righthander.

He is average as a fielder and, despite an average move to first, five of nine basestealers were thrown out when Wendell was pitching in 1995.

HOW HE PERFORMED IN '95

The eccentric righthander got an extended big-league audition for the first time, and despite a couple of miserable outings, he pitched better than expected. Working almost exclusively in middle relief, he showed durability and better-than-expected strikeout numbers, although location problems led to a staggering 11 homers and he couldn't seem to get a lefthander out. Turk, hitless in seven trips last year, is now 1-for-16 as a batter in the majors.

WHAT TO EXPECT IN '96

While Wendell isn't a candidate for closing or for the rotation, he pitched decently in 1995 and could sneak into the bullpen again. He has settled down his wild antics and can be effective if he keeps the ball low consistently.

ANTHONY YOUNG

Position: RP
Bats: R **Throws:** R
Ht: 6'2" **Wt:** 200
Opening Day Age: 30
Born: 1/19/1966
Drafted: NYN87 39/978
ML Seasons: 5

Overall Statistics

	G	GS	GF	SV	W	L	ERA	IP	H	R	ER	HR	BB	SO
95 CHN	32	1	8	2	3	4	3.70	41.1	47	20	17	5	14	15
Career	153	51	55	20	12	45	3.84	426.2	435	225	182	37	145	226

1995 Situational Statistics

	W	L	ERA	SV	IP	BB	SO		AB	HR	RBI	BA	OBA	SLG
Home	2	2	4.15	1	21.2	12	8	LHB	59	0	2	.271	.358	.339
Road	1	2	3.20	1	19.2	2	7	RHB	104	5	18	.298	.354	.529
Apr-Jun	0	2	6.48	1	8.1	5	5	ScPos	54	0	11	.241	.339	.296
Jul-Oct	3	2	3.00	1	33.0	9	10	Clutch	37	1	6	.270	.341	.405

SCOUTING REPORT

Young still throws with a high three-quarter to overhand delivery. His sinking fastball has good movement but is of average-minus velocity after his surgery.

Anthony has a plus curve that he could use more often, an average-minus changeup, and an average-minus forkball that he doesn't use as often as he used to. His fielding and holding runners skills are mediocre.

HOW HE PERFORMED IN '95

Young returned early from "Tommy John" elbow surgery and worked out of the Cubs' bullpen. He got some duty as a setup man, but couldn't consistently rely on his sinker. Poor control hounded Anthony, who allowed 13 doubles and five homers.

Three of five runners were successful stealing against Young. He was 2-for-3 at bat after coming into 1995 with a .146 career average. He is quick and has been used as a pinch-runner.

WHAT TO EXPECT IN '96

Despite his good arm, Young hasn't produced in the major leagues, and may need to return to the minors to continue his recovery from his very serious injury. It's clear now that his role in the majors, if he has one, is as a middle reliever.

CHICAGO CUBS: TOP PROSPECTS

TERRY ADAMS

Bats: R Throws: R Opening Day Age: 23
Ht: 6-3 Wt: 180 Born: 3/6/1973
Position: P Drafted: 1991 #3 CHN

YR TEAM	LG/CLASS	G	GS	GF	SV	W	L	ERA	IP	H	HR	BB	SO	O/BA
93 Daytona	FSL/A	13	13	0	0	3	5	4.97	70.2	78	2	43	35	.288
94 Daytona	FSL/A	39	7	21	7	9	10	4.38	84.1	87	5	46	64	.266
95 Iowa	AMAS/AAA	7	0	6	5	0	0	0.00	6.1	3	0	2	10	.130
95 Orlando	SOU/AA	37	0	30	19	2	3	1.43	37.2	23	2	16	26	.177
95 Chicago	NL/MAJ	18	0	7	1	1	1	6.50	18.0	22	0	10	15	.289

As a starter, he had an ERA approaching 5.00. When moved to the bullpen in 1994, he blossomed and is now considered the closer of the future. Long regarded the hardest thrower in the organization, Adams refined the command of his mid-90's fastball and slider, posted 19 saves, and was among the Southern League leaders when promoted. He struck out the side in his Triple-A debut, picked up five saves in seven appearances there, and was summoned to Chicago at the age of just 22. Confidence and a lack of a breaking pitch led to a 6.50 ERA with the Cubs. Adams allowed just one unearned run in his last 18 outings for Orlando and finished second in the organization in saves.

DARREN BURTON

Bats: S Throws: R Opening Day Age: 24
Ht: 6-1 Wt: 185 Born: 9/16/1972
Position: OF Drafted: 1990 #3 KC

YR TEAM	LG/CLASS	G	AB	R	H	2B	3B	HR	RBI	SB	BA	OBA
93 Wilmington	CARO/A	134	549	82	152	23	5	10	45	30	.277	.334
94 Memphis	SOU/AA	97	373	55	95	12	3	3	37	10	.255	.316
95 Omaha	AMAS/AAA	2	5	0	0	0	0	0	0	0	.000	.000
95 Orlando	SOU/AA	62	222	40	68	16	2	4	21	7	.306	.382
95 Wichita	TEX/AA	41	163	13	39	9	1	1	20	6	.239	.295

Highly regarded, but a major disappointment in Kansas City, Burton was waived at age 21 and picked up by the Cubs. The switch-hitter immediately responded, hitting for the cycle July 18 and batting a career-high .306 for his new organization. Burton is a switch-hitting athlete who plays a solid center field and can run, but he has swiped just 23 bases the last two years after nabbing 30 in 1993. He also needs to hit the ball on the ground more often to take advantage of his speed.

MATT FRANCO

Bats: L Throws: R Opening Day Age: 27
Ht: 6-3 Wt: 195 Born: 8/19/1969
Position: 3B Drafted: 1987 #6 CHN

YR TEAM	LG/CLASS	G	AB	R	H	2B	3B	HR	RBI	SB	BA	OBA
93 Orlando	SOU/AA	68	237	31	75	20	1	7	37	3	.316	.393
93 Iowa	AMAS/AAA	62	199	24	58	17	4	5	29	4	.291	.342
94 Iowa	AMAS/AAA	128	437	63	121	32	4	11	71	3	.277	.353
95 Iowa	AMAS/AAA	121	455	51	128	28	5	6	58	1	.281	.331
95 Chicago	NL/MAJ	16	17	0	5	1	0	0	1	0	.294	.294

Originally a third basemen, the 26-year-old spent much of the past five years at first base before moving back to the hot corner last season. A decent fielder with soft hands, Franco has made his reputation with the bat. He has hit .280 the last three years at Triple-A with 97 doubles, has a good understanding of the strike zone, and doesn't have a problem hitting lefthanders. However, the nine-year veteran has reached double figures in home runs just twice and does not move very swiftly. Franco served as a pinch-hitter for Chicago in September.

DOUG GLANVILLE

Bats: R Throws: R Opening Day Age: 26
Ht: 6-2 Wt: 170 Born: 8/25/1970
Position: CF Drafted: 1991 #1 CHN

YR TEAM	LG/CLASS	G	AB	R	H	2B	3B	HR	RBI	SB	BA	OBA
93 Daytona	FSL/A	61	239	47	70	10	1	2	21	18	.293	.374
93 Orlando	SOU/AA	73	296	42	78	14	4	9	40	15	.264	.292
94 Orlando	SOU/AA	130	483	53	127	22	2	5	52	26	.263	.301
95 Iowa	AMAS/AAA	112	419	48	113	16	2	4	37	13	.270	.299

The 25-year-old former first-round pick has not progressed as hoped with the bat. Glanville has not become the leadoff hitter hoped because of a mediocre swing, a lack of patience, and a rather poor stolen base percentage (59% the last 3 years). After a very strong Arizona League last winter, the University of Penn graduate reported to Iowa, but posted just a .299 on-base percentage and hit about .225 the second half. Defensively, Glanville is superb, covering lots of ground and showing a very strong arm.

JASON HART

Bats: R Throws: R Opening Day Age: 24
Ht: 6-0 Wt: 195 Born: 11/14/1971
Position: P Drafted: NDFA 12-30-93 CHN

YR TEAM	LG/CLASS	G	GS	GF	SV	W	L	ERA	IP	H	HR	BB	SO	O/BA
94 Peoria	MID/A	20	0	10	3	4	2	3.62	37.1	29	4	7	33	.207
94 Daytona	FSL/A	26	0	23	12	3	3	1.69	37.1	26	1	6	39	.186
95 Orlando	SOU/AA	14	0	10	3	0	1	2.12	17.0	14	0	4	20	.233
95 Daytona	FSL/A	37	0	34	24	0	3	2.21	40.2	29	2	18	50	.192

Hart had a fantastic season at Daytona, leading the Florida State League in saves the first half of the season. He posted saves in 11 consecutive outings at one point and allowed no earned runs in his last 21 outings before being promoted. He was almost as effective at Orlando, finishing the season with 8.1 scoreless innings while striking out 12. The 23-year-old may not have the heat to close in the big leagues, but his devastating slider and command makes him perfect for a set-up role.

MIKE HUBBARD

Bats: R Throws: R Opening Day Age: 25
Ht: 6-1 Wt: 180 Born: 2/16/1971
Position: C Drafted: 1992 #7 CHN

YR TEAM	LG/CLASS	G	AB	R	H	2B	3B	HR	RBI	SB	BA	OBA
93 Daytona	FSL/A	68	245	25	72	10	3	1	20	10	.294	.348
94 Orlando	SOU/AA	104	357	52	102	13	3	11	39	7	.286	.351
95 Iowa	AMAS/AAA	75	254	28	66	6	3	5	23	6	.260	.325
95 Chicago	NL/MAJ	15	23	2	4	0	0	0	1	0	.174	.240

Hubbard's best attributes are his speed and athleticism, two attributes that make it possible for him to move out from behind the plate and play somewhere in the infield. He has good tools behind the plate and a decent arm, but he needs to refine them. Offensively, the 24-year-old has hit .273 in his four-year career and shown some pop, but his production may not be enough to make him an everyday player.

CHICAGO CUBS: TOP PROSPECTS

ROBIN JENNINGS

Bats: L Throws: L Opening Day Age: 24
Ht: 6-2 Wt: 200 Born: 4/11/1972
Position: OF Drafted: 1991 #33 CHN

YR	TEAM	LG/CLASS	G	AB	R	H	2B	3B	HR	RBI	SB	BA	OBA
93	Peoria	MID/A	132	474	64	146	29	5	3	65	11	.308	.372
94	Daytona	FSL/A	128	476	54	133	24	5	8	60	2	.279	.344
95	Orlando	SOU/AA	132	490	71	145	27	7	17	79	7	.296	.355

Jennings may have been the biggest surprise in the organization in 1995. He had always hit for a high average and made contact, but showed unexpected power last year, hitting ten homers in the first two months of the season. He finished first in the organization in RBI and second in home runs. A solid outfielder with a very good arm, the lefthanded hitter doesn't back down against southpaws, batting over .300 against them last year. The 1995 Southern League All-Star finished second in the Midwest League in batting in 1993 while leading the loop with 20 outfield assists.

BROOKS KIESCHNICK

Bats: L Throws: R Opening Day Age: 24
Ht: 6-4 Wt: 228 Born: 6/6/1972
Position: LF Drafted: 1993 #1 CHN

YR	TEAM	LG/CLASS	G	AB	R	H	2B	3B	HR	RBI	SB	BA	OBA
93	Cubs	GULF/R	3	9	0	2	1	0	0	0	0	.222	.222
93	Daytona	FSL/A	6	22	1	4	2	0	0	2	0	.182	.217
93	Orlando	SOU/AA	25	91	12	31	8	0	2	10	1	.341	.388
94	Orlando	SOU/AA	126	468	57	132	25	3	14	55	3	.282	.332
95	Iowa	AMAS/AAA	138	505	61	149	30	1	23	73	2	.295	.370

There is no doubt that Kieschnick is the best hitting prospect in the entire organization. The 23-year-old led the American Association in homers, hits and extra-base hits while earning a berth on the league All-Star squad. The former University of Texas pitcher/DH was consistent from start to finish, has a cannon for an arm, and made just two errors in left field. He still needs work tracking down fly balls. The lefthanded swinger still has some adjustments to make against southpaws, but there is no doubt that his power to all fields is his ticket to the major leagues.

JON RATLIFF

Bats: R Throws: R Opening Day Age: 24
Ht: 6-5 Wt: 200 Born: 12/22/1971
Position: P Drafted: 1993 #2 CHN

YR	TEAM	LG/CLASS	G	GS	GF	SV	W	L	ERA	IP	H	HR	BB	SO	O/BA
93	Geneva	NYP/A	3	3	0	0	1	1	3.21	14.0	12	0	8	7	.218
93	Daytona	FSL/A	8	8	0	0	2	4	3.95	41.0	50	0	23	15	.311
94	Daytona	FSL/A	8	8	0	0	3	2	3.50	54.0	64	5	5	17	.298
94	Iowa	AMAS/AAA	5	4	0	0	1	3	5.40	28.1	39	7	7	10	.325
94	Orlando	SOU/AA	12	12	0	0	1	9	5.63	62.1	78	4	26	19	.313
95	Orlando	SOU/AA	26	25	1	0	10	5	3.47	140.0	143	9	42	94	.267

Although Ratliff has a career record under .500 and an ERA of 4.08, he is considered one of the best pitchers in the organization. After a severe ingrown toenail hindered his progress in '94, the 23-year-old had a solid season at Double-A last year. He made four consecutive starts without allowing a run at one point, but also had several outings where he failed to get past the fifth inning. Ratliff throws in the upper-80's with good control and also uses a slider and changeup.

KENNIE STEENSTRA

Bats: R Throws: R Opening Day Age: 26
Ht: 6-5 Wt: 220 Born: 10/13/1970
Position: P Drafted: 1992 #11 CHN

YR	TEAM	LG/CLASS	G	GS	GF	SV	W	L	ERA	IP	H	HR	BB	SO	O/BA
93	Daytona	FSL/A	13	13	0	0	5	3	2.55	81.1	64	2	12	57	.219
93	Iowa	AMAS/AAA	1	1	0	0	1	0	6.75	6.2	9	2	4	6	.321
93	Orlando	SOU/AA	14	14	0	0	8	3	3.59	100.1	103	4	25	60	.266
94	Orlando	SOU/AA	23	23	0	0	9	7	2.61	158.1	146	12	39	83	.246
94	Iowa	AMAS/AAA	3	3	0	0	1	2	13.15	13.0	24	2	4	10	.400
95	Iowa	AMAS/AAA	29	26	1	0	9	12	3.89	171.1	174	15	48	96	.266

Steenstra puts hitters off balance, holds runners close, and keeps the ball on the ground. He has posted a 42-30 record with a 3.23 ERA in his four-year career. He also won his last 25 collegiate decisions at Wichita State. The 25-year-old is not a flame thrower despite his size and will have to show outstanding command and location to get a future shot with the Cubs.

AMAURY TELEMACO

Bats: R Throws: R Opening Day Age: 22
Ht: 6-3 Wt: 180 Born: 1/19/1974
Position: P Drafted: NDFA 5-23-91 CHN

YR	TEAM	LG/CLASS	G	GS	GF	SV	W	L	ERA	IP	H	HR	BB	SO	O/BA
93	Peoria	MID/A	23	23	0	0	8	11	3.45	143.2	129	9	54	133	.241
94	Daytona	FSL/A	11	11	0	0	7	3	3.40	76.2	62	4	23	59	.221
94	Orlando	SOU/AA	12	12	0	0	3	5	3.45	62.2	56	6	20	49	.239
95	Orlando	SOU/AA	22	22	0	0	8	8	3.29	147.2	112	13	42	151	.211

Although Telemaco doesn't throw a 90+-mph heater, he still finished second in the Southern League (and first in the organization) in strikeouts despite missing the first month of the season due to the strike. In addition, the young 22-year-old led league starters in baserunners/9 IP (9.63) and was second in average against (.211). Only 22, the Dominican native has a projectable body, live arm, good breaking stuff, and excellent command.

PEDRO VALDES

Bats: L Throws: L Opening Day Age: 23
Ht: 6-1 Wt: 160 Born: 6/29/1973
Position: OF Drafted: 1990 #13 CHN

YR	TEAM	LG/CLASS	G	AB	R	H	2B	3B	HR	RBI	SB	BA	OBA
93	Peoria	MID/A	65	234	33	74	11	1	7	36	2	.316	.339
93	Daytona	FSL/A	60	230	27	66	16	1	8	49	3	.287	.313
94	Orlando	SOU/AA	116	365	39	103	14	4	1	37	2	.282	.322
95	Orlando	SOU/AA	114	426	57	128	28	3	7	68	3	.300	.359

Selected to the Southern League All-Star team in his second year with the club, the 22-year-old Valdes is considered one of the purest hitters in the organization. He doesn't back down against lefties, but his uppercut swing hasn't generated many home runs. He also walks too infrequently and can't steal bases. Defensively, Valdes is adequate with a fairly good throwing arm.

THE SCOUTING REPORT: 1996

CHICAGO CUBS: OTHERS TO WATCH

BRANT BROWN Bats: L Throws: L Ht: 6-3 Wt: 220
Born: 6/22/1971 Drafted: 1992 #2 CHN Position: 1B

YR TEAM	LG/CLASS	G	AB	R	H	2B	3B	HR	RBI	SB	BA	OBA
95 Orlando	SOU/AA	121	446	67	121	27	4	6	53	8	.271	.332

Brown, a Mark Grace wannabe, is smooth around the bag, but has not developed as a hitter, lacking in power, patience and ability to hit southpaws.

PAT CLINE Bats: R Throws: R Ht: 6-3 Wt: 220
Born: 10/9/1974 Drafted: 1993 #7 CHN Position: C

YR TEAM	LG/CLASS	G	AB	R	H	2B	3B	HR	RBI	SB	BA	OBA
95 Rockford	MID/A	112	390	65	106	27	0	13	77	6	.272	.377

The top young catcher has big-time power (neutralized by a spacious home park) and a strong arm, but must refine his skills behind the dish.

TODD HANEY Bats: R Throws: R Ht: 5-9 Wt: 165
Born: 7/30/1965 Drafted: 1987 #38 SEA Position: 2B

YR TEAM	LG/CLASS	G	AB	R	H	2B	3B	HR	RBI	SB	BA	OBA
95 Iowa	AMAS/AAA	90	326	38	102	20	2	4	30	2	.313	.376
95 Chicago	NL/MAJ	25	73	11	30	8	0	2	6	0	.411	.463

Haney, a .293 career minor league hitter, impressed the Cubs with a .411 average in 73 at-bats, but he has only played second base in his career.

DAVID HUTCHESON Bats: R Throws: R Ht: 6-2 Wt: 185
Born: 8/29/1971 Drafted: 1993 #22 CHN Position: P

YR TEAM	LG/CLASS	G	GS	GF	SV	W	L	ERA	IP	H	HR	BB	SO	O/BA
95 Orlando	SOU/AA	28	27	1	0	8	10	4.01	168.1	178	23	45	103	.275

An offspeed pitcher with command, Hutcheson was not as tough as '94 when he tied for the Florida State League with 14 wins and pitched three consecutive shutouts.

JASON MAXWELL Bats: R Throws: R Ht: 6-0 Wt: 175
Born: 3/21/1972 Drafted: 1993 #75 CHN Position: SS

YR TEAM	LG/CLASS	G	AB	R	H	2B	3B	HR	RBI	SB	BA	OBA
95 Daytona	FSL/A	117	388	66	102	13	3	10	58	12	.263	.368

The Florida State League All-Star made great strides with the bat and glove in '95, leading league shortstops in fielding, but projects as a utility player down the road.

BOBBY MORRIS Bats: L Throws: R Ht: 6-0 Wt: 180
Born: 11/22/1972 Drafted: 1993 #10 CHN Position: 2B

YR TEAM	LG/CLASS	G	AB	R	H	2B	3B	HR	RBI	SB	BA	OBA
95 Daytona	FSL/A	95	344	44	106	18	2	2	55	22	.308	.385

Hal's brother is an outstanding hitter, finishing second in the Midwest League in 1994 (.354) and fifth last year, but has not made the grade at second base and probably doesn't have the punch for the outfield.

KEVIN ORIE Bats: R Throws: R Ht: 6-4 Wt: 215
Born: 9/1/1972 Drafted: 1993 #3 CHN Position: 3B

YR TEAM	LG/CLASS	G	AB	R	H	2B	3B	HR	RBI	SB	BA	OBA
95 Daytona	FSL/A	119	409	54	100	17	4	9	51	5	.244	.333

Orie, a power-hitting prospect who missed virtually all of 1994 with wrist surgery, finished up a subpar 1995 season with a very strong August.

STEVE RAIN Bats: R Throws: R Ht: 6-6 Wt: 225
Born: 6/2/1975 Drafted: 1993 #12 CHN Position: P

YR TEAM	LG/CLASS	G	GS	GF	SV	W	L	ERA	IP	H	HR	BB	SO	O/BA
95 Rockford	MID/A	53	0	51	23	5	2	1.21	59.1	38	0	23	66	.186

Considered not good enough to make the rotation, Rain established himself as the closer with an upper-80's fastball and slider and didn't allow an earned run in his first 14 and his last 18 games.

ROBERTO RIVERA Bats: L Throws: L Ht: 6-0 Wt: 175
Born: 1/1/1969 Drafted: NDFA 1-24-88 CLE Position: P

YR TEAM	LG/CLASS	G	GS	GF	SV	W	L	ERA	IP	H	HR	BB	SO	O/BA
95 Orlando	SOU/AA	49	0	14	6	6	2	2.38	68.0	50	4	11	34	.207
95 Chicago	NL/MAJ	7	0	2	0	0	0	5.40	5.0	8	1	2	2	.381

Rivera, a Cleveland castoff, throws strikes; his Double-A success the past two years led to a September call in '95.

JASON RYAN Bats: S Throws: R Ht: 6-2 Wt: 180
Born: 1/23/1976 Drafted: 1994 #9 CHN Position: P

YR TEAM	LG/CLASS	G	GS	GF	SV	W	L	ERA	IP	H	HR	BB	SO	O/BA
95 Daytona	FSL/A	26	26	0	0	11	5	3.48	134.2	128	10	54	98	.250

Ryan, just 20, throws hard and uses an assortment of pitches that will improve once he gains command.

SCOTT SAMUELS Bats: L Throws: R Ht: 5-11 Wt: 190
Born: 5/19/1971 Drafted: 1992 #9 FLO Position: OF

YR TEAM	LG/CLASS	G	AB	R	H	2B	3B	HR	RBI	SB	BA	OBA
95 Orlando	SOU/AA	5	21	3	6	1	0	1	4	2	.286	.375
95 Daytona	FSL/A	112	388	92	127	29	12	2	42	38	.327	.435

A washout with the Marlins, Samuels scrapped the power-hitting approach and finished among the top three in six Florida State League categories last season.

BRIAN STEPHENSON Bats: R Throws: R Ht: 6-3 Wt: 205
Born: 7/17/1973 Drafted: 1994 #2 CHN Position: P

YR TEAM	LG/CLASS	G	GS	GF	SV	W	L	ERA	IP	H	HR	BB	SO	O/BA
95 Daytona	FSL/A	26	26	0	0	10	9	3.96	150.0	145	7	58	109	.256

Stephenson, whose father and grandfather played in the major leagues, just took up pitching a few years ago but throws hard and has a devastating curve—when it's under control.

TANYON STURTZE Bats: R Throws: R Ht: 6-5 Wt: 190
Born: 10/12/1970 Drafted: 1990 #28 OAK Position: P

YR TEAM	LG/CLASS	G	GS	GF	SV	W	L	ERA	IP	H	HR	BB	SO	O/BA
95 Iowa	AMAS/AAA	23	17	0	0	4	7	6.80	86.0	108	18	42	48	.314
95 Chicago	NL/MAJ	2	0	0	0	0	0	9.00	2.0	2	1	1	0	.250

Sturtze, a Rule V pickup from Oakland, has a live arm, but has had limited success due to lack of command.

DAX WINSLETT Bats: R Throws: R Ht: 6-1 Wt: 200
Born: 1/1/1972 Drafted: 1993 #2 LA Position: P

YR TEAM	LG/CLASS	G	GS	GF	SV	W	L	ERA	IP	H	HR	BB	SO	O/BA
95 Vero Beach	FSL/A	14	13	0	0	6	4	3.18	85.0	87	7	21	59	.263
95 Daytona	FSL/A	12	12	0	0	6	2	2.28	67.0	61	4	18	52	.245

Acquired from the Dodgers for Willie Banks, the 23-year-old combines a loose arm with good command.

CINCINNATI REDS

BRET BOONE

Position: 2B
Bats: R **Throws:** R
Ht: 5'10" **Wt:** 180
Opening Day Age: 26
Born: 4/6/1969
Drafted: SEA90 5/134
ML Seasons: 4

SCOUTING REPORT

Bret is basically a line-drive hitter who has developed some power over his first two seasons in the major leagues. He likes to go after pitches out over the plate and will hit them where they are pitched. With just average speed, Boone will never be a big basestealing threat and sometimes runs too aggressively. While all of Bret's defensive tools—range, hands, throwing arm strength, and throwing accuracy—rate as slightly above-average, he is a better defensive player because of his intelligence, hustle, and steadiness. He makes all of the routine plays and more than his share of spectacular ones.

Boone is always in the game while playing second base, adjusting his position from hitter to hitter and using unorthodox positioning to compensate for his lack of great mobility. His most notable trait is to play well behind the infield line on artificial turf with no runners on base; this allows Bret to cover more ground while taking advantage of the turf's bounce.

HOW HE PERFORMED IN '95

It was an odd season. At the plate, Boone struggled from the start, and only July saved him from disastrous final totals. He hit .367 with 10 home runs in July, but batted just .243 the rest of the year. Although Bret kept saying that he felt he would break out of his slump sooner or later, he never really did.

Bret reached career highs in home runs and doubles, but still went 194 at-bats without a long ball from July 29 to the last day of the season. The normally free-swinging Boone did walk 41 times, nearly doubling his career total, but still had a problem with strikeouts.

Boone's defensive play last year erased any lingering doubts about his ability to field his position. He didn't make an error until July 8, finished the year with only four errors and led all NL second basemen in fielding percentage.

WHAT TO EXPECT IN '96

While Boone is better than a .267 hitter, he probably won't match his '94 average of .320 again. But a 20-homer, 80-RBI season is not out of the question by any means for the former Mariners' prospect, and he should be a quality regular for several seasons—He has come a long way from Lou Piniella's doghouse in Seattle to become the regular second sacker on a championship team.

Overall Statistics

	G	AB	R	H	2B	3B	HR	RBI	SB	CS	BB	SO	BA	OBA
95 CIN	138	513	63	137	34	2	15	68	5	1	41	84	.267	.326
Career	355	1294	168	352	75	6	43	189	11	9	86	244	.272	.323

1995 Situational Statistics

	AB	HR	RBI	BA	OBA	SLG		AB	HR	RBI	BA	OBA	SLG
Home	244	6	35	.225	.306	.369	LHP	123	4	22	.252	.293	.439
Road	269	9	33	.305	.345	.483	RHP	390	11	46	.272	.336	.426
Apr-Jun	223	4	25	.274	.328	.381	ScPos	145	3	50	.228	.291	.366
Jul-Oct	290	11	43	.262	.324	.466	Clutch	71	3	9	.254	.303	.408

How He Compares to Other Batters

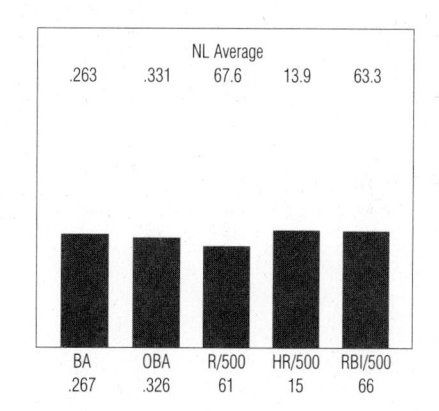

	BA	OBA	R/500	HR/500	RBI/500
NL Average	.263	.331	67.6	13.9	63.3
	.267	.326	61	15	66

Where He Hits the Ball

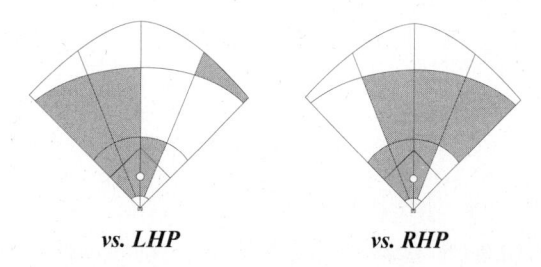

vs. LHP   vs. RHP

THE SCOUTING REPORT: 1996

CINCINNATI REDS

JEFF BRANSON

Positions: 3B/SS//2B/1B
Bats: L **Throws:** R
Ht: 6'0" **Wt:** 180
Opening Day Age: 29
Born: 1/26/1967
Drafted: CIN88 1/45
ML Seasons: 4

SCOUTING REPORT

Branson is a straightaway hitter with some power. One of his strong suits is an ability to slap at pitches he can't really handle and foul them off. Usually, Jeff can do this until he gets something more desirable to hit. His favorite pitch is fastball low and over the plate. Defensively, Jeff has average major-league tools. While he doesn't make many spectacular stops at third, he doesn't screw up many simple plays, either.

He is an average runner who does not steal. While Branson does not bunt for hits, he has sacrificed effectively when he sees the bunt sign.

HOW HE PERFORMED IN '95

Branson and Mark Lewis began their year-long platoon at third base when the season was less than a week old. The Reds made Willie Greene the scapegoat for their 0-6 start and promptly sent the youngster back to the minors.

Jeff, being the lefthanded hitter, received the most playing time. He finished with his second-highest at-bat total of his career and his season closely followed that of '93, when he also had gotten more playing time.

In 1993, Branson hit .296 before the All-Star break, then hit only .211 after it as he wore down as the season progressed. The same pattern repeated in '95, though not as dramatically. However, Jeff did hit for most of his power from July onward.

Although he had never shown any sign of being able to hit double figures in home runs, neither had many players before the recent offensive explosion. The most he'd hit before previously was six in '94. Jeff was a very ordinary hitter on the road, but enjoyed the friendly power alleys of Riverfront Stadium. He is viewed with justification as a straight platoon player and is not likely to ever expand his role. His range was well above-average last year, as was his .970 fielding percentage.

WHAT TO EXPECT IN '96

He is a fan favorite, but it's a little hard to understand why. Though Jeff is a good utility player, he's weak as a starter when playing a power position. The Reds have several candidates to replace the now-departed Lewis in the platoon, or to replace Branson altogether. Former Reds' star Chris Sabo and prospects Pokey Reese and the misused Greene could all start at the hot corner in '96.

Overall Statistics

	G	AB	R	H	2B	3B	HR	RBI	SB	CS	BB	SO	BA	OBA
95 CIN	122	331	43	86	18	2	12	45	2	1	44	69	.260	.345
Career	377	936	113	243	44	5	21	98	6	3	73	174	.260	.311

1995 Situational Statistics

	AB	HR	RBI	BA	OBA	SLG		AB	HR	RBI	BA	OBA	SLG
Home	149	9	24	.268	.327	.523	LHP	38	0	4	.158	.238	.211
Road	182	3	21	.253	.358	.363	RHP	293	12	41	.273	.358	.464
Apr-Jun	116	4	14	.276	.344	.466	ScPos	86	2	32	.233	.374	.349
Jul-Oct	215	8	31	.251	.345	.419	Clutch	46	1	3	.196	.245	.261

How He Compares to Other Batters

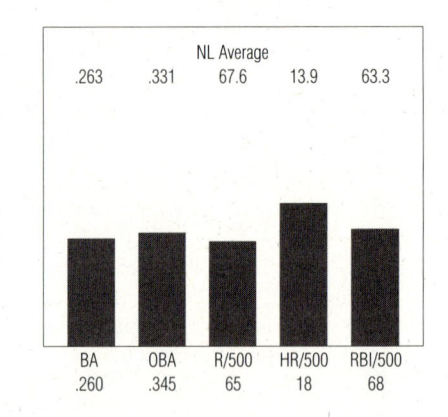

NL Average: .263 .331 67.6 13.9 63.3

BA	OBA	R/500	HR/500	RBI/500
.260	.345	65	18	68

Where He Hits the Ball

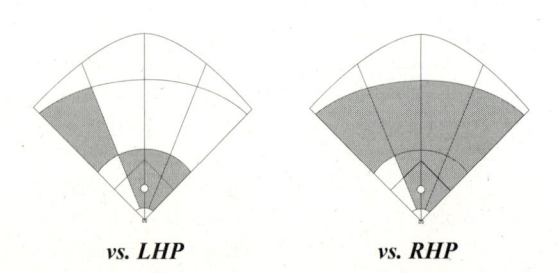

vs. LHP   vs. RHP

CINCINNATI REDS

JEFF BRANTLEY

Position: RP
Bats: R **Throws:** R
Ht: 5'11" **Wt:** 180
Opening Day Age: 32
Born: 9/5/1963
Drafted: SF85 6/134
ML Seasons: 8

SCOUTING REPORT

The diminutive Brantley is very aggressive and not afraid to challenge hitters from his three-quarter delivery. His three pitches (fastball, slider, and splitter) are all average, but he mixes them well and doesn't fool around. His fastball sinks and bores into righthanders, and Jeff's splitter is thrown hard. He has a tendency to give up home runs for two reasons: a desire to keep the ball in the strike zone and occasional problems with hanging pitches.

Only three runners attempted to steal on Brantley all year long, largely because of his plus move to first and quick delivery to home. Jeff is an average fielder.

In three at-bats during '95, Brantley was hitless. He is now a .119 career hitter in 67 at-bats and is a mediocre bunter.

HOW HE PERFORMED IN '95

Used as a starter, middleman, and late reliever during his career, Brantley spent '95 as the main closer on his team for the first time. He responded by eclipsing his career high in saves by nine. Jeff had 19 saves in 1990, but hadn't had more than 15 in any year since then. Some have said he wasn't capable of shouldering the full-time load, but Brantley proved to be one of the league's better late-inning relievers.

Although he allowed 11 homers, which is high for a closer, most of them came when the Reds were up a few runs and didn't hurt the team. He converted 28 of 32 save opportunities (88%), a rate better than that of his Cincinnati bullpen mates. The Reds were 49-7 when Brantley got into the game and won 25 straight games in which he appeared after their 0-6 start. Jeff didn't lose a game until July 5, when he gave up a three-run homer to Barry Bonds in the ninth inning.

While Brantley doesn't overpower hitters, he can mix his pitches well, using good location and striking out nearly a batter an inning. He allowed only 17 non-intentional walks in '95.

WHAT TO EXPECT IN '96

Jeff will be the late-inning man again for at least another year. The Reds believe Hector Carrasco ultimately will take over the closer's job, but he's still a year or two away. If the Reds don't strip their team too badly in the off-season, Brantley should post 25-30 saves in '96.

Overall Statistics

	G	GS	GF	SV	W	L	ERA	IP	H	R	ER	HR	BB	SO
95 CIN	56	0	49	28	3	2	2.82	70.1	53	22	22	11	20	62
Career	405	18	213	85	38	28	3.12	641.0	556	242	222	67	267	509

1995 Situational Statistics

	W	L	ERA	SV	IP	BB	SO		AB	HR	RBI	BA	OBA	SLG
Home	1	2	3.86	12	37.1	6	27	LHB	118	7	15	.229	.316	.449
Road	2	0	1.64	16	33.0	14	35	RHB	139	4	12	.187	.214	.295
Apr-Jun	3	0	2.62	12	34.1	9	31	ScPos	54	1	15	.148	.222	.204
Jul-Oct	0	2	3.00	16	36.0	11	31	Clutch	154	7	19	.188	.257	.351

How He Compares to Other Pitchers

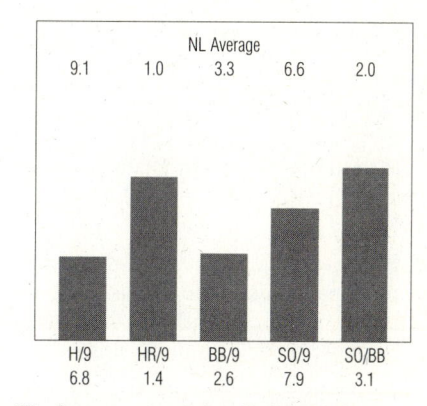

NL Average: 9.1, 1.0, 3.3, 6.6, 2.0

	H/9	HR/9	BB/9	SO/9	SO/BB
	6.8	1.4	2.6	7.9	3.1

How He Compares to Other Relief Pitchers

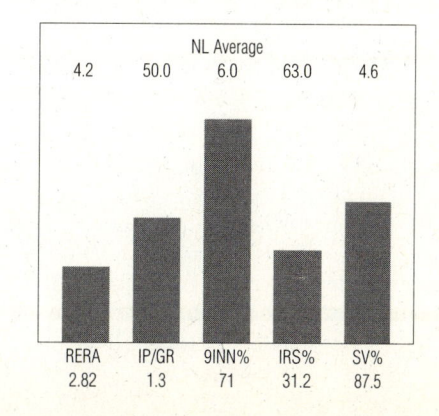

NL Average: 4.2, 50.0, 6.0, 63.0, 4.6

	RERA	IP/GR	9INN%	IRS%	SV%
	2.82	1.3	71	31.2	87.5

THE SCOUTING REPORT: 1996

CINCINNATI REDS

DAVE BURBA

Position: RP/SP
Bats: R **Throws:** R
Ht: 6'4" **Wt:** 220
Opening Day Age: 29
Born: 7/7/1966
Drafted: SEA87 2/33
ML Seasons: 6

SCOUTING REPORT

Burba has a good arm and will throw four pitches from a high three-quarter delivery: fastball, slider, change and split-finger. He uses all four as a starter but relies on just the fastball and splitter as a reliever.

Dave's heater is above-average with good movement downward. He will also cut the fastball. His plus splitter is thrown very hard. His breaking and off-speed stuff needs work; while Burba throws an average curve, he needs to develop better command of the pitch. His change-up is average but not used enough. The burly Burba is slow off the mound, making him a slightly below-average fielder, but throws well on bunts. He is average at holding runners: of the 11 attempting stolen bases against Dave in '95, eight were successful.

HOW HE PERFORMED IN '95

Burba was a throw-in for the Reds in the Deion Sanders-Mark Portugal trade. The thinking at the time was that he would provide another arm in the bullpen and could start if the Reds needed somebody to fill in, but he outpitched the celebrated and more highly-paid Portugal.

After making four appearances out of the bullpen, Dave got his first start on August 3 and was in the rotation from then on, winning three consecutive starts. The third one was a complete-game shutout against Houston where he had a no-hitter for 7.2 innings.

Overall, Burba made nine starts, all with the Reds, and 43 relief appearances. He was 4-2 with a 2.41 ERA as a starter and 6-2 with a 4.04 ERA in the bullpen. Burba suffered mild tendinitis in his right shoulder late in the season and had to miss one start, but went right back in the rotation. With the Giants, Dave did not bat. After the trade to Cincy, he was 1-for-15 with nine strikeouts, although he did lay down four sacrifices. Burba is a .140 career hitter in 50 trips.

WHAT TO EXPECT IN '96

Burba is in the Reds' plans for '96, and may play a bigger role than any other player they received in the trade. Darren Lewis is already gone and Mark Portugal and his hefty salary may be unloaded. Dave will begin the year in the rotation and will have to pitch his way out of it. With the way he finished last season, that doesn't seem likely.

Overall Statistics

	G	GS	GF	SV	W	L	ERA	IP	H	R	ER	HR	BB	SO
95 SF/CIN	52	9	7	0	10	4	3.97	106.2	90	50	47	9	51	96
Career	214	27	46	1	27	22	4.28	391.1	366	203	186	38	180	335

1995 Situational Statistics

	W	L	ERA	SV	IP	BB	SO		AB	HR	RBI	BA	OBA	SLG
Home	4	1	2.41	0	59.2	27	48	LHB	157	5	29	.274	.365	.433
Road	6	3	5.94	0	47.0	24	48	RHB	238	4	19	.197	.282	.294
Apr-Jun	3	2	4.50	0	36.0	18	41	ScPos	108	3	38	.241	.352	.370
Jul-Oct	7	2	3.69	0	70.2	33	55	Clutch	91	2	12	.187	.312	.297

How He Compares to Other Pitchers

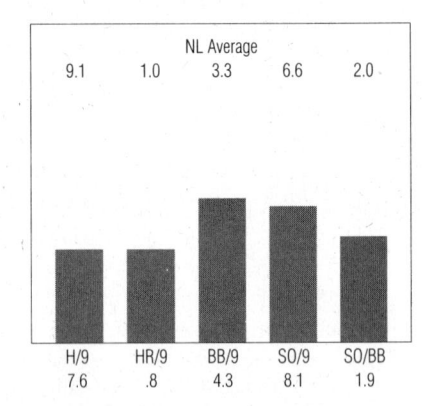

NL Average: H/9 9.1, HR/9 1.0, BB/9 3.3, SO/9 6.6, SO/BB 2.0
H/9 7.6, HR/9 .8, BB/9 4.3, SO/9 8.1, SO/BB 1.9

How He Compares to Other Relief Pitchers

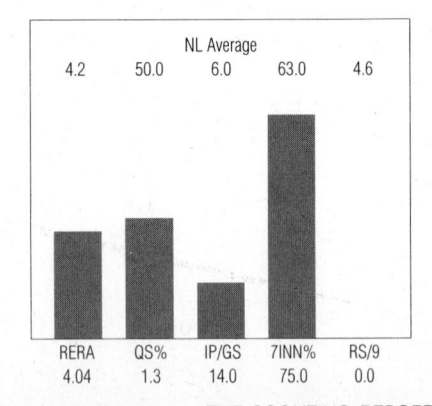

NL Average: RERA 4.2, QS% 50.0, IP/GS 6.0, 7INN% 63.0, RS/9 4.6
RERA 4.04, QS% 1.3, IP/GS 14.0, 7INN% 75.0, RS/9 0.0

CINCINNATI REDS

RON GANT

Position: OF
Bats: R **Throws:** R
Ht: 6' " **Wt:** 192
Opening Day Age: 31
Born: 3/2/1965
Drafted: ATL83 4/100
ML Seasons: 8

SCOUTING REPORT

After missing all of the 1994 season with a broken leg, Gant came back with above-average speed although he has an uneven stride following the injury.

Still a first-ball fastball hitter, Gant has a good idea of the strike zone. He likes the pitch down and in, but shows power to all fields. Although he often bunts for hits, he did not do this very well in '95.

Ron's throwing strength and accuracy rate as slightly below-average, suiting him best for left field. His range is average-plus and his hands average.

HOW HE PERFORMED IN '95

Chalk another one up for Reds' GM Jim Bowden. He took a chance on Gant when nobody else would and it paid off very big. Ron ranked among league leaders in home runs most of the year and hit many of them in critical situations. He had slugged four game-winning, extra-inning homers by July 2, tying the single-season major-league record set by Willie Mays.

Gant never had much of a problem with the right leg he broke after the '93 season, although he needed a cortisone shot to relieve knee swelling during spring training. There appeared to be few ill effects, as Ron stole 11 bases in the first seven weeks of the season. Gant said the only time his leg acted up was when he ran full speed and had to stop suddenly, so he compensated by trying to slide headfirst at all times.

The strong-armed slugger hit only one home run in September and October, which probably cost him a shot at the MVP award. One serious problem last year was a rise in strikeouts; Ron fanned in well over a quarter of his at-bats, a significant rise over his previous rate.

He threw out seven runners last year, charging balls aggressively to make up for a lack of overall throwing ability.

WHAT TO EXPECT IN '96

Although Bowden badly wanted Ron back, Ron signed a five-year deal with St. Louis in December. The wisdom of this move remains to be seen—as good as Gant is now, he'll still be collecting big paychecks at age 35, and a lot can happen in half a decade. He has to hit very well in order to earn that money, which he should do this season in St. Louis.

Overall Statistics

	G	AB	R	H	2B	3B	HR	RBI	SB	CS	BB	SO	BA	OBA
95 CIN	119	410	79	113	19	4	29	88	23	8	74	108	.276	.386
Career	977	3602	594	949	177	31	176	568	180	76	374	708	.263	.334

1995 Situational Statistics

	AB	HR	RBI	BA	OBA	SLG		AB	HR	RBI	BA	OBA	SLG
Home	189	12	42	.275	.390	.524	LHP	84	7	17	.250	.413	.536
Road	221	17	46	.276	.383	.579	RHP	326	22	71	.282	.379	.558
Apr-Jun	194	17	47	.299	.409	.629	ScPos	114	9	61	.298	.433	.614
Jul-Oct	216	12	41	.255	.365	.486	Clutch	55	7	18	.418	.508	.855

How He Compares to Other Batters

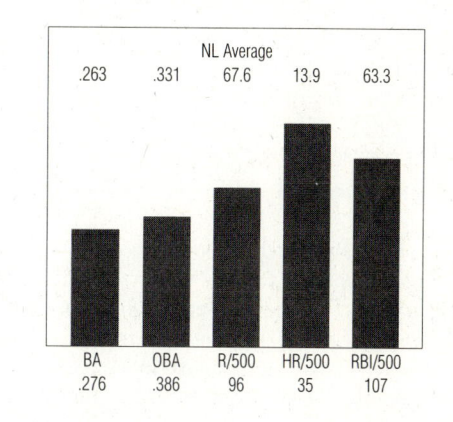

NL Average: .263 .331 67.6 13.9 63.3

	BA	OBA	R/500	HR/500	RBI/500
	.276	.386	96	35	107

Where He Hits the Ball

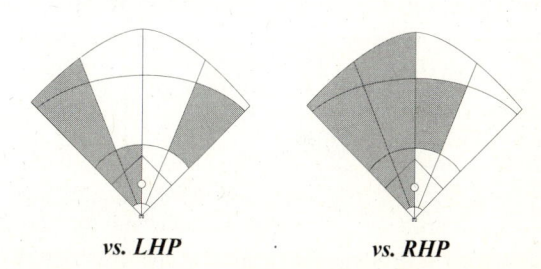

vs. LHP   vs. RHP

THE SCOUTING REPORT: 1996

CINCINNATI REDS

BARRY LARKIN

Position: SS
Bats: R **Throws:** R
Ht: 6'0" **Wt:** 185
Opening Day Age: 31
Born: 4/28/1964
Drafted: CIN85 1/4
ML Seasons: 10

SCOUTING REPORT
While Larkin isn't as flashy a defensive player as other shortstops, many regard him as the best defensive middle infielder in the league. He is solid in every aspect of the game.

Barry's hands, range, arm strength, and throwing accuracy are all plus. He is capable of spectacular plays as well as the routine ones and turns the double play effectively. Although he often throws off the wrong foot to get the ball to first sooner, Larkin has the arm to get away with it.

Larkin is now in his 30s but still has above-average speed and is an outstanding runner and basestealer. Barry has plus power and likes to drive low pitches, making outstanding contact with good discipline.

HOW HE PERFORMED IN '95
Larkin was voted the 1995 National League MVP despite competition from more powerful hitters. The voting showed that offense, defense, and leadership were important in the selection process, and Barry had plenty of all of those things to spare.

First of all, he can just hit. Take out his 3-for-50 slump in June while playing through a thumb injury he suffered when hit by a Darryl Kile pitch, and Larkin hit .348 with a slugging percentage of nearly .550. He had more walks than strikeouts for the fourth consecutive season.

The most surprising aspect of his '95 season, however, was his stolen base total. Larkin hadn't swiped more than 26 in a season since 1990 and his previous high was 40 in 1988. Barry credited his running to an improved off-season diet which had allowed him to lose 10 pounds. Although Larkin lost the stolen base title to Quilvio Veras, he was caught stealing only five times, 16 fewer than Veras.

Larkin is the heart and soul as well as the clubhouse leader of the Reds. When Cincinnati was having trouble closing out the NL Central title, he called a team meeting and ripped his teammates for coasting through the last weeks of the schedule.

WHAT TO EXPECT IN '96
Still the best shortstop in the game without a doubt, Larkin has been healthy for two straight years and is in the prime of his career. He's entering the final year of his contract and, if he has another season like '95, he may well wind up the highest-paid player in the game. A class act and one of the best.

Overall Statistics

	G	AB	R	H	2B	3B	HR	RBI	SB	CS	BB	SO	BA	OBA
95 CIN	131	496	98	158	29	6	15	66	51	5	61	49	.319	.394
Career	1176	4429	711	1322	222	44	102	537	239	41	449	431	.298	.364

1995 Situational Statistics

	AB	HR	RBI	BA	OBA	SLG		AB	HR	RBI	BA	OBA	SLG
Home	253	8	34	.328	.424	.498	LHP	111	8	20	.288	.370	.577
Road	243	7	32	.309	.360	.486	RHP	385	7	46	.327	.400	.468
Apr-Jun	188	6	29	.282	.391	.468	ScPos	110	6	54	.345	.453	.591
Jul-Oct	308	9	37	.341	.395	.506	Clutch	68	2	11	.397	.494	.559

How He Compares to Other Batters

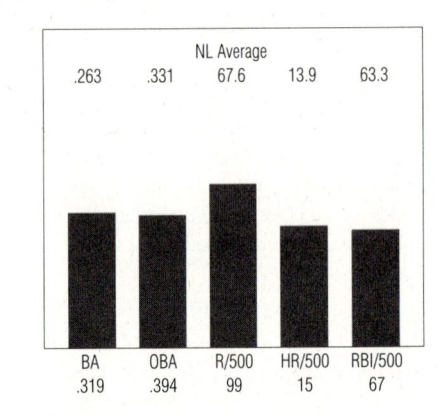

NL Average
.263 .331 67.6 13.9 63.3

BA	OBA	R/500	HR/500	RBI/500
.319	.394	99	15	67

Where He Hits the Ball

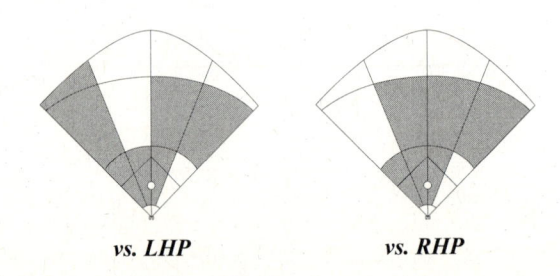

vs. LHP   vs. RHP

CINCINNATI REDS

DARREN LEWIS

Position: OF
Bats: R **Throws:** R
Ht: 6'0" **Wt:** 180
Opening Day Age: 28
Born: 8/28/1967
Drafted: OAK88 19/463
ML Seasons: 6

SCOUTING REPORT

A Gold Glove centerfielder, Darren Lewis has above-average hands and range and gets a very good jump on fly balls. Defensively, his only down side is below-average arm strength.

Lewis is an above-average runner who accelerates quickly but is inconsistent on the bases. He has the ability to leg out doubles and triples.

The only thing slow about Darren is his bat. Lack of bat speed and power forces him to take pitches to the opposite field. While Lewis likes high pitches over the plate, he cannot catch up to a good fastball or figure out a hard slider. At times, he has shown good plate discipline but, in general, he does not walk often.

HOW HE PERFORMED IN '95

Speed and defense were about all that Lewis offered in '95, especially to the Reds. Lewis hit .252 for the Giants through late July before being traded to Cincinnati. He was the Reds' starting center fielder for about a week, but didn't hit a lick and quickly lost the job to Thomas Howard. While Darren had never been much of a power hitter, the Reds certainly expected him to provide more than the three extra-base hits, all doubles, that he hit in 163 at-bats with Cincinnati.

D-Lew, his nickname from his days in San Francisco, had better success with the Giants. While in San Francisco he stole 27 bases in 38 attempts. In Cincinnati he swiped 11 sacks, but was also caught stealing an ugly 11 times. If he doesn't steal bases, Darren is practically useless on offense.

Lewis didn't let his problems at the plate affect his fielding, showing excellent mobility in the field and finishing third among NL outfielders with a .994 fielding percentage. His mediocre total of five assists is about Darren's usual.

WHAT TO EXPECT IN '96

Lewis was a decent hitter in the minors, but it has become painfully obvious that he'll never be much of an offensive player in the bigs. His contract demands cost him his job with the Reds in December, but his speed and defense got him a job for '96 with the White Sox.

How valuable is Lewis? If he couldn't beat out Thomas Howard for a starting spot in Cincinnati in '95, expect him to bat low in the Sox' order this year and contribute little except in the field.

Overall Statistics

	G	AB	R	H	2B	3B	HR	RBI	SB	CS	BB	SO	BA	OBA
95 SF/CIN	132	472	66	118	13	3	1	24	32	18	34	57	.250	.311
Career	579	2022	303	503	58	23	9	135	151	61	189	227	.249	.319

1995 Situational Statistics

	AB	HR	RBI	BA	OBA	SLG		AB	HR	RBI	BA	OBA	SLG
Home	220	1	14	.236	.306	.282	LHP	104	0	3	.231	.270	.288
Road	252	0	10	.262	.315	.310	RHP	368	1	21	.255	.322	.299
Apr-Jun	250	0	13	.256	.303	.304	ScPos	86	0	22	.267	.333	.291
Jul-Oct	222	1	11	.243	.319	.288	Clutch	64	0	5	.344	.440	.359

How He Compares to Other Batters

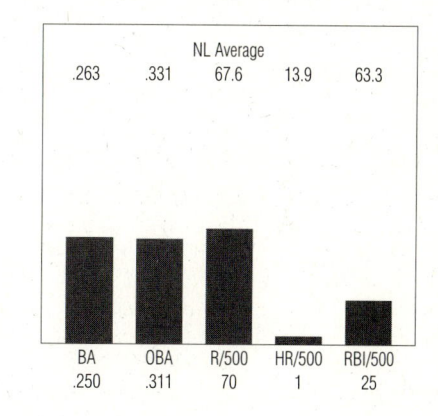

NL Average: .263 .331 67.6 13.9 63.3

BA	OBA	R/500	HR/500	RBI/500
.250	.311	70	1	25

Where He Hits the Ball

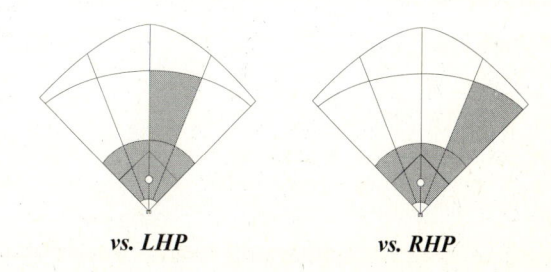

vs. LHP   vs. RHP

THE SCOUTING REPORT: 1996

CINCINNATI REDS

HAL MORRIS

Position: 1B
Bats: L **Throws:** L
Ht: 6'3" **Wt:** 200
Opening Day Age: 30
Born: 4/9/1965
Drafted: NYA86 7/210
ML Seasons: 8

SCOUTING REPORT

William Harold Morris twitches around in the batting box, shuffles his feet, and then uses his outstanding vision and quick wrists to adjust to whatever a pitcher delivers. He will hit almost anything thrown in the strike zone, preferring pitches over the plate whether they're high or low.

Mostly a straightaway and opposite-field hitter, Hal will occasionally turn on a fat pitch inside. He makes good contact despite his unconventional hitting mechanics. With mediocre speed, he rarely attempts to steal or bunt. While Morris is just an average fielder, he has improved. His range is now slightly above-average, as are his hands. Hal has also improved his ability to scoop throws out of the dirt, but has an average arm.

HOW HE PERFORMED IN '95

Morris struggled badly through the first few weeks of the season, starting off 1-for-26, then pulled his left hamstring running out a grounder in Atlanta. That injury dogged him most of the first half.

After coming off the disabled list at the All-Star break, Morris bounced back and eventually produced typical seasonal numbers. Hal's batting average after the break was only slightly lower than his .313 career average entering '95. Despite his relatively poor '95, Hal still ranks eighth among active players in batting average.

WHAT TO EXPECT IN '96

Morris' re-signing with the Reds was somewhat of a surprise. He had served as the Reds' player representative, and it was thought that the team would let him become a free agent as a result of the players' strike.

However, Hal is deeply loyal to the Reds. Asked during the playoffs about the possibility that he wouldn't be back, Morris broke down. He makes his off-season home in the northern Kentucky suburbs, wants to play for new manager Ray Knight, and was very happy to re-up with Cincinnati.

He does not hit with the home run punch usually expected of a first baseman, rarely walks, and does not steal bases. However, .300 hitters with doubles power have real value. When Morris is healthy he's one of the top first basemen in the league, and his career hitting stats stack up with those of more highly-regarded Mark Grace. If healthy, Hal will have another fine season in '96.

Overall Statistics

	G	AB	R	H	2B	3B	HR	RBI	SB	CS	BB	SO	BA	OBA
95 CIN	101	359	53	100	25	2	11	51	1	1	29	58	.279	.333
Career	702	2394	327	737	149	13	55	330	34	18	210	330	.308	.363

1995 Situational Statistics

	AB	HR	RBI	BA	OBA	SLG		AB	HR	RBI	BA	OBA	SLG
Home	161	6	26	.335	.378	.559	LHP	68	0	7	.221	.274	.294
Road	198	5	25	.232	.298	.364	RHP	291	11	44	.292	.347	.488
Apr-Jun	110	3	17	.209	.241	.327	ScPos	111	1	33	.216	.313	.306
Jul-Oct	249	8	34	.309	.372	.506	Clutch	54	3	11	.241	.311	.444

How He Compares to Other Batters

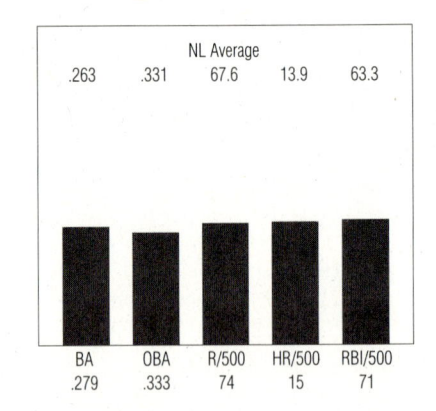

NL Average: BA .263, OBA .331, R/500 67.6, HR/500 13.9, RBI/500 63.3

BA .279, OBA .333, R/500 74, HR/500 15, RBI/500 71

Where He Hits the Ball

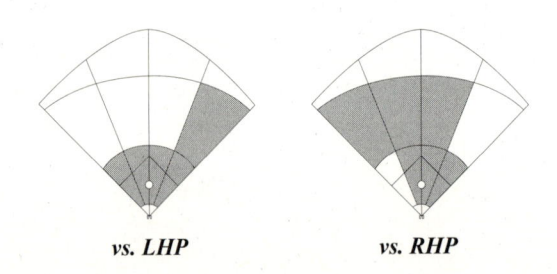

vs. LHP

vs. RHP

CINCINNATI REDS

MARK PORTUGAL

Position: SP
Bats: R **Throws:** R
Ht: 6'0" **Wt:** 190
Opening Day Age: 33
Born: 10/30/1962
Drafted: MIN 10/23/80
ML Seasons: 11

SCOUTING REPORT

Mark throws from a three-quarter angle, bringing home four pitches with well above-average control. His slightly below-average fastball is usually thrown to sink and has good life, but Portugal will also throw a four-seamer at times.

His average curve has good rotation, and Mark also possesses an average slider. His best pitch is an outstanding change-up that ranks as one of the top deception pitches in baseball. Portugal changes speeds very well and is a smart pitcher.

Despite his build, Mark is a plus fielder. He is just average at holding runners, and 15 of 17 trying to steal against him in '95 were successful. Just a .138 hitter last season in 58 at-bats, Mark is a .197 lifetime hitter with two home runs. He is an efficient sacrifice bunter.

HOW HE PERFORMED IN '95

When the Reds traded Deion Sanders and two minor leaguers to get Portugal last July, they thought they were getting a top pitcher who could lead the team to the World Series. However, Mark made anything but a positive first impression on his new teammates. In his first two starts, Portugal allowed 17 hits and 11 earned runs in only 5.1 innings. He rebounded after that, going 6-3 the rest of the season and averaging six innings a start with an ERA of 3.62 in August and 1.80 in September. He made seven quality starts in the last two months of the season.

Portugal allowed leadoff hitters to hit .329 against him while he was with the Reds. He allowed 79 hits, but only 22 extra base hits, including seven home runs in nearly 78 innings in Cincinnati. Overall, his numbers with the Reds weren't that bad, but fans got down on him because of his first few starts.

WHAT TO EXPECT IN '96

The frugal Reds wanted to unload Portugal's $4 million salary but had trouble finding takers for the paychecks attached to their pitchers. As a result, although Mark is not a #1 or #2 starter, he'll be in the rotation and will have to assume a key role if the Reds succeed in trading John Smiley, David Wells, or both.

Overall Statistics

	G	GS	GF	SV	W	L	ERA	IP	H	R	ER	HR	BB	SO
95 SF/CIN	31	31	0	0	11	10	4.01	181.2	185	91	81	17	56	96
Career	259	201	23	5	84	67	3.81	1340.0	1285	623	567	135	487	856

1995 Situational Statistics

	W	L	ERA	SV	IP	BB	SO		AB	HR	RBI	BA	OBA	SLG
Home	4	6	3.52	0	99.2	30	59	LHB	340	5	32	.256	.321	.356
Road	7	4	4.61	0	82.0	26	37	RHB	365	12	47	.268	.319	.430
Apr-Jun	5	2	3.66	0	83.2	28	50	ScPos	171	5	58	.263	.349	.404
Jul-Oct	6	8	4.32	0	98.0	28	46	Clutch	47	0	2	.234	.308	.234

How He Compares to Other Pitchers

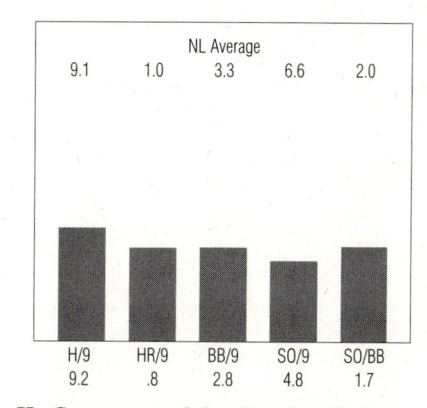

NL Average: H/9 9.1, HR/9 1.0, BB/9 3.3, SO/9 6.6, SO/BB 2.0

H/9	HR/9	BB/9	SO/9	SO/BB
9.2	.8	2.8	4.8	1.7

How He Compares to Other Starting Pitchers

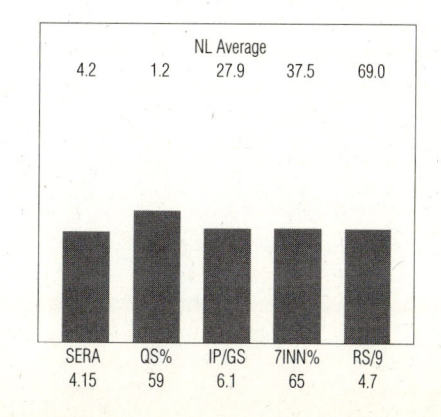

NL Average: 4.2, 1.2, 27.9, 37.5, 69.0

SERA	QS%	IP/GS	7INN%	RS/9
4.15	59	6.1	65	4.7

CINCINNATI REDS

REGGIE SANDERS

Position: OF
Bats: R **Throws:** R
Ht: 6'1" **Wt:** 180
Opening Day Age: 28
Born: 12/1/1967
Drafted: CIN87 7/180
ML Seasons: 5

SCOUTING REPORT

Sanders has above-average power and will blast a well-placed fastball a million miles, but off-speed pitches have flustered Reggie for his entire career. He prefers the ball down and in, where he will pull it. Strikeouts are a constant problem, although he did make better contact in '95, as he had led the league in whiffs the season before.

One of the best right fielders in the league, Sanders has an above-average arm in strength and accuracy. His range and hands are plus as well.

Reggie is an above-average runner and a smart basestealer. He does not try to steal every time he reaches, but instead waits until he has a good opportunity. He rarely bunts.

HOW HE PERFORMED IN '95

Sanders got only five at-bats in spring training because of a minor leg injury, but came back well in the first month of the regular season, hitting over .300 by late May.

In '95, the soft-spoken Sanders had the All-Star year many have predicted for him since he first came up. He had his best average by over 30 points and also set career highs in doubles, home runs, RBIs and stolen bases. Reggie ranked among the NL's top ten hitters in nine key offensive categories, and was the club's most consistent day-in, day-out performer. Improvement against righthanders (40 points in batting average from '94, plus much more power) was key to Sanders' success.

He started every game the first half of the year and was named "National League Mid-Season MVP" by Baseball America. Reggie then hit .354 with eight homers in August, but just .253 with middling power in September.

Sanders finally started to get recognition as a top defensive outfielder. He can cover as much ground as any right fielder in the league, and his arm ranks near the top as well: Reggie tied for fourth in the league with 12 assists.

WHAT TO EXPECT IN '96

Sanders is now regarded as an All-Star but could be even better if he could make more consistent contact against righthanders. Power hitters are allowed to strike out, but once every four at bats may be a bit much. If he can learn to hit mediocre breaking pitches, Reggie could have a true monster season.

Overall Statistics

	G	AB	R	H	2B	3B	HR	RBI	SB	CS	BB	SO	BA	OBA
95 CIN	133	484	91	148	36	6	28	99	36	12	69	122	.306	.397
Career	503	1805	315	501	98	24	78	283	101	39	209	461	.278	.355

1995 Situational Statistics

	AB	HR	RBI	BA	OBA	SLG		AB	HR	RBI	BA	OBA	SLG
Home	240	9	45	.296	.378	.517	LHP	104	8	24	.365	.447	.692
Road	244	19	54	.316	.415	.639	RHP	380	20	75	.289	.383	.547
Apr-Jun	216	13	49	.315	.398	.602	ScPos	147	7	68	.299	.441	.531
Jul-Oct	268	15	50	.299	.396	.560	Clutch	70	1	10	.200	.317	.286

How He Compares to Other Batters

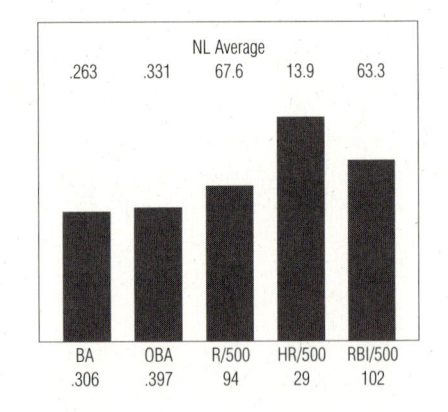

NL Average: .263 .331 67.6 13.9 63.3

BA	OBA	R/500	HR/500	RBI/500
.306	.397	94	29	102

Where He Hits the Ball

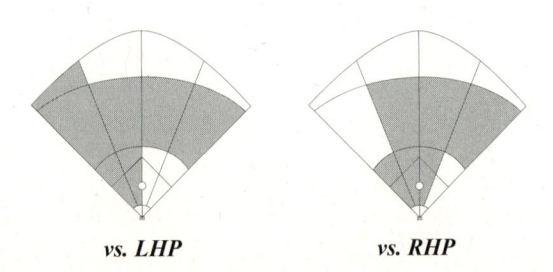

vs. LHP   vs. RHP

CINCINNATI REDS

BENITO SANTIAGO

Positions: C//1B
Bats: R **Throws:** R
Ht: 6'1" **Wt:** 185
Opening Day Age: 31
Born: 3/9/1965
Drafted: SD 9/1/82
ML Seasons: 10

SCOUTING REPORT
Benito remains a free swinger at bat, but his plate discipline has improved somewhat in the past two seasons. A low-ball hitter with decent bat speed and some power, he has been much more effective facing lefties the last few years, but hardly saw them in '95—not because he was rigidly platooned, but because the Reds saw so few southpaws. He is an adequate baserunner but no longer steals or bunts.

Behind the mask, Santiago's formerly plus tools, especially his famously strong arm, are now average.

HOW HE PERFORMED IN '95
Santiago's season started slowly. He got only 34 at-bats before bone chips in his right elbow landed him on the disabled list for two months. However, he was one of the hottest hitters in the league in his first two weeks after coming off the DL in early July. He hit nearly .500 in that stretch and wound up hitting .347 for the month. It was easily his most productive month, as he hit five home runs and drove in 19, nearly half his season totals in both categories.

After several mediocre seasons at bat, including a '93 campaign that saw Santiago bottom out at .230, he has regained some of his value in the last two seasons, hitting for power, working on making better contact, and showing surprising selectivity. Benny was surprisingly productive against righties in '95.

Benito made just two errors in '95 and had a .996 fielding percentage that rated best among NL catchers. Unfortunately, he slumped in his strongest area, throwing, with only 28% of potential thieves being sent to the bench. He also committed six passed balls. He had thrown out 43% of potential basestealers in '94 and 29% the season before that; part of his decline is attributable to his surgery.

WHAT TO EXPECT IN '96
The Reds will not bring him back in '96. The club did not offer Santiago arbitration in December, making him a free agent. After a dip in his career which almost ended it, he's put together two straight solid, if unspectacular, seasons. While Benito will never again be the horse he once was, he is valuable enough to warrant a starting job somewhere.

Overall Statistics

	G	AB	R	H	2B	3B	HR	RBI	SB	CS	BB	SO	BA	OBA
95 CIN	81	266	40	76	20	0	11	44	2	2	24	48	.286	.351
Career	1110	3944	436	1034	177	23	120	510	75	57	225	709	.262	.303

1995 Situational Statistics

	AB	HR	RBI	BA	OBA	SLG		AB	HR	RBI	BA	OBA	SLG
Home	144	7	23	.333	.398	.576	LHP	62	3	14	.355	.444	.597
Road	122	4	21	.230	.296	.377	RHP	204	8	30	.265	.321	.451
Apr-Jun	34	1	1	.324	.361	.500	ScPos	68	3	34	.338	.434	.588
Jul-Oct	232	10	43	.280	.350	.483	Clutch	34	0	2	.235	.297	.324

How He Compares to Other Batters

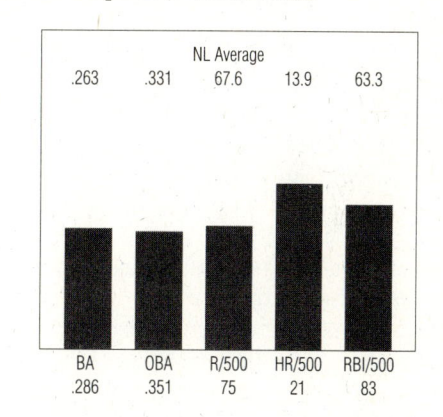

NL Average: .263   .331   67.6   13.9   63.3

BA	OBA	R/500	HR/500	RBI/500
.286	.351	75	21	83

Where He Hits the Ball

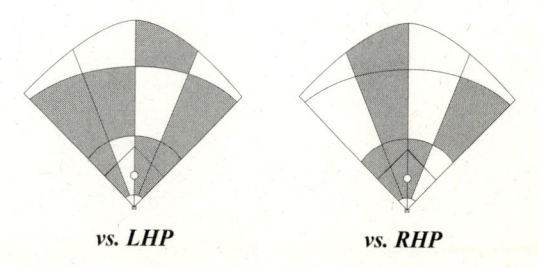

vs. LHP   vs. RHP

THE SCOUTING REPORT: 1996

CINCINNATI REDS

PETE SCHOUREK

Position: SP
Bats: L **Throws:** L
Ht: 6'5" **Wt:** 195
Opening Day Age: 26
Born: 5/10/1969
Drafted: NYN87 3/56
ML Seasons: 5

SCOUTING REPORT
The lanky lefty throws from three-quarters, with his best pitch a well above-average change-up. Pete disguises the pitch very well with his motion, varying the delivery little from that of his fastball. When he's throwing the change effectively, Pete makes the best hitters in the NL look like Little Leaguers. Schourek sinks and cuts his fastball with now-average, improved velocity, and also has a curve ranking slightly above-average.

An average fielder off the mound, Pete has a decent move but pays attention to runners—12 of 19 trying to steal while he was on the mound were thrown out.

HOW HE PERFORMED IN '95
It's safe to say that Schourek had the best season of any player who was waived in 1994. It's hard to believe the Reds got him for just $1 that April. Three Reds were mentioned as MVP candidates (Ron Gant, Reggie Sanders, and eventual winner Barry Larkin), but Schourek should have gotten more support. All season, he was the glue that held the starting rotation together. With Jose Rijo hurting and the Reds trying out Kevin Jarvis, C.J. Nitkowski, Tim Pugh, replacement player Rick Reed, et al., Schourek stabilized the staff like a veteran. His longest winless streak all year was four starts in June (two losses and two no-decisions).

Schourek also proved himself to be a big-game pitcher with his playoff performance, despite never having been close to postseason play before. Pete allowed only two earned runs in 14.1 innings against the Braves in the NLCS after having won Game One of the Division Series against the Dodgers.

Batting a very respectable .220 with 12 sacrifice bunts, Schourek was Cincinnati's best hitting pitcher and raised his career average to .163.

WHAT TO EXPECT IN '96
It's hard to imagine where the Reds would be without Pete. However, GM Jim Bowden said he wouldn't go to arbitration with anyone and intended to trade all the arb-eligible players that he couldn't sign. While the loss of Ron Gant hurt the Reds, Schourek was just as important to the team's success in '95 and could be even more important in '96, especially with Jose Rijo out until at least the All-Star break. If the Reds let Pete go, it could be as big a mistake as when the Mets gave him away.

Overall Statistics

	G	GS	GF	SV	W	L	ERA	IP	H	R	ER	HR	BB	SO
95 CIN	29	29	0	0	18	7	3.22	190.1	158	72	68	17	45	160
Career	149	86	16	2	41	33	4.14	622.1	635	310	286	57	206	428

1995 Situational Statistics

	W	L	ERA	SV	IP	BB	SO		AB	HR	RBI	BA	OBA	SLG
Home	13	2	1.86	0	106.2	21	90	LHB	90	4	12	.267	.316	.433
Road	5	5	4.95	0	83.2	24	70	RHB	603	13	55	.222	.276	.347
Apr-Jun	6	4	3.72	0	75.0	22	65	ScPos	115	2	45	.304	.368	.435
Jul-Oct	12	3	2.89	0	115.1	23	95	Clutch	47	0	0	.191	.224	.213

How He Compares to Other Pitchers

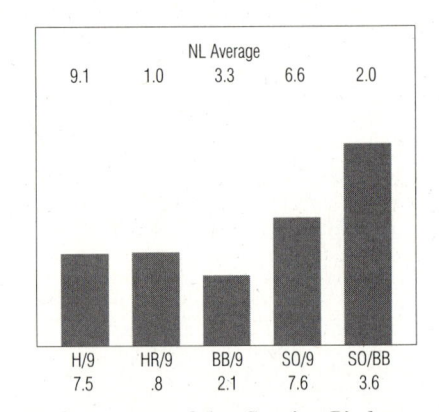

NL Average: H/9 9.1, HR/9 1.0, BB/9 3.3, SO/9 6.6, SO/BB 2.0
Schourek: H/9 7.5, HR/9 .8, BB/9 2.1, SO/9 7.6, SO/BB 3.6

How He Compares to Other Starting Pitchers

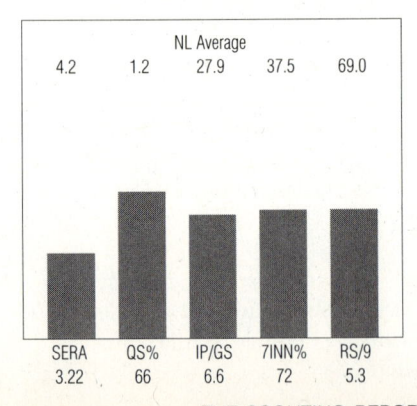

NL Average: SERA 4.2, QS% 1.2, IP/GS 27.9, 7INN% 37.5, RS/9 69.0
Schourek: SERA 3.22, QS% 66, IP/GS 6.6, 7INN% 72, RS/9 5.3

378   THE SCOUTING REPORT: 1996

CINCINNATI REDS

JOHN SMILEY

Position: SP
Bats: L **Throws:** L
Ht: 6'4" **Wt:** 195
Opening Day Age: 31
Born: 3/17/1965
Drafted: PIT83 12/300
ML Seasons: 10

SCOUTING REPORT

While Smiley doesn't have overpowering stuff, he is a smart pitcher who sets up hitters well. His fastball and curve are only average, while his slider and turned-over change-up rate slightly above par. John will sink the fastball and also cut it into the fists of righthanded hitters.

He tucks his head into his shoulder when he delivers the pitch, coming from a three-quarter motion out of a high leg kick. Probably because of this protracted delivery, nine of 13 men trying to steal while John was pitching in '95 were successful despite his acceptable move to first. He is an average fielder.

HOW HE PERFORMED IN '95

Smiley can't get a break from Reds' fans, who are still upset over his first season with the Reds. If his '95 performance can't convince the faithful that he's a good pitcher, nothing can.

John had his best season since 1992. He won one more game and lost five fewer than during the strike-shortened '94 season while also allowing his fewest hits per inning in three years. He ranked among the league leaders in inducing ground ball double plays. When he needed a grounder, Smiley simply threw his overhand curve or slider in order to get the hitters to bang the ball into the turf. For most of last summer, he simply wasn't walking anybody. However, in September, he had a 5.01 ERA and walked 10 men in six games—a lot for John.

John has never been a good hitter, and he hit only .164 last season. However, two of his nine hits surprisingly left the yard. His lifetime average is only .141, and he isn't much of a bunter either. In the field, Smiley didn't commit an error in 30 chances, and turned three double plays.

WHAT TO EXPECT IN '96

Smiley will become a free agent after the 1996 season, which lowers his potential trade value significantly. He's had two straight solid seasons and his only bad year in the last five came in '93 when he had arm problems. Despite the fact that he's one of the better lefthanded starters in the majors, the Reds may decide to trade John in order to unload his salary or lose him to free agency in a year.

Overall Statistics

	G	GS	GF	SV	W	L	ERA	IP	H	R	ER	HR	BB	SO
95 CIN	28	27	0	0	12	5	3.46	176.2	173	72	68	11	39	124
Career	300	220	21	4	102	75	3.67	1536.0	1451	689	627	139	401	993

1995 Situational Statistics

	W	L	ERA	SV	IP	BB	SO		AB	HR	RBI	BA	OBA	SLG
Home	4	4	4.00	0	72.0	23	55	LHB	102	4	14	.225	.298	.392
Road	8	1	3.10	0	104.2	16	69	RHB	557	7	51	.269	.307	.377
Apr-Jun	7	1	3.32	0	78.2	18	46	ScPos	152	3	50	.257	.306	.388
Jul-Oct	5	4	3.58	0	98.0	21	78	Clutch	50	1	4	.180	.196	.240

How He Compares to Other Pitchers

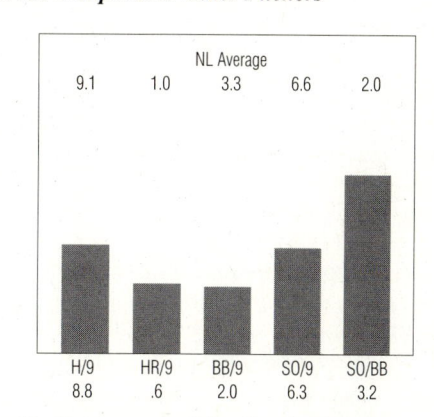

NL Average: H/9 9.1, HR/9 1.0, BB/9 3.3, SO/9 6.6, SO/BB 2.0
John Smiley: H/9 8.8, HR/9 .6, BB/9 2.0, SO/9 6.3, SO/BB 3.2

How He Compares to Other Starting Pitchers

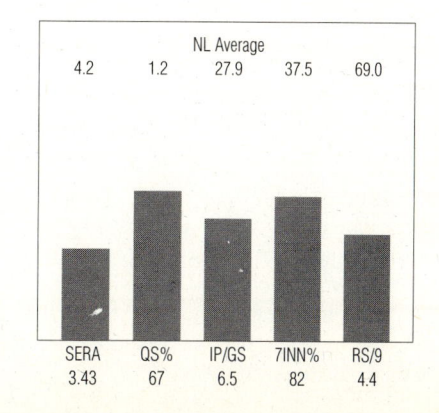

NL Average: SERA 4.2, QS% 1.2, IP/GS 27.9, 7INN% 37.5, RS/9 69.0
John Smiley: SERA 3.43, QS% 67, IP/GS 6.5, 7INN% 82, RS/9 4.4

THE SCOUTING REPORT: 1996

CINCINNATI REDS

DAVID WELLS

Position: SP
Bats: L **Throws:** L
Ht: 6'3" **Wt:** 225
Opening Day Age: 32
Born: 5/20/1963
Drafted: TOR82 2/30
ML Seasons: 9

SCOUTING REPORT

A lefthander with a plus fastball, Wells threw harder than some Reds fans had expected and also displayed a plus curve. His average change-up could be better, but David tips off the pitch with his motion. Wells, who has a high three-quarter delivery, has average control. He doesn't give up too many walks but does occasionally have problems falling behind in the count. If he walks hitters in bunches, it's a tipoff that David doesn't have his best stuff.

Since he is slow getting the ball to the plate, Wells is below-average at holding runners: 19 tried to steal against David in '95, 13 successfully. He is big and lacks mobility, making him a minus fielder.

HOW HE PERFORMED IN '95

The Reds gave up a lot to pry Wells away from Detroit in August (their 1994 top draft pick C.J. Nitkowski, and, after the season, former Indians' #1 choice Mark Lewis), but David certainly helped solidify their pitching staff down the stretch. He became an instant favorite in the clubhouse as the tattooed lefthander played practical jokes and kept things relaxed with his offbeat humor.

Wells led the Reds with three complete games despite being with the team for only two months. Two of those came in consecutive starts, both against the Cardinals. Coming into 1994, he had thrown only two complete games in 101 career starts. In the last two years, David has tossed 11 complete games, even though he missed significant time in '94 with an elbow injury that required surgery. He joined Pete Schourek and John Smiley as a dominating lefthanded threesome in the Cincinnati rotation late in the season.

Wells was an All-Star with the Tigers in '95, posting a 10-3 record and 3.04 ERA with the moribund Detroit club before being dealt to the NL. While David had spent his entire career in the American League before the trade and had never hit, he managed to collect four hits in 28 at-bats (.143). He laid down just one successful sacrifice.

WHAT TO EXPECT IN '96

The Reds traded for Wells in part to match up against the Braves' lefthanded hitters, but in the off-season the club decided to move his salary. Despite the shortened season, his 203 innings of '95 were a career high, and he'll be asked to pile up the innings this year for Baltimore.

Overall Statistics

	G	GS	GF	SV	W	L	ERA	IP	H	R	ER	HR	BB	SO
95 DET/CIN	29	29	0	0	16	8	3.24	203.0	194	88	73	23	53	133
Career	314	144	65	13	79	61	3.77	1188.2	1149	554	498	133	320	792

1995 Situational Statistics

	W	L	ERA	SV	IP	BB	SO		AB	HR	RBI	BA	OBA	SLG
Home	12	2	2.98	0	114.2	27	77	LHB	147	4	16	.245	.277	.422
Road	4	6	3.57	0	88.1	26	56	RHB	627	19	60	.252	.304	.410
Apr-Jun	6	3	3.26	0	91.0	28	55	ScPos	153	3	48	.275	.356	.418
Jul-Oct	10	5	3.21	0	112.0	25	78	Clutch	69	1	3	.246	.297	.362

How He Compares to Other Pitchers

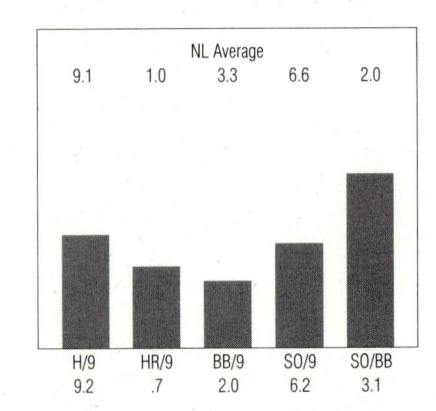

NL Average
H/9 9.1 | HR/9 1.0 | BB/9 3.3 | SO/9 6.6 | SO/BB 2.0
9.2 | .7 | 2.0 | 6.2 | 3.1

How He Compares to Other Starting Pitchers

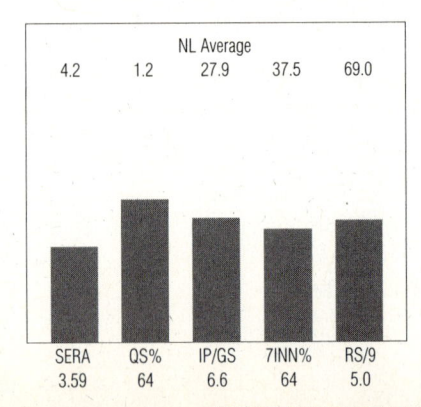

NL Average
SERA 4.2 | QS% 1.2 | IP/GS 27.9 | 7INN% 37.5 | RS/9 69.0
3.59 | 64 | 6.6 | 64 | 5.0

CINCINNATI REDS

ERIC ANTHONY

Positions: OF/1B
Bats: L **Throws:** L
Ht: 6'2" **Wt:** 195
Opening Day Age: 28
Born: 11/8/1967
Drafted: HOU86 34/795
ML Seasons: 7

Overall Statistics

	G	AB	R	H	2B	3B	HR	RBI	SB	CS	BB	SO	BA	OBA
95 CIN	47	134	19	36	6	0	5	23	2	1	13	30	.269	.327
Career	556	1740	209	399	70	6	64	242	22	12	173	417	.229	.298

1995 Situational Statistics

	AB	HR	RBI	BA	OBA	SLG		AB	HR	RBI	BA	OBA	SLG
Home	71	3	13	.254	.253	.408	LHP	17	1	5	.294	.286	.471
Road	63	2	10	.286	.400	.444	RHP	117	4	18	.265	.333	.419
Apr-Jun	58	4	13	.328	.375	.586	ScPos	47	1	19	.255	.333	.362
Jul-Oct	76	1	10	.224	.291	.303	Clutch	22	1	8	.273	.320	.455

SCOUTING REPORT

Eric Anthony loves to pull the ball, jumping on pitches down and in. He has above-average power.

Although he is just adequate as a fielder, Eric is used at all three outfield positions as well as first base. He has average hands, throwing strength, and arm accuracy, but possesses minus range largely because of below-par speed.

HOW HE PERFORMED IN '95

After coming over from the Mariners, Anthony was injury-plagued the entire season, spending time on the disabled list three different times for three different reasons.

Eric had acceptable home run and RBI totals considering his playing time. As evidence of his raw power, he hit two of the three longest home runs by Reds' players last season and hit only the fourth right-field red seat (upper deck) home run in Riverfront Stadium by a lefthanded hitter.

WHAT TO EXPECT IN '96

Anthony is a guy who could play a lot more if he could stay healthy, although he's never put up the kind of numbers that ensure a starting job. He'll have to earn a regular spot in '96, but that's still not out of the question considering his power potential.

HECTOR CARRASCO

Position: RP
Bats: R **Throws:** R
Ht: 6'2" **Wt:** 175
Opening Day Age: 26
Born: 10/22/1969
Drafted: NYN 32088
ML Seasons: 2

Overall Statistics

	G	GS	GF	SV	W	L	ERA	IP	H	R	ER	HR	BB	SO
95 CIN	64	0	28	5	2	7	4.12	87.1	86	45	40	1	46	64
Career	109	0	57	11	7	13	3.38	143.2	128	62	54	4	76	105

1995 Situational Statistics

	W	L	ERA	SV	IP	BB	SO		AB	HR	RBI	BA	OBA	SLG
Home	1	1	3.20	2	39.1	19	25	LHB	140	0	18	.300	.392	.386
Road	1	6	4.88	3	48.0	27	39	RHB	195	1	18	.226	.309	.282
Apr-Jun	2	3	2.85	5	41.0	20	21	ScPos	92	0	33	.239	.361	.283
Jul-Oct	0	4	5.24	0	46.1	26	43	Clutch	165	0	16	.255	.339	.321

SCOUTING REPORT

The overhand-delivering Carrasco has great stuff but will not consistently succeed without better command of his pitches.

He throws both a two-seam sinking fastball and a four-seam rising heater, both of which are outstanding in velocity. He also cuts the fastball. Hector throws an above-average slider and an above-average, very hard splitter. A minus fielder, Carrasco as an average move to first but is quick to home. Four tried to steal against him, all successfully; he was hitless in seven at-bats.

HOW HE PERFORMED IN '95

Carrasco's ERA jumped nearly two full runs from his rookie season but he pitched well until the last month, allowing 34 hits and 21 walks in his last 30 innings. Hector seemed to miss Jose Rijo's presence. Rijo took Carrasco under his wing in '94, and Hector's late-season '95 slide coincided with Rijo's elbow surgery and, therefore, absence from the clubhouse.

WHAT TO EXPECT IN '96

Carrasco has had only two seasons above Class A. He throws hard and hasn't had arm problems yet; assuming he can throw a few more strikes, he can graduate into the closer's role in a year or two.

THE SCOUTING REPORT: 1996

CINCINNATI REDS

MARIANO DUNCAN

Positions: 2B/SS/1B//OF/3B
Bats: R **Throws:** R
Ht: 6'0" **Wt:** 185
Opening Day Age: 33
Born: 3/13/1963
Drafted: LA 1/17/82
ML Seasons: 10

Overall Statistics

	G	AB	R	H	2B	3B	HR	RBI	SB	CS	BB	SO	BA	OBA
95 PHI/CIN	81	265	36	76	14	2	6	36	1	3	5	62	.287	.297
Career	1081	3938	521	1031	185	34	78	410	164	51	180	758	.262	.298

1995 Situational Statistics

	AB	HR	RBI	BA	OBA	SLG		AB	HR	RBI	BA	OBA	SLG
Home	118	3	18	.314	.328	.466	LHP	114	2	17	.298	.322	.430
Road	147	3	18	.265	.272	.388	RHP	151	4	19	.278	.277	.417
Apr-Jun	135	2	13	.281	.283	.385	ScPos	65	1	26	.308	.306	.446
Jul-Oct	130	4	23	.292	.312	.462	Clutch	46	1	7	.326	.326	.500

SCOUTING REPORT

Mariano can hit close to .300 by swinging at nearly every pitch—he never sees a pitch he doesn't like, no matter how bad that pitch is. He is a straight-away hitter with some power who prefers low pitches; he is really awful on breaking pitchers of all types. He has plus baserunning speed.

Defensively, second base is his best position, where he displays average-plus range and decent hands. He can play also third, short, or left field in a pinch.

HOW HE PERFORMED IN '95

Mariano began '95 in Philadelphia, hitting .286 with three home runs—and no walks!—in 186 at-bats before being traded for a minor-leaguer in August. The Braves wanted him, and Cincinnati claimed Mariano just so Atlanta couldn't.

Duncan was decent off the pine for the Reds, but he doesn't hit righthanders well enough or field well enough (even though he appeared at all four infield positions) to play every day. He walked only five times all year, all in Cincinnati.

WHAT TO EXPECT IN '96

A useful player who is better off the bench than starting, he will ply his trade in the Bronx in '96.

LENNY HARRIS

Positions: 3B/1B//OF/2B
Bats: L **Throws:** R
Ht: 5'10" **Wt:** 195
Opening Day Age: 31
Born: 10/28/1964
Drafted: CIN83 5/108
ML Seasons: 8

Overall Statistics

	G	AB	R	H	2B	3B	HR	RBI	SB	CS	BB	SO	BA	OBA
95 CIN	101	197	32	41	8	3	2	16	10	1	14	20	.208	.259
Career	822	2042	256	553	71	11	12	172	84	34	149	172	.271	.322

1995 Situational Statistics

	AB	HR	RBI	BA	OBA	SLG		AB	HR	RBI	BA	OBA	SLG
Home	90	0	4	.178	.242	.211	LHP	17	1	2	.235	.278	.471
Road	107	2	12	.234	.274	.393	RHP	180	1	14	.206	.258	.294
Apr-Jun	117	0	11	.222	.264	.308	ScPos	47	0	12	.234	.260	.340
Jul-Oct	80	2	5	.188	.253	.313	Clutch	36	1	3	.111	.154	.222

SCOUTING REPORT

Harris is what you'd expect out of a utility infielder, pinch-hitter, and pinch-runner. His tools are mediocre defensively and he is a slightly above-average runner who doesn't make many mistakes on the bases.

Lenny likes down and in fastballs and will pull but doesn't have much power. He is a frequent and excellent bunter, both for hits and sacrifices.

HOW HE PERFORMED IN '95

Just about the only positive in Lenny's '95 season was the fact that he hit his first two home runs in over two years.

Harris slumped badly in the middle of the year, hitting just .163 over 116 at-bats during June, July and August, and his overall batting average dipped 102 points. Of course, it's unwise to read much into small at-bat totals, but Harris won't be getting 500 plate appearances to get into the groove in the future. If he can't hit off the bench, he's gone.

WHAT TO EXPECT IN '96

Harris has had less than 200 at-bats in each of the last three seasons, so he's likely to be asked to sign a minor-league contract and do well in spring training in order to make a big-league club.

CINCINNATI REDS

XAVIER HERNANDEZ

Position: RP
Bats: L **Throws:** R
Ht: 6'2" **Wt:** 185
Opening Day Age: 30
Born: 8/16/1965
Drafted: TOR86 4/107
ML Seasons: 7

Overall Statistics

	G	GS	GF	SV	W	L	ERA	IP	H	R	ER	HR	BB	SO
95 CIN	59	0	19	3	7	2	4.60	90.0	95	47	46	8	31	84
Career	312	7	107	28	29	20	3.76	485.2	450	225	203	42	186	404

1995 Situational Statistics

	W	L	ERA	SV	IP	BB	SO		AB	HR	RBI	BA	OBA	SLG
Home	5	1	4.61	0	41.0	11	41	LHB	127	5	23	.315	.393	.528
Road	2	1	4.59	3	49.0	20	43	RHB	221	3	18	.249	.304	.353
Apr-Jun	5	0	4.54	3	41.2	19	41	ScPos	98	1	29	.276	.336	.378
Jul-Oct	2	2	4.66	0	48.1	12	43	Clutch	85	3	9	.224	.290	.353

SCOUTING REPORT

He once threw a hard sinker with Houston, but Hernandez now relies on a straight, average four-seam fastball. His out pitch is a slightly above-average splitter. From a high three-quarter delivery, Xavier also features a bit below-average slider and change-up.

An average fielder, Hernandez is quick to home and has a slightly plus move. Only five runners tried to steal on him in '95 in 90 innings, all successfully.

HOW HE PERFORMED IN '95

Hernandez posted back-to-back years with sub-3.00 ERAs in his first two seasons for Houston, but Xavier's ERA was 5.85 in '94 and he didn't improve much in '95. He pitched a bit better as the year went on before losing it after August. He allowed 14 earned runs over 10 innings during September and October. Hitless in eight at-bats last year, Xavier is now 1-for-35 (.028) in his career.

WHAT TO EXPECT IN '96

Hernandez is still striking out people at the same rate he always has, so there's some hope he can regain his 1992-93 form. However, he's going to have to turn it on pretty quick to avoid being just another middle reliever.

THOMAS HOWARD

Position: OF
Bats: B **Throws:** R
Ht: 6'2" **Wt:** 200
Opening Day Age: 31
Born: 12/11/1964
Drafted: SD86 1/11
ML Seasons: 6

Overall Statistics

	G	AB	R	H	2B	3B	HR	RBI	SB	CS	BB	SO	BA	OBA
95 CIN	113	281	42	85	15	2	3	26	17	8	20	37	.302	.350
Career	556	1464	185	395	70	10	21	140	56	33	95	258	.270	.313

1995 Situational Statistics

	AB	HR	RBI	BA	OBA	SLG		AB	HR	RBI	BA	OBA	SLG
Home	127	1	13	.307	.369	.402	LHP	19	0	0	.158	.273	.263
Road	154	2	13	.299	.333	.403	RHP	262	3	26	.313	.356	.412
Apr-Jun	71	0	5	.282	.354	.366	ScPos	64	1	23	.297	.361	.406
Jul-Oct	210	3	21	.310	.348	.414	Clutch	51	0	8	.353	.389	.471

SCOUTING REPORT

Thomas is a low-ball hitter who has a little power batting lefthanded. He is an above-average runner who will steal and bunt. Howard plays plenty of center field, but it isn't his best position. He has above-average range, average hands, but a slightly below-average arm.

HOW HE PERFORMED IN '95

Howard began the season as the Reds' fourth outfielder but wound up as the regular in center. He hit .313 after Deion Sanders was traded, beating out newly-acquired Darren Lewis for the everyday spot. "Tank"—his nickname since collegiate days at Ball State—enjoyed his best season. His batting average was a career high by 25 points. However, Thomas' offensive gifts are limited. He provides singles and stolen bases, but doesn't walk and lacks power and lefthanders bamboozle him. He showed good range playing all three outfield spots last year, but threw out just two runners.

WHAT TO EXPECT IN '96

Howard's big break came when the Reds released Darren Lewis. Thomas is arbitration-eligible, but won't get a multi-million dollar salary from the Reds. If hustling center field prospect Steve Gibralter has a good spring, Howard could end up playing left field in '96.

THE SCOUTING REPORT: 1996

CINCINNATI REDS

MIKE JACKSON

Position: RP
Bats: R **Throws:** R
Ht: 6'1" **Wt:** 185
Opening Day Age: 31
Born: 12/22/1964
Drafted: PHI84* S2/44
ML Seasons: 10

Overall Statistics

	G	GS	GF	SV	W	L	ERA	IP	H	R	ER	HR	BB	SO
95 CIN	40	0	10	2	6	1	2.39	49.0	38	13	13	5	19	41
Career	550	7	194	38	46	50	3.30	738.0	578	301	271	72	322	651

1995 Situational Statistics

	W	L	ERA	SV	IP	BB	SO		AB	HR	RBI	BA	OBA	SLG
Home	4	0	1.78	2	25.1	9	22	LHB	63	2	3	.206	.333	.349
Road	2	1	3.04	0	23.2	10	19	RHB	115	3	15	.217	.266	.383
Apr-Jun	1	0	7.36	0	7.1	3	6	ScPos	47	2	14	.213	.321	.404
Jul-Oct	5	1	1.51	2	41.2	16	35	Clutch	83	2	6	.193	.247	.313

SCOUTING REPORT

Depending mostly on hard stuff, Jackson has lost some of his former sharpness in the past two seasons. His fastball has plus velocity but is straight up in the zone; his slider and splitfinger are rated average. He now has a change and uses his splitter less often.

An acceptable fielder, Mike shut down opposing runners convincingly in '95, allowing only two stolen bases. He rapped a single in four at-bats, raising his career average to .185.

HOW HE PERFORMED IN '95

On the DL until early June with tendinitis in his right shoulder, Jackson was Cincinnati's best relief pitcher for most of the year after his return. It took him a few outings to get started, but he was impressive after the All-Star break. Despite the injury, Jackson still showed enough zip on his fastball to dominate hitters.

WHAT TO EXPECT IN '96

When he's healthy, he's awfully good—one of the best setup pitchers in the game—but Mike has been on the disabled list with arm problems for two seasons in a row now. He'll should pitch effectively this year in Riverfront—or somewhere else if not brought back by the Reds.

KEVIN JARVIS

Position: SP/RP
Bats: L **Throws:** R
Ht: 6'2" **Wt:** 200
Opening Day Age: 26
Born: 8/1/1969
Drafted: CIN91 21/561
ML Seasons: 2

Overall Statistics

	G	GS	GF	SV	W	L	ERA	IP	H	R	ER	HR	BB	SO
95 CIN	19	11	2	0	3	4	5.70	79.0	91	56	50	13	32	33
Career	25	14	2	0	4	5	5.96	96.2	113	70	64	17	37	43

1995 Situational Statistics

	W	L	ERA	SV	IP	BB	SO		AB	HR	RBI	BA	OBA	SLG
Home	0	3	7.51	0	44.1	17	20	LHB	115	6	18	.278	.368	.461
Road	3	1	3.12	0	34.2	15	13	RHB	197	7	30	.299	.352	.487
Apr-Jun	3	4	5.23	0	63.2	24	22	ScPos	90	3	35	.222	.279	.367
Jul-Oct	0	0	7.04	0	15.1	8	11	Clutch	7	2	2	.429	.500	1.286

SCOUTING REPORT

Scouts feel Jarvis should be better than he has shown so far. He has two slightly above-average overhand fastballs: the four-seamer rides up and the two-seamer sinks effectively.

Kevin's change-up is slightly above-average and he throws an average curve and slider to complete his package. Although Jarvis has a quick delivery and had a plus move to first in the past, all 13 men trying to steal against him were successful. He is a slightly above-average fielder. At bat, he was just 3-for-21 (.125) last year, striking out eight times.

HOW HE PERFORMED IN '95

Jarvis was surprisingly effective in the early part of the season, peaking with a two-hit shutout of the Padres which was the first complete game by any pitcher in '95.

Kevin faded after his quick start, though, and was out of the rotation by the All-Star break—and in the minors shortly after that. Command and concentration were his big problems.

WHAT TO EXPECT IN '96

The Reds are still high on Jarvis, who has pitched consistently well as a starter in the minors. He'll get a shot at starting if Dave Burba or Mark Portugal falter early.

CINCINNATI REDS

MARK LEWIS

Positions: 3B//2B/SS
Bats: R **Throws:** R
Ht: 6'1" **Wt:** 190
Opening Day Age: 26
Born: 11/30/1969
Drafted: CLE88 1/2
ML Seasons: 5

Overall Statistics

	G	AB	R	H	2B	3B	HR	RBI	SB	CS	BB	SO	BA	OBA
95 CIN	81	171	25	58	13	1	3	30	0	3	21	33	.339	.407
Career	321	1023	110	278	56	2	10	103	10	10	63	167	.272	.313

1995 Situational Statistics

	AB	HR	RBI	BA	OBA	SLG		AB	HR	RBI	BA	OBA	SLG
Home	93	1	13	.312	.385	.430	LHP	115	2	22	.357	.409	.513
Road	78	2	17	.372	.433	.538	RHP	56	1	8	.304	.403	.411
Apr-Jun	81	2	14	.383	.414	.556	ScPos	45	1	26	.422	.517	.644
Jul-Oct	90	1	16	.300	.402	.411	Clutch	31	0	4	.323	.405	.387

SCOUTING REPORT

Primarily an opposite-field hitter, Mark Lewis has some power, choosing fastballs down and over the plate. He is an average runner.

Lewis' arm is slightly above-average in strength, which helps him at third and shortstop. His range, hands, and throwing accuracy all rate average.

HOW HE PERFORMED IN '95

Lewis played almost exclusively in a platoon role, starting all 35 games the Reds played against lefty starters. He was in the lineup only five times against righties, with some of those games coming late in the season when Jeff Branson slumped. Filling in at three positions (third, short, second), Lewis was a valuable reserve.

WHAT TO EXPECT IN '96

How old is too old to become an everyday player? Lewis is 26 but will get every chance to start at shortstop with Detroit in '96.

One hitless streak with Cleveland in '94 put Mark in the category of a failed prospect, but Tigers obtained him (along with C.J. Nitkowski) in the David Wells trade. It's likely that Mark will also be benefit from the advice of his new manager, Buddy Bell, who was an outstanding infielder during his playing days in Texas and Cincinnati.

CHUCK McELROY

Position: RP
Bats: L **Throws:** L
Ht: 6'0" **Wt:** 160
Opening Day Age: 28
Born: 10/1/1967
Drafted: PHI86 8/192
ML Seasons: 7

Overall Statistics

	G	GS	GF	SV	W	L	ERA	IP	H	R	ER	HR	BB	SO
95 CIN	44	0	11	0	3	4	6.02	40.1	46	29	27	5	15	27
Career	315	0	89	14	16	18	3.43	354.2	331	162	135	25	177	295

1995 Situational Statistics

	W	L	ERA	SV	IP	BB	SO		AB	HR	RBI	BA	OBA	SLG
Home	2	2	7.08	0	20.1	8	10	LHB	60	3	15	.283	.348	.533
Road	1	2	4.95	0	20.0	7	17	RHB	98	2	23	.296	.352	.429
Apr-Jun	1	2	6.17	0	11.2	5	7	ScPos	46	2	34	.413	.474	.609
Jul-Oct	2	2	5.97	0	28.2	10	20	Clutch	36	2	7	.306	.419	.556

SCOUTING REPORT

McElroy has a now-average sinking fastball that does not have the velocity it once did. He pairs it with an average slider, throwing with a three-quarter motion. An average fielder and average when holding runners, four men tried to steal against him in '95, three successfully. Hitless in three trips last year, Chuck has an excellent .258 career average in 31 at-bats.

HOW HE PERFORMED IN '95

The only similarity between his '95 season and that of former Cubs' teammate Greg Maddux was that both caught the chicken pox. McElroy was bad from the start of the year and never regained his '94 form, when he posted a 2.34 ERA and five saves. McElroy stayed with the Reds because there were no other lefthanded relief pitchers who could pitch at the big-league level. The Reds tried Brad Pennington after acquiring him from Baltimore, but he was even worse.

WHAT TO EXPECT IN '96

McElroy was so bad last season that manager Davey Johnson wouldn't use him against lefthanders in the playoffs. Since southpaw relievers who have any stuff are so scarce, Chuck shouldn't be scratched out entirely for '96. He's only 28, so there's still time to straighten things out.

CINCINNATI REDS

TIM PUGH

Position: RP/SP
Bats: R **Throws:** R
Ht: 6'6" **Wt:** 225
Opening Day Age: 29
Born: 1/26/1967
Drafted: CIN89 6/160
ML Seasons: 4

Overall Statistics

	G	GS	GF	SV	W	L	ERA	IP	H	R	ER	HR	BB	SO
95 CIN	28	12	4	0	6	5	3.84	98.1	100	46	42	13	32	38
Career	76	55	7	0	23	25	4.63	355.2	407	200	183	39	130	174

1995 Situational Statistics

	W	L	ERA	SV	IP	BB	SO		AB	HR	RBI	BA	OBA	SLG
Home	1	1	3.94	0	45.2	15	18	LHB	152	3	11	.204	.282	.309
Road	5	4	3.76	0	52.2	17	20	RHB	223	10	30	.309	.354	.507
Apr-Jun	4	1	3.64	0	54.1	19	19	ScPos	78	2	29	.269	.359	.462
Jul-Oct	2	4	4.09	0	44.0	13	19	Clutch	14	0	2	.286	.333	.357

SCOUTING REPORT

Tim throws from low three quarters with a slightly below-average sinking fastball. His best pitch is a well above-average palmball (sometimes called a "slip" pitch); he has a slightly below-average slider as well. Pugh can throw pretty hard when he wants to, but credited his '95 renaissance to not trying to overpower every hitter. This improved his often inconsistent control.

Tim is a minus fielder, slow off the mound, but average at holding runners: 10 tried to steal off him in '95, seven successfully. Pugh hit .143 in 28 at-bats.

HOW HE PERFORMED IN '95

Pugh had his best season, in a slightly different fashion than expected. He started 12 games but was more effective in relief, allowing one earned run in his first 15 bullpen innings, earning a promotion to the rotation. After winning his first three starts, Tim dropped his last three, earning a demotion to Triple-A.

WHAT TO EXPECT IN '96

If the Reds unload Mark Portugal or John Smiley (or both), Pugh will get a chance to start. He has a 3.18 career ERA in the minors and may have turned a corner.

JOSE RIJO

Position: SP
Bats: R **Throws:** R
Ht: 6'1" **Wt:** 200
Opening Day Age: 30
Born: 5/13/1965
Drafted: NYA 8/1/80
ML Seasons: 12

Overall Statistics

	G	GS	GF	SV	W	L	ERA	IP	H	R	ER	HR	BB	SO
95 CIN	14	14	0	0	5	4	4.17	69.0	76	33	32	6	22	62
Career	332	260	33	3	111	87	3.16	1786.0	1602	718	628	132	634	1556

1995 Situational Statistics

	W	L	ERA	SV	IP	BB	SO		AB	HR	RBI	BA	OBA	SLG
Home	2	3	5.06	0	32.0	8	31	LHB	128	4	14	.328	.387	.500
Road	3	1	3.41	0	37.0	14	31	RHB	139	2	14	.245	.287	.353
Apr-Jun	3	4	4.58	0	57.0	17	49	ScPos	61	1	21	.279	.329	.410
Jul-Oct	2	0	2.25	0	12.0	5	13	Clutch	7	1	1	.286	.286	.857

SCOUTING REPORT

Rijo's plus, overhand, four-seam fastball bores into righthanded hitters. It's now his best pitch. His once-fearsome slider is now slightly above-average and hangs more often than in the past. Jose also throws a slightly above-average splitter and an average change. An average fielder, Rijo saw eight men steal against him in eight tries during '95. Jose batted .136 last year and is a good hitter (.193 career) and bunter.

HOW HE PERFORMED IN '95

A calcium formation in his right elbow finally caught up with Rijo in '95. He didn't allow a run during spring training but was hittable during the season. In June, Jose was disabled with what was thought to be tendinitis. He was activated and received a cortisone shot but made just four starts before being sidelined for good July 19. Although Rijo hoped the elbow would naturally heal, he eventually underwent "Tommy John" surgery.

WHAT TO EXPECT IN '96

The '96 season is a giant question mark for a guy whose out pitch has been a wicked slider. On schedule with his rehabilitation, Rijo could be back after the All-Star break. However, Davey Johnson hinted late in the season that Jose's career might be over.

CINCINNATI REDS

EDDIE TAUBENSEE

Positions: C//1B
Bats: L **Throws:** R
Ht: 6'3" **Wt:** 205
Opening Day Age: 27
Born: 10/31/1968
Drafted: CIN86 6/150
ML Seasons: 5

Overall Statistics

	G	AB	R	H	2B	3B	HR	RBI	SB	CS	BB	SO	BA	OBA
95 CIN	80	218	32	62	14	2	9	44	2	2	22	52	.284	.354
Career	370	1056	115	269	50	6	31	143	7	3	94	221	.255	.316

1995 Situational Statistics

	AB	HR	RBI	BA	OBA	SLG		AB	HR	RBI	BA	OBA	SLG
Home	96	4	18	.260	.343	.458	LHP	28	2	10	.250	.344	.464
Road	122	5	26	.303	.363	.516	RHP	190	7	34	.289	.355	.495
Apr-Jun	119	4	20	.252	.323	.445	ScPos	79	4	38	.342	.404	.582
Jul-Oct	99	5	24	.323	.391	.545	Clutch	34	1	6	.294	.385	.471

SCOUTING REPORT

Eddie could be a full-time starter if he improved his defense. He has average range and hands, but sometimes loses his concentration behind the mask and misses easy pitches. His arm has slightly above-average strength with average accuracy.

A decent fastball hitter down and in, Eddie will pull if he can. He is a below-average runner and rarely bunts.

HOW HE PERFORMED IN '95

Taubensee became the everyday catcher in early May when Benito Santiago was disabled with a sore right elbow. He improved considerably as a full-time player, batting around .270 while Santiago was out. Taubensee again had defensive problems, committing two errors in his first seven games and six on the year, and his inability to catch a key pitch hurt the Reds in the NLCS against the Braves. He threw out just 11 of 53 (21%) trying to steal.

WHAT TO EXPECT IN '96

Taubensee can hit, so he'll always get a shot at a position where there aren't very many good hitters around. He's also a lefthanded hitter, which gives him an advantage in a platoon situation. He's arbitration-eligible, however, and therefore might not be back with the Reds.

JEROME WALTON

Positions: OF//1B
Bats: R **Throws:** R
Ht: 6'1" **Wt:** 175
Opening Day Age: 30
Born: 7/8/1965
Drafted: CHN86* 2/36
ML Seasons: 7

Overall Statistics

	G	AB	R	H	2B	3B	HR	RBI	SB	CS	BB	SO	BA	OBA
95 CIN	102	162	32	47	12	1	8	22	10	7	17	25	.290	.368
Career	523	1424	220	376	68	8	21	116	58	29	127	254	.264	.330

1995 Situational Statistics

	AB	HR	RBI	BA	OBA	SLG		AB	HR	RBI	BA	OBA	SLG
Home	95	4	12	.263	.333	.474	LHP	98	6	9	.306	.391	.541
Road	67	4	10	.328	.416	.597	RHP	64	2	13	.266	.329	.500
Apr-Jun	88	5	10	.273	.327	.489	ScPos	30	1	11	.233	.324	.400
Jul-Oct	74	3	12	.311	.414	.568	Clutch	34	1	5	.118	.139	.235

SCOUTING REPORT

Walton has some power and likes the fastball down and over the plate. He is an above-average runner but not a good percentage basestealer. A decent outfielder, Jerome can play all three outfield positions but appears most comfortable in left now.

HOW HE PERFORMED IN '95

Walton's season highlight was quite possibly becoming the first player ever to hit home runs on consecutive pitches in two games. He won the Reds' May 6 game with a homer in the bottom of the ninth and led off the next day with another four-bagger. Jerome hadn't seen this much action since '91 and, although used mostly as a backup outfielder, he proved that he deserved the playing time. Walton's eight home runs were a career high, three more than he hit in '89 when he was Rookie of the Year with the Cubs.

WHAT TO EXPECT IN '96

Although he was looking for a new home for '96, Walton has salvaged his career over the last two seasons, showing he can still hit while providing speed and defense. Finding a job as a fourth outfielder should be no problem this year, but Jerome is not going to be an everyday player again.

CINCINNATI REDS: TOP PROSPECTS

TIM BELK
Bats: R Throws: R Opening Day Age: 26
Ht: 6-3 Wt: 200 Born: 4/6/1970
Position: 1B Drafted: 1992 #16 CIN

YR TEAM	LG/CLASS	G	AB	R	H	2B	3B	HR	RBI	SB	BA	OBA
93 Winston-Sal	CARO/A	134	509	89	156	23	3	14	65	9	.306	.372
94 Chattanooga	SOU/AA	118	411	64	127	35	3	10	86	13	.309	.392
94 Indianapolis	AMAS/AAA	6	18	1	2	1	0	0	0	0	.111	.158
95 Indianapolis	AMAS/AAA	57	193	30	58	11	0	4	18	2	.301	.360

Belk was hit in the face with a pitch in mid-May and did not return until late July. He got a late start due to the strike and began in left field, but was moved back to his natural position of first base soon after. The 25-year-old had a breakthrough season in '94 and has hit .300 in his four-year career with good strike zone judgment, but lacks the power to be a first baseman or the defensive ability to play the outfield.

AARON BOONE
Bats: R Throws: R Opening Day Age: 23
Ht: 6-2 Wt: 190 Born: 3/9/1973
Position: 3B Drafted: 1994 #3 CIN

YR TEAM	LG/CLASS	G	AB	R	H	2B	3B	HR	RBI	SB	BA	OBA
94 Billings	PIO/R	67	256	48	70	15	5	7	55	6	.273	.362
95 Chattanooga	SOU/AA	23	66	6	15	3	0	0	3	2	.227	.274
Winston-Sal	CARO/A	108	395	61	103	19	14	50	11	.261	.345

Boone hopes to use good defense, a strong arm, speed, and power to join brother Brett in the major leagues one day. He lasted just three weeks at Double-A last year before going to Class-A where his home run output was influenced greatly by a hitters' park. Some doubt he will supply the power needed for the hot corner and lacks the agility to play elsewhere.

CHAD FOX
Bats: R Throws: R Opening Day Age: 26
Ht: 6-2 Wt: 180 Born: 9/3/1970
Position: P Drafted: 1992 #24 CIN

YR TEAM	LG/CLASS	G	GS	GF	SV	W	L	ERA	IP	H	HR	BB	SO	O/BA
93 Chston-WV	SAL/A	27	26	0	0	9	12	5.37	135.2	138	7	97	81	.268
94 Winston-Sal	CARO/A	25	25	0	0	12	5	3.86	156.1	121	18	94	137	.216
95 Chattanooga	SOU/AA	20	17	1	0	4	5	5.06	80	76	2	52	56	.250

Fox has a better arm than his numbers indicate, but the former NAIA pitcher lacks command. Another member of the 40-man roster hurt by the strike, the 25-year-old pitched seven innings just twice all season and picked up his last win June 16. He has some pop on his fastball and a good slider, but needs work on his off-speed pitches. Fox has averaged nearly six walks per nine innings during his career.

STEVE GIBRALTER
Bats: R Throws: R Opening Day Age: 23
Ht: 6-0 Wt: 170 Born: 10/9/1972
Position: CF Drafted: 1990 #6 CIN

YR TEAM	LG/CLASS	G	AB	R	H	2B	3B	HR	RBI	SB	BA	OBA
93 Chattanooga	SOU/AA	132	477	65	113	25	3	11	47	7	.237	.276
94 Chattanooga	SOU/AA	133	460	71	124	28	3	14	63	10	.270	.345
95 Indianapolis	AMAS/AAA	79	263	49	83	19	3	18	63	0	.316	.381
Cincinnati	NL/MAJ	4	3	0	1	0	0	0	0	0	.333	.333

An outstanding center fielder who plays the game with all-out hustle, Gibralter blossomed with the stick in '95 after two mediocre years in Double-A. He was leading the minor leagues with a .616 slugging percentage and pacing the American Association in homers and RBI when he suffered a season-ending thumb injury in mid-July while sliding into a base. After winning Midwest League MVP honors in '92 (.306, 32 2B, 19 HR), Gibralter, now 23, batted .253 in two seasons with Chattanooga.

WILLIE GREENE
Bats: L Throws: R Opening Day Age: 25
Ht: 5-11 Wt: 184 Born: 9/23/1971
Position: 3B Drafted: 1989 #1 PIT

YR TEAM	LG/CLASS	G	AB	R	H	2B	3B	HR	RBI	SB	BA	OBA
93 Indianapolis	AMAS/AAA	98	341	62	91	19	0	22	58	2	.267	.362
93 Cincinnati	NL/MAJ	15	50	7	8	1	1	2	5	0	.160	.189
94 Cincinnati	NL/MAJ	16	37	5	8	2	0	0	3	0	.216	.318
94 Indianapolis	AMAS/AAA	114	435	77	124	24	1	23	80	8	.285	.367
95 Indianapolis	AMAS/AAA	91	325	57	79	12	2	19	45	3	.243	.324
Cincinnati	NL/MAJ	8	19	1	2	0	0	0	0	0	.105	.227

Given the third base job in spring training, Greene did not hold the job long and soon found himself back at Triple-A. An elbow injury forced him to the bench, but he showed outstanding power when healthy, hitting three homers in one game in late August. The 24-year-old has not progressed as hoped at the hot corner and played some left field last season.

CHAD MOTTOLA
Bats: R Throws: R Opening Day Age: 24
Ht: 6-3 Wt: 215 Born: 10/15/1971
Position: RF Drafted: 1992 #1 CIN

YR TEAM	LG/CLASS	G	AB	R	H	2B	3B	HR	RBI	SB	BA	OBA
93 Winston-Sal	CARO/A	137	493	76	138	25	3	21	91	13	.280	.361
94 Chattanooga	SOU/AA	118	402	44	97	19	1	7	41	9	.241	.294
95 Indianapolis	AMAS/AAA	69	239	40	62	11	1	8	37	8	.259	.315
Chattanooga	SOU/AA	51	181	32	53	13	1	10	39	1	.293	.342

A prototypical right fielder, the 23-year-old has good range and an outstanding arm, throwing out 11 runners in 69 games for Indianapolis in 1995. He can hit for power and is very fast, although he's not a big stolen base threat. After a poor '94 campaign, Mottola repeated Double-A last year, started to turn on the ball, and practically matched his previous season's output in 51 games before being sent to Indianapolis in mid-June. He still has work to do with the bat, but 1995 was a huge success for the former first-rounder.

CINCINNATI REDS: TOP PROSPECTS

ERIC OWENS
Bats: R Throws: R Opening Day Age: 25
Ht: 6-1 Wt: 184 Born: 2/3/1971
Position: 2B Drafted: 1992 #5 CIN

YR TEAM	LG/CLASS	G	AB	R	H	2B	3B	HR	RBI	SB	BA	OBA
93 Winston-Sal	CARO/A	122	487	74	132	25	4	10	63	21	.271	.343
94 Chattanooga	SOU/AA	134	523	73	133	17	3	3	36	38	.254	.325
95 Indianapolis	AMAS/AAA	108	427	86	134	24	8	12	63	33	.314	.388
Cincinnati	NL/MAJ	2	2	0	2	0	0	0	1	0	1.000	1.000

Playing his third position in three years, Owens won 1995 Rookie-of-the-Year and MVP honors in the American Association. His season ended in mid-August because of knee surgery, but he's expected at full strength this spring. The 24-year-old led the league in steals, runs and triples and finished third in batting. Considered an overachiever with a great work ethic, Owens showed in '95 that he can play in the big leagues, although he still needs some work at second base.

POKEY REESE
Bats: R Throws: R Opening Day Age: 23
Ht: 6-0 Wt: 160 Born: 6/10/1973
Position: SS Drafted: 1991 #1 CIN

YR TEAM	LG/CLASS	G	AB	R	H	2B	3B	HR	RBI	SB	BA	OBA
93 Chattanooga	SOU/AA	102	345	35	73	17	4	3	37	8	.212	.258
94 Chattanooga	SOU/AA	134	484	77	130	23	4	12	49	21	.269	.336
95 Indianapolis	AMAS/AAA	89	343	51	82	21	1	10	46	8	.239	.316

Great range, soft hands, an outstanding arm, and good bat speed are the qualities the 22-year-old Reese takes to the field every night. However, he's still prone to blow an easy play and needs to be more consistent with the bat. After a great start Reese slumped badly, then missed a month with an ankle injury and hit only .200 after his return. The former first-round pick has drifted away from making contact and using all fields in favor of trying for home runs, an approach that may need to change.

ROGER SALKELD
Bats: R Throws: R Opening Day Age: 25
Ht: 6-5 Wt: 215 Born: 3/6/1971
Position: P Drafted: 1989 #1 SEA

YR TEAM	LG/CLASS	G	GS	GF	SV	W	L	ERA	IP	H	HR	BB	SO	O/BA
93 Jacksonville	SOU/AA	14	14	0	0	4	3	3.27	77.0	71	8	29	56	.244
93 Seattle	AL/MAJ	3	2	0	0	0	0	2.51	14.1	10	0	4	13	.179
94 Calgary	PCL/AAA	13	13	0	0	3	7	6.15	67.1	74	11	39	54	.277
94 Seattle	AL/MAJ	13	13	0	0	2	5	7.17	59.0	76	7	45	46	.314
95 Indianapolis	AMAS/AAA	20	20	0	0	12	4	4.22	119	96	13	57	86	.223
Tacoma	PCL/AAA	4	3	1	1	1	0	1.80	15	8	0	7	11	.154

The former Seattle first-rounder was acquired in mid-May for Tim Belcher. He posted an impressive won-loss record, held opponents to a .223 batting average (best among league starters), but was also the recipient of great run support. He won six straight starts and eight straight decisions at one point, but his 1993 pre-shoulder injury velocity was seen only on rare occasions as he relied more on his breaking ball.

SCOTT SULLIVAN
Bats: R Throws: R Opening Day Age: 25
Ht: 6-3 Wt: 210 Born: 3/13/1971
Position: P Drafted: 1993 #2 CIN

YR TEAM	LG/CLASS	G	GS	GF	SV	W	L	ERA	IP	H	HR	BB	SO	O/BA
93 Billings	PIO/R	18	7	9	3	5	0	1.67	54.0	33	1	25	79	.174
94 Chattanooga	SOU/AA	34	13	16	7	11	7	3.41	121.1	101	8	40	111	.220
95 Indianapolis	AMAS/AAA	44	0	21	1	4	3	3.53	58	51	2	24	54	.232
Cincinnati	NL/MAJ	3	0	1	0	0	0	4.91	3	4	0	2	2	.267

It took the former Auburn walk-on less than two years to make it to the major leagues. The sidearmer throws 90 mph, throws a tough slider and is a competitor. He was Chattanooga's top starter in '94 before moving to the closer role, but he was used as a set-up man last season. After holding lefthanders to a .199 average in '94, Sullivan struggled against them in 1995, a cause for concern. Although righties batted just .208 in 1995, Sullivan's total opposing average was .282.

PAT WATKINS
Bats: R Throws: R Opening Day Age: 24
Ht: 6-2 Wt: 185 Born: 9/2/1972
Position: RF Drafted: 1993 #1 CIN

YR TEAM	LG/CLASS	G	AB	R	H	2B	3B	HR	RBI	SB	BA	OBA
93 Billings	PIO/R	66	235	46	63	10	3	6	30	15	.268	.335
94 Winston-Sal	CARO/A	132	524	107	152	24	5	27	83	31	.290	.369
95 Chattanooga	SOU/AA	105	358	57	104	26	2	12	57	5	.291	.352
Winston-Sal	CARO/A	27	107	14	22	3	1	4	13	1	.206	.269

A vision problem was thought to be the culprit of an early-season slump that led to his return to Winston-Salem. However, after a brief adjustment period, Watkins started to hit, returned to Chattanooga and hit about .320 the rest of the way. Regarded as a five-tool talent who has played all three outfield positions, the 23-year-old's stolen bases fell from 31 to six last season. Watkins, like Mottola, is a good right fielder with a cannon. He knows how to play the game.

NIGEL WILSON
Bats: L Throws: L Opening Day Age: 26
Ht: 6-1 Wt: 170 Born: 1/12/1970
Position: OF Drafted: NDFA 7-30-87, by TOR

YR TEAM	LG/CLASS	G	AB	R	H	2B	3B	HR	RBI	SB	BA	OBA
93 Edmonton	PCL/AAA	96	370	66	108	26	7	17	68	8	.292	.351
93 Florida	NL/MAJ	7	16	0	0	0	0	0	0	0	.000	.000
94 Edmonton	PCL/AAA	87	314	50	97	24	1	12	62	2	.309	.369
95 Indianapolis	AMAS/AAA	82	304	53	95	27	3	17	51	5	.313	.356
Cincinnati	NL/MAJ	5	7	0	0	0	0	0	0	0	.000	.000

The Marlins' first pick in the expansion draft has been a major disappointment. Wilson, acquired on waivers in April, still has outstanding bat speed and played last year with a renewed dedication. After a slow start, the 25-year-old lost about 20 pounds and played a very good left field, hit well and had two 5-hit games during the season. He showed power, although he was greatly aided by a hitter-friendly park in Indianapolis, but an inability to learn the strike zone may keep him from ever using his tremendous gifts.

THE SCOUTING REPORT: 1996

CINCINNATI REDS: OTHERS TO WATCH

CEDRIC ALLEN Bats: L Throws: L Ht: 5-10 Wt: 183
Born: 1/13/1972 Drafted: 1994 #32 CIN Pos: P

YR TEAM	LG/CLASS	G	GS	GF	SV	W	L	ERA	IP	H	HR	BB	SO	O/BA
95 Chlston-WV	SAL/A	27	27	0	0	13	7	2.85	170.1	143	8	46	108	.231

Not overpowering, Allen had a great second half and used a pitchers' park to lead the organization in wins while finishing second in ERA.

RAY BROWN Bats: L Throws: R Ht: 6-2 Wt: 205
Born: 7/30/1972 Drafted: 1994 #28 CIN Pos: 1B

YR TEAM	LG/CLASS	G	AB	R	H	2B	3B	HR	RBI	SB	BA	OBA
95 Chlston-WV	SAL/A	6	17	3	2	1	0	0	0	0	.118	.286
95 Win-Salem	CARO/A	122	445	63	118	26	0	19	77	3	.265	.354

The 1994 Pioneer League MVP has good pop and hits to all fields, but was aided by a hitter-friendly park in 1995 and made 19 errors.

JOHNNY CARVAJAL Bats: R Throws: R Ht: 5-10 Wt: 165
Born: 7/24/1974 Drafted: NDFA 9-25-92 CIN Pos: 2B

YR TEAM	LG/CLASS	G	AB	R	H	2B	3B	HR	RBI	SB	BA	OBA
95 Chlston-WV	SAL/A	135	486	78	128	18	5	0	42	44	.263	.347

A slick fielder with fast feet but a suspect bat, Carvajal put together a 21-game hit streak late to finish strong.

DECOMBA CONNER Bats: R Throws: R Ht: 5-10 Wt: 184
Born: 7/17/1973 Drafted: 1994 #7 CIN Pos: OF

YR TEAM	LG/CLASS	G	AB	R	H	2B	3B	HR	RBI	SB	BA	OBA
95 Chlston-WV	SAL/A	91	308	55	81	10	7	5	40	22	.263	.346
95 Princeton	APPY/R	6	16	2	2	2	0	0	5	2	.125	.250

Conner, owner of a Puckett-like body, was the 1994 Appalachian League MVP and has plus skills in every area except throwing.

TODD ETLER Bats: R Throws: R Ht: 6-0 Wt: 205
Born: 4/18/1974 Drafted: 1992 #4 CIN Pos: P

YR TEAM	LG/CLASS	G	GS	GF	SV	W	L	ERA	IP	H	HR	BB	SO	O/BA
95 Win-Salem	CARO/A	24	23	0	0	6	12	3.69	153.2	148	13	49	78	.261

One of the best young pitchers in the system, Etler has good command of three pitchers and keeps the ball down.

EMILIANO GIRON Bats: R Throws: R Ht: 6-2 Wt: 000
Born: 1/5/1972 Drafted: NDFA 1-10-90 CIN Pos: P

YR TEAM	LG/CLASS	G	L	ERA	IP	H	HR	BB	SO	O/BA
95 Chlston-WV	SAL/A	30	0 28 20	0 0 0.94	28.2	12	0	8	39	.122
95 Win-Salem	CARO/A	17	0 11 0	2 2 2.30	27.1	23	1	10	29	.213

The tall, thin 23-year-old used a 93 mph fastball to pitch scoreless ball in his first 23 outings for Charleston-WV.

CURT LYONS Bats: R Throws: R Ht: 6-5 Wt: 228
Born: 10/17/1974 Drafted: 1992 #7 CIN Pos: P

YR TEAM	LG/CLASS	G	GS	GF	SV	W	L	ERA	IP	H	HR	BB	SO	O/BA
95 Win-Salem	CARO/A	26	26	0	0	9	9	2.98	160.1	139	10	67	122	.239

A four-year pro at the age of 21, Lyons is big, throws hard and was impressive in '95.

RICKY MAGDALENO Bats: R Throws: R Ht: 6-1 Wt: 170
Born: 7/6/1974 Drafted: 1992 #3 CIN Pos: SS

YR TEAM	LG/CLASS	G	AB	R	H	2B	3B	HR	RBI	SB	BA	OBA
95 Indianapolis	AMAS/AAA	4	8	1	1	0	0	1	1	0	.125	.125
95 Chattanooga	SOU/AA	11	40	2	7	2	0	1	2	0	.175	.250
95 Win-Salem	CARO/A	91	309	30	69	13	1	7	40	3	.223	.261

Highly ranked by Reds GM Jim Bowden, the 21-year-old is best known for his defense but had a subpar year both in the field and at the plate.

MARCUS MOORE Bats: S Throws: R Ht: 6-5 Wt: 204
Born: 11/2/1970 Drafted: 1989 #17 CAL Pos: P

YR TEAM	LG/CLASS	G	GS	GF	SV	W	L	ERA	IP	H	HR	BB	SO	O/BA
95 Indianapolis	AMAS/AAA	7	1	2	1	1	0	4.97	12.2	13	0	14	6	.277
95 Chattanooga	SOU/AA	36	0	8	2	6	1	4.98	43.1	31	6	34	57	.204

Moore, still young, hit 100 mph on the radar gun last summer and made strides with his attitude, but still needs command.

NICK MORROW Bats: R Throws: R Ht: 5-11 Wt: 180
Born: 4/17/1972 Drafted: 1994 #30 CIN Pos: OF

YR TEAM	LG/CLASS	G	AB	R	H	2B	3B	HR	RBI	SB	BA	OBA
95 Chlston-WV	SAL/A	139	467	67	117	28	8	9	54	41	.251	.358

He needs to make better contact, but Morrow is multi-skilled and his numbers were affected by a tough pitchers' park.

CHRIS REED Bats: R Throws: R Ht: 6-3 Wt: 206
Born: 8/25/1973 Drafted: 1991 #7 CIN Pos: P

YR TEAM	LG/CLASS	G	GS	GF	SV	W	L	ERA	IP	H	HR	BB	SO	O/BA
95 Win-Salem	CARO/A	24	24	0	0	10	7	3.32	149.0	116	11	68	104	.216

The club's top winner had the staff's best curve and was very tough when he stayed ahead in the count.

JASON ROBBINS Bats: R Throws: R Ht: 6-3 Wt: 195
Born: 12/20/1972 Drafted: NDFA 6-7-93 CIN Pos: P

YR TEAM	LG/CLASS	G	GS	GF	SV	W	L	ERA	IP	H	HR	BB	SO	O/BA
95 Win-Salem	CARO/A	23	23	0	0	9	6	3.06	141.0	113	16	42	106	.219

The 1994 Pioneer League All-Star (11-1, 3.15 ERA) had a strong second half, improving the command of his split-finger fastball.

TOBY RUMFIELD Bats: R Throws: R Ht: 6-3 Wt: 190
Born: 9/4/1972 Drafted: 1991 #2 CIN Pos: 1B

YR TEAM	LG/CLASS	G	AB	R	H	2B	3B	HR	RBI	SB	BA	OBA
95 Chattanooga	SOU/AA	92	273	32	72	12	1	8	53	0	.264	.329

The converted catcher can pound fastballs but has problems with off-speed pitches and adds little on defense.

BRETT TOMKO Bats: R Throws: R Ht: 6-4 Wt: 205
Born: 4/7/1973 Drafted: 1995 #1 CIN Pos: P

YR TEAM	LG/CLASS	G	GS	GF	SV	W	L	ERA	IP	H	HR	BB	SO	O/BA
95 Chlston-WV	SAL/A	9	7	0	0	4	2	1.84	49.0	41	1	9	46	.228

The Division II Player-of-the-Year from Florida Southern combines a 92-mph fastball with a good change, but he has had rotator cuff tendinitis.

COLORADO ROCKIES

JASON BATES

Positions: 2B/SS/3B
Bats: B **Throws:** R
Ht: 5'11" **Wt:** 170
Opening Day Age: 25
Born: 1/5/1971
Drafted: COL92 7/207
ML Seasons: 1

SCOUTING REPORT
A line-drive switch-hitter who hits out of a crouch lefthanded and out of a deep crouch righthanded, Jason is a low-ball swinger with a little power both ways. He has average speed but does not utilize it well when stealing.

At second base, Bates has a strong arm, minus range, but good hands. This combination will probably make him into a utility player, since he has the ability to make the long throw from short and his range won't be a big factor at third.

HOW HE PERFORMED IN '95
In his first major-league go-around, Bates held down the Rockies' regular second base job for much of the early season after Roberto Mejia proved a bust at the position for the third straight year.

Although Bates maintained an average over .300 through the end of May, his starting opportunities decreased dramatically in late June when he suffered an injury to his left wrist and consequently went into a tailspin, garnering just four hits in his next 37 at-bats.

Don Baylor, desperate for offense at the top of the order, turned to Eric Young at second. Young hit well in the leadoff spot and Jason never got his job back.

During the rest of the campaign, Bates saw limited action but showed some versatility, making eleven starts at third and nine at shortstop in addition to his 55 at second. He made only five errors all season.

A switch-hitter, Jason didn't get many appearances against lefthanders and didn't do much against them anyway; his on-base and slugging were much stronger against righthanders.

WHAT TO EXPECT IN '96
As can be said about almost all of his teammates, Bates' offensive numbers are dramatically better at Coors Field than on the road. The poor performance he turned in during road games in '95 calls into question exactly how good a hitter Jason is at this point.

It seems likely that Bates, seen prior to the '95 season as a platoon partner for Vinny Castilla at third base, will occupy a utility role at the start of '96. Despite the fact that the Rockies like Jason, there's no regular job open for him right now.

Overall Statistics

	G	AB	R	H	2B	3B	HR	RBI	SB	CS	BB	SO	BA	OBA
95 COL	116	322	42	86	17	4	8	46	3	6	42	70	.267	.355
Career	116	322	42	86	17	4	8	46	3	6	42	70	.267	.355

1995 Situational Statistics

	AB	HR	RBI	BA	OBA	SLG		AB	HR	RBI	BA	OBA	SLG
Home	157	4	28	.325	.411	.510	LHP	71	2	10	.183	.284	.324
Road	165	4	18	.212	.301	.333	RHP	251	6	36	.291	.375	.446
Apr-Jun	189	6	25	.270	.358	.434	ScPos	73	1	36	.370	.505	.548
Jul-Oct	133	2	21	.263	.351	.398	Clutch	48	1	3	.146	.268	.271

How He Compares to Other Batters

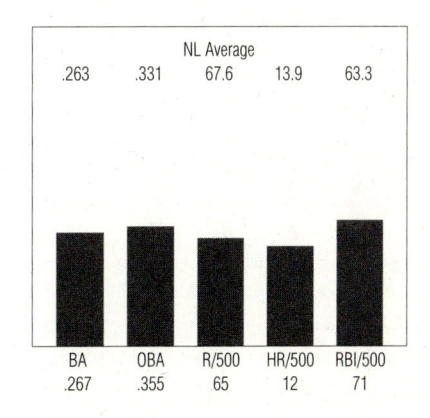

NL Average: .263 .331 67.6 13.9 63.3

BA	OBA	R/500	HR/500	RBI/500
.267	.355	65	12	71

Where He Hits the Ball

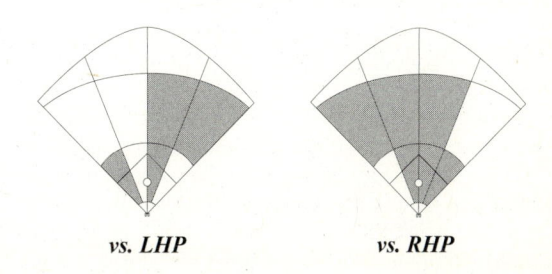

vs. LHP   vs. RHP

THE SCOUTING REPORT: 1996

COLORADO ROCKIES

DANTE BICHETTE

Position: OF
Bats: R **Throws:** R
Ht: 6'3" **Wt:** 215
Opening Day Age: 32
Born: 11/18/1963
Drafted: CAL84 17/424
ML Seasons: 8

SCOUTING REPORT
In his element at the plate, Bichette has a short, quick stroke which is obviously well-adapted to Coors Field. He loves low, inside pitches which he can jerk over the left field fence. Dante's speed on the basepaths is now minus but he is still trying to steal—not very effectively. Once a good right fielder, Dante's defense has seriously deteriorated in recent years. The move to left field in '95 (due to the acquisition of Larry Walker) didn't help, as his range was clearly minus. His formerly strong arm is also now minus, although his throws are accurate and his hands are average.

HOW HE PERFORMED IN '95
Bichette's offensive numbers improved when he moved to Mile High Stadium for the '93 season, and they took another big leap last year at Coors Field. Bichette led the league in home runs and RBI and finished third in batting average, trailing only Tony Gwynn at .368 and Mike Piazza at .346. Dante finished near the top in almost every major offensive category and ended up second in MVP voting to the Reds' Barry Larkin.

Slugging his first homer at Coors Field off the Mets' Mike Remlinger to win the new park's 14-inning inaugural game, Bichette hit his first 17 homers of '95 at home and finished with 31 homers in Colorado and only nine on the road.

His overall road performance was an improvement over past years, but is still dramatically below his spectacular Coors Field numbers and far from the kind of performance one would expect of an MVP.

His defense was a mixed bag. Dante made just three errors and threw out nine baserunners on the season, but showed mobility as poor as that of any NL outfielder.

WHAT TO EXPECT IN '96
Bichette played the '95 season on a one-year contract after nearly not signing with the Rockies. Last November, Dante signed a new, incentive-laden three-year, $11.1-million deal. The contract reflects the club's concern about his nagging left knee problem. Bichette's production has improved over a three-year period and, barring injury, there's no reason to believe that Dante will not continue to put up impressive offensive numbers in friendly Coors Field. Of course, so would quite a few other hitters if they played in Denver.

Overall Statistics

	G	AB	R	H	2B	3B	HR	RBI	SB	CS	BB	SO	BA	OBA
95 COL	139	579	102	197	38	2	40	128	13	9	22	96	.340	.364
Career	820	2966	413	858	183	15	126	488	88	42	129	556	.289	.320

1995 Situational Statistics

	AB	HR	RBI	BA	OBA	SLG		AB	HR	RBI	BA	OBA	SLG
Home	302	31	83	.377	.397	.755	LHP	149	14	40	.336	.377	.691
Road	277	9	45	.300	.329	.473	RHP	430	26	88	.342	.360	.595
Apr-Jun	239	9	37	.335	.360	.536	ScPos	158	16	93	.367	.385	.722
Jul-Oct	340	31	91	.344	.368	.679	Clutch	76	4	20	.303	.325	.539

How He Compares to Other Batters

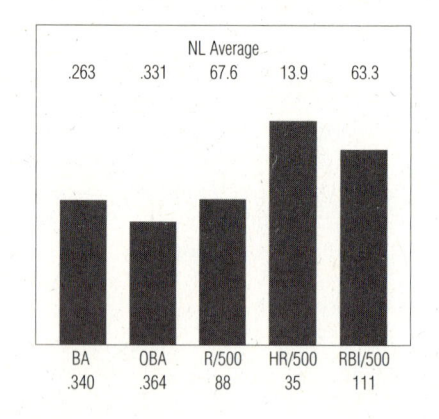

NL Average: .263 .331 67.6 13.9 63.3

BA	OBA	R/500	HR/500	RBI/500
.340	.364	88	35	111

Where He Hits the Ball

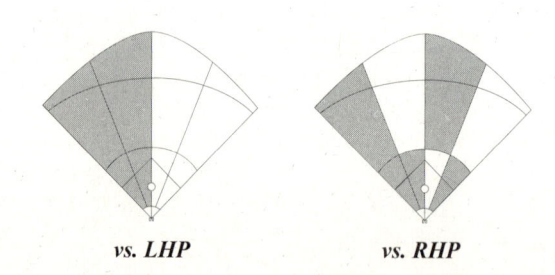

vs. LHP   vs. RHP

COLORADO ROCKIES

VINNY CASTILLA

Positions: 3B//SS
Bats: R **Throws:** R
Ht: 6'1" **Wt:** 175
Opening Day Age: 28
Born: 7/4/1967
Drafted: MEX 3/7/89
ML Seasons: 5

SCOUTING REPORT
Castilla hits with an uppercut swing and is a dead high fastball hitter. This makes him a good match for his home park, where pitchers have trouble with the bite on their breaking pitches in the thin air and where routine fly balls go a long way. Vinny stopped trying to pull everything and learned to go to right-center in '95. He is a slow baserunner and a terrible basestealer. At third, Castilla has soft hands and his range is adequate. His arm is strong with average accuracy.

HOW HE PERFORMED IN '95
Castilla was probably the most pleasant surprise of '95 for the Rockies. He hadn't played that much third base prior to the season, but he worked hard in winter ball to prepare himself for an anticipated platoon arrangement with Jason Bates to replace the departed Charlie Hayes. However, Vinny quickly established himself as an offensive force and took over the job full-time. He had worked on his power stroke in the spring, which paid off as he over .300 in every full month except September—with consistent home-run pop. Castilla even started the All-Star game when Matt Williams was injured.

All of the "Blake Street Bombers"—Bichette, Walker, Galarraga, and Castilla—had their offensive production inflated by Coors Field, but the differential is most dramatic in Vinny's case: all of his offensive numbers were far below the league average on the road.

Castilla's 32 home runs established a new major-league record for home runs by a Mexican national, breaking the mark previously held by Aurelio Rodriguez, another third baseman, who hit 19 for Washington in 1970. This past December, Vinny returned to play winter ball in his native country and was treated as a conquering hero.

The transition to third base went relatively smoothly. While Castilla did make 15 errors and had occasional erratic spurts, he worked very hard and charged bunts effectively.

WHAT TO EXPECT IN '96
Castilla's huge home/road differential and his dramatic improvement over previous personal bests in almost every offensive category raise a red flag about his potential for '96. However, at age 28, Vinny is in his prime and, of course, will be playing at friendly Coors again.

Overall Statistics

	G	AB	R	H	2B	3B	HR	RBI	SB	CS	BB	SO	BA	OBA
95 COL	139	527	82	163	34	2	32	90	2	8	30	87	.309	.347
Career	317	1015	136	297	55	10	44	139	6	14	51	161	.293	.327

1995 Situational Statistics

	AB	HR	RBI	BA	OBA	SLG		AB	HR	RBI	BA	OBA	SLG
Home	274	23	58	.383	.413	.730	LHP	134	12	35	.388	.417	.769
Road	253	9	32	.229	.277	.383	RHP	393	20	55	.282	.324	.494
Apr-Jun	226	12	38	.314	.342	.558	ScPos	130	3	52	.285	.308	.446
Jul-Oct	301	20	52	.306	.352	.568	Clutch	72	3	8	.236	.282	.444

How He Compares to Other Batters

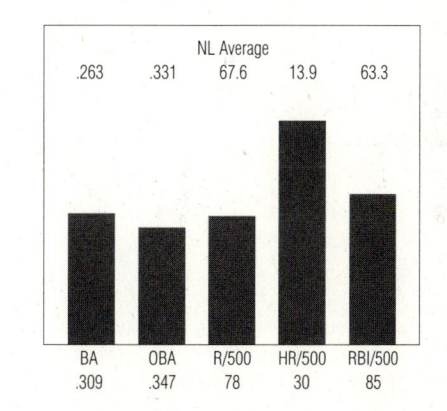

NL Average: .263 .331 67.6 13.9 63.3

	BA	OBA	R/500	HR/500	RBI/500
	.309	.347	78	30	85

Where He Hits the Ball

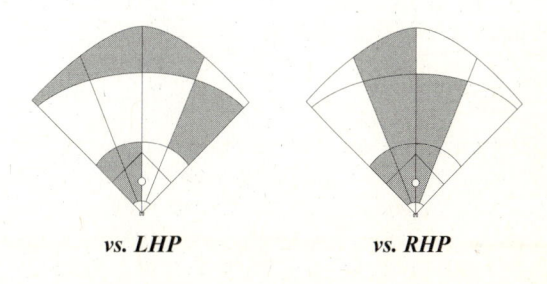

vs. LHP   vs. RHP

COLORADO ROCKIES

ANDRES GALARRAGA

Position: 1B
Bats: R **Throws:** R
Ht: 6'3" **Wt:** 235
Opening Day Age: 34
Born: 6/18/1961
Drafted: MON 1/19/79
ML Seasons: 11

SCOUTING REPORT

Free-swinging Galarraga stands at the plate with a very open stance and steps into the pitch. He likes to go after the ball when it's high and out over the plate and can clobber a mistake. However, Andres will also chase bad pitches and can be worked effectively on the outside corner. He has well below-average speed but is a surprisingly effective base thief. Galarraga does not bunt.

Despite his lack of speed and below-average range, Andres is a decent first baseman. He has good, soft hands and scoops throws out of the dirt extremely well. Galarraga's throwing arm is both strong and very accurate.

HOW HE PERFORMED IN '95

Galarraga had another outstanding offensive year for the Rockies. While his average dipped significantly for the second straight season, he again hit for power and knocked in runs. Beginning the season slowly, Andres struck out 43 times in April and May, which helped contribute to his league-leading total. It was the fourth time, but the first since 1990, that Galarraga had paced the NL in whiffs.

This early slump prompted some grumbling from the Rockies' front office that Galarraga had lost too much weight in the off-season. However, once the weather warmed up, so did Andres.

Galarraga appeared in 143 games, his highest total since 1990, avoiding the nagging injuries that have cut into his recent seasons. Of the four "Blake Street Bombers" (the others being Bichette, Castilla and Walker), Andres was one who benefitted least from hitter-friendly Coors Field, although he performed better at home. The Big Cat's throwing arm and good ability to receive throws helped him participate in more double plays than any other first baseman. However, Galarraga also paced everyone at his position in errors, fielding .991, a well below-average percentage for a first sacker.

WHAT TO EXPECT IN '96

Galarraga is a fan favorite as well as a key element in the Rockies' offensive scheme. However, he's not a superstar and turns 35 in June. Andres had hit poorly for four straight years before coming to the thin air of Colorado; as long he can stay injury-free and play half his games in Denver, look for him to produce for several more years.

Overall Statistics

	G	AB	R	H	2B	3B	HR	RBI	SB	CS	BB	SO	BA	OBA
95 COL	143	554	89	155	29	3	31	106	12	2	32	146	.280	.331
Career	1308	4848	669	1371	267	23	200	761	81	46	310	1171	.283	.334

1995 Situational Statistics

	AB	HR	RBI	BA	OBA	SLG		AB	HR	RBI	BA	OBA	SLG
Home	273	18	55	.297	.355	.571	LHP	137	10	33	.270	.327	.562
Road	281	13	51	.263	.307	.452	RHP	417	21	73	.283	.333	.494
Apr-Jun	223	12	39	.274	.337	.489	ScPos	157	9	72	.293	.356	.541
Jul-Oct	331	19	67	.284	.327	.526	Clutch	82	5	12	.280	.330	.524

How He Compares to Other Batters

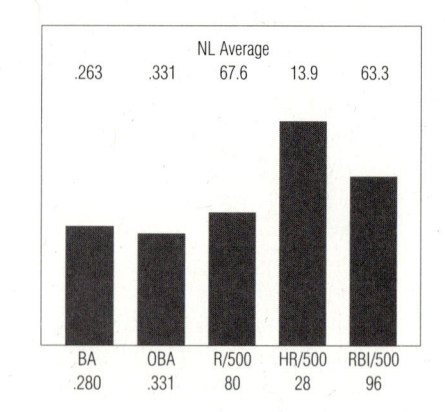

NL Average: .263 | .331 | 67.6 | 13.9 | 63.3

BA .280 | OBA .331 | R/500 80 | HR/500 28 | RBI/500 96

Where He Hits the Ball

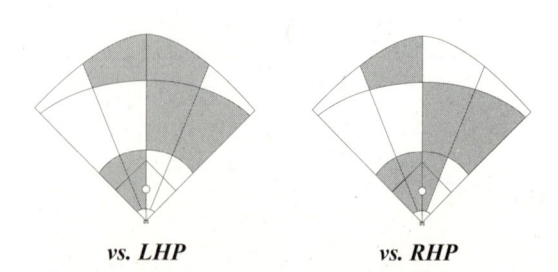

vs. LHP   vs. RHP

COLORADO ROCKIES

JOE GIRARDI

Position: C
Bats: R **Throws:** R
Ht: 5'11" **Wt:** 195
Opening Day Age: 31
Born: 10/14/1964
Drafted: CHN86 5/116
ML Seasons: 7

SCOUTING REPORT

Girardi is a good contact hitter who accepts his lack of power and will go with the pitch to the opposite field. He likes the pitch out over the plate as most Rockies hitters do. Joe is very aggressive with the bat and rarely goes deep into the count, but he is adept at moving a runner along via the hit-and-run or the bunt. Girardi is a slightly below-average runner, but will occasionally try to steal anyway.

Joe has outstanding tools behind the plate. His well above-average range behind the plate is due both to quick feet and good agility. He also has good hands and throws well, with a strong and very accurate arm.

HOW HE PERFORMED IN '95

Girardi started off with a bang, posting a four-hit performance on Opening Day and hitting safely in 17 of his first 18 games. In April and May, he batted .328, but tailed off as catching 81% of the team's innings began to wear him down. He did set career highs in home runs, runs and runs batted in—middling as they were. He stayed relatively healthy for a change, appearing in over 100 games for the first time since 1990.

Often batting in the #2 slot, Girardi led the team in sacrifice bunts (12), tying for fifth in the NL. However, he had a very poor on-base average for someone hitting so high. As was true with many Rockies, his offense shone at home and but was much less impressive on the road. Once his hitting began to decline, the Rockies focused on trying to find a suitable backup for Joe, but only the late-season call-up of Jayhawk Owens proved profitable.

Behind the plate, Girardi had some trouble throwing out runners (33 of 131, 27%), ranking just below league-average, but many Rockies' pitchers are very poor at holding runners. Joe committed only five passed balls in '95.

WHAT TO EXPECT IN '96

The Rockies traded Girardi to the New York Yankees in November, partly on the strength of Owens' performance in September. The poor performance of Rockies' starters may have called into question Girardi's ability to handle the staff and may have influenced management's decision to deal him. He's a solid if unspectacular receiver who should soldier on for another year or two.

Overall Statistics

	G	AB	R	H	2B	3B	HR	RBI	SB	CS	BB	SO	BA	OBA
95 COL	125	462	63	121	17	2	8	55	3	3	29	76	.262	.308
Career	608	1995	218	536	79	14	18	190	22	18	127	285	.269	.315

1995 Situational Statistics

	AB	HR	RBI	BA	OBA	SLG		AB	HR	RBI	BA	OBA	SLG
Home	247	6	41	.291	.333	.417	LHP	116	1	10	.250	.310	.302
Road	215	2	14	.228	.278	.293	RHP	346	7	45	.266	.307	.379
Apr-Jun	192	2	25	.292	.335	.380	ScPos	125	2	46	.336	.391	.424
Jul-Oct	270	6	30	.241	.288	.344	Clutch	72	0	9	.306	.351	.319

How He Compares to Other Batters

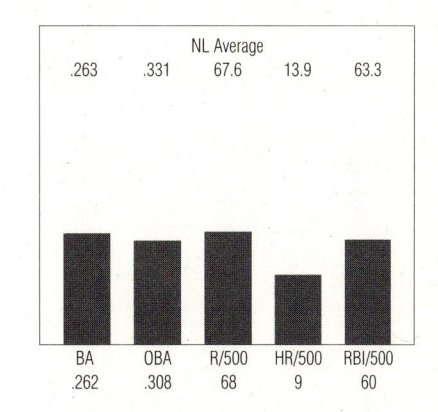

NL Average: .263 .331 67.6 13.9 63.3

	BA	OBA	R/500	HR/500	RBI/500
	.262	.308	68	9	60

Where He Hits the Ball

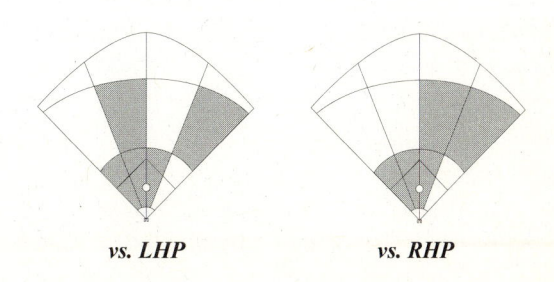

vs. LHP   vs. RHP

COLORADO ROCKIES

DARREN HOLMES

Position: RP
Bats: R **Throws:** R
Ht: 6'0" **Wt:** 199
Opening Day Age: 29
Born: 4/25/1966
Drafted: LA84 16/415
ML Seasons: 6

SCOUTING REPORT
Holmes is one of the more gifted short relievers in the NL. Coming to the plate with a high three-quarter to overhand delivery, Darren throws a slightly above-average fastball that he also cuts. He also uses an average slider and an occasional change-up to set up his out pitch, a well above-average curve with a sharp downward break.

Control can be a problem at times for Holmes; Often, his curve breaks so well that umpires don't call strikes on it: as a result, Darren has to rely on the slider. Bouts of inconsistency have kept the potentially dominating reliever from claiming the Rockies closer's job all to himself.

A below-average fielder, Holmes is average at holding runners: seven stole against him in ten tries during '95. He was hitless in his only '95 at-bat and is 0-for-2 lifetime with three successful sacrifices.

HOW HE PERFORMED IN '95
After spending parts of '93 and '94 in the minors, Darren was an integral part of the Colorado bullpen in '95. He took up some of the slack created by Bruce Ruffin's injury-plagued season and wound up leading the team in saves. His 68 appearances were fifth in the league; his ERA was considerably improved over that of the previous two seasons. Holmes blew just four save opportunities and allowed only 24% of inherited runners to score. Always a slow starter, Darren pitched poorly in May but quite well the next two months, picking up ten of his saves in a July that included a 15-inning scoreless streak.

Surprisingly, he did better at Coors Field than on the road. However, his tendency to get behind in the count drove both Manager Don Baylor and the fans nuts. In the last two months, Holmes didn't get many save chances and was not effective.

WHAT TO EXPECT IN '96
The Rockies re-signed Holmes in November and intend to divide the save chances between him and a hopefully-healed Ruffin. If Ruffin can't do the job and Darren is asked to take full responsibility, problems with location might become a problem for Holmes. He has fallen apart under the pressure of full-time closer duty before, and had an aching right elbow as recently as '94.

Overall Statistics

	G	GS	GF	SV	W	L	ERA	IP	H	R	ER	HR	BB	SO
95 COL	68	0	33	14	6	1	3.24	66.2	59	26	24	3	28	61
Career	254	0	133	51	14	16	4.11	297.2	290	147	136	22	121	263

1995 Situational Statistics

	W	L	ERA	SV	IP	BB	SO		AB	HR	RBI	BA	OBA	SLG
Home	3	0	2.95	9	39.2	12	38	LHB	106	2	16	.179	.264	.311
Road	3	1	3.67	5	27.0	16	23	RHB	143	1	10	.280	.350	.357
Apr-Jun	5	0	2.86	3	28.1	12	25	ScPos	80	1	22	.225	.316	.325
Jul-Oct	1	1	3.52	11	38.1	16	36	Clutch	138	1	14	.225	.304	.283

How He Compares to Other Pitchers

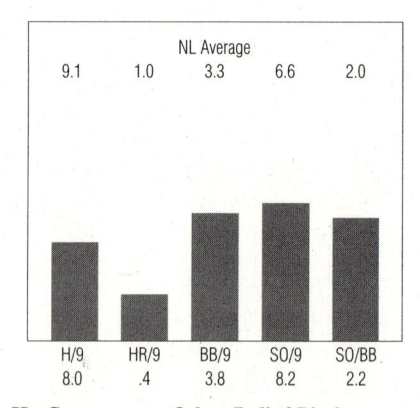

NL Average: H/9 9.1, HR/9 1.0, BB/9 3.3, SO/9 6.6, SO/BB 2.0

Holmes: H/9 8.0, HR/9 .4, BB/9 3.8, SO/9 8.2, SO/BB 2.2

How He Compares to Other Relief Pitchers

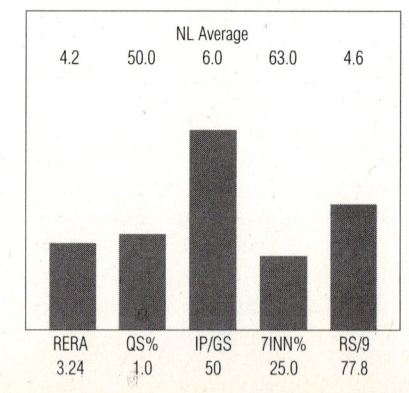

NL Average: RERA 4.2, QS% 50.0, IP/GS 6.0, 7INN% 63.0, RS/9 4.6

Holmes: RERA 3.24, QS% 1.0, IP/GS 50, 7INN% 25.0, RS/9 77.8

COLORADO ROCKIES

MIKE KINGERY

Positions: OF//1B
Bats: L **Throws:** L
Ht: 6'0" **Wt:** 180
Opening Day Age: 35
Born: 3/29/1961
Drafted: KC 8/27/79
ML Seasons: 9

SCOUTING REPORT

Kingery will slash line drives to all fields, making good contact and habitually walking as often as he strikes out. Although he doesn't have great power, he can occasionally pop the ball out. Mike will lay down the sacrifice as well as bunt for a base hit. He is a decent basestealer due to plus speed.

He has good defensive skills and can play all three outfield positions. Mike has good mobility but doesn't get to a lot of fly balls in center (partly due to the unusual nature of a mile-high stadium, he must play very deep), slightly above-average hands, and throws with slightly above-par accuracy. Tremendous hustle is perhaps Kingery's greatest attribute. He plays hard both in the outfield and on the bases, and concedes nothing at bat.

HOW HE PERFORMED IN '95

After a surprising .349 performance in '94, Mike began the season as Colorado's everyday center fielder while Ellis Burks was recovering from surgery. He initially responded well to this added responsibility, batting .353 through May, but tailed off and hit only .242 for the remainder of the season. Unlike most Rockies, he hit as well on the road as at home. What Kingery produced in '95 is very comparable to what he has done for most of his career. He is an unspectacular offensive player with some positives and can play a key defensive position.

The Rockies were fortunate that Kingery stepped forward and took command in the outfield in the early going. With Bichette's lack of range in left, and the large dimensions of Coors Field, Kingery had a lot of ground to cover in center. His fielding was always good, and often spectacular, and Mike never let any offensive problems interfere with his defense. He threw out four runners last year, but also made four errors.

WHAT TO EXPECT IN '96

The Rockies allowed Kingery to file for free-agency in November and he signed with the Pittsburgh Pirates. One of the reasons the veteran became expendable was the emergence of Trenidad Hubbard as the current fourth outfielder and, possibly, center fielder of the future. Mike, who is 35, will be a good fit on Jim Leyland's club, serving as a fourth outfielder who can start if needed.

Overall Statistics

	G	AB	R	H	2B	3B	HR	RBI	SB	CS	BB	SO	BA	OBA
95 COL	119	350	66	94	18	4	8	37	13	5	45	40	.269	.351
Career	702	1758	260	478	96	24	27	192	43	27	168	219	.272	.334

1995 Situational Statistics

	AB	HR	RBI	BA	OBA	SLG		AB	HR	RBI	BA	OBA	SLG
Home	166	4	19	.265	.372	.428	LHP	44	0	4	.227	.358	.273
Road	184	4	18	.272	.330	.397	RHP	306	8	33	.275	.350	.431
Apr-Jun	162	5	19	.284	.383	.438	ScPos	83	1	28	.229	.330	.325
Jul-Oct	188	3	18	.255	.322	.388	Clutch	55	3	5	.255	.328	.436

How He Compares to Other Batters

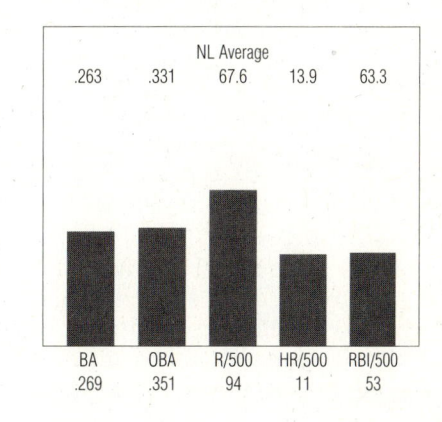

NL Average: .263 / .331 / 67.6 / 13.9 / 63.3

BA	OBA	R/500	HR/500	RBI/500
.269	.351	94	11	53

Where He Hits the Ball

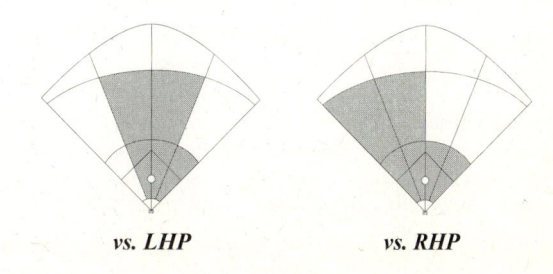

vs. LHP   vs. RHP

THE SCOUTING REPORT: 1996

COLORADO ROCKIES

CURT LESKANIC

Position: RP
Bats: R **Throws:** R
Ht: 6'0" **Wt:** 180
Opening Day Age: 27
Born: 4/2/1968
Drafted: CLE89 7/203
ML Seasons: 3

SCOUTING REPORT
Aggressive, hard-throwing Leskanic has a high three-quarter to overhand delivery which he uses to bring home three plus pitches: a sinking fastball that could use more movement, an average-plus curve, and a slider that rates as one of the best in the league. Leskanic also shows a change-up.

Curtis has average control and a bulldog attitude and will pitch inside at any time. He also sports a good move to first base: only eight tried to steal against him in '95, six successfully. His fielding is slightly below-average because Leskanic falls off to the first base side in his follow-through.

HOW HE PERFORMED IN '95
Curtis opened the season on the big-league roster for the first time and spent the whole season making up for two previous years of lost time. Utilized as a swingman in 1993-94 by the Rockies, Leskanic worked exclusively in relief in '95. And he worked hard, leading the majors in appearances. He earned the save in the Rockies wild-card clincher on October 1 against the Giants.

After a slow start, Curtis was 5-2 with 10 saves and a 2.82 ERA from June through the end of the season. He gained Don Baylor's confidence gradually and ended the year as part of the Colorado bullpen committee. Leskanic allowed only 13% of inherited runners to score, and three times entered games with the bases loaded and allowed no one to score.

While Curtis is very durable, and can be used effectively on back-to-back days, he cannot pitch for long stretches because his all-out attitude leads to quickly deteriorating stuff.

Some Rockies' trivia, indicating a staff historically short on strikeout stuff: Leskanic's 107 strikeouts marked only the fourth time in the Rockies three-year history that one of their pitchers had recorded at least 100 strikeouts.

WHAT TO EXPECT IN '96
Look for Leskanic to be the "can-do" guy again in the bullpen. The Rockies bullpen will likely remain a committee affair and will be called on often due to a less-than-stellar starting rotation. While he probably won't be the closer, Curtis will see plenty of action as the guy sent out to stop a rally or prevent an uprising. He is a horse.

Overall Statistics

	G	GS	GF	SV	W	L	ERA	IP	H	R	ER	HR	BB	SO
95 COL	76	0	27	10	6	3	3.40	98.0	83	38	37	7	33	107
Career	102	11	30	10	8	9	4.31	177.1	169	92	85	16	70	154

1995 Situational Statistics

	W	L	ERA	SV	IP	BB	SO		AB	HR	RBI	BA	OBA	SLG
Home	4	1	3.33	7	51.1	12	47	LHB	154	4	19	.247	.330	.403
Road	2	2	3.47	3	46.2	21	60	RHB	214	3	17	.210	.256	.308
Apr-Jun	2	1	3.74	3	45.2	18	54	ScPos	101	1	24	.188	.282	.277
Jul-Oct	4	2	3.10	7	52.1	15	53	Clutch	187	3	18	.214	.275	.326

How He Compares to Other Pitchers

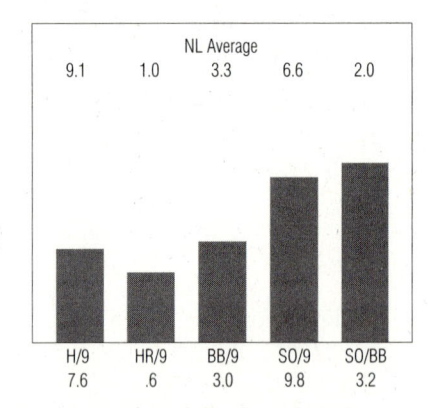

NL Average: 9.1 / 1.0 / 3.3 / 6.6 / 2.0

H/9	HR/9	BB/9	SO/9	SO/BB
7.6	.6	3.0	9.8	3.2

How He Compares to Other Relief Pitchers

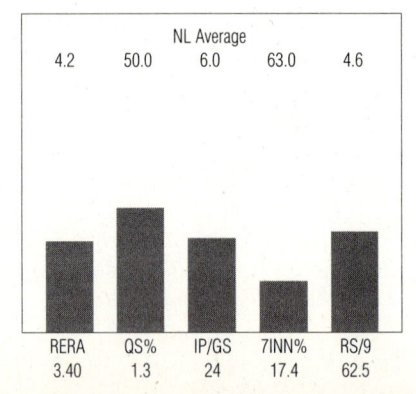

NL Average: 4.2 / 50.0 / 6.0 / 63.0 / 4.6

RERA	QS%	IP/GS	7INN%	RS/9
3.40	1.3	24	17.4	62.5

COLORADO ROCKIES

STEVE REED

Position: RP
Bats: R **Throws:** R
Ht: 6'2" **Wt:** 200
Opening Day Age: 30
Born: 3/11/1966
Drafted: SF 6/24/88
ML Seasons: 4

SCOUTING REPORT

Reed pitches underhand. The unorthodox delivery is a big part of his success and, paradoxically, why it took him so long to get a chance. Coming from underneath and across his body with lots of motion in his windup, he's hard to pick up and absolute hell on righthanded hitters. Steve has a slightly below-average sinking fastball and three other average pitches: a sweeping curve, a slider and a change-up. Good control makes all of his pitches much more effective.

In the past, Reed had struggled with lefthanders, but in '95 he worked the corners against them effectively, throwing sinkers away and then sliders in on the hands. Due to his awkward delivery, his ability to hold runners has been poor. However, only seven tried to steal on Steve in '95, and four were thrown out. He is an average fielder. His one hit in three trips last season was Reed's first ever in 14 career at-bats.

HOW HE PERFORMED IN '95

The former Giants' prospect was another member of the relief corps that kept the team in the pennant race when their starters foundered. He had his most successful year in the majors in '95, largely because of major improvements at home and against lefthanders. For the first time, Steve pitched well at home, but for the third straight season, he posted an ERA under 2.00 in road games. What he could do in a neutral park is something few seem to have contemplated—the Giants probably don't want to think about it either.

Reed led the Rockies' staff with a .203 opponents' average and, during a stretch from July 3 to August 13, he allowed just one earned run in 21.2 innings. On the season, he allowed only a quarter of inherited runners to score. However, he continued to pay for his infrequent control mistakes, giving up his share of home runs on fat pitches to righties.

WHAT TO EXPECT IN '96

Reed is a very successful pitcher when he is able to move the ball around effectively. If he continues to shut down lefthanders, Steve should again be outstanding in a setup role for the Rockies in '96. The abilities of the durable Reed will be especially in demand if the performance of the team's starting rotation does not improve.

Overall Statistics

	G	GS	GF	SV	W	L	ERA	IP	H	R	ER	HR	BB	SO
95 COL	71	0	15	3	5	2	2.14	84.0	61	24	20	8	21	79
Career	214	0	42	9	18	9	3.41	248.0	233	109	94	32	80	192

1995 Situational Statistics

	W	L	ERA	SV	IP	BB	SO		AB	HR	RBI	BA	OBA	SLG
Home	5	1	3.07	2	41.0	12	44	LHB	99	1	7	.202	.295	.263
Road	0	1	1.26	1	43.0	9	35	RHB	202	7	24	.203	.236	.327
Apr-Jun	1	1	2.48	3	32.2	7	37	ScPos	71	2	23	.239	.321	.324
Jul-Oct	4	1	1.93	0	51.1	14	42	Clutch	107	4	9	.178	.239	.336

How He Compares to Other Pitchers

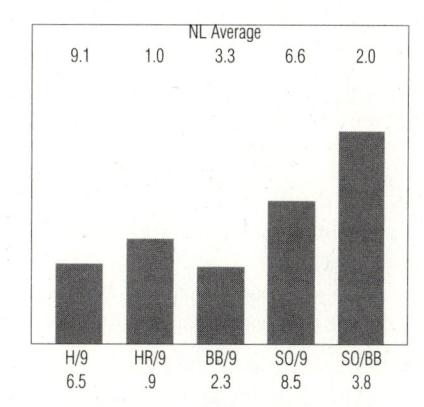

NL Average: H/9 9.1, HR/9 1.0, BB/9 3.3, SO/9 6.6, SO/BB 2.0

H/9 6.5 | HR/9 .9 | BB/9 2.3 | SO/9 8.5 | SO/BB 3.8

How He Compares to Other Relief Pitchers

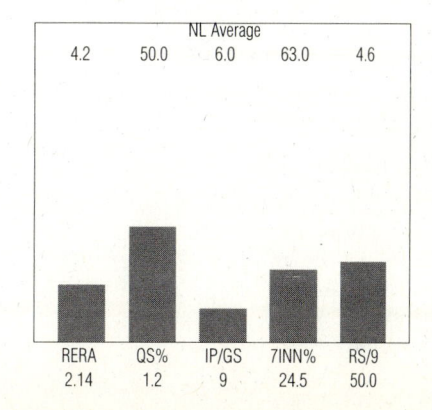

NL Average: RERA 4.2, QS% 50.0, IP/GS 6.0, 7INN% 63.0, RS/9 4.6

RERA 2.14 | QS% 1.2 | IP/GS 9 | 7INN% 24.5 | RS/9 50.0

COLORADO ROCKIES

KEVIN RITZ

Position: SP
Bats: R **Throws:** R
Ht: 6'4" **Wt:** 195
Opening Day Age: 30
Born: 6/8/1965
Drafted: DET85 S4/85
ML Seasons: 6

SCOUTING REPORT

Kevin has a live arm, which is why he has gotten many chances despite limited success prior to '95. He comes to the plate with a high three-quarter delivery. Ritz made big improvements last season. He used to get hit hard in Detroit because he often hung his slightly below-average curve. In order to correct the problem, Kevin developed a circle change-up which has become a plus deception pitch; he throws the bender less frequently now.

Ritz also uses his average slider more often than previously, and continues to throw a plus sinking fastball. His periodic struggles with command have become less common, but Kevin's control rates average at best. He now uses a slide step to hold runners better; however, he is still subpar and 18 out of 22 were successful stealing with Ritz pitching in '95. He is an average fielder.

He snapped a 0-22 lifetime mark at bat with a single in May. However, Kevin isn't intimidating anyone yet: he hit .188 in 48 at-bats with 20 strikeouts to raise his career mark to .132.

HOW HE PERFORMED IN '95

Ritz's disastrous August (0-5, 6.12) marred an otherwise surprising season. He provided a reliable if unspectacular presence to an injury-plagued rotation. Almost unbelievably for a playoff team, Kevin was the only Rockies' pitcher to post double-digit victories. He was durable and made great strides against righthanders, who had entered the year with a .292 career average against him. However, improved control also meant more home runs allowed. Kevin is still working out some of the kinks in his game and, like most of his Rockies' mound mates, didn't particularly appreciate working in Coors Field.

Ritz' struggles in August prompted the Rockies to try him in the bullpen briefly, and Kevin had a fine September, with a 2.94 ERA. He was 2-1 in four starts and notched two saves in two relief appearances.

WHAT TO EXPECT IN '96

Unless the Rockies' front office can find several reliable starters, Ritz will be asked to shoulder a heavy load. On most clubs, he would be a #3 or #4 starter but, with the possibility of Bret Saberhagen being sidelined for the season, Kevin could battle Bill Swift for the #1 role.

Overall Statistics

	G	GS	GF	SV	W	L	ERA	IP	H	R	ER	HR	BB	SO
95 COL	31	28	3	2	11	11	4.21	173.1	171	91	81	16	65	120
Career	96	75	10	2	22	35	5.14	424.0	453	267	242	28	224	298

1995 Situational Statistics

	W	L	ERA	SV	IP	BB	SO		AB	HR	RBI	BA	OBA	SLG
Home	5	4	5.42	2	76.1	31	56	LHB	295	3	34	.295	.378	.386
Road	6	7	3.25	0	97.0	34	64	RHB	364	13	55	.231	.288	.393
Apr-Jun	6	3	3.58	0	75.1	27	53	ScPos	160	6	73	.325	.399	.481
Jul-Oct	5	8	4.68	2	98.0	38	67	Clutch	13	0	3	.231	.286	.231

How He Compares to Other Pitchers

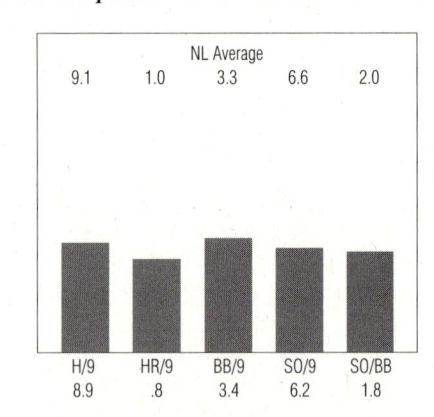

NL Average: H/9 9.1, HR/9 1.0, BB/9 3.3, SO/9 6.6, SO/BB 2.0

H/9 8.9, HR/9 .8, BB/9 3.4, SO/9 6.2, SO/BB 1.8

How He Compares to Other Starting Pitchers

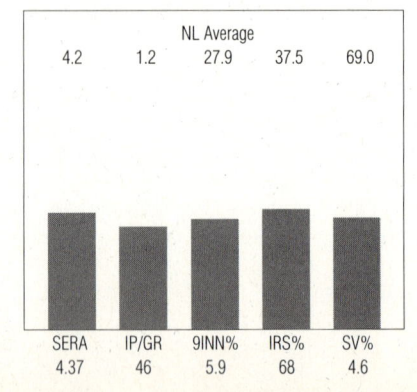

NL Average: SERA 4.2, IP/GR 1.2, 9INN% 27.9, IRS% 37.5, SV% 69.0

SERA 4.37, IP/GR 46, 9INN% 5.9, IRS% 68, SV% 4.6

COLORADO ROCKIES

BRET SABERHAGEN

Position: SP
Bats: R **Throws:** R
Ht: 6'1" **Wt:** 195
Opening Day Age: 31
Born: 4/11/1964
Drafted: KC82 19/480
ML Seasons: 12

SCOUTING REPORT

Two-time Cy Young Award-winning righthander Saberhagen delivers the ball to the plate from a three-quarter angle against lefthanders but will drop to low three quarters against righthanders.

He has simply outstanding control and challenges all hitters. Bret's fastball rates well above-average. He throws three different varieties of the pitch: a two-seam sinker, a four-seam riser, and a cutter. Saberhagen also throws a plus curve. His change-up, which he turns over, also is plus but isn't used all that much. When Bret is healthy, his pitches are rated even higher. Being around the plate and not giving in to hitters means that Saberhagen will give up the occasional home run; he can get away with that because he walks so few.

Bret has quick feet that give him an above-average ability to hold runners: only five tested Saberhagen in '95, four successfully. He is a superb fielder with a 1989 Gold Glove on his mantle. Hitting, however, is minus; Bret batted only .102 last year.

HOW HE PERFORMED IN '95

Saberhagen joined Colorado on July 31 after a surprising trade with the Mets. Rockies' fans were ecstatic when Bret won his first start against the Dodgers, salvaging the final game of a crucial series. Unfortunately, that was the high point of his tenure with Colorado; he was not healthy and managed only a 2-1 record and an unsightly 6.28 ERA in nine starts with his new team.

Without much starting pitching to begin with, the Rockies did not have the luxury of allowing him to heal and continued to use Bret even though he was experiencing pain in his shoulder.

WHAT TO EXPECT IN '96

This gambit came home to roost, as it was learned in the off-season that despite surgery in October to repair a torn labrum in the shoulder, Saberhagen could spend the entire year recovering. He has continued to experience pain in the shoulder after the procedure, and at least one doctor has recommended that Bret undergo additional surgery.

If Saberhagen is lost for the year, it would be a major blow to the Rockies. If healthy, he will anchor a suspect staff; if he can't pitch, Colorado must get by with same undependable group as they used for most of '95.

Overall Statistics

	G	GS	GF	SV	W	L	ERA	IP	H	R	ER	HR	BB	SO
95 NYN/COL	25	25	0	0	7	6	4.18	153.0	165	78	71	21	33	100
Career	337	309	13	1	141	100	3.26	2227.2	2100	880	807	177	421	1510

1995 Situational Statistics

	W	L	ERA	SV	IP	BB	SO		AB	HR	RBI	BA	OBA	SLG
Home	4	3	4.84	0	83.2	19	61	LHB	277	8	26	.235	.279	.394
Road	3	3	3.38	0	69.1	14	39	RHB	328	13	41	.305	.353	.482
Apr-Jun	5	2	3.24	0	86.0	17	50	ScPos	125	5	45	.256	.314	.456
Jul-Oct	2	4	5.37	0	67.0	16	50	Clutch	27	0	2	.148	.179	.259

How He Compares to Other Pitchers

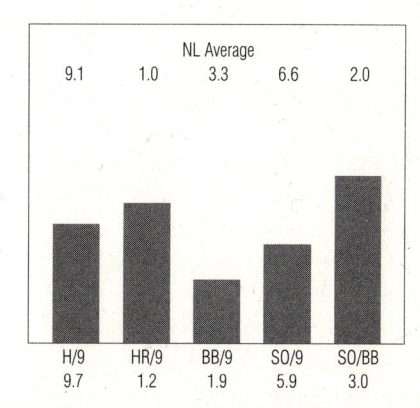

NL Average: H/9 9.1, HR/9 1.0, BB/9 3.3, SO/9 6.6, SO/BB 2.0
H/9 9.7, HR/9 1.2, BB/9 1.9, SO/9 5.9, SO/BB 3.0

How He Compares to Other Starting Pitchers

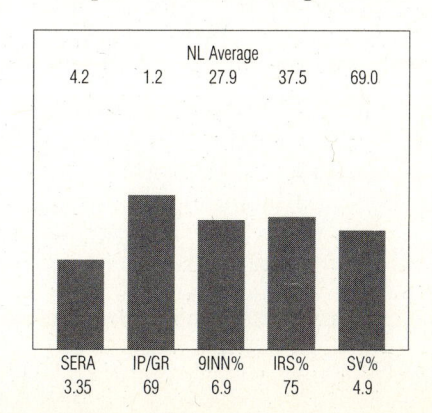

NL Average: SERA 4.2, IP/GR 1.2, 9INN% 27.9, IRS% 37.5, SV% 69.0
SERA 3.35, IP/GR 69, 9INN% 6.9, IRS% 75, SV% 4.9

THE SCOUTING REPORT: 1996

COLORADO ROCKIES

BILL SWIFT

Position: SP
Bats: R **Throws:** R
Ht: 6'0" **Wt:** 180
Opening Day Age: 34
Born: 10/27/1961
Drafted: SEA84 1/2
ML Seasons: 10

SCOUTING REPORT
Ground ball specialist Bill Swift uses a three-quarter delivery to throw three slightly above-average pitches. A sinking fastball is Swift's out pitch due to its excellent low movement. He also throws a quick-breaking slider that he uses in strikeout situations. Although Bill also has a forkball in his arsenal, recent arm problems have limited its use.

Perhaps Swift's biggest skill is an ability to set up hitters. He keeps the ball low and moves it around the strike zone. Bill has average control and a plus ability to hold runners: nine tried to steal on him last year, only four successfully. He is considered a Gold-Glove caliber fielder, and batted .194 last year with his first-ever home run. Swift is a .211 career hitter who bunts fairly well.

HOW HE PERFORMED IN '95
Signed as a free-agent by the Rockies at the beginning of spring training, Swift quickly became the number one starter but had shoulder problems from the outset. He spent two tours on the DL, one lasting more than a month. Bill struggled through April and May with a 1-1 record and a horrendous 8.75 ERA, walking 20 in his first 39 innings before being disabled. After returning from the injured list, he posted a 5-1 record and 3.37 ERA in June and July, but his shoulder had begun to ache again and, as a result, Swift missed the entire month of August.

In September, Swift returned to form, recording critical back-to-back victories against the Giants and Dodgers within five days.

WHAT TO EXPECT IN '96
It would be nice to blame Bill's problems on adjusting to Coors Field, but his performance last year on the road was poor as well. Unexpected problems with hitters from both sides, but especially righthanders, bedeviled him at times. It's a question whether his oft-injured shoulder can handle the workload he is given.

Swift is 34 and has been hampered by injuries much of his career. If healthy, Swift is a good #2 starter who will give a team 100-150 innings of work per year. However, it's clear that he cannot handle the 233-inning workload that the Giants asked of him in 1993.

Overall Statistics

	G	GS	GF	SV	W	L	ERA	IP	H	R	ER	HR	BB	SO
95 COL	19	19	0	0	9	3	4.94	105.2	122	62	58	12	43	68
Career	353	178	64	25	78	62	3.62	1371.1	1397	629	551	83	425	656

1995 Situational Statistics

	W	L	ERA	SV	IP	BB	SO		AB	HR	RBI	BA	OBA	SLG
Home	4	1	5.01	0	55.2	24	38	LHB	213	6	31	.319	.401	.484
Road	5	2	4.86	0	50.0	19	30	RHB	199	6	27	.271	.321	.412
Apr-Jun	3	2	6.62	0	53.0	30	39	ScPos	93	4	46	.387	.448	.634
Jul-Oct	6	1	3.25	0	52.2	13	29	Clutch	10	0	1	.200	.200	.200

How He Compares to Other Pitchers

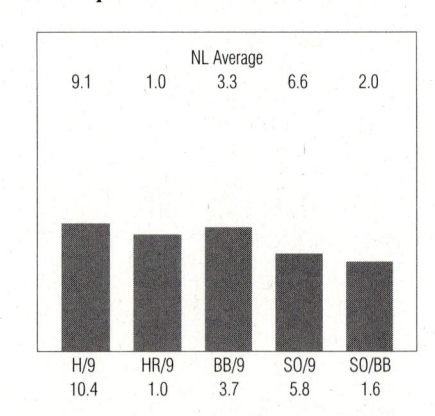

NL Average: 9.1 | 1.0 | 3.3 | 6.6 | 2.0

H/9: 10.4 | HR/9: 1.0 | BB/9: 3.7 | SO/9: 5.8 | SO/BB: 1.6

How He Compares to Other Starting Pitchers

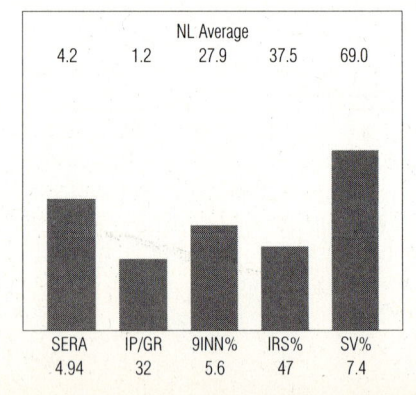

NL Average: 4.2 | 1.2 | 27.9 | 37.5 | 69.0

SERA: 4.94 | IP/GR: 32 | 9INN%: 5.6 | IRS%: 47 | SV%: 7.4

COLORADO ROCKIES

LARRY WALKER

Position: OF
Bats: L **Throws:** R
Ht: 6'2" **Wt:** 185
Opening Day Age: 29
Born: 12/1/1966
Drafted: MON 11/14/84
ML Seasons: 7

SCOUTING REPORT

Walker has a short, smooth stroke and excellent bat speed. A good fastball hitter, Larry can also clobber the breaking ball and makes surprisingly good contact for someone who produces so much power. In true Rockies' fashion, Walker likes the pitch high and out over the plate and is not concerned with going deep into the count. Larry is a slightly above-average baserunner, and continues to leg out hits and steal bases with surprising effectiveness for a man of his size. He does not bunt.

Walker's defensive skills in right field are all plus. Although Larry is still celebrated for his arm, shoulder injuries have taken some of the power out of his throwing.

HOW HE PERFORMED IN '95

Signed as a free-agent in early April (the same day as Bill Swift), Walker was a key part of the offensive fireworks supplied by the Blake Street Bombers. He gave immediate notice of his value by hitting three doubles on Opening Day. Despite an August batting slump, he hit with consistent power all season. Larry's career-high 36 home runs ranked second in the NL and broke a 48-year-old record held by Jeff Heath for most four-baggers in a season by a Canadian-born player.

As with most of the Rockies' hitters, Walker had unbelievable numbers at home but only so-so stats on the road. His away-game performance was somewhat inferior to what Larry had done in the past while playing for Montreal: whether this was a fluke or whether Coors Field got Walker into bad habits will be shown in time. He was more aggressive at the plate than usual in '95, drawing just 36 non-intentional walks.

Larry's presence in right field improved the Colorado defense, although former right fielder Dante Bichette had some problems adjusting to left. Tying for second among NL outfielders with 13 assists, Walker made just three errors.

WHAT TO EXPECT IN '96

Only 29 at the beginning of the season, Walker is in the right place at the right time. Assuming he improves his performance when traveling, he could enjoy MVP-caliber performance. Larry is a complete player—his booming home runs to right field have endeared him to Colorado fans, and his defense and baserunning are still strong.

Overall Statistics

	G	AB	R	H	2B	3B	HR	RBI	SB	CS	BB	SO	BA	OBA
95 COL	131	494	96	151	31	5	36	101	16	3	49	72	.306	.381
Career	805	2860	464	817	178	21	135	485	114	38	313	546	.286	.361

1995 Situational Statistics

	AB	HR	RBI	BA	OBA	SLG		AB	HR	RBI	BA	OBA	SLG
Home	248	24	59	.343	.401	.730	LHP	141	7	30	.319	.389	.532
Road	246	12	42	.268	.361	.484	RHP	353	29	71	.300	.378	.637
Apr-Jun	199	17	38	.322	.396	.653	ScPos	130	6	59	.277	.407	.523
Jul-Oct	295	19	63	.295	.371	.576	Clutch	68	5	15	.279	.383	.574

How He Compares to Other Batters

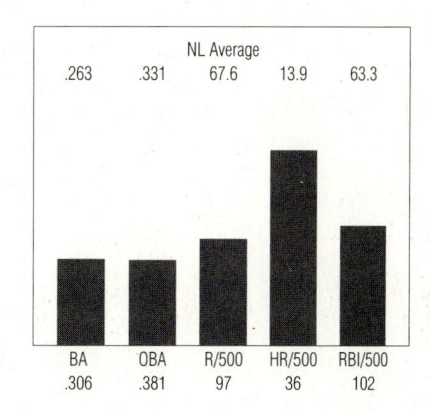

NL Average: BA .263 | OBA .331 | R/500 67.6 | HR/500 13.9 | RBI/500 63.3

Walker: BA .306 | OBA .381 | R/500 97 | HR/500 36 | RBI/500 102

Where He Hits the Ball

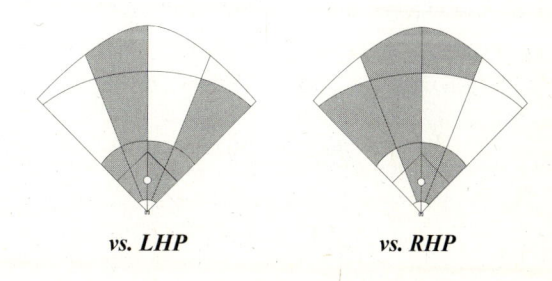

vs. LHP   vs. RHP

THE SCOUTING REPORT: 1996

COLORADO ROCKIES

WALT WEISS

Position: SS
Bats: B **Throws:** R
Ht: 6'0" **Wt:** 175
Opening Day Age: 32
Born: 11/28/1963
Drafted: OAK85 1/11
ML Seasons: 9

SCOUTING REPORT
Wily switch-hitter Weiss has no power and poor bat speed but can make good contact to all fields. He is a disciplined hitter and works the walk well, but he can easily be overpowered. A smart baserunner with plus speed, Walt has become a more aggressive basestealer, and has been quite effective. He is an outstanding sacrifice bunter who will also try to bunt for hits.

Though Weiss has only average range at shortstop, he compensates with good hands and good positioning. He is able to uncork strong, accurate throws from the hole or from behind second base, and Walt is willing to dive for the ball.

HOW HE PERFORMED IN '95
Adaptability has become the hallmark of Weiss' career, as he seems to pick up new talents depending on how he's used. Placed in the #8 spot for most of last year, Weiss took advantage of being pitched around and drew a career-high 98 walks. That set a team record and ranked second in the NL behind Barry Bonds; Walt thereby finished fourth in the league in on-base average. He also set a career mark in stolen bases with 15 in '95. His ability to reach base was a bonus for a player paid mostly for defense—he even led off for a time.

Even in Colorado, though, Walt couldn't show power. He hit his first home run in 750 at-bats on September 20 against San Diego; up to that point, he had experienced the third-longest long ball drought among active players behind fellow powerhouses Rafael Belliard and Otis Nixon.

In the field, Weiss finished fourth among NL shortstops with a .974 fielding percentage. He was a model of consistency in a sometimes erratic infield and earned his pay for that reason alone. One of his specialties is the over-the-shoulder grab in left field, an especially valuable play when one considers left fielder Dante Bichette's limited range.

WHAT TO EXPECT IN '96
After allowing the 32-year-old Weiss to file for free-agency, the Rockies re-signed him in November. His presence will insure some stability in the infield, and the offense he provides is gravy. Although plagued by injuries earlier in his career, he has stayed in the lineup everyday the last three seasons.

Overall Statistics

	G	AB	R	H	2B	3B	HR	RBI	SB	CS	BB	SO	BA	OBA
95 COL	137	427	65	111	17	3	1	25	15	3	98	57	.260	.403
Career	933	2958	351	745	102	16	11	226	66	26	392	391	.252	.341

1995 Situational Statistics

	AB	HR	RBI	BA	OBA	SLG		AB	HR	RBI	BA	OBA	SLG
Home	217	0	20	.281	.429	.323	LHP	114	0	2	.263	.387	.298
Road	210	1	5	.238	.375	.319	RHP	313	1	23	.259	.409	.329
Apr-Jun	199	0	12	.251	.375	.312	ScPos	100	0	23	.180	.394	.240
Jul-Oct	228	1	13	.268	.426	.329	Clutch	61	0	5	.246	.412	.262

How He Compares to Other Batters

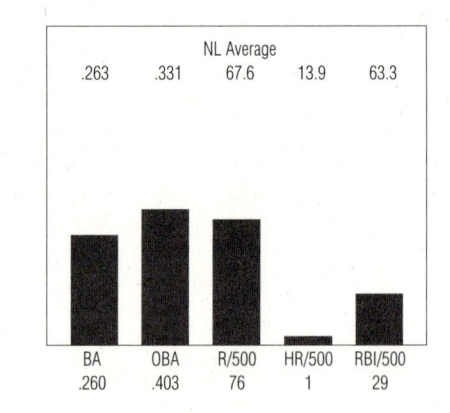

NL Average: BA .263, OBA .331, R/500 67.6, HR/500 13.9, RBI/500 63.3

BA .260, OBA .403, R/500 76, HR/500 1, RBI/500 29

Where He Hits the Ball

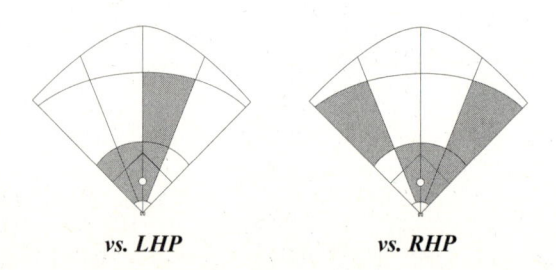

vs. LHP   vs. RHP

COLORADO ROCKIES

ERIC YOUNG

Positions: 2B/OF
Bats: R **Throws:** R
Ht: 5'9" **Wt:** 180
Opening Day Age: 28
Born: 5/18/1967
Drafted: LA89 46/1123
ML Seasons: 4

SCOUTING REPORT
Young's problem is that he hits like an infielder but doesn't have the glove for second base. An aggressive contact hitter with a good eye, he can be overmatched by good pitchers. He has some gap power, but his primary asset aside from his batting average is his good speed and ability to steal bases.

Eric has minus arm strength from the outfield, but his big problem is accuracy: it is poor whether he's playing left field or second base. He has hard hands, once again much more of a problem in the infield. His range at second is adequate and he is fair in the pivot.

HOW HE PERFORMED IN '95
Young was the Rockies' original second baseman back in '93, but he hadn't played there very often since being shifted to the outfield at that season's All-Star break.

Last June 22, however, Eric was moved back to the infield in an attempt to get some offense at the top of the order. Second-base prospect Roberto Mejia had again flopped and Jason Bates was mired in an injury-related slump.

Young took the opportunity and ran with it, never looking back. He hit .406 in July and .404 after September 1, and his 35 stolen bases ranked sixth in the league. Again showing a good eye, Eric took his share of walks and cut his strikeouts. He also worked out some of his old problems with righthanders and hit for good average on the road, if not for power.

Speed was again a factor for him, as Young tied for the league lead in triples and beat out eight bunt singles. His stolen base success rate was a career high.

His play at second base was bad enough to get him out of the infield two years ago and hasn't improved that much. Although he's fast and can get to a lot of ground balls, Young made 11 errors, fielding a far-below-par .973. His post-season problems with the glove were not an illusion.

WHAT TO EXPECT IN '96
His '95 performance and the Rockies' failure to lure Craig Biggio to Coors Field indicate that Young is likely to start the season as the regular second baseman again, despite defensive deficiencies that he hasn't yet conquered.

Overall Statistics

	G	AB	R	H	2B	3B	HR	RBI	SB	CS	BB	SO	BA	OBA
95 COL	120	366	68	116	21	9	6	36	35	12	49	29	.317	.404
Career	403	1216	196	344	51	18	17	119	101	39	158	96	.283	.369

1995 Situational Statistics

	AB	HR	RBI	BA	OBA	SLG		AB	HR	RBI	BA	OBA	SLG
Home	169	5	22	.331	.430	.533	LHP	125	4	21	.400	.449	.648
Road	197	1	14	.305	.380	.421	RHP	241	2	15	.274	.382	.382
Apr-Jun	67	0	7	.149	.275	.194	ScPos	84	1	27	.262	.357	.369
Jul-Oct	299	6	29	.355	.434	.535	Clutch	52	0	2	.404	.523	.538

How He Compares to Other Batters

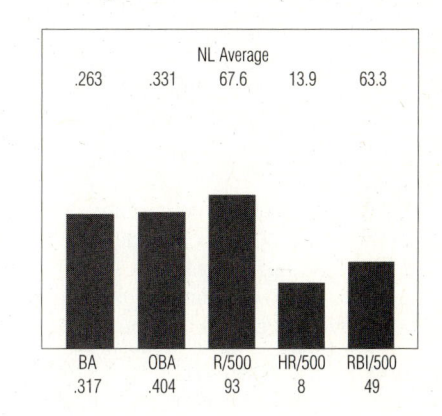

NL Average: .263 .331 67.6 13.9 63.3

BA .317 | OBA .404 | R/500 93 | HR/500 8 | RBI/500 49

Where He Hits the Ball

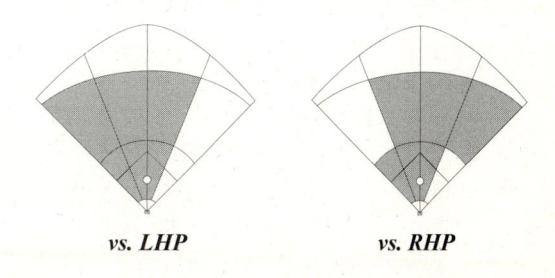

vs. LHP   vs. RHP

THE SCOUTING REPORT: 1996

COLORADO ROCKIES

ROGER BAILEY

Position: RP/SP
Bats: R **Throws:** R
Ht: 6'1" **Wt:** 180
Opening Day Age: 25
Born: 10/3/1970
Drafted: COL92 3/95
ML Seasons: 1

Overall Statistics

	G	GS	GF	SV	W	L	ERA	IP	H	R	ER	HR	BB	SO
95 COL	39	6	9	0	7	6	4.98	81.1	88	49	45	9	39	33
Career	39	6	9	0	7	6	4.98	81.1	88	49	45	9	39	33

1995 Situational Statistics

	W	L	ERA	SV	IP	BB	SO		AB	HR	RBI	BA	OBA	SLG
Home	5	2	6.65	0	46.0	21	15	LHB	129	1	16	.256	.373	.388
Road	2	4	2.80	0	35.1	18	18	RHB	182	8	29	.302	.355	.527
Apr-Jun	2	3	3.57	0	35.1	19	19	ScPos	94	3	35	.277	.369	.457
Jul-Oct	5	3	6.07	0	46.0	20	14	Clutch	45	0	5	.311	.448	.467

SCOUTING REPORT

Bailey comes to the plate from high three-quarters with an average, sinking fastball that he also cuts, but Roger's best pitch is a plus change-up. His curve is slightly below-average, featuring a late, small break.

Bailey needs good control to be effective, because his stuff isn't that good. He is adequate at holding runners on and fielding: five runners stole bases in six attempts against Roger during '95. He batted .125 (2-for-16) with three sacrifice bunts.

HOW HE PERFORMED IN '95

The rookie righthander opened the season with Colorado as a middle reliever, earning his first win May 7 and posted a 2.04 ERA that month. However, he lost then four in a row out of the pen and was sent down in July. After returning in early August, Roger won four of six starts but did not pitch all that well in those games.

WHAT TO EXPECT IN '96

Bailey will start '96 in the bullpen. Given Don Baylor's quick hook, he should see plenty of action. If Roger improves his control, he could eventually find a spot in the Rockies' rotation. His performance, especially in road games, was encouraging.

ELLIS BURKS

Position: OF
Bats: R **Throws:** R
Ht: 6'2" **Wt:** 200
Opening Day Age: 31
Born: 9/11/1964
Drafted: BOS83* 1/20
ML Seasons: 9

Overall Statistics

	G	AB	R	H	2B	3B	HR	RBI	SB	CS	BB	SO	BA	OBA
95 COL	103	278	41	74	10	6	14	49	7	3	39	72	.266	.359
Career	1013	3720	589	1044	202	40	137	534	109	57	366	658	.281	.347

1995 Situational Statistics

	AB	HR	RBI	BA	OBA	SLG		AB	HR	RBI	BA	OBA	SLG
Home	141	8	32	.291	.387	.567	LHP	104	5	18	.327	.397	.567
Road	137	6	17	.241	.331	.423	RHP	174	9	31	.230	.338	.454
Apr-Jun	113	5	15	.239	.333	.442	ScPos	91	3	35	.253	.337	.440
Jul-Oct	165	9	34	.285	.377	.533	Clutch	49	1	12	.224	.278	.388

SCOUTING REPORT

Burks is a high fastball hitter with power who goes with the pitch. Unfortunately, Ellis is not the hitter he used to be due to a severe 1994 wrist injury. He is still an above-average baserunner.

He has above-average skills (range, hands, arm strength and throwing accuracy) in center field, and Burks throws well enough to play right.

HOW HE PERFORMED IN '95

His year began disabled, recovering from wrist surgery. On his return, Ellis struggled through May and early June. He then found his stroke and had a good second half while tearing up lefthanders.

However, like many Rockies' players, he did little on the road. Only four of Ellis' homers came with men on, and he was a .207 pinch-hitter. Perhaps most seriously, he struck out at a frightening pace.

Dante Bichette's poor range in left stretched Burks' ability to cover ground. Ellis also threw out just three runners.

WHAT TO EXPECT IN '96

Burks needs a great spring to justify his hefty paycheck, especially with Trenidad Hubbard in the wings. If Ellis becomes trade bait, his salary—and wrist—might be difficult to peddle.

COLORADO ROCKIES

MARVIN FREEMAN

Position: SP
Bats: R **Throws:** R
Ht: 6'7" **Wt:** 200
Opening Day Age: 32
Born: 4/10/1963
Drafted: PHI84 2/49
ML Seasons: 9

Overall Statistics

	G	GS	GF	SV	W	L	ERA	IP	H	R	ER	HR	BB	SO
95 COL	22	18	0	0	3	7	5.89	94.2	122	64	62	15	41	61
Career	194	54	31	5	28	19	4.21	462.0	461	230	216	42	191	311

1995 Situational Statistics

	W	L	ERA	SV	IP	BB	SO		AB	HR	RBI	BA	OBA	SLG
Home	2	3	7.01	0	52.2	22	32	LHB	194	8	34	.351	.419	.567
Road	1	4	4.50	0	42.0	19	29	RHB	190	7	21	.284	.347	.447
Apr-Jun	2	6	6.38	0	60.2	27	40	ScPos	110	3	34	.245	.323	.364
Jul-Oct	1	1	5.03	0	34.0	14	21	Clutch	0	0	0	.000	.000	.000

SCOUTING REPORT

When healthy, Freeman has a plus fastball, an above-average slider and a good splitter. However, arm problems have sapped a great deal of his velocity and hampered his control.

An adequate fielder, he used to hold runners reasonably well. However, in '95, 14 men stole bases in 16 tries with Marvin on the mound.

HOW HE PERFORMED IN '95

After a sensational '94 (10-2, 2.80 ERA), Freeman disappointed. Struggling with an aching elbow for most of '95, Marvin tried to tough it out but never found a groove and was, at times, awful. The Rockies finally shut him down in early September to undergo surgery. Despite his poor showing, Freeman remained a fan favorite.

He batted just .087 (2-for-23), striking out 16 times, but figured in one interesting note. On May 23, Freeman hit his second career homer, off Chicago's Kevin Foster. Several innings later, Foster returned the favor by taking Marvin downtown.

WHAT TO EXPECT IN '96

If Marvin recovers from surgery and has a good spring, he should be in the Rockies' rotation. However, Colorado may not have the luxury of giving him all the time he needs to fully recover.

JOE GRAHE

Position: SP/RP
Bats: R **Throws:** R
Ht: 6'1" **Wt:** 196
Opening Day Age: 28
Born: 8/14/1967
Drafted: CAL89 2/39
ML Seasons: 6

Overall Statistics

	G	GS	GF	SV	W	L	ERA	IP	H	R	ER	HR	BB	SO
95 COL	17	9	0	0	4	3	5.08	56.2	69	42	32	6	27	27
Career	174	34	97	45	21	26	4.46	367.2	411	207	182	26	165	188

1995 Situational Statistics

	W	L	ERA	SV	IP	BB	SO		AB	HR	RBI	BA	OBA	SLG
Home	3	1	6.55	0	33.0	16	19	LHB	110	3	14	.309	.382	.436
Road	1	2	3.04	0	23.2	11	8	RHB	119	3	17	.294	.374	.445
Apr-Jun	3	2	3.15	0	34.1	16	13	ScPos	63	3	26	.302	.373	.492
Jul-Oct	1	1	8.06	0	22.1	11	14	Clutch	7	1	1	.286	.375	.714

SCOUTING REPORT

Using a high three-quarter delivery, Grahe throws three slightly below-average pitches: a sinking fastball, a curve, and a change-up. His out pitch is an above-average palmball.

A fast worker, Joe must stay ahead in the count and keep the ball low to be successful. His ability to field and hold runners is average: eight stole against Grahe last year in 11 attempts. In his first major-league at-bats, Joe was 5-for-12 (.417).

HOW HE PERFORMED IN '95

Signed to a minor-league contract during the off-season, Grahe was called up May 20 to shore up the Rockies' pitching. After a few relief appearances, he moved into the rotation and promptly tossed 15 scoreless innings.

However, Joe hadn't been used as a starter in four years and couldn't handle the workload; a sore shoulder sidelined him from mid-July until the end of August. He saw limited duty in September. Even when healthy, Grahe struggled with control.

WHAT TO EXPECT IN '96

Grahe needs a great spring to land a job in the Rockies' rotation, otherwise it's middle relief—or Triple-A.

COLORADO ROCKIES

BRYAN HICKERSON

Position: RP
Bats: L **Throws:** L
Ht: 6'2" **Wt:** 195
Opening Day Age: 32
Born: 10/13/1963
Drafted: MIN86 7/169
ML Seasons: 5

Overall Statistics

	G	GS	GF	SV	W	L	ERA	IP	H	R	ER	HR	BB	SO
95 CHN/COL	56	0	13	1	3	3	8.57	48.1	69	52	46	8	28	40
Career	209	36	31	2	21	21	4.72	404.1	451	221	212	52	143	279

1995 Situational Statistics

	W	L	ERA	SV	IP	BB	SO		AB	HR	RBI	BA	OBA	SLG
Home	3	0	8.19	0	29.2	15	27	LHB	78	1	15	.295	.389	.423
Road	0	3	9.16	1	18.2	13	13	RHB	130	7	32	.354	.429	.569
Apr-Jun	2	2	6.29	0	24.1	10	21	ScPos	60	2	41	.450	.542	.700
Jul-Oct	1	1	10.88	1	24.0	18	19	Clutch	74	0	8	.216	.284	.284

SCOUTING REPORT

Using a deceptive, wrist-wrapping delivery and a three-quarter motion, Hickerson throws four pitches. His below-average fastball has good life; he occasionally cuts the fastball. Bryan's average, big-breaking curve and minus turned-over change-up set up his out pitch, a plus forkball.

He holds runners on well with a good move and is an average fielder. Seven tried to steal against him in '95, four successfully. He was 2-for-3 in '95 with three RBI but is a .149 career batter.

HOW HE PERFORMED IN '95

He joined the Rockies July 31 following an undistinguished tour with the Cubs. The change of scenery didn't improve Hickerson's game: he worked 16.2 innings for Colorado, compiling a miserable 11.88 ERA.

Bryan wasn't really that bad; take away a nine-run inning on June 25 (he was preserving a worn-out Cubs' bullpen during a blowout), and his numbers look better. Hickerson, a workhorse, will take the ball without asking questions.

WHAT TO EXPECT IN '96

The Rockies released him after the playoffs. Bryan still has time left providing he is able to recover the form he showed with San Francisco.

MIKE MUNOZ

Position: RP
Bats: L **Throws:** L
Ht: 6'2" **Wt:** 190
Opening Day Age: 30
Born: 7/12/1965
Drafted: LA86 3/74
ML Seasons: 7

Overall Statistics

	G	GS	GF	SV	W	L	ERA	IP	H	R	ER	HR	BB	SO
95 COL	64	0	19	2	2	4	7.42	43.2	54	38	36	9	27	37
Career	232	0	60	5	9	11	5.06	176.0	185	107	99	18	108	117

1995 Situational Statistics

	W	L	ERA	SV	IP	BB	SO		AB	HR	RBI	BA	OBA	SLG
Home	2	0	9.00	0	25.0	15	21	LHB	84	5	19	.286	.351	.512
Road	0	4	5.30	2	18.2	12	16	RHB	92	4	19	.326	.438	.543
Apr-Jun	1	2	3.74	2	21.2	15	19	ScPos	57	3	30	.351	.435	.579
Jul-Oct	1	2	11.05	0	22.0	12	18	Clutch	70	2	10	.286	.386	.414

SCOUTING REPORT

Munoz throws from three-quarters. He has a plus turned-over change-up; his out pitch is a plus forkball. Mike's slightly below-average fastball tails away from righthanded batters; his curve is average. Mike's control suffered in '95 from pitching at 5280 feet.

Munoz' good move to first gives him the ability to holding runners: just three tried to steal against Mike in '95. He is an average fielder and 1-for-3 at bat in his career with two walks.

HOW HE PERFORMED IN '95

The best way to describe his season is to quote the Rockies' broadcasters: "Munoz is warming up again." Working four consecutive games five different times, Mike showed the wear and tear. He allowed only one home run over his first 28.2 innings of work but then served up four homers in his next 6.2 innings.

He couldn't get untracked all year. Of course, it's hard to establish consistency when facing one or two men at a time.

WHAT TO EXPECT IN '96

The Rockies re-signed Munoz in December. His ability to work effectively with little rest makes him a vital part of the Rockies' bullpen.

COLORADO ROCKIES

JAYHAWK OWENS

Position: C
Bats: R **Throws:** R
Ht: 6'1" **Wt:** 200
Opening Day Age: 27
Born: 2/10/1969
Drafted: MIN90 3/52
ML Seasons: 3

Overall Statistics

	G	AB	R	H	2B	3B	HR	RBI	SB	CS	BB	SO	BA	OBA
95 COL	18	45	7	11	2	0	4	12	0	0	2	15	.244	.286
Career	57	143	23	32	7	1	7	19	1	0	11	48	.224	.291

1995 Situational Statistics

	AB	HR	RBI	BA	OBA	SLG		AB	HR	RBI	BA	OBA	SLG
Home	23	3	5	.261	.320	.652	LHP	16	2	9	.500	.529	1.000
Road	22	1	7	.227	.250	.455	RHP	29	2	3	.103	.156	.310
Apr-Jun	0	0	0	.000	.000	.000	ScPos	8	1	8	.500	.545	1.125
Jul-Oct	45	4	12	.244	.286	.556	Clutch	3	0	0	.333	.333	.333

SCOUTING REPORT
Owens hits to all fields and has some power. Although he likes the high pitch, his slow bat can be overpowered and he strikes out often.

Jayhawk is mobile behind the plate, but has slightly below-average speed on the bases. He features a plus arm with a quick release and has above-average hands.

HOW HE PERFORMED IN '95
Jayhawk spent most of the season in the minors, batting .294 at Colorado Springs with 12 homers and 48 RBI, but so impressed the Rockies when he came up in August that the club dealt Joe Girardi in the off-season.

On August 6, Owens made an especially auspicious debut, going 4-for-4 with two home runs and three RBIs. In 16 games behind the plate, he threw out five of eight runners trying to steal and allowed just one passed ball.

WHAT TO EXPECT IN '96
Owens will probably platoon behind the plate with winter acquisition Jeff Reed. The Rockies hope Jayhawk can deliver on his early promise, but many feel he may be best as a backup and not a front-line catcher.

LANCE PAINTER

Position: RP
Bats: L **Throws:** L
Ht: 6'1" **Wt:** 195
Opening Day Age: 28
Born: 7/21/1967
Drafted: SD90 25/681
ML Seasons: 3

Overall Statistics

	G	GS	GF	SV	W	L	ERA	IP	H	R	ER	HR	BB	SO
95 COL	33	1	7	1	3	0	4.37	45.1	55	23	22	9	10	36
Career	58	21	10	1	9	8	5.58	158.0	198	100	98	23	45	93

1995 Situational Statistics

	W	L	ERA	SV	IP	BB	SO		AB	HR	RBI	BA	OBA	SLG
Home	3	0	5.60	0	27.1	9	18	LHB	65	1	7	.292	.370	.431
Road	0	0	2.50	1	18.0	1	18	RHB	121	8	20	.298	.320	.579
Apr-Jun	0	0	13.50	0	6.0	4	4	ScPos	53	3	19	.264	.304	.528
Jul-Oct	3	0	2.97	1	39.1	6	32	Clutch	27	0	0	.185	.267	.222

SCOUTING REPORT
Lance varies between throwing three-quarters and sidearm against righthanders, dropping down full sidearm against lefties, with an average fastball and curve. His out pitch is a plus turned-over change-up that benefits from his deceptive motion. His control is average. His plus move to first keeps runners close; only two men attempted to steal on him in '95. Painter is an adequate fielder. Just 1-for-9 at bat (.111), he is a .175 career hitter.

HOW HE PERFORMED IN '95
The young lefty had an up-and-down year. He opened the season disabled and pitched terribly after being activated, earning a trip to Triple-A in May. Recalled June 5, Painter was ineffective before being shipped out again.

Brought up for good in mid-July, Lance pitched respectably. He was especially tough on the first batter he faced, retiring 85%. He allowed seven homers in just 27.1 innings at home, but Painter was outstanding in road contests.

WHAT TO EXPECT IN '96
He is expected to make the team, but a poor spring might land Lance at Triple-A. Painter has not established consistency in the majors but hasn't really had a chance to.

THE SCOUTING REPORT: 1996

COLORADO ROCKIES

BRYAN REKAR

Position: SP
Bats: R **Throws:** R
Ht: 6'3" **Wt:** 205
Opening Day Age: 23
Born: 6/3/1972
Drafted: COL93 2/70
ML Seasons: 1

Overall Statistics

	G	GS	GF	SV	W	L	ERA	IP	H	R	ER	HR	BB	SO
95 COL	15	14	0	0	4	6	4.98	85.0	95	51	47	11	24	60
Career	15	14	0	0	4	6	4.98	85.0	95	51	47	11	24	60

1995 Situational Statistics

	W	L	ERA	SV	IP	BB	SO		AB	HR	RBI	BA	OBA	SLG
Home	1	3	8.53	0	38.0	8	25	LHB	166	3	23	.307	.364	.458
Road	3	3	2.11	0	47.0	16	35	RHB	171	8	23	.257	.299	.462
Apr-Jun	0	0	0.00	0	0.0	0	0	ScPos	80	4	35	.313	.372	.563
Jul-Oct	4	6	4.98	0	85.0	24	60	Clutch	20	1	3	.300	.318	.550

SCOUTING REPORT

Rekar delivers with a high leg kick and a three-quarter motion, throwing five pitches with good control. Bryan has an average-plus sinking fastball, an average curve, and an average slider. He also shows a change-up curve and works a plus straight change into the mix effectively. An average fielder, just two runners stole against him in four attempts.

HOW HE PERFORMED IN '95

Rookie Rekar had a dream season, shooting through three levels in the Rockies' organization and assuming a spot in the Colorado rotation. He won his major-league debut on July 19 and began his career by going 3-0 that month.

He struggled after his hot start but impressed with his poise, control, and mix of pitches. Like his teammates, Bryan was infinitely more effective away from Coors Field's unfriendly confines. Hitting was a problem; Rekar managed only one hit in 26 at-bats (.038) with four sacrifice bunts.

WHAT TO EXPECT IN '96

The Rockies have found a pitcher: Don Baylor was particularly impressed with Rekar's willingness to challenge hitters and pitch inside. With some guidance and patience, Bryan should become the Rockies' first homemade pitching star.

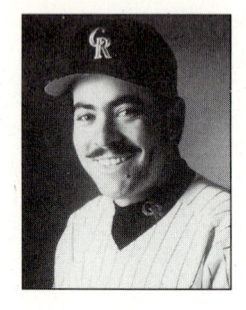

ARMANDO REYNOSO

Position: SP
Bats: R **Throws:** R
Ht: 6'0" **Wt:** 186
Opening Day Age: 29
Born: 5/1/1966
Drafted: MEX 3/15/89
ML Seasons: 5

Overall Statistics

	G	GS	GF	SV	W	L	ERA	IP	H	R	ER	HR	BB	SO
95 COL	20	18	0	0	7	7	5.32	93.0	116	61	55	12	36	40
Career	68	63	2	1	25	23	4.61	365.1	413	214	187	45	133	194

1995 Situational Statistics

	W	L	ERA	SV	IP	BB	SO		AB	HR	RBI	BA	OBA	SLG
Home	2	3	6.63	0	38.0	15	15	LHB	163	6	27	.301	.365	.491
Road	5	4	4.42	0	55.0	21	25	RHB	204	6	30	.328	.397	.515
Apr-Jun	1	0	4.35	0	10.1	7	2	ScPos	92	2	38	.326	.434	.478
Jul-Oct	6	7	5.44	0	82.2	29	38	Clutch	11	0	0	.182	.182	.182

SCOUTING REPORT

The crafty Reynoso lacks outstanding stuff but works the angles. He usually comes from high three-quarters but will throw each of his six pitches from several angles.

His arsenal includes an above-average slider with a short, quick break. Armando also throws an average change-up and forkball, a slightly below-average curve and slow curve, and a minus fastball.

Reynoso has good control and one of the best moves in the league: 14 men tried to steal against him in '95, but five were thrown out. His fielding is well above-average. Just 4-for-30 (.133) at bat, he's a .126 career hitter and a poor bunter.

HOW HE PERFORMED IN '95

His effectiveness was limited in '95 while he continued to recover from reconstructive elbow surgery. On June 18, Armando made his first appearance in the majors in 13 months, ending up the Rockies' fifth starter. Used sparingly because of his tender arm, Reynoso struggled with control and gopher balls.

WHAT TO EXPECT IN '96

The Rockies re-signed Armando in late December. The team plans to use him in the rotation provided his elbow is sound.

COLORADO ROCKIES

BRUCE RUFFIN

Position: RP
Bats: B **Throws:** L
Ht: 6'2" **Wt:** 205
Opening Day Age: 32
Born: 10/4/1963
Drafted: PHI85 2/34
ML Seasons: 10

Overall Statistics

	G	GS	GF	SV	W	L	ERA	IP	H	R	ER	HR	BB	SO
95 COL	37	0	19	11	0	1	2.12	34.0	26	8	8	1	19	23
Career	375	152	89	32	53	75	4.19	1176.1	1272	627	547	84	518	738

1995 Situational Statistics

	W	L	ERA	SV	IP	BB	SO		AB	HR	RBI	BA	OBA	SLG
Home	0	1	3.57	2	17.2	8	14	LHB	33	0	2	.242	.324	.273
Road	0	0	0.55	9	16.1	11	9	RHB	84	1	8	.214	.333	.262
Apr-Jun	0	0	1.13	8	16.0	8	13	ScPos	35	1	10	.200	.317	.286
Jul-Oct	0	1	3.00	3	18.0	11	10	Clutch	61	1	9	.279	.371	.344

SCOUTING REPORT

Ruffin now delivers three-quarters rather than dropping sidearm. He has a plus sinking fastball that he can also cut. Bruce's plus hard slider has a late break; he also has a slightly below-average turned-over change.

Ruffin has learned to throw strikes and has developed a slide-step to hold runners. Two of four trying to steal against him in '95 were retired. His fielding is slightly below-average and he's a weak .082 career hitter (0-for-2 last season).

HOW HE PERFORMED IN '95

Bruce began with seven saves and a 1.29 ERA in his first 12 appearances. However, he ended up on the DL for the first time ever on May 29 with a sore elbow. He returned June 17, pitching just two innings before returning to the injured roll until late August. Ruffin had a great September, with three saves and 1.88 ERA.

WHAT TO EXPECT IN '96

The Rockies will split closer duties between Bruce and Darren Holmes, but management prefers Ruffin in that role because he has been more consistent. Who would have thought the once-unpredictable Ruffin would ever be considered "consistent"?

JOHN VANDERWAL

Positions: 1B/OF
Bats: L **Throws:** L
Ht: 6'1" **Wt:** 180
Opening Day Age: 29
Born: 4/29/1966
Drafted: MON87 5/70
ML Seasons: 5

Overall Statistics

	G	AB	R	H	2B	3B	HR	RBI	SB	CS	BB	SO	BA	OBA
95 COL	105	101	15	35	8	1	5	21	1	1	16	23	.347	.432
Career	428	700	86	176	30	9	20	94	12	5	84	138	.251	.331

1995 Situational Statistics

	AB	HR	RBI	BA	OBA	SLG		AB	HR	RBI	BA	OBA	SLG
Home	45	2	13	.400	.500	.711	LHP	5	0	2	.400	.400	.600
Road	56	3	8	.304	.371	.500	RHP	96	5	19	.344	.434	.594
Apr-Jun	42	2	12	.429	.529	.690	ScPos	22	1	15	.409	.563	.682
Jul-Oct	59	3	9	.288	.358	.525	Clutch	37	0	4	.297	.350	.351

SCOUTING REPORT

VanderWal is an aggressive, first-ball fastball hitter who likes the pitch low and inside. He has average speed, some power and good discipline at the plate. While he is most valued as a pinch-hitter, he also shows all-around average skills at first base and left field.

HOW HE PERFORMED IN '95

John set the major-league record for most pinch hits in a season, collecting 28, batting .389 in the pinch with four home runs and 17 RBI.

He struggled in July and August, batting just .200, but came back strong in the last month. He made only five starts all year, batting just .188 in those games. However, he was so feared coming off the bench that his entrance was responsible for six pitching changes by opposing managers.

WHAT TO EXPECT IN '96

VanderWal will continue to be the Rockies' premier bench player, although he's highly unlikely to ever match his '95 production. While John will probably never be a starter, Don Baylor loves to have him around to torment opposing managers.

COLORADO ROCKIES: TOP PROSPECTS

JOHN BURKE
Bats: S Throws: R Opening Day Age: 26
Ht: 6-4 Wt: 220 Born: 2/9/1970
Position: P Drafted: 1992 #1 COL

YR TEAM	LG/CLASS	G	GS	GF	SV	W	L	ERA	IP	H	HR	BB	SO	O/BA
93 Central Val	CAL/A	20	20	0	0	7	8	3.18	119.0	104	5	64	114	.234
93 Colo Spngs	PCL/AAA	8	8	0	0	3	2	3.14	48.2	44	0	23	38	.250
94 Colo Spngs	PCL/AAA	8	0	3	0	0	0	19.64	11.0	16	0	22	6	.340
94 Asheville	SAL/A	4	4	0	0	0	1	1.06	17.0	5	1	5	16	.089
95 Colo Spngs	PCL/AAA	19	17	1	1	7	1	4.55	87.0	79	7	48	65	.245

An interesting story. Burke was the Rockies' first-ever draft choice and reached Triple-A in 1993, but mysteriously lost his control the following season and spent most of 1994 in extended spring training. The 25-year-old regained his command last year and won five consecutive starts before nagging shoulder problems landed him on the disabled list twice the rest of the way. Burke brings the ball in the 90's and has a devastating breaking pitch—when he can command it.

CRAIG COUNSELL
Bats: L Throws: R Opening Day Age: 26
Ht: 6-0 Wt: 177 Born: 8/21/1970
Position: SS Drafted: 1992 #11 COL

YR TEAM	LG/CLASS	G	AB	R	H	2B	3B	HR	RBI	SB	BA	OBA
93 Central Val	CAL/A	131	471	79	132	26	3	5	59	14	.280	.401
94 New Haven	EAST/AA	83	300	47	84	20	1	5	37	4	.280	.366
95 Colo Spngs	PCL/AAA	118	399	60	112	22	6	5	53	10	.281	.336
95 Colorado	NL/MAJ	3	1	0	0	0	0	0	0	0	.000	.500

Counsell is a solid hitter with bat speed who makes contact and can hit southpaws. He does not have any particularly outstanding tools, but has a solid reputation with the glove. Although he has a .279 career average and more walks than strikeouts, it should be noted that most of his hitting came in extremely hitter-friendly Colorado Springs last season.

BRENT CROWTHER
Bats: R Throws: R Opening Day Age: 24
Ht: 6-4 Wt: 220 Born: 5/15/1972
Position: P Drafted: 1994 #7 COL

YR TEAM	LG/CLASS	G	GS	GF	SV	W	L	ERA	IP	H	HR	BB	SO	O/BA
94 Bend	NWST/A	13	9	1	0	3	5	4.66	56.0	68	2	24	44	.291
95 Colo Spngs	PCL/AAA	1	1	0	0	0	1	7.50	6.0	11	1	2	1	.407
95 Salem	CARO/A	12	12	0	0	3	6	2.76	78.1	70	4	25	60	.241
95 Asheville	SAL/A	15	15	0	0	12	3	2.28	98.2	79	4	25	72	.217

Virtually unknown at season's start, the Canadian quickly grabbed the Rockies' attention. Using a fastball/slider combination with average velocity and incredible sink, Crowther won 12 straight starts at one point, the longest such streak in the minor leagues, and led the entire minor leagues in shutouts. The organization was so impressed by his poise and determination they promoted him to Triple-A as post-season insurance. The 24-year-old ended up leading the entire organization in wins and strikeouts.

ANGEL ECHEVARRIA
Bats: R Throws: R Opening Day Age: 25
Ht: 6-4 Wt: 215 Born: 5/25/1971
Position: OF Drafted: 1992 #17 COL

YR TEAM	LG/CLASS	G	AB	R	H	2B	3B	HR	RBI	SB	BA	OBA
93 Central Val	CAL/A	104	358	45	97	16	2	6	52	6	.271	.356
94 Central Val	CAL/A	50	192	28	58	8	1	6	35	2	.302	.341
94 New Haven	EAST/AA	58	205	25	52	6	0	8	32	2	.254	.308
95 New Haven	EAST/AA	124	453	78	136	30	1	21	100	8	.300	.382

Echevarria, an avid listener and a very popular player, became much more selective in 1995 (despite the importance of this facet of the game, many young hitters fail to learn it). The end result showed an Eastern League All-Star selection, a three-home run game, the league's top average in June (.412). He paced his league in RBI and set franchise records in RBI, doubles, and outfield assists (20). Despite the impressive assist total, the 24-year-old is not considered top shelf in the field and some feel he can not handle the breaking pitch.

DERRICK GIBSON
Bats: R Throws: R Opening Day Age: 21
Ht: 6-2 Wt: 238 Born: 2/5/1975
Position: OF Drafted: 1993 #13 COL

YR TEAM	LG/CLASS	G	AB	R	H	2B	3B	HR	RBI	SB	BA	OBA
93 Rockies	ARIZ/R	34	119	13	18	2	2	0	10	3	.151	.203
94 Bend	NWST/A	73	284	47	75	19	5	12	57	14	.264	.350
95 Asheville	SAL/A	135	506	91	148	16	10	32	115	31	.292	.350

Any remaining doubts about Gibson's potential were erased in 1995. After a .180 April average, the former Auburn linebacker recruit heated up. Although he played in one of the best hitters' parks in his league, Gibson led the minors with 11 homers in June, had a 16-game hitting streak, homered in four straight games and even had an inside-the-park homer. He hit about .340 the second half, led the minor leagues in RBI, and became only the third minor league player since 1987 to hit 30 home runs and steal 30 bases in the same season (Greg Vaughn and Ruben Rivera are the others). The still inexperienced 20-year-old should improve as he matures; he still needs plenty of work in the outfield.

TRENIDAD HUBBARD
Bats: R Throws: R Opening Day Age: 30
Ht: 5-8 Wt: 180 Born: 5/11/1966
Position: CF Drafted: 1986 #12 HOU

YR TEAM	LG/CLASS	G	AB	R	H	2B	3B	HR	RBI	SB	BA	OBA
93 Colo Spngs	PCL/AAA	117	439	83	138	24	8	7	56	33	.314	.387
94 Colo Spngs	PCL/AAA	79	320	78	116	22	5	8	38	28	.363	.441
94 Colorado	NL/MAJ	18	25	3	7	1	1	1	3	0	.280	.357
95 Colo Spngs	PCL/AAA	123	480	102	163	29	7	12	66	37	.340	.416
95 Colorado	NL/MAJ	24	58	13	18	4	0	3	9	2	.310	.394

Since joining the Colorado organization in 1993, the 29-year-old Hubbard has batted .340 with 75 doubles, 20 triples, 27 homers, 160 RBI, 98 stolen bases and 152 walks in 319 minor league games. In 1995, he led the minor leagues with a .442 average in July, put together a team-record 29-game hitting streak (second-longest in the minors) and batted .340 with runners in scoring position. With that resume and a fine defensive reputa-

COLORADO ROCKIES: TOP PROSPECTS

tion, it was no surprise that Hubbard gave the Rockies a much-needed boost down the stretch. Obviously, hitter-friendly Colorado Springs aided Hubbard's offense. He hit .270 with 16 homers in his first seven years.

DAVID KENNEDY

Bats: R Throws: R Opening Day Age: 26
Ht: 6-4 Wt: 215 Born: 9/3/1970
Position: 1B Drafted: 1991 #6 CAL

YR TEAM	LG/CLASS	G	AB	R	H	2B	3B	HR	RBI	SB	BA	OBA
93 Boise	NWST/A	74	248	53	59	14	2	10	49	2	.238	.394
94 St. Paul	NOR/I	25	72	13	21	6	1	4	15	2	.292	.370
95 New Haven	EAST/AA	128	484	75	148	22	2	22	96	4	.306	.372

A sore-armed pitcher in the Angels farm system, Kennedy converted to first base, was released, surfaced in the Northern League in '94, and signed with the Rockies last year. He did extremely well last season considering he had never played full-season ball before. The slugger was second in the Eastern League in homers and RBI and fifth in batting, batted .338 with runners in scoring position (including 7-for-12 with the bases loaded) and landed an All-Star berth. As his 16 errors attest, the 25-year-old needs work at first base.

QUINTON McCRACKEN

Bats: S Throws: R Opening Day Age: 26
Ht: 5-8 Wt: 170 Born: 3/16/1970
Position: OF Drafted: 1992 #25 COL

YR TEAM	LG/CLASS	G	AB	R	H	2B	3B	HR	RBI	SB	BA	OBA
93 Central Val	CAL/A	127	483	94	141	17	7	2	58	60	.292	.390
94 New Haven	EAST/AA	136	544	94	151	27	4	5	39	36	.278	.338
95 Color Spngs	PCL/AAA	61	244	55	88	14	6	3	28	17	.361	.418
95 New Haven	EAST/AA	55	221	33	79	11	4	1	26	26	.357	.419
95 Colorado	NL/MAJ	3	1	0	0	0	0	0	0	0	.000	.000

Returned to Double-A, perhaps unfairly, for a second season, McCracken let his bat do the talking. He led the Eastern League in batting up until the time he was finally summoned to Triple-A in late June. A former cornerback and second baseman at Duke University, the 25-year-old hit even better at Colorado Springs and ended up with the minor leagues' third-best overall average (.359). A switch-hitter with patience who can run, McCracken's uppercut swing is not advantageous for a speed player. Defensively, the ex-infielder is still making some adjustments, but has the skills to be more than adequate.

JOEL MOORE

Bats: L Throws: R Opening Day Age: 24
Ht: 6-2 Wt: 200 Born: 8/13/1972
Position: P Drafted: 1993 #3 COL

YR TEAM	LG/CLASS	G	GS	GF	SV	W	L	ERA	IP	H	HR	BB	SO	O/BA
93 Bend	NWST/A	15	15	0	0	4	7	3.21	89.2	75	2	31	79	.228
94 Central Val	CAL/A	25	24	0	0	11	8	4.53	133.0	149	8	64	89	.282
95 New Haven	EAST/AA	27	26	0	0	16	3.20	157.1	156	8	67	102	.262

When Moore is pitching well, as he did the second half of 1995, he keeps hitters off balance with a sweeping curveball and excellent change that make his fastball look quicker than average. The Eastern League's top winner captured his last seven decisions, lowering his ERA from 4.06 to 3.20 in the process, and was pitching shutout ball in a playoff start at Portland when he blew out his elbow. The former Bradley star and college team-mate of Bryan Rekar underwent Tommy John surgery and may not pitch in 1996.

NEIFI PEREZ

Bats: S Throws: R Opening Day Age: 21
Ht: 6-0 Wt: 175 Born: 6/2/1975
Position: SS Drafted: NDFA 11-9-92 COL

YR TEAM	LG/CLASS	G	AB	R	H	2B	3B	HR	RBI	SB	BA	OBA
93 Bend	NWST/A	75	296	35	77	11	4	3	32	19	.260	.306
94 Central Val	CAL/A	134	506	64	121	16	7	1	35	9	.239	.284
95 Colo Spngs	PCL/AAA	11	36	4	10	4	0	0	2	1	.278	.278
95 New Haven	EAST/AA	116	427	59	108	28	3	5	43	5	.253	.295

Perez, a free swinger and bad-ball hitter, gets down the line quickly but is not a stolen base threat. A switch-hitter with little pop, Perez is much better with a glove on his hand. The 20-year-old was one of the youngest players in the Eastern League, but displayed good range, a very strong arm and a quick release. He made just 18 errors in '95, down from 39 the previous season. Perez has hit .250 in his career with just 75 walks and nine home runs.

EDGARDO VELAZQUEZ

Bats: R Throws: R Opening Day Age: 20
Ht: 6-0 Wt: 170 Born: 12/15/1975
Position: CF Drafted: 1993 #10 COL

YR TEAM	LG/CLASS	G	AB	R	H	2B	3B	HR	RBI	SB	BA	OBA
93 Rockies	ARIZ/R	39	147	20	36	4	2	2	20	7	.245	.315
94 Asheville	SAL/A	119	447	50	106	22	3	11	39	9	.237	.278
95 Salem	CARO/A	131	497	74	149	25	6	13	69	7	.300	.352

Velazquez, who has just turned 20, made great strides in his second full professional season. He improved his batting average 63 points and showed more power and a better understanding of the strike zone. He went from below-average in center field to outstanding, with a very strong and accurate arm. Although he is not a burner on the basepaths, the nephew of Roberto Clemente has first-step quickness and good instincts and could come close to the five-tool talent the scouts projected when he was signed.

JAMEY WRIGHT

Bats: R Throws: R Opening Day Age: 21
Ht: 6-6 Wt: 205 Born: 12/24/1974
Position: P Drafted: 1993 #1 COL

YR TEAM	LG/CLASS	G	GS	GF	SV	W	L	ERA	IP	H	HR	BB	SO	O/BA
93 Rockies	ARIZ/R	8	8	0	0	1	3	4.00	36.0	35	1	9	26	.243
94 Asheville	SAL/A	28	27	0	0	7	14	5.97	143.1	188	6	59	103	.329
95 New Haven	EAST/AA	1	1	0	0	0	1	9.00	3.0	6	0	3	0	.375
95 Salem	CARO/A	26	26	0	0	10	8	2.47	171.0	160	7	72	95	.251

Wright undoubtedly has the best arm in the system and combines a projectable body with a 93-mph fastball with sink. This combination yielded just 19 extra-base hits in 1995, an unbelievable feat considering that the Salem park is one of the best hitters' parks in the league. The 20-year-old had nine wins by mid-season, but went nearly two months before he got his tenth despite lowering his ERA from 2.73 to 2.48 in the eight starts. Wright finished second in the Carolina League in innings, lasting 6+ in 13 of his last 14 starts, and ranked fifth in ERA. Wright's breaking pitches and changeup are far from perfected.

THE SCOUTING REPORT: 1996

COLORADO ROCKIES: OTHERS TO WATCH

GARVIN ALSTON   Bats: R   Throws: R   Ht: 6-2   Wt: 188
Born: 12/8/1971   Drafted: 1992 #10 COL   Position: P

YR TEAM	LG/CLASS	G	GS	GF	SV	W	L	ERA	IP	H	HR	BB	SO	O/BA
95 New Haven	EAST/AA	47	0	20	6	4	4	2.84	66.2	47	1	26	73	.199

Alston, a live arm with a 90+ mph fastball, could become a top closer.

IVAN ARTEAGA   Bats: L   Throws: R   Ht: 6-2   Wt: 220
Born: 7/20/1972   Drafted: NDFA 5-11-89 MON   Position: P

YR TEAM	LG/CLASS	G	GS	GF	SV	W	L	ERA	IP	H	HR	BB	SO	O/BA
95 New Haven	EAST/AA	14	11	0	0	2	4	5.56	34.0	36	3	21	18	.271

A power pitcher still learning on the mound since being converted from first base, Arteaga was shut down by shoulder problems that required surgery.

VINCENTE GARCIA   Bats: R   Throws: R   Ht: 6-0   Wt: 170
Born: 2/14/1975   Drafted: NDFA 5-18-93 COL   Position: 2B

YR TEAM	LG/CLASS	G	AB	R	H	2B	3B	HR	RBI	SB	BA	OBA
95 Salem	CARO/A	119	457	62	111	26	1	10	41	5	.243	.322

Young and talented with some punch, Garcia hasn't hit for average or stolen many bases the last two years.

TODD HELTON   Bats: L   Throws: L   Ht: 6-2   Wt: 195
Born: 8/20/1973   Drafted: 1995 # COL   Position: 1B

YR TEAM	LG/CLASS	G	AB	R	H	2B	3B	HR	RBI	SB	BA	OBA
95 Asheville	SAL/A	54	201	24	51	11	1	1	15	1	.254	.339

The 1995 first-rounder and former Tennessee quarterback came with a power reputation, but didn't show it in his first year.

BOBBY JONES   Bats: R   Throws: L   Ht: 6-0   Wt: 175
Born: 4/11/1972   Drafted: 1991 #44 MIL   Position: P

YR TEAM	LG/CLASS	G	GS	GF	SV	W	L	ERA	IP	H	HR	BB	SO	O/BA
95 Colo Sprgs	PCL/AAA	11	8	0	0	1	2	7.30	40.2	50	5	33	48	.305
95 New Haven	EAST/AA	27	8	9	3	5	2	2.58	73.1	61	4	36	70	.230

Jones is young and has both a good arm and a much-needed ability to get lefthanders out.

TERRY JONES   Bats: S   Throws: R   Ht: 5-10   Wt: 160
Born: 2/15/1971   Drafted: 1993 #40 COL   Position: OF

YR TEAM	LG/CLASS	G	AB	R	H	2B	3B	HR	RBI	SB	BA	OBA
95 New Haven	EAST/AA	124	472	78	127	12	1	1	26	51	.269	.327

The Eastern League's fastest player led the league in steals and swiped a minor league-high 18 bags in June, but needs to get on base more, hit the ball on the ground, and improve his defense.

MIKE KUSIEWICZ   Bats: R   Throws: L   Ht: 6-2   Wt: 185
Born: 11/1/1976   Drafted: 1994 #5 COL   Position: P

YR TEAM	LG/CLASS	G	GS	GF	SV	W	L	ERA	IP	H	HR	BB	SO	O/BA
95 Salem	CARO/A	1	1	0	0	0	0	1.50	6.0	7	0	0	7	.292
95 Asheville	SAL/A	21	21	0	0	8	4	2.06	122.1	92	6	34	103	.208

In his first professional season, the crafty lefty led the South Atlantic League in ERA and was 5-0, 1.22 ERA at hitter-friendly Asheville.

DOUG MILLION   Bats: L   Throws: L   Ht: 6-4   Wt: 175
Born: 10/13/1975   Drafted: 1994 #1 COL   Position: P

YR TEAM	LG/CLASS	G	GS	GF	SV	W	L	ERA	IP	H	HR	BB	SO	O/BA
95 Salem	CARO/A	24	23	0	0	5	7	4.62	111.0	111	6	79	85	.266

Million throws a curve that drops off the table, but in an attempt to improve his average velocity he put on 35 pounds—which led to a shoulder strain in late April.

JOHN MYROW   Bats: R   Throws: R   Ht: 6-0   Wt: 177
Born: 2/11/1972   Drafted: 1993 #9 COL   Position: OF

YR TEAM	LG/CLASS	G	AB	R	H	2B	3B	HR	RBI	SB	BA	OBA
95 New Haven	EAST/AA	96	353	52	87	18	1	3	50	16	.246	.308

A solid defensive outfielder with good tools, Myrow's bat and understanding of the strike zone have kept him back.

LLOYD PEEVER   Bats: R   Throws: R   Ht: 5-11   Wt: 185
Born: 9/15/1971   Drafted: 1992 #4 COL   Position: P

YR TEAM	LG/CLASS	G	GS	GF	SV	W	L	ERA	IP	H	HR	BB	SO	O/BA
95 Colo Spngs	PCL/AAA	8	8	0	0	3	2	5.36	42.0	45	5	16	25	.273

Continued shoulder problems kept Peever, one of the organization's most preferred pitchers, on the sidelines in '95.

TOM SCHMIDT   Bats: R   Throws: R   Ht: 6-3   Wt: 200
Born: 2/12/1973   Drafted: 1992 #24 COL   Position: 3B

YR TEAM	LG/CLASS	G	AB	R	H	2B	3B	HR	RBI	SB	BA	OBA
95 New Haven	EAST/AA	115	423	55	92	25	3	6	49	2	.217	.265

A power hitter with a good glove, Schmidt has not hit for average or shown the power expected.

CHRIS SEXTON   Bats: R   Throws: R   Ht: 5-11   Wt: 180
Born: 8/3/1971   Drafted: 1993 #11 CIN   Position: SS

YR TEAM	LG/CLASS	G	AB	R	H	2B	3B	HR	RBI	SB	BA	OBA
95 New Haven	EAST/AA	1	3	0	0	0	0	0	0	0	.000	.000
95 Win-Salem	CARO/A	4	15	3	6	0	0	1	5	0	.400	.526
95 Salem	CARO/A	123	461	81	123	16	6	4	32	14	.267	.390

Acquired from the Reds last April for Marcus Moore, Sexton gets on base and has sure hands, but doesn't have projectable tools.

MARK STRITTMATTER   Bats: R   Throws: R   Ht: 6-1   Wt: 200
Born: 4/4/1969   Drafted: 1992 #28 COL   Position: C

YR TEAM	LG/CLASS	G	AB	R	H	2B	3B	HR	RBI	SB	BA	OBA
95 Colo Sprgs	PCL/AAA	5	17	1	5	2	0	0	3	0	.294	.294
95 New Haven	EAST/AA	90	288	44	70	12	1	7	42	1	.243	.359

Strittmatter, an outstanding receiver with a good arm, is not much of the hitter.

JOHN THOMSON   Bats: R   Throws: R   Ht: 6-3   Wt: 175
Born: 10/1/1973   Drafted: 1993 #7 COL   Position: P

YR TEAM	LG/CLASS	G	GS	GF	SV	W	L	ERA	IP	H	HR	BB	SO	O/BA
95 New Haven	EAST/AA	26	24	0	0	7	8	4.18	131.1	132	8	56	82	.261

Tall and lanky, Thomson will rely on spotting three pitches unless his average velocity increases.

DOUG WALLS   Bats: L   Throws: R   Ht: 6-3   Wt: 200
Born: 3/21/1974   Drafted: 1993 #4 COL   Position: P

YR TEAM	LG/CLASS	G	GS	GF	SV	W	L	ERA	IP	H	HR	BB	SO	O/BA
95 Salem	CARO/A	15	15	0	0	5	5	3.84	79.2	61	10	49	79	.212

Walls, a hard thrower with great stuff but little command, went down in late June with a rotator cuff injury.

FLORIDA MARLINS

KURT ABBOTT

Position: SS
Bats: R **Throws:** R
Ht: 6'0" **Wt:** 170
Opening Day Age: 26
Born: 6/2/1969
Drafted: OAK89 15/400
ML Seasons: 3

SCOUTING REPORT
Despite decent power, Abbott is not a productive hitter because of two things: a desire to pull everything and poor strike-zone judgment. Both of them contribute to his big problem with strikeouts and lead to very poor on-base percentages.

He is a very mobile and dependable fielder, with adequate range and sure hands. However, Kurt's arm has just average strength and below-par accuracy. It is possible that he may move to third base in the future, and he was also used in the outfield during his minor-league career.

Abbott has plus speed but rarely steals bases. He will occasionally try to beat out a bunt and does not hit into many double plays.

HOW HE PERFORMED IN '95
Kurt didn't play until May 6, starting the season on the DL because of a pulled right hamstring, but appeared almost every day after being activated. He connected for a pro-high 17 homers in '95. It was a year of promise for the former Oakland farmhand. Abbott does his best hitting in June; during both '94 and '95, it was by far his best month. Although he has problems with slumps, Kurt has posted similar first- and second-half totals in both seasons. He has been more successful against righthanders than lefties so far in his career.

Although he has serious problems getting the bat on the ball, Abbott did double his walks in '95 and cut his strikeouts a bit, evincing some hope for the future and pleasing the Florida management. However, manager Rene Lachemann said that Kurt still needs to learn to play the "little game" more intelligently.

Poor throwing led to 19 errors last season, the third-highest total in the league. Abbott's fielding percentage of .959 was one of the lowest for a shortstop in the majors, and he didn't get to as many balls as he had in '94.

WHAT TO EXPECT IN '96
Due to his poor on-base average but good power potential, Abbott will bat low in order this season, probably in the #7 spot. Florida wants him to hit for higher average—if he can do that, he'll be more valuable and prolong his tenure as a regular shortstop, although there are still defensive problems he needs to iron out.

Overall Statistics

	G	AB	R	H	2B	3B	HR	RBI	SB	CS	BB	SO	BA	OBA
95 FLO	120	420	60	107	18	7	17	60	4	3	36	110	.255	.318
Career	241	826	112	208	36	10	29	102	9	3	55	228	.252	.304

1995 Situational Statistics

	AB	HR	RBI	BA	OBA	SLG		AB	HR	RBI	BA	OBA	SLG
Home	207	12	34	.295	.355	.556	LHP	119	3	13	.244	.297	.395
Road	213	5	26	.216	.281	.352	RHP	301	14	47	.259	.325	.475
Apr-Jun	151	8	25	.265	.309	.497	ScPos	90	3	41	.244	.371	.433
Jul-Oct	269	9	35	.249	.322	.428	Clutch	68	2	9	.191	.313	.309

How He Compares to Other Batters

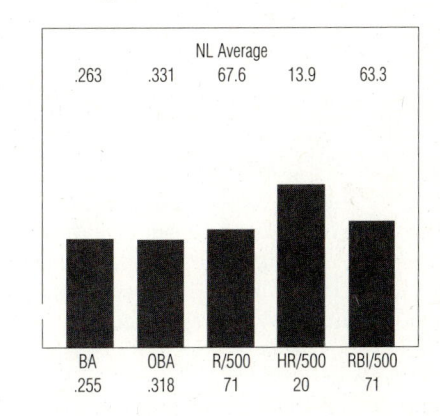

NL Average: .263 .331 67.6 13.9 63.3

BA	OBA	R/500	HR/500	RBI/500
.255	.318	71	20	71

Where He Hits the Ball

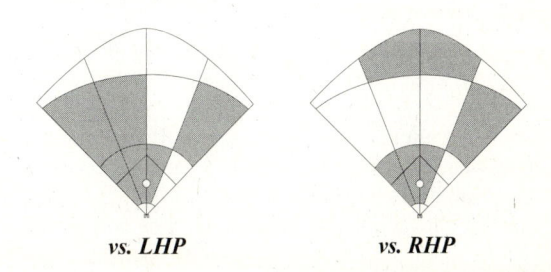

vs. LHP   vs. RHP

THE SCOUTING REPORT: 1996

FLORIDA MARLINS

JOHN BURKETT

Position: SP
Bats: R **Throws:** R
Ht: 6'2" **Wt:** 205
Opening Day Age: 31
Born: 11/28/1964
Drafted: SF83 6/148
ML Seasons: 7

SCOUTING REPORT
Burkett is a sinker-slider-forkball pitcher who has average stuff overall and depends on his control, his fielders, and his supporting batters to produce results, as do most pitchers of his type. He delivers from high three quarters to three quarters with a bit below-average fastball which sinks and tails into righthanded hitters. He will also cut his fastball and will use his average forkball to fool hitters looking for the fastball. His breaking pitchers, a slider and a big curve, are also average.

John is above-average at holding runners and is an average fielder: only 12 baserunners attempting to steal while he was on the mound in '95, with eight making it safely. A notoriously weak hitter, Burkett hit .106 (7-for-66) with 23 strikeouts last season, which raised his career average to a miserable .076.

HOW HE PERFORMED IN '95
Dealt by San Francisco to Texas in December 1994, Burkett figured in an unusual episode when his new team, the Rangers, strangely didn't offer him a contract in April after the strike and he became a free agent. Signing a two-year contract with Florida the next day, he became the Marlins' opening day starter.

John got off to a weak start, although he didn't pitch really badly until June. His early-season struggles, however, were due more to a lack of support than his pitching, and he rebounded to a 7-4 record in June and August. Overall, he had some problems with control, leading to a career-high walk rate and a career-high 22 home runs allowed. Righthanded hitters were very successful against John, which they usually aren't. It's seems clear now that he is a journeyman who can't afford to lose much more of his stuff.

WHAT TO EXPECT IN '96
The Marlins' brain trust did not feel that Burkett could be the rotation anchor on a contending team—which the Fish aspire to be soon—so they went out and pursued big-ticket free-agent pitchers in the off-season, eventually signing AL refugees Kevin Brown and Al Leiter. John will start the '96 season as the #3 starter in the Florida rotation. If he can provide the team with another season of 30 starts and league-average ERA or so, he will be fulfilling expectations.

Overall Statistics

	G	GS	GF	SV	W	L	ERA	IP	H	R	ER	HR	BB	SO
95 FLO	30	30	0	0	14	14	4.30	188.1	208	95	90	22	57	126
Career	193	187	2	1	81	56	3.90	1185.2	1233	562	514	106	302	717

1995 Situational Statistics

	W	L	ERA	SV	IP	BB	SO		AB	HR	RBI	BA	OBA	SLG
Home	7	7	4.42	0	95.2	33	65	LHB	361	6	39	.274	.338	.418
Road	7	7	4.18	0	92.2	24	61	RHB	376	16	47	.290	.339	.489
Apr-Jun	5	7	5.50	0	70.1	25	48	ScPos	172	5	58	.244	.350	.395
Jul-Oct	9	7	3.58	0	118.0	32	78	Clutch	71	1	7	.324	.385	.451

How He Compares to Other Pitchers

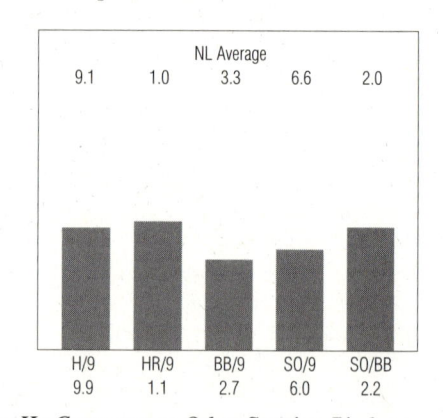

NL Average

H/9	HR/9	BB/9	SO/9	SO/BB
9.1	1.0	3.3	6.6	2.0
9.9	1.1	2.7	6.0	2.2

How He Compares to Other Starting Pitchers

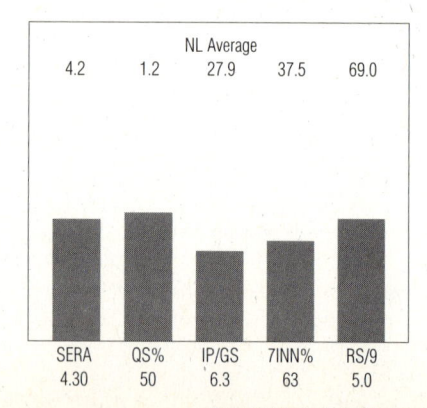

NL Average

SERA	QS%	IP/GS	7INN%	RS/9
4.2	1.2	27.9	37.5	69.0
4.30	50	6.3	63	5.0

FLORIDA MARLINS

CHUCK CARR

Position: OF
Bats: B **Throws:** R
Ht: 5'10" **Wt:** 155
Opening Day Age: 28
Born: 8/10/1967
Drafted: CIN86 9/228
ML Seasons: 6

SCOUTING REPORT

A player with plus speed who fails to use this asset to maximum advantage, Carr is a line-drive hitter with very little power who like fastballs up and over the plate. He will bunt often, both for sacrifices and hits, but he does not bunt particularly well. Formerly a switch-hitter, he gave up switch-hitting in August, batting righthanded exclusively thereafter. His batting line against righthanded pitchers clearly shows why he made the change, as his average dropped more than 100 points against them compared to the previous season.

In center field, Chuck displays plus range with average-plus hands but has minus arm strength and makes inaccurate throws. He did throw out eight runners last season, however, improving substantially from his previous rate.

HOW HE PERFORMED IN '95

Carr started '95 ice-cold and was hitting only .170 in mid-May when he missed a month with a strained left hamstring. He continued to struggle when he returned, eventually losing his starting job to Jesus Tavarez in August. He did not steal bases efficiently last year and, despite plus speed and playing in a big ballpark, Chuck does not hit many triples.

Despite the fact that his batting average plunged 36 points, his on-base average was a career-high .330. He also cut his strikeouts impressively and more than doubled his walks from '94 despite having over 100 fewer plate appearances.

WHAT TO EXPECT IN '96

Chuck was very popular with the Marlins' fans during his tenure in Miami, but that popularity didn't extend to his teammates and the Florida front office. Both felt that he made too many mental mistakes on the field as well as fundamental mistakes like missing the cutoff man on throws. He also didn't respond to the team's coaching on how he could improve as leadoff hitter, thus punching his ticket out of town.

Florida thus traded Carr to Milwaukee over the winter and signed free-agent center fielder Devon White to a big contract to replace him. Chuck could end up as Milwaukee's leadoff hitter and center fielder in '96, since the Brewers lack both. He probably won't be any better than he was in Florida, though, unless the trade and the cold weather shocks him into improving his game.

Overall Statistics

	G	AB	R	H	2B	3B	HR	RBI	SB	CS	BB	SO	BA	OBA
95 FLO	105	308	54	70	20	0	2	20	25	11	46	49	.227	.330
Career	391	1369	199	347	61	4	8	95	127	43	126	204	.253	.319

1995 Situational Statistics

	AB	HR	RBI	BA	OBA	SLG		AB	HR	RBI	BA	OBA	SLG
Home	151	1	9	.265	.353	.351	LHP	116	2	8	.310	.403	.466
Road	157	1	11	.191	.308	.274	RHP	192	0	12	.177	.286	.219
Apr-Jun	107	0	8	.196	.307	.234	ScPos	67	0	17	.239	.391	.343
Jul-Oct	201	2	12	.244	.342	.353	Clutch	45	0	4	.244	.386	.333

How He Compares to Other Batters

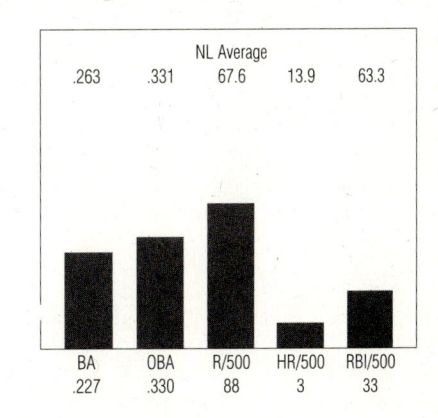

NL Average: .263 / .331 / 67.6 / 13.9 / 63.3

BA .227 OBA .330 R/500 88 HR/500 3 RBI/500 33

Where He Hits the Ball

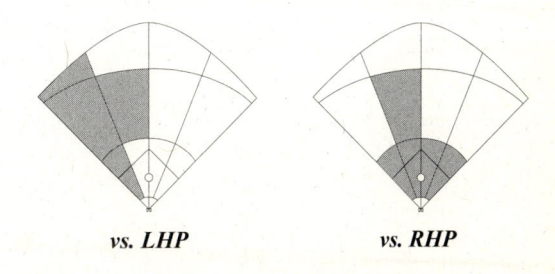

vs. LHP   vs. RHP

FLORIDA MARLINS

GREG COLBRUNN

Position: 1B
Bats: R **Throws:** R
Ht: 6'0" **Wt:** 190
Opening Day Age: 26
Born: 7/26/1969
Drafted: MON87 8/148
ML Seasons: 4

SCOUTING REPORT
Greg is a line-drive hitter with a quick bat who can hit fastballs hard to all fields, although he will pull inside pitches. Greg makes reasonably good contact for a power hitter, primarily because his power comes from hitting the ball hard on a line, not lifting pitches for long fly balls.

Previously a minus runner due to serious knee problems, he improved dramatically in '95 and showed his knee had healed completely, running with average speed and stealing a very surprising 11 bases in 14 tries. He does not bunt.

At first base, Colbrunn's surgically-rebuilt arm has rebounded to average strength and accuracy, and he has soft hands with somewhat above-average range. He fielded .996 last year, making just five errors.

HOW HE PERFORMED IN '95
Greg had a big power year in '95, easily wiping out his previous career high of 13 homers (Class A, 1990) and was reasonably consistent after a slow start. The team was unhappy with his power and run production in the first half, though, and he basically saved his job with an impressive second-half surge.

However, his already poor plate discipline worsened, leading to a very poor on-base average. He did this in spite of a terrible slump against left-handers, whom he had hit well previously, but he hit righties very hard.

WHAT TO EXPECT IN '96
Last season was Colbrunn's first full season unmarred by injury, and he responded to the good health by improving substantially at bat, at first base, and on the basepaths. Despite his unexpectedly weak performance against southpaws, the team has no immediate plans to platoon him. The first base job is his to lose and, if he can continue to play like he did in '95, he will be a fixture in Miami for several more years.

All in all, Colbrunn fulfilled every reasonable expectation anyone could have had for him. It would be surprising if he took another step forward. On the other hand, last season was the first time since 1990 that Greg got more than 400 at-bats and, at the young age of 26, he still has plenty of time to improve if he works hard on his weak points.

Overall Statistics

	G	AB	R	H	2B	3B	HR	RBI	SB	CS	BB	SO	BA	OBA
95 FLO	138	528	70	146	22	1	23	89	11	3	22	69	.277	.311
Career	307	1004	114	277	49	1	35	161	19	8	43	163	.276	.309

1995 Situational Statistics

	AB	HR	RBI	BA	OBA	SLG		AB	HR	RBI	BA	OBA	SLG
Home	260	12	41	.281	.314	.446	LHP	144	3	14	.215	.257	.326
Road	268	11	48	.272	.308	.459	RHP	384	20	75	.299	.331	.500
Apr-Jun	207	8	33	.271	.301	.415	ScPos	147	8	70	.333	.386	.531
Jul-Oct	321	15	56	.280	.317	.477	Clutch	84	4	14	.226	.298	.393

How He Compares to Other Batters

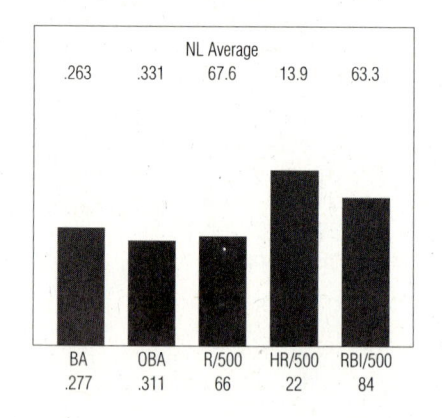

NL Average: .263 .331 67.6 13.9 63.3

BA .277 | OBA .311 | R/500 66 | HR/500 22 | RBI/500 84

Where He Hits the Ball

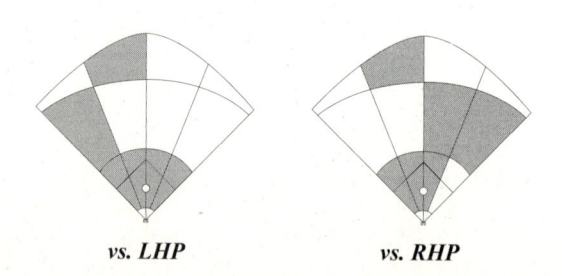

vs. LHP   vs. RHP

FLORIDA MARLINS

JEFF CONINE

Positions: OF/1B
Bats: R **Throws:** R
Ht: 6'1" **Wt:** 205
Opening Day Age: 29
Born: 6/27/1966
Drafted: KC87 58/1226
ML Seasons: 5

SCOUTING REPORT
A low fastball devotee who wields a quick bat, Conine can hit both lefties and righties well. Pitchers can climb the ladder with him, however, and will sometimes strike him out with eye-level fastballs. Jeff has worked hard to be more disciplined at the plate, but the Marlins' reliance on his bat means that he'll continue to swing from the heels. He's no threat to steal and has slightly below-average speed.

Conine plays the two least-demanding defensive positions (left field and first base) with drive but mediocre skill. His range and hands are plus at first, but slightly below that in the pasture. Jeff's arm strength and accuracy rate just average.

HOW HE PERFORMED IN '95
Conine enjoyed his third straight strong season in Florida, reaching career highs in homers, RBI (finishing fourth in the league), and walks, and pacing the NL with 12 sacrifice flies. He has increased his power production each season. Jeff also added a mid-season highlight, becoming the All-Star Game MVP by hitting a game-winning homer off the AL's Steve Ontiveros.

Working on correcting one of his few flaws, Conine sliced his strikeout rate a bit. He lifted his career average to an even .300, hitting lefthanders with excellent power and also raising his lifetime mark against righthanders to a fine .296. Jeff had his consecutive games streak interrupted last year at a league-leading 307 due to a severe hamstring pull. He had played in every game in Marlins history to that point.

Defense has never been Jeff's strong point. He threw out seven from left field last year, but again did not show good range and made five errors. He also saw some time at first base, and is slightly better defensively there. However, Conine is likely to see continued action in the pasture due to the emergence of first sacker Greg Colbrunn.

WHAT TO EXPECT IN '96
The Marlins' best day-in, day-out player, he assumed some of the veteran leadership mantle when Gary Sheffield went out. A durable, popular player who works hard every day—and produces—is a pretty good guy to lead a club. Although Conine isn't a superstar, he is a very good, dependable, and likeable player.

Overall Statistics

	G	AB	R	H	2B	3B	HR	RBI	SB	CS	BB	SO	BA	OBA
95 FLO	133	483	72	146	26	2	25	105	2	0	66	94	.302	.379
Career	447	1640	220	492	84	13	55	277	5	4	168	349	.300	.363

1995 Situational Statistics

	AB	HR	RBI	BA	OBA	SLG		AB	HR	RBI	BA	OBA	SLG
Home	243	13	52	.350	.414	.564	LHP	120	9	24	.317	.407	.592
Road	240	12	53	.254	.345	.475	RHP	363	16	81	.298	.369	.496
Apr-Jun	189	13	41	.328	.429	.598	ScPos	149	7	80	.322	.408	.537
Jul-Oct	294	12	64	.286	.346	.469	Clutch	74	2	19	.230	.348	.365

How He Compares to Other Batters

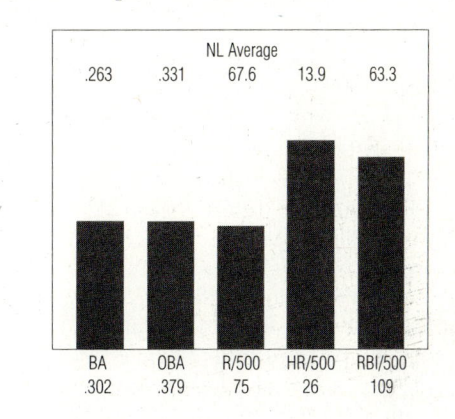

NL Average: .263 | .331 | 67.6 | 13.9 | 63.3

BA .302 | OBA .379 | R/500 75 | HR/500 26 | RBI/500 109

Where He Hits the Ball

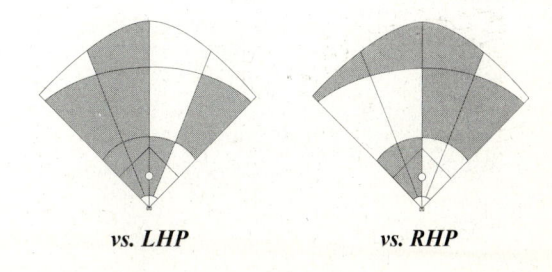

vs. LHP   vs. RHP

THE SCOUTING REPORT: 1996

FLORIDA MARLINS

CHRIS HAMMOND

Position: SP
Bats: L **Throws:** L
Ht: 6'1" **Wt:** 190
Opening Day Age: 30
Born: 1/21/1966
Drafted: CIN86* 6/148
ML Seasons: 6

SCOUTING REPORT
Coming to the plate from high three quarters, Chris throws four pitches with average control. His slightly minus sinking fastball tails into left-handers. Hammond also has an average curve and slider, but his best pitch is an plus change-up that baffles hitters and gets Chris many of his strikeouts.

Rated average as a fielder, he is plus at holding runners. Just seven dared to steal against Hammond last year, and all seven were thrown out! He had an outstanding year at bat, hitting .271 with a grand-slam homer (against Shane Reynolds) in 48 at-bats, and is now hitting .215 in 214 career at-bats with four home runs. He had five sacrifice hits as well.

HOW HE PERFORMED IN '95
While falling a bit short in the majors of the 15-1 season he enjoyed at Triple-A in 1990, Hammond has proven to be a real find for Florida. Despite being disabled twice during '95, first with a strained side muscle and later due to tendinitis in his left biceps, he enjoyed a fine season.

Historically a fast starter who pitches poorly in the last two months, Chris filled this pattern again in '95. He is a good pitcher who can be overpowering in stretches, and Hammond notched a 1.74 ERA in May and was 6-3 with a 2.69 ERA in June and July before sliding off the mountain in the last two months.

Most of the trouble he experienced in August and September was injury-related. Though he both significantly increased his strikeout rate and cut his walks in '95, he did allow 16 free passes in his last 35 innings, as he came back too soon from the August biceps injury and couldn't locate his pitches. Chris did have good run support (5.7 per game, ranking fifth in the NL), and is taking full advantage of his spacious home park.

WHAT TO EXPECT IN '96
While Florida feels Hammond will be very good if he can stay healthy all year, they have real doubts about his durability. As a result, the club signed two new starting pitchers for '95. Allowed to assume a #3 or #4 starter role, Chris could be extremely valuable without having to carry the load himself.

Overall Statistics

	G	GS	GF	SV	W	L	ERA	IP	H	R	ER	HR	BB	SO
95 FLO	25	24	0	0	9	6	3.80	161.0	157	73	68	17	47	126
Career	121	116	1	0	38	41	4.13	683.2	697	344	314	59	251	407

1995 Situational Statistics

	W	L	ERA	SV	IP	BB	SO		AB	HR	RBI	BA	OBA	SLG
Home	5	3	3.15	0	80.0	20	71	LHB	106	2	12	.217	.259	.321
Road	4	3	4.44	0	81.0	27	55	RHB	507	15	53	.264	.327	.432
Apr-Jun	5	2	2.27	0	67.1	18	46	ScPos	141	1	36	.184	.282	.270
Jul-Oct	4	4	4.90	0	93.2	29	80	Clutch	44	2	10	.386	.426	.636

How He Compares to Other Pitchers

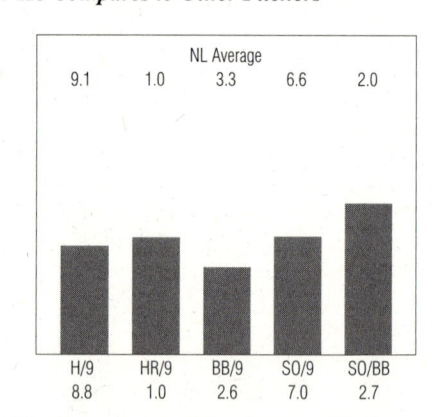

NL Average: H/9 9.1, HR/9 1.0, BB/9 3.3, SO/9 6.6, SO/BB 2.0

Hammond: H/9 8.8, HR/9 1.0, BB/9 2.6, SO/9 7.0, SO/BB 2.7

How He Compares to Other Starting Pitchers

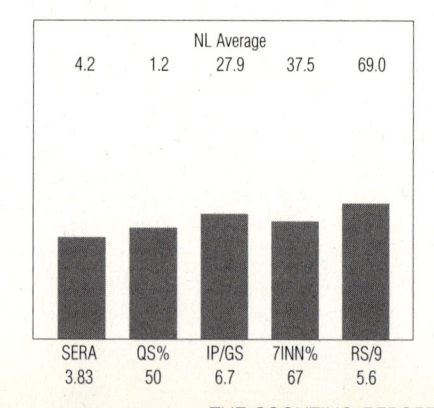

NL Average: SERA 4.2, QS% 1.2, IP/GS 27.9, 7INN% 37.5, RS/9 69.0

Hammond: SERA 3.83, QS% 50, IP/GS 6.7, 7INN% 67, RS/9 5.6

FLORIDA MARLINS

CHARLES JOHNSON

Position: C
Bats: R **Throws:** R
Ht: 6'2" **Wt:** 215
Opening Day Age: 24
Born: 7/20/1971
Drafted: FLO92 1/28
ML Seasons: 2

SCOUTING REPORT

The strong and athletic Johnson has a long swing, which makes him a pull hitter even when he tries to take down and over the plate pitches the other way. As a result, he will strike out often, but his power also commands respect. He has catcher speed on the basepaths and will ground into double plays, but isn't bad at the little game: Charles will take walks and can lay down the sacrifice bunt effectively.

As promising as his offense is, it's his work behind the plate that makes Johnson so appealing. A strong and accurate arm, combined with slightly above-par range and hands and surprisingly polished game-calling skills for a youngster, are his calling cards. He's already one of the best defensive catchers in the game.

HOW HE PERFORMED IN '95

Spending '95 as the best Rookie of the Year candidate that nobody noticed, Johnson was extremely impressive both at bat and behind the bat and is already positioning himself to be an All-Star. His 41.4% rate of throwing out runners (36 of 87) was the best in the NL. In addition, Charles showed superior pitch-blocking skills and handled a young pitching staff well.

He started out poorly, batting just .188 in May and .225 in June. However, Florida was very patient and resisted the temptation to send him to Triple-A, letting him ride out his slump. Charles got hot in July and hit well for the rest of the year. Unfortunately, his second half was truncated by injuries. On August 7, a Bret Saberhagen pitch broke Charles' right hand, and Johnson did not play until September 1.

Undaunted, he came back and was hitting .327 in the last month with three homers before he was again hit in the hand, this time by Philadelphia's Chuck Ricci. That errant pitch ended Charles' season.

WHAT TO EXPECT IN '96

The front office expects Johnson to continue his fine second-half play for a full year. Whether he will always be a slow starter remains to be seen but, given his power and polished defense, Charles belongs in the lineup even if he's still learning to hit major-league pitching. It's important to remember that '95 was only Johnson's third professional season. He's going to be a very, very good player.

Overall Statistics

	G	AB	R	H	2B	3B	HR	RBI	SB	CS	BB	SO	BA	OBA
95 FLO	97	315	40	79	15	1	11	39	0	2	46	71	.251	.351
Career	101	326	45	84	16	1	12	43	0	2	47	75	.258	.355

1995 Situational Statistics

	AB	HR	RBI	BA	OBA	SLG		AB	HR	RBI	BA	OBA	SLG
Home	157	3	12	.229	.313	.318	LHP	83	3	12	.289	.417	.470
Road	158	8	27	.272	.388	.500	RHP	232	8	27	.237	.326	.388
Apr-Jun	165	5	19	.188	.289	.315	ScPos	79	1	25	.253	.358	.367
Jul-Oct	150	6	20	.320	.418	.513	Clutch	47	2	6	.234	.315	.404

How He Compares to Other Batters

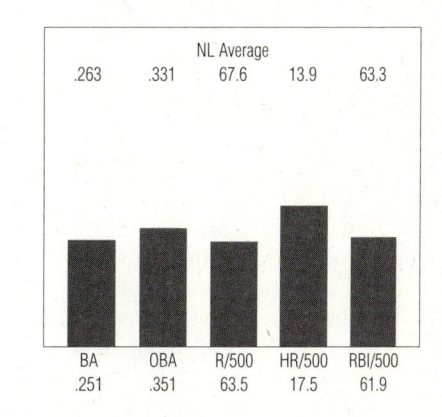

NL Average: .263 .331 67.6 13.9 63.3

BA .251 | OBA .351 | R/500 63.5 | HR/500 17.5 | RBI/500 61.9

Where He Hits the Ball

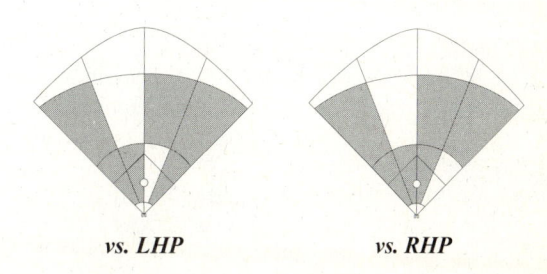

vs. LHP   vs. RHP

FLORIDA MARLINS

ROBB NEN

Position: RP
Bats: R **Throws:** R
Ht: 6'4" **Wt:** 200
Opening Day Age: 26
Born: 11/28/1969
Drafted: TEX87 34/831
ML Seasons: 3

SCOUTING REPORT
A young righthander with an explosive fastball, Nen is still learning the ropes of his vocation—closing games. He delivers from high three quarters, unleashing his four-seam fastball with good (mid-90s or better) velocity and good movement. He is essentially a two-pitch pitcher and will snap off a well above-average, hard slider when ahead in the count. Like most power relief pitchers, he neither needs nor throws off-speed stuff.

Robb is an average fielder on the mound. Due to his protracted delivery, all 11 basestealing attempts were successful in '95. He did not bat last year and is hitless in seven trips in his career.

HOW HE PERFORMED IN '95
Nen began and ended the '95 season cold, but he fashioned a hot streak in the middle. By June 30, he was a miserable 0-5 with a 4.30 ERA, having blown almost as many leads (three) as he had saved (four). Nen's early-season woes were of concern to the Marlins because they didn't know what the problem was. He wasn't pitching that badly, but he was allowing hits and home runs in key situations: the first batters he faced had compiled a lofty .385 average against him and he had allowed five home runs in only 31.2 innings before the mid-summer break.

Robb made an adjustment in his delivery and got into a groove with better control after the All-Star break, saving 19 games while blowing only three saves—mostly on the strength of a strong August (13.2 scoreless innings, nine saves). He allowed only one round-tripper after the break while fanning nearly 11 batters per nine innings. Then in September, his early-season problems returned and he allowed eight runs in 11.2 innings.

WHAT TO EXPECT IN '96
In '95, Nen converted 23 of 29 save opportunities (79%), which is not a good percentage for a top relief pitcher. In '94, his first full season in the majors, he was a perfect 15-for-15 in save situations after he was handed the closer's job. The most plausible explanation of his inconsistency is inexperience—he has tremendous talent and the right makeup to be a top-flight closer. The additional wisdom he will garner with experience should allow him to dominate hitters for years to come.

Overall Statistics

	G	GS	GF	SV	W	L	ERA	IP	H	R	ER	HR	BB	SO
95 FLO	62	0	54	23	0	7	3.29	65.2	62	26	24	6	23	68
Career	130	4	87	38	7	13	4.26	179.2	171	91	85	18	86	167

1995 Situational Statistics

	W	L	ERA	SV	IP	BB	SO		AB	HR	RBI	BA	OBA	SLG
Home	0	5	4.30	11	37.2	13	39	LHB	121	3	16	.273	.336	.471
Road	0	2	1.93	12	28.0	10	29	RHB	133	3	12	.218	.283	.346
Apr-Jun	0	5	4.30	4	29.1	11	26	ScPos	83	2	21	.205	.272	.313
Jul-Oct	0	2	2.48	19	36.1	12	42	Clutch	154	5	23	.240	.308	.416

How He Compares to Other Pitchers

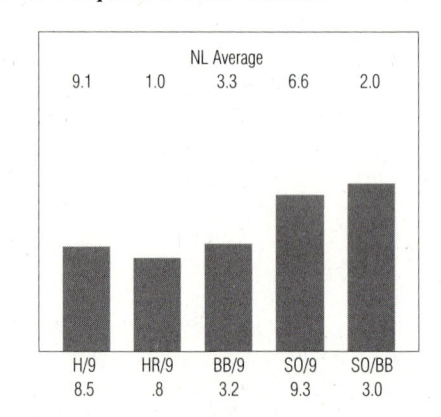

NL Average: 9.1 | 1.0 | 3.3 | 6.6 | 2.0

H/9	HR/9	BB/9	SO/9	SO/BB
8.5	.8	3.2	9.3	3.0

How He Compares to Other Relief Pitchers

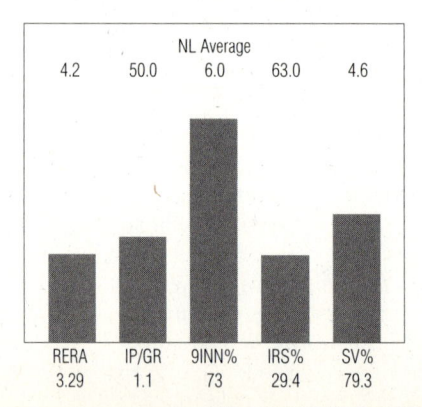

NL Average: 4.2 | 50.0 | 6.0 | 63.0 | 4.6

RERA	IP/GR	9INN%	IRS%	SV%
3.29	1.1	73	29.4	79.3

FLORIDA MARLINS

TERRY PENDLETON

Position: 3B
Bats: B **Throws:** R
Ht: 5'9" **Wt:** 180
Opening Day Age: 35
Born: 7/16/1960
Drafted: SL82 7/179
ML Seasons: 12

SCOUTING REPORT

A switch-hitter with decent power, Terry likes pitches up and out over the plate when hitting righthanded and down and over the plate when hitting lefthanded. He is a slow runner who no longer steals. He does not bunt.

In the field, Pendleton plays third with a quick first step and somewhat above-average range. His hands are a bit above-par, but his arm is now weak although his throwing is accurate and he turns the double play well. He made 18 errors last season, leading to a mediocre .952 fielding percentage. A winner of three Gold Gloves in his career, his defense at the hot corner is still respectable.

HOW HE PERFORMED IN '95

Pendleton had a surprisingly good comeback season after being signed as a free-agent by the Marlins in April '95. He recaptured a great deal of his offensive value in Florida, hitting especially well in Miami. A large part of the comeback was freedom from the back and leg injuries he suffered from in '94 in Atlanta, allowing him to drive the ball better. He also hit more than 40 points better than his career average against lefthanders.

Starting the season slowly, Terry exploded after Memorial Day. He hit a robust .366 in June, following that by clubbing ten of his 14 home runs in the last three months of the season. While he has never been a very patient hitter, his plate discipline returned to normal levels last year after an abrupt drop in 1994, boosting his on-base average by 59 points.

WHAT TO EXPECT IN '96

The Marlins are very appreciate of the Pendleton's leadership on the field and in the clubhouse. However, there is some concern about the shoulder problems which bothered Terry all last year, causing him to make soft throws to first. Nonetheless, Florida exercised the option in Pendleton's contract for '96, and he'll be starting every day at the hot corner as the Fighting Fish struggle towards contending status.

Even though he has worn the teal togs of the Marlins for only one season, he is unquestionably the veteran leader of the young team. At 35, he should be able to produce at his '95 level for another year unless injuries drag him down.

Overall Statistics

	G	AB	R	H	2B	3B	HR	RBI	SB	CS	BB	SO	BA	OBA
95 FLO	133	513	70	149	32	1	14	78	1	2	38	84	.290	.339
Career	1611	6114	772	1673	311	38	125	825	122	55	418	805	.274	.318

1995 Situational Statistics

	AB	HR	RBI	BA	OBA	SLG		AB	HR	RBI	BA	OBA	SLG
Home	267	8	43	.318	.351	.491	LHP	149	3	23	.336	.359	.456
Road	246	6	35	.260	.327	.382	RHP	364	11	55	.272	.332	.431
Apr-Jun	208	4	30	.293	.332	.418	ScPos	134	4	59	.321	.414	.478
Jul-Oct	305	10	48	.289	.344	.452	Clutch	85	1	12	.294	.365	.400

How He Compares to Other Batters

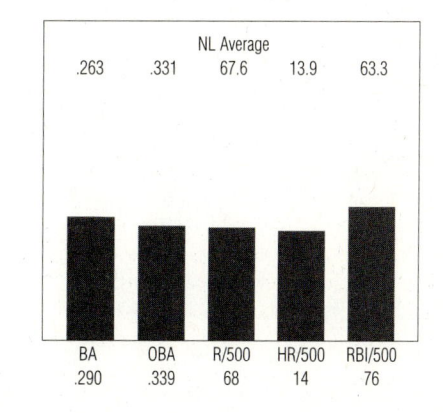

NL Average
.263   .331   67.6   13.9   63.3

BA   OBA   R/500 HR/500 RBI/500
.290 .339   68   14   76

Where He Hits the Ball

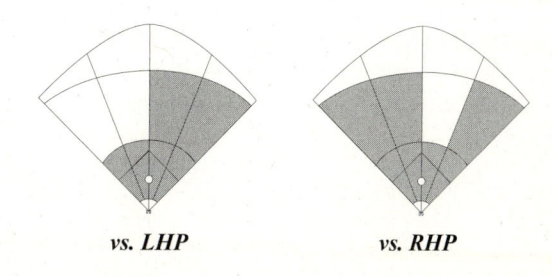

vs. LHP   *vs. RHP*

THE SCOUTING REPORT: 1996

FLORIDA MARLINS

PAT RAPP

Position: SP
Bats: R **Throws:** R
Ht: 6'3" **Wt:** 195
Opening Day Age: 28
Born: 7/13/1967
Drafted: SF89 15/388
ML Seasons: 4

SCOUTING REPORT

Using a cross-body, three-quarter delivery, Rapp throws four pitches with inconsistent control. His plus fastball is thrown three ways: he will sink it, throw a high four-seamer (which often gets whacked), and will cut the fastball as well. Unfortunately, none of his other pitches match up. His curve and change are nothing special and Rapp has problems controlling them. Pat also has an average slider, but doesn't use it that much.

Although he has an average move, his delivery makes it hard to run and Pat has now led the NL in runners caught two straight seasons (credit also due to Charles Johnson: 15 of 20 trying to steal against him were thrown out during '95). Rapp is an average fielder. Just 6-for-56 at bat (.107) with nine sacrifices, he's a .131 career hitter.

HOW HE PERFORMED IN '95

After pitching erratically for over two years in Florida's rotation, Pat had a big second half in '95, putting together all of his gifts in the way they needed to be assembled. At the break, Rapp was just 3-5 with a 4.95 ERA. However, he went 11-2, 2.28 afterward, pitching as well as anyone in the league, including Greg Maddux.

After a 5-1 mark in August—despite walking 21 men in 36 innings—his often wobbly control stabilized in September when Pat went 5-0 with a 1.24 ERA and just nine walks in 43.2 innings. He mixed his pitches much better and kept the ball low in the strike zone to good effect. By working hitters below the belt, he nearly sawed his home run rate in half. Pat had allowed one long ball per ten innings during '94, but last season, Rapp's .54 homers per game ranked third-best in the league behind Maddux and Tom Glavine.

WHAT TO EXPECT IN '96

The off-season acquisitions of Al Leiter and Kevin Brown indicate that Rapp will serve as the Marlins' third or fourth starter. In one way, this is good: Pat won't be forced into a marquee role, thus continuing his development in a low-pressure situation. While a continuation of his '95 second-half performance is unlikely, Rapp should be fine if he keeps the ball down and walks the control tightrope a bit better.

Overall Statistics

	G	GS	GF	SV	W	L	ERA	IP	H	R	ER	HR	BB	SO
95 FLO	28	28	0	0	14	7	3.44	167.1	158	72	64	10	76	102
Career	71	69	2	0	25	23	3.80	404.2	399	196	171	30	190	237

1995 Situational Statistics

	W	L	ERA	SV	IP	BB	SO		AB	HR	RBI	BA	OBA	SLG
Home	6	4	3.55	0	78.2	25	52	LHB	293	4	25	.242	.347	.355
Road	8	3	3.35	0	88.2	51	50	RHB	332	6	35	.262	.334	.346
Apr-Jun	3	4	4.48	0	62.1	31	38	ScPos	163	2	41	.209	.317	.264
Jul-Oct	11	3	2.83	0	105.0	45	64	Clutch	10	1	2	.400	.571	.900

How He Compares to Other Pitchers

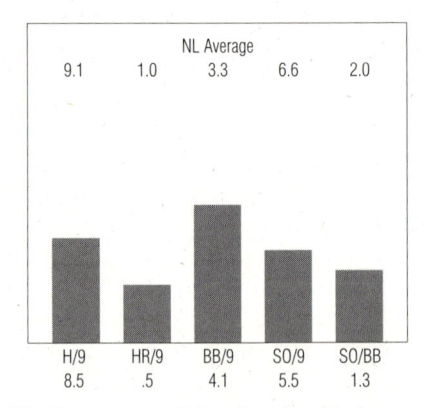

NL Average: 9.1 / 1.0 / 3.3 / 6.6 / 2.0

H/9	HR/9	BB/9	SO/9	SO/BB
8.5	.5	4.1	5.5	1.3

How He Compares to Other Starting Pitchers

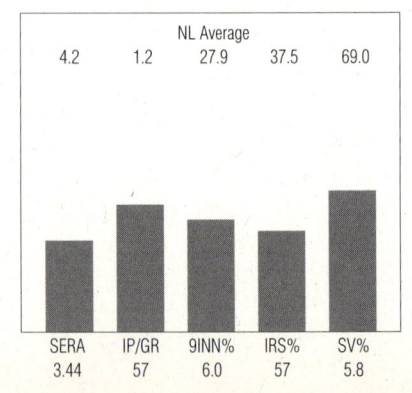

NL Average: 4.2 / 1.2 / 27.9 / 37.5 / 69.0

SERA	IP/GR	9INN%	IRS%	SV%
3.44	57	6.0	57	5.8

FLORIDA MARLINS

GARY SHEFFIELD

Position: OF
Bats: R **Throws:** R
Ht: 5'11" **Wt:** 190
Opening Day Age: 27
Born: 11/18/1968
Drafted: MIL86 1/6
ML Seasons: 8

SCOUTING REPORT

Sheffield has conclusively shown that he is one of the most fearsome hitters in the major leagues. He is a strong pull hitter with blinding bat speed, picking on low and inside fastballs and turning them around in a hurry. He has average speed now but is a decent basestealer, enjoying his best year as a thief and grounding into just three double plays during '95.

In right field, Gary is less able. He has an average arm and adequate hands; he displayed a bit below-par range in '95—an improvement over his first season in the outfield. Although he threw out five runners, he also made seven errors, fielding a very poor .942. While his defense is cause for some concern, it's very possible that he will improve as he's played less than 150 games in the outfield in his career.

HOW HE PERFORMED IN '95

Again, Sheffield saw another fine season ripped apart by injuries. He didn't play between June 10 and August 31 due to a torn ligament in his right thumb. When he came back September 1, facing Greg Swindell, Gary hit the first pitch he saw 426 feet, pounding pitchers from then to the end of the season to the tune of a .343 average with 10 homers and 27 runs batted in in only 70 at-bats.

He was very consistent against both lefties and righties, but did not show much power at Joe Robbie Stadium, which was a tough home-run park in '95. Partly due to the respect pitchers have for his power and partly due to his increased discipline at the plate in the past two years, he posted an eye-popping on-base average in '95.

WHAT TO EXPECT IN '96

The Marlins have real concern about Sheffield's ability to stay in the lineup, his outspoken comments in the media, and his off-field problems. He was shot in the shoulder in October 1995 while at a traffic light in Tampa. Although he was not seriously injured, the incident was frightening enough, especially when combined with other allegations reported by the media.

Since his run at the Triple Crown in 1992 in San Diego, Sheffield has proven that he is one of the best hitters in baseball, with virtually no offensive weaknesses—except staying healthy.

Overall Statistics

	G	AB	R	H	2B	3B	HR	RBI	SB	CS	BB	SO	BA	OBA
95 FLO	63	213	46	69	8	0	16	46	19	4	55	45	.324	.467
Career	730	2696	399	774	139	12	117	430	96	43	298	295	.287	.361

1995 Situational Statistics

	AB	HR	RBI	BA	OBA	SLG		AB	HR	RBI	BA	OBA	SLG
Home	102	4	17	.333	.481	.490	LHP	61	3	8	.328	.488	.525
Road	111	12	29	.315	.455	.676	RHP	152	13	38	.322	.459	.612
Apr-Jun	143	6	19	.315	.459	.483	ScPos	51	6	34	.294	.519	.667
Jul-Oct	70	10	27	.343	.484	.800	Clutch	33	2	8	.303	.468	.485

How He Compares to Other Batters

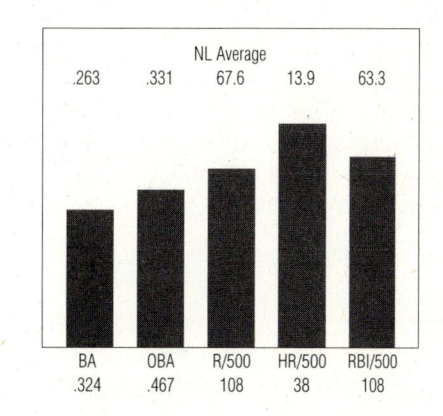

NL Average: .263 .331 67.6 13.9 63.3

BA .324 OBA .467 R/500 108 HR/500 38 RBI/500 108

Where He Hits the Ball

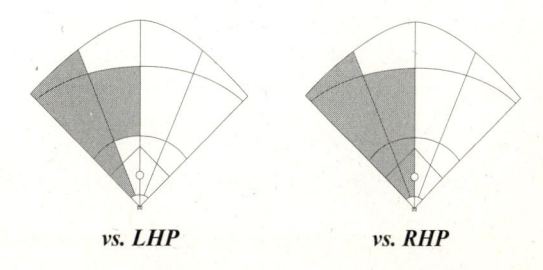

vs. LHP   vs. RHP

FLORIDA MARLINS

QUILVIO VERAS

Positions: 2B//OF
Bats: B **Throws:** R
Ht: 5'9" **Wt:** 170
Opening Day Age: 24
Born: 4/3/1971
Drafted: NYN 11/22/89
ML Seasons: 1

SCOUTING REPORT
A line-drive hitter without much power, Quilvio likes to pick on low fastballs from the left side but will hack at anything high and over the plate while batting righthanded. He is extremely patient at bat, displaying excellent discipline for a young player. His swing appears to have recovered after a '94 shoulder injury. Blessed with slightly above-average speed, Veras proved an extremely aggressive basestealer in '95 but is not yet polished in the art and should improve. Quilvio will also bunt for hits.

Veras has slightly above-average range and hands at second base with an average arm and is outstanding on the pivot.

HOW HE PERFORMED IN '95
Veras did what he was supposed to do and more in '95, leading the majors in stolen bases and establishing himself as a Rookie of the Year candidate (finishing third). He got on base, played good defense, and improved as the year went on.

When the Marlins acquired Quilvio from the Mets, they knew of his speed and defensive ability but were concerned about his hitting. After some problems, Veras eventually did, batting over .300 during both August and September. Quilvio also chipped in by tying for third in the NL in walks and leaned into pitches in order to get hit. As a result, his on-base average ranked just outside the league's top ten. Veras ran opponents crazy, stealing third base 14 times.

There's room to improve, of course. Quilvio led the league in caught stealing as well as steals and, although he bunted often, he was not particularly good at it.

He contributed in a big way on defense. Making nine errors, Quilvio finished in the middle with a .986 fielding percentage. He showed fine mobility, footwork and coordination, helping the Marlins finish second in the league in double plays.

WHAT TO EXPECT IN '96
Although he possesses outstanding leadoff skills, the Marlins are not happy with Veras' caught stealing totals and feel he might be better suited for the #2 spot. However, hitting in front of Gary Sheffield might hurt his running, as Sheffield is not fond of runners moving when he bats. As long as Veras stays healthy, he's going to be a fine player for a long time no matter where he hits.

Overall Statistics

	G	AB	R	H	2B	3B	HR	RBI	SB	CS	BB	SO	BA	OBA
95 FLO	124	440	86	115	20	7	5	32	56	21	80	68	.261	.384
Career	124	440	86	115	20	7	5	32	56	21	80	68	.261	.384

1995 Situational Statistics

	AB	HR	RBI	BA	OBA	SLG		AB	HR	RBI	BA	OBA	SLG
Home	195	2	19	.267	.396	.369	LHP	119	3	10	.244	.362	.370
Road	245	3	13	.257	.375	.376	RHP	321	2	22	.268	.392	.374
Apr-Jun	192	3	13	.234	.364	.323	ScPos	86	2	24	.209	.369	.314
Jul-Oct	248	2	19	.282	.400	.411	Clutch	68	0	4	.279	.402	.426

How He Compares to Other Batters

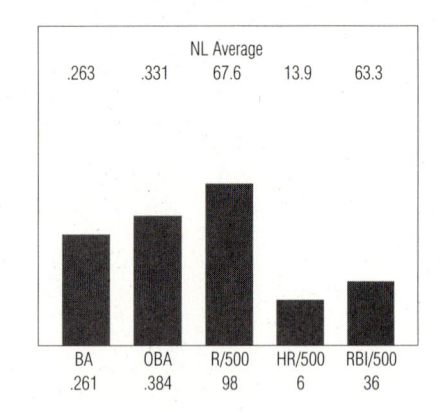

NL Average: .263 .331 67.6 13.9 63.3

BA	OBA	R/500	HR/500	RBI/500
.261	.384	98	6	36

Where He Hits the Ball

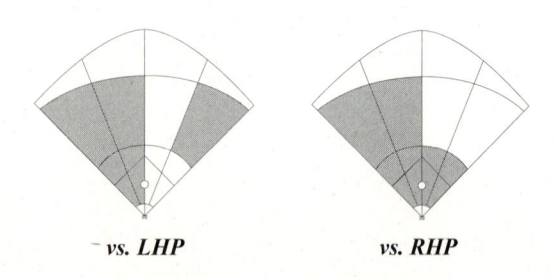

vs. LHP   vs. RHP

FLORIDA MARLINS

DAVE WEATHERS

Position: SP/RP
Bats: R **Throws:** R
Ht: 6'3" **Wt:** 205
Opening Day Age: 26
Born: 9/25/1969
Drafted: TOR88 3/82
ML Seasons: 5

SCOUTING REPORT
Weathers throws three average pitches from high three quarters. Although David used to throw a four-seam fastball, he has junked it in favor of a two-seam sinker. While he throws hard enough to get strikeouts, he cannot effectively set up his fastball. Weathers lacks command of his average slider, and his change-up doesn't often fool anyone. Hitters end up sitting on David's fastball, and they can get around on it.

To make things worse, David's command has gotten worse in the last two seasons. Despite being a ground ball pitcher, David has hung plenty of sliders and pays for those mistakes. Walks are also a serious problem.

He is an average fielder. Despite a quick delivery to home, nine of twelve men trying to steal were successful. Weathers fanned in 17 of his 26 at-bats last year, batting .154, which raised his career average to a weak .100. He is a decent bunter, however.

HOW HE PERFORMED IN '95
David spent the year shuttling back and forth between the Marlins' bullpen and the rotation. He failed to perform well in either role, and may have pitched his way back to the minors. After three relief appearances to begin the season, Weathers made seven straight starts before suffering a cut right pinky June 25 in Cincinnati. He missed nearly three weeks with the injury.

After he returned, David assumed a swing role. He ended up 3-4 with a 5.57 ERA in his 15 starts, but was even worse (7.64) from the bullpen. In 90 innings, he walked nearly as many men as he had in 125 innings in '94. In addition, Weathers allowed nearly a home run per game last season.

He might be in the wrong ballpark. Weathers is nearly two runs better pitching on artificial turf than on grass in his career; His lifetime ERA on real stuff is 5.97.

WHAT TO EXPECT IN '96
If David makes the club this season, it will be as a long reliever unless one of the starters is hurt. The Marlins may decide that the burly pitcher needs more time at Triple-A to improve. If he can't locate the slider better, or develop another pitch, David is going to be forgotten.

Overall Statistics

	G	GS	GF	SV	W	L	ERA	IP	H	R	ER	HR	BB	SO
95 FLO	28	15	0	0	4	5	5.98	90.1	104	68	60	8	52	60
Career	83	45	6	0	15	20	5.48	289.0	347	193	176	26	143	182

1995 Situational Statistics

	W	L	ERA	SV	IP	BB	SO		AB	HR	RBI	BA	OBA	SLG
Home	2	1	7.43	0	36.1	27	16	LHB	143	2	21	.315	.438	.441
Road	2	4	5.00	0	54.0	25	44	RHB	209	6	34	.282	.356	.411
Apr-Jun	2	3	5.25	0	48.0	27	30	ScPos	104	1	43	.337	.459	.423
Jul-Oct	2	2	6.80	0	42.1	25	30	Clutch	15	0	6	.400	.500	.400

How He Compares to Other Pitchers

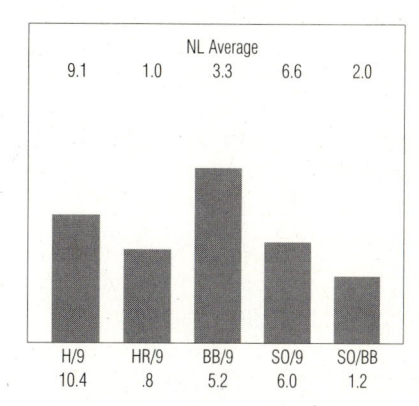

NL Average: H/9 9.1, HR/9 1.0, BB/9 3.3, SO/9 6.6, SO/BB 2.0
Weathers: H/9 10.4, HR/9 .8, BB/9 5.2, SO/9 6.0, SO/BB 1.2

How He Compares to Other Starting Pitchers

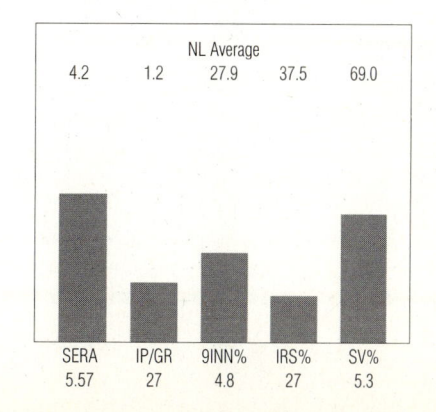

NL Average: SERA 4.2, IP/GR 1.2, 9INN% 27.9, IRS% 37.5, SV% 69.0
Weathers: SERA 5.57, IP/GR 27, 9INN% 4.8, IRS% 27, SV% 5.3

THE SCOUTING REPORT: 1996

FLORIDA MARLINS

ALEX ARIAS

Positions: SS/3B//2B
Bats: R **Throws:** R
Ht: 6'3" **Wt:** 185
Opening Day Age: 28
Born: 11/20/1967
Drafted: CHN87 2/62
ML Seasons: 4

Overall Statistics

	G	AB	R	H	2B	3B	HR	RBI	SB	CS	BB	SO	BA	OBA
95 FLO	94	216	22	58	9	2	3	26	1	0	22	20	.269	.337
Career	281	677	67	181	25	3	5	68	2	2	69	70	.267	.339

1995 Situational Statistics

	AB	HR	RBI	BA	OBA	SLG		AB	HR	BA	OBA	SLG
Home	95	2	17	.316	.394	.432	LHP	50	0	4 .220	.310	.300
Road	121	1	9	.231	.291	.322	RHP	166	3	22 .283	.346	.392
Apr-Jun	95	2	8	.274	.355	.389	ScPos	67	1	22 .299	.359	.403
Jul-Oct	121	1	18	.264	.324	.355	Clutch	44	0	7 .273	.340	.318

SCOUTING REPORT

Arias' biggest asset is his versatility. He can play second base, shortstop, or third base decently and has some hitting ability, unlike many utility infielders with good gloves. His defensive tools are average in all respects.

At the plate, Alex is a straightaway hitter who likes fastballs up and over the plate. He has little power but makes contact and will take the walk. Despite good steal totals in the minors, he has done nothing on the bases in the major leagues with his average speed.

HOW HE PERFORMED IN '95

Arias had another good season of the pine for Florida, hitting .316 in 38 pinch-hit at-bats. Alex might have been a solid everyday shortstop if he got the right break. It doesn't look like that will happen now but, if he gets the chance to play regularly, he could surprise people.

WHAT TO EXPECT IN '96

The Marlins are happy with the package Alex gives them, and Arias will return as an infield backup in '96. He will probably get more playing time at short and third in '96 due to the dismissal of Jerry Browne.

WILLIE BANKS

Position: SP/RP
Bats: R **Throws:** R
Ht: 6'1" **Wt:** 190
Opening Day Age: 27
Born: 2/27/1969
Drafted: MIN87 1/3
ML Seasons: 5

Overall Statistics

	G	GS	GF	SV	W	L	ERA	IP	H	R	ER	HR	BB	SO
95 CH/LA/FL	25	15	2	0	2	6	5.66	90.2	106	71	57	14	58	62
Career	100	83	7	0	26	35	5.03	488.2	532	311	273	54	241	344

1995 Situational Statistics

	W	L	ERA	SV	IP	BB	SO		AB	HR	RBI	BA	OBA	SLG
Home	2	2	5.14	0	49.0	27	32	LHB	164	8	33	.293	.376	.457
Road	0	4	6.26	0	41.2	31	30	RHB	197	6	28	.294	.404	.452
Apr-Jun	0	1	12.96	0	16.2	14	14	ScPos	107	6	51	.299	.422	.486
Jul-Oct	2	5	4.01	0	74.0	44	48	Clutch	28	1	7	.357	.500	.536

SCOUTING REPORT

Banks has two plus pitches, a slow curve and a change, to go with his average four-seam fastball. He delivers overhand but lacks control and has frightening bouts of inconsistency and to problems with gopher balls.

Willie has an average move but has plenty of runners to worry about: 11 ran in '95, ten successfully. He is an average fielder but hit .269 (7-for-26) and is a .179 career batter. He's a good athlete who can pinch-run, and he bunts well.

HOW HE PERFORMED IN '95

Banks started '95 with Chicago but came to spring training out of shape. The Cubs were angry and used him 10 times in garbage relief (15.43 ERA) before giving him to L.A. in June. With the Dodgers, he was 0-2, 4.03 in six starts before being waived in August. With the Marlins, he made nine more starts and went 2-3, 4.32.

WHAT TO EXPECT IN '96

Florida wanted Banks back for '96 as a spot starter/long reliever but didn't have room, losing him to Philadelphia on a waiver claim. With the combat-weary Phillies' staff and with Johnny Podres' tutelage, he will get the chance to convert his talent into performance.

FLORIDA MARLINS

JERRY BROWNE

Positions: OF/2B//3B
Bats: B **Throws:** R
Ht: 5'10" **Wt:** 170
Opening Day Age: 30
Born: 2/13/1966
Drafted: TEX 3/3/83
ML Seasons: 10

Overall Statistics

	G	AB	R	H	2B	3B	HR	RBI	SB	CS	BB	SO	BA	OBA
95 FLO	77	184	21	47	4	0	1	17	1	1	25	20	.255	.346
Career	982	3190	431	866	135	25	23	288	73	45	393	325	.271	.351

1995 Situational Statistics

	AB	HR	RBI	BA	OBA	SLG		AB	HR	RBI	BA	OBA	SLG
Home	111	0	9	.270	.354	.288	LHP	46	0	4	.174	.283	.174
Road	73	1	8	.233	.333	.301	RHP	138	1	13	.283	.367	.333
Apr-Jun	71	1	9	.197	.296	.254	ScPos	48	0	16	.208	.316	.208
Jul-Oct	113	0	8	.292	.377	.319	Clutch	42	0	2	.167	.286	.167

SCOUTING REPORT

Jerry is a rare utility player who can play all outfield positions as well as third and the middle infield positions. He has good plate discipline and is an outstanding bunter, but Jerry has no power and has only average speed now. His defensive tools are average across the board.

HOW HE PERFORMED IN '95

Browne slumped some in '95, disappointing the Marlins, largely because of two injuries that hampered his mobility. He missed almost all of June with a pulled left quadricep, and then went down for two weeks beginning August 19 after pulling his right quad.

Jerry spent most of his time last season at second base, making 21 starts, but also started games at third and all three outfield spots.

WHAT TO EXPECT IN '96

Only 30, Browne is younger than he seems because he made his big-league debut so young at age 20 in 1986. With erratic performance when he got a chance to play regularly, Browne became typecast as a utility player much earlier than most players.

Florida let Browne go free after the season, signing Craig Grebeck to handle the reserve duties at second base in '96.

ANDRE DAWSON

Position: OF
Bats: R **Throws:** R
Ht: 6'3" **Wt:** 195
Opening Day Age: 41
Born: 7/10/1954
Drafted: MON75 11/250
ML Seasons: 20

Overall Statistics

	G	AB	R	H	2B	3B	HR	RBI	SB	CS	BB	SO	BA	OBA
95 FLO	79	226	30	58	10	3	8	37	0	0	9	45	.257	.305
Career	2585	9869	1367	2758	501	98	436	1577	314	109	587	1496	.279	.323

1995 Situational Statistics

	AB	HR	RBI	BA	OBA	SLG		AB	HR	RBI	BA	OBA	SLG
Home	110	1	13	.218	.250	.309	LHP	80	4	18	.313	.333	.563
Road	116	7	24	.293	.354	.552	RHP	146	4	19	.226	.290	.363
Apr-Jun	100	4	15	.230	.278	.430	ScPos	68	4	27	.250	.308	.441
Jul-Oct	126	4	22	.278	.326	.437	Clutch	44	0	0	.159	.213	.182

SCOUTING REPORT

Andre retains some of his power on low, inside fastballs, especially from southpaws. He is way too eager to swing, though, and doesn't have the bat speed to catch up to good hard stuff. His legendary bad knees prevent him from running at all well.

He's a disaster in the outfield due to those same knees. Last season, he threw out just three runners and made eight errors, fielding .907 on the season. All defensive tools are now clearly minus.

HOW HE PERFORMED IN '95

In his last 518 at-bats (1994–95), Dawson's batting only .247 with 24 homers, 98 strikeouts, and 14 non-intentional walks. He can still hit lefthanders. If he doesn't have to play against righties, Andre can still be helpful in a platoon situation.

WHAT TO EXPECT IN '96

Dawson was not on Florida's winter roster in order to make room for prospects. He wants to play one more year; that the Marlins want him back for '96 says a lot about Andre's popularity and leadership. The team is very concerned about its attendance drop and is trying to make some high-profile moves to bolster fan interest.

THE SCOUTING REPORT: 1996

FLORIDA MARLINS

STEVE DECKER

Positions: C//1B
Bats: R **Throws:** R
Ht: 6'3" **Wt:** 205
Opening Day Age: 30
Born: 10/25/1965
Drafted: SF88 23/542
ML Seasons: 5

Overall Statistics

	G	AB	R	H	2B	3B	HR	RBI	SB	CS	BB	SO	BA	OBA
95 FLO	51	133	12	30	2	1	3	13	1	0	19	22	.226	.318
Career	168	478	31	101	12	2	11	47	1	1	45	86	.211	.281

1995 Situational Statistics

	AB	HR	RBI	BA	OBA	SLG		AB	HR	RBI	BA	OBA	SLG
Home	64	2	8	.281	.347	.422	LHP	29	1	3	.241	.313	.379
Road	69	1	5	.174	.293	.232	RHP	104	2	10	.221	.320	.308
Apr-Jun	26	0	1	.192	.333	.231	ScPos	32	0	8	.219	.308	.219
Jul-Oct	107	3	12	.234	.314	.346	Clutch	18	0	3	.222	.318	.222

SCOUTING REPORT
Steve is a line-drive hitter with minus power who likes to swing at low fastballs. He has catcher speed on the basepaths.

Defensively, Decker's tools are average in all categories behind the plate. He threw out 12 of 38 baserunners (32%) in '95 and blocked pitches very efficiently.

HOW HE PERFORMED IN '95
Spending the entire '95 season with the Marlins after spending '94 in the minors, Steve played defense adequately but just isn't hitting enough to keep a solid grip on a reserve job. He can hit the occasional long ball and will take the walk, but Steve has had almost a full season's worth of major-league at-bats without encouraging anyone to take a chance on him since the Giants gave his 200-plus at-bats in 1995.

WHAT TO EXPECT IN '96
At age 30, Steve has lost his chance, it seems, at ever fulfilling his promise. Florida doesn't have any backup of consequence for Charles Johnson, so Decker will fight for the #2 job in '96 with Bob Natal.

MARK GARDNER

Position: RP/SP
Bats: R **Throws:** R
Ht: 6'1" **Wt:** 190
Opening Day Age: 34
Born: 3/1/1962
Drafted: MON85 8/192
ML Seasons: 7

Overall Statistics

	G	GS	GF	SV	W	L	ERA	IP	H	R	ER	HR	BB	SO
95 FLO	39	11	7	1	5	5	4.49	102.1	109	60	51	14	43	87
Career	170	128	13	1	41	48	4.38	813.1	771	425	396	92	316	593

1995 Situational Statistics

	W	L	ERA	SV	IP	BB	SO		AB	HR	RBI	BA	OBA	SLG
Home	3	3	4.82	0	56.0	26	41	LHB	168	6	16	.274	.378	.440
Road	2	2	4.08	1	46.1	17	46	RHB	233	8	36	.270	.328	.455
Apr-Jun	1	4	5.82	0	38.2	23	32	ScPos	104	1	33	.240	.347	.365
Jul-Oct	4	1	3.68	1	63.2	20	55	Clutch	48	1	6	.292	.358	.438

SCOUTING REPORT
Mark is a garden-variety veteran righthander, delivering from three-quarters with a sinking fastball which tails a little with a bit below-average velocity. He also employs an average curve and average change-up to complement his fastball.

Gardner is a minus fielder on the mound with an average move to first: 11 of 16 basestealers were successful taking off against him in '95. He was 4-for-21 last year with four sacrifice hits, and is a poor hitter, with a .114 career average.

HOW HE PERFORMED IN '95
Gardner spent his second year with the Marlins as a swingman. He isn't horrible but isn't anything special, either. His strikeout rate rose unexpectedly last year, but he walked more as well and continued to get bombed by the long ball.

WHAT TO EXPECT IN '96
Mark can fill in on the Marlins' staff in the same role—really, multiple roles—in '96. Florida values his versatility and his willingness to take the ball whenever needed. He's getting a bit old to be counted on heavily, though.

FLORIDA MARLINS

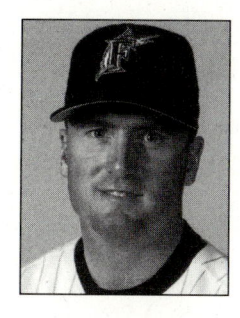

TOMMY GREGG

Positions: OF//1B
Bats: L **Throws:** L
Ht: 6'1" **Wt:** 190
Opening Day Age: 32
Born: 7/29/1963
Drafted: PIT85 7/164
ML Seasons: 8

Overall Statistics

	G	AB	R	H	2B	3B	HR	RBI	SB	CS	BB	SO	BA	OBA
95 FLO	72	156	20	37	5	0	6	20	3	1	16	33	.237	.313
Career	433	861	85	209	39	2	20	88	13	11	70	156	.243	.301

1995 Situational Statistics

	AB	HR	RBI	BA	OBA	SLG		AB	HR	RBI	BA	OBA	SLG
Home	76	2	4	.184	.250	.276	LHP	11	0	3	.182	.231	.273
Road	80	4	16	.287	.370	.488	RHP	145	6	17	.241	.319	.393
Apr-Jun	54	3	9	.222	.313	.444	ScPos	44	1	14	.250	.327	.341
Jul-Oct	102	3	11	.245	.313	.353	Clutch	39	1	4	.256	.341	.333

SCOUTING REPORT
At bat, Gregg is an opposite-field fastball hitter with some power, preferring pitches up and over the plate. More effective against righthanded pitching, Tommy is a platoon hitter. He has minus speed and doesn't steal often.

Defensively, Tommy has a very weak arm with minus accuracy, minus range and average hands.

HOW HE PERFORMED IN '95
Gregg hit .386 at Charlotte with eight homers in 31 games, and then hit two homers in his first 23 at-bats for Florida. Of course, he cooled off considerably after that, batting just .216 in 111 at-bats between June 1 and August 31 before a strong finish. It didn't help that Tommy was just 4-for-28 as a pinch-hitter in '95.

WHAT TO EXPECT IN '96
Tommy was signed to a Triple-A contract for '96 and will shuttle between the bushes and the bigs again—if he's lucky—adding to his 861 at-bats in his eight years in the majors. Joe Orsulak will take his role as a reserve outfielder and a lefthanded bat off the bench in Miami this summer.

RICHIE LEWIS

Position: RP
Bats: R **Throws:** R
Ht: 5'10" **Wt:** 170
Opening Day Age: 30
Born: 1/25/1966
Drafted: MON87 4/44
ML Seasons: 4

Overall Statistics

	G	GS	GF	SV	W	L	ERA	IP	H	R	ER	HR	BB	SO
95 FLO	21	1	6	0	0	1	3.75	36.0	30	15	15	9	15	32
Career	125	3	29	0	8	9	4.40	174.0	173	104	85	24	103	146

1995 Situational Statistics

	W	L	ERA	SV	IP	BB	SO		AB	HR	RBI	BA	OBA	SLG
Home	0	1	2.82	0	22.1	11	13	LHB	55	3	9	.200	.323	.436
Road	0	0	5.27	0	13.2	4	19	RHB	79	6	14	.241	.294	.557
Apr-Jun	0	1	4.58	0	17.2	5	18	ScPos	33	3	17	.273	.415	.667
Jul-Oct	0	0	2.95	0	18.1	10	14	Clutch	24	3	7	.167	.333	.542

SCOUTING REPORT
The diminutive righty uses his curveball as his out pitch: a plus pitch in the past, it's now average. He delivers from three quarters with a slightly short sinking fastball and also will throw an average slider and change.

Quick to home and possessing a plus move, only three baserunners ran on him last year. He has made five errors in his career, posting a poor .881 fielding average. Richie fanned in his only '95 at-bat and is 1-for-8 in his career.

HOW HE PERFORMED IN '95
Lewis had three stints with the Marlins as a middle and short reliever in '95. He allowed a remarkable nine homers in 36 innings, but again showed his trademark good stuff, fanning almost a batter per inning. His stats were misleadingly good as the homers he allowed seemed to come at the worst times.

WHAT TO EXPECT IN '96
Frustrated with his inconsistency, the Fish bade Lewis farewell after the season. At 30, the diminutive righty will certainly get another chance. Lewis can pitch and might be better off as a starter or with a new organization.

THE SCOUTING REPORT: 1996

FLORIDA MARLINS

TERRY MATHEWS

Position: RP
Bats: L **Throws:** R
Ht: 6'2" **Wt:** 200
Opening Day Age: 31
Born: 10/5/1964
Drafted: TEX87 7/129
ML Seasons: 4

Overall Statistics

	G	GS	GF	SV	W	L	ERA	IP	H	R	ER	HR	BB	SO
95 FLO	57	0	14	3	4	4	3.38	82.2	70	32	31	9	27	72
Career	155	4	38	4	12	9	3.91	225.1	217	101	98	22	85	170

1995 Situational Statistics

	W	L	ERA	SV	IP	BB	SO		AB	HR	RBI	BA	OBA	SLG
Home	2	2	2.74	1	46.0	12	42	LHB	119	4	16	.227	.328	.387
Road	2	2	4.17	2	36.2	15	30	RHB	179	5	24	.240	.279	.385
Apr-Jun	2	0	2.93	2	40.0	14	28	ScPos	71	2	31	.282	.388	.451
Jul-Oct	2	4	3.80	1	42.2	13	44	Clutch	99	3	17	.273	.339	.434

SCOUTING REPORT

A sinker-slider pitcher with plus velocity, Mathews comes from high three-quarters and also possesses an average curve, slider, and change. His fastball sinks and tails into righthanded hitters.

With a quick delivery, Terry is effective at holding runners, and seven of 12 basestealers were cut down against Mathews in '95. Coming into '95 he was 3-for-6 at the plate; last year he went 6-for-13 to raise his career average to .474! He batted in three runs during '95 and smacked two doubles. In college, Terry was a pitcher/first baseman/DH. He is not a good fielder off the mound.

HOW HE PERFORMED IN '95

Mathews resurrected his career with a fine season. He could always pitch, and now is fully recovered from his 1992 elbow miseries. He was quite streaky in '95, and was much more effective in home games and night contests.

WHAT TO EXPECT IN '96

The Marlins' workhorse in '95 will be the #1 setup pitcher for closer Robb Nen in '96. While he's not going to graduate to anything more important, Mathews is very valuable in his role.

YORKIS PEREZ

Position: RP
Bats: L **Throws:** L
Ht: 6'0" **Wt:** 180
Opening Day Age: 28
Born: 9/30/1967
Drafted: MIN 2/23/83
ML Seasons: 3

Overall Statistics

	G	GS	GF	SV	W	L	ERA	IP	H	R	ER	HR	BB	SO
95 FLO	69	0	11	1	2	6	5.21	46.2	35	29	27	6	28	47
Career	116	0	22	1	6	6	4.32	91.2	70	48	44	10	44	91

1995 Situational Statistics

	W	L	ERA	SV	IP	BB	SO		AB	HR	RBI	BA	OBA	SLG
Home	1	2	1.67	1	32.1	13	34	LHB	83	3	10	.157	.286	.325
Road	1	4	13.19	0	14.1	15	13	RHB	89	3	13	.247	.352	.449
Apr-Jun	0	2	6.65	1	23.0	17	27	ScPos	50	1	12	.180	.300	.280
Jul-Oct	2	4	3.80	0	23.2	11	20	Clutch	89	4	13	.247	.402	.427

SCOUTING REPORT

The slender southpaw comes from three-quarters with a sinking fastball of now-average velocity which tails into lefthanded hitters. He also features an average slider and forkball.

Quick to home, Yorkis is poor at holding runners. Seven of eight men stole successfully in '95. He is hitless in four career at-bats and is an average fielder.

HOW HE PERFORMED IN '95

Perez' ERA rose by over a run and a half from '94 despite peripheral numbers not that different from those he had posted the year before. Used often for just one or two hitters, Yorkis fell into a quandary—when you pitch to one or two hitters at a time, it's hard to establish consistency, and his control problems sank him.

WHAT TO EXPECT IN '96

Yorkis will be back in the Marlins' bullpen in '96, but if he doesn't learn to get the ball over the plate, he will run out of chances pretty soon. If he does harness his stuff, he could be a very good situational lefty.

FLORIDA MARLINS

JESUS TAVAREZ

Position: OF
Bats: B **Throws:** R
Ht: 6'0" **Wt:** 170
Opening Day Age: 25
Born: 3/26/1971
Drafted: SEA 6/8/89
ML Seasons: 2

Overall Statistics

	G	AB	R	H	2B	3B	HR	RBI	SB	CS	BB	SO	BA	OBA
95 FLO	63	190	31	55	6	2	2	13	7	5	16	27	.289	.346
Career	80	229	35	62	6	2	2	17	8	6	17	32	.271	.323

1995 Situational Statistics

	AB	HR	RBI	BA	OBA	SLG		AB	HR	RBI	BA	OBA	SLG
Home	103	1	9	.301	.348	.408	LHP	24	0	2	.250	.296	.292
Road	87	1	4	.276	.344	.333	RHP	166	2	11	.295	.354	.386
Apr-Jun	39	0	2	.205	.244	.231	ScPos	38	1	12	.395	.467	.500
Jul-Oct	151	2	11	.311	.371	.411	Clutch	34	0	2	.235	.297	.294

SCOUTING REPORT

A line-drive hitter who likes fastballs over the plate, Tavarez has a little power to go with his somewhat above-average speed. His range is acceptable in center but he has a weak arm with minus accuracy.

Although he threw out just one runner all year, Jesus didn't make an error. Although he switch-hits, Tavarez is not going to play much against left-handers.

HOW HE PERFORMED IN '95

Of the four outfield prospects the Marlins took in the expansion draft, three (Carl Everett, Nigel Wilson, and Darrell Whitmore) are now out of the picture. Tavarez remains and was a pleasant surprise for the Marlins at bat in '95, beating out weak-hitting regular Chuck Carr in center field.

Jesus looks to be a decent reserve, with some pop, some speed, and the range to play all three outfield spots.

WHAT TO EXPECT IN '96

With the acquisition of star center fielder Devon White, Tavarez will be a backup in '96. If he gets a break someday, he could play regularly for a few teams and should at least be around for awhile on the bench.

RANDY VERES

Position: RP
Bats: R **Throws:** R
Ht: 6'3" **Wt:** 190
Opening Day Age: 30
Born: 11/25/1965
Drafted: MIL85* S1/2
ML Seasons: 4

Overall Statistics

	G	GS	GF	SV	W	L	ERA	IP	H	R	ER	HR	BB	SO
95 FLO	47	0	15	1	4	4	3.88	48.2	46	25	21	6	22	31
Career	86	1	29	2	5	9	3.99	108.1	105	53	48	14	44	60

1995 Situational Statistics

	W	L	ERA	SV	IP	BB	SO		AB	HR	RBI	BA	OBA	SLG
Home	3	0	3.38	0	21.1	7	17	LHB	65	4	13	.262	.395	.462
Road	1	4	4.28	1	27.1	15	14	RHB	118	2	19	.246	.287	.314
Apr-Jun	2	2	2.42	1	26.0	11	18	ScPos	65	2	27	.308	.402	.400
Jul-Oct	2	2	5.56	0	22.2	11	13	Clutch	67	3	19	.313	.359	.463

SCOUTING REPORT

Basically a two-pitch pitcher, Veres' sinking fastball is a bit above-average in velocity with plus movement. He also depends on a plus curveball, delivered from a three-quarter angle. He has never been able to set up hitters well enough to get strikeouts despite his stuff.

Veres was hitless in three at-bats last year. Five of six runners stole against him in '95 despite an average move to first. He is an average fielder.

HOW HE PERFORMED IN '95

The journeyman righty hung around for most of the season in the Florida bullpen. He wasn't horrible against lefthanders and, although used sparingly, Randy pitched pretty well in every month but August; that month, he was disabled with a cut right hand. A fringe pitcher, Veres has never had particularly good control; he has to be better in that regard than he was in '95 to survive for very long.

WHAT TO EXPECT IN '96

There was talk that Veres had a tired arm late in the year. If he's back this year, he will have to impress in spring training to retain his bullpen job.

FLORIDA MARLINS: TOP PROSPECTS

JOEL ADAMSON
Bats: L Throws: L Opening Day Age: 25
Ht: 6-4 Wt: 180 Born: 7/2/1971
Position: P Drafted: 1990 #7 PHI

YR TEAM	LG/CLASS	G	GS	GF	SV	W	L	ERA	IP	H	HR	BB	SO	O/BA
93 HIGH Desert	CAL/A	22	20	1	0	5	5	4.58	129.2	160	13	30	72	.302
93 Edmonton	PCL/AAA	5	5	0	0	1	2	6.92	26.0	39	5	13	7	.355
94 Portland	EAST/AA	33	11	16	7	5	6	4.34	91.1	95	9	32	59	.265
95 Charlotte	INT/AAA	19	18	0	0	8	4	3.29	115.0	113	12	20	80	.256

The southpaw was acquired from the Phillies in the Danny Jackson deal on the day of the expansion draft in 1992. Despite missing time with shoulder tendinitis, Adamson won a career-high eight games in 1995 and finished fourth in the organization with a 3.29 ERA. The 24-year-old is not overpowering, but held lefthanded hitters to a .214 average last season.

WILSON HEREDIA
Bats: R Throws: R Opening Day Age: 24
Ht: 6-0 Wt: 165 Born: 3/30/1972
Position: P Drafted: NDFA 2-26-90 TEX

YR TEAM	LG/CLASS	G	GS	GF	SV	W	L	ERA	IP	H	HR	BB	SO	O/BA
93 Charlotte	FSL/A	34	0	29	15	1	5	3.72	38.2	30	0	20	26	.217
94 Tulsa	TEX/AA	18	1	5	0	3	2	3.77	43.0	35	6	8	53	.222
95 Okla City	AMAS/AAA	8	7	0	0	1	4	6.82	31.2	40	3	25	21	.317
95 Portland	EAST/AA	4	4	0	0	4	0	2.00	27.0	22	2	14	19	.224
95 Tulsa	TEX/AA	8	7	1	1	4	2	3.18	45.1	42	4	21	34	.251

Heredia was acquired from the Rangers in August for Bobby Witt. The Dominican native has spent most of his career as a reliever, and began the '95 season in the Texas bullpen. He was soon sent to Triple-A, where he struggled as a starter before a June demotion to Double-A. The 23-year-old pitched well for Tulsa, winning four of his last five before the trade. Heredia, assigned to Portland, won all four of his starts as Marlins property. He has a good curveball and mixes his pitches well.

ANDY LARKIN
Bats: R Throws: R Opening Day Age: 22
Ht: 6-4 Wt: 181 Born: 6/27/1974
Position: P Drafted: 1992 #25 FLO

YR TEAM	LG/CLASS	G	GS	GF	SV	W	L	ERA	IP	H	HR	BB	SO	O/BA
93 Elmira	NYP/A	14	14	0	0	5	7	2.97	88.0	74	1	23	89	.225
94 Kane Cty	MID/A	21	21	0	0	9	7	2.83	140.0	125	6	27	125	.238
95 Portland	EAST/AA	9	9	0	0	1	2	3.38	40.0	29	5	11	23	.209

Larkin's 1994 season established him as one of the top hurlers in the system. He jumped over Class-A Brevard County in 1995 and began the season with 14 scoreless innings in his first two starts. Soon after, elbow problems cropped up that disabled him twice and limited him to nine starts all season. The 21-year-old features a 93-mph fastball with good movement, a power curveball, great control, good poise, and an excellent work ethic.

MATT MANTEI
Bats: R Throws: R Opening Day Age: 23
Ht: 6-1 Wt: 181 Born: 7/7/1973
Position: P Drafted: 1991 #25 SEA

YR TEAM	LG/CLASS	G	GS	GF	SV	W	L	ERA	IP	H	HR	BB	SO	O/BA
93 Bellingham	NWST/A	26	0	21	12	1	1	5.96	25.2	26	2	15	34	.260
94 Appleton	MID/A	48	0	43	26	5	1	2.06	48.0	42	2	21	70	.240
95 Charlotte	INT/AAA	6	0	1	0	0	1	2.57	7.0	1	0	5	10	.050
95 Portland	EAST/AA	8	0	4	1	1	0	2.38	11.1	10	0	5	15	.244
95 Florida	NL/MAJ	12	0	3	0	0	1	4.73	13.1	12	1	13	15	.245

Mantei emerged as a power reliever in 1994 in the Seattle system. He placed second in the Midwest League in saves, relief points and SO/9 IP ratio (13.13). After being selected by the Marlins in the Rule 5 draft, the 22-year-old suffered a back injury before the 1995 season and spent some time in the minors rehabbing. He made it to the majors in mid-June, but was shut down in late July with another injury.

BILLY McMILLON
Bats: L Throws: L Opening Day Age: 24
Ht: 5-11 Wt: 172 Born: 11/17/1971
Position: OF Drafted: 1993 #8 FLO

YR TEAM	LG/CLASS	G	AB	R	H	2B	3B	HR	RBI	SB	BA	OBA
93 Elmira	NYP/A	57	226	38	69	14	2	6	35	5	.305	.398
94 Kane Cty	MID/A	137	496	88	125	25	3	17	101	7	.252	.366
95 Portland	EAST/AA	141	518	92	162	29	3	14	93	15	.313	.423

After leading the Midwest League in RBI and walks in 1994, the Clemson product went on to have an All-Star season in Double-A in '95. He led the organization in homers and RBI, paced the Eastern League in hits and on-base percentage and finished third in average, and tied for third in the minor leagues with 96 walks. The 23-year-old really poured it on in the second half, batting .338 after June 1. The lefthanded swinger hit .332 with 12 homers against righthanded pitchers. Although McMillon is good hitter with a sweet swing, he is a below-average outfielder who has difficulty reading flyballs.

KURT MILLER
Bats: R Throws: R Opening Day Age: 24
Ht: 6-5 Wt: 200 Born: 8/24/1972
Position: P Drafted: 1990 #1 PIT

YR TEAM	LG/CLASS	G	GS	GF	SV	W	L	ERA	IP	H	HR	BB	SO	O/BA
93 Tulsa	TEX/AA	18	18	0	0	6	8	5.06	96.0	102	8	45	68	.268
93 Edmonton	PCL/AAA	9	9	0	0	3	3	4.50	48.0	42	2	34	19	.258
94 Edmonton	PCL/AAA	23	23	0	0	7	13	6.88	125.2	164	18	64	58	.318
94 Florida	NL/MAJ	4	4	0	0	1	3	8.10	20.0	26	3	7	11	.317
95 Charlotte	INT/AAA	22	22	0	0	8	11	4.62	126.2	143	13	55	83	.290

A former Pirates first-round pick, Miller was traded to the Rangers in 1991 and then to the Marlins in 1993. Although he has great stuff and a textbook power-pitcher delivery, Miller has been a disappointment. Early in his career, he appeared to be on the fast track to the majors, going 21-18, 2.93 ERA in his first three years with the Pirates and Rangers. However, he has not been the same pitcher since, with a poor 25-38 mark and a 5.56 ERA from 1993–95. The 23-year-old got off to a good start in '95, posting a 2.31 ERA through the end of May, but his ERA was 5.56 the rest of the year.

FLORIDA MARLINS: TOP PROSPECTS

RALPH MILLIARD
Bats: R Throws: R Opening Day Age: 22
Ht: 5-10 Wt: 160 Born: 12/30/1973
Position: 2B Drafted: NDFA 7-26-92 FLO

YR TEAM	LG/CLASS	G	AB	R	H	2B	3B	HR	RBI	SB	BA	OBA
93 Marlins	GULF/R	53	192	35	45	15	0	0	25	11	.234	.354
94 Kane Cty	MID/A	133	515	97	153	34	2	8	67	10	.297	.384
95 Portland	EAST/AA	128	464	104	124	22	3	11	40	22	.267	.393

The exciting 21-year-old native of Curacao (in the Caribbean) has drawn comparisons to Willie Randolph. He has a good glove and fine range, although his instincts aren't up to those of the Yankee All-Star. In 1994, Milliard led the Midwest League in runs and finished among the league leaders in several other categories. He had an All-Star year in 1995, as his 104 runs led the Eastern League and were the fourth most in the minors, but he struggled the second half after changing his game to aim for home runs. He also compiled a team-record 19-game hitting streak.

JAY POWELL
Bats: R Throws: R Opening Day Age: 24
Ht: 6-4 Wt: 220 Born: 1/9/1972
Position: P Drafted: 1993 #1 BAL

YR TEAM	LG/CLASS	G	GS	GF	SV	W	L	ERA	IP	H	HR	BB	SO	O/BA
93 Albany	SAL/A	6	6	0	0	0	2	4.55	27.2	29	0	13	29	.274
94 Frederick	CARO/A	26	20	2	1	7	7	4.96	123.1	132	13	54	87	.269
95 Portland	EAST/AA	50	0	44	24	5	4	1.87	53.0	42	2	15	53	.219
95 Florida	NL/MAJ	9	0	1	0	0	0	1.08	8.1	7	0	6	4	.241

The Mississippi product was the Orioles' first pick in 1993, but was slow to develop as a starting pitcher and was dealt to Florida in 1994 for Bret Barberie. In '95, Powell was converted to a closer, scrapped his curve, and used his mid-90s-mph sinking fastball and 88 mph power slider to dominate Eastern League hitters. The Double-A All-Star led the league in saves and was extremely tough on righthanders, holding them to a .181 average. If you subtract Powell's two bad outings, his seasonal ERA would have been 0.70; this is one reason he was named the organization's Pitcher of the Year.

EDGAR RENTERIA
Bats: R Throws: R Opening Day Age: 21
Ht: 6-1 Wt: 172 Born: 8/7/1975
Position: SS Drafted: NDFA 1-14-92 FLO

YR TEAM	LG/CLASS	G	AB	R	H	2B	3B	HR	RBI	SB	BA	OBA
93 Kane County	MID/A	116	384	40	78	8	0	1	35	7	.203	.268
94 Brevard Cty	FSL/A	128	439	46	111	15	1	0	36	5	.253	.307
95 Portland	EAST/AA	135	508	70	147	15	7	7	68	30	.289	.329

The 20-year-old from Colombia was the Marlin's 1995 organization Player of the Year and teamed with Ralph Milliard to form one of the best middle infield combinations in the minors. Renteria, the youngest player in the Eastern League, placed fourth in the loop in hits and stolen bases. He is built like Tony Fernandez and plays like him in the field, with plus range, quick feet, outstanding instincts and a strong arm. He also has some pop in his bat, although with his speed, he may be better served by hitting more balls on the ground.

MARC VALDES
Bats: R Throws: R Opening Day Age: 24
Ht: 6-0 Wt: 170 Born: 12/20/1971
Position: P Drafted: 1993 #1 FLO

YR TEAM	LG/CLASS	G	GS	GF	SV	W	L	ERA	IP	H	HR	BB	SO	O/BA
93 Elmira	NYP/A	3	3	0	0	0	2	5.59	9.2	8	0	7	15	.222
94 Kane Cty	MID/A	11	11	0	0	7	4	2.95	76.1	62	3	21	68	.221
94 Portland	EAST/AA	15	15	0	0	8	4	2.55	99.0	77	5	39	70	.214
95 Charlotte	INT/AAA	27	27	0	0	9	13	4.86	170.1	189	19	59	104	.291
95 Florida	NL/MAJ	3	3	0	0	0	0	14.14	7.0	17	1	9	2	.459

Valdes, Florida's first pick in 1993, had a great year at two levels in 1994, finishing with a 15-8 record. The 23-year-old advanced to Charlotte last year after just 15 Double-A starts but had a down season, losing six straight starts at one point, allowing plenty of hits and leading his league in losses. On the positive side, Valdes was a workhorse, finishing fourth in the International League in innings, and put together three consecutive strong starts in August that got him a promotion to the parent club in September. Valdes throws an above-average sinking fastball, a hard slider, and a changeup. The key to his success is keeping the ball down to induce ground balls.

MATT WHISENANT
Bats: S Throws: L Opening Day Age: 25
Ht: 6-3 Wt: 215 Born: 6/8/1971
Position: P Drafted: 1989 #18 PHI

YR TEAM	LG/CLASS	G	GS	GF	SV	W	L	ERA	IP	H	HR	BB	SO	O/BA
93 Kane Cty	MID/A	15	15	0	0	2	6	4.69	71.0	68	3	56	74	.260
94 Brevard Cty	FSL/A	28	26	0	0	6	9	3.38	160.0	125	7	82	103	.218
95 Portland	EAST/AA	23	22	0	0	10	6	3.50	128.2	106	8	65	107	.231

The big southpaw is a strikeout pitcher but often struggles with his control. He has always been tough to hit; his lifetime opponents' batting average is .224. Whisenant had a solid year in 1995, finishing fourth in the organization in wins and strikeouts and sixth in ERA. He was murder on lefties, holding them to a .160 average. If the 24-year-old can improve his control, he should become a bona fide big league starter.

DARRELL WHITMORE
Bats: L Throws: R Opening Day Age: 27
Ht: 6-1 Wt: 210 Born: 11/18/1968
Position: OF Drafted: 1990 #3 CLE

YR TEAM	LG/CLASS	G	AB	R	H	2B	3B	HR	RBI	SB	BA	OBA
93 Edmonton	PCL/AAA	73	273	52	97	24	2	9	62	11	.355	.399
93 Florida	NL/MAJ	76	250	24	51	8	2	4	19	4	.204	.249
94 Edmonton	PCL/AAA	115	421	72	119	24	5	20	61	14	.283	.347
94 Florida	NL/MAJ	9	22	1	5	1	0	0	0	0	.227	.320
95 Florida	NL/MAJ	27	58	6	11	2	0	1	2	0	.190	.250

Whitmore was selected from the Indians in the expansion draft and soon was regarded as a potential impact player after a few solid years in the organization. However, the .295 career hitter has not been able to hit in three stints the major league level and the 26-year-old former West Virginia defensive back missed much of '95 with a shoulder problem.

FLORIDA MARLINS: OTHERS TO WATCH

ANTONIO ALFONSECA   Bats: R   Throws: R   Ht: 6-4   Wt: 160
Born: 4/16/1972   Drafted: NDFA 7-3-89 MON   Position: P

YR TEAM	LG/CLASS	G	GS	GF	SV	W	L	ERA	IP	H	HR	BB	SO	O/BA
95 Portland	EAST/AA	19	17	0	0	9	3	3.64	96.1	81	6	42	75	.229

The Dominican-native is best known for having 12 fingers and toes, but in the future he may be better known for his 92 mph fastball and wicked slider.

LUIS CASTILLO   Bats: S   Throws: R   Ht: 5-11   Wt: 146
Born: 9/12/1975   Drafted: NDFA 8-19-92 FLO   Position: 2B

YR TEAM	LG/CLASS	G	AB	R	H	2B	3B	HR	RBI	SB	BA	OBA
95 Kane County	MID/A	89	340	71	111	4	4	0	23	41	.326	.419

The 20-year-old has all the tools except power and plays second base like a shortstop, but he missed the second half with a separated left shoulder.

WILL CUNNANE   Bats: R   Throws: R   Ht: 6-2   Wt: 165
Born: 4/24/1974   Drafted: NDFA 8-31-92 FLO   Position: P

YR TEAM	LG/CLASS	G	GS	GF	SV	W	L	ERA	IP	H	HR	BB	SO	O/BA
95 Portland	EAST/AA	21	21	0	0	9	2	3.67	117.2	120	10	34	83	.264

A non-drafted free agent in 1992, the 21-year-old is a hard thrower with great control and a 23-8 career record with a 2.51 ERA.

TODD DUNWOODY   Bats: L   Throws: L   Ht: 6-2   Wt: 185
Born: 4/11/1975   Drafted: 1993 #7 FLO   Position: OF

YR TEAM	LG/CLASS	G	AB	R	H	2B	3B	HR	RBI	SB	BA	OBA
95 Kane Cty	MID/A	132	494	89	140	20	8	14	89	39	.283	.355

Dunwoody, a Midwest League All-Star, is a five-tool talent who finished among the organization leaders in the triple crown categories, but hit only .180 after August 1.

LOU LUCCA   Bats: R   Throws: R   Ht: 5-11   Wt: 210
Born: 10/13/1970   Drafted: 1992 #32 FLO   Position: 3B

YR TEAM	LG/CLASS	G	AB	R	H	2B	3B	HR	RBI	SB	BA	OBA
95 Portland	EAST/AA	112	388	57	107	28	1	9	64	4	.276	.377

The Oklahoma State product, who has an unusual but effective throwing motion, is a good third baseman who hits for average with doubles power.

BRIAN MEADOWS   Bats: R   Throws: R   Ht: 6-4   Wt: 210
Born: 11/21/1975   Drafted: 1994 #4 FLO   Position: P

YR TEAM	LG/CLASS	G	GS	GF	SV	W	L	ERA	IP	H	HR	BB	SO	O/BA
95 Kane County	MID/A	26	26	0	0	9	9	4.22	147.0	163	11	41	103	.281

The highly-regarded 19-year-old power pitcher has a great curve, but was less dominant in his first full season than he was in rookie ball in 1994.

REYNOL MENDOZA   Bats: R   Throws: R   Ht: 6-0   Wt: 215
Born: 10/27/1970   Drafted: 1992 #7 FLO   Position: P

YR TEAM	LG/CLASS	G	GS	GF	SV	W	L	ERA	IP	H	HR	BB	SO	O/BA
95 Portland	EAST/AA	27	27	0	0	9	10	3.43	168.0	163	6	69	120	.262

A groundball pitcher who is not overpowering, Mendoza placed second in the system in strikeouts and fifth in ERA.

KEVIN MILLAR   Bats: R   Throws: R   Ht: 6-1   Wt: 195
Born: 9/24/1971   Drafted: Position: 1B

YR TEAM	LG/CLASS	G	AB	R	H	2B	3B	HR	RBI	SB	BA	OBA
95 Brevard Cty	FSL/A	129	459	53	132	32	2	13	68	4	.288	.388

Millar is a dead pull hitter with a compact swing and good power.

CLEMENTE NUNEZ   Bats: R   Throws: R   Ht: 5-11   Wt: 181
Born: 2/10/1975   Drafted: NDFA 12-10-91 FLO   Position: P

YR TEAM	LG/CLASS	G	GS	GF	SV	W	L	ERA	IP	H	HR	BB	SO	O/BA
95 Brevard Cty	FSL/A	19	19	0	0	12	6	2.48	123.1	99	3	22	79	.216

Nunez, the starting pitcher in the Florida State League All-Star game, is not overpowering, but led the organization in wins and ERA and threw a no-hitter before missing most of the second half with shoulder stiffness.

VICTOR RODRIGUEZ   Bats: R   Throws: R   Ht: 6-2   Wt: 185
Born: 10/25/1976   Drafted: 1994 #2 FLO   Position: SS

YR TEAM	LG/CLASS	G	AB	R	H	2B	3B	HR	RBI	SB	BA	OBA
95 Kane Cty	MID/A	127	472	65	111	9	1	0	43	18	.235	.295

A second-round pick from Puerto Rico in 1994, Rodriguez is a contact hitter with no power, but is a vacuum cleaner at shortstop.

JOHNNY ROSKOS   Bats: R   Throws: R   Ht: 5-11   Wt: 198
Born: 11/19/1974   Drafted: 1993 #2 FLO   Position: C

YR TEAM	LG/CLASS	G	AB	R	H	2B	3B	HR	RBI	SB	BA	OBA
95 Kane Cty	MID/A	114	418	74	124	36	3	12	88	2	.297	.364

Roskos is still learning the finer points of catching, but he hits for average, drives in runs and legged out 36 doubles in '95.

CHRIS SHEFF   Bats: R   Throws: R   Ht: 6-3   Wt: 210
Born: 2/4/1971   Drafted: 1992 #10 FLO   Position: OF

YR TEAM	LG/CLASS	G	AB	R	H	2B	3B	HR	RBI	SB	BA	OBA
95 Portland	EAST/AA	131	471	85	130	25	7	12	91	23	.276	.372

The Pepperdine product had his most productive year at the plate in 1995 and is a 80% basestealer over his career, but he needs to pull the ball more to realize his power potential.

AARON SMALL   Bats: R   Throws: R   Ht: 6-5   Wt: 200
Born: 11/23/1971   Drafted: 1989 #23 TOR   Position: P

YR TEAM	LG/CLASS	G	GS	GF	SV	W	L	ERA	IP	H	HR	BB	SO	O/BA
95 Syracuse	INT/AAA	1	0	0	0	0	0	5.40	1.2	3	1	1	2	.375
95 Charlotte	INT/AAA	33	0	17	10	2	1	2.88	40.2	36	2	10	31	.229
95 Florida	NL/MAJ	7	0	1	0	1	0	1.42	6.1	7	1	6	5	.269

The former Blue Jays farm hand, who has a live arm, notched ten saves for Charlotte in '95 and posted a 2.10 ERA after July 1.

BRYAN WARD   Bats: L   Throws: L   Ht: 6-2   Wt: 210
Born: 1/28/1972   Drafted: 1993 #20 FLO   Position: P

YR TEAM	LG/CLASS	G	GS	GF	SV	W	L	ERA	IP	H	HR	BB	SO	O/BA
95 Portland	EAST/AA	20	11	5	2	7	3	4.50	72.0	70	9	31	71	.245
95 Brevard Cty	FSL/A	11	11	0	0	5	1	2.88	72.0	68	5	17	65	.249

The lefthander led the organization in wins and strikeouts and pitched much better at home (1.67 ERA) than on the road (5.90 ERA).

EDDIE ZOSKY   Bats: R   Throws: R   Ht: 6-0   Wt: 175
Born: 2/10/1968   Drafted: 1989 #1 TOR   Position: SS

YR TEAM	LG/CLASS	G	AB	R	H	2B	3B	HR	RBI	SB	BA	OBA
95 Charlotte	INT/AAA	92	312	27	77	15	2	3	42	2	.247	.265
95 Florida	NL/MAJ	6	5	0	1	0	0	0	0	0	.200	.200

Once thought to be Toronto's shortstop of the future, Zosky's future in the big leagues is as a utility man.

HOUSTON ASTROS

JEFF BAGWELL

Position: 1B
Bats: R **Throws:** R
Ht: 6'0" **Wt:** 195
Opening Day Age: 27
Born: 5/27/1968
Drafted: BOS89 6/110
ML Seasons: 5

SCOUTING REPORT

Although Bagwell was unable to repeat his outstanding '94, his abilities didn't change. An plus hitter across the board, Jeff doesn't swing at many bad pitches, even while slumping. He has good power, knows the strike zone well and hits with punch to all fields. Jeff likes pitches both up and over the plate and down and in. Despite slightly below-average speed, Bagwell runs intelligently and uses surprise to be an effective base stealer.

Bagwell has worked hard to become one of the NL's top defensive first basemen. His range and hands are above-average and he is very aggressive when fielding bunts. (Sometimes, he ends up on the third base side of the mound.) In addition, his arm and accuracy are slightly above-average.

HOW HE PERFORMED IN '95

After a monstrous '94, which culminated in a MVP award, Bagwell couldn't get untracked for the first two months of '95. His rather unorthodox batting stance, the long layoff caused by the strike, and the lack of a full spring training all conspired against him, and Jeff was hitting .183 on May 31. However, he soon regained his stroke, knocking in 31 runs during July to set an Astros' monthly record.

As usual, he spent time on the disabled list. For the third straight year, he suffered a broken right hand: this time, Brian Williams nailed him with a pitch on July 30. After missing all of August, Jeff returned outfitted with a special pad to protect the oft-injured hand. The pad was successfully tested when Bagwell was plunked by Xavier Hernandez. Being hit by pitches is part of the risk Jeff takes with his aggressive swing.

Bagwell's lack of early-season hitting success did not affect the other facets of his game: One of Jeff's strongest attributes is that he does not get down on himself if he's slumping. For the fourth straight year, he stole over ten bases, and he finished second in Gold Glove voting.

WHAT TO EXPECT IN '96

While it will be difficult to duplicate the year he had in '94, a full spring of preparation should help Bagwell return to prominence as one of the game's top offensive players. However, the risk of permanent damage to his hand is significant, and it will be a surprise if he can ever play 160 games again in a season.

Overall Statistics

	G	AB	R	H	2B	3B	HR	RBI	SB	CS	BB	SO	BA	OBA
95 HOU	114	448	88	130	29	0	21	87	12	5	79	102	.290	.399
Career	684	2523	434	771	158	16	113	469	57	23	365	453	.306	.395

1995 Situational Statistics

	AB	HR	RBI	BA	OBA	SLG		AB	HR	RBI	BA	OBA	SLG
Home	221	10	41	.285	.408	.489	LHP	84	2	15	.298	.439	.440
Road	227	11	46	.295	.390	.502	RHP	364	19	72	.288	.389	.508
Apr-Jun	224	9	35	.259	.371	.446	ScPos	137	5	62	.270	.421	.423
Jul-Oct	224	12	52	.321	.426	.545	Clutch	76	4	15	.276	.421	.474

How He Compares to Other Batters

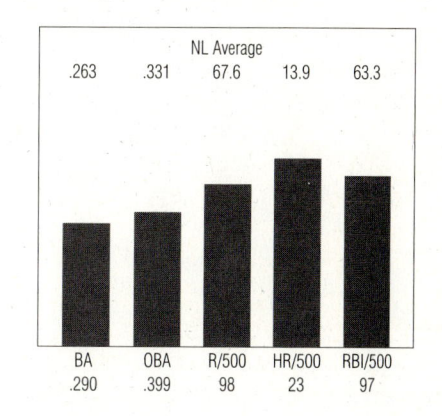

NL Average: .263 .331 67.6 13.9 63.3

BA	OBA	R/500	HR/500	RBI/500
.290	.399	98	23	97

Where He Hits the Ball

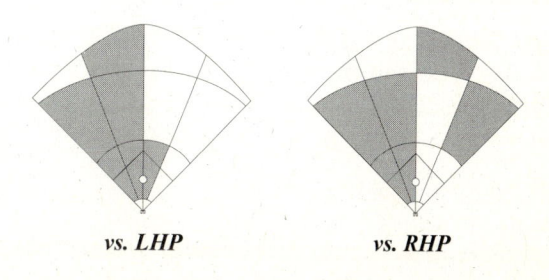

vs. LHP   vs. RHP

THE SCOUTING REPORT: 1996

HOUSTON ASTROS

DEREK BELL

Position: OF
Bats: R **Throws:** R
Ht: 6'2" **Wt:** 200
Opening Day Age: 27
Born: 12/11/1968
Drafted: TOR87 2/49
ML Seasons: 5

SCOUTING REPORT

Despite years of experience in center field, Bell was used almost exclusively by the Astros as a right fielder during '95. While his range and hands are slightly above-average, Derek's arm strength and accuracy are only average.

The free-swinging Bell has slightly above-average power. He likes pitches down and on the inside half of the plate. Overall, Bell is an average-plus hitter who has worked on shortening his stroke when he has two strikes on him.

Derek is an above-average runner and a very good basestealer who can take the extra base without much trouble. Although he's fast enough to bunt for hits, he doesn't lay the ball down.

HOW HE PERFORMED IN '95

Bell provided much-needed offensive punch for the Astros, setting career highs in batting average and RBI as he took over the cleanup spot. However, his extra-base pop was clearly not enough for him to bat fourth regularly.

He was, however, a model of consistency, hitting over .300 every month of the season. Going back to '94, Derek has now hit over .300 for eight consecutive months. He tied Jeff Bagwell for the new club record, batting in 31 runs during July.

Although Derek is far from being a patient hitter, he has become smarter, cutting his strikeouts each of the last two years after whiffing 122 times in '93. While Bell hit 35 homers in 1993-94, he concentrated on putting the ball in play during '95. That contact approach sliced his power but created more productive at-bats. Sometimes, Derek even changed bats during plate appearances if he felt the pitcher's approach had varied.

Derek has speed and range more than adequate for right field, but how best to utilize his strengths poses a quandary. He doesn't have a right fielder's arm, does not hit for extra bases, and rarely walks.

WHAT TO EXPECT IN '96

Bell missed the final month of '95 with a torn thigh muscle but should be fully recovered for the start of '96. With his maturity as a hitter, another fine season is not unlikely. However, Derek may have trouble improving his power production in the spacious Astrodome. Houston has to put some thought into how best to use Bell, a talented but incomplete player.

Overall Statistics

	G	AB	R	H	2B	3B	HR	RBI	SB	CS	BB	SO	BA	OBA
95 HOU	112	452	63	151	21	2	8	86	27	9	33	71	.334	.385
Career	449	1617	218	471	66	6	45	228	87	26	106	320	.291	.342

1995 Situational Statistics

	AB	HR	RBI	BA	OBA	SLG		AB	HR	RBI	BA	OBA	SLG
Home	219	3	33	.306	.379	.374	LHP	100	2	28	.410	.455	.510
Road	233	5	53	.361	.390	.506	RHP	352	6	58	.313	.365	.423
Apr-Jun	233	3	44	.343	.391	.442	ScPos	152	2	78	.309	.373	.428
Jul-Oct	219	5	42	.324	.379	.443	Clutch	74	1	12	.297	.349	.378

How He Compares to Other Batters

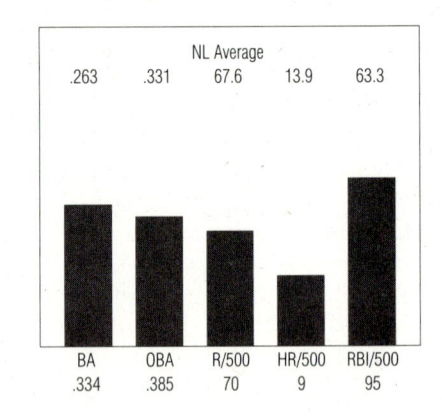

NL Average
.263 .331 67.6 13.9 63.3

BA OBA R/500 HR/500 RBI/500
.334 .385 70 9 95

Where He Hits the Ball

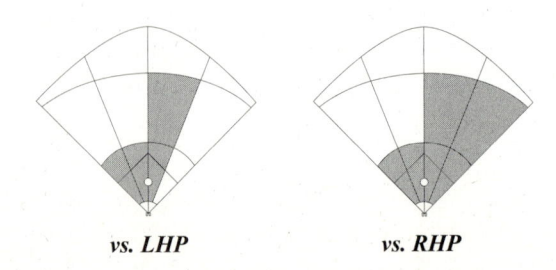

vs. LHP   vs. RHP

HOUSTON ASTROS

CRAIG BIGGIO

Position: 2B
Bats: R **Throws:** R
Ht: 5'11" **Wt:** 185
Opening Day Age: 30
Born: 12/14/1965
Drafted: HOU87 1/22
ML Seasons: 8

SCOUTING REPORT

Biggio is one of the top defensive second basemen in the National League. He has above-average hands and range, which he augments with average-plus arm strength and throwing accuracy. Over the past few years, Craig has improved in the field and won his second Gold Glove last season.

Biggio is also one of the loop's top offensive players. An plus hitter with a discerning eye, he likes both breaking balls and fastballs up and over the plate. Mostly a line-drive hitter in his early years, Craig has now developed significant home run pop. Although he is an aggressive runner with good smarts on the bases, his speed is only slightly above-average.

HOW HE PERFORMED IN '95

The '95 season was an exceptional one for the NL's All-Star second baseman. Craig paced the league in runs and was among the league leaders in walks, on-base percentage, hits, and stolen bases. In addition, Biggio has perfected the art of being hit by pitches, leading the league and setting a club record by being plunked 22 times.

Craig ranks as one of the top leadoff hitters in the game with his outstanding ability to reach base and his fine baserunning. However, Brian Hunter's arrival meant that Biggio spent most of the season batting second. In that role, Craig demonstrated good hit-and-run ability. In addition, his power made him an effective third-place hitter.

Although Biggio was hampered most of the season by an assortment of nagging leg injuries, he played in almost every game, as usual. He stole over 30 bases for the third time, leading the Astros in that category for the second straight year, and showed broad-based development in several areas.

WHAT TO EXPECT IN '96

Biggio signed a lucrative, multi-year deal with the Astros after being the most sought-after position player on the market in the off-season. Considering the club's financial instability, Craig's presence means a great deal towards ensuring the future of baseball in Houston. His performance might not again scale the heights of '95, but Biggio should remain one of the best infielders in the game.

Overall Statistics

	G	AB	R	H	2B	3B	HR	RBI	SB	CS	BB	SO	BA	OBA
95 HOU	141	553	123	167	30	2	22	77	33	8	80	85	.302	.406
Career	1055	3880	615	1105	221	24	79	389	196	65	475	574	.285	.369

1995 Situational Statistics

	AB	HR	RBI	BA	OBA	SLG		AB	HR	RBI	BA	OBA	SLG
Home	265	6	31	.275	.402	.411	LHP	107	7	18	.383	.493	.626
Road	288	16	46	.326	.411	.549	RHP	446	15	59	.283	.384	.448
Apr-Jun	220	7	32	.273	.395	.441	ScPos	146	4	51	.260	.365	.370
Jul-Oct	333	15	45	.321	.414	.511	Clutch	109	2	13	.284	.376	.394

How He Compares to Other Batters

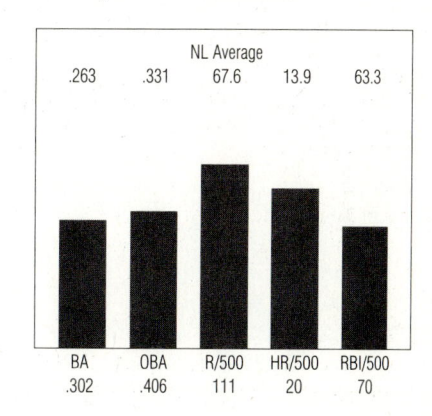

NL Average: BA .263, OBA .331, R/500 67.6, HR/500 13.9, RBI/500 63.3

Biggio: BA .302, OBA .406, R/500 111, HR/500 20, RBI/500 70

Where He Hits the Ball

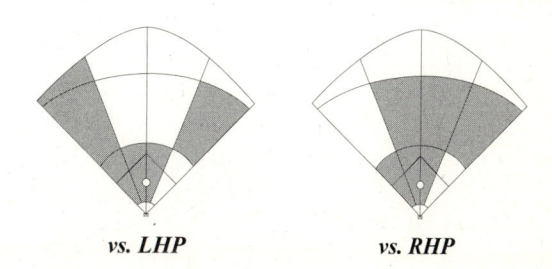

vs. LHP   vs. RHP

THE SCOUTING REPORT: 1996

HOUSTON ASTROS

DOUG DRABEK

Position: SP
Bats: R **Throws:** R
Ht: 6'1" **Wt:** 185
Opening Day Age: 33
Born: 7/25/1962
Drafted: CHA83 11/279
ML Seasons: 10

SCOUTING REPORT

Drabek is no longer the pitcher he was with Pittsburgh a few seasons ago, but he still puts in a good day's work on the mound. He never had great velocity, but always used his intelligence and guile to retire National League hitters.

However, experience and craft can only go so far when your pitches are declining. Doug throws from three-quarters but his two-seam fastball is now rated as a slightly below-average pitch. He has three other pitches, all rated average: a curve, slider and change-up. Drabek's curve, in particular, has declined sharply.

The former Cy Young award winner still helps himself out on the mound with his good fielding. Although Doug is rated slightly above-average at holding runners, a high total of 31 men tried to steal bases against him last year, with 21 of them being successful.

HOW HE PERFORMED IN '95

Drabek followed a fine '94 season with a disappointing '95. He has now pitched poorly in two of his three campaigns in Houston and had a miserable 5.74 ERA on the road last year. His earned run average was the worst in his career and his innings per start fell a full inning from his average of the previous five years.

On the positive side, Doug fashioned a strikeout-to-walk ratio that matched his career average, he doesn't seem to have been injured, and he still possesses one of the best work ethics in the NL. However, even though he was able to win ten games, Drabek was inconsistent all year and has apparently been replaced as the staff ace by Shane Reynolds.

Doug had an excellent year at the plate, hitting .233 average with eight sacs and leading Astros' pitchers with eight RBI. He is now a .164 career hitter in 658 at-bats.

WHAT TO EXPECT IN '96

Drabek is no longer thought of as Houston's best starting pitcher. He has a guaranteed contract through 1996 with a club option for 1997. With the Astros' stated desire to pare down the payroll and the emergence of several young pitchers, Houston may attempt to move Doug in the off-season. If not, he could be traded during the year if the club falls out of contention early. He is still capable of being a #2 starter for many clubs.

Overall Statistics

	G	GS	GF	SV	W	L	ERA	IP	H	R	ER	HR	BB	SO
95 HOU	31	31	0	0	10	9	4.77	185.0	205	104	98	18	54	143
Career	314	305	3	0	130	103	3.32	2081.2	1932	840	767	175	546	1317

1995 Situational Statistics

	W	L	ERA	SV	IP	BB	SO		AB	HR	RBI	BA	OBA	SLG
Home	4	6	3.95	0	100.1	27	91	LHB	380	10	44	.289	.344	.439
Road	6	3	5.74	0	84.2	27	52	RHB	348	8	52	.273	.329	.414
Apr-Jun	4	5	4.62	0	76.0	29	69	ScPos	179	4	72	.341	.429	.508
Jul-Oct	6	4	4.87	0	109.0	25	74	Clutch	30	1	1	.133	.235	.267

How He Compares to Other Pitchers

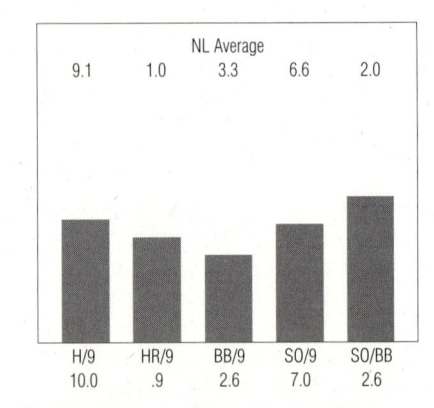

NL Average: H/9 9.1, HR/9 1.0, BB/9 3.3, SO/9 6.6, SO/BB 2.0

H/9 10.0, HR/9 .9, BB/9 2.6, SO/9 7.0, SO/BB 2.6

How He Compares to Other Starting Pitchers

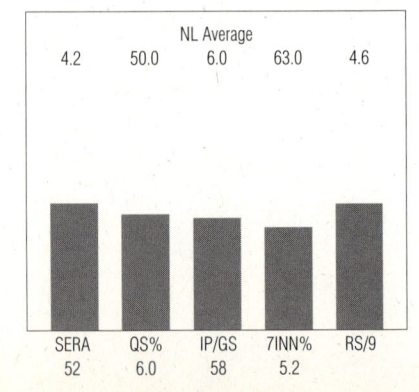

NL Average: SERA 4.2, QS% 50.0, IP/GS 6.0, 7INN% 63.0, RS/9 4.6

SERA 52, QS% 6.0, IP/GS 58, 7INN% 5.2

HOUSTON ASTROS

TONY EUSEBIO

Position: C
Bats: R **Throws:** R
Ht: 6'2" **Wt:** 180
Opening Day Age: 28
Born: 4/27/1967
Drafted: HOU 5/30/85
ML Seasons: 3

SCOUTING REPORT
Eusebio is an average hitter who likes the fastball down and will often go to the opposite field against lefthanders. Although his power and power production are only average, Eusebio gets in his cuts and does not get cheated at the plate. He reminds some scouts of former Pirates' receiver Manny Sanguillen.

Tony has average speed that makes him one of the faster catchers in the league, but he isn't much of a threat to steal.

Make no mistake about it—Eusebio won the catcher's spot with his bat, not his glove. Behind the plate, his mobility and his hands earn only an average rating. While Tony has a strong arm, he is not polished defensively; due to a mediocre release, he rates only average in arm strength and accuracy.

HOW HE PERFORMED IN '95
It's taken nine years of pro ball to do it, but Eusebio has finally shown he can handle an everyday catching assignment in the major leagues. After coming to spring training out of shape, Tony began the season sharing playing time with Scott Servais. However, Eusebio soon won the starting job as he demonstrated that his .296 average of '94 was no fluke, and Servais was traded to Chicago in late June.

Eusebio hit .327 in May, .338 in June and .333 in July. He tired late in the season, however, as the Astros were unable to find even an adequate back-up catcher.

Despite his opposite-field ability, Tony has good power and was fourth on the team in runs batted in. He was one of Houston's top pinch-hitters, tallying seven hits with six RBI and one home run in 16 at-bats. However, hitting the ball hard isn't always good; Tony also grounded into a team-high 12 double plays.

The league doesn't seem to respect Eusebio's arm yet. Fully 95 baserunners, a very high total, ran against him; Tony threw out 29 of them (31%).

WHAT TO EXPECT IN '96
Eusebio is a solid offensive player, which should guarantee him a majority of the playing time in '96. His ability to drive in runs helps offset his defensive liabilities, but he will have to improve behind the plate in order to be regarded as an above-average player overall.

Overall Statistics

	G	AB	R	H	2B	3B	HR	RBI	SB	CS	BB	SO	BA	OBA
95 HOU	113	368	46	110	21	1	6	58	0	2	31	59	.299	.354
Career	178	546	68	159	31	2	11	88	0	3	45	100	.291	.343

1995 Situational Statistics

	AB	HR	RBI	BA	OBA	SLG		AB	HR	RBI	BA	OBA	SLG
Home	182	5	28	.286	.332	.423	LHP	88	1	13	.273	.323	.386
Road	186	1	30	.312	.374	.398	RHP	280	5	45	.307	.363	.418
Apr-Jun	128	2	25	.328	.371	.438	ScPos	115	2	51	.313	.378	.452
Jul-Oct	240	4	33	.283	.345	.396	Clutch	78	2	15	.321	.364	.474

How He Compares to Other Batters

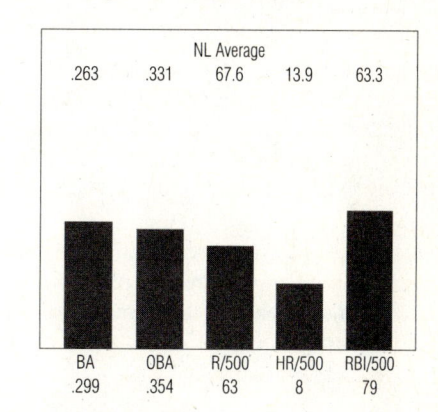

NL Average
.263 .331 67.6 13.9 63.3

BA   OBA   R/500 HR/500 RBI/500
.299 .354 63   8   79

Where He Hits the Ball

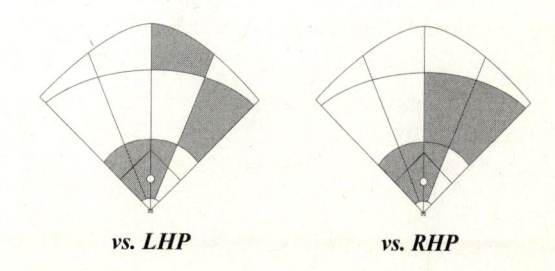

vs. LHP   vs. RHP

THE SCOUTING REPORT: 1996

HOUSTON ASTROS

MIKE HAMPTON

Position: SP
Bats: R **Throws:** L
Ht: 5'10" **Wt:** 180
Opening Day Age: 23
Born: 9/9/1972
Drafted: SEA90 6/161
ML Seasons: 3

SCOUTING REPORT
Finesse lefty Mike Hampton uses a three-quarter delivery and a four-pitch arsenal. Hampton's out pitch is an average slider, which he sets up with two of his better offerings - a curve and a change-up, both slightly above-average. Mike also throws a sinking two-seam fastball, currently slightly below-average in velocity.

Hampton is a bit above-average as a fielder. He needs to improve his ability to hold baserunners, as 18 of 24 basestealing attempts were successful against Hampton, high numbers for a lefthander.

HOW HE PERFORMED IN '95
Hampton began the season as the Astros' biggest question mark in the starting rotation, but soon established himself as one of the most dependable and effective pitchers on the staff.

The former Mariners' pitcher, who came to Houston in trade for the now-nearly forgotten Eric Anthony, spent '94 as a middle reliever before moving into the rotation last season. Coming into '95, Hampton had made just 19 starts above Class A, but he took to his new assignment with panache.

Consistent work allowed Mike to improve his control: he cut his walks per nine innings to three, an improvement of more than two walks from his previous career average. He also had the lowest opponents' batting average of any Houston starter.

Not everything was rosy. Hampton did have a slump in August, allowing 16 runs in a 25-inning span, and pitched much more effectively in Houston than on the road. In the dome, he allowed just a .238 average and three homers; in road games, it was .254 and 10 dingers.

Hampton is an inexperienced hitter. However, he is an aggressive baserunner and has the speed to take the extra base. He led the staff with seven runs scored and batted a respectable .146 (7-for-48), although he only laid down four sacrifice bunts.

WHAT TO EXPECT IN '96
Hampton demonstrated remarkable maturity in his first full season as a starter, showing outstanding knowledge of how to pitch for someone of his age and his experience. He is only 23 years old and, assuming he continues to improve, Mike should be a solid performer with Houston for years to come. Obviously, he's lucky to be pitching in the friendly Astrodome.

Overall Statistics

	G	GS	GF	SV	W	L	ERA	IP	H	R	ER	HR	BB	SO
95 HOU	24	24	0	0	9	8	3.35	150.2	141	73	56	13	49	115
Career	81	27	9	1	12	12	3.92	209.0	215	112	91	20	82	147

1995 Situational Statistics

	W	L	ERA	SV	IP	BB	SO		AB	HR	RBI	BA	OBA	SLG
Home	4	4	2.47	0	80.0	22	71	LHB	114	3	14	.272	.341	.412
Road	5	4	4.33	0	70.2	27	44	RHB	458	10	46	.240	.300	.352
Apr-Jun	2	3	2.08	0	43.1	10	37	ScPos	141	5	47	.227	.301	.383
Jul-Oct	7	5	3.86	0	107.1	39	78	Clutch	30	0	1	.233	.281	.233

How He Compares to Other Pitchers

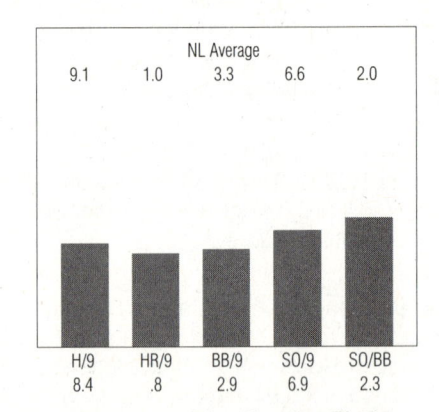

NL Average: H/9 9.1, HR/9 1.0, BB/9 3.3, SO/9 6.6, SO/BB 2.0
Hampton: H/9 8.4, HR/9 .8, BB/9 2.9, SO/9 6.9, SO/BB 2.3

How He Compares to Other Starting Pitchers

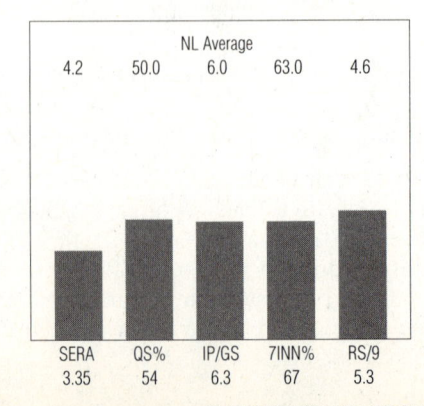

NL Average: SERA 4.2, QS% 50.0, IP/GS 6.0, 7INN% 63.0, RS/9 4.6
Hampton: SERA 3.35, QS% 54, IP/GS 6.3, 7INN% 67, RS/9 5.3

HOUSTON ASTROS

MIKE HENNEMAN

Position: RP
Bats: R **Throws:** R
Ht: 6'4" **Wt:** 205
Opening Day Age: 34
Born: 12/11/1961
Drafted: DET84 4/104
ML Seasons: 9

SCOUTING REPORT
The veteran righthander has an assortment of pitches that he shows with a varying delivery. Sometimes Mike comes in three-quarters, sometimes lower. He has above-average control, but the confusing delivery is Henneman's biggest asset now that his stuff has declined. His fastball is slightly below-average in velocity but has above-average life and sink. Henneman also has an average slider. His out pitch is a slightly above-average splitter, which Mike throws often. He did not bat with the Astros in his NL action; he fanned in his only big-league at bat back in 1987. Henneman is an average fielder. When holding runners, he has a quick release to the plate but only an average move to first base. Only two men tried to steal against Mike last year, one successfully—an excellent performance for a righthanded reliever who throws frequent splitfingers and sinkers with his delivery.

HOW HE PERFORMED IN '95
Henneman bounced back strongly from a disappointing '94 to post 18 saves (in 20 chances) and a 1.53 ERA for the Tigers, for whom he had toiled in relief his whole career. He was acquired by the Astros on August 10 to replace the injured John Hudek as their closer for the stretch drive. The deal with Houston was Detroit's only option, as Henneman greatly diminished his trade value by talking retirement unless he could play close to his Texas residence.

Mike was hit very hard in '94 and looked finished, but a megabucks guaranteed contract kept him on the '95 Tigers' roster. He surprised many by pitching better than he had in years, albeit in relatively few, short outings.

Mike didn't have much of a chance to close anything as Houston promptly embarked on an eleven-game losing streak a few days after he after he arrived. When given the opportunity, however, he pitched effectively, saving six games.

WHAT TO EXPECT IN '96
Henneman became a free agent after the '95 season amidst continuing rumors that he might retire. With the anticipated return of '94 closer John Hudek from his circulatory problem and with hard-throwing Todd Jones as insurance, the Astros should be in good hands even if Mike elects to go elsewhere or to go home.

Overall Statistics

	G	GS	GF	SV	W	L	ERA	IP	H	R	ER	HR	BB	SO
95 DET/HOU	50	0	44	26	0	2	2.15	50.1	45	12	12	1	13	43
Career	512	0	387	162	57	35	3.05	690.2	645	273	234	41	254	499

1995 Situational Statistics

	W	L	ERA	SV	IP	BB	SO		AB	HR	RBI	BA	OBA	SLG
Home	0	0	1.13	15	24.0	6	23	LHB	98	1	13	.286	.330	.388
Road	0	2	3.08	11	26.1	7	20	RHB	89	0	13	.191	.255	.225
Apr-Jun	0	1	2.11	14	21.1	7	17	ScPos	52	0	23	.288	.328	.327
Jul-Oct	0	1	2.17	12	29.0	6	26	Clutch	130	1	20	.223	.287	.285

How He Compares to Other Pitchers

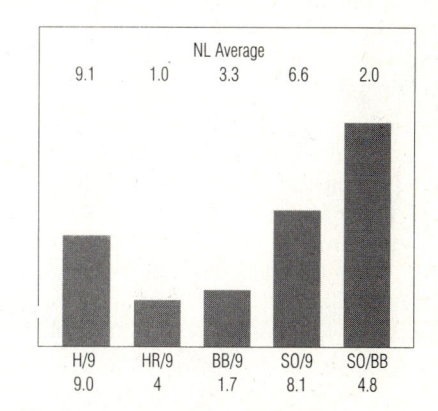

NL Average: H/9 9.1, HR/9 1.0, BB/9 3.3, SO/9 6.6, SO/BB 2.0
Henneman: H/9 9.0, HR/9 .4, BB/9 1.7, SO/9 8.1, SO/BB 4.8

How He Compares to Other Relief Pitchers

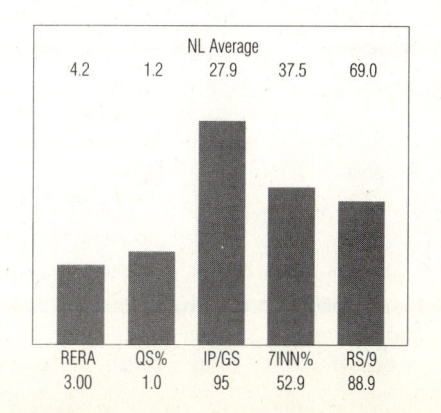

NL Average: RERA 4.2, QS% 1.2, IP/GS 27.9, 7INN% 37.5, RS/9 69.0
Henneman: RERA 3.00, QS% 1.0, IP/GS 95, 7INN% 52.9, RS/9 88.9

HOUSTON ASTROS

BRIAN HUNTER

Position: OF
Bats: R **Throws:** R
Ht: 6'4" **Wt:** 180
Opening Day Age: 25
Born: 3/5/1971
Drafted: HOU89 3/35
ML Seasons: 2

SCOUTING REPORT

Hunter has already shown the ability to be an excellent leadoff hitter for years to come. While he is only an average hitter overall, he uses his above-average speed not only to take the extra base and steal, but also to beat out infield hits. However, he does not yet bunt.

Brian has slightly below-average power and needs to reduce his strikeout totals and increase his walks. He is a first-ball, fastball hitter who likes the heater down in the zone. While Hunter still needs experience to excel, he clearly has the tools to perform at the major-league level.

He can already play center in the bigs. Brian covers the power alleys in the spacious Astrodome with plus range and slightly above-average hands. As he learns the hitters, he will be able to better position himself to make up for an only average arm.

HOW HE PERFORMED IN '95

Hunter was expected to be Houston's '95 opening day centerfielder when the trade of Steve Finley opened up the position. However, the shortened spring training did not provide him with the opportunity to display his talents and Brian began the year at Triple-A.

The Astros' slow start led to Hunter's recall from Tucson on June 13 (he was batting .329), a move that proved a much-needed jumpstart for the club. When an Omar Olivares pitch broke his right hand on July 4, Brian went onto the disabled list with a .374 average and 26 runs in 21 games. He was unable to maintain that torrid pace after returning from the injury but finished with a fine rookie year.

To become one of the better leadoff hitters in baseball, Hunter must first improve his batting eye. Although he didn't draw many walks for Houston, he has showed decent patience in the minors. Brian is a good basestealer now, and should improve as he learns the pitchers and gains experience.

Brain showed outstanding range in the 'dome, and his eight assists tied him for second among NL center fielders.

WHAT TO EXPECT IN '96

The sky is the limit for Hunter, who is likely to improve his strike-zone judgment with experience, improving his value in the #1 slot. He's already set on defense. Brian appears has a chance to stake his claim as one of the best at his position in baseball.

Overall Statistics

	G	AB	R	H	2B	3B	HR	RBI	SB	CS	BB	SO	BA	OBA
95 HOU	78	321	52	97	14	5	2	28	24	7	21	52	.302	.346
Career	84	345	54	103	15	5	2	28	26	8	22	58	.299	.341

1995 Situational Statistics

	AB	HR	RBI	BA	OBA	SLG		AB	HR	RBI	BA	OBA	SLG
Home	153	0	10	.275	.313	.333	LHP	80	0	9	.287	.344	.375
Road	168	2	18	.327	.375	.452	RHP	241	2	19	.307	.346	.402
Apr-Jun	82	1	10	.378	.433	.488	ScPos	75	0	26	.293	.349	.400
Jul-Oct	239	1	18	.276	.315	.364	Clutch	54	1	5	.352	.386	.519

How He Compares to Other Batters

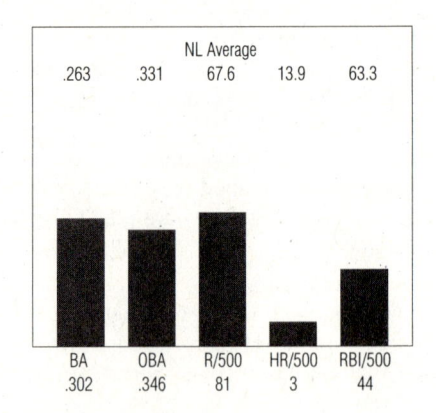

	BA	OBA	R/500	HR/500	RBI/500
NL Average	.263	.331	67.6	13.9	63.3
	.302	.346	81	3	44

Where He Hits the Ball

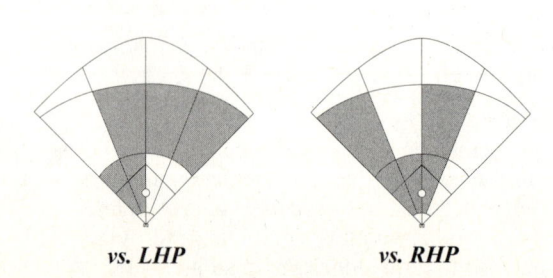

vs. LHP   vs. RHP

HOUSTON ASTROS

TODD JONES

Position: RP
Bats: L **Throws:** R
Ht: 6'3" **Wt:** 200
Opening Day Age: 27
Born: 4/24/1968
Drafted: HOU89 2/27
ML Seasons: 3

SCOUTING REPORT

Jones, rumored to be a closer since coming to Houston in '93, pitches well for the most part but suffers from bouts of inconsistency.

The burly reliever uses a high three-quarter delivery, throwing across his body. Todd's #1 pitch is an above-average fastball that bores in on righthanded hitters. He complements this with a curve that is slightly above-average. Jones rounds out the repertoire with an average change-up.

Todd is decent at holding runners; ten men tried to steal against him last year—not a high number in 100 innings—but nine were successful. His fielding skills are average; 1-for-5 at bat last year, Todd is now 3-for-10 in his career.

HOW HE PERFORMED IN '95

Jones began the season as the Astros' setup man and ended it the same way, with a difficult detour in the middle. Todd, expected to assume closing duties in '94, instead spent the season setting up for surprise closer John Hudek. Jones had ended that season not allowing a run after July 26 and extended the streak to May 14, 1995, a span of 28 innings.

However, trouble was ahead. When Hudek suffered a season-ending circulation injury in June, Jones was thrust into the closer's role. Even though Todd led Houston with 14 saves and pitched well in July, he began to struggle in early August. When the Astros acquired Mike Henneman, Jones returned to setting up.

On the year, Todd ranked eighth in the NL in appearances and third in relief innings, working in the busiest bullpen in the league. He didn't have any problems with velocity in '95, but he struggled with command. In addition to his high walk total, he hit six batters and flung five wild pitches.

Jones may have just been tired, as he seemed to have his worst location problems in August and September—he hadn't pitched this many innings since working as a starter in 1990.

WHAT TO EXPECT IN '96

Jones is valuable due to his strong arm, good stuff, and willingness to take the ball. If he improves his control, he'll be even better. If Hudek is unable to bounce back from injury, Todd may get another the chance to be Houston's closer. He's still too young to be permanently labeled as a setup pitcher.

Overall Statistics

	G	GS	GF	SV	W	L	ERA	IP	H	R	ER	HR	BB	SO
95 HOU	68	0	40	15	6	5	3.07	99.2	89	38	34	8	52	96
Career	143	0	68	22	12	9	2.96	209.2	169	75	69	15	93	184

1995 Situational Statistics

	W	L	ERA	SV	IP	BB	SO		AB	HR	RBI	BA	OBA	SLG
Home	3	4	2.86	5	50.1	26	57	LHB	164	3	16	.268	.376	.396
Road	3	1	3.28	10	49.1	26	39	RHB	211	5	27	.213	.304	.332
Apr-Jun	4	1	1.76	4	46.0	19	40	ScPos	118	2	35	.212	.374	.331
Jul-Oct	2	4	4.19	11	53.2	33	56	Clutch	219	3	25	.224	.333	.324

How He Compares to Other Pitchers

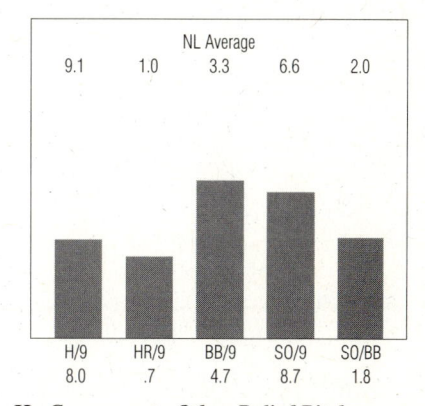

NL Average: H/9 9.1, HR/9 1.0, BB/9 3.3, SO/9 6.6, SO/BB 2.0

H/9 8.0, HR/9 .7, BB/9 4.7, SO/9 8.7, SO/BB 1.8

How He Compares to Other Relief Pitchers

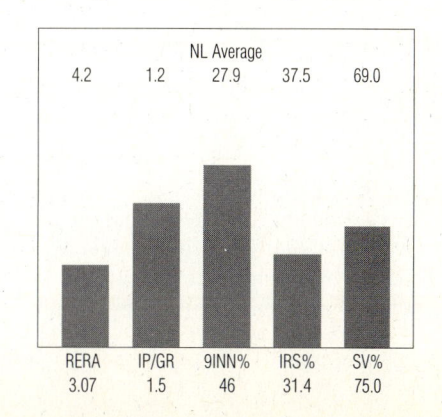

NL Average: 4.2, 1.2, 27.9, 37.5, 69.0

RERA 3.07, IP/GR 1.5, 9INN% 46, IRS% 31.4, SV% 75.0

HOUSTON ASTROS

DAVE MAGADAN

Positions: 3B/1B
Bats: L **Throws:** R
Ht: 6'3" **Wt:** 190
Opening Day Age: 33
Born: 9/30/1962
Drafted: NYN83 4/32
ML Seasons: 10

SCOUTING REPORT
Magadan has stayed in the major leagues with his hitting ability, which tends to offset his molasses legs and less-than-stellar glovework.

He likes the ball up and away and looks to extend his arms at the plate. Dave has average bat speed and hits the ball straight away. Because of his terrific patience, Magadan can bat second in the order, but he is not a particularly good bunter and is a below-average runner. In addition, he has below-average power.

As expected, the Astros were unable to replace slick-fielding Ken Caminiti with the Magadan-Craig Shipley platoon arrangement used in '95. Magadan has slightly below-average range and hands at the hot corner with an average arm.

HOW HE PERFORMED IN '95
Magadan, a free agent coming into '95, was picked up by the Astros late in spring training when injuries and Phil Nevin's slow development created a void at third base. He hit for his best average since '90 but chipped in little else for Houston.

While Dave can certainly hit singles, he again failed to provide the power or run production associated with his position. He posted his best on-base percentage ever in '95, largely because of an unusually high number of bases on balls: He annually walks more than he strikes out.

While Magadan's consistently high on-base percentages would suit him to the second position in the order, his lack of speed tended to clog up Houston's baserunning. His two stolen bases tied Dave's career high. The veteran did have some fine stretches, batting .361 in June and .419 after September 1. However, he is habitually at his worst in August, and true to form hit just .247 in August of '95.

Magadan is adequate, but nothing special, at third. His best defensive position is actually first base, but he simply doesn't produce enough offense to challenge for that spot.

WHAT TO EXPECT IN '96
The Astros expressed a desire to find an everyday third baseman for '96. Therefore, Magadan, a free-agent, inked a one-year contract with the Cubs in December, his fifth club in five years. While Dave is a good hitter with some other strengths, he's also difficult to use effectively due to his shortcomings.

Overall Statistics

	G	AB	R	H	2B	3B	HR	RBI	SB	CS	BB	SO	BA	OBA
95 HOU	127	348	44	109	24	0	2	51	2	1	71	56	.313	.428
Career	1039	3102	398	901	164	11	29	372	9	5	537	392	.290	.393

1995 Situational Statistics

	AB	HR	RBI	BA	OBA	SLG		AB	HR	RBI	BA	OBA	SLG
Home	157	0	24	.344	.447	.414	LHP	35	0	4	.171	.237	.200
Road	191	2	27	.288	.412	.387	RHP	313	2	47	.329	.446	.422
Apr-Jun	106	1	15	.292	.445	.406	ScPos	101	0	49	.327	.474	.416
Jul-Oct	242	1	36	.322	.419	.397	Clutch	74	0	10	.216	.356	.243

How He Compares to Other Batters

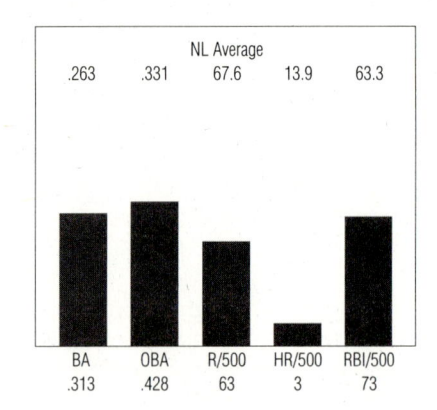

NL Average: .263 .331 67.6 13.9 63.3

BA .313 | OBA .428 | R/500 63 | HR/500 3 | RBI/500 73

Where He Hits the Ball

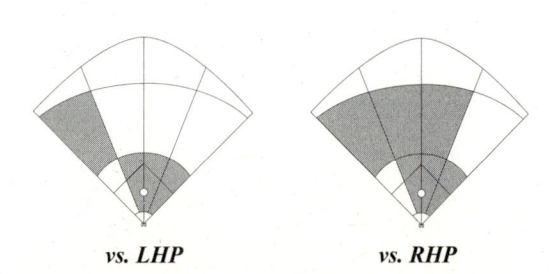

vs. LHP   vs. RHP

HOUSTON ASTROS

ORLANDO MILLER

Position: SS
Bats: R **Throws:** R
Ht: 6'1" **Wt:** 180
Opening Day Age: 27
Born: 1/13/1969
Drafted: NYA 9/17/87
ML Seasons: 2

SCOUTING REPORT
Miller's role for the Astros is to provide solid defense in the middle of the infield without being a liability at the bottom of the batting order.

While he has slightly above-average range and hands, Orlando is erratic defensively. Most baseball people feel he will settle down and perform better with increased experience. The strength and accuracy of Miller's throwing arm rank as average.

Orlando is an average hitter who likes the fastball down in the strike zone and over the plate. However, he is extremely aggressive at the dish and walks so rarely that his on-base percentages are habitually awful. He showed average power last season, but had some sock in the minor leagues.

He has average speed and is both an infrequent and poor basestealer. He sacrifices effectively when asked, which is not often.

HOW HE PERFORMED IN '95
The Astros took a chance on Miller in '95, giving him a shot to win the regular shortstop job after trading the incumbent, Andujar Cedeno. Orlando responded by playing decent defense and providing some offense.

His free-swinging tendency is evidenced by poor strikeout and walk numbers: of his 24 career walks, 10 are intentional because he bats eighth most of the time. After racking up 93 extra-base hits during 215 games in 1993–94 at Tucson, Orlando did not display much power for Houston. While the cavernous Astrodome held down Miller's production, swinging at bad pitches didn't help any. However, he hit just .180 during July, striking out 25 times in 100 at-bats.

Orlando's season ended early when he severely sprained his right knee on August 15 in an infield collision with Philadelphia's Tom Marsh. Although the injury lingered longer than anyone expected, keeping Miller nailed to the bench during the club's playoff drive, he is expected to recover in '96.

WHAT TO EXPECT IN '96
With a year's experience under his belt, Miller could improve his power numbers, but he isn't going to be a helpful offensive player unless he improves his batting eye. With Class A prospect Bry Nelson years away, Orlando's challenge comes from Ray Holbert, acquired from San Diego over the winter, and from holdover Ricky Gutierrez.

Overall Statistics

	G	AB	R	H	2B	3B	HR	RBI	SB	CS	BB	SO	BA	OBA
95 HOU	92	324	36	85	20	1	5	36	3	4	22	71	.262	.319
Career	108	364	39	98	20	2	7	45	4	4	24	83	.269	.327

1995 Situational Statistics

	AB	HR	RBI	BA	OBA	SLG		AB	HR	RBI	BA	OBA	SLG
Home	158	1	18	.234	.275	.316	LHP	72	0	7	.250	.316	.361
Road	166	4	18	.289	.359	.434	RHP	252	5	29	.266	.320	.381
Apr-Jun	187	3	23	.305	.343	.439	ScPos	82	1	28	.244	.354	.305
Jul-Oct	137	2	13	.204	.288	.292	Clutch	63	0	5	.270	.333	.317

How He Compares to Other Batters

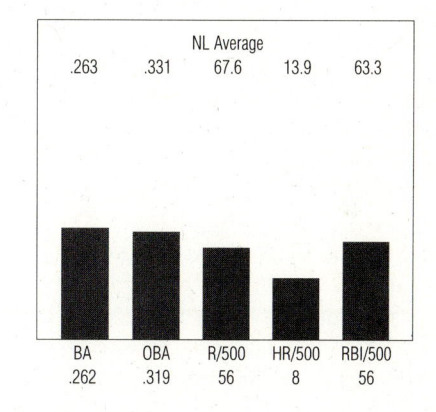

NL Average: .263 .331 67.6 13.9 63.3

BA .262 | OBA .319 | R/500 56 | HR/500 8 | RBI/500 56

Where He Hits the Ball

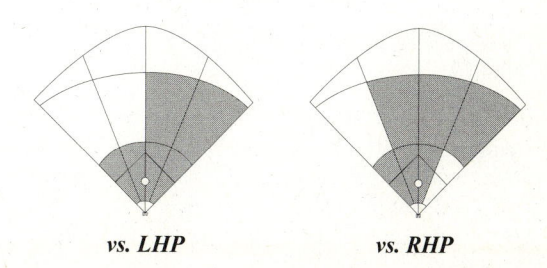

vs. LHP   vs. RHP

HOUSTON ASTROS

JAMES MOUTON

Position: OF
Bats: R **Throws:** R
Ht: 5'9" **Wt:** 175
Opening Day Age: 27
Born: 12/19/1968
Drafted: HOU91 12/183
ML Seasons: 2

SCOUTING REPORT
The athletically gifted Mouton is an average hitter who likes the fastball down in the zone. James has a quick bat and will take pitches but tends to have problems with breaking balls. He has shown leadoff skills in the minor leagues. However, Mouton has not produced as much power as his potential would suggest. One of Houston's fastest runners, Mouton has above-average speed. He is an excellent basestealer who tries to bunt for hits, but is very unsuccessful at it.

Though Mouton's best position is right field and he can play center, he played left field in '95 due to the emergence of Derek Bell. James does not have an exceptional throwing arm, ranking only average in strength and accuracy. What he does possess are slightly above-average hands and range, which he uses cover the gaps in the Astrodome outfield.

HOW HE PERFORMED IN '95
After a disappointing '94 rookie campaign in which he hit just .245 with two homers, Mouton started last season as the odd man out due to the arrival of Derek Bell and Phil Plantier from San Diego. However, he played well when called on, and with the mid-season trades of Plantier and Luis Gonzalez, Mouton found himself with more playing time, mostly in left field. He made 68 starts on the year, getting plenty of additional duty as a pinch-hitter and late-inning defensive replacement.

James responded with decent hitting and flawless defense. Mouton improved in just about every offensive category and fit the Astros' plan of speed and defense. James has excellent speed as well as a little power. However, he fanned 43 times in 182 at-bats against righthanders and is hitting just .214 against them over his two major-league seasons.

A converted second baseman, Mouton does not throw especially well. He had only four outfield assists in '95. However, he did not commit an error all season while making at least ten starts at each outfield position.

WHAT TO EXPECT IN '96
The promising Mouton should continue to improve his game as he gains experience. He has fine raw skills, and has a chance to develop into a solid major-league outfielder. However, James' problem making contact against righthanded pitching are serious enough that it could limit him to a platoon role.

Overall Statistics

	G	AB	R	H	2B	3B	HR	RBI	SB	CS	BB	SO	BA	OBA
95 HOU	104	298	42	78	18	2	4	27	25	8	25	59	.262	.326
Career	203	608	85	154	29	2	6	43	49	13	52	128	.253	.320

1995 Situational Statistics

	AB	HR	RBI	BA	OBA	SLG		AB	HR	RBI	BA	OBA	SLG
Home	155	2	10	.265	.329	.387	LHP	116	3	10	.328	.381	.483
Road	143	2	17	.259	.323	.364	RHP	182	1	17	.220	.292	.308
Apr-Jun	90	2	10	.256	.316	.411	ScPos	77	1	22	.234	.355	.312
Jul-Oct	208	2	17	.264	.330	.361	Clutch	57	2	8	.193	.277	.351

How He Compares to Other Batters

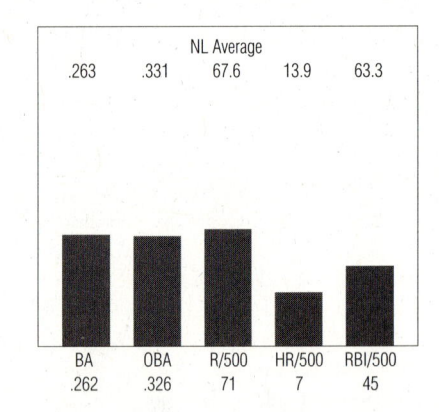

	BA	OBA	R/500	HR/500	RBI/500
NL Average	.263	.331	67.6	13.9	63.3
	.262	.326	71	7	45

Where He Hits the Ball

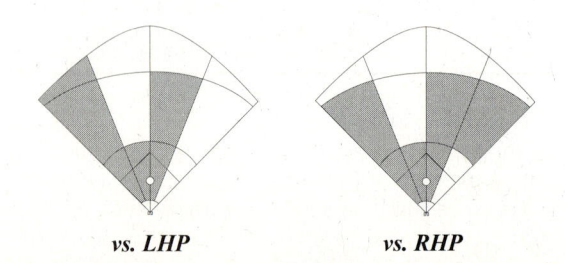

vs. LHP   vs. RHP

HOUSTON ASTROS

SHANE REYNOLDS

Position: SP
Bats: R **Throws:** R
Ht: 6'3" **Wt:** 210
Opening Day Age: 28
Born: 3/26/1968
Drafted: HOU89 5/72
ML Seasons: 4

SCOUTING REPORT
While Reynolds has emerged as the Astros' top starter, he still has bouts of inconsistency, although he is often outstanding. Shane uses an overhand motion, delivering the ball across his body at times. His fastball is average, improving at times to slightly above-average. When effective, the heater bores in on righthanded hitters with a sinking action and good life. To complement the fastball, Reynolds mixes in an average split-finger pitch and a slightly above-average curve. An extreme ground-ball pitcher, Shane has above-average control and rarely walks anybody.

Reynolds is an average fielder and average at holding runners: 16 of 22 potential basestealers were successful against Shane during '95.

HOW HE PERFORMED IN '95
A third-round pick in 1989, Reynolds struggled through three years of mediocre performance in the Houston chain. During '92, he began to find his control. He cut down his walks, and by the time he made the majors for good in '94, Shane had settled down comfortably to a superb five-to-one strikeout-to-walk ratio. Last year, in his second full season, he showed that he is close to assuming a place among the NL's best pitchers.

Last year, he ranked second to perennial Cy Young award winner Greg Maddux in fewest walks per nine innings and was among the league leaders in earned run average and strikeouts.

However, there are problems to iron out. Shane struggled late in the year, compiling a 4.99 ERA in his last 11 starts. He must improve his performance on the road, and cannot afford to leave hittable fastballs high in the strike zone, as he allowed 15 homers in '95 despite being a groundball pitcher.

One thing Reynolds certainly doesn't do well is hit. Last season, he struck out 28 times in 60 at-bats and batted just .117. He is a good bunter, however, leading the team with ten sacrifice hits.

WHAT TO EXPECT IN '96
With his continued improvement, the Astros are counting on Reynolds to be their staff ace in '96. The abilities he has demonstrated at the major-league level bode well for his future prospects. Pitchers with his control and consistency—and there aren't that many—often end up with trophies on their mantles.

Overall Statistics

	G	GS	GF	SV	W	L	ERA	IP	H	R	ER	HR	BB	SO
95 HOU	30	30	0	0	10	11	3.47	189.1	196	87	73	15	37	175
Career	76	50	5	0	19	19	3.50	349.2	377	159	136	27	70	305

1995 Situational Statistics

	W	L	ERA	SV	IP	BB	SO		AB	HR	RBI	BA	OBA	SLG
Home	4	4	2.82	0	83.0	14	89	LHB	354	6	34	.260	.299	.381
Road	6	7	3.98	0	106.1	23	86	RHB	391	9	40	.266	.300	.399
Apr-Jun	4	5	3.23	0	69.2	16	62	ScPos	190	3	58	.247	.299	.384
Jul-Oct	6	6	3.61	0	119.2	21	113	Clutch	63	1	5	.286	.297	.413

How He Compares to Other Pitchers

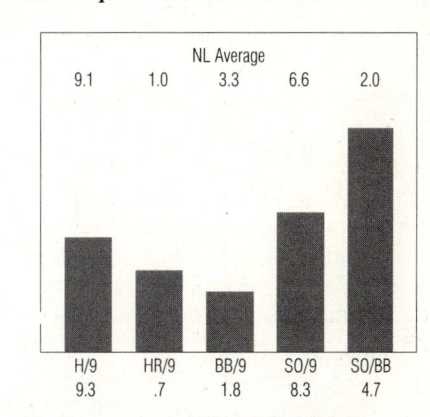

NL Average
9.1   1.0   3.3   6.6   2.0

H/9   HR/9   BB/9   SO/9   SO/BB
9.3   .7   1.8   8.3   4.7

How He Compares to Other Relief Pitchers

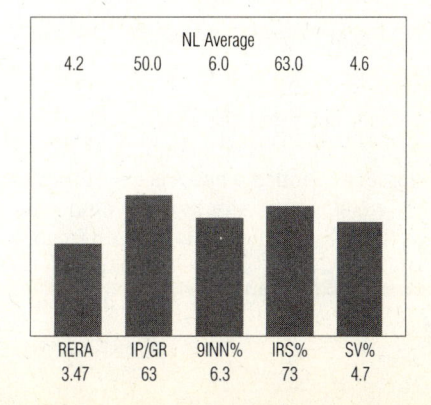

NL Average
4.2   50.0   6.0   63.0   4.6

RERA   IP/GR   9INN%   IRS%   SV%
3.47   63   6.3   73   4.7

THE SCOUTING REPORT: 1996

HOUSTON ASTROS

GREG SWINDELL

Position: SP/RP
Bats: R **Throws:** L
Ht: 6'2" **Wt:** 225
Opening Day Age: 31
Born: 1/2/1965
Drafted: CLE86 1/2
ML Seasons: 10

SCOUTING REPORT

There has been a noticeable drop in the velocity of Swindell's four-seam fastball over the last few seasons. In past years the pitch used to average 90-91 MPH, but now clocks in at a below-average 84-88.

Because of this drop-off, Greg has had to alter his game and now works as an off-speed, finesse-type pitcher. Unfortunately, the rest of his offerings (curve, slider and change-up) are just average. He throws from three-quarters with decent control; however, sometimes his location is too good, given the lack of power in his pitches, and Swindell gives up more than his fair share of home runs.

He is an average fielder with only average ability at holding runners. Greg's delivery does tend to slow down a runner's first step, though, and last year, only 14 of the 26 baserunners who tried to steal with him on the mound were successful.

HOW HE PERFORMED IN '95

Once again, Swindell failed to deliver the performance that the Astros and their fans have expected since he signed a large contract before the '93 season. He was up and down all year, eventually landing in the bullpen.

On August 26, Greg lost his fifth game in a row. From that point on, six of his last nine appearances came in relief, and he became something of a non-person during the playoff drive.

In the 17 starts in which he won or got a no-decision, he worked six or more innings 11 times and notched an ERA of 3.31. However, in his nine losses, he posted a 7.17 ERA and was not able to get past the second inning twice. Swindell ranked tenth among NL pitchers in fewest walks per nine innings but was also sixth in home runs allowed.

A decent hitter, Greg batted .240 with three doubles in 50 at-bats last season and laid down six sacrifice bunts. Swindell now has a .188 career average.

WHAT TO EXPECT IN '96

Swindell has not pitched effectively for Houston, either as a starter or from the bullpen. His name is the first one mentioned whenever payroll reduction is discussed, since he is one of the club's highest-paid players. This is the final year of Greg's lucrative contract. If he shows anything in spring training, he could be dealt quickly just to unload his salary.

Overall Statistics

	G	GS	GF	SV	W	L	ERA	IP	H	R	ER	HR	BB	SO
95 HOU	33	26	3	0	10	9	4.47	153.0	180	86	76	21	39	96
Career	272	262	3	0	102	94	3.80	1748.1	1839	823	739	188	372	1188

1995 Situational Statistics

	W	L	ERA	SV	IP	BB	SO		AB	HR	RBI	BA	OBA	SLG
Home	5	5	3.78	0	85.2	14	62	LHB	111	1	9	.234	.265	.324
Road	5	4	5.35	0	67.1	25	34	RHB	495	20	72	.311	.353	.507
Apr-Jun	5	3	4.05	0	66.2	18	39	ScPos	127	6	60	.299	.358	.535
Jul-Oct	5	6	4.80	0	86.1	21	57	Clutch	33	0	2	.273	.333	.424

How He Compares to Other Pitchers

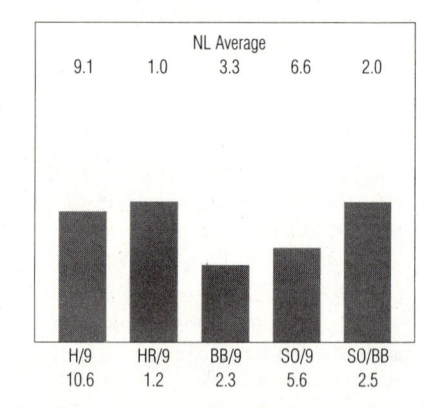

NL Average: H/9 9.1, HR/9 1.0, BB/9 3.3, SO/9 6.6, SO/BB 2.0
Swindell: H/9 10.6, HR/9 1.2, BB/9 2.3, SO/9 5.6, SO/BB 2.5

How He Compares to Other Starting Pitchers

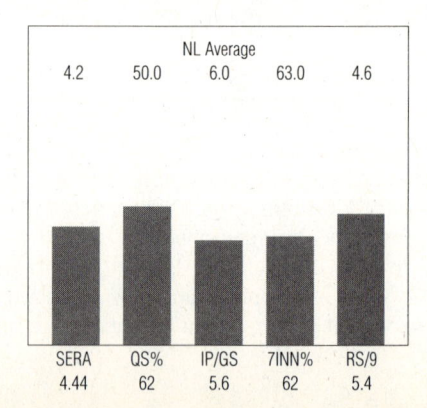

NL Average: SERA 4.2, QS% 50.0, IP/GS 6.0, 7INN% 63.0, RS/9 4.6
Swindell: SERA 4.44, QS% 62, IP/GS 5.6, 7INN% 62, RS/9 5.4

HOUSTON ASTROS

DAVE VERES

Position: RP
Bats: R **Throws:** R
Ht: 6'2" **Wt:** 195
Opening Day Age: 29
Born: 10/19/1966
Drafted: OAK86* 4/89
ML Seasons: 2

SCOUTING REPORT
While Veres' three pitches don't dazzle anyone, he has been effective for Houston and can and will pitch often. Using an overhand motion and cross-body delivery, Dave has average control of a slider, a splitter, and a four-seam fastball that runs in on righthanded hitters. All three offerings are of major-league average quality. Veres is decent at holding runners and, in '95, four of the nine who tried to steal bases while he was pitching were thrown out. Dave is an average fielder but, coming up empty in five trips to the plate last season, is now batting .143 in seven career tries.

HOW HE PERFORMED IN '95
Veres, who had spent eight and a half years in the minors before coming up in '94, followed his fine rookie season by becoming the workhorse of the Astros' bullpen last year. He led all NL relievers in innings pitched and was second in appearances as Dave developed a reputation as one of the game's better set-up pitchers.

A starter for most of his minor-league career, Dave moved to relief in '91. He always had good bite on his pitches, but until recently had poor control—at Class A in '87, he threw 29 wild pitches. However, Veres always kept the ball low, which got ground balls and prevented homers, and by '93, his control had improved.

Dave provided Houston with consistent middle and setup work last year. While he was unable to maintain the nearly perfect control he displayed in '94, he didn't allow many bases on balls and his strikeout rate improved significantly.

Unlike most Houston pitchers, he did not overly benefit from pitching at home in the Astrodome, posting better totals in road games in '95. Dave worked extremely well with short rest last season and didn't really have a bad month.

WHAT TO EXPECT IN '96
Veres performs well in an unglamorous role. He has not racked up saves, but the Astros have had other pitchers to take care of that. A capable pitcher, Dave was dealt to Montreal in the off-season. He should appear often in '96, as Felipe Alou's starters complete few games. He has shown he can handle a heavy workload, but any increase of his '95 schedule may stretch the upper limits of his arm.

Overall Statistics

	G	GS	GF	SV	W	L	ERA	IP	H	R	ER	HR	BB	SO
95 HOU	72	0	15	1	5	1	2.26	103.1	89	29	26	5	30	94
Career	104	0	22	2	8	4	2.31	144.1	128	42	37	9	37	122

1995 Situational Statistics

	W	L	ERA	SV	IP	BB	SO		AB	HR	RBI	BA	OBA	SLG
Home	2	0	2.52	0	50.0	17	43	LHB	139	3	6	.237	.333	.360
Road	3	1	2.03	1	53.1	13	51	RHB	231	2	25	.242	.276	.312
Apr-Jun	3	1	2.06	0	43.2	13	38	ScPos	98	0	25	.194	.281	.245
Jul-Oct	2	0	2.41	1	59.2	17	56	Clutch	162	3	16	.228	.278	.315

How He Compares to Other Pitchers

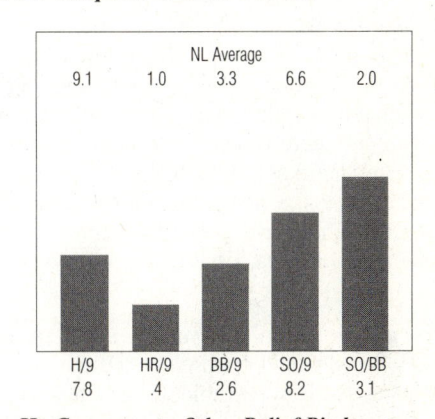

NL Average: 9.1 | 1.0 | 3.3 | 6.6 | 2.0

H/9	HR/9	BB/9	SO/9	SO/BB
7.8	.4	2.6	8.2	3.1

How He Compares to Other Relief Pitchers

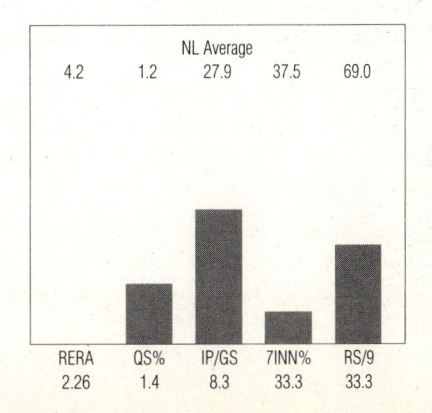

NL Average: 4.2 | 1.2 | 27.9 | 37.5 | 69.0

RERA	QS%	IP/GS	7INN%	RS/9
2.26	1.4	8.3	33.3	33.3

HOUSTON ASTROS

PAT BORDERS

Positions: C//DH
Bats: R **Throws:** R
Ht: 6'2" **Wt:** 190
Opening Day Age: 32
Born: 5/14/1963
Drafted: TOR82 6/134
ML Seasons: 8

Overall Statistics

	G	AB	R	H	2B	3B	HR	RBI	SB	CS	BB	SO	BA	OBA
95 KC/HOU	63	178	15	37	8	1	4	13	0	0	9	29	.208	.246
Career	804	2473	219	624	135	10	57	282	6	6	120	391	.252	.287

1995 Situational Statistics

	AB	HR	RBI	BA	OBA	SLG		AB	HR	RBI	BA	OBA	SLG
Home	86	1	5	.174	.220	.267	LHP	89	2	6	.225	.266	.348
Road	92	3	8	.239	.271	.391	RHP	89	2	7	.191	.226	.315
Apr-Jun	83	4	10	.253	.271	.446	ScPos	51	0	7	.137	.228	.176
Jul-Oct	95	0	3	.168	.225	.232	Clutch	33	0	2	.242	.286	.303

SCOUTING REPORT

Behind the plate, Borders once-impressive arm strength has deteriorated and is now rated slightly below-average. His throwing accuracy and range are also slightly below-average while his hands are average. Borders likes low fastballs. His raw power is average, but his power production is subpar because he does not have good discipline. As with most older catchers, Pat's speed is very poor.

HOW HE PERFORMED IN '95

Borders was acquired on August 11 from K.C. when the Astros found themselves without an adequate backup for Tony Eusebio. He was hitting .231 at the time of the trade but was unable to get on track for Houston, hitting only .114 in eleven games. Pat's main contribution was leadership, demonstrated during a late-season brawl with the Reds in which he was one of the first players off the bench to defend his teammates. Defensively, Pat was able to retire 12 of the 27 runners that attempted to steal.

WHAT TO EXPECT IN '96

With Houston's catching situation in good hands with Tony Eusebio and Rick Wilkins, free-agent Borders was not expected to be back in '96. He should catch on with someone else as a reserve.

DOUG BROCAIL

Position: RP/SP
Bats: L **Throws:** R
Ht: 6'5" **Wt:** 220
Opening Day Age: 28
Born: 5/16/1967
Drafted: SD86* 1/12
ML Seasons: 4

Overall Statistics

	G	GS	GF	SV	W	L	ERA	IP	H	R	ER	HR	BB	SO
95 HOU	36	7	12	1	6	4	4.19	77.1	87	40	36	10	22	39
Career	75	34	16	1	10	17	4.64	236.2	268	138	122	29	74	135

1995 Situational Statistics

	W	L	ERA	SV	IP	BB	SO		AB	HR	RBI	BA	OBA	SLG
Home	4	1	3.83	0	42.1	11	21	LHB	131	5	19	.313	.384	.473
Road	2	3	4.63	1	35.0	11	18	RHB	180	5	23	.256	.297	.406
Apr-Jun	1	0	3.80	1	21.1	3	11	ScPos	74	3	32	.270	.368	.446
Jul-Oct	5	4	4.34	0	56.0	19	28	Clutch	47	1	3	.255	.340	.383

SCOUTING REPORT

Using a high three-quarter motion, he delivers a four-pitch repertoire. Doug's fastball and slider are slightly above-average, while his curve and splitter are only average. He lacks a change-up.

Although Brocail has only an average pickoff move, he compensates somewhat by being quick to home plate. However, eight of nine potential base-stealers were successful against Doug in '95. His defense is plus.

HOW HE PERFORMED IN '95

Brocail, part of the big trade between Houston and San Diego before the '95 season, served as both a long reliever and spot starter for the Astros and pitched his best ball ever.

Doug was more effective in relief, compiling a 4-1 record with a 3.09 ERA in 27 games. He retired over 80% of the first batters he faced and earned first major league save on June 16.

Brocail batted .250 in sixteen at-bats with a triple, even pinch-hitting once. He is now hitting .196 for his career.

WHAT TO EXPECT IN '96

Brocail is an effective reliever who, with the anticipated shake-up of the Astros' starting rotation, may get another opportunity to win a starting job.

HOUSTON ASTROS

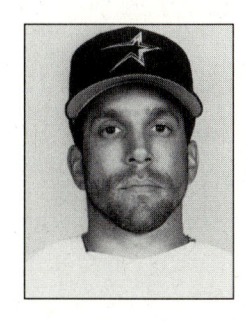

JOHN CANGELOSI

Positions: OF//P
Bats: B **Throws:** L
Ht: 5'8" **Wt:** 150
Opening Day Age: 33
Born: 3/10/1963
Drafted: CHA82* 4/91
ML Seasons: 9

Overall Statistics

	G	AB	R	H	2B	3B	HR	RBI	SB	CS	BB	SO	BA	OBA
95 HOU	90	201	46	64	5	2	2	18	21	5	48	42	.318	.457
Career	716	1373	232	341	45	11	9	96	130	48	265	221	.248	.377

1995 Situational Statistics

	AB	HR	RBI	BA	OBA	SLG		AB	HR	RBI	BA	OBA	SLG
Home	114	2	11	.333	.453	.421	LHP	33	2	5	.303	.410	.545
Road	87	0	7	.299	.461	.356	RHP	168	0	13	.321	.465	.363
Apr-Jun	42	2	4	.262	.415	.405	ScPos	51	1	17	.275	.449	.353
Jul-Oct	159	0	14	.333	.468	.390	Clutch	57	0	7	.263	.425	.298

SCOUTING REPORT

Cangelosi concentrated on making contact and going the opposite way in '95. While he likes fastballs over the plate and away, pitchers can jam John with inside stuff. He knows that his role is to get on base and takes plenty of walks. Cangelosi's speed is slightly above-average. The veteran started games at all three outfield positions but is best suited to left or center because his arm strength and accuracy are below-average. He has average-plus hands and can cover the gaps with his slightly above-average range.

HOW HE PERFORMED IN '95

Cangelosi quickly became one of manager Terry Collins' favorite players, showing hustle and an incredible ability to get on base. John's batting average, patience, and outstanding stolen base rate helped maintain the Astros' speed-dependent offense. Aside from filling in where expected, John even pitched a scoreless inning in June against Chicago.

WHAT TO EXPECT IN '96

Cangelosi will be hard-pressed to repeat his fine year, but is a good reserve outfielder nonetheless. While he is a free agent going into 1996, John's game is best suited to the Astros' style of speed and defense.

JIM DOUGHERTY

Position: RP
Bats: R **Throws:** R
Ht: 6'0" **Wt:** 210
Opening Day Age: 28
Born: 3/8/1968
Drafted: HOU90 27/703
ML Seasons: 1

Overall Statistics

	G	GS	GF	SV	W	L	ERA	IP	H	R	ER	HR	BB	SO
95 HOU	56	0	11	0	8	4	4.92	67.2	76	37	37	7	25	49
Career	56	0	11	0	8	4	4.92	67.2	76	37	37	7	25	49

1995 Situational Statistics

	W	L	ERA	SV	IP	BB	SO		AB	HR	RBI	BA	OBA	SLG
Home	3	1	4.50	0	32.0	12	19	LHB	87	5	23	.425	.510	.678
Road	5	3	5.30	0	35.2	13	30	RHB	173	2	19	.225	.273	.306
Apr-Jun	3	0	3.75	0	36.0	14	24	ScPos	81	3	37	.321	.383	.494
Jul-Oct	5	4	6.25	0	31.2	11	25	Clutch	77	2	12	.325	.404	.442

SCOUTING REPORT

Dougherty has an underhand/sidearm delivery that may be his greatest asset. His two-seam fastball is below-average in velocity but has sinking action. Jim also has an average change-up and a slightly below-average slider.

Although Jim is quick to the plate, six runners stole against him in seven tries—his delivery makes him an easy mark for good runners. He is an average fielder and was 1-for-8 as a hitter in '95.

HOW HE PERFORMED IN '95

Dougherty made it to the majors after a successful minor-league career. He led two leagues in saves, pacing the Texas League in '93 and the PCL in '94.

Jim worked in the middle with Houston, leading the relief corps with eight victories. As with most righthanded sidewinders, he had a serious problem with lefty swingers, who find that his sidearm motion makes his offering easy to pick up.

WHAT TO EXPECT IN '96

With experience, he should solidify his role as a middle reliever with Houston. If, that is, he can get lefthanded hitters out occasionally. If not, he will be relegated to one- or two-out appearances against righthanded hitters who can't or won't be pinch-hit for.

HOUSTON ASTROS

RICKY GUTIERREZ

Positions: SS//3B
Bats: R **Throws:** R
Ht: 6'1" **Wt:** 175
Opening Day Age: 25
Born: 5/23/1970
Drafted: BAL88 2/30
ML Seasons: 3

Overall Statistics

	G	AB	R	H	2B	3B	HR	RBI	SB	CS	BB	SO	BA	OBA
95 HOU	52	156	22	43	6	0	0	12	5	0	10	33	.276	.321
Career	275	869	125	219	27	7	6	66	11	9	92	184	.252	.328

1995 Situational Statistics

	AB	HR	RBI	BA	OBA	SLG		AB	HR	RBI	BA	OBA	SLG
Home	70	0	6	.257	.297	.271	LHP	40	0	2	.250	.250	.275
Road	86	0	6	.291	.340	.349	RHP	116	0	10	.284	.344	.328
Apr-Jun	10	0	0	.100	.100	.100	ScPos	43	0	12	.279	.347	.326
Jul-Oct	146	0	12	.288	.335	.329	Clutch	34	0	0	.235	.235	.265

SCOUTING REPORT

Gutierrez is a slightly below-average hitter with below-average power. He goes after pitches low in the strike zone, usually taking middle of the plate and outside fastballs to the opposite field. He has average baserunning speed but is a poor basestealer. An adequate fielder at shortstop, Ricky displays a slightly above-average arm with average accuracy. His range and hands are average.

HOW HE PERFORMED IN '95

Gutierrez, an off-season acquisition from San Diego, was unable to win the starting shortstop position and did not display much consistency in spot duty. Sent to the minors to regain his form, he returned in August when Orlando Miller was injured. Playing every day for the last six weeks of the season, he filled in adequately both offensively and defensively during the Astros' stretch drive. He didn't provide much offense besides the occasional single, however.

WHAT TO EXPECT IN '96

If Miller struggles this year, Gutierrez will be given a another shot at the starting job. However, he must be more consistent defensively and reduce his strikeouts. While he's a long shot ever to be a regular player again, Ricky can be a valuable backup.

DEAN HARTGRAVES

Position: RP
Bats: R **Throws:** L
Ht: 6'0" **Wt:** 185
Opening Day Age: 29
Born: 8/12/1966
Drafted: HOU87 20/522
ML Seasons: 1

Overall Statistics

	G	GS	GF	SV	W	L	ERA	IP	H	R	ER	HR	BB	SO
95 HOU	40	0	11	0	2	0	3.22	36.1	30	14	13	2	16	24
Career	40	0	11	0	2	0	3.22	36.1	30	14	13	2	16	24

1995 Situational Statistics

	W	L	ERA	SV	IP	BB	SO		AB	HR	RBI	BA	OBA	SLG
Home	2	0	0.45	0	20.0	7	14	LHB	56	0	9	.232	.295	.375
Road	0	0	6.61	0	16.1	9	10	RHB	76	2	9	.224	.318	.342
Apr-Jun	0	0	3.48	0	10.1	5	4	ScPos	42	0	14	.310	.412	.429
Jul-Oct	2	0	3.12	0	26.0	11	20	Clutch	42	1	8	.190	.300	.333

SCOUTING REPORT

Dean normally comes from three-quarters but will drop lower in certain situations. Like most borderline lefthanders, he lacks great stuff. His out pitch, thrown often, is a slightly above-average splitter. Hartgraves also has an average slider and an average-minus two-seam sinking fastball. Dean is slightly above-average in holding runners because of his quickness to home and is an average defensive player. Only one runner stole on him last year. He was 0-for-2 at bat.

HOW HE PERFORMED IN '95

Hartgraves was recalled from the minors twice as part of the Astros' search for an effective lefty reliever. Like teammate Dave Veres a year ago, Dean made his major-league debut following eight seasons in the minors. He acclimated himself to pitching in the Astrodome, not allowing a single earned run in 22 games. On the road, however, he was atrocious. He did not pitch between September 3-24 due to food poisoning and was ineffective in three appearances after returning.

WHAT TO EXPECT IN '96

Effective lefthanded pitchers are a valuable commodity. If Hartgraves, a fairly marginal talent, can improve his road performance, he could earn a steady living for several years.

HOUSTON ASTROS

JOHN HUDEK

Position: RP
Bats: B **Throws:** R
Ht: 6'1" **Wt:** 200
Opening Day Age: 29
Born: 8/8/1966
Drafted: CHA88 10/249
ML Seasons: 2

Overall Statistics

	G	GS	GF	SV	W	L	ERA	IP	H	R	ER	HR	BB	SO
95 HOU	19	0	16	7	2	2	5.40	20.0	19	12	12	3	5	29
Career	61	0	49	23	2	4	3.79	59.1	43	26	25	8	23	68

1995 Situational Statistics

	W	L	ERA	SV	IP	BB	SO		AB	HR	RBI	BA	OBA	SLG
Home	2	1	4.76	2	11.1	2	16	LHB	33	3	9	.364	.400	.788
Road	0	1	6.23	5	8.2	3	13	RHB	44	0	1	.159	.213	.182
Apr-Jun	2	2	5.40	7	20.0	5	29	ScPos	23	1	7	.130	.167	.391
Jul-Oct	0	0	0.00	0	0.0	0	0	Clutch	49	1	8	.245	.315	.429

SCOUTING REPORT
Hudek pitches with no windup and a three-quarter motion. His mechanics are poor overall, but John has a well above-average fastball that he can throw to rise or sink. He has two other pitches: an average slider with a small break and a middling splitfinger that he seldom throws. Hudek's control is just average.

John was 1-for-1 last year, his first big-league at-bat. He is average at fielding his position, but just one runner stole against him in '95.

HOW HE PERFORMED IN '95
Hudek's meteoric rise as a rookie closer was the '94 Astros' biggest surprise. His future appeared bright until a circulation problem in his pitching arm ended his season last June 23. Nobody knows what caused the injury or whether he will be able to come back again—velocity is his game.

WHAT TO EXPECT IN '96
The health of Hudek is the biggest question mark on the Houston staff entering '96. If he can regain the form he showed in '94, the Astros' bullpen will again be a dependable part of the team. If Hudek falters, look for Todd Jones to get the call.

DARRYL KILE

Position: SP
Bats: R **Throws:** R
Ht: 6'5" **Wt:** 185
Opening Day Age: 27
Born: 12/2/1968
Drafted: HOU87 30/782
ML Seasons: 5

Overall Statistics

	G	GS	GF	SV	W	L	ERA	IP	H	R	ER	HR	BB	SO
95 HOU	25	21	1	0	4	12	4.96	127.0	114	81	70	5	73	113
Career	140	115	6	0	40	47	4.09	725.1	687	380	330	54	371	549

1995 Situational Statistics

	W	L	ERA	SV	IP	BB	SO		AB	HR	RBI	BA	OBA	SLG
Home	1	8	5.82	0	60.1	38	51	LHB	216	3	32	.250	.386	.319
Road	3	4	4.18	0	66.2	35	62	RHB	259	2	25	.232	.324	.336
Apr-Jun	3	7	5.00	0	72.0	35	57	ScPos	148	1	49	.250	.374	.297
Jul-Oct	1	5	4.91	0	55.0	38	56	Clutch	24	1	2	.292	.346	.500

SCOUTING REPORT
Former All-Star Kile's career is suffering because he walks too many and compensates for falling behind in the count by making his pitches too good. Although he is durable, Darryl lacks confidence.

This is a shame, because he has two tremendous pitches. His live, well above-average fastball bores in on righthanded hitters and sinks. Kile's well above-average curve is one of the best; he also has an average change-up. He throws with a compact, three-quarter delivery.

Kile is quick to home with an average move: 11 of 15 potential basestealers were successful in '95. His fielding is average. He was 4-for-36 at bat (.111), raising his career average to just .102.

HOW HE PERFORMED IN '95
Darryl hurled himself out of the Astros' rotation and back to Tucson on August 12. He ranked among league leaders in an unholy trinity: walks, hit batsmen, and wild pitches. He walked seven in a game three times and tied an Astros' record by plunking three batters in one contest.

WHAT TO EXPECT IN '96
If Kile improves his control, he could again reach All-Star status. If not, Houston has other young arms waiting for the chance to step up.

THE SCOUTING REPORT: 1996

HOUSTON ASTROS

DERRICK MAY

Positions: OF//1B
Bats: L **Throws:** R
Ht: 6'4" **Wt:** 210
Opening Day Age: 27
Born: 7/14/1968
Drafted: CHN86 1/9
ML Seasons: 6

Overall Statistics

	G	AB	R	H	2B	3B	HR	RBI	SB	CS	BB	SO	BA	OBA
95 MIL/HOU	110	319	44	90	18	2	9	50	5	1	24	42	.282	.333
Career	494	1563	194	441	78	6	37	237	24	9	103	165	.282	.326

1995 Situational Statistics

	AB	HR	RBI	BA	OBA	SLG		AB	HR	RBI	BA	OBA	SLG
Home	168	4	30	.262	.335	.411	LHP	39	0	5	.256	.293	.333
Road	151	5	20	.305	.331	.464	RHP	280	9	45	.286	.339	.450
Apr-Jun	122	1	10	.254	.289	.336	ScPos	99	5	43	.263	.339	.455
Jul-Oct	197	8	40	.299	.359	.497	Clutch	56	2	13	.321	.381	.500

SCOUTING REPORT

Derrick is a pull hitter against both lefthanded and righthanded pitching. A slightly above-average hitter, he has some power. May has below-average speed, which hurts him on the bases and in the field. His range and hands are both slightly below-average, and Derrick has a weak and inaccurate arm.

HOW HE PERFORMED IN '95

May rebounded from an unusually slow first half with Milwaukee, giving Houston a late-season charge. Hitting just .248 for the Brewers, Derrick was donated to the Astros on June 20. Initially, manager Terry Collins used him to provide pop off the bench and for occasional duty in left field, but by September, May was playing every day against righthanders. He hit .321 with five homers in the last month. Derrick batted .301 for Houston with 12 pinch-RBI, increasing his playing time when Derek Bell was hurt. While May hit well for the Astros, he rarely walked and didn't dazzle in left field. Despite his early-season slump and September jolt, '95 added up to another typical Derrick May season.

WHAT TO EXPECT IN '96

May provides some punch, but mediocre defense limits his flexibility. He should continue as a pinch-hitter/reserve outfielder in '96.

CRAIG SHIPLEY

Positions: 3B/SS//2B/1B
Bats: R **Throws:** R
Ht: 6'1" **Wt:** 175
Opening Day Age: 33
Born: 1/7/1963
Drafted: LA 5/28/84
ML Seasons: 8

Overall Statistics

	G	AB	R	H	2B	3B	HR	RBI	SB	CS	BB	SO	BA	OBA
95 HOU	92	232	23	61	8	1	3	24	6	1	8	28	.263	.291
Career	409	967	102	259	42	5	12	95	25	12	33	134	.268	.298

1995 Situational Statistics

	AB	HR	RBI	BA	OBA	SLG		AB	HR	RBI	BA	OBA	SLG
Home	121	1	6	.231	.264	.281	LHP	118	1	11	.280	.293	.356
Road	111	2	18	.297	.322	.414	RHP	114	2	13	.246	.289	.333
Apr-Jun	83	1	9	.277	.315	.349	ScPos	59	1	21	.254	.303	.356
Jul-Oct	149	2	15	.255	.277	.342	Clutch	46	0	2	.304	.353	.348

SCOUTING REPORT

At third, Craig has slightly above-average hands but average range, arm strength, and throwing accuracy. Although Shipley was once a shortstop and still plays there on occasion, he no longer has the quickness to play the position well. Craig is very aggressive at bat and likes high fastballs over the plate. Once a switch-hitter, Shipley now bats exclusively from the right with slightly below-average power production. He is an average runner, but a decent percentage base stealer. Craig does not bunt often.

HOW HE PERFORMED IN '95

As the righthanded half of the Astros' third-base platoon, Shipley was unable to match the career year he enjoyed with San Diego in '94. Reverting to his career averages in most offensive categories, he was still successful as a pinch-hitter, collecting nine hits in 24 at-bats. However, Craig led Houston by grounding into 13 double plays.

He made just two errors at third base. Although he also filled in at shortstop and second base, Shipley's performance there was adequate at best.

WHAT TO EXPECT IN '96

Shipley is not going to be the Astros everyday third baseman in '96. His best role is a spot player and late-inning replacement.

HOUSTON ASTROS

MIKE SIMMS

Positions: 1B/OF
Bats: R **Throws:** R
Ht: 6'4" **Wt:** 185
Opening Day Age: 29
Born: 1/12/1967
Drafted: HOU85 6/144
ML Seasons: 5

Overall Statistics

	G	AB	R	H	2B	3B	HR	RBI	SB	CS	BB	SO	BA	OBA
95 HOU	50	121	14	31	4	0	9	24	1	2	13	28	.256	.341
Career	132	293	37	67	12	0	14	45	3	2	33	84	.229	.312

1995 Situational Statistics

	AB	HR	RBI	BA	OBA	SLG		AB	HR	RBI	BA	OBA	SLG
Home	59	5	15	.254	.302	.542	LHP	55	6	14	.291	.350	.673
Road	62	4	9	.258	.373	.484	RHP	66	3	10	.227	.333	.379
Apr-Jun	3	0	0	.000	.250	.000	ScPos	40	2	12	.175	.320	.325
Jul-Oct	118	9	24	.263	.343	.525	Clutch	19	1	3	.158	.292	.368

SCOUTING REPORT

An inability to hit righthanders has kept Mike limited to platoon duty in the majors. However, he has above-average raw power and is patient at bat. Simms has slightly below-average speed, rarely steals, and does not bunt. Mike shows slightly below-average range and hands at first base but displays slightly below-average arm strength and accuracy. He can also play left or right field when needed.

HOW HE PERFORMED IN '95

Simms' contract was purchased from Triple-A Tucson last August 1. He replaced two key injured players: Jeff Bagwell at first base and, later, Derek Bell in right field. After several disappointing call-ups in years past, Mike filled in admirably for the Astros in '95, displaying good power and run production. He had shortened his swing and, as a result, showed remarkable opposite field power—even in the spacious Astrodome. Defensively, Simms was adequate at first base but lacks the speed and arm to play right field.

WHAT TO EXPECT IN '96

Simms made quite an impression last year. It appears he has established himself as a major-league hitter, but his limited defensive ability will continue to keep him on the bench.

JEFF TABAKA

Position: RP
Bats: R **Throws:** L
Ht: 6'2" **Wt:** 195
Opening Day Age: 32
Born: 1/17/1964
Drafted: MON86 2/43
ML Seasons: 2

Overall Statistics

	G	GS	GF	SV	W	L	ERA	IP	H	R	ER	HR	BB	SO
95 SD/HOU	34	0	6	0	1	0	3.23	30.2	27	11	11	2	17	25
Career	73	0	16	1	4	1	4.40	71.2	59	40	35	3	44	57

1995 Situational Statistics

	W	L	ERA	SV	IP	BB	SO		AB	HR	RBI	BA	OBA	SLG
Home	0	0	3.50	0	18.0	9	13	LHB	42	0	4	.190	.333	.238
Road	1	0	2.84	0	12.2	8	12	RHB	69	2	8	.275	.351	.406
Apr-Jun	0	0	7.11	0	6.1	5	6	ScPos	40	0	8	.175	.283	.200
Jul-Oct	1	0	2.22	0	24.1	12	19	Clutch	19	0	3	.263	.440	.263

SCOUTING REPORT

Tabaka uses a high three-quarter delivery to bring home his four-pitch arsenal. His best offering is a slightly above-average four-seam fastball that looks like a screwball when he turns it over. Jeff's other pitches are an average slider and change and a slightly below-average curve. While Tabaka has quality stuff, his control isn't good enough overall, although he locates the slider and change-up effectively. Tabaka's fielding and ability to hold runners are average. Both runners trying to steal against him in '95 were retired. He was hitless in one try during '95 after doubling in his first major-league at-bat in '94.

HOW HE PERFORMED IN '95

Tabaka spent eight years in the minors before finally making the majors in '94. The Astros acquired him from San Diego last July as part of their quest for quality lefthanded relief. Jeff fit the bill, appearing in 22 games for Houston with a 1.54 ERA, allowing opponents to hit only .190 and allowing only one of 13 inherited runners to score.

WHAT TO EXPECT IN '96

The Astros will probably give Tabaka significant work in '96. Though he pitched well last season, Jeff is really just a journeyman.

HOUSTON ASTROS

MILT THOMPSON

Position: OF
Bats: L **Throws:** R
Ht: 5'11" **Wt:** 170
Opening Day Age: 37
Born: 1/5/1959
Drafted: ATL79* 2/29
ML Seasons: 12

Overall Statistics

	G	AB	R	H	2B	3B	HR	RBI	SB	CS	BB	SO	BA	OBA
95 HOU	92	132	14	29	9	0	2	19	4	2	14	37	.220	.297
Career	1297	3695	488	1022	154	37	47	354	213	65	329	622	.277	.338

1995 Situational Statistics

	AB	HR	RBI	BA	OBA	SLG		AB	HR	RBI	BA	OBA	SLG
Home	62	0	9	.226	.329	.339	LHP	5	0	0	.000	.000	.000
Road	70	2	10	.214	.267	.329	RHP	127	2	19	.228	.308	.346
Apr-Jun	53	0	6	.226	.293	.321	ScPos	37	1	18	.324	.422	.514
Jul-Oct	79	2	13	.215	.300	.342	Clutch	42	0	6	.214	.358	.262

SCOUTING REPORT
Thompson likes medium-velocity pitches down and over the plate and is no longer able to catch up to good hard stuff. A slightly below-average hitter, Milt's power is average at best. Once quite fast, Thompson is now 37 and has average speed.

At one time, Milt played center field. However, he now has average range and hands with minus arm strength and accuracy, making him best suited for the corner outfield positions.

HOW HE PERFORMED IN '95
In his 12th major-league season, Thompson found his playing time reduced due to Houston's acquisitions of Derrick May and John Cangelosi. Milt still served as the Astros' top pinch-hitter.

The lack of consistent work resulted in a noticeable drop-off in offensive production, but Thompson paced the Astros with 13 pinch hits and 11 pinch RBI. Thompson's greatest asset at this point in his career was his ability to mentor Houston's young outfielders.

WHAT TO EXPECT IN '96
A free agent after the '95 season, Milt may not be back with the Astros this year. Although his outlook for '96 is uncertain, he can probably contribute for another year as a fifth outfielder.

RICK WILKINS

Positions: C//1B
Bats: L **Throws:** R
Ht: 6'2" **Wt:** 210
Opening Day Age: 28
Born: 6/4/1967
Drafted: CHN86 23/582
ML Seasons: 5

Overall Statistics

	G	AB	R	H	2B	3B	HR	RBI	SB	CS	BB	SO	BA	OBA
95 CH/HO	65	202	30	41	3	0	7	19	0	0	46	61	.203	.351
Career	470	1408	193	358	69	4	58	175	9	9	183	355	.254	.344

1995 Situational Statistics

	AB	HR	RBI	BA	OBA	SLG		AB	HR	RBI	BA	OBA	SLG
Home	87	3	7	.195	.330	.310	LHP	38	1	3	.158	.327	.237
Road	115	4	12	.209	.366	.330	RHP	164	6	16	.213	.356	.341
Apr-Jun	162	6	14	.191	.343	.315	ScPos	65	1	13	.200	.357	.262
Jul-Oct	40	1	5	.250	.380	.350	Clutch	31	0	0	.065	.256	.065

SCOUTING REPORT
Wilkins is a low-ball pull hitter with some power and good bat speed. However, trouble with breaking pitches makes Rick a below-average hitter overall. His speed is minus but better than many catchers. Defensive is Rick's forte. He has average hands, plus mobility and blocks the ball well. Shoulder problems have diminished what once was a strong arm; his throwing strength and accuracy now rate slightly below-average. Wilkins has a good release.

HOW HE PERFORMED IN '95
In an effort to break a logjam in their outfield, Houston traded Luis Gonzalez and Scott Servais to Chicago for Wilkins on June 28. However, Rick was almost immediately disabled with a cervical disk problem and didn't return until September. Wilkins followed a disappointing '94 with another off-year at the plate. His '93 numbers (.303, 30 HR, 73 RBI) now seem a distant memory. He still throws effectively, however, nailing 23 of 67 men trying to steal (34%).

WHAT TO EXPECT IN '96
Rick should be recovered from his neck injury by the time spring training begins. If he can even approach the offensive numbers he put up three years ago, Wilkins should provide the Astros with half of a formidable platoon.

HOUSTON ASTROS: TOP PROSPECTS

BOB ABREU
Bats: L Throws: R Opening Day Age: 22
Ht: 6-0 Wt: 160 Born: 3/11/1974
Position: OF Drafted: NDFA 8-21-90 HOU

YR TEAM	LG/CLASS	G	AB	R	H	2B	3B	HR	RBI	SB	BA	OBA
93 Osceola	FSL/A	129	474	62	134	21	17	5	55	10	.283	.352
94 Jackson	TEX/AA	118	400	61	121	25	9	16	73	12	.303	.368
95 Tucson	PCL/AAA	114	415	72	126	24	17	10	75	16	.304	.395

Abreu has been one of the top hitting prospects in the organization since coming over from Venezuela in 1991. An alley hitter who led the minor leagues with 17 triples last season, the 21-year-old will improve his power numbers once he fills out and gets out of the spacious parks in Jackson and Tucson where he has spent the last two years. The Astros are concerned about his defense, the number of times he strikes out and his ability to hit lefthanders, but he batted .355 with some pop against southpaws last season, a rise of over 100 points from '94. He also increased his assist total from three to 18.

RAUL CHAVEZ
Bats: R Throws: R Opening Day Age: 23
Ht: 5-11 Wt: 175 Born: 3/18/1973
Position: C Drafted: NDFA 1-10-90 HOU

YR TEAM	LG/CLASS	G	AB	R	H	2B	3B	HR	RBI	SB	BA	OBA
93 Osceola	FSL/A	58	197	13	45	5	1	0	16	1	.228	.261
94 Jackson	TEX/AA	89	251	17	55	7	0	1	22	1	.219	.273
95 Tucson	PCL/AAA	32	103	14	27	5	0	0	10	0	.262	.325
95 Jackson	TEX/AA	58	188	16	54	8	0	4	25	0	.287	.323

Chavez, originally a shortstop, was moved behind the plate because of his shotgun arm and reflexes. He quickly impressed, gunning down 61% of all basestealers in an injury-shortened 1993, 34% the following year and nearly 50% last season, drawing comparisons to another former Jackson catcher, Todd Hundley. The Venezuelan, although still young, has not been as quick to adapt with the bat. After two very poor years in 1992-93, Chavez hit for a decent average at both stops last year. However, he is not very selective and has little punch.

RYAN CREEK
Bats: R Throws: R Opening Day Age: 24
Ht: 6-1 Wt: 180 Born: 9/24/1972
Position: P Drafted: 1992 #35 HOU

YR TEAM	LG/CLASS	G	GS	GF	SV	W	L	ERA	IP	H	HR	BB	SO	O/BA
93 Astros	GULF/R	12	11	1	1	7	3	2.34	69.1	53	0	30	62	.211
94 Quad City	MID/A	21	15	3	0	3	5	4.99	74.0	86	6	41	66	.294
95 Jackson	TEX/AA	26	24	1	0	9	7	3.63	143.2	137	11	64	120	.255

Although Creek was Jackson's opening night starter, many thought the 23-year-old, who had arm problems the previous year, would be sent to Class-A after the strike was settled. But Creek showed plus velocity, a great curve at times and was so dominant on occasions that he lasted the entire season in Jackson. Much better the first half—he had a 1.93 ERA in the middle of June—Creek also enjoyed his home starts at pitcher-friendly Jackson. He was very effective against lefthanders because his fastball runs up and away.

KEVIN GALLAHER
Bats: R Throws: R Opening Day Age: 28
Ht: 6-3 Wt: 190 Born: 8/1/1968
Position: P Drafted: NDFA 5-8-91 HOU

YR TEAM	LG/CLASS	G	GS	GF	SV	W	L	ERA	IP	H	HR	BB	SO	O/BA
93 Osceola	FSL/A	21	21	0	0	7	3	3.80	135.0	132	7	57	93	.254
93 Jackson	TEX/AA	4	4	0	0	0	2	2.63	24.0	14	3	10	30	.175
94 Jackson	TEX/AA	18	18	0	0	6	3	3.91	106.0	88	5	67	112	.226
94 Tucson	PCL/AAA	9	9	0	0	3	4	5.37	53.2	55	5	25	58	.266
95 Tucson	PCL/AAA	3	3	0	0	1	1	6.43	14.0	19	1	9	11	.333
95 Kissimmee	FSL/A	7	7	0	0	1	1	5.71	17.1	8	0	24	21	.136
95 Jackson	TEX/AA	6	6	0	0	2	2	3.40	42.1	31	1	23	28	.204

When healthy, Gallaher throws 90+ mph with a knee-buckling curveball. Unfortunately, a shoulder problem kept him in extended spring training until mid-June and he never showed his old velocity upon return; he seemed to overuse his breaking ball. Even though Gallaher is 27 years old, he didn't start pitching until his senior year at St. Bonaventure. He has major league stuff and just needs to be healthy and more fundamentally sound to crack the big leagues.

DAVE HAJEK
Bats: R Throws: R Opening Day Age: 29
Ht: 5-10 Wt: 165 Born: 10/14/1967
Position: 2B Drafted: NDFA 8-9-89 HOU

YR TEAM	LG/CLASS	G	AB	R	H	2B	3B	HR	RBI	SB	BA	OBA
93 Jackson	TEX/AA	110	332	50	97	20	2	5	27	6	.292	.328
94 Tucson	PCL/AAA	129	484	71	157	29	5	7	70	12	.324	.362
95 Tucson	PCL/AAA	131	502	99	164	37	4	4	79	12	.327	.373
95 Houston	NL/MAJ	5	2	0	0	0	0	0	0	1	.000	.333

Hajek has played every position in the field except catcher and has batted .299 in a six-year career but receives little respect. Tabbed as a utility player early in his career, Hajek has impressed the last two years playing second base every day in Triple-A. The 28-year-old has hit for average consistently while developing a reputation as an outstanding defensive player with great range who can turn the double play. He is extremely tough to strike out and performs in the clutch. Hajek has hit over .350 with runners in scoring position each of the last two years. Last season he appeared in replacement games in the spring before getting a September callup.

RICHARD HIDALGO
Bats: R Throws: R Opening Day Age: 21
Ht: 6-2 Wt: 175 Born: 7/2/1975
Position: OF Drafted: NDFA 7-2-91 HOU

YR TEAM	LG/CLASS	G	AB	R	H	2B	3B	HR	RBI	SB	BA	OBA
93 Asheville	SAL/A	111	403	49	109	23	3	10	55	21	.270	.324
94 Quad City	MID/A	124	476	68	139	47	6	12	76	12	.292	.331
95 Jackson	TEX/AA	133	489	59	130	28	6	14	59	8	.266	.309

Hidalgo's strong throwing arm is deadly accurate. He led the entire minor leagues in outfield assists with 30 in 1993 and 23 in 1994. The Venezuelan should be an above-average right fielder once he gains more experience tracking fly balls. Offensively, the Texas League's youngest player in 1995 has bat speed, 25 home run potential, and decent speed, but showed a tendency to chase the breaking ball out of the strike zone a little too often. He set a Midwest League record with 47 doubles in '94.

THE SCOUTING REPORT: 1996

HOUSTON ASTROS: TOP PROSPECTS

CHRIS HOLT
Bats: R Throws: R Opening Day Age: 25
Ht: 6-4 Wt: 205 Born: 9/18/1971
Position: P Drafted: 1992 #4 HOU

YR TEAM	LG/CLASS	G	GS	GF	SV	W	L	ERA	IP	H	HR	BB	SO	O/BA
93 Quad City	MID/A	26	26	0	0	11	10	2.27	186.1	162	10	54	176	.229
94 Jackson	TEX/AA	26	25	0	0	10	9	3.45	167.0	169	11	22	111	.265
95 Tucson	PCL/AAA	20	19	0	0	5	8	4.10	118.2	155	5	32	69	.326
95 Jackson	TEX/AA	5	5	0	0	2	2	1.67	32.1	27	2	5	24	.225

The big 24-year-old throws a soft fastball, but has pinpoint control and an ability to work the lower half of the plate. Because of the strike Holt did not join Jackson until May and was summoned to Triple-A after 15 scoreless innings later that month. Although he was racked at a .326 clip at Tucson, he allowed just five homers and 32 walks and had the league's ninth-best ERA. The minor league's complete game leader in 1993 and BB/9 IP leader in '94, Holt has walked as many as three hitters in a game just four times in the last two years.

DOUG MLICKI
Bats: R Throws: R Opening Day Age: 25
Ht: 6-3 Wt: 175 Born: 4/23/1971
Position: P Drafted: 1992 #13 HOU

YR TEAM	LG/CLASS	G	GS	GF	SV	W	L	ERA	IP	H	HR	BB	SO	O/BA
93 Osceola	FSL/A	26	23	0	0	11	10	3.91	158.2	158	16	65	111	.268
94 Jackson	TEX/AA	23	23	0	0	13	7	3.38	138.2	107	20	54	130	.211
95 Tucson	PCL/AAA	6	6	0	0	1	2	5.56	34.0	44	3	6	22	.306
95 Jackson	TEX/AA	16	16	0	0	8	3	2.79	96.2	73	6	33	72	.209

Mlicki is unusual in that he has been much more effective against lefthanded hitters the past two years and has yielded many more fly ball outs than ground ball outs, which is curious since the 24-year-old has only average velocity and relies on major-league quality curveballs and changeups. After a very strong '94, Mlicki returned to Jackson last season and won five straight starts. After allowing two earned runs or fewer in 11 of his 16 Double-A starts he was promoted to Tucson where he pitched well after surrendering ten runs in his first appearance.

TONY MOUNCE
Bats: L Throws: L Opening Day Age: 21
Ht: 6-2 Wt: 185 Born: 2/8/1975
Position: P Drafted: 1994 #9 HOU

YR TEAM	LG/CLASS	G	GS	GF	SV	W	L	ERA	IP	H	HR	BB	SO	O/BA
94 Astros	GULF/R	11	11	0	0	4	2	2.72	59.2	56	1	18	72	.250
95 Quad City	MID/A	25	25	0	0	16	8	2.43	159.0	118	6	57	143	.205

Mounce followed up an impressive pro debut, leading the Gulf Coast League in strikeouts and SO/9 IP (10.86), by pacing the Midwest League in wins, finishing second in strikeouts, and ending third in ERA. Mounce, a '95 All-Star, features a great curveball and upper-80's heater, and started the season with 19 scoreless innings. He fanned ten or more hitters in three of his first five starts and, after having occasional control problems the first half of the season, improved his command in the second half.

TYRONE NARCISSE
Bats: R Throws: R Opening Day Age: 24
Ht: 6-5 Wt: 205 Born: 2/4/1972
Position: P Drafted: 1990 #9 SD

YR TEAM	LG/CLASS	G	GS	GF	SV	W	L	ERA	IP	H	HR	BB	SO	O/BA
93 Asheville	SAL/A	29	29	0	0	6	12	4.38	160.1	173	11	66	114	.283
94 Osceola	FSL/A	26	26	0	0	7	11	4.87	146.0	153	7	57	86	.276
95 Jackson	TEX/AA	27	27	0	0	5	14	3.24	163.2	140	8	60	93	.234

Narcisse got such poor run support he led the Texas League in losses despite fashioning the league's third-best ERA. He allowed three runs or fewer in 18 of his 27 starts but sported just a 4-9 record in those games. Released by the Padres after two years in the Arizona League because he had only one pitch, a fastball, Narcisse proved a pleasant surprise for Houston. Although his mechanics still need work, the 24-year-old has developed a pretty good slider to complement his low-90 mph heat. He hasn't missed a start in the last three years although his record is only 18-37.

BILLY WAGNER
Bats: L Throws: L Opening Day Age: 25
Ht: 5-10 Wt: 180 Born: 7/25/1971
Position: P Drafted: 1993 #1 HOU

YR TEAM	LG/CLASS	G	GS	GF	SV	W	L	ERA	IP	H	HR	BB	SO	O/BA
93 Auburn	NYP/A	7	7	0	0	1	3	4.08	28.2	25	2	25	31	.231
94 Quad City	MID/A	26	26	0	0	8	9	3.29	153.0	99	9	91	204	.188
95 Tucson	PCL/AAA	13	13	0	0	5	3	3.18	76.1	70	3	32	80	.245
95 Jackson	TEX/AA	12	12	0	0	2	2	2.57	70.0	49	7	36	77	.199
95 Houston	NL/MAJ	1	0	0	0	0	0	0.00	0.1	0	0	0	0	.000

Wagner, selected to Howe Sportsdata's Minor League All-Star team, had an even better season than his impressive record indicates. He did not pick up his first decision until May 11, although he had left five of his first six starts with leads that his bullpen didn't hold. The 24-year-old, who still needs better command of his breaking pitches to supplement his 95-mph fastball, was often unhittable, holding Texas League opponents to three hits or fewer four times. At Triple-A, Wagner threw scoreless ball four times, including his last two starts, and fanned ten twice.

DONNE WALL
Bats: R Throws: R Opening Day Age: 29
Ht: 6-1 Wt: 180 Born: 7/11/1967
Position: P Drafted: 1989 #20 HOU

YR TEAM	LG/CLASS	G	GS	GF	SV	W	L	ERA	IP	H	HR	BB	SO	O/BA
93 Tucson	PCL/AAA	25	22	2	0	6	4	3.83	131.2	147	11	35	89	.283
94 Tucson	PCL/AAA	26	24	0	0	11	8	4.43	148.1	171	9	35	84	.293
95 Tucson	PCL/AAA	28	28	0	0	17	6	3.30	177.1	190	5	32	119	.277
95 Houston	NL/MAJ	6	5	0	0	3	1	5.55	24.1	33	5	5	16	.320

After three full years at Tucson, Wall was finally given a shot with Houston in September after winning Pacific Coast League MVP honors and winning the league's pitching Triple Crown. Wall is a control artist, averaging just 1.95 BB/9 IP for his career. This is the main reason he has gone 72-41, 3.44 ERA in seven years, because the 28-year-old is not overpowering. He uses five pitches and will throw sidearm.

HOUSTON ASTROS: OTHERS TO WATCH

MANNY BARRIOS Bats: R Throws: R Ht: 6-0 Wt: 145
Born: 9/21/1974 Drafted: NDFA 1-27-93 HOU Position: P

YR TEAM	LG/CLASS	G	GS	GF	SV	W	L	ERA	IP	H	HR	BB	SO	O/BA
95 Quad City	MID/A	50	0	48	23	1	5	2.25	52.0	44	1	17	55	.226

The hard-throwing Barrios picked up 13 saves in the second half and turned his career around after going 0-6, 5.95 ERA for the same club in '94.

KARY BRIDGES Bats: L Throws: R Ht: 5-10 Wt: 165
Born: 10/27/1971 Drafted: 1993 #8 HOU Position: 2B

YR TEAM	LG/CLASS	G	AB	R	H	2B	3B	HR	RBI	SB	BA	OBA
95 Jackson	TEX/AA	118	418	56	126	22	4	3	43	10	.301	.372

The scrappy Bridges has versatility, makeup, bat control and a knack for big hits, but he is not the defender the similar Dave Hajek is.

RAMON CASTRO Bats: R Throws: R Ht: 6-3 Wt: 195
Born: 3/1/1976 Drafted: 1994 #1 HOU Position: C

YR TEAM	LG/CLASS	G	AB	R	H	2B	3B	HR	RBI	SB	BA	OBA
95 Kissimmee	FSL/A	36	120	6	25	5	0	0	8	0	.208	.250
95 Auburn	NYP/A	63	224	40	67	17	0	9	49	0	.299	.358

The 1994 first-rounder's tools, a powerful bat and throwing arm, were too raw for full season ball, but he finished third in the New York–Penn home run chase.

SCOTT ELARTON Bats: R Throws: R Ht: 6-8 Wt: 225
Born: 2/23/1976 Drafted: 1994 #2 HOU Position: P

YR TEAM	LG/CLASS	G	GS	GF	SV	W	L	ERA	IP	H	HR	BB	SO	O/BA
95 Quad City	MID/A	26	26	0	0	13	7	4.45	149.2	149	12	71	112	.259

Elarton, a big kid with a strong arm, improved his command greatly in the second half and posted an ERA just over 3.00 in his last 15 starts.

TIM FORKNER Bats: L Throws: R Ht: 5-11 Wt: 180
Born: 3/28/1973 Drafted: 1993 #12 HOU Position: 3B

YR TEAM	LG/CLASS	G	AB	R	H	2B	3B	HR	RBI	SB	BA	OBA
95 Kissimmee	FSL/A	89	296	42	84	20	4	1	34	4	.284	.408
95 Jackson	TEX/AA	35	119	19	32	11	0	3	23	1	.269	.379

A solid hitter with a compact swing and excellent strike zone judgment, Forkner has little power, slow feet and defensive problems.

OSCAR HENRIQUEZ Bats: R Throws: R Ht: 6-4 Wt: 175
Born: 1/28/1974 Drafted: NDFA 5-20-91 HOU Position: P

YR TEAM	LG/CLASS	G	GS	GF	SV	W	L	ERA	IP	H	HR	BB	SO	O/BA
95 Kissimmee	FSL/A	20	0	7	1	3	4	5.04	44.2	40	2	30	36	.240

Henriquez, one of the best young arms in the system, eased his 95-mph fastball back after recovering from a mysterious life-threatening illness in 1994.

RUSS JOHNSON Bats: R Throws: R Ht: 5-10 Wt: 185
Born: 2/22/1973 Drafted: 1994 #3 HOU Position: SS

YR TEAM	LG/CLASS	G	AB	R	H	2B	3B	HR	RBI	SB	BA	OBA
95 Jackson	TEX/AA	132	475	65	118	16	2	9	53	10	.248	.327

The 1994 Southeastern Conference Player-of-the-Year at LSU (.410, 17 HR) didn't show the bat the system had hoped but far exceeded expectations with the glove, committing just five errors the last three months.

RICH LOISELLE Bats: R Throws: R Ht: 6-5 Wt: 225
Born: 1/12/1972 Drafted: 1991 #39 SD Position: P

YR TEAM	LG/CLASS	G	GS	GF	SV	W	L	ERA	IP	H	HR	BB	SO	O/BA
95 Las Vegas	PCL/AAA	8	7	0	0	2	2	7.24	27.1	36	5	9	16	.303
95 Tucson	PCL/AAA	2	1	0	0	0	0	2.61	10.1	8	0	4	4	.200
95 Memphis	SOU/AA	13	13	0	0	6	3	3.55	78.2	82	5	33	48	.259

Acquired from the Padres in mid-season in the Phil Plantier trade, Loiselle has a live arm.

JOHANN LOPEZ Bats: R Throws: R Ht: 6-2 Wt: 170
Born: 4/4/1975 Drafted: NDFA 7-2-91 HOU Position: P

YR TEAM	LG/CLASS	G	GS	GF	SV	W	L	ERA	IP	H	HR	BB	SO	O/BA
95 Kissimmee	FSL/A	18	12	3	1	5	5	2.61	69.0	55	3	25	67	.219

Lopez, who can bring it in the 90-mph range and also has a change, curve and splitter, put together a 23-inning scoreless streak last season.

HECTOR MERCADO Bats: L Throws: L Ht: 6-3 Wt: 205
Born: 4/29/1974 Drafted: 1992 #14 HOU Position: P

YR TEAM	LG/CLASS	G	GS	GF	SV	W	L	ERA	IP	H	HR	BB	SO	O/BA
95 Kissimmee	FSL/A	19	17	0	0	6	8	3.46	104.0	96	2	37	75	.247
95 Jackson	TEX/AA	8	7	0	0	1	4	7.80	30.0	36	5	32	20	.300

Highly regarded but showing few results in Double-A, the 21-year-old features a slow breaking ball, but lacks command.

TONY MITCHELL Bats: S Throws: R Ht: 6-4 Wt: 225
Born: 10/14/1970 Drafted: 1989 #35 PIT Position: OF

YR TEAM	LG/CLASS	G	AB	R	H	2B	3B	HR	RBI	SB	BA	OBA
95 Jackson	TEX/AA	96	331	45	88	17	2	19	61	1	.266	.335

A power hitter from both sides of the plate, Mitchell is not a good defensive player and has a lackluster work ethic.

MELVIN MORA Bats: R Throws: R Ht: 5-10 Wt: 160
Born: 2/2/1972 Drafted: NDFA 3-30-91 HOU Position: OF

YR TEAM	LG/CLASS	G	AB	R	H	2B	3B	HR	RBI	SB	BA	OBA
95 Tucson	PCL/AAA	2	5	3	3	0	1	0	1	1	.600	.714
95 Jackson	TEX/AA	123	467	63	139	32	0	3	45	22	.298	.350

A versatile outfielder who can also play second base, Mora can run and finished strong for the Generals but doesn't have eye-popping defensive skills at any position.

ALVIN MORMAN Bats: L Throws: L Ht: 6-3 Wt: 210
Born: 1/6/1969 Drafted: 1991 #44 HOU Position: P

YR TEAM	LG/CLASS	G	GS	GF	SV	W	L	ERA	IP	H	HR	BB	SO	O/BA
95 Tucson	PCL/AAA	45	0	10	3	5	1	3.91	48.1	50	6	20	36	.281

The hard-throwing Morman, a supreme pitching prospect two years ago, has been sidetracked by nagging shoulder problems and inconsistency.

JHONNY PEREZ Bats: R Throws: R Ht: 5-10 Wt: 150
Born: 10/23/1976 Drafted: NDFA 7-2-93 HOU Position: SS

YR TEAM	LG/CLASS	G	AB	R	H	2B	3B	HR	RBI	SB	BA	OBA
95 Kissimmee	FSL/A	65	214	24	58	12	0	4	31	23	.271	.358

Wiry and strong with bat speed, instincts and work ethic, the 19-year-old plays older than his years, but went out twice in '95 with shoulder problems.

THE SCOUTING REPORT: 1996

LOS ANGELES DODGERS

BRETT BUTLER

Position: OF
Bats: L **Throws:** L
Ht: 5'10" **Wt:** 160
Opening Day Age: 38
Born: 6/15/1957
Drafted: ATL79 22/573
ML Seasons: 15

SCOUTING REPORT

Butler does all the things dead-ball era ballplayers did. He stands on top of the plate, chokes up on the bat, and tries to slap the ball to any field. He runs hard, plays strong defense, and is baseball's best bunter. Opposing outfielders play him shallow and to the left field line, while the infield corners play in on the grass until there are two strikes. Some third basemen expect Brett to lay the ball down at any time. Although pitchers try to overpower Butler inside, he has excellent discipline and will usually make a pitcher throw him something to hit. If he doesn't get a good pitch, he'll just take the walk.

Butler still has the fine speed and well-above average range necessary to cover a wide area, and he has only made four errors in the last two years. However, Brett's throwing has become a problem. He has plus accuracy, but clearly a minus arm. Time has made Butler's throwing possibly the weakest of all NL center fielders.

HOW HE PERFORMED IN '95

After bitter free-agent negotiations with the Dodgers, Butler signed a one-year contract with the Mets. Beset by family illness, however, he started poorly and fell out of favor in New York. Towards midsummer Butler began to produce, but the Mets decided to go with youth and, to everyone's surprise, dealt Butler back to the Dodgers at the end of August.

Although he hit only .274 with Los Angeles, Brett was a critical figure in the Dodgers' playoff drive. He walked 24 times in 39 games after the trade, providing his usual spark at the top of the lineup. Overall, he led the NL with 43 infield hits and 19 bunt singles. Butler showed he can still chop the ball to any particular spot, and he knows every pitcher's ability to field the bunt.

Although Brett once again showed well above-average range in 1995, he would probably welcome the addition of mobile corner outfielders so that he doesn't have to cover so much territory.

WHAT TO EXPECT IN '96

The Dodgers have several young center field prospects in the pipeline. Ultimately, however, the team felt the kids weren't ready to step in, and signed Butler to a one-year contract for 1996. There is no reason to believe Brett can't continue to be productive both ways in '96.

Overall Statistics

	G	AB	R	H	2B	3B	HR	RBI	SB	CS	BB	SO	BA	OBA
95 NYN/LA	129	513	78	154	18	9	1	38	32	8	67	51	.300	.377
Career	2074	7706	1285	2243	268	127	54	552	535	244	1078	845	.291	.379

1995 Situational Statistics

	AB	HR	RBI	BA	OBA	SLG		AB	HR	RBI	BA	OBA	SLG
Home	253	0	19	.296	.376	.344	LHP	130	1	11	.277	.358	.369
Road	260	1	19	.304	.378	.408	RHP	383	0	27	.308	.384	.379
Apr-Jun	215	0	19	.256	.333	.307	ScPos	106	0	36	.274	.390	.302
Jul-Oct	298	1	19	.332	.408	.426	Clutch	98	0	8	.296	.378	.327

How He Compares to Other Batters

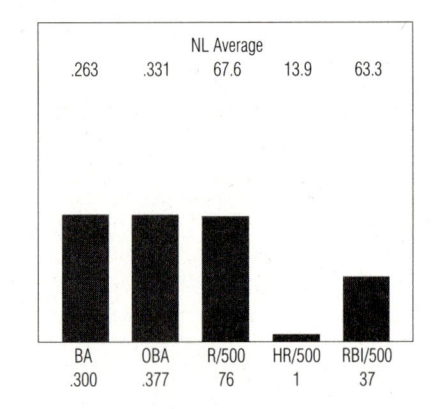

NL Average
.263 .331 67.6 13.9 63.3

BA .300 | OBA .377 | R/500 76 | HR/500 1 | RBI/500 37

Where He Hits the Ball

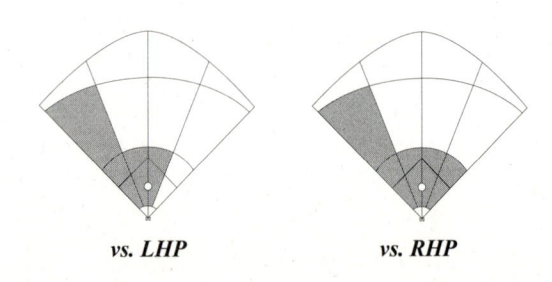

vs. LHP   vs. RHP

LOS ANGELES DODGERS

TOM CANDIOTTI

Position: SP
Bats: R **Throws:** R
Ht: 6'3" **Wt:** 205
Opening Day Age: 38
Born: 8/31/1957
Drafted: VICT 7/17/79
ML Seasons: 12

SCOUTING REPORT

Tom throws from a three-quarter angle with control that ranks above-average for someone who depends on throwing the knuckleball. He is essentially a two-pitch guy, throwing fastballs and knucklers almost exclusively. He survives even more now on craft and guile, as he has less velocity and stamina than in his earlier years. Knuckleballs make up about 75% of his offerings. His knuckler, which rates as plus, is hard to catch due to its very late break. Tom's fastball is minus and he will cut it at times. Candiotti has an average curve and occasionally shows a slider just to confuse the hitter. He struggled against the Rockies in Denver: the altitude had an adverse effect on his prime pitch, which won't knuckle when a mile high.

Candiotti has had problems with baserunners in the past, but this year, even with Piazza struggling behind the plate, had 13 of 23 potential basestealers thrown out. Although Tom is slow to the plate, he has a quick move to first. He is an average fielder.

HOW HE PERFORMED IN '95

Candiotti has been the premier knuckleballer in baseball since Phil Niekro retired. However, he didn't have a banner season in 1995, though he pitched better than his record indicates. He received the lowest run support of all Dodger starters (3.4 runs per game) and the porous Dodgers' defense allowed a league-leading 19 unearned runs to score against Candiotti.

As befits an aging workhorse, Candiotti generally tires as the season progresses. He did not pitch well late in '95, allowing five home runs in his last six starts. Tom's career ERA in September and October is 4.20, a half a run higher than his totals in any other month. He pitched just one complete game last year, further taxing an already shallow Dodgers' bullpen.

At the dish, Candiotti is no bargain. He was 6-for-55 (.109) last season and is now hitting .122 lifetime. Tom doesn't bunt well.

WHAT TO EXPECT IN '96

Now a free agent, Candiotti is entering the twilight of his career. The 12-year veteran hasn't had a winning record since 1990, and he barely averaged six innings a start in '95. Although he pitches every five days without fail, throwing a pitch that is easy on the arm, Tom may not return to the Dodgers in 1996.

Overall Statistics

	G	GS	GF	SV	W	L	ERA	IP	H	R	ER	HR	BB	SO
95 LA	30	30	0	0	7	14	3.50	190.1	187	93	74	18	58	141
Career	331	319	4	0	117	124	3.47	2165.1	2054	960	834	167	707	1428

1995 Situational Statistics

	W	L	ERA	SV	IP	BB	SO		AB	HR	RBI	BA	OBA	SLG
Home	3	9	3.35	0	102.0	29	75	LHB	322	7	25	.264	.338	.385
Road	4	5	3.67	0	88.1	29	66	RHB	410	11	58	.249	.298	.383
Apr-Jun	4	6	3.08	0	87.2	28	57	ScPos	187	6	62	.209	.295	.342
Jul-Oct	3	8	3.86	0	102.2	30	84	Clutch	72	3	7	.236	.317	.403

How He Compares to Other Pitchers

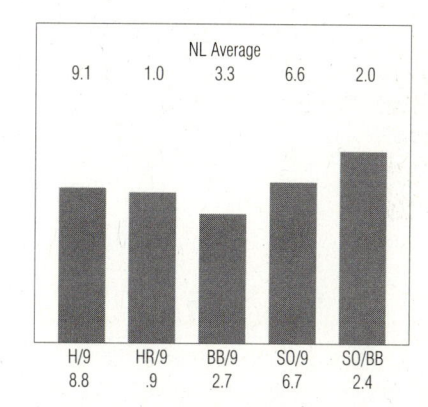

NL Average: 9.1 | 1.0 | 3.3 | 6.6 | 2.0

H/9 8.8 | HR/9 .9 | BB/9 2.7 | SO/9 6.7 | SO/BB 2.4

How He Compares to Other Starting Pitchers

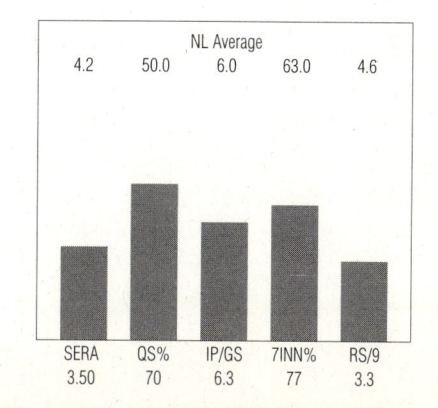

NL Average: 4.2 | 50.0 | 6.0 | 63.0 | 4.6

SERA 3.50 | QS% 70 | IP/GS 6.3 | 7INN% 77 | RS/9 3.3

LOS ANGELES DODGERS

DELINO DESHIELDS

Position: 2B
Bats: L **Throws:** R
Ht: 6'1" **Wt:** 170
Opening Day Age: 27
Born: 1/15/1969
Drafted: MON87 1/12
ML Seasons: 6

SCOUTING REPORT
DeShields finally showed signs of becoming the second baseman the Dodgers wanted him to be in the latter part of 1995. He began to use his above-average speed more constructively at the plate, hitting the ball into the ground and collecting more infield hits than he'd gotten in any previous season. He is a spray hitter to all fields and likes the ball low and over the plate. Despite occasional bursts of power, Delino does not have much raw pop. DeShields doesn't bunt for hits as often as he might, considering his speed. DeShields has plus range and turns the double play on a consistent basis. His arm is of average strength and accuracy. However, Delino committed a career-high 11 errors last season.

HOW HE PERFORMED IN '95
DeShields has been hampered by slumps and injuries in his two years with the Dodgers. In 1995, he lost his job at second base to Chad Fonville after a slow start, only to regain it later when Fonville moved to shortstop. A late charge saved Delino's season stats and probably his job. Patience and speed give DeShields the ability to bat leadoff, second, sixth, or even eighth. However, he strikes out a lot and is often inconsistent. After a .148 July (usually one of his best months), Delino came on strong, hitting almost .300 in the last six weeks. He has been remarkably consistent against pitchers throwing from either side during his career, but in 1995 DeShields slumped dramatically lefthanders: his average dropped 70 points against them from the previous season in his worst performance against portsiders to date. Delino was the Dodgers' top base thief in 1995, and, as usual, had a good stolen base percentage. He does not ground into many double plays.

WHAT TO EXPECT IN '96
Despite DeShields' inconsistent play and injury problems, he's likely to return to L.A. in 1996. He's still just 27 and could easily have a breakthrough year if he stays healthy. Los Angeles isn't thick in middle-infield prospects, either. However, if Delino is going to have that big season, he's going to have to have it sometime soon. In three of his six seasons, he's batted .256 or lower, and has only hit double figures in doubles and homers once apiece. If he doesn't hit for average or for power, that puts a pretty big burden on his defense.

Overall Statistics

	G	AB	R	H	2B	3B	HR	RBI	SB	CS	BB	SO	BA	OBA
95 LA	127	425	66	109	18	3	8	37	39	14	63	83	.256	.353
Career	754	2818	426	764	108	31	33	251	253	91	404	555	.271	.363

1995 Situational Statistics

	AB	HR	RBI	BA	OBA	SLG		AB	HR	RBI	BA	OBA	SLG
Home	205	2	15	.210	.332	.283	LHP	121	2	11	.207	.273	.314
Road	220	6	22	.300	.374	.450	RHP	304	6	26	.276	.383	.391
Apr-Jun	231	4	16	.251	.345	.351	ScPos	75	1	29	.360	.479	.440
Jul-Oct	194	4	21	.263	.363	.392	Clutch	80	1	8	.225	.287	.262

How He Compares to Other Batters

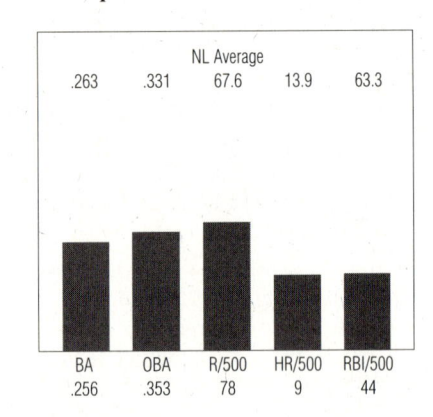

NL Average
BA	OBA	R/500	HR/500	RBI/500
.263	.331	67.6	13.9	63.3

BA	OBA	R/500	HR/500	RBI/500
.256	.353	78	9	44

Where He Hits the Ball

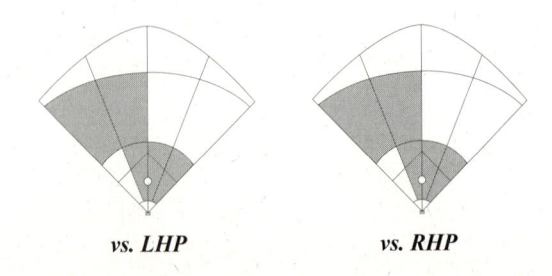

vs. LHP   vs. RHP

464   THE SCOUTING REPORT: 1996

LOS ANGELES DODGERS

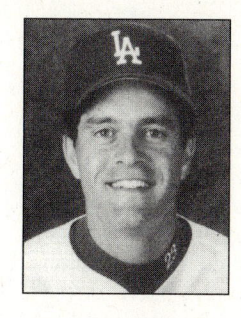

ERIC KARROS

Position: 1B
Bats: R **Throws:** R
Ht: 6'4" **Wt:** 205
Opening Day Age: 28
Born: 11/4/1967
Drafted: LA88 5/140
ML Seasons: 5

SCOUTING REPORT
Like many righthanded power hitters, Karros likes fastballs high and over the plate where he can extend his arms. Eric also can handle low, inside pitches with good bat speed. He has good power to all fields, but most of his home runs came off lefthanders and went to left field. He stands up straight in the box and covers the plate well.

Karros has minus running ability and is a poor percentage base stealer. He does not bunt, either for hits or to sacrifice.

He has average range and hands and has improved his handling of throws from his erratic infielders. His arm is well above-average in strength for the position, with average accuracy.

HOW HE PERFORMED IN '95
Although he hit with power his first three big-league seasons, Karros' batting average and run production was mediocre at best until last season. His bat sparked the Dodgers from wire to wire, and some believed Eric was the team's MVP. With Mike Piazza out at the beginning of the year, Karros hit .359 through May 31 to carry Los Angeles until the power-hitting catcher returned.

Eric has always mashed lefties, but a dramatic improvement against righthanders was the key to his good performance last season. He took more bases on balls last year than in any previous campaign, and it continued success with righties might force pitchers to be more conservative with Karros, leading to more walks.

Eric was a much better fielder in '95 than he had been previously, although he's never going to be a Gold Glover. He made only seven errors in '95.

WHAT TO EXPECT IN '96
Karros will be hard pressed to remain at his new level. His career record is uneven, and many players have their best years at age 27. In order to be an outstanding offensive player, he must avoid hacking at too many bad pitches and continue to go deeper in the count.

The handsome Karros is a management and fan favorite, and should be the club's starting first baseman for the next several years. Los Angeles doesn't have a quality first base prospect in their system, and the front office will be very pleased if Eric can maintain his '95 pace in the future.

Overall Statistics

	G	AB	R	H	2B	3B	HR	RBI	SB	CS	BB	SO	BA	OBA
95 LA	143	551	83	164	29	3	32	105	4	4	61	115	.298	.369
Career	575	2135	271	566	108	7	89	320	8	9	162	359	.265	.317

1995 Situational Statistics

	AB	HR	RBI	BA	OBA	SLG		AB	HR	RBI	BA	OBA	SLG
Home	263	19	51	.293	.370	.548	LHP	124	4	17	.315	.384	.484
Road	288	13	54	.302	.369	.524	RHP	427	28	88	.293	.365	.550
Apr-Jun	237	14	46	.312	.379	.544	ScPos	145	8	72	.345	.441	.600
Jul-Oct	314	18	59	.287	.362	.529	Clutch	74	7	19	.338	.479	.689

How He Compares to Other Batters

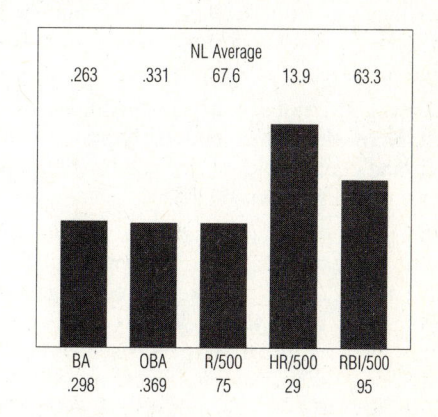

NL Average: BA .263, OBA .331, R/500 67.6, HR/500 13.9, RBI/500 63.3

Karros: BA .298, OBA .369, R/500 75, HR/500 29, RBI/500 95

Where He Hits the Ball

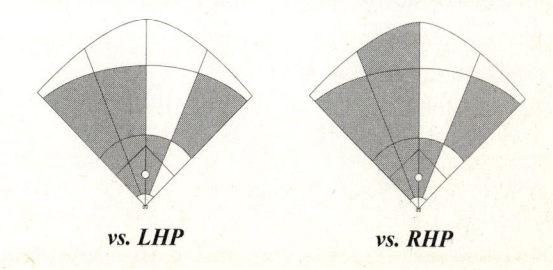

vs. LHP   vs. RHP

THE SCOUTING REPORT: 1996

LOS ANGELES DODGERS

ROBERTO KELLY

Position: OF
Bats: R **Throws:** R
Ht: 6'4" **Wt:** 185
Opening Day Age: 31
Born: 10/1/1964
Drafted: NYA 2/21/82
ML Seasons: 9

SCOUTING REPORT
An aggressive, low-fastball hitter with above-average power in past years, Roberto declined precipitously at bat last season. He displayed little of the punch that the Dodgers were expecting from him when they acquired him from Montreal for Henry Rodriguez in May. He had trouble with off-speed pitches and did not produce against righthanders. He has never been a patient hitter, seldom walking and striking out often. However, Kelly doesn't whiff as often as he once did. Although he still has plus speed, Roberto does not use it well on the bases and seldom bunts. Kelly didn't show he was capable of covering center field for Los Angeles, and after Brett Butler was acquired, Roberto ended up in left field. Kelly has had plus range with well above-average hands and average arm strength and accuracy during his career.

HOW HE PERFORMED IN '95
Kelly was targeted as the all-around center fielder the Dodgers needed during the last off-season, when longtime fixture Brett Butler signed with the Mets. However, Roberto had a very poor '95 season for L.A. and his performance has seriously damaged his career.

Despite his good mobility and his good defense in the past, Kelly showed exceptionally poor range in both left and center field in '95, and threw out just three baserunners all season.

Something was wrong with his bat as well. On September 1, Kelly was batting .267 with four home runs. He hit .329 and smacked three dingers the rest of the way but, all in all, '95 was a very disappointing year for Roberto. His on-base percentage, never a strong point, was intolerable in 1995, and for the second straight season his basestealing hurt his team. Roberto stopped hitting for power four years ago, has declined on the bases, and gets on base at a well below-average pace. That's hardly an impressive record.

WHAT TO EXPECT IN '96
Kelly's future is now in doubt. If he can't play center field any longer, he may not be around. He has not proven that he can hit enough to play left field in the major leagues, especially at a veteran's salary. Roberto was without a home in December, although it likely some team with a weak outfield will want to give him a chance to prove '95 was an aberration. At a greatly reduced price, of course.

Overall Statistics

	G	AB	R	H	2B	3B	HR	RBI	SB	CS	BB	SO	BA	OBA
95 MON/LA	136	504	58	140	23	2	7	57	19	10	22	79	.278	.312
Career	962	3535	495	1006	173	20	81	395	210	74	242	633	.285	.333

1995 Situational Statistics

	AB	HR	RBI	BA	OBA	SLG		AB	HR	RBI	BA	OBA	SLG
Home	236	2	21	.280	.309	.360	LHP	117	2	14	.299	.331	.436
Road	268	5	36	.276	.314	.384	RHP	387	5	43	.271	.306	.354
Apr-Jun	237	2	23	.270	.308	.338	ScPos	124	0	46	.315	.374	.371
Jul-Oct	267	5	34	.285	.315	.404	Clutch	76	3	16	.329	.350	.539

How He Compares to Other Batters

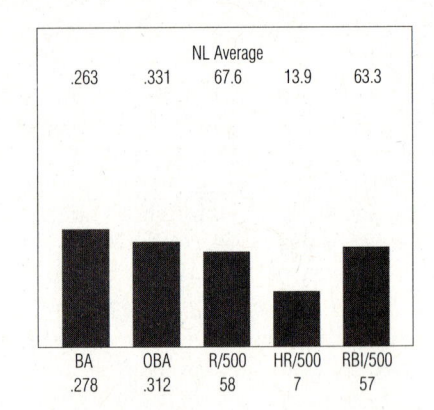

	BA	OBA	R/500	HR/500	RBI/500
NL Average	.263	.331	67.6	13.9	63.3
	.278	.312	58	7	57

Where He Hits the Ball

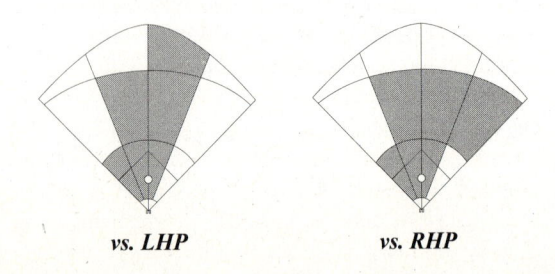

vs. LHP   vs. RHP

LOS ANGELES DODGERS

RAMON MARTINEZ

Position: SP
Bats: R **Throws:** R
Ht: 6'4" **Wt:** 165
Opening Day Age: 28
Born: 3/22/1968
Drafted: LA 9/1/84
ML Seasons: 8

SCOUTING REPORT
Martinez has a three-quarter delivery, which he uses to unload a plus fastball that sinks and bores in on righthanded batters. He will occasionally use a cut fastball against lefthanded hitters. His fastball has almost returned to his early-1990s level. Ramon has an outstanding circle change, which dips low and away to righthanded hitters. In addition, Martinez throws an average, big overhand curve that breaks straight down. His slider works better against lefthanders, but is mostly for show. The thin, agile Martinez is quick off the mound, rating as a plus fielder. Despite being rather slow to home, he has a quick move to first base. Just 12 of 21 basestealers were successful against Ramon last season.

HOW HE PERFORMED IN '95
Martinez, a Dodgers' rookie at 20, had thrown 369 major-league innings by age 22. For a young, skinny pitcher, this workload appears to have been excessive, and Ramon quickly began to lose his fastball. Plagued by arm problems, he did not pitch especially well in 1992–94.

However, he re-emerged in '95. Following a long layoff due to the strike, a rested and strong Martinez was Los Angeles' most consistent starter. In an exciting year for Dodgers fans, Ramon provided one of the highlights on July 14 by no-hitting the Florida Marlins at Dodger Stadium. Martinez was masterful and did not allow a runner until a walk in the eighth.

While Ramon can still blow away batters, he is no longer the overpowering strikeout artist of old. Instead, he is more likely to use off-speed stuff in key situations. In previous years, Martinez had gotten tired in the later months, getting hit quite hard in August and September. However, last season he was 6-1 after July 31 with a 3.20 ERA.

He hit .172 last year (11 for 64) but did lay down 13 sacrifice bunts, which tied him with Jose Vizcaino for the third-highest total in the NL.

WHAT TO EXPECT IN '96
The Dodgers want Martinez, a free agent, back to anchor the staff. He seems recovered from his ailments, has become a smarter pitcher and, at 28, appears to have good years ahead. However, Ramon may not be capable of shouldering a 35-start workload, and may never get back to where he was in 1990.

THE SCOUTING REPORT: 1996

Overall Statistics

	G	GS	GF	SV	W	L	ERA	IP	H	R	ER	HR	BB	SO
95 LA	30	30	0	0	17	7	3.66	206.1	176	95	84	19	81	138
Career	201	198	0	0	91	63	3.48	1327.2	1166	582	513	114	509	970

1995 Situational Statistics

	W	L	ERA	SV	IP	BB	SO		AB	HR	RBI	BA	OBA	SLG
Home	8	5	3.57	0	118.1	37	74	LHB	315	8	34	.254	.363	.381
Road	9	2	3.78	0	88.0	44	64	RHB	446	11	48	.215	.265	.343
Apr-Jun	7	5	4.39	0	84.0	41	54	ScPos	156	5	62	.263	.351	.410
Jul-Oct	10	2	3.16	0	122.1	40	84	Clutch	48	2	6	.229	.302	.375

How He Compares to Other Pitchers

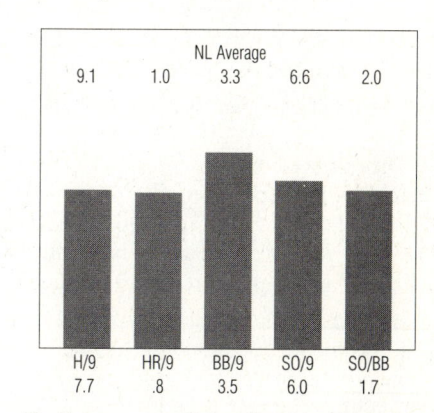

NL Average

H/9	HR/9	BB/9	SO/9	SO/BB
9.1	1.0	3.3	6.6	2.0
7.7	.8	3.5	6.0	1.7

How He Compares to Other Starting Pitchers

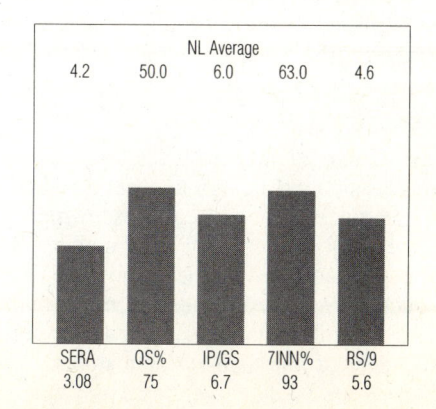

NL Average

SERA	QS%	IP/GS	7INN%	RS/9
4.2	50.0	6.0	63.0	4.6
3.08	75	6.7	93	5.6

LOS ANGELES DODGERS

RAUL MONDESI

Position: OF
Bats: R **Throws:** R
Ht: 5'11" **Wt:** 202
Opening Day Age: 25
Born: 3/12/1971
Drafted: LA 6/6/88
ML Seasons: 3

SCOUTING REPORT

Raul can drive the ball to all fields with power and is fast enough to beat out infield hits. He has excellent bat speed and a relatively short swing. Mondesi is a high fastball hitter who has problems with inside off-speed pitches. He continues to struggle, surprisingly, against lefthanded pitchers.

A lack of patience at the plate causes Raul to swing at the first pitch much too often, helping pitchers by getting himself out.

The still-young Mondesi used his outstanding legs more wisely last year. He has average-plus speed and is a well above-average baserunner, but Raul is rather slow out of the batters box.

Mondesi has the strongest outfield arm in all of baseball, along with one of most accurate. He has plus range and well above-average hands.

HOW HE PERFORMED IN '95

While Raul Mondesi has the tools most players only dream about, he is working to refine his gifts into performance. In '95, his second big-league season, he continued the process impressively, joining the All-Star team for the first time and helping his team make the playoffs.

Mondesi started hot and was batting .320 on July 1. Unfortunately, he hit just .258 the rest of the way, although he showed consistent power all year. While Raul still has a poor on-base percentage, he doubled his walk total from that of his rookie campaign. Mondesi improved his stolen base rate by 30 percent in 1995 and is a future 30-30 candidate.

Defense may be Raul's strongest point. He opened the year in center field, but soon returned to right, again showing the devastating arm that opponents are increasingly reluctant to test. For the second straight year he led the majors with 16 outfield assists and showed much better range than he had as a rookie, using his mobility to cut off balls in the gap.

WHAT TO EXPECT IN '96

Mondesi is one of the most exciting players in baseball. He's young enough to eventually become a bona fide superstar, and he could easily move into the elite inner circle of MVP-type sluggers if he improves his command of the strike zone. Amazingly enough, Mondesi never hit more than 12 homers in any minor-league season, and has an excellent chance of improving as he matures.

Overall Statistics

	G	AB	R	H	2B	3B	HR	RBI	SB	CS	BB	SO	BA	OBA
95 LA	139	536	91	153	23	6	26	88	27	4	33	96	.285	.328
Career	293	1056	167	311	53	15	46	154	42	13	53	190	.295	.329

1995 Situational Statistics

	AB	HR	RBI	BA	OBA	SLG		AB	HR	RBI	BA	OBA	SLG
Home	257	13	45	.288	.330	.502	LHP	112	5	16	.250	.315	.473
Road	279	13	43	.283	.326	.491	RHP	424	21	72	.295	.331	.502
Apr-Jun	241	13	37	.320	.368	.568	ScPos	127	10	61	.283	.347	.591
Jul-Oct	295	13	51	.258	.295	.437	Clutch	77	1	8	.273	.326	.377

How He Compares to Other Batters

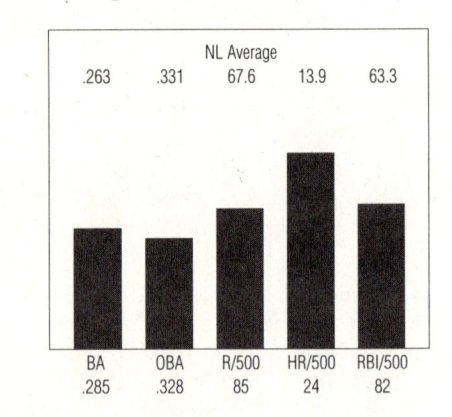

NL Average: .263 .331 67.6 13.9 63.3

BA .285 | OBA .328 | R/500 85 | HR/500 24 | RBI/500 82

Where He Hits the Ball

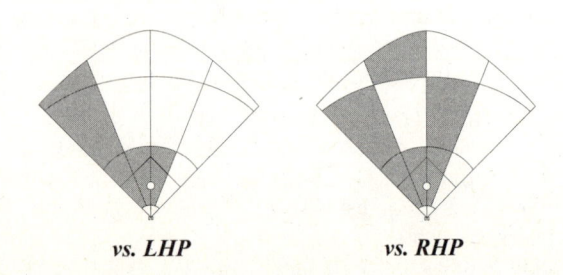

vs. LHP   vs. RHP

LOS ANGELES DODGERS

HIDEO NOMO

Position: SP
Bats: R **Throws:** R
Ht: 6'2" **Wt:** 210
Opening Day Age: 27
Born: 8/31/1968
Drafted: LA 2/18/95
ML Seasons: 1

SCOUTING REPORT

Using a whirling, look-at-my-uniform-number, full-twist delivery not seen since the days of Luis Tiant, Hideo Nomo brings the ball home from an overhand to three-quarters release point, depending on the pitch. A wrist wrap just adds to the deception NL hitters have come to fear.

Hideo has an average-plus fastball which drops as it reaches the plate. His fastball has deceptive speed thanks to his delivery. However, the velocity on his heater dropped in the second half of the year, probably due to overuse. Nomo's out pitch is his devastating plus forkball, of which he has excellent command. He will occasionally throw a minus curve as a waste pitch.

With his long delivery, Nomo has serious problems holding runners despite an average move to first. Runners took off every chance they could get, stealing 30 bases in 35 tries while Nomo was pitching, the highest raw total in the league. Despite his delivery, Nomo is an average fielder.

At the plate, Hideo was 6-for-66 (.091) and fanned in exactly half his at-bats. He laid down just five sacrifices.

HOW HE PERFORMED IN '95

Using his excellent command and that baffling delivery, Japanese "rookie" righthander Hideo Nomo led the NL in strikeouts and opponents' batting average and helped restore excitement to baseball in '95.

Nomo, a five-year veteran of the Kintetsu Buffaloes, was plagued by elbow trouble in Japan, and the Dodgers brought him along slowly. After a start at Class-A, Hideo came to L.A. on May 2 and was an immediate sensation. He was wild at he beginning of the year but settled down quickly; in June, he was a spectacular 6-0 with an 0.89 ERA.

WHAT TO EXPECT IN '96

If Rookie-of-the-Year Nomo does experience a sophomore slump, it may be because of Tommy Lasorda's pattern of allowing his good starting pitchers to pitch deep into many games. Nomo seemed visibly tired in the last month of the season.

Some say Nomo will lose effectiveness when batters figure out his unusual delivery. However, Nomo will have also learned about NL batters' weaknesses, and he is a quick enough study to adapt and prosper.

Overall Statistics

	G	GS	GF	SV	W	L	ERA	IP	H	R	ER	HR	BB	SO
95 LA	28	28	0	0	13	6	2.54	191.1	124	63	54	14	78	236
Career	28	28	0	0	13	6	2.54	191.1	124	63	54	14	78	236

1995 Situational Statistics

	W	L	ERA	SV	IP	BB	SO		AB	HR	RBI	BA	OBA	SLG
Home	8	2	1.73	0	99.0	40	113	LHB	310	8	27	.200	.287	.326
Road	5	4	3.41	0	92.1	38	123	RHB	371	6	26	.167	.255	.253
Apr-Jun	6	1	2.05	0	83.1	41	109	ScPos	156	3	42	.192	.337	.327
Jul-Oct	7	5	2.92	0	108.0	37	127	Clutch	53	1	2	.113	.266	.170

How He Compares to Other Pitchers

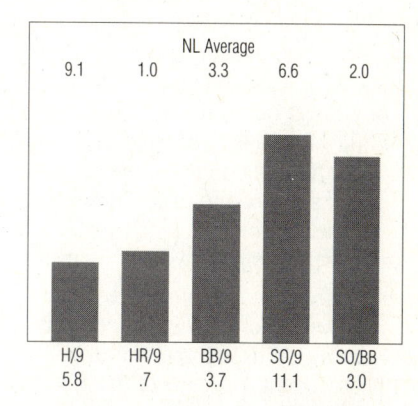

NL Average: 9.1 / 1.0 / 3.3 / 6.6 / 2.0

H/9	HR/9	BB/9	SO/9	SO/BB
5.8	.7	3.7	11.1	3.0

How He Compares to Other Starting Pitchers

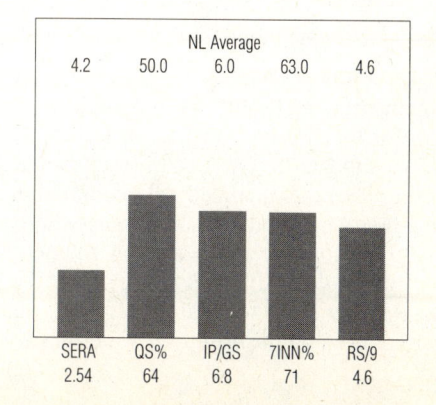

NL Average: 4.2 / 50.0 / 6.0 / 63.0 / 4.6

SERA	QS%	IP/GS	7INN%	RS/9
2.54	64	6.8	71	4.6

THE SCOUTING REPORT: 1996

LOS ANGELES DODGERS

JOSE OFFERMAN

Position: SS
Bats: B **Throws:** R
Ht: 6'0" **Wt:** 150
Opening Day Age: 27
Born: 11/8/1968
Drafted: LA 7/24/86
ML Seasons: 6

SCOUTING REPORT

Defense draws attention to Offerman—for all the wrong reasons. Although he has outstanding tools, he has not produced good results in the field. Jose has well above-average range, can make outstanding plays, and owns a very strong arm with average accuracy. However, he is constantly confounded by below-average hands and serious lapses in concentration. His fundamentals are not good, and as a result, Offerman's defense has gotten worse, not better, over the years.

A natural righthanded hitter, Jose has done well after adopting switch-hitting. In the classic pattern, he likes low pitches batting lefty and higher offerings from the right side. Offerman made better contact in 1995 than he had ever done before, showing gap power from both sides. He is a good bunter with good baserunning speed.

HOW HE PERFORMED IN '95

While Offerman hit well in 1995, miserable baserunning and wretched defense forced him to the bench by the end of the year and ultimately out of the Dodgers' plans for good.

Offerman, batting at the top of the order, hit .353 through the end of May and even made the All-Star team. From July onward, however, Offerman sagged. While he made decent contact and drew plenty of walks, his ridiculous stolen base numbers doomed him as a top-of-the-order hitter. Offerman stole 30 bases as recently as 1993, making his recent lack of baserunning prowess 472baffling.

Defensively, Offerman has almost become a joke. His 35 errors were the most in baseball in '95 by far. The pitching staff became increasingly frustrated with Offerman, who made 25 errors in his last 80 games, and ultimately wound up at the end of Tommy Lasorda's long bench. He batted just eight times after September 1.

WHAT TO EXPECT IN '96

The signing of Greg Gagne was the final writing on the wall for Jose in Los Angeles. In December, he was shipped to Kansas City for Billy Brewer, a disappointing young lefthanded reliever. While this means a brand new start for Offerman, who could well jumpstart his career in a new environment, the specifics of the deal still amaze. When was the last time an All-Star shortstop was traded for a middle reliever not even on the 40-player roster during the winter?

Overall Statistics

	G	AB	R	H	2B	3B	HR	RBI	SB	CS	BB	SO	BA	OBA
95 LA	119	429	69	123	14	6	4	33	2	7	69	67	.287	.389
Career	579	1967	257	503	65	24	8	160	61	39	264	324	.256	.344

1995 Situational Statistics

	AB	HR	RBI	BA	OBA	SLG		AB	HR	RBI	BA	OBA	SLG
Home	207	2	18	.280	.389	.372	LHP	123	1	7	.301	.403	.390
Road	222	2	15	.293	.389	.378	RHP	306	3	26	.281	.384	.369
Apr-Jun	218	1	15	.321	.429	.422	ScPos	89	0	26	.258	.394	.337
Jul-Oct	211	3	18	.251	.347	.327	Clutch	60	0	7	.283	.434	.317

How He Compares to Other Batters

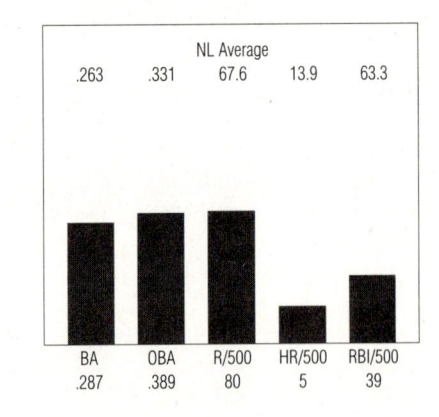

NL Average: .263 .331 67.6 13.9 63.3

BA	OBA	R/500	HR/500	RBI/500
.287	.389	80	5	39

Where He Hits the Ball

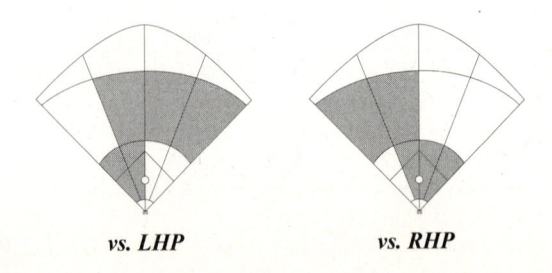

vs. LHP   vs. RHP

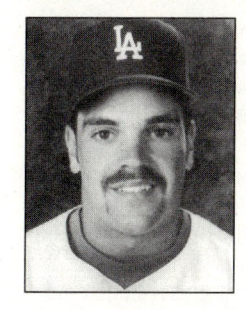

LOS ANGELES DODGERS

MIKE PIAZZA

Position: C
Bats: R **Throws:** R
Ht: 6'3" **Wt:** 200
Opening Day Age: 27
Born: 9/4/1968
Drafted: LA88 61/1390
ML Seasons: 4

SCOUTING REPORT
Piazza has the plate discipline of a grizzled veteran with the power of the young, quick athlete he is. Mike works to get the count to his advantage and uses a quick bat to drive his pitch to any field. He especially likes pitches out over the plate; Piazza is one of the strongest players in baseball. Although Mike has become susceptible to high, inside fastballs, there are only a few pitchers that can get that pitch by him. Piazza is now trying to take those inside deliveries to the opposite field. As befits his position, Piazza has minus speed. He is a smart runner, but is strictly station-to-station on the bases. Defense is the only truly weak area of Piazza's game. He has minus range and poor mobility behind the plate, and his throws are frequently not accurate. He does, however have plus arm strength, and his throwing accuracy may improve with experience.

HOW HE PERFORMED IN '95
In just three years, Mike has shown himself to be a star of the first order, and he had his best season yet in '95. His batting average and slugging percentage were by far his best ever.

He put up MVP numbers, battling Tony Gwynn for the batting title and finishing third in the NL in slugging percentage despite missing a month with a torn thumb ligament. With Piazza out from May 10 to June 3, the Dodgers played sub-.500 ball.

Reversing his usual pattern, this was the first year that Piazza hit better against lefthanders than righthanders. In addition, for the first time, he hit for far more power in road games (23 homers, .384 average) than at home. He doesn't take many walks, because Mike feels his job is to hit, and did strike out more often in '95 than he had previously.

His throws to second have become more erratic, and working with a pitching staff known for its slow deliveries, Mike is easy to steal on. He tossed out just 25% of potential base thieves in '95.

WHAT TO EXPECT IN '96
Piazza's offensive output is amazing considering the wear and tear associated with catching. Mike is still learning how to play the position, and his career seems limitless. A hard worker who leads his team by example, Piazza should remain the best catcher in baseball for several more years as long as he remains healthy.

Overall Statistics

	G	AB	R	H	2B	3B	HR	RBI	SB	CS	BB	SO	BA	OBA
95 LA	112	434	82	150	17	0	32	93	1	0	39	80	.346	.400
Career	389	1455	232	469	62	2	92	304	5	7	122	243	.322	.375

1995 Situational Statistics

	AB	HR	RBI	BA	OBA	SLG		AB	HR	RBI	BA	OBA	SLG
Home	205	9	36	.302	.364	.463	LHP	89	8	15	.326	.362	.607
Road	229	23	57	.384	.432	.734	RHP	345	24	78	.351	.409	.606
Apr-Jun	136	13	36	.390	.439	.728	ScPos	112	9	60	.357	.421	.661
Jul-Oct	298	19	57	.326	.382	.550	Clutch	61	4	10	.361	.458	.623

How He Compares to Other Batters

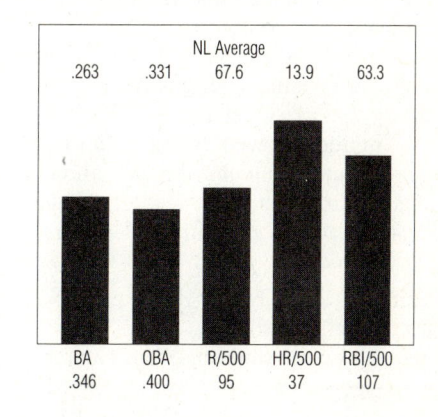

NL Average: .263 .331 67.6 13.9 63.3

BA	OBA	R/500	HR/500	RBI/500
.346	.400	95	37	107

Where He Hits the Ball

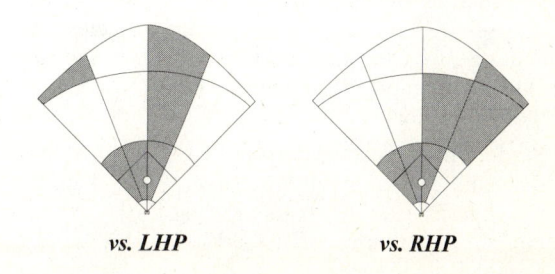

vs. LHP   vs. RHP

LOS ANGELES DODGERS

KEVIN TAPANI

Position: SP
Bats: R **Throws:** R
Ht: 6'0" **Wt:** 180
Opening Day Age: 32
Born: 2/18/1964
Drafted: OAK86 2/40
ML Seasons: 7

SCOUTING REPORT
Kevin has a high kick and an easy three-quarter motion. Tapani will use any of his five pitches at any time, but he must have good control in order to work the corners: he doesn't have the good stuff to win if he is not sharp. Kevin's average-plus sinking fastball moves almost straight down. He has a plus forkball, but Tapani's curve, slider, and change-up are all average-minus deliveries. He never did throw especially hard, and Tapani's pitches now seem to have lost some of their bite.

With his high kick, Tapani has trouble holding runners. In Minnesota, 15 baserunners stole against him in 16 tries, but in Los Angeles, only six of nine were successful. It's likely that runners weren't familiar with his motion, accounting for their lack of aggressiveness. Kevin is an average fielder.

He hit a respectable .176 with the Dodgers, taking his first 14 major-league trips to the plate.

HOW HE PERFORMED IN '95
The veteran righthander was finally traded last July 31 after years of rumors that had him leaving Minnesota. Tapani was supposed to fill the fourth starter role on the Dodgers, but pitched ineffectively and was eventually dropped from the rotation, getting only five starts over the final six weeks. Kevin allowed well over a hit an inning in Los Angeles, and while he did not allow many walks, his control was poor. He served up eight home runs in eleven starts with the Dodgers.

Tapani works best when he paints the corners. While adjusting to the National League strike zone might have been a problem, Kevin never established that he could work the edges consistently with the Dodgers.

WHAT TO EXPECT IN '96
Tapani has always been a second-half pitcher, but he failed to continue that pattern in 1995. Kevin was a free agent, and his return to Los Angeles was contingent on the money he would seek and the club's evaluation of its own pitching prospects in the high minors.

Kevin's three best years were 1990–92, his first three full campaigns in the majors. Since then, he has experienced three years of rising ERAs and declining overall effectiveness. He is durable and should have at least a couple of seasons left in some club's rotation.

Overall Statistics

	G	GS	GF	SV	W	L	ERA	IP	H	R	ER	HR	BB	SO
95 MIN/LA	33	31	0	0	10	13	4.96	190.2	227	116	105	29	48	131
Career	197	191	1	0	79	65	4.10	1235.2	1305	605	563	118	273	769

1995 Situational Statistics

	W	L	ERA	SV	IP	BB	SO		AB	HR	RBI	BA	OBA	SLG
Home	5	6	5.68	0	95.0	22	63	LHB	419	15	56	.284	.329	.480
Road	5	7	4.23	0	95.2	26	68	RHB	351	14	48	.308	.349	.496
Apr-Jun	4	8	4.56	0	92.2	19	63	ScPos	198	7	72	.288	.342	.449
Jul-Oct	6	5	5.33	0	98.0	29	68	Clutch	38	0	2	.263	.317	.395

How He Compares to Other Pitchers

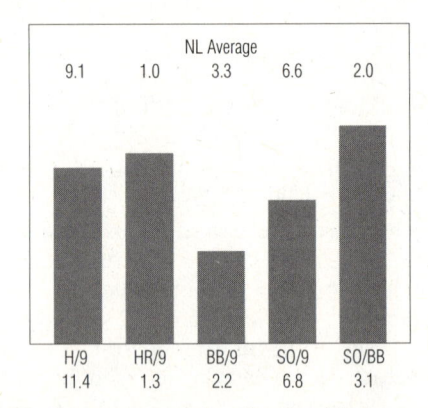

NL Average: 9.1 / 1.0 / 3.3 / 6.6 / 2.0

H/9	HR/9	BB/9	SO/9	SO/BB
11.4	1.3	2.2	6.8	3.1

How He Compares to Other Starting Pitchers

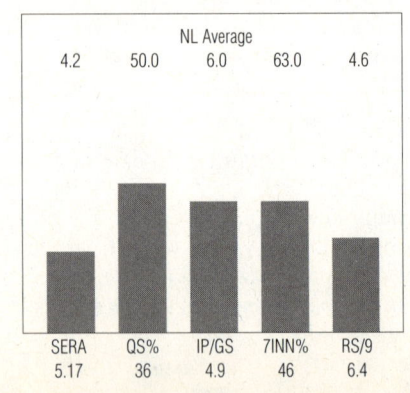

NL Average: 4.2 / 50.0 / 6.0 / 63.0 / 4.6

SERA	QS%	IP/GS	7INN%	RS/9
5.17	36	4.9	46	6.4

LOS ANGELES DODGERS

ISMAEL VALDES

Position: SP/RP
Bats: R **Throws:** R
Ht: 6'3" **Wt:** 185
Opening Day Age: 22
Born: 8/21/1973
Drafted: LA 6/14/91
ML Seasons: 2

SCOUTING REPORT
Ismael fires to the plate from three-quarters with long arm action. He has a plus sinking fastball that is equally hard to hit from both sides of the plate. He has three other pitches, the best being an outstanding change-up. Valdes' big rolling curve has improved to average, and he also has an average hard slider that jams lefthanded batters.

As a result of Valdes' improvement in holding baserunners, opponents did not take off at will as they had in '94. Ten runners stole against Ismael in 14 attempts, a much-reduced number. He has a minus move to first but comes to the plate quickly, and is an average fielder.

HOW HE PERFORMED IN '95
It was a breakthrough year from Valdes, who is young, improving, and underrated by those who don't see him enough. A victim of the porous Dodgers' defense, he pitched much better than his record would indicate.

Ismael had spent 1994 as a starter in the minors and a middleman in Los Angeles. Last season, the Mexican native became a member of the Dodgers' "international" rotation in mid-May and did an excellent job. His ERA as a starter was 3.05 and he won five straight games in June.

Valdes ranked fourth in the National League in ERA, hits allowed per nine innings, and opponents' batting average. The only area of concern for him was a tendency to give up home runs early in his starts, which knocked him out of games in which he was actually pitching well otherwise.

As the year progressed, Ismael began to throw more off-speed pitches in crucial situations. This ability should make Valdes even better as he gets more experience. Right now, even with his career just beginning, he knows how to pitch.

He clearly could stand to improve at the plate, though. Ismael hit just .097 in 62 at-bats, striking out 26 times, and he's not a good bunter.

WHAT TO EXPECT IN '96
Young, smart, and able to learn from mistakes, Valdes has a very bright future. If he pitched on another team he might be a number one starter, but he is now the #3 behind Martinez and Nomo. That might be a good thing, as it will keep the pressure off Valdes as he matures.

Overall Statistics

	G	GS	GF	SV	W	L	ERA	IP	H	R	ER	HR	BB	SO
95 LA	33	27	1	1	13	11	3.05	197.2	168	76	67	17	51	150
Career	54	28	8	1	16	12	3.07	226.0	189	86	77	19	61	178

1995 Situational Statistics

	W	L	ERA	SV	IP	BB	SO		AB	HR	RBI	BA	OBA	SLG
Home	6	5	2.30	0	98.0	21	78	LHB	352	13	38	.227	.292	.389
Road	7	6	3.79	1	99.2	30	72	RHB	385	4	30	.229	.263	.301
Apr-Jun	5	3	2.53	1	81.2	28	66	ScPos	155	6	53	.239	.289	.387
Jul-Oct	8	8	3.41	0	116.0	23	84	Clutch	94	3	9	.234	.298	.340

How He Compares to Other Pitchers

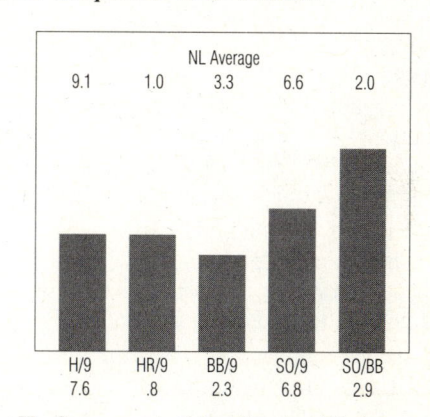

	H/9	HR/9	BB/9	SO/9	SO/BB
NL Average	9.1	1.0	3.3	6.6	2.0
	7.6	.8	2.3	6.8	2.9

How He Compares to Other Starting Pitchers

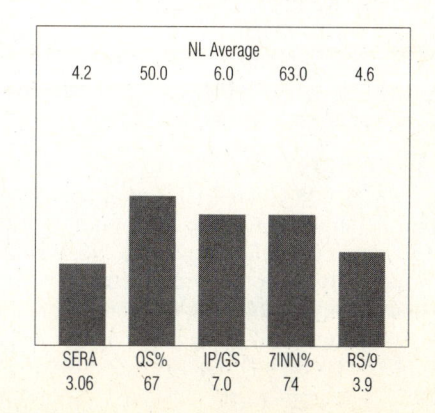

	SERA	QS%	IP/GS	7INN%	RS/9
NL Average	4.2	50.0	6.0	63.0	4.6
	3.06	67	7.0	74	3.9

LOS ANGELES DODGERS

TIM WALLACH

Positions: 3B//1B
Bats: R **Throws:** R
Ht: 6'3" **Wt:** 200
Opening Day Age: 38
Born: 9/14/1957
Drafted: MON79 1/10
ML Seasons: 16

SCOUTING REPORT
Wallach has a long, uppercut swing with decent bat speed. He now has trouble getting around on good fastballs. A low-ball hitter, he can look pretty bad on off-speed pitches. He has only occasional power, and doesn't make contact on a consistent basis. With his recent history of back and leg ailments, it's no surprise that Wallach is a minus runner. Tim provides solid, if unspectacular, third base work. He now has just average range but well above-average hands. His average-minus arm strength is teamed with well above-average accuracy. Despite the pinpoint throws he delivers, however, it is increasingly apparent that he can no longer turn the double play.

HOW HE PERFORMED IN '95
The veteran had an excellent 1994 comeback season, but was hampered last year by injuries and might be finished as an everyday player. Wallach was in and out of the lineup in '95 with nagging ailments. He missed nearly a month with a bulging disc in his back and tore a knee ligament in August. He returned on September 11, however, and ran off a hot streak. All his offensive totals were down from 1994, which is to be expected considering Wallach's age and ailments. Although his on-field contributions were slight, Tim was viewed as a team leader by his fellow Dodgers for playing hard and coming back quickly from his injuries.

He collected his 2,000th hit last September 22, and will finish with over 250 home runs. While he has never had an MVP-type season, Tim was for many years a good hitter and a fine fielder.

Steady defense, in fact, is why Tommy Lasorda continued to write "Wallach, 3B" on the lineup card. Tim solidified a shaky left side of the infield and gave Dodger pitchers confidence that one infielder, at least, could handle the ball cleanly. However, his once-outstanding range wasn't that good in '95, and Tim's 10 double plays were the lowest of any regular third baseman in the majors.

WHAT TO EXPECT IN '96
Wallach's future is cloudy. His age, poor offense, and injuries should preclude him from everyday duty. He signed with the Angels for '96, where he will purportedly platoon with Japanese refugee Jack Howell. As mediocre as Wallach's production was in 1995, it was still better than what he had delivered in 1993. Or 1992. Or 1991.

Overall Statistics

	G	AB	R	H	2B	3B	HR	RBI	SB	CS	BB	SO	BA	OBA
95 LA	97	327	24	87	22	2	9	38	0	0	27	69	.266	.326
Career	2110	7747	871	2003	422	35	248	1083	50	65	619	1228	.259	.317

1995 Situational Statistics

	AB	HR	RBI	BA	OBA	SLG		AB	HR	RBI	BA	OBA	SLG
Home	168	4	18	.232	.284	.357	LHP	85	4	13	.259	.315	.459
Road	159	5	20	.302	.369	.503	RHP	242	5	25	.269	.330	.417
Apr-Jun	129	3	14	.264	.331	.403	ScPos	78	2	25	.256	.354	.436
Jul-Oct	198	6	24	.268	.323	.444	Clutch	52	1	6	.288	.362	.500

How He Compares to Other Batters

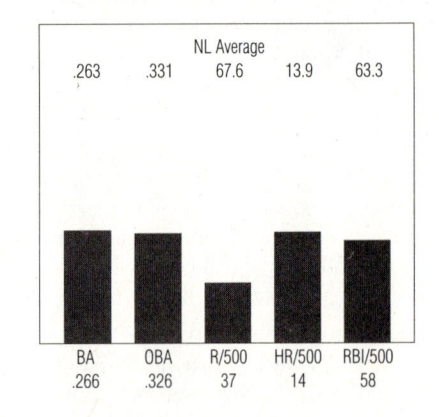

NL Average
.263 .331 67.6 13.9 63.3

BA	OBA	R/500	HR/500	RBI/500
.266	.326	37	14	58

Where He Hits the Ball

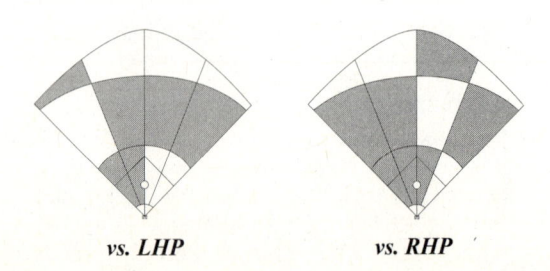

vs. LHP   vs. RHP

LOS ANGELES DODGERS

TODD WORRELL

Position: RP
Bats: R **Throws:** R
Ht: 6'5" **Wt:** 215
Opening Day Age: 36
Born: 9/28/1959
Drafted: SL82 1/21
ML Seasons: 9

SCOUTING REPORT

Worrell has a three-quarter to low three-quarter delivery, throwing slightly across his body. Both his fastballs are well above-average: a two seam fastball that sinks effectively and a rising four-seamer. His arm troubles seem to be behind him, as Todd's fastball returned to its 90-plus, pre-surgery range. Although he no longer throws the hard slider much, Worrell now throws an average slurve-type curve as well as an infrequent, minus change-up.

Worrell does not hold runners well at all. Ten runners tried to steal against Todd in '95 and all were successful. He is a minus fielder, and an 0-for-2 performance at the plate means he is now 2-for-27 (.074) in his career.

HOW HE PERFORMED IN '95

After two years of frustration, Worrell finally had the year the Dodgers had been waiting for since they signed him in 1993. His arm troubles seem to be behind him and Todd stayed strong as a result of being used judiciously.

He came through with the closer's performance that the Dodgers needed to win, setting a Dodgers' record with 32 saves and blowing just four save opportunities. Worrell's performance was the best the team has had from a closer in many years. He didn't allow an earned run until after July 4, by which time he was 12 for 12 in save chances. However, he was horrid in July and August (5.17 ERA in 24.1 innings), getting hit hard before finishing with 12.1 scoreless innings in September.

He has allowed exactly four home runs per season in four of the last five years. Todd also rarely walks anyone and rarely flings wild pitches. However, he does have bouts of poor control, especially if he does not have the fastball. If the heat isn't working, Worrell does not have much to count on.

WHAT TO EXPECT IN '96

The Dodgers want Todd to anchor their bullpen again in '96—the pitcher of May, June, and September '95, that is, not the one they saw in 1993-94. While his comeback was stunning and he served as one of the league's better closers last year, there is a hazard involved in re-signing the aging, streaky, and injury-plagued Worrell.

Overall Statistics

	G	GS	GF	SV	W	L	ERA	IP	H	R	ER	HR	BB	SO
95 LA	59	0	53	32	4	1	2.02	62.1	50	15	14	4	19	61
Career	480	0	334	177	44	40	2.86	568.2	478	197	181	48	209	501

1995 Situational Statistics

	W	L	ERA	SV	IP	BB	SO		AB	HR	RBI	BA	OBA	SLG
Home	3	1	3.21	18	33.2	7	39	LHB	112	1	9	.179	.248	.223
Road	1	0	0.63	14	28.2	12	22	RHB	114	3	15	.263	.317	.377
Apr-Jun	1	0	0.00	12	25.2	5	25	ScPos	59	1	19	.237	.319	.322
Jul-Oct	3	1	3.44	20	36.2	14	36	Clutch	168	4	24	.220	.273	.315

How He Compares to Other Pitchers

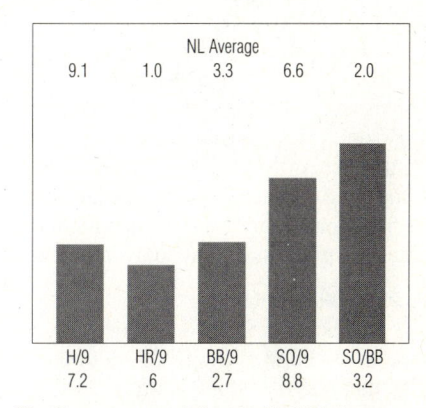

NL Average: H/9 9.1, HR/9 1.0, BB/9 3.3, SO/9 6.6, SO/BB 2.0

H/9 7.2, HR/9 .6, BB/9 2.7, SO/9 8.8, SO/BB 3.2

How He Compares to Other Relief Pitchers

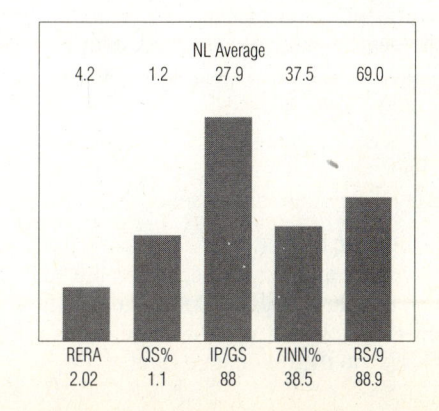

NL Average: RERA 4.2, QS% 1.2, IP/GS 27.9, 7INN% 37.5, RS/9 69.0

RERA 2.02, QS% 1.1, IP/GS 88, 7INN% 38.5, RS/9 88.9

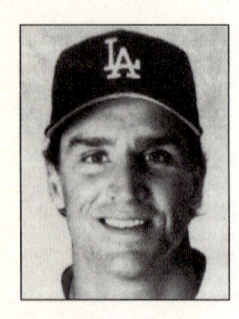

LOS ANGELES DODGERS

BILLY ASHLEY

Position: OF
Bats: R **Throws:** R
Ht: 6'7" **Wt:** 220
Opening Day Age: 25
Born: 7/11/1970
Drafted: LA88 2/62
ML Seasons: 4

Overall Statistics

	G	AB	R	H	2B	3B	HR	RBI	SB	CS	BB	SO	BA	OBA
95 LA	81	215	17	51	5	0	8	27	0	0	25	88	.237	.320
Career	126	353	23	83	11	0	10	33	0	0	32	135	.235	.301

1995 Situational Statistics

	AB	HR	RBI	BA	OBA	SLG		AB	HR	RBI	BA	OBA	SLG
Home	117	6	22	.299	.373	.479	LHP	68	2	5	.279	.329	.382
Road	98	2	5	.163	.255	.245	RHP	147	6	22	.218	.316	.367
Apr-Jun	164	8	25	.256	.342	.421	ScPos	50	3	22	.220	.369	.440
Jul-Oct	51	0	2	.176	.246	.216	Clutch	26	0	1	.154	.290	.192

SCOUTING REPORT
Ashley is a low fastball hitter who cuts at pitches over the plate. However, he has a big swing with lots of holes and too often waves at pitches out of the strike zone. He's particularly weak at hitting curves and is generally a mistake hitter. Billy is big, slow, lumbering runner who poses no threat to steal. He has minus range, is not a particularly good fielder, and has a minus arm with average accuracy.

HOW HE PERFORMED IN '95
Ashley began the year as the starting Dodgers' left fielder, touted as a one of the Dodgers of the future. However, that future won't come until Ashley learns to hit a major-league curve.

Billy has big power, even against righthanders, who he struggles against. However, Ashley's biggest contribution to the '95 Dodgers was the strikeout. Many, many strikeouts.

He showed decent mobility in left field last year— better than expected—but threw out just three runners. Billy didn't bunt all season.

WHAT TO EXPECT IN '96
Ashley will get another chance at the left field job. However, until he makes better contact, his future is problematic. He hasn't yet translated his success at Albuquerque to the big-league level.

PEDRO ASTACIO

Position: RP/SP
Bats: R **Throws:** R
Ht: 6'2" **Wt:** 174
Opening Day Age: 26
Born: 11/28/1969
Drafted: LA 11/21/87
ML Seasons: 4

Overall Statistics

	G	GS	GF	SV	W	L	ERA	IP	H	R	ER	HR	BB	SO
95 LA	48	11	7	0	7	8	4.24	104.0	103	53	49	12	29	80
Career	113	76	7	0	32	30	3.66	521.1	490	233	212	45	164	353

1995 Situational Statistics

	W	L	ERA	SV	IP	BB	SO		AB	HR	RBI	BA	OBA	SLG
Home	4	3	4.04	0	49.0	16	43	LHB	192	8	24	.260	.322	.458
Road	3	5	4.42	0	55.0	13	37	RHB	203	4	25	.261	.309	.365
Apr-Jun	1	6	4.59	0	66.2	22	48	ScPos	91	1	33	.242	.308	.396
Jul-Oct	6	2	3.62	0	37.1	7	32	Clutch	82	2	10	.268	.307	.366

SCOUTING REPORT
Astacio has an unorthodox delivery, slinging the ball across his body at a high three-quarter angle. His fastball is an average-plus sinker. Pedro's curve and slow curve are average, but his straight change is well above-average. He turns it over effectively against lefthanders. Although Astacio once threw many different pitches at different speeds, he has cut down on those that didn't work.

Pedro is plus at holding runners and fielding; seven of 13 potential basestealers were thrown out last season. He entered '95 as a career .120 hitter, then hit .125 to continue the pattern.

HOW HE PERFORMED IN '95
Astacio started the season as the Dodgers' #4 starter and ended the year in middle relief. He struggled early in the year, as he usually does, and was demoted to the bullpen after eleven starts.

As a starter, Astacio could not control his off-speed pitches and his fastball didn't move. However, he improved in relief.

WHAT TO EXPECT IN '96
Astacio should begin this year in the rotation. He pitched well under pennant pressure and the team felt his mechanics had improved. However, he may return to middle relief if he slumps again.

LOS ANGELES DODGERS

JOHN CUMMINGS

Position: RP
Bats: L **Throws:** L
Ht: 6'3" **Wt:** 200
Opening Day Age: 26
Born: 5/10/1969
Drafted: SEA90 8/215
ML Seasons: 3

Overall Statistics

	G	GS	GF	SV	W	L	ERA	IP	H	R	ER	HR	BB	SO
95 SEA/LA	39	0	11	0	3	1	4.06	44.1	46	24	20	3	17	25
Career	66	16	13	0	5	11	5.30	154.2	171	101	91	16	70	77

1995 Situational Statistics

	W	L	ERA	SV	IP	BB	SO		AB	HR	RBI	BA	OBA	SLG
Home	2	0	4.57	0	21.2	8	8	LHB	62	1	7	.306	.328	.387
Road	1	1	3.57	0	22.2	9	17	RHB	110	2	12	.245	.328	.382
Apr-Jun	0	0	11.81	0	5.1	7	4	ScPos	47	1	17	.234	.361	.340
Jul-Oct	3	1	3.00	0	39.0	10	21	Clutch	42	1	3	.238	.304	.381

SCOUTING REPORT
John Cummings has a three-quarter delivery but comes sidearm to some lefthanders. His average-minus fastball sinks and tails away from righties, but tends to tail in to lefthanders and become hittable. Cummings' change-up is just average. His big-breaking curve is a plus offering, although John is not thought to be related to "Candy" Cummings, credited with inventing the pitch in the 1880s. John's control is just average. A deceptive delivery makes him plus at holding runners, and only two tried to steal against him. An average fielder, he went hitless in three trips to the plate.

HOW HE PERFORMED IN '95
Cummings was a disappointment with the Mariners, but coming to the Dodgers improved his chances of staying in the majors. Lefthanded relief has recently been a sinkhole for Los Angeles. Although he had some trouble, he gave the Dodgers something they haven't had since Steve Howe left: a lefthanded reliever with decent stuff.

WHAT TO EXPECT IN '96
After pitching well in the pennant race, Cummings has the inside track at the top lefthanded bullpen spot in '96. However, if John doesn't get people out consistently, he will fight for a job with Joey Eischen.

CHAD FONVILLE

Positions: 2B/SS/OF
Bats: B **Throws:** R
Ht: 5'6" **Wt:** 155
Opening Day Age: 25
Born: 3/5/1971
Drafted: SF92 11/299
ML Seasons: 1

Overall Statistics

	G	AB	R	H	2B	3B	HR	RBI	SB	CS	BB	SO	BA	OBA
95 MON/LA	102	320	43	89	6	1	0	16	20	7	23	42	.278	.328
Career	102	320	43	89	6	1	0	16	20	7	23	42	.278	.328

1995 Situational Statistics

	AB	HR	RBI	BA	OBA	SLG		AB	HR	RBI	BA	OBA	SLG
Home	147	0	4	.265	.312	.279	LHP	87	0	4	.241	.275	.276
Road	173	0	12	.289	.342	.324	RHP	233	0	12	.292	.348	.313
Apr-Jun	35	0	1	.343	.361	.371	ScPos	64	0	16	.281	.352	.313
Jul-Oct	285	0	15	.270	.325	.295	Clutch	43	0	1	.140	.196	.140

SCOUTING REPORT
Many feel Chad is the fastest player in baseball. He handles the bat well and likes to slap the ball to the left side of the infield. Fonville is also an excellent bunter and collected 18 infield hits, most drag bunts. He has literally no power and rarely walks, making his overall offensive value questionable despite that excellent speed. Even with his speed, Fonville only has average range. His arm is neither strong nor accurate enough for full-time shortstop duty. He is working in the Arizona Fall league on defensive fundamentals, which are lacking at this point.

HOW HE PERFORMED IN '95
Rookie Fonville was one of baseball's biggest surprises in '95. A Giants' prospect drafted by the Expos, Chad didn't work out in Montreal but played a key part in the Dodgers' pennant run. After playing second base and left field, Fonville took Jose Offerman's job on September 2. However, while Chad has some defensive value, he doesn't project as an everyday shortstop.

WHAT TO EXPECT IN '96
The Dodgers may try Fonville at second base, but utility duty looks to be his best bet. He's probably not going to play the infield regularly in '96 unless others are injured.

THE SCOUTING REPORT: 1996

LOS ANGELES DODGERS

MARK GUTHRIE

Position: RP
Bats: B **Throws:** R
Ht: 6'4" **Wt:** 195
Opening Day Age: 30
Born: 9/22/1965
Drafted: MIN87 7/165
ML Seasons: 7

Overall Statistics

	G	GS	GF	SV	W	L	ERA	IP	H	R	ER	HR	BB	SO
95 MIN/LA	60	0	14	0	5	5	4.21	62.0	66	33	29	6	25	67
Career	264	43	59	8	29	29	4.17	509.1	546	263	236	49	183	407

1995 Situational Statistics

	W	L	ERA	SV	IP	BB	SO		AB	HR	RBI	BA	OBA	SLG
Home	2	2	4.65	0	31.0	15	33	LHB	94	2	13	.245	.297	.319
Road	3	3	3.77	0	31.0	10	34	RHB	147	4	19	.293	.377	.449
Apr-Jun	3	3	5.10	0	30.0	9	38	ScPos	71	2	27	.324	.429	.465
Jul-Oct	2	2	3.38	0	32.0	16	29	Clutch	103	3	10	.252	.319	.388

SCOUTING REPORT

Guthrie comes to the plate from three-quarters with a high leg kick. Much of his success is due to his deceptive delivery, and he must keep the ball low and away. Mark's best pitch is his well above-average forkball. He has a minus fastball that sinks and tails into lefthanders and a big-breaking curve which he sometimes changes speeds on. In addition, Guthrie occasionally shows a slider to lefties.

He is slow to home but has a good move to first. Seven runners tried to steal against him, five successfully. Mark is an average fielder. In his one 1995 at-bat—his first ever—Guthrie was hitless.

HOW HE PERFORMED IN '95

Guthrie came to Dodgers from Minnesota midway through the season. He had problems facing righthanded batters, and in '95 he allowed a majority of his baserunners against them. After a few shaky outings, he settled down, striking out a hitter per inning.

WHAT TO EXPECT IN '96

Guthrie has a good chance return to the Dodgers' bullpen in '96, but he must show more control and get out righties more consistently, or he will end up fighting with John Cummings and Joey Eischen for a job.

CHRIS GWYNN

Positions: OF//1B
Bats: L **Throws:** L
Ht: 6' " **Wt:** 200
Opening Day Age: 31
Born: 10/13/1964
Drafted: LA85 1/10
ML Seasons: 9

Overall Statistics

	G	AB	R	H	2B	3B	HR	RBI	SB	CS	BB	SO	BA	OBA
95 LA	67	84	8	18	3	2	1	10	0	0	6	23	.214	.272
Career	518	917	111	247	32	11	16	108	2	4	61	143	.269	.313

1995 Situational Statistics

	AB	HR	RBI	BA	OBA	SLG		AB	HR	RBI	BA	OBA	SLG
Home	42	1	4	.214	.292	.310	LHP	2	0	0	.000	.000	.000
Road	42	0	6	.214	.250	.357	RHP	82	1	10	.220	.278	.341
Apr-Jun	55	0	6	.255	.317	.382	ScPos	25	0	8	.200	.250	.280
Jul-Oct	29	1	4	.138	.188	.241	Clutch	26	1	7	.346	.419	.538

SCOUTING REPORT

Gwynn is a line-drive hitter with average bat speed. Rarely ever used against lefthanded pitchers, he likes the high fastballs righthanders throw, especially when he can extend his arms. Chris struggles against curves and has problems with anything low and inside.

He is average in throwing accuracy but below-average in arm strength and, in fact, all other defensive areas. Gwynn has average-minus speed.

HOW HE PERFORMED IN '95

Gwynn was used almost exclusively as a pinch-hitter against righthanded hurlers in 1995. He and Mitch Webster were usually the first men off the Dodgers' bench. However, leg injuries hampered Gwynn all year and he was not effective. He provided no power, speed, or the ability to get on base. Chris isn't much of an outfielder and, if he doesn't hit, he has no role.

WHAT TO EXPECT IN '96

If he plays for Los Angeles in 1996, it will be in his usual role as a pinch-hitter. Luckily for Chris, Tommy Lasorda is faithful to his role players and believes that an injury-free Gwynn can still be productive. However, every year he doesn't hit brings him closer to Palookaville.

LOS ANGELES DODGERS

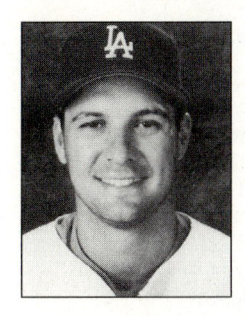

DAVE HANSEN

Position: 3B
Bats: L **Throws:** R
Ht: 6'0" **Wt:** 180
Opening Day Age: 27
Born: 11/24/1968
Drafted: LA86 2/47
ML Seasons: 6

Overall Statistics

	G	AB	R	H	2B	3B	HR	RBI	SB	CS	BB	SO	BA	OBA
95 LA	100	181	19	52	10	0	1	14	0	0	28	28	.287	.384
Career	414	734	68	194	31	0	12	77	1	3	90	110	.264	.345

1995 Situational Statistics

	AB	HR	RBI	BA	OBA	SLG		AB	HR	RBI	BA	OBA	SLG
Home	77	0	4	.273	.371	.273	LHP	13	0	1	.154	.250	.231
Road	104	1	10	.298	.393	.423	RHP	168	1	13	.298	.395	.369
Apr-Jun	72	1	5	.264	.384	.361	ScPos	54	0	12	.241	.344	.296
Jul-Oct	109	0	9	.303	.384	.358	Clutch	37	0	4	.162	.311	.216

SCOUTING REPORT
Dave Hansen is an aggressive hitter who makes good contact and will spray the ball around. He is a low ball, line-drive specialist with good plate discipline. He has not had many at-bats against left-handers, but might do well against them given a chance. Dave has below-average speed and poses no threat to steal. At third base, Hansen has good hands and a very accurate throwing arm of average strength. He has average range around the bag.

HOW HE PERFORMED IN '95
Dave has hit .318 for the Dodgers since 1993. With Tim Wallach hurt and ineffective in '95, it seemed that Hansen might get a real shot at playing third base. However, it seemed everyone but Hansen received a chance at the hot corner, which meant Dave was again relegated to pinch-hitting duty. He's a decent hitter, getting on base consistently although he has little speed or power.

WHAT TO EXPECT IN '96
Hansen isn't as good with the glove as the departed Wallach but is better suited for third base than anyone else currently on the Dodgers' roster. If the Dodgers don't sign a free-agent third baseman, this might be Dave's year to prove himself.

CARLOS HERNANDEZ

Position: C
Bats: R **Throws:** R
Ht: 5'11" **Wt:** 185
Opening Day Age: 28
Born: 5/24/1967
Drafted: LA 10/10/84
ML Seasons: 6

Overall Statistics

	G	AB	R	H	2B	3B	HR	RBI	SB	CS	BB	SO	BA	OBA
95 LA	45	94	3	14	1	0	2	8	0	0	7	25	.149	.216
Career	221	464	29	105	14	0	9	40	1	1	21	78	.226	.267

1995 Situational Statistics

	AB	HR	RBI	BA	OBA	SLG		AB	HR	RBI	BA	OBA	SLG
Home	55	1	3	.145	.203	.200	LHP	37	2	7	.243	.282	.432
Road	39	1	5	.154	.233	.256	RHP	57	0	1	.088	.175	.088
Apr-Jun	57	0	0	.088	.188	.088	ScPos	30	2	8	.133	.257	.367
Jul-Oct	37	2	8	.243	.263	.432	Clutch	19	1	3	.263	.333	.421

SCOUTING REPORT
Carlos has a short, compact swing with occasional power. He doesn't get enough at-bats to show any his offensive skills, however, and is one of the slowest players in baseball. The defensive skills Hernandez displays keep him employed in the big leagues. He has plus arm with average accuracy, augmented by average range and hands. He calls a good game.

HOW HE PERFORMED IN '95
Hernandez has had the misfortune to play behind Mike Piazza, the best catcher in baseball. Nevertheless, Carlos has stuck with the Dodgers for four full seasons. Offensively, last season was Hernandez' worst. His especially poor hitting can be attributed to a lack of work, as he made only 22 starts. Most of his appearances came as a late-inning defensive replacement. Carlos' real value lies in his defense and hard work. He threw out 11 of 23 enemy basestealers in '95.

WHAT TO EXPECT IN '96
Hernandez is never going to be a starter in the majors. He has a much stronger arm and is defensively more proficient than Piazza, but won't hit enough to play regularly even though he did hit .300 five times in the minors.

LOS ANGELES DODGERS

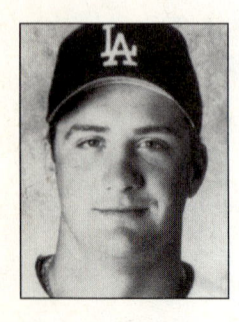

TODD HOLLANDSWORTH

Position: OF
Bats: L **Throws:** L
Ht: 6'2" **Wt:** 195
Opening Day Age: 22
Born: 4/20/1973
Drafted: LA91 1/80
ML Seasons: 1

Overall Statistics

	G	AB	R	H	2B	3B	HR	RBI	SB	CS	BB	SO	BA	OBA
95 LA	41	103	16	24	2	0	5	13	2	1	10	29	.233	.304
Career	41	103	16	24	2	0	5	13	2	1	10	29	.233	.304

1995 Situational Statistics

	AB	HR	RBI	BA	OBA	SLG		AB	HR	RBI	BA	OBA	SLG
Home	43	3	6	.279	.333	.512	LHP	31	1	2	.194	.286	.290
Road	60	2	7	.200	.284	.317	RHP	72	4	11	.250	.313	.444
Apr-Jun	4	0	0	.000	.000	.000	ScPos	24	0	8	.292	.357	.292
Jul-Oct	99	5	13	.242	.315	.414	Clutch	12	1	1	.250	.500	.500

SCOUTING REPORT

Hollandsworth is a promising hitter who has a compact swing and is expected to develop plus power in the majors. A low-ball, fastball hitter, Todd struggles against lefthanders and often swings at bad pitches. Strike-zone judgment may be Hollandsworth's biggest problem. He struck out once in every 4.4 at-bats in the minors and rarely walked. He has average speed. Defense is a big part of Todd's game. He has well above-average throwing accuracy, although his arm strength is just average. Plus range and hands enable Hollandsworth to play either left or center.

HOW HE PERFORMED IN '95

Following an exceptional spring training, Hollandsworth was a surprise member of the Dodgers' opening-day roster. Unfortunately, he went down almost immediately with a broken thumb and didn't collect his first hit until July 14. Todd is very aggressive in the field, occasionally making mistakes due to overeager play. He didn't collect an assist in 1995.

WHAT TO EXPECT IN '96

He may begin the year as the Dodgers' full-time left fielder, and at worst, should be platooning with Billy Ashley. Todd is not likely to be an outstanding hitter in '96 but should improve with experience.

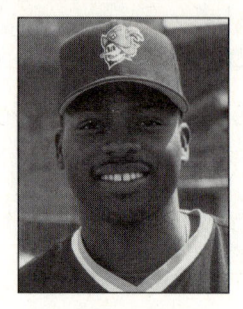

GAREY INGRAM

Positions: 3B//2B/OF
Bats: R **Throws:** R
Ht: 5'11" **Wt:** 180
Opening Day Age: 25
Born: 7/25/1970
Drafted: LA89 47/1146
ML Seasons: 2

Overall Statistics

	G	AB	R	H	2B	3B	HR	RBI	SB	CS	BB	SO	BA	OBA
95 LA	44	55	5	11	2	0	0	3	3	0	9	8	.200	.313
Career	70	133	15	33	3	0	3	11	3	0	16	30	.248	.329

1995 Situational Statistics

	AB	HR	RBI	BA	OBA	SLG		AB	HR	RBI	BA	OBA	SLG
Home	28	0	2	.214	.313	.214	LHP	27	0	1	.259	.375	.296
Road	27	0	1	.185	.313	.259	RHP	28	0	2	.143	.250	.179
Apr-Jun	40	0	3	.250	.375	.300	ScPos	15	0	3	.200	.333	.200
Jul-Oct	15	0	0	.067	.125	.067	Clutch	13	0	0	.154	.267	.231

SCOUTING REPORT

A line-drive hitter who goes with the pitch, Ingram has limited offensive skills. He doesn't do much besides hit singles and struggles mightily against righthanded pitchers. Ingram's best asset is his above-average speed, but he does not steal or bunt as often as he might.

As a second baseman, Ingram is average in all defensive areas. As a third baseman, however, Garey is below par in every way. This limits his usefulness as a utility player.

HOW HE PERFORMED IN '95

The 25-year-old Ingram found himself in L.A. last summer because of injuries to regular third-sacker Tim Wallach. Garey ended up hitting just .246 at Triple-A Albuquerque in 1995, his fourth straight season spent at Double-A or higher.

Ingram doesn't have the arm a third baseman needs and made eight errors in just 12 games at the hot corner. He did not hit for power and looked bad against off-speed pitches.

WHAT TO EXPECT IN '96

It's unlikely that he will start '96 with the Dodgers. He hasn't proven much in the minors, and it's time for him to start hitting if he wants to have a career other than as a spare part.

LOS ANGELES DODGERS

ANTONIO OSUNA

Position: RP
Bats: R **Throws:** R
Ht: 5'11" **Wt:** 160
Opening Day Age: 22
Born: 4/12/1973
Drafted: LA 6/12/91
ML Seasons: 1

Overall Statistics

	G	GS	GF	SV	W	L	ERA	IP	H	R	ER	HR	BB	SO
95 LA	39	0	8	0	2	4	4.43	44.2	39	22	22	5	20	46
Career	39	0	8	0	2	4	4.43	44.2	39	22	22	5	20	46

1995 Situational Statistics

	W	L	ERA	SV	IP	BB	SO		AB	HR	RBI	BA	OBA	SLG
Home	0	1	2.11	0	21.1	6	22	LHB	58	1	4	.276	.417	.379
Road	2	3	6.56	0	23.1	14	24	RHB	104	4	15	.221	.268	.375
Apr-Jun	1	2	8.16	0	14.1	11	9	ScPos	37	0	13	.351	.444	.432
Jul-Oct	1	2	2.67	0	30.1	9	37	Clutch	105	1	14	.248	.304	.324

SCOUTING REPORT

Strong-armed Antonio Osuna comes to batters from three-quarters. He throws a plus fastball that rises into righthanders. Antonio also has a average-minus curve and an average change-up. Osuna is an average fielder and well as average at holding runners at first. Four men tried to steal off Antonio, three successfully, in 1995.

HOW HE PERFORMED IN '95

Originally a catcher, Osuna was moved to the mound in 1991 because of his outstanding arm. Antonio is still very inexperienced and is basically a one-pitch pitcher. If he develops another above-average delivery, Osuna will be a dominant force. He has averaged over a strikeout per inning since converting to pitching, both in the minors and majors.

Osuna's biggest problem is inconsistent control. He had the usual problems associated with hard-throwing youngsters, walking too many hitters and getting burned on 'get-me-over" fastballs. He was hitless in two at-bats.

WHAT TO EXPECT IN '96

The Dodgers' organization feels Antonio will be their closer in the coming years and will bring him along slowly. He may well begin '96 in Triple-A as he has only 25 games of experience at that level.

MITCH WEBSTER

Position: OF
Bats: B **Throws:** L
Ht: 6'0" **Wt:** 185
Opening Day Age: 36
Born: 5/16/1959
Drafted: LA77 23/581
ML Seasons: 13

Overall Statistics

	G	AB	R	H	2B	3B	HR	RBI	SB	CS	BB	SO	BA	OBA
95 LA	54	56	6	10	1	1	1	3	0	0	4	14	.179	.246
Career	1265	3419	504	900	150	55	70	342	160	73	325	578	.263	.330

1995 Situational Statistics

	AB	HR	RBI	BA	OBA	SLG		AB	HR	RBI	BA	OBA	SLG
Home	26	0	0	.269	.345	.346	LHP	37	1	3	.189	.231	.351
Road	30	1	3	.100	.156	.233	RHP	19	0	0	.158	.273	.158
Apr-Jun	31	1	2	.161	.188	.290	ScPos	15	0	1	.000	.118	.000
Jul-Oct	25	0	1	.200	.310	.280	Clutch	21	0	0	.190	.227	.286

SCOUTING REPORT

The straightaway-hitting Webster makes good contact, going with the pitch to produce line drives. He has no power, but has shown reasonable strike-zone judgment in the past. He has minus speed but is an average baserunner. Webster rarely gets into the field, but isn't bad out there. At one time, Mitch showed well above-average range, but now ranks only average in that category. His arm has minus strength but is very accurate and he has well above-average hands.

HOW HE PERFORMED IN '95

Tommy Lasorda loves to keep veterans on his bench—sometimes well past their prime. Such is the case with Mitch Webster, possibly the worst regular pinch-hitter on any major league roster in '95. A solid emergency swinger in the past, Mitch's production fell off considerably. A broken right hand hampered Mitch, who, to his credit, continued to play. Though a switch-hitter, he batted only righthanded while recovering from the injury.

WHAT TO EXPECT IN '96

With the slew of young, talented outfielders in the Dodger organization, it's unlikely that Webster will have a job in '96. With Lasorda, however, you never know.

LOS ANGELES DODGERS TOP PROSPECTS

KYM ASHWORTH
Bats: L Throws: L Opening Day Age: 20
Ht: 6-3 Wt: 185 Born: 7/31/1976
Position: P Drafted: NDFA 12-12-92 LAN

YR TEAM	LG/CLASS	G	GS	GF	SV	W	L	ERA	IP	H	HR	BB	SO	O/BA
93 Great Falls	PIO/R	11	11	0	0	3	3	2.44	59.0	43	4	14	52	.198
94 Bakersfield	CAL/A	24	24	0	0	6	7	3.95	127.2	112	9	69	109	.241
94 San Antonio	TEX/AA	1	1	0	0	0	1	4.50	4.0	5	0	0	6	.278
95 Vero Beach	FSL/A	24	24	0	0	7	4	3.53	120.0	111	8	64	97	.253

Ashworth, a native Australian and part of the Dodgers heralded international scouting efforts, has mound maturity that belies his age. The big 19-year-old lefthander has a good curveball which he mixes in well with a mid-80's fastball that is gaining in velocity as he fills out. Ashworth also has a great pickoff move to first base. A lack of command prevented Ashworth from pitching past the sixth inning in 23 of his 24 starts.

MIGUEL CAIRO
Bats: R Throws: R Opening Day Age: 22
Ht: 6-1 Wt: 160 Born: 5/4/1974
Position: 2B Drafted: NDFA 9-20-90 LAN

YR TEAM	LG/CLASS	G	AB	R	H	2B	3B	HR	RBI	SB	BA	OBA
93 Vero Beach	FSL/A	90	346	50	109	10	1	1	23	23	.315	.378
94 Bakersfield	CAL/A	133	533	76	155	23	4	2	48	44	.291	.338
95 San Antonio	TEX/AA	107	435	53	121	20	1	1	41	33	.278	.323

A solid contact hitter with above-average speed, Cairo's fine season included a trip to the mid-season Texas-Mexican League All-Star game. Consistently one of the toughest batters in the league to strike out, the Venezuelan native fanned just once every 14.81 at-bats, second-best in the Texas League. However, Cairo is not an ideal leadoff man as he rarely walks and wastes his speed by hitting too many fly balls. Defensively, the converted shortstop has excellent range and a strong arm.

JUAN CASTRO
Bats: R Throws: R Opening Day Age: 24
Ht: 5-10 Wt: 163 Born: 6/20/1972
Position: SS Drafted: NDFA 6-13-91 LAN

YR TEAM	LG/CLASS	G	AB	R	H	2B	3B	HR	RBI	SB	BA	OBA
93 San Antonio	TEX/AA	118	424	55	117	23	8	7	41	12	.276	.325
94 San Antonio	TEX/AA	123	445	55	128	25	4	4	44	4	.288	.334
95 Albuquerque	PCL/AAA	104	341	51	91	18	4	3	43	4	.267	.307
95 Los Angeles	NL/MAJ	11	4	0	1	0	0	0	0	0	.250	.400

Considered the best defensive middle infielder in the organization, Castro has a great glove and the strong arm necessary to make the throw from deep in the hole. The Mexican native is not a big hitter, but took a step offensively this year by hitting to right field rather than trying to pull everything, which helped him bat .301 the final two months of the season.

ROGER CEDENO
Bats: S Throws: R Opening Day Age: 22
Ht: 6-1 Wt: 165 Born: 8/16/1974
Position: OF Drafted: NDFA 3-3-91 LAN

YR TEAM	LG/CLASS	G	AB	R	H	2B	3B	HR	RBI	SB	BA	OBA
93 San Antonio	TEX/AA	122	465	70	134	12	8	4	30	28	.288	.352
93 Albuquerque	PCL/AAA	6	18	1	4	1	1	0	4	0	.222	.333
94 Albuquerque	PCL/AAA	104	383	84	123	18	5	4	49	30	.321	.395
95 Albuquerque	PCL/AAA	99	367	67	112	19	9	2	44	23	.305	.393
95 Los Angeles	NL/MAJ	40	42	4	10	2	0	0	3	1	.238	.283

A switch-hitting center fielder with great speed, Cedeno has finished among the league leaders in steals each of his four seasons, placing fourth in the Pacific Coast League in '95. But the Venezuelan native, a .305 career hitter with 121 stolen bases, could better utilize his speed by hitting more balls on the ground. His uppercut swing produced just two homers in the hitter-friendly PCL and he has but 12 in a four-year career. Just 21 last year, Cedeno has excellent defensive tools, and his three errors in 1995 were the lowest total of his career.

KARIM GARCIA
Bats: L Throws: L Opening Day Age: 21
Ht: 6-0 Wt: 200 Born: 10/29/1975
Position: OF Drafted: NDFA 7-16-92 LAN

YR TEAM	LG/CLASS	G	AB	R	H	2B	3B	HR	RBI	SB	BA	OBA
93 Bakersfield	CAL/A	123	460	61	111	20	9	19	54	5	.241	.299
94 Vero Beach	FSL/A	121	452	72	120	28	10	21	84	8	.265	.319
95 Albuquerque	PCL/AAA	124	474	88	151	26	10	20	91	12	.319	.369
95 Los Angeles	NL/MAJ	13	20	1	4	0	0	0	0	0	.200	.200

Despite skipping Double-A entirely, Garcia finished among the Pacific Coast League leaders in each of the Triple Crown categories in his Triple-A debut and was selected to Howe Sportsdata's Minor League All-Star team. The Mexican native hit over .300 in each month and drove in 50 runs the last two months of the season. The league's youngest hitter has tremendous power and above-average speed and needs only to improve his strike zone judgement to be an impact player in the major leagues. A corner outfielder with a good arm, Garcia is far from polished in the field, leading the league in errors for the second time in three years.

WILTON GUERRERO
Bats: R Throws: R Opening Day Age: 22
Ht: 5-11 Wt: 145 Born: 10/24/1974
Position: SS Drafted: NDFA 10-14-91 LAN

YR TEAM	LG/CLASS	G	AB	R	H	2B	3B	HR	RBI	SB	BA	OBA
93 Great Falls	PIO/R	66	256	44	76	5	1	0	21	20	.297	.364
94 Vero Beach	FSL/A	110	402	55	118	11	4	1	32	23	.294	.341
95 Albuquerque	PCL/AAA	14	49	10	16	1	1	0	2	2	.327	.340
95 San Antonio	TEX/AA	95	382	53	133	13	6	0	26	21	.348	.390

There are doubts about Guerrero's true age, but nobody questions his ability to hit. After finishing fifth in batting in 1994, the Dominican native won the Texas League batting crown last year, posting 41 multiple-hit games and hitting streaks of 13 and 23 games. The Double-A All-Star is one of the fastest players in the organization but a poor percentage basestealer. In the field he shows good range and a strong arm, but often struggles with the routine play.

LOS ANGELES DODGERS TOP PROSPECTS

PAUL KONERKO
Bats: R Throws: R Opening Day Age: 20
Ht: 6-3 Wt: 210 Born: 3/5/1976
Position: C Drafted: 1994 #1 LAN

YR TEAM	LG/CLASS	G	AB	R	H	2B	3B	HR	RBI	SB	BA	OBA
94 Yakima	NWST/A	67	257	25	74	15	2	6	58	1	.288	.379
95 San Bernardino	CAL/A	118	448	77	124	21	1	19	77	3	.277	.362

Konerko, the Dodgers' first-round pick in 1994, posted a fine offensive season in the advanced California League despite being one of its youngest players. Good hitting mechanics combined with patience at the plate made the big backstop a tough out, although his average tailed off the final month of the season. The 20-year-old is not advanced defensively, leading the league in errors and throwing out just 20% of opposing baserunners.

MIKE METCALFE
Bats: S Throws: R Opening Day Age: 23
Ht: 5-10 Wt: 175 Born: 1/2/1973
Position: SS Drafted: 1994 #3 LAN

YR TEAM	LG/CLASS	G	AB	R	H	2B	3B	HR	RBI	SB	BA	OBA
94 Bakersfield	CAL/A	69	275	44	78	10	0	0	18	41	.284	.350
95 Vero Beach	FSL/A	120	435	86	131	13	3	3	35	60	.301	.386
95 San Antonio	TEX/AA	10	41	10	10	1	0	0	2	1	.244	.347

Metcalfe, an aggressive player with great speed, recovered from a spring car accident that left his upper body badly bruised to lead the organization in steals, but also led the entire minor leagues in times caught stealing. The Miami product, a spray hitter with good strike zone judgement, finished third in the Florida State League in runs and seventh in batting. The third-round 1994 pick is reliable in the field but may not have the arm to play shortstop.

WILLIS OTANEZ
Bats: R Throws: R Opening Day Age: 23
Ht: 5-11 Wt: 150 Born: 4/19/1973
Position: 3B Drafted: NDFA 2-10-90 LAN

YR TEAM	LG/CLASS	G	AB	R	H	2B	3B	HR	RBI	SB	BA	OBA
93 Bakersfield	CAL/A	95	325	34	85	11	2	10	39	1	.262	.324
94 Vero Beach	FSL/A	131	476	77	132	27	1	19	72	4	.277	.350
95 Vero Beach	FSL/A	92	354	39	92	24	0	10	53	1	.260	.314
95 San Antonio	TEX/AA	27	100	8	24	4	1	1	7	0	.240	.278

Otanez is capable of hitting the ball a long way, but spent the better part of three seasons in the pitcher-friendly Florida State League before finally getting a late season promotion to Double-A last season. Just 22 despite five years of professional experience, Otanez needs to learn to hit to all fields. The Native Dominican is a converted shortstop, and has soft hands and a great arm at the hot corner.

CHAN HO PARK
Bats: R Throws: R Opening Day Age: 23
Ht: 6-2 Wt: 185 Born: 6/30/1973
Position: P Drafted: NDFA 1-14-94 LAN

YR TEAM	LG/CLASS	G	GS	GF	SV	W	L	ERA	IP	H	HR	BB	SO	O/BA
94 Los Angeles	NL/MAJ	2	0	1	0	0	0	11.25	4.0	5	1	5	6	.294
94 San Antonio	TEX/AA	20	20	0	0	5	7	3.55	101.1	91	4	57	100	.241
95 Albuquerque	PCL/AAA	23	22	0	0	6	7	4.91	110.0	93	10	76	101	.233
95 Los Angeles	NL/MAJ	2	1	0	0	0	0	4.50	4.0	2	1	2	7	.143

Blessed with great stuff, Park is still learning how to pitch. His arsenal includes a mid-90's fastball, slider, and curve, which, combined with an unusual delivery, led to a Pacific Coast League-leading total of 8.17 strikeouts per nine innings. Lack of command has led to inconsistency on the mound for the Korean native, however: after posting a 3-0 record with a 1.83 ERA in July, the 22-year-old went 1-3 with an 8.78 ERA in August.

GARY RATH
Bats: L Throws: L Opening Day Age: 23
Ht: 6-2 Wt: 185 Born: 1/10/1973
Position: P Drafted: 1994 #2 LAN

YR TEAM	LG/CLASS	G	GS	GF	SV	W	L	ERA	IP	H	HR	BB	SO	O/BA
94 Vero Beach	FSL/A	13	11	0	0	5	6	2.73	62.2	55	3	23	50	.239
95 Albuquerque	PCL/AAA	8	8	0	0	3	5	5.08	39.0	46	4	20	23	.299
95 San Antonio	TEX/AA	18	18	0	0	13	3	2.77	117.0	96	6	48	81	.225

A First Team All-American out of Mississippi State, Rath was the Dodgers' second-round pick in 1994. The big lefthander throws a mid-80's moving fastball along with a decent curve, which overpowered Texas League hitters. Rath led the league in ERA and tied for the lead in wins, despite pitching the last month-and-a-half in Triple-A. The 23-year-old was extremely tough on lefthanders and is a polished pitcher who needs only to sharpen his control.

FELIX RODRIGUEZ
Bats: R Throws: R Opening Day Age: 23
Ht: 6-1 Wt: 190 Born: 12/5/1972
Position: P Drafted: NDFA 10-17-89 LAN

YR TEAM	LG/CLASS	G	GS	GF	SV	W	L	ERA	IP	H	HR	BB	SO	O/BA
93 Vero Beach	FSL/A	32	20	7	0	8	8	3.75	132.0	109	15	71	80	.225
94 San Antonio	TEX/AA	26	26	0	0	6	8	4.03	136.1	106	8	88	126	.219
95 Albuquerque	PCL/AAA	14	11	0	0	3	2	4.24	51.0	52	5	26	46	.269
95 Los Angeles	NL/MAJ	11	0	5	0	1	1	2.53	10.2	11	2	5	5	.275

Rodriguez, a catcher his first two years in the organization, has a great arm but limited pitching experience. Featuring a live fastball and slider, the Dominican native needs to round out his arsenal with an off-speed pitch if he's to break into the Dodger rotation. Leadoff batters frequently reach against him, forcing the 23-year-old to constantly pitch with men on base. This might suggest a concentration problem.

LOS ANGELES DODGERS: OTHERS TO WATCH

HENRY BLANCO Bats: R Throws: R Ht: 5-11 Wt: 168
Born: 8/29/1971 Drafted: NDFA 11-12-89 LA Position: 3B

YR TEAM	LG/CLASS	G	AB	R	H	2B	3B	HR	RBI	SB	BA	OBA
95 Albuquerque	PCL/AAA	29	97	11	22	4	1	2	13	0	.227	.294
95 San Antonio	TEX/AA	88	302	37	77	18	4	12	48	1	.255	.328

Blanco, a good fielder with a great arm, set career marks in runs, homers, and RBI last season.

MIKE BUSCH Bats: R Throws: R Ht: 6-5 Wt: 241
Born: 7/7/1968 Drafted: 1990 #4 LA Position: 3B

YR TEAM	LG/CLASS	G	AB	R	H	2B	3B	HR	RBI	SB	BA	OBA
95 Albuquerque	PCL/AAA	121	443	68	119	32	1	18	62	2	.269	.341
95 Los Angeles	NL/MAJ	13	17	3	4	0	0	3	6	0	.235	.235

The former replacement player and ex-football tight end can hit the ball a long way, but is a defensive liability at either corner infield position.

DARREN DREIFORT Bats: R Throws: R Ht: 6-2 Wt: 205
Born: 5/18/1972 Drafted: 1993 #1 LA Position: P

Dreifort, the second overall pick in the 1993 draft, missed all of '95 due to elbow problems.

JOEY EISCHEN Bats: L Throws: L Ht: 6-1 Wt: 190
Born: 5/25/1970 Drafted: 1989 #3 TEX Position: P

YR TEAM	LG/CLASS	G	GS	GF	SV	W	L	ERA	IP	H	HR	BB	SO	O/BA
95 Ottawa	INT/AAA	11	0	3	0	2	1	1.72	15.2	9	0	8	13	.173
95 Albuquerque	PCL/AAA	13	0	6	2	3	0	0.00	16.1	8	0	3	14	.145
95 Los Angeles	NL/MAJ	17	0	8	0	0	0	3.10	20.1	19	1	11	15	.232

Acquired from the Expos in the Roberto Kelly deal, Eischen was a 16-game winner in 1993, and throws a fastball, curve, and changeup.

RICK GORECKI Bats: R Throws: R Ht: 6-3 Wt: 180
Born: 8/27/1973 Drafted: 1991 #18 LA Position: P

YR TEAM	LG/CLASS	G	GS	GF	SV	W	L	ERA	IP	H	HR	BB	SO	O/BA
95 Vero Beach	FSL/A	6	5	0	0	1	2	0.67	27.0	19	0	9	24	.200
95 Los Angeles	NL/MAJ	0	0	0	0	0	0	0.00	0.0	0	0	0	0	.000

Gorecki, a 22-year-old with an outstanding curveball, missed most of the '95 season due to a hernia.

KEN HUCKABY Bats: R Throws: R Ht: 6-1 Wt: 205
Born: 1/27/1971 Drafted: 1991 #21 LA Position: C

YR TEAM	LG/CLASS	G	AB	R	H	2B	3B	HR	RBI	SB	BA	OBA
95 Albuquerque	PCL/AAA	89	278	30	90	16	2	1	40	2	.324	.359

An outstanding defensive catcher, Huckaby nailed 42% of opposing baserunners last year, and set career marks in slugging and on-base percentage.

RYAN LUZINSKI Bats: R Throws: R Ht: 6-0 Wt: 215
Born: 8/22/1973 Drafted: 1992 #1 LA Position: C

YR TEAM	LG/CLASS	G	AB	R	H	2B	3B	HR	RBI	SB	BA	OBA
95 Vero Beach	FSL/A	38	134	15	45	12	0	5	23	1	.336	.375
95 San Antonio	TEX/AA	44	144	18	33	5	0	1	9	1	.229	.304

Son of ex-major leaguer Greg, the Dodgers' first selection in the 1992 draft has big league power, but struggled both in the field and at the plate in '95.

JESUS MARTINEZ Bats: L Throws: L Ht: 6-2 Wt: 145
Born: 3/13/1974 Drafted: NDFA 8-22-90 LAN Position: P

YR TEAM	LG/CLASS	G	GS	GF	SV	W	L	ERA	IP	H	HR	BB	SO	O/BA
95 Albuquerque	PCL/AAA	2	0	1	0	1	1	4.50	4.0	4	0	4	5	.308
95 San Antonio	TEX/AA	24	24	0	0	6	9	3.54	139.2	129	6	71	83	.251

The younger brother of Ramon and Pedro, Jesus is a lean left-hander who throws hard, but lacks command.

KEVIN PINCAVITCH Bats: R Throws: R Ht: 5-11 Wt: 180
Born: 7/5/1970 Drafted: NDFA 6-14-92 LAN Position: P

YR TEAM	LG/CLASS	G	GS	GF	SV	W	L	ERA	IP	H	HR	BB	SO	O/BA
95 San Brndino	CAL/A	3	0	0	0	2	0	2.70	10.0	8	1	6	10	.205
95 Vero Beach	FSL/A	32	13	5	2	10	7	1.66	124.2	83	7	48	103	.187

A smart pitcher who works both sides of the plate, Pincavitch throws a fastball, curve, and changeup, and led the Florida State League in ERA.

JOSE PRADO Bats: R Throws: R Ht: 6-2 Wt: 195
Born: 5/9/1972 Drafted: 1993 #7 LA Position: P

YR TEAM	LG/CLASS	G	GS	GF	SV	W	L	ERA	IP	H	HR	BB	SO	O/BA
95 San Antonio	TEX/AA	28	22	3	1	7	11	3.48	144.2	126	9	64	93	.236

A 15-game winner in '94, Prado battled control problems with his curve last year, but hurled quality starts in eight of his last nine outings.

DAVE PYC Bats: L Throws: L Ht: 6-3 Wt: 235
Born: 2/11/1971 Drafted: 1992 #22 LA Position: P

YR TEAM	LG/CLASS	G	GS	GF	SV	W	L	ERA	IP	H	HR	BB	SO	O/BA
95 Albuquerque	PCL/AAA	1	1	0	0	0	1	3.86	7.0	7	1	2	3	.250
95 San Antonio	TEX/AA	26	26	0	0	12	6	3.38	157.0	170	6	49	78	.277

The big lefthander mixes his pitches well, but struggles against left-handed batters.

BRIAN RICHARDSON Bats: R Throws: R Ht: 6-2 Wt: 190
Born: 8/31/1975 Drafted: 1992 #10 LA Position: 3B

YR TEAM	LG/CLASS	G	AB	R	H	2B	3B	HR	RBI	SB	BA	OBA
95 San Brndino	CAL/A	127	462	68	131	18	1	12	58	17	.284	.341

The California native, one of the youngest players in the California League, is a good fielder with a strong arm and developing power.

ADAM RIGGS Bats: R Throws: R Ht: 6-0 Wt: 190
Born: 10/4/1972 Drafted: 1994 #22 LA Position: 2B

YR TEAM	LG/CLASS	G	AB	R	H	2B	3B	HR	RBI	SB	BA	OBA
95 San Brndino	CAL/A	134	542	111	196	39	5	24	106	31	.362	.431

An aggressive player struggling tremendously trying to make the switch from the outfield to second base, Riggs led the California League in batting while pacing the minors in hits, runs and total bases and finishing second in batting and extra-base hits.

DAVID YOCUM Bats: L Throws: L Ht: 6-0 Wt: 175
Born: 6/10/1974 Drafted: 1995 # LA Position: P

YR TEAM	LG/CLASS	G	GS	GF	SV	W	L	ERA	IP	H	HR	BB	SO	O/BA
95 Vero Beach	FSL/A	8	7	0	0	2	1	2.96	27.1	22	2	12	20	.224

The first-round draft pick out of Florida State, a Second-Team All-American, was a draft-eligible sophomore who went 12-2.

MONTREAL EXPOS

SCOUTING REPORT

A plus hitter, both for average and power, Alou likes fastballs from the middle half of the plate in. He is an aggressive hitter and will wave at bad breaking balls on occasion. Moises, now the club's big power threat, no longer bunts or engages in the hit-and-run.

Alou's 1993 broken leg has robbed him of much of what was above-average speed. He still runs all-out, but Moises now only has average speed on the bases and is no longer a stolen base threat.

His range has also slipped; previously, Moises was an outstanding right fielder, now he is only an adequate left fielder. His range and hands both rate slightly above-par; his throwing strength and accuracy are just average.

HOW HE PERFORMED IN '95

Before surgery on both his shoulders, which effectively knocked him out for the last two months of the season, Alou was having a successful season in the media black hole of Montreal. As the only certifiable star in an Expos' lineup shorn of Larry Walker and Marquis Grissom, his production (batting average, RBI, and home runs) was similar to what he had shown in the full seasons of '92 and '93. However, Moises was often pitched around and could not match his outstanding '94 campaign.

Alou played through June and July despite injuries to his right bicep and left rotator cuff. However, on August 14, he crashed into an outfield wall in Philadelphia and suffered a right shoulder injury that required season-ending surgery. The Expos slipped from the wildcard race at the same time that Alou was injured; his absence left a gaping hole in the middle of the lineup that could not be filled.

He started games at all three outfield spots in '95, but Alou threw out just five runners and did not show great mobility at any position.

WHAT TO EXPECT IN '96

Alou is expected to be fully recovered this spring. Although probably best used in the #3 spot, Moises is currently the only legitimate cleanup hitter that the Expos have. If he can stay healthy, he should again enjoy a steady and productive season. At 29, it's more likely to resemble his 1993 level, not his superb 1994.

MOISES ALOU

Position: OF
Bats: R **Throws:** R
Ht: 6'3" **Wt:** 185
Opening Day Age: 29
Born: 7/3/1966
Drafted: PIT86* 1/2
ML Seasons: 5

Overall Statistics

	G	AB	R	H	2B	3B	HR	RBI	SB	CS	BB	SO	BA	OBA
95 MON	93	344	48	94	22	0	14	58	4	3	29	56	.273	.342
Career	467	1609	256	475	110	14	63	277	44	17	134	221	.295	.351

1995 Situational Statistics

	AB	HR	RBI	BA	OBA	SLG		AB	HR	RBI	BA	OBA	SLG
Home	151	4	25	.245	.331	.384	LHP	82	5	19	.341	.409	.622
Road	193	10	33	.295	.351	.518	RHP	262	9	39	.252	.321	.408
Apr-Jun	204	8	34	.294	.347	.475	ScPos	98	2	42	.357	.432	.500
Jul-Oct	140	6	24	.243	.335	.436	Clutch	50	1	8	.280	.308	.400

How He Compares to Other Batters

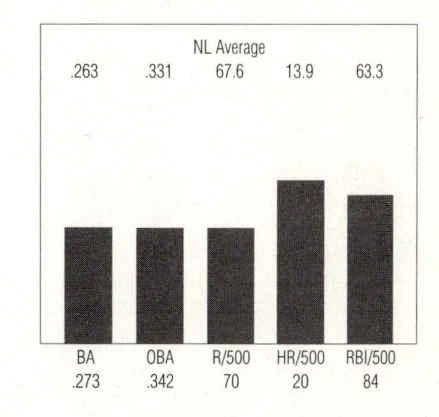

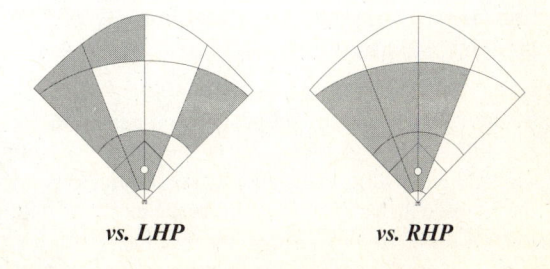

NL Average: .263 .331 67.6 13.9 63.3

BA	OBA	R/500	HR/500	RBI/500
.273	.342	70	20	84

Where He Hits the Ball

vs. LHP   vs. RHP

THE SCOUTING REPORT: 1996

MONTREAL EXPOS

SEAN BERRY

Positions: 3B//1B
Bats: R **Throws:** R
Ht: 5'11" **Wt:** 200
Opening Day Age: 30
Born: 3/22/1966
Drafted: KC86* S1/9
ML Seasons: 6

SCOUTING REPORT
Sean hits with average power and has just fair strike zone judgment. However, he makes contact and hits low fastballs very well. Best against left-handers in the past, Berry has become much more effective against righties recently.

Sean has slightly above-average speed and has been an outstanding basestealer in the past. However, he slumped in this area in '95 but is a smart runner. When asked, Berry will bunt, although not for hits.

The Expos have never liked Sean's glovework, despite his slightly above-average tools across the board.

HOW HE PERFORMED IN '95
One of the mysteries of the Montreal Expos is why Sean Berry has not become an everyday player. Manager Felipe Alou again elected to play Berry sporadically in '95, giving him only 77 starts. Instead, Alou opted to give significant playing time to Shane Andrews and Mike Grudzielanek, who may be marginally better fielders but are both significantly weaker hitters at this point.

Berry led Expos' regulars by hitting .333 with runners in scoring position. He also hit extremely well in road games and on grass fields—good reason for a move elsewhere. Sean has showed a tendency to heat up as the year proceeds, doing most of his damage in the hot summer months of July and August. He batted over .400 in each of those months last season.

Aside from his bizarre baserunning slump (he had stolen an excellent 26 bases in 28 attempts in 1993-94), Berry has also experienced a sharp drop in his bases on balls as his batting average has risen each of the last two years. However, Sean has hit for power at a very consistent rate.

His .948 fielding percentage in '95 (12 errors) ranked with the major-league average at the position. However, as he has in the past, Berry was more mobile than the normal third sacker.

WHAT TO EXPECT IN '96
Sean's performance in '94 proved that he should be a regular. Unfortunately, Berry never fully convinced Felipe Alou of his ability. Traded to Houston this winter for reliever Dave Veres, Sean will take over at third for Dave Magadan. While his offense can be expected to dip a bit, Berry is a good player who continues to confound the skeptics.

Overall Statistics

	G	AB	R	H	2B	3B	HR	RBI	SB	CS	BB	SO	BA	OBA
95 MON	103	314	38	100	22	1	14	55	3	8	25	53	.318	.367
Career	391	1073	143	299	61	6	40	154	31	11	106	212	.279	.344

1995 Situational Statistics

	AB	HR	RBI	BA	OBA	SLG		AB	HR	RBI	BA	OBA	SLG
Home	157	5	26	.268	.322	.414	LHP	74	1	13	.284	.372	.405
Road	157	9	29	.369	.411	.643	RHP	240	13	42	.329	.365	.567
Apr-Jun	111	2	19	.234	.294	.333	ScPos	81	4	42	.333	.385	.568
Jul-Oct	203	12	36	.365	.409	.635	Clutch	52	2	3	.269	.309	.404

How He Compares to Other Batters

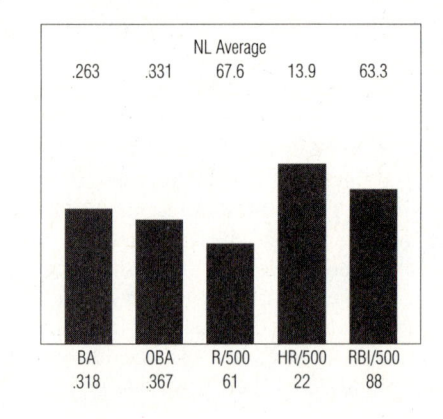

NL Average: .263 .331 67.6 13.9 63.3

BA	OBA	R/500	HR/500	RBI/500
.318	.367	61	22	88

Where He Hits the Ball

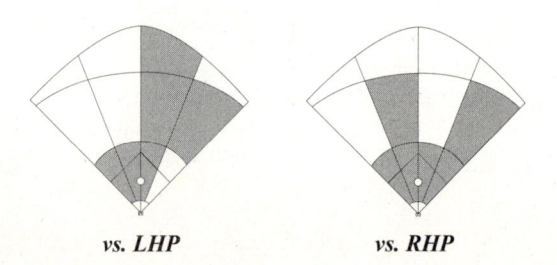

vs. LHP   vs. RHP

MONTREAL EXPOS

SCOUTING REPORT
Despite Cordero's fine tools, his erratic play and, apparently, a hard-to-reach nature have soured the Expos on him. Wil can jerk pitches effectively against lefthanded pitchers with slightly plus power. He likes high fastballs over the plate, but swung at too many bad pitches in '95, getting himself out. Cordero strides into the ball and gets hit by pitches often. Wil is a slightly above-average runner and has been a decent basestealer in the past despite a poor '95 showing. He does not bunt to take advantage of his speed. Defense has been the main criticism of Cordero, who has adequate range at shortstop and slightly above-average hands. His arm strength and accuracy also rate slightly above-average, but Wil has experienced stretches of abysmal throwing.

HOW HE PERFORMED IN '95
During his fine '94 season, Cordero was hailed as the Expos' shortstop for the rest of the century. By last August, he had been dumped to left field, a position he had never before played. The reason given was an erratic arm, but his range had deteriorated as well; it seemed that almost any ball hit to Wil's left automatically went through for a single. As a left fielder, his range was poor except on balls hit in front of him, where he was able to come in effectively. In fact, he made several outstanding catches on such plays.

Cordero's offensive statistics appeared close to those he totaled in '94, but he lost some power and experienced a substantial increase in strikeouts. In addition, Wil went an incredible 109 plate appearances late in the year without driving in a run.

Used as a #2 or #3 hitter most of the season, he hit for good average but does not appear ideally tailored for either slot, lacking exceptional ability to make contact or good power. He is probably an ideal #6 hitter, but the Expos are already loaded with #6 hitters.

WHAT TO EXPECT IN '96
The Expos are not going to return Cordero to shortstop, but they cannot afford to play him regularly in the outfield. Wil might move to third base, where he would not have time to "think" his throws into wild tosses. Despite his frustrating inconsistency, Cordero is still an extremely promising player who is only 24 with time—and the need—to improve.

WIL CORDERO

Positions: SS/OF
Bats: R **Throws:** R
Ht: 6'2" **Wt:** 185
Opening Day Age: 24
Born: 10/3/1971
Drafted: MON 5/25/88
ML Seasons: 4

Overall Statistics

	G	AB	R	H	2B	3B	HR	RBI	SB	CS	BB	SO	BA	OBA
95 MON	131	514	64	147	35	2	10	49	9	5	36	88	.286	.341
Career	424	1530	202	425	101	8	37	178	37	11	120	241	.278	.338

1995 Situational Statistics

	AB	HR	RBI	BA	OBA	SLG		AB	HR	RBI	BA	OBA	SLG
Home	247	2	23	.291	.356	.417	LHP	124	3	19	.306	.360	.476
Road	267	8	26	.281	.326	.423	RHP	390	7	30	.279	.335	.403
Apr-Jun	233	3	23	.292	.359	.416	ScPos	109	2	36	.266	.349	.376
Jul-Oct	281	7	26	.281	.326	.423	Clutch	66	0	6	.242	.333	.318

How He Compares to Other Batters

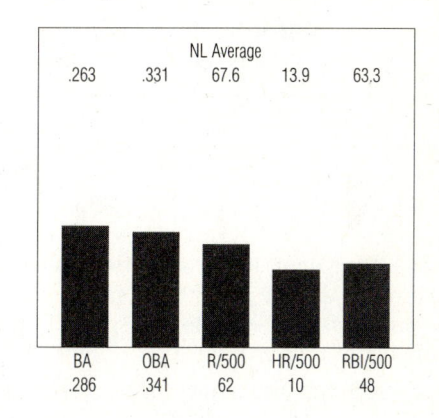

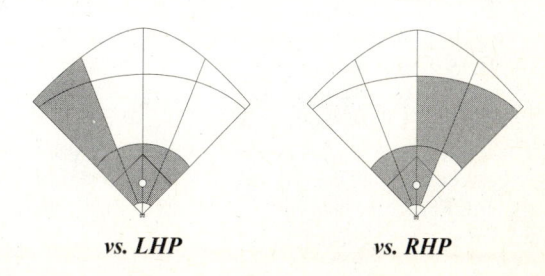

NL Average
.263   .331   67.6   13.9   63.3

BA   OBA   R/500   HR/500   RBI/500
.286 .341   62   10   48

Where He Hits the Ball

vs. LHP   *vs. RHP*

THE SCOUTING REPORT: 1996

MONTREAL EXPOS

JEFF FASSERO

Position: SP
Bats: L **Throws:** L
Ht: 6'1" **Wt:** 180
Opening Day Age: 33
Born: 1/5/1963
Drafted: SL84 22/554
ML Seasons: 5

SCOUTING REPORT

Fassero throws from a three-quarter angle with better-than-average stuff for a southpaw. His slightly above-average fastball, thrown to sink, tails in on lefthanders. Jeff also has a slightly above-par curve and forkball as well as an average curve.

Control is a problem for Fassero. All pitches but his curve rate minus in location; Jeff has average control over the bender. Due to his inability to get the ball where he wants it consistently, Fassero goes deep into the count—he compounds this by being a slow worker.

He is an average fielder, but with a high leg kick and a poor pickoff move, Jeff does not hold runners well. As a result, he allowed the most stolen bases among Expos' starters in '95; 26 stole against him in 38 attempts. Among NL pitchers, only Steve Avery had more runners take off. Like other Montreal pitchers, he is a poor hitter, but Jeff is the best bunter of the group. He batted just .070 in '95 (4-for-57), duplicating his previous career average, but laid down eight successful sacrifices.

HOW HE PERFORMED IN '95

One of the top pitchers in the NL during the season's early weeks (6-1, 2.91 ERA through May 30), Fassero floundered for the remainder of the season and lost five of his last six. In early June, he became the first NL pitcher to win seven games, but was 6-13 the rest of the way with an ERA of nearly 5.00. A well-publicized run-in with pitching coach Joe Kerrigan in July (concerning his attitude and approach) did not help the situation, and the Expos' poor finish appeared to take some of the enthusiasm out of Fassero's game.

Although Jeff was better than usual against lefthanders, he allowed righthanders to do uncommonly well, especially in the power department. He allowed more walks than anyone on the Expos' staff.

WHAT TO EXPECT IN '96

Before last season, Fassero had four straight years of sub-3.00 ERAs, both as a starter and a reliever. There is reason to believe that he can recover his effectiveness, particularly if the Expos can stabilize their defense. He is healthy and still throws well, but must improve his command.

Overall Statistics

	G	GS	GF	SV	W	L	ERA	IP	H	R	ER	HR	BB	SO
95 MON	30	30	0	0	13	14	4.33	189.0	207	102	91	15	74	164
Career	228	66	62	10	43	37	3.16	618.1	565	258	217	37	219	528

1995 Situational Statistics

	W	L	ERA	SV	IP	BB	SO		AB	HR	RBI	BA	OBA	SLG
Home	6	10	4.65	0	110.1	52	97	LHB	108	0	10	.185	.229	.231
Road	7	4	3.89	0	78.2	22	67	RHB	623	15	79	.300	.368	.453
Apr-Jun	7	5	3.51	0	77.0	24	73	ScPos	180	3	69	.283	.364	.411
Jul-Oct	6	9	4.90	0	112.0	50	91	Clutch	42	2	4	.238	.256	.429

How He Compares to Other Pitchers

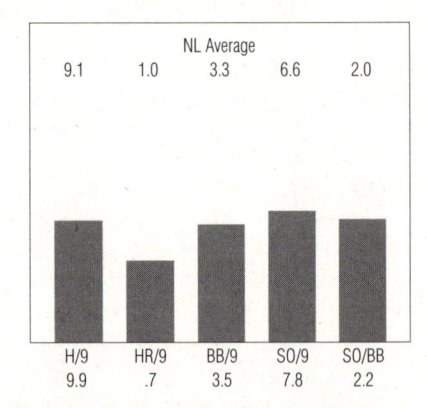

NL Average: H/9 9.1, HR/9 1.0, BB/9 3.3, SO/9 6.6, SO/BB 2.0
Fassero: H/9 9.9, HR/9 .7, BB/9 3.5, SO/9 7.8, SO/BB 2.2

How He Compares to Other Starting Pitchers

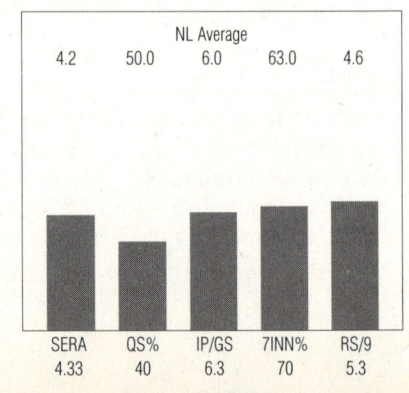

NL Average: SERA 4.2, QS% 50.0, IP/GS 6.0, 7INN% 63.0, RS/9 4.6
Fassero: SERA 4.33, QS% 40, IP/GS 6.3, 7INN% 70, RS/9 5.3

MONTREAL EXPOS

DARRIN FLETCHER

Position: C
Bats: L **Throws:** R
Ht: 6'2" **Wt:** 195
Opening Day Age: 29
Born: 10/3/1966
Drafted: LA87 6/144
ML Seasons: 7

SCOUTING REPORT
Darrin has power and makes decent contact, especially on fastballs down and over the plate, where he can extend his arms. He does not strike or walk often, but Fletcher hits well enough to make the overall offensive package quite good for a catcher. A very slow runner, Fletcher hasn't stolen a base in the majors. He has effectively bunted for sacrifices on occasion.

Montreal doesn't think much of Darrin's defense, as evidenced by their decision to carry three catchers despite Fletcher being the clear regular. Usually, he is spelled in the late innings of close games. All of Darrin's defensive tools rate average except for slightly below-average arm strength. He has, however, improved his throwing accuracy.

HOW HE PERFORMED IN '95
Fletcher contributed significantly to the great season the Expos had in '94. However, while he continued to hit effectively last year, his habitually mediocre defense stuck out on a team shorn thin of other major-league talent. The club could no longer support his poor glovework. Not known as a great handler of pitchers, he has also had a poor history of throwing runners out. However, Fletcher no longer whips throws into center field regularly, and the 33% success rate he experienced in '95 (36 of 119) was the best of his career.

Darrin is painfully slow and is often pinch-run for. His forte is offense, as over a normal season he hits 15 home runs and drives in 60-70 runs. Felipe Alou was forced to bat Fletcher high in the order because of injuries to other Expos' hitters. A majority of his plate appearances came batting fifth, but Darrin saw action in the cleanup slot as well. As he showed during '94, he can best contribute hitting sixth or seventh, because of his lack of speed clogs up the basepaths.

WHAT TO EXPECT IN '96
There is no other starting catcher in sight for the Expos; Tim Laker and Tim Spehr are backups at best. Fletcher can contribute on a strong offensive team, but on a team that needs outstanding pitching to win, his below-average defensive abilities are exposed. This does not bode well for the Expos, as they aren't likely to add much hitting for '96.

Overall Statistics

	G	AB	R	H	2B	3B	HR	RBI	SB	CS	BB	SO	BA	OBA
95 MON	110	350	42	100	21	1	11	45	0	1	32	23	.286	.351
Career	482	1420	125	367	78	5	34	203	0	4	112	135	.258	.315

1995 Situational Statistics

	AB	HR	RBI	BA	OBA	SLG		AB	HR	RBI	BA	OBA	SLG
Home	163	3	23	.282	.350	.429	LHP	44	1	8	.227	.333	.341
Road	187	8	22	.289	.351	.460	RHP	306	10	37	.294	.353	.461
Apr-Jun	134	5	16	.284	.358	.448	ScPos	103	3	36	.214	.320	.359
Jul-Oct	216	6	29	.287	.346	.444	Clutch	52	1	7	.269	.345	.385

How He Compares to Other Batters

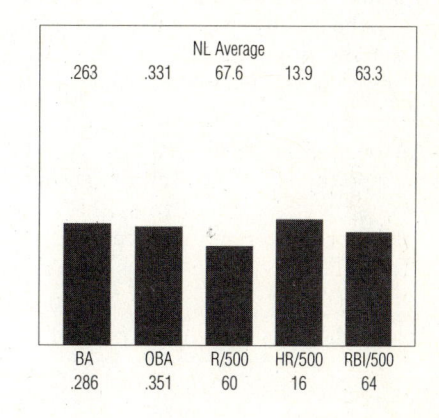

NL Average: .263 | .331 | 67.6 | 13.9 | 63.3

BA	OBA	R/500	HR/500	RBI/500
.286	.351	60	16	64

Where He Hits the Ball

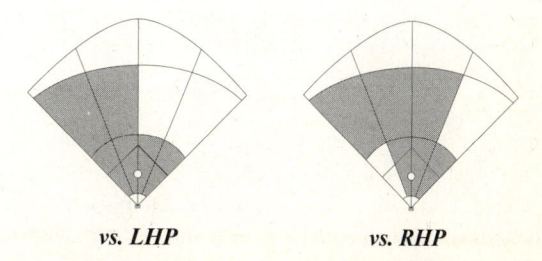

vs. LHP   vs. RHP

MONTREAL EXPOS

GIL HEREDIA

Position: RP/SP
Bats: R **Throws:** R
Ht: 6'1" **Wt:** 190
Opening Day Age: 30
Born: 10/26/1965
Drafted: SF87 9/230
ML Seasons: 5

SCOUTING REPORT

Delivering from straight overhand, Heredia doesn't throw that hard any longer. His slightly below-average fastball has average tailing life and is always thrown to sink. Gil also delivers an average slider, but his best pitch is a slightly plus forkball that has almost enough velocity to be considered a splitfinger fastball.

His control is average; although he doesn't walk many hitters, Heredia occasionally gets into trouble falling behind in the count. Mostly a groundball pitcher, Gil stays out of home run trouble.

Coming to the plate quickly, Heredia is average at holding runners: 21 runners tried larceny with Gil on the mound last year, 16 were successful. He is an average fielder and was probably the best hitter among Expos' pitchers. A .218 career hitter, he batted .182 last year. Heredia also sacrifices effectively.

HOW HE PERFORMED IN '95

The veteran righthander started the season in the Expos' rotation, but was shifted to the bullpen in late June and then re-inserted for a few starts in August. Gil won just two of his final ten starts and had an ERA over 5.00 while in the rotation.

However, Heredia's ERA was just 1.32 as a reliever. Although he pitched well, Gil was never given an opportunity to be a closer despite the season-long struggles of Mel Rojas. Felipe Alou used Heredia in middle relief and seemed to waste his talents in situations where games were already out of hand.

It is not clear whether simply moving out of the rotation is what made Gil effective: he has been a far superior pitcher in the second half of the season for his entire career although the difference was much greater than usual in '95. One problem with using Heredia in late-inning relief situations is that he has no platoon advantage. In fact, Gil has allowed righthanders to hit for much more power than lefthanders in his career.

WHAT TO EXPECT IN '96

Heredia signed with Texas this winter, where he will probably continue to work in a swing role. Before last season, he was equally effective in starting and relief and, given the fairly weak and injury-prone Rangers' rotation, Gil could make 15-20 starts for his new club this summer.

Overall Statistics

	G	GS	GF	SV	W	L	ERA	IP	H	R	ER	HR	BB	SO
95 MON	40	18	5	1	5	6	4.31	119.0	137	60	57	7	21	74
Career	126	39	20	3	17	16	3.99	329.1	359	159	146	26	75	211

1995 Situational Statistics

	W	L	ERA	SV	IP	BB	SO		AB	HR	RBI	BA	OBA	SLG
Home	3	2	4.85	0	42.2	9	27	LHB	203	4	20	.296	.306	.414
Road	2	4	4.01	1	76.1	12	47	RHB	267	3	30	.288	.340	.356
Apr-Jun	3	4	5.28	0	61.1	13	42	ScPos	110	2	42	.355	.414	.455
Jul-Oct	2	2	3.28	1	57.2	8	32	Clutch	21	0	2	.381	.435	.381

How He Compares to Other Pitchers

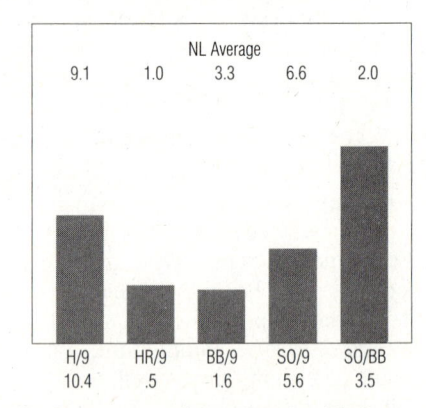

NL Average: H/9 9.1, HR/9 1.0, BB/9 3.3, SO/9 6.6, SO/BB 2.0
Heredia: H/9 10.4, HR/9 .5, BB/9 1.6, SO/9 5.6, SO/BB 3.5

How He Compares to Other Starting Pitchers

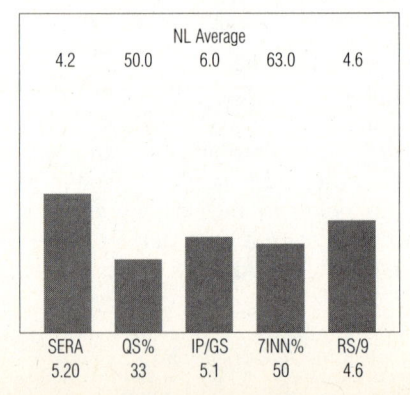

NL Average: SERA 4.2, QS% 50.0, IP/GS 6.0, 7INN% 63.0, RS/9 4.6
Heredia: SERA 5.20, QS% 33, IP/GS 5.1, 7INN% 50, RS/9 4.6

MONTREAL EXPOS

MIKE LANSING

Positions: 2B//SS
Bats: R **Throws:** R
Ht: 6'0" **Wt:** 180
Opening Day Age: 27
Born: 4/3/1968
Drafted: MIA90 3/155
ML Seasons: 3

SCOUTING REPORT
Lansing is an average hitter with some pull power who likes fastballs down in the zone and middle-in. Mike has a bit above-average—but deceptive—speed and is an outstanding baserunner. His major-league career stolen base success rate is 79%, consistent with his minor-league record. A decent sacrifice bunter, Lansing only laid down one bunt in '95.

In the field, Mike is somewhat above-average in range, arm, accuracy and hands at second base. One of the top defensive second baseman the NL, Mike is outstanding on the double play. Each erratic throw delivered to second by scatter-armed shortstop Wil Cordero only emphasized Lansing's skills. When Cordero was replaced by Mark Grudzielanek, Lansing benefitted.

Originally a shortstop, Mike has played both short and third in Montreal, but he is now established as the regular at the keystone position.

HOW HE PERFORMED IN '95
As the Expos returned from the West Coast in August, Lansing kick-started the debate on Quebec sovereignty by opining that plane announcements should not be made in French. As a result, Lansing was unmercifully booed by the few French-speaking fans who showed up for the rest of the Expos' home games.

The controversy obscured the fact that Lansing was the Expos' most consistent player in '95. While he's no Jeff Kent in the hitting department, Lansing is a capable stickman with a little pop; his club-leading 62 RBIs set a team record for second basemen. His 27 steals also paced Montreal.

WHAT TO EXPECT IN '96
If Lansing progresses as a hitter, he could establish himself as an All-Star candidate. He showed class by apologizing for his intemperate remarks and by not knocking the fans when they booed him. In 1996, Mike might even hear cheers from the Montreal partisans if he continues his excellent play.

Originally drafted out of college by the independent Miami Miracle in 1990, Lansing has been an overachiever for most of his career. After an excellent year in Double-A in '92, he jumped over Triple-A to the majors. At 28 with three years of big-league experience, he still could improve somewhat.

Overall Statistics

	G	AB	R	H	2B	3B	HR	RBI	SB	CS	BB	SO	BA	OBA
95 MON	127	467	47	119	30	2	10	62	27	4	28	65	.255	.299
Career	374	1352	155	365	80	5	18	142	62	17	104	158	.270	.327

1995 Situational Statistics

	AB	HR	RBI	BA	OBA	SLG		AB	HR	RBI	BA	OBA	SLG
Home	243	4	27	.259	.295	.366	LHP	107	4	19	.271	.322	.421
Road	224	6	35	.250	.305	.420	RHP	360	6	43	.250	.292	.383
Apr-Jun	166	4	22	.229	.283	.355	ScPos	124	6	54	.323	.374	.548
Jul-Oct	301	6	40	.269	.308	.412	Clutch	70	1	10	.286	.333	.414

How He Compares to Other Batters

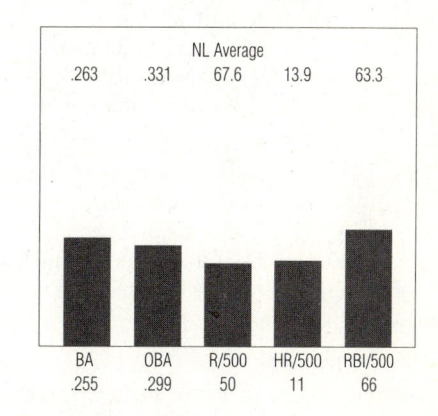

	BA	OBA	R/500	HR/500	RBI/500
NL Average	.263	.331	67.6	13.9	63.3
	.255	.299	50	11	66

Where He Hits the Ball

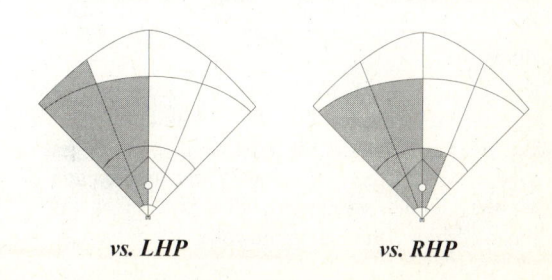

vs. LHP   vs. RHP

THE SCOUTING REPORT: 1996

MONTREAL EXPOS

PEDRO MARTINEZ

Position: SP
Bats: R **Throws:** R
Ht: 5'11" **Wt:** 150
Opening Day Age: 24
Born: 7/25/1971
Drafted: LA 6/18/88
ML Seasons: 4

SCOUTING REPORT
A pitcher with a fastball with good (mid-90s) velocity and good life, Pedro delivers his #1 pitch from three quarters, striking fear in the hearts of many skittish righthanded batters who know his heater will most often run inside to them. He will also bore and sink the two-seamer. Martinez breaking pitch is an average-plus curve, but his change-up is a solid plus pitch.

Pedro is both quick to home and quick to first, especially for a righthander. He was extremely successful holding runners on base last year: 22 baserunners tried to steal against him, but 13 were thrown out. He is one of the worst-hitting pitchers in baseball, though, batting .111 last year with five sacrifices and 30 strikeouts in 63 at-bats. He now boasts(?) a career average of less than .100, very poor for a starting pitcher.

HOW HE PERFORMED IN '95
The Expos' most consistent pitcher in '95, Martinez was often the club's only hope for a win in a series during the season's last two months. His well-known penchant for pitching high and tight kept batters loose. However, the reputation he has for this type of pitching, and the resulting warnings by umpires, have caused Pedro to alter the location of his pitches.

Martinez appeared to have altered his style in the latter part of the season. This extra care may have cost him some of his effectiveness, as he allowed a club-high 21 home runs. Of course, being taken deep is an occupational risk when one throws hard fastballs up in the zone.

WHAT TO EXPECT IN '96
When Martinez works up and in, he is an extremely effective pitcher. However, his hit batsmen (11 in '95, third highest in the NL, and a league-leading 11 in the short '94 season) and close pitches have made Martinez a marked man with certain umpires.

The challenge is for Pedro to deal with this problem without forsaking the inside fastball. If he can, Martinez might be the first Expos' 20-game winner since Ross Grimsley. At the tender age of 24, the slender young pitcher has a great future ahead of him if he can avoid injury and overuse.

Overall Statistics

	G	GS	GF	SV	W	L	ERA	IP	H	R	ER	HR	BB	SO
95 MON	30	30	0	0	14	10	3.51	194.2	158	79	76	21	66	174
Career	121	56	22	3	35	21	3.25	454.1	355	173	164	37	169	443

1995 Situational Statistics

	W	L	ERA	SV	IP	BB	SO		AB	HR	RBI	BA	OBA	SLG
Home	6	7	3.59	0	105.1	43	100	LHB	363	8	33	.220	.307	.364
Road	8	3	3.43	0	89.1	23	74	RHB	334	13	36	.234	.297	.410
Apr-Jun	5	4	3.22	0	81.0	27	72	ScPos	119	2	44	.244	.359	.353
Jul-Oct	9	6	3.72	0	113.2	39	102	Clutch	50	1	5	.280	.333	.480

How He Compares to Other Pitchers

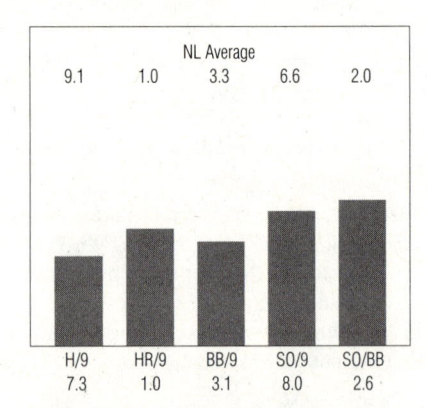

NL Average: 9.1 | 1.0 | 3.3 | 6.6 | 2.0

H/9: 7.3 | HR/9: 1.0 | BB/9: 3.1 | SO/9: 8.0 | SO/BB: 2.6

How He Compares to Other Starting Pitchers

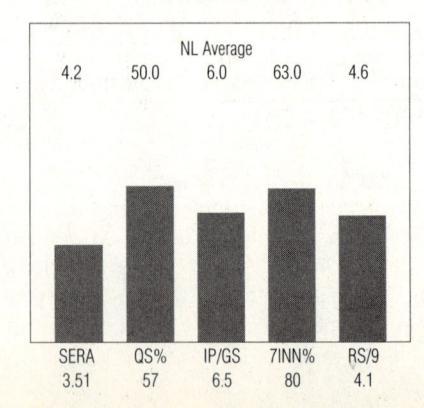

NL Average: 4.2 | 50.0 | 6.0 | 63.0 | 4.6

SERA: 3.51 | QS%: 57 | IP/GS: 6.5 | 7INN%: 80 | RS/9: 4.1

MONTREAL EXPOS

CARLOS PEREZ

Position: SP/RP
Bats: L **Throws:** L
Ht: 6'3" **Wt:** 195
Opening Day Age: 24
Born: 4/14/1971
Drafted: MON 12/19/87
ML Seasons: 1

SCOUTING REPORT

Perez depends on his plus control and on turning over his average-velocity fastball to give it screwball action away from righthanded hitters—who still hit him pretty hard last year. The southpaw delivers from three-quarters and also features an average forkball and average change-up, which he had good command of. He will show a slightly below par slider as well.

An average fielder with a mediocre move for a lefthander, 14 of the 21 runners who tried to steal against him were successful in '95. At the plate, Perez hit pretty well in early going but he slumped as the season progressed. He ended up at .133 with a double, a triple, and a home run but only four sacrifice bunts.

HOW HE PERFORMED IN '95

The demonstrative Perez pitched very well in his rookie year and was the only Expos' player to make the All-Star team. Unfortunately, two incidents not connected with his pitching destroyed the last month and a half of his season. On August 22, irate over a borderline fair/foul home run call at Olympic Stadium, Perez bumped umpire Bill Hohn. After the resulting suspension, Carlos was ineffective. He then was charged with sexual assault in Atlanta in mid-September and did not pitch again.

Before these two incidents, Carlos was the second-best pitcher on the Expos' staff behind ace Pedro Martinez. Probably named to the All-Star team ahead of Martinez only because of his crowd-pleasing antics after striking out batters, Perez's actions began to wear thin late in the season. However, these antics notwithstanding, Carlos had an outstanding rookie season.

WHAT TO EXPECT IN '96

With a serious criminal charge hanging over his head in the off-season, Perez's future is uncertain. If he returns to duty, Carlos will need to keep silencing lefty swingers but also do something to keep righty hitters from taking him deep if he wants to thrive in the majors.

A return to the pitching effectiveness that he displayed before the All-Star break is not out of the question. However, his maturity as an individual is in question, and this may derail him as it did his brother Pascual.

Overall Statistics

	G	GS	GF	SV	W	L	ERA	IP	H	R	ER	HR	BB	SO
95 MON	28	23	2	0	10	8	3.69	141.1	142	61	58	18	28	106
Career	28	23	2	0	10	8	3.69	141.1	142	61	58	18	28	106

1995 Situational Statistics

	W	L	ERA	SV	IP	BB	SO		AB	HR	RBI	BA	OBA	SLG
Home	9	3	2.86	0	88.0	16	63	LHB	101	1	5	.178	.224	.277
Road	1	5	5.06	0	53.1	12	43	RHB	451	17	51	.275	.315	.448
Apr-Jun	7	2	2.93	0	61.1	11	50	ScPos	135	5	37	.193	.247	.356
Jul-Oct	3	6	4.28	0	80.0	17	56	Clutch	23	0	0	.130	.259	.130

How He Compares to Other Pitchers

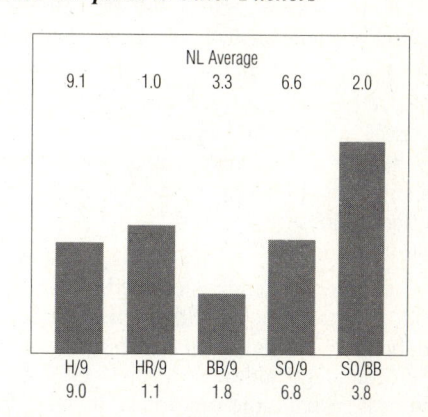

	H/9	HR/9	BB/9	SO/9	SO/BB
NL Average	9.1	1.0	3.3	6.6	2.0
	9.0	1.1	1.8	6.8	3.8

How He Compares to Other Starting Pitchers

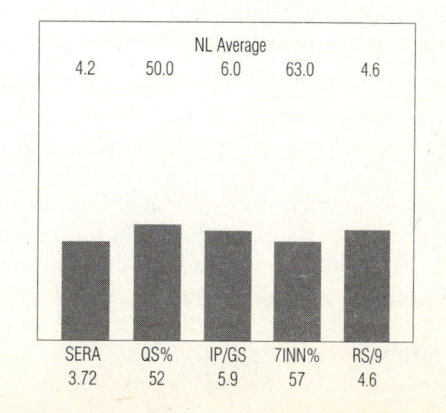

	SERA	QS%	IP/GS	7INN%	RS/9
NL Average	4.2	50.0	6.0	63.0	4.6
	3.72	52	5.9	57	4.6

THE SCOUTING REPORT: 1996

MONTREAL EXPOS

MEL ROJAS

Position: RP
Bats: R **Throws:** R
Ht: 5'11" **Wt:** 175
Opening Day Age: 29
Born: 12/10/1966
Drafted: MON 11/7/85
ML Seasons: 6

SCOUTING REPORT
Below-average control continues to bedevil Rojas. He comes overhand with good velocity and keeps the ball low, but both his slightly above-average slider and his well above-average splitter tend to run wild at times. Mel does have good command of his slightly plus fastball.

Rated average as a fielder, Rojas has a decent move but all 11 trying to steal against him last year were successful—he tends to lose concentration on the mound. Attitude has also been a concern. As one scout remarked, "He's got to get his head screwed on right. If he isn't used he gripes, and if he's used too much, he bitches."

Hitless in six trips last season, Rojas is an .080 (4-for-50) lifetime batter with 30 strikeouts. He's not a good bunter.

HOW HE PERFORMED IN '95
After spending several years lobbying for full-time closer duty, Mel was thrust into the role in '95 when John Wetteland left for the Yankees. Although he racked up his saves, Rojas had streaks of ineffectiveness and unexpected problems with hitters from both sides of the plate. He blew nine saves.

Mel's ERA has climbed alarmingly over the last three years, as has his walks-to-innings-pitched ratio. Although he improved in one very critical area, slicing his home runs allowed from 11 in '94 to just two, Rojas also doubled his wild pitches and nearly doubled his hit batters.

Rojas' difficulties generally stemmed from walking the leadoff hitter, who would often steal second. With nobody on, Mel allowed the opposition a .391 on-base percentage; although he did well with runners on base, usually the run got in anyway. There were many times when Rojas was effective. Unfortunately, he couldn't string them together, and the resulting inconsistency made it hard for Felipe Alou to count on him.

WHAT TO EXPECT IN '96
Prior to '95, Rojas was probably the best set-up pitcher in the NL. However, his first season as a full-time closer was less than spectacular. Rojas is still the only real candidate the Expos have to close games and is almost certain to re-assume the role in '96. Perhaps a year of experience as a closer will benefit Mel and he will return to his previous consistent form.

Overall Statistics

	G	GS	GF	SV	W	L	ERA	IP	H	R	ER	HR	BB	SO
95 MON	59	0	48	30	1	4	4.12	67.2	69	32	31	2	29	61
Career	311	0	144	73	22	19	3.00	428.2	367	161	143	30	151	326

1995 Situational Statistics

	W	L	ERA	SV	IP	BB	SO		AB	HR	RBI	BA	OBA	SLG
Home	1	1	4.19	13	34.1	9	33	LHB	127	1	17	.268	.367	.362
Road	0	3	4.05	17	33.1	20	28	RHB	136	1	17	.257	.333	.331
Apr-Jun	1	2	4.11	12	30.2	14	29	ScPos	89	0	29	.247	.346	.303
Jul-Oct	0	2	4.14	18	37.0	15	32	Clutch	186	2	31	.263	.358	.355

How He Compares to Other Pitchers

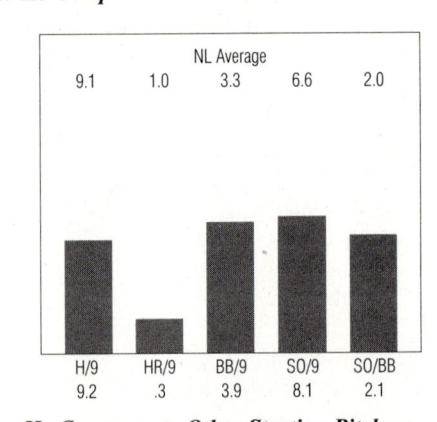

	H/9	HR/9	BB/9	SO/9	SO/BB
NL Average	9.1	1.0	3.3	6.6	2.0
	9.2	.3	3.9	8.1	2.1

How He Compares to Other Starting Pitchers

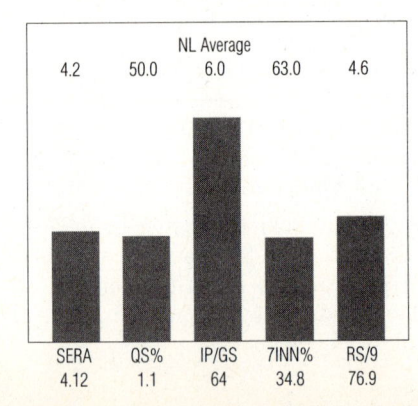

	SERA	QS%	IP/GS	7INN%	RS/9
NL Average	4.2	50.0	6.0	63.0	4.6
	4.12	1.1	64	34.8	76.9

MONTREAL EXPOS

DAVID SEGUI

Positions: 1B/OF
Bats: B **Throws:** L
Ht: 6'1" **Wt:** 170
Opening Day Age: 29
Born: 7/19/1966
Drafted: BAL87 19/455
ML Seasons: 6

SCOUTING REPORT

A plus hitter with some power, David makes good contact and is a straightaway hitter from both sides. From the left side, he'll stroke the low fastball out over the plate, and prefers the down and away fastball while hitting righthanded. He can't catch up to good, high fastballs. Although he lacks the big power ideally found in a first baseman, Segui offers some other assets, including a good attitude, hard play—one scout refers to him as a "ball-buster"—and strong defense. He is a good sacrifice bunter. With average range and arm and average-plus hands, David is a good-fielding first baseman. In addition, he can fill in as a left fielder (although not well). One thing he can't add is speed. An average runner, Segui is a below-par basestealer.

HOW HE PERFORMED IN '95

One of the few pleasant surprises for the Expos last season, Segui was one of the team's best players after coming from the Mets in early June. Hitting over .300 against both lefthanders and righties and doing well with runners in scoring position, he lived up to the potential expected of him in both Baltimore and New York.

He was hitting .329 for New York when Montreal came calling. After injuries to Cliff Floyd and Henry Rodriguez, the Expos needed someone to play first, and Segui was acquired June 8. Segui ended the season with career highs in nearly every offensive category. Fanning just 28 times in 383 at-bats for Montreal, David had hitting streaks of 18 and 13 games during the season. Used in the #2, #3, and #4 spots in the batting order, Segui was comfortable in all of them. Although he's usually a slow finisher and his average declined after July, he hit seven homers and drove in 35 runs in August and September.

However, despite good bat control, Segui doesn't get on base often enough to be that helpful in the #2 spot and doesn't have enough power for the middle of the order slots. On a good team, he'd probably hit seventh.

WHAT TO EXPECT IN '96

If David's can reprise his '95 performance, he will be a good everyday first baseman—the position has been a problem for the Expos since Andres Galarraga left. With his great bat control he'll probably hit second this season behind Rondell White.

Overall Statistics

	G	AB	R	H	2B	3B	HR	RBI	SB	CS	BB	SO	BA	OBA
95 NY/MO	130	456	68	141	25	4	12	68	2	7	40	47	.309	.367
Career	609	1766	218	478	92	5	37	225	6	9	174	200	.271	.335

1995 Situational Statistics

	AB	HR	RBI	BA	OBA	SLG		AB	HR	RBI	BA	OBA	SLG
Home	234	6	36	.295	.353	.432	LHP	112	2	17	.330	.403	.464
Road	222	6	32	.324	.381	.491	RHP	344	10	51	.302	.354	.459
Apr-Jun	148	3	18	.331	.402	.480	ScPos	118	4	55	.305	.384	.483
Jul-Oct	308	9	50	.299	.348	.451	Clutch	61	2	7	.180	.301	.311

How He Compares to Other Batters

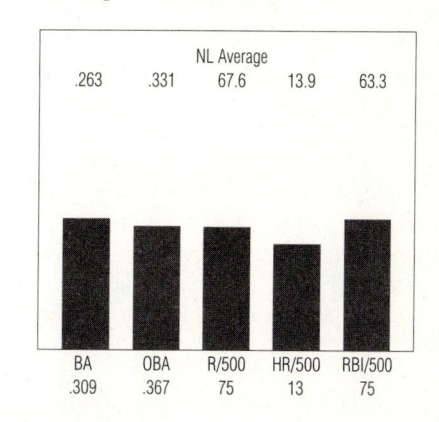

NL Average: .263 .331 67.6 13.9 63.3

BA	OBA	R/500	HR/500	RBI/500
.309	.367	75	13	75

Where He Hits the Ball

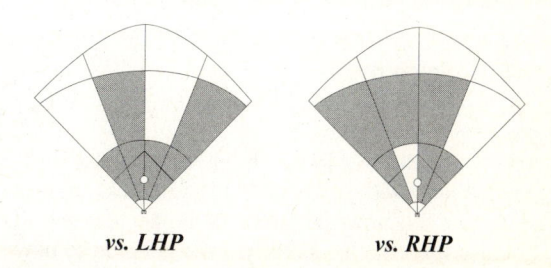

vs. LHP   vs. RHP

THE SCOUTING REPORT: 1996

MONTREAL EXPOS

TONY TARASCO

Position: OF
Bats: L **Throws:** R
Ht: 6'0" **Wt:** 185
Opening Day Age: 25
Born: 12/9/1970
Drafted: ATL88 17/372
ML Seasons: 3

SCOUTING REPORT
Tony has a problem reputation, but his talent makes him worth the gamble. He just average pull power but is strong and will take low, middle-away fastballs deep to all fields. Strike-zone judgment is a problem. An average-plus runner, Tarasco is both smart and tough on the bases.

Tony has a strong and relatively accurate arm. His throwing, his plus range and average-plus hands make him a natural for right field.

HOW HE PERFORMED IN '95
Tarasco came out of the gate like gangbusters, hitting safely in the first 11 games at a .444 clip. He was hitting over .300 until late May and remained effective until the midpoint of the season, but then faded badly.

As aggressive a hitter as he was early in the season, he became just as passive in the second half—often taking called third strikes or getting weak swings when he managed to put the ball in play. It's possible that Tarasco was just tired; he had not played regularly for the last three seasons.

Hard to believe, Tony led the Expos in walks last year, although a great portion of them were incidental. He was used in two seemingly incompatible lineup spots in '95: first and seventh. He hit seven home runs as a leadoff hitter but reached base at a mediocre .333 clip.

The toughest player to double up in the NL, hitting into just two twin killings, Tony was an outstanding basestealer who went in hard to the bases at all times. An early-season collision at home plate with big Charles Johnson made all the highlight films.

After starting the year in left field, Tarasco was shifted to right and ended up playing 102 games there. He got to balls in the gap, but had problems with line drives in the corner. His defense was a mixed bag all around, as Tony threw out seven runners but made five errors.

WHAT TO EXPECT IN '96
Tarasco may have difficulty holding on to a regular job with Moises Alou, Henry Rodriguez, and Cliff Floyd all returning from the injured list. However, he has untested potential and deserves another season of full-time play to see what he can do, but he must hit lefthanders better if he is going to play every day.

Overall Statistics

	G	AB	R	H	2B	3B	HR	RBI	SB	CS	BB	SO	BA	OBA
95 MON	126	438	64	109	18	4	14	40	24	3	51	78	.249	.329
Career	237	605	86	153	26	4	19	61	29	4	60	100	.253	.321

1995 Situational Statistics

	AB	HR	RBI	BA	OBA	SLG		AB	HR	RBI	BA	OBA	SLG
Home	230	7	19	.252	.323	.404	LHP	89	1	7	.247	.287	.337
Road	208	7	21	.245	.336	.404	RHP	349	13	33	.249	.339	.421
Apr-Jun	216	8	23	.287	.351	.472	ScPos	93	3	26	.280	.404	.430
Jul-Oct	222	6	17	.212	.308	.338	Clutch	63	0	3	.175	.243	.206

How He Compares to Other Batters

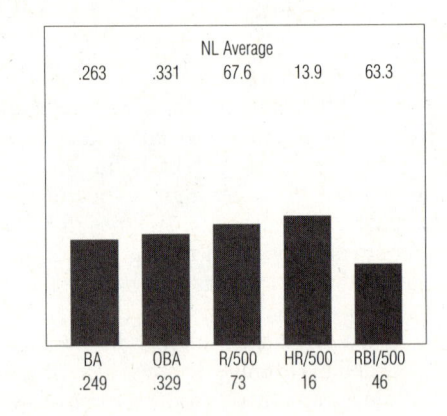

NL Average
.263 .331 67.6 13.9 63.3

BA OBA R/500 HR/500 RBI/500
.249 .329 73 16 46

Where He Hits the Ball

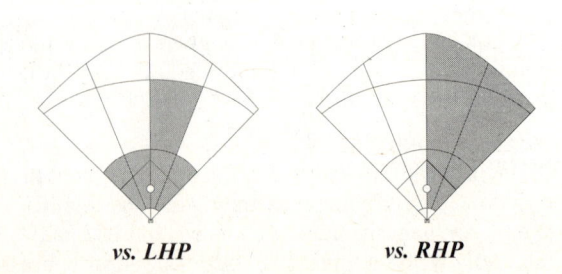

vs. LHP   vs. RHP

MONTREAL EXPOS

RONDELL WHITE

Position: OF
Bats: R **Throws:** R
Ht: 6'1" **Wt:** 205
Opening Day Age: 24
Born: 2/23/1972
Drafted: MON90 2/24
ML Seasons: 3

SCOUTING REPORT
With plus range and hands, White is a prototypical centerfielder. He has slightly above-average arm strength with average accuracy. He didn't get to as many fly balls as he could have in '95, but that should improve as he learns to position himself better.

An above-average hitter with tremendous power potential, White likes low fastballs on the inside half of the plate; he is a line-drive hitter to all fields but will add more pull power as he matures. Although he strikes out often now, Rondell is expected to make better contact when he learns how pitchers work the count. White has plus speed and showed tremendous basestealing ability; he will run singles into doubles with gusto.

HOW HE PERFORMED IN '95
Young Rondell was given the almost-impossible job of replacing Marquis Grissom in center field and at the top of the Expos' order, but he acquitted himself well. Rondell punished lefties and held his own against most righties. A poor final week dropped his average to .295, but he batted over .300 in four of the five full months. Despite being the leadoff batter in nearly 60 games, White still managed to drive in a respectable 57 runs. Despite his speed, Rondell was not as aggressive as he could have been. There were many times during the season that the situation called for a stolen base but White did not run.

He improved significantly as a defensive player over the course of the season. In the first half, he appeared tentative on drives hit over his head, allowing many to go for extra bases. However, in the second half, he was more aggressive. In particular, when Cordero was moved to left and White was forced to cover more ground, Rondell seemed to gain confidence and showed his greatest improvement as a fielder. However, he threw out just five runners, and many baserunners went from second to home on singles with impunity.

WHAT TO EXPECT IN '96
There is little White cannot do on a baseball field. He should improve substantially in all facets of the game and could become a big star if he doesn't get hurt. Although the Expos expect Rondell to add power shortly, he will probably spend the '96 season as a leadoff hitter before he moves down in the order.

Overall Statistics

	G	AB	R	H	2B	3B	HR	RBI	SB	CS	BB	SO	BA	OBA
95 MON	130	474	87	140	33	4	13	57	25	5	41	87	.295	.356
Career	193	644	112	186	46	6	17	85	27	8	57	121	.289	.352

1995 Situational Statistics

	AB	HR	RBI	BA	OBA	SLG		AB	HR	RBI	BA	OBA	SLG
Home	232	6	29	.306	.383	.457	LHP	122	2	18	.377	.437	.549
Road	242	7	28	.285	.330	.471	RHP	352	11	39	.267	.328	.435
Apr-Jun	139	7	24	.309	.391	.561	ScPos	111	2	45	.234	.326	.369
Jul-Oct	335	6	33	.290	.341	.424	Clutch	69	3	11	.232	.289	.464

How He Compares to Other Batters

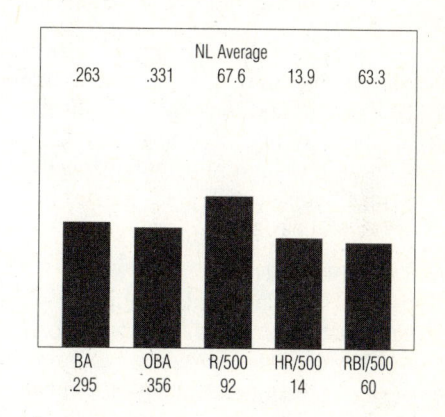

NL Average: .263 .331 67.6 13.9 63.3

BA	OBA	R/500	HR/500	RBI/500
.295	.356	92	14	60

Where He Hits the Ball

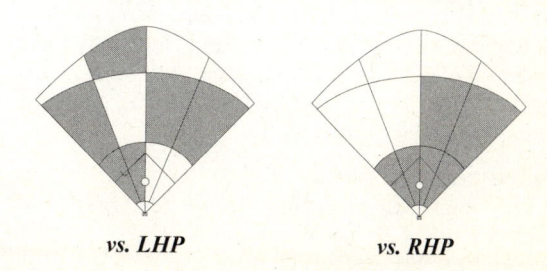

vs. LHP   vs. RHP

THE SCOUTING REPORT: 1996

MONTREAL EXPOS

SHANE ANDREWS

Positions: 3B/1B
Bats: R **Throws:** R
Ht: 6'1" **Wt:** 215
Opening Day Age: 24
Born: 8/28/1971
Drafted: MON90 1/11
ML Seasons: 1

Overall Statistics

	G	AB	R	H	2B	3B	HR	RBI	SB	CS	BB	SO	BA	OBA
95 MON	84	220	27	47	10	1	8	31	1	1	17	68	.214	.271
Career	84	220	27	47	10	1	8	31	1	1	17	68	.214	.271

1995 Situational Statistics

	AB	HR	RBI	BA	OBA	SLG		AB	HR	RBI	BA	OBA	SLG
Home	102	2	13	.225	.279	.353	LHP	64	2	12	.203	.288	.359
Road	118	6	18	.203	.264	.398	RHP	156	6	19	.218	.263	.385
Apr-Jun	92	4	12	.217	.298	.413	ScPos	71	5	28	.239	.325	.521
Jul-Oct	128	4	19	.211	.250	.352	Clutch	30	1	5	.233	.351	.433

SCOUTING REPORT

A very patient hitter with some power, Shane likes the fastball up and over the plate, but pitchers moved the ball around on him effectively last season. He can play both first and third well. Although Andrews has slightly below-average speed, he has average tools in the field, he hustles, has quick reflexes, and has a good first step.

HOW HE PERFORMED IN '95

The Expos have a track record of first-year players enjoying productive seasons (Cordero, Lansing, White), and they counted on Andrews to follow this tradition. Given many opportunities, however, Shane was the biggest disappointment on a team chock full of them. Appearing hesitant at the plate, particularly with runners in scoring position, Andrews would often take a called third strike in a key situation. A better fielder than Sean Berry, Andrews made 38 starts at third base despite hitting 100 points lower than Berry. He also played 28 games at first, but failed to impress defensively.

WHAT TO EXPECT IN '96

The Expos will give him another opportunity to show he belongs, but Shane must be more aggressive at the plate or he is likely to spend the summer in Ottawa.

CLIFF FLOYD

Positions: 1B//OF
Bats: L **Throws:** L
Ht: 6'4" **Wt:** 220
Opening Day Age: 23
Born: 12/5/1972
Drafted: MON91 1/14
ML Seasons: 3

Overall Statistics

	G	AB	R	H	2B	3B	HR	RBI	SB	CS	BB	SO	BA	OBA
95 MON	29	69	6	9	1	0	1	8	3	0	7	22	.130	.221
Career	139	434	52	110	20	4	6	51	13	3	31	94	.253	.307

1995 Situational Statistics

	AB	HR	RBI	BA	OBA	SLG		AB	HR	RBI	BA	OBA	SLG
Home	29	1	5	.103	.212	.207	LHP	7	0	2	.286	.286	.286
Road	39	0	3	.154	.233	.179	RHP	61	1	6	.115	.217	.180
Apr-Jun	51	1	8	.176	.263	.255	ScPos	21	1	8	.333	.364	.524
Jul-Oct	17	0	0	.000	.105	.000	Clutch	13	0	0	.000	.000	.000

SCOUTING REPORT

Floyd is a very promising hitter with plus raw power and a good stroke, but he needs lots of work. Like most lefthanded power hitters, he loves low fastballs. Defensively, Cliff is slightly below-average in arm strength, range, and hands and does not throw accurately. He can play either right or first; neither well.

HOW HE PERFORMED IN '95

After a promising debut in '94, Floyd was expected to be one of the Expos' outstanding youngsters. Instead, last season was a disaster. Batting just .173 on May 15, he collided with Todd Hundley and suffered a shattered left wrist. An ill-advised return in September saw Cliff go hitless in 17 at-bats.

Cliff's play at first base was below-average, and poor footwork caused his wrist injury as he could not get out of Hundley's way. Despite somewhat above-average speed, Floyd rarely ran because he was rarely on base.

WHAT TO EXPECT IN '96

Floyd must prove he is a major leaguer. Fortunately for him, the Expos have several positions open. A move to left field is possible; the real question is whether he can hit. He's still very young, so don't be surprised if he breaks loose.

MONTREAL EXPOS

MARK GRUDZIELANEK

Positions: SS/3B/2B
Bats: R **Throws:** R
Ht: 6'1" **Wt:** 185
Opening Day Age: 25
Born: 6/30/1970
Drafted: MON91 12/295
ML Seasons: 1

Overall Statistics

	G	AB	R	H	2B	3B	HR	RBI	SB	CS	BB	SO	BA	OBA
95 MON	78	269	27	66	12	2	1	20	8	3	14	47	.245	.300
Career	78	269	27	66	12	2	1	20	8	3	14	47	.245	.300

1995 Situational Statistics

	AB	HR	RBI	BA	OBA	SLG		AB	HR	RBI	BA	OBA	SLG
Home	112	1	11	.330	.375	.455	LHP	70	0	9	.343	.387	.400
Road	157	0	9	.185	.247	.217	RHP	199	1	11	.211	.270	.286
Apr-Jun	152	1	11	.250	.305	.329	ScPos	69	0	18	.217	.341	.217
Jul-Oct	117	0	9	.239	.294	.299	Clutch	43	0	4	.209	.261	.279

SCOUTING REPORT
Mark is a straightaway hitter with some power who likes fastballs down and over the plate. He has average speed on the basepaths but is a good basestealer when he picks his spots.

Defensively, the jury is out on whether Grudzielanek will be a big-league shortstop. He showed better range than Cordero but made ten errors in a limited number of appearances. He is better at third but can also play second; his tools in the field are all average.

HOW HE PERFORMED IN '95
A spring surprise, the G-man jumped from Double-A to Montreal in '95. Used at third base early in the season, he was sent to Ottawa for nearly two months in July. On his return in August, he was handed the shortstop job when Wil Cordero was banished to left field. Mark's offense before and after the trip to Triple-A was nearly identical.

WHAT TO EXPECT IN '96
Unless Grudzielanek proves this spring that he can play shortstop, the Expos may have to trade for one. Mark does have offensive potential and might be capable of hitting close to .300 if he plays regularly.

GREG HARRIS

Position: RP
Bats: B **Throws:** R
Ht: 6'0" **Wt:** 175
Opening Day Age: 40
Born: 11/2/1955
Drafted: NYN 9/17/76
ML Seasons: 15

Overall Statistics

	G	GS	GF	SV	W	L	ERA	IP	H	R	ER	HR	BB	SO
95 MON	45	0	12	0	2	3	2.61	48.1	45	18	14	6	16	47
Career	703	98	266	54	74	90	3.69	1467.0	1329	689	601	129	652	1141

1995 Situational Statistics

	W	L	ERA	SV	IP	BB	SO		AB	HR	RBI	BA	OBA	SLG
Home	0	1	3.00	0	24.0	7	18	LHB	83	3	10	.289	.344	.422
Road	2	2	2.22	0	24.1	9	29	RHB	101	3	11	.208	.279	.386
Apr-Jun	0	0	3.00	0	15.0	2	14	ScPos	64	1	14	.188	.268	.250
Jul-Oct	2	3	2.43	0	33.1	14	33	Clutch	30	0	3	.300	.432	.400

SCOUTING REPORT
Greg delivers from three-quarters with a slightly short fastballs with some sinking and tailing action. He can also call upon an average curve and slider. On September 28, Greg became the first major-leaguer to pitch both lefthanded and righthanded in the same game since 1888, something he had wanted to do for a long time. He walked one hitter and retired one as a southpaw.

As befits a switch-pitcher, Greg also switch-hits. He had a single in three trips and is a .221 lifetime hitter in 68 at-bats. An average fielder, Harris does not hold runners well: eight men stole in ten tries during '95.

HOW HE PERFORMED IN '95
The oldest pitcher in the league had a productive year, leading the Expos' staff in ERA and doing fine work in the middle innings. However, Harris had trouble in game situations, twice forcing in winning runs, once with a hit batsman and once with a walk.

WHAT TO EXPECT IN '96
Greg figures in Montreal's '96 plans. At the least, he can absorb innings. The Expos hope that he can regain his previous form and become an effective setup pitcher again.

MONTREAL EXPOS

BUTCH HENRY

Position: SP
Bats: L **Throws:** L
Ht: 6'1" **Wt:** 195
Opening Day Age: 27
Born: 10/7/1968
Drafted: CIN87 15/388
ML Seasons: 4

Overall Statistics

	G	GS	GF	SV	W	L	ERA	IP	H	R	ER	HR	BB	SO
95 MON	21	21	0	0	7	9	2.84	126.2	133	47	40	11	28	60
Career	103	80	5	1	24	30	3.81	502.2	550	234	213	52	117	273

1995 Situational Statistics

	W	L	ERA	SV	IP	BB	SO		AB	HR	RBI	BA	OBA	SLG
Home	2	4	2.25	0	52.0	11	30	LHB	99	1	6	.273	.314	.384
Road	5	5	3.25	0	74.2	17	30	RHB	385	10	37	.275	.316	.410
Apr-Jun	3	5	3.48	0	67.1	15	29	ScPos	105	3	31	.248	.311	.381
Jul-Oct	4	4	2.12	0	59.1	13	31	Clutch	33	1	3	.273	.316	.424

SCOUTING REPORT

Butch pitches from the stretch at all times, using no windup and a standard three-quarter delivery. When healthy, he throws an average-minus sinking fastball with average life and tailing action but average-plus control. Henry also throws an average slider, an average-plus change-up, and an average curve that he controls well. Average-plus at holding runners, seven of 15 men trying to steal on Butch were tossed out last season. He is an average fielder but batted just .048 (2-for-42) in '95.

HOW HE PERFORMED IN '95

Despite a 7-9 record, Henry was effective. Plagued by lack of support in early outings, Butch was outstanding in July and August. When he went on the disabled list on August 18 with the NL's sixth-best ERA, the Expos' slide from wild-card contention began—no starter besides Pedro Martinez could pick up the slack. Henry is one of few major-league starters to have consecutive season of sub 3.00 ERA's.

WHAT TO EXPECT IN '96

Operated on August 22 for a torn left medial collateral ligament, Henry was waived in October and claimed by Boston. He may need all of '96 to rehabilitate.

TIM LAKER

Position: C
Bats: R **Throws:** R
Ht: 6'3" **Wt:** 195
Opening Day Age: 26
Born: 11/27/1969
Drafted: MON88 7/154
ML Seasons: 3

Overall Statistics

	G	AB	R	H	2B	3B	HR	RBI	SB	CS	BB	SO	BA	OBA
95 MON	64	141	17	33	8	1	3	20	0	1	14	38	.234	.306
Career	135	273	28	60	13	2	3	31	3	2	18	68	.220	.271

1995 Situational Statistics

	AB	HR	RBI	BA	OBA	SLG		AB	HR	RBI	BA	OBA	SLG
Home	72	1	11	.236	.317	.361	LHP	67	2	10	.209	.260	.358
Road	69	2	9	.232	.293	.377	RHP	74	1	10	.257	.345	.378
Apr-Jun	67	1	13	.179	.253	.299	ScPos	31	0	16	.323	.436	.452
Jul-Oct	74	2	7	.284	.354	.432	Clutch	19	1	4	.211	.286	.474

SCOUTING REPORT

Tim is a minus, straightaway hitter with almost no power who strikes out often and doesn't walk much. Laker bunts well but has below-average speed.

Behind the plate, Tim has a strong arm which has streaks of poor accuracy. However, slightly above-average hands and range mean that he gets plenty of duty for the Expos.

HOW HE PERFORMED IN '95

Laker, one of Darrin Fletcher's two backups, hit .298 in July and August, which only partially made up for a poor start and finish. His season at the plate was disappointing. Often used to spell Fletcher against lefthanded pitchers, Tim barely kept his head above water in that situation.

While a better handler of pitchers than Fletcher, Laker is even worse throwing out runners despite a good arm. His 25% success rate last year meant that teams could almost run at will. While not a basestealer, Laker is called on to pinch-run for the even slower Fletcher.

WHAT TO EXPECT IN '96

Unless he can improves against lefthanders or ratchets up his catching skills, Laker will remain a second- or third-string catcher despite opportunity to move up.

MONTREAL EXPOS

DAVE LEIPER

Position: RP
Bats: L **Throws:** L
Ht: 6'1" **Wt:** 160
Opening Day Age: 33
Born: 6/18/1962
Drafted: OAK82 S1/22
ML Seasons: 7

Overall Statistics

	G	GS	GF	SV	W	L	ERA	IP	H	R	ER	HR	BB	SO
95 OK/MO	50	0	10	2	1	3	3.22	44.2	39	18	16	5	19	22
Career	231	0	57	7	10	7	3.66	253.0	242	120	103	21	105	137

1995 Situational Statistics

	W	L	ERA	SV	IP	BB	SO		AB	HR	RBI	BA	OBA	SLG
Home	1	2	2.45	0	29.1	11	15	LHB	76	2	8	.197	.274	.303
Road	0	1	4.70	2	15.1	8	7	RHB	93	3	15	.258	.343	.430
Apr-Jun	1	1	2.95	0	21.1	12	7	ScPos	39	1	16	.256	.356	.385
Jul-Oct	0	2	3.47	2	23.1	7	15	Clutch	56	2	8	.268	.349	.446

SCOUTING REPORT
Throwing from a three-quarter angle, Dave has a fastball with minus velocity but good movement. His best pitch is a plus turned-over change-up; Leiper also has an average curve. His control is average.

An above-average fielder, Dave is just average at holding runners on base. All three basestealing attempts against him in '95 were successful. He was hitless in his only Expos' at-bat.

HOW HE PERFORMED IN '95
Acquired in July from Oakland, Leiper pitched effectively. With the lowest average-against of all Expos' pitchers (.200), he was used several times in save situations when Mel Rojas faltered.

Dave can be brought into any situation that requires a lefty and still remain to pitch to a few righthanded hitters—he's really not bad against them. However, Leiper does give up gopher balls.

WHAT TO EXPECT IN '96
Leiper, who played for three Canadian teams in '95 (Montreal, Ottawa and Edmonton), would like to stay with one for the entire season. If he pitches up to his '95 form, Dave will be the Expos' top lefty reliever in '96.

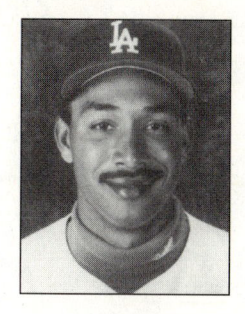

HENRY RODRIGUEZ

Positions: OF/1B
Bats: L **Throws:** L
Ht: 6'1" **Wt:** 180
Opening Day Age: 28
Born: 11/8/1967
Drafted: LA 7/14/85
ML Seasons: 4

Overall Statistics

	G	AB	R	H	2B	3B	HR	RBI	SB	CS	BB	SO	BA	OBA
95 LA/MON	45	138	13	33	4	1	2	15	0	1	11	28	.239	.293
Career	278	766	77	186	35	3	21	101	1	2	47	155	.243	.286

1995 Situational Statistics

	AB	HR	RBI	BA	OBA	SLG		AB	HR	RBI	BA	OBA	SLG
Home	82	1	8	.195	.247	.256	LHP	32	0	3	.219	.257	.250
Road	56	1	7	.304	.361	.429	RHP	106	2	12	.245	.304	.349
Apr-Jun	108	2	15	.259	.314	.370	ScPos	38	0	12	.237	.318	.316
Jul-Oct	30	0	0	.167	.219	.167	Clutch	24	1	7	.250	.345	.458

SCOUTING REPORT
A hitter with poor strike-zone judgment, Henry has some power but is unlikely to ever hit enough to compensate for his lack of defense. In left field, he has minus arm strength and accuracy and slightly below-average range and hands. He can also play right field and first base. Rodriguez is very slow.

HOW HE PERFORMED IN '95
Henry smashed four home runs in the final game of spring training, but after that his '95 was all downhill. In one of Kevin Malone's worst deals, Montreal acquired Rodriguez and Jeff Treadway on May 23 for Roberto Kelly and Joey Eischen. Treadway retired in September, and Henry hit the disabled list in June 2 with a fractured right tibia.

In his first game with the Expos, Rodriguez hit a game-winning homer. After that, he hit under .200 with no homers. After returning in September, he was still hobbling; it was obvious he should not have come back.

WHAT TO EXPECT IN '96
Henry should fill the role of a left-handed pinch-hitter and fourth outfielder for the Expos this season. Then again, he might not—he's really a borderline player.

THE SCOUTING REPORT: 1996

MONTREAL EXPOS

KIRK RUETER

Position: SP
Bats: L **Throws:** L
Ht: 6'3" **Wt:** 190
Opening Day Age: 25
Born: 12/1/1970
Drafted: MON91 19/477
ML Seasons: 3

Overall Statistics

	G	GS	GF	SV	W	L	ERA	IP	H	R	ER	HR	BB	SO
95 MON	9	9	0	0	5	3	3.23	47.1	38	17	17	3	9	28
Career	43	43	0	0	20	6	3.83	225.1	229	110	96	19	50	109

1995 Situational Statistics

	W	L	ERA	SV	IP	BB	SO		AB	HR	RBI	BA	OBA	SLG
Home	2	2	3.71	0	26.2	8	14	LHB	21	0	0	.143	.182	.143
Road	3	1	2.61	0	20.2	1	14	RHB	149	3	15	.235	.278	.322
Apr-Jun	0	2	10.57	0	7.2	3	5	ScPos	27	1	11	.296	.367	.444
Jul-Oct	5	1	1.82	0	39.2	6	23	Clutch	8	0	0	.000	.111	.000

SCOUTING REPORT

Kirk used to throw straight overhand, which made his pitches easy to read. He now throws from a three-quarter angle. The gangly lefty has a minus fastball and relies on a slightly above-average change-up and an average curve. His control has improved and he is one of the fastest-working pitchers in the league.

Rueter helps himself by being above-average in fielding and holding runners. Only three runners went on him last season, one successfully. He was hitless in 16 at-bats in '95.

HOW HE PERFORMED IN '95

After being sent down in May, Rueter pitched well at Ottawa and became the Expos' most consistent pitcher in September. His highlight was a one-hit shutout against the Giants. Rueter often weakens in the fifth or sixth inning, and Felipe Alou yanks him at the first sign of trouble. However, Kirk was a markedly better pitcher in '95.

WHAT TO EXPECT IN '96

Kirk appeared to get over the hump in '95 and should be in the Expos' rotation in '96. Rueter, Jeff Fassero and Carlos Perez make the Expos one of few staffs with a majority of lefthanded starters.

F. P. SANTANGELO

Positions: OF//2B
Bats: B **Throws:** R
Ht: 5'10" **Wt:** 165
Opening Day Age: 28
Born: 10/24/1967
Drafted: MON89 20/514
ML Seasons: 1

Overall Statistics

	G	AB	R	H	2B	3B	HR	RBI	SB	CS	BB	SO	BA	OBA
95 MON	35	98	11	29	5	1	1	9	1	1	12	9	.296	.384
Career	35	98	11	29	5	1	1	9	1	1	12	9	.296	.384

1995 Situational Statistics

	AB	HR	RBI	BA	OBA	SLG		AB	HR	RBI	BA	OBA	SLG
Home	61	1	8	.328	.423	.459	LHP	32	0	3	.281	.361	.406
Road	37	0	1	.243	.317	.297	RHP	66	1	6	.303	.395	.394
Apr-Jun	0	0	0	.000	.000	.000	ScPos	21	0	8	.333	.440	.429
Jul-Oct	98	1	9	.296	.384	.398	Clutch	11	0	0	.091	.231	.091

SCOUTING REPORT

An average runner, F.P. plays several positions, primarily left and right field, with average range and hands. His throwing strength and accuracy rate slightly below-par.

Santangelo doesn't have much power. Hitting the ball the opposite way when batting righthanded, F.P. will pull at times from the left side of the plate. He will take the walk and makes good contact.

HOW HE PERFORMED IN '95

A career minor-leaguer who had spent four years at Triple-A, Santangelo may have been called up as a reward for dedicated service to the organization. However, F.P. acquitted himself very well, hitting nearly 40 points above his '95 average at Ottawa and playing four different positions (second base plus outfield).

A line-drive, spray hitter to all fields, Santangelo showed some promise. He made several good defensive plays in the outfield, and was a great improvement over Wil Cordero in left.

WHAT TO EXPECT IN '96

He could win a season-long utility job with the Expos off his late-season showing. A better-than-average defender, F.P. was 3-for-9 as a pinch-hitter for Montreal and could be a valuable bench player.

MONTREAL EXPOS

TIM SCOTT

Position: RP
Bats: R **Throws:** R
Ht: 6'2" **Wt:** 185
Opening Day Age: 29
Born: 11/16/1966
Drafted: LA84 2/51
ML Seasons: 5

Overall Statistics

	G	GS	GF	SV	W	L	ERA	IP	H	R	ER	HR	BB	SO
95 MON	62	0	15	2	2	0	3.98	63.1	52	30	28	6	23	57
Career	194	0	57	4	18	5	3.61	227.0	213	101	91	14	96	190

1995 Situational Statistics

	W	L	ERA	SV	IP	BB	SO		AB	HR	RBI	BA	OBA	SLG
Home	0	0	2.41	2	33.2	12	30	LHB	110	5	16	.236	.325	.445
Road	2	0	5.76	0	29.2	11	27	RHB	124	1	12	.210	.290	.290
Apr-Jun	0	0	4.13	2	28.1	10	28	ScPos	89	1	19	.169	.292	.236
Jul-Oct	2	0	3.86	0	35.0	13	29	Clutch	115	3	14	.191	.282	.330

SCOUTING REPORT

Tim throws overhand: his sinking fastball is now average as is his change-up. The best pitch he throws is a slightly above-average curve; he also has a slider and splitter. Scott is annually one of the worst in baseball at holding runners, and last season 22 stole in 23 attempts! Tim's an average fielder; his one hit last year in four at-bats was his first ever.

HOW HE PERFORMED IN '95

The righty was a model of consistency—at least in the first week of July. In four consecutive appearances, Scott hit the first batter he faced. He led the team in appearances; with the lowest opponents' batting average allowed on the staff, Tim showed he could be effective.

However, baserunners run at will against him, a poor trait for a relief pitcher. This helps account for his high ERA, which rose well over a run from '94, but the real culprits were the six homers he allowed; Tim hadn't allowed any in '94.

WHAT TO EXPECT IN '96

Scott is a pretty good set-up pitcher. However, he's never going to get out of that job and can't afford to slip any further.

DAVE SILVESTRI

Positions: 2B/SS//1B/3B/DH/OF
Bats: R **Throws:** R
Ht: 6'0" **Wt:** 180
Opening Day Age: 28
Born: 9/29/1967
Drafted: HOU88 3/52
ML Seasons: 4

Overall Statistics

	G	AB	R	H	2B	3B	HR	RBI	SB	CS	BB	SO	BA	OBA
95 NY/MO	56	93	16	21	6	0	3	11	2	0	13	36	.226	.321
Career	82	145	26	33	7	3	5	18	2	1	22	51	.228	.327

1995 Situational Statistics

	AB	HR	RBI	BA	OBA	SLG		AB	HR	RBI	BA	OBA	SLG
Home	43	0	5	.233	.382	.349	LHP	37	1	7	.216	.295	.324
Road	50	3	6	.220	.259	.420	RHP	56	2	4	.232	.338	.429
Apr-Jun	21	1	4	.095	.259	.238	ScPos	25	1	8	.280	.355	.480
Jul-Oct	72	2	7	.264	.341	.431	Clutch	15	0	0	.133	.278	.133

SCOUTING REPORT

An erstwhile shortstop prospect, Dave is now typecast as a utility player with the bat but not the glove for infield duty. He has a decent arm and adequate range but suspect hands defensively. Offensively, he has some raw power and is an average runner.

HOW HE PERFORMED IN '95

Silvestri came to the Expos in July after an .095 average and a broken hand ruined his time in the Bronx. He was a utility player and pinch-hitter in Montreal. However, Dave had a serious problem with contact in '95, fanning in more than one third of his at-bats.

Used at all four infield positions as well as left field, Silvestri did not impress at any position. He did not get enough at-bats to show what he could do with consistent playing time.

WHAT TO EXPECT IN '96

Silvestri's best hope for a big-league career may be to develop into a Dave Hansen-type pinch-hitter. Because he has shown in the minors that he can hit for power, Dave might yet fashion a career in the majors. However, mediocre defense and problems making contact will prevent him from being an everyday player.

MONTREAL EXPOS: TOP PROSPECTS

ISRAEL ALCANTARA
Bats: R Throws: R Opening Day Age: 22
Ht: 6-2 Wt: 165 Born: 5/6/1973
Position: 3B Drafted: NDFA 7-2-90 MON

YR TEAM	LG/CLASS	G	AB	R	H	2B	3B	HR	RBI	SB	BA	OBA
93 Burlington	MID/A	126	470	65	115	26	3	18	73	6	.245	.283
94 Wst Plm Bch	FSL/A	125	471	65	134	26	4	15	69	9	.285	.324
95 Harrisburg	EAST/AA	71	237	25	50	12	2	10	29	1	.211	.280
95 W Palm Bch	FSL/A	39	134	16	37	7	2	3	22	3	.276	.329

Alcantara struggled in his jump to Double-A, striking out 32 times in his first 66 at-bats and displaying a questionable attitude. He was finally demoted in mid-July despite leading the club in homers. The 22-year-old has big-time power, but has no idea of the strike zone, has made 131 errors in his four-year career, and has poor fundamentals.

YAMIL BENITEZ
Bats: R Throws: R Opening Day Age: 23
Ht: 6-2 Wt: 180 Born: 10/5/1972
Position: OF Drafted: NDFA 10-26-89 MON

YR TEAM	LG/CLASS	G	AB	R	H	2B	3B	HR	RBI	SB	BA	OBA
93 Burlington	MID/A	111	411	70	112	21	5	15	61	18	.273	.323
94 Harrisburg	EAST/AA	126	475	58	123	18	4	17	91	18	.259	.311
95 Montreal	NL/MAJ	14	39	8	15	2	1	2	7	0	.385	.400
95 Ottawa	INT/AAA	127	474	66	123	24	6	18	69	14	.259	.324

Benitez, Montreal's best upper-level hitting prospect, finished third in the organization in home runs and RBI and pounded a couple of homers in 39 major league at-bats. The 22-year-old Puerto Rican has above average tools across the board, but he needs to better learn the strike zone. Benitez, who has a huge uppercut in his swing, led his league in strikeouts two straight seasons.

HIRAM BOCACHICA
Bats: R Throws: R Opening Day Age: 20
Ht: 5-11 Wt: 165 Born: 3/4/1976
Position: SS Drafted: 1994 #1 MON

YR TEAM	LG/CLASS	G	AB	R	H	2B	3B	HR	RBI	SB	BA	OBA
94 Expos	GULF/R	43	168	31	47	9	0	5	16	11	.280	.346
95 Albany	SAL/A	96	380	65	108	20	10	2	30	47	.284	.381

After injuring his ankle a week into the season and sitting out a month, Bocachica returned and extended a season-opening hitting streak to 17 games. An exciting player with gap power, excellent speed, a strong arm, and good range, the 19-year-old was third in the South Atlantic League in steals with an organization-high 47. However, the 1994 first-rounder had problems in the field, committing a minor league-high 58 errors in just 94 games—numbers not uncommon for a young shortstop.

STEVE FALTEISEK
Bats: R Throws: R Opening Day Age: 24
Ht: 6-2 Wt: 200 Born: 1/28/1972
Position: P Drafted: 1992 #10 MON

YR TEAM	LG/CLASS	G	GS	GF	SV	W	L	ERA	IP	H	HR	BB	SO	O/BA
93 Burlington	MID/A	14	14	0	0	3	5	5.90	76.1	86	4	35	63	.284
94 W Palm Bch	FSL/A	27	24	0	0	9	4	2.54	159.2	144	3	49	91	.240
95 Ottawa	INT/AAA	3	3	0	0	2	0	1.17	23.0	17	0	5	18	.213
95 Harrisburg	EAST/AA	25	25	0	0	9	6	2.95	168.0	152	3	64	112	.245

After a poor start (0-2, 6.46 ERA) Falteisek won six straight decisions, had 19 quality starts in his final 23 appearances, and finished second in the Eastern League in ERA. The South Alabama product, by far the Senators' most productive pitcher, was second in the organization in ERA, wins, and strikeouts. Falteisek, just 23, is not overpowering and relies on great command and keeping the ball down. He finished the year with a four-hit shutout for Ottawa.

SCOTT GENTILE
Bats: R Throws: R Opening Day Age: 25
Ht: 5-11 Wt: 210 Born: 12/21/1970
Position: P Drafted: 1992 #4 MON

YR TEAM	LG/CLASS	G	GS	GF	SV	W	L	ERA	IP	H	HR	BB	SO	O/BA
93 W Palm Bch	FSL/A	25	25	0	0	8	9	4.03	138.1	132	8	54	108	.253
94 Harrisburg	EAST/AA	6	2	1	0	0	1	17.42	10.1	16	1	25	14	.348
94 W Palm Bch	FSL/A	53	1	40	26	5	2	1.93	65.1	44	0	19	90	.190
95 Harrisburg	EAST/AA	37	0	26	11	2	2	3.44	49.2	36	3	15	48	.200

Gentile finished 1994 with a 43-inning scoreless streak but allowed 11 runs in his first four appearances in 1995. Soon after, however, he allowed just two runs in 31 innings before injuring his elbow in mid-July and landing on the disabled list for a month. Because of the strike, reporting to camp out of shape, and the elbow problem, scouts rarely saw the 90+-mph fastball and a hard slider that Gentile throws.

VLADIMIR GUERRERO
Bats: R Throws: R Opening Day Age: 20
Ht: 6-2 Wt: 158 Born: 2/9/1976
Position: OF Drafted: NDFA 3-1-93 MON

YR TEAM	LG/CLASS	G	AB	R	H	2B	3B	HR	RBI	SB	BA	OBA
94 Expos	GULF/R	37	137	24	43	13	3	5	25	0	.314	.366
95 Albany	SAL/A	110	421	77	140	21	10	16	63	12	.333	.383

Guerrero, a five-tool talent, followed up his fine debut in 1994 with a monster year at Albany. Despite playing in a park that favors pitchers, he finished with double-digit doubles, triples, home runs and steals, leading the league in batting and finishing third in slugging (.544). The 19-year-old, who was selected to the post-season All-Star team and had his season end early because of a minor knee problem, also showed one of the best arms in his league.

MONTREAL EXPOS: TOP PROSPECTS

CURTIS PRIDE

Bats: L Throws: R Opening Day Age: 27
Ht: 5-11 Wt: 195 Born: 12/17/1968
Position: OF Drafted: 1986 #10 NYN

YR TEAM	LG/CLASS	G	AB	R	H	2B	3B	HR	RBI	SB	BA	OBA
93 Harrisburg	EAST/AA	50	180	51	64	6	3	15	39	21	.356	.404
93 Ottawa	INT/AAA	69	262	55	79	11	4	6	22	29	.302	.388
93 Montreal	NL/MAJ	10	9	3	4	1	1	1	5	1	.444	.444
94 W Palm Bch	FSL/A	3	8	5	6	1	0	1	3	2	.750	.833
94 Ottawa	INT/AAA	82	300	56	77	16	4	9	32	22	.257	.345
95 Montreal	NL/MAJ	48	63	10	11	1	0	0	2	3	.175	.235
95 Ottawa	INT/AAA	42	154	25	43	8	3	4	24	8	.279	.339

Signed as a six-year free agent from the Mets' organization after the 1992 season, Pride has been a productive hitter in his three years as an Expo farmhand. However, injuries and a stockpile of talent at the major league level have kept him in the minors. In 1995 the lefthanded-hitter added what might be the final piece to his game as he hit southpaws better than righthanders for the first time in his career.

CURT SCHMIDT

Bats: R Throws: R Opening Day Age: 26
Ht: 6-6 Wt: 223 Born: 3/16/1970
Position: P Drafted: 1992 #41 MON

YR TEAM	LG/CLASS	G	GS	GF	SV	W	L	ERA	IP	H	HR	BB	SO	O/BA
93 W Palm Bch	FSL/A	44	2	22	5	4	6	3.17	65.1	63	3	25	51	.248
93 Expos	GULF/R	1	1	0	0	1	0	0.00	5.0	1	0	0	7	.063
94 Harrisburg	EAST/AA	53	0	26	5	6	2	1.88	71.2	51	4	29	75	.202
95 Montreal	NL/MAJ	11	0	0	0	0	6.97	10.1	15	1	9	7	.357
95 Ottawa	INT/AAA	41	0	38	15	5	0	2.22	52.2	40	1	18	38	.219

The hard-throwing Schmidt, a big righthander with nasty breaking stuff, induces lots of ground balls. He gave up just one run in 21 innings during one mid-season stretch and converted saves in five straight games when given a chance to close in August. After a very impressive '94 campaign, the 25-year-old began the '95 season in Montreal but was sent to Triple-A after three outings.

EVERETT STULL

Bats: R Throws: R Opening Day Age: 24
Ht: 6-3 Wt: 195 Born: 8/24/1971
Position: P Drafted: 1992 #3 MON

YR TEAM	LG/CLASS	G	GS	GF	SV	W	L	ERA	IP	H	HR	BB	SO	O/BA
93 Burlington	MID/A	15	15	0	0	4	9	3.83	82.1	68	8	59	85	.226
94 W Palm Bch	FSL/A	27	26	0	0	10	9	3.31	147.0	116	3	78	165	.220
95 Harrisburg	EAST/AA	24	24	0	0	3	12	5.54	126.2	114	12	79	132	.243

After finishing second in the Florida State League in strikeouts and winning nine of his last 12 decisions, great things were expected from Stull, a big guy with a 90+-mph fastball. However, he lost nine of his first ten decisions last year and had trouble with his mechanics nearly all season. The 24-year-old did show signs of his promise, pitching a two-hitter and striking out 14 in one start, and he still managed to lead the organization in strikeouts, but he had plenty of outings when he couldn't get through the third inning.

UGUETH URBINA

Bats: R Throws: R Opening Day Age: 22
Ht: 6-2 Wt: 170 Born: 2/15/1974
Position: P Drafted: NDFA 11-90 MON

YR TEAM	LG/CLASS	G	GS	GF	SV	W	L	ERA	IP	H	HR	BB	SO	O/BA
93 Burlington	MID/A	16	16	0	0	10	1	1.99	108.1	78	7	36	107	.200
93 Harrisburg	EAST/AA	11	11	0	0	4	5	3.99	70.0	66	5	32	45	.259
94 Harrisburg	EAST/AA	21	21	0	0	9	3	3.28	120.2	96	11	43	86	.218
95 Montreal	NL/MAJ	7	4	0	0	2	2	6.17	23.1	26	6	14	15	.280
95 Ottawa	INT/AAA	13	11	0	0	6	2	3.04	68.0	46	1	26	55	.191
95 W Palm Bch	FSL/A	2	2	0	0	1	0	0.00	9.0	4	0	1	11	.143

Urbina, the best pitching prospect in the organization, began the year in the Florida State League rehabbing a tender shoulder. After dropping his first decision upon his arrival in Triple-A, the Venezuelan native ripped off six consecutive wins and fashioned a 26⅓ scoreless innings streak. The 21-year-old features a mid-90's fastball and in his five-year career has limited batters to a .218 average.

JOSE VIDRO

Bats: S Throws: R Opening Day Age: 21
Ht: 5-11 Wt: 175 Born: 8/27/1974
Position: 2B Drafted: 1992 #6 MON

YR TEAM	LG/CLASS	G	AB	R	H	2B	3B	HR	RBI	SB	BA	OBA
93 Burlington	MID/A	76	287	39	69	19	0	2	34	3	.240	.317
94 W Palm Bch	FSL/A	125	465	57	124	30	2	4	49	8	.267	.344
95 Harrisburg	EAST/AA	64	246	33	64	16	2	4	38	3	.260	.315
95 W Palm Bch	FSL/A	44	163	20	53	15	2	3	24	0	.325	.360

A middle infielder with good pop in his bat, Vidro put together hitting streaks of 12 and 15 games last season. Additionally, he had 35 multiple-hit games despite missing a month of the season with a torn ligament in his left thumb. A switch-hitter and a good fielder, the Puerto Rican native is a better hitter from the left side of the plate.

GABE WHITE

Bats: L Throws: L Opening Day Age: 24
Ht: 6-2 Wt: 200 Born: 11/20/1971
Position: P Drafted: 1990 #3 MON

YR TEAM	LG/CLASS	G	GS	GF	SV	W	L	ERA	IP	H	HR	BB	SO	O/BA
93 Harrisburg	EAST/AA	16	16	0	0	7	2	2.16	100.0	80	4	28	80	.221
93 Ottawa	INT/AAA	6	6	0	0	2	1	3.12	40.1	38	3	6	28	.242
94 W Palm Bch	FSL/A	1	1	0	0	1	0	1.50	6.0	2	0	1	4	.105
94 Ottawa	INT/AAA	14	14	0	0	8	3	5.05	73.0	77	11	28	63	.270
94 Montreal	NL/MAJ	7	5	2	1	1	1	6.08	23.2	24	4	11	17	.261
95 Montreal	NL/MAJ	19	1	8	0	1	2	7.01	25.2	26	7	9	25	.260
95 Ottawa	INT/AAA	12	12	0	0	2	3	3.90	62.1	58	5	10	37	.244

The Expos' third pick in their heralded 1990 draft, White shuttled back and forth between Montreal and Ottawa and never found his stride in 1995. Plagued by an inconsistent curveball, his fastball and changeup became more hittable pitches. In his three previous minor league seasons the big lefthander had been 32-14.

MONTREAL EXPOS: OTHERS TO WATCH

DEREK AUCOIN Bats: R Throws: R Ht: 6-7 Wt: 226
Born: 3/27/1970 Drafted: NDFA 7-17-89 MON Position: P

YR TEAM	LG/CLASS	G	GS	GF	SV	W	L	ERA	IP	H	HR	BB	SO	O/BA
95 Harrisburg	EAST/AA	29	0	10	1	2	4	4.96	52.2	52	3	28	48	.259

Set to become a six-year free agent and leave the organization, Aucoin found his command and a nasty slider, won the International League championship clincher, and landed on the 40-man roster.

JAKE BENZ Bats: L Throws: L Ht: 5-9 Wt: 162
Born: 2/27/1972 Drafted: 1994 #15 MON Position: P

YR TEAM	LG/CLASS	G	GS	GF	SV	W	L	ERA	IP	H	HR	BB	SO	O/BA
95 W Palm Bch	FSL/A	44	0	38	22	0	2	1.17	54.0	44	0	18	48	.227

A diminutive lefty with four pitches he can throw for strikes, Benz led the organization in saves.

KIRK BULLINGER Bats: R Throws: R Ht: 6-2 Wt: 170
Born: 10/28/1969 Drafted: 1992 #32 SL Position: P

YR TEAM	LG/CLASS	G	GS	GF	SV	W	L	ERA	IP	H	HR	BB	SO	O/BA
95 Harrisburg	EAST/AA	56	0	39	7	5	3	2.42	67.0	61	4	25	42	.242

A ground ball pitcher with a good slider, Jim Bullinger's brother went 14 consecutive appearances without allowing a run last year.

JOLBERT CABRERA Bats: R Throws: R Ht: 6-0 Wt: 177
Born: 12/8/1972 Drafted: NDFA 7-3-90 MON Position: SS

YR TEAM	LG/CLASS	G	AB	R	H	2B	3B	HR	RBI	SB	BA	OBA
95 Harrisburg	EAST/AA	9	35	4	10	2	0	0	1	3	.286	.306
95 W Palm Bch	FSL/A	103	357	62	102	23	2	1	25	19	.286	.364

A good athlete with a quick first step, Cabrera hits to all fields and is improving defensively.

BRAD FULLMER Bats: L Throws: R Ht: 6-1 Wt: 185
Born: 1/17/1975 Drafted: 1993 #4 MON Position: 3B

YR TEAM	LG/CLASS	G	AB	R	H	2B	3B	HR	RBI	SB	BA	OBA
95 Albany	SAL/A	123	468	69	151	38	4	8	67	10	.323	.387

The South Atlantic League's number two hitter, who missed all of '94 with a rotator cuff injury, has one of the quickest bats in the organization.

ROD HENDERSON Bats: R Throws: R Ht: 6-4 Wt: 195
Born: 3/11/1971 Drafted: 1992 #2 MON Position: P

YR TEAM	LG/CLASS	G	GS	GF	SV	W	L	ERA	IP	H	HR	BB	SO	O/BA
95 Harrisburg	EAST/AA	12	12	0	0	3	6	4.31	56.1	51	4	18	53	.236

Henderson, a former top prospect, had his season end in July due to shoulder problems.

BOB HENLEY Bats: R Throws: R Ht: 6-2 Wt: 190
Born: 1/30/1973 Drafted: 1991 #27 MON Position: C

YR TEAM	LG/CLASS	G	AB	R	H	2B	3B	HR	RBI	SB	BA	OBA
95 Albany	SAL/A	102	335	45	94	20	1	3	46	1	.281	.436

A good-hitting catcher with alley power, Henley finished second in the South Atlantic League in on-base percentage. Defensively, he has a good arm with a quick release.

JOSE PANIAGUA Bats: R Throws: R Ht: 6-1 Wt: 160
Born: 8/20/1973 Drafted: NDFA 8-18-90 MON Position: P

YR TEAM	LG/CLASS	G	GS	GF	SV	W	L	ERA	IP	H	HR	BB	SO	O/BA
95 Harrisburg	EAST/AA	25	25	0	0	7	12	5.34	126.1	140	9	62	89	.285

Paniagua, who had six quality starts in his last seven starts, throws fairly hard but mainly relies on mixing his pitches.

MATT RALEIGH Bats: R Throws: R Ht: 5-11 Wt: 205
Born: 7/18/1970 Drafted: 1992 #14 MON Position: 1B

YR TEAM	LG/CLASS	G	AB	R	H	2B	3B	HR	RBI	SB	BA	OBA
95 W Palm Bch	FSL/A	66	179	29	37	11	0	2	18	4	.207	.401

A wrist injury was a big reason Raleigh slipped from a Midwest League-high 34 homers in 1994 to two last year.

FERNANDO SEGUIGNOL Bats: S Throws: R Ht: 6-5 Wt: 179
Born: 1/19/1975 Drafted: NDFA 1-29-93 NYA Position: OF

YR TEAM	LG/CLASS	G	AB	R	H	2B	3B	HR	RBI	SB	BA	OBA
95 Albany	SAL/A	121	457	59	95	22	2	12	66	12	.208	.260

One of the players acquired from the Yankees in the John Wetteland deal, Seguignol is an athlete with power potential who had a subpar '95.

DAROND STOVALL Bats: S Throws: L Ht: 6-1 Wt: 185
Born: 1/3/1973 Drafted: 1991 #9 SL Position: OF

YR TEAM	LG/CLASS	G	AB	R	H	2B	3B	HR	RBI	SB	BA	OBA
95 W Palm Bch	FSL/A	121	461	52	107	22	2	4	51	18	.232	.297

Stovall, a good defensive center fielder, has a big swing and tries to pull most pitches.

B.J. WALLACE Bats: R Throws: L Ht: 6-4 Wt: 195
Born: 5/18/1971 Drafted: 1992 #1 MON Position: P

YR TEAM	LG/CLASS	G	GS	GF	SV	W	L	ERA	IP	H	HR	BB	SO	O/BA
Did not play due to injury														

The third player selected in the 1992 draft, Wallace missed the entire 1995 season with elbow problems.

NEIL WEBER Bats: L Throws: L Ht: 6-5 Wt: 205
Born: 12/6/1972 Drafted: 1993 #10 MON Position: P

YR TEAM	LG/CLASS	G	GS	GF	SV	W	L	ERA	IP	H	HR	BB	SO	O/BA
95 Harrisburg	EAST/AA	28	28	0	0	6	11	5.01	152.2	157	16	90	119	.271

The big lefthander finished fifth in the organization in strikeouts, but lacks command and overpowering stuff.

JASON WOODRING Bats: R Throws: R Ht: 6-3 Wt: 190
Born: 4/2/1974 Drafted: 1993 #60 MON Position: P

YR TEAM	LG/CLASS	G	GS	GF	SV	W	L	ERA	IP	H	HR	BB	SO	O/BA
95 Albany	SAL/A	48	0	39	16	1	1	2.66	50.2	46	0	20	50	.238

Woodring mixes in a changeup with his fastball/curveball arsenal and finished third in the organization in saves.

ESTEBAN YAN Bats: R Throws: R Ht: 6-4 Wt: 180
Born: 6/22/1974 Drafted: NDFA 11-21-90 ATL Position: P

YR TEAM	LG/CLASS	G	GS	GF	SV	W	L	ERA	IP	H	HR	BB	SO	O/BA
95 W Palm Bch	FSL/A	24	21	1	1	6	8	3.07	137.2	139	3	33	89	.265

Yan has a great arm and throws a low 90's fastball with movement, allowing three earned runs or less in 17 of his 21 starts.

NEW YORK METS

EDGARDO ALFONZO

Positions: 3B/2B//SS
Bats: R **Throws:** R
Ht: 5'11" **Wt:** 185
Opening Day Age: 22
Born: 8/11/1973
Drafted: NYN 2/19/91
ML Seasons: 1

SCOUTING REPORT
A very aggressive player who showed excellent strike-zone judgment in the minors, Alfonzo made good contact in '95 but didn't hit for power, run well, or walk. A straightaway hitter, Edgardo must learn to pull more and lay off pitches he can't hit. Despite above-average speed, Edgardo is not a good basestealer. He will lay down the bunt, but could improve in this area as well.

Although he is expected to become a solid regular, he hasn't yet found an everyday defensive position. At both second and third base, Alfonzo shows good hands and adequate range. His throwing arm is very strong and accurate as well.

HOW HE PERFORMED IN '95
Alfonzo's came to the majors touted as a strong offensive player, but his punch seemed to vanished when he got to the bigs. No power and a remarkably low walk total combined for a fairly small offensive package for third base, where he was used most by the Mets.

However, Edgardo was playing in the Eastern League in '94. Making the jump from Double-A isn't easy, especially when doing it in the Big Apple. He is expected to be a better hitter when he learns how major-league pitchers work hitters.

Edgardo played three infield positions for New York. In 29 games at second base during '95, Alfonzo made just one error despite showing sub-average range. He got to balls more frequently while used at third, but he made six miscues in 57 contests. He didn't play much shortstop, and won't for New York with Jose Vizcaino and young Rey Ordonez around.

Edgardo's last day as a regular was August 10; that week, a herniated disc was found in his back. He had experienced back trouble in the past and, it is possible that this injury was a factor in his loss of power. He returned in mid-September and got a few at-bats in spot duty.

WHAT TO EXPECT IN '96
The Mets' infield is a question mark for '96, but Alfonzo's quick bat and "gamer" attitude impressed Dallas Green last season. Edgardo is likely to be in the lineup somewhere for New York; he played well in winter ball and appears fully recovered from the back problem. If his plate discipline improves with experience, he could become a force for the Mets.

Overall Statistics

	G	AB	R	H	2B	3B	HR	RBI	SB	CS	BB	SO	BA	OBA
95 NYN	101	335	26	93	13	5	4	41	1	1	12	37	.278	.301
Career	101	335	26	93	13	5	4	41	1	1	12	37	.278	.301

1995 Situational Statistics

	AB	HR	RBI	BA	OBA	SLG		AB	HR	RBI	BA	OBA	SLG
Home	167	0	16	.281	.315	.335	LHP	98	2	15	.286	.314	.418
Road	168	4	25	.274	.287	.429	RHP	237	2	26	.274	.296	.367
Apr-Jun	162	3	21	.259	.274	.383	ScPos	81	2	36	.321	.352	.543
Jul-Oct	173	1	20	.295	.326	.382	Clutch	61	0	4	.295	.377	.311

How He Compares to Other Batters

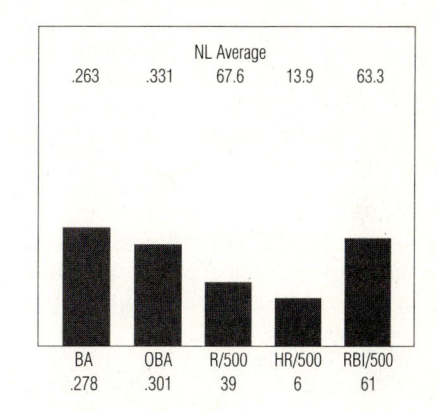

NL Average
.263   .331   67.6   13.9   63.3

BA	OBA	R/500	HR/500	RBI/500
.278	.301	39	6	61

Where He Hits the Ball

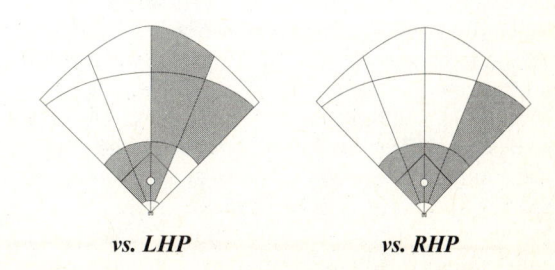

vs. LHP   vs. RHP

THE SCOUTING REPORT: 1996

NEW YORK METS

RICO BROGNA

Position: 1B
Bats: L **Throws:** L
Ht: 6'2" **Wt:** 202
Opening Day Age: 25
Born: 4/18/1970
Drafted: DET88 1/26
ML Seasons: 3

SCOUTING REPORT
Brogna shows good line-drive power but has some trouble with breaking balls. Like most lefthanded power hitters, his favorite pitches are fastballs down and in. The past year revealed a weakness against left-handed pitching, as Rico did all his heavy work against righties and may end up platooning if he can't fix this disparity. Below-average footspeed makes his baserunning average for his position, and he's not much of a bunter.

Brogna's fieldwork is what draws attention. His above-average range, throwing and aggressive play at first base draw many comparisons to Keith Hernandez. He was hampered a bit by a bad knee (he had surgery after the season), but still made all the plays around the bag.

HOW HE PERFORMED IN '95
Brogna followed his surprising 1994 rookie year with a solid 1995 performance that justified the trade of David Segui to Montreal. For most of the year, he was the big gun in the New York lineup.

While his production dipped slightly, Rico still led the Mets in slugging percentage. He also struck out a lot, leading the team in whiffs by a large margin. He drew just enough walks to compile an on-base percentage close to the league average, but is far from a patient hitter. His professional high in bases on balls is 50.

WHAT TO EXPECT IN '96
Brogna is set as the Mets' first baseman for the immediate future. He could increase his value by making better contact and improving his production against lefthanders. His overall offense is not quite up to par for his position; the club will need more from his bat to transform itself into a contender.

Rico is still young enough to improve and he continues to develop at the plate. Originally with the Tigers organization, he never had a breakthrough season in his six years as Detroit property. His best minor-league average was .273, and the 22 homers Brogna slugged last year were his highest total as a professional. Whether Rico can maintain the power pace and improve the other parts of his offense are the key questions. He's still valuable if he doesn't, but he needs to boost his production if he is to be a solid middle-of-the-order hitter in an improved lineup for the Mets.

Overall Statistics

	G	AB	R	H	2B	3B	HR	RBI	SB	CS	BB	SO	BA	OBA
95 NYN	134	495	72	143	27	2	22	76	0	0	39	111	.289	.342
Career	182	652	91	194	39	4	30	99	1	0	48	145	.298	.347

1995 Situational Statistics

	AB	HR	RBI	BA	OBA	SLG		AB	HR	RBI	BA	OBA	SLG
Home	243	13	43	.292	.351	.510	LHP	118	2	14	.229	.272	.339
Road	252	9	33	.286	.333	.460	RHP	377	20	62	.308	.363	.531
Apr-Jun	199	9	30	.291	.340	.482	ScPos	135	4	52	.267	.353	.430
Jul-Oct	296	13	46	.287	.344	.486	Clutch	88	6	18	.341	.420	.614

How He Compares to Other Batters

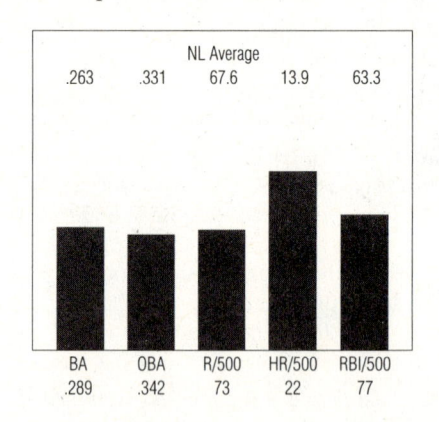

NL Average: .263 .331 67.6 13.9 63.3

BA	OBA	R/500	HR/500	RBI/500
.289	.342	73	22	77

Where He Hits the Ball

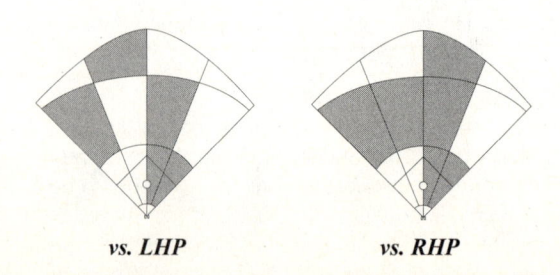

vs. LHP   vs. RHP

NEW YORK METS

CARL EVERETT

Position: OF
Bats: B **Throws:** R
Ht: 6'0" **Wt:** 190
Opening Day Age: 25
Born: 6/3/1970
Drafted: NYA90 1/10
ML Seasons: 3

SCOUTING REPORT
A line-drive hitter, Everett was particularly fond of first-pitch fastballs before a sudden onset of discipline late last season. He regained some of his speed last season, beating out infield rollers, but is not yet much of a baserunner and won't hit high in the order unless he can steal bases more effectively. However, Carl does bunt for hits, with the drag bunt a specialty.

Carl regularly racks up high outfield assists totals with what most feel is an average arm. He has average-plus range and charges balls well, two factors in his throwing success. Last year, he nailed eight runners for New York in just 79 games. Most scouts feel Everett lacks sufficient speed to play center field, however.

HOW HE PERFORMED IN '95
Everett began the season as the Mets' right fielder, but was sent down to Norfolk on May 15, batting a lowly .193. The club brought him back July 24 and was rewarded for the promotion, as Carl was a real factor in the club's strong second half and reassumed playing right field on an everyday basis. Dallas Green, who had questioned Everett's work ethic earlier in the year, batted him third over the last ten weeks, showing a high regard for the youngster's power potential.

The key to Everett's improvement was patience at the plate. He hacked at everything in sight during the first half, accepting just three bases on balls in his first 83 at-bats through July 31. Carl abruptly changed his approach, however, and his on-base percentage shot up. However, most of the improvement came against righties; "Poochy" had serious problems against lefthanders.

WHAT TO EXPECT IN '96
The upbeat finish to 1995 makes for an optimistic outlook for this year. Carl has at least a chance to break through to stardom if he improves his production against lefthanders and shows some more power. Everett's range and throwing make him an exciting player in right field, but the jury is out as to whether he will hit enough to play there. While he has terrific tools, Carl is still a step away from translating his abilities into game-winning production on the field and in the lineup.

Overall Statistics

	G	AB	R	H	2B	3B	HR	RBI	SB	CS	BB	SO	BA	OBA
95 NYN	79	289	48	75	13	1	12	54	2	5	39	67	.260	.352
Career	106	359	55	88	14	1	14	60	7	5	43	91	.245	.329

1995 Situational Statistics

	AB	HR	RBI	BA	OBA	SLG		AB	HR	RBI	BA	OBA	SLG
Home	138	9	24	.312	.410	.551	LHP	100	4	14	.210	.269	.400
Road	151	3	30	.212	.296	.331	RHP	189	8	40	.286	.392	.455
Apr-Jun	57	3	6	.193	.233	.386	ScPos	95	4	46	.305	.405	.505
Jul-Oct	232	9	48	.276	.378	.448	Clutch	48	1	3	.208	.296	.313

How He Compares to Other Batters

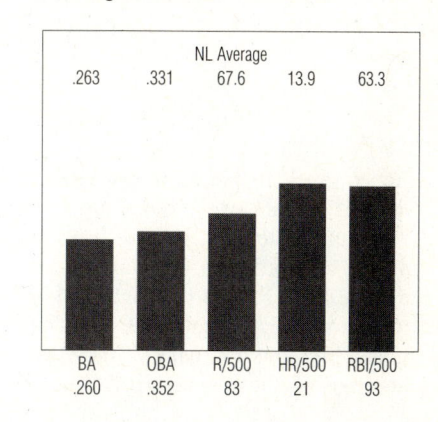

NL Average: .263 .331 67.6 13.9 63.3

BA .260 OBA .352 R/500 83 HR/500 21 RBI/500 93

Where He Hits the Ball

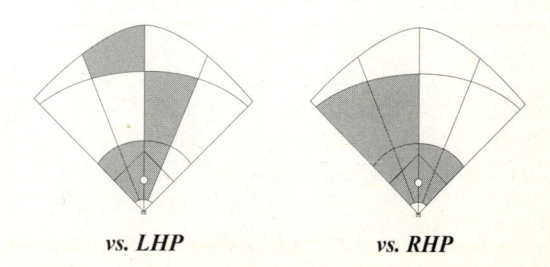

vs. LHP   vs. RHP

NEW YORK METS

JOHN FRANCO

Position: RP
Bats: L **Throws:** L
Ht: 5'10" **Wt:** 180
Opening Day Age: 35
Born: 9/17/1960
Drafted: LA81 6/125
ML Seasons: 12

SCOUTING REPORT
Franco uses four pitches, throwing from a low three-quarter motion with average control. His sinking fastball, circle change-up, and splitfinger fastball are now all of average big-league quality. The sinker, especially, is extremely hittable if it rises. However, his pitches are more effective late in the count because batters have to look for his out pitch—a plus, nasty slider.

John is a bit above-average with his glove, but really helps himself with his excellent ability at keeping runners planted firmly on the bag: only two opponents even tried to run against him in '95. He didn't bat all season, and is just a .100 career hitter in 30 at-bats.

HOW HE PERFORMED IN '95
New York's terrible play in the first half of the season caused the veteran reliever to barely miss a seventh 30-save season. There weren't many save opportunities before mid-July, and Franco was simply not sharp due to rust. When the young Mets emerged from their cocoons to enjoy a successful second half, John, by then the oldest player on the roster, snapped back into form as he posted 18 saves in his final 21 appearances. His 295 career saves are the most of any lefthanded pitcher in major-league history.

Overall, Franco saved 29 games in 36 opportunities (81%), a decent but not exceptional ratio for any club not bordering Lake Erie. He was tough on inherited runners, stranding 16 out of 21. He was basically the same John Franco the Mets had in '94, posting close-to-identical numbers. Batters can get on base against him, but not many of those eventually end up crossing the plate. Lefthanded hitters hit for a higher average against him for the third straight year, but they didn't hit for much power.

WHAT TO EXPECT IN '96
John's been healthy and at full strength for two seasons, and there's no reason not to expect a third year of the same quality, as manager Dallas Green has used him carefully over that period. With Green coming back this season, there should be no change in Franco's working conditions in '96. He lacks the dominating heat of the best closers, but is still a championship-quality late man.

Overall Statistics

	G	GS	GF	SV	W	L	ERA	IP	H	R	ER	HR	BB	SO
95 NYN	48	0	41	29	5	3	2.44	51.2	48	17	14	4	17	41
Career	661	0	526	295	68	54	2.62	822.0	752	290	239	46	315	600

1995 Situational Statistics

	W	L	ERA	SV	IP	BB	SO		AB	HR	RBI	BA	OBA	SLG
Home	4	1	2.51	18	32.1	8	23	LHB	32	0	3	.281	.314	.344
Road	1	2	2.33	11	19.1	9	18	RHB	159	4	17	.245	.310	.377
Apr-Jun	2	1	3.18	8	22.2	9	18	ScPos	51	1	15	.196	.250	.294
Jul-Oct	3	2	1.86	21	29.0	8	23	Clutch	156	3	18	.237	.306	.353

How He Compares to Other Pitchers

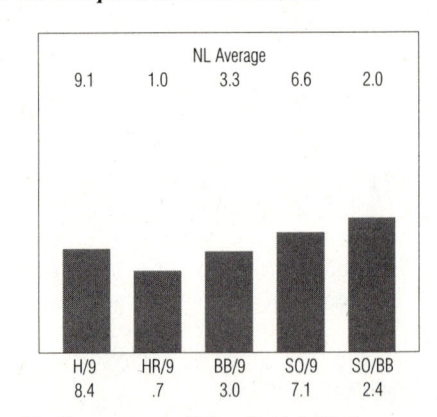

NL Average: 9.1 / 1.0 / 3.3 / 6.6 / 2.0

H/9	HR/9	BB/9	SO/9	SO/BB
8.4	.7	3.0	7.1	2.4

How He Compares to Other Relief Pitchers

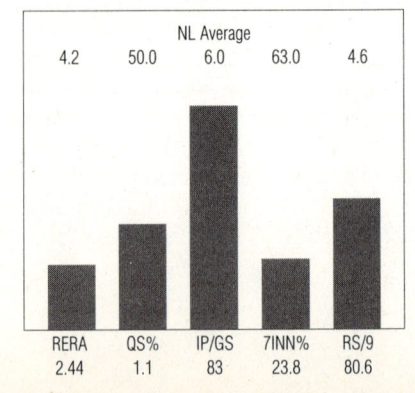

NL Average: 4.2 / 50.0 / 6.0 / 63.0 / 4.6

RERA	QS%	IP/GS	7INN%	RS/9
2.44	1.1	83	23.8	80.6

NEW YORK METS

PETE HARNISCH

Position: SP
Bats: B **Throws:** R
Ht: 6'1" **Wt:** 195
Opening Day Age: 29
Born: 9/23/1966
Drafted: BAL87 3/27
ML Seasons: 8

SCOUTING REPORT

Harnisch uses an odd hesitation in his three-quarter delivery that makes his pitches just that much harder to pick up. Not that he needs the help: when he's healthy, Pete's arsenal is loaded.

He has an average fastball that can be thrown either on the fists of righthanders or with explosive sinking motion. Harnisch also has a well above-average, hard, sharp-breaking slider and an average change-up and curve. Unfortunately, two years of injuries have diminished his stuff somewhat.

A battler on the mound, Pete tries to throw every pitch on the black. He has inconsistent control, however, which has been made worse by arm problems. Harnisch is one of the few pitchers unafraid to get his uniform dirty, and generally looks pretty sloppy.

Pete is ungainly-looking as a fielder as well. He's slow off the mound and has a poor follow-through. He does not hold runners well; in '95, 17 tried to steal against Harnisch and 12 were successful. He is a poor hitter, carrying a .130 lifetime mark into 1995 that got worse when he batted .091 in 33 at-bats.

HOW HE PERFORMED IN '95

In '94, Harnisch missed time because of a torn biceps tendon. Last year, things got more serious. He tore a muscle in his throwing shoulder at the start of August, and underwent season-ending surgery. Before the injury, he pitched pretty effectively despite an awful won-lost record, compiling the second-lowest ERA among Mets' starters. He was close to his career average of 6.1 innings per start.

Pete did his share in '95 to enhance Shea Stadium's reputation as a pitcher's park, with his road ERA doubling his home total. He struck out hitters far more frequently in Queens, which could be the result of the park's poor nighttime visibility and his deceptive, hesitation-filled pitching motion.

WHAT TO EXPECT IN '96

Given a full off-season, chances are good that the shoulder will heal, allowing Harnisch to resume his spot in the rotation. He's now the senior member of the starting staff and the team's highest-paid player. New York fans hope that he'll earn that money in '96, but age and injury have a way of dashing such hopes.

Overall Statistics

	G	GS	GF	SV	W	L	ERA	IP	H	R	ER	HR	BB	SO
95 NYN	18	18	0	0	2	8	3.68	110.0	111	55	45	13	24	82
Career	186	185	1	0	63	63	3.72	1151.0	1032	520	476	106	448	867

1995 Situational Statistics

	W	L	ERA	SV	IP	BB	SO		AB	HR	RBI	BA	OBA	SLG
Home	1	4	2.73	0	66.0	12	53	LHB	195	6	26	.308	.357	.503
Road	1	4	5.11	0	44.0	12	29	RHB	230	7	24	.222	.253	.370
Apr-Jun	1	5	4.13	0	72.0	17	51	ScPos	102	2	37	.275	.350	.431
Jul-Oct	1	3	2.84	0	38.0	7	31	Clutch	22	0	2	.364	.375	.500

How He Compares to Other Pitchers

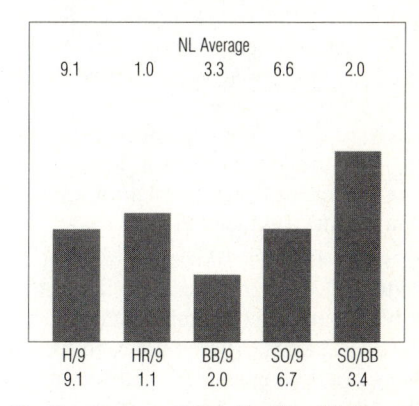

NL Average: H/9 9.1 | HR/9 1.0 | BB/9 3.3 | SO/9 6.6 | SO/BB 2.0

Harnisch: H/9 9.1 | HR/9 1.1 | BB/9 2.0 | SO/9 6.7 | SO/BB 3.4

How He Compares to Other Starting Pitchers

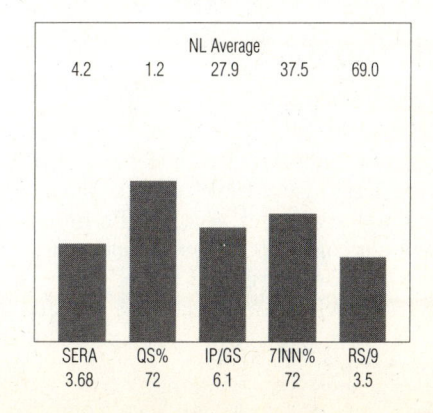

NL Average: SERA 4.2 | QS% 1.2 | IP/GS 27.9 | 7INN% 37.5 | RS/9 69.0

Harnisch: SERA 3.68 | QS% 72 | IP/GS 6.1 | 7INN% 72 | RS/9 3.5

THE SCOUTING REPORT: 1996

NEW YORK METS

TODD HUNDLEY

Position: C
Bats: B **Throws:** R
Ht: 5'11" **Wt:** 170
Opening Day Age: 26
Born: 5/27/1969
Drafted: NYN87 2/39
ML Seasons: 6

SCOUTING REPORT

Like most switch-hitters, Hundley likes the low inside pitch from the left side and higher offerings from the right side. His swing has gotten quicker lately, with his overall bat speed now ranking as above-average. Todd has above-average power and has improved his strike-zone judgment. On the basepaths, he is a catcher and runs like one, taking one deliberate base at a time.

Hundley's defense has remained a constant plus. He showed solid mechanics and average hands behind the plate to go with slightly below-average mobility and blocking ability and a good rapport with the pitching staff. Some of the blame for a below-average success rate at throwing out basestealers (24%) must go to the Mets' young mound corps, which is unseasoned at holding runners. However, Todd doesn't dazzle with his arm (average strength with average-minus accuracy).

HOW HE PERFORMED IN '95

Developing into a solid hitter, Todd finally fulfilled the Mets' long-held expectations by jumping into the upper class of National League receivers last year. Todd's batting average jumped over 40 points in '95 and his on-base average jumped nearly 80. He did not hit for more power, but simply had more productive at-bats, hitting more singles and drawing more walks. There was a dramatic improvement against lefthanded pitching as well as a solid gain against righthanded pitchers.

It appears that Hundley's season could have been even better. He was hitting everything in sight during July, but unfortunately sprained his left wrist on the 22nd in a home-plate collision with Colorado's Eric Young and was placed on the disabled list two days later. Todd returned September 6, but his momentum had been lost. While his September performance was decent, it fell quite a bit short of his July pace.

WHAT TO EXPECT IN '96

Hundley underwent surgery to fix the injured wrist for good in October. Expected to recover fully, he faces a critical season. The challenge is to continue to hit as well as he did in '95 while grooming a very raw pitching staff. If he can succeed in both areas, he will be recognized as one of the better catchers in baseball. And if he does succeed both ways, the Mets will take a big step toward their promising future.

Overall Statistics

	G	AB	R	H	2B	3B	HR	RBI	SB	CS	BB	SO	BA	OBA
95 NYN	90	275	39	77	11	0	15	51	1	0	42	64	.280	.382
Career	491	1468	169	338	61	4	50	187	7	2	121	307	.230	.293

1995 Situational Statistics

	AB	HR	RBI	BA	OBA	SLG		AB	HR	RBI	BA	OBA	SLG
Home	125	6	20	.272	.384	.456	LHP	60	3	12	.300	.391	.533
Road	150	9	31	.287	.379	.507	RHP	215	12	39	.274	.379	.470
Apr-Jun	149	7	30	.262	.371	.443	ScPos	66	4	36	.333	.453	.545
Jul-Oct	126	8	21	.302	.395	.532	Clutch	49	2	12	.245	.406	.408

How He Compares to Other Batters

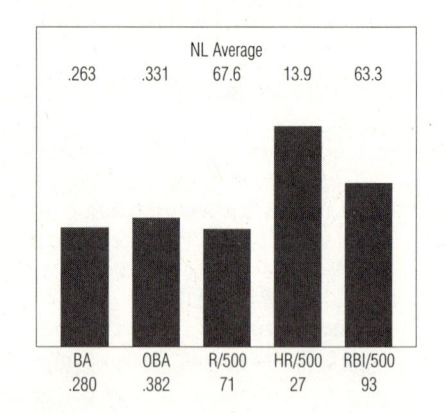

NL Average: .263 .331 67.6 13.9 63.3

BA .280 | OBA .382 | R/500 71 | HR/500 27 | RBI/500 93

Where He Hits the Ball

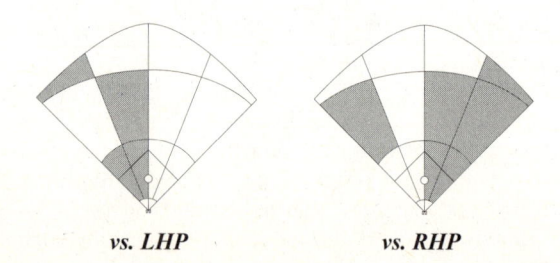

vs. LHP   vs. RHP

THE SCOUTING REPORT: 1996

NEW YORK METS

BOBBY JONES

Position: SP
Bats: R **Throws:** R
Ht: 6'4" **Wt:** 210
Opening Day Age: 26
Born: 2/10/1970
Drafted: NYN91 2/36
ML Seasons: 3

SCOUTING REPORT
Jones is a standard, three-quarter-throwing finesse pitcher who must keep his command sharp in order to survive. His fastball is not very, but does sink and he can work the pitch to spots. He also throws an average slider and change. His plus curveball is his highest-rated pitch, and when thrown for strikes makes the rest of the repertoire better.

When he's in a groove, he fools opponents by moving the ball around and changing speeds. Jones is smart and sets up hitters well. When he doesn't, Bobby's pitches look fat to hitters.

HOW HE PERFORMED IN '95
After an outstanding rookie season in 1994, the league started to catch on to Jones last year. Batters slugged over 70 points higher and his ERA climbed by a full run. More alarming is the fact that his ERA rose as the season went on. Through June, Bobby averaged over seven innings per start; from July on, he went fewer than six.

In 1994 Jones was mediocre at Shea but unhittable on the road. Last year he was pounded in away games, but was more effective inside Shea's hard-to-reach fences.

Bobby really suffered once a batter reached first base. His move to first is decent, but his motion is easy to read and opponents ran wild last year, stealing 24 bases in 27 attempts. To be fair, neither Mets' catcher has outstanding throwing skills. Worry over this constant theft threat produced hittable deliveries with runners on first.

Bobby led the NL with 18 sacrifice bunts but fanned 25 times in 56 at-bats while hitting .161.

WHAT TO EXPECT IN '96
The one positive 1995 development for Jones was a sharp rise in his strikeout rate. He had ten games in which he whiffed six or more batters and was noticeably more effective in those contests. He must make that type of game a more frequent occurrence this season in order to succeed.

Jones spent fewer than two full seasons in the minors and has not experienced much failure. If he can adjust to his problems, Bobby can hold a job as a third or fourth starter. However, with the Mets' supply of pitching talent in the high minors, he must establish himself to avoid being relegated to the bullpen or getting a ticket out of town.

Overall Statistics

	G	GS	GF	SV	W	L	ERA	IP	H	R	ER	HR	BB	SO
95 NYN	30	30	0	0	10	10	4.19	195.2	209	107	91	20	53	127
Career	63	63	0	0	24	21	3.71	417.1	427	217	172	36	131	242

1995 Situational Statistics

	W	L	ERA	SV	IP	BB	SO		AB	HR	RBI	BA	OBA	SLG
Home	5	3	3.28	0	96.0	20	63	LHB	347	9	34	.248	.299	.406
Road	5	7	5.06	0	99.2	33	64	RHB	415	11	60	.296	.346	.443
Apr-Jun	4	5	3.01	0	95.2	17	60	ScPos	183	2	64	.240	.303	.355
Jul-Oct	6	5	5.31	0	100.0	36	67	Clutch	69	1	7	.217	.239	.319

How He Compares to Other Pitchers

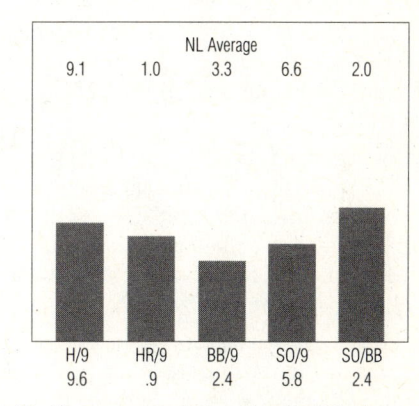

	H/9	HR/9	BB/9	SO/9	SO/BB
NL Average	9.1	1.0	3.3	6.6	2.0
Jones	9.6	.9	2.4	5.8	2.4

How He Compares to Other Starting Pitchers

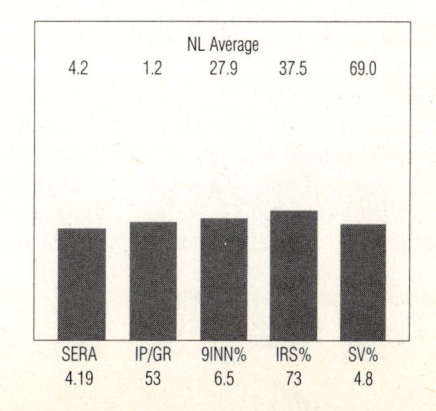

	SERA	IP/GR	9INN%	IRS%	SV%
NL Average	4.2	1.2	27.9	37.5	69.0
Jones	4.19	53	6.5	73	4.8

NEW YORK METS

JEFF KENT

Position: 2B
Bats: R **Throws:** R
Ht: 6'1" **Wt:** 185
Opening Day Age: 28
Born: 3/7/1968
Drafted: TOR89 21/523
ML Seasons: 4

SCOUTING REPORT
Kent has excellent power for his position. He can drive the ball and will go with the pitch, but he's a little too much in love with home runs and wastes some at-bats trying to uppercut pitches.

He is a bit on the slow side on the bases, and cannot help the offense much by taking extra bases. His doubles total is rather low considering his power. Jeff does not bunt. Jeff's defense grades out as average, except for his arm, which is very strong for a second baseman.

HOW HE PERFORMED IN '95
Kent is one of the last holdovers from the "old" Mets. Unfortunately, he mouthed off a little too much in his early days with the club, and as a result has never been too popular with the front office.

He hits for a decent average and was second on the club in home runs last year. However, Jeff strikes out often and his low walk count holds down his on-base percentage. This weakness, combined with lack of sparkle in the field, keeps Kent from being ranked in the upper tier of second basemen.

Like many hitters who strike out often, Kent is much more productive in day games. Last year, he hit .317 with eight homers over just 123 at-bats in the sunshine.

Jeff hurt his standing in 1995 with a lack of RBI production. Promoted to the cleanup spot following the trade of Bobby Bonilla, Kent did not take to the new role. He only drove in 45 runners besides himself with 131 hits, and fifteen of his twenty homers came with the bases empty.

In the field, Kent displayed average range and made 10 errors, placing in the middle of the pack among NL second basemen with a .984 fielding percentage. He has acquired a very poor defensive reputation, but Jeff is truly not as bad as many people think.

WHAT TO EXPECT IN '96
Kent has likely worn a Mets uniform for the last time. Joe McIlvaine has been trying to unload him, just as he shipped out so many others in the past who were not farm-bred by the Mets. However, Jeff is talented and will likely be a starter wherever he ends up—especially if he can keep his mouth shut.

Overall Statistics

	G	AB	R	H	2B	3B	HR	RBI	SB	CS	BB	SO	BA	OBA
95 NYN	125	472	65	131	22	3	20	65	3	3	29	89	.278	.327
Career	474	1688	235	459	91	10	66	263	10	14	109	337	.272	.326

1995 Situational Statistics

	AB	HR	RBI	BA	OBA	SLG		AB	HR	RBI	BA	OBA	SLG
Home	243	11	33	.284	.336	.494	LHP	133	3	10	.248	.306	.376
Road	229	9	32	.271	.319	.432	RHP	339	17	55	.289	.336	.499
Apr-Jun	212	9	24	.274	.330	.453	ScPos	136	4	45	.199	.271	.331
Jul-Oct	260	11	41	.281	.325	.473	Clutch	85	5	7	.271	.340	.494

How He Compares to Other Batters

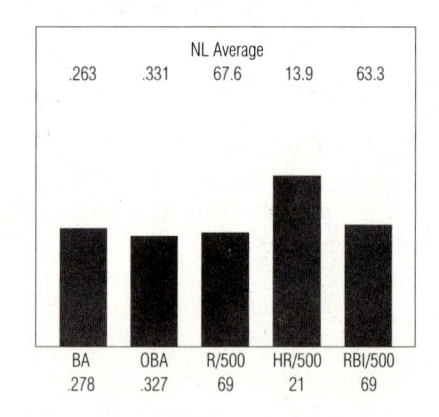

NL Average: .263 .331 67.6 13.9 63.3

BA	OBA	R/500	HR/500	RBI/500
.278	.327	69	21	69

Where He Hits the Ball

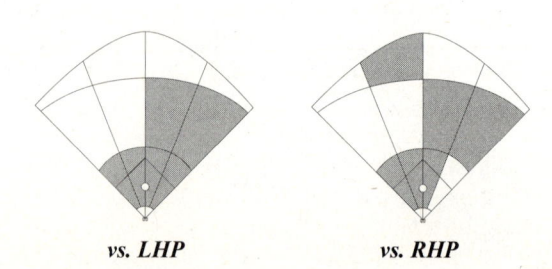

vs. LHP   vs. RHP

NEW YORK METS

DAVE MLICKI

Position: SP
Bats: R **Throws:** R
Ht: 6'4" **Wt:** 185
Opening Day Age: 27
Born: 6/8/1968
Drafted: CLE90 19/460
ML Seasons: 3

SCOUTING REPORT

Inconsistent control means Mlicki does not get the most out of his four-pitch inventory. Dave has an average-plus sinking fastball, which he can turn over, as well as a decent curve and change. His fourth offering is an average slider. This combo means a tough day for hitters when Dave gets the ball where he wants it consistently. Some days in 1995 he did, and some days he didn't. He throws from a standard three-quarter angle. Like most New York pitchers, Dave had a stolen base problem, as 17 of 20 opposition runners were successful. He's a bit light with the glove and even less helpful at the plate. Although Mlicki laid down 12 sacrifice hits, he batted an abominable .051, garnering just two hits in 39 at-bats.

HOW HE PERFORMED IN '95

Mlicki's first major-league season was a roller-coaster ride. He started off decently, got roughed up in mid-season, then came back to finish well. It was an encouraging debut for Mlicki, a former Indians' farmhand who missed most of 1993 after undergoing serious shoulder surgery.

After a 4-1 start, Dave went 0-4 and was banished to the bullpen. However, an opportunity for redemption came when Pete Harnisch tore up his shoulder in early August. Mlicki returned to the rotation and had his best month of the season in August, finishing with a decent September.

Mlicki ended up a close second to Bobby Jones on the Mets' staff in strikeouts. In between the Ks, however, he saw a lot of baserunners, and lefties were a particular problem for him.

Overall, the club had to be pleased with Mlicki, who had a winning record and an ERA near the league average. He demonstrated that he could come back strong after a cold streak and profit from the experience. The trade bringing him and Jerry DiPoto to New York for Jeromy Burnitz looks mighty good at this point.

WHAT TO EXPECT IN '96

Despite his encouraging rookie season, Mlicki can't yet be complacent. He will be pushed hard by the mound talent the Mets are bringing up, and will have to improve on his 1995 performance in order to maintain a slot in the starting rotation. Dave also has to hope that his shoulder is mended for good. If healthy, Mlicki is at the very least capable of filling a swing role.

Overall Statistics

	G	GS	GF	SV	W	L	ERA	IP	H	R	ER	HR	BB	SO
95 NYN	29	25	1	0	9	7	4.26	160.2	160	82	76	23	54	123
Career	36	32	1	0	9	9	4.28	195.2	194	102	93	28	76	146

1995 Situational Statistics

	W	L	ERA	SV	IP	BB	SO		AB	HR	RBI	BA	OBA	SLG
Home	4	3	3.66	0	83.2	26	62	LHB	275	12	33	.309	.382	.509
Road	5	4	4.91	0	77.0	28	61	RHB	350	11	41	.214	.264	.354
Apr-Jun	4	4	3.99	0	70.0	19	48	ScPos	141	5	51	.248	.343	.418
Jul-Oct	5	3	4.47	0	90.2	35	75	Clutch	42	2	6	.214	.313	.405

How He Compares to Other Pitchers

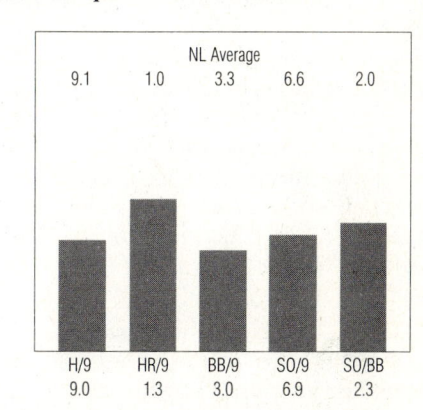

	H/9	HR/9	BB/9	SO/9	SO/BB
NL Average	9.1	1.0	3.3	6.6	2.0
	9.0	1.3	3.0	6.9	2.3

How He Compares to Other Starting Pitchers

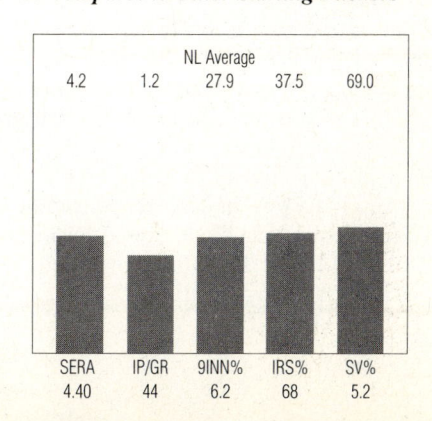

	SERA	IP/GR	9INN%	IRS%	SV%
NL Average	4.2	1.2	27.9	37.5	69.0
	4.40	44	6.2	68	5.2

NEW YORK METS

JOE ORSULAK

Positions: OF//1B
Bats: L **Throws:** L
Ht: 6'1" **Wt:** 186
Opening Day Age: 33
Born: 5/31/1962
Drafted: PIT80 7/153
ML Seasons: 12

SCOUTING REPORT
Joe is a singles hitter who is good at putting the ball into play. He can guide his Louisville Slugger toward pitches anywhere in the strike zone with excellent bat control. However, Orsulak is at the age where skills begin to erode, and the strikeout total is creeping up as his bat speed decreases. Due to his tendency to simply put the stick on the ball, his raw power is measured with a microscope.

Orsulak used to be a burner on the bases but now is a minus runner. He is awfully slow for an outfielder, but so far has compensated for receding speed by good positioning and by being a quick read. He's got good hands and so catches everything he can get to.

HOW HE PERFORMED IN '95
Joe has played 12 seasons in the majors, rarely putting together above-average totals. He's currently an aging platoon player whose mobility is almost gone. His on-base percentage is poor, and combined with a total lack of power, Orsulak is an anomaly among outfielders—a slow singles hitter who doesn't get on base much.

A close look, however, reveals some clearly positive traits. His defensive skills are still good enough for him to play the outfield corners, and Orsulak ranks as an outstanding contact hitter and hit-and-run man. If the situation calls for a single, he can hit righthanded pitching as well as almost anyone. Another positive is his personality. Joe is well-liked by all, and has been a major factor in team cohesiveness.

Last season, he threw out three runners on the bases. Joe is no longer asked to play center field, and showed his best range in right.

WHAT TO EXPECT IN '96
Pushed out of the picture in New York due to the emergence of younger players, Orsulak will likely see significant playing time in Florida. The Fighting Fish have had problems with bench depth and currently employ two starting outfielders with checkered injury histories. Joe has often been mentioned as coach material, and the leadership he will bring to his new club will be valued by management. However, it's questionable whether he merits 290 at-bats again in any situation.

Overall Statistics

	G	AB	R	H	2B	3B	HR	RBI	SB	CS	BB	SO	BA	OBA
95 NYN	108	290	41	82	19	2	1	37	1	3	19	35	.283	.323
Career	1268	3926	523	1091	168	35	54	379	92	58	284	347	.278	.328

1995 Situational Statistics

	AB	HR	RBI	BA	OBA	SLG		AB	HR	RBI	BA	OBA	SLG
Home	126	1	22	.325	.353	.437	LHP	25	0	6	.160	.185	.200
Road	164	0	15	.250	.300	.323	RHP	265	1	31	.294	.336	.389
Apr-Jun	123	0	14	.301	.336	.374	ScPos	66	1	34	.348	.402	.485
Jul-Oct	167	1	23	.269	.314	.371	Clutch	79	1	16	.266	.302	.418

How He Compares to Other Batters

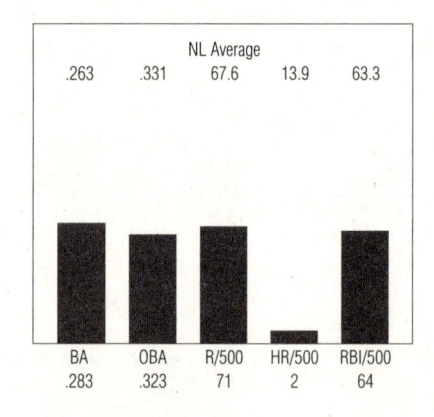

NL Average: .263 .331 67.6 13.9 63.3

BA	OBA	R/500	HR/500	RBI/500
.283	.323	71	2	64

Where He Hits the Ball

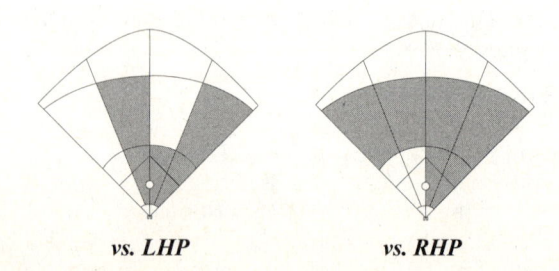

vs. LHP   vs. RHP

NEW YORK METS

BILL PULSIPHER

Position: SP
Bats: L **Throws:** L
Ht: 6'3" **Wt:** 210
Opening Day Age: 22
Born: 10/9/1973
Drafted: NYN91 3/66
ML Seasons: 1

SCOUTING REPORT
Pulsipher throws from a low three-quarter angle. He has an average-plus fastball with good sinking motion and also has the confidence to ride the heat up in the strike zone. His best weapon is a plus sharp curve, which he will throw at any time, though his control of it is a bit shaky. He also uses a change, which is not much softer than his fastball and tends to hang.

Potential is the what gets everyone excited about this kid. He's got a great arm, and if he can learn to change speeds more effectively and iron out some kinks in his control, Pulsipher projects as a #2 starter on what promises to be a powerful New York staff.

Last season, Pulsipher batted just .105, fanning in half of his 38 at-bats. He is an average fielder.

HOW HE PERFORMED IN '95
June 17 was the first day of the revolution for the Mets: Bill Pulsipher's graduation date from the minors. He was the first of the team's set of future franchise pitchers to be called up, serving as the bellwether of a process that will reshape the team.

"The Pulse's" first start included a five-run first inning, but the young righty got comfortable in a hurry. He was so dominant against lefthanded batters that most every opponent stacked their lineup with righthanders. The quality lefties who were left in to face him did almost nothing, and the righties didn't do too much better. Bill was tough on runners as well, with five of the 14 men attempting steals being thrown out.

His ERA showed steady improvement throughout the season. By August, he was holding offenses to fewer than one baserunner an inning. Pulsipher had an uncomfortable September, when he was affected by a sprained elbow ligament. With the Mets out of the race, Bill sat out after September 11, but is reported to have fully recovered without any surgery.

WHAT TO EXPECT IN '96
Bill will be just 22 this season and should continue to improve if he doesn't abuse his arm. Like Jason Isringhausen, he has had two straight years of over 200 innings at a tender age. This year, Pulsipher is likely to make 30 starts. The losing record he compiled in 1995 may be his last, as the team should improve along with him.

Overall Statistics

	G	GS	GF	SV	W	L	ERA	IP	H	R	ER	HR	BB	SO
95 NYN	17	17	0	0	5	7	3.98	126.2	122	58	56	11	45	81
Career	17	17	0	0	5	7	3.98	126.2	122	58	56	11	45	81

1995 Situational Statistics

	W	L	ERA	SV	IP	BB	SO		AB	HR	RBI	BA	OBA	SLG
Home	4	4	3.76	0	69.1	21	39	LHB	68	1	6	.250	.311	.368
Road	1	3	4.24	0	57.1	24	42	RHB	410	10	45	.256	.326	.385
Apr-Jun	1	2	4.71	0	21.0	14	16	ScPos	132	4	43	.280	.329	.409
Jul-Oct	4	5	3.83	0	105.2	31	65	Clutch	58	4	9	.310	.375	.534

How He Compares to Other Pitchers

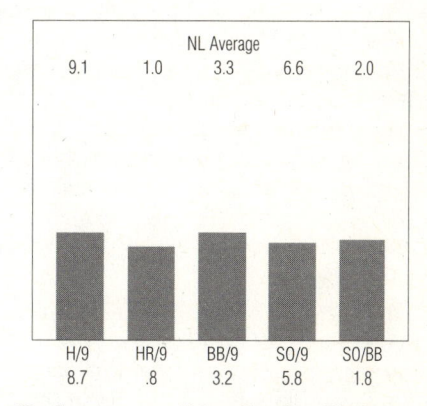

NL Average: 9.1 / 1.0 / 3.3 / 6.6 / 2.0

H/9	HR/9	BB/9	SO/9	SO/BB
8.7	.8	3.2	5.8	1.8

How He Compares to Other Starting Pitchers

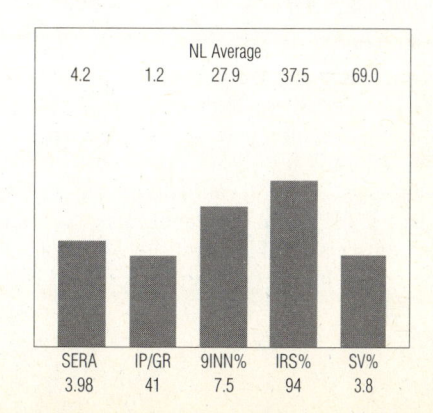

NL Average: 4.2 / 1.2 / 27.9 / 37.5 / 69.0

SERA	IP/GR	9INN%	IRS%	SV%
3.98	41	7.5	94	3.8

NEW YORK METS

RYAN THOMPSON

Position: OF
Bats: R **Throws:** R
Ht: 6'3" **Wt:** 200
Opening Day Age: 28
Born: 11/4/1967
Drafted: TOR87 13/335
ML Seasons: 4

SCOUTING REPORT
Thompson likes to hack at first-pitch fastballs. Typical of switch-hitters, he prefers low pitches from the left and high pitches from the right. He's a better hitter against lefties, but from both sides of the plate he tends to pull off the ball. He gets himself out way too much due to a poor understanding of the strike zone. Ryan has the range to play right field but is really not fleet enough for center. He has a mediocre arm with average-minus accuracy. When he does get on base he's an asset, with a reputation as a smart runner despite his average speed. He seldom bunts, either for hits or to move teammates along.

HOW HE PERFORMED IN '95
Thompson had another frustrating year. He missed two months of the season with hamstring problems, got hot in June, and then was awful the remainder of the year. Again, he failed to deliver on his potential.

While his batting average increased by 26 points over 1994, the rise came entirely on the strength of the one hot month. Aside from June, Thompson batted a lowly .212. Add a big drop in home run production and a decline in an already terrible strikeout-to-walk ratio, and the result is a player who is regressing, not progressing. Few teams can afford to carry such a rally-killer in the lineup. He threw out four runners last season and showed above-average range in the outfield. However, Ryan's glovework hardly makes up for his disappointing offense.

Despite the presence of young outfield prospects, Thompson got a lot of playing time in September as management took one last good look before deciding his fate. Unfortunately for Ryan, his September numbers fell into the "ship-him" range.

WHAT TO EXPECT IN '96
New York has a group of exciting young home-grown outfielders to try out this year, and they also inked former White Sox' center fielder Lance Johnson. There is no reason for the club to try to solve the mystery of Ryan Thompson. He's had 1,000 major league at-bats and hasn't yet shown that he can play. At this point, he'll have to hope someone picks him up as a spare part, and he may have to return to Triple-A to prove that he deserves a shot.

Overall Statistics

	G	AB	R	H	2B	3B	HR	RBI	SB	CS	BB	SO	BA	OBA
95 NYN	75	267	39	67	13	0	7	31	3	1	19	77	.251	.306
Career	283	997	127	238	53	4	39	126	8	11	74	276	.239	.300

1995 Situational Statistics

	AB	HR	RBI	BA	OBA	SLG		AB	HR	RBI	BA	OBA	SLG
Home	150	3	17	.240	.278	.353	LHP	73	2	7	.288	.333	.425
Road	117	4	14	.265	.341	.410	RHP	194	5	24	.237	.296	.361
Apr-Jun	104	5	16	.308	.345	.490	ScPos	69	1	22	.232	.287	.319
Jul-Oct	163	2	15	.215	.282	.307	Clutch	38	0	3	.237	.293	.316

How He Compares to Other Batters

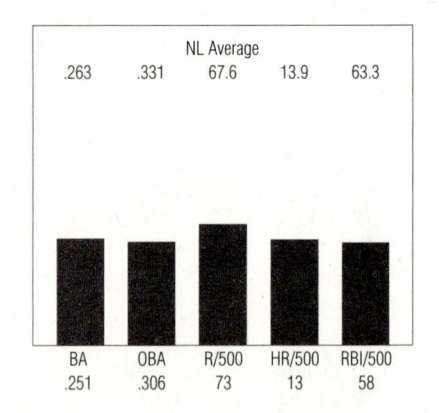

NL Average
.263 .331 67.6 13.9 63.3

BA .251   OBA .306   R/500 73   HR/500 13   RBI/500 58

Where He Hits the Ball

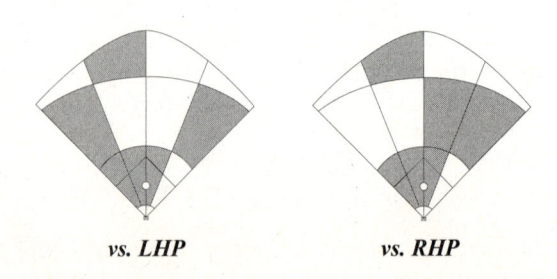

vs. LHP   vs. RHP

NEW YORK METS

JOSE VIZCAINO

Positions: SS//2B
Bats: B **Throws:** R
Ht: 6'1" **Wt:** 150
Opening Day Age: 28
Born: 3/26/1968
Drafted: LA 2/18/86
ML Seasons: 7

SCOUTING REPORT
The shortstop is a pure singles hitter who likes first-pitch fastballs. He's the standard highball on the right, lowball on the left switch-hitter, but hits better from the right side. Many of Jose's hits are line drives that just clear the infield, as he has little power. Decent bat control makes him a serviceable hit-and-run man batting second, even though he strikes out regularly. He can bunt for hits and laid down 13 sacrifices last season. Vizcaino is above-average in range, arm and accuracy, and has soft hands. While he can play three infield spots, his tools are best at shortstop. He's a smart guy who plays hard and uses his head on the bases despite just average speed. Jose is never going to be a prolific basestealer, but he improved his success rate by leaps and bounds in 1995.

HOW HE PERFORMED IN '95
Vizcaino was one of the few constants in "The Year The Mets Remade Themselves." He led the team in innings, at-bats, and hits while playing fine defense.

One thing that was not constant was Jose's position in the batting order. Ejected from the leadoff spot he occupied during 1994, Vizcaino hit either second or in the lower third of the lineup. Wherever he batted, his offense was up a couple of notches from the previous year, and Jose got stronger as the season progressed. His worst months were April and May, and he collected 21 of his extra-base hits after June.

The respectable offensive figures were pumped by Vizcaino's sudden mastery of lefthanded pitchers. He also performed well with men on base. As a result he drove in 56 runs, an impressive total for a singles-hitting shortstop. If Jose could hit for better power or draw some walks, he'd be a complete package at shortstop.

WHAT TO EXPECT IN '96
As good as Jose has looked at times, the presence of prospect Rey Ordonez is a factor. Ordonez is a spectacular defensive player and will likely get a shot at the job in the next year. Vizcaino, re-signed this winter by New York, will probably play most of the time at short this year. He should provide his usual good range and kick in some production at bat, and has carved out a spot for himself in the majors for several more years.

Overall Statistics

	G	AB	R	H	2B	3B	HR	RBI	SB	CS	BB	SO	BA	OBA
95 NYN	135	509	66	146	21	5	3	56	8	3	35	76	.287	.332
Career	612	1961	224	527	69	17	11	172	27	25	137	271	.269	.315

1995 Situational Statistics

	AB	HR	RBI	BA	OBA	SLG		AB	HR	RBI	BA	OBA	SLG
Home	263	2	31	.289	.339	.369	LHP	130	0	9	.346	.388	.385
Road	246	1	25	.285	.324	.362	RHP	379	3	47	.266	.313	.359
Apr-Jun	206	1	21	.262	.311	.325	ScPos	125	1	50	.320	.371	.392
Jul-Oct	303	2	35	.304	.347	.393	Clutch	97	0	13	.247	.282	.299

How He Compares to Other Batters

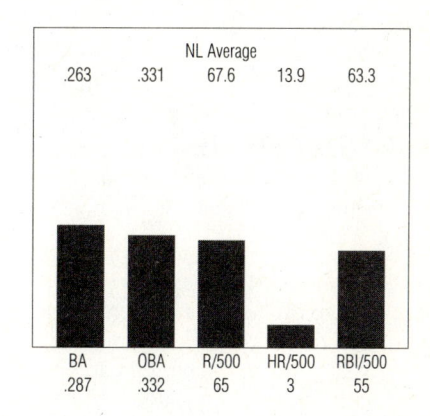

NL Average: .263 .331 67.6 13.9 63.3

BA .287 | OBA .332 | R/500 65 | HR/500 3 | RBI/500 55

Where He Hits the Ball

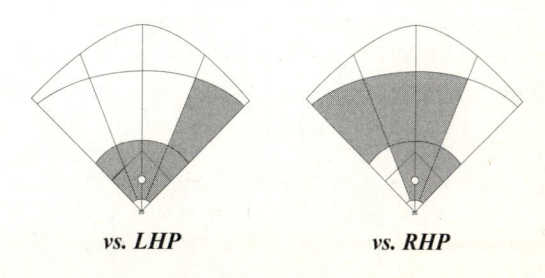

vs. LHP   vs. RHP

NEW YORK METS

TIM BOGAR

Positions: SS/3B/1B//2B/OF
Bats: R **Throws:** R
Ht: 6'2" **Wt:** 198
Opening Day Age: 29
Born: 10/28/1966
Drafted: NYN87 9/212
ML Seasons: 3

Overall Statistics

	G	AB	R	H	2B	3B	HR	RBI	SB	CS	BB	SO	BA	OBA
95 NYN	78	145	17	42	7	0	1	21	1	0	9	25	.290	.329
Career	206	402	41	100	20	0	6	51	2	1	27	65	.249	.299

1995 Situational Statistics

	AB	HR	RBI	BA	OBA	SLG		AB	HR	RBI	BA	OBA	SLG
Home	60	0	4	.233	.292	.283	LHP	77	1	16	.377	.400	.494
Road	85	1	17	.329	.356	.412	RHP	68	0	5	.191	.253	.206
Apr-Jun	42	1	6	.214	.267	.286	ScPos	41	1	20	.293	.388	.390
Jul-Oct	103	0	15	.320	.355	.388	Clutch	27	1	9	.333	.379	.481

SCOUTING REPORT

As a hitter, Bogar likes the ball up and out over the plate and will go with the pitch. He's a singles hitter who doesn't walk much, bunt often, or steal bases.

Tim is an average fielder in most every way and is a bit slow-footed. A strong arm is his one notable defensive feature. He does play hard, increasing his longevity as a utility player.

HOW HE PERFORMED IN '95

Bogar had a huge offensive improvement this year and belied his previous reputation as an all-glove, no-bat player. His at-bats increased each month of the season as he hit his way into the lineup. Tim feasted on lefthanded pitching, and even his poor .191 average against righties was still an improvement on his previous performance. Bogar played all four infield positions, specializing in the left side, but didn't impress anywhere in the field.

WHAT TO EXPECT IN '96

The better bat has solidified Tim's position as the team's utility infielder. He may even get some more pinch-hitting assignments against lefthanded pitching, but unless he can add walks, power, or speed, he's not going to start.

DAMON BUFORD

Position: OF
Bats: R **Throws:** R
Ht: 5'10" **Wt:** 170
Opening Day Age: 25
Born: 6/12/1970
Drafted: BAL90 11/283
ML Seasons: 3

Overall Statistics

	G	AB	R	H	2B	3B	HR	RBI	SB	CS	BB	SO	BA	OBA
95 BAL/NYN	68	168	30	34	5	0	4	14	10	8	25	35	.202	.318
Career	125	249	50	53	10	0	6	23	12	10	34	55	.213	.318

1995 Situational Statistics

	AB	HR	RBI	BA	OBA	SLG		AB	HR	RBI	BA	OBA	SLG
Home	88	2	7	.182	.270	.284	LHP	56	2	5	.268	.388	.393
Road	80	2	7	.225	.366	.325	RHP	112	2	9	.170	.284	.259
Apr-Jun	32	0	2	.063	.205	.063	ScPos	35	1	11	.229	.362	.343
Jul-Oct	136	4	12	.235	.346	.360	Clutch	23	0	1	.261	.393	.348

SCOUTING REPORT

Buford shows quick hands at the plate and hits line drives but tends to go after high, outside pitches that he can't handle due to poor arm extension. His speed has not been an asset on the bases so far, and Damon lacks the confidence to challenge opponents, although he bunted for hits last year with some success. Damon has well above-average range in the outfield, albeit with a weak, inaccurate arm. His hands are average-minus.

HOW HE PERFORMED IN '95

Buford, the "other" player in the Bobby Bonilla deal, started the season with the Orioles but was demoted in May, hitting just .062. The Mets, on the other hand, began playing him immediately after acquiring him.

After a weak August, Damon finished strong in September. He has a good rep as a defender, and unlike many of his Met teammates, will take the base on balls when it's offered. However, his overall offensive skills do not seem to be starter-grade.

WHAT TO EXPECT IN '96

Damon will have to keep up his September hitting pace to get much playing time. He turns 26 this year, the age when many players make their biggest year-to-year improvement.

NEW YORK METS

REID CORNELIUS

Position: SP/RP
Bats: R **Throws:** R
Ht: 6'0" **Wt:** 200
Opening Day Age: 25
Born: 6/2/1970
Drafted: MON88 11/284
ML Seasons: 1

Overall Statistics

	G	GS	GF	SV	W	L	ERA	IP	H	R	ER	HR	BB	SO
95 MO/NY	18	10	1	0	3	7	5.53	66.2	75	44	41	11	30	39
Career	18	10	1	0	3	7	5.53	66.2	75	44	41	11	30	39

1995 Situational Statistics

	W	L	ERA	SV	IP	BB	SO		AB	HR	RBI	BA	OBA	SLG
Home	2	3	4.81	0	33.2	14	23	LHB	132	7	22	.311	.361	.538
Road	1	4	6.27	0	33.0	16	16	RHB	128	4	18	.266	.368	.414
Apr-Jun	0	0	8.00	0	9.0	5	4	ScPos	67	2	25	.194	.337	.284
Jul-Oct	3	7	5.15	0	57.2	25	35	Clutch	3	0	0	.333	.600	.333

SCOUTING REPORT
Cornelius throws from a high three-quarter, nearly overhand, angle, but he lacks power stuff. His average-minus fastball sinks a bit. He has a decent change-up; his curveball, which he throws often, is his best pitch. Unfortunately, Cornelius has a tendency to hang the bender.

Reid's fielding is no asset, and 11 of 17 runners were successful stealing against him, about par for Mets' pitchers.

HOW HE PERFORMED IN '95
Reid was acquired June 8 from Montreal for David Segui. When the Mets shipped Bret Saberhagen to the Rockies, Cornelius was brought up to fill the open spot in the rotation, but did not remind anyone of the pitcher he replaced.

Control has long been Reid's problem; as a result, he had a rough two months in New York, losing five games in a row in the middle of his stay with the Mets. Cornelius hit just .100 with no sacrifice bunts.

WHAT TO EXPECT IN '96
Reid's tenure with the Mets will be brief if he doesn't turn things around quickly this year. On a team rich in good arms, he may struggle just to be considered a fifth starter.

JERRY DIPOTO

Position: RP
Bats: R **Throws:** R
Ht: 6'2" **Wt:** 200
Opening Day Age: 27
Born: 5/24/1968
Drafted: CLE89 2/71
ML Seasons: 3

Overall Statistics

	G	GS	GF	SV	W	L	ERA	IP	H	R	ER	HR	BB	SO
95 NYN	58	0	26	2	4	6	3.78	78.2	77	41	33	2	29	49
Career	111	0	53	13	8	10	3.70	150.2	160	76	62	3	69	99

1995 Situational Statistics

	W	L	ERA	SV	IP	BB	SO		AB	HR	RBI	BA	OBA	SLG
Home	0	1	3.43	1	39.1	11	31	LHB	122	0	14	.270	.364	.311
Road	4	5	4.12	1	39.1	18	18	RHB	166	2	24	.265	.321	.361
Apr-Jun	0	3	6.91	0	28.2	10	24	ScPos	85	1	36	.306	.415	.353
Jul-Oct	4	3	1.98	2	50.0	19	25	Clutch	117	0	18	.308	.399	.359

SCOUTING REPORT
A true finesse pitcher, DiPoto is an effective package when his control is sharp. A three-quarter, wraparound delivery makes his average-plus fastball, which bores in on righties, and his average splitter harder to pick up. Jerry also has a slider which he throws only for show. DiPoto's defense is decent and he held runners pretty well: nine tried to steal against him, but only five succeeded.

HOW HE PERFORMED IN '95
DiPoto's season mirrored that of the team as a whole: smacked around a lot early, he was quite effective during the second half. His ERA through June was 6.28, but over the rest of the season was 1.98. He even picked up a couple of saves in September. He kept the ball in the park, tallying the lowest home run rate of any Mets' pitcher by far.

Jerry was hitless in five at-bats, his first major-league plate experience.

WHAT TO EXPECT IN '96
A good follow-up to his strong 1995 finish should place DiPoto in the righthanded setup slot. He appeared much more comfortable in late-game situations than Doug Henry did last year.

NEW YORK METS

DOUG HENRY

Position: RP
Bats: R **Throws:** R
Ht: 6'4" **Wt:** 185
Opening Day Age: 32
Born: 12/10/1963
Drafted: MIL85 8/185
ML Seasons: 5

Overall Statistics

	G	GS	GF	SV	W	L	ERA	IP	H	R	ER	HR	BB	SO
95 NYN	51	0	20	4	3	6	2.96	67.0	48	23	22	7	25	62
Career	230	0	149	65	12	18	3.72	254.1	227	115	105	28	111	200

1995 Situational Statistics

	W	L	ERA	SV	IP	BB	SO		AB	HR	RBI	BA	OBA	SLG
Home	2	2	3.12	1	34.2	10	28	LHB	99	2	12	.182	.287	.263
Road	1	4	2.78	3	32.1	15	34	RHB	143	5	16	.210	.265	.378
Apr-Jun	1	3	5.06	2	21.1	7	20	ScPos	60	3	23	.217	.364	.417
Jul-Oct	2	3	1.97	2	45.2	18	42	Clutch	128	5	22	.258	.322	.430

SCOUTING REPORT

The righthander works from the stretch, throwing a better-than-average slider and a serviceable change from a three-quarter angle. He's best with his sinking fastball, which he controls well enough to throw inside to batters.

Doug grades out as average in his overall control and fielding, and five runners stole against him in seven tries. He singled in his one at-bat last year, his first in the majors.

HOW HE PERFORMED IN '95

Henry had a good ERA in 1995, but his dominant statistics lead one to wonder why his overall performance wasn't better. Not many pitchers are 3-6 when the opposition hits under .200.

The reason for his relative failure is the same as it was in Milwaukee: in tough late-inning situations, Henry loses his edge. He is merely ordinary with the game on the line. Given some save chances in May and June, he had a 5.89 ERA and was 1-3, losing any further opportunities.

WHAT TO EXPECT IN '96

The obvious move is for the Mets to have Henry work earlier in games, where there is less pressure. He is a valuable middle-inning reliever but won't ever be a good closer.

JASON ISRINGHAUSEN

Position: SP
Bats: R **Throws:** R
Ht: 6'3" **Wt:** 195
Opening Day Age: 23
Born: 9/7/1972
Drafted: NYN91 46/1157
ML Seasons: 1

Overall Statistics

	G	GS	GF	SV	W	L	ERA	IP	H	R	ER	HR	BB	SO
95 NYN	14	14	0	0	9	2	2.81	93.0	88	29	29	6	31	55
Career	14	14	0	0	9	2	2.81	93.0	88	29	29	6	31	55

1995 Situational Statistics

	W	L	ERA	SV	IP	BB	SO		AB	HR	RBI	BA	OBA	SLG
Home	5	2	2.92	0	52.1	17	36	LHB	183	3	15	.301	.363	.388
Road	4	0	2.66	0	40.2	14	19	RHB	163	3	11	.202	.264	.288
Apr-Jun	0	0	0.00	0	0.0	0	0	ScPos	87	1	20	.172	.279	.241
Jul-Oct	9	2	2.81	0	93.0	31	55	Clutch	23	0	0	.217	.280	.217

SCOUTING REPORT

Jason has full command of his fastball and curve. The average-plus fastball, thrown three-quarters, bores into righties when thrown low and runs when thrown high. He's also not afraid to work inside. His plus curveball has a downward, 12-to-6 o'clock break. His slider is average, his change is hittable, and his splitter is under development.

Despite an average-plus move to first, Isringhausen allowed 22 steals in 26 attempts. Jason's fielding is an asset, and he batted .148 with four sacrifices in 27 tries.

HOW HE PERFORMED IN '95

Drafted low and signed as a position player in 1991, Isringhausen was converted to the mound. Last July 17, he capped a quick ascent by winning his first big-league game. He compiled the lowest ERA among Mets starters and dominated righthanders. Jason had some problems with lefties, but most of their hits were singles, and he didn't walk many.

WHAT TO EXPECT IN '96

Isringhausen began 1995 in Double-A. Now he's a staff ace in the big leagues. New York is likely to improve and Isringhausen will be a big factor. The Mets must watch his arm, though, as Jason has pitched 418 innings over the past two seasons.

NEW YORK METS

CHRIS JONES

Positions: OF//1B
Bats: R **Throws:** R
Ht: 6'2" **Wt:** 205
Opening Day Age: 30
Born: 12/16/1965
Drafted: CIN84 3/59
ML Seasons: 5

Overall Statistics

	G	AB	R	H	2B	3B	HR	RBI	SB	CS	BB	SO	BA	OBA
95 NYN	79	182	33	51	6	2	8	31	2	1	13	45	.280	.327
Career	292	583	89	158	22	10	17	74	16	7	34	159	.271	.310

1995 Situational Statistics

	AB	HR	RBI	BA	OBA	SLG		AB	HR	RBI	BA	OBA	SLG
Home	72	4	10	.194	.266	.375	LHP	84	3	10	.250	.286	.417
Road	110	4	21	.336	.367	.527	RHP	98	5	21	.306	.361	.510
Apr-Jun	68	4	9	.338	.423	.559	ScPos	41	3	26	.341	.375	.610
Jul-Oct	114	4	22	.246	.264	.412	Clutch	43	3	14	.349	.442	.628

SCOUTING REPORT

Jones fits the mold of a fringe player perfectly. He's a bit below average in all categories except for his range, where he gets a good first step. He can hit for some power as long as the pitch is a high fastball over the plate, but is a very impatient hitter who strikes out often and rarely walks.

He has average-minus speed and isn't a basestealer. Jones is most comfortable in right field, where he has shown serviceable mobility. Chris totaled three outfield assists last season.

HOW HE PERFORMED IN '95

Jones has been marginal his entire career but had a productive season with the Mets as a spare outfielder and pinch-hitter. Chris hit .400 in 25 pinch-hit at-bats to lead the National League and smacked three homers in the emergency role. His season pattern was contrary to that of the club as a whole; his best months were May and June, when the Metropolitans were the dregs of the league.

WHAT TO EXPECT IN '96

Expect Jones to spend more time on the bench as the Mets audition their younger outfielders. He should still have a role off the bench in the late innings, however.

BLAS MINOR

Position: RP
Bats: R **Throws:** R
Ht: 6'3" **Wt:** 195
Opening Day Age: 30
Born: 3/20/1966
Drafted: PIT88 6/148
ML Seasons: 4

Overall Statistics

	G	GS	GF	SV	W	L	ERA	IP	H	R	ER	HR	BB	SO
95 NYN	35	0	10	1	4	2	3.66	46.2	44	21	19	6	13	43
Career	118	0	30	4	12	9	4.44	162.0	168	83	80	18	48	144

1995 Situational Statistics

	W	L	ERA	SV	IP	BB	SO		AB	HR	RBI	BA	OBA	SLG
Home	4	1	4.30	1	23.0	4	23	LHB	70	1	9	.286	.324	.429
Road	0	1	3.04	0	23.2	9	20	RHB	104	5	10	.231	.298	.423
Apr-Jun	3	2	3.96	0	25.0	8	25	ScPos	43	1	13	.209	.346	.349
Jul-Oct	1	0	3.32	1	21.2	5	18	Clutch	51	1	2	.196	.293	.314

SCOUTING REPORT

Blas has a minus-velocity fastball with good sinking action. He also employs an average change and slider, getting his strikeouts because of the precision with which he locates the slider. Minor is working on a knuckleball. He throws from a three-quarters motion with average control.

Half of the six runners trying to steal off Minor were gunned down. He has a well above-average move to first, and is an average fielder. Blas was hitless in two trips to the plate, and is now 2-for-12 in his career.

HOW HE PERFORMED IN '95

Minor was used sparingly by Dallas Green in 1995, and was just on the good side of mediocre. His only notoriety was having the highest strikeout rate of any Mets' pitcher with more than 25 innings pitched despite lacking a killer fastball. Blas was a background performer with most of his mound time spent in middle relief.

WHAT TO EXPECT IN '96

With the new arms arriving on the club, Minor may have a difficult time clinging to any position at all with New York. However, he has had two good seasons in the majors out of three, and is certainly employable in middle relief somewhere.

THE SCOUTING REPORT: 1996

NEW YORK METS

BILL SPIERS

Positions: 3B//2B
Bats: L **Throws:** R
Ht: 6'2" **Wt:** 190
Opening Day Age: 29
Born: 6/5/1966
Drafted: MIL87 1/13
ML Seasons: 7

Overall Statistics

	G	AB	R	H	2B	3B	HR	RBI	SB	CS	BB	SO	BA	OBA
95 NYN	63	72	5	15	2	1	0	11	0	1	12	15	.208	.314
Career	620	1764	236	448	59	18	16	189	52	27	132	275	.254	.307

1995 Situational Statistics

	AB	HR	RBI	BA	OBA	SLG		AB	HR	RBI	BA	OBA	SLG
Home	31	0	8	.355	.475	.419	LHP	3	0	1	.667	.750	1.000
Road	41	0	3	.098	.174	.146	RHP	69	0	10	.188	.293	.232
Apr-Jun	24	0	2	.167	.276	.292	ScPos	22	0	10	.318	.320	.318
Jul-Oct	48	0	9	.229	.333	.250	Clutch	27	0	3	.185	.267	.185

SCOUTING REPORT
Spiers does best swinging at low pitches. He has little power but will draw some walks. He has average range and hands, but his bum shoulder has led to a spate of weak, inaccurate throws.

HOW HE PERFORMED IN '95
Spiers' stuck with the club all year despite playing only 62 innings in the field (during which he made six errors). His hitting was as anemic as his fielding.

Apparently the Mets were too busy making deals and moving prospects to find a functional utility man, and Spiers just blended into the bench. Twice during the year, he was disabled with a strained rotator cuff, not a good injury for a utility infielder to suffer.

There was a time when Billy was considered a comer. A #1 draft choice by the Brewers in 1987, he was a starting big-league shortstop two years later. However, injuries and inconsistency at the plate stalled him after a good 1991 season, and now he's just hanging on.

WHAT TO EXPECT IN '96
After several poor seasons, one would think the ride was over for Spiers, but one might have thought that a year or two ago as well.

KELLY STINNETT

Position: C
Bats: R **Throws:** R
Ht: 5'11" **Wt:** 195
Opening Day Age: 26
Born: 2/14/1970
Drafted: CLE89 10/281
ML Seasons: 2

Overall Statistics

	G	AB	R	H	2B	3B	HR	RBI	SB	CS	BB	SO	BA	OBA
95 NYN	77	196	23	43	8	1	4	18	2	0	29	65	.219	.338
Career	124	346	43	81	14	3	6	32	4	0	40	93	.234	.332

1995 Situational Statistics

	AB	HR	RBI	BA	OBA	SLG		AB	HR	RBI	BA	OBA	SLG
Home	95	1	5	.179	.316	.263	LHP	76	3	10	.224	.330	.368
Road	101	3	13	.257	.359	.396	RHP	120	1	8	.217	.343	.308
Apr-Jun	51	2	6	.275	.383	.431	ScPos	50	1	14	.220	.371	.360
Jul-Oct	145	2	12	.200	.322	.297	Clutch	34	0	5	.206	.250	.294

SCOUTING REPORT
Even though he has limited power, Stinnett tries to muscle pitches. He does best with inside stuff which he can pull. Kelly does not bunt and has experienced serious problems making contact. He has a strong arm but never knows where the ball will end up. While Stinnett is mobile behind the plate, hands of stone cancel out his average-plus range and blocking skills.

HOW HE PERFORMED IN '95
Stinnett had a rough second year in 1995. He treaded water as Todd Hundley's backup into late July, with fair hitting in limited action. Then Hundley went down for six weeks and Stinnett got put into the fire, where he was toasted. Everyday duty doesn't suit Kelly, who just hasn't hit yet. Righthanders simply killed him, though he can at least provide some punch against lefties. In addition, he had defensive problems. In 67 games, 72 bases were stolen on him, with an 81% success rate.

WHAT TO EXPECT IN '96
Stinnett may be a marginal backup, but a contender needs a little more quality than Kelly offers. Though the Mets should be looking for a replacement, they are very thin in catching in the high minors.

NEW YORK METS: TOP PROSPECTS

JUAN ACEVEDO

Bats: R Throws: R Opening Day Age: 26
Ht: 6-2 Wt: 195 Born: 5/5/1970
Position: P Drafted: 1992 #14 COL

YR TEAM	LG/CLASS	G	GS	GF	SV	W	L	ERA	IP	H	HR	BB	SO	O/BA
93 Central Val	CAL/A	27	20	3	0	9	8	4.40	118.2	119	8	58	107	.263
94 New Haven	EAST/AA	26	26	0	0	17	6	2.37	174.2	142	16	38	161	.219
95 Colorado	NL/MAJ	17	11	0	0	4	6	6.44	65.2	82	15	20	40	.343
95 Norfolk	INT/AAA	2	2	0	0	0	0	0.00	3.0	0	0	1	2	.000
95 Colo Spgs	PCL/AAA	3	3	0	0	1	6	6.14	14.2	18	0	7	7	.316

Acquired from the Rockies in the Bret Saberhagen deal, Acevedo had a breakout year in 1994 when he led the Eastern League in wins and ERA and was selected its Pitcher of the Year. He started last season in the Colorado rotation. The Mexican native is very poised on the mound and features a 90+-mph fastball with excellent movement, a split-finger pitch, and a slurve. The 25-year-old saw limited time late in the year due to elbow tendinitis and ribcage problems, but he's expected back at full strength this season.

OMAR GARCIA

Bats: R Throws: R Opening Day Age: 24
Ht: 6-0 Wt: 192 Born: 11/16/1971
Position: 1B Drafted: 1989 #18 NYN

YR TEAM	LG/CLASS	G	AB	R	H	2B	3B	HR	RBI	SB	BA	OBA
93 St.Lucie	FSL/A	129	485	73	156	17	7	3	76	25	.322	.392
94 Binghamton	EAST/AA	64	246	38	88	14	4	5	42	3	.358	.407
94 Norfolk	INT/AAA	67	227	28	55	9	2	0	28	7	.242	.295
95 Norfolk	INT/AAA	115	430	55	133	21	7	3	64	3	.309	.336
95 Binghamton	EAST/AA	5	19	4	10	1	1	0	1	0	.526	.609

Garcia is a righthanded version of former Met Dave Magadan. In his second stint at Norfolk, he proved he could hit Triple-A pitching, posting four hitting streaks of eight games or more including a 15-game streak in May. He had 31 multiple-hit games, including two games with five hits, and led the organization in batting. For disciplinary reasons, the 23-year-old was demoted to Double-A the last week of the season. That issue and his lack of power put his future with the organization in doubt.

BUTCH HUSKEY

Bats: R Throws: R Opening Day Age: 24
Ht: 6-3 Wt: 240 Born: 11/10/1971
Position: 3B Drafted: 1989 #7 NYN

YR TEAM	LG/CLASS	G	AB	R	H	2B	3B	HR	RBI	SB	BA	OBA
93 Binghamton	EAST/AA	139	526	72	132	23	1	25	98	11	.251	.312
93 New York	NL/MAJ	13	41	2	6	1	0	0	3	0	.146	.159
94 Norfolk	INT/AAA	127	474	59	108	23	3	10	57	16	.228	.285
95 New York	NL/MAJ	28	90	8	17	1	0	3	11	1	.189	.267
95 Norfolk	INT/AAA	109	394	66	112	18	1	28	87	8	.284	.355

Rebounding from a dismal 1994 season, Huskey regained his power stroke to force his way back into the Mets' plans. By losing weight and opening his stance, the 24-year-old increased his bat speed and enjoyed his finest season, which was especially satisfying since he played in Harbor Park, the best pitchers' park in the league. Huskey never went more than two games without a hit and his 12 homers and 36 RBI in July led all minor leaguers. The Oklahoma native led the International League in homers and finished second in RBI and slugging and was named the league's Most Valuable Player. Huskey, also

named to Howe Sportsdata's All-Star squad, played every day at third base for the Mets in September before injuring his wrist. He is adequate at best at the hot corner, and played some first base and left field during the season.

ERIC LUDWICK

Bats: R Throws: R Opening Day Age: 24
Ht: 6-5 Wt: 210 Born: 12/14/1971
Position: P Drafted: 1993 #2 NYN

YR TEAM	LG/CLASS	G	GS	GF	SV	W	L	ERA	IP	H	HR	BB	SO	O/BA
93 Pittsfield	NYP/A	10	10	0	0	4	3	3.18	51.0	51	0	18	40	.259
94 St. Lucie	FSL/A	27	27	0	0	7	13	4.55	150.1	162	6	77	77	.282
95 Norfolk	INT/AAA	4	3	0	0	1	1	5.85	20.0	22	3	7	9	.275
95 Binghamton	EAST/AA	23	22	0	0	12	5	2.95	143.1	108	9	68	131	.212

Seldom mentioned as one of the club's top prospects, Ludwick led the organization in wins and finished third in strikeouts last season. A second-round draft pick in 1993, the big righthander suffered through a terrible 1994, losing velocity and leading the Florida State League in losses. But in 1995 the UNLV product won six of his first seven decisions, including back-to-back shutouts in June, and regained the velocity that made him among the hardest throwers in the system. Ludwick also has a decent slider and changeup.

ALEX OCHOA

Bats: R Throws: R Opening Day Age: 24
Ht: 6-0 Wt: 185 Born: 3/29/1972
Position: RF Drafted: 1991 #3 BAL

YR TEAM	LG/CLASS	G	AB	R	H	2B	3B	HR	RBI	SB	BA	OBA
93 Frederick	CARO/A	137	532	84	147	29	5	13	90	34	.276	.341
94 Bowie	EAST/AA	134	519	77	156	25	2	14	82	28	.301	.355
95 New York	NL/MAJ	11	37	7	11	1	0	0	6	1	.297	.333
95 Rochester	INT/AAA	91	336	41	92	18	2	8	46	17	.274	.328
95 Norfolk	INT/AAA	34	123	17	38	6	2	2	15	7	.309	.377

Acquired from the Orioles in the Bobby Bonilla deal, Ochoa is a fine athlete with speed and an outstanding arm in right field. The 23-year-old is a line drive hitter who had hitting streaks of 11 and 13 games during the season, but did not show the consistent power expected of him. The Miami native has good baserunning instincts and has swiped 128 bases in 582 games. Ochoa hit .360 during the International League playoffs and was selected to the post-season All-Star team.

REY ORDONEZ

Bats: R Throws: R Opening Day Age: 24
Ht: 5-9 Wt: 159 Born: 1/11/1972
Position: SS Drafted: Cuban lottery 10-29-93

YR TEAM	LG/CLASS	G	AB	R	H	2B	3B	HR	RBI	SB	BA	OBA
93 St. Paul	NOR/I	15	60	10	17	4	0	0	7	3	.283	.317
94 St. Lucie	FSL/A	79	314	47	97	21	2	0	40	11	.309	.336
94 Binghamton	EAST/AA	48	191	22	50	10	2	1	20	4	.262	.279
95 Norfolk	INT/AAA	125	439	49	94	21	4	2	50	11	.214	.261

Despite playing just 48 games at Double-A in 1994, Ordonez was sent to Norfolk last year, and he struggled all year at the plate. However, despite his hitting problems, the Mets feel Ordonez will be a quality player. Defensively, he compares to Ozzie Smith, and is considered the best minor leaguer to come along at the position in many years. The Cuban native has a "swing from the heels" approach, and hit .218 or less in four

NEW YORK METS: TOP PROSPECTS

separate months of the season, including an International League low .172 in July. He is also not a good baserunner, being thrown out in 13 of 24 steal attempts last year.

RICKY OTERO

Bats: S Throws: R Opening Day Age: 24
Ht: 5-7 Wt: 150 Born: 4/15/1972
Position: OF Drafted: 1990 #45 NYN

YR TEAM	LG/CLASS	G	AB	R	H	2B	3B	HR	RBI	SB	BA	OBA
93 Binghamton	EAST/AA	124	503	63	133	21	10	2	54	29	.264	.322
94 Binghamton	EAST/AA	128	531	96	156	31	9	7	57	33	.294	.355
95 New York	NL/MAJ	35	51	5	7	2	0	0	1	2	.137	.185
95 Norfolk	INT/AAA	72	295	37	79	8	6	1	23	16	.268	.331

Otero shuttled back and forth between New York and Norfolk and had a disappointing year in 1995. A very capable leadoff man with surprising power for his size, he is one of the fastest players in the organization. A switch-hitter who hits equally well from both sides of the plate, the Puerto Rican native has a lifetime .291 average in his five-year career and covers a lot of ground in the outfield.

JAY PAYTON

Bats: R Throws: R Opening Day Age: 23
Ht: 5-10 Wt: 190 Born: 11/22/1972
Position: OF Drafted: 1994 #3 NYN

YR TEAM	LG/CLASS	G	AB	R	H	2B	3B	HR	RBI	SB	BA	OBA
94 Pittsfield	NYP/A	58	219	47	80	16	2	3	37	10	.365	.439
94 Binghamton	EAST/AA	8	25	3	7	1	0	0	1	1	.280	.357
95 Norfolk	INT/AAA	50	196	33	47	11	4	4	30	11	.240	.284
95 Binghamton	EAST/AA	85	357	59	123	20	3	14	54	16	.345	.395

Propelled by hitting streaks of 11, 14 and 25-games, Payton won his second batting title in as many years in 1995. Named the Eastern League's Rookie of the Year and Most Valuable Player, only a promotion following the All-Star game (in which he had two hits) kept him from making a triple-crown run. After hitting .297 his first month in Triple-A, the offensive numbers of the Georgia Tech product took a nosedive in August. The 23-year-old had off-season surgery on his right elbow but is expected back at full strength. Payton plays center field now, but a mediocre arm could push him to left.

ROBERT PERSON

Bats: R Throws: R Opening Day Age: 27
Ht: 5-11 Wt: 180 Born: 1/8/1969
Position: P Drafted: 1989 #24 CLE

YR TEAM	LG/CLASS	G	GS	GF	W	L	ERA	IP	H	HR	BB	SO	O/BA
93 High Desert	CAL/A	28	26	1	0	12	10	4.69	169.0	184	13	48	107	.271
94 Binghamton	EAST/AA	31	23	4	0	9	6	3.45	159.0	124	18	68	130	.219
95 New York	NL/MAJ	3	1	0	0	1	0	0.75	12.0	5	1	2	10	.119
95 Norfolk	INT/AAA	5	4	0	0	2	1	4.50	32.0	30	2	13	33	.244
95 Binghamton	EAST/AA	26	7	13	7	5	4	3.11	66.2	46	4	25	65	.197

Person began the year in the bullpen, but after giving up runs in nine of his first 19 appearances, he returned to the starting rotation. After a couple of starts to stretch out his arm, the 27-year-old won four of five decisions before earning a promotion to Norfolk. A very hard thrower, the righthander has averaged 7.96 strikeouts per nine innings in his two seasons with the Mets and has three other pitches he can throw for strikes.

PETE WALKER

Bats: R Throws: R Opening Day Age: 27
Ht: 6-2 Wt: 184 Born: 4/8/1969
Position: P Drafted: 1990 #7 NYN

YR TEAM	LG/CLASS	G	GS	GF	SV	W	L	ERA	IP	H	HR	BB	SO	O/BA
93 Binghamton	EAST/AA	45	10	33	19	4	9	3.44	99.1	89	6	46	89	.244
94 St. Lucie	FSL/A	3	0	2	0	0	0	2.25	4.0	3	1	1	5	.200
94 Norfolk	INT/AAA	37	0	19	3	2	4	3.97	47.2	48	3	24	42	.270
95 New York	NL/MAJ	13	0	10	0	1	0	4.58	17.2	24	3	5	5	.329
95 Norfolk	INT/AAA	34	1	25	8	5	2	3.91	48.1	51	4	16	39	.274

Despite the modest save total, Walker had a good season in the bullpen for Norfolk. In early June when he was promoted to the majors, the 26-year-old had a 4-0 record with five saves and a 1.04 ERA. However, upon returning to Triple-A, he gave up 17 runs in just 12 innings. Once that rough stretch was completed, the Connecticut product finished August by hurling 12 scoreless innings over nine consecutive outings to re-establish himself. Walker throws a 92 mph fastball and a slider.

PAUL WILSON

Bats: R Throws: R Opening Day Age: 23
Ht: 6-5 Wt: 235 Born: 3/28/1973
Position: P Drafted: 1994 #1 NYN

YR TEAM	LG/CLASS	G	GS	GF	SV	W	L	ERA	IP	H	HR	BB	SO	O/BA
94 Mets	GULF/R	3	3	0	0	2	3	3.00	12.0	8	0	4	13	.190
94 St. Lucie	FSL/A	8	8	0	0	5	5	5.06	37.1	32	3	17	37	.230
95 Norfolk	INT/AAA	10	10	0	0	5	3	2.85	66.1	59	3	20	67	.242
95 Binghamton	EAST/AA	16	16	0	0	6	3	2.17	120.1	89	5	24	127	.208

The number-one pick in the 1994 draft finally delivered his first win on May third and never looked back. He hurled 14 consecutive quality starts at Binghamton and was the starting pitcher in the Double-A All-Star game. The Florida State product continued to dominate after being promoted to Norfolk, tossing a complete game shutout over Richmond in the playoffs. Named the Pitcher of the Year in the Eastern League, he led the loop in ERA. The big righthander has great command of both a moving mid-90's fastball and a sharp slider.

PRESTON WILSON

Bats: R Throws: R Opening Day Age: 22
Ht: 6-2 Wt: 193 Born: 7/19/1974
Position: OF Drafted: 1992 #1 NYN

YR TEAM	LG/CLASS	G	AB	R	H	2B	3B	HR	RBI	SB	BA	OBA
93 Kingsport	APPY/R	66	259	44	60	10	0	16	48	6	.232	.302
93 Pittsfield	NYP/A	8	29	6	16	3	1	1	12	1	.552	.576
94 Columbia	SAL/A	131	474	55	108	17	4	14	58	13	.228	.262
95 Columbia	SAL/A	111	442	70	119	26	5	20	61	20	.269	.311

The ninth player drafted in 1992, Wilson turned the corner in 1995. The South Carolina native began the year on the disabled list due to elbow problems and started his season 0-for-20 with eight strikeouts. Batting .205 at the end of June, Wilson went on a 24-game hitting streak and led the South Atlantic League in batting for the month of July (.356). Mookie Wilson's son has tremendous bat speed and finished second in the organization in home runs. A third baseman in '94, Wilson moved to right field last season where he displayed a strong arm.

NEW YORK METS: OTHERS TO WATCH

PAUL BYRD — Bats: R Throws: R Ht: 6-1 Wt: 185
Born: 12/3/1970 1991 #4 CLE Drafted: Position: P

YR TEAM	LG/CLASS	G	GS	GF	SV	W	L	ERA	IP	H	HR	BB	SO	O/BA
95 New York	NL/MAJ	17	0	6	0	2	0	2.05	22.0	18	1	7	26	.222
95 Norfolk	INT/AAA	22	10	10	6	3	5	2.79	87.0	71	6	21	61	.227

The 25-year-old, acquired from the Indians last winter, used a curveball and changeup to pitch effectively last season.

ALBERTO CASTILLO — Bats: R Throws: R Ht: 6-0 Wt: 184
Born: 2/10/1970 Drafted: NDFA 4-15-87 NYN Position: C

YR TEAM	LG/CLASS	G	AB	R	H	2B	3B	HR	RBI	SB	BA	OBA
95 New York	NL/MAJ	13	29	2	3	0	0	0	1	.103	.212	
95 Norfolk	INT/AAA	69	217	23	58	13	1	4	31	2	.267	.346

An excellent defensive catcher, Castillo also displayed some pop with his bat.

ARNOLD GOOCH — Bats: R Throws: R Ht: 6-2 Wt: 195
Born: 11/12/1976 Drafted: 1994 #6 COL Position: P

YR TEAM	LG/CLASS	G	GS	GF	SV	W	L	ERA	IP	H	HR	BB	SO	O/BA
95 Asheville	SAL/A	21	21	0	0	5	8	2.94	128.2	111	8	57	117	.234
95 Columbia	SAL/A	6	6	0	0	2	3	4.46	38.1	39	3	15	34	.258

The 19-year-old Gooch, the "other" pitcher acquired in the Saberhagen deal, has a live arm with a plus fastball.

CHARLIE GREENE — Bats: R Throws: R Ht: 6-1 Wt: 177
Born: 1/23/1971 Drafted: 1991 #20 SD Position: C

YR TEAM	LG/CLASS	G	AB	R	H	2B	3B	HR	RBI	SB	BA	OBA
95 Norfolk	INT/AAA	27	88	6	17	3	0	0	4	0	.193	.286
95 Binghamton	EAST/AA	100	346	26	82	13	0	2	34	2	.237	.276

An outstanding catcher who handles pitchers well, Greene led the International League by throwing out 68% of opposing baserunners.

JASON HARDTKE — Bats: S Throws: R Ht: 5-10 Wt: 175
Born: 9/15/1971 Drafted: 1990 #5 CLE Position: 2B

YR TEAM	LG/CLASS	G	AB	R	H	2B	3B	HR	RBI	SB	BA	OBA
95 Norfolk	INT/AAA	4	7	1	2	1	0	0	1	.286	.444	
95 Binghamton	EAST/AA	121	455	65	130	42	4	4	52	6	.286	.375

A middle infielder with a potent bat, he led the minor leagues in doubles and finished seventh in the organization in batting.

ERIK HILJUS — Bats: R Throws: R Ht: 6-5 Wt: 230
Born: 12/25/1972 Drafted: 1991 #6 NYN Position: P

YR TEAM	LG/CLASS	G	GS	GF	SV	W	L	ERA	IP	H	HR	BB	SO	O/BA
95 Binghamton	EAST/AA	10	10	0	0	2	4	5.86	55.1	60	8	32	40	.278
95 St. Lucie	FSL/A	17	17	0	0	8	4	2.99	111.1	85	4	50	98	.219

A big righthander with a major league fastball and decent curve, Hiljus finished fourth in the organization in strikeouts.

SEAN JOHNSTON — Bats: L Throws: L Ht: 6-4 Wt: 187
Born: 6/28/1976 Drafted: 1994 #4 NYN Position: P

YR TEAM	LG/CLASS	G	GS	GF	SV	W	L	ERA	IP	H	HR	BB	SO	O/BA
95 Columbia	SAL/A	23	22	0	0	11	6	3.03	148.1	132	6	63	105	.245

The highly-regarded 19-year-old lefthander, who throws heat along with a plus curve and change, finished tied for second in the organization in wins and ninth in ERA.

AARON LEDESMA — Bats: R Throws: R Ht: 6-2 Wt: 200
Born: 6/3/1971 Drafted: 1990 #2 NYN Position: 3B

YR TEAM	LG/CLASS	G	AB	R	H	2B	3B	HR	RBI	SB	BA	OBA
95 New York	NL/MAJ	21	33	4	8	0	0	0	3	0	.242	.359
95 Norfolk	INT/AAA	56	201	26	60	12	1	0	28	6	.299	.335

Originally a shortstop, the six-year veteran can play any infield position and has a lifetime .286 average.

TERRENCE LONG — Bats: L Throws: L Ht: 6-1 Wt: 179
Born: 2/29/1976 Drafted: 1994 #2 NYN Position: OF

YR TEAM	LG/CLASS	G	AB	R	H	2B	3B	HR	RBI	SB	BA	OBA
95 Columbia	SAL/A	55	178	27	35	1	2	2	13	8	.197	.309
95 Pittsfield	NYP/A	51	187	24	48	9	4	4	31	11	.257	.324

The 20th player selected in the 1994 draft is a potential 30-30 man, but a weak throwing arm may relegate him to first base.

CHRIS ROBERTS — Bats: R Throws: L Ht: 5-10 Wt: 185
Born: 6/25/1971 Drafted: 1992 #2 NYN Position: P

YR TEAM	LG/CLASS	G	GS	GF	SV	W	L	ERA	IP	H	HR	BB	SO	O/BA
95 Norfolk	INT/AAA	25	25	0	0	7	13	5.52	150.0	197	24	58	88	.328

After winning 26 games his first two seasons, Roberts had a rough season in which he led the International League in losses and home runs allowed.

JEFF TAM — Bats: R Throws: R Ht: 6-1 Wt: 185
Born: 8/19/1970 Drafted: NDFA 6-28-93 NYN Position: P

YR TEAM	LG/CLASS	G	GS	GF	SV	W	L	ERA	IP	H	HR	BB	SO	O/BA
95 Binghamton	EAST/AA	14	0	7	3	0	2	4.50	18.0	20	1	4	9	.278
95 Mets	GULF/R	2	1	0	0	0	0	3.00	3.0	2	0	1	2	.200

Tam, a sinker/slider pitcher who keeps the ball down, has allowed just one home run in 122.1 innings, but missed most of '95 with knee and finger injuries.

DEREK WALLACE — Bats: R Throws: R Ht: 6-3 Wt: 200
Born: 9/1/1971 Drafted: 1992 #1 CHN Position: P

YR TEAM	LG/CLASS	G	GS	GF	SV	W	L	ERA	IP	H	HR	BB	SO	O/BA
95 Binghamton	EAST/AA	15	0	11	2	0	1	5.28	15.1	11	1	9	8	.224
95 Wichita	TEX/AA	26	0	18	6	4	3	4.40	43.0	51	5	13	24	.298

Acquired in the Jason Jacome deal, the hard-throwing Wallace was the 11th player selected in the 1992 draft; he features a fastball and slider but has not lived up to expectations.

MIKE WELCH — Bats: L Throws: R Ht: 6-2 Wt: 207
Born: 8/25/1972 Drafted: 1993 #3 NYN Position: P

YR TEAM	LG/CLASS	G	GS	GF	SV	W	L	ERA	IP	H	HR	BB	SO	O/BA
95 Binghamton	EAST/AA	1	0	1	0	0	0	0.00	1.0	0	0	0	2	.000
95 St. Lucie	FSL/A	44	6	33	15	4	5	5.40	70.0	96	7	18	51	.330

The organization's leader in saves had trouble in the rotation, but his 90+ mph fastball and curve put together a 16-inning scoreless streak that included a win and 12 saves.

JULIO ZORRILLA — Bats: S Throws: R Ht: 5-11 Wt: 156
Born: 2/20/1975 Drafted: NDFA 7-12-92 NYN Position: 2B

YR TEAM	LG/CLASS	G	AB	R	H	2B	3B	HR	RBI	SB	BA	OBA
95 Columbia	SAL/A	133	518	65	143	15	3	0	31	42	.276	.315

The switch-hitting South Atlantic League All-Star is an exciting player and he led the organization in steals, but needs to be more patient.

THE SCOUTING REPORT: 1996

PHILADELPHIA PHILLIES

RICKY BOTTALICO

Position: RP
Bats: L **Throws:** R
Ht: 6'1" **Wt:** 200
Opening Day Age: 26
Born: 8/26/1969
Drafted: PHI 7/21/91
ML Seasons: 2

SCOUTING REPORT
A clear up-and-comer, Bottalico is a hard-throwing, hard-nosed young pitcher with a bright future. He delivers from a three-quarter angle with a good, mid-90s fastball and a plus, hard, late-breaking slider. Ricky challenges each hitter and doesn't worry about throwing any off-speed pitches. With his velocity, he doesn't need an off-speed pitch in order to pitch short relief. He also doesn't have to have pinpoint control to succeed, since he is tough to catch up with even if he makes a mistake in the strike zone.

With good control and hard-to-hit stuff, Ricky doesn't have to be concerned too much with baserunners. Six of nine stole successfully on his average move last year, not unusual for righthanded power pitchers. He is an average fielder. At the plate, Bottalico went 0-for-5 with one sac hit in his first time facing big-league pitching.

HOW HE PERFORMED IN '95
One of those guys whose unlikely stories keep thousands of minor-leaguers dreaming of the big time, Bottalico is a converted catcher who was undrafted out of Central Connecticut State University. The Phillies signed him as an amateur free agent in 1991 when he was playing in a semi-pro league. He has made steady progress since then, blossoming in 1995 as an intimidating reliever.

Bottalico fanned a batter per inning in the majors in '95 as he had done consistently in the minor leagues, and he was remarkably steady all season for a rookie. He allowed no runs and only four hits in 10 unhittable appearances in June. He held the league to an incredible .167 batting average with only 14 extra-base hits in 300 at-bats.

As Ricky showed he was capable of dominating major-league hitters, his workload increased as a setup pitcher for Heathcliff Slocumb. This resulted in reduced effectiveness and with a bout with tendinitis in late August, but he recovered to close out the season in fine form.

WHAT TO EXPECT IN '96
With Slocumb a prime trade candidate for the rebuilding Phillies, Bottalico's path to becoming the future closer in Philadelphia is charted. The Phils don't think he is quite ready for that high-stress job, though, so he will start 1996 as a setup pitcher. He should ascend to the closer's role sometime in 1996 or 1997.

Overall Statistics

	G	GS	GF	SV	W	L	ERA	IP	H	R	ER	HR	BB	SO
95 PHI	62	0	20	1	5	3	2.46	87.2	50	25	24	7	42	87
Career	65	0	23	1	5	3	2.38	90.2	53	25	24	7	43	90

1995 Situational Statistics

	W	L	ERA	SV	IP	BB	SO		AB	HR	RBI	BA	OBA	SLG
Home	3	2	1.88	0	48.0	23	54	LHB	111	3	15	.180	.324	.288
Road	2	1	3.18	1	39.2	19	33	RHB	189	4	22	.159	.246	.254
Apr-Jun	3	1	1.19	1	30.1	17	26	ScPos	73	4	32	.247	.417	.452
Jul-Oct	2	2	3.14	0	57.1	25	61	Clutch	204	4	23	.162	.260	.260

How He Compares to Other Pitchers

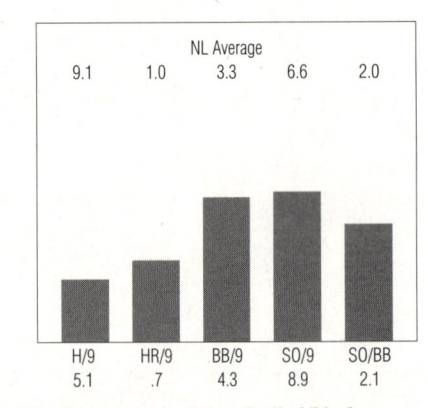

NL Average: H/9 9.1, HR/9 1.0, BB/9 3.3, SO/9 6.6, SO/BB 2.0
Bottalico: H/9 5.1, HR/9 .7, BB/9 4.3, SO/9 8.9, SO/BB 2.1

How He Compares to Other Relief Pitchers

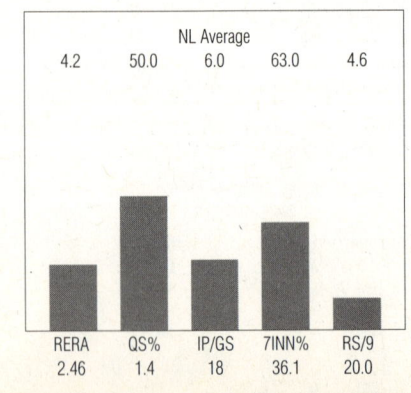

NL Average: RERA 4.2, QS% 50.0, IP/GS 6.0, 7INN% 63.0, RS/9 4.6
Bottalico: RERA 2.46, QS% 1.4, IP/GS 18, 7INN% 36.1, RS/9 20.0

PHILADELPHIA PHILLIES

DARREN DAULTON

Position: C
Bats: L **Throws:** R
Ht: 6'2" **Wt:** 195
Opening Day Age: 34
Born: 1/3/1962
Drafted: PHI80 25/629
ML Seasons: 12

SCOUTING REPORT

Darren is the prototype of a lefthanded power hitter, liking low fastballs he can pull and lift with his uppercut swing. He has superb discipline at bat, forcing pitchers to come into him or to walk him, and he will take high or outside pitches to the opposite field with power if forced to.

Always a good athlete, Daulton has average running speed despite his age, position, and injury history. Behind the plate, he has a plus, accurate arm with a quick release, although he has long arm action (which is unusual for a good catcher). His mobility is now sub-par due to countless knee injuries, but he has average hands and handles pitchers very well.

HOW HE PERFORMED IN '95

As for the Phillies, the '95 season was a lost one for Darren. While he hit for a decent average, both his slugging and on-base dropped dramatically. Age combined with the wear-and-tear of playing the toughest position almost every day ground him down—he started at catcher for 93 of the Phillies' 112 games before his injury. More rest would probably have helped, but manager Jim Fregosi wrote his name on the lineup card every day and Daulton never complained.

The frustrating '95 season ended on August 25th when he tore his right anterior cruciate ligament on the basepaths, knocking him out for the rest of the season. This was doubly frustrating, since he was doing his best hitting of the year at the time. He underwent his eighth surgery on his right knee in September and also had his left shoulder surgically repaired.

WHAT TO EXPECT IN '96

This will be a critical season for the Phillies' team leader. While Daulton is an asset even if he plays like he did in '95, he's not going to lead his mates back into contention at that level. Dutch is a tough player driven to succeed; his teammates look to him for both leadership and production. A move to first base would be best for his bat, but that option is blocked by Greg Jefferies.

If forced to catch every day in '96, Daulton's performance will look a lot more like 1995 than 1992–94. With more rest, he should hit better, but his big power days are probably behind him now.

Overall Statistics

	G	AB	R	H	2B	3B	HR	RBI	SB	CS	BB	SO	BA	OBA
95 PHI	98	342	44	85	19	3	9	55	3	0	55	52	.249	.359
Career	1020	3223	440	785	176	17	123	525	44	9	546	647	.244	.354

1995 Situational Statistics

	AB	HR	RBI	BA	OBA	SLG		AB	HR	RBI	BA	OBA	SLG
Home	176	7	29	.256	.370	.460	LHP	111	2	23	.243	.358	.387
Road	166	2	26	.241	.347	.337	RHP	231	7	32	.251	.359	.407
Apr-Jun	178	6	31	.242	.358	.399	ScPos	111	2	41	.252	.370	.396
Jul-Oct	164	3	24	.256	.359	.402	Clutch	57	1	7	.228	.397	.333

How He Compares to Other Batters

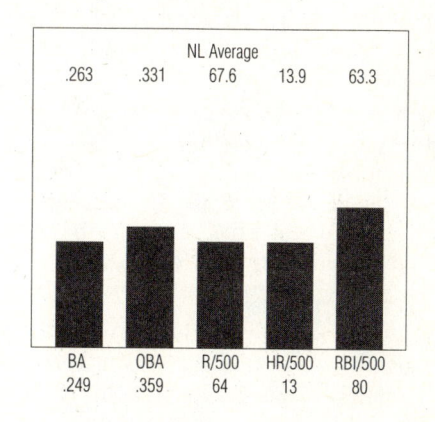

	BA	OBA	R/500	HR/500	RBI/500
NL Average	.263	.331	67.6	13.9	63.3
	.249	.359	64	13	80

Where He Hits the Ball

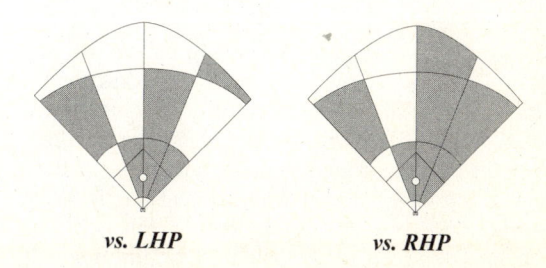

vs. LHP   vs. RHP

PHILADELPHIA PHILLIES

LENNY DYKSTRA

Position: OF
Bats: L **Throws:** L
Ht: 5'10" **Wt:** 167
Opening Day Age: 33
Born: 2/10/1963
Drafted: NYN81 12/315
ML Seasons: 11

SCOUTING REPORT
After embarrassing National League pitchers and catchers for several years, Lenny was the one who was embarrassed by his performance last season. Although still a plus runner, he has slowed down some on the basepaths, and his defensive play deteriorated as well. He has always had a very weak arm with poor accuracy, but his formerly excellent range has now diminished.

Dykstra was a good inside fastball hitter until his back problems prevented him from turning on inside pitches. He was an excellent situational hitter, very disciplined, and would take pitches as a leadoff hitter when needed.

HOW HE PERFORMED IN '95
Practically nothing went right for Dykstra in '95. He didn't hit well, didn't generate any power, and didn't steal much or steal effectively. He missed 22 games with an inflamed joint between the vertebrae in his lower back, a chronic problem that has clouded his future. Just when he was hitting with some authority again (12 extra-base hits in 100 at-bats in July), he went down for the count at the end of July with an arthritic knee which required surgery.

Unhappy with his play in center field, the Phillies moved Dykstra to left field in mid-season, blaming the move on limited mobility due to his back problems. While he accepted the change, he wants badly to return to center field, although the front office was auditioning replacements for him.

WHAT TO EXPECT IN '96
Previously the cock-of-the-walk, Dykstra's strut was stunted by his disastrous '95 season. After hearing publicly-expressed doubts in the off-season about his ability to return to center and his commitment to a rigorous conditioning program, Lenny assured everyone that he was ready, willing, and able to make a big comeback.

Barring a trade or free-agent signing, the Phils' regular job in center field in '96 is Dykstra's for the taking. If he shows his old form, everyone will be happy and all will be forgotten. If he's not 100% physically and struggles at the plate or in the field, it's going to be a tough adjustment for Dykstra. Neither his attitude nor his temper will help him cope with adversity. He has been healthy for only two of the last six seasons, and while he has obvious talent, it will inevitably erode as he ages.

Overall Statistics

	G	AB	R	H	2B	3B	HR	RBI	SB	CS	BB	SO	BA	OBA
95 PHI	62	254	37	67	15	1	2	18	10	5	33	28	.264	.353
Career	1238	4425	781	1263	275	40	78	391	282	71	614	478	.285	.374

1995 Situational Statistics

	AB	HR	RBI	BA	OBA	SLG		AB	HR	RBI	BA	OBA	SLG
Home	131	2	10	.237	.306	.344	LHP	88	1	9	.307	.380	.398
Road	123	0	8	.293	.400	.366	RHP	166	1	9	.241	.339	.331
Apr-Jun	154	0	10	.260	.341	.299	ScPos	53	0	15	.302	.391	.396
Jul-Oct	100	2	8	.270	.371	.440	Clutch	44	0	3	.205	.286	.273

How He Compares to Other Batters

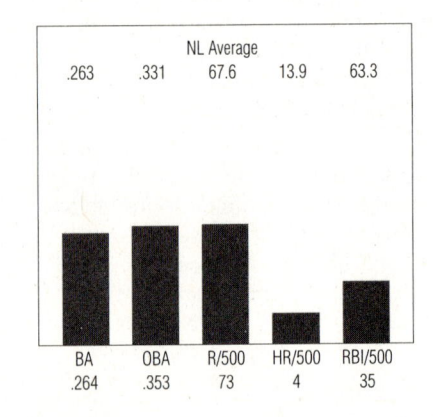

NL Average: .263 .331 67.6 13.9 63.3

BA	OBA	R/500	HR/500	RBI/500
.264	.353	73	4	35

Where He Hits the Ball

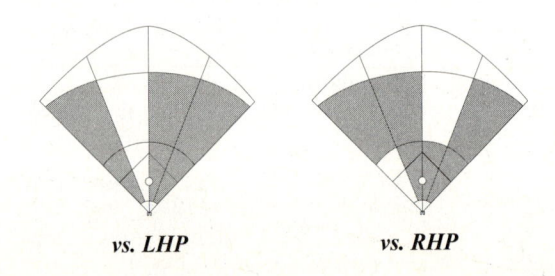

vs. LHP   vs. RHP

PHILADELPHIA PHILLIES

JIM EISENREICH

Position: OF
Bats: L **Throws:** L
Ht: 5'11" **Wt:** 195
Opening Day Age: 36
Born: 4/18/1959
Drafted: MIN80 16
ML Seasons: 12

SCOUTING REPORT
Eisenreich is a tough out: a good line-drive hitter with some power. He has a quick bat and will go with the pitch to the any field, liking pitches out over the plate best. He is a plus baserunner and good percentage basestealer who has stolen 21 bases in 23 tries in the past three seasons.

In the field, Jim can play either right or left field with plus range. Although his arm isn't very strong any more, it is accurate. He has good hands, almost never makes an error (four miscues in his last 426 games in the field), and can still play center field in an emergency.

HOW HE PERFORMED IN '95
Hitting .406 in May and .345 in June, Eisenreich was in the odd position of leading the league in hitting for a short while even though he was a platoon player. Despite his performance, he was moved to left field after the acquisition of Mark Whiten in late July. In fact, Jim wouldn't have seen a lot of playing time after that if Lenny Dykstra hadn't been disabled for the rest of the year. He displayed unusual power, posting his career high in home runs in 1995. Jim has hit .300 or better every year since coming to Philadelphia in '93.

Aside from the inevitable slowing with age, the only aspect of Eisenreich's game to go south is his ability to hit lefthanders. He has not hit them well in the past two years and is really a platoon player now.

WHAT TO EXPECT IN '96
It's hard to be critical of Eisenreich: he is an unassuming professional, doing whatever he is asked without a complaint and usually doing it well. He is very popular with both the fans and with his teammates, a real advantage on a tough team and in a tough town like Philly.

Jim was re-signed by the Phillies in December and will reprise his '95 role. He can start against righthanded pitching in left or right field, he will hit line drives like clockwork, and he will take a walk or steal a base whenever needed. He might not hit as well as he did last season, but he should continue as a good platoon hitter and extremely valuable role-player for several more seasons. Eisenreich has been a great story as a big-leaguer and is always a class act.

Overall Statistics

	G	AB	R	H	2B	3B	HR	RBI	SB	CS	BB	SO	BA	OBA
95 PHI	129	377	46	119	22	2	10	55	10	0	38	44	.316	.375
Career	1084	3173	390	915	175	33	46	389	88	37	247	339	.288	.337

1995 Situational Statistics

	AB	HR	RBI	BA	OBA	SLG		AB	HR	RBI	BA	OBA	SLG
Home	183	5	29	.333	.392	.508	LHP	75	0	9	.213	.287	.253
Road	194	5	26	.299	.359	.423	RHP	302	10	46	.341	.398	.517
Apr-Jun	161	3	24	.360	.420	.503	ScPos	110	1	43	.300	.379	.382
Jul-Oct	216	7	31	.282	.342	.435	Clutch	73	1	7	.247	.321	.315

How He Compares to Other Batters

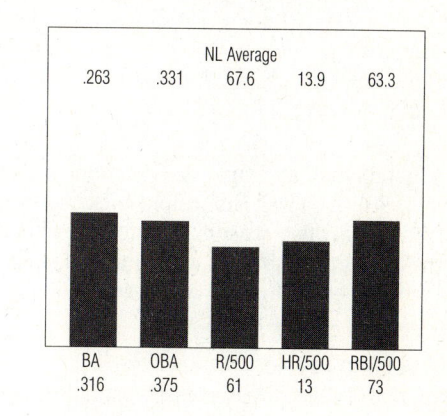

NL Average
.263 .331 67.6 13.9 63.3

BA OBA R/500 HR/500 RBI/500
.316 .375 61 13 73

Where He Hits the Ball

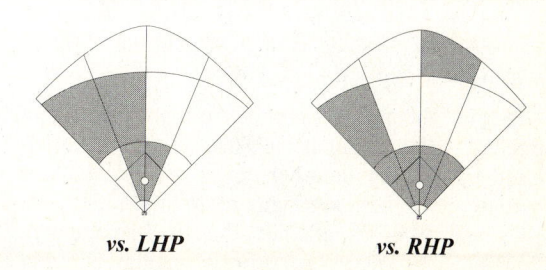

vs. LHP   vs. RHP

PHILADELPHIA PHILLIES

TYLER GREEN

Position: SP
Bats: R **Throws:** R
Ht: 6'5" **Wt:** 185
Opening Day Age: 26
Born: 2/18/1970
Drafted: PHI91 1/10
ML Seasons: 2

SCOUTING REPORT

A big righthander, Green delivers from a three-quarter angle across his body. He is essentially a two-pitch pitcher, with a slightly above-average fastball that is hittable in the strike zone and a good, hard knuckle curve that freezes hitters. He also shows a below-average change-up. When Tyler gets his knuckle curve over consistently, his fastball looks quicker and he gets the batters to take many weak swings. When he can't get the knuckle curve over, hitters wait for a fastball in the zone and hit it hard. To say that his control is erratic is to be kind.

For a righthander on the Phillies' staff, Green held runners tolerably well, allowing ten steals in 17 attempts. His fielding is a bit below par. He went 8-for-44 (.182) at the plate with one home run last season.

HOW HE PERFORMED IN '95

Based on his 8-3 record in May and June, Tyler was selected to the NL All-Star team as a rookie—quite an honor. After taking his bow, he fell off the stage in the second half, failing to win another game all year and getting pounded for an astronomical earned run average. He needs to learn to set up hitters better; they laid off the breaking pitch in the second half, forcing him to come in with other pitches

After a good year at Triple-A Scranton-Wilkes-Barre in 1993, the 1991 first-round pick has been hammered the last two seasons. He doesn't give up too many home runs, but he gets burned on fastballs when he's behind in the count, which is quite often.

WHAT TO EXPECT IN '96

Will the real Tyler Green please stand up? The Phillies' chances of returning to contention will be substantially increased if Green shows the form he displayed in the first half of '95. If he pitches like he did after the All-Star break, he's likely to see more time in Triple-A as his stock in the Phillies' organization drops rapidly.

Green has the ability but needs to mature a lot as a pitcher to be a consistent major-league starter. Until he develops another plus pitch or develops better control, he'll see many more ups and downs. It's no secret in Philadelphia that the management thinks his problems are mostly mental and not physical.

Overall Statistics

	G	GS	GF	SV	W	L	ERA	IP	H	R	ER	HR	BB	SO
95 PHI	26	25	0	0	8	9	5.31	140.2	157	86	83	15	66	85
Career	29	27	1	0	8	9	5.41	148.0	173	95	89	16	71	92

1995 Situational Statistics

	W	L	ERA	SV	IP	BB	SO		AB	HR	RBI	BA	OBA	SLG
Home	4	5	5.85	0	64.2	32	50	LHB	224	7	40	.304	.402	.464
Road	4	4	4.86	0	76.0	34	35	RHB	318	8	35	.280	.342	.412
Apr-Jun	8	4	2.75	0	88.1	38	55	ScPos	142	4	60	.296	.398	.437
Jul-Oct	0	5	9.63	0	52.1	28	30	Clutch	32	0	3	.375	.459	.500

How He Compares to Other Pitchers

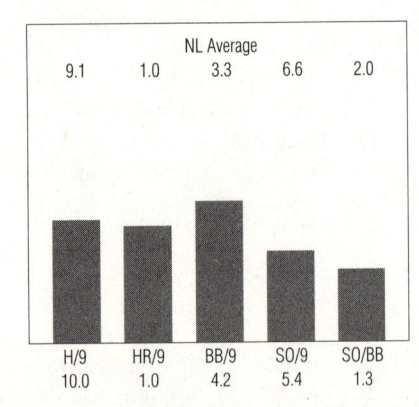

NL Average: H/9 9.1, HR/9 1.0, BB/9 3.3, SO/9 6.6, SO/BB 2.0

His values: H/9 10.0, HR/9 1.0, BB/9 4.2, SO/9 5.4, SO/BB 1.3

How He Compares to Other Starting Pitchers

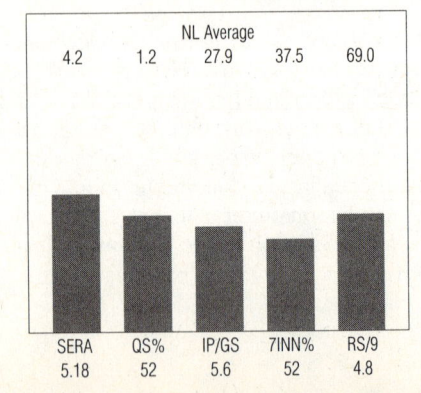

NL Average: SERA 4.2, QS% 1.2, IP/GS 27.9, 7INN% 37.5, RS/9 69.0

His values: SERA 5.18, QS% 52, IP/GS 5.6, 7INN% 52, RS/9 4.8

PHILADELPHIA PHILLIES

CHARLIE HAYES

Position: 3B
Bats: R **Throws:** R
Ht: 6'0" **Wt:** 190
Opening Day Age: 30
Born: 5/29/1965
Drafted: SF83 3/96
ML Seasons: 8

SCOUTING REPORT
The best aspects of Hayes' game are all defensive, as he is one of the better third baseman on the field. He has a plus arm, although his throws are erratic at times, and he reads ground balls very well. His plus range has diminished somewhat, but his good hands make him a pleasure to watch in the field as he scoops up hard-hit balls with catlike reflexes.

At the plate, Charlie is a first-ball, fastball hitter with not very good plate discipline. He likes the pitch inside, tries to pull too many pitches, and doesn't hit breaking pitches well. On the basepaths, Hayes is a minus runner who does not steal often nor especially well. He has enough power to hit any fastball out of the park, but he doesn't do it often enough to be a star at a power position.

HOW HE PERFORMED IN '95
All in all, Charlie had a very good season and was considered by many fans and writers as the most valuable player on the Phillies in their disappointing year. He started 141 of 144 games in his second tour of duty with the Phillies. He also showed increased maturity as a hitter in '95, posting a career high in walks and attaining easily the best K/W ratio of his career. If this improvement continues, he may be able to offset somewhat for a few years the inevitable decline in hitting skills as he ages. Considering the ballpark, he had a better year than in 1994 with the Rockies in friendly Mile High Stadium. Of course, he will never again reach the heights he scaled in 1993 in Denver.

WHAT TO EXPECT IN '96
Hayes is a good player but is also seriously overrated. He was a free agent last winter and wanted a multi-year guaranteed deal from the Phillies, who were unwilling to commit that much money. On the old market, he would easily get what he was looking for; in the new market, he may have to settle for a one-year deal or for a relatively small base salary. He will start at the hot corner for someone in '96, but he won't get any better than he was in '95 unless he returns to a good hitters' park.

Overall Statistics

	G	AB	R	H	2B	3B	HR	RBI	SB	CS	BB	SO	BA	OBA
95 PHI	141	529	58	146	30	3	11	85	5	1	50	88	.276	.340
Career	941	3370	361	904	175	13	94	452	32	26	212	560	.268	.312

1995 Situational Statistics

	AB	HR	RBI	BA	OBA	SLG		AB	HR	RBI	BA	OBA	SLG
Home	257	6	45	.288	.354	.432	LHP	147	3	25	.313	.388	.476
Road	272	5	40	.265	.326	.382	RHP	382	8	60	.262	.321	.380
Apr-Jun	210	6	44	.295	.381	.443	ScPos	180	4	77	.283	.345	.433
Jul-Oct	319	5	41	.263	.310	.382	Clutch	88	2	14	.261	.327	.409

How He Compares to Other Batters

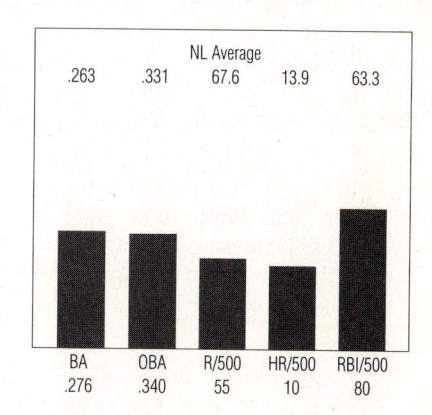

NL Average
.263 .331 67.6 13.9 63.3

BA	OBA	R/500	HR/500	RBI/500
.276	.340	55	10	80

Where He Hits the Ball

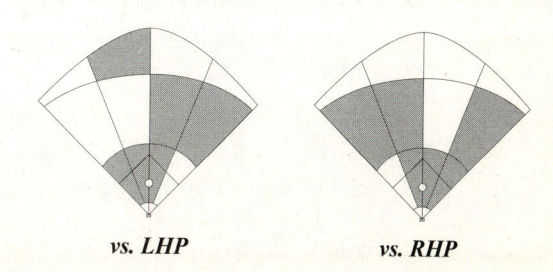

vs. LHP   vs. RHP

THE SCOUTING REPORT: 1996

PHILADELPHIA PHILLIES

GREGG JEFFERIES

Positions: 1B/OF
Bats: B **Throws:** R
Ht: 5'11" **Wt:** 175
Opening Day Age: 28
Born: 8/1/1967
Drafted: NYN85 1/20
ML Seasons: 9

SCOUTING REPORT

Gregg is a line-drive hitting machine, a player who has found his level and does several things very well. He is a good contact hitter from both sides of the plate with a quick bat and a short stroke. He can handle pitches, especially fastballs, in any part of the strike zone.

As a runner, Jefferies has slowed down somewhat and now has about average speed. His nine stolen bases in '95 were the lowest in any full season of his major-league career.

At first base, his arm, accuracy, and range are all a little below-average and he has minus hands. However, being a little below par at first doesn't hurt your team defensively anywhere nearly as badly as being well below par in left field.

HOW HE PERFORMED IN '95

Signed to a huge free-agent contract after 1994 and moved to left field by the Phillies, Gregg tried hard but just couldn't play the position. The experiment lasted half the season and didn't work out well at all. With no experience in the pasture, Gregg misread many fly balls, displaying had poor range and a weak arm. Worse, his hitting suffered as well until he went on an offensive tear after being moved back to first base, finishing the year strongly at the plate.

Jefferies has hit now .300 or better three years in a row, but his average has dropped steadily since its peak of .342 in 1993. He is also taking fewer walks and his home-run rate dropped dramatically last season in a big home-run year.

WHAT TO EXPECT IN '96

It is very likely that Jefferies will continue to hit as he did the past few years: .300-plus average, 10–15 home runs, and 25–35 doubles and triples. Unfortunately for him, that's not what the Phillies need the most. They need a big bopper in the middle of their lineup, but that guy almost certainly needs to play first base, leaving Jefferies out of the mix. If the Phils can make a deal for him, they will, but it won't be easy moving his big contract.

Barring a trade, Greg will continue to do for the Phillies exactly what he has shown he can do. To ask any more from him is foolish. The Phils are paying him power-hitter money, but that doesn't make him a power hitter.

Overall Statistics

	G	AB	R	H	2B	3B	HR	RBI	SB	CS	BB	SO	BA	OBA
95 PHI	114	480	69	147	31	2	11	56	9	5	35	26	.306	.349
Career	976	3738	522	1106	214	18	91	474	149	42	325	247	.296	.352

1995 Situational Statistics

	AB	HR	RBI	BA	OBA	SLG		AB	HR	RBI	BA	OBA	SLG
Home	211	4	31	.327	.383	.464	LHP	151	4	15	.351	.390	.510
Road	269	7	25	.290	.322	.435	RHP	329	7	41	.286	.331	.419
Apr-Jun	168	4	16	.262	.317	.405	ScPos	114	2	41	.254	.321	.342
Jul-Oct	312	7	40	.330	.367	.471	Clutch	90	2	12	.322	.371	.456

How He Compares to Other Batters

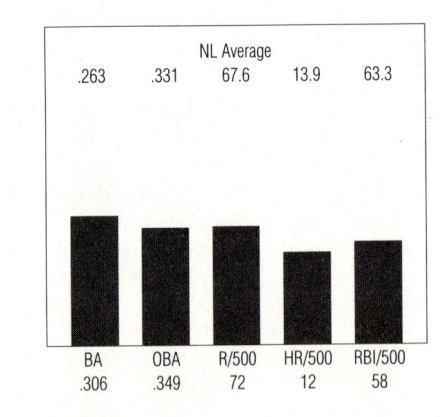

	BA	OBA	R/500	HR/500	RBI/500
NL Average	.263	.331	67.6	13.9	63.3
	.306	.349	72	12	58

Where He Hits the Ball

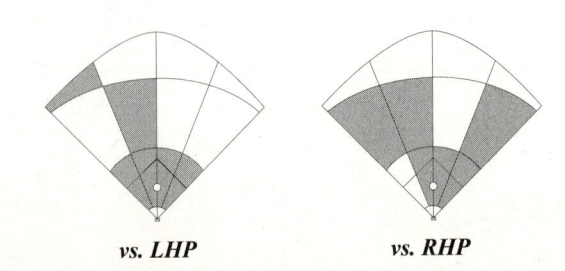

vs. LHP   vs. RHP

PHILADELPHIA PHILLIES

MIKE MIMBS

Position: SP/RP
Bats: L **Throws:** L
Ht: 6'2" **Wt:** 180
Opening Day Age: 27
Born: 2/13/1969
Drafted: LA90 24/645
ML Seasons: 1

SCOUTING REPORT
A southpaw who depends on his oft-used plus change-up to retire hitters, Mimbs delivers from a three-quarter angle with longish arm action. His fastball is a tad below-average in velocity with some tailing action into lefthanded hitters; his curve lacks sharpness and is therefore minus.

With a quick delivery to home plate and the natural advantage of being lefthanded, Mimbs is very good at keeping runners honest. Only 11 tried to run on him in '95, and seven were retired. He is an average fielder. Mike hit .143 (5-for-35) with eight sacrifice bunts in his debut season.

HOW HE PERFORMED IN '95
Released in the spring of '93 after three years in the Dodgers' system, Mimbs hooked on with St. Paul in the independent Northern League. After going 8-2 with a 3.20 ERA, he signed with Montreal in January '94. After a decent season at Double-A Harrisburg, he was plucked off the Expos' roster in the Rule V draft by the Phillies.

Mimbs got his chance when several of the veteran Phillies' starters went down with injuries early in the year. He started off well as the #5 starter (3-1 in May with a 3.09 ERA), but a slump in June and July shunted him to the bullpen. He pitched well in relief and eventually was put back in the rotation at the end of the season.

Completely shutting down lefthanded hitters, Mike also held righties to a tolerable level of damage. His problem has always been control; when he can hit his fastball and drop his curve where he wants, he's a much more effective pitcher.

WHAT TO EXPECT IN '96
Mike is almost certain to get another audition for the Phillies' rotation in '96. With the added experience under his belt, he could take advantage of the chance and win 15 games. If he fails as a starter, he should still stick around as a valuable middle reliever. There's no guarantee that he'll ever put it all together, but he has a decent chance to develop into a solid major-league starter. His twin brother Mark, another refugee from the Dodgers' minor-league system, was drafted by Texas in the Rule V draft last December.

Overall Statistics

	G	GS	GF	SV	W	L	ERA	IP	H	R	ER	HR	BB	SO
95 PHI	35	19	6	1	9	7	4.15	136.2	127	70	63	10	75	93
Career	35	19	6	1	9	7	4.15	136.2	127	70	63	10	75	93

1995 Situational Statistics

	W	L	ERA	SV	IP	BB	SO		AB	HR	RBI	BA	OBA	SLG
Home	6	6	4.52	1	85.2	46	62	LHB	98	1	11	.214	.325	.306
Road	3	1	3.53	0	51.0	29	31	RHB	410	9	52	.259	.354	.383
Apr-Jun	6	2	3.74	0	67.1	30	40	ScPos	123	4	52	.244	.361	.390
Jul-Oct	3	5	4.54	1	69.1	45	53	Clutch	44	0	4	.205	.271	.295

How He Compares to Other Pitchers

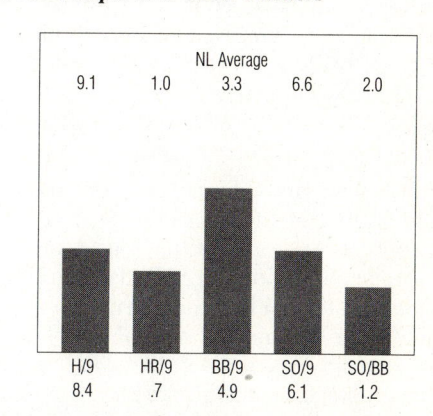

NL Average: H/9 9.1, HR/9 1.0, BB/9 3.3, SO/9 6.6, SO/BB 2.0
Mimbs: H/9 8.4, HR/9 .7, BB/9 4.9, SO/9 6.1, SO/BB 1.2

How He Compares to Other Starting Pitchers

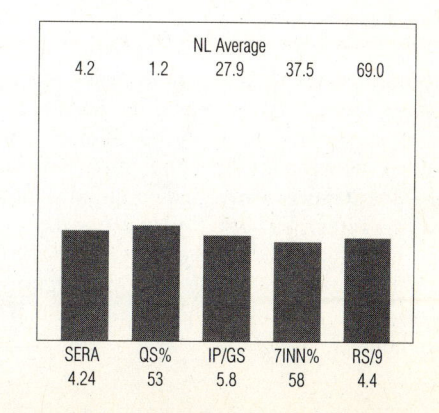

NL Average: SERA 4.2, QS% 1.2, IP/GS 27.9, 7INN% 37.5, RS/9 69.0
Mimbs: SERA 4.24, QS% 53, IP/GS 5.8, 7INN% 58, RS/9 4.4

THE SCOUTING REPORT: 1996

PHILADELPHIA PHILLIES

MICKEY MORANDINI

Position: 2B
Bats: L **Throws:** R
Ht: 5'11" **Wt:** 170
Opening Day Age: 29
Born: 4/22/1966
Drafted: PHI88 4/120
ML Seasons: 6

SCOUTING REPORT

While he has developed into a good hitter for a middle infielder, Morandini's forte has always been his defense. He is a Gold Glover at second base, with a plus arm, plus range, and soft hands. He excels in the pivot, turning many double plays that most other second basemen wouldn't make. He had post-season surgery on his right elbow, but that shouldn't affect him negatively in '96.

An aggressive line-drive hitter who chokes up on the bat, Mickey makes good contact and goes with pitch well. He likes fastballs out over the plate that he can line into the gaps.

Mickey is an average runner who doesn't steal often. His career stolen base percentage in the majors is excellent, but he has had less success in that area the past two years.

HOW HE PERFORMED IN '95

How many second basemen lead their team in doubles? Morandini did in '95. He also led the team in triples. He is a fine player who always hustles. He doesn't walk often, however, making him less valuable at the top of the order, and his K/W ratio went from 1:1 in 1994 to 2:1 in 1995 as he hit for more power. It's pretty clear now that he cannot hit left-handers well, but his glove will probably keep him away from a platoon arrangement.

The Phillies gave Kevin Jordan a try-out at second base late last season after he hit .310 at Triple-A. This wasn't due to dissatisfaction with Morandini, it was an attempt to find out if Jordan can play in the majors and if the Phils could afford to make a big trade while Morandini was at the peak of his career. The management didn't like what they saw of Jordan, however, reducing the chances of their trading the incumbent.

WHAT TO EXPECT IN '96

Rumor had it that the Phillies had placed their All-Star second baseman on the trading block in the off-season. Second base is one of the few areas the Philadelphia system has a surfeit of talent, with Morandini, Kevin Jordan, and prospect Dave Doster. Morandini is a valuable commodity at this stage of his career, so he will play every day if the Phillies move him. His offense is likely to decline somewhat as he enters his 30s, but his superb defense should keep him in the starting lineup for years to come.

Overall Statistics

	G	AB	R	H	2B	3B	HR	RBI	SB	CS	BB	SO	BA	OBA
95 PHI	127	494	65	140	34	7	6	49	9	6	42	80	.283	.350
Career	584	2019	256	537	92	33	16	161	56	18	170	314	.266	.328

1995 Situational Statistics

	AB	HR	RBI	BA	OBA	SLG		AB	HR	RBI	BA	OBA	SLG
Home	242	3	25	.302	.370	.426	LHP	105	1	14	.229	.287	.343
Road	252	3	24	.266	.330	.409	RHP	389	5	35	.298	.367	.437
Apr-Jun	195	4	25	.287	.347	.436	ScPos	107	2	44	.346	.441	.542
Jul-Oct	299	2	24	.281	.351	.405	Clutch	89	2	8	.225	.307	.360

How He Compares to Other Batters

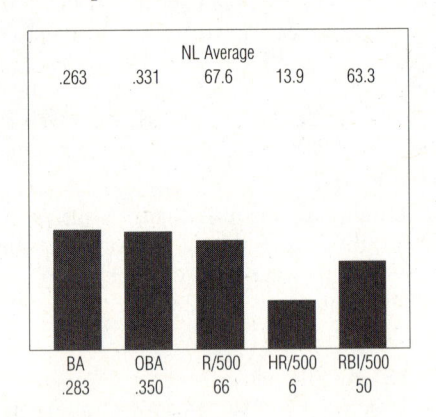

NL Average: .263 .331 67.6 13.9 63.3

BA	OBA	R/500	HR/500	RBI/500
.283	.350	66	6	50

Where He Hits the Ball

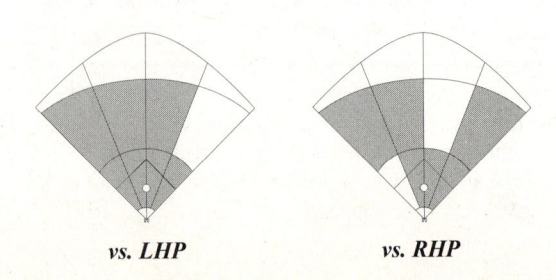

vs. LHP   vs. RHP

PHILADELPHIA PHILLIES

PAUL QUANTRILL

Position: SP
Bats: L **Throws:** R
Ht: 6'1" **Wt:** 175
Opening Day Age: 27
Born: 11/3/1968
Drafted: BOS89 8/163
ML Seasons: 4

SCOUTING REPORT

A pitcher with a rubber arm, Quantrill always takes the ball and serves quietly in whatever role he's asked. He has a standard three-quarter delivery for a righthanded sinkerballer, with average-plus velocity and good movement on his trademark pitch.

The problem is that Paul doesn't have any plus pitches. He shows a curve and change, and his slider is just average. He has excellent control—maybe too good, for his stuff isn't good enough to survive anywhere but at the very bottom of the strike zone. When his sinker is above the knees, it gets hit hard. He seemed to have better movement and velocity on is sinker at times last season, but couldn't sustain it.

Another problem with Quantrill is that he is very poor at holding runners. Given the number of hits he allows, this is a serious flaw, and 20 of 24 basestealers were successful against him last year. He is an average fielder and a terrible hitter (.100 career BA), although he laid down seven sacs in '95.

HOW HE PERFORMED IN '95

After disappointing the Phillies when they acquired him in 1994 from Boston, Paul improved enough to spend the full season with the big club. He stayed in the Phillies' battered rotation most of the season, leading the team in wins, starts, and innings pitched. However, he was also one of the battered by year's end. Lefthanded hitters have hit well over .300 with power against him the past two years, a trend which will shorten his days in the rotation if he doesn't develop a countermeasure.

The fact is that Quantrill would not be starting many games for a good team. He has been a better pitcher on grass than on turf, but the difference has not been so dramatic as with some other sinkerballers, so the move back to the turf-short AL probably won't have a dramatic effect.

WHAT TO EXPECT IN '96

Dealt to the Blue Jays in December for prospects Howard Battle and Rico Jordan, Quantrill will get another chance in the American League. He's never going to be a good pitcher, but he could fashion a couple of years of 30 starts with a league-average ERA if he's lucky. Of course, he could also get pounded back to middle relief if his control isn't sharp or if he doesn't develop a decent off-speed pitch.

Overall Statistics

	G	GS	GF	SV	W	L	ERA	IP	H	R	ER	HR	BB	SO
95 PHI	33	29	1	0	11	12	4.67	179.1	212	102	93	20	44	103
Career	144	44	28	3	22	30	4.16	419.2	482	224	194	41	118	221

1995 Situational Statistics

	W	L	ERA	SV	IP	BB	SO		AB	HR	RBI	BA	OBA	SLG
Home	5	6	4.82	0	97.0	30	57	LHB	308	10	44	.351	.396	.558
Road	6	6	4.48	0	82.1	14	46	RHB	411	10	49	.253	.293	.384
Apr-Jun	7	3	4.22	0	74.2	15	45	ScPos	192	8	77	.276	.350	.479
Jul-Oct	4	9	4.99	0	104.2	29	58	Clutch	45	3	8	.289	.385	.511

How He Compares to Other Pitchers

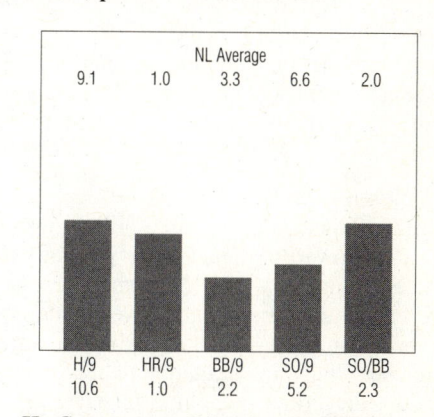

NL Average: H/9 9.1, HR/9 1.0, BB/9 3.3, SO/9 6.6, SO/BB 2.0
Quantrill: H/9 10.6, HR/9 1.0, BB/9 2.2, SO/9 5.2, SO/BB 2.3

How He Compares to Other Starting Pitchers

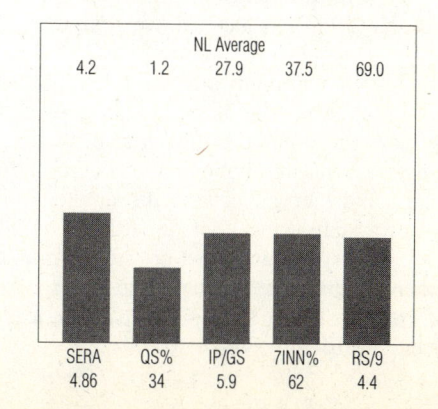

NL Average: SERA 4.2, QS% 1.2, IP/GS 27.9, 7INN% 37.5, RS/9 69.0
Quantrill: SERA 4.86, QS% 34, IP/GS 5.9, 7INN% 62, RS/9 4.4

PHILADELPHIA PHILLIES

CURT SCHILLING

Position: SP
Bats: R **Throws:** R
Ht: 6'5" **Wt:** 205
Opening Day Age: 29
Born: 11/14/1966
Drafted: BOS86* 2/39
ML Seasons: 8

SCOUTING REPORT
Curt is a bulldog pitcher who delivers from high three-quarters with a wrist wrap, unleashing a plus fastball which sinks and bores into righthanded hitters. He also has a plus, hard slider, an average change-up (which he palms), and an average forkball. He has good control for a power pitcher.

Once good at holding runners, Schilling has been easy to run on the past two injury-plagued seasons. Even though he varies his time to home to keep runners off-balance, 11 of 13 basestealers were successful in '95. He is an average fielder and a decent hitter (.175 with 5 sac hits in '95).

HOW HE PERFORMED IN '95
Schilling was enjoying a very good year in '95. He was punching out a hitter per inning, walking very few hitters, allowing very few hits, and in general displaying the dominating form of 1992–93. He was the top dog on a pitching staff that had taken the league by storm. Alas, it was not to last.

He missed his first start of the season on July 23 due to inflammation and tendinitis in his right shoulder and was placed on the DL two days later, finally going under the knife in late August. He had arthroscopic surgery to repair a small tear in his rotator cuff and to remove a bone spur from his right shoulder.

WHAT TO EXPECT IN '96
The Phillies expected to re-sign Schilling over the winter at a lower pay rate than previously. If healthy, Schilling can win 15 games easily. "If healthy," of course, are the first two words heard whenever anyone talks about Philadelphia starting pitchers. Schilling's rehabilitation schedule called for him to start throwing again in January.

However, Curt has pitched 200+ innings only once in his career (1993), he has had two straight injury-plagued seasons now, he will be 29 in '96, and he will try to pitch through any injury or pain that doesn't disable him. That makes him a good candidate to blaze through the league once or twice, impressing everyone into believing he's come all the way back, and then go down with another injury. That's not a statement about his attitude or commitment, it's a statement about physical limitations and the inherent dangers in trying to throw a baseball at speeds of over 90 mph past major league-hitters every fifth day.

Overall Statistics

	G	GS	GF	SV	W	L	ERA	IP	H	R	ER	HR	BB	SO
95 PHI	17	17	0	0	7	5	3.57	116.0	96	52	46	12	26	114
Career	206	95	60	13	43	42	3.56	805.0	731	348	318	64	241	618

1995 Situational Statistics

	W	L	ERA	SV	IP	BB	SO		AB	HR	RBI	BA	OBA	SLG
Home	1	4	3.94	0	48.0	16	53	LHB	172	8	23	.238	.303	.413
Road	6	1	3.31	0	68.0	10	61	RHB	265	4	20	.208	.243	.298
Apr-Jun	5	3	3.26	0	91.0	12	85	ScPos	83	2	27	.217	.287	.325
Jul-Oct	2	2	4.68	0	25.0	14	29	Clutch	40	5	10	.350	.400	.725

How He Compares to Other Pitchers

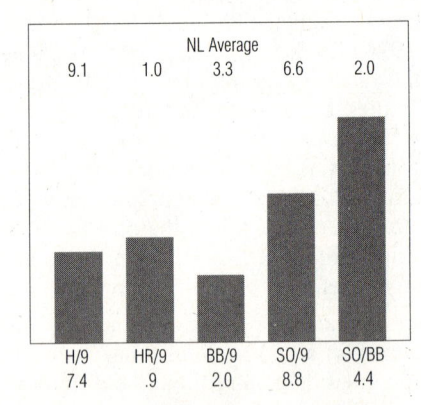

NL Average: H/9 9.1, HR/9 1.0, BB/9 3.3, SO/9 6.6, SO/BB 2.0

Schilling: H/9 7.4, HR/9 .9, BB/9 2.0, SO/9 8.8, SO/BB 4.4

How He Compares to Other Starting Pitchers

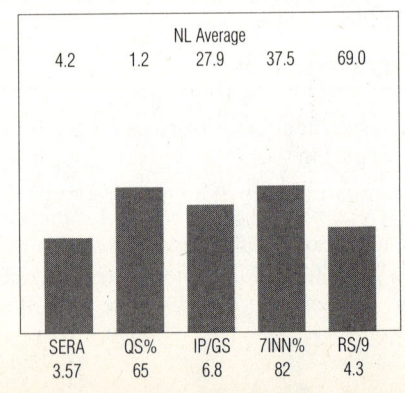

NL Average: SERA 4.2, QS% 1.2, IP/GS 27.9, 7INN% 37.5, RS/9 69.0

Schilling: SERA 3.57, QS% 65, IP/GS 6.8, 7INN% 82, RS/9 4.3

PHILADELPHIA PHILLIES

HEATHCLIFF SLOCUMB

Position: RP
Bats: R **Throws:** R
Ht: 6'3" **Wt:** 210
Opening Day Age: 29
Born: 6/7/1966
Drafted: NYN 7/10/84
ML Seasons: 5

SCOUTING REPORT

Slocumb delivers from high three-quarters to overhand with a jerky motion, unleashing both two-seam and four-seam fastballs with good velocity and a good, very hard slider, which is his out pitch. He also will throw an average splitter to give the hitters something else to worry about.

In the past, Heathcliff had so much movement on his fastballs that he couldn't get them over consistently enough. He solved that problem by keeping his pitches consistently low in the strike zone in the first half, meaning that his mistakes were not hit hard. In the second half, however, he got more pitches up and made more mistakes, although he only allowed an incredible two homers on the season.

Quick to home and with a decent move, Slocumb is very hard to run on. Only five runners tried to in '95, although four were successful. He is also quick off the mound and is a good fielder.

HOW HE PERFORMED IN '95

Getting his chance to save games very early in the season when Norm Charlton showed he wasn't ready, Heathcliff made the most of it. He was almost untouchable in the first half, saving 20 games before July, going unscored-upon in June, making the All-Star team for the first time and even picking up the win in the mid-summer classic.

Like his team's early-season hot streak, though, Slocumb's first-half performance was not to last. He posted a 4.54 ERA from July 1 onward, was hammered for 21 hits in 11 innings in August, and saved only 12 more games as his team sank out of the pennant race. In reality, he wasn't that bad, but the hard liners that were hit right at his teammates in the first half went into the gaps in the second half.

WHAT TO EXPECT IN '96

On the trading block over the winter, not due to poor performance but because of his greatly increased value, Slocumb may find himself closing games for someone besides the Phillies in '96. He's capable of 30-35 saves again with a good club, but a 40-save season is probably asking too much. He's now proven that he's a good pitcher and a bona fide closer, but he has yet to show that he can be a dominant pitcher for a full season.

Overall Statistics

	G	GS	GF	SV	W	L	ERA	IP	H	R	ER	HR	BB	SO
95 PHI	61	0	54	32	5	6	2.89	65.1	64	26	21	2	35	63
Career	225	0	111	34	16	12	3.64	274.1	279	133	111	11	134	204

1995 Situational Statistics

	W	L	ERA	SV	IP	BB	SO		AB	HR	RBI	BA	OBA	SLG
Home	4	1	3.19	13	31.0	20	32	LHB	107	0	5	.224	.331	.243
Road	1	5	2.62	19	34.1	15	31	RHB	142	2	25	.282	.366	.366
Apr-Jun	1	0	0.91	20	29.2	15	24	ScPos	75	2	28	.307	.416	.427
Jul-Oct	4	6	4.54	12	35.2	20	39	Clutch	198	2	27	.247	.341	.303

How He Compares to Other Pitchers

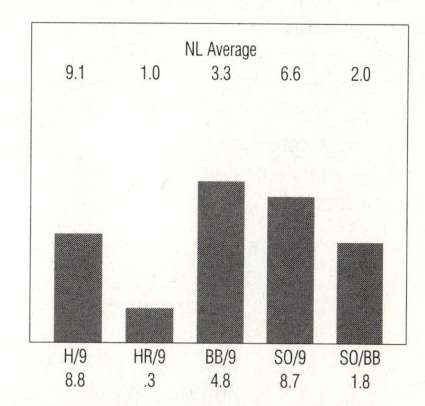

NL Average: H/9 9.1 | HR/9 1.0 | BB/9 3.3 | SO/9 6.6 | SO/BB 2.0

Slocumb: H/9 8.8 | HR/9 .3 | BB/9 4.8 | SO/9 8.7 | SO/BB 1.8

How He Compares to Other Relief Pitchers

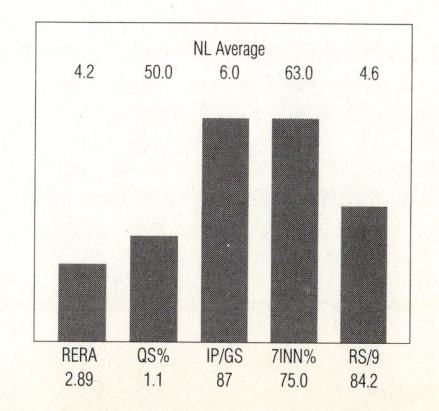

NL Average: RERA 4.2 | QS% 50.0 | IP/GS 6.0 | 7INN% 63.0 | RS/9 4.6

Slocumb: RERA 2.89 | QS% 1.1 | IP/GS 87 | 7INN% 75.0 | RS/9 84.2

THE SCOUTING REPORT: 1996

PHILADELPHIA PHILLIES

KEVIN STOCKER

Position: SS
Bats: B **Throws:** R
Ht: 6'1" **Wt:** 175
Opening Day Age: 26
Born: 2/13/1970
Drafted: PHI91 2/54
ML Seasons: 3

SCOUTING REPORT
A disciplined switch-hitter with no power, Kevin chokes up on the bat and goes with the pitch. He has good bat control and is a plus bunter, especially when laying down the sacrifice. He is an average runner and a good percentage basestealer who doesn't run often.

In the field, Stocker has an average arm with a quick release, average-to-above range, and good hands. All of this sounds like an impressive package for a shortstop.

HOW HE PERFORMED IN '95
Unfortunately, for a good part of the '95 season, Stocker was the worst hitter playing regularly in the major leagues. What a disappointment! No one thought that he could be that bad, but he certainly was. Previously a bright spot on an aging team, he is now a gigantic question mark as the Phillies struggle to rebuild. By the end of his miserable season, his work ethic was being questioned and his future as a major-league regular was clouded.

Kevin started slow and struggled badly for the whole first half, finally raising his average above water with a decent July. Stocker didn't really do anything different in '95, he just did everything less well while the baseball gods who had turned so many soft liners into bloop hits in the past now watched those same soft liners drop harmlessly into opposing fielders' gloves.

WHAT TO EXPECT IN '96
If Stocker hits .250-.260, he's helping the team. Regrettably, after his '95 performance, that's not a given anymore. The Phils acquired utility player Mike Benjamin in the off-season to give them a tolerable alternative to another campaign like Stocker's last, but Benjamin is nothing more than a reserve.

At age 26, Kevin has time to mature and to improve. He'll need to do both pretty quickly to avoid becoming a footnote to the Phillies' magical 1993 season. Stocker's 1993-94 seasons were completely out of character with his professional record, so a drop in performance was to be expected. However, the drop off the cliff was a shocker. He should improve somewhat, but it's now clear that he won't ever fulfill the expectations he raised when he first came to the majors.

Overall Statistics

	G	AB	R	H	2B	3B	HR	RBI	SB	CS	BB	SO	BA	OBA
95 PHI	125	412	42	90	14	3	1	32	6	1	43	75	.218	.304
Career	277	942	126	248	37	8	5	91	13	3	117	159	.263	.357

1995 Situational Statistics

	AB	HR	RBI	BA	OBA	SLG		AB	HR	RBI	BA	OBA	SLG
Home	209	1	23	.196	.292	.278	LHP	115	0	9	.217	.268	.252
Road	203	0	9	.241	.317	.271	RHP	297	1	23	.219	.317	.283
Apr-Jun	170	0	20	.212	.313	.247	ScPos	109	0	31	.174	.326	.229
Jul-Oct	242	1	12	.223	.297	.293	Clutch	71	1	5	.239	.353	.310

How He Compares to Other Batters

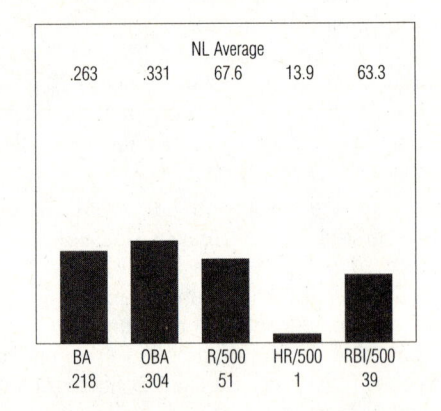

NL Average: .263 .331 67.6 13.9 63.3

BA .218 | OBA .304 | R/500 51 | HR/500 1 | RBI/500 39

Where He Hits the Ball

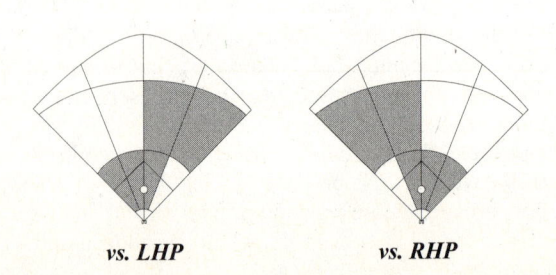

vs. LHP   vs. RHP

PHILADELPHIA PHILLIES

ANDY VAN SLYKE

Position: OF
Bats: L **Throws:** R
Ht: 6'2" **Wt:** 192
Opening Day Age: 35
Born: 12/21/1960
Drafted: SL79 1/6
ML Seasons: 13

SCOUTING REPORT
Andy is now a shadow of the player who was a star with the Pirates' in the early 1990s. His skills have deteriorated in almost every area due to age and serious back problems. He has altered his swing due to his injuries and now shows little of the line-drive power he used to have. He has good discipline at bat, not uncommon with smart older players who can't hit the good fastball anymore, but doesn't hit lefthanders well. Defensively, Andy can still play center field adequately. He has good hands and somewhat below-average range, but has always played his position very deep. His arm is now also a bit below-average although his throws are very accurate. With average speed, Van Slyke doesn't run often but is a good percentage basestealer who has not been thrown out in 14 attempts in 1994–95.

HOW HE PERFORMED IN '95
A prime example of the owners' determination not to sign aging veterans to expensive contracts, Andy was stuck in the refugee camp in Homestead, Florida, until the end of the spring. He signed with Baltimore but washed out quickly in the AL, hitting a meager .159 in 17 games and being disabled twice before being traded to Philadelphia in June for Gene Harris.

With the Phillies, he started off fast, hitting a home run in his first game, then went on the DL after his second game. He returned in mid-July to play an undistinguished center field for most of the rest of the year.

WHAT TO EXPECT IN '96
The open question about Van Slyke in the off-season was whether he was going to retire. Since he did not announce his retirement after the season, whether he starts preparing for a career in the broadcast booth—as has been mentioned in the media—will depend on whether someone makes him an offer.

At this point, Andy is not a good player, really, despite his reputation. If he could adapt to a reserve role and to the concomitant reduction in pay, he would be worth a roster slot. If not, he can start in center field only for a desperate team which has no good alternative. The Phils fit that bill last year when Dykstra was hobbled, but if Lenny's conditioning program works, there won't be any room at the Vet for the veteran Van Slyke in '96.

Overall Statistics

	G	AB	R	H	2B	3B	HR	RBI	SB	CS	BB	SO	BA	OBA
95 BAL/PHI	80	277	32	62	11	2	6	24	7	0	33	56	.224	.309
Career	1658	5711	835	1562	293	91	164	792	245	59	667	1063	.274	.349

1995 Situational Statistics

	AB	HR	RBI	BA	OBA	SLG		AB	HR	RBI	BA	OBA	SLG
Home	143	1	9	.203	.283	.280	LHP	59	0	5	.169	.275	.271
Road	134	5	15	.246	.335	.410	RHP	218	6	19	.239	.318	.362
Apr-Jun	69	4	10	.174	.260	.362	ScPos	68	0	13	.162	.298	.191
Jul-Oct	208	2	14	.240	.325	.337	Clutch	60	1	2	.200	.294	.300

How He Compares to Other Batters

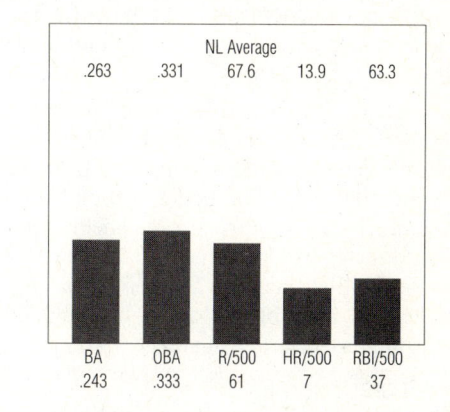

NL Average: .263 .331 67.6 13.9 63.3

BA .243 OBA .333 R/500 61 HR/500 7 RBI/500 37

Where He Hits the Ball

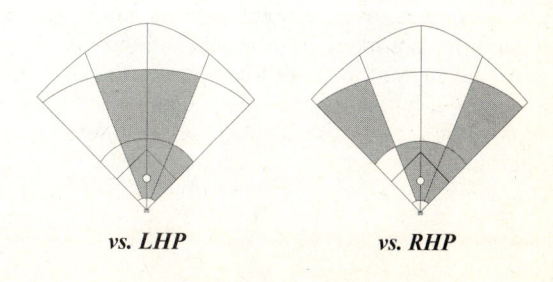

vs. LHP   vs. RHP

PHILADELPHIA PHILLIES

MARK WHITEN

Positions: OF//DH
Bats: B **Throws:** R
Ht: 6'3" **Wt:** 210
Opening Day Age: 29
Born: 11/25/1966
Drafted: TOR86* 5/130
ML Seasons: 6

SCOUTING REPORT
Whiten is a strong switch-hitter with good power from both sides of the plate. A fastball hitter, especially when out over the plate, he likes pitches low when hitting lefthanded and high when hitting righthanded. He doesn't hit for average against southpaws, but he has become more selective at the plate as he has gained experience.

Mark is a slightly above-average runner and a decent basestealer. Where he shines, of course, is on defense. He has an unbelievably strong and accurate arm in right field, the kind that scares enemy runners and coaches into timid, station-to-station advancement. His range is average or better in right field, but his hands are below par and he will juggle base hits at times.

HOW HE PERFORMED IN '95
Poor play, a hamstring injury, and a very bad attitude got Whiten a ticket out of Boston in a hurry in '95. After being demoted to Triple-A Pawtucket, he was dealt to the ailing Phillies for Dave Hollins in late July in an exchange of problem players. Whiten hit several long, loud home runs for the Phillies and provided almost the only power they had for the last two months of the season.

So far, so good. But Whiten isn't really that good. He is not a bona fide cleanup hitter by any means and has hit over 20 home runs only once in his big-league career. He would be better batting sixth in the order, where his good power but mediocre average and on-base would be more than acceptable. Unless the Phillies acquire another good hitter, though, he will probably be asked to shoulder a middle-of-the-order burden again.

WHAT TO EXPECT IN '96
The Phillies are counting on the second-half Mark Whiten to bolster their lineup again in '96. Talented but very inconsistent, he can help a team as he did in Philadelphia, or he can hurt a team as he did in Boston. It's not likely he will generate the kind of power he showed in August and September over a full season, but he can easily hit enough to be an asset offensively while playing stellar defense in right field.

Overall Statistics

	G	AB	R	H	2B	3B	HR	RBI	SB	CS	BB	SO	BA	OBA
95 BOS/PHI92	320	51	77	13	1	12	47	8	0	39	86	.241	.324
Career	633	2219	320	569	82	19	71	294	55	28	243	472	.256	.330

1995 Situational Statistics

	AB	HR	RBI	BA	OBA	SLG		AB	HR	RBI	BA	OBA	SLG
Home	177	5	26	.243	.350	.373	LHP	110	6	15	.209	.285	.400
Road	143	7	21	.238	.290	.434	RHP	210	6	32	.257	.345	.400
Apr-Jun	92	1	8	.185	.240	.239	ScPos	106	2	31	.255	.355	.358
Jul-Oct	228	11	39	.263	.356	.465	Clutch	62	4	12	.226	.294	.468

How He Compares to Other Batters

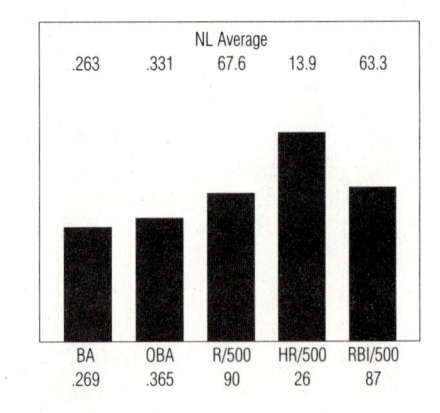

NL Average: BA .263, OBA .331, R/500 67.6, HR/500 13.9, RBI/500 63.3

Player: BA .269, OBA .365, R/500 90, HR/500 26, RBI/500 87

Where He Hits the Ball

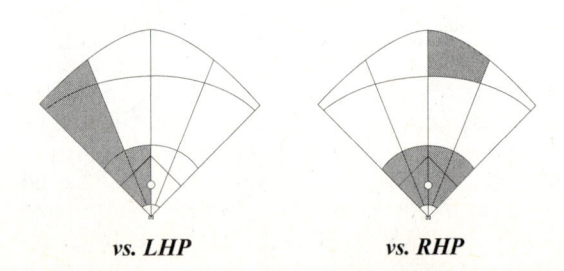

vs. LHP   vs. RHP

PHILADELPHIA PHILLIES

TOBY BORLAND

Position: RP
Bats: R **Throws:** R
Ht: 6'6" **Wt:** 186
Opening Day Age: 26
Born: 5/29/1969
Drafted: PHI87 26/702
ML Seasons: 2

Overall Statistics

	G	GS	GF	SV	W	L	ERA	IP	H	R	ER	HR	BB	SO
95 PHI	50	0	18	6	1	3	3.77	74.0	81	37	31	3	37	59
Career	74	0	25	7	2	3	3.32	108.1	112	47	40	4	51	85

1995 Situational Statistics

	W	L	ERA	SV	IP	BB	SO		AB	HR	RBI	BA	OBA	SLG
Home	1	2	5.56	3	34.0	19	22	LHB	121	1	16	.298	.368	.347
Road	0	1	2.25	3	40.0	18	37	RHB	171	2	19	.263	.365	.368
Apr-Jun	0	0	6.86	1	21.0	16	13	ScPos	92	1	29	.272	.389	.370
Jul-Oct	1	3	2.55	5	53.0	21	46	Clutch	113	1	10	.257	.361	.327

SCOUTING REPORT
Borland comes from the side with a deceptive, long-arm delivery. He is a sinker-slider pitcher who will show a curveball. His sinker has slightly above-average velocity with good movement down and away from righties; his slider has a quick, late break.

Toby is a good fielder and gets lots of practice with all the grounders hit against him. Like most righthanded sidewinders, he is easy to run on: opponents were 7-for-7 stealing against him. He is 1-for-8 as a big-league hitter.

HOW HE PERFORMED IN '95
Borland started the season poorly and missed some time in June with a strained ribcage, but he came back and pitched much better after he returned. He seemed to find his control after he came back from the injury.

WHAT TO EXPECT IN '96
Borland established himself as a major-league reliever in 1995, but he has to improve in several areas if he is going to have an important role in the future. While his ERA was good enough and he allowed very few home runs, he must cut down on his excessive walks and wild pitches if he is going to be called in key situations.

KEVIN ELSTER

Positions: SS//1B/3B/2B
Bats: R **Throws:** R
Ht: 6'2" **Wt:** 180
Opening Day Age: 31
Born: 8/3/1964
Drafted: NYN84* 2/28
ML Seasons: 9

Overall Statistics

	G	AB	R	H	2B	3B	HR	RBI	SB	CS	BB	SO	BA	OBA
95 NYA/PHI	36	70	11	13	5	1	1	9	0	0	8	19	.186	.272
Career	580	1674	177	368	80	7	35	183	10	6	151	267	.220	.284

1995 Situational Statistics

	AB	HR	RBI	BA	OBA	SLG		AB	HR	RBI	BA	OBA	SLG
Home	27	1	4	.259	.355	.481	LHP	32	0	3	.188	.278	.281
Road	43	0	5	.140	.220	.233	RHP	38	1	6	.184	.267	.368
Apr-Jun	17	0	0	.118	.167	.176	ScPos	20	0	8	.200	.280	.350
Jul-Oct	53	1	9	.208	.302	.377	Clutch	8	0	2	.250	.385	.500

SCOUTING REPORT
Elster is the quintessential veteran playing out the string after his skills have deteriorated. Formerly a good defensive shortstop who played regularly for years despite low batting averages because he had some pop in his bat, he has lost what he had due to age and serious shoulder surgery.

A steady shortstop now with below-average range, Elster will play any infield position if asked. He is a decent runner but does not steal.

HOW HE PERFORMED IN '95
Kevin started 1995 with the Yankees, was released after hitting .118 in 10 games, hooked up with K.C. at Triple-A, was released after hitting .238 in 11 games, then was acquired by the Phils in mid-season when the team was desperately unhappy with Kevin Stocker's play. Elster started 14 games at short and also made his big-league debuts at first and third base while with the Phillies.

WHAT TO EXPECT IN '96
Elster didn't play as badly as one might have expected last season, but little was expected other that he not boot routine grounders when in the field. Someone will probably give him another chance to play in 1996, but he hasn't ever hit above .241 in the majors.

PHILADELPHIA PHILLIES

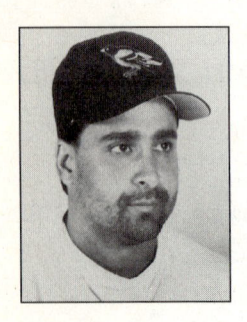

SID FERNANDEZ

Position: SP
Bats: L **Throws:** L
Ht: 6'1" **Wt:** 220
Opening Day Age: 33
Born: 10/12/1962
Drafted: LA81 4/73
ML Seasons: 13

Overall Statistics

	G	GS	GF	SV	W	L	ERA	IP	H	R	ER	HR	BB	SO
95 BAL/PHI	19	18	1	0	6	5	4.56	92.2	84	51	47	20	38	110
Career	295	288	2	1	110	90	3.35	1798.2	1367	722	670	185	687	1663

1995 Situational Statistics

	W	L	ERA	SV	IP	BB	SO		AB	HR	RBI	BA	OBA	SLG
Home	4	1	3.88	0	46.1	12	53	LHB	51	1	2	.137	.200	.196
Road	2	4	5.24	0	46.1	26	57	RHB	307	19	45	.251	.327	.495
Apr-Jun	0	4	7.67	0	27.0	16	29	ScPos	73	4	25	.260	.337	.507
Jul-Oct	6	1	3.29	0	65.2	22	81	Clutch	17	0	0	.235	.278	.235

SCOUTING REPORT
Throwing from three-quarters or lower out of his uniform, Fernandez' now-average fastball seems quicker than it is. He kills lefties with a big-breaking curveball and slow curve and turns over a change-up to righties. He is a poor athlete and a minus fielder.

Offensively, Sid was a woeful 1-for-23 at bat in 1995, well below his career average though. Opposing runners ran wild on his slow delivery, stealing 20 bases in 23 tries.

HOW HE PERFORMED IN '95
The Orioles bought out his expensive contract in July after seven awful starts, and Fernandez made a smart move by signing with the pitching-poor Phillies. After losing his first game, he was crowned NL Pitcher of the Month in August. Of course, that was too good to be true. Fernandez finished the year with nagging arm and shoulder problems.

WHAT TO EXPECT IN '96
Fernandez signed a low-base-salary, incentive-heavy deal with the Phillies in November, so he'll get to show that he can start more than 15 games without breaking down. His gopher ball problem with righthanded hitters is worrisome, though, even if he gets every lefty out in the future.

KEVIN FLORA

Positions: OF//DH
Bats: R **Throws:** R
Ht: 6'0" **Wt:** 180
Opening Day Age: 26
Born: 6/10/1969
Drafted: CAL87 4/57
ML Seasons: 2

Overall Statistics

	G	AB	R	H	2B	3B	HR	RBI	SB	CS	BB	SO	BA	OBA
95 CAL/PHI	26	76	13	16	3	0	2	7	1	0	4	23	.211	.250
Career	29	84	14	17	3	0	2	7	2	0	5	28	.202	.247

1995 Situational Statistics

	AB	HR	RBI	BA	OBA	SLG		AB	HR	RBI	BA	OBA	SLG
Home	45	2	7	.244	.306	.444	LHP	39	0	1	.154	.214	.154
Road	31	0	0	.161	.161	.161	RHP	37	2	6	.270	.289	.514
Apr-Jun	1	0	0	.000	.000	.000	ScPos	18	0	3	.167	.167	.222
Jul-Oct	75	2	7	.213	.253	.333	Clutch	16	2	4	.375	.412	.813

SCOUTING REPORT
With his good speed, Kevin can play either in the infield or outfield. He has had problems defensively in both places, which has cut down on his playing time. Because he was labeled a liability at second base, he was converted to the outfield by the Angels. He has failed to impress in the pasture, though, as his inexperience has shown in his defensive play.

At the plate, Kevin is a line-drive, fastball hitter who goes well with the pitch. He has some power and is an excellent basestealer.

HOW HE PERFORMED IN '95
Flora came to the Phillies in the Dave Gallagher deal and was given a chance to play a bit due to the injuries to Dykstra and Van Slyke. He failed to impress the Phils' brain trust, however, and was outrighted after the season. Refusing assignment, he re-signed a minor-league deal with the Angels.

WHAT TO EXPECT IN '96
Despite good minor-league batting records, Flora just hasn't caught a break. Strikes out way too much, though, for someone without much power, which could keep him from ever hitting well enough to make it. Right now, he's on the verge of becoming a career Triple-A player.

PHILADELPHIA PHILLIES

TOMMY GREENE

Position: SP/RP
Bats: R **Throws:** R
Ht: 6'5" **Wt:** 225
Opening Day Age: 28
Born: 4/6/1967
Drafted: ATL85 1/14
ML Seasons: 7

Overall Statistics

	G	GS	GF	SV	W	L	ERA	IP	H	R	ER	HR	BB	SO
95 PHI	11	6	3	0	0	5	8.29	33.2	45	32	31	6	20	24
Career	117	95	7	0	38	24	4.10	619.0	581	303	282	60	236	450

1995 Situational Statistics

	W	L	ERA	SV	IP	BB	SO		AB	HR	RBI	BA	OBA	SLG
Home	0	3	7.25	0	22.1	9	16	LHB	70	3	16	.357	.451	.614
Road	0	2	10.32	0	11.1	11	8	RHB	71	3	15	.282	.373	.493
Apr-Jun	0	0	11.57	0	2.1	0	1	ScPos	57	4	27	.298	.359	.579
Jul-Oct	0	5	8.04	0	31.1	20	23	Clutch	4	0	1	.750	.800	1.000

SCOUTING REPORT

Tommy throws from high three-quarters with good arm action, just like he did before his injuries. His formerly impressive velocity hasn't returned, however, and he has only an average change-up and minus curve and slider to accompany his now-mediocre fastball.

Greene had trouble holding runners, allowing 6 of 8 to steal on him. He is a good fielder and a good hitter despite going 0-for-8 last season, hitting .219 with 4 homers in his career.

HOW HE PERFORMED IN '95

Shoulder troubles got in Tommy's way in 1995 for the third year in the last four, straining his relationship with the front office. Greene refused major surgery while maintaining he was in a lot of pain; the Phillies clearly thought much of his problem was above his neck, not below. He struggled to get anything over the plate that wasn't hit hard.

WHAT TO EXPECT IN '96

The big question is whether he will ever be 100% healthy again. Greene was a good—but not great—pitcher when healthy, but it is very unlikely he will ever return to his 1991 or 1993 form again. If he can't throw hard, he isn't going to get big-league hitters out.

JEFF JUDEN

Position: SP
Bats: R **Throws:** R
Ht: 6'7" **Wt:** 245
Opening Day Age: 25
Born: 1/19/1971
Drafted: HOU89 1/12
ML Seasons: 4

Overall Statistics

	G	GS	GF	SV	W	L	ERA	IP	H	R	ER	HR	BB	SO
95 PHI	13	10	0	0	2	4	4.02	62.2	53	31	28	6	31	47
Career	25	18	1	0	3	11	4.92	113.1	105	73	62	14	54	87

1995 Situational Statistics

	W	L	ERA	SV	IP	BB	SO		AB	HR	RBI	BA	OBA	SLG
Home	1	1	4.46	0	34.1	19	24	LHB	90	3	14	.300	.396	.444
Road	1	3	3.49	0	28.1	12	23	RHB	136	3	13	.191	.294	.316
Apr-Jun	0	0	0.00	0	0.0	0	0	ScPos	57	0	18	.211	.338	.298
Jul-Oct	2	4	4.02	0	62.2	31	47	Clutch	13	0	1	.385	.429	.462

SCOUTING REPORT

Jeff is a very big righthander who throws from three-quarters or lower with a now-average fastball that is too straight. He cuts his fastball to compensate, has an average slider and shows a curve.

Slow to home and with a big motion, runners went to town against him, stealing 14 bases in 16 tries. A minus fielder and a terrible hitter, Jeff was just 1-for-18 with 3 sacrifices at the plate, with his only hit being a surprise grand slam homer.

HOW HE PERFORMED IN '95

Overall, Juden didn't pitch that badly after his call-up. He shut down righthanded hitters but was hammered by lefthanders, a pattern which is fatal for starting pitchers in a platoon era. He was also outstanding in night games (2.13 ERA) but very bad during the day (6.93 ERA), a pattern which won't help him in San Fran if it holds true.

WHAT TO EXPECT IN '96

Traded to San Francisco after the season for Mike Benjamin, Juden has now been unceremoniously dumped by two organizations frustrated with his conditioning and his attitude. He clearly has talent and potential, and it is way too early to write him off at age 25.

THE SCOUTING REPORT: 1996

PHILADELPHIA PHILLIES

TONY LONGMIRE

Position: OF
Bats: L **Throws:** R
Ht: 6'1" **Wt:** 197
Opening Day Age: 27
Born: 8/12/1968
Drafted: PIT86 8/186
ML Seasons: 3

Overall Statistics

	G	AB	R	H	2B	3B	HR	RBI	SB	CS	BB	SO	BA	OBA
95 PHI	59	104	21	37	7	0	3	19	1	1	11	19	.356	.419
Career	139	256	32	73	18	0	3	37	3	2	21	47	.285	.340

1995 Situational Statistics

	AB	HR	RBI	BA	OBA	SLG		AB	HR	RBI	BA	OBA	SLG
Home	53	2	15	.434	.492	.642	LHP	21	1	5	.524	.593	.762
Road	51	1	4	.275	.345	.373	RHP	83	2	14	.313	.367	.446
Apr-Jun	55	2	9	.382	.433	.564	ScPos	31	2	18	.452	.500	.710
Jul-Oct	49	1	10	.327	.404	.449	Clutch	28	2	9	.357	.438	.643

SCOUTING REPORT

Considered a good hitting prospect for years, Longmire has been slow to develop due to injuries. Tony hits breaking balls well but does not have good plate discipline. With a long swing, he can be overmatched by good fastballs although he has some power. Defensively, Longmire is a corner outfielder without the arm to play right field everyday. He has above-average range and can fill in in center field in an emergency. With slightly below-average speed and previous leg problems, he doesn't steal very often.

HOW HE PERFORMED IN '95

Longmire may have found his eventual role as a lefthanded pinch-hitter and reserve outfielder. He led the team with 11 pinch-hit runs batted in, the Phillies' most since 1979. Unfortunately, he fractured his left wrist in early August while diving for a ball, ending his season. He finished 10-for-33 as a pinch-hitter with 3 homers.

WHAT TO EXPECT IN '96

Tony clearly isn't a .356 hitter as he was last year, but he also isn't a .237 hitter as he was in 1994. He could develop into a good role player, but expectations of his being a solid regular outfielder are overly optimistic.

TOM MARSH

Position: OF
Bats: R **Throws:** R
Ht: 6'2" **Wt:** 180
Opening Day Age: 30
Born: 12/27/1965
Drafted: PHI88 15/406
ML Seasons: 3

Overall Statistics

	G	AB	R	H	2B	3B	HR	RBI	SB	CS	BB	SO	BA	OBA
95 PHI	43	109	13	32	3	1	3	15	0	1	4	25	.294	.316
Career	93	252	23	62	7	4	5	34	0	2	7	49	.246	.266

1995 Situational Statistics

	AB	HR	RBI	BA	OBA	SLG		AB	HR	RBI	BA	OBA	SLG
Home	53	1	3	.283	.296	.377	LHP	56	1	5	.268	.305	.357
Road	56	2	12	.304	.333	.464	RHP	53	2	10	.321	.327	.491
Apr-Jun	37	2	8	.297	.297	.514	ScPos	34	1	11	.294	.306	.382
Jul-Oct	72	1	7	.292	.325	.375	Clutch	15	0	3	.200	.250	.200

SCOUTING REPORT

Tom is a very aggressive contact hitter with some power, feasting on fastballs high and over the plate. However, like many hitters of this type, he lacks the good plate discipline needed to get good pitches to hit. However, he has average speed on the basepaths and will steal an occasional base.

In the outfield, Marsh displays average range in left with an average-plus arm in left field. He can play right field if needed but is not as good there.

HOW HE PERFORMED IN '95

Marsh walked four times and fanned 25 last season, thereby improving his major-league K/W numbers! Not a .294 hitter except at Triple-A Scranton, where he holds the franchise record for career homers and extra-base hits. He was disabled in mid-August with a concussion and cervical strain after being kneed in the head in Houston while breaking up a DP, but he came back just 15 days later.

WHAT TO EXPECT IN '96

Tom always plays hard, always hustles and is a good Triple-A player, but he will be lucky to ever see 100 at-bats in the majors again. A fringe role player at best.

PHILADELPHIA PHILLIES

RUSS SPRINGER

Position: RP/SP
Bats: R **Throws:** R
Ht: 6'4" **Wt:** 195
Opening Day Age: 27
Born: 11/7/1968
Drafted: NYA89 6/181
ML Seasons: 4

Overall Statistics

	G	GS	GF	SV	W	L	ERA	IP	H	R	ER	HR	BB	SO
95 CAL/PHI	33	6	6	1	1	2	5.29	78.1	82	48	46	16	35	70
Career	79	20	20	3	4	10	5.99	200.0	226	135	133	36	91	141

1995 Situational Statistics

	W	L	ERA	SV	IP	BB	SO		AB	HR	RBI	BA	OBA	SLG
Home	0	1	6.23	0	39.0	18	35	LHB	134	5	18	.306	.415	.493
Road	1	1	4.35	1	39.1	17	35	RHB	170	11	34	.241	.307	.500
Apr-Jun	0	2	6.53	1	30.1	12	27	ScPos	75	6	30	.240	.352	.533
Jul-Oct	1	0	4.50	0	48.0	23	43	Clutch	20	4	8	.300	.481	.900

SCOUTING REPORT

Springer has a cross-body motion from low three quarters and a straight fastball with average-plus velocity. He throws an average-minus curve and will show a change. His control has been very poor in the majors.

Russ allowed 8 of 9 baserunners to steal successfully in 1995, which will have to improve if he's to pitch in the NL. He fanned once and sacrificed once in his first two ML at-bats and is an adequate fielder.

HOW HE PERFORMED IN '95

Despite being regarded as a good prospect, Springer pitched himself out of the AL. With the Phils, he came on strong—as have many young pitchers—dramatically improving his control and striking out 32 in 27 innings. He did allow five homers in 27 innings, which is a sign that his stuff isn't good enough to be in the strike zone.

WHAT TO EXPECT IN '96

The Phillies like Springer, so he will get every chance to stick and could even be tried out as a starter. He will have to solve his problems with lefty hitters if he is going to start games, otherwise his only role will be in middle relief. Some potential, but a good chance he'll relapse.

GARY VARSHO

Position: OF
Bats: L **Throws:** R
Ht: 5'11" **Wt:** 190
Opening Day Age: 34
Born: 6/20/1961
Drafted: CHN82 6/107
ML Seasons: 8

Overall Statistics

	G	AB	R	H	2B	3B	HR	RBI	SB	CS	BB	SO	BA	OBA
95 PHI	72	103	7	26	1	1	0	11	2	0	7	17	.252	.310
Career	571	837	101	204	41	11	10	84	27	5	55	146	.244	.294

1995 Situational Statistics

	AB	HR	RBI	BA	OBA	SLG		AB	HR	RBI	BA	OBA	SLG
Home	56	0	3	.214	.279	.214	LHP	4	0	0	.250	.250	.250
Road	47	0	8	.298	.346	.362	RHP	99	0	11	.253	.312	.283
Apr-Jun	64	0	6	.297	.333	.297	ScPos	34	0	10	.265	.316	.294
Jul-Oct	39	0	5	.179	.273	.256	Clutch	33	0	6	.212	.341	.242

SCOUTING REPORT

A good fastball hitter but with no power, Varsho puts the ball in play. He is a good pinch-hitter with the ability to keep in shape and come off the bench—that's what keeps him in the big leagues.

In the outfield, Gary has adequate range and average hands but a poor arm. He has decent speed but no longer attempts to steal.

HOW HE PERFORMED IN '95

A bit player with a good attitude, Varsho is the kind of guy managers love. He'll do anything asked of him without complaining. However, he's just not that much of a hitter, with little power and not much patience. Amazingly, he managed only two extra-base hits with no homers in 103 at-bats in 1995, despite being platooned almost exclusively. He is a good percentage basestealer, though, running his career record to 27 steals in 34 tries in 1995.

WHAT TO EXPECT IN '96

Varsho can hang around like this for years, adding to his pension time, as long as he hits .250 and if he recovers some of his previous line-drive power.

THE SCOUTING REPORT: 1996 — 547

PHILADELPHIA PHILLIES

LENNY WEBSTER

Position: C
Bats: R **Throws:** R
Ht: 5'9" **Wt:** 185
Opening Day Age: 31
Born: 2/10/1965
Drafted: MIN85 21/535
ML Seasons: 7

Overall Statistics

	G	AB	R	H	2B	3B	HR	RBI	SB	CS	BB	SO	BA	OBA
95 PHI	49	150	18	40	9	0	4	14	0	0	16	27	.267	.337
Career	242	577	66	151	35	1	14	67	1	2	62	83	.262	.339

1995 Situational Statistics

	AB	HR	RBI	BA	OBA	SLG		AB	HR	RBI	BA	OBA	SLG
Home	76	1	6	.263	.325	.368	LHP	48	1	5	.250	.345	.396
Road	74	3	8	.270	.349	.446	RHP	102	3	9	.275	.333	.412
Apr-Jun	44	0	3	.205	.271	.250	ScPos	43	0	9	.209	.320	.209
Jul-Oct	106	4	11	.292	.364	.472	Clutch	27	0	2	.259	.333	.296

SCOUTING REPORT
A decent veteran backup catcher, Lenny has good hands and a plus arm, but he has a slow release and his throws are frequently off-target. At the plate, he is a high, inside fastball hitter with some power and good discipline although he has a slow bat. He runs like most veteran catchers do.

HOW HE PERFORMED IN '95
Webster has some power, takes a walk, and hits for a decent average. He's not an exceptionally good defensive catcher, but he's not an embarrassment, either. Lenny got a lot of playing time at the end of the season when Darren Daulton went down, but not much beforehand: that's a function of his manager more than a statement about Lenny's skills.

WHAT TO EXPECT IN '96
The Phillies were shopping Webster around last fall, and there's a good chance they'll deal him and let prospect Mike Lieberthal, who is out of options, take over the #2 job. If not, Webster will probably stick with the Phils as insurance against another Daulton injury or a flop by Lieberthal.

MIKE WILLIAMS

Position: RP/SP
Bats: R **Throws:** R
Ht: 6'2" **Wt:** 190
Opening Day Age: 26
Born: 7/29/1969
Drafted: PHI90 14/374
ML Seasons: 4

Overall Statistics

	G	GS	GF	SV	W	L	ERA	IP	H	R	ER	HR	BB	SO
95 PHI	33	8	7	0	3	3	3.29	87.2	78	37	32	10	29	57
Career	67	25	11	0	7	11	4.42	217.2	218	120	107	25	78	124

1995 Situational Statistics

	W	L	ERA	SV	IP	BB	SO		AB	HR	RBI	BA	OBA	SLG
Home	1	1	4.03	0	44.2	16	38	LHB	145	6	17	.193	.280	.372
Road	2	2	2.51	0	43.0	13	19	RHB	182	4	20	.275	.323	.418
Apr-Jun	0	1	4.70	0	30.2	12	22	ScPos	92	2	24	.152	.257	.250
Jul-Oct	3	2	2.53	0	57.0	17	35	Clutch	18	0	3	.222	.375	.444

SCOUTING REPORT
Mike is a classic three-quarters sinker-slider pitcher with adequate stuff who needs good control to be effective. In addition to his two primary pitches, he will also throw an average-minus change-up.

Opposing runners were 9-for-11 when stealing last year, an area he needs to improve on although some of that was due to the Phillies' catchers. Although he was only 2-for-16 at the plate last season, Mike laid down seven sacrifice bunts, thus fulfilling his offensive duties. He is a decent fielder off the mound.

HOW HE PERFORMED IN '95
On his fourth try in as many years, Williams got it right last season and turned in a good year as a spot starter/long reliever. However, 1995 was as good as he's ever going to be.

WHAT TO EXPECT IN '96
Williams' role is the classic middle reliever who gets some occasional starts when the pitching staff is struggling. If the Phillies continue to keep him in that role, he can contribute. If he gets put in the rotation for an extended period, he's probably going to get hit hard.

PHILADELPHIA PHILLIES: TOP PROSPECTS

DAVE DOSTER

Bats: R Throws: R Opening Day Age: 26
Ht: 5-10 Wt: 185 Born: 10/8/1970
Position: 2B Drafted: 1993 #27 PHI

YR TEAM	LG/CLASS	G	AB	R	H	2B	3B	HR	RBI	SB	BA	OBA
93 Spartanburg	SAL/A	60	223	34	61	15	0	3	20	1	.274	.353
93 Clearwater	FSL/A	9	28	4	10	3	1	0	2	0	.357	.400
94 Clearwater	FSL/A	131	480	76	135	42	4	13	74	12	.281	.362
95 Reading	EAST/AA	139	551	84	146	39	3	21	79	11	.265	.333

Doster, a steady second baseman who makes all of the plays in the field, has excellent power for a middle infielder. Building on an outstanding season in 1994, Doster broke the Reading club record with 39 doubles last season while leading the Eastern League in total bases (254) and extra-base hits. The Indiana State product went 37 games without an error in one 193 chance-stretch and is adept at turning the double play. The 25-year-old capped his fine season with a stellar playoff, hitting .361 with six home runs and 14 RBI in eight games.

BOBBY ESTALELLA

Bats: R Throws: R Opening Day Age: 22
Ht: 6-1 Wt: 200 Born: 8/23/1974
Position: C Drafted: 1992 #22 PHI

YR TEAM	LG/CLASS	G	AB	R	H	2B	3B	HR	RBI	SB	BA	OBA
93 Martinsvlle	APPY/R	35	122	14	36	11	0	3	19	0	.295	.377
93 Clearwater	FSL/A	11	35	4	8	0	0	0	4	0	.229	.270
94 Spartanburg	SAL/A	86	299	34	65	19	1	9	41	0	.217	.290
24 Clearwater	FSL/A	13	46	3	12	1	0	2	9	0	.261	.300
95 Reading	EAST/AA	10	34	5	8	1	0	2	9	0	.235	.333
95 Clearwater	FSL/A	117	404	61	105	24	1	15	58	0	.260	.350

An agile receiver with a quick release, Estalella reaped the benefits of off-season conditioning with his best offensive season in 1995. Playing in the pitcher-friendly Florida State League, the Miami native used his compact swing to smack 15 home runs, the fifth highest total in the league. The 21-year-old threw out 41% of opposing baserunners and was selected to the post-season All-Star team. He was promoted to Reading in late August and hit two grand slams in his first week there.

WAYNE GOMES

Bats: R Throws: R Opening Day Age: 23
Ht: 6-0 Wt: 215 Born: 1/15/1973
Position: P Drafted: 1993 #1 PHI

YR TEAM	LG/CLASS	G	GS	GF	SV	W	L	ERA	IP	H	HR	BB	SO	O/BA
93 Batavia	NYP/A	5	0	3	0	1	0	1.23	7.1	1	0	8	11	.042
93 Clearwater	FSL/A	9	0	8	4	0	1	1.17	7.2	4	0	9	13	.143
94 Clearwater	FSL/A	23	21	0	0	6	8	4.74	104.1	85	5	82	102	.222
95 Reading	EAST/AA	22	22	0	0	7	4	3.96	104.2	89	8	70	102	.230

Gomes, the fourth player selected in the 1993 draft, successfully made the jump to Double-A last season. The 23-year-old converted reliever has the best fastball in the organization and also throws a curve and an occasional changeup, but still needs much better command. Gomes made just one start between May 11 and June 24 due to stomach and groin injuries.

MIKE GRACE

Bats: R Throws: R Opening Day Age: 26
Ht: 6-4 Wt: 210 Born: 6/20/1970
Position: P Drafted: 1991 #10 PHI

YR TEAM	LG/CLASS	G	GS	GF	SV	W	L	ERA	IP	H	HR	BB	SO	O/BA
91 Batavia	NYP/A	6	6	0	0	1	2	1.39	32.1	20	3	14	36	.189
91 Spartanburg	SAL/A	6	6	0	0	3	1	1.89	33.1	24	1	9	23	.211
92 Spartanburg	SAL/A	6	6	0	0	1	4	4.94	27.1	25	3	8	21	.238
94 Spartanburg	SAL/A	15	15	0	0	5	5	4.82	80.1	84	6	20	45	.269
95 Scnton-WB	INT/AAA	2	2	0	0	2	0	1.59	17.0	17	0	2	13	.258
95 Reading	EAST/AA	24	24	0	0	13	6	3.54	147.1	137	13	35	118	.245
95 Philadelphia	NL/MAJ	2	2	0	0	1	1	3.18	11.1	10	0	4	7	.238

In his career Grace has had three elbow operations, including one which caused him to miss the entire 1993 season. The 25-year-old did not miss a start in the minors last year, but ended the season disabled again after making his major league debut. He won seven of his last eight decisions and was leading the Eastern League in wins when promoted to Scranton. He won both starts there and was summoned to the big leagues. Grace is not overpowering, but has excellent control and throws in the upper-80's.

RICH HUNTER

Bats: R Throws: R Opening Day Age: 22
Ht: 6-1 Wt: 180 Born: 9/25/1974
Position: P Drafted: 1993 #14 PHI

YR TEAM	LG/CLASS	G	GS	GF	SV	W	L	ERA	IP	H	HR	BB	SO	O/BA
93 Martinsvlle	APPY/R	13	9	1	0	0	6	9.55	49.0	82	9	27	36	.380
94 Martinsvlle	APPY/R	18	0	8	5	3	2	4.50	38.0	31	3	9	39	.220
95 Reading	EAST/AA	3	3	0	0	3	0	2.05	22.0	14	1	6	17	.177
95 Clearwater	FSL/A	9	9	0	0	6	0	2.93	58.1	62	3	7	46	.276
95 Piedmont	SAL/A	15	15	0	0	10	2	2.77	104.0	79	9	19	80	.207

The Phillies' 1995 Pitcher of the Year led the minors with 19 wins and did not lose a game after June 3. He excelled at three levels and picked up his 20th win the Eastern League playoffs. He allowed three runs or fewer in 20 of 27 starts and pitched at least six innings 25 times. The 21-year-old succeeds with excellent control, changes speeds, and is extremely poised on the mound. He also helps himself by being a good fielder and holding runners well.

KEVIN JORDAN

Bats: R Throws: R Opening Day Age: 27
Ht: 6-1 Wt: 185 Born: 10/9/1969
Position: 2B Drafted: 1990 #20 NYA

YR TEAM	LG/CLASS	G	AB	R	H	2B	3B	HR	RBI	SB	BA	OBA
93 Albany	EAST/AA	135	513	87	145	33	4	16	87	8	.283	.344
94 Scnton-WB	INT/AAA	81	314	44	91	22	1	12	57	0	.290	.348
95 Scnton-WB	INT/AAA	106	410	61	127	29	4	5	60	3	.310	.361
95 Philadelphia	NL/MAJ	24	54	6	10	1	0	2	6	0	.185	.228

A career .297 hitter, Jordan once again posted a solid season at the plate in '95, finishing fifth in the International League in doubles and seventh in batting. Primarily a ground ball hitter, the Nebraska product does have gap power, and is considered a smart baserunner despite declining stolen base totals. The rap on Jordan is poor defense, but the All-Star second baseman has improved his range and his .976 fielding percentage in 1995 was the highest of his six-year career.

PHILADELPHIA PHILLIES: TOP PROSPECTS

MIKE LIEBERTHAL

Bats: R Throws: R Opening Day Age: 24
Ht: 6-0 Wt: 170 Born: 1/18/1972
Position: C Drafted: 1990 #1 PHI

YR TEAM	LG/CLASS	G	AB	R	H	2B	3B	HR	RBI	SB	BA	OBA
93 Scnton-WB	INT/AAA	112	382	35	100	17	0	7	40	2	.262	.313
94 Scnton-WB	INT/AAA	84	296	23	69	16	0	1	32	1	.233	.286
94 Phila	NL/MAJ	24	79	6	21	3	1	1	5	0	.266	.301
95 Scnton-WB	INT/AAA	85	278	44	78	20	2	6	42	1	.281	.388
95 Philadelphia	NL/MAJ	16	47	1	12	2	0	0	4	0	.255	.327

Lieberthal, the third player drafted in 1990, had his finest offensive season last year, setting career marks in runs, RBI, slugging and on-base percentage despite being slowed by a hip pointer injury. The 24-year-old has good strike zone judgement and some gap power but has never reached double digits in home runs. The California native has an excellent defensive reputation, yet threw out just 22% of opposing baserunners at Scranton and allowed 15 passed balls in his two stops last year.

CARLTON LOEWER

Bats: S Throws: R Opening Day Age: 23
Ht: 6-6 Wt: 220 Born: 9/24/1973
Position: P Drafted: 1994 #1 PHI

YR TEAM	LG/CLASS	G	GS	GF	SV	W	L	ERA	IP	H	HR	BB	SO	O/BA
95 Reading	EAST/AA	8	8	0	0	4	1	2.16	50.0	42	3	31	35	.235
95 Clearwater	FSL/A	20	20	0	0	7	5	3.30	114.2	124	6	36	83	.274

The 1994 first-round pick did not make his professional debut until last season but was very impressive at two stops. He struggled early at Clearwater, but pitched very well in his last five starts before being promoted to Reading where he had five outstanding appearances in his last six starts. The 22-year-old features a fastball in the low 90's with good movement, a curveball, and a changeup, but still struggles with his control.

WENDELL MAGEE

Bats: R Throws: R Opening Day Age: 24
Ht: 6-0 Wt: 225 Born: 8/3/1972
Position: OF Drafted: 1994 #12 PHI

YR TEAM	LG/CLASS	G	AB	R	H	2B	3B	HR	RBI	SB	BA	OBA
94 Batavia	NYP/A	63	229	42	64	12	4	2	35	10	.279	.335
95 Reading	EAST/AA	39	136	17	40	9	1	3	21	3	.294	.379
95 Clearwater	FSL/A	96	388	67	137	24	5	6	46	7	.353	.405

Magee, slated for a utility role until injuries opened up a starting spot, blossomed into one of the best batting prospects in the Florida State League last year. A hard worker with big league power potential, the former football player at Samford (AL) makes good contact and only once went two games without a hit at Clearwater. The 23-year-old All-Star won the batting title and finished second in slugging and fourth in on-base percentage. Despite having above-average speed, Magee is a poor percentage basestealer and needs to work on his defensive play, as he committed ten errors in left field.

RYAN NYE

Bats: R Throws: R Opening Day Age: 23
Ht: 6-2 Wt: 195 Born: 6/24/1973
Position: P Drafted: 1994 #2 PHI

YR TEAM	LG/CLASS	G	GS	GF	SV	W	L	ERA	IP	H	HR	BB	SO	O/BA
94 Batavia	NYP/A	13	12	0	0	7	2	2.64	71.2	64	3	15	71	.229
95 Clearwater	FSL/A	27	27	0	0	12	7	3.40	167.0	164	8	33	116	.259

Nye, a tough competitor, finished the year on a hot streak by winning seven of his last eight decisions, including his final four starts of the season. Selected out of Texas Tech in 1994, Nye has just an average fastball, but complements it with a sinker and a plus slider and has good command of all three pitches. The big righthander spun two three-hitters during the year, and finished third in the Florida State League in wins and innings pitched.

SCOTT ROLEN

Bats: R Throws: R Opening Day Age: 21
Ht: 6-4 Wt: 210 Born: 4/4/1975
Position: 3B Drafted: 1993 #2 PHI

YR TEAM	LG/CLASS	G	AB	R	H	2B	3B	HR	RBI	SB	BA	OBA
93 Martinsvlle	APPY/R	25	80	8	25	5	0	0	12	3	.313	.429
94 Spartanburg	SAL/A	138	513	83	151	34	5	14	72	6	.294	.363
95 Reading	EAST/AA	20	76	16	22	3	0	3	15	1	.289	.353
95 Clearwater	FSL/A	66	238	45	69	13	2	10	39	4	.290	.392

Scouts love the package Rolen brings to the park each night: a compact swing that generates power to all fields, a powerful but still developing body, quick reflexes, soft hands and a very strong arm. A member of the Howe Sportsdata All-Teenager team, Rolen spent the first half of the season on the sidelines with a broken hamate bone in his left hand, but wasted no time to get back in the groove when activated. Although extremely young and talented, Rolen still needs work at the hot corner and is only an average base runner.

GENE SCHALL

Bats: R Throws: R Opening Day Age: 26
Ht: 6-3 Wt: 190 Born: 6/5/1970
Position: OF Drafted: 1991 #4 PHI

YR TEAM	LG/CLASS	G	AB	R	H	2B	3B	HR	RBI	SB	BA	OBA
93 Reading	EAST/AA	82	285	51	93	12	4	15	60	2	.326	.394
93 Scnton-WB	INT/AAA	40	139	16	33	6	1	4	16	4	.237	.355
94 Scnton-WB	INT/AAA	127	463	54	132	35	4	16	89	9	.285	.358
95 Scnton-WB	INT/AAA	92	320	52	100	25	4	12	63	0	.313	.415
95 Philadelphia	NL/MAJ	24	65	2	15	2	0	0	5	0	.231	.306

For the second straight season, Schall ripped Triple-A pitching. A productive RBI man with good bat speed, the Villanova product finished second in the International League in on-base percentage, fourth in slugging, and fifth in batting. The 25-year-old led league first basemen in errors in 1994 with 14, but committed just four last year splitting time between first base and the outfield.

PHILADELPHIA PHILLIES: OTHERS TO WATCH

MATT BEECH Bats: L Throws: L Ht: 6-2 Wt: 190
Born: 1/20/1972 Drafted: 1994 #7 PHI Position: P

YR TEAM	LG/CLASS	G	GS	GF	SV	W	L	ERA	IP	H	HR	BB	SO	O/BA
95 Reading	EAST/AA	14	13	0	0	2	4	2.96	79.0	67	7	33	70	.225
95 Clearwater	FSL/A	15	15	0	0	9	4	4.19	86.0	87	5	30	85	.268

A crafty lefthander with a fastball, curve and slider, Beech is consistently around the plate and he led the organization in KS.

ROB BUTLER Bats: L Throws: L Ht: 5-11 Wt: 185
Born: 4/10/1970 Drafted: NDF 9-24-90 TOR Position: OF

YR TEAM	LG/CLASS	G	AB	R	H	2B	3B	HR	RBI	SB	BA	OBA
95 Scnton-WB	INT/AAA	92	327	46	98	16	4	3	35	5	.300	.355

Acquired from the Blue Jays, Butler was the International League's best hitter in June and does well against southpaws.

ANDY CARTER Bats: L Throws: L Ht: 6-5 Wt: 190
Born: 11/9/1968 Drafted: 1987 #36 PHI Position: P

YR TEAM	LG/CLASS	G	GS	GF	SV	W	L	ERA	IP	H	HR	BB	SO	O/BA
95 Scnton-WB	INT/AAA	14	1	5	0	1	2	4.35	20.2	17	2	13	18	.230
95 Philadelphia	NL/MAJ	4	0	1	0	0	0	6.14	7.1	4	3	2	6	.167

The big lefthander saw limited action due to a broken thumb from a brawl, but has been tough on lefties the past two seasons.

BLAKE DOOLAN Bats: R Throws: R Ht: 6-0 Wt: 178
Born: 2/11/1969 Drafted: 1992 #32 PHI Position: P

YR TEAM	LG/CLASS	G	GS	GF	SV	W	L	ERA	IP	H	HR	BB	SO	O/BA
95 Reading	EAST/AA	60	0	45	16	11	5	2.22	73.0	63	3	27	50	.238

A former outfielder, Doolan keeps the ball down and he led the Eastern League in appearances.

ROB GRABLE Bats: R Throws: R Ht: 6-2 Wt: 200
Born: 1/20/1970 Drafted: 1991 #25 DET Position: OF

YR TEAM	LG/CLASS	G	AB	R	H	2B	3B	HR	RBI	SB	BA	OBA
95 Scnton-WB	INT/AAA	26	83	7	19	4	0	3	11	3	.229	.297
95 Reading	EAST/AA	103	353	71	106	24	1	16	67	15	.300	.408

After missing most of '94 with a hand injury, Grable switched from third base to the outfield and had the best offensive season of his five-year career.

BRONSON HEFLIN Bats: R Throws: R Ht: 6-3 Wt: 195
Born: 8/29/1971 Drafted: 1994 #37 PHI Position: P

YR TEAM	LG/CLASS	G	GS	GF	SV	W	L	ERA	IP	H	HR	BB	SO	O/BA
95 Reading	EAST/AA	1	0	1	0	0	0	0.00	1.0	0	0	1	2	.000
95 Clearwater	FSL/A	57	0	44	21	2	3	2.95	61.0	52	3	21	84	.228

Mixing an average fastball with a good slider, Heflin led all minor league relievers with a 12.39 SO/9 IP ratio.

DAN HELD Bats: R Throws: R Ht: 6-0 Wt: 200
Born: 10/7/1970 Drafted: 1993 #42 PHI Position: 1B

YR TEAM	LG/CLASS	G	AB	R	H	2B	3B	HR	RBI	SB	BA	OBA
95 Reading	EAST/AA	2	4	2	2	1	0	1	3	1	.500	.667
95 Clearwater	FSL/A	134	489	82	133	35	1	21	82	2	.272	.366

A good defensive first baseman with an all-or-nothing swing, Held led the Florida State League in home runs and set a Clearwater record by getting hit by a pitch 19 times.

RICK HOLIFIELD Bats: L Throws: L Ht: 6-2 Wt: 165
Born: 3/25/1970 Drafted: 1988 #21 TOR Position: OF

YR TEAM	LG/CLASS	G	AB	R	H	2B	3B	HR	RBI	SB	BA	OBA
95 Scnton-WB	INT/AAA	76	223	32	46	6	3	3	24	21	.206	.297
95 Reading	EAST/AA	30	93	18	23	3	1	1	5	5	.247	.397

The 26-year-old provides quickness and defense, but an uppercut swing neutralizes his speed—Holifield's best asset.

RYAN KARP Bats: L Throws: L Ht: 6-4 Wt: 205
Born: 4/5/1970 Drafted: 1992 #7 NYA Position: P

YR TEAM	LG/CLASS	G	GS	GF	SV	W	L	ERA	IP	H	HR	BB	SO	O/BA
95 Scnton-WB	INT/AAA	13	13	0	0	7	1	4.20	81.1	81	6	31	73	.255
95 Reading	EAST/AA	7	7	0	0	1	2	3.06	47.0	44	4	15	37	.256
95 Philadelphia	NL/MAJ	1	0	0	0	0	0	4.50	2.0	1	0	3	2	.143

A master at changing speeds but has had shoulder problems.

BRIAN KOELLING Bats: R Throws: R Ht: 6-1 Wt: 185
Born: 6/11/1969 Drafted: 1991 #14 CIN Position: 2B

YR TEAM	LG/CLASS	G	AB	R	H	2B	3B	HR	RBI	SB	BA	OBA
95 Scnton-WB	INT/AAA	16	53	5	14	1	0	0	3	3	.264	.273
95 Chattanooga	SOU/AA	107	432	71	128	21	7	3	44	30	.296	.358

Acquired from the Reds for Mariano Duncan, Koelling has good speed and can play both second base and shortstop, but has never established himself above Double-A.

FRED McNAIR Bats: R Throws: R Ht: 6-4 Wt: 215
Born: 1/31/1970 Drafted: 1989 #9 SEA Position: DH

YR TEAM	LG/CLASS	G	AB	R	H	2B	3B	HR	RBI	SB	BA	OBA
95 Scnton-WB	INT/AAA	9	25	1	6	1	0	0	2	0	.240	.310
95 Reading	EAST/AA	108	395	64	107	24	1	23	68	3	.271	.339

Acquired from the Mariners in 1994 for Shawn Boskie, McNair drives the ball to all fields and led the EL in home runs.

JASON MOLER Bats: R Throws: R Ht: 6-1 Wt: 195
Born: 10/29/1969 Drafted: 1992 #3 PHI Position: 3B

YR TEAM	LG/CLASS	G	AB	R	H	2B	3B	HR	RBI	SB	BA	OBA
95 Reading	EAST/AA	22	83	17	22	3	0	2	14	2	.265	.354

Moler, a converted catcher, is a solid hitter but missed much of last season due to a broken leg.

CHUCK RICCI Bats: R Throws: R Ht: 6-2 Wt: 180
Born: 11/20/1968 Drafted: 1987 #5 BAL Position: P

YR TEAM	LG/CLASS	G	GS	GF	SV	W	L	ERA	IP	H	HR	BB	SO	O/BA
95 Scnton-WB	INT/AAA	68	0	48	25	4	3	2.49	65.0	48	6	24	66	.203
95 Philadelphia	NL/MAJ	7	0	3	0	1	0	1.80	10.0	9	0	3	9	.273

The 27-year-old led the International League in games and saves by keeping the ball down and working out of jams.

SCOTT SHORES Bats: R Throws: R Ht: 6-1 Wt: 190
Born: 2/4/1972 Drafted: 1994 #5 PHI Position: OF

YR TEAM	LG/CLASS	G	AB	R	H	2B	3B	HR	RBI	SB	BA	OBA
95 Clearwater	FSL/A	133	460	74	117	23	5	7	52	30	.254	.345

Drafted twice before the Phillies selected him in 1994, Shores has above-average speed, a good arm, and surprising pop.

JON ZUBER Bats: L Throws: L Ht: 6-1 Wt: 175
Born: 12/10/1969 Drafted: 1992 #11 PHI Position: 1B

YR TEAM	LG/CLASS	G	AB	R	H	2B	3B	HR	RBI	SB	BA	OBA
95 Scnton-WB	INT/AAA	119	418	53	120	19	5	3	50	1	.287	.360

A smooth-fielding first baseman, Zuber has gap power and finished tenth in the organization in batting.

PITTSBURGH PIRATES

JAY BELL

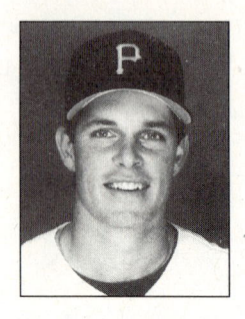

Positions: SS//3B
Bats: R **Throws:** R
Ht: 6'1" **Wt:** 180
Opening Day Age: 30
Born: 12/11/1965
Drafted: MIN84 1/8
ML Seasons: 10

SCOUTING REPORT
Bell is one of the better all-around shortstops in the majors. He employs a strong and accurate arm that allows him to successfully gun down batters from both the hole and from behind second base. Although Jay's range is diminishing and now is below par, he knows NL hitters and positions himself very well. In addition, his good, soft hands allow him to hold on to nearly everything he reaches.

A high-ball hitter, Bell continues to improve at the plate. He has average bat speed but knows how to handle the stick, with an ability to hit to all fields, hit-and-run, bunt effectively, and take pitches—both in order to let runners steal and to look for the walk when necessary. An intelligent, alert runner despite a tad below-average speed, Jay regularly turns singles into doubles but steals infrequently and ineffectively.

HOW HE PERFORMED IN '95
He started '95 slower than a turtle ankle-deep in molasses: on June 24, Bell was hitting only .198. From that date, however, the hits started to flow. In fact, after the All-Star break, Bell batted .292 with eight of his home runs. This second-half charge has become more pronounced for Bell in recent years.

All in all, his final .262 average ranked as Jay's lowest in five years but wasn't far from his career mark. Bell met or approached career norms in most other offensive categories.

He still strikes out more than he should. Bell's 110 whiffs during '95 means that he has now exceeded the century mark four times. However, Jay has always been a excellent bunter and set the team record with 39 sacrifice hits in '91. Asked to provide power to a punchless Pirates' lineup last year, he sacrificed just three times.

In '95, Bell made only 14 errors and ranked third in fielding percentage for NL shortstops, including a career-best string of 44 errorless games.

WHAT TO EXPECT IN '96
The current edition of the Pirates is built around Bell's talents. It will be interesting to see if he remains with the Bucs as his $4 million per year contract, which runs through '97, is a burden on the financially troubled club. With Carlos Garcia (a shortstop in the minors) able to take over, Pittsburgh may yet opt to trade Jay for economic reasons.

Overall Statistics

	G	AB	R	H	2B	3B	HR	RBI	SB	CS	BB	SO	BA	OBA
95 PIT	138	530	79	139	28	4	13	55	2	5	55	110	.262	.336
Career	1071	4002	598	1070	220	43	70	390	58	37	403	759	.267	.337

1995 Situational Statistics

	AB	HR	RBI	BA	OBA	SLG		AB	HR	RBI	BA	OBA	SLG
Home	260	8	25	.227	.303	.377	LHP	144	7	17	.306	.387	.535
Road	270	5	30	.296	.367	.430	RHP	386	6	38	.246	.316	.355
Apr-Jun	208	3	14	.221	.319	.298	ScPos	135	3	40	.230	.331	.333
Jul-Oct	322	10	41	.289	.347	.472	Clutch	91	0	9	.264	.337	.341

How He Compares to Other Batters

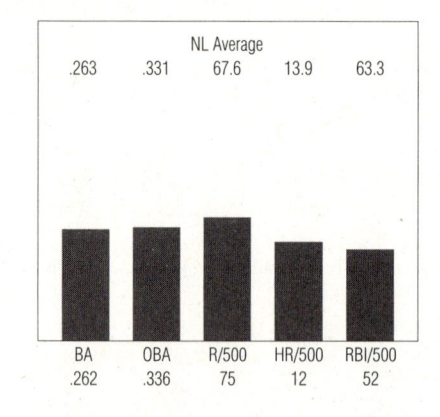

NL Average: .263 / .331 / 67.6 / 13.9 / 63.3

BA .262 | OBA .336 | R/500 75 | HR/500 12 | RBI/500 52

Where He Hits the Ball

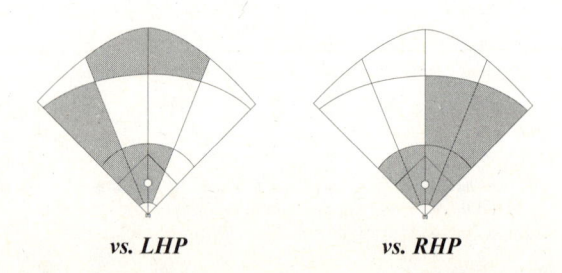

vs. LHP   vs. RHP

PITTSBURGH PIRATES

JACOB BRUMFIELD

Position: OF
Bats: R **Throws:** R
Ht: 6'0" **Wt:** 170
Opening Day Age: 30
Born: 5/27/1965
Drafted: CHN83 7/164
ML Seasons: 4

SCOUTING REPORT
Jacob is the Pirates' most exciting baserunner. He flies around the bases with well above-average speed and is a joy to watch running out a double or triple. A constant threat to steal every time he reaches, Brumfield rattles many pitchers when he is on base. A high fastball hitter, Jacob likes to turn on inside pitches and can occasionally pull with power. He will bunt for the hit, but does not often sacrifice.

He covered ground in center field last year, showing well above-average range. Despite his good hands, Brumfield appeared tentative at times and had occasional problems fielding the position. His arm strength and accuracy are just average.

HOW HE PERFORMED IN '95
Formerly a reserve with Cincinnati, Jacob Brumfield joined the Pirates and played his way off the bench. His 92 starts in center were a career high, and he set personal bests in almost every category. While not an exceptional hitter, he is good from both sides of the plate and is consistent from year-to-year. Jacob was clearly the Bucs' best baserunner, pacing the team in steals and legging out 18 infield hits (including three bunt singles). In mid-September he became the first Pirates' player in eight seasons to steal home without the aid of a double-steal.

Brumfield was involved in baseball's most bone-jarring outfield collision last year, a spectacular July 25 full-speed smashup with Dave Clark. Amazingly, Jacob held the ball and stayed in the lineup despite some cuts and bruises. The next month was his best of the season, as he batted .313 and scored 27 runs in 30 August contests.

He threw out eight runners from center but also made eight errors, fielding a far-below-league-average .969. Early in the year, Brumfield played timidly, but improved as the year progressed. When he plays the outfield with the same abandon he shows on the bases, Jacob is at his best.

WHAT TO EXPECT IN '96
Brumfield could become a permanent outfield fixture. Last year he shared center field with several others, but a .280 average, 30 doubles and 30 steals—numbers which aren't out of the question—would give Brumfield a job all to himself. He'll have to fight this spring with new arrival Mike Kingery to get a chance to put up those numbers.

Overall Statistics

	G	AB	R	H	2B	3B	HR	RBI	SB	CS	BB	SO	BA	OBA
95 PIT	116	402	64	109	23	2	4	26	22	12	37	71	.271	.339
Career	311	826	146	224	50	7	14	62	54	23	75	140	.271	.335

1995 Situational Statistics

	AB	HR	RBI	BA	OBA	SLG		AB	HR	RBI	BA	OBA	SLG
Home	208	4	17	.279	.351	.404	LHP	124	1	6	.298	.326	.419
Road	194	0	9	.263	.327	.330	RHP	278	3	20	.259	.345	.345
Apr-Jun	139	1	11	.245	.335	.331	ScPos	82	1	22	.256	.354	.366
Jul-Oct	263	3	15	.285	.341	.388	Clutch	68	2	7	.309	.392	.485

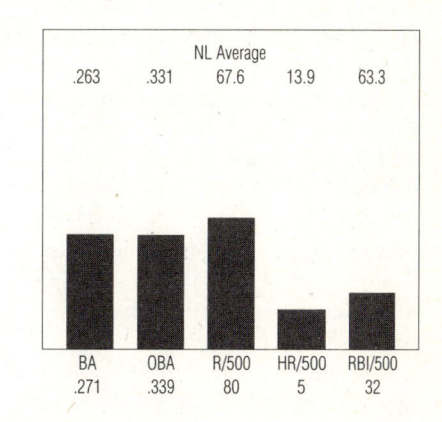

How He Compares to Other Batters

NL Average: .263 / .331 / 67.6 / 13.9 / 63.3

BA .271 | OBA .339 | R/500 80 | HR/500 5 | RBI/500 32

Where He Hits the Ball

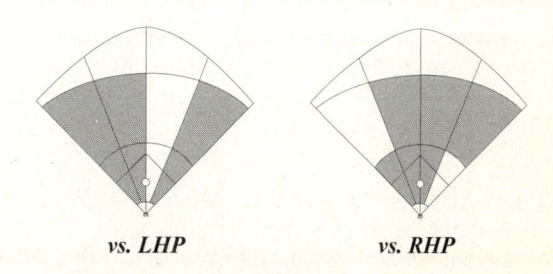

vs. LHP — vs. RHP

THE SCOUTING REPORT: 1996

PITTSBURGH PIRATES

CARLOS GARCIA

Positions: 2B/SS
Bats: R **Throws:** R
Ht: 6'1" **Wt:** 185
Opening Day Age: 28
Born: 10/15/1967
Drafted: PIT 1/9/87
ML Seasons: 6

SCOUTING REPORT

Carlos has a quick bat, likes inside fastballs, and is rarely overmatched by anyone. Good wrists allow him to pop an occasional pitch out of the park, but the free-swinging Garcia won't truly harness his productivity until he can make contact more consistently. He is most effective when keeping his stroke and backswing compact.

An effective sacrifice bunter when asked, Garcia does not walk enough to hit near the top of the order and is no longer asked to hit leadoff.

Ordinarily, Carlos runs as fast as any of his teammates. However, he played much of last year with both an injured knee and a strained hamstring which cut down on his speed. He is a smart runner.

Garcia has fine defensive tools, including well above-average hands, plus range, and a good, strong arm. While he is a fine defender at second base, Carlos is even better at shortstop (his minor-league position) due to his arm and range behind second base.

HOW HE PERFORMED IN '95

Garcia compiled his best batting average yet in his third major-league campaign despite a horrible start that saw him hitting just .217 on June 4. At that point, Carlos went on a 21-game hitting streak, batting .359 during the stretch. Garcia's hitting string was the second longest in the NL last year.

While his batting average has climbed, his power numbers have declined. Carlos clubbed 12 homers in '93 but has smacked just six in each of the last two years. However, his RBI total was more than respectable for a guy batting eighth much of the time.

Garcia entered the season recovering from a knee injury sustained in winter ball. He wore a brace for much of the year, and as a result, didn't run the way he had in 1993-94 when he led the team in steals.

Although Carlos doesn't have the range of his predecessor Jose Lind, he moves well to his left and chases pop flies well. A natural shortstop, Garcia is still learning how to play second.

WHAT TO EXPECT IN '96

Garcia is a dedicated worker. A return to double-digit numbers in both homers and steals would make him a complete player. He will play second as long as Jay Bell continues at shortstop; should Bell be dealt, Carlos will take his place.

Overall Statistics

	G	AB	R	H	2B	3B	HR	RBI	SB	CS	BB	SO	BA	OBA
95 PIT	104	367	41	108	24	2	6	50	8	4	25	55	.294	.340
Career	381	1392	174	385	65	11	24	130	44	24	73	208	.277	.317

1995 Situational Statistics

	AB	HR	RBI	BA	OBA	SLG		AB	HR	RBI	BA	OBA	SLG
Home	200	4	31	.315	.365	.450	LHP	105	1	12	.295	.342	.371
Road	167	2	19	.269	.309	.383	RHP	262	5	38	.294	.339	.439
Apr-Jun	178	3	23	.281	.321	.416	ScPos	93	1	40	.290	.361	.452
Jul-Oct	189	3	27	.307	.357	.423	Clutch	43	0	5	.186	.308	.256

How He Compares to Other Batters

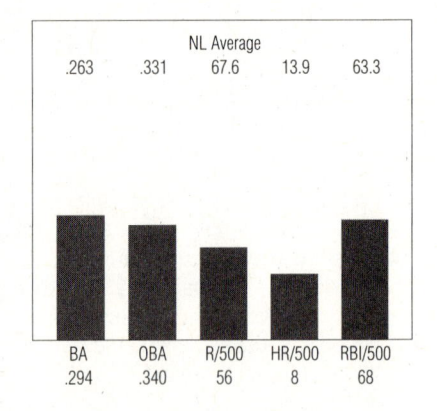

NL Average
.263 .331 67.6 13.9 63.3

BA	OBA	R/500	HR/500	RBI/500
.294	.340	56	8	68

Where He Hits the Ball

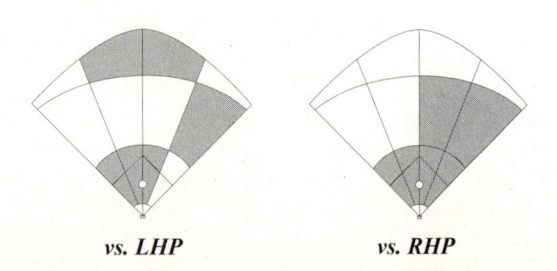

vs. LHP   vs. RHP

PITTSBURGH PIRATES

MARK JOHNSON

Position: 1B
Bats: L **Throws:** L
Ht: 6'4" **Wt:** 230
Opening Day Age: 28
Born: 10/17/1967
Drafted: PIT90 20/537
ML Seasons: 1

SCOUTING REPORT
The big first sacker swings for downtown on nearly every cut. When he hits the ball, it can clear any fence, but Johnson's problem is making contact. He is a show at the dish, with a wide-open stance, a lifted right leg, a coiled swing, and a big follow-through. Unfortunately, Mark has so many holes in his swing, and is so impatient, that pitchers learned quickly to pick him apart. He will have to improve his defense to stay in the majors. Johnson has average hands but minus range. While he can make the occasional diving stop, he has trouble following up due to a throwing arm that rates slightly below par in strength and accuracy. He lumbers around the bases with below-average speed, but Mark has never been timid about stealing bases and had unexpected success.

HOW HE PERFORMED IN '95
Johnson jumped to the majors without playing an inning of Triple-A, having spent three seasons in the Southern League. Mark began sharing first base with Rich Aude early in '95 when Orlando Merced moved to the outfield. Despite good power, Johnson had trouble adjusting to the majors, batting only .194 in his first 26 games. Slow improvement raised his average to a season-high .258 by July 4. Included was a four-game span in June where he clubbed three homers.

After the All-Star break, everything fell apart. Johnson went 10-for-80 in his next 27 games and found himself optioned to Calgary, where his season ended on August 24 due to a broken thumb. Pitchers, especially lefthanders, found Mark susceptible to change-ups and anything thrown down and away.

Johnson can provide much-needed power to the Pirates' lineup. His home runs were a key contribution, but must be complemented by more than a .208 batting average. His .986 fielding percentage was the lowest among NL regular first basemen as he got to few balls and made eight errors.

WHAT TO EXPECT IN '96
Johnson's power is impressive, but the club's signing of Charlie Hayes in the off-season means that former third sacker Jeff King could move across the diamond. If this happens, it will probably push either Mark or fellow first-base hopeful Rich Aude out of the organization.

Overall Statistics

	G	AB	R	H	2B	3B	HR	RBI	SB	CS	BB	SO	BA	OBA
95 PIT	79	221	32	46	6	1	13	28	5	2	37	66	.208	.326
Career	79	221	32	46	6	1	13	28	5	2	37	66	.208	.326

1995 Situational Statistics

	AB	HR	RBI	BA	OBA	SLG		AB	HR	RBI	BA	OBA	SLG
Home	100	7	14	.210	.352	.460	LHP	22	1	4	.182	.217	.364
Road	121	6	14	.207	.302	.388	RHP	199	12	24	.211	.336	.427
Apr-Jun	123	9	20	.252	.363	.520	ScPos	62	2	13	.113	.211	.226
Jul-Oct	98	4	8	.153	.278	.296	Clutch	34	1	1	.176	.300	.294

How He Compares to Other Batters

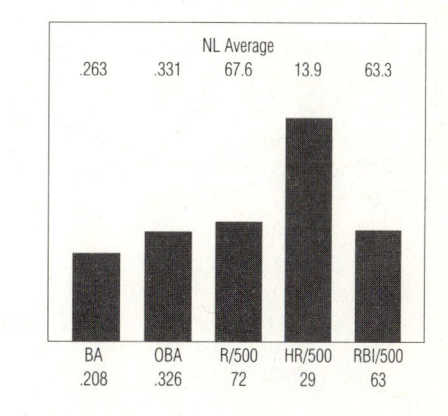

NL Average: BA .263, OBA .331, R/500 67.6, HR/500 13.9, RBI/500 63.3

Player: BA .208, OBA .326, R/500 72, HR/500 29, RBI/500 63

Where He Hits the Ball

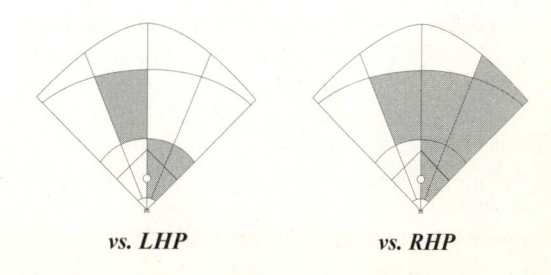

vs. LHP   vs. RHP

THE SCOUTING REPORT: 1996

PITTSBURGH PIRATES

JEFF KING

Positions: 3B/1B//2B/SS
Bats: R **Throws:** R
Ht: 6'1" **Wt:** 175
Opening Day Age: 31
Born: 12/26/1964
Drafted: PIT86 1/1
ML Seasons: 7

SCOUTING REPORT
King continues to improve as a hitter. He stands straight as a string at the plate, lashing pitches all over the field. Although he isn't a big home-run threat, Jeff improved last year at driving pitches, getting the most out of his average bat speed and power. King has become a more patient hitter and walks nearly as often as he strikes out.

A smart runner with minus speed, King rarely gets thrown out going for extra base. He steals only occasionally but did bunt for three hits in '95.

He can play any infield position, but has spent most of his time at third base. Wherever he plays, Jeff has well above-average hands, but his range is slightly below par. Although King throws sidearm, which causes occasional problems with accuracy, he has good arm strength.

HOW HE PERFORMED IN '95
Jeff is a solid threat in the Pirates' lean attack, leading the club in homers and RBI despite missing two weeks with a wrist injury. He batted clean-up last season in nearly 75 percent of his starts and responded well to the challenge, with a career-high 18 round-trippers (a huge increase over '94) and an RBI count rating as the second-best of his career. He hit righties better than lefties, reversing his '94 performance. Jeff's greatest surprise came on August 8 in San Francisco when he became the first Bucco in 101 years to club two homers in one inning.

Despite leading the '95 Pirates with 17 errors, Jeff proved once again to be a solid defensive player. His natural position is third base, but he said he is now more comfortable at first. He played all four infield positions in '95, an uncommon achievement.

WHAT TO EXPECT IN '96
The Pirates have signed King for the next two years and are expected to build the club around him and Jay Bell. Jeff's unpretentious attitude, continuing improvement, and growing versatility make him valuable. However, he is now 31 and has not been the healthiest of players. He will likely play first for the Bucs in '96 because of the signing of veteran free-agent Charlie Hayes.

Overall Statistics

	G	AB	R	H	2B	3B	HR	RBI	SB	CS	BB	SO	BA	OBA
95 PIT	122	445	61	118	27	2	18	87	7	4	55	63	.265	.342
Career	739	2570	328	657	137	12	69	382	32	24	226	310	.256	.314

1995 Situational Statistics

	AB	HR	RBI	BA	OBA	SLG		AB	HR	RBI	BA	OBA	SLG
Home	222	7	41	.239	.306	.410	LHP	112	7	19	.241	.348	.509
Road	223	11	46	.291	.377	.502	RHP	333	11	68	.273	.340	.438
Apr-Jun	150	6	35	.287	.377	.493	ScPos	137	3	60	.263	.351	.409
Jul-Oct	295	12	52	.254	.323	.437	Clutch	77	2	13	.247	.337	.403

How He Compares to Other Batters

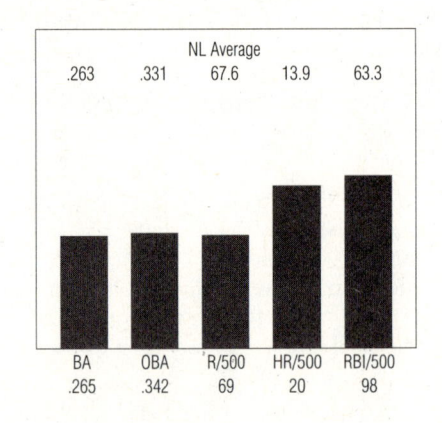

NL Average: BA .263 | OBA .331 | R/500 67.6 | HR/500 13.9 | RBI/500 63.3

Jeff King: BA .265 | OBA .342 | R/500 69 | HR/500 20 | RBI/500 98

Where He Hits the Ball

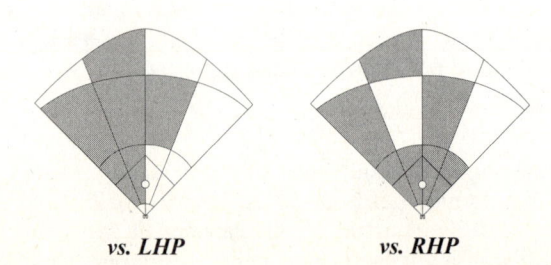

vs. LHP   vs. RHP

PITTSBURGH PIRATES

NELSON LIRIANO

Positions: 2B//3B/SS
Bats: B **Throws:** R
Ht: 5'10" **Wt:** 172
Opening Day Age: 31
Born: 6/3/1964
Drafted: TOR 11/1/82
ML Seasons: 8

SCOUTING REPORT
The aggressive, switch-hitting Liriano jumps at more pitches from the left side and is slightly more effective there. Once a spray hitter with negligible power, Nelson has become more effective at pulling the ball. Liriano has above-average speed, but does not steal bases often or effectively and rarely bunts for hits. Defensively, he is an adequate utility infielder. Nelson's arm is still accurate, although it has lost some zip and is now somewhat below par in strength. His range is average. However, at times, Liriano has trouble with grounders hit right at him; his hands rate average-minus.

HOW HE PERFORMED IN '95
The veteran vagabond performed very well in his first season with Pittsburgh, becoming the team's surprise success.

Liriano made solid contributions both offensively and defensively, leading the team in hitting with runners in scoring position and filling in at three infield spots. He served as the club's most frequently-used pinch-hitter, going 9-for-37 as an emergency batter.

He used his legs to beat out 12 infield hits during the season, but just one of them was a bunt. Oddly, despite moving from the hitting paradise of Mile High Stadium to Pittsburgh, Nelson lifted his batting average over 30 points last year and hit with more power. However, his base on balls total dropped by nearly half. He enjoyed the best game of his career August 18 against the Marlins when he socked his first career grand slam and banged in a career-high five RBI.

Providing versatility in the infield, Liriano started 51 games at second base, three at third, and one at shortstop. The Pirates signed him as added bench strength, but Nelson proved far more rewarding than just another warm body. He can run, switch-hit, and play fair defense.

WHAT TO EXPECT IN '96
This season, Liriano will again serve as the Pirates' utility infielder but would be a fine replacement should injuries befall either Carlos Garcia or Jay Bell. Formerly a starter with the Blue Jays in the 1980s, Nelson has now played for five teams in six years, but may finally settle down in Pittsburgh. He has changed a lot in the last two seasons but may have some more improvement left in him.

Overall Statistics

	G	AB	R	H	2B	3B	HR	RBI	SB	CS	BB	SO	BA	OBA
95 PIT	107	259	29	74	12	1	5	38	2	2	24	34	.286	.347
Career	623	1894	263	498	85	25	21	199	57	30	192	259	.263	.331

1995 Situational Statistics

	AB	HR	RBI	BA	OBA	SLG		AB	HR	RBI	BA	OBA	SLG
Home	101	2	14	.257	.333	.356	LHP	46	3	11	.283	.340	.500
Road	158	3	24	.304	.356	.424	RHP	213	2	27	.286	.349	.376
Apr-Jun	75	1	9	.267	.337	.360	ScPos	74	2	32	.365	.412	.554
Jul-Oct	184	4	29	.293	.351	.413	Clutch	65	2	11	.262	.329	.446

How He Compares to Other Batters

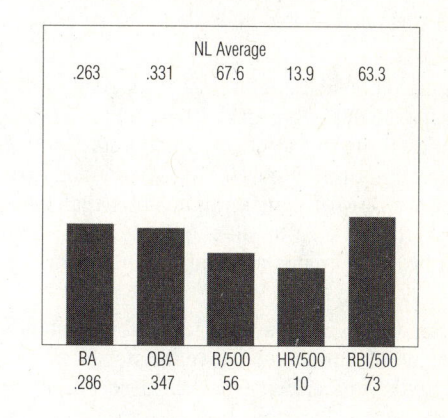

NL Average
.263 .331 67.6 13.9 63.3

BA .286 | OBA .347 | R/500 56 | HR/500 10 | RBI/500 73

Where He Hits the Ball

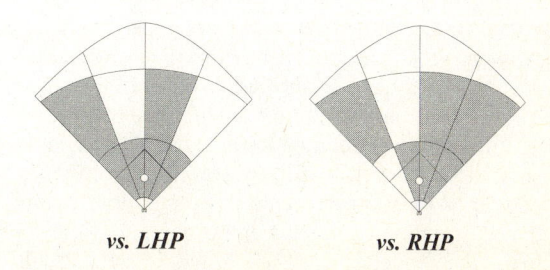

vs. LHP   vs. RHP

THE SCOUTING REPORT: 1996

PITTSBURGH PIRATES

ESTEBAN LOAIZA

Position: SP
Bats: R **Throws:** R
Ht: 6'4" **Wt:** 190
Opening Day Age: 24
Born: 12/31/1971
Drafted: PIT 3/12/91
ML Seasons: 1

SCOUTING REPORT

Loaiza throws from high three quarters. His average-plus live fastball sinks effectively, but his best pitch is a tight, plus slider with a sharp, quick break. When he spots those pitches effectively, Loaiza can be extremely effective.

Although Esteban has above-average control, he had problems getting ahead in the count and grooved some long home run balls. He lacks game-to-game consistency and lost some strength as the season went on. He is well above-average with the glove but is just average at holding runners. Of the 27 men who tried to steal bases when Loaiza was pitching, 19 were successful. Esteban was 10 for 52 at bat (.192) with a double, a triple, and seven sacrifice bunts.

HOW HE PERFORMED IN '95

Loaiza was originally set to start the season at Triple-A, but injuries created an opportunity for him. Not only did Esteban make the Pirates' staff, he stayed with the team all year and tied for the NL lead in starts. While he may have been rushed, Loaiza was needed, and he looks to be an emerging talent.

It was an inconsistent campaign. Esteban won his major-league debut on April 29, but in his next start surrendered eight earned runs and didn't win his second game until June 10. Ten days later, Loaiza started a string of four straight wins that carried him into the All-Star break at 6-3. He was 2-6 after the midsummer hiatus and didn't win after August 22.

He came to the majors with a rep for outstanding control, and for much of the year Esteban was very stingy with walks. However, he passed 17 men in 32.1 September innings. Loaiza topped all Bucs' pitchers by surrendering 21 homers. Worse yet, he led the league in runs (and earned runs) allowed.

WHAT TO EXPECT IN '96

At worst, Esteban looked like the green rookie he was in '95; at best, he showed flashes of brilliance. The still-inexperienced Loaiza will open the season as Pittsburgh's second or third starter. He has outstanding stuff but is still a thrower, rather than a pitcher. With improvements in preparation, confidence, stamina, and concentration, and time to learn the tendencies of NL hitters, Esteban will turn his outstanding arm into results. The Pirates have time.

Overall Statistics

	G	GS	GF	SV	W	L	ERA	IP	H	R	ER	HR	BB	SO
95 PIT	32	31	0	0	8	9	5.16	172.2	205	115	99	21	55	85
Career	32	31	0	0	8	9	5.16	172.2	205	115	99	21	55	85

1995 Situational Statistics

	W	L	ERA	SV	IP	BB	SO		AB	HR	RBI	BA	OBA	SLG
Home	3	6	5.01	0	88.0	28	50	LHB	298	6	46	.279	.359	.409
Road	5	3	5.31	0	84.2	27	35	RHB	385	15	57	.317	.347	.506
Apr-Jun	5	3	6.03	0	68.2	16	35	ScPos	178	2	76	.348	.396	.466
Jul-Oct	3	6	4.59	0	104.0	39	50	Clutch	23	0	0	.174	.296	.174

How He Compares to Other Pitchers

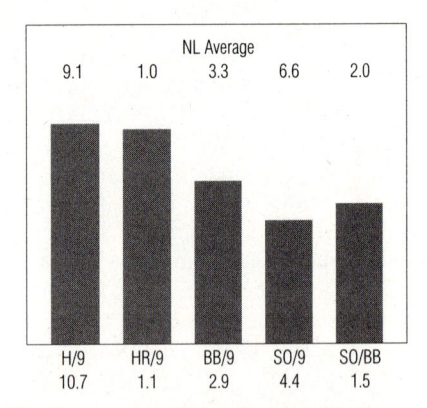

NL Average: H/9 9.1, HR/9 1.0, BB/9 3.3, SO/9 6.6, SO/BB 2.0

Loaiza: H/9 10.7, HR/9 1.1, BB/9 2.9, SO/9 4.4, SO/BB 1.5

How He Compares to Other Starting Pitchers

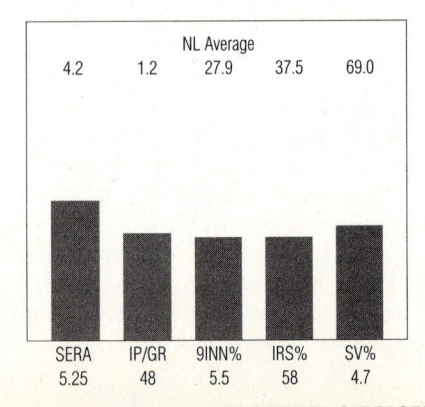

NL Average: SERA 4.2, IP/GR 1.2, 9INN% 27.9, IRS% 37.5, SV% 69.0

Loaiza: SERA 5.25, IP/GR 48, 9INN% 5.5, IRS% 58, SV% 4.7

PITTSBURGH PIRATES

ALBERT MARTIN

Position: OF
Bats: L **Throws:** L
Ht: 6'2" **Wt:** 220
Opening Day Age: 28
Born: 11/24/1967
Drafted: ATL85 7/198
ML Seasons: 4

SCOUTING REPORT
The former Braves' minor-leaguer has enjoyed a good career with the Pirates, hitting for average each of his three seasons but with inconsistent extra-base pop. Martin has excellent bat speed and will drive low, inside fastballs over the right field fence. Unfortunately, Al tries to pull every pitch, even against lefthanders, who bamboozle him. He might be better if he attempted to use the whole field on outside pitches.

A good runner with plus speed, Martin has become a legitimate stolen base threat and could still improve, although he must pick his spots better.

Although Al can play both left and center field, he is considerably better in left. His range is plus at that position but minus in center. Martin has average hands and an average throwing arm, so speedsters challenge him for the extra base.

HOW HE PERFORMED IN '95
Al's excellent '93 and disappointing '94 seasons were totally dissimilar, so he split the difference last year. He entered '95 with a lifetime batting average of .281 and he hit .280. His home run total was at his career average. About the only area of noticeable improvement Martin showed was a career-high stolen base count.

Martin missed the last month of '94 with a serious wrist injury, the effects of which carried into last season and limited Al to an impoverished .215 batting average through June 30. Martin's season was saved by a great second half: he batted .329 following the All-Star break.

One serious problem is Al's inability to do anything against southpaws; he could be headed for a permanent platoon role if he doesn't turn that around. Although Martin batted .297 with eight homers in '95 as a leadoff man, he might be better used lower in the order if he can hit for power consistently. He lacks the discipline to be an exceptional top-of-the-lineup man.

WHAT TO EXPECT IN '96
Martin's power production last year was a major disappointment. The Bucs need 15-20 homers and eighty RBI a year from Martin, who they regard as an offensive catalyst if healthy. To reach his apex, Al has to do something against lefthanded pitching. Otherwise, he is doomed to marginal everyday totals and, eventually, reserve duty.

Overall Statistics

	G	AB	R	H	2B	3B	HR	RBI	SB	CS	BB	SO	BA	OBA
95 PIT	124	439	70	124	25	3	13	41	20	11	44	92	.282	.351
Career	361	1207	204	340	63	16	40	140	51	26	120	275	.282	.348

1995 Situational Statistics

	AB	HR	RBI	BA	OBA	SLG		AB	HR	RBI	BA	OBA	SLG
Home	224	8	24	.308	.362	.482	LHP	68	1	7	.132	.145	.176
Road	215	5	17	.256	.339	.400	RHP	371	12	34	.310	.385	.491
Apr-Jun	191	6	15	.215	.302	.346	ScPos	96	2	24	.219	.324	.323
Jul-Oct	248	7	26	.335	.389	.516	Clutch	76	2	6	.237	.326	.355

How He Compares to Other Batters

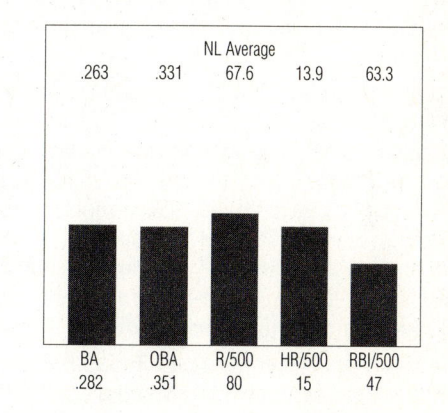

NL Average: .263 / .331 / 67.6 / 13.9 / 63.3

BA .282 | OBA .351 | R/500 80 | HR/500 15 | RBI/500 47

Where He Hits the Ball

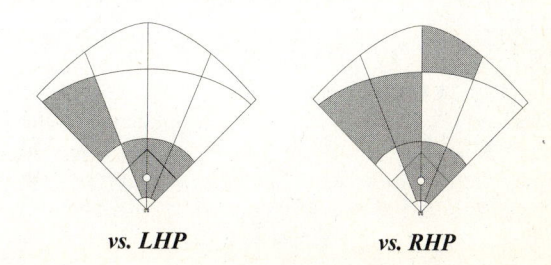

vs. LHP   vs. RHP

PITTSBURGH PIRATES

ORLANDO MERCED

Positions: OF/1B
Bats: B **Throws:** R
Ht: 6'0" **Wt:** 180
Opening Day Age: 29
Born: 11/2/1966
Drafted: PIT 2/25/85
ML Seasons: 6

SCOUTING REPORT

With his quick bat, Orlando is developing power, especially to center and right-center field. While Merced is becoming more disciplined, he will still chase the pitch in the dirt on occasion. Over the years, he has improved his handling of the low, inside fastball and can now punch that pitch to any part of the field.

He is a smart runner despite slightly below-average speed and could steal more often than he does, as he is 11 for 13 in basestealing attempts over the last two seasons. Orlando does not bunt.

Merced plays both first base and right field for the Pirates but is more effective in the infield. His range at first is well above-average, but below par in the outfield. He has average hands and minus arm strength with average accuracy.

HOW HE PERFORMED IN '95

Merced has become the Pirates' top overall offensive threat. For the second time in the past three seasons, he hit .300. Orlando's hit, double, homer and RBI totals were all career highs, as he led club regulars in several categories and finished second in most others.

Merced tried switch-hitting for a couple of seasons but now hits exclusively lefthanded. While he had a pronounced advantage against righties last year, he does not plan a return to the right side of the plate. Lefthanders gave Orlando even more trouble than usual, but he showed unexpected power against them. He usually loses steam late in the season, but in '95 Merced hit .330 in August with 29 RBI and then .299 in the final month.

He was scheduled to play first base in '95 but spent most of his time in right field. Merced played the position far more aggressively than in the past, charging base hits and shallow pop flies with abandon. He registered eight outfield assists with a stronger and more accurate arm than he had previously shown in his best defensive season.

WHAT TO EXPECT IN '96

Merced is constantly rumored as trade bait, but the Pirates re-signed him this winter. He is likely to play right field and occasionally back up at first base. A smart player, Orlando has improved in almost every way in the past few years and is justifiably popular in Pittsburgh.

Overall Statistics

	G	AB	R	H	2B	3B	HR	RBI	SB	CS	BB	SO	BA	OBA
95 PIT	132	487	75	146	29	4	15	83	7	2	52	74	.300	.365
Career	656	2160	327	609	122	18	48	314	27	14	288	349	.282	.366

1995 Situational Statistics

	AB	HR	RBI	BA	OBA	SLG		AB	HR	RBI	BA	OBA	SLG
Home	242	8	47	.306	.376	.479	LHP	120	5	17	.225	.301	.408
Road	245	7	36	.294	.354	.457	RHP	367	10	66	.324	.386	.488
Apr-Jun	180	4	23	.272	.323	.417	ScPos	140	6	70	.336	.402	.543
Jul-Oct	307	11	60	.316	.389	.498	Clutch	83	3	14	.253	.376	.446

How He Compares to Other Batters

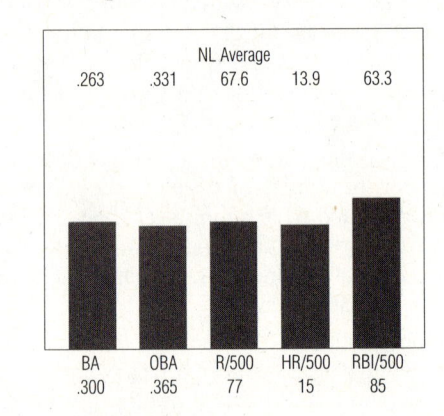

NL Average
.263   .331   67.6   13.9   63.3

BA	OBA	R/500	HR/500	RBI/500
.300	.365	77	15	85

Where He Hits the Ball

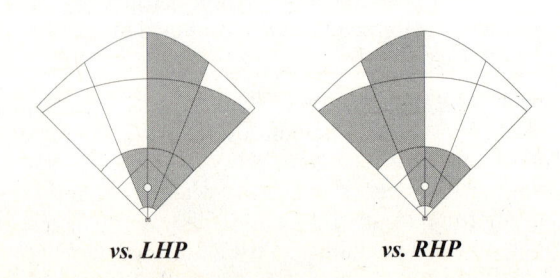

vs. LHP   vs. RHP

PITTSBURGH PIRATES

DAN MICELI

Position: RP
Bats: R **Throws:** R
Ht: 6'1" **Wt:** 185
Opening Day Age: 25
Born: 9/9/1970
Drafted: KC 3/7/90
ML Seasons: 3

SCOUTING REPORT
From a compact, three-quarter delivery, Miceli fires a blazing, well above-average sinking fastball. He must keep the pitch down in the zone to stay ahead in the count and avoid the home run. Dan uses the fastball most of the time, because both his slider and change-up are minus pitches that are still under construction. One of them, at least, must improve.

Because of poor skills at holding baserunners, ten of 12 basestealing attempts were successful against Miceli in '95. He is also below-par with the glove. Hitless in one trip in '95, he is hitless in four big-league at-bats.

HOW HE PERFORMED IN '95
Despite just two major-league saves entering the year, Miceli opened last season as the Pirates' closer and threw pure smoke. In his first 14 appearances, he notched seven saves, allowing just two earned runs.

His only problem early in the year was surrendering the key homer. In fact, he allowed five in his first 27 appearances. Fortunately, he had another string of 27 games between July 12 and September 17 when he permitted none, but he then gave up two more in the season's last two weeks.

Effective into the middle of July, Dan posted six saves in the twelve innings he hurled immediately after the All-Star game. After that, Miceli began to tire and his year took a downturn, especially after Labor Day, posting a 10.61 ERA in his last nine games.

Miceli's 21 saves were the most by a Bucs' reliever since 1989. However, he allowed 11 of 25 inherited runners to score, far too many for a closer, and must improve against lefthanders. His platoon differential was huge and might make it difficult to use Dan as a closer if it continues.

WHAT TO EXPECT IN '96
Miceli has obvious talent and will continue as the Pirates' closer. He must improve his durability in order to remain a successful finisher for the entire campaign, however. With at least one more pitch, he will be far more effective. Success will also come more quickly for Dan if he gets ahead in the count consistently. Concentration is still a problem for Dan, who has the closer's mentality but must learn simply to relax and let his talent shine.

Overall Statistics

	G	GS	GF	SV	W	L	ERA	IP	H	R	ER	HR	BB	SO
95 PIT	58	0	51	21	4	4	4.66	58.0	61	30	30	7	28	56
Career	95	0	61	23	6	5	5.06	90.2	95	52	51	12	42	87

1995 Situational Statistics

	W	L	ERA	SV	IP	BB	SO		AB	HR	RBI	BA	OBA	SLG
Home	2	1	4.06	12	31.0	18	27	LHB	91	5	20	.363	.460	.626
Road	2	3	5.33	9	27.0	10	29	RHB	135	2	19	.207	.275	.304
Apr-Jun	1	2	3.57	10	22.2	6	25	ScPos	80	4	35	.262	.364	.488
Jul-Oct	3	2	5.35	11	35.1	22	31	Clutch	140	5	25	.271	.342	.429

How He Compares to Other Pitchers

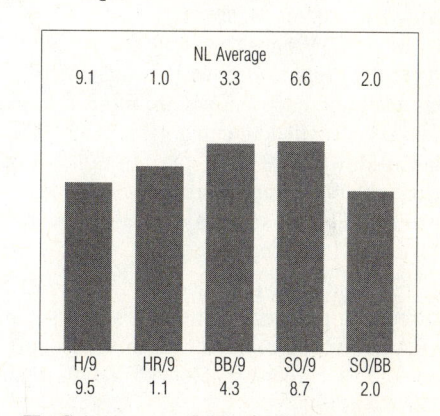

NL Average: 9.1 / 1.0 / 3.3 / 6.6 / 2.0

H/9: 9.5 | HR/9: 1.1 | BB/9: 4.3 | SO/9: 8.7 | SO/BB: 2.0

How He Compares to Other Relief Pitchers

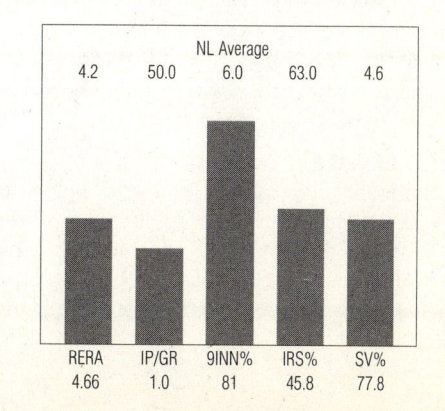

NL Average: 4.2 / 50.0 / 6.0 / 63.0 / 4.6

RERA: 4.66 | IP/GR: 1.0 | 9INN%: 81 | IRS%: 45.8 | SV%: 77.8

PITTSBURGH PIRATES

DENNY NEAGLE

Position: SP
Bats: L **Throws:** L
Ht: 6'4" **Wt:** 200
Opening Day Age: 27
Born: 9/13/1968
Drafted: MIN89 3/85
ML Seasons: 5

SCOUTING REPORT

Neagle is a true believer in Pirates' pitching coach Ray Miller's creed: "work fast, throw strikes, and change speeds." Adherence to this philosophy made him a big winner last season. Denny, coming from three quarters to low three quarters, throws a well above-average change-up that is easily his best pitch. The offering is deceptive and gets him plenty of strikeouts. His average-plus slow curve is also an effective pitch. An average curve and average-minus sinking fastball complete his arsenal. All of his pitches are more effective because Neagle has good command of them and he jumps ahead in the count consistently. He changes speeds extremely well. Although he is slow to home, Denny is quick to first base, resulting in 11 of 24 runners who tried to steal against Neagle in '95 being put out. An excellent fifth infielder, he covers the mound well. Denny smashed a grand slam homer and three doubles last season, but fanned 26 times in 74 at-bats and hit just .122. He's not a particularly good bunter.

HOW HE PERFORMED IN '95

Neagle was the Pirates' top pitcher in '95. The league's first ten-game winner, he was named to the All-Star team and ended up compiling career highs in almost every statistical categories. Denny started his season slowly, but won five straight through June 1. By the midsummer break, he was clearly in the top echelon of NL starters with a 9-4 record and a 3.34 ERA in 16 starts.

His offensive support declined in the second half and a tired arm reduced his numbers to 4-4 with a 3.63 ERA. However, in mid-September, Neagle recovered with a career-high ten strikeouts against the Giants.

For the season, Neagle was undefeated pitching in Pittsburgh. His walks-per-nine innings ratio was third-best in the league behind those of Greg Maddux and Shane Reynolds, although he did lead the NL in hits allowed.

WHAT TO EXPECT IN '96

The confident and talented Neagle opens this season as the Bucs' ace. Having shared the league lead in innings pitched in '95 and pitching consistently well, he is fully capable of repeating or bettering his performance and making several more All-Star appearances.

Overall Statistics

	G	GS	GF	SV	W	L	ERA	IP	H	R	ER	HR	BB	SO
95 PIT	31	31	0	0	13	8	3.43	209.2	221	91	80	20	45	150
Career	167	71	23	3	29	30	4.35	534.1	547	275	258	60	181	436

1995 Situational Statistics

	W	L	ERA	SV	IP	BB	SO		AB	HR	RBI	BA	OBA	SLG
Home	6	0	3.56	0	81.0	20	58	LHB	126	5	14	.270	.348	.484
Road	7	8	3.36	0	128.2	25	92	RHB	683	15	66	.274	.305	.391
Apr-Jun	9	3	2.90	0	96.1	20	64	ScPos	161	1	56	.267	.322	.379
Jul-Oct	4	5	3.89	0	113.1	25	86	Clutch	51	1	4	.157	.228	.294

How He Compares to Other Pitchers

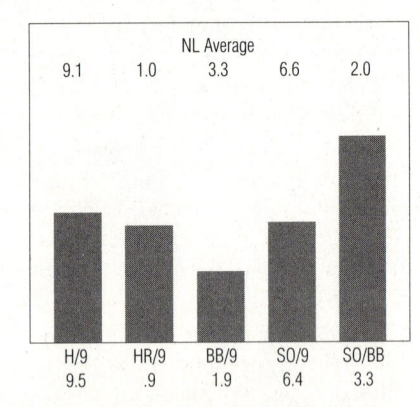

NL Average: H/9 9.1, HR/9 1.0, BB/9 3.3, SO/9 6.6, SO/BB 2.0

Neagle: H/9 9.5, HR/9 .9, BB/9 1.9, SO/9 6.4, SO/BB 3.3

How He Compares to Other Starting Pitchers

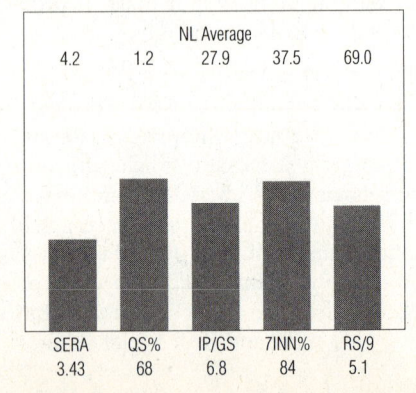

NL Average: SERA 4.2, QS% 27.9, IP/GS 37.5, 7INN% 69.0, RS/9 (1.2)

Neagle: SERA 3.43, QS% 68, IP/GS 6.8, 7INN% 84, RS/9 5.1

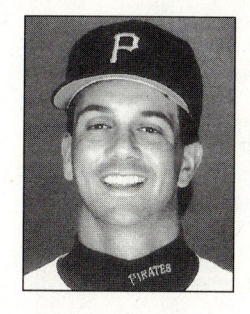

PITTSBURGH PIRATES

PAUL WAGNER

Position: SP/RP
Bats: R **Throws:** R
Ht: 6'3" **Wt:** 205
Opening Day Age: 28
Born: 11/14/1967
Drafted: PIT89 13/314
ML Seasons: 4

SCOUTING REPORT
The still-young Wagner has a good arm and great potential. Unfortunately, he has not yet mastered the art of pitching in the major leagues. Using a three-quarter delivery, he fires a better-than-average fastball that bores in on righthanders. Paul will also cut the fastball to give it extra movement. He also has an above-par slider with a sharp, quick, late break. His curve is just an average pitch, but the Pirates and many in baseball feel Wagner should throw the bender more often.

Despite his good stuff, Paul has not learned to change speeds. Indeed, his only off-speed delivery is a below-average circle change. If he can ever master the art of deception, he could be truly dangerous.

A plus fielder around the mound, Wagner has a below-average move to first base. Concentration is also a key issue for Wagner to work on, as 25 runners stole on him in 30 tries. Paul is a good hitter. He entered 1995 with a .183 average and last year batted .214 with six sacrifices.

HOW HE PERFORMED IN '95
Wagner's '95 highlight came on August 29 when he no-hit the Rockies for 8.2 innings. Unfortunately, he lost his bid for history on Andres Galarraga's weak infield single. It would have been the seventh no-hitter in Pirates' history, but luck was not on Paul's side. He led the league in losses, becoming the first Pittsburgh pitcher since 1985 to do so. In Mid-May, Wagner was 0-5 with an 8.49 ERA; a month later, he stood at 1-10.

Despite the horrid start, he didn't pitch that badly. Control was a problem, but so was support: the Pirates scored one run or fewer in nine of Paul's starts.

WHAT TO EXPECT IN '96
Wagner improved after the All-Star game and was used in relief much of the second half in '95. Jim Leyland still thinks Paul is best suited to the rotation—if he can develop a change-up to go along with the rest of his fine pitches.

Paul is likely to be Pittsburgh's second or third starter, providing he adds that off-speed delivery. If he does, he could challenge Denny Neagle for the title of staff ace. If he doesn't, Paul may find himself in the bullpen for good.

Overall Statistics

	G	GS	GF	SV	W	L	ERA	IP	H	R	ER	HR	BB	SO
95 PIT	33	25	1	1	5	16	4.80	165.0	174	96	88	18	72	120
Career	112	60	15	3	22	32	4.45	439.0	462	238	217	40	169	325

1995 Situational Statistics

	W	L	ERA	SV	IP	BB	SO		AB	HR	RBI	BA	OBA	SLG
Home	4	9	5.10	1	83.0	38	63	LHB	283	5	33	.276	.364	.378
Road	1	7	4.50	0	82.0	34	57	RHB	354	13	54	.271	.343	.472
Apr-Jun	1	10	5.68	0	69.2	36	48	ScPos	180	6	69	.267	.350	.467
Jul-Oct	4	6	4.15	1	95.1	36	72	Clutch	34	1	3	.294	.324	.382

How He Compares to Other Pitchers

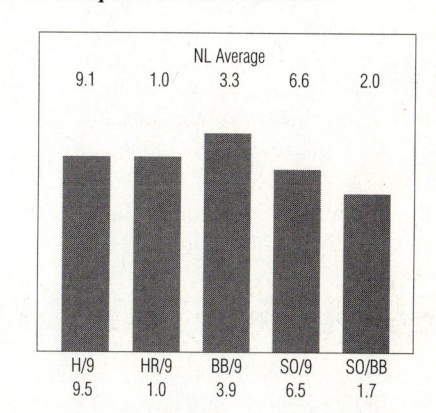

NL Average: 9.1 / 1.0 / 3.3 / 6.6 / 2.0

H/9	HR/9	BB/9	SO/9	SO/BB
9.5	1.0	3.9	6.5	1.7

How He Compares to Other Starting Pitchers

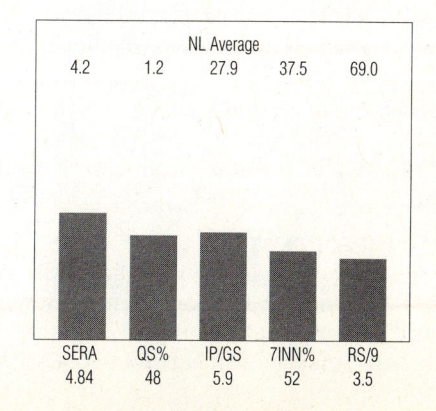

NL Average: 4.2 / 1.2 / 27.9 / 37.5 / 69.0

SERA	QS%	IP/GS	7INN%	RS/9
4.84	48	5.9	52	3.5

THE SCOUTING REPORT: 1996

PITTSBURGH PIRATES

RICH AUDE

Position: 1B
Bats: R **Throws:** R
Ht: 6'5" **Wt:** 180
Opening Day Age: 24
Born: 7/13/1971
Drafted: PIT89 2/48
ML Seasons: 2

Overall Statistics

	G	AB	R	H	2B	3B	HR	RBI	SB	CS	BB	SO	BA	OBA
95 PIT	42	109	10	27	8	0	2	19	1	2	6	20	.248	.287
Career	55	135	11	30	9	0	2	23	1	2	7	27	.222	.261

1995 Situational Statistics

	AB	HR	RBI	BA	OBA	SLG		AB	HR	RBI	BA	OBA	SLG
Home	54	1	6	.167	.182	.278	LHP	61	1	11	.279	.313	.426
Road	55	1	13	.327	.383	.473	RHP	48	1	8	.208	.255	.313
Apr-Jun	70	2	11	.271	.320	.429	ScPos	38	0	14	.237	.256	.316
Jul-Oct	39	0	8	.205	.225	.282	Clutch	13	0	2	.231	.333	.231

SCOUTING REPORT

The big kid hit well in the minors and can hammer the inside fastball with power, but he has experienced constant trouble with breaking pitches in the majors. Aude must improve his plate discipline in order to take advantage of his power.

Rich displays average fielding skills all the way around, except for slightly below-par range. He is a slow runner.

HOW HE PERFORMED IN '95

Aude opened the season platooning at first base with Mark Johnson. Rich batted .333 in his first 18 games but things went quickly downhill and he was returned to Triple-A on July 1. While in Calgary, Aude accepted the challenge of battling back, clubbing nine homers 42 RBIs before rejoining the Pirates in September.

Rich may be no more than a year or two away from a rewarding big-league career. If he doesn't stick with Pittsburgh, an expansion team will be his destination.

WHAT TO EXPECT IN '96

Aude may have lost his shot at first base with Charlie Hayes moving Jeff King to first. However, continued improvement in his power hitting and fielding will eventually win him a job somewhere.

JASON CHRISTIANSEN

Position: RP
Bats: R **Throws:** L
Ht: 6'5" **Wt:** 230
Opening Day Age: 26
Born: 9/21/1969
Drafted: PIT 7/1/91
ML Seasons: 1

Overall Statistics

	G	GS	GF	SV	W	L	ERA	IP	H	R	ER	HR	BB	SO
95 PIT	63	0	13	0	1	3	4.15	56.1	49	28	26	5	34	53
Career	63	0	13	0	1	3	4.15	56.1	49	28	26	5	34	53

1995 Situational Statistics

	W	L	ERA	SV	IP	BB	SO		AB	HR	RBI	BA	OBA	SLG
Home	0	1	3.56	0	30.1	18	33	LHB	81	2	18	.210	.330	.346
Road	1	2	4.85	0	26.0	16	20	RHB	128	3	16	.250	.355	.391
Apr-Jun	1	0	1.35	0	20.0	9	14	ScPos	68	2	28	.265	.418	.412
Jul-Oct	0	3	5.70	0	36.1	25	39	Clutch	87	3	13	.241	.391	.437

SCOUTING REPORT

Jason's strong, live arm should keep him in the majors for some time. Using a three-quarter delivery, he throws an average fastball that tails in on left-handers. His average curve and forkball set up his best pitch, an average-plus slider with a hard, fast break. He must have better control in order to win.

Jason is an average fielder who has an average move to first. Four of seven potential basestealers were successful running on him. Jason fanned in his only plate appearance last year.

HOW HE PERFORMED IN '95

Christiansen led the pitching staff with 63 appearances, all in relief. Jason's year was split between a terrific start and a poor second half. He didn't allow a run in his first eight outings and surrendered just two tallies during his opening 23 appearances.

After that, things went south, largely due to heavy use. Christiansen's ERA skyrocketed close to double digits in the second half before levelling at 6.10 after strong efforts in his last eight outings.

WHAT TO EXPECT IN '96

Christiansen will stay in the bullpen, working mostly in middle relief. He will get the occasional call against a dangerous lefty in key situations.

PITTSBURGH PIRATES

DAVE CLARK

Position: OF
Bats: L **Throws:** R
Ht: 6'2" **Wt:** 200
Opening Day Age: 33
Born: 9/3/1962
Drafted: CLE83 1/11
ML Seasons: 10

Overall Statistics

	G	AB	R	H	2B	3B	HR	RBI	SB	CS	BB	SO	BA	OBA
95 PIT	77	196	30	55	6	0	4	24	3	3	24	38	.281	.359
Career	603	1464	189	387	54	6	49	212	15	10	155	319	.264	.333

1995 Situational Statistics

	AB	HR	RBI	BA	OBA	SLG		AB	HR	RBI	BA	OBA	SLG
Home	88	2	13	.284	.363	.398	LHP	23	1	4	.348	.464	.565
Road	108	2	11	.278	.355	.352	RHP	173	3	20	.272	.344	.347
Apr-Jun	119	3	17	.336	.392	.462	ScPos	57	2	21	.263	.362	.421
Jul-Oct	77	1	7	.195	.312	.234	Clutch	31	1	7	.290	.353	.419

SCOUTING REPORT

Dave is a very aggressive hitter who can rip high, inside fastballs. However, he is fooled by breaking stuff and often chases pitches in his eyes. He has minus speed and is a poor baserunner.

No matter what outfield position he plays, he's a gamble. Dave has poor range, especially going back, and a relatively weak arm. Despite poor tools, he always plays at full intensity.

HOW HE PERFORMED IN '95

In three full seasons with the Pirates, Clark has batted .278 with some power. Dave started 24 games in left field and 20 in right, but was a liability in both spots. He suffered a broken left collarbone in a ferocious collision with Jacob Brumfield in late July and missed seven weeks. Although Clark was hitting a confident .314 at the time, he batted just .150 in 40 at-bats upon his return.

WHAT TO EXPECT IN '96

This is the final year of Dave's contract and may be his last with the Pirates. Since Jim Leyland uses everybody on the team, Clark will get some starts, but only the NL's worst team would pencil him in 44 times a season.

MIDRE CUMMINGS

Position: OF
Bats: B **Throws:** R
Ht: 6'1" **Wt:** 190
Opening Day Age: 24
Born: 10/14/1971
Drafted: MIN90 2/29
ML Seasons: 3

Overall Statistics

	G	AB	R	H	2B	3B	HR	RBI	SB	CS	BB	SO	BA	OBA
95 PIT	59	152	13	37	7	1	2	15	1	0	13	30	.243	.303
Career	96	274	29	62	12	1	3	30	1	0	21	57	.226	.282

1995 Situational Statistics

	AB	HR	RBI	BA	OBA	SLG		AB	HR	RBI	BA	OBA	SLG
Home	51	1	5	.255	.333	.392	LHP	17	1	1	.176	.176	.353
Road	101	1	10	.238	.287	.317	RHP	135	1	14	.252	.318	.341
Apr-Jun	15	0	0	.267	.353	.333	ScPos	37	0	13	.270	.386	.405
Jul-Oct	137	2	15	.241	.297	.343	Clutch	32	0	0	.188	.278	.188

SCOUTING REPORT

Cummings, a talent waiting to arrive, never fails to baffle the Pirates' coaching staff. He is an undisciplined hitter who loves fastballs and anything inside, but struggles with breaking balls and off-speed stuff. During '95, Midre appeared to have lost some of his power and speed. He lacks a good first step and is now just an average runner.

He has terrific outfield skills, with slightly above-average range, soft hands, and a strong and accurate arm.

HOW HE PERFORMED IN '95

Midre has been a major disappointment to the Pirates. Ticketed for a starting berth in right field during spring training, Cummings failed due to weak hitting, poor fielding, and a horrible attitude. He was on his way to Triple-A after just 15 at-bats. He returned in late July and saw action at all three outfield positions, playing his best ball in September.

WHAT TO EXPECT IN '96

Cummings, once considered a replacement for Barry Bonds, must play his way onto the roster this spring. Regarded as the jewel of the Bucs' farm system a couple years ago, Midre is in grave danger of being forgotten.

PITTSBURGH PIRATES

MIKE DYER

Position: RP
Bats: R **Throws:** R
Ht: 6'3" **Wt:** 195
Opening Day Age: 29
Born: 9/8/1966
Drafted: MIN86* 4/87
ML Seasons: 3

Overall Statistics

	G	GS	GF	SV	W	L	ERA	IP	H	R	ER	HR	BB	SO
95 PIT	55	0	15	0	4	5	4.34	74.2	81	40	36	9	30	53
Career	85	12	22	4	9	13	4.70	161.0	170	95	84	12	79	103

1995 Situational Statistics

	W	L	ERA	SV	IP	BB	SO		AB	HR	RBI	BA	OBA	SLG
Home	2	2	3.46	0	41.2	14	23	LHB	94	4	19	.362	.444	.564
Road	2	3	5.45	0	33.0	16	30	RHB	194	5	21	.242	.315	.361
Apr-Jun	1	1	4.65	0	31.0	14	27	ScPos	92	1	31	.250	.369	.326
Jul-Oct	3	4	4.12	0	43.2	16	26	Clutch	66	2	9	.273	.355	.394

SCOUTING REPORT

Durability is one of Dyer's strengths, as he is willing and able to work three or four consecutive games. Using a herky-jerky, three-quarter delivery, he brings home a plus sinking fastball. He has a plus change-up but rarely uses it because he likes to overpower hitters. This causes control troubles.

Dyer also has an average slider and curve. An average-minus fielder, he holds runners poorly. During '95, 11 runners tried to steal against Mike, eight successfully. He was a surprising 4-for-7 at bat after one unsuccessful at-bat in '94.

HOW HE PERFORMED IN '95

Dyer made his big-league debut with Minnesota in 1989, then missed almost all of 1990-91 after shoulder surgery. Hooking up with Pittsburgh in '94, he led Pirates' relievers in innings pitched in '95. However, he was hammered by lefthanded hitters and will have to learn to get them out to pitch in the majors.

WHAT TO EXPECT IN '96

There is no assurance that Dyer will be on the team past training camp but, if he makes the team, he'll be reasonably effective and could improve if he uses his change more often.

ANGELO ENCARNACION

Position: C
Bats: R **Throws:** R
Ht: 5'8" **Wt:** 180
Opening Day Age: 22
Born: 4/18/1973
Drafted: PIT 6/1/90
ML Seasons: 1

Overall Statistics

	G	AB	R	H	2B	3B	HR	RBI	SB	CS	BB	SO	BA	OBA
95 PIT	58	159	18	36	7	2	2	10	1	1	13	28	.226	.285
Career	58	159	18	36	7	2	2	10	1	1	13	28	.226	.285

1995 Situational Statistics

	AB	HR	RBI	BA	OBA	SLG		AB	HR	RBI	BA	OBA	SLG
Home	72	2	7	.194	.284	.306	LHP	42	2	4	.286	.302	.524
Road	87	0	3	.253	.286	.356	RHP	117	0	6	.205	.279	.265
Apr-Jun	36	0	3	.361	.378	.417	ScPos	35	0	6	.229	.357	.257
Jul-Oct	123	2	7	.187	.259	.309	Clutch	18	0	0	.167	.211	.167

SCOUTING REPORT

The athletic youngster has a terrific arm with a quick release, firing throws to the bag with plus accuracy. It's already one of the best guns in the game. Encarnacion catches solidly, and is very quick handling balls near the plate. Experience will improve Angelo's pitch selection and ability to handle the staff.

He hits with an open stance and loves to jerk inside fastballs. However, pitchers work him low and away, taking advantage of his impatience. Blessed with slightly above-average speed, Angelo also has good bunting skills.

HOW HE PERFORMED IN '95

Encarnacion, with 70 games above Class A entering '95, made an impressive showing with Pittsburgh. He had two separate stints with the Bucs, hitting .361 in 36 at-bats in his first trial, but a very humble .187 in his second.

Defensively, he showed remarkable skills, nailing 19 of 57 would-be thieves and picking two runners off first.

WHAT TO EXPECT IN '96

Encarnacion may be the Bucs' opening-day catcher. However, he can't hit .187 and hold the position.

PITTSBURGH PIRATES

JOHN ERICKS

Position: SP
Bats: R **Throws:** R
Ht: 6'7" **Wt:** 220
Opening Day Age: 28
Born: 6/16/1967
Drafted: SL88 1/22
ML Seasons: 1

Overall Statistics

	G	GS	GF	SV	W	L	ERA	IP	H	R	ER	HR	BB	SO
95 PIT	19	18	0	0	3	9	4.58	106.0	108	59	54	7	50	80
Career	19	18	0	0	3	9	4.58	106.0	108	59	54	7	50	80

1995 Situational Statistics

	W	L	ERA	SV	IP	BB	SO		AB	HR	RBI	BA	OBA	SLG
Home	3	4	4.30	0	67.0	27	56	LHB	209	4	23	.282	.363	.383
Road	0	5	5.08	0	39.0	23	24	RHB	201	3	29	.244	.322	.348
Apr-Jun	0	1	6.00	0	6.0	2	3	ScPos	105	1	42	.333	.440	.467
Jul-Oct	3	8	4.50	0	100.0	48	77	Clutch	33	0	5	.364	.417	.394

SCOUTING REPORT
John throws a slightly above-average fastball that bores into righthanded batters. Using a three-quarter motion, he wraps his wrist before delivering the ball. The righthander's curve, slider, and change-up rate average-minus. Control is a problem for Ericks; he has not learned how to set up hitters. He is still adjusting to decreased velocity following severe shoulder injuries.

An average fielder, he has an average move to first, with 14 of 23 basestealers successful in '95. He was a poor 3-for-31 at bat (.097).

HOW HE PERFORMED IN '95
Once a very hard thrower, given up on by the Cardinals after a 1992 shoulder problem, John worked through the minors and ended up in Pittsburgh. He debuted on June 24, won his first game ten days later, and hurled his first complete game four days after that. On September 12 against the Padres, Ericks struck out a career-high nine batters.

WHAT TO EXPECT IN '96
The Pirates are banking on Ericks to bolster the rotation, although they are concerned about his shoulder and will handle him carefully.

JON LIEBER

Position: SP/RP
Bats: L **Throws:** R
Ht: 6'3" **Wt:** 220
Opening Day Age: 25
Born: 4/2/1970
Drafted: KC92 5/44
ML Seasons: 2

Overall Statistics

	G	GS	GF	SV	W	L	ERA	IP	H	R	ER	HR	BB	SO
95 PIT	21	12	3	0	4	7	6.32	72.2	103	56	51	7	14	45
Career	38	29	3	0	10	14	4.76	181.1	219	118	96	19	39	116

1995 Situational Statistics

	W	L	ERA	SV	IP	BB	SO		AB	HR	RBI	BA	OBA	SLG
Home	2	6	7.90	0	41.0	11	29	LHB	134	6	24	.396	.415	.619
Road	2	1	4.26	0	31.2	3	16	RHB	164	1	24	.305	.344	.390
Apr-Jun	2	7	7.48	0	55.1	10	34	ScPos	83	1	40	.386	.406	.518
Jul-Oct	2	0	2.60	0	17.1	4	11	Clutch	32	0	4	.313	.333	.438

SCOUTING REPORT
Jon has outstanding control, especially for a young pitcher. He throws from three quarters to low three quarters, his best pitch is a slightly above-average fastball which he can sink or cut. Lieber also has an average slider and a change-up that still needs work.

An unskilled fielder, Jon is average at holding runners: 11 of 15 were successful stealing against him in '95. He was 1-for-21 at the plate with 14 strikeouts and no sacrifices.

HOW HE PERFORMED IN '95
Lieber, the Bucs' opening day starter due to his fine '94 rookie season, had a miserable sophomore campaign. Demoted to Calgary, he posted a 7.01 ERA. Many felt that Lieber had let success go to his head: he put on weight, lost concentration, and appeared lost on the mound. The bright spots: Jon had a 1.50 ERA in nine relief appearances and did not allow a homer in his final 29 innings.

WHAT TO EXPECT IN '96
While Lieber throws strikes, he can't afford another year like '95. He had lost weight and was working out in Pittsburgh over the winter, determined to fulfill his early promise.

PITTSBURGH PIRATES

JEFF McCURRY

Position: RP
Bats: R **Throws:** R
Ht: 6'7" **Wt:** 210
Opening Day Age: 26
Born: 1/21/1970
Drafted: PIT90 14/376
ML Seasons: 1

Overall Statistics

	G	GS	GF	SV	W	L	ERA	IP	H	R	ER	HR	BB	SO
95 PIT	55	0	10	1	1	4	5.02	61.0	82	38	34	9	30	27
Career	55	0	10	1	1	4	5.02	61.0	82	38	34	9	30	27

1995 Situational Statistics

	W	L	ERA	SV	IP	BB	SO		AB	HR	RBI	BA	OBA	SLG
Home	1	1	7.08	0	34.1	20	14	LHB	85	3	13	.388	.475	.612
Road	0	3	2.36	1	26.2	10	13	RHB	158	6	27	.310	.391	.500
Apr-Jun	0	2	4.44	0	26.1	13	8	ScPos	78	3	30	.282	.417	.513
Jul-Oct	1	2	5.45	1	34.2	17	19	Clutch	55	1	8	.309	.406	.527

SCOUTING REPORT

His out pitch is a plus slider. Throwing from three quarters, Jeff has a slightly odd, jerky motion and snaps his wrist while releasing the ball. McCurry's sinking fastball rates average. Both his curve and change-up are used for show; development of a third pitch will be critical for him.

Average at fielding and holding runners, Jeff saw four of eight steal successfully against him. He was hitless in three trips to the plate.

HOW HE PERFORMED IN '95

McCurry's rookie season was a roller-coaster ride. He allowed four runs in his debut but didn't allow a run in his next ten appearances. He was up and down most of the season. Jeff pitched almost exclusively in middle relief, as befits a pitcher with no Triple-A experience.

WHAT TO EXPECT IN '96

McCurry seemed to lose some stamina and pitched poorly late in the year. He was waived to the Tigers in November. Jeff could pitch often for the undercapitalized Tigers' pitching staff, but control troubles make ascension to an important role unlikely.

STEVE PARRIS

Position: SP
Bats: R **Throws:** R
Ht: 6'0" **Wt:** 190
Opening Day Age: 28
Born: 12/17/1967
Drafted: PHI89 5/118
ML Seasons: 1

Overall Statistics

	G	GS	GF	SV	W	L	ERA	IP	H	R	ER	HR	BB	SO
95 PIT	15	15	0	0	6	6	5.38	82.0	89	49	49	12	33	61
Career	15	15	0	0	6	6	5.38	82.0	89	49	49	12	33	61

1995 Situational Statistics

	W	L	ERA	SV	IP	BB	SO		AB	HR	RBI	BA	OBA	SLG
Home	4	3	4.70	0	46.0	17	35	LHB	140	5	18	.243	.342	.393
Road	2	3	6.25	0	36.0	16	26	RHB	175	7	26	.314	.378	.509
Apr-Jun	1	0	4.82	0	9.1	3	10	ScPos	59	5	30	.288	.397	.576
Jul-Oct	5	6	5.45	0	72.2	30	51	Clutch	10	0	0	.200	.200	.300

SCOUTING REPORT

Parris is still recovering from a serious arm injury that cost him all of 1994. He uses a three-quarter delivery and hangs his banner on a slightly above-average fastball. His slider is average and his curve needs work. Learning to set up hitters is a priority for Parris, who has average control but must stay ahead in the count.

He is an average-plus fielder and holds runners effectively: of 15 who tried to steal in '95, eight were thrown out. Steve hit a credible .250 last year (7-for-28).

HOW HE PERFORMED IN '95

Parris opened the season with Double-A Carolina. He made his debut June 26, beating the Cubs, his boyhood favorites. Steve ran off 16 consecutive scoreless innings in mid-July, a string highlighted by a nine-strikeout game against the Braves July 12.

Suffering from a sore arm, Parris was bombed in early September and was then rested for the remainder of the season.

WHAT TO EXPECT IN '96

Parris will be given every chance to nail down a spot in the rotation. However, the Pirates will take precautions to avoid further arm troubles.

PITTSBURGH PIRATES

STEVE PEGUES

Position: OF
Bats: R **Throws:** R
Ht: 6'2" **Wt:** 190
Opening Day Age: 27
Born: 5/21/1968
Drafted: DET87 2/21
ML Seasons: 2

Overall Statistics

	G	AB	R	H	2B	3B	HR	RBI	SB	CS	BB	SO	BA	OBA
95 PIT	82	171	17	42	8	0	6	16	1	2	4	36	.246	.263
Career	100	207	19	55	10	0	6	18	2	2	6	41	.266	.286

1995 Situational Statistics

	AB	HR	RBI	BA	OBA	SLG		AB	HR	RBI	BA	OBA	SLG
Home	83	5	10	.229	.244	.446	LHP	117	3	12	.248	.254	.385
Road	88	1	6	.261	.280	.352	RHP	54	3	4	.241	.281	.426
Apr-Jun	76	2	6	.289	.305	.461	ScPos	37	0	8	.081	.098	.108
Jul-Oct	95	4	10	.211	.227	.347	Clutch	37	1	4	.270	.263	.351

SCOUTING REPORT

Steve uses the whole field when hitting. He has plus bat speed and can crack an occasional high fastball into the stands. Unfortunately, he wraps his bat, which slows down his swing, and overaggressiveness at the plate and an inconsistent backswing lead to slumps.

Despite just average speed, Pegues is a good baserunner and was an effective base thief in the minors. Steve is an adequate outfielder with a slightly below-average arm and average range. He can play all three outfield positions.

HOW HE PERFORMED IN '95

Pegues spent '95, his first full season in the majors, as a fifth outfielder. Most of his action came against lefthanded pitching. His season highlight was clubbing two homers (his first two career shots) on June 19 against San Francisco.

With runners in scoring position, Pegues was especially poor, and his very poor plate discipline made him easy to pitch to in most key situations.

WHAT TO EXPECT IN '96

Seattle inked Steve to a minor-league deal last winter and will bring him to camp this spring with a chance to make the big-league roster. However, his value is questionable.

DAN PLESAC

Position: RP
Bats: L **Throws:** L
Ht: 6'5" **Wt:** 210
Opening Day Age: 34
Born: 2/4/1962
Drafted: MIL83 1/26
ML Seasons: 10

Overall Statistics

	G	GS	GF	SV	W	L	ERA	IP	H	R	ER	HR	BB	SO
95 PIT	58	0	16	3	4	4	3.58	60.1	53	26	24	3	27	57
Career	534	14	311	137	37	45	3.49	702.0	648	300	272	65	247	605

1995 Situational Statistics

	W	L	ERA	SV	IP	BB	SO		AB	HR	RBI	BA	OBA	SLG
Home	2	2	3.77	1	28.2	14	26	LHB	81	2	16	.222	.298	.383
Road	2	2	3.41	2	31.2	13	31	RHB	143	1	9	.245	.329	.322
Apr-Jun	2	0	2.49	2	25.1	14	21	ScPos	62	0	20	.274	.392	.371
Jul-Oct	2	4	4.37	1	35.0	13	36	Clutch	104	2	14	.269	.361	.375

SCOUTING REPORT

The veteran lefthander uses a three-quarter delivery to throw an average-plus fastball that is often straight, but he will cut it and sink it. Plesac throws an average palmball as an off-speed pitch, getting strikeouts with a good, sharp slider.

Dan has average control but loses velocity and location when overused. With a deceptive move to first, he holds runners well: just two runners tried to steal against him in '95. He is a poor fielder. Plesac was 1-for-4 last year, collecting his first major-league hit.

HOW HE PERFORMED IN '95

Plesac was two different pitchers in '95. He opened the season with 13 consecutive scoreless games and, at the All-Star break, Dan was 3-0 with a 2.08 ERA. Frequent appearances, however, caused a slump. Although he allowed just three earned runs in his last 16 games, Plesac was 1-4 with a 5.10 ERA after the midsummer break. This pattern duplicated his '94 showing with the Cubs.

WHAT TO EXPECT IN '96

Plesac showed that he still has the stuff to get the job done in middle relief, and Pirates' manager Jim Leyland likes to carry three lefties in his pen.

THE SCOUTING REPORT: 1996

PITTSBURGH PIRATES

DON SLAUGHT

Position: C
Bats: R **Throws:** R
Ht: 6'1" **Wt:** 190
Opening Day Age: 37
Born: 9/11/1958
Drafted: KC80 8/172
ML Seasons: 14

Overall Statistics

	G	AB	R	H	2B	3B	HR	RBI	SB	CS	BB	SO	BA	OBA
95 PIT	35	112	13	34	6	0	0	13	0	0	9	8	.304	.361
Career	1231	3800	388	1075	225	28	71	440	18	15	291	533	.283	.337

1995 Situational Statistics

	AB	HR	RBI	BA	OBA	SLG		AB	HR	RBI	BA	OBA	SLG
Home	56	0	9	.393	.460	.446	LHP	25	0	4	.280	.357	.400
Road	56	0	4	.214	.254	.268	RHP	87	0	9	.310	.362	.345
Apr-Jun	31	0	5	.290	.313	.387	ScPos	28	0	11	.286	.355	.321
Jul-Oct	81	0	8	.309	.378	.346	Clutch	20	0	2	.350	.409	.400

SCOUTING REPORT

The injury-prone veteran is an excellent hitter when healthy. He is disciplined and well-prepared at the plate. A good contact hitter, Slaught prefers his pitches high and inside, but lacks a quick bat and has no power.

While Don has good hands, he blocks pitches poorly and has minus range. His arm isn't strong but he has good accuracy on his throws. He is an extremely slow runner.

HOW HE PERFORMED IN '95

Slaught's sixth season with Pittsburgh drained away on the disabled list due to a badly strained right hamstring. Don has batted .300 or better four times with the Pirates. However, he's never had much power and last year failed to homer. With the Pirates, Slaught has averaged just 80 games played per season. He started just 30 last year and threw out only five of 37 potential basestealers.

WHAT TO EXPECT IN '96

Don has reached the end of the line with Pittsburgh. He is going to move on, possibly to join an American League team as a backup receiver and DH. In that role, he should be valuable.

JOHN WEHNER

Positions: OF/3B//C/SS
Bats: R **Throws:** R
Ht: 6'3" **Wt:** 204
Opening Day Age: 28
Born: 6/29/1967
Drafted: PIT88 7/174
ML Seasons: 5

Overall Statistics

	G	AB	R	H	2B	3B	HR	RBI	SB	CS	BB	SO	BA	OBA
95 PIT	52	107	13	33	0	3	0	5	3	1	10	17	.308	.361
Career	175	375	43	97	14	3	0	19	9	1	35	67	.259	.320

1995 Situational Statistics

	AB	HR	RBI	BA	OBA	SLG		AB	HR	RBI	BA	OBA	SLG
Home	60	0	3	.350	.379	.383	LHP	45	0	3	.289	.346	.378
Road	47	0	2	.255	.340	.340	RHP	62	0	2	.323	.373	.355
Apr-Jun	12	0	0	.417	.417	.417	ScPos	20	0	4	.150	.296	.150
Jul-Oct	95	0	5	.295	.355	.358	Clutch	25	0	1	.280	.367	.280

SCOUTING REPORT

The gung-ho Wehner will do anything and play anywhere to stay in the majors. Whether playing infield or outfield, he displays adequate range, but hustles and gets the job done with his average hands and arm.

John has a slow bat and good fastballs zip right by him. As a result, he crouches and uses an odd, open stance to get at pitches earlier. A good runner despite average speed, Wehner is daring on the bases.

HOW HE PERFORMED IN '95

The Pirates' Mr. Versatility played the infield, the outfield, and even caught a game—and did it all without committing an error. He added some stick as well.

As he has in the past, Wehner bounced between the majors and Triple-A, settling in with the Pirates for good on July 24. Surprisingly solid hitting (his average climbed as high .407) made John valuable.

WHAT TO EXPECT IN '96

Wehner's ability to play any defensive position should assure him a spot on the roster. A high batting average would keep him around for years, but John can't afford a prolonged batting slump.

PITTSBURGH PIRATES

RICK WHITE

Position: SP/RP
Bats: R **Throws:** R
Ht: 6'4" **Wt:** 215
Opening Day Age: 27
Born: 12/23/1968
Drafted: PIT90 15/403
ML Seasons: 2

Overall Statistics

	G	GS	GF	SV	W	L	ERA	IP	H	R	ER	HR	BB	SO
95 PIT	15	9	2	0	2	3	4.75	55.0	66	33	29	3	18	29
Career	58	14	25	6	6	8	4.21	130.1	145	68	61	12	35	67

1995 Situational Statistics

	W	L	ERA	SV	IP	BB	SO		AB	HR	RBI	BA	OBA	SLG
Home	0	2	5.86	0	27.2	9	15	LHB	104	1	17	.317	.374	.433
Road	2	1	3.62	0	27.1	9	14	RHB	117	2	13	.282	.333	.376
Apr-Jun	0	1	3.80	0	23.2	10	11	ScPos	64	1	28	.266	.342	.406
Jul-Oct	2	2	5.46	0	31.1	8	18	Clutch	11	0	1	.273	.385	.364

SCOUTING REPORT

White is struggling to regain the control that got him to the majors. He uses a three-quarter to low three-quarter delivery with a wrist wrap.

His out pitch is a well above-average curve which he sets up with an average fastball. Rick will also show a slider, a change, and a change-up curve. He must change speeds more effectively.

He has a good move to first and only two runners tried to steal on Rick last year, but he is a minus fielder and a poor hitter (.067 in '95 and 2-for-28 lifetime).

HOW HE PERFORMED IN '95

White got off on the wrong foot by reporting to training camp overweight. A sprained right elbow then knocked him onto the DL. Rick bounced between the majors and minors, working as a starter and reliever. He spent September in Pittsburgh, compiling an unattractive 5.81 ERA in six starts and suffering from elbow pain.

WHAT TO EXPECT IN '96

White wasn't in a good position with the Pirates at the end of the season, and his future got cloudier when it was determined that he needed reconstructive elbow surgery. Rick's career is in serious jeopardy.

KEVIN YOUNG

Positions: 3B//1B
Bats: R **Throws:** R
Ht: 6'3" **Wt:** 210
Opening Day Age: 26
Born: 6/16/1969
Drafted: PIT90 7/187
ML Seasons: 4

Overall Statistics

	G	AB	R	H	2B	3B	HR	RBI	SB	CS	BB	SO	BA	OBA
95 PIT	56	181	13	42	9	0	6	22	1	3	8	53	.232	.268
Career	266	759	68	177	40	5	13	84	4	7	54	169	.233	.290

1995 Situational Statistics

	AB	HR	RBI	BA	OBA	SLG		AB	HR	RBI	BA	OBA	SLG
Home	97	5	17	.258	.311	.495	LHP	64	3	8	.156	.191	.313
Road	84	1	5	.202	.216	.250	RHP	117	3	14	.274	.310	.419
Apr-Jun	32	1	2	.250	.273	.375	ScPos	40	2	16	.175	.280	.375
Jul-Oct	149	5	20	.228	.267	.383	Clutch	41	0	3	.171	.227	.268

SCOUTING REPORT

Kevin hacks his bat like a golf club and makes poor contact because of his long swing. He likes fastballs over the plate but wrestles with low, inside pitches. An average runner, Young is a poor basestealer.

He is a dandy fielder at both first and third. He dares batters to smash the ball by him, covering each bag with plus range. He has soft hands and an average arm.

HOW HE PERFORMED IN '95

If Kevin could hit the way he fields, he would be an annual All-Star; he covers third base as well as anyone in the league. His eleven assists at the hot corner on June 25 tied the single-game record.

Unfortunately, he may be doomed to a career in the minors if he cannot improve his .233 lifetime average. Batting a pitiful .188 last August 16, Kevin changed his batting stance and promptly went 11 for his next 22. However, he hit poorly in September.

WHAT TO EXPECT IN '96

Charlie Hayes' signing with Pittsburgh could spell the end for Young, who has to hit better to even hold a utility job with the Pirates.

PITTSBURGH PIRATES: TOP PROSPECTS

JERMAINE ALLENSWORTH
Bats: R Throws: R Opening Day Age: 24
Ht: 5-11 Wt: 180 Born: 1/11/1972
Position: CF Drafted: 1993 #2 PIT

YR TEAM	LG/CLASS	G	AB	R	H	2B	3B	HR	RBI	SB	BA	OBA
93 Welland	NYP/A	67	263	44	81	16	4	1	32	18	.308	.390
94 Carolina	SOU/AA	118	452	63	109	26	8	1	34	16	.241	.315
95 Calgary	PCL/AAA	51	190	46	60	13	4	3	11	13	.316	.375
Carolina	SOU/AA	56	219	37	59	14	2	1	14	13	.269	.357

Allensworth can play center field in the major leagues now and he showed considerable improvement with the bat in 1995. He's swiped 60 bases in his three-year career, but has hit just six home runs. He could be more selective and bunt more often, but the 1992 Welland MVP did hit .316 in his first taste of Triple-A.

TREY BEAMON
Bats: L Throws: R Opening Day Age: 22
Ht: 6-3 Wt: 195 Born: 2/11/1974
Position: OF Drafted: 1992 #4 PIT

YR TEAM	LG/CLASS	G	AB	R	H	2B	3B	HR	RBI	SB	BA	OBA
93 Augusta	SAL/A	104	373	64	101	18	6	0	45	19	.271	.360
94 Carolina	SOU/AA	112	434	69	140	18	9	5	47	24	.323	.375
95 Calgary	PCL/AAA	118	452	74	151	29	5	5	62	18	.334	.387

After winning the Southern League batting crown as the league's youngest hitter in 1994, Beamon finished third in the Pacific Coast League bat race last season. A pure hitter who makes consistent contact, the 21-year-old hit nearly .370 in the second half last season, faring equally well against right and lefthanded pitching. The four-year pro has good speed, but has not shown much power. Beamon is below-average in both right and left field.

LOU COLLIER
Bats: R Throws: R Opening Day Age: 22
Ht: 5-10 Wt: 170 Born: 8/21/1973
Position: SS Drafted: 1992 #33 PIT

YR TEAM	LG/CLASS	G	AB	R	H	2B	3B	HR	RBI	SB	BA	OBA
93 Welland	NYP/A	50	201	35	61	6	2	1	19	8	.303	.356
94 Augusta	SAL/A	85	318	48	89	17	4	7	40	32	.280	.345
94 Salem	CARO/A	43	158	25	42	4	1	6	16	5	.266	.348
95 Lynchburg	CARO/A	114	399	68	110	19	3	4	38	31	.276	.365

Collier may be the most exciting player in the organization. He can hit and run, has some pop and possesses a very strong throwing arm. He cut down on his strikeouts and nearly doubled his walks last season, but hit more than twice as many flyballs than ground balls, a bad sign for a "speed" player. Defensively, his arm is his best tool. Questions persist about his range and errors (a remarkable 80 in the last two years).

ELMER DESSENS
Bats: R Throws: R Opening Day Age: 24
Ht: 6-0 Wt: 190 Born: 1/13/1972
Position: P Drafted: Purchased 4-95 MEX

YR TEAM	LG/CLASS	G	GS	GF	SV	W	L	ERA	IP	H	HR	BB	SO	O/BA
95 Carolina	SOU/AA	27	27	0	0	15	8	2.49	152.0	170	10	21	68	.284

None of the Mudcats' coaches had ever seen Dessens pitch before he arrived last season. The Mexican native was purchased from the Mexican League in April, went to Double-A, and did not allow more than one earned run in any of his first ten starts. He led the Southern League in wins and ERA, did not allow a walk in ten of 12 starts during one stretch, and was selected to the post-season All-Star team. The 23-year-old has a below-average fastball and allowed more hits than innings pitched, but showed great location, threw strikes and kept the ball down, inducing many double plays.

MICAH FRANKLIN
Bats: S Throws: R Opening Day Age: 23
Ht: 6-0 Wt: 195 Born: 4/25/1972
Position: OF Drafted: 1990 #3 NYN

YR TEAM	LG/CLASS	G	AB	R	H	2B	3B	HR	RBI	SB	BA	OBA
93 Chston-WV	SAL/A	102	343	56	90	14	4	17	68	6	.262	.374
93 Winston-Sal	CARO/A	20	69	10	16	1	1	3	6	0	.232	.346
94 Winston-Sal	CARO/A	42	150	44	45	7	0	21	44	7	.300	.424
94 Chattanooga	SOU/AA	79	279	46	77	17	0	10	40	2	.276	.375
95 Calgary	PCL/AAA	110	358	64	105	28	0	21	71	3	.293	.372

Franklin, another Pirates corner outfield prospect, has decent skills, with a powerful bat being his best. He finished second in the Pacific Coast League in slugging (.547) and was third in homers. The 23-year-old, already with his third organization, is just adequate in the outfield and chases too many pitches out of the strike zone. A switch-hitter, Franklin has fared much better against southpaws the last two seasons. He made news in 1994 by hitting 21 homers in his first 42 games at Winston-Salem.

FREDDY GARCIA
Bats: R Throws: R Opening Day Age: 23
Ht: 6-2 Wt: 186 Born: 8/1/1972
Position: 3B Drafted: NDFA 5-16-91 TOR

YR TEAM	LG/CLASS	G	AB	R	H	2B	3B	HR	RBI	SB	BA	OBA
93 Medicne Hat	PIO/R	72	264	47	63	8	2	11	42	4	.239	.319
94 St. Cathrnes	NYP/A	73	260	46	74	10	2	13	40	1	.285	.366
95 Pittsburgh	NL/MAJ	42	57	5	8	1	1	0	1	0	.140	.246

This Rule V selectee is thought to be the first player in baseball history to jump from a short-season league directly to the major leagues. After leading the New York–Penn League in homers in 1994, the Pirates acquired the 23-year-old and kept him on their roster all season. Garcia will return to the minor leagues this season. His best tools are a quick, powerful bat and a strong throwing arm, but he is obviously very inexperienced.

PITTSBURGH PIRATES: TOP PROSPECTS

JOHN HOPE
Bats: R Throws: R Opening Day Age: 25
Ht: 6-3 Wt: 206 Born: 12/21/1970
Position: P Drafted: 1989 #3 PIT

YR TEAM	LG/CLASS	G	GS	GF	SV	W	L	ERA	IP	H	HR	BB	SO	O/BA
93 Carolina	SOU/AA	21	20	0	0	9	4	4.37	111.1	123	7	29	66	.284
93 Buffalo	AMAS/AAA	4	4	0	0	2	1	6.33	21.1	30	4	2	6	.337
93 Pittsburgh	NL/MAJ	7	7	0	0	0	2	4.03	38.0	40	2	8	8	.267
94 Buffalo	AMAS/AAA	18	17	0	0	4	9	3.87	100.0	98	8	23	54	.253
94 Pittsburgh	NL/MAJ	9	0	1	0	0	0	5.79	14.0	18	1	4	6	.310
95 Pittsburgh	NL/MAJ	3	0	0	0	0	0	30.86	2.1	8	0	4	2	.615
Calgary	PCL/AAA	13	13	0	0	7	1	2.79	80.2	76	3	11	41	.250

The former second-round pick, who had overcome career-threatening shoulder surgery in 1990, got off to a great start in 1995, going 7-1 with a league-best 2.49 ERA by the end of May. Then a bout with shoulder tendinitis limited the 24-year-old to just two starts the rest of the season. Although he hasn't regained his pre-injury, 90-mph velocity, Hope has outstanding control and is successful because he keeps the ball down.

JASON KENDALL
Bats: R Throws: R Opening Day Age: 21
Ht: 6-0 Wt: 170 Born: 6/26/1974
Position: C Drafted: 1992 #1 PIT

YR TEAM	LG/CLASS	G	AB	R	H	2B	3B	HR	RBI	SB	BA	OBA
93 Augusta	SAL/A	102	366	43	101	17	4	1	40	8	.276	.325
94 Salem	CARO/A	101	371	68	118	19	2	7	66	14	.318	.406
94 Carolina	SOU/AA	13	47	6	11	2	0	0	6	0	.234	.294
95 Carolina	SOU/AA	117	429	87	140	26	1	8	71	10	.326	.414

Barring injury, Kendall could easily skip Triple-A this season and take over behind the plate for the Pirates. Defensively, the Southern League MVP's worst tool is an above-average throwing arm, which is now pain-free after earlier troubles. Offensively, Kendall is a .301 career hitter who has finished second in batting in the Carolina and Southern Leagues the last two years. In addition, the Howe Sportsdata All-Star rarely whiffs—he has been the toughest batter in his league to strike out each of the last three years—and is a run producer (.354 with runners in scoring position last year) with good speed for a catcher.

RAMON MOREL
Bats: R Throws: R Opening Day Age: 21
Ht: 6-2 Wt: 170 Born: 8/15/1974
Position: P Drafted: NDFA 5-29-91 PIT

YR TEAM	LG/CLASS	G	GS	GF	SV	W	L	ERA	IP	H	HR	BB	SO	O/BA
93 Welland	NYP/A	16	16	0	0	7	8	4.21	77.0	90	7	21	51	.286
94 Augusta	SAL/A	28	27	0	0	10	7	2.83	168.2	157	8	24	152	.243
95 Pittsburgh	NL/MAJ	5	0	0	0	0	1	2.84	6.1	6	0	2	3	.300
Carolina	SOU/AA	10	10	0	0	3	3	3.52	69.0	71	4	10	34	.267
Lynchburg	CARO/A	12	12	0	0	3	7	3.47	72.2	80	2	13	44	.283

The biggest asset for Ramon, the Pirates' top pitching prospect, is his ability to throw strikes. He didn't walk more than two batters in any start all season, featuring a fastball that varied in velocity from 85 to 93 mph. He also throws a slider and changeup. Just 21, Morel has a chance to fill out his tall, lean frame and add more consistent velocity in the future.

CHARLES PETERSON
Bats: R Throws: R Opening Day Age: 21
Ht: 6-3 Wt: 200 Born: 5/8/1974
Position: OF Drafted: 1993 #1 PIT

YR TEAM	LG/CLASS	G	AB	R	H	2B	3B	HR	RBI	SB	BA	OBA
93 Pirates	GULF/R	49	188	28	57	11	3	1	23	8	.303	.374
94 Augusta	SAL/A	108	415	55	106	14	6	4	40	27	.255	.316
95 Carolina	SOU/AA	20	70	13	23	3	1	0	7	2	.329	.415
Lynchburg	CARO/A	107	391	61	107	9	4	7	51	31	.274	.345

The most physically gifted player in the entire organization, Peterson, from rural South Carolina, has a powerful body, sprinter speed and a very strong arm, although he is still very raw. The 21-year-old impressed the organization with the way he handled two levels in '95 and made the Carolina League All-Star team, but has not shown the power expected of him despite an uppercut swing. Peterson is still learning how to play the outfield.

MATT RUEBEL
Bats: L Throws: L Opening Day Age: 26
Ht: 6-2 Wt: 180 Born: 10/16/1969
Position: P Drafted: 1991 #4 PIT

YR TEAM	LG/CLASS	G	GS	GF	SV	W	L	ERA	IP	H	HR	BB	SO	O/BA
93 Salem	CARO/A	19	1	4	0	1	4	5.94	33.1	34	6	32	29	.262
93 Augusta	SAL/A	23	7	6	0	5	5	2.42	63.1	51	2	34	50	.219
94 Salem	CARO/A	21	13	0	0	6	6	3.44	86.1	87	9	27	72	.260
94 Carolina	SOU/AA	6	3	0	0	1	1	6.61	16.1	28	3	3	14	.389
95 Carolina	SOU/AA	27	27	0	0	13	5	2.76	169.1	150	7	45	136	.236

Reubel, the biggest surprise in the organization last year, won as many games in 1995 as he did in his previous two years combined. Featuring a mid-80's fastball, great curve, and decent change, the 25-year-old learned how to pitch inside and spot his pitches better. A Southern League All-Star, Reubel finished among the league leaders in ERA, wins and strikeouts and was second in the Pirate organization in wins and strikeouts.

MATT RYAN
Bats: R Throws: R Opening Day Age: 24
Ht: 6-5 Wt: 190 Born: 3/20/1972
Position: P Drafted: 1993 #28 PIT

YR TEAM	LG/CLASS	G	GS	GF	SV	W	L	ERA	IP	H	HR	BB	SO	O/BA
93 Welland	NYP/A	16	0	12	5	0	1	2.08	17.1	11	0	12	25	.157
93 Pirates	GULF/R	9	0	5	2	1	1	2.33	19.1	17	0	9	20	.243
94 Augusta	SAL/A	33	0	31	13	2	1	1.14	39.1	29	0	7	49	.190
94 Salem	CARO/A	25	0	16	7	2	2	1.91	28.1	27	0	8	13	.252
95 Calgary	PCL/AAA	5	0	4	1	0	0	1.93	4.2	5	0	1	2	.278
Carolina	SOU/AA	44	0	38	26	2	1	1.57	46.0	33	0	19	23	.202

Some scouts say Ryan has the best sinker in baseball, and his 5:1 groundball/flyball ratio and zero career home runs allowed make a strong case. He tops out at 88 mph on the gun, but has held hitters to a .210 average in his three-year career. Although he struggled in the Southern League playoffs, the 23-year-old finished the season with 16.1 scoreless innings in which he allowed six hits and two walks. His season would have been more impressive had he not missed a month's duty with a sore shoulder.

PITTSBURGH PIRATES: OTHERS TO WATCH

JIMMY ANDERSON Bats: L Throws: L Ht: 6-1 Wt: 180
Born: 1/22/1976 Drafted: 1994 #9 PIT Position: P

YR TEAM	LG/CLASS	G	GS	GF	SV	W	L	ERA	IP	H	HR	BB	SO	O/BA
95 Lynchburg	CARO/A	10	9	1	0	1	5	4.13	52.1	56	1	21	32	.280
95 Augusta	SAL/A	14	14	0	0	4	2	1.53	76.2	51	1	31	75	.190

The best young pitcher in the system has had success with a 90-mph fastball, slider and changeup.

JEFF CONGER Bats: L Throws: L Ht: 6-0 Wt: 185
Born: 8/6/1971 Drafted: 1990 #8 PIT Position: CF

YR TEAM	LG/CLASS	G	AB	R	H	2B	3B	HR	RBI	SB	BA	OBA
95 Carolina	SOU/AA	39	128	15	37	6	1	1	17	8	.289	.378
95 Lynchburg	CARO/A	90	318	44	84	13	5	3	23	26	.264	.345

A "classic" center fielder who can steal bases, Conger hit well for the first time in 1995.

JAY CRANFORD Bats: R Throws: R Ht: 6-3 Wt: 175
Born: 4/7/1971 Drafted: 1992 #23 PIT Position: 3B

YR TEAM	LG/CLASS	G	AB	R	H	2B	3B	HR	RBI	SB	BA	OBA
95 Carolina	SOU/AA	93	288	30	66	12	1	5	42	3	.229	.348

An intense, highly-regarded competitor, Cranford struggled in the field and at the plate in 1995.

KANE DAVIS Bats: R Throws: R Ht: 6-3 Wt: 180
Born: 6/25/1975 Drafted: 1993 #16 PIT Position: P

YR TEAM	LG/CLASS	G	GS	GF	SV	W	L	ERA	IP	H	HR	BB	SO	O/BA
95 Augusta	SAL/A	26	25	0	0	12	6	3.75	139.1	136	4	43	78	.251

The 12-game winner has a projectable body, a live arm, and good command.

JOSE GUILLEN Bats: R Throws: R Ht: 5-11 Wt: 165
Born: 5/17/1976 Drafted: NDFA 9-22-92 PIT Position: OF

YR TEAM	LG/CLASS	G	AB	R	H	2B	3B	HR	RBI	SB	BA	OBA
95 Augusta	SAL/A	10	34	6	8	1	1	2	6	0	.235	.316
95 Erie	NYP/A	66	258	41	81	17	1	12	46	1	.314	.367

The NYP All-Star and home run leader is young and has a strong arm, but is a typical Dominican free swinger.

CHAD HERMANSEN Bats: R Throws: R Ht: 6-2 Wt: 185
Born: 9/10/1977 Drafted: 1995 #1 PIT Position: SS

YR TEAM	LG/CLASS	G	AB	R	H	2B	3B	HR	RBI	SB	BA	OBA
95 Pirates	GULF/R	24	92	14	28	10	1	3	17	0	.304	.363
95 Erie	NYP/A	44	165	30	45	8	3	6	25	4	.273	.354

The 1995 first-rounder dominated two short-season leagues last summer.

ROB LEARY Bats: L Throws: L Ht: 6-3 Wt: 195
Born: 7/9/1971 Drafted: 1991 #29 OAK Position: 1B

YR TEAM	LG/CLASS	G	AB	R	H	2B	3B	HR	RBI	SB	BA	OBA
95 Carolina	SOU/AA	67	243	38	74	14	3	6	42	3	.305	.405
95 Lynchburg	CARO/A	63	208	42	54	9	0	8	31	9	.260	.398

The former Northern League slugger hit for average and showed power and a good eye at two levels in 1995.

JOE MAKSIVISH Bats: R Throws: R Ht: 6-4 Wt: 180
Born: 8/14/1971 Drafted: 1994 #37 PIT Position: P

YR TEAM	LG/CLASS	G	GS	GF	SV	W	L	ERA	IP	H	HR	BB	SO	O/BA
95 Augusta	SAL/A	26	0	26	20	2	1	2.12	29.2	23	0	9	33	.211

The sidearmer with a sinking 85-mph fastball was leading the South Atlantic League in saves when elbow surgery ended his season in early July.

CHRIS PETERS Bats: L Throws: L Ht: 6-1 Wt: 170
Born: 1/28/1972 Drafted: 1993 #40 PIT Position: P

YR TEAM	LG/CLASS	G	GS	GF	SV	W	L	ERA	IP	H	HR	BB	SO	O/BA
95 Carolina	SOU/AA	2	2	0	0	2	0	1.29	14.0	9	0	2	7	.170
95 Lynchburg	CARO/A	24	24	0	0	11	5	2.43	144.2	126	5	35	132	.236

Featuring a curveball, excellent control and an ability to keep the ball down, Peters finished among the Carolina League leaders in wins, ERA, strikeouts and shutouts.

KEVIN PICKFORD Bats: L Throws: L Ht: 6-3 Wt: 200
Born: 3/12/1975 Drafted: 1993 #4 PIT Position: P

YR TEAM	LG/CLASS	G	GS	GF	SV	W	L	ERA	IP	H	HR	BB	SO	O/BA
95 Lynchburg	CARO/A	4	4	0	0	0	3	4.94	27.1	31	5	0	15	.284
95 Augusta	SAL/A	16	16	0	0	7	3	2.00	85.2	85	5	16	59	.258

A finesse pitcher who relies on command and an upper-80's fastball, Pickford won his first six decisions in 1995.

MARC PISCIOTTA Bats: R Throws: R Ht: 6-5 Wt: 240
Born: 8/7/1970 Drafted: 1991 #20 PIT Position: P

YR TEAM	LG/CLASS	G	GS	GF	SV	W	L	ERA	IP	H	HR	BB	SO	O/BA
95 Carolina	SOU/AA	56	0	27	9	6	4	4.15	69.1	60	2	45	57	.238

Pisciotta can bring it at 95 mph, but has no command or off-speed pitches.

KEVIN POLCOVICH Bats: R Throws: R Ht: 5-9 Wt: 165
Born: 6/28/1970 Drafted: 1992 #32 PIT Position: SS

YR TEAM	LG/CLASS	G	AB	R	H	2B	3B	HR	RBI	SB	BA	OBA
95 Calgary	PCL/AAA	62	213	31	60	8	1	3	27	5	.282	.336
95 Carolina	SOU/AA	64	221	27	70	8	0	3	18	10	.317	.369

Polcovich is a solid shortstop with good speed and range who surprised the organization with his bat.

KEVIN RYCHEL Bats: R Throws: R Ht: 5-9 Wt: 176
Born: 9/24/1971 Drafted: 1989 #7 PIT Position: P

YR TEAM	LG/CLASS	G	GS	GF	SV	W	L	ERA	IP	H	HR	BB	SO	O/BA
95 Calgary	PCL/AAA	10	0	3	0	0	1	10.38	8.2	14	3	6	4	.359
95 Carolina	SOU/AA	40	0	14	1	3	2	3.33	51.1	35	1	24	60	.198

Rychel has a 90+-mph sinking fastball and major league stuff when he's on, and got off to a great start before hurting his arm.

CHANCE SANFORD Bats: L Throws: R Ht: 5-10 Wt: 165
Born: 6/2/1972 Drafted: 1992 #29 PIT Position: 2B

YR TEAM	LG/CLASS	G	AB	R	H	2B	3B	HR	RBI	SB	BA	OBA
95 Carolina	SOU/AA	16	36	6	10	3	1	3	10	3	.278	.381
95 Lynchburg	CARO/A	16	66	8	22	4	0	3	14	1	.333	.392
95 Pirates	GULF/R	6	19	2	4	0	0	1	1	0	.211	.286

A solid hitter who needs work at second base, the 1994 Carolina League All-Star missed most of '95 with an elbow injury.

ST. LOUIS CARDINALS

SCOTT COOPER

Position: 3B
Bats: L **Throws:** R
Ht: 6'3" **Wt:** 200
Opening Day Age: 28
Born: 10/13/1967
Drafted: BOS86 2/69
ML Seasons: 6

SCOUTING REPORT
Cooper has improved at taking pitches the other way, and will now offer at low pitches both inside and outside. He isn't as effective against high fastballs due to a slow bat. Scott lacks the ability to pull the ball and is what scouts call a "straight-away" hitter.

While Cooper has impressed defensively at third base in the past, his skills seem to have deteriorated. He is a minus runner with minus range, throws with average strength and average-minus accuracy, and has average-minus hands. Some of Cooper's throwing problems could be a result of his 1994 shoulder surgery.

HOW HE PERFORMED IN '95
If there was a "Disappointment of the Year" award for the Redbirds, Cooper probably would have won it in 1995. A good fielder and decent hitter while in Boston, Scott's incredibly bad season has seriously, if not irreparably, damaged his career. As is his pattern, he began the season hot and was hitting .310 on May 10. However, Cooper hit just .206 the rest of the way.

A native of St. Louis, Scott was said to be pressing. He experienced a sharp rise in strikeouts and by September he had been relegated to riding the pine while the Cardinals explored other options. Cooper's slump last season can't be attributed to any one factor, but his shoulder problems appear to robbed him of some bat speed.

He doesn't add anything on the bases, and last season he made 18 errors and fielded just .945 at the hot corner, ranking sixth among league third sackers.

WHAT TO EXPECT IN '96
The Cardinals are probably not going to tender Cooper a contract, which makes him a free agent. They may re-sign him simply because there's nobody else: once highly-touted prospect Jose Oliva, who came over from the Braves in 1995, was even worse than Cooper.

New Cardinals' skipper Tony LaRussa knows a lot about Cooper from the AL and could get him restarted. Scott, a two-time All-Star, is a much better player than he showed in 1995. As one veteran observer of the Cardinals remarked, "Cooper is a great candidate to pull a Galarraga on us if he leaves."

Overall Statistics

	G	AB	R	H	2B	3B	HR	RBI	SB	CS	BB	SO	BA	OBA
95 SL	118	374	29	86	18	2	3	40	0	3	49	85	.230	.321
Career	517	1642	185	446	88	11	30	196	6	9	176	267	.272	.343

1995 Situational Statistics

	AB	HR	RBI	BA	OBA	SLG		AB	HR	RBI	BA	OBA	SLG
Home	189	1	20	.228	.320	.302	LHP	97	0	18	.206	.316	.268
Road	185	2	20	.232	.322	.324	RHP	277	3	22	.238	.323	.329
Apr-Jun	200	2	20	.265	.365	.350	ScPos	100	0	35	.210	.314	.300
Jul-Oct	174	1	20	.190	.269	.270	Clutch	60	0	10	.183	.351	.250

How He Compares to Other Batters

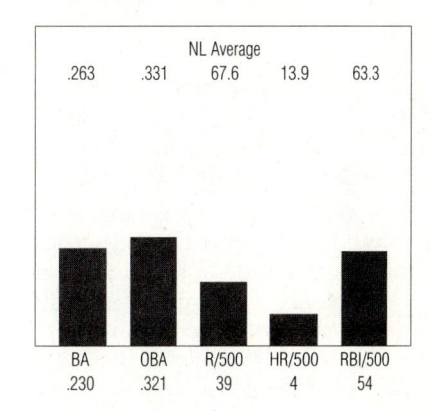

	BA	OBA	R/500	HR/500	RBI/500
NL Average	.263	.331	67.6	13.9	63.3
	.230	.321	39	4	54

Where He Hits the Ball

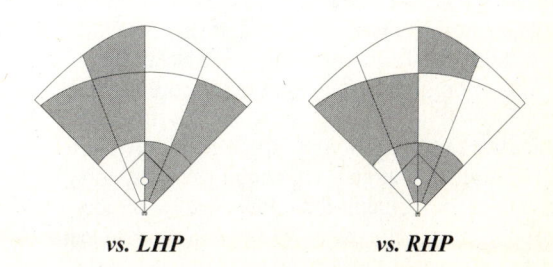

vs. LHP   vs. RHP

THE SCOUTING REPORT: 1996

ST. LOUIS CARDINALS

TRIPP CROMER

Positions: SS/2B
Bats: R **Throws:** R
Ht: 6'2" **Wt:** 165
Opening Day Age: 28
Born: 11/21/1967
Drafted: SL89 3/66
ML Seasons: 3

SCOUTING REPORT
Roy Bunyan Cromer III is a weak hitter with poor bat speed. He likes high pitches over the plate, but tries to pull the ball incessantly and swings at a lot of things he can't possibly hit. Tripp rarely bunts, either for a base hit or to sacrifice. He is an average runner who doesn't clog the bases but poses no threat to steal.

Cromer can play both shortstop and second base, featuring above-average range at both spots. His arm is average but he has plus accuracy, and his hands are well above-average. Tripp is a good athlete and a tough competitor who is a very smart defensive player.

HOW HE PERFORMED IN '95
Ozzie Smith's season-long injury problems made Cromer a starter for the first time in the majors. He showed some skills, but he had a rough rookie campaign overall.

While Cromer hadn't come up to the Cardinals with great offensive expectations, he had batted .275 and .274 in his two full seasons of Triple-A. Therefore, his poor showing at the bat in 1995 ranks as a disappointment. He socked a few extra-base hits, but since he doesn't know the strike zone or how to work the pitchers into giving him a pitch to hit, Tripp posted an intolerably low on-base percentage, even for a middle infielder.

Cromer is a good infielder who turns the double play very well at both shortstop and second base. He has the arm and glove to play either place, although he did commit 16 errors at shortstop last season, giving him a mediocre .960 fielding percentage. It's clear that Tripp could stick as a utility player because of his defensive ability and occasional power, but he's got so many holes in his bat that he isn't likely to used as a pinch-hitter.

WHAT TO EXPECT IN '96
The Cardinals were in a bind at shortstop after the season ended, not knowing if Ozzie Smith could return strong in 1996 and not being sure that Cromer is capable of hitting enough to stay in the lineup. Utility duty is probably his immediate future, but he might get another shot at an everyday job in the majors sometime in the future. The December trade for Giants' shortstop Royce Clayton appears to have answered those questions.

Overall Statistics

	G	AB	R	H	2B	3B	HR	RBI	SB	CS	BB	SO	BA	OBA
95 SL	105	345	36	78	19	0	5	18	0	0	14	66	.226	.261
Career	117	368	38	80	19	0	5	18	0	0	15	72	.217	.253

1995 Situational Statistics

	AB	HR	RBI	BA	OBA	SLG		AB	HR	RBI	BA	OBA	SLG
Home	164	2	8	.250	.291	.354	LHP	84	2	6	.190	.222	.345
Road	181	3	10	.204	.233	.298	RHP	261	3	12	.238	.273	.318
Apr-Jun	175	5	11	.246	.283	.389	ScPos	60	0	11	.133	.208	.150
Jul-Oct	170	0	7	.206	.238	.259	Clutch	47	0	3	.234	.245	.277

How He Compares to Other Batters

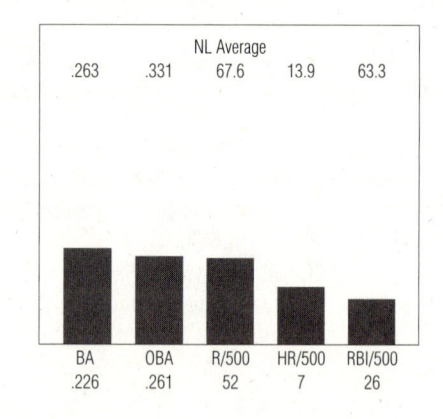

NL Average: .263 .331 67.6 13.9 63.3

BA .226 | OBA .261 | R/500 52 | HR/500 7 | RBI/500 26

Where He Hits the Ball

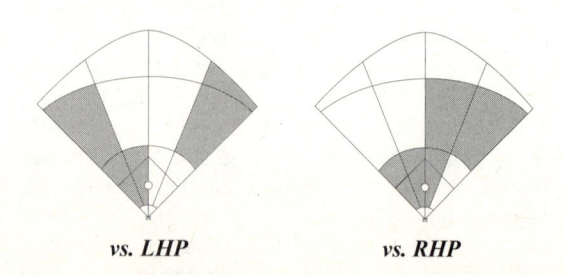

vs. LHP | vs. RHP

ST. LOUIS CARDINALS

BERNARD GILKEY

Position: OF
Bats: R **Throws:** R
Ht: 6'0" **Wt:** 170
Opening Day Age: 29
Born: 9/24/1966
Drafted: SL 8/22/84
ML Seasons: 6

SCOUTING REPORT

Bernard Gilkey hits the ball hard to all fields with plus power. This means lots of extra-base hits, and it also means lots of double-play balls (17 in 1995) despite his plus speed. Gilkey is a smart baserunner, but doesn't steal as often as he might, and only bunted a couple of times last season.

Gilkey's throwing arm is average in strength for a left fielder but above-average in accuracy. He has plus range in left, charges balls well, and has plus hands.

HOW HE PERFORMED IN '95

After a poor 1994, Gilkey wasn't tendered a contract by St. Louis, but they re-signed him for $600,000 less than he had made before. Bernard's big 1995 season would normally mean he would get a healthy increase for 1996, but that may not be true in the new economic climate.

Gilkey has batted .298 or higher in three of his four big-league seasons. As in the past, he hit much better on the road than he did at Busch Stadium. In a favorable park for hitters and on a contending team, he would probably be a star.

Although Bernard hit in each of the top five lineup spots, he was used most of the time last season as in the leadoff slot. This is not utilize his talents best, however, as he is a first-ball fastball hitter and doesn't take as many pitches in the top spot as he might. Gilkey's power may suit him best to batting third or fifth.

Bernard is a surehanded outfielder who registered a career-high ten assists last year, leading the Cardinals' strong-armed flychasers in baserunners nailed for the third straight season. He did this despite missing time with a strained right elbow. Gilkey made only three errors in '95.

WHAT TO EXPECT IN '96

The Cardinals were expected to re-sign Gilkey in the off-season, possibly to a multi-year deal. He is seen as a cornerstone for rebuilding the team, and even if he doesn't get any better than he is now, Bernard is a quality regular. However, should the Cardinals find someone else with better leadoff skills, Gilkey could move down in the lineup where his power would put to better use in an RBI slot.

Overall Statistics

	G	AB	R	H	2B	3B	HR	RBI	SB	CS	BB	SO	BA	OBA
95 SL	121	480	73	143	33	4	17	69	12	6	42	70	.298	.358
Career	593	2133	319	602	126	18	52	250	80	45	223	291	.282	.354

1995 Situational Statistics

	AB	HR	RBI	BA	OBA	SLG		AB	HR	RBI	BA	OBA	SLG
Home	238	5	36	.277	.342	.445	LHP	106	2	15	.311	.378	.472
Road	242	12	33	.318	.375	.533	RHP	374	15	54	.294	.353	.495
Apr-Jun	222	8	36	.311	.352	.464	ScPos	95	0	43	.326	.451	.453
Jul-Oct	258	9	33	.287	.364	.512	Clutch	83	3	16	.277	.341	.470

How He Compares to Other Batters

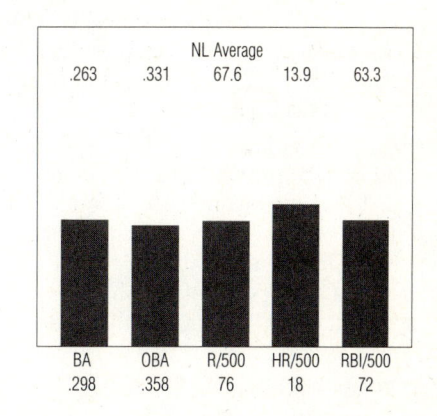

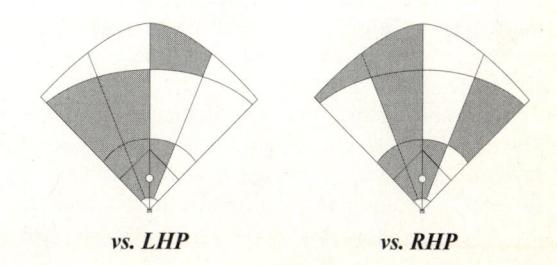

NL Average				
.263	.331	67.6	13.9	63.3

BA	OBA	R/500	HR/500	RBI/500
.298	.358	76	18	72

Where He Hits the Ball

vs. LHP   vs. RHP

THE SCOUTING REPORT: 1996

ST. LOUIS CARDINALS

TOM HENKE

Position: RP
Bats: R **Throws:** R
Ht: 6'5" **Wt:** 215
Opening Day Age: 37
Born: 12/21/1957
Drafted: TEX80 S4/67
ML Seasons: 13

SCOUTING REPORT
Henke throws overhand with good stuff. However, he occasionally drops down sidearm against tough righthanders. His fastball is a four-seamer with average velocity now. He has good command of his plus split-finger pitch, and throws a slider that has lost some of its bite. He used to throw all of his pitches harder, but he has retained effectiveness by improving his control and command as he has lost some velocity.

HOW HE PERFORMED IN '95
Henke decided to pitch for the Cardinals in 1995 largely because he's from Missouri. All he did in his first NL season was win the Rolaids Relief Award with a fourth-place team, enjoying a season that was, in its own way, as good as any in his career.

Tom is no longer the overpowering pitcher he was with the Blue Jays several years ago, but last year he allowed just two homers—his lowest total in over ten years. Lefthanders can't touch Henke, hitting .205 or under against him every year since 1990. His 1995 performance is especially impressive considering that the 37-year-old Henke had missed a month during the 1994 season because of a bulging disk in his back.

Coming to a speedier league, Henke found NL runners willing to test his slow pickoff move and long delivery, and last year 13 of 15 basestealers were successful against him. However, when opponents hit .209, such baserunning damage can't be too worrisome and his problems with basestealers aren't at all uncommon for righthanded power pitchers.

Tom was hitless in his only at-bat last year, his first trip to the plate in the majors.

WHAT TO EXPECT IN '96
St. Louis wanted him back after 1995, but Henke may want to retire at the peak of his game and spend more time with his family. If he returns for one more season, he'll be the closer while the Cardinals groom hot prospect T.J. Mathews to take his place in 1997. Henke is now fifth on the all-time saves list with 311 for his career and could get serious consideration as a Hall of Fame candidate if he adds to his career totals with another season like 1995.

Overall Statistics

	G	GS	GF	SV	W	L	ERA	IP	H	R	ER	HR	BB	SO
95 TEX	37	0	31	15	3	6	3.79	38.0	33	16	16	6	12	39
Career	590	0	501	275	40	41	2.73	735.1	565	241	223	62	237	813

1995 Situational Statistics

	W	L	ERA	SV	IP	BB	SO		AB	HR	RBI	BA	OBA	SLG
Home	1	2	2.21	9	33.2	6	25	LHP	72	4	15	.208	.293	.486
Road	2	4	5.60	6	29.0	6	14	RHP	70	2	10	.257	.288	.400
Apr-Jun	2	3	4.43	6	33.2	6	24	ScPos	38	4	22	.263	.293	.684
Jul-Oct	1	3	3.06	9	29.0	6	15	Clutch	101	6	24	.238	.310	.505

How He Compares to Other Pitchers

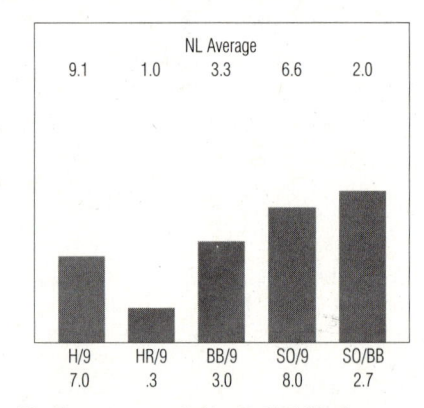

NL Average: 9.1 / 1.0 / 3.3 / 6.6 / 2.0

H/9	HR/9	BB/9	SO/9	SO/BB
7.0	.3	3.0	8.0	2.7

How He Compares to Other Relief Pitchers

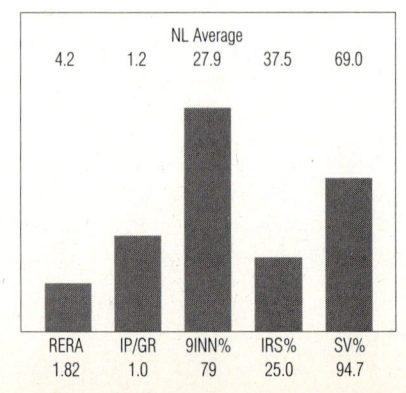

NL Average: 4.2 / 1.2 / 27.9 / 37.5 / 69.0

RERA	IP/GR	9INN%	IRS%	SV%
1.82	1.0	79	25.0	94.7

THE SCOUTING REPORT: 1996

ST. LOUIS CARDINALS

DANNY JACKSON

Position: SP
Bats: R **Throws:** L
Ht: 6'0" **Wt:** 205
Opening Day Age: 34
Born: 1/5/1962
Drafted: KC82* S1/1
ML Seasons: 13

SCOUTING REPORT
Danny uses a compact, cross-body delivery and throws from a three-quarter angle. He has above-average control of three pitches: a plus sinking fastball that Jackson also cuts, a good, big, hard slider, and an average circle change. His pickoff move is well above-average, but over the last two seasons 23 of 28 runners have been successful stealing against Jackson. Danny's assortment of sliders and sinkers, hard pitches for a catcher to unload quickly, doesn't help. He is an average fielder. Jackson came into '95 with a .120 career average in 368 at-bats, but did bat .161 last summer, with two doubles—one of which the Cardinals wish he hadn't hit.

HOW HE PERFORMED IN '95
Jackson had undergone surgery for thyroid cancer during the previous off-season, and although he's been pronounced healthy, the operations' effects plagued him throughout his worst big-league season.

Danny signed a big free-agent contract with the Cardinals for '95 and wanted to fulfill their expectations. As a result, he pitched despite being weak from his medication for much of the year. Often he fared well for the first five innings, only to fall apart quickly. In June, Jackson sat out for two weeks in order to regain his energy. Danny needs strength to throw his hard slider, but obviously didn't have much in the early portion of last season, allowing an almost unbelievable 34 doubles and 10 homers in just 100.2 innings.

However, he did begin to pitch effectively after coming back from the injured list. Jackson was 2-2 in July with a 2.79 ERA in 39.1 innings. Unfortunately, his run of good fortune and good performance ended on August 6, when Jackson severely sprained an ankle rounding second base after doubling against Chicago. Danny tried to come back a few days later, but the ankle hurt so much that he had to leave the game and missed the rest of the season.

WHAT TO EXPECT IN '96
Danny will come back healthy and strong this spring, and there's no reason he can't still be a decent lefthanded starter: Jackson has come back from the ash heap before. He could be successful with a good team, and the Cardinals are sure to be significantly improved in '96.

Overall Statistics

	G	GS	GF	SV	W	L	ERA	IP	H	R	ER	HR	BB	SO
95 SL	19	19	0	0	2	12	5.90	100.2	120	82	66	10	48	52
Career	323	307	8	1	109	121	3.88	1968.2	1979	979	848	119	772	1166

1995 Situational Statistics

	W	L	ERA	SV	IP	BB	SO		AB	HR	RBI	BA	OBA	SLG
Home	1	5	6.26	0	46.0	21	24	LHB	58	1	10	.259	.348	.362
Road	1	7	5.60	0	54.2	27	28	RHB	338	9	62	.311	.386	.494
Apr-Jun	0	8	8.08	0	49.0	28	28	ScPos	116	3	57	.319	.386	.474
Jul-Oct	2	4	3.83	0	51.2	20	24	Clutch	25	1	6	.400	.423	.600

How He Compares to Other Pitchers

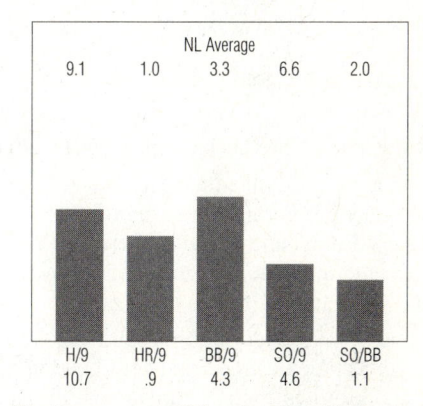

NL Average: H/9 9.1, HR/9 1.0, BB/9 3.3, SO/9 6.6, SO/BB 2.0
Jackson: H/9 10.7, HR/9 .9, BB/9 4.3, SO/9 4.6, SO/BB 1.1

How He Compares to Other Starting Pitchers

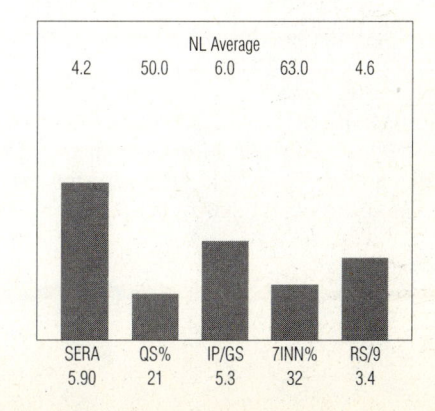

NL Average: SERA 4.2, QS% 50.0, IP/GS 6.0, 7INN% 63.0, RS/9 4.6
Jackson: SERA 5.90, QS% 21, IP/GS 5.3, 7INN% 32, RS/9 3.4

ST. LOUIS CARDINALS

BRIAN JORDAN

Position: OF
Bats: R **Throws:** R
Ht: 6'1" **Wt:** 205
Opening Day Age: 29
Born: 3/29/1967
Drafted: SL88 3/29
ML Seasons: 4

SCOUTING REPORT

Brian Jordan is one of the best pure athletes in the game. He is a plus runner with well above-average range in right field. His arm strength and accuracy are both average, and he has plus hands. Jordan always hustles in the outfield, and suffers some injuries due to his all-out play.

Brian is a pull hitter who likes the ball low and inside. He swings at bad pitches, however, and does not use much of the field. Despite his good wheels, Jordan does not bunt.

HOW HE PERFORMED IN '95

It was Jordan's first full major-league season, and only the second of his eight years in pro ball in which he has played over 100 games. Brian has suffered serious injuries in three different years, and missed significant time in other years in order to play football.

However, he was healthy and focused on the diamond in 1995, and played very well. Jordan contributed on the bases, hit with power, and hit well against lefties and, especially, righties.

The problems Brian has on offense center around command of the strike zone. He finished third on the Cardinals in whiffs, but just sixth in walks; his mediocre on-base percentage would have been even worse had he not been plunked by 11 pitches.

Jordan is a second-half hitter. He was batting just .212 last May 23, but improved significantly in the later stages. From June on, he hit between .296 and .318 each month with very consistent power production.

Brian mostly worked out of right field last year, but also played center 13 times, and could end up there if Ray Lankford is traded. Jordan made just one error all season, but had only four assists.

WHAT TO EXPECT IN '96

Jordan signed a long-term baseball-only contract last year, a step viewed as a major commitment by both Jordan and St. Louis. One more step forward on the field would make him star material. However, Brian turns 29 as this season begins, and if he's going to explode, it has to happen soon.

Overall Statistics

	G	AB	R	H	2B	3B	HR	RBI	SB	CS	BB	SO	BA	OBA
95 SL	131	490	83	145	20	4	22	81	24	9	22	79	.296	.339
Career	306	1084	147	300	47	16	42	162	41	20	60	202	.277	.323

1995 Situational Statistics

	AB	HR	RBI	BA	OBA	SLG		AB	HR	RBI	BA	OBA	SLG
Home	259	14	53	.313	.357	.541	LHP	121	5	21	.273	.328	.455
Road	231	8	28	.277	.319	.429	RHP	369	17	60	.304	.343	.499
Apr-Jun	221	9	38	.281	.322	.480	ScPos	131	5	57	.321	.385	.527
Jul-Oct	269	13	43	.309	.353	.494	Clutch	85	2	15	.235	.286	.376

How He Compares to Other Batters

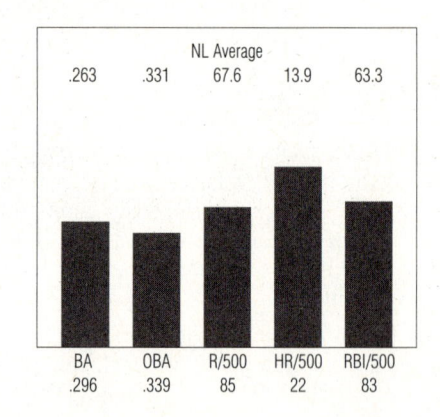

NL Average
.263 .331 67.6 13.9 63.3

BA OBA R/500 HR/500 RBI/500
.296 .339 85 22 83

Where He Hits the Ball

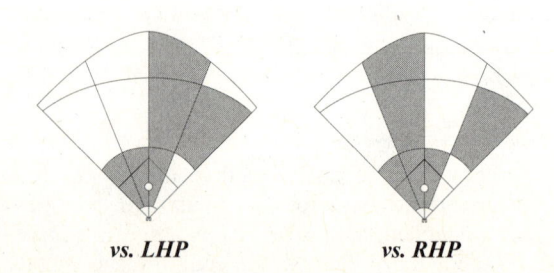

vs. LHP   vs. RHP

ST. LOUIS CARDINALS

RAY LANKFORD

Position: OF
Bats: L **Throws:** L
Ht: 5'11" **Wt:** 180
Opening Day Age: 28
Born: 6/5/1967
Drafted: SL87 3/72
ML Seasons: 6

SCOUTING REPORT

Lankford is a down-and-in fastball hitter who has good power but gets tied up by off-speed pitches. He is generally weak against lefthanders. Although he can bunt, he did not lay the ball down at all last year.

Ray is a plus runner. He usually shows above-average range in center but last year Lankford didn't get to his usual number of fly balls. His hands are well above-average, and Ray's arm is average for center field with average accuracy.

HOW HE PERFORMED IN '95

Ray had another up and down season. He paced the Cardinals in doubles, home runs, runs batted in, stolen bases, and walks, but also led the team in strikeouts, finishing sixth in the league and fanning at a rate near his career average.

There are periods where Lankford is an automatic out, and there are periods in which he's one of the best players in the game. After batting just .208 with one homer in August, the streaky Lankford homered in four straight games during September, finished on a hot streak. From the start of September through the season's end, he hit for a .356 average with ten four-baggers.

He raised his batting average against lefthanders last year by 107 points, but knocked out just two homers against them. In recent years, he has hit much better at Busch Stadium than on the road, conforming to a career pattern of hitting much better on artificial turf.

Although Lankford's raw stolen base totals have fallen dramatically in the past three seasons, he was far more successful when stealing in 1995 than he had ever been before.

WHAT TO EXPECT IN '96

Lankford is always likely to be a hot and cold player at the plate who will strike out a lot. If Ray hits with extra-base punch, he's very valuable; if not, he's an average player. There was talk that the Cardinals would trade over the winter to acquire a starting pitcher or a power-hitting infielder, but St. Louis has little in the pipeline to replace his bat at a key defensive position. Morever, his skills fit his park and team well—a move to the AL or to a grass park might diminish his value.

Overall Statistics

	G	AB	R	H	2B	3B	HR	RBI	SB	CS	BB	SO	BA	OBA
95 SL	132	483	81	134	35	2	25	82	24	8	63	110	.277	.360
Career	711	2596	416	695	150	32	83	351	143	78	328	622	.268	.351

1995 Situational Statistics

	AB	HR	RBI	BA	OBA	SLG		AB	HR	RBI	BA	OBA	SLG
Home	237	16	48	.308	.387	.612	LHP	142	3	29	.275	.354	.444
Road	246	9	34	.248	.333	.419	RHP	341	22	53	.279	.362	.543
Apr-Jun	233	8	30	.270	.341	.459	ScPos	125	9	61	.304	.414	.608
Jul-Oct	250	17	52	.284	.377	.564	Clutch	74	4	15	.311	.372	.554

How He Compares to Other Batters

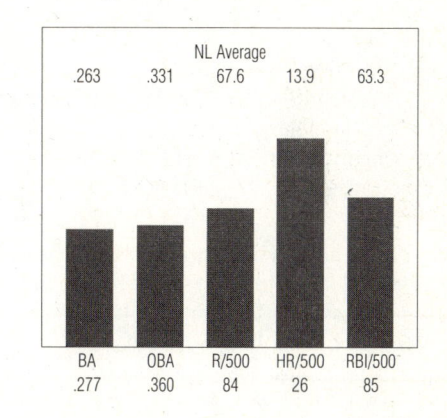

NL Average: .263 .331 67.6 13.9 63.3

BA	OBA	R/500	HR/500	RBI/500
.277	.360	84	26	85

Where He Hits the Ball

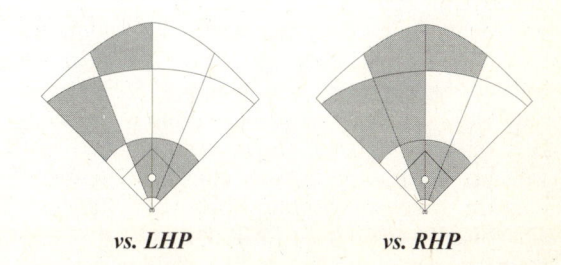

vs. LHP   vs. RHP

THE SCOUTING REPORT: 1996

ST. LOUIS CARDINALS

JOHN MABRY

Positions: 1B/OF
Bats: L **Throws:** R
Ht: 6'4" **Wt:** 195
Opening Day Age: 25
Born: 10/17/1970
Drafted: SL91 10/155
ML Seasons: 2

SCOUTING REPORT
Mabry has average punch and uses the whole field as a hitter, but he is expected to develop more power as he gains experience. He likes high pitches out over the plate, but is a very aggressive hitter who swings at too many marginal offerings.

John is an average-minus runner who won't be stealing bases in the majors. He did not bunt last season.

He has a plus arm with well above-average accuracy, making him a good right fielder. Mabry's range and hands are average, although he does not accelerate especially well. Despite being raw at first base, he performed adequately at the position for St. Louis in 1995.

HOW HE PERFORMED IN '95
First-year player Mabry was one of the Cardinals' few bright spots in a dismal '95 season. He flourished at the plate, hitting well in the second half and leading the Cardinals in batting average, despite learning a new position at the big-league level.

Due to St. Louis' logjam of quality outfielders, Mabry ended up spending 73 games at first base, becoming the regular there after Todd Zeile was dealt to Chicago. Mabry did not have an inning of pro experience at first base prior to 1995, but he didn't embarrass himself while learning the new position.

Although John homered in three straight games in August, he does not project as a big home-run hitter; his professional high in long balls is 16. He makes decent contact, however, and stood in well against lefthanders last year. Mabry's 1995 on-base percentage was only fair because he didn't take many walks. This is consistent for him: he's never taken more than 32 bases on balls in a season.

WHAT TO EXPECT IN '96
For Mabry to be truly productive, he's going to have to hit for a high average and either draw more walks or rack up more extra-base hits. If he forces pitchers to come into him by being more selective, he should hit for better power. He would be more valuable defensively in the outfield, because his plus arm is not so important at first base. It's possible an off-season trade for Ray Lankford would clear the way for him to play right field in 1996.

Overall Statistics

	G	AB	R	H	2B	3B	HR	RBI	SB	CS	BB	SO	BA	OBA
95 SL	129	388	35	119	21	1	5	41	0	3	24	45	.307	.347
Career	135	411	37	126	24	1	5	44	0	3	26	49	.307	.348

1995 Situational Statistics

	AB	HR	RBI	BA	OBA	SLG		AB	HR	RBI	BA	OBA	SLG
Home	204	2	22	.324	.368	.412	LHP	100	2	14	.330	.362	.420
Road	184	3	19	.288	.323	.397	RHP	288	3	27	.299	.342	.399
Apr-Jun	124	0	9	.298	.323	.371	ScPos	92	2	35	.293	.367	.380
Jul-Oct	264	5	32	.311	.358	.420	Clutch	72	0	10	.375	.432	.472

How He Compares to Other Batters

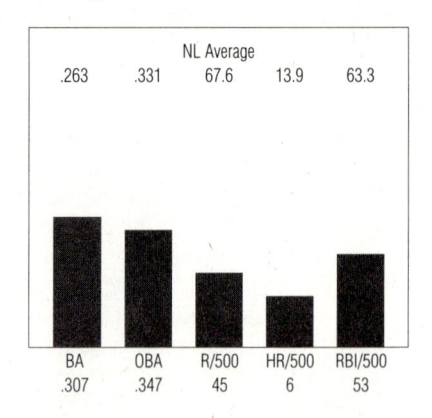

NL Average: .263 .331 67.6 13.9 63.3

BA	OBA	R/500	HR/500	RBI/500
.307	.347	45	6	53

Where He Hits the Ball

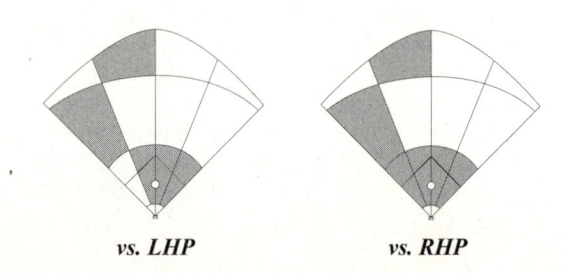

vs. LHP   vs. RHP

ST. LOUIS CARDINALS

MIKE MORGAN

Position: SP
Bats: R **Throws:** R
Ht: 6'3" **Wt:** 195
Opening Day Age: 36
Born: 10/8/1959
Drafted: OAK78 1/4
ML Seasons: 15

SCOUTING REPORT
Veteran righty Mike Morgan comes to the plate using a high three-quarters delivery. His sinking fastball is now a minus pitch, and his other three offerings (curve, slider, changeup) are average at best. Mike no longer has much velocity and relies on his experience to be effective by changing speeds, using all four pitches, and spotting his fastball to make it appear quicker.

He is quick to home and has a plus move to first, but last year 16 of 20 potential basestealers were successful against Morgan. He is an average fielder and a terrible hitter. Mike's 2-for-38 performance at the plate in 1995 lowered his career average to an very poor .090 mark in 385 at-bats.

HOW HE PERFORMED IN '95
Morgan had a miserable 1994 season and opened last year on the disabled list with Chicago. He didn't fit into the Cubs' plans though, and when he was activated May 25, it was only to be showcased for a trade. The Cardinals, desperate for healthy veteran hurlers, picked him up June 16 for Todd Zeile. Mike, happy to go someplace he was wanted, was doubly blessed that day as his wife delivered a baby girl.

Morgan went 5-6 for his new club with a 3.88 ERA. As he had been in Chicago, Mike was popular among his teammates and provided a stabilizing influence on a struggling team.

He was much improved against lefthanded hitters last year, shaving over 100 points from the batting average he had allowed them in 1994. Morgan needs to have good control to win, and last year didn't walk many people, but he left a few too many pitches high in the strike zone. He doesn't have the stuff to afford that any longer.

WHAT TO EXPECT IN '96
Morgan has been in the major leagues for parts of 15 seasons, but has only two winning records in that time. He can probably hang around pitching for a few more years if he wants to; he's already worn the uniforms of eight big-league clubs, but the Cardinals like him and wanted him back for 1996. With his age and talents, he could go either way this year. Another typical veteran pitcher's year of 10-15 wins with league-average ERA is possible, but the line between that and getting bombed out of the rotation isn't very distinct at his age.

Overall Statistics

	G	GS	GF	SV	W	L	ERA	IP	H	R	ER	HR	BB	SO
95 CHN/SL	21	21	0	0	7	7	3.56	131.1	133	56	52	12	34	61
Career	366	306	22	3	102	144	3.98	2045.2	2101	1001	904	176	689	1012

1995 Situational Statistics

	W	L	ERA	SV	IP	BB	SO		AB	HR	RBI	BA	OBA	SLG
Home	4	4	2.69	0	73.2	12	34	LHB	225	5	22	.271	.343	.400
Road	3	3	4.68	0	57.2	22	27	RHB	266	7	28	.271	.305	.395
Apr-Jun	3	3	3.07	0	44.0	10	25	ScPos	123	3	38	.203	.280	.293
Jul-Oct	4	4	3.81	0	87.1	24	36	Clutch	21	1	1	.143	.217	.286

How He Compares to Other Pitchers

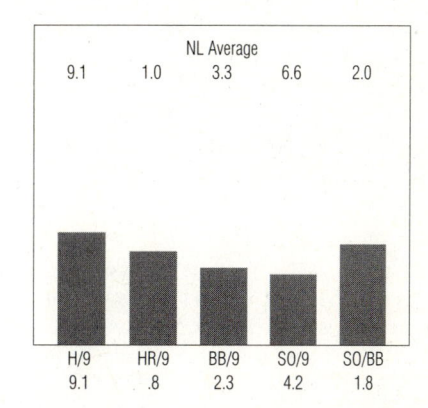

NL Average: H/9 9.1, HR/9 1.0, BB/9 3.3, SO/9 6.6, SO/BB 2.0

Morgan: H/9 9.1, HR/9 .8, BB/9 2.3, SO/9 4.2, SO/BB 1.8

How He Compares to Other Starting Pitchers

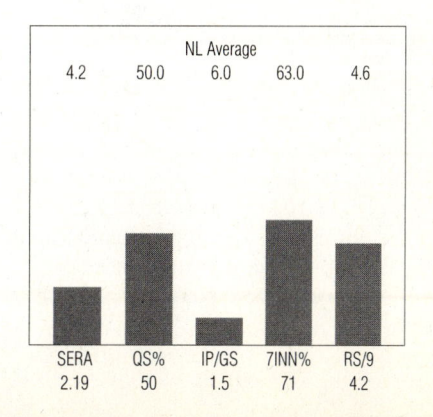

NL Average: SERA 4.2, QS% 50.0, IP/GS 6.0, 7INN% 63.0, RS/9 4.6

Morgan: SERA 2.19, QS% 50, IP/GS 1.5, 7INN% 71, RS/9 4.2

ST. LOUIS CARDINALS

DONOVAN OSBORNE

Position: SP
Bats: B **Throws:** L
Ht: 6'2" **Wt:** 195
Opening Day Age: 26
Born: 6/21/1969
Drafted: SL90 1/13
ML Seasons: 3

SCOUTING REPORT

Lefthander Donovan Osborne's delivery ranges from three-quarters to high three-quarters depending on the pitch and hitter. He has an average-minus fastball that has good sinking and running action. His curve and slider are average but his best pitch, a changeup, is well above-average. He doesn't get many strikeouts, but when his control is working, Osborne effectively throws off a hitter's timing.

Donovan's fielding is average, as is his move to first base. However, ten runners were thrown out trying to steal last year in 18 tries with Osborne on the hill.

HOW HE PERFORMED IN '95

Osborne missed all of 1994 after reconstructive shoulder surgery. Before the surgery, he had established a reputation as a decent lefthander who won with control rather than velocity. Upon his return in 1995, Osborne struggled with health problems but ended the season looking much like the hurler who recorded a 21-16 mark in 1992-93.

He began 1995 in the Cardinals' rotation, but he made just four starts before hitting the DL on May 15 with a sore elbow. After returning two months later, he struggled, and by September 1, was 0-6 with a 4.73 ERA. Poor location and sub-average velocity led to 15 homers allowed in just 72.1 innings.

However, in September, Osborne was a different pitcher. In his last six starts, he recorded a 4-0 record and a 2.18 ERA in 41 innings, fanning 30 and allowing just nine walks and two long balls in that span. Some said the big obstacle he had overcome was his own confidence.

Donovan came into the year with a .159 career average, and then stayed consistent by hitting .161.

WHAT TO EXPECT IN '96

Anyone recently disabled with both shoulder and elbow problems can hardly be considered a sure thing, but if Osborne is reasonably healthy and rested, he can be counted on to pitch well. He's not capable of being a #1 or #2 starter, but he goes after hitters and remains the ranking lefthander in the St. Louis rotation. And the Cardinals aren't in a position to bury anyone who has any chance of being effective.

Overall Statistics

	G	GS	GF	SV	W	L	ERA	IP	H	R	ER	HR	BB	SO
95 SL	19	19	0	0	4	6	3.81	113.1	112	58	48	17	34	82
Career	79	74	2	0	25	22	3.78	448.0	458	222	188	49	119	269

1995 Situational Statistics

	W	L	ERA	SV	IP	BB	SO		AB	HR	RBI	BA	OBA	SLG
Home	3	2	3.52	0	61.1	17	39	LHB	73	3	8	.274	.369	.534
Road	1	4	4.15	0	52.0	17	43	RHB	357	14	43	.258	.304	.437
Apr-Jun	0	1	4.09	0	22.0	5	13	ScPos	97	2	30	.237	.313	.351
Jul-Oct	4	5	3.74	0	91.1	29	69	Clutch	25	1	3	.320	.346	.520

How He Compares to Other Pitchers

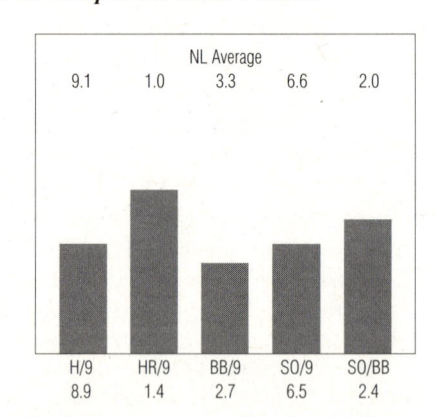

NL Average: 9.1 | 1.0 | 3.3 | 6.6 | 2.0

H/9: 8.9 | HR/9: 1.4 | BB/9: 2.7 | SO/9: 6.5 | SO/BB: 2.4

How He Compares to Other Starting Pitchers

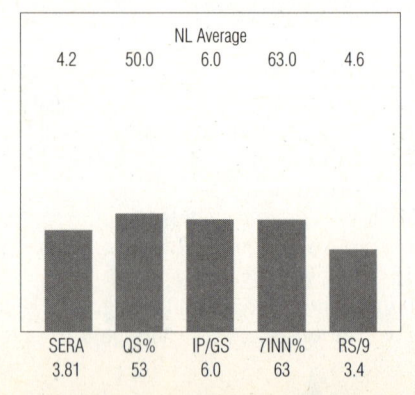

NL Average: 4.2 | 50.0 | 6.0 | 63.0 | 4.6

SERA: 3.81 | QS%: 53 | IP/GS: 6.0 | 7INN%: 63 | RS/9: 3.4

ST. LOUIS CARDINALS

TOM PAGNOZZI

Position: C
Bats: R **Throws:** R
Ht: 6'0" **Wt:** 190
Opening Day Age: 33
Born: 7/30/1962
Drafted: SL83 8/208
ML Seasons: 9

SCOUTING REPORT
Defense has always been Pagnozzi's strong suit, resulting in three Gold Gloves at catcher in his career. However, age and injury are taking their toll. He now has an average-plus throwing arm with average accuracy, although he has annually ranked among the league's most successful at retiring baserunners. Behind the plate, his mobility is now average and Pagnozzi has above-average hands.

His offense is not nearly as strong. Tom likes fastballs down in the strike zone and over the plate, but has little power and ends up hitting most pitches straightaway—a fatal problem if one doesn't have lots of power, especially in a big ballpark. He is one of the slowest runners in the league after numerous knee ailments.

HOW HE PERFORMED IN '95
It was a lost year for Pagnozzi. He didn't hit well when he was in the lineup, and went down July 18 with a left knee injury, getting only 17 at-bats the rest of the season.

Pagnozzi has been a good line-drive hitter with some line-drive power in recent years. However, in 1995, he posted career lows in nearly every category. Although Tom smacked some doubles early in the year, he wasn't doing much else and suffered through a horrendous 4-for-50 slump in June.

When he tore a tendon in his left knee in July, it was the third straight year Pagnozzi had suffered a knee problem; Tom has not played 100 games in a season since 1992. He attempted to return to action last August, but was forced out after a handful of games when the knee began to ache again.

Behind the plate, he again did a good job of throwing, nailing 37% of enemy basestealers (28 of 76). He made but two errors and allowed only one passed ball.

WHAT TO EXPECT IN '96
The Cardinals don't have any catching help in the high minors. Barring a trade, it's up to Pagnozzi to try to stay healthy. When he's able to play, he's one of the better defensive receivers in baseball, and can chip in a little with the bat. However, chronic knee problems are perhaps the worst thing a catcher has to deal with, making his future as a regular questionable.

Overall Statistics

	G	AB	R	H	2B	3B	HR	RBI	SB	CS	BB	SO	BA	OBA
95 SL	62	219	17	47	14	1	2	15	0	1	11	31	.215	.254
Career	732	2279	188	577	118	11	29	247	14	20	150	328	.253	.299

1995 Situational Statistics

	AB	HR	RBI	BA	OBA	SLG		AB	HR	RBI	BA	OBA	SLG
Home	115	1	8	.252	.295	.357	LHP	33	0	1	.242	.286	.394
Road	104	1	7	.173	.209	.269	RHP	186	2	14	.210	.249	.301
Apr-Jun	163	0	8	.215	.250	.282	ScPos	44	1	12	.182	.229	.250
Jul-Oct	56	2	7	.214	.267	.411	Clutch	38	1	3	.079	.143	.158

How He Compares to Other Batters

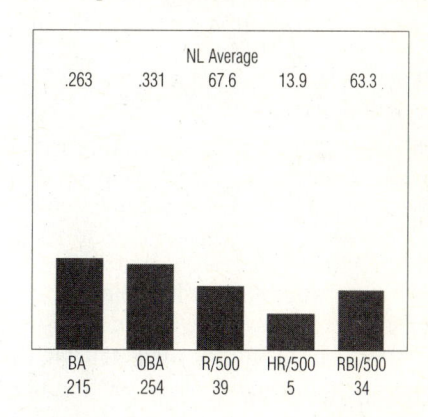

NL Average: .263 / .331 / 67.6 / 13.9 / 63.3

BA .215 | OBA .254 | R/500 39 | HR/500 5 | RBI/500 34

Where He Hits the Ball

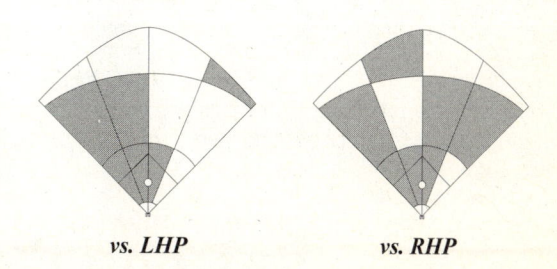

vs. LHP | vs. RHP

ST. LOUIS CARDINALS

MARK PETKOVSEK

Position: SP/RP
Bats: R **Throws:** R
Ht: 6'0" **Wt:** 185
Opening Day Age: 30
Born: 11/18/1965
Drafted: TEX87 3/29
ML Seasons: 3

SCOUTING REPORT

Mark Petkovsek comes at hitters with a smooth, high three-quarter motion. His best pitch is his plus curve, which he will throw at any time. His fastball has below-average velocity but sinks well. Mark can also run his fastball in effectively on righthanded hitters. His changeup is average. Inconsistent command and control were usually Petkovsek's biggest problems last year.

Mark holds runners well and is quick to home. Of the 17 runners who tried to steal against him last year, ten were thrown out by Cardinals' catchers. His fielding is above-average, but he batted just .081 in 37 at-bats.

HOW HE PERFORMED IN '95

Despite pitching at Triple-A since 1989, Petkovsek had only one major-league start and 30 appearances to his credit prior to last year. The nine-year professional threw a no-hitter for Tucson in 1994, but was he allowed to leave the Astros organization that winter as a free agent. He began 1995 in St. Louis' bullpen, but he was moved into the rotation when other hurlers failed. At season's end, the rookie had tied for the Cardinals' staff lead in starts. On a grim team in a down year, he was one of the bright spots.

Mark is a finesse pitcher whose control varies from outstanding to miserable; he was too often either very good or very bad. He had a game in which he allowed 10 earned runs and a game in which he registered 10 strikeouts. He pitched a shutout and was involved in several blowouts. He did have his share of strong outings, however, and almost by default, ranked as the Cardinals' most reliable starter.

WHAT TO EXPECT IN '96

Despite his success in 1995, Mark is unlikely to be in the starting rotation for the majority of 1996. More likely, Petkovsek, who has a 37-45 career record at Triple-A, will work as a swingman/spot starter if he isn't bombed back to the minors. For now, however, new manager Tony LaRussa has few options. The moribund Cardinals are one of those clubs where a pitcher of Petkovsek's stuff and pedigree can get another chance.

Overall Statistics

	G	GS	GF	SV	W	L	ERA	IP	H	R	ER	HR	BB	SO
95 SL	26	21	1	0	6	6	4.00	137.1	136	71	61	11	35	71
Career	56	22	10	0	9	7	5.08	179.0	200	112	101	22	48	91

1995 Situational Statistics

	W	L	ERA	SV	IP	BB	SO		AB	HR	RBI	BA	OBA	SLG
Home	4	1	2.92	0	77.0	16	35	LHB	231	4	33	.290	.327	.424
Road	2	5	5.37	0	60.1	19	36	RHB	289	7	29	.239	.303	.363
Apr-Jun	3	2	3.79	0	40.1	9	13	ScPos	118	4	52	.305	.358	.475
Jul-Oct	3	4	4.08	0	97.0	26	58	Clutch	32	0	3	.250	.333	.313

How He Compares to Other Pitchers

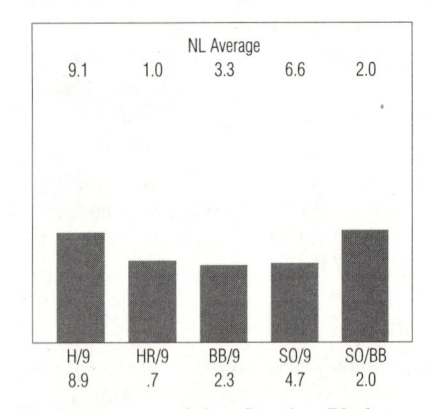

NL Average: H/9 9.1, HR/9 1.0, BB/9 3.3, SO/9 6.6, SO/BB 2.0
Petkovsek: H/9 8.9, HR/9 .7, BB/9 2.3, SO/9 4.7, SO/BB 2.0

How He Compares to Other Starting Pitchers

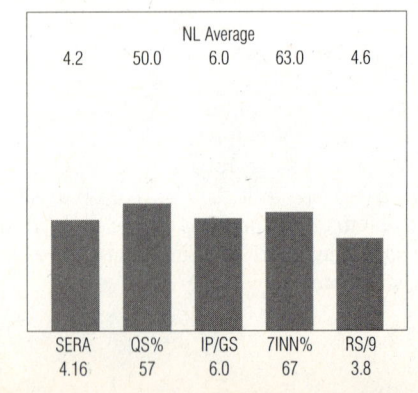

NL Average: SERA 4.2, QS% 50.0, IP/GS 6.0, 7INN% 63.0, RS/9 4.6
Petkovsek: SERA 4.16, QS% 57, IP/GS 6.0, 7INN% 67, RS/9 3.8

ST. LOUIS CARDINALS

ALLEN WATSON

Position: SP
Bats: L **Throws:** L
Ht: 6'3" **Wt:** 195
Opening Day Age: 25
Born: 11/18/1970
Drafted: SL91 2/21
ML Seasons: 3

SCOUTING REPORT

Not many lefthanders have stuff like Watson's. He throws across his body with a three-quarter motion, bringing home a four-seam fastball with average velocity that sometimes rides too high. His slider is an above-average offering, and his circle change, which he uses often, is well above-average. However, scouts feel that he may throw the change too much. His control is inconsistent.

Watson has what scouts call a "balk move" to first base, but it worked last year, as eleven of the 20 men who tried to steal against Allen were thrown out. His fielding is also plus, and Allen hit an astonishing .417 (15-for-36) last season to raise his career average to .270 in 100 at-bats. He is speedy and quick off the mound, but nobody in the organization is yet considering a conversion to the outfield.

HOW HE PERFORMED IN '95

Watson continued to struggle in his third big-league season. He got 19 starts mainly because the Cardinals desperately needed healthy pitchers. Unfortunately, Watson couldn't convert the opportunity into good performance.

Control is still a major problem for Watson, who does not set up hitters well and leaves too many hittable fastballs up in the strike zone. NL hitters rapped out 17 homers against him, tops on the Cardinals' staff. Watson's strikeout frequency has dropped in each of the last two years and his strikeout-to-walk ratio has gotten progressively worse as well.

Watson improved against lefthanders last season, but he allowed righthanders to bat over .300 off him for the second straight time. He missed a month last season with tendinitis in his left biceps, but pitched equally poorly before and after being disabled.

WHAT TO EXPECT IN '96

Although he's likely to be in the majors again this year, Allen would probably benefit from a year back at Louisville to improve his command. He was brought up very quickly, making just 33 starts above Single-A ball before reaching the majors in 1993. Pitchers with good stuff from the left side aren't given up on quickly, however, and Watson will get more than a few chances to establish himself as a bona fide big-league pitcher.

Overall Statistics

	G	GS	GF	SV	W	L	ERA	IP	H	R	ER	HR	BB	SO
95 SL	21	19	1	0	7	9	4.96	114.1	126	68	63	17	41	49
Career	59	56	2	0	19	21	5.07	316.0	346	194	178	43	122	172

1995 Situational Statistics

	W	L	ERA	SV	IP	BB	SO		AB	HR	RBI	BA	OBA	SLG
Home	6	4	4.86	0	63.0	26	22	LHB	75	3	11	.200	.286	.387
Road	1	5	5.08	0	51.1	15	27	RHB	367	14	43	.302	.365	.496
Apr-Jun	1	2	8.17	0	25.1	8	11	ScPos	99	1	33	.222	.304	.354
Jul-Oct	6	7	4.04	0	89.0	33	38	Clutch	14	0	1	.143	.368	.214

How He Compares to Other Pitchers

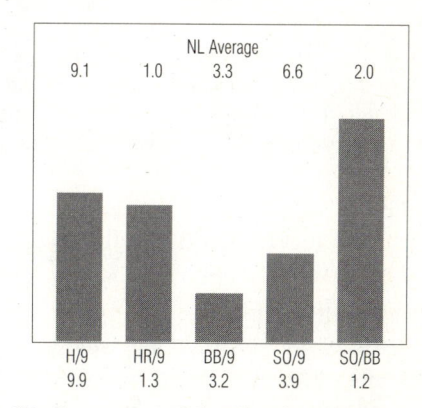

NL Average: H/9 9.1, HR/9 1.0, BB/9 3.3, SO/9 6.6, SO/BB 2.0
Watson: H/9 9.9, HR/9 1.3, BB/9 3.2, SO/9 3.9, SO/BB 1.2

How He Compares to Other Starting Pitchers

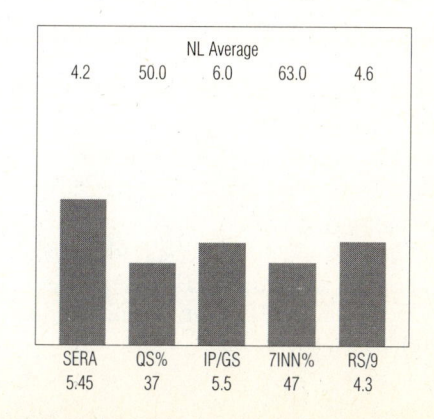

NL Average: SERA 4.2, QS% 50.0, IP/GS 6.0, 7INN% 63.0, RS/9 4.6
Watson: SERA 5.45, QS% 37, IP/GS 5.5, 7INN% 47, RS/9 4.3

ST. LOUIS CARDINALS

RENE AROCHA

Position: RP
Bats: R **Throws:** R
Ht: 6'0" **Wt:** 180
Opening Day Age: 30
Born: 2/24/1966
Drafted: SL 11/21/91
ML Seasons: 3

Overall Statistics

	G	GS	GF	SV	W	L	ERA	IP	H	R	ER	HR	BB	SO
95 SL	41	0	13	0	3	5	3.99	49.2	55	24	22	6	18	25
Career	118	36	38	11	18	17	3.87	320.2	346	155	138	35	70	183

1995 Situational Statistics

	W	L	ERA	SV	IP	BB	SO		AB	HR	RBI	BA	OBA	SLG
Home	1	1	3.47	0	23.1	7	12	LHB	94	3	13	.255	.317	.383
Road	2	4	4.44	0	26.1	11	13	RHB	91	3	14	.341	.413	.582
Apr-Jun	3	4	3.79	0	35.2	15	14	ScPos	58	1	22	.259	.348	.379
Jul-Oct	0	1	4.50	0	14.0	3	11	Clutch	129	3	23	.310	.384	.481

SCOUTING REPORT

When he's healthy, Arocha relies on a full bag of pitches. He throws a hard slider with a sharp break, an average moving fastball, and an average curve. He lacks a change-up but does have an average-plus forkball.

Rene isn't quick off the hill, but he worked on his average pickoff move last year, resulting in six of eight basestealers being cut down.

HOW HE PERFORMED IN '95

If Arocha wasn't the Cardinals' most disappointing pitcher, he was near the top of the list. After saving 11 games in 12 chances in 1994, Rene became second banana last season to Tom Henke and blew all seven of his save opportunities.

Opponents slugged .481 against him on the year. On July 31, Arocha was disabled with a strained right elbow and missed the rest of the season. Hitless in one trip at the plate in 1995, Rene is 7-for-68 (.103) in his career but is a decent bunter.

WHAT TO EXPECT IN '96

He's not going to be the closer in 1996 unless several other plans fall through. However, if Arocha is healthy, he should be effective in middle relief and could fill in as a spot starter.

ALLEN BATTLE

Position: OF
Bats: R **Throws:** R
Ht: 6'0" **Wt:** 170
Opening Day Age: 27
Born: 11/29/1968
Drafted: SL91 14/259
ML Seasons: 1

Overall Statistics

	G	AB	R	H	2B	3B	HR	RBI	SB	CS	BB	SO	BA	OBA
95 SL	61	118	13	32	5	0	0	2	3	3	15	26	.271	.358
Career	61	118	13	32	5	0	0	2	3	3	15	26	.271	.358

1995 Situational Statistics

	AB	HR	RBI	BA	OBA	SLG		AB	HR	RBI	BA	OBA	SLG
Home	51	0	1	.294	.368	.373	LHP	44	0	1	.273	.360	.273
Road	67	0	1	.254	.351	.269	RHP	74	0	1	.270	.357	.338
Apr-Jun	8	0	1	.250	.250	.250	ScPos	21	0	2	.286	.375	.286
Jul-Oct	110	0	1	.273	.365	.318	Clutch	29	0	1	.172	.273	.241

SCOUTING REPORT

Allen is an aggressive, high-ball hitter. He doesn't have great bat speed and lacks pull power, but he hits with some pop. He has been a basestealer in the minors and has average-plus speed, but does not bunt for hits.

Defensively, Battle is ordinary. His arm is accurate but it is not that strong. Allen has average-minus range despite his speed but does have average-plus hands.

HOW HE PERFORMED IN '95

Battle opened the year with the Cardinals, but was just 7-for-34 (.206) when sent to Louisville on May 9. Recalled for good on July 4, he hit much better, making 23 starts through year's end. He was better as a starter, going 3-for-21 as a pinch-hitter.

Battle showed some patience at the plate, but he did not run as well or often as advertised. He was used at all three outfield positions and made just one error.

WHAT TO EXPECT IN '96

It is unlikely that Battle will ever be good enough to play every day in the majors, but he is a legitimate .270 hitter with some other positives and could become a valuable reserve.

ST. LOUIS CARDINALS

DAVID BELL

Positions: 2B//3B
Bats: R **Throws:** R
Ht: 5'10" **Wt:** 170
Opening Day Age: 23
Born: 9/14/1972
Drafted: CLE90 9/190
ML Seasons: 1

Overall Statistics

	G	AB	R	H	2B	3B	HR	RBI	SB	CS	BB	SO	BA	OBA
95 CLE/SL	41	146	13	36	7	2	2	19	1	2	4	25	.247	.275
Career	41	146	13	36	7	2	2	19	1	2	4	25	.247	.275

1995 Situational Statistics

	AB	HR	RBI	BA	OBA	SLG		AB	HR	RBI	BA	OBA	SLG
Home	76	1	11	.211	.256	.303	LHP	36	0	3	.361	.395	.389
Road	70	1	8	.286	.296	.429	RHP	110	2	16	.209	.235	.355
Apr-Jun	2	0	0	.000	.000	.000	ScPos	38	0	12	.211	.262	.237
Jul-Oct	144	2	19	.250	.278	.368	Clutch	25	0	4	.160	.192	.200

SCOUTING REPORT

David has minus range and hands at second base. His arm is average with average accuracy. He has more experience at third base and is decent defensively there.

He likes low and inside pitches, but will swing at almost anything. Bell has average speed and didn't bunt last year. His power has developed some and could be a factor in the future.

HOW HE PERFORMED IN '95

St. Louis dumped Ken Hill's salary on Cleveland July 27, and picked up Bell in the bargain. David then became the Cardinals' regular second baseman for the last six weeks of the season.

Buddy's son, who has the trademark family hustle, beat up on NL lefthanders but didn't walk at all and fanned often. He lacks speed and projects to line-drive power at best. Bell fielded just .957 at second base, making seven errors.

WHAT TO EXPECT IN '96

Bell's scrappy play and hitting against lefties may get him a lot of duty this season. However, unless he improves his defense and his strike zone judgment, David projects as a utilityman: he won't hit enough to play third and lacks the defense for second.

RICH DELUCIA

Position: RP
Bats: R **Throws:** R
Ht: 6'0" **Wt:** 180
Opening Day Age: 31
Born: 10/7/1964
Drafted: SEA86 6/141
ML Seasons: 6

Overall Statistics

	G	GS	GF	SV	W	L	ERA	IP	H	R	ER	HR	BB	SO
95 SL	56	1	8	0	8	7	3.39	82.1	63	38	31	9	36	76
Career	161	49	27	1	27	34	4.53	437.1	424	239	220	64	186	323

1995 Situational Statistics

	W	L	ERA	SV	IP	BB	SO		AB	HR	RBI	BA	OBA	SLG
Home	4	3	4.02	0	40.1	17	41	LHB	112	5	15	.241	.358	.455
Road	4	4	2.79	0	42.0	19	35	RHB	184	4	21	.196	.266	.277
Apr-Jun	2	3	3.95	0	41.0	15	36	ScPos	79	2	27	.241	.295	.354
Jul-Oct	6	4	2.83	0	41.1	21	40	Clutch	95	5	12	.200	.336	.400

SCOUTING REPORT

Rich DeLucia uses a smooth three-quarters delivery for what is essentially a two-pitch arsenal. He has an average fastball that he usually sinks and often tries to tail away from lefthanded hitters. Rich's slider, an above-average pitch, gets most of his strikeouts. DeLucia has a quick move to home and holds runners well. He is an average fielder.

HOW HE PERFORMED IN '95

That DeLucia, a middle reliever, led St. Louis in wins in 1995 said a lot about the team's starting pitching. DeLucia enjoyed a fine comeback season after being drafted by the Cardinals over the winter. He fanned nearly a man an inning but he also allowed 20 extra-base hits and experienced some control problems. A former starter with the Mariners, Rich jump-started his sagging career with a 19-save season at Indianapolis in 1994.

Four of seven runners trying to steal were unsuccessful against Rich. He collected a respectable two hits in ten at-bats in his first big-league offensive experience.

WHAT TO EXPECT IN '96

Middle relief suits DeLucia well. If he's used in a more demanding role in the future, his performance is almost certain to suffer.

ST. LOUIS CARDINALS

TONY FOSSAS

Position: RP
Bats: L **Throws:** L
Ht: 6'0" **Wt:** 195
Opening Day Age: 38
Born: 9/23/1957
Drafted: TEX79 12/303
ML Seasons: 8

Overall Statistics

	G	GS	GF	SV	W	L	ERA	IP	H	R	ER	HR	BB	SO
95 SL	58	0	20	0	3	0	1.47	36.2	28	6	6	1	10	40
Career	385	0	114	5	14	10	3.84	293.1	293	141	125	23	116	224

1995 Situational Statistics

	W	L	ERA	SV	IP	BB	SO		AB	HR	RBI	BA	OBA	SLG
Home	2	0	0.44	0	20.1	4	22	LHB	72	0	8	.181	.203	.250
Road	1	0	2.76	0	16.1	6	18	RHB	59	1	7	.254	.348	.339
Apr-Jun	1	0	1.02	0	17.2	6	17	ScPos	40	0	14	.300	.396	.375
Jul-Oct	2	0	1.89	0	19.0	4	23	Clutch	64	0	4	.188	.235	.234

SCOUTING REPORT

Tony has stuff typical of your usual 38-year-old lefthander. His fastball, delivered from a standard three-quarter angle, is well below-average but has decent movement. Fossas uses the heater (sic) to set up his slider, an average pitch with a big, slow break.

Although he is average-plus at holding runners, Tony is very slow to the plate. His fielding is average. Fossas has never batted in the major leagues.

HOW HE PERFORMED IN '95

Fossas, the quintessential one-out lefty, was unscored on in his first 21 games last season while hurling only 11.2 innings. He pitched well, clamping down on lefties and keeping the ball in the park. Not a single runner tried to steal on him.

He didn't get a chance at the majors until he was past thirty, but now Fossas has spent most of the last seven years spending big-league meal money.

WHAT TO EXPECT IN '96

It's possible that Fossas could notch totals like he did in 1995, but there is always the chance he could get bombed out of baseball even pitching 40 innings a season and facing mostly lefthanders.

SCOTT HEMOND

Positions: C//2B
Bats: R **Throws:** R
Ht: 6'0" **Wt:** 205
Opening Day Age: 30
Born: 11/18/1965
Drafted: OAK86 1/12
ML Seasons: 7

Overall Statistics

	G	AB	R	H	2B	3B	HR	RBI	SB	CS	BB	SO	BA	OBA
95 SL	57	118	11	17	1	0	3	9	0	0	12	31	.144	.233
Career	298	607	79	132	30	0	12	58	23	13	65	162	.217	.295

1995 Situational Statistics

	AB	HR	RBI	BA	OBA	SLG		AB	HR	RBI	BA	OBA	SLG
Home	71	3	8	.225	.304	.366	LHP	27	1	3	.222	.364	.370
Road	47	0	1	.021	.130	.021	RHP	91	2	6	.121	.190	.187
Apr-Jun	35	1	2	.057	.154	.143	ScPos	22	0	6	.227	.333	.227
Jul-Oct	83	2	7	.181	.266	.265	Clutch	15	0	0	.133	.235	.133

SCOUTING REPORT

Hemond has a slow bat and is overmatched by a good fastball. He can hit pitches that hang up and over the plate. He is now an average runner and rarely bunts.

Scott has a plus arm behind the plate with average accuracy. He can fill in at first, second, and third with decent range and hands at all positions.

HOW HE PERFORMED IN '95

The majors' only catcher/second baseman had a dismal 1995 offensively. He struck out often, didn't draw walks or hit for power, and batted an incredible .021 (1-for-47) on the road. Speed is one reason Hemond has stuck around in the majors, but it's impossible to steal bases when you don't get any hits.

Scott's throwing at catcher is why he is still employed. In 1995, he tossed out an outstanding 43% of enemy basestealers, a number consistent with his career.

WHAT TO EXPECT IN '96

Hemond's average has fallen from .256 to .222 to .144 in three years. He should be thanking his lucky stars that Tony LaRussa has taken over in St. Louis, since LaRussa likes fringe players who can fill in at multiple positions.

ST. LOUIS CARDINALS

T. J. MATHEWS
Position: RP
Bats: R **Throws:** R
Ht: 6'2" **Wt:** 200
Opening Day Age: 26
Born: 1/9/1970
Drafted: SL92 36/1007
ML Seasons: 1

Overall Statistics

	G	GS	GF	SV	W	L	ERA	IP	H	R	ER	HR	BB	SO
95 SL	23	0	12	2	1	1	1.52	29.2	21	7	5	1	11	28
Career	23	0	12	2	1	1	1.52	29.2	21	7	5	1	11	28

1995 Situational Statistics

	W	L	ERA	SV	IP	BB	SO		AB	HR	RBI	BA	OBA	SLG
Home	1	0	0.56	0	16.0	3	15	LHB	29	0	3	.207	.361	.207
Road	0	1	2.63	2	13.2	8	13	RHB	76	1	6	.197	.237	.263
Apr-Jun	0	0	0.00	0	0.0	0	0	ScPos	32	0	7	.125	.200	.156
Jul-Oct	1	1	1.52	2	29.2	11	28	Clutch	56	0	5	.232	.317	.268

SCOUTING REPORT
T.J. comes at hitters from a low three-quarter angle with a deceptive delivery. His fastball has slightly above-average velocity and is very effective because of its good sink. He has an average slider with a long, sweeping break. Mathews' control is average and, though his move to first is also average, seven runners stole against him in seven tries. T.J. is a well above-average fielder. He was hitless in two tries last year.

HOW HE PERFORMED IN '95
Recalled from Triple-A on July 27, he threw eight scoreless relief innings to start his big-league career. Mathews had spent three seasons as a starter before moving to the bullpen at Louisville last spring, going 9-4 with a 2.70 ERA before his recall. Allowing just one home run in 29.1 innings in your big-league debut gets you noticed. Although Mathews isn't an especially hard thrower, his ball moves and he has consistently gotten strikeouts in the minors.

WHAT TO EXPECT IN '96
T.J. is viewed as closer material and will have a full season of setup duties. However, he doesn't have classic closer stuff and might be better in the rotation. Wherever he ends up, he's a competitive, quality prospect who just needs experience.

JOSE OLIVA
Positions: 3B//1B
Bats: R **Throws:** R
Ht: 6'1" **Wt:** 150
Opening Day Age: 25
Born: 3/3/1971
Drafted: TEX 11/12/87
ML Seasons: 2

Overall Statistics

	G	AB	R	H	2B	3B	HR	RBI	SB	CS	BB	SO	BA	OBA
95 ATL/SL	70	183	15	26	5	0	7	20	0	0	12	46	.142	.202
Career	89	242	24	43	10	0	13	31	0	1	19	56	.178	.242

1995 Situational Statistics

	AB	HR	RBI	BA	OBA	SLG		AB	HR	RBI	BA	OBA	SLG
Home	95	2	11	.126	.192	.232	LHP	57	2	5	.105	.164	.211
Road	88	5	9	.159	.213	.341	RHP	126	5	15	.159	.219	.317
Apr-Jun	78	4	10	.154	.205	.359	ScPos	50	1	11	.080	.145	.140
Jul-Oct	105	3	10	.133	.200	.229	Clutch	37	1	3	.162	.162	.243

SCOUTING REPORT
Although he has legitimate power, Oliva lacks any kind of plate discipline. He hits down and in fastballs, but tries to pull everything and is helpless against breaking balls or off-speed pitches. Even in the minors, he struck out four times as often as he walked. He doesn't run well, and won't be a threat on the bases.

Jose has a strong arm at third base with average accuracy. His range is poor and his hands below-average. In addition, questions have been raised about Jose's conditioning and makeup.

HOW HE PERFORMED IN '95
Oliva couldn't crack Atlanta's lineup. Rotting away on the Braves' bench, he was pried loose on August 25 by St. Louis, for whom he played third base most of September.

Scott Cooper's poor year created a huge opportunity that Jose couldn't capitalize on. He was just 9-for-74 (.122) with two home runs after the trade, which certainly didn't inspire the Cardinals.

WHAT TO EXPECT IN '96
He's obviously got major-league power, but unless he can show a dramatic improvement in plate discipline, he won't be around long. Raw tools won't get him anywhere if he doesn't develop.

THE SCOUTING REPORT: 1996

ST. LOUIS CARDINALS

JOSE OQUENDO

Positions: 2B/SS//3B/OF
Bats: B **Throws:** R
Ht: 5'10" **Wt:** 160
Opening Day Age: 32
Born: 7/4/1963
Drafted: NYN 4/15/79
ML Seasons: 12

Overall Statistics

	G	AB	R	H	2B	3B	HR	RBI	SB	CS	BB	SO	BA	OBA
95 SL	88	220	31	46	8	3	2	17	1	1	35	21	.209	.316
Career	1190	3202	339	821	104	24	14	254	35	33	448	376	.256	.346

1995 Situational Statistics

	AB	HR	RBI	BA	OBA	SLG		AB	HR	RBI	BA	OBA	SLG
Home	100	0	7	.230	.369	.330	LHP	54	2	6	.204	.317	.426
Road	120	2	10	.192	.269	.275	RHP	166	0	11	.211	.316	.259
Apr-Jun	125	1	11	.224	.340	.304	ScPos	40	1	13	.325	.417	.550
Jul-Oct	95	1	6	.189	.284	.295	Clutch	43	0	3	.186	.300	.233

SCOUTING REPORT

Versatility in the field allows Jose Oquendo to stay employed. He has plus range and hands at both second base and shortstop, and his arm has average strength and accuracy.

Jose's bat speed and raw power are poor. He hits the ball up the middle, mostly picking on high pitches over the plate. Heel problems have robbed him of some speed, although he is still a plus runner. He rarely steals or bunts.

HOW HE PERFORMED IN '95

Injuries to other Cardinals infielders gave Oquendo a chance to play in 1995. He hadn't played that much since 1991, and his bat showed why. Jose's only offensive plus is good strike-zone judgment. He has four steals in four years, but, oddly, pitchers still hold him close at first base.

Oquendo is a surehanded infielder. On a good (or healthy) team, however, he wouldn't see nearly as much action.

WHAT TO EXPECT IN '96

Jose was a free agent. If he does return to the Cards, it will be at a greatly reduced salary. Oquendo's just-finished long-term contract, which netted him $2 million a year, was another example of an overly generous contract for a non-key player.

JEFF PARRETT

Position: RP
Bats: R **Throws:** R
Ht: 6'3" **Wt:** 200
Opening Day Age: 34
Born: 8/26/1961
Drafted: MIL83 9/236
ML Seasons: 9

Overall Statistics

	G	GS	GF	SV	W	L	ERA	IP	H	R	ER	HR	BB	SO
95 SL	59	0	17	0	4	7	3.64	76.2	71	33	31	8	28	71
Career	440	11	172	22	53	40	3.84	658.1	608	311	281	59	314	552

1995 Situational Statistics

	W	L	ERA	SV	IP	BB	SO		AB	HR	RBI	BA	OBA	SLG
Home	3	1	3.29	0	41.0	14	33	LHB	96	2	7	.219	.315	.365
Road	1	6	4.04	0	35.2	14	38	RHB	196	6	28	.255	.307	.393
Apr-Jun	2	2	4.96	0	32.2	14	30	ScPos	73	3	28	.260	.341	.452
Jul-Oct	2	5	2.66	0	44.0	14	41	Clutch	106	3	16	.302	.364	.453

SCOUTING REPORT

Jeff throws across his body from a high three-quarter angle. All of his pitches are average, but his command of them is subpar. Parrett sinks or cuts the fastball; his slider and splitter break erratically. In 1995 six of seven runners stole successfully against Jeff. His fielding is average.

HOW HE PERFORMED IN '95

Parrett spent 1994 bouncing around the Royals' system. Signed by the Cardinals for 1995, he started the year poorly, with a 7.50 ERA after 13 games, but eventually rebounded.

Jeff led St. Louis in appearances and struck out nearly a batter per inning. He had some control problems, flinging seven wild pitches, tops on the staff. He also allowed opponents 24 extra-base hits. All in all, though, it was a comeback season for Parrett.

He was 1-for-2 at the plate after entering 1995 with an .088 average in 34 at-bats.

WHAT TO EXPECT IN '96

Parrett will be lucky to hang on much longer. He's had serious elbow problems and, even when healthy, has rarely been indispensable. A quality team might not even take a chance on him, but there are lots of desperate teams looking for pitching.

ST. LOUIS CARDINALS

GERONIMO PENA

Position: 2B
Bats: B **Throws:** R
Ht: 6'1" **Wt:** 170
Opening Day Age: 29
Born: 3/29/1967
Drafted: SL 8/9/84
ML Seasons: 6

Overall Statistics

	G	AB	R	H	2B	3B	HR	RBI	SB	CS	BB	SO	BA	OBA
95 SL	32	101	20	27	6	1	1	8	3	2	16	30	.267	.367
Career	373	1001	161	264	60	8	29	122	54	22	111	251	.264	.346

1995 Situational Statistics

	AB	HR	RBI	BA	OBA	SLG		AB	HR	RBI	BA	OBA	SLG
Home	47	1	4	.234	.327	.383	LHP	29	0	1	.379	.486	.621
Road	54	0	4	.296	.400	.370	RHP	72	1	7	.222	.318	.278
Apr-Jun	34	1	5	.324	.385	.441	ScPos	15	0	6	.267	.350	.333
Jul-Oct	67	0	3	.239	.358	.343	Clutch	23	0	4	.174	.286	.217

SCOUTING REPORT

Geronimo has some power, but can't catch up to most righthanders' good fastballs. He will walk, bunt, and can pop the ball out of the park. He is a smart runner but has just average speed.

At second base, Pena has above-average range but is erratic with the glove. His throwing is decent, and he is sharp on the pivot.

HOW HE PERFORMED IN '95

Forgive Geronimo if he gets up and punches the jukebox, since it plays the same broken record over and over. Once again, he couldn't stay healthy, and has probably played his last game for St. Louis. Geronimo was disabled three times in '95, with a fractured left tibia, a strained right hamstring and, finally, torn cartilage in his left knee that required season-ending surgery. As a result of the injuries, Pena had no time to get his rhythm, missing most of the summer.

WHAT TO EXPECT IN '96

Given his injuries and resulting inconsistency, Pena may have to start in Triple-A this year. He's still a talented hitter and underrated defensive player, and would be a fine everyday second baseman, if...

DANNY SHEAFFER

Positions: C//1B/3B
Bats: R **Throws:** R
Ht: 6' " **Wt:** 185
Opening Day Age: 34
Born: 8/2/1961
Drafted: BOS81* 1/20
ML Seasons: 5

Overall Statistics

	G	AB	R	H	2B	3B	HR	RBI	SB	CS	BB	SO	BA	OBA
95 SL	76	208	24	48	10	1	5	30	0	0	23	38	.231	.306
Career	234	616	67	141	24	2	11	79	2	5	43	80	.229	.277

1995 Situational Statistics

	AB	HR	RBI	BA	OBA	SLG		AB	HR	RBI	BA	OBA	SLG
Home	93	2	12	.290	.380	.452	LHP	73	1	13	.205	.310	.301
Road	115	3	18	.183	.242	.287	RHP	135	4	17	.244	.304	.393
Apr-Jun	57	3	13	.211	.286	.404	ScPos	51	2	26	.255	.400	.431
Jul-Oct	151	2	17	.238	.314	.344	Clutch	39	1	5	.256	.356	.385

SCOUTING REPORT

Veteran receiver Danny Sheaffer likes low pitches that catch the plate. He has some power, but is generally a very impatient hitter and one of the league's slowest runners. Sheaffer has an average throwing arm which is slightly below-average in accuracy. His range and hands are average-minus, but what he lacks in ability, Danny tries to make up for in grit and aggressiveness. He is fearless during home-plate collisions.

HOW HE PERFORMED IN '95

Sheaffer played 67 games behind the dish for St. Louis because of Tom Pagnozzi's injury problems. He didn't play especially well, but the alternatives were worse.

Danny showed decent sock last year and took a surprisingly high number of walks. However, at age 34 he won't be improving much. He tossed out just 18 of 78 basestealers last season (23%), but provided decent game-calling skills and displayed his hard-driving attitude.

WHAT TO EXPECT IN '96

Sheaffer isn't really any better than lots of other guys just like him at Triple-A. On the basis of his 1995 performance, though, he'll probably stick as a backup in the majors in 1996.

ST. LOUIS CARDINALS

OZZIE SMITH

Position: SS
Bats: B **Throws:** R
Ht: 5'11" **Wt:** 150
Opening Day Age: 41
Born: 12/26/1954
Drafted: SD77 4/86
ML Seasons: 18

Overall Statistics

	G	AB	R	H	2B	3B	HR	RBI	SB	CS	BB	SO	BA	OBA
95 SL	44	156	16	31	5	1	0	11	4	3	17	12	.199	.282
Career	2491	9169	1221	2396	392	67	26	775	573	143	1047	580	.261	.337

1995 Situational Statistics

	AB	HR	RBI	BA	OBA	SLG		AB	HR	RBI	BA	OBA	SLG
Home	97	0	7	.175	.283	.216	LHP	35	0	2	.143	.205	.200
Road	59	0	4	.237	.281	.288	RHP	121	0	9	.215	.304	.256
Apr-Jun	68	0	3	.250	.320	.294	ScPos	37	0	11	.216	.311	.297
Jul-Oct	88	0	8	.159	.255	.205	Clutch	27	0	3	.259	.364	.296

SCOUTING REPORT

At his advanced age, most of Smith's arm strength is gone. He has compensated for his minus arm for years with a very quick release, but now he loops his throws to first base. His range and hands are still average-plus and Ozzie positions himself well.

His speed has deteriorated to just average. A slap hitter, Smith likes high pitches over the plate while batting righthanded, and low inside pitches left-handed.

HOW HE PERFORMED IN '95

When Smith started for the Cardinals on April 26, he became the oldest opening-day shortstop in 45 years. He didn't play well, but he was still voted to the All-Star team by the fans for the 12th time, even though he missed most of the year after undergoing arthroscopic shoulder surgery on May 31. Smith contributed little on offense and made seven errors in just 41 games at shortstop.

WHAT TO EXPECT IN '96

If an outside doctor clears him for duty, Smith's option kicks in for 1996. Ozzie is a smart player and his feel for the shortstop position is still better than almost anyone else's. The acquisition of Royce Clayton in December, though, means his starting days are over.

TOM URBANI

Position: SP/RP
Bats: L **Throws:** L
Ht: 6'1" **Wt:** 190
Opening Day Age: 28
Born: 1/21/1968
Drafted: SL90 14/357
ML Seasons: 3

Overall Statistics

	G	GS	GF	SV	W	L	ERA	IP	H	R	ER	HR	BB	SO
95 SL	24	13	2	0	3	5	3.70	82.2	99	40	34	11	21	52
Career	62	32	6	0	7	15	4.48	225.0	270	132	112	27	68	128

1995 Situational Statistics

	W	L	ERA	SV	IP	BB	SO		AB	HR	RBI	BA	OBA	SLG
Home	1	3	3.75	0	36.0	6	27	LHB	74	3	6	.243	.300	.459
Road	2	2	3.66	0	46.2	15	25	RHB	251	8	29	.323	.366	.470
Apr-Jun	2	3	3.83	0	44.2	12	27	ScPos	73	2	21	.247	.295	.370
Jul-Oct	1	2	3.55	0	38.0	9	25	Clutch	24	0	0	.375	.423	.500

SCOUTING REPORT

Tom uses five pitches, although none of them is better than average. He throws from a three-quarter angle with passable control. Urbani's fastball has average-minus velocity, and he sinks, cuts, and turns it over to compensate. His curve, slider, change-up, and looping change-up curve are average.

HOW HE PERFORMED IN '95

Urbani was in and out of the rotation in '95: it seemed that every time he had a bad start, he was demoted to the bullpen. Righthanders have hit over .300 against Tom in each of his three years in the majors. He doesn't walk many but has serious problems with gopher balls.

He tries to help himself in other ways. Urbani has a fine pickoff move and a quick release. Only seven men ran against him in 1995, and three were thrown out. He hit .316 last season with a home run, raising his career average to .254. Tom's fielding is well above-average.

WHAT TO EXPECT IN '96

Urbani's role is always going to be as a spot starter/long reliever. As such, he has value if he can pitch as well as he did in '95. But he'll always be on the bubble.

ST. LOUIS CARDINALS: TOP PROSPECTS

BRIAN BARBER
Bats: R Throws: R Opening Day Age: 23
Ht: 6-1 Wt: 172 Born: 3/4/1973
Position: P Drafted: 1991 #3 SL

YR TEAM	LG/CLASS	G	GS	GF	SV	W	L	ERA	IP	H	HR	BB	SO	O/BA
93 Arkansas	TEX/AA	24	24	0	0	9	8	4.02	143.1	154	19	56	126	.278
93 Louisville	AMAS/AAA	1	1	0	0	0	1	4.76	5.2	4	0	4	5	.200
94 Louisville	AMAS/AAA	19	18	1	1	4	7	5.38	85.1	79	7	46	95	.248
94 Arkansas	TEX/AA	6	6	0	0	1	3	3.25	36.0	31	4	16	54	.230
95 St. Louis	NL/MAJ	9	4	2	0	2	1	5.22	29.1	31	4	16	27	.279
95 Louisville	AMAS/AAA	20	19	0	0	6	5	4.70	107.1	105	14	40	94	.254

One of three first-round picks in the Cardinals' impact draft of 1991, the hard-throwing Barber was expected to move through the system quickly. However, he's lost some velocity, which has forced him to become more of a pitcher. Barber uses his slider more often now and finished fourth in the American Association last season in strikeouts. He made his big league debut last year at age 22. Barber is 32-39, 4.29 ERA in his five-year minor league career, but has averaged a strikeout per inning.

ALAN BENES
Bats: R Throws: R Opening Day Age: 24
Ht: 6-5 Wt: 215 Born: 1/21/1972
Position: P Drafted: 1993 #1 SL

YR TEAM	LG/CLASS	G	GS	GF	SV	W	L	ERA	IP	H	HR	BB	SO	O/BA
93 Glens Falls	NYP/A	7	7	0	0	0	4	3.65	37.0	39	2	14	29	.269
94 Savannah	SAL/A	4	4	0	0	2	0	1.48	24.1	21	1	7	24	.241
94 St. Pete	FSL/A	11	11	0	0	7	1	1.61	78.1	55	0	15	69	.197
94 Arkansas	TEX/AA	13	13	0	0	7	2	2.98	87.2	58	8	26	75	.188
94 Louisville	AMAS/AAA	2	2	0	0	1	0	2.93	15.1	10	1	4	16	.175
95 St. Louis	NL/MAJ	3	3	0	0	1	2	8.44	16.0	24	2	4	20	.343
95 Louisville	AMAS/AAA	11	11	0	0	4	2	2.41	56.0	37	5	14	54	.185

After establishing himself as one of the top pitching prospects in the game in 1994, Benes began 1995 on a roll. Leading the American Association with 35 strikeouts in five starts through the end of April, he also had a 1.74 ERA. However, the big righthander then came down with stiffness in his right forearm, which sent him to the DL for over three months. The Cardinals' first-round pick in 1993 was fully recovered by August and made his major league debut a month later. The Creighton product throws strikes and has a top-notch slider and the best fastball in the organization.

JEFF BERBLINGER
Bats: R Throws: R Opening Day Age: 25
Ht: 6-0 Wt: 190 Born: 11/19/1970
Position: 2B Drafted: 1993 #8 SL

YR TEAM	LG/CLASS	G	AB	R	H	2B	3B	HR	RBI	SB	BA	OBA
93 Glens Falls	NYP/A	38	138	26	43	9	0	2	21	9	.312	.368
93 St.Pete	FSL/A	19	70	7	13	1	0	0	5	3	.186	.250
94 Savannah	SAL/A	132	479	86	142	27	7	8	67	24	.296	.390
95 Arkansas	TEX/AA	87	332	66	106	15	4	5	29	16	.319	.417

The only full-time player in the organization to bat over .300, Berblinger played well at Double-A before his season ended prematurely due to a stress fracture in his leg. The Kansas product led the Texas League in runs scored for a time and was batting .391 in July before being knocked out of the lineup. The 25-year-old is a steady fielder adept at turning the double play, but had questionable range even before the injury.

TERRY BRADSHAW
Bats: L Throws: R Opening Day Age: 27
Ht: 6-0 Wt: 180 Born: 2/3/1969
Position: OF Drafted: 1990 #10 SL

YR TEAM	LG/CLASS	G	AB	R	H	2B	3B	HR	RBI	SB	BA	OBA
93 St.Pete	FSL/A	125	461	84	134	25	6	5	51	43	.291	.402
94 Arkansas	TEX/AA	114	425	65	119	25	8	10	52	13	.280	.362
94 Louisville	AMAS/AAA	22	80	16	20	4	0	4	8	5	.250	.318
95 St. Louis	NL/MAJ	19	44	6	10	1	1	0	2	1	.227	.261
95 Louisville	AMAS/AAA	111	389	65	110	24	8	8	42	20	.283	.372

Bradshaw, an exciting player who hits to all fields, had a solid but unspectacular '95 campaign and was shaky during a brief mid-season promotion to St. Louis. Forced to sit out the entire 1992 season with a torn knee ligament, the Norfolk State product has worked hard to transform from speed demon to all-around ballplayer. The 27-year-old is considered a good defensive center fielder, but tied for the American Association lead with eight errors.

JOHN FRASCATORE
Bats: R Throws: R Opening Day Age: 26
Ht: 6-1 Wt: 200 Born: 2/4/1970
Position: P Drafted: 1991 #28 SL

YR TEAM	LG/CLASS	G	GS	GF	SV	W	L	ERA	IP	H	HR	BB	SO	O/BA
93 Springfield	MID/A	27	26	1	0	7	12	3.78	157.1	157	6	33	126	.259
94 Arkansas	TEX/AA	12	12	0	0	7	3	3.10	78.1	76	3	15	63	.251
94 Louisville	AMAS/AAA	13	12	0	0	8	3	3.39	85.0	82	3	33	58	.255
94 St. Louis	NL/MAJ	1	1	0	0	0	1	16.20	3.1	7	2	2	2	.438
95 St. Louis	NL/MAJ	14	4	3	0	1	1	4.41	32.2	39	3	16	21	.298
95 Louisville	AMAS/AAA	28	10	15	5	2	8	3.95	82.0	89	5	34	55	.273

One of the top winners in the Cardinals organization in '94, Frascatore was hit hard in 1995, allowing five or more runs in half of his ten starts before being sent to the bullpen. The move paid off as the hard-throwing 26-year-old recorded five saves and a 2.25 ERA in 18 games in relief. The C.W. Post product had previously posted a 23-save season for Savannah in 1992.

MIKE GULAN
Bats: R Throws: R Opening Day Age: 25
Ht: 6-1 Wt: 190 Born: 12/18/1970
Position: 3B Drafted: 1992 #2 SL

YR TEAM	LG/CLASS	G	AB	R	H	2B	3B	HR	RBI	SB	BA	OBA
93 Springfield	MID/A	132	455	81	118	28	4	23	76	8	.259	.321
94 St. Pete	FSL/A	120	466	39	113	30	2	8	56	2	.242	.282
95 Arkansas	TEX/AA	64	242	47	76	16	3	12	48	4	.314	.358
95 Louisville	AMAS/AAA	58	195	21	46	10	4	5	27	2	.236	.281

Selected as the organization's Player of the Year, Gulan is a great prospect both at the plate and in the field. A high school football star, the Kent State product has big-time power, with 41% of his hits going for extra-bases in '95. He finished third among Cardinal farmhands in both homers and RBI. However, strikeouts are a big concern; Gulan has fanned 348 times the last three years with just 81 walks. Defensively, he has excellent range and a solid glove at the hot corner that few minor leaguers can match.

THE SCOUTING REPORT: 1996

ST. LOUIS CARDINALS: TOP PROSPECTS

AARON HOLBERT
Bats: R Throws: R Opening Day Age: 23
Ht: 6-0 Wt: 160 Born: 1/9/1973
Position: SS Drafted: 1990 #2 SL

YR TEAM	LG/CLASS	G	AB	R	H	2B	3B	HR	RBI	SB	BA	OBA
93 St.Pete	FSL/A	121	457	60	121	18	3	2	31	45	.265	.312
94 Arkansas	TEX/AA	59	233	41	69	10	6	2	19	9	.296	.340
94 Cardinals	ARIZ/R	5	12	3	2	0	0	0	0	2	.167	.286
95 Louisville	AMAS/AAA	112	401	57	103	16	4	9	40	14	.257	.297

Despite a hamstring injury that landed him briefly on the DL, Holbert had a relatively injury-free year in '95. The defensive whiz has been beset with knee, ankle, and shoulder problems in his six-year career. Known for his arm and range, the 23-year-old led the American Association in errors, topping the 30 mark in miscues for the fourth time. At the plate Holbert set career marks in total bases, homers and RBI. He had seven dingers in his first five years combined.

STEVE MONTGOMERY
Bats: R Throws: R Opening Day Age: 25
Ht: 6-4 Wt: 200 Born: 12/25/1970
Position: P Drafted: 1992 #3 SL

YR TEAM	LG/CLASS	G	GS	GF	SV	W	L	ERA	IP	H	HR	BB	SO	O/BA
93 St.Pete	FSL/A	14	5	7	3	2	1	2.66	40.2	33	2	9	34	.221
93 Arkansas	TEX/AA	6	6	0	0	3	3	3.94	32.0	34	2	12	19	.270
94 Arkansas	TEX/AA	50	9	19	2	4	5	3.28	107.0	97	10	33	73	.241
95 Arkansas	TEX/AA	55	0	53	36	5	2	3.25	61.0	52	6	22	56	.231

In his second season with Arkansas, Montgomery stepped into the closer's role and tied the all-time Texas League record for saves. A former starter with a fastball, slider, and curve, the big righthander proved quite durable in his new role as he led the league in games pitched, finishing 53 of the 55 games he appeared in. He was roughed up a few times early in the year, but posted a 2.15 ERA the last three months. The Pepperdine product is not overpowering, but works quickly and had enough velocity and movement to average 8.26 strikeouts per nine innings.

MARK SWEENEY
Bats: L Throws: L Opening Day Age: 27
Ht: 6-1 Wt: 195 Born: 10/26/1969
Position: OF Drafted: 1991 #10 CAL

YR TEAM	LG/CLASS	G	AB	R	H	2B	3B	HR	RBI	SB	BA	OBA
93 Palm Sprngs	CAL/A	66	245	41	87	18	3	4	47	9	.355	.449
93 Midland	TEX/AA	51	188	41	67	13	4	2	9	32	1	.356	.444
94 Vancouver	PCL/AAA	103	344	59	98	12	3	8	49	3	.285	.394
94 Midland	TEX/AA	14	50	13	15	3	0	3	18	1	.300	.403
95 Vancouver	PCL/AAA	69	226	48	78	14	2	7	59	3	.345	.452
95 St. Louis	NL/MAJ	37	77	5	21	2	0	2	13	1	.273	.348
95 Louisville	AMAS/AAA	22	76	15	28	8	0	2	22	2	.368	.468

Acquired from the Angels in the John Habyan deal, Sweeney played in the Triple-A All-Star game and had the finest season of his five-year career. Switched from the outfield to first base after the deal, the University of Maine product handled himself well, but is still learning the position. At the plate the 26-year-old has good strike zone judgement and uses the whole field. The .310 career hitter, third in the minor leagues with a .355 average in 1993, was among the minor league leaders in average and on-base percentage last season when promoted to St. Louis.

BRET WAGNER
Bats: L Throws: L Opening Day Age: 23
Ht: 6-0 Wt: 190 Born: 4/17/1973
Position: P Drafted: 1994 #1 SL

YR TEAM	LG/CLASS	G	GS	GF	SV	W	L	ERA	IP	H	HR	BB	SO	O/BA
94 New Jersey	NYP/A	3	3	0	0	0	1	5.11	12.1	10	0	4	10	.204
94 Savannah	SAL/A	7	7	0	0	4	1	1.23	44.0	27	2	6	43	.175
95 St. Pburg	FSL/A	17	17	0	0	5	4	2.12	93.1	77	3	28	59	.228
95 Arkansas	TEX/AA	6	6	0	0	1	2	3.19	36.2	34	1	18	31	.241

The Cardinals' first-round pick in 1994 out of Wake Forest, Wagner is a hard thrower with a great pitcher's makeup. He's not afraid to pitch inside with his fastball and slider and is particularly tough on lefthanders. Wagner spent three weeks on the disabled list with a sore shoulder, and he was used carefully upon his return, pitching past the sixth inning just three times in his final 17 starts.

JAY WITASICK
Bats: R Throws: R Opening Day Age: 24
Ht: 6-4 Wt: 205 Born: 8/28/1972
Position: P Drafted: 1993 #3 SL

YR TEAM	LG/CLASS	G	GS	GF	SV	W	L	ERA	IP	H	HR	BB	SO	O/BA
93 Johnson Cty	APPY/R	12	12	0	0	4	3	4.12	67.2	65	8	19	74	.246
93 Savannah	SAL/A	1	1	0	0	1	0	4.50	6.0	7	0	2	8	.280
94 Madison	MID/A	18	18	0	0	10	4	2.32	112.1	74	5	42	141	.189
95 St. Pburg	FSL/A	18	18	0	0	7	7	2.74	105.0	80	4	36	109	.208
95 Arkansas	TEX/AA	7	7	0	0	2	4	6.88	34.0	46	4	16	26	.317

A tough competitor who throws strikes, Witasick recovered from a strained back which prematurely ended his '94 season. The big righthander hit his stride in his final four starts in St. Petersburg last season, allowing just one earned run in 28 innings while striking out 32. Featuring a fastball, slider, and changeup, the 23-year-old finished third in the organization in strikeouts, but struggled in Double-A, allowing 17 runs in his last 14 innings.

DMITRI YOUNG
Bats: S Throws: R Opening Day Age: 23
Ht: 6-2 Wt: 215 Born: 10/11/1973
Position: OF Drafted: 1991 #1 SL

YR TEAM	LG/CLASS	G	AB	R	H	2B	3B	HR	RBI	SB	BA	OBA
93 St. Pete	FSL/A	69	270	31	85	13	3	5	43	3	.315	.369
93 Arkansas	TEX/AA	45	166	13	41	11	2	3	21	4	.247	.294
94 Arkansas	TEX/AA	125	453	53	123	33	2	8	54	0	.272	.330
95 Arkansas	TEX/AA	97	367	54	107	18	6	10	62	2	.292	.347
95 Louisville	AMAS/AAA	2	7	3	2	0	0	0	0	0	.286	.375

It was an eventful year for Young, the fourth player selected in the 1991 draft. He was arrested in the spring after a barroom brawl and his attitude problems resurfaced late in the year when he was suspended for attacking a fan. In between the white lines, the switch-hitter still has great bat speed and enjoyed another productive season, although the organization is still waiting for Young to exhibit his explosive power. The 22-year-old has shifted between first base, third base and the outfield his entire career, and was adequate at best playing left field last season.

ST. LOUIS CARDINALS: OTHERS TO WATCH

MIKE BADOREK   Bats: R Throws: R   Ht: 6-5 Wt: 230
Born: 5/15/1969   Drafted: 1991 #16 SL   Position: P

YR TEAM	LG/CLASS	G	GS	GF	SV	W	L	ERA	IP	H	HR	BB	SO	O/BA
95 Arkansas	TEX/AA	18	17	1	1	7	5	4.35	101.1	119	4	30	50	.295

Badorek, a ground ball pitcher who won his first seven decisions, underwent season-ending arthroscopic surgery to remove bone spurs from his elbow.

CORY BAILEY   Bats: R Throws: R   Ht: 6-1 Wt: 210
Born: 1/24/1971   Drafted: 1991 #18 BOS   Position: P

YR TEAM	LG/CLASS	G	GS	GF	SV	W	L	ERA	IP	H	HR	BB	SO	O/BA
95 St. Louis	NL/MAJ	3	0	0	0	0	0	7.36	3.2	2	0	2	5	.154
95 Louisville	AMAS/AAA	55	0	40	25	5	3	4.55	59.1	51	6	30	49	.232

Acquired in the Scott Cooper deal, Bailey keeps the ball down and led the American Association in saves.

MIKE BUSBY   Bats: R Throws: R   Ht: 6-4 Wt: 215
Born: 12/27/1972   Drafted: 1991 #18 SL   Position: P

YR TEAM	LG/CLASS	G	GS	GF	SV	W	L	ERA	IP	H	HR	BB	SO	O/BA
95 Arkansas	TEX/AA	20	20	0	0	7	6	3.29	134.0	125	8	35	95	.241
95 Louisville	AMAS/AAA	6	6	0	0	2	2	3.29	38.1	28	2	11	26	.206

Selected as the organization's Pitcher of the Year, Busby rebounded from tendinitis to finish fourth in the Texas League in ERA.

DAN CHOLOWSKY   Bats: R Throws: R   Ht: 6-0 Wt: 195
Born: 10/30/1970   Drafted: 1991 #5 SL   Position: OF

YR TEAM	LG/CLASS	G	AB	R	H	2B	3B	HR	RBI	SB	BA	OBA
95 Arkansas	TEX/AA	54	190	41	59	12	0	7	35	7	.311	.398
95 Louisville	AMAS/AAA	76	238	27	52	9	1	7	25	10	.218	.326

The Cal-Berkeley product combines good power and decent speed with the ability to play in both the infield and outfield.

KEITH CONWAY   Bats: R Throws: L   Ht: 6-2 Wt: 200
Born: 5/8/1973   Drafted: 1993 #24 SL   Position: P

YR TEAM	LG/CLASS	G	GS	GF	SV	W	L	ERA	IP	H	HR	BB	SO	O/BA
95 Savannah	SAL/A	60	0	26	10	7	2	1.46	74.0	49	1	26	87	.188

A big lefthander with good control, Conway throws a mid-80's fastball, along with a slider and changeup and assumed the closer's role in late July.

RAY DAVIS   Bats: R Throws: R   Ht: 6-1 Wt: 225
Born: 2/6/1973   Drafted: 1991 #65 SL   Position: P

YR TEAM	LG/CLASS	G	GS	GF	SV	W	L	ERA	IP	H	HR	BB	SO	O/BA
95 Arkansas	TEX/AA	21	18	1	0	7	6	4.50	110.0	112	14	30	70	.265

The big righthander won six straight decisions and hurled 11 quality starts in 18 chances a year ago.

FRANK GARCIA   Bats: R Throws: R   Ht: 5-11 Wt: 170
Born: 3/5/1974   Drafted: NDFA 1-17-94 SLN   Position: P

YR TEAM	LG/CLASS	G	GS	GF	SV	W	L	ERA	IP	H	HR	BB	SO	O/BA
95 St. Pburg	FSL/A	16	0	8	1	0	1	10.26	16.2	27	1	18	8	.346
95 Savannah	SAL/A	34	0	32	24	0	3	3.16	37.0	26	3	15	41	.188

The Dominican native overpowered South Atlantic League hitters with his 90 mph fastball and was leading the league in saves at the time of his promotion.

RICK HEISERMAN   Bats: R Throws: R   Ht: 6-7 Wt: 220
Born: 2/22/1973   Drafted: 1994 #2 CLE   Position: P

YR TEAM	LG/CLASS	G	GS	GF	SV	W	L	ERA	IP	H	HR	BB	SO	O/BA
95 Kinston	CARO/A	19	19	0	0	9	3	3.74	113.0	97	13	42	86	.235
95 St. Pburg	FSL/A	6	5	1	0	2	3	5.46	28.0	28	2	11	18	.269

Acquired from the Indians in the Ken Hill deal, Heiserman is a huge righthander with a big sweeping curveball.

KEITH JOHNS   Bats: R Throws: R   Ht: 6-1 Wt: 175
Born: 7/19/1971   Drafted: 1992 #6 SL   Position: 2B

YR TEAM	LG/CLASS	G	AB	R	H	2B	3B	HR	RBI	SB	BA	OBA
95 Arkansas	TEX/AA	111	396	69	111	13	2	2	28	14	.280	.369
95 Louisville	AMAS/AAA	5	10	0	0	0	0	0	0	0	.000	.000

A smooth fielder with excellent leadoff skills, Johns had three hitting streaks of ten or more games last year.

ANTHONY LEWIS   Bats: L Throws: L   Ht: 5-11 Wt: 185
Born: 2/2/1971   Drafted: 1989 #8 SL   Position: OF

YR TEAM	LG/CLASS	G	AB	R	H	2B	3B	HR	RBI	SB	BA	OBA
95 Arkansas	TEX/AA	115	407	55	102	21	3	24	85	0	.251	.326

The organization's leader in homers and RBI, the lefthanded-hitting Lewis hangs in well versus southpaws and has a good arm in right field.

SEAN LOWE   Bats: R Throws: R   Ht: 6-2 Wt: 205
Born: 3/29/1971   Drafted: 1992 #1 SL   Position: P

YR TEAM	LG/CLASS	G	GS	GF	SV	W	L	ERA	IP	H	HR	BB	SO	O/BA
95 Arkansas	TEX/AA	24	24	0	0	9	8	4.88	129.0	143	2	64	77	.287

The Cardinals' first-round draft pick in 1992, Lowe is a ground-ball pitcher with good stuff but lacks command.

JOE MCEWING   Bats: R Throws: R   Ht: 5-10 Wt: 170
Born: 10/19/1972   Drafted: 1992 #28 SL   Position: 2B

YR TEAM	LG/CLASS	G	AB	R	H	2B	3B	HR	RBI	SB	BA	OBA
95 St. Pburg	FSL/A	75	281	33	64	13	0	1	23	2	.228	.289
95 Arkansas	TEX/AA	42	121	16	30	4	0	2	12	3	.248	.305

A gutty player who gets the most out of his talent, McEwing can play both infield and outfield.

BRIAN RUPP   Bats: R Throws: R   Ht: 6-5 Wt: 185
Born: 9/20/1971   Drafted: 1992 #43 SL   Position: 1B

YR TEAM	LG/CLASS	G	AB	R	H	2B	3B	HR	RBI	SB	BA	OBA
95 St. Pburg	FSL/A	90	325	30	90	12	2	0	23	0	.277	.334
95 Arkansas	TEX/AA	23	77	10	25	3	0	0	6	0	.325	.373

A good hitter with above-average speed, Rupp batted .337 the final two months of the season and plays multiple positions.

SCOTT SIMMONS   Bats: R Throws: L   Ht: 6-2 Wt: 200
Born: 8/15/1969   Drafted: 1991 #17 SL   Position: P

YR TEAM	LG/CLASS	G	GS	GF	SV	W	L	ERA	IP	H	HR	BB	SO	O/BA
95 Arkansas	TEX/AA	22	22	0	0	11	9	3.43	139.0	145	9	28	73	.274
95 Louisville	AMAS/AAA	2	2	0	0	0	2	8.00	9.0	11	3	1	2	.289

The leading fielder among Texas League pitchers, Simmons gets outs consistently with ground balls, throws strikes, and cuts down the running game.

THE SCOUTING REPORT: 1996

SAN DIEGO PADRES

ANDY ASHBY

Position: SP
Bats: R **Throws:** R
Ht: 6'5" **Wt:** 180
Opening Day Age: 28
Born: 7/11/1967
Drafted: PHI 5/4/86
ML Seasons: 5

SCOUTING REPORT

Ashby has a live arm, delivering from a high three-quarter angle. Both Andy's fastball and curve are plus pitches. The fastball sinks and he has learned to cut it effectively, eliminating the need to develop a slider. His curve has a tight rotation and a hard break. He needs to work on his change-up, which is slightly below-average.

While Ashby's control improved in 1995, he still goes deep into the count against too many hitters, which allows them to sit on his fastball. He does not walk an inordinate amount of men.

Andy's ability to hold runners improved to an average level with the development of a slide step. While 27 runners, a high number, attempted to steal on Ashby, ten were thrown out. His fielding is average. While he is not much of a hitter, batting .163 in 49 at-bats last year, his total of 17 sacrifice bunts ranked second in the NL.

HOW HE PERFORMED IN '95

After the Padres traded Andy Benes to Seattle on July 31, Ashby became San Diego's #1 starter. Despite an 11-29 career record entering '95, Andy had earned the responsibility, and by October had enjoyed by far his best season.

It was an encouraging year for Ashby, who finished among the league's top ten in ERA (third) and games started (first). A starter in the classic six-innings-per-game mold, he had enjoyed some success in the Phillies' system, but only last year translated it into major-league results.

He allowed both half a hit and half a walk more per nine innings in '95 than in '94. However, when in trouble, Ashby could rely on his ability to overpower hitters and he finished eighth best in the NL in Ks. Only in May did he have prolonged periods of ineffectiveness; he was outstanding from then on. All in all, Andy developed a great deal as a pitcher last year.

WHAT TO EXPECT IN '96

One of manager Bruce Bochy's biggest questions will be whether Ashby should continue as the team's top starter or move into the #2 spot behind Joey Hamilton. If Andy improves his command just that little bit more, he could be even better than in '95. However, in order to be a true staff ace, Ashby will have to go a bit deeper into games and show he can finish what he starts.

Overall Statistics

	G	GS	GF	SV	W	L	ERA	IP	H	R	ER	HR	BB	SO
95 SD	31	31	0	0	12	10	2.94	192.2	180	79	63	17	62	150
Career	105	92	3	1	23	39	4.46	559.0	576	313	277	63	201	398

1995 Situational Statistics

	W	L	ERA	SV	IP	BB	SO		AB	HR	RBI	BA	OBA	SLG
Home	7	3	2.21	0	93.2	32	86	LHB	325	5	29	.274	.336	.378
Road	5	7	3.64	0	99.0	30	64	RHB	387	12	40	.235	.308	.362
Apr-Jun	5	4	3.32	0	78.2	30	68	ScPos	159	2	47	.239	.339	.321
Jul-Oct	7	6	2.68	0	114.0	32	82	Clutch	41	1	3	.171	.244	.268

How He Compares to Other Pitchers

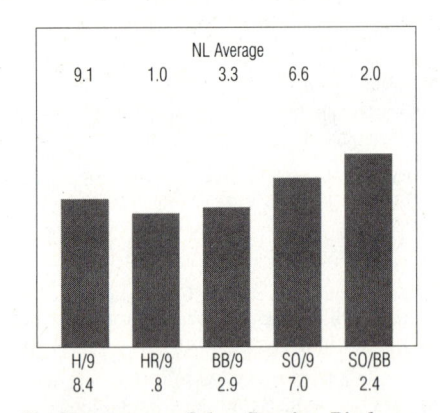

NL Average: H/9 9.1, HR/9 1.0, BB/9 3.3, SO/9 6.6, SO/BB 2.0
Ashby: H/9 8.4, HR/9 .8, BB/9 2.9, SO/9 7.0, SO/BB 2.4

How He Compares to Other Starting Pitchers

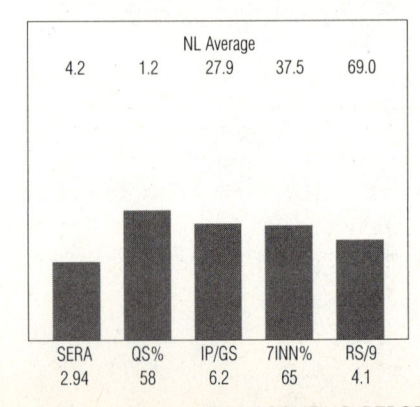

NL Average: SERA 4.2, QS% 1.2, IP/GS 27.9, 7INN% 37.5, RS/9 69.0
Ashby: SERA 2.94, QS% 58, IP/GS 6.2, 7INN% 65, RS/9 4.1

SAN DIEGO PADRES

BRAD AUSMUS

Positions: C//1B
Bats: R **Throws:** R
Ht: 5'11" **Wt:** 185
Opening Day Age: 26
Born: 4/14/1969
Drafted: NYA87 46/1152
ML Seasons: 3

SCOUTING REPORT

Ausmus improved greatly in all areas of his game in 1995, gaining confidence and the respect of his new manager. Brad is a patient line-drive hitter who has learned to go with the pitch and will use the whole field. Although he hangs in very well on breaking balls, he can still be overmatched by a good fastball. Ausmus likes the ball over the plate. He has average speed—good for a catcher—will steal often, and even bunted for five hits last season.

As a catcher, Brad is above-average in nearly every area: he has a quick throwing release, quick feet and soft hands. Ausmus' throwing accuracy is also above-average. Game-calling is not yet Brad's strongest point, but it is improving.

HOW HE PERFORMED IN '95

Ausmus may have had a career year at the dish in '95. His .293 average was more than 40 points better than the year before, and in fact was Brad's best average since '91 in Class A. He performed well in the first half of the season, and improved significantly in the second. In August, Brad batted a .424 with 13 walks, totaling a spectacular .514 on-base percentage for the month. For the year, Ausmus improved his batting average 70 points against lefthanders and 35 versus righties and hit especially well on the road.

With improved discipline in '95, Brad kicked in a good amount of offense even without much power. He showed surprising basestealing skills, moved runners along, and got some key hits. With the Padres', he is a seventh- or eighth-place hitter. When not starting, Ausmus was occasionally used as a pinch-hitter and runner.

However, the Padres are probably most gratified by his improved defense. In 1995, Ausmus threw out 40% of runners (34 of 85) trying to steal on him, a percentage ranking second-best in the NL. He has become a good pitch blocker, keeping wild pitches in front of him and keeping runners honest. Overall, Ausmus displayed the sort of ability that justified the Padres' trade for him in 1993.

WHAT TO EXPECT IN '96

If Brad maintains his pace at the plate and on the field, he figures to be the Padres' regular catcher for the next several seasons. He has already exceeded most people's expectations, and might even give a little bit more.

Overall Statistics

	G	AB	R	H	2B	3B	HR	RBI	SB	CS	BB	SO	BA	OBA
95 SD	103	328	44	96	16	4	5	34	16	5	31	56	.293	.353
Career	253	815	107	219	36	6	17	70	23	6	67	147	.269	.324

1995 Situational Statistics

	AB	HR	RBI	BA	OBA	SLG		AB	HR	RBI	BA	OBA	SLG
Home	173	2	15	.266	.326	.370	LHP	70	3	7	.314	.415	.500
Road	155	3	19	.323	.383	.458	RHP	258	2	27	.287	.336	.388
Apr-Jun	151	1	12	.298	.335	.397	ScPos	69	1	27	.290	.369	.391
Jul-Oct	177	4	22	.288	.368	.424	Clutch	51	1	3	.196	.305	.275

How He Compares to Other Batters

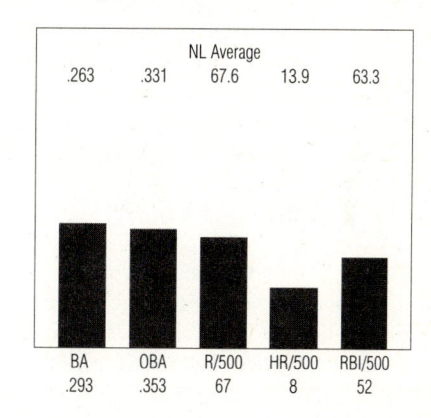

	BA	OBA	R/500	HR/500	RBI/500
NL Average	.263	.331	67.6	13.9	63.3
	.293	.353	67	8	52

Where He Hits the Ball

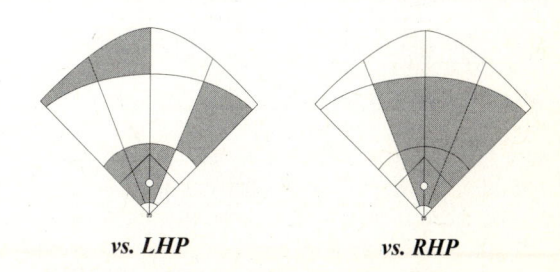

vs. LHP   vs. RHP

SAN DIEGO PADRES

WILLIE BLAIR

Position: RP/SP
Bats: R **Throws:** R
Ht: 6'1" **Wt:** 185
Opening Day Age: 30
Born: 12/18/1965
Drafted: TOR86 11/289
ML Seasons: 6

SCOUTING REPORT

Blair comes to the plate with a high three-quarters delivery. His best pitch is an average-plus fastball that has consistent, but insubstantial, sinking action. He also cuts the fastball occasionally. Willie has four other pitches: an average curve (which he now uses infrequently), an average, hard slider (which has replaced the curve in his repertoire) and a forkball and change-up that are minus pitches which he needs to improve.

Most importantly, Blair's control needs work in order for him to be an effective pitcher. He simply can't afford to fall behind as often as he does without having great stuff.

Quickness to the plate gives him an above-average ability to hold runners. Eight of 14 runners trying to bases with Blair pitching were thrown out in '95. He is an average fielder but a miserable hitter; he came up empty in all 24 trips to the plate last year, fanning 17 times.

HOW HE PERFORMED IN '95

Blair is one of those players who seems to hang on even though his performance is never much better than average. He was signed by the Padres after Colorado released him prior to spring training.

However, despite his 6-15 mark with Colorado in 1993-94, Blair obviously has talent. He had a good season in '95, working in a variety of roles. The Padres used him primarily as a middle reliever, but they also gave him some spot starts late in the season. Blair responded to steady work by posting his first winning record in the majors. However, his performance on the road was atrocious, as evidenced by his ERA away from Jack Murphy Stadium.

His most glaring weakness was an inability to get outs with runners in scoring position. Another problem was a late-season spate of gophers: after allowing only four homers in his first 32 games, Willie allowed seven in his final eight appearances.

WHAT TO EXPECT IN '96

Blair will probably make the team again this season as a long reliever and spot starter. The Padres are working with him to reduce the number of walks he allows. He has been with five major league clubs in six years, all of whom loved his arm, but so far have not been rewarded with consistent performance.

Overall Statistics

	G	GS	GF	SV	W	L	ERA	IP	H	R	ER	HR	BB	SO
95 SD	40	12	11	0	7	5	4.34	114.0	112	60	55	11	45	83
Career	200	50	39	3	23	35	4.75	521.0	592	314	275	56	189	339

1995 Situational Statistics

	W	L	ERA	SV	IP	BB	SO		AB	HR	RBI	BA	OBA	SLG
Home	3	1	3.20	0	59.0	24	41	LHB	161	5	23	.273	.376	.441
Road	4	4	5.56	0	55.0	21	42	RHB	267	6	38	.255	.306	.375
Apr-Jun	1	0	5.06	0	26.2	8	21	ScPos	83	4	46	.373	.449	.554
Jul-Oct	6	5	4.12	0	87.1	37	62	Clutch	54	0	6	.259	.328	.259

How He Compares to Other Pitchers

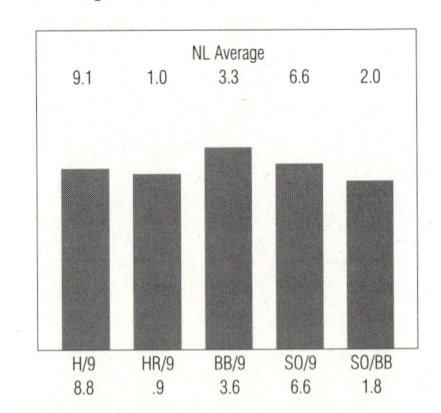

NL Average: 9.1 / 1.0 / 3.3 / 6.6 / 2.0

H/9	HR/9	BB/9	SO/9	SO/BB
8.8	.9	3.6	6.6	1.8

How He Compares to Other Relief Pitchers

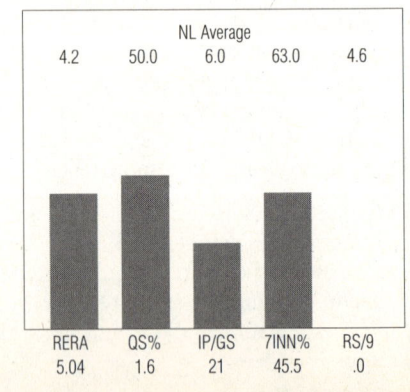

NL Average: 4.2 / 50.0 / 6.0 / 63.0 / 4.6

RERA	QS%	IP/GS	7INN%	RS/9
5.04	1.6	21	45.5	.0

SAN DIEGO PADRES

KEN CAMINITI

Position: 3B
Bats: B **Throws:** R
Ht: 6'0" **Wt:** 200
Opening Day Age: 32
Born: 4/21/1963
Drafted: HOU84 4/71
ML Seasons: 9

SCOUTING REPORT
Caminiti is a very aggressive, first-ball, fastball hitter who can turn on the inside pitch and pull it 400 feet. A switch-hitter, he likes the ball low when batting lefthanded and high when righthanded. He has never been an overly patient hitter, but has begun to take more pitches. He is now a minus baserunner due to nagging knee problems. Due to his lack of speed and role as a run producer, Ken does not bunt. At third base, his arm strength and hands are well above-average. The accuracy of his throws and his range are slightly above-average. This package is very well regarded; many think Caminiti is the best defensive third baseman in the game.

HOW HE PERFORMED IN '95
Caminiti came to the Padres in the eleven-player trade with the Astros in December, 1994. He had a career year, setting personal highs in batting average, home runs, RBI, and walks while finishing among the league's top ten in several categories.

He has more power from the left side of the plate but hits for a higher average from the right. In September, Ken amazed the baseball world by homering from both sides of the plate three times in one week, which had never been done before.

While Caminiti suffered a June swoon, he came alive over the last two months, batting .329 with 12 home runs and 40 runs batted in. He showed average basestealing skills, took a goodly amount of walks, and was very consistent, hitting nearly identically at home and on the road and batting over .290 in every month but June.

Although Caminiti has generally been known for fine defense at third base rather than for his bat, he committed 27 errors at the position in '95. At times, he would follow an outstanding grab of a hard liner by booting a routine grounder on the next play. His fielding impressed overall, though, because he won his first Gold Glove.

WHAT TO EXPECT IN '96
Caminiti's defense should get back to normal in '96 as he continues to make the adjustment to grass from turf. His offensive numbers will probably drop off from last season's career highs, but he should remain a key run producer. If Ken bats in 94 runs again, San Diego could contend; if he slumps, there aren't many other Padres' hitters to pick up the slack.

Overall Statistics

	G	AB	R	H	2B	3B	HR	RBI	SB	CS	BB	SO	BA	OBA
95 SD	143	526	74	159	33	0	26	94	12	5	69	94	.302	.380
Career	1091	3967	483	1055	213	13	101	539	51	27	367	658	.266	.328

1995 Situational Statistics

	AB	HR	RBI	BA	OBA	SLG		AB	HR	RBI	BA	OBA	SLG
Home	261	16	51	.303	.364	.525	LHP	169	10	32	.331	.374	.574
Road	265	10	43	.302	.395	.502	RHP	357	16	62	.289	.383	.485
Apr-Jun	219	11	40	.279	.344	.475	ScPos	146	8	68	.288	.424	.500
Jul-Oct	307	15	54	.319	.405	.541	Clutch	71	1	4	.254	.400	.352

How He Compares to Other Batters

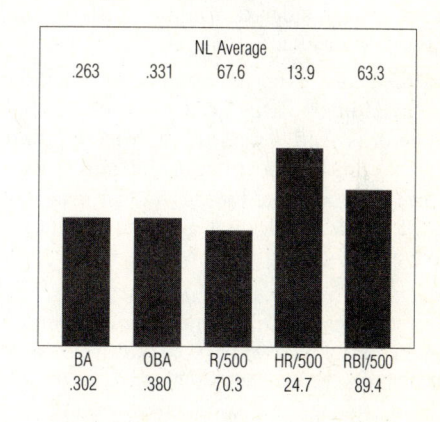

NL Average: .263 .331 67.6 13.9 63.3

BA	OBA	R/500	HR/500	RBI/500
.302	.380	70.3	24.7	89.4

Where He Hits the Ball

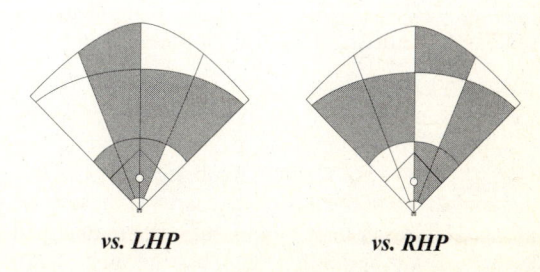

vs. LHP   vs. RHP

THE SCOUTING REPORT: 1996

SAN DIEGO PADRES

ANDUJAR CEDENO

Positions: SS//3B
Bats: R **Throws:** R
Ht: 6'1" **Wt:** 170
Opening Day Age: 26
Born: 8/21/1969
Drafted: HOU 10/1/86
ML Seasons: 6

SCOUTING REPORT
Cedeno has plus raw power. If only he were an intelligent hitter, he could turn that power into results. Unfortunately, Cedeno is thoroughly undisciplined and has a long swing with lots of holes. He likes the pitch over the plate, but doesn't see many of them because he'll chase plenty of poor offerings. This makes fat fastballs a rarity. He has above-average speed on the bases and uses his legs in the field. Although Andujar is an erratic fielder, he has well above-average range and a fine arm at shortstop. His throwing accuracy and fielding ability are average overall, but unreliable. Despite outstanding talent, Cedeno has been an underachiever and must improve both his hitting and fielding in order to remain a regular in the majors.

HOW HE PERFORMED IN '95
Cedeno, one product of the big '94 trade with the Astros, was a major disappointment for the Padres at shortstop. He hit 40 points lower than his major-league average and batted .185 from July on, continuing a career-long pattern of poor second-half performance. Considered a comer just two years ago, Andujar's production has dipped alarmingly.

The Padres began experimenting with other shortstops (Ray Holbert, Bip Roberts, and even Archi Cianfrocco) as Andujar's batting woes continued. After five years in the majors, he still does not know the strike zone and struck out in nearly one-quarter of his at-bats. He has good power but is not selective enough to get good pitches to hit.

In particular, Cedeno fares poorly against right-handed pitching. He still exhibits good speed but, because he rarely gets on base, is out of practice on the bases and is a poor basestealer.

As a fielder, he continued to have problems last year with lapses of concentration. Andujar committed 16 errors on the season, ending with a .965 fielding percentage that ranked him ninth among regular NL shortstops. That's not good enough.

WHAT TO EXPECT IN '96
Cedeno is going to have to prove himself in spring training to continue as the Padres' starting shortstop. If he does hold on to his job, he will probably bat eighth until he proves he can move runners along. That won't happen without more maturity in Andujar's hitting philosophy, but he may learn from experience. If not, he'll have time to ponder his approach from the bench.

Overall Statistics

	G	AB	R	H	2B	3B	HR	RBI	SB	CS	BB	SO	BA	OBA
95 SD	120	390	42	82	16	2	6	31	5	3	28	92	.210	.271
Career	512	1716	191	414	92	10	37	185	21	14	128	418	.241	.300

1995 Situational Statistics

	AB	HR	RBI	BA	OBA	SLG		AB	HR	RBI	BA	OBA	SLG
Home	180	3	14	.217	.290	.289	LHP	96	2	9	.271	.314	.385
Road	210	3	17	.205	.254	.324	RHP	294	4	22	.190	.258	.282
Apr-Jun	201	6	24	.234	.272	.368	ScPos	100	3	26	.280	.365	.400
Jul-Oct	189	0	7	.185	.270	.243	Clutch	62	1	2	.226	.294	.339

How He Compares to Other Batters

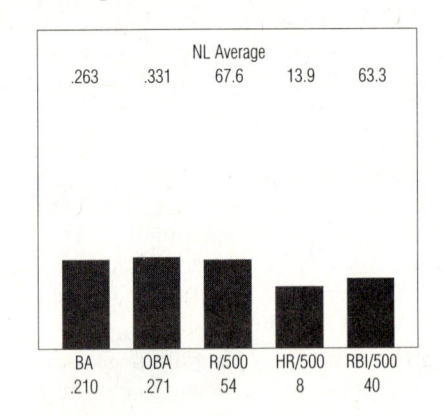

NL Average: .263 .331 67.6 13.9 63.3

BA .210 | OBA .271 | R/500 54 | HR/500 8 | RBI/500 40

Where He Hits the Ball

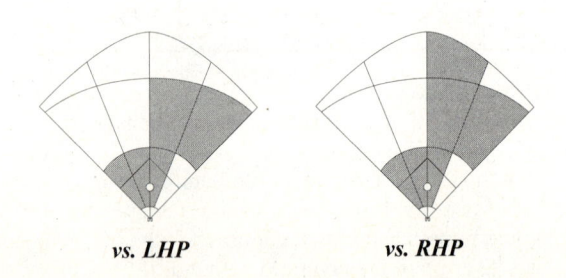

vs. LHP | vs. RHP

SAN DIEGO PADRES

GLENN DISHMAN

Position: SP
Bats: R **Throws:** L
Ht: 6'1" **Wt:** 195
Opening Day Age: 25
Born: 11/5/1970
Drafted: SD 5/23/93
ML Seasons: 1

SCOUTING REPORT
Dishman comes to the plate from low three-quarters to three-quarters, a very tough delivery on left-handed hitters. He has a well above-average change-up, but only an average-minus sinking fastball and slider. The change makes Glenn's other pitches look faster, but he needs to have good control to win because of his lack of stuff.

He is plus at holding runners: only eight runners tried to steal against Dishman in '95, with four being thrown out. He is also a plus fielder. Glenn batted .200 in 30 at-bats, laying down four sacrifices but whiffing 13 times.

HOW HE PERFORMED IN '95
Dishman was signed by the Padres as an undrafted free agent out of TCU in 1993. He shot through the minors, was called up by San Diego in June, and finished the season as the Padres' fourth starter.

He started out well, compiling a 2.60 ERA in June and July, but struggled after that, allowing more than seven runs per game in the final two months.

Dishman's struggles are not that surprising; he has less than two full years of minor-league experience, and never stayed in one league long enough for hitters to get comfortable with him. Major-league batters are far better, obviously, than the ones he rolled over at Double-A and Triple-A. In addition, '95 was Glenn's first experience of failure as a professional and he needs to adjust.

While Glenn was very effective against lefties, he didn't see many of them. Righthanders ate him for lunch, and the tactic of stacking righthanded hitters against him became a real problem for Dishman.

WHAT TO EXPECT IN '96
Dishman could make tremendous strides this season if the Padres are patient with him. The coaching staff will have him working on his control and pitch selection in spring training. He could be a good lefthanded complement to Andy Ashby and Joey Hamilton, and should see duty as the Padres' third or fourth starter unless he has a disastrous spring.

If he can't get it started in Arizona, look for Glenn to open the year in the bullpen or in the minors for additional seasoning, and for veteran Fernando Valenzuela to make more emergency starts.

Overall Statistics

	G	GS	GF	SV	W	L	ERA	IP	H	R	ER	HR	BB	SO
95 SD	19	16	1	0	4	8	5.01	97.0	104	60	54	11	34	43
Career	19	16	1	0	4	8	5.01	97.0	104	60	54	11	34	43

1995 Situational Statistics

	W	L	ERA	SV	IP	BB	SO		AB	HR	RBI	BA	OBA	SLG
Home	2	3	4.57	0	43.1	16	17	LHB	68	1	7	.162	.293	.294
Road	2	5	5.37	0	53.2	18	26	RHB	306	10	40	.304	.354	.464
Apr-Jun	1	1	3.27	0	11.0	1	4	ScPos	77	3	38	.299	.406	.494
Jul-Oct	3	7	5.23	0	86.0	33	39	Clutch	20	0	0	.150	.261	.250

How He Compares to Other Pitchers

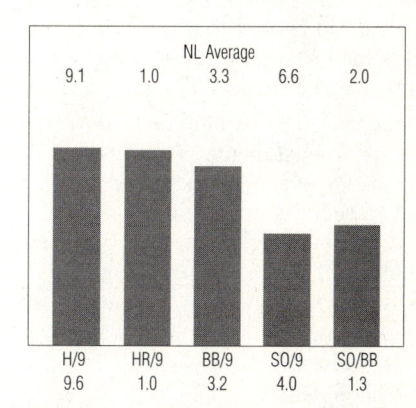

NL Average: H/9 9.1, HR/9 1.0, BB/9 3.3, SO/9 6.6, SO/BB 2.0
Dishman: H/9 9.6, HR/9 1.0, BB/9 3.2, SO/9 4.0, SO/BB 1.3

How He Compares to Other Starting Pitchers

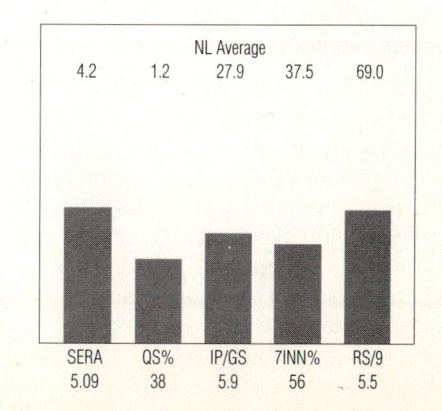

NL Average: SERA 4.2, QS% 1.2, IP/GS 27.9, 7INN% 37.5, RS/9 69.0
Dishman: SERA 5.09, QS% 38, IP/GS 5.9, 7INN% 56, RS/9 5.5

THE SCOUTING REPORT: 1996

SAN DIEGO PADRES

STEVE FINLEY

Position: OF
Bats: L **Throws:** L
Ht: 6'2" **Wt:** 175
Opening Day Age: 31
Born: 3/12/1965
Drafted: BAL87 14/325
ML Seasons: 7

SCOUTING REPORT
Finley chokes up on the bat and likes the ball low in the strike zone. He has developed some power in the last few years and is an above-average contact hitter against breaking balls, but can be overmatched by a hard fastball. Although Steve's home run potential is limited by his contact-type swing, he is strong and has good alley power.

Finley possesses plus speed and is a very intelligent runner and basestealer. He will lay down the bunt, but Steve isn't as good as he might be at either sacrificing or bunting for hits.

He is one of the top centerfielders in the National League and can also play right if needed. (He began his career as a right fielder in Baltimore.) Finley has well above-average range and hands, and gets a good jump on the ball because of his speed, playing very shallow. His arm strength and accuracy are both above-average.

HOW HE PERFORMED IN '95
Another member of the '94 Houston-San Diego megatrade, Finley enjoyed a fine season in '95, his first with the Padres after four years in Houston. He finished in the league's top 10 in runs, hits, triples, stolen bases, and at-bats.

The Padres moved Steve into the leadoff spot after Bip Roberts' August injury. While his on-base percentage was not great, it was his best ever. Finley managed to score a career-high 104 runs and hit more than 20 points higher than his career average. Finley batted .350 over July and August but tailed off in September.

Finley ran often and effectively in '95. He also lived up to his billing as an excellent defensive outfielder, winning his first Gold Glove. He has an strong arm, throwing out eight runners during the season. His speed allows him to make plenty of spectacular catches, plays that might not be so spectacular if he didn't play so close to the infield.

WHAT TO EXPECT IN '96
Should Bip Roberts come back healthy this spring, Finley will probably drop back to the more natural #2 spot in the batting order. However, if the Bipster is not up to the job, Steve may be asked to lead off again. He won't be great in the role, but Finley works hard and should be a major contributor to the Padres for several years.

Overall Statistics

	G	AB	R	H	2B	3B	HR	RBI	SB	CS	BB	SO	BA	OBA
95 SD	139	562	104	167	23	8	10	44	36	12	59	62	.297	.366
Career	919	3364	486	935	132	55	47	292	185	64	262	390	.278	.331

1995 Situational Statistics

	AB	HR	RBI	BA	OBA	SLG		AB	HR	RBI	BA	OBA	SLG
Home	255	4	17	.275	.350	.384	LHP	187	3	9	.326	.388	.433
Road	307	6	27	.316	.379	.450	RHP	375	7	35	.283	.355	.413
Apr-Jun	236	4	17	.267	.343	.369	ScPos	103	2	34	.301	.422	.408
Jul-Oct	326	6	27	.319	.382	.457	Clutch	91	2	10	.319	.364	.407

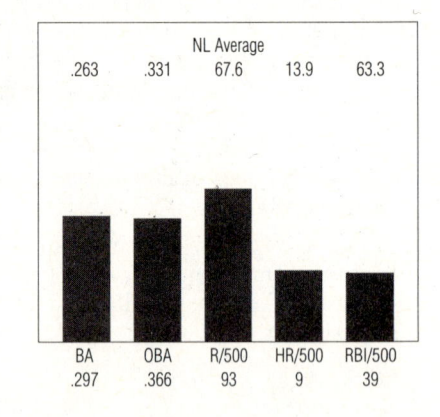

How He Compares to Other Batters

NL Average: .263 / .331 / 67.6 / 13.9 / 63.3

BA	OBA	R/500	HR/500	RBI/500
.297	.366	93	9	39

Where He Hits the Ball

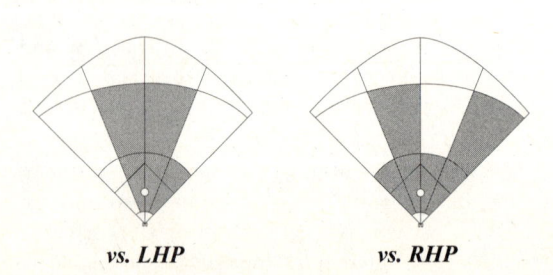

vs. LHP   vs. RHP

THE SCOUTING REPORT: 1996

SAN DIEGO PADRES

TONY GWYNN

Position: OF
Bats: L **Throws:** L
Ht: 5'11" **Wt:** 200
Opening Day Age: 35
Born: 5/9/1960
Drafted: SD81 4/58
ML Seasons: 14

SCOUTING REPORT

Gwynn has an inside-out swing to the opposite field and excellent bat control. Tony has struck out fewer than twenty times each of the last five years, an unprecedented achievement in modern baseball. While he doesn't walk often, he doesn't any waste at-bats. He is a good situational hitter and adjusts well to any kind of pitching. He doesn't have over-the-fence power, but he lashes line drives to the gap with regularity.

His speed on the bases, once well above-average, has dipped to slightly below-average as he has aged and put on weight. However, he is still an outstanding percentage basestealer. Tony does not bunt.

In right field, Gwynn shows average range but gets a good jump on the ball. He enhances his fielding performance with plus hands, average arm strength and plus throwing accuracy. He doesn't look like a good outfielder, but he is.

HOW HE PERFORMED IN '95

What more can be said about one of the game's greatest hitters? Gwynn claims he sees the ball rotating as it comes toward him, making it possible for him to judge what the pitcher is throwing, see how the fielders are positioned and wait until the last moment before deciding to swing. He possesses a dedicated work ethic, spending hours studying videotapes of his at-bats and of opposing pitchers' deliveries. If he feels he has had a bad game, he will spend extra time in the batting cage to correct any problems immediately.

As a result of all his hard work, he won his sixth NL batting title, tied for the major-league lead in hits, had the most multi-hit games in the majors and, for the first time, drove in 90 runs.

Although not as fast as he once was, he can still steal a base when he needs to. Padres' fans have begun to complain about his weight, but Gwynn still is a good defensive player who can make the big catch. He collected eight assists from right field and made only two errors.

WHAT TO EXPECT IN '96

Look for Gwynn to be among the league leaders again in batting and hits. At 35, he should play for several more years, at least long enough to get 3,000 hits. And he might even get 3,500 at the pace he's set.

Overall Statistics

	G	AB	R	H	2B	3B	HR	RBI	SB	CS	BB	SO	BA	OBA
95 SD	135	535	82	197	33	1	9	90	17	5	35	15	.368	.404
Career	1830	7144	1073	2401	384	80	87	804	285	112	625	344	.336	.388

1995 Situational Statistics

	AB	HR	RBI	BA	OBA	SLG		AB	HR	RBI	BA	OBA	SLG
Home	266	5	45	.387	.420	.511	LHP	188	2	27	.330	.365	.404
Road	269	4	45	.349	.388	.457	RHP	347	7	63	.389	.424	.527
Apr-Jun	224	5	40	.344	.393	.478	ScPos	137	4	82	.394	.454	.569
Jul-Oct	311	4	50	.386	.412	.489	Clutch	80	3	18	.387	.443	.550

How He Compares to Other Batters

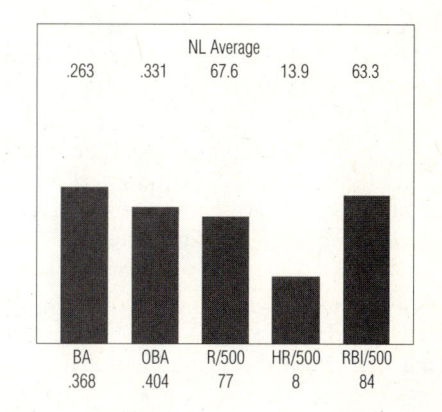

NL Average: .263 .331 67.6 13.9 63.3

BA	OBA	R/500	HR/500	RBI/500
.368	.404	77	8	84

Where He Hits the Ball

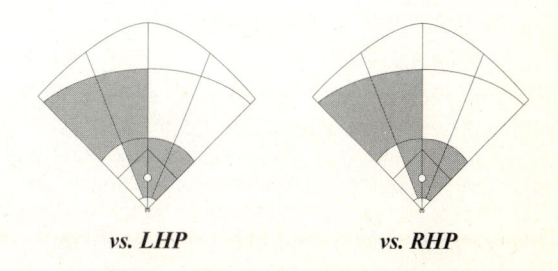

vs. LHP   vs. RHP

THE SCOUTING REPORT: 1996

SAN DIEGO PADRES

JOEY HAMILTON

Position: SP
Bats: R **Throws:** R
Ht: 6'4" **Wt:** 220
Opening Day Age: 25
Born: 9/9/1970
Drafted: SD91 1/8
ML Seasons: 2

SCOUTING REPORT
Using a cross-body, low three-quarter motion, Joey Hamilton comes hard at righthanders. His delivery is distracting to them, but his willingness to pitch inside is even more so. Despite the intimidation factor, Joey lacks a high hard heater. A plus sinking fastball with fine movement is Hamilton's bread and butter. The pitch induces plenty of weak swings from hitters due to its break and life. His other pitches are not as strong: Joey's slider is average, his curve is currently minus, and a slightly below-average change-up is being renovated.

Hamilton throws with average control. Despite a quick delivery to the plate, his move to first is slow. However, half of the 16 men trying to steal against Joey last year were tossed out. His fielding rates as slightly below-average.

HOW HE PERFORMED IN '95
In his first full season in the majors, Hamilton was impressive, to say the least. He ranked among the league's top pitchers in several categories despite a poor won-lost mark.

The Padres pushed him quickly through the minors but he hasn't appeared overmatched. Joey averaged nearly seven innings a start in '95, displaying both brilliance and inexperience.

Hamilton's celebrated aggressiveness led to 11 hit batters last year, tied for third in the NL. His bulldog attitude needs to be tempered: Hamilton needs to learn to pace himself better in late and close situations.

Some of Hamilton's problems were out of his control. He got poor run support from his teammates and little help from the Padres bullpen. Perhaps Joey's greatest weakness is his miserable hitting; he went 0-for-57 to start his career before getting his first major-league hit last summer. In '95, Hamilton batted .106 in 65 at-bats with 38 strikeouts. He's a poor bunter.

WHAT TO EXPECT IN '96
Hamilton has already secured a job as his team's number two starter. Pairing him with Andy Ashby gives the Padres the makings of a fine one-two punch on the mound. If he continues to improve at his current rate, look for Hamilton to be pitching like a staff ace in a year or two. He's never going to be a dominating strikeout pitcher, but Joey has already shown he can get big-league hitters out.

Overall Statistics

	G	GS	GF	SV	W	L	ERA	IP	H	R	ER	HR	BB	SO
95 SD	31	30	1	0	6	9	3.08	204.1	189	89	70	17	56	123
Career	47	46	1	0	15	15	3.05	313.0	287	129	106	24	85	184

1995 Situational Statistics

	W	L	ERA	SV	IP	BB	SO		AB	HR	RBI	BA	OBA	SLG
Home	3	6	2.84	0	107.2	28	62	LHB	337	9	36	.231	.293	.350
Road	3	3	3.35	0	96.2	28	61	RHB	430	8	42	.258	.316	.358
Apr-Jun	3	2	2.73	0	89.0	20	48	ScPos	161	2	58	.267	.333	.360
Jul-Oct	3	7	3.36	0	115.1	36	75	Clutch	80	1	5	.313	.375	.375

How He Compares to Other Pitchers

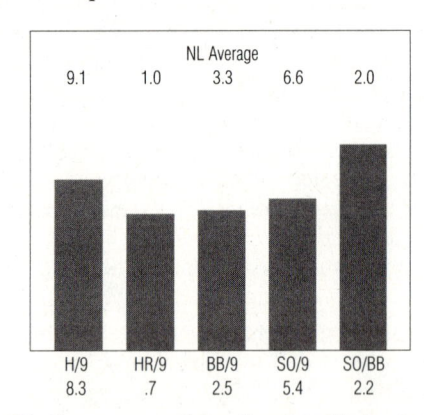

	H/9	HR/9	BB/9	SO/9	SO/BB
NL Average	9.1	1.0	3.3	6.6	2.0
	8.3	.7	2.5	5.4	2.2

How He Compares to Other Starting Pitchers

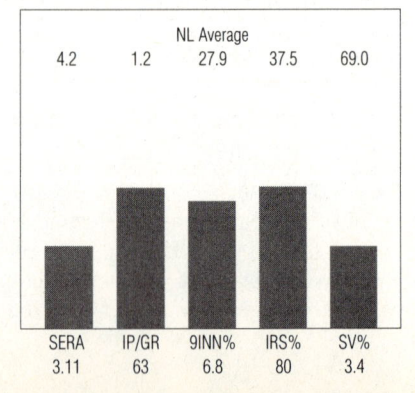

	SERA	IP/GR	9INN%	IRS%	SV%
NL Average	4.2	1.2	27.9	37.5	69.0
	3.11	63	6.8	80	3.4

SAN DIEGO PADRES

TREVOR HOFFMAN

Position: RP
Bats: R **Throws:** R
Ht: 6'1" **Wt:** 200
Opening Day Age: 28
Born: 10/13/1967
Drafted: CIN89 11/290
ML Seasons: 3

SCOUTING REPORT

Hard-throwing converted shortstop Hoffman comes to the plate with a high leg kick and a motion ranging from straight overhand to high three-quarters. Hoffman's fastball is above-average in velocity but tends to be straight. A well-above average hard slider is Trevor's out pitch.

He uses his mediocre curve and change-up rarely, just letting hitters know that he can throw them. He is very aggressive and will throw inside. Trevor's control has improved, and now rates as plus.

A protracted delivery has meant trouble with holding runners in the past, but last year just two runners tried to steal bases against him, one successfully. Hoffman helps himself by being an above-average fielder and a decent hitter: he was 1-for-2 at bat in '95, and is 2-for-12 in his career.

HOW HE PERFORMED IN '95

While Hoffman had his best save total of his three-year career and improved in some important ways, '95 wasn't close to perfect. At times, Trevor was the league's dominant reliever. At other times, his inexperience clearly showed and he got rocked. He compiled a 2.11 ERA over the last two months of the season, aiding the Padres' playoff drive, and allowed only one earned run in September.

Unfortunately, he also had awful streaks. Just a few bad outings can ugly up a reliever's totals, and almost every time a closer struggles, it's significant. A big problem for Hoffman in '95 was a loss of concentration with runners aboard. Opponents batted just .235 against Trevor with the bases empty, but 90 points higher when runners were on base.

Before last season, Hoffman had walked more than three and a half hitters per nine innings. In '95, he cut that total by over a full base on balls; however, getting more pitches over also means the risk of allowing more home runs, and Trevor gave up 10 of them.

WHAT TO EXPECT IN '96

Hoffman has the pitches and mentality necessary to be one of the league's dominant short relievers. However, he must improve on last year's up-and-down performance. If Hoffman can adjust, he should be a top major-league closer for a number of years.

Overall Statistics

	G	GS	GF	SV	W	L	ERA	IP	H	R	ER	HR	BB	SO
95 SD	55	0	51	31	7	4	3.88	53.1	48	25	23	10	14	52
Career	169	0	118	56	15	14	3.52	199.1	167	84	78	24	73	199

1995 Situational Statistics

	W	L	ERA	SV	IP	BB	SO		AB	HR	RBI	BA	OBA	SLG
Home	6	1	3.00	15	27.0	7	25	LHB	99	3	9	.202	.282	.313
Road	1	3	4.78	16	26.1	7	27	RHB	105	7	17	.267	.287	.533
Apr-Jun	4	2	4.58	10	19.2	6	18	ScPos	44	4	18	.273	.385	.591
Jul-Oct	3	2	3.48	21	33.2	8	34	Clutch	140	5	20	.243	.293	.400

How He Compares to Other Pitchers

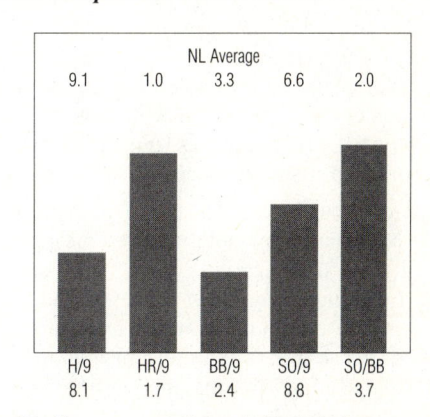

NL Average: H/9 9.1, HR/9 1.0, BB/9 3.3, SO/9 6.6, SO/BB 2.0
Hoffman: H/9 8.1, HR/9 1.7, BB/9 2.4, SO/9 8.8, SO/BB 3.7

How He Compares to Other Relief Pitchers

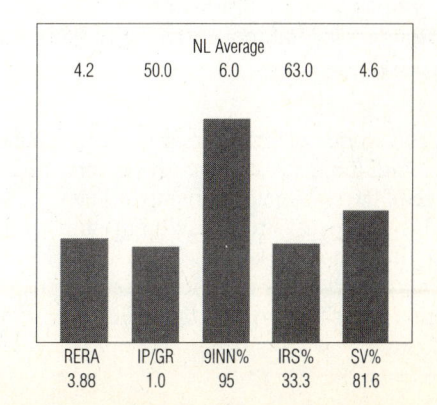

NL Average: RERA 4.2, IP/GR 50.0, 9INN% 6.0, IRS% 63.0, SV% 4.6
Hoffman: RERA 3.88, IP/GR 1.0, 9INN% 95, IRS% 33.3, SV% 81.6

SAN DIEGO PADRES

PHIL PLANTIER

Position: OF
Bats: L **Throws:** R
Ht: 6'0" **Wt:** 175
Opening Day Age: 27
Born: 1/27/1969
Drafted: BOS87 12/292
ML Seasons: 6

SCOUTING REPORT
Plantier hits from a deep crouch with an uppercut swing that produces a lot of fly balls: some end up as home runs, more end up as outs. He likes the ball low and inside and can turn on that pitch with ease. On the bases, Phil shows below-average speed. He does not bunt. His range in left field is well below-average and he uses below-average hands to try to catch it. His arm strength rates as average, but Plantier has slightly below-average throwing accuracy. His best defensive position is certainly designated hitter. He's never been tried at first base in either the majors or the minors, but that is always possible if he regains his power stroke.

HOW HE PERFORMED IN '95
Plantier was traded by the Padres to the Astros in the massive December '94 trade, then returned last July. He was a disappointment in Houston and even more so on his return to Jack Murphy Stadium. Despite setting up residence in San Diego a few years ago, Plantier has appeared out of his rhythm at bat for his hometown club.

A streaky hitter, Phil is not providing enough offense to play on a regular basis. His production has fallen off dramatically since he slammed a career-best 34 homers and knocked in 100 runs in '93. He takes plenty of walks, but has to hit a lot of home runs in order to justify a space in the lineup.

Even before that great '93 season in San Diego, Plantier had alternately tantalized and disappointed the Red Sox organization for several seasons, leading two minor leagues in home runs but alternating hot and cold streaks while in Boston. Phil has one of the strangest batting stances in baseball, which may account for his inconsistency at the plate.

Plantier threw out five baserunners in '95, but also made four errors and looked typically bad in both left and right field.

WHAT TO EXPECT IN '96
The Padres released Plantier in November and he signed with the Detroit Tigers. If he can't take advantage of the right field overhang in Tiger Stadium with his uppercut stroke and pull hitting, then there's little hope for a comeback. Expect him to see duty as a platoon DH unless he produces enough to force his way into the lineup on a regular basis.

Overall Statistics

	G	AB	R	H	2B	3B	HR	RBI	SB	CS	BB	SO	BA	OBA
95 HOU/SD	76	216	33	55	6	0	9	34	1	1	28	48	.255	.339
Career	485	1531	218	378	74	2	79	243	11	10	196	390	.247	.336

1995 Situational Statistics

	AB	HR	RBI	BA	OBA	SLG		AB	HR	RBI	BA	OBA	SLG
Home	93	1	5	.215	.311	.290	LHP	45	3	8	.333	.404	.556
Road	123	8	29	.285	.359	.496	RHP	171	6	26	.234	.321	.368
Apr-Jun	46	4	11	.239	.333	.500	ScPos	71	3	27	.296	.398	.465
Jul-Oct	170	5	23	.259	.340	.382	Clutch	34	2	2	.118	.268	.294

How He Compares to Other Batters

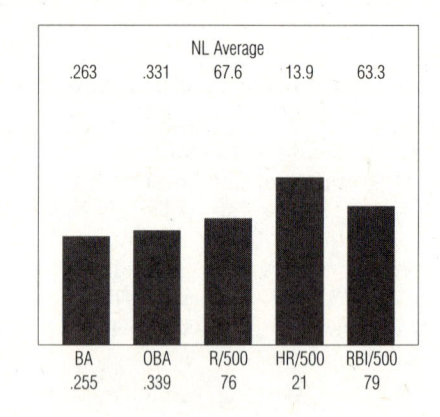

NL Average: .263 | .331 | 67.6 | 13.9 | 63.3

BA .255 | OBA .339 | R/500 76 | HR/500 21 | RBI/500 79

Where He Hits the Ball

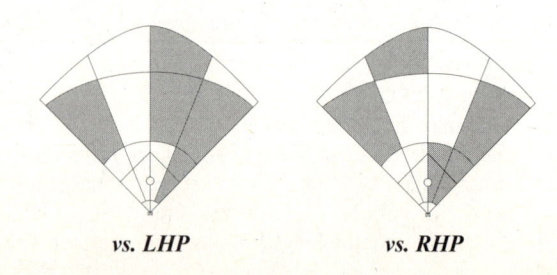

vs. LHP   vs. RHP

SAN DIEGO PADRES

JODY REED

SCOUTING REPORT

Jody Reed is one of baseball's best defensive second basemen. While his range is slightly below-average, he more than makes up for it with terrific positioning. Jody has average hands and below-average arm strength, but balances those skills with a quick release and well above-average throwing accuracy. He is especially good in the pivot on the double play. Though not as productive as he was in Boston, Reed is a line-drive contact hitter who has learned to use the whole field. He is excellent on the hit-and-run due to his discipline at the plate and is a good sacrifice bunter. He has below-average speed on the bases and is not a good basestealer.

HOW HE PERFORMED IN '95

Reed solidified the Padres' infield in '95 with his fine play at second base. Although he hit 20 points under his career average, he more than earned his keep on defense.

Jody began the season platooning with Bip Roberts at second but soon became the everyday second baseman due to the Bipster's injuries. Eventually, Reed made 118 starts at second base. As usual, he got to a well above-average number of ground balls and was very steady. On the season, Jody made just four errors, fielding an exceptional .994.

Reed is not a particularly good hitter anymore. He doesn't have the Green Monster to rifle doubles off now and has seen his power production drop to almost nothing. However, he will take the walk, doesn't give up at-bats, and hit well with runners in scoring position and in late-and-close situations. Only once in his career has he struck out more often than he has walked.

Jody rebounded against lefthanders last year but sagged 40 points against righthanders and continued his normal pattern of hitting better on grass than turf.

WHAT TO EXPECT IN '96

When San Diego failed in their quest to bring Craig Biggio westward, the club decided to re-ink Reed for two more seasons. He may benefit from settling down, having been with four clubs in the previous four seasons after twice turning down long-term deals. While Jody is not an exceptional hitter, he provides more than enough on defense to stay in the lineup and should have a couple of more years of regular duty left in his career.

Positions: 2B//SS
Bats: R **Throws:** R
Ht: 5'9" **Wt:** 170
Opening Day Age: 33
Born: 7/26/1962
Drafted: BOS84 8/198
ML Seasons: 9

Overall Statistics

	G	AB	R	H	2B	3B	HR	RBI	SB	CS	BB	SO	BA	OBA
95 SD	131	445	58	114	18	1	4	40	6	4	59	38	.256	.348
Career	1086	3947	515	1088	241	10	25	335	35	37	473	339	.276	.355

1995 Situational Statistics

	AB	HR	RBI	BA	OBA	SLG		AB	HR	RBI	BA	OBA	SLG
Home	212	4	23	.278	.384	.382	LHP	131	0	9	.290	.400	.366
Road	233	0	17	.236	.313	.279	RHP	314	4	31	.242	.325	.312
Apr-Jun	133	1	11	.248	.371	.301	ScPos	103	1	36	.291	.449	.359
Jul-Oct	312	3	29	.260	.337	.340	Clutch	71	0	5	.296	.383	.352

How He Compares to Other Batters

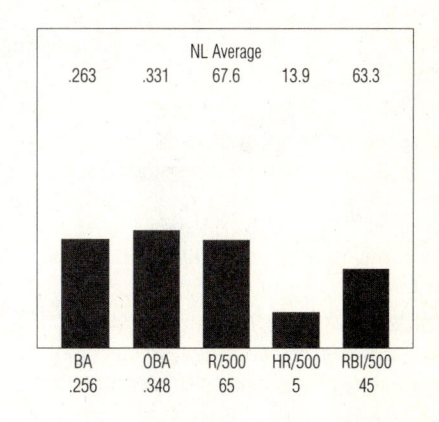

NL Average: .263 .331 67.6 13.9 63.3

	BA	OBA	R/500	HR/500	RBI/500
	.256	.348	65	5	45

Where He Hits the Ball

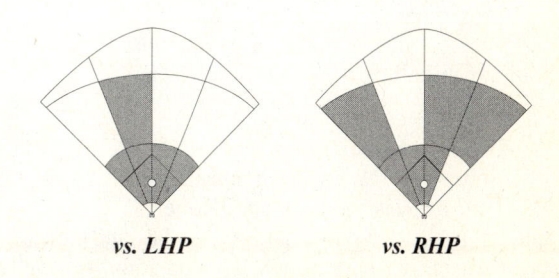

vs. LHP   vs. RHP

SAN DIEGO PADRES

BIP ROBERTS

Positions: OF/2B//SS
Bats: B **Throws:** R
Ht: 5'7" **Wt:** 160
Opening Day Age: 32
Born: 10/27/1963
Drafted: PIT82 S1/13
ML Seasons: 9

SCOUTING REPORT
Roberts is an aggressive hitter who uses the whole field. He does not have much power and can't hit good fastballs. Most of his damage is done against breaking pitches. He has well above-average baserunning speed and is also a fine basestealer. Roberts is a good bunter, but does not lay the ball down as often as he might. Bip plays three positions (left field, second base, and third base) showing above-average range in the outfield but below-average range in the infield. He has below-average hands and arm strength but average accuracy, although missing the cutoff man is a problem for him. Over the last few seasons, Bip has become increasingly prone to injuries, suffering quadricep, leg, thumb, shoulder, and wrist problems since 1993.

HOW HE PERFORMED IN '95
Roberts' season ended on September 12 when an Andy Ashby warm-up pitch fractured Bip's right leg. This was a shame for Roberts, who came into '95 as a .351 hitter during September. However, the year-ending injury was just part of a frustratingly short season for Bip. He had earlier been sidelined twice by a strained right quadricep.

When healthy, the Padres' leadoff hitter had another fine season at bat and on the bases. Although he has hit only five home runs in the past three seasons, he provides speed and usually hits .300. However, his walk total has declined each of the last two seasons and is no longer adequate for a top-of-the-order hitter.

A versatile player, Roberts can play decently at almost any position in the infield or outfield. In left field, Bip threw out just two baserunners in 48 games, but got to plenty of fly balls.

Roberts achieved some additional fame this past season as the star of a hilarious television commercial promoting Major League Baseball. In the ad, Bip mistakes the estimated price of Robin Roberts' rookie baseball card for that of his own.

WHAT TO EXPECT IN '96
Look for the Padres to use Roberts in the leadoff role, if he's healthy, and as their starting left fielder. Besides his speed, perhaps Roberts' greatest quality is that he plays hard every day and never makes excuses. Unfortunately, he is injury-prone and aging. If he plays regularly, he should hit close to .300 again and steal more than 20 bases.

Overall Statistics

	G	AB	R	H	2B	3B	HR	RBI	SB	CS	BB	SO	BA	OBA
95 SD	73	296	40	90	14	0	2	25	20	2	17	36	.304	.346
Career	897	3082	516	915	145	27	25	232	218	79	312	405	.297	.363

1995 Situational Statistics

	AB	HR	RBI	BA	OBA	SLG		AB	HR	RBI	BA	OBA	SLG
Home	172	2	18	.308	.335	.390	LHP	79	0	3	.253	.306	.278
Road	124	0	7	.298	.360	.347	RHP	217	2	22	.323	.361	.406
Apr-Jun	208	1	19	.317	.372	.389	ScPos	63	1	24	.381	.458	.460
Jul-Oct	88	1	6	.273	.281	.330	Clutch	51	1	10	.333	.393	.490

How He Compares to Other Batters

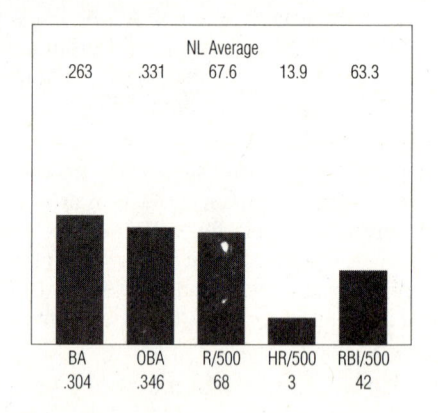

NL Average: BA .263, OBA .331, R/500 67.6, HR/500 13.9, RBI/500 63.3

Bip: BA .304, OBA .346, R/500 68, HR/500 3, RBI/500 42

Where He Hits the Ball

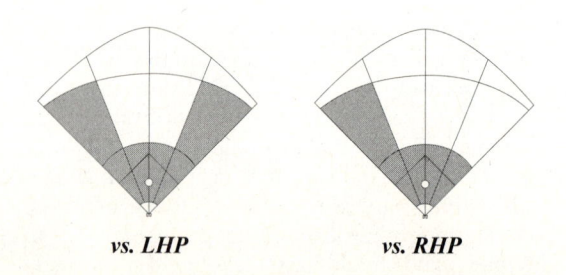

vs. LHP   vs. RHP

SAN DIEGO PADRES

ANDRES BERUMEN

Position: RP
Bats: R **Throws:** R
Ht: 6'2" **Wt:** 210
Opening Day Age: 24
Born: 4/5/1971
Drafted: KC89 28/699
ML Seasons: 1

Overall Statistics

	G	GS	GF	SV	W	L	ERA	IP	H	R	ER	HR	BB	SO
95 SD	37	0	17	1	2	3	5.68	44.1	37	29	28	3	36	42
Career	37	0	17	1	2	3	5.68	44.1	37	29	28	3	36	42

1995 Situational Statistics

	W	L	ERA	SV	IP	BB	SO		AB	HR	RBI	BA	OBA	SLG
Home	2	1	3.74	1	21.2	18	22	LHB	67	2	19	.239	.398	.358
Road	0	2	7.54	0	22.2	18	20	RHB	97	1	12	.216	.347	.278
Apr-Jun	2	2	5.57	1	21.0	16	24	ScPos	54	0	27	.333	.458	.407
Jul-Oct	0	1	5.79	0	23.1	20	18	Clutch	50	2	10	.220	.344	.340

SCOUTING REPORT
The strong-armed young righthander needs to develop command, maturity, and an off-speed pitch to make it in the majors. Berumen already has an above-average, rising four-seam fastball and a well above-average, but inconsistent, slider that breaks very quickly. His curve is minus.

Andres throws with very poor control from a three-quarter angle. He is an average fielder but had real trouble holding baserunners: nine runners stole bases against Berumen in ten tries, a common pattern for young, righthanded power pitchers.

HOW HE PERFORMED IN '95
Berumen spent his first season in the majors as a middle reliever. Although he has plenty to learn, he could soon be an excellent addition to the Padres' pitching staff. Berumen allows more than his fair share of walks but also averaged nearly a strikeout per inning. He needs to work on shutting down a team with runners on base; half of the runners he inherited scored.

WHAT TO EXPECT IN '96
His curve and breaking pitches have potential, but Andres needs more seasoning—perhaps a full season—in the minors. His control—or lack of same—will make or break him.

DOUG BOCHTLER

Position: RP
Bats: R **Throws:** R
Ht: 6'3" **Wt:** 205
Opening Day Age: 25
Born: 7/5/1970
Drafted: MON89 9/228
ML Seasons: 1

Overall Statistics

	G	GS	GF	SV	W	L	ERA	IP	H	R	ER	HR	BB	SO
95 SD	34	0	11	1	4	4	3.57	45.1	38	18	18	5	19	45
Career	34	0	11	1	4	4	3.57	45.1	38	18	18	5	19	45

1995 Situational Statistics

	W	L	ERA	SV	IP	BB	SO		AB	HR	RBI	BA	OBA	SLG
Home	3	2	4.03	0	22.1	10	21	LHB	56	2	8	.250	.364	.446
Road	1	2	3.13	1	23.0	9	24	RHB	103	3	12	.233	.292	.369
Apr-Jun	0	0	3.38	0	5.1	2	5	ScPos	46	1	13	.239	.333	.326
Jul-Oct	4	4	3.60	1	40.0	17	40	Clutch	80	3	13	.250	.337	.387

SCOUTING REPORT
Bochtler has a deceptive, jerky, long-arm motion and delivers three-quarters to overhand. He has a plus fastball and three other average pitches (hard slider, change-up, and splitfinger). Doug is easy to run on and an average fielder. Seven of 11 bases-tealing attempts were successful against Bochtler last season; he was hitless in two at-bats.

HOW HE PERFORMED IN '95
Doug started the year in the minors, was called up in early May, sent back down six days later, and returned to stay in July.

He averaged just less than one strikeout per inning but had an awful September (11 ER in 11 IP). Bruce Bochy used him in relatively low-stress mopup and setup roles, allowing Bochtler to finish ten games in non-save situations. Doug was sent to San Diego in 1993 (with Andy Ashby and Brad Ausmus) for Bruce Hurst and Greg Harris. Criticized at the time, that deal now looks awfully good deal for the Padres.

WHAT TO EXPECT IN '96
Look for Bochtler to become the Padres second reliever behind Trevor Hoffman and be used as Hoffman's set-up pitcher. Four pitches and a confusing delivery make him a comer.

SAN DIEGO PADRES

ARCHI CIANFROCCO

Positions: 1B/SS//OF/2B/3B
Bats: R **Throws:** R
Ht: 6'5" **Wt:** 200
Opening Day Age: 29
Born: 10/6/1966
Drafted: MON87 7/122
ML Seasons: 4

Overall Statistics

	G	AB	R	H	2B	3B	HR	RBI	SB	CS	BB	SO	BA	OBA
95 SD	51	118	22	31	7	0	5	31	0	2	11	28	.263	.333
Career	292	792	86	191	31	4	27	122	7	2	42	202	.241	.285

1995 Situational Statistics

	AB	HR	RBI	BA	OBA	SLG		AB	HR	RBI	BA	OBA	SLG
Home	58	1	10	.224	.308	.310	LHP	36	0	7	.250	.325	.278
Road	60	4	21	.300	.358	.583	RHP	82	5	24	.268	.337	.524
Apr-Jun	0	0	0	.000	.000	.000	ScPos	31	4	29	.452	.526	.903
Jul-Oct	118	5	31	.263	.333	.449	Clutch	21	2	14	.238	.360	.619

SCOUTING REPORT

Angelo Dominic Cianfrocco has a slow bat but some power. He likes to pick on high, inside fastballs, but is overaggressive at the dish and can be overmatched by good heat. He is an extremely slow baserunner but doesn't make many mistakes.

Archi is an average fielder with a strong arm but below-average range. He can play all the infield positions, though not that well, and even started two games as the Padres' right fielder.

HOW HE PERFORMED IN '95

Cianfrocco started the season in Triple-A and did not appear in a major-league game until July. However, manager Bruce Bochy found him a reliable reserve. He became Bochy's "can do" guy with runners in scoring position, batting .452 in 31 at-bats. Archi has decent power but strikes out much more than he walks, although he cut down dramatically on whiffs and increased his bases on balls in '95.

WHAT TO EXPECT IN '96

Cianfrocco will probably make the team as a pinch-hitter and reserve player. His set of strengths and weaknesses is not often found in a utility player; if he can play as he did in '95, he could have a long career in that role.

PHIL CLARK

Positions: OF//1B
Bats: R **Throws:** R
Ht: 6'0" **Wt:** 180
Opening Day Age: 27
Born: 5/6/1968
Drafted: DET86 1/18
ML Seasons: 4

Overall Statistics

	G	AB	R	H	2B	3B	HR	RBI	SB	CS	BB	SO	BA	OBA
95 SD	75	97	12	21	3	0	2	7	0	2	8	18	.216	.278
Career	261	540	62	150	30	0	17	65	4	4	27	75	.278	.319

1995 Situational Statistics

	AB	HR	RBI	BA	OBA	SLG		AB	HR	RBI	BA	OBA	SLG
Home	43	1	6	.233	.314	.349	LHP	67	1	6	.179	.240	.254
Road	54	1	1	.204	.246	.278	RHP	30	1	1	.300	.364	.433
Apr-Jun	33	1	3	.364	.371	.485	ScPos	24	0	5	.167	.290	.208
Jul-Oct	64	1	4	.141	.233	.219	Clutch	22	0	1	.136	.174	.182

SCOUTING REPORT

Clark is an above-average fastball hitter who likes to hack at inside pitches. He is also a better-than-average mistake hitter who has some bat speed. In '95, he had some trouble with his swing.

Phil is a minus runner and does not bunt. He will attempt a steal only when begged to do so. He can play first, third, left field, right field, and even catch. Clark's arm is average in strength and accuracy but he has minus range and hands.

HOW HE PERFORMED IN '95

Clark is a versatile utility player. In 1995, he was used often as either a pinch-hitter or as a defensive substitute in double switches. However, this slight use never gave him a chance to get into a rhythm at the plate.

If he got 400 at-bats in a season, Phil could conceivably hit 25 home runs. However, he would provide no speed and wouldn't walk often.

WHAT TO EXPECT IN '96

The Padres released him in the off-season and Clark signed with Boston. If he makes the team, he will be a 24th or 25th man at best. He'll never be a regular and may not be productive again as a reserve.

SAN DIEGO PADRES

BRYCE FLORIE

Position: RP
Bats: R **Throws:** R
Ht: 6'0" **Wt:** 185
Opening Day Age: 25
Born: 5/21/1970
Drafted: SD88 5/110
ML Seasons: 2

Overall Statistics

	G	GS	GF	SV	W	L	ERA	IP	H	R	ER	HR	BB	SO
95 SD	47	0	10	1	2	2	3.01	68.2	49	30	23	8	38	68
Career	56	0	14	1	2	2	2.77	78.0	57	31	24	8	41	76

1995 Situational Statistics

	W	L	ERA	SV	IP	BB	SO		AB	HR	RBI	BA	OBA	SLG
Home	0	1	2.78	1	32.1	21	32	LHB	107	2	10	.206	.328	.280
Road	2	1	3.22	0	36.1	17	36	RHB	135	6	24	.200	.312	.378
Apr-Jun	1	0	2.81	0	32.0	18	30	ScPos	84	1	25	.179	.320	.250
Jul-Oct	1	2	3.19	1	36.2	20	38	Clutch	101	5	15	.188	.328	.337

SCOUTING REPORT

Florie delivers the ball with a delivery ranging from low three-quarters to sidearm, depending on the hitter and the pitch. His sinking fastball has slightly above-average velocity. His curveball and slider are a bit below-average, and his change-up definitely needs work.

While Bryce has no problems with movement or velocity, control of all his pitches is below-average. He must improve in this area to be effective. His fielding is average, as is his move, but righthanders with his delivery are easy to run on: all 12 stealing against Florie last year were successful.

HOW HE PERFORMED IN '95

Florie spent his first full season in the big leagues in 1995. Working almost exclusively in middle relief, he finished 10 games and cut down his walks dramatically. He had a consistent season except for a short stretch in April, pitching better with runners on base, a helpful trait in a reliever.

WHAT TO EXPECT IN '96

Bryce should help out considerably this year in middle relief and could end up as Trevor Hoffman's backup if Doug Bochtler does not work out. The promising Florie has a good enough arm to become a key element in the Padres' relief corps.

RAY HOLBERT

Positions: SS//2B/OF
Bats: R **Throws:** R
Ht: 6'0" **Wt:** 170
Opening Day Age: 25
Born: 9/25/1970
Drafted: SD88 3/58
ML Seasons: 2

Overall Statistics

	G	AB	R	H	2B	3B	HR	RBI	SB	CS	BB	SO	BA	OBA
95 SD	63	73	11	13	2	1	2	5	4	0	8	20	.178	.277
Career	68	78	12	14	2	1	2	5	4	0	8	24	.179	.273

1995 Situational Statistics

	AB	HR	RBI	BA	OBA	SLG		AB	HR	RBI	BA	OBA	SLG
Home	32	1	4	.219	.286	.313	LHP	39	2	5	.154	.214	.359
Road	41	1	1	.146	.271	.293	RHP	34	0	0	.206	.341	.235
Apr-Jun	20	0	0	.100	.308	.100	ScPos	14	1	4	.071	.316	.286
Jul-Oct	53	2	5	.208	.263	.377	Clutch	7	0	0	.143	.143	.143

SCOUTING REPORT

Holbert is a line-drive hitter who goes with the pitch. However, he needs to make better contact in order to become an everyday player. He has above-average speed on the basepaths and could be a fine basestealer. Ray is also an effective bunter.

He shines defensively at shortstop, with above-average range and well above-average hands. Ray also sports a strong, accurate arm.

HOW HE PERFORMED IN '95

Holbert hit .300 in '94 at Triple-A Las Vegas and ended up as Andujar Cedeno's backup. Although Ray is a good defensive shortstop, but may not provide enough offense to make an impact. He will not hit for power but could be valuable offensively if he cuts down on his strikeouts. A grand slam in July was the highlight of his year at the plate.

WHAT TO EXPECT IN '96

The Padres traded Holbert to the Astros last winter for Pedro A. Martinez. Barring an outstanding spring or a Houston trade, look for him to begin the year in Triple-A with the possibility of a callup if Orlando Miller has problems in the field.

SAN DIEGO PADRES

BRIAN JOHNSON

Positions: C//1B
Bats: R **Throws:** R
Ht: 6'2" **Wt:** 210
Opening Day Age: 28
Born: 1/8/1968
Drafted: NYA89 15/415
ML Seasons: 2

Overall Statistics

	G	AB	R	H	2B	3B	HR	RBI	SB	CS	BB	SO	BA	OBA
95 SD	68	207	20	52	9	0	3	29	0	0	11	39	.251	.287
Career	104	300	27	75	13	1	6	45	0	0	16	60	.250	.286

1995 Situational Statistics

	AB	HR	RBI	BA	OBA	SLG		AB	HR	RBI	BA	OBA	SLG
Home	84	1	8	.250	.281	.310	LHP	63	1	11	.270	.314	.365
Road	123	2	21	.252	.291	.358	RHP	144	2	18	.243	.275	.326
Apr-Jun	71	3	14	.282	.338	.451	ScPos	51	2	24	.275	.339	.451
Jul-Oct	136	0	15	.235	.260	.279	Clutch	41	3	15	.341	.349	.659

SCOUTING REPORT
Johnson is a good fastball hitter with some power. He is very aggressive at the plate and will pull inside pitches. Brian has slightly below-average speed on the bases but isn't called on to run often.

Behind the plate, he shows an above-average arm with average accuracy. Although his range is just average, Johnson has well above-average hands.

HOW HE PERFORMED IN '95
Johnson played the role of a backup catcher perfectly in '95 but may end up permanently stuck with that role. He's not going to beat out Brad Ausmus at this rate. Brian would often start a day game after a night game and made appearances in the late innings. He was 5-for-12 (.417) as a pinch-hitter.

He draws few walks, but shows occasional power. Behind the plate, he threw out 29% of runners trying to steal and allowed slightly more wild pitches and passed balls than average.

WHAT TO EXPECT IN '96
Johnson will begin his third season as a backup with little hope of expanding his job. In order to hold his position and maybe move up, Brian must improve his defense or his offense substantially.

SCOTT LIVINGSTONE

Positions: 1B/3B//2B
Bats: L **Throws:** R
Ht: 6'0" **Wt:** 190
Opening Day Age: 30
Born: 7/15/1965
Drafted: DET88 2/56
ML Seasons: 5

Overall Statistics

	G	AB	R	H	2B	3B	HR	RBI	SB	CS	BB	SO	BA	OBA
95 SD	99	196	26	66	15	0	5	32	2	1	15	22	.337	.380
Career	430	1184	138	346	64	3	15	139	8	10	72	141	.292	.329

1995 Situational Statistics

	AB	HR	RBI	BA	OBA	SLG		AB	HR	RBI	BA	OBA	SLG
Home	87	1	13	.345	.406	.460	LHP	21	1	3	.524	.524	.714
Road	109	4	19	.330	.359	.514	RHP	175	4	29	.314	.365	.463
Apr-Jun	35	1	5	.229	.222	.343	ScPos	53	1	28	.377	.397	.509
Jul-Oct	161	4	27	.360	.412	.522	Clutch	38	2	8	.342	.386	.526

SCOUTING REPORT
Livingstone is a high fastball hitter who hits line drives and makes good contact. He has average-minus speed, no power and lacks patience at the plate, meaning he depends on hitting frequent singles. He does not bunt.

A former starting third baseman with Detroit, Scott has below-average range at first base but well above-average hands. His arm strength and throwing accuracy are both average.

HOW HE PERFORMED IN '95
Livingstone is trapped by circumstance in San Diego: due to Ken Caminiti's durability, Scott will not see much action at third base and, because of his limited power, he does not hit enough to start at first. He is an adequate player at best and appears to have found his niche as a reserve.

In this role, he had an outstanding season. Despite limited power, Scott drove in runs and hit .360 in 161 at-bats from July on. He also hit .326 (14-for-43) as a pinch-hitter.

WHAT TO EXPECT IN '96
Livingstone signed a new contract with the Padres in December and will remain with the team as one of its primary reserves. He has now hit .270 or higher in each of his five major-league seasons.

SAN DIEGO PADRES

MARC NEWFIELD

Position: OF
Bats: R **Throws:** R
Ht: 6'4" **Wt:** 205
Opening Day Age: 23
Born: 10/19/1972
Drafted: SEA90 1/6
ML Seasons: 3

Overall Statistics

	G	AB	R	H	2B	3B	HR	RBI	SB	CS	BB	SO	BA	OBA
95 SEA/SD	45	140	13	33	8	1	4	21	0	0	5	24	.236	.267
Career	79	244	21	55	12	1	6	32	0	1	9	36	.225	.258

1995 Situational Statistics

	AB	HR	RBI	BA	OBA	SLG		AB	HR	RBI	BA	OBA	SLG
Home	70	1	8	.200	.233	.286	LHP	57	2	7	.281	.328	.474
Road	70	3	13	.271	.301	.500	RHP	83	2	14	.205	.224	.337
Apr-Jun	85	3	14	.188	.225	.329	ScPos	35	1	16	.314	.351	.457
Jul-Oct	55	1	7	.309	.333	.491	Clutch	22	0	4	.227	.227	.318

SCOUTING REPORT

Newfield is a promising young hitter with line-drive power, above-average bat speed and a good stroke. He has average baserunning speed. Originally a first baseman, Marc is still learning to play left field. His arm strength is slightly below-average. His throwing accuracy, range and hands are all average.

HOW HE PERFORMED IN '95

Newfield, Seattle's top draft pick in 1990, was perhaps the key reason San Diego would trade Andy Benes to the Mariners. He struggled in Triple-A and with the Mariners early in '95 but, after the trade, batted .343 for Triple-A Las Vegas and earned a callup to the Padres. Mark is an excellent contact hitter yet is quite aggressive. He does not walk often, though, and hasn't yet shown great power. Newfield will have to hit his way into the starting lineup, but he should be able to do that.

WHAT TO EXPECT IN '96

Newfield will probably start the season in Triple-A. If Marc, who is still very young, shows he is ready to hit at the major-league level and neither Eddie Williams or Roberto Petagine work out, Newfield could end up at first base. He is an excellent hitting prospect.

MELVIN NIEVES

Positions: OF//1B
Bats: B **Throws:** R
Ht: 6'2" **Wt:** 186
Opening Day Age: 24
Born: 12/28/1971
Drafted: ATL 5/20/88
ML Seasons: 4

Overall Statistics

	G	AB	R	H	2B	3B	HR	RBI	SB	CS	BB	SO	BA	OBA
95 SD	98	234	32	48	6	1	14	38	2	3	19	88	.205	.276
Career	139	319	38	66	8	1	17	46	2	3	27	126	.207	.279

1995 Situational Statistics

	AB	HR	RBI	BA	OBA	SLG		AB	HR	RBI	BA	OBA	SLG
Home	111	5	17	.153	.207	.306	LHP	56	5	9	.179	.246	.464
Road	123	9	21	.252	.336	.520	RHP	178	9	29	.213	.285	.404
Apr-Jun	121	5	16	.207	.279	.364	ScPos	75	2	23	.187	.238	.307
Jul-Oct	113	9	22	.204	.272	.478	Clutch	42	4	9	.214	.250	.500

SCOUTING REPORT

Nieves is a fastball hitter who is easily fooled by breaking pitches. Although he has fine power, Melvin has a swing full of holes, makes poor contact, and lacks patience at the plate. He is a slightly below-average runner.

In the pasture, Nieves has below-average range and does not get a good jump. Melvin's arm strength is above-average but he displays only average accuracy. His hands are slightly below-average.

HOW HE PERFORMED IN '95

Nieves spent his first full season in the majors in '95 and began playing the outfield on a regular basis after Bip Roberts was injured. Despite showing some strengths, Melvin did not have an impressive year. The overaggressive Nieves struck out in 38 percent of his at-bats. He still produced a .419 slugging percentage, however, as nearly a third of his hits were home runs. The Padres used him at all three outfield spots, but left field was Melvin's best position, where he threw out five baserunners.

WHAT TO EXPECT IN '96

Until he shows greater discipline at bat, Nieves will be relegated to a reserve role. He provides a home run threat, when he connects, but that's not often enough.

THE SCOUTING REPORT: 1996

SAN DIEGO PADRES

ROBERTO PETAGINE

Positions: 1B//OF
Bats: L **Throws:** L
Ht: 6'1" **Wt:** 170
Opening Day Age: 24
Born: 6/7/1971
Drafted: HOU 2/13/90
ML Seasons: 2

Overall Statistics

	G	AB	R	H	2B	3B	HR	RBI	SB	CS	BB	SO	BA	OBA
95 SD	89	124	15	29	8	0	3	17	0	0	26	41	.234	.367
Career	97	131	15	29	8	0	3	17	0	0	27	44	.221	.354

1995 Situational Statistics

	AB	HR	RBI	BA	OBA	SLG		AB	HR	RBI	BA	OBA	SLG
Home	45	2	8	.244	.460	.467	LHP	13	0	1	.231	.412	.308
Road	79	1	9	.228	.299	.316	RHP	111	3	16	.234	.361	.378
Apr-Jun	80	2	14	.287	.430	.450	ScPos	34	1	14	.265	.432	.353
Jul-Oct	44	1	3	.136	.240	.227	Clutch	39	3	9	.231	.348	.487

SCOUTING REPORT

A disciplined low-ball hitter, Petagine is expected to develop power as he gains experience. He is quite slow on the bases and is no threat to steal, but sacrificed successfully both times he was asked to do so in '95.

At first base, his range, hands, arm strength and throwing accuracy are all average.

HOW HE PERFORMED IN '95

Petagine came to San Diego last winter in the megadeal with Houston. He spent a considerable portion of the year in the majors, batting .355 through May but only .194 the rest of the way. The Padres sent him to the minors twice—although he drew plenty of walks, Roberto's strikeout problems were disillusioning.

A first baseman by nature, Petagine is trying to learn to play right field, and it may be necessary for Roberto to develop utility skills in order to stick around in the big leagues.

WHAT TO EXPECT IN '96

Unless he has a great spring, Petagine will likely start the season in the minors to re-establish his batting stroke. The Padres could make Petagine their starting first baseman or use him as trade bait. His problem is mediocre power at a power position.

SCOTT SANDERS

Position: SP
Bats: R **Throws:** R
Ht: 6'4" **Wt:** 220
Opening Day Age: 27
Born: 3/25/1969
Drafted: SD 90 2/32
ML Seasons: 3

Overall Statistics

	G	GS	GF	SV	W	L	ERA	IP	H	R	ER	HR	BB	SO
95 SD	17	15	0	0	5	5	4.30	90.0	79	46	43	14	31	88
Career	49	44	2	1	12	16	4.48	253.1	236	141	126	28	102	234

1995 Situational Statistics

	W	L	ERA	SV	IP	BB	SO		AB	HR	RBI	BA	OBA	SLG
Home	4	2	5.11	0	56.1	20	53	LHB	134	5	19	.276	.355	.485
Road	1	3	2.94	0	33.2	11	35	RHB	212	9	21	.198	.253	.344
Apr-Jun	5	4	4.11	0	72.1	25	61	ScPos	61	3	26	.311	.353	.541
Jul-Oct	0	1	5.09	0	17.2	6	27	Clutch	14	0	0	.000	.176	.000

SCOUTING REPORT

Sanders uses a three-quarter delivery to bring home a sinking fastball that is slightly above-average but needs more movement. His hard slider is well above-average. When he's on, Sanders gets strikeouts and groundouts. If the sinker doesn't sink, however, he gets hammered.

His auxiliary pitches aren't much. Scott must improve his average change-up to better set up hitters; his curve is only for show. He has average control and does well holding runners on: five of eight potential basestealers in '95 were thrown out. Quick feet make Sanders a well above-average fielder.

HOW HE PERFORMED IN '95

Sanders' disappointing season ended on the disabled list. A sprained elbow ligament (originally diagnosed as soreness) shelved him from mid-July onward except for two games in early September.

Scott improved against lefties significantly in '95. He also did well at the plate, batting .296 after he entered last year hitting just .104 for his career.

WHAT TO EXPECT IN '96

Sanders is a contender for the fourth or fifth spot in the Padres' rotation. He has stay healthy and eliminate the fat pitches that end up as extra-base hits. If he does, he could win 15 games.

SAN DIEGO PADRES

FERNANDO VALENZUELA

Position: SP/RP
Bats: L **Throws:** L
Ht: 5'11" **Wt:** 195
Opening Day Age: 35
Born: 11/1/1960
Drafted: MEX 1978
ML Seasons: 15

Overall Statistics

	G	GS	GF	SV	W	L	ERA	IP	H	R	ER	HR	BB	SO
95 SD	29	15	5	0	8	3	4.98	90.1	101	53	50	16	34	57
Career	402	375	10	2	158	133	3.49	2669.1	2435	1164	1036	197	1038	1918

1995 Situational Statistics

	W	L	ERA	SV	IP	BB	SO		AB	HR	RBI	BA	OBA	SLG
Home	4	2	5.23	0	43.0	12	29	LHB	63	1	4	.317	.377	.460
Road	4	1	4.75	0	47.1	22	28	RHB	286	15	44	.283	.345	.514
Apr-Jun	2	2	6.49	0	34.2	10	17	ScPos	90	4	29	.200	.295	.378
Jul-Oct	6	1	4.04	0	55.2	24	40	Clutch	5	0	2	.600	.500	.800

SCOUTING REPORT

Valenzuela has a full windup with an open, three-quarter delivery. Fernando nibbles constantly and gets by on experience.

He cuts his minus fastball so it rides in on the fists of righthanders and turns over a change-up so it is like a soft screwball. His curve and straight change-up are thrown only for show. Fernando still has decent control and does an average job of holding runners on and fielding his position. Four of eight were thrown out trying to steal on him in '95.

HOW HE PERFORMED IN '95

Valenzuela, the world's oldest 35-year-old, was signed by the Padres last spring to draw more Hispanic fans to the park. Used as a starter and a reliever, he posted his first winning season in the majors since 1987.

While Fernando struggled in the first half (6.49 ERA), he rebounded in the second. He batted .250 and hit two home runs to extend his lead among active pitchers with 10 career homers. Valenzuela is still a decent bunter and laid down three sacrifices.

WHAT TO EXPECT IN '96

The Padres have re-signed Valenzuela and will continue to use him as a spot starter and reliever.

RON VILLONE

Position: RP
Bats: L **Throws:** L
Ht: 6'3" **Wt:** 230
Opening Day Age: 26
Born: 1/16/1970
Drafted: SEA92 1/14
ML Seasons: 1

Overall Statistics

	G	GS	GF	SV	W	L	ERA	IP	H	R	ER	HR	BB	SO
95 SEA/SD	38	0	15	1	2	3	5.80	45.0	44	31	29	11	34	63
Career	38	0	15	1	2	3	5.80	45.0	44	31	29	11	34	63

1995 Situational Statistics

	W	L	ERA	SV	IP	BB	SO		AB	HR	RBI	BA	OBA	SLG
Home	1	2	5.56	0	22.2	15	31	LHB	47	2	11	.298	.492	.468
Road	1	1	6.04	1	22.1	19	32	RHB	126	9	24	.238	.326	.492
Apr-Jun	0	2	7.91	0	19.1	23	26	ScPos	54	3	25	.278	.412	.463
Jul-Oct	2	1	4.21	1	25.2	11	37	Clutch	77	5	16	.312	.391	.558

SCOUTING REPORT

Villone has a jerky, deceptive motion and a high three-quarter delivery. His above-average fastball bores in on righthanders, and Ron also has an average slider. However, his best pitch is an outstanding change-up that drops like a forkball. Villone's control is currently below-average.

A minus fielder, Villone has a good flip throw to first but doesn't pay attention to runners at times. However, just four runners tried to steal on him, and three were gunned down. Ron was hitless in his only '95 at-bat.

HOW HE PERFORMED IN '95

Ron came to San Diego in the Andy Benes trade. He received a warm welcome from the fans, who liked his hard stuff and gamer attitude. Villone is unafraid to pitch inside, even if it's due to bad location. At times, Ron didn't look ready for the majors—he struck out well over a batter per inning, but struggled some with righthanders.

WHAT TO EXPECT IN '96

Villone has plus stuff and tremendous potential. Lefties with heat are hard to find, and Ron will get a year or two to hone his game in middle relief.

SAN DIEGO PADRES

BRIAN WILLIAMS

Position: RP/SP
Bats: R **Throws:** R
Ht: 6'3" **Wt:** 205
Opening Day Age: 27
Born: 2/15/1969
Drafted: HOU90 2/31
ML Seasons: 5

Overall Statistics

	G	GS	GF	SV	W	L	ERA	IP	H	R	ER	HR	BB	SO
95 SD	44	6	7	0	3	10	6.00	72.0	79	54	48	3	38	75
Career	124	42	21	3	20	26	4.99	340.2	370	215	189	31	163	238

1995 Situational Statistics

	W	L	ERA	SV	IP	BB	SO		AB	HR	RBI	BA	OBA	SLG
Home	1	4	5.52	0	29.1	16	35	LHB	111	0	17	.279	.403	.351
Road	2	6	6.33	0	42.2	22	40	RHB	172	3	23	.279	.362	.384
Apr-Jun	1	5	5.76	0	25.0	14	32	ScPos	84	3	39	.321	.458	.452
Jul-Oct	2	5	6.13	0	47.0	24	43	Clutch	78	2	16	.333	.458	.423

SCOUTING REPORT

Williams, a power pitcher, throws with a high three-quarter delivery. He has an above-average fastball that tends to straighten out when it's thrown high and a plus curve that breaks downward.

An average change-up is also part of Brian's arsenal along with a minus slider that gets hit hard. He has below-average control which must improve for him to be successful. Four runners tried to steal in '95 on Brian's adequate move to first, with two being thrown out. He is an average fielder.

HOW HE PERFORMED IN '95

After coming over from Houston last December, Williams suffered through an awful year with a career-worst record and ERA. August was particularly hellish for him (17 earned runs in 10.1 innings).

WHAT TO EXPECT IN '96

The Padres could keep Williams in the bigs and hope he rebounds or send him to the minors to work out his problems. He has promise, but has yet to show it with San Diego. Like many young power pitchers, Brian yet has to learn how to pitch to take advantage of his gifts. At 27, he could go either way.

EDDIE WILLIAMS

Position: 1B
Bats: R **Throws:** R
Ht: 6'0" **Wt:** 175
Opening Day Age: 31
Born: 11/1/1964
Drafted: NYN83 1/4
ML Seasons: 7

Overall Statistics

	G	AB	R	H	2B	3B	HR	RBI	SB	CS	BB	SO	BA	OBA
95 SD	97	296	35	77	11	1	12	47	0	0	23	47	.260	.320
Career	263	806	111	218	37	2	30	109	1	4	70	135	.270	.336

1995 Situational Statistics

	AB	HR	RBI	BA	OBA	SLG		AB	HR	RBI	BA	OBA	SLG
Home	138	4	19	.268	.342	.420	LHP	118	7	19	.288	.341	.500
Road	158	8	28	.253	.300	.430	RHP	178	5	28	.242	.306	.376
Apr-Jun	155	5	23	.277	.327	.432	ScPos	93	2	33	.237	.298	.355
Jul-Oct	141	7	24	.241	.312	.418	Clutch	53	1	7	.264	.304	.340

SCOUTING REPORT

Williams, who stands coiled like a spring at the plate, has lots of holes in his swing and does not make especially good contact. However, he is a good mistake hitter, especially on fastballs out over the plate, and has above-average bat speed. He was less successful in '95 than in the previous year as pitchers adjusted to his strengths.

Eddie has below-average baserunning speed. He has below-average range but average hands, arm strength and throwing accuracy at first base. Given his current, bulked-up appearance, it's hard to imagine that he used to play third base in the major leagues.

HOW HE PERFORMED IN '95

Williams has come back from the dead with San Diego and has proven that his power is legitimate. However, after a decent first half, he suffered a strained hamstring July 31 and hit just two homers from that point on. The late-season slump led San Diego to platoon Eddie with Roberto Petagine.

WHAT TO EXPECT IN '96

Williams is likely to see a reduced role with the team unless he has a particularly good spring, or unless no other first base options are available.

THE SCOUTING REPORT: 1996

SAN DIEGO PADRES: TOP PROSPECTS

GABE ALVAREZ

Bats: R Throws: R Opening Day Age: 22
Ht: 6-1 Wt: 185 Born: 3/6/1974
Position: SS Drafted: 1995 #2 SD

YR TEAM	LG/CLASS	G	AB	R	H	2B	3B	HR	RBI	SB	BA	OBA
95 Memphis	SOU/AA	2	9	0	5	1	0	0	4	0	.556	.600
95 Ranch Cuca	CAL/A	59	212	41	73	17	2	6	36	1	.344	.431

A three-year starter at shortstop for USC, Alvarez was named to the All-Pac-10 squad three times and was a two-time All-American. A third-round pick of the A's out of high school, the Mexican native was the Padres' second-round choice last June. He excelled for Rancho Cucamonga, never going four games in a row without a hit and putting together hitting streaks of 11 and 12 games. Alvarez was promoted to Memphis for the last few games of the season and the playoffs. He has a quick bat and good power for a shortstop, though despite a great arm and better than average range, a move to third base could be in his future.

HOMER BUSH

Bats: R Throws: R Opening Day Age: 23
Ht: 5-11 Wt: 180 Born: 11/11/1972
Position: 2B Drafted: 1991 #8 SD

YR TEAM	LG/CLASS	G	AB	R	H	2B	3B	HR	RBI	SB	BA	OBA
93 Waterloo	MID/A	130	472	63	152	19	3	5	51	39	.322	.349
94 Ranch Cuca	CAL/A	39	161	37	54	10	3	0	16	9	.335	.383
94 Wichita	TEX/AA	59	245	35	73	11	4	3	14	20	.298	.333
95 Memphis	SOU/AA	108	432	53	121	12	5	7	37	34	.280	.307

Bush, a pure hitter with excellent speed, is a great athlete who batted leadoff last year. He could also become a solid number two hitter. Since he has little power, he must contain his swing, drive balls into the gaps, and let his speed create doubles and triples. The 23-year-old must be more selective and learn to draw more walks while cutting down on his strikeouts. Bush has improved greatly on defense and has good range at second base.

RAUL CASANOVA

Bats: R Throws: R Opening Day Age: 24
Ht: 6-0 Wt: 192 Born: 8/24/1972
Position: C Drafted: 1990 #8 NYN

YR TEAM	LG/CLASS	G	AB	R	H	2B	3B	HR	RBI	SB	BA	OBA
93 Waterloo	MID/A	76	227	32	58	12	0	6	30	0	.256	.321
94 Ranch Cuca	CAL/A	123	471	83	160	27	2	23	120	1	.340	.403
95 Memphis	SOU/AA	89	306	42	83	18	0	12	44	4	.271	.330

Casanova is a switch-hitting catcher with power, the most highly sought-after commodity in baseball. Acquired from the Mets as part of the Tony Fernandez deal in 1992, the 23-year-old came out of nowhere in 1994 to win the California League batting title and rank second in RBI to earn MVP honors. Hampered by ankle injuries last season, he did not put up huge numbers but showed he could hit Double-A pitching. The Puerto Rican native handles pitchers well and is solid behind the plate, but doesn't throw well—Casanova has a great arm, but it can be erratic and he threw out just 30.7% of opposing base-stealers last year.

BEN DAVIS

Bats: S Throws: R Opening Day Age: 19
Ht: 6-4 Wt: 195 Born: 3/10/1977
Position: C Drafted: 1995 #1 SD

YR TEAM	LG/CLASS	G	AB	R	H	2B	3B	HR	RBI	SB	BA	OBA
95 Idaho Falls	PIO/R	52	197	36	55	8	3	5	46	0	.279	.338

Davis was the second overall pick in last June's draft after a stellar high school career in Pennsylvania. He has all the tools to be an outstanding defensive catcher and has the kind of rocket arm that opposing teams fear. Offensively, he is a switch-hitter who could provide some power. Davis made a solid pro debut last summer at Idaho Falls and was named to the Pioneer League All-Star team.

DUSTIN HERMANSON

Bats: R Throws: R Opening Day Age: 23
Ht: 6-3 Wt: 195 Born: 12/21/1972
Position: P Drafted: 1994 #1 SD

YR TEAM	LG/CLASS	G	GS	GF	SV	W	L	ERA	IP	H	HR	BB	SO	O/BA
94 Wichita	TEX/AA	16	0	14	8	1	0	0.43	21.0	13	0	6	30	.176
94 Las Vegas	PCL/AAA	7	0	7	3	0	0	6.14	7.1	6	1	5	6	.222
95 Las Vegas	PCL/AAA	31	0	22	11	0	1	3.50	36.0	35	5	29	42	.245
95 San Diego	NL/MAJ	26	0	6	0	3	1	6.82	31.2	35	8	22	19	.280

The former Kent State standout was the third overall pick in the '94 draft. After an impressive debut at Wichita that summer, Hermanson was considered the top closer prospect in baseball, ready to step in and help the Padres right away. After seven scoreless outings with five saves for Las Vegas, the 23-year-old was summoned to San Diego in early May. After a good start for the Padres, his mechanics got fouled up and he was pounded mercilessly. Shipped back to Las Vegas, he never regained his confidence or his slider. When on his game, Hermanson has great control of a mid-90's fastball with good movement—and that hard slider.

MARC KROON

Bats: S Throws: R Opening Day Age: 23
Ht: 6-2 Wt: 175 Born: 4/2/1973
Position: P Drafted: 1991 #4 NYN

YR TEAM	LG/CLASS	G	GS	GF	SV	W	L	ERA	IP	H	HR	BB	SO	O/BA
93 Capital Cty	SAL/A	29	19	8	2	2	11	3.47	124.1	123	6	70	122	.269
94 RanchCuca	CAL/A	26	26	0	0	11	6	4.83	143.1	143	14	81	153	.260
95 Memphis	SOU/AA	22	19	2	7	5	3.51	115.1	90	12	61	123	.211
95 San Diego	NL/MAJ	2	0	1	0	0	1	10.80	1.2	1	0	2	2	.200

Kroon, a pure power pitcher with a high-90's fastball, also has an above-average slider and a developing circle change. His fastball/slider combination could turn him into an overpowering reliever, but he could also develop into a dominant starter if he can change speeds better. Kroon, who will be just 23 on Opening Day, gets rattled on the mound and isn't good at handling adversity. He needs to work on his control and learn not to rely on his fastball too much. Kroon led the Southern League in opponents' batting average (.211) and strikeouts per nine innings (9.55).

SAN DIEGO PADRES: TOP PROSPECTS

DEREK LEE

Bats: R Throws: R Opening Day Age: 21
Ht: 6-5 Wt: 220 Born: 9/6/1975
Position: 1B Drafted: 1993 #1 SD

YR TEAM	LG/CLASS	G	AB	R	H	2B	3B	HR	RBI	SB	BA	OBA
93 Padres	ARIZ/R	15	52	11	17	1	1	2	5	4	.327	.397
93 Ranch Cuca	CAL/A	20	73	13	20	5	1	1	10	0	.274	.369
94 Ranch Cuca	CAL/A	126	442	66	118	19	2	8	53	18	.267	.336
95 Memphis	SOU/AA	2	9	0	1	0	0	0	1	0	.111	.111
95 Ranch Cuca	CAL/A	128	502	82	151	25	2	23	95	14	.301	.366

The nephew of former Padre Leron Lee led the Padres' farm system in home runs and RBI last year. Playing against mostly older competition in the California League, the 20-year-old was one of the league's most dangerous hitters. He has excellent bat speed and will continue to hit with great power as he matures physically. The former first-round pick is trying to learn to hit the ball to all fields and needs to cut down on his strikeouts. Lee is athletic enough to play the outfield and has been tried at third, but is most comfortable at first, where he should develop into a solid defensive player.

RAY MCDAVID

Bats: L Throws: R Opening Day Age: 25
Ht: 6-3 Wt: 195 Born: 7/20/1971
Position: CF Drafted: 1989 #8 SD

YR TEAM	LG/CLASS	G	AB	R	H	2B	3B	HR	RBI	SB	BA	OBA
93 Wichita	TEX/AA	126	441	65	119	18	5	11	55	33	.270	.371
94 Las Vegas	PCL/AAA	128	476	85	129	24	6	13	62	24	.271	.370
94 San Diego	NL/MAJ	9	28	2	7	1	0	0	2	1	.250	.276
95 Las Vegas	PCL/AAA	52	166	28	45	8	1	5	27	7	.271	.393
95 Padres	ARIZ/R	9	28	13	13	2	1	1	6	3	.464	.583
95 San Diego	NL/MAJ	11	17	2	3	0	0	0	0	1	.176	.263

At one time McDavid was considered one of the top outfield prospects in the game, but his stock has slipped over the last few seasons. While he is not going to be the 30-30 man some hoped for, he is still a decent hitter with good speed and some power. The 24-year-old is a superb athlete and a good defensive center-fielder. Last May he ruptured thumb ligaments sliding into second base and didn't return to full-time duty until August.

HEATH MURRAY

Bats: L Throws: L Opening Day Age: 23
Ht: 6-4 Wt: 205 Born: 4/19/1973
Position: P Drafted: 1994 #3 SD

YR TEAM	LG/CLASS	G	GS	GF	SV	W	L	ERA	IP	H	HR	BB	SO	O/BA
94 Spokane	NWST/A	15	15	0	0	5	6	2.90	99.1	101	6	18	78	.268
95 Memphis	SOU/AA	14	14	0	0	4	3	3.38	71	83	1	42	71	.267
95 Ranch Cuca	CAL/A	14	14	0	0	9	4	3.12	92.1	80	5	38	81	.240

Murray led the Padres' farm system in wins and was second in strikeouts and third in ERA last year. The 22-year-old lefthander got off to a great start at Rancho Cucamonga and in mid-June was leading the league in wins and innings pitched while ranking third in strikeouts. This earned him a promotion to Memphis where he continued to impress. In 28 starts, he pitched five or more innings 23 times and gave up more than three earned runs only six times. Murray, the Padres' third-round pick in '94 out of Michigan, features a fastball in the 88–90 mph range.

TODD SCHMITT

Bats: R Throws: R Opening Day Age: 26
Ht: 6-2 Wt: 170 Born: 2/12/1970
Position: P Drafted: NDFA 6-17-92 SD

YR TEAM	LG/CLASS	G	GS	GF	SV	W	L	ERA	IP	H	HR	BB	SO	O/BA
93 Waterloo	MID/A	51	0	47	25	1	4	1.99	58.2	41	0	33	76	.192
94 Ranch Cuca	CAL/A	53	0	50	29	2	4	1.95	50.2	43	2	24	45	.235
95 Las Vegas	PCL/AAA	12	0	8	2	0	2	7.82	12.2	16	0	9	6	.327
95 Memphis	SOU/AA	26	0	24	18	0	0	1.30	27.2	18	2	11	27	.189

After pitching at Grand Valley State in Michigan, Schmitt went undrafted and signed with the Padres as a free agent. He led the California League in saves in 1994 after finishing among his league's leaders the previous two seasons. The 26-year-old converted 18 of 19 save opportunities for Memphis last year to earn a June promotion to Las Vegas, where a minor elbow injury limited him to just 12 appearances. Schmitt throws his fastball and curve from two different arm angles and also has a very tough split-finger curve.

JASON THOMPSON

Bats: L Throws: L Opening Day Age: 25
Ht: 6-4 Wt: 200 Born: 6/13/1971
Position: 1B Drafted: 1993 #9 SD

YR TEAM	LG/CLASS	G	AB	R	H	2B	3B	HR	RBI	SB	BA	OBA
93 Spokane	NWST/A	66	240	36	72	25	1	7	38	3	.300	.389
94 Ranch Cuca	CAL/A	68	253	57	91	19	2	13	63	1	.360	.443
94 Wichita	TEX/AA	63	215	35	56	17	2	8	46	0	.260	.352
95 Memphis	SOU/AA	137	475	62	129	20	1	20	64	7	.272	.352

Thompson, one of the Padres' top power prospects, was second in the farm system in homers last year and was named Memphis' MVP. The Arizona product tied for third in the Southern League in home runs and was fifth in HR/AB (1/23.75). While he has legitimate major league caliber power, he strikes out too much and tries to pull everything he sees. The 24-year-old does have a good eye at the plate and will take a walk. Defensively, Thompson is solid and has good hands, though he does not have great range.

JORGE VELANDIA

Bats: R Throws: R Opening Day Age: 21
Ht: 5-9 Wt: 160 Born: 1/12/1975
Position: SS Drafted: NDFA 1-15-92 DET

YR TEAM	LG/CLASS	G	AB	R	H	2B	3B	HR	RBI	SB	BA	OBA
93 Fayetteville	SAL/A	37	106	15	17	4	0	0	11	5	.160	.266
93 Niagara Fls	NYP/A	72	212	30	41	11	0	1	22	22	.193	.258
94 Lakeland	FSL/A	22	60	8	14	4	0	0	3	0	.233	.299
94 Springfield	MID/A	98	290	42	71	14	0	4	36	5	.245	.302
95 Las Vegas	PCL/AAA	66	206	25	54	12	3	0	25	0	.262	.309
95 Memphis	SOU/AA	63	186	23	38	10	2	4	17	0	.204	.262

Velandia, a slick-fielding shortstop, came to the Padres from the Tigers as part of the Gene Harris trade in 1994. The Venezuelan native has great hands and is very quick in the field. He makes all the routine plays as well as some spectacular ones and could play defense in the majors right now. The 21-year-old's weakness is his bat. While he has some potential at the plate, he hits too many fly balls and gives away plenty of at-bats. Velandia was slumping offensively when injuries forced a promotion to Las Vegas, but he responded and hit better in Triple-A than he did in Double-A.

SAN DIEGO PADRES: OTHERS TO WATCH

ROBBIE BECKETT Bats: R Throws: L Ht: 6-5 Wt: 235
Born: 7/16/1972 Drafted: 1990 #1 SD Position: P

YR TEAM	LG/CLASS	G	GS	GF	SV	W	L	ERA	IP	H	HR	BB	SO	O/BA
95 Memphis	SOU/AA	36	8	11	0	3	4	4.80	86.1	65	3	73	98	.208

While he has overpowering stuff including a 90+-mph fastball and tough breaking pitch, Beckett has struggled mightily with his control.

JULIO BRUNO Bats: R Throws: R Ht: 5-11 Wt: 190
Born: 10/15/1972 Drafted: NDFA 11-7-89 SD Position: 3B

YR TEAM	LG/CLASS	G	AB	R	H	2B	3B	HR	RBI	SB	BA	OBA
95 Las Vegas	PCL/AAA	38	139	13	34	6	1	0	6	1	.245	.284
95 Memphis	SOU/AA	59	196	16	53	6	3	2	25	3	.270	.303
95 San Diego	NL/MAJ	0	0	0	0	0	0	0	0	0	.000	.000

A good defensive third baseman with power potential, Bruno battled injuries all season before finally finding his stroke in August at Memphis.

SHANE DENNIS Bats: R Throws: L Ht: 6-3 Wt: 200
Born: 7/3/1971 Drafted: 1994 #7 SD Position: P

YR TEAM	LG/CLASS	G	GS	GF	SV	W	L	ERA	IP	H	HR	BB	SO	O/BA
95 R Cuca	CAL/A	11	11	0	0	8	2	2.51	79.0	63	8	22	77	.218
95 Clinton	MID/A	14	14	0	0	3	9	3.87	86.0	68	5	35	80	.211

A third team All-American at Wichita State, the son of former big leaguer Don Dennis led the Padres' farm system in strikeouts last year.

SEAN FESH Bats: L Throws: L Ht: 6-2 Wt: 165
Born: 11/3/1972 Drafted: 1991 #66 HOU Position: P

YR TEAM	LG/CLASS	G	GS	GF	SV	W	L	ERA	IP	H	HR	BB	SO	O/BA
95 Tucson	PCL/AAA	10	0	1	0	1	0	1.35	13.1	11	0	3	7	.224
95 Las Vegas	PCL/AAA	30	0	11	1	2	1	3.32	38.0	53	2	16	18	.327

The sidearming lefthanded reliever was acquired from the Astros, completing the blockbuster trade made last December.

BILLY HALL Bats: S Throws: R Ht: 5-9 Wt: 180
Born: 6/17/1969 Drafted: 1991 #18 SD Position: 2B

YR TEAM	LG/CLASS	G	AB	R	H	2B	3B	HR	RBI	SB	BA	OBA
95 Las Vegas	PCL/AAA	86	249	42	56	3	1	1	22	22	.225	.282

The Wichita State product has a career .295 average and great speed, but poor fielding may prevent him from ever being a major league regular.

GREG LAROCCA Bats: R Throws: R Ht: 5-11 Wt: 185
Born: 11/10/1972 Drafted: 1994 #10 SD Position: SS

YR TEAM	LG/CLASS	G	AB	R	H	2B	3B	HR	RBI	SB	BA	OBA
95 Memphis	SOU/AA	2	7	0	1	0	0	0	0	0	.143	.143
95 R Cuca	CAL/A	125	466	77	150	36	5	8	74	15	.322	.393

A versatile infielder out of UMass, LaRocca is a solid all-around player named to the California League All-Star squad.

JOSE MARTINEZ Bats: R Throws: R Ht: 6-2 Wt: 155
Born: 4/1/1971 Drafted: NDFA 12-11-88 NYN Position: P

YR TEAM	LG/CLASS	G	GS	GF	SV	W	L	ERA	IP	H	HR	BB	SO	O/BA
95 Las Vegas	PCL/AAA	27	25	0	0	6	10	4.75	151.2	156	9	44	64	.269

Martinez, part of the Gary Sheffield trade, does not throw hard and has not had the same success in Triple-A that he had in the lower levels.

ROB MATTSON Bats: L Throws: R Ht: 6-1 Wt: 190
Born: 11/18/1966 Drafted: NDFA 10-10-90 ATL Position: P

YR TEAM	LG/CLASS	G	GS	GF	SV	W	L	ERA	IP	H	HR	BB	SO	O/BA
95 Memphis	SOU/AA	30	28	1	0	12	13	4.11	201.2	199	20	73	139	.266

After pitching in the Netherlands in 1994, Mattson returned as a knuckle-balling replacement player and was second in the system in wins and fourth in strikeouts.

TERRIC MCFARLIN Bats: S Throws: R Ht: 6-0 Wt: 160
Born: 4/6/1969 Drafted: NDFA 9-13-90 LA Position: P

YR TEAM	LG/CLASS	G	GS	GF	SV	W	L	ERA	IP	H	HR	BB	SO	O/BA
95 Las Vegas	PCL/AAA	58	2	20	7	7	6	3.96	122.2	120	11	59	85	.259

A hard-throwing reliever, McFarlin tied for third in the Pacific Coast League in games pitched and was sixth in ERA.

JUAN MELO Bats: S Throws: R Ht: 6-3 Wt: 185
Born: 11/5/1976 Drafted: NDFA 6-15-93 SD Position: SS

YR TEAM	LG/CLASS	G	AB	R	H	2B	3B	HR	RBI	SB	BA	OBA
95 Clinton	MID/A	134	479	65	135	32	1	5	46	12	.282	.333

The 19-year-old Dominican is a switch-hitter with some pop from both sides of the plate and is a decent shortstop with a good arm.

SEAN MULLIGAN Bats: R Throws: R Ht: 6-2 Wt: 205
Born: 4/25/1970 Drafted: 1991 #5 SD Position: C

YR TEAM	LG/CLASS	G	AB	R	H	2B	3B	HR	RBI	SB	BA	OBA
95 Las Vegas	PCL/AAA	101	339	34	93	20	1	7	43	0	.274	.340
95 San Diego	NL/MAJ	0	0	0	0	0	0	0	0	0	.000	.000

The Illinois product is a solid defensive catcher with a little pop in his bat.

PAUL RUSSO Bats: R Throws: R Ht: 5-11 Wt: 215
Born: 8/26/1969 Drafted: 1990 #19 MIN Position: 3B

YR TEAM	LG/CLASS	G	AB	R	H	2B	3B	HR	RBI	SB	BA	OBA
95 Las Vegas	PCL/AAA	44	148	17	44	10	0	4	19	0	.297	.333
95 Memphis	SOU/AA	45	122	19	38	9	1	6	18	1	.311	.421

Russo, a Triple-A veteran, is a power-hitting third baseman who can also play first and has hit .275 with 97 home runs in his career.

KERRY TAYLOR Bats: R Throws: R Ht: 6-3 Wt: 200
Born: 1/25/1971 Drafted: NDFA 6-26-89 MIN Position: P

YR TEAM	LG/CLASS	G	GS	GF	SV	W	L	ERA	IP	H	HR	BB	SO	O/BA
95 Las Vegas	PCL/AAA	8	8	0	0	2	2	4.38	37.0	44	3	21	21	.299
95 San Diego	NL/MAJ	0	0	0	0	0	0	0.00	0.0	0	0	0	0	.000

Taylor led the Pacific Coast League in strikeouts in '94 and has a decent fastball and a good curve and slider, but suffered from a sore elbow last year.

TIM WORRELL Bats: R Throws: R Ht: 6-4 Wt: 215
Born: 7/5/1967 Drafted: 1989 #19 SD Position: P

YR TEAM	LG/CLASS	G	GS	GF	SV	W	L	ERA	IP	H	HR	BB	SO	O/BA
95 Las Vegas	PCL/AAA	10	3	0	0	2	6.00	24.0	27	1	17	18	.273	
95 R Cuca	CAL/A	9	3	2	1	0	2	5.16	22.2	25	2	6	17	.266
95 San Diego	NL/MAJ	9	0	4	0	1	0	4.73	13.1	16	2	6	13	.291

Todd Worrell's brother, Tim had just established himself with the Padres when he blew out his elbow and spent last season trying to work his way back.

THE SCOUTING REPORT: 1996

SAN FRANCISCO GIANTS

ROD BECK

Position: RP
Bats: R **Throws:** R
Ht: 6'1" **Wt:** 215
Opening Day Age: 27
Born: 8/3/1968
Drafted: OAK86 13/327
ML Seasons: 5

SCOUTING REPORT
Beck throws from three quarters with an open delivery and does not hide the ball well. His fastball has fallen off to a bit below major-league average; a sinker, it is now several feet slower than two years ago.

His slider is average, and Rod needs to feature it more often as too many first-ball fastballs got tagged hard last season. His forkball is top-notch, breaking down and in to righthanders, moving late and hard when it's working.

Although Beck is poor at holding runners, he compensates by having a quick move to the plate. Just four runners tried to steal against him in '95, three successfully. He does not field his position particularly well.

HOW HE PERFORMED IN '95
In '95 Rod was third in the NL in saves with 33 but also led both leagues with 10 blown saves. That is significant for Beck, who has blown only 18 opportunities in his five-year career. The fourth-youngest pitcher to reach 100 saves, he trails only Lee Smith and Randy Myers with 109 saves over the last three years.

The major problem in '95 was the abrupt absence of a reliable setup pitcher, the role Mike Jackson had held in 1993–94. Beck had to pitch in the eighth inning nearly a dozen times and was frequently lit up in those outings. From July 9-28 he allowed fully 15 of his 29 earned runs all year; without that stretch, he would have been 5-2 with 32 saves and a 2.37 ERA.

Unscored on in 11 of his last 12 outings, he appeared to regain his old form in August. An unusual fact: he made only 37 relief appearances in his minor-league career, essentially becoming a relief pitcher at the major-league level.

WHAT TO EXPECT IN '96
At 27 years of age and arbitration-eligible, the all-time franchise leader in saves will return for two more seasons. Ace Adams and Frank Linzy are the only Giants to lead the team in saves five straight years; Beck will surely join that group.

At just over $2 million in '95, Beck was still a bargain among top-shelf, established closers. His pitching pattern seemed to become predictable in the middle of the season; he said that he has found "patterns and mechanics" to correct. A deeper bullpen will take care of a lot of Rod's problems.

Overall Statistics

	G	GS	GF	SV	W	L	ERA	IP	H	R	ER	HR	BB	SO
95 SF	60	0	52	33	5	6	4.45	58.2	60	31	29	7	21	42
Career	280	0	222	127	14	15	2.80	331.0	281	110	103	36	75	292

1995 Situational Statistics

	W	L	ERA	SV	IP	BB	SO		AB	HR	RBI	BA	OBA	SLG
Home	5	3	4.54	16	35.2	15	25	LHB	109	3	22	.275	.333	.404
Road	0	3	4.30	17	23.0	6	17	RHB	116	4	13	.259	.328	.379
Apr-Jun	4	2	2.79	12	29.0	9	21	ScPos	59	2	26	.237	.333	.373
Jul-Oct	1	4	6.07	21	29.2	12	21	Clutch	158	7	33	.297	.363	.475

How He Compares to Other Pitchers

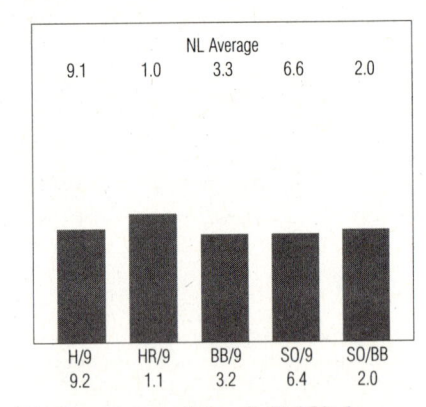

NL Average: H/9 9.1, HR/9 1.0, BB/9 3.3, SO/9 6.6, SO/BB 2.0
Beck: H/9 9.2, HR/9 1.1, BB/9 3.2, SO/9 6.4, SO/BB 2.0

How He Compares to Other Relief Pitchers

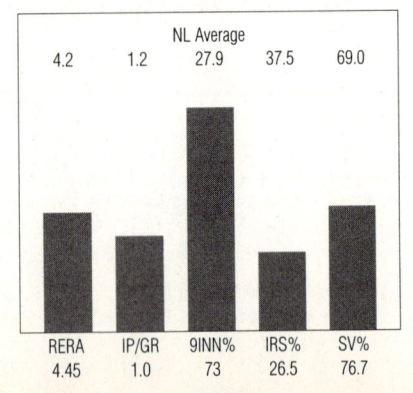

NL Average: RERA 4.2, IP/GR 1.2, 9INN% 27.9, IRS% 37.5, SV% 69.0
Beck: RERA 4.45, IP/GR 1.0, 9INN% 73, IRS% 26.5, SV% 76.7

SAN FRANCISCO GIANTS

BARRY BONDS

Position: OF
Bats: L **Throws:** L
Ht: 6'1" **Wt:** 185
Opening Day Age: 31
Born: 7/24/1964
Drafted: PIT85 1/6
ML Seasons: 10

SCOUTING REPORT

If you were asked to design the perfect ballplayer, he'd look a lot like Barry Bonds. A plus runner and a top-notch basestealer, he is an outstanding blend of power and speed.

The intimidating Bonds stands on top of the plate and chokes up. He has as much bat speed as anyone in the game and adjusts well, not only during a game, but during an at-bat. He can hit any pitch with his short stroke and terrific discipline, which makes Barry one of the best situational hitters in baseball.

His arm strength is average now in left field but his accuracy and range both remain plus. This, combined with the great jump he gets on fly balls, allows Barry to control baserunners well. He has well above-average hands and rarely makes errors. His outfield play reduces the number of doubles in the NL by about one a week.

HOW HE PERFORMED IN '95

Most players would call Barry's "off-year" a career year: he led the NL in on-base percentage and walks, ranked second in runs, and placed in the top ten in many other categories. Bonds suffered during Matt Williams' absence, as he averaged a walk per game with Williams out, although he still hit 17 homers and drove in 52 runs during those 69 games. He led the NL in intentional walks for the fourth straight year while recording the third 30-30 season of his career.

Half of Barry's homers in '95 tied or gave the Giants the lead, and 13 came in the seventh inning or later. Although Bonds had easily the worst August of his career, hitting .204 with only four homers, he still managed an excellent .393 on-base average.

One of the many categories in which Bonds ranked among NL leaders was outfield assists; he nailed 12 errant baserunners in '95.

WHAT TO EXPECT IN '96

To watch Barry is to believe he can win a game at any time. His 4-for-5, five-RBI, two-homer performance on June 30, with Williams out of the lineup, was a signal moment. In that game, he mashed a three-run, upper-deck blast before the largest crowd of the year, then came out and blew kisses to the crowd just days after having been booed for misplaying a line drive to left. There is seemingly no limit to his ability.

Overall Statistics

	G	AB	R	H	2B	3B	HR	RBI	SB	CS	BB	SO	BA	OBA
95 SF	144	506	109	149	30	7	33	104	31	10	120	83	.294	.431
Career	1425	5020	999	1436	306	48	292	864	340	103	931	795	.286	.398

1995 Situational Statistics

	AB	HR	RBI	BA	OBA	SLG		AB	HR	RBI	BA	OBA	SLG
Home	238	16	51	.307	.475	.605	LHP	138	5	28	.268	.388	.478
Road	268	17	53	.284	.389	.552	RHP	368	28	76	.304	.447	.614
Apr-Jun	220	13	45	.309	.419	.577	ScPos	117	4	57	.325	.517	.538
Jul-Oct	286	20	59	.283	.441	.577	Clutch	80	7	29	.350	.519	.738

How He Compares to Other Batters

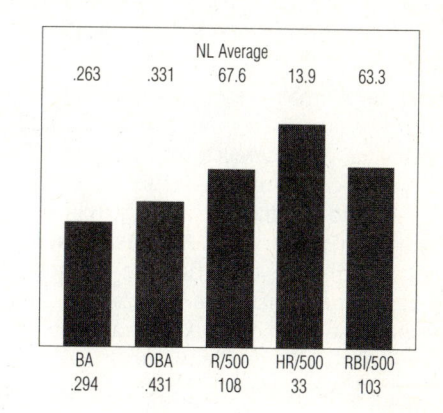

NL Average: BA .263, OBA .331, R/500 67.6, HR/500 13.9, RBI/500 63.3

Bonds: BA .294, OBA .431, R/500 108, HR/500 33, RBI/500 103

Where He Hits the Ball

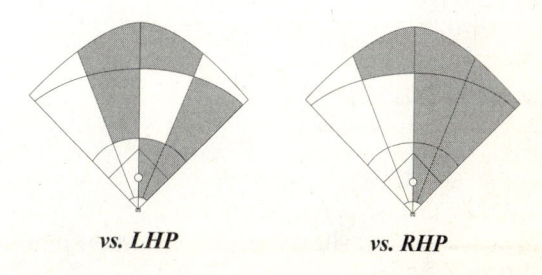

vs. LHP   vs. RHP

THE SCOUTING REPORT: 1996

SAN FRANCISCO GIANTS

MARK CARREON

Positions: 1B/OF
Bats: R **Throws:** L
Ht: 6'0" **Wt:** 194
Opening Day Age: 32
Born: 7/19/1963
Drafted: NYN81 7/185
ML Seasons: 9

SCOUTING REPORT
Formerly an outfielder, Carreon ended the season playing a new position: first base. Mark has a strong arm but required time to adjust to the shorter, quicker throws of the infield. His hands are just average and his range below that, but Carreon learned to position himself and had dramatically improved by the season's end.

Mark has a quick bat with decent big-league power; aggressive at the dish, he uses the whole field to advantage and is the best breaking-ball hitter on the Giants' roster. It is easy to see when he is out-of-sync, as he constantly adjusts his feet in the batter's box. Carreon is never a quiet hitter, though, and usually moves both feet just as the pitcher is releasing the ball.

Although he possesses average baserunning speed, he has stolen just one base in the last three seasons.

HOW HE PERFORMED IN '95
Every roster has a couple of players who could have been regulars if they just got 400 at-bats or 25 starts. Most wind up stuck in a twilight zone, but all of these semi-regulars got a boost out of Carreon's success in '95.

In his previous eight seasons, Mark had totaled under 1200 at-bats; used mostly as an emergency swinger, he has eight career pinch-homers, one of the top marks in the majors. However, when J.R. Phillips failed to produce in '95, Carreon got an opportunity to play every day. As a result, he set career highs in almost every offensive category. He worked very hard to make more consistent contact and dramatically sliced his strikeout rate, though he has never walked often in the majors.

Mark batted at least .279 in every full month and knocked in 21 runs during July. He then followed by hitting .329 in August and finishing off the year with five more homers in September, including his career night on September 29 in Colorado (four hits and six runs batted in).

WHAT TO EXPECT IN '96
At 32, he may have finally become a regular. Dusty Baker said that signing Mark was the most important thing the Giants had to do in the off-season, and the club inked Carreon for '96 during the playoffs. The Giants will give him a chance to prove that his '95 productivity as a starter at first base was no fluke.

Overall Statistics

	G	AB	R	H	2B	3B	HR	RBI	SB	CS	BB	SO	BA	OBA
95 SF	117	396	53	119	24	0	17	65	0	1	23	37	.301	.343
Career	619	1578	190	435	74	2	58	224	9	7	107	204	.276	.324

1995 Situational Statistics

	AB	HR	RBI	BA	OBA	SLG		AB	HR	RBI	BA	OBA	SLG
Home	191	7	29	.267	.311	.429	LHP	97	3	11	.309	.330	.454
Road	205	10	36	.332	.373	.546	RHP	299	14	54	.298	.347	.502
Apr-Jun	98	6	11	.286	.352	.510	ScPos	111	0	40	.315	.363	.387
Jul-Oct	298	11	54	.305	.340	.483	Clutch	66	2	11	.303	.365	.470

How He Compares to Other Batters

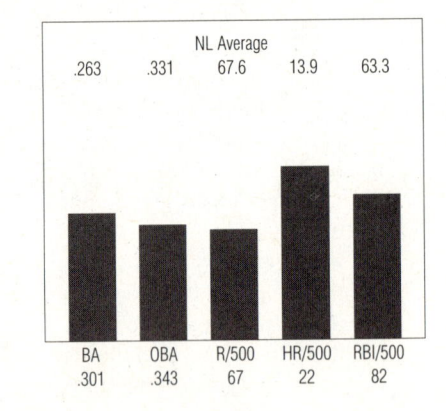

NL Average: .263 .331 67.6 13.9 63.3

BA	OBA	R/500	HR/500	RBI/500
.301	.343	67	22	82

Where He Hits the Ball

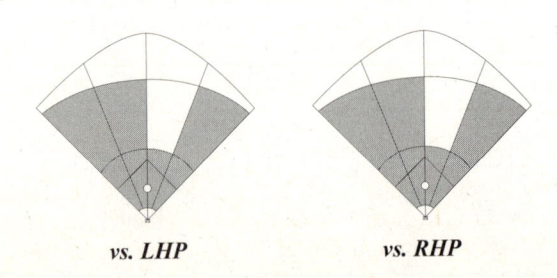

vs. LHP   vs. RHP

624 THE SCOUTING REPORT: 1996

SAN FRANCISCO GIANTS

ROYCE CLAYTON

Position: SS
Bats: R **Throws:** R
Ht: 6'0" **Wt:** 175
Opening Day Age: 26
Born: 1/2/1970
Drafted: SF88 1/15
ML Seasons: 5

SCOUTING REPORT
One of the better young shortstops in the game, Clayton has a plus arm and a quick release from the hole but only average throwing accuracy. He has well above-average range and soft, sure hands, is aggressive and charges ground balls well. Despite just average speed, Royce has improved his base stealing and runs often. He rarely bunts, but does so effectively for sacrifices. Overall, Clayton's offense is somewhat below par for a major-league hitter, but is above par for a shortstop. With fair bat speed and an inside-out swing, he is a high-ball hitter who likes the ball out over the plate, punching it to the opposite field much of the time. He can be locked up by a good hard fastball, though, and chases too many pitches off the plate.

HOW HE PERFORMED IN '95
Royce turned in a solid year with career highs in runs, doubles, and steals while equalling his career high of walks. Unfortunately, he also set a career high with 109 whiffs, ninth highest in the NL. His 24 steals made him a member of the first Giants' foursome since 1915 (with Bonds, Hill, and Lewis) to steal 20 or more in the same season.

With 93 double plays turned, Clayton ranked second in the NL behind Walt Weiss. The Giants' rotating parade of second baseman in '95 brings Royce's ability more clearly into focus. His .969 fielding percentage ranked sixth in the league, however, despite a 30-game errorless string between August 11 and September 14.

WHAT TO EXPECT IN '96
Early in the season he showed more plate discipline than in the past, but Royce wound up with only 38 walks—his .298 on-base average needs serious improvement. The Giants brought up Rich Aurilia (obtained from Texas in the John Burkett trade a year ago), and the rookie's brief exposure in '95 convinced the Giants they could afford to trade Clayton to St. Louis for three pitchers.

While Royce will have the benefit of continuing to play on real grass this year in the revamped Busch Stadium, he will also shoulder the burden of following an all-time legend at short. Cleared for duty by Cardinals' doctors, Ozzie Smith will be back for '96. Although it will be strange to see the Wizard backing up Clayton, it would be stranger still to see Clayton acquired just to ride the bench.

Overall Statistics

	G	AB	R	H	2B	3B	HR	RBI	SB	CS	BB	SO	BA	OBA
95 SF	138	509	56	124	29	3	5	58	24	9	38	109	.244	.298
Career	506	1790	179	445	72	18	18	184	66	26	133	343	.249	.302

1995 Situational Statistics

	AB	HR	RBI	BA	OBA	SLG		AB	HR	RBI	BA	OBA	SLG
Home	251	2	23	.215	.272	.291	LHP	104	4	11	.260	.304	.423
Road	258	3	35	.271	.324	.391	RHP	405	1	47	.240	.297	.321
Apr-Jun	212	2	33	.241	.320	.349	ScPos	141	1	52	.255	.308	.333
Jul-Oct	297	3	25	.246	.282	.337	Clutch	90	1	9	.211	.268	.278

How He Compares to Other Batters

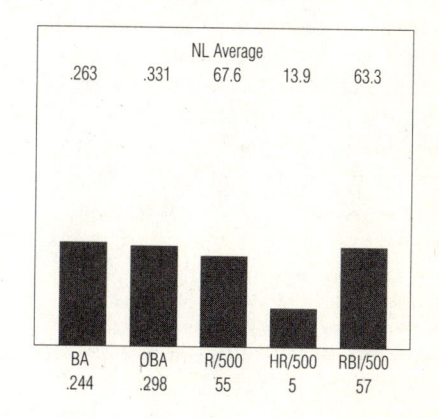

NL Average: .263 | .331 | 67.6 | 13.9 | 63.3

	BA	OBA	R/500	HR/500	RBI/500
	.244	.298	55	5	57

Where He Hits the Ball

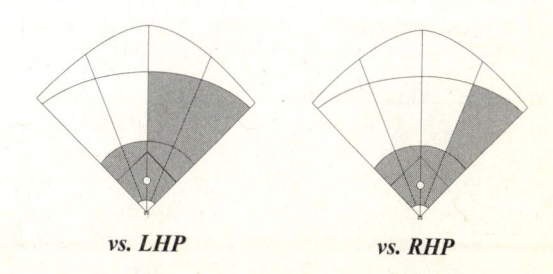

vs. LHP   vs. RHP

THE SCOUTING REPORT: 1996

SAN FRANCISCO GIANTS

GLENALLEN HILL

Position: OF
Bats: R **Throws:** R
Ht: 6'3" **Wt:** 210
Opening Day Age: 31
Born: 3/22/1965
Drafted: TOR83 9/219
ML Seasons: 7

SCOUTING REPORT

Although he has a somewhat slow first step, Glenallen accelerates effectively and has average-plus speed. He is a proficient basestealer and has improved his success rate.

Hill also shows good speed in the outfield but, again, does not get a very good jump on the ball. His range is above-average because of his speed and he tends to catch most everything he gets to. His average arm strength and accuracy belie the ten outfield assists he had in '95; some of Glenallen's assists came as a result of those slow jumps.

The strong Hill hits with as still a bat as anyone in the NL. A fastball hitter, he likes the ball over the plate and has good opposite field power. Although he will go the other way at times, he has problems making contact and rarely walks.

HOW HE PERFORMED IN '95

Another member of the "if I could just play every day" club, Hill blossomed into a fine major-league hitter in 1994-95. Well-renowned for his power, he hit one of the longest home runs ever seen in Shea Stadium, a ball that arched above the light standards, carried over the left-center field bleachers, and hit in the rear of the player's parking lot, bouncing over the rear fence and trees and into the main parking lot.

Aside from this display, Glenallen also set career bests in most significant offensive categories as he topped 400 at-bats for the first time in his career. However, he had some poor streaks and struggled at times with righthanders. Despite his occasional slumps, however, Hill hit five or more homers in every full month except during a miserable June (.232, one homer).

His stolen base success rate was seventh-best in the league, and he tied for sixth in outfield assists. Popular with his teammates, Glenallen was the only protection Barry Bonds had in the lineup for half of '95, and he came through impressively.

WHAT TO EXPECT IN '96

After some serious give-and-take, Hill re-signed with the Giants last winter for two years and he should be the right fielder for at least that long. Although the Giants courted Bernard Gilkey, Hill was the hitter manager Dusty Baker really wanted, and now he will have him for the foreseeable future.

Overall Statistics

	G	AB	R	H	2B	3B	HR	RBI	SB	CS	BB	SO	BA	OBA
95 SF	132	497	71	131	29	4	24	86	25	5	39	98	.264	.317
Career	595	1929	270	501	90	13	88	284	77	28	149	427	.260	.313

1995 Situational Statistics

	AB	HR	RBI	BA	OBA	SLG		AB	HR	RBI	BA	OBA	SLG
Home	234	13	49	.261	.316	.496	LHP	91	8	22	.308	.357	.615
Road	263	11	37	.266	.318	.471	RHP	406	16	64	.254	.308	.453
Apr-Jun	225	8	40	.253	.316	.427	ScPos	159	7	60	.239	.332	.459
Jul-Oct	272	16	46	.272	.318	.529	Clutch	99	4	20	.212	.250	.424

How He Compares to Other Batters

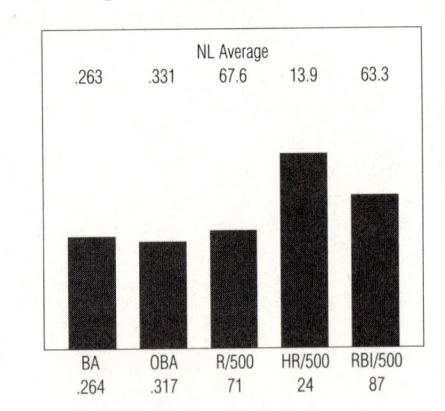

NL Average: BA .263, OBA .331, R/500 67.6, HR/500 13.9, RBI/500 63.3

BA .264, OBA .317, R/500 71, HR/500 24, RBI/500 87

Where He Hits the Ball

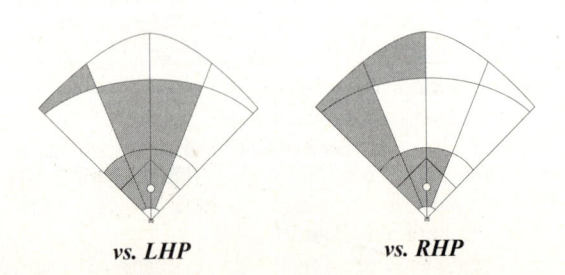

vs. LHP   vs. RHP

SAN FRANCISCO GIANTS

MARK LEITER

Position: SP
Bats: R **Throws:** R
Ht: 6'3" **Wt:** 200
Opening Day Age: 32
Born: 4/13/1963
Drafted: BAL83* 4/103
ML Seasons: 6

SCOUTING REPORT
Mark throws five pitches, using a three-quarter motion. His hard, sinking fastball is a plus pitch; he also has an average, hard curveball and an average, slightly tight slider which he sets up well with the inside fastball.

He prefers to use his forkball as an off-speed pitch, but it is slightly below-average. Mark has also had a circle change for some time, which he has just begun to gain game-use confidence in.

One of Leiter's strong points is a willingness to pitch inside and move hitters off the plate. His good control is another bright spot and, while just average at fielding and holding runners on, he knows how to pitch and is learning to control his emotions. Eleven of 16 basestealing attempts were successful against Leiter in '95. A miserable hitter, Mark was just 6-for-61 (.098) and fanned 33 times although he did lay down nine sacrifices.

HOW HE PERFORMED IN '95
Mark's tale is one of the truly heartwarming stories of 1995, or any year. He was nearly out of baseball a couple of years ago, released by Detroit after missing most of spring training due to the illness and, later, death of his infant son.

The Angels took a chance on him after the '94 season started but let him escape via free agency. The Giants were truly grateful for this—Mark, who signed as a long reliever, became the workhorse of the Giants staff, ranking second in the NL in complete games and leading the staff in wins, starts, innings, and strikeouts. Getting very comfortable in a new league, Leiter did not forsake his hard-driving style. As a result, he led the senior circuit with 17 hit batsmen.

When things did not go well, Leiter maintained his perspective, reminding all that baseball is a game, not life and death—as well he knows. Both a gentleman and a fierce competitor, Mark was a breath of fresh air for the Giants.

WHAT TO EXPECT IN '96
Mark turns a young 33 just after opening day. He has only thrown 1,225 innings in his 11 professional seasons, having missed three years due to injury. As a result, he might have many years left in his arm. The Giants re-signed him last winter for two years and will likely make Leiter the Opening Day starter in 1996.

Overall Statistics

	G	GS	GF	SV	W	L	ERA	IP	H	R	ER	HR	BB	SO
95 SF	30	29	0	0	10	12	3.82	195.2	185	91	83		195	129
Career	178	81	35	3	38	38	4.35	670.2	669	351	324		792	36469

1995 Situational Statistics

	W	L	ERA	SV	IP	BB	SO		AB	HR	RBI	BA	OBA	SLG
Home	5	5	3.87	0	100.0	29	71	LHB	314	9	33	.239	.321	.382
Road	5	7	3.76	0	95.2	26	58	RHB	415	10	48	.265	.316	.402
Apr-Jun	3	5	4.16	0	75.2	25	38	ScPos	154	0	59	.325	.396	.429
Jul-Oct	7	7	3.60	0	120.0	30	91	Clutch	65	1	4	.185	.232	.277

How He Compares to Other Pitchers

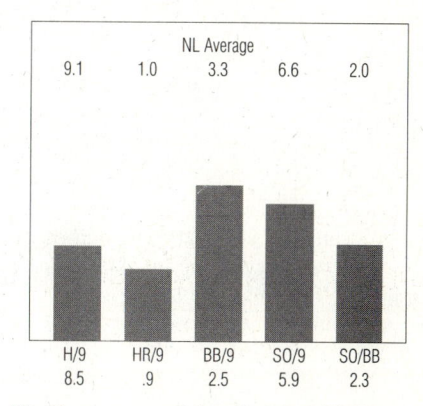

NL Average: H/9 9.1, HR/9 1.0, BB/9 3.3, SO/9 6.6, SO/BB 2.0
Leiter: H/9 8.5, HR/9 .9, BB/9 2.5, SO/9 5.9, SO/BB 2.3

How He Compares to Other Starting Pitchers

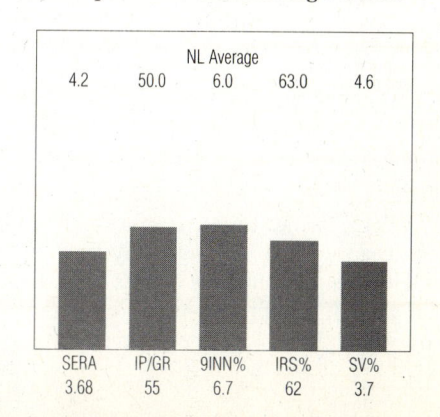

NL Average: SERA 4.2, IP/GR 50.0, 9INN% 6.0, IRS% 63.0, SV% 4.6
Leiter: SERA 3.68, IP/GR 55, 9INN% 6.7, IRS% 62, SV% 3.7

SAN FRANCISCO GIANTS

KIRT MANWARING

Position: C
Bats: R **Throws:** R
Ht: 5'11" **Wt:** 185
Opening Day Age: 30
Born: 7/15/1965
Drafted: SF86 2/31
ML Seasons: 9

SCOUTING REPORT
Everything about Manwaring's defense behind the plate is sterling. He has a well above-average arm with plus accuracy and a quick release to go with very good footwork. Kirt's range on popups is just average, but he will hustle and sacrifice his body to make a play.

He has good, soft hands, giving Giants' pitchers the confidence to throw breaking stuff in the dirt with runners on third. A 1993 Gold Glove winner, Manwaring handles pitchers very well.

Kirt has poor bat speed, almost no power, and strikes out often. A line-drive hitter who chokes up a bit on the bat, he likes balls over the plate but can be overpowered by good hard stuff. Kirt sacrifices effectively, a good thing to do if you're a weak hitter. He has poor speed on the basepaths.

HOW HE PERFORMED IN '95
His '95 looked a lot like his '94: a career .247 hitter, Kirt hit .251 after registering a .250 mark the year before. Once again, he shouldered a heavy load behind the plate. His 118 games caught ranked second in the NL and Manwaring logged over 75% of the Giants' total innings caught—despite San Francisco carrying three receivers all season.

Manwaring played most of the second half of the season with five broken ribs on his throwing side, but he played with the pain and made the plays. He threw out just 23% (21 of 91) of enemy baserunners last year, an indication of the effect of playing with his injury. After throwing out 44% of potential stealers in '93, his success has dipped by 10 percentage points in each of the last two years.

Kirt ran hot-and-cold in '95, with a career-high 10-game streak in late July (.382) and a .333 string at season's end. He began the year 10-for-50 and then went 10-for-52 June 24 through July 18.

WHAT TO EXPECT IN '96
When Kirt opens the '96 season behind the plate, he will tie a franchise record held by Bob Brenly and Tom Haller with five straight openers at catcher.

"Man-O-War" is like his namesake—all heart. A straight-ahead guy, he is immensely popular with the pitching staff. As long as he hits .250, handles pitchers well, and improves his throwing a bit, he will be a regular backstop for several more seasons.

Overall Statistics

	G	AB	R	H	2B	3B	HR	RBI	SB	CS	BB	SO	BA	OBA
95 SF	118	379	21	95	15	2	4	36	1	0	27	72	.251	.314
Career	660	1990	165	492	77	12	15	193	8	8	144	315	.247	.308

1995 Situational Statistics

	AB	HR	RBI	BA	OBA	SLG		AB	HR	RBI	BA	OBA	SLG
Home	183	4	16	.268	.320	.383	LHP	85	3	7	.247	.312	.447
Road	196	0	20	.235	.309	.286	RHP	294	1	29	.252	.315	.299
Apr-Jun	151	1	14	.265	.323	.325	ScPos	105	0	29	.210	.304	.248
Jul-Oct	228	3	22	.241	.308	.338	Clutch	58	0	3	.241	.308	.259

How He Compares to Other Batters

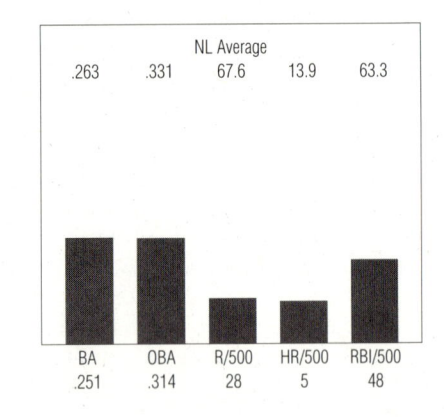

NL Average: .263 .331 67.6 13.9 63.3

BA	OBA	R/500	HR/500	RBI/500
.251	.314	28	5	48

Where He Hits the Ball

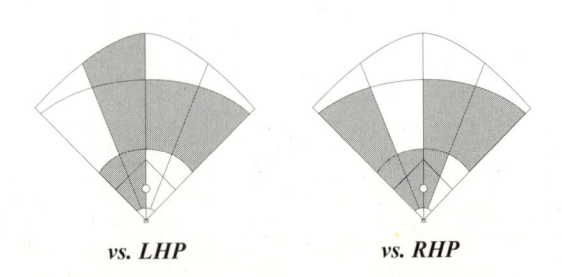

vs. LHP   vs. RHP

SAN FRANCISCO GIANTS

TERRY MULHOLLAND

Position: SP/RP
Bats: R **Throws:** L
Ht: 6'3" **Wt:** 200
Opening Day Age: 33
Born: 3/9/1963
Drafted: SF84 2/24
ML Seasons: 9

SCOUTING REPORT

Terry throws three-quarters out of a long, high-kicking windup. He has developed the best pickoff move in the game: he is extremely quick with his "A" move, and his flat-footed snap to both first and second requires extraordinary arm strength. Unfortunately, despite that muscular wing, Terry has lost all of the power behind his pitches—his fastball is minus, even though he can both cut and sink it. His curve, slider and change-up are all somewhat below par now. His control is excellent; in fact, it's too good given his stuff. Hitters know that he's going to be around the plate and wait for a pitch to hammer. Mulholland is an average fielder but a wretched hitter, batting .102 in 49 at-bats last year with 22 strikeouts. His career average is just .081; he does not bunt well, either.

HOW HE PERFORMED IN '95

It was a bitterly disappointing year, causing Terry to strongly consider retirement. On his Opening day start in Atlanta, Mulholland surrendered six consecutive hits before recording his first out and allowed six runs in the first two frames.

This foreshadowed the rest of the season. He had a nine-game losing streak and dropped a career-worst 13 games. On June 7, both Mulholland and the Giants admitted he was pitching in pain, and Terry subsequently had four floating bone chips removed from his pitching elbow.

Mulholland made a rehab start 16 days after the surgery. However, he was moved to the bullpen for three weeks before coming back to the rotation August 18. From August 23 through September 9, Mulholland was an encouraging 3-0 with a 3.30 ERA, but he finished on an 0-3 skein with a 5.21 ERA. One thing he did, was limit base-runner movement. Only seven runners dared to steal, and six were thrown out. Terry also picked off five.

WHAT TO EXPECT IN '96

Whatever Terry's future holds, it won't be in Giants garb. Age and innings have taken their toll. Although he is just 33, he has over 2,000 innings and a couple of surgeries on his left arm. Mulholland will probably find work again in '96: look at how long Jim Deshaies and Scott Sanderson have hung on. However, another year even remotely like 1994 or 1995 will have him thinking seriously about his second career.

Overall Statistics

	G	GS	GF	SV	W	L	ERA	IP	H	R	ER	HR	BB	SO
95 SF	29	24	2	0	5	13	5.80	149.0	190	112	96	25	38	65
Career	230	197	14	0	68	78	4.24	1318.1	1385	684	621	127	330	706

1995 Situational Statistics

	W	L	ERA	SV	IP	BB	SO		AB	HR	RBI	BA	OBA	SLG
Home	2	5	4.66	0	65.2	17	30	LHB	108	3	17	.278	.317	.407
Road	3	8	6.70	0	83.1	21	35	RHB	499	22	80	.321	.363	.513
Apr-Jun	2	6	7.04	0	47.1	15	12	ScPos	135	3	67	.363	.403	.511
Jul-Oct	3	7	5.22	0	101.2	23	53	Clutch	29	0	1	.207	.233	.276

How He Compares to Other Pitchers

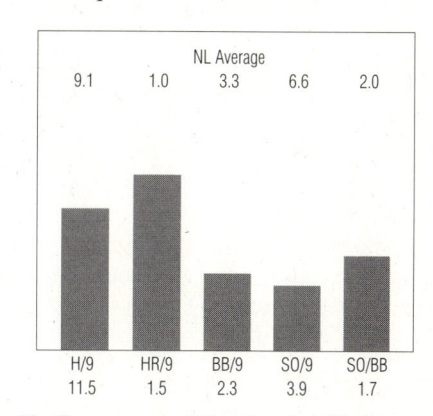

NL Average

H/9	HR/9	BB/9	SO/9	SO/BB
9.1	1.0	3.3	6.6	2.0
11.5	1.5	2.3	3.9	1.7

How He Compares to Other Starting Pitchers

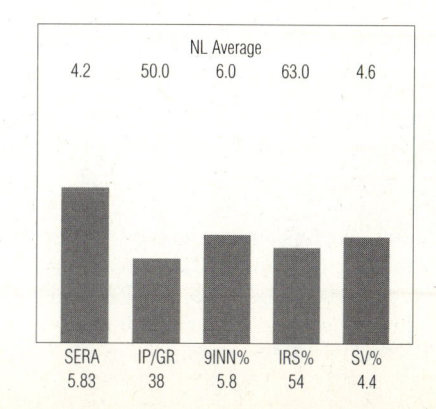

NL Average

SERA	IP/GR	9INN%	IRS%	SV%
4.2	50.0	6.0	63.0	4.6
5.83	38	5.8	54	4.4

SAN FRANCISCO GIANTS

DEION SANDERS

Position: OF
Bats: L **Throws:** L
Ht: 6'1" **Wt:** 195
Opening Day Age: 28
Born: 8/9/1967
Drafted: NYA88 27/781
ML Seasons: 7

SCOUTING REPORT
Sanders is probably the fastest runner in the game. However, he is not an outstanding basestealer and led the NL in times caught stealing in '94, although Deion does leg singles into doubles and doubles into triples quite effectively.

He has outstanding acceleration and displays well above-average range in the outfield, due to the fact that his speed lets him outrun his lapses in judgment. Sanders plays very deep in center and is poor at going back, but has good hands and often makes plays by simply outrunning the ball. He has an accurate arm but throws very poorly.

An aggressive slash-hitter with good bat speed, he has some power on low inside fastballs, but Deion helps pitchers out by chasing too many breaking balls out of the zone. He does not walk nearly enough to bat leadoff despite his speed.

HOW HE PERFORMED IN '95
The "Prime Time" tour made a couple of stops in '95, adding Cincinnati and San Francisco to the itinerary. This made three teams in just over a year—not counting football—that Sanders had played for. He season ended early with an ankle injury that required minor surgery; the Giants generously allowed him to leave the team before the end of the season to start his football season earlier.

After the trade, Giants' hitting coach Bobby Bonds seemed to help Deion out; Sanders started 5-for-31 with San Francisco, but hit .311 and slugged .444 over his last 40 games. Although Deion did a pretty good job at the plate for the Giants (.285 average, five homers in 214 at-bats), he had a baserunning slump and did not prove to be the box-office draw the team had hoped.

In the outfield, he threw out just two runners all season and made five errors, but Sanders tracked down plenty of fly balls.

WHAT TO EXPECT IN '96
The Giants said they had a $2 million-plus deal on the table, plus incentives, but never heard a reply or returned phone call from Deion's agent. The club then went out and signed Stan Javier for less than they offered Sanders and designated "Prime Time" for assignment to Phoenix. Deion declined assignment and thus became a free agent. Look for "Neon Deion" to hook on with a team that has a lot of cash available and, one presumes, the patience to put up with him.

Overall Statistics

	G	AB	R	H	2B	3B	HR	RBI	SB	CS	BB	SO	BA	OBA
95 CIN/SF	85	343	48	92	11	8	6	28	24	9	27	60	.268	.327
Career	494	1583	249	418	57	36	33	141	127	46	121	275	.264	.320

1995 Situational Statistics

	AB	HR	RBI	BA	OBA	SLG		AB	HR	RBI	BA	OBA	SLG
Home	159	3	12	.289	.350	.440	LHP	89	0	7	.213	.268	.337
Road	184	3	16	.250	.307	.364	RHP	254	6	21	.287	.348	.421
Apr-Jun	114	1	8	.246	.307	.333	ScPos	61	0	21	.262	.347	.377
Jul-Oct	229	5	20	.279	.337	.432	Clutch	53	0	4	.226	.276	.321

How He Compares to Other Batters

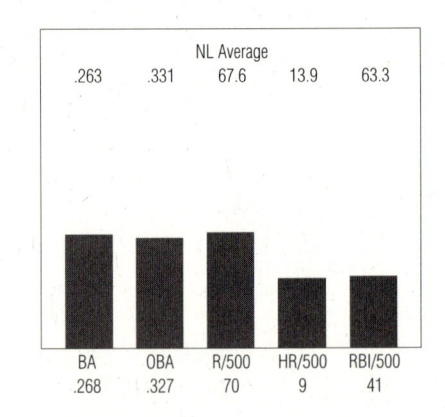

	BA	OBA	R/500	HR/500	RBI/500
NL Average	.263	.331	67.6	13.9	63.3
	.268	.327	70	9	41

Where He Hits the Ball

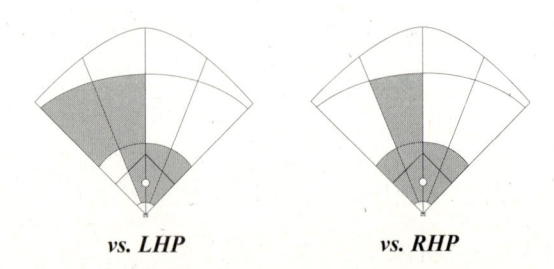

vs. LHP   vs. RHP

SAN FRANCISCO GIANTS

ROBBY THOMPSON

Position: 2B
Bats: R **Throws:** R
Ht: 5'11" **Wt:** 170
Opening Day Age: 33
Born: 5/10/1962
Drafted: SF83 S1/2
ML Seasons: 10

SCOUTING REPORT

Serious back and shoulder injuries have robbed Thompson of many of his skills. Now a shadow of his former self, Robby is now a minus baserunner, his arm strength and accuracy are just average, and his range has seriously declined. Thompson compensates for decreased mobility with his knowledge of hitters and excellent positioning and is still one of the best in the business in the double-play pivot. As a hitter, he has always liked high fastballs but now will have to show that he can still turn on the inside pitch. Robby does take the outside pitch the other way with some authority. He has never walked often during his career and strikes out frequently.

HOW HE PERFORMED IN '95

In Hideo Nomo's major-league debut on May 2, with the attendant huge following from Japan, Robby hit a three-run shot off the Dodgers' Greg Hansell to tie the game at three in the bottom of the 15th inning. Barry Bonds and Matt Williams completed the improbable comeback as the Giants won 4-3.

That was the high point of Thompson's season. Not long after, his shoulder miseries returned and he wound up missing significant playing time for the second straight year. After playing at half-strength for much of '95, he finally underwent surgery on September 23 on his left rotator cuff and shoulder.

Before his injuries began in '94, Thompson had played 128 games or more for the Giants every year between 1986 and 1993. He had nagging aches and pains during that time but now the maladies have turned more serious—career-threateningly serious.

WHAT TO EXPECT IN '96

Robby is signed through '96 with a club option for '97. The Giants decided two years ago they could not afford both Thompson and Will Clark, so they kept their second baseman. At the time it seemed like a sensible decision, as Robby provided steady defense and had come off a career offensive year, but everything has been a nightmare since for both Thompson and the team.

If he makes the lineup on April 1 at Atlanta, only two Giants in history will have made more opening day starts than Thompson's 11. But it may be Robby's last with San Francisco unless he can recapture the magic of 1991–93.

Overall Statistics

	G	AB	R	H	2B	3B	HR	RBI	SB	CS	BB	SO	BA	OBA
95 SF	95	336	51	75	15	0	8	23	1	2	42	76	.223	.317
Career	1241	4385	636	1139	227	38	114	437	101	60	415	918	.260	.331

1995 Situational Statistics

	AB	HR	RBI	BA	OBA	SLG		AB	HR	RBI	BA	OBA	SLG
Home	170	4	10	.212	.306	.324	LHP	77	1	5	.247	.363	.338
Road	166	4	13	.235	.328	.355	RHP	259	7	18	.216	.302	.340
Apr-Jun	135	2	10	.215	.293	.319	ScPos	69	3	18	.275	.412	.420
Jul-Oct	201	6	13	.229	.332	.353	Clutch	59	3	8	.186	.273	.390

How He Compares to Other Batters

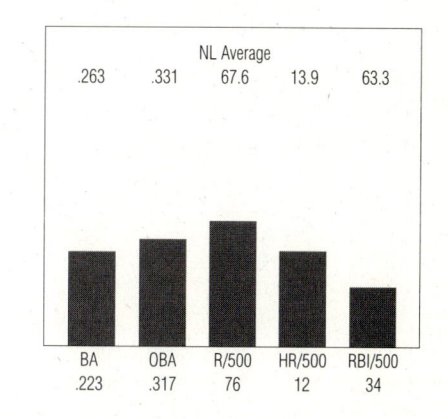

NL Average: BA .263, OBA .331, R/500 67.6, HR/500 13.9, RBI/500 63.3

Robby: BA .223, OBA .317, R/500 76, HR/500 12, RBI/500 34

Where He Hits the Ball

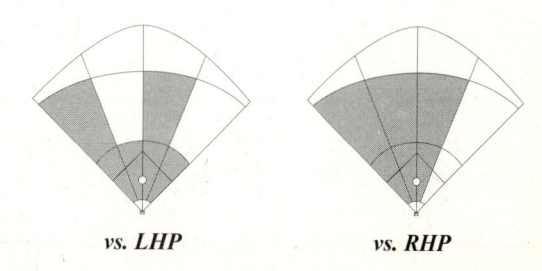

vs. LHP | vs. RHP

SAN FRANCISCO GIANTS

WILLIAM VAN LANDINGHAM

Position: SP
Bats: R **Throws:** R
Ht: 6'2" **Wt:** 210
Opening Day Age: 25
Born: 7/16/1970
Drafted: SF91 3/141
ML Seasons: 2

SCOUTING REPORT

The righthander comes with a big motion, delivering three-quarters to low three-quarters depending on the hitter. He throws a plus rising four-seam fastball as his out pitch. VanLandingham's fastball has a great amount of live natural movement—jumping, diving, and darting in all directions. His fastball moves so much that it took Kirt Manwaring several outings to realize he should not set up off the edge of the plate, but rather in the center so that VanLandingham's fastball will catch the edges with its natural movement.

He complements the heat with an average slider with a fairly tight break and an average change-up in which he is developing confidence. William's control rates as plus, and his fielding is about par, but he is poor in controlling runners, primarily due to his prolonged delivery. In '95, 17 runners tried to steal on VanLandingham, 13 successfully.

HOW HE PERFORMED IN '95

The absolutely unflappable "Young William" (as he is known to his teammates) suffered no sophomore jinx last year despite several injuries. He strained a rib muscle on opening day, and missed 38 games while mending; on September 10, VanLandingham ended his season prematurely by straining a groin muscle running out a sacrifice bunt.

Between those ailments, William pitched extremely well. He had poor support in the early going, and didn't win in his first seven starts despite pitching some good games. However, VanLandingham's season turned around and he went 6-1, 3.40, over his final 13 starts beginning July 1. A couple of unusual streaks: William hasn't been beaten at Candlestick (9-0, 2.45 ERA in 17 starts) and is undefeated during the day (12-0, 3.12 ERA in 24 starts) over his two-year career. Luckily for VanLandingham, San Francisco is scheduled to play 51 day games at home in '96.

Although he fanned in 24 of his 46 '95 at-bats, he did bat .152, smacking two doubles and his first major-league home run. He is a poor bunter.

WHAT TO EXPECT IN '96

The Giants need a big, complete season from William in '96. He should be the club's second or third starter and Dusty Baker will count on him heavily. He only had 14 minor-league starts above Single-A, and thus can be expected to continue his learning at the big-league level.

Overall Statistics

	G	GS	GF	SV	W	L	ERA	IP	H	R	ER	HR	BB	SO
95 SF	18	18	0	0	6	3	3.67	122.2	124	58	50	14	40	95
Career	34	32	1	0	14	5	3.61	206.2	194	95	83	18	83	151

1995 Situational Statistics

	W	L	ERA	SV	IP	BB	SO		AB	HR	RBI	BA	OBA	SLG
Home	5	0	3.05	0	73.2	20	58	LHB	215	4	22	.302	.352	.428
Road	1	3	4.59	0	49.0	20	37	RHB	255	10	30	.231	.295	.392
Apr-Jun	0	2	4.94	0	27.1	10	23	ScPos	92	5	37	.228	.315	.457
Jul-Oct	6	1	3.30	0	95.1	30	72	Clutch	60	1	5	.267	.313	.350

How He Compares to Other Pitchers

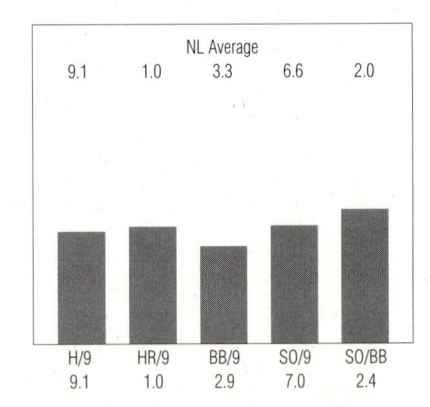

	H/9	HR/9	BB/9	SO/9	SO/BB
NL Average	9.1	1.0	3.3	6.6	2.0
	9.1	1.0	2.9	7.0	2.4

How He Compares to Other Starting Pitchers

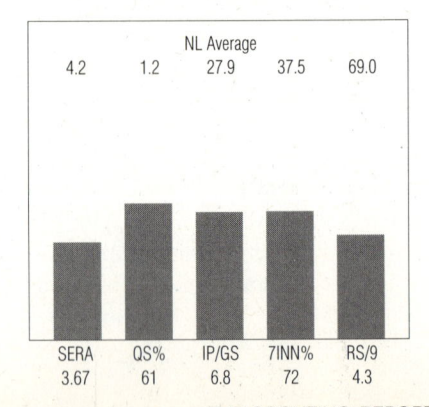

	SERA	QS%	IP/GS	7INN%	RS/9
NL Average	4.2	1.2	27.9	37.5	69.0
	3.67	61	6.8	72	4.3

SAN FRANCISCO GIANTS

MATT WILLIAMS

Position: 3B
Bats: R **Throws:** R
Ht: 6'2" **Wt:** 205
Opening Day Age: 30
Born: 11/28/1965
Drafted: SF86 1/3
ML Seasons: 9

SCOUTING REPORT

Matt has tremendous bat speed, of course, and standing close to the plate, he is able to turn on inside pitches easily while covering the outer portion of the strike zone.

Pitchers try to bust him inside to move him off the plate, then throw breaking balls down and away. However, Williams has learned over the last two years to take those pitches to right field with authority. This is one of the keys to his success.

Williams is also a deserving Gold Glover, playing top-notch defense. He has soft hands, well above-average range, a plus arm with plus accuracy, and the ability to come in on the ball extremely well despite very poor baserunning speed. Thankfully, he has stopped trying to steal bases.

HOW HE PERFORMED IN '95

What if? What if they played 162 games in '94? What if Matt had stayed healthy last year?

Williams was leading the NL in all three triple crown categories when he broke his foot with a foul ball June 3. Despite missing nearly half of the '95 the season with the injury, Matt remained the league leader in homers for almost half his time on the disabled list.

Through mid-May, he had hit 62 homers in his last 157 games. When injured, he was leading the league in seven major offensive categories as well as in fielding percentage. During May, Matt batted .405, slugged .811, and had a .451 on-base average. On August 19, he returned from the injured list and pinch-hit. The next day, he homered deep into the second deck in Philadelphia on the first pitch he saw from Jeff Juden.

Williams has mashed lefthanders over the last few seasons, hitting .328 against them in '93, .298 the next season, and .377 in '95.

WHAT TO EXPECT IN '96

He's still only 29 years old and the best may be yet to come. Drafted as a shortstop, Matt still plays third with a shortstop's hand and an aggressive, charge-the-ball mentality. His frequent long home runs make a sound unlike those launched by any other hitter in the big leagues.

Williams, a linchpin of the Giants' formidable offense, is signed through 1998. A truly humble and pleasant man, he is the National League's version of Cal Ripken.

Overall Statistics

	G	AB	R	H	2B	3B	HR	RBI	SB	CS	BB	SO	BA	OBA
95 SF	76	283	53	95	17	1	23	65	2	0	30	58	.336	.399
Career	1015	3735	525	970	163	24	225	647	28	25	233	781	.260	.306

1995 Situational Statistics

	AB	HR	RBI	BA	OBA	SLG		AB	HR	RBI	BA	OBA	SLG
Home	120	9	22	.325	.394	.617	LHP	53	6	16	.377	.468	.811
Road	163	14	43	.344	.403	.669	RHP	230	17	49	.326	.383	.609
Apr-Jun	134	13	35	.381	.436	.754	ScPos	75	7	40	.307	.433	.600
Jul-Oct	149	10	30	.295	.367	.550	Clutch	43	2	10	.395	.480	.628

How He Compares to Other Batters

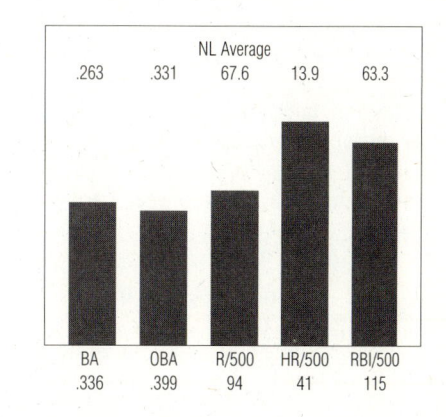

NL Average: .263 | .331 | 67.6 | 13.9 | 63.3

BA	OBA	R/500	HR/500	RBI/500
.336	.399	94	41	115

Where He Hits the Ball

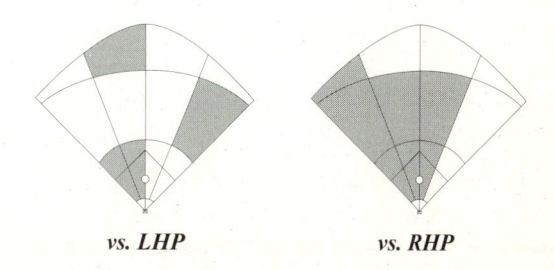

vs. LHP   vs. RHP

THE SCOUTING REPORT: 1996

SAN FRANCISCO GIANTS

SHAWN BARTON

Position: RP
Bats: R **Throws:** L
Ht: 6'3" **Wt:** 195
Opening Day Age: 32
Born: 5/14/1963
Drafted: PHI84 21/542
ML Seasons: 2

Overall Statistics

	G	GS	GF	SV	W	L	ERA	IP	H	R	ER	HR	BB	SO
95 SF	52	0	11	1	4	1	4.26	44.1	37	22	21	3	19	22
Career	66	0	13	1	4	2	3.97	56.2	47	27	25	4	26	26

1995 Situational Statistics

	W	L	ERA	SV	IP	BB	SO		AB	HR	RBI	BA	OBA	SLG
Home	3	0	2.59	0	24.1	9	13	LHB	61	0	9	.246	.319	.295
Road	1	1	6.30	1	20.0	10	9	RHB	95	3	14	.232	.324	.368
Apr-Jun	1	0	2.12	0	17.0	6	6	ScPos	44	0	19	.318	.400	.386
Jul-Oct	3	1	5.60	1	27.1	13	16	Clutch	80	2	11	.200	.290	.313

SCOUTING REPORT

Barton has a stylish three-quarter delivery and relies on an assortment of breaking pitches. His fastball is minus but tails away from lefties. His out pitches are an average slider and a nearly-overhand curve. Like all Dick Pole disciples, Shawn is working a straight change into his repertoire.

He fielded his position flawlessly; six runners tried to steal with Barton pitching, four were thrown out. In his only plate appearance, he sacrificed successfully.

HOW HE PERFORMED IN '95

Persistence pays off! Barton hadn't sniffed major-league air since late '92, when he had a 12-inning cup of Seattle's finest coffee. The lefty joined the Giants May 20 and finished tied for second on the club in appearances. Barton's ERA, a fine 2.15 on August 2, ballooned after he allowed 14 earned runs in his final 15 innings. He may have just been tired; his 69.1 combined innings this year were Shawn's most since '88.

WHAT TO EXPECT IN '96

Dusty Baker showed a lot of confidence in Barton, who may be the top lefty in the pen until the much younger Ricky Pickett or Doug Creek show sustained major-league ability.

JOSE BAUTISTA

Position: RP/SP
Bats: R **Throws:** R
Ht: 6'1" **Wt:** 205
Opening Day Age: 31
Born: 7/25/1964
Drafted: NYN 4/25/81
ML Seasons: 7

Overall Statistics

	G	GS	GF	SV	W	L	ERA	IP	H	R	ER	HR	BB	SO
95 SF	52	6	19	0	3	8	6.44	100.2	120	77	72	24	26	45
Career	243	48	78	3	27	36	4.59	563.1	596	302	287	88	142	277

1995 Situational Statistics

	W	L	ERA	SV	IP	BB	SO		AB	HR	RBI	BA	OBA	SLG
Home	1	5	5.26	0	53.0	12	23	LHB	156	9	35	.333	.391	.577
Road	2	3	7.74	0	47.2	14	22	RHB	251	15	47	.271	.309	.542
Apr-Jun	2	4	5.24	0	55.0	14	23	ScPos	98	5	52	.357	.443	.571
Jul-Oct	1	4	7.88	0	45.2	12	22	Clutch	62	3	10	.306	.358	.581

SCOUTING REPORT

Always around the plate, using a three-quarter to low three-quarter delivery, control is probably Jose's downfall. He relies heavily on a slightly below-average fastball early in the count, which he cuts and sinks. His out pitch, a hard splitter, is plus. He also throws an average hard slider and a minus curve.

A decent fielder, Jose is average at holding runners. Last season, four of five basestealing attempts succeeded against him. Bautista, 0-for-18 last year, is now 4-for-41 (.098) in his career. He bunts poorly.

HOW HE PERFORMED IN '95

Unremittingly dreadful in '95, opponents scored on Jose in eight straight outings from June 17-July 15. He allowed four runs on four hits (including back-to-back homers) in one inning on Opening Day, setting the tone for the season. Jose's 24 home runs allowed ranked fourth in the league, an amazing feat considering his innings pitched.

WHAT TO EXPECT IN '96

To his credit, Bautista never lost self-confidence and gave his best despite hostile crowd reaction. He's not as bad as he was in '95, but he won't return to his 1993-94 form with the Cubs.

SAN FRANCISCO GIANTS

MIKE BENJAMIN

Positions: 3B/SS//2B
Bats: R **Throws:** R
Ht: 6'3" **Wt:** 195
Opening Day Age: 30
Born: 11/22/1965
Drafted: SF87 3/74
ML Seasons: 7

Overall Statistics

	G	AB	R	H	2B	3B	HR	RBI	SB	CS	BB	SO	BA	OBA
95 SF	68	186	19	41	6	0	3	12	11	1	8	51	.220	.256
Career	299	637	79	125	26	3	13	51	21	1	36	142	.196	.250

1995 Situational Statistics

	AB	HR	RBI	BA	OBA	SLG		AB	HR	RBI	BA	OBA	SLG
Home	97	1	5	.186	.210	.237	LHP	37	1	2	.270	.325	.432
Road	89	2	7	.258	.305	.371	RHP	149	2	10	.208	.239	.268
Apr-Jun	72	2	8	.333	.351	.458	ScPos	42	0	8	.238	.304	.262
Jul-Oct	114	1	4	.149	.198	.202	Clutch	37	0	1	.189	.211	.216

SCOUTING REPORT

He plays three infield positions well. Mike's accuracy, range and hands are all average, but a plus arm and the ability to fill in at second, shortstop or third make him useful.

Benjamin is not blindingly fast, but he has above-average speed and is a smart baserunner. Not much of a hitter, Benjamin chokes up and crouches quite a bit, spraying line drives around the field with little power.

HOW HE PERFORMED IN '95

Andy Warhol was right again. Benji got his 15 minutes of fame—and a spot in the record books—by going 6-for-7 June 14 in Chicago, capping a three-day spree of 14 hits. During the rest of the season, however, he was a rock-solid .182. Mike got an extended opportunity to play when Matt Williams broke his foot, and played like a utility infielder.

WHAT TO EXPECT IN '96

The Phillies, who haven't employed a true utility infielder in years, traded Jeff Juden and Tommy Eason for Benjamin in October. He will likely see most of his duty as a late-inning defensive sub for Philadelphia unless Kevin Stocker flops again.

JAMIE BREWINGTON

Position: SP
Bats: R **Throws:** R
Ht: 6'4" **Wt:** 180
Opening Day Age: 24
Born: 9/28/1971
Drafted: SF92 10/271
ML Seasons: 1

Overall Statistics

	G	GS	GF	SV	W	L	ERA	IP	H	R	ER	HR	BB	SO
95 SF	13	13	0	0	6	4	4.54	75.1	68	38	38	8	45	45
Career	13	13	0	0	6	4	4.54	75.1	68	38	38	8	45	45

1995 Situational Statistics

	W	L	ERA	SV	IP	BB	SO		AB	HR	RBI	BA	OBA	SLG
Home	3	2	3.51	0	41.0	25	24	LHB	135	2	12	.200	.335	.296
Road	3	2	5.77	0	34.1	20	21	RHB	142	6	22	.289	.373	.486
Apr-Jun	0	0	0.00	0	0.0	0	0	ScPos	69	1	27	.232	.400	.348
Jul-Oct	6	4	4.54	0	75.1	45	45	Clutch	9	1	1	.222	.364	.556

SCOUTING REPORT

A tall, slender righthander with a Dave Stewartish on-field demeanor, Jamie has an average fastball, curve, slider and change. He throws from three quarters. Then again, he hadn't pitched above Class A before '95, so to have four average major-league pitches at his experience level is no embarrassment. Too often, Brewington's fastball, which bores in on righties, stays up in the zone. His control is poor.

Average at holding runners and fielding his position (four of eight basestealers were successful). Jamie was 5-for-23 (.217) in '95, with four sacrifice bunts.

HOW HE PERFORMED IN '95

After going 8-3 with a 3.06 ERA at Double-A, Jamie was called up July 23 to take the traded Mark Portugal's rotation spot. Brewington won his debut in Miami the next night. He finished with six wins, tied for second on the club, despite problems with walks and a late-season slide.

WHAT TO EXPECT IN '96

The Giants used 25 pitchers last year; within that motley crew, Brewington was a bright spot because he often worked out of self-imposed control trouble. His poise is already good, and Jamie appears to have a bright future in San Francisco.

THE SCOUTING REPORT: 1996

SAN FRANCISCO GIANTS

MARK DEWEY

Position: RP
Bats: R **Throws:** R
Ht: 6'0" **Wt:** 185
Opening Day Age: 31
Born: 1/3/1965
Drafted: SF87 23/594
ML Seasons: 5

Overall Statistics

	G	GS	GF	SV	W	L	ERA	IP	H	R	ER	HR	BB	SO
95 SF	27	0	5	0	1	0	3.13	31.2	30	12	11	2	17	32
Career	127	0	51	8	6	4	3.37	165.2	164	65	62	9	61	111

1995 Situational Statistics

	W	L	ERA	SV	IP	BB	SO		AB	HR	RBI	BA	OBA	SLG
Home	0	0	3.20	0	19.2	8	22	LHB	36	2	7	.389	.488	.639
Road	1	0	3.00	0	12.0	9	10	RHB	82	0	8	.195	.280	.256
Apr-Jun	1	0	4.07	0	24.1	11	30	ScPos	37	0	13	.216	.388	.243
Jul-Oct	0	0	0.00	0	7.1	6	2	Clutch	47	0	5	.298	.365	.362

SCOUTING REPORT

Dewey slings the ball, coming in three quarters to lefties but dropping down sidearm against righties. His sinking fastball is average. Mark has a minus slider uses a forkball as a change of pace.

He has well above-average control, and Mark fields his position extremely well. He is also among the Giants' best at holding runners, due to a good move: only four tried to steal last year, two successfully. Hitless in his only '95 at-bat, he's 1-for-4 lifetime.

HOW HE PERFORMED IN '95

A potential closer several years ago, Mark served as a middle and setup reliever for the '95 Giants. He has now pitched effectively in that role for three straight seasons. After suffering a stress fracture of a rib last June 16, Dewey missed 80 games. As the team's player representative, he incurred management's ire by strongly opposing the callup of replacement player Joel Chimelis after Matt Williams' injury.

WHAT TO EXPECT IN '96

Dewey is a useful reliever, especially when called upon to face a righthanded lineup. If he doesn't start retiring lefty hitters better than in '95 though, he won't see a lot of late-inning work.

RIKKERT FANEYTE

Position: OF
Bats: R **Throws:** R
Ht: 6'1" **Wt:** 170
Opening Day Age: 26
Born: 5/31/1969
Drafted: SF90 19/446
ML Seasons: 3

Overall Statistics

	G	AB	R	H	2B	3B	HR	RBI	SB	CS	BB	SO	BA	OBA
95 SF	46	86	7	17	4	1	0	4	1	0	11	27	.198	.289
Career	72	127	10	22	7	1	0	8	1	0	16	42	.173	.266

1995 Situational Statistics

	AB	HR	RBI	BA	OBA	SLG		AB	HR	RBI	BA	OBA	SLG
Home	49	0	1	.224	.345	.265	LHP	33	0	3	.182	.250	.212
Road	37	0	3	.162	.205	.270	RHP	53	0	1	.208	.311	.302
Apr-Jun	19	0	1	.263	.364	.263	ScPos	21	0	3	.095	.174	.095
Jul-Oct	67	0	3	.179	.267	.269	Clutch	26	0	1	.308	.333	.308

SCOUTING REPORT

The third native of Holland to play in the majors (Bert Blyleven and Win Remmerswal preceded him), Rikkert is a fairly undisciplined line-drive hitter who is susceptible to breaking pitches. He likes low fastballs and will inside-out pitches to right field.

Faneyte, a slightly above-average runner, can play left or center field. His range and hands are plus, and his accurate arm has average strength but is not powerful enough to enable Rikkert to play right.

HOW HE PERFORMED IN '95

This was the first year Faneyte appeared in more games in San Francisco than in the minors. However, he's never been given a chance to simply play. He made three starts in center field between Darren Lewis' departure and Deion Sanders' arrival and, on five-minutes notice after the trade was announced, doubled to lead off the game and score the first run.

WHAT TO EXPECT IN '96

Rikkert could a Jacob Brumfield-type player, contributing speed and defense off the bench. However, he must improve with the bat; 42 whiffs in 127 major-league at-bats is not the way to earn playing time.

SAN FRANCISCO GIANTS

CHRIS HOOK

Position: RP
Bats: R **Throws:** R
Ht: 6'5" **Wt:** 230
Opening Day Age: 27
Born: 8/4/1968
Drafted: CIN 6/14/89
ML Seasons: 1

Overall Statistics

	G	GS	GF	SV	W	L	ERA	IP	H	R	ER	HR	BB	SO
95 SF	45	0	14	0	5	1	5.50	52.1	55	33	32	7	29	40
Career	45	0	14	0	5	1	5.50	52.1	55	33	32	7	29	40

1995 Situational Statistics

	W	L	ERA	SV	IP	BB	SO		AB	HR	RBI	BA	OBA	SLG
Home	5	0	4.55	0	31.2	16	21	LHB	61	0	4	.197	.380	.246
Road	0	1	6.97	0	20.2	13	19	RHB	140	7	34	.307	.363	.521
Apr-Jun	3	0	3.90	0	27.2	12	22	ScPos	54	4	35	.333	.480	.630
Jul-Oct	2	1	7.30	0	24.2	17	18	Clutch	69	2	12	.217	.308	.333

SCOUTING REPORT

His low three-quarter-to-sidearm motion presented no mystery to righties in '95, but it presented serious problems for lefthanded hitters. He throws a sinker and a cut fastball as well as a slider, but all are below-average. The best thing Chris throws is a solid, plus forkball.

He's just average at holding runners and fielding, not unexpected for a pitcher his size. Eight runners tried to steal against him in '95, seven successfully. Hook was hitless in three at-bats.

HOW HE PERFORMED IN '95

Hook began his major-league tenure pitching effectively, but saw his ERA jump from a 3.86 mark in his 14 innings to 6.35 in his next 17 frames. Chris was 5-0 when sent down in mid-July, but was recalled just 10 days later when newly acquired Luis Aquino made his obligatory visit to the DL.

WHAT TO EXPECT IN '96

Hook too often put himself in trouble with walks last year; he must show more command and control to keep from collecting a lot of frequent-flier miles in '96.

TOM LAMPKIN

Positions: C//OF
Bats: L **Throws:** R
Ht: 5'11" **Wt:** 180
Opening Day Age: 32
Born: 3/4/1964
Drafted: CLE86 11/265
ML Seasons: 6

Overall Statistics

	G	AB	R	H	2B	3B	HR	RBI	SB	CS	BB	SO	BA	OBA
95 SF	65	76	8	21	2	0	1	9	2	0	9	8	.276	.360
Career	215	380	41	82	13	2	6	41	11	4	43	53	.216	.296

1995 Situational Statistics

	AB	HR	RBI	BA	OBA	SLG		AB	HR	RBI	BA	OBA	SLG
Home	38	1	4	.211	.318	.289	LHP	9	0	1	.111	.200	.111
Road	38	0	5	.342	.405	.395	RHP	67	1	8	.299	.382	.373
Apr-Jun	33	1	4	.273	.368	.394	ScPos	18	1	9	.333	.500	.556
Jul-Oct	43	0	5	.279	.354	.302	Clutch	30	0	2	.200	.273	.233

SCOUTING REPORT

He runs like a catcher and has strictly garden-variety tools behind the plate. Tom is a line-drive type hitter who goes with the pitch. He has a pretty slow bat and is susceptible to hard stuff inside.

HOW HE PERFORMED IN '95

Tom began the year as the Giants' 25th man, but ended it with a secure job. He ranked as the Giants' second most frequent pinch-hitter, but was not too successful (8-for-39, .205, 4 RBI). However, Tom was 8-for-22 (.364) in his six starts. His average was by far his best in the majors, ranking 75 points above his previous career average.

He threw out three of five would-be base stealers, and spent six games in left field as a late-inning replacement. It was the first non-catcher duty of Lampkin's six-year major-league career.

WHAT TO EXPECT IN '96

Lefthanded-hitting catchers generally have work if they want it. Tom handles pitchers fairly well, has accepted his role as a backup, and will be the #2 catcher in San Francisco next year, since Jeff Reed has signed with the Rockies.

SAN FRANCISCO GIANTS

DAVID MCCARTY

Positions: 1B//OF
Bats: R **Throws:** L
Ht: 6'5" **Wt:** 215
Opening Day Age: 26
Born: 11/23/1969
Drafted: MIN91 1/3
ML Seasons: 3

Overall Statistics

	G	AB	R	H	2B	3B	HR	RBI	SB	CS	BB	SO	BA	OBA
95 MIN/SF37		75	11	17	4	1	0	6	1	1	6	22	.227	.289
Career	179	556	68	126	27	5	3	39	5	8	32	134	.227	.277

1995 Situational Statistics

	AB	HR	RBI	BA	OBA	SLG		AB	HR	RBI	BA	OBA	SLG
Home	46	0	6	.217	.275	.304	LHP	40	0	2	.275	.370	.350
Road	29	0	0	.241	.313	.310	RHP	35	0	4	.171	.189	.257
Apr-Jun	55	0	4	.218	.279	.309	ScPos	22	0	5	.182	.240	.182
Jul-Oct	20	0	2	.250	.318	.300	Clutch	12	0	2	.583	.615	.750

SCOUTING REPORT

The 6'5" first baseman needs to put on some serious muscle in his upper body. He hits line drives off high fastballs but has little power for a man his size. Dave's speed as a runner is average, as are his defensive tools at first base.

HOW HE PERFORMED IN '95

McCarty attended Stanford, so last year was something of a homecoming for him. Always a solid minor-league hitter (.307 average, with walks and power), big-league pitching has been a mystery up until now.

A disappointment in Minnesota, McCarty was dealt to the Reds' system June 8. Six weeks later, the Giants acquired him. Dave hit .344 last year with 12 homers in the minors, but hit quite poorly in the show. He and Mark Carreon give the Giants two righthanded-hitting and lefty-throwing first basemen, a real oddity.

WHAT TO EXPECT IN '96

The Giants have re-signed Carreon and Glenallen Hill for '96, which leaves little space for McCarty. However, Dave is only 25 and should still have time to develop, although he isn't likely to be a power hitter in the majors.

JOHN PATTERSON

Position: 2B
Bats: B **Throws:** R
Ht: 5'9" **Wt:** 160
Opening Day Age: 29
Born: 2/11/1967
Drafted: SF88 25/594
ML Seasons: 4

Overall Statistics

	G	AB	R	H	2B	3B	HR	RBI	SB	CS	BB	SO	BA	OBA
95 SF	95	205	27	42	5	3	1	14	4	2	14	41	.205	.294
Career	228	564	74	121	16	5	5	52	22	7	35	113	.215	.289

1995 Situational Statistics

	AB	HR	RBI	BA	OBA	SLG		AB	HR	RBI	BA	OBA	SLG
Home	106	1	6	.170	.285	.245	LHP	25	1	1	.160	.250	.280
Road	99	0	8	.242	.306	.303	RHP	180	0	13	.211	.300	.272
Apr-Jun	107	0	6	.187	.237	.234	ScPos	46	0	12	.239	.375	.370
Jul-Oct	98	1	8	.224	.350	.316	Clutch	45	0	3	.156	.269	.244

SCOUTING REPORT

Patterson is very quick on the pivot at second and has a decent arm for a middle infielder. His range and hands are below-average, though, and he cheats up the middle since he does not go to his left very well. He is a plus baserunner.

JP is a line-drive switch-hitter who stands in a crouch and likes the pitch low and over the plate. He has poor plate discipline, walking only 30 times in 190 games over the past two seasons.

HOW HE PERFORMED IN '95

Patterson flat did not hit in '95. His chief offensive contribution is being plunked by pitches; John was drilled 12 times after being hit 11 times in '94. He effectively turns his back from an inside pitch while batting lefty, bending his knee into the strike zone and taking one for the team. A fractured wrist in September was the fourth serious injury of his career.

WHAT TO EXPECT IN '96

The disappointing Patterson was outrighted to Phoenix over the winter to create room on the 40-player roster. Because of his versatility and speed, John may make the club in '96, but it's also possible he may move on to a reserve job somewhere else.

SAN FRANCISCO GIANTS

J. R. PHILLIPS

Positions: 1B//OF
Bats: L **Throws:** L
Ht: 6'1" **Wt:** 185
Opening Day Age: 25
Born: 4/29/1970
Drafted: CAL88 3/91
ML Seasons: 3

Overall Statistics

	G	AB	R	H	2B	3B	HR	RBI	SB	CS	BB	SO	BA	OBA
95 SF	92	231	27	45	9	0	9	28	1	1	19	69	.195	.256
Career	118	285	29	55	10	1	11	35	2	1	20	87	.193	.245

1995 Situational Statistics

	AB	HR	RBI	BA	OBA	SLG		AB	HR	RBI	BA	OBA	SLG
Home	125	5	16	.192	.235	.328	LHP	30	1	6	.233	.281	.333
Road	106	4	12	.198	.280	.377	RHP	201	8	22	.189	.252	.353
Apr-Jun	145	4	13	.131	.192	.234	ScPos	71	3	21	.183	.266	.352
Jul-Oct	86	5	15	.302	.362	.547	Clutch	47	1	4	.234	.265	.362

SCOUTING REPORT

The strapping first baseman has a lot of holes in his swing, his bat is slow and he has serious problems making contact. Like many lefthanded hitters, J.R. has well above-average power on low, inside fastballs.

The surprise was his fielding. While his range is still somewhat below-average and he has a slow first step, Phillips has a strong arm, soft and sure hands, and uncanny suppleness for a big man. He stretches as well as any first baseman in the league.

HOW HE PERFORMED IN '95

Phillips batted .278 when he made contact, but struck out far more often than he hit safely. It's hard to start any slower than J.R. did, going 10-for-99 to begin the '95 season. After starting 29 of the first 32 games, he started only 25 more all year.

After his hideous start, Phillips became a crowd favorite because of the dignity he displayed through a very difficult half-season. In his final 38 games, J.R. hit an encouraging .305 with five homers.

WHAT TO EXPECT IN '96

The Giants' re-signing of Mark Carreon indicates they were not convinced by J.R.'s closing rush. Phillips will compete with Dave McCarty for a bench job this spring.

JEFF REED

Position: C
Bats: L **Throws:** R
Ht: 6'2" **Wt:** 190
Opening Day Age: 33
Born: 11/12/1962
Drafted: MIN80 1/12
ML Seasons: 12

Overall Statistics

	G	AB	R	H	2B	3B	HR	RBI	SB	CS	BB	SO	BA	OBA
95 SF	66	113	12	30	2	0	0	9	0	0	20	17	.265	.376
Career	722	1760	136	411	71	6	20	147	2	3	187	263	.234	.306

1995 Situational Statistics

	AB	HR	RBI	BA	OBA	SLG		AB	HR	RBI	BA	OBA	SLG
Home	65	0	5	.308	.438	.323	LHP	8	0	0	.250	.455	.250
Road	48	0	4	.208	.283	.229	RHP	105	0	9	.267	.369	.286
Apr-Jun	52	0	2	.269	.367	.288	ScPos	28	0	9	.286	.459	.286
Jul-Oct	61	0	7	.262	.384	.279	Clutch	30	0	1	.300	.417	.333

SCOUTING REPORT

Adequate defensively, Jeff has well above-average hands, an arm of average strength and accuracy, but poor mobility behind the plate.

Reed runs like a 16-year veteran catcher. For a fairly big man, he has limited power, choking up and spraying the ball the other way. He likes the ball out over the plate or away, helping to compensate for his slow bat.

HOW HE PERFORMED IN '95

Reed backed up Kirt Manwaring for the third straight season. Jeff started 24 games, hitting well in this role (.304 with seven RBI) and nearly doubled his walks last season. Locked into platoon duty, he had just eight at-bats against lefties.

He threw out an excellent 43% of would-be base stealers on the season (12 of 28).

WHAT TO EXPECT IN '96

The Giants allowed Jeff to become a free agent in the off-season and he signed with the Colorado Rockies, replacing Joe Girardi. Watch him carefully in Denver even though the former #1 draft pick has only 20 career homers in 1760 at-bats. Expect a career high in home runs from him, almost all of them over Coors Field's invitingly short right field porch.

THE SCOUTING REPORT: 1996

SAN FRANCISCO GIANTS

STEVE SCARSONE

Positions: 3B/2B/1B
Bats: R **Throws:** R
Ht: 6'2" **Wt:** 170
Opening Day Age: 29
Born: 4/11/1966
Drafted: PHI86* 2/34
ML Seasons: 4

Overall Statistics

	G	AB	R	H	2B	3B	HR	RBI	SB	CS	BB	SO	BA	OBA
95 SF	80	233	33	62	10	3	11	29	3	2	18	82	.266	.333
Career	194	469	73	121	27	3	15	57	3	5	34	146	.258	.314

1995 Situational Statistics

	AB	HR	RBI	BA	OBA	SLG		AB	HR	RBI	BA	OBA	SLG
Home	128	7	17	.227	.298	.461	LHP	71	3	7	.324	.364	.549
Road	105	4	12	.314	.376	.495	RHP	162	8	22	.241	.320	.444
Apr-Jun	85	7	14	.318	.376	.635	ScPos	63	2	16	.206	.301	.349
Jul-Oct	148	4	15	.236	.309	.385	Clutch	40	3	7	.275	.341	.525

SCOUTING REPORT
Average in virtually all his tools, Scarsone has learned to expand his role over the years and now plays several positions. He did not amaze defensively at any position, however, and won't hold a job if he doesn't provide some offense.

A solid fastball hitter, Steve likes the ball middle-in and can jump on hard stuff inside. He is very impatient and susceptible to breaking stuff, which he cannot hit but tries to anyway.

HOW HE PERFORMED IN '95
It wasn't exactly a breakthrough year, but Steve had career highs in most every offensive category. His 11 homers were particularly notable, as his career total coming into the year was four. Scarsone was hot early, homering in five straight starts, and going 5-for-5 on May 21. Steve feasted on lefthanded pitching, but had an incredibly high strikeout rate. This is worrisome if the Giants want to give him significant duty in the future.

WHAT TO EXPECT IN '96
The valuable Scarsone will be the first man Dusty Baker turns to if Robby Thompson continues to have physical problems. By playing first, second, third, shortstop and even serving as emergency catcher, Steve is almost two players in one roster slot.

SCOTT SERVICE

Position: RP
Bats: R **Throws:** R
Ht: 6'6" **Wt:** 230
Opening Day Age: 29
Born: 2/26/1967
Drafted: PHI 8/24/85
ML Seasons: 5

Overall Statistics

	G	GS	GF	SV	W	L	ERA	IP	H	R	ER	HR	BB	SO
95 SF	28	0	6	0	3	1	3.19	31.0	18	11	11	4	20	30
Career	73	0	16	2	6	5	4.75	96.2	92	56	51	13	45	95

1995 Situational Statistics

	W	L	ERA	SV	IP	BB	SO		AB	HR	RBI	BA	OBA	SLG
Home	0	0	3.55	0	12.2	9	13	LHB	35	0	5	.171	.392	.229
Road	3	1	2.95	0	18.1	11	17	RHB	67	4	10	.179	.267	.388
Apr-Jun	0	0	0.00	0	0.0	0	0	ScPos	27	1	11	.259	.421	.370
Jul-Oct	3	1	3.19	0	31.0	20	30	Clutch	49	4	11	.224	.333	.510

SCOUTING REPORT
The big, rawboned righthander throws from low three-quarters to sidearm with long arm action. His fastball is slightly below-average but sinks and bores in on righty hitters, helping Scott get groundball outs. Service's slurve-curve is a minus pitch, with his slider and forkball rated average. In general, his control is ordinary. He has an average move to first, but just four men tried to steal against him in '95, two successfully. Scott is a decent fielder. Going 0-for-1 last year, he now has one hit in ten career at-bats.

HOW HE PERFORMED IN '95
Service has over 1,000 minor-league innings under his belt. After joining the Giants July 22, he took over the setup role and led the team in appearances from that point with 28. He retired 20 of 28 first batters faced, stranded 13 of 18 inherited runners and notched a 2.66 ERA in his final 17 appearances. His ERA was nearly two runs better than his previous career average. Curiously, control was a weakness.

WHAT TO EXPECT IN '96
Scott has the experience and craftiness to be an effective setup pitcher if he doesn't put too many enemy hitters on base via the walk.

SAN FRANCISCO GIANTS

SERGIO VALDEZ

Position: SP
Bats: R **Throws:** R
Ht: 6'0" **Wt:** 165
Opening Day Age: 31
Born: 9/7/1964
Drafted: MON 1/20/83
ML Seasons: 8

Overall Statistics

	G	GS	GF	SV	W	L	ERA	IP	H	R	ER	HR	BB	SO
95 SF	13	11	0	0	4	5	4.75	66.1	78	43	35	12	17	29
Career	116	31	28	0	12	20	5.06	302.2	332	194	170	46	109	190

1995 Situational Statistics

	W	L	ERA	SV	IP	BB	SO		AB	HR	RBI	BA	OBA	SLG
Home	3	2	5.24	0	34.1	9	15	LHB	129	8	19	.302	.350	.574
Road	1	3	4.22	0	32.0	8	14	RHB	133	4	18	.293	.338	.451
Apr-Jun	0	0	0.00	0	0.0	0	0	ScPos	58	2	26	.328	.400	.517
Jul-Oct	4	5	4.75	0	66.1	17	29	Clutch	28	3	3	.286	.310	.679

SCOUTING REPORT

Valdez comes three-quarters out of a full and very fluid windup—although many pitchers are called stylish, Valdez certainly qualifies.

His fastball is somewhat below-average but sinks well; his average hard slider has good movement and rates as his best pitch. Sergio's forkball and change are both average, giving him four decent pitches to go with improved, plus control. Valdez is an average fielder and holds runners creditably. Ten ran against Valdez, six successfully. A .133 career batter, he hit .095 in 21 at-bats in '95.

HOW HE PERFORMED IN '95

Recalled from Triple-A July 19, Sergio threw five perfect innings in his first '95 start and ended up a mainstay in an injury-riddled and ineffective San Francisco rotation. Twice in '95, he was charged by enemy hitters who took exception to inside deliveries, but in both cases the batter was ejected and Sergio picked up a win.

WHAT TO EXPECT IN '96

Although he's only 30, Sergio enters his 15th professional season in '96. Valdez will probably not be in the rotation out of spring training, but if history is an indicator, he will fill in for several members of the Giants' rotation before the season ends.

TREVOR WILSON

Position: SP
Bats: L **Throws:** L
Ht: 6'0" **Wt:** 190
Opening Day Age: 29
Born: 6/7/1966
Drafted: SF85 8/186
ML Seasons: 7

Overall Statistics

	G	GS	GF	SV	W	L	ERA	IP	H	R	ER	HR	BB	SO
95 SF	17	17	0	0	3	4	3.92	82.2	82	42	36	8	38	38
Career	154	115	12	0	41	46	3.87	720.1	657	342	310	61	300	425

1995 Situational Statistics

	W	L	ERA	SV	IP	BB	SO		AB	HR	RBI	BA	OBA	SLG
Home	2	1	3.14	0	43.0	23	20	LHB	47	0	3	.255	.345	.319
Road	1	3	4.76	0	39.2	15	18	RHB	258	8	24	.271	.357	.407
Apr-Jun	3	3	3.79	0	54.2	21	24	ScPos	69	3	20	.174	.262	.333
Jul-Oct	0	1	4.18	0	28.0	17	14	Clutch	16	0	1	.250	.400	.313

SCOUTING REPORT

Wilson throws from a three-quarter to high three-quarter angle with a high leg kick. His fastball has lost a few feet due to several shoulder surgeries, but Trevor cuts and sinks it effectively.

Currently, Wilson relies on his well above-average change as his out pitch. His big slider rates average. A decent fielder, he has a plus move and holds runners well. Just six men attempted to steal on him in '95, three successfully. A .176 lifetime hitter, Wilson sacrifices effectively and batted .233 in '95.

HOW HE PERFORMED IN '95

Wilson returned to the Giants in '95, taking less money than other teams offered, but was sidelined for much of a fourth straight year. His final appearance came August 12, when he struck out the Cubs' Brian McRae to begin the game and immediately left with a rotator cuff strain that required season-ending surgery.

WHAT TO EXPECT IN '96

He has another long rehab ahead. At age 30, the hard-working Wilson may yet make it back, but it remains to be seen whether any big-league team will take a chance on him in '96.

THE SCOUTING REPORT: 1996

SAN FRANCISCO GIANTS: TOP PROSPECTS

RICH AURILIA

Bats: R Throws: R Opening Day Age: 24
Ht: 6-0 Wt: 170 Born: 9/2/1971
Position: SS Drafted: 1992 #24 TEX

YR TEAM	LG/CLASS	G	AB	R	H	2B	3B	HR	RBI	SB	BA	OBA
93 Charlotte	FSL/A	122	440	80	136	16	5	5	56	15	.309	.408
94 Tulsa	TEX/AA	129	458	67	107	18	6	12	57	10	.234	.315
95 San Fran	NL/MAJ	9	19	4	9	3	0	2	4	1	.474	.476
Phoenix	PCL/AAA	71	258	42	72	12	0	5	34	2	.279	.361
Shreveport	TEX/AA	64	226	29	74	17	1	4	42	10	.327	.398

Acquired from the Rangers in the John Burkett deal last winter, Aurilia was the leader of the Shreveport club that won the Texas League championship. He hit .382 with runners in scoring position, over .400 against lefthanders, and .350 with 15 doubles away from pitcher-friendly Shreveport before departing for Phoenix in mid-June. The 24-year-old performed well at Triple-A. In the field, he had the highest range factor of any Double-A shortstop, in spite of his reputation for having sure hands but questionable mobility.

STEVE BOURGEOIS

Bats: R Throws: R Opening Day Age: 23
Ht: 6-1 Wt: 220 Born: 8/4/1972
Position: P Drafted: 1993 #23 SF

YR TEAM	LG/CLASS	G	GS	GF	SV	W	L	ERA	IP	H	HR	BB	SO	O/BA
93 Everett	NWST/A	15	15	0	0	5	3	4.21	77.0	62	7	44	77	.219
94 Clinton	MID/A	20	20	0	0	8	5	3.64	106.1	97	16	54	88	.244
94 San Jose	CAL/A	7	7	0	0	4	0	5.40	36.2	40	4	22	27	.282
95 Phoenix	PCL/AAA	6	5	0	0	1	3	3.38	34	38	2	13	23	.275
Shreveport	TEX/AA	22	22	0	0	12	3	2.85	145	140	8	53	91	.260

Bourgeois may be the biggest surprise in the organization. He would have been in San Francisco by July had he not been a replacement player during the spring. The 23-year-old is not overwhelming, but got into better shape last season, improved his command, and spotted his pitches expertly enough to earn Texas League Pitcher of the Year honors. He also led the organization in wins and ERA while finishing second in strikeouts. The low-round draft selection also held his own after an early August promotion to Triple-A. Bourgeois led all minor league pitchers with 11 hits in 1995, batting .306 with a homer and nine RBI in 36 at-bats.

JAY CANIZARO

Bats: R Throws: R Opening Day Age: 22
Ht: 5-10 Wt: 175 Born: 7/4/1973
Position: 2B Drafted: 1993 #6 SF

YR TEAM	LG/CLASS	G	AB	R	H	2B	3B	HR	RBI	SB	BA	OBA
93 SF	ARIZ/R	49	180	34	47	10	6	3	41	12	.261	.337
94 San Jose	CAL/A	126	464	77	117	16	2	15	69	12	.252	.324
95 Shreveport	TEX/AA	126	440	83	129	25	7	12	60	16	.293	.379

Canizaro has posted impressive power numbers the last two years despite playing in pitchers' parks. He batted .323 with 16 doubles and seven homers on the road last season and was consistent all year, leading to a post-season All-Star berth. Defensively, the 22-year-old is above-average with a very strong arm. He has played shortstop several times during his career.

JACOB CRUZ

Bats: L Throws: L Opening Day Age: 23
Ht: 6-0 Wt: 175 Born: 1/28/1973
Position: OF Drafted: 1994 #2 SF

YR TEAM	LG/CLASS	G	AB	R	H	2B	3B	HR	RBI	SB	BA	OBA
94 San Jose	CAL/A	31	118	14	29	7	0	0	12	0	.246	.305
95 Shreveport	TEX/AA	127	458	88	136	33	1	13	77	9	.297	.383

Cruz is a high average hitter with gap power to both alleys, but his uppercut swing could lead to more homers as he matures. He finished second in the Texas League in both runs and doubles, hit close to .350 the first two months of the season, and was selected to the post-season All-Star squad. Defensively, Cruz committed just one error, and possessed the best outfield throwing arm on his club.

SHAWN ESTES

Bats: R Throws: L Opening Day Age: 23
Ht: 6-2 Wt: 200 Born: 2/28/1973
Position: P Drafted: 1991 #1 SEA

YR TEAM	LG/CLASS	G	GS	GF	SV	W	L	ERA	IP	H	HR	BB	SO	O/BA
93 Appleton	MID/A	19	18	0	0	5	9	7.24	83.1	108	3	52	65	.305
94 Mariners	ARIZ/R	5	5	0	0	0	3	3.15	20.0	16	0	6	31	.205
94 Appleton	MID/A	5	4	1	0	0	2	4.58	19.2	19	1	17	28	.271
95 San Fran	NL/MAJ	3	3	0	0	0	3	6.75	17	16	2	5	14	.229
Shreveport	TEX/AA	4	4	0	0	2	0	2.01	22	14	1	10	18	.184
San Jose	CAL/A	9	8	0	0	5	2	2.17	49	32	1	17	61	.188
Wisconsin	MID/A	2	2	0	0	0	0	0.90	10	5	0	5	11	.156
Burlington	MID/A	4	4	0	0	0	4	4.11	15	13	2	12	22	.224

Estes, acquired from the Mariners along with Wilson Delgado for Salomon Torres, made the major leagues after starting the year in low Class-A ball. Winless in 1994 and suffering from shoulder problems, the 22-year-old regained a 90+-mph fastball and an impressive curve last season, and improved his command. "Buck" was overpowering at times in four different stops prior to his arrival in the majors.

MARCUS JENSEN

Bats: S Throws: R Opening Day Age: 23
Ht: 6-4 Wt: 195 Born: 12/14/1972
Position: C Drafted: 1990 #3 SF

YR TEAM	LG/CLASS	G	AB	R	H	2B	3B	HR	RBI	SB	BA	OBA
93 Clinton	MID/A	104	324	53	85	24	2	11	56	1	.262	.389
94 San Jose	CAL/A	118	418	56	101	18	0	7	47	1	.242	.345
95 Shreveport	TEX/AA	95	321	55	91	22	8	4	45	0	.283	.362

Although Jensen is improving as a hitter, defense is his ticket to the major leagues. The 23-year-old threw out 52% of all base stealers last season, best in the Texas League, and is solid at blocking pitches and calling a game. Offensively, he hasn't generated the power his size suggests and he seems more comfortable batting from the left side, but the 1991 first-round pick is selective—perhaps to a fault.

SAN FRANCISCO GIANTS: TOP PROSPECTS

BILL MUELLER
Bats: S Throws: R Opening Day Age: 25
Ht: 5-11 Wt: 173 Born: 3/17/1971
Position: 3B Drafted: 1993 #17 SF

YR TEAM	LG/CLASS	G	AB	R	H	2B	3B	HR	RBI	SB	BA	OBA
93 Everett	NWST/A	58	200	31	60	8	2	1	24	13	.300	.425
94 San Jose	CAL/A	120	431	79	130	20	9	5	72	4	.302	.435
95 Phoenix	PCL/AAA	41	172	23	51	13	6	2	19	0	.297	.365
Shreveport	TEX/AA	88	330	56	102	16	2	1	39	6	.309	.407

Mueller is a pesky hitter who will do anything to get on base. He showed a knack for driving in runs last season, batting over .360 at both stops with runners in scoring position and nearly .380 with two out. An overachiever in the Pete Rose mold, the 24-year-old has no outstanding tools, but hits from both sides of the plate and makes the plays in the field.

RICKY PICKETT
Bats: L Throws: L Opening Day Age: 26
Ht: 6-0 Wt: 185 Born: 1/19/1970
Position: P Drafted: 1992 #29 CIN

YR TEAM	LG/CLASS	G	GS	GF	SV	W	L	ERA	IP	H	HR	BB	SO	O/BA
93 Chston-WV	SAL/A	44	1	5	0	1	2	6.75	44.0	42	1	48	65	.246
94 Chrstn-WV	SAL/A	28	0	19	13	1	1	1.98	27.1	14	1	20	48	.143
94 Winston-Sal	CARO/A	21	0	17	4	2	1	3.75	24.0	16	0	23	33	.188
95 Chattanooga	SOU/AA	40	0	19	9	4	5	3.28	46	22	3	44	69	.140
Shreveport	TEX/AA	14	0	9	3	2	0	1.71	21	9	1	9	23	.125

Pickett may be the key player acquired from the Reds in the Deion Sanders deal. He has been impossible to hit and will arrive in the major leagues as soon as he does two things: gain command of his 95-mph fastball and work on another pitch. He had an 11-inning hitless streak during the season and led all minor league relievers in average against (.135) while finishing second in SO/9 IP (12.24). His career totals show a .179 average against with 279 strikeouts and 172 walks in 217 innings.

JOE ROSSELLI
Bats: R Throws: L Opening Day Age: 23
Ht: 6-1 Wt: 170 Born: 5/28/1972
Position: P Drafted: 1990 #5 SF

YR TEAM	LG/CLASS	G	GS	GF	SV	W	L	ERA	IP	H	HR	BB	SO	O/BA
93 Shreveport	TEX/AA	4	4	0	0	0	1	3.13	23.0	22	1	7	19	.247
94 Shreveport	TEX/AA	14	14	0	0	7	2	1.89	90.2	67	2	17	54	.206
94 Phoenix	PCL/AAA	13	13	0	0	1	8	4.94	74.2	96	10	15	35	.322
95 San Fran	NL/MAJ	9	5	0	0	2	1	8.70	30	39	5	20	7	.342
Phoenix	PCL/AAA	13	13	0	0	4	3	4.99	79	94	8	12	34	.299

The 1992 California League Pitcher of the Year (11-4, 2.41 ERA) has been held back by arm problems and an inability to get righthanders out. However, his best pitch, a slider, is extremely effective against lefties. After missing virtually all of 1993 because of shoulder surgery, Rosselli was the most impressive pitcher at Shreveport in '94 before being promoted to Phoenix, where he pitched decently but got little support.

STEVE SODERSTROM
Bats: R Throws: R Opening Day Age: 23
Ht: 6-3 Wt: 215 Born: 4/3/1972
Position: P Drafted: 1993 #1 SF

YR TEAM	LG/CLASS	G	GS	GF	SV	W	L	ERA	IP	H	HR	BB	SO	O/BA
94 San Jose	CAL/A	8	8	0	0	2	3	4.20	40.2	34	2	26	40	.233
95 Shreveport	TEX/AA	22	22	0	0	9	5	3.41	116	106	6	51	91	.241

Soderstrom may be the best pitching prospect on a Shreveport staff full of good young arms. He made great strides last season after missing most of his first two years with elbow and shoulder problems. He started and finished strong despite missing a month with a shoulder strain. The Fresno State product has a power pitcher's frame, but has not yet completely regained his 90 mph fastball.

CARLOS VALDEZ
Bats: R Throws: R Opening Day Age: 24
Ht: 5-11 Wt: 165 Born: 12/26/1971
Position: P Drafted: NDFA 4-6-90 SF

YR TEAM	LG/CLASS	G	GS	GF	SV	W	L	ERA	IP	H	HR	BB	SO	O/BA
93 Clinton	MID/A	35	2	14	3	4	7	3.99	90.1	74	6	44	85	.224
94 San Jose	CAL/A	36	17	10	0	8	6	4.51	123.2	109	7	61	116	.240
95 San Fran	NL/MAJ	11	0	3	0	0	1	6.14	14	19	1	8	7	.322
Phoenix	PCL/AAA	18	0	12	2	1	0	2.76	29	29	2	13	30	.250
Shreveport	TEX/AA	22	3	8	5	3	2	1.27	64	40	0	14	51	.180

Valdez split his first four years between the rotation and bullpen with moderate success, but pitched exclusively as a reliever in 1995. His outstanding breaking ball, which consistently produces ground balls, and a decent fastball dominated Double-A hitters, held their own at the next level, and eventually got the 23-year-old to the major leagues.

KEITH WILLIAMS
Bats: R Throws: R Opening Day Age: 23
Ht: 6-0 Wt: 190 Born: 4/21/1972
Position: OF Drafted: 1993 #9 SF

YR TEAM	LG/CLASS	G	AB	R	H	2B	3B	HR	RBI	SB	BA	OBA
93 Everett	NWST/A	75	288	57	87	21	5	12	49	21	.302	.407
94 San Jose	CAL/A	128	504	91	151	30	8	21	97	4	.300	.373
95 Phoenix	PCL/AAA	24	83	7	25	4	1	2	14	0	.301	.341
Shreveport	TEX/AA	75	275	39	84	20	1	9	55	5	.305	.351

This 23-year-old doesn't do anything impressively except put up impressive numbers by season's end. He has hit over .300 in each of his three pro years, shows good power potential to all fields, runs well, and plays a solid outfield. His numbers have been hurt by playing in pitcher-friendly parks the past two years. Williams set a club record for homers at San Jose in 1994 and hit .336 with 12 doubles and six homers in road games last season.

SAN FRANCISCO GIANTS: OTHERS TO WATCH

MARVIN BENARD   Bats: L Throws: L   Ht: 5-10 Wt: 180
Born: 1/20/1971   Drafted: 1992 #50 SF   Position: OF

YR TEAM	LG/CLASS	G	AB	R	H	2B	3B	HR	RBI	SB	BA	OBA
95 San Fran	NL/MAJ	13	34	5	13	2	0	1	4	1	.382	.400
95 Phoenix	PCL/AAA	111	378	70	115	14	6	6	32	10	.304	.390

Benard, a .299 career hitter who can hit southpaws but packs little sock, is a decent outfielder with a good arm.

DAN CARLSON   Bats: R Throws: R   Ht: 6-1 Wt: 185
Born: 1/26/1970   Drafted: 1989 #33 SF   Position: P

YR TEAM	LG/CLASS	G	GS	GF	SV	W	L	ERA	IP	H	HR	BB	SO	O/BA
95 Phoenix	PCL/AAA	23	22	1	0	9	5	4.27	132.2	138	11	66	93	.277

Carlson has led three different leagues in wins, getting by with an average fastball and a very good breaking pitch.

EDWIN CORPS   Bats: R Throws: R   Ht: 5-11 Wt: 180
Born: 11/3/1972   Drafted: NDFA 12-5-93 SF   Position: P

YR TEAM	LG/CLASS	G	GS	GF	SV	W	L	ERA	IP	H	HR	BB	SO	O/BA
95 Shreveport	TEX/AA	27	27	0	0	13	6	3.86	165.2	195	16	41	53	.298

The Texas League All-Star doesn't throw hard and gives up hits, but he throws strikes and wins.

KEITH FOULKE   Bats: R Throws: R   Ht: 6-1 Wt: 195
Born: 10/19/1972   Drafted: 1994 #10 SF   Position: P

YR TEAM	LG/CLASS	G	GS	GF	SV	W	L	ERA	IP	H	HR	BB	SO	O/BA
95 San Jose	CAL/A	28	26	0	0	13	6	3.50	177.1	166	16	32	168	.247

The Cal League All-Star has great control of a 90-mph fastball, but was much more effective at extremely pitcher-friendly San Jose than on the road.

JESSE IBARRA   Bats: S Throws: R   Ht: 6-3 Wt: 195
Born: 7/12/1972   Drafted: 1994 #7 SF   Position: 1B

YR TEAM	LG/CLASS	G	AB	R	H	2B	3B	HR	RBI	SB	BA	OBA
95 San Jose	CAL/A	3	9	1	3	2	0	0	4	0	.333	.400
95 Burlington	MID/A	129	437	72	144	30	1	34	96	1	.330	.434

The Midwest League MVP led the minors in slugging and was second in homers, clubbing a minor league-leading 12 in August, but was aided greatly by the hitter-friendly park in Burlington.

DAX JONES   Bats: R Throws: R   Ht: 6-0 Wt: 170
Born: 8/4/1970   Drafted: 1991 #6 SF   Position: OF

YR TEAM	LG/CLASS	G	AB	R	H	2B	3B	HR	RBI	SB	BA	OBA
95 Phoenix	PCL/AAA	112	404	47	108	21	3	2	45	11	.267	.319

Jones is a solid outfielder with a good arm, a decent bat, and speed, but has not exhibited enough pop to advance to the next level.

CALVIN MURRAY   Bats: R Throws: R   Ht: 5-11 Wt: 185
Born: 7/30/1971   Drafted: 1992 #1 SF   Position: CF

YR TEAM	LG/CLASS	G	AB	R	H	2B	3B	HR	RBI	SB	BA	OBA
95 Phoenix	PCL/AAA	13	50	8	9	1	0	4	10	2	.180	.236
95 Shreveport	TEX/AA	110	441	77	104	17	3	2	29	56	.236	.329

The former first-rounder could take over in center field now, but his bat has too many holes and an unproductive uppercut.

ARMANDO RIOS   Bats: L Throws: L   Ht: 5-9 Wt: 178
Born: 9/13/1971   Drafted: NDFA 1-6-94 SF   Position: RF

YR TEAM	LG/CLASS	G	AB	R	H	2B	3B	HR	RBI	SB	BA	OBA
95 San Jose	CAL/A	128	488	76	143	34	3	8	75	51	.293	.382

The San Jose MVP is small, but had the best arm in the California League, great speed, and a quick bat which would have generated better power numbers in a less pitcher-friendly park.

BENJI SIMONTON   Bats: R Throws: R   Ht: 6-1 Wt: 225
Born: 5/12/1972   Drafted: 1992 #3 SF   Position: 1B

YR TEAM	LG/CLASS	G	AB	R	H	2B	3B	HR	RBI	SB	BA	OBA
95 Shreveport	TEX/AA	38	108	18	33	9	3	4	30	3	.306	.377
95 San Jose	CAL/A	61	225	38	65	9	6	8	37	7	.289	.412

Simonton, an outstanding power-hitting prospect selected as a Rule V pick by the Red Sox in 1994, didn't make it in the outfield with Boston, returned to the Giants, and shifted to first base.

CHRIS SINGLETON   Bats: L Throws: L   Ht: 6-2 Wt: 195
Born: 8/15/1972   Drafted: 1993 #2 SF   Position: OF

YR TEAM	LG/CLASS	G	AB	R	H	2B	3B	HR	RBI	SB	BA	OBA
95 San Jose	CAL/A	94	405	55	112	13	5	2	31	33	.277	.313

The talented but raw 23-year-old has great speed and works hard, but needs to play better defense and take more pitches.

ANDY TAULBEE   Bats: R Throws: R   Ht: 6-4 Wt: 210
Born: 10/5/1972   Drafted: 1994 #3 SF   Position: P

YR TEAM	LG/CLASS	G	GS	GF	SV	W	L	ERA	IP	H	HR	BB	SO	O/BA
95 Shreveport	TEX/AA	14	14	0	0	4	5	3.95	86.2	107	5	27	38	.307
95 San Jose	CAL/A	10	9	0	0	3	2	3.02	62.2	50	7	22	33	.226

Despite his size, Taulbee is a finesse pitcher who wins with good control; he split '95 at two levels.

DOUG VANDERWEELE   Bats: R Throws: R   Ht: 6-3 Wt: 200
Born: 3/18/1970   Drafted: 1991 #7 SF   Position: P

YR TEAM	LG/CLASS	G	GS	GF	SV	W	L	ERA	IP	H	HR	BB	SO	O/BA
95 Phoenix	PCL/AAA	11	4	1	0	2	4	6.10	38.1	57	9	11	20	.354
95 Shreveport	TEX/AA	13	9	0	0	5	2	2.52	64.1	61	3	13	22	.257

Vanderweele is not overpowering, relying on command and location, but was effective at Double-A last season before being pounded at Triple-A.

STEVE WHITAKER   Bats: L Throws: L   Ht: 6-6 Wt: 225
Born: 4/15/1970   Drafted: 1991 #1 SF   Position: P

YR TEAM	LG/CLASS	G	GS	GF	SV	W	L	ERA	IP	H	HR	BB	SO	O/BA
95 Phoenix	PCL/AAA	16	13	0	0	5	7.00	54.0	72	2	36	30	.335
95 Shreveport	TEX/AA	4	3	0	0	2	0	3.86	16.1	17	0	10	10	.288
95 San Jose	CAL/A CAL/A2	0	1	1	0	0	4.50	6.0	7	0	2	2	.292

The strike, coupled with shoulder and groin problems, prevented the former first-rounder from getting out of the blocks in 1995.

CHRIS WIMMER   Bats: R Throws: R   Ht: 5-11 Wt: 170
Born: 9/25/1970   Drafted: 1992 #8 SF   Position: 2B

YR TEAM	LG/CLASS	G	AB	R	H	2B	3B	HR	RBI	SB	BA	OBA
95 Phoenix	PCL/AAA	132	449	55	118	23	4	2	44	13	.263	.325

Wimmer, a defensive standout, has had two streaks of 50+ errorless games in his career, but his bat remains a major question mark despite a big 1995 second half.

Other Veteran Players

This section includes brief notes on every player who played in the major-leagues in 1995 and who is not found elsewhere in the book. This is because the player has either retired, is apparently at the end of his career, was injured for most of 1995, or is likely to spend most or all of 1996 in the minors. Also included are a few veteran players who spent the whole season on the major-league DL. All players are shown with the last 1995 major-league team they played for.

A few of these players still have enough potential to make an impact, but most of them won't play in the majors in 1996 or won't contribute much if they do. Because of the shortened spring training and the expansion of rosters at the start of the season, fully 247 players made their major-league debut last season. Many of those will never play in the big leagues again. Of course, there will always be a few surprises.

AMERICAN LEAGUE

Baltimore Orioles

JARVIS BROWN—Minor league veteran hit .148 in 27 at-bats with the Orioles. Pinch-running and late-inning defensive work is his future in the majors, if he has one.

JIM DEDRICK—A middling middle-relief prospect, Dedrick got into six games with Baltimore last year, allowing eight hits and six walks in 7.2 innings. His best hope is as a 10th or 11th pitcher.

JOHN DESILVA—Allowing three home runs and seven walks in 8.2 innings, spread over two games, is no way to convince anyone you're ready to pitch in the majors. DeSilva has decent stuff but isn't in the Orioles' plans.

MARK EICHHORN—Missed the entire season after undergoing right rotator cuff surgery. Eichhorn throws harder than your usual sidearmer, and a full comeback is questionable at age 35.

MIKE HARTLEY—What a long, strange trip it's been for Hartley, who has been with six different clubs—including a year playing in Japan—over the last five seasons. He's a marginal righty middle reliever who landed in Boston and Baltimore for a total of eight games in 1995, posting a 5.14 ERA in 14 innings. Seventh organization in six years coming right up.

ALAN MILLS—After two years as the Orioles' top righthanded middle reliever, Mills slumped terribly in 1995, racking up a 7.43 ERA in 21 games while walking 18 in 23 innings. Back at Triple-A, he pitched just once before being shut down for the year. The book on Mills is that he throws very hard but has no idea of how to set up hitters.

Boston Red Sox

BRIAN BARK—A former Braves' farmhand, Bark got into three games with the Red Sox, pitching 2.1 innings without distinction. Being lefthanded is his only marker.

JUAN BELL—He is running out of teams to disappoint. Bell hit .154 in 26 at-bats with the Red Sox, and will have to start at Triple-A again this spring.

WES CHAMBERLAIN—He came to Boston amidst high expectations, but Chamberlain hit poorly over the last two years and has played himself out of the organization. In 1995, he batted .119 in 42 at-bats with one home run. He could re-emerge as a platoon player for a team down on its luck, since he has some talent.

ERIC GUNDERSON—Three organizations (Mets, Mariners, and Red Sox) had possession of Gunderson last year despite a spotty career record. He had a 5.11 ERA in 12.1 innings spread over 19 games. Gunderson will likely get more chances since he's a portsider.

JOEL JOHNSTON—The Red Sox thought they could turn Johnston's live arm into good performance. They were wrong, just like the Yankees and Pirates were before them. Johnston pitched four innings for the Red Sox and allowed five runs; at Triple-A Pawtucket, he fashioned a 6.59 ERA in 42 innings before moving on to the Rockies' organization, where he was 2-2, 5.96 in 23 innings.

DEREK LILLIQUIST—Southpaw reliever Lilliquist had a 6.26 ERA in 28 games with the BoSox (pitching just 23 innings), but has had good seasons in the majors and could again.

JEFF PIERCE—The former White Sox and Reds prospect opened the year with the Red Sox but was sent back to Triple-A May 27 after compiling an 0-3 mark and 6.60 ERA in 15 innings. Still thought of as a "hopeful" and was on Boston's 40-player winter roster.

KARL "TUFFY" RHODES—Went 2-for-16 for the Cubs before they waived him to Boston. Rhodes then hit .080 with the Sox before he was sent to Triple-A, where batted .285 as a half-time player. Rhodes has a little power and some speed but is a horrid outfielder who has king-sized holes in his swing. Little future except as a platoon DH/bench player.

OTHER VETERAN PLAYERS

CARLOS RODRIGUEZ—A reserve infielder who batted .333 with the Red Sox (10-for-30). He's a decent defensive player but is now 28 and hasn't been on the major-league roster the last two winters despite stints with the big club.

RICH ROWLAND—Went 5-for-29 with 11 strikeouts for the Red Sox before once again hitting the bushes, where he is likely to remain for the balance of his career.

KEITH SHEPHERD—Allowed four runs in one inning with the Red Sox. Some talent but very unlucky: he missed all of 1994 after a batted ball shattered his kneecap.

TERRY SHUMPERT—Couldn't stick with Boston, batting .234 as an infrequently-used utility infielder. Won't ever be a starter in the majors, but has enough positives that he could again stick as a deep backup.

TIM VANEGMOND—Went 0-1 in four games with the Red Sox. Not that bad, but probably going to be a Triple-A pitcher for most of his career with Boston.

California Angels

ANDY ALLANSON—Veteran reserve catcher hit .171 in 82 at-bats with three homers for California but was released after the season. Could still hook on with a team lacking depth behind the plate.

ERIK BENNETT—Pitched one-third of an inning for the 1995 Angels, making his major-league debut in his seventh year in the organization. However, he was waived and finished the year at Tucson in the Astros' organization. Righthanded reliever, nothing special.

ROD CORREIA—Correia is a utility infielder at best and won't add any offense. He batted a thin .303 at Triple-A and went 5-for-21 with the Angels.

TIM FORTUGNO—Longtime minor-league lefthander pitched for the White Sox in 1995 and wasn't bad, faring well for the first two months before overuse and a string of bad outings lifted his ERA to 5.59 in 38.2 innings (over 37 games). Traded to California in the Abbott deal, he returned to Triple-A.

RENE GONZALES—Gonzales, now 34, keeps going back to Triple-A and keeps getting cups of coffee in the majors, in 1995 with the Angels, where he went 6-for-18 with a homer. Could be a sixth infielder for some club.

MARK HOLZEMER—Although he has rarely pitched well in the minors, Holzemer keeps getting chances because he is lefthanded and has a good arm. He had a 5.40 ERA in 12 games with the 1995 Angels and ended the year pitching middle relief in Vancouver.

JOSE LIND—Jumped Kansas City in early June and went AWOL for a few weeks, by which point most people had forgotten about him—including the Royals. The Angels signed him and stuck him in the lineup for a few games before deciding that he wasn't the answer. Hit .236 in 140 at-bats; his career may be over.

CARLOS MARTINEZ—The former White Sox and Indians infielder made an unexpected return to the majors in 1995 but didn't stay long, hitting .180 in 61 at-bats with one home run. Hard to envision much of a future for him.

RICH MONTELEONE—Came back from Japan just in time to board the Angels' sinking ship. He allowed two runs in nine innings as a middle reliever and might get another job in 1996.

SCOTT SANDERSON—Most of his 1995 action involved cheering on his Angels teammates, as a back problem that required surgery sidelined him for all but seven starts. He didn't pitch badly, allowing just four walks in 39 innings, but Sanderson can't be counted on for much at his age.

DICK SCHOFIELD—Started the season with the Dodgers, for whom he went 1-for-10, and ended it with the Angels, for whom he was 5-for-20. He could be still be a utilityman somewhere, but more likely Schofield is done.

CHRIS TURNER—A fine athlete who hasn't been able to get over the hump, Turner has lost a chance to be the Angels' regular catcher and might have to start over in another organization. He was just 1-for-10 with California before retreating to Triple-A, where he batted .266.

MITCH WILLIAMS—Retired again, involuntarily, after being released by the Angels, for whom he walked 21 men in 10.2 innings.

Chicago White Sox

ROD BOLTON—Bolton has had a couple of trials with the White Sox but showed a lack of stuff and control both in 1993 and 1995. His best bet is to start again with another organization; had an 8.18 ERA in 22 innings with Chicago last summer.

DOUG BRADY—Brady played in spring replacement games and later in the year had a 30-game hitting streak at Nashville before going 4-for-21 with the White Sox. He can run and hit singles but is mediocre defensively, doesn't walk, and has little power. Played college ball at Liberty University.

OTHER VETERAN PLAYERS

ATLEE HAMMAKER—Didn't pitch badly at Triple-A in 1995, but the Sox seemed afraid to use him, bringing him in 13 times but allowing him to pitch just six innings (in which he walked eight) before shipping him back to Nashville. The story looks about over for the 37-year-old lefty.

JOHN KRUK—His illness and the 1995 layoff left him with only a fraction of his old line-drive power, but Kruk could probably hit .300 with 70 walks a year in his sleep. He's chosen to retire, however.

ISIDRO MARQUEZ—The submarining righthander started the 1995 season with the White Sox but allowed three home runs in 6.2 innings and was quickly sent down, even though he had struck out eight batters. He has pitched well in the minors but might not get another shot.

Cleveland Indians

RUBEN AMARO—Speed and defense have some value, because Amaro has proven that he can't hit major-league pitching. In 1995, he batted .200 in 60 at-bats, but he still made the post-season roster. Let go afterward by the World Champions; more likely to spend most of 1996 in Triple-A than the big leagues.

BUD BLACK—Didn't show much with the Indians (4-2, 6.85 in 47 innings) and appears finished. He fanned 43 and walked only 16, but was waived in July and, by the postseason, had assumed the role of "player-coach."

JOHN FARRELL—Brought up for one game in September, the oft-injured Farrell pitched 4.2 innings for Cleveland without incident. No future in the majors if he continues to pitch.

BROOK FORDYCE—The former Mets catching prospect went 1-for-2 for New York before being waived to the Cleveland organization, where he hit .250 in 176 at-bats for Triple-A Buffalo. His best hope is as a backup, but that even that doesn't look good now. A third-round pick in 1989.

JULIO FRANCO—Signed a deal with Cleveland in early December. Julio didn't have a great year in Japan in 1995, but he can still hit and should help the Indians as a DH/first baseman.

JASON GRIMSLEY—Grimsley is an arm which hasn't got a clue of how to pitch in the major leagues. He walked 32 in 34 innings with the Indians.

JESSE LEVIS—Went 6-for-18 with the Indians, but spent most of the year at Triple-A, where he's likely to spend many more summers. Not a bad player, but doesn't look impressive enough in any area to break through without some luck.

BILLY RIPKEN—Cal's younger sibling has become a crack defensive shortstop, which might win him a utility job in the majors this year. He hit .292 at Buffalo before going 7-for-17 with two homers for the Indians. Ripken is still just 31.

EDDIE "SCOOTER" TUCKER—It's too bad Tucker won't have a career—he's got a good nickname. The catcher played in two cities in 1995, getting two hits in seven tries for Houston but going 0-for-20 with Cleveland.

Detroit Tigers

PAT AHEARNE—Ahearne, a control pitcher with a very short fastball, made three starts and one relief appearance for the Tigers. His 11.70 ERA and .400 opposition average in 10 innings were enough to convince Detroit that Ahearne isn't nearly ready.

MIKE GARDINER—Had one of the year's odder injuries, missing time with a severe allergy. That was his key distinction, as his pitching (20 earned runs in 12.1 innings) won't keep even the Tigers interested.

KIRK GIBSON—Retired in September and can look back on a strong career that included more than one comeback after people thought he was finished.

GREG GOHR—At one time Detroit's top pitching prospect, the hard-throwing Gohr missed most of the season because of injury. However, he came back in September and made 10 relief appearances for the Tigers, giving up just one earned run in 10.1 innings. He may get a chance at the closer's job this spring.

JOE HALL—"Do-It-All" Hall played well at Toledo but was just 2-for-15 with the Tigers. Runs fairly well and can hit a little, but couldn't grab a job. Is beginning to fit the pattern of a Triple-A star.

DWAYNE HENRY—Believe it or not, he saved five games in ten appearances for the Tigers in the last month of the season despite a 6.23 ERA. Is as likely to be their closer in 1996 as is John Hiller.

MIKE MOORE—Was released by the Tigers in late August but still tied for the AL lead in losses. His campaign (5-15, 7.53) was one of the worst in modern memory. Presumably, his career is over.

SEAN WHITESIDE—Pitched 3.2 innings for the Tigers, allowing six earned runs. The young lefty spent most of the year at Double-A. He had been on the 40-player roster last spring and is viewed as something of a

OTHER VETERAN PLAYERS

prospect although his records have been unimpressive to date.

Kansas City Royals

SCOTT ANDERSON—Anderson, a replacement player, hadn't pitched in the majors since 1990, but he did get a win in 1995 despite a 5.33 ERA in 25 innings. No future.

TOM BROWNING—Made two starts for the Royals, pitching 10 innings and allowing nine runs. It would take quite an optimist to see him pitching effectively ever again.

JIM CONVERSE—Traded to Kansas City mid-season, Converse had a 6.56 ERA in 23 innings of middle relief, and even the shortage of lefthanders in the big leagues doesn't mean he'll have a job in the future. Converse has pitched well in Class A, but was promoted way too quickly by Seattle, probably damaging what might have been a decent career.

CHRIS EDDY—Following the 1994 season, Eddy, a young reliever in the Kansas City system, was chosen by the Athletics in the Rule V draft. After six appearances covering 3.2 innings with Oakland, he was returned to the Royals' organization, where he pitched 21 undistinguished games at Triple and Double-A. Eddy is a strikeout pitcher but has some control problems.

JEFF GROTEWOLD—10-for-36 as a pinch-hitter for the Royals, but couldn't stick. Grotewold, who has little defensive value at any spot, is a prototypical 25th player and thus is highly unlikely to have a much of a career.

PHIL HIATT—Dealt to the Tigers in late September as payment for Juan Samuel. Hiatt has power but swings at everything and can't run; a transplant to the outfield proved disastrous. Might get some time at third base for the Tigers, but is more likely to head back to Triple-A. Batted .204 in 113 at-bats for Kansas City before the trade.

FELIX JOSE—Jose started the year with Kansas City but was cut loose after a 4-for-30 start. Signed to the Cubs' Iowa affiliate, he was again dumped just two weeks later. He can't play the outfield or run the bases well, but Jose might still have some bat left if he chooses to come back.

DOUG LINTON—Linton appeared in seven games for Kansas City, pitching 22 innings, before the Royals let him go. He compiled a 7.25 ERA and allowed four home runs. He'll be on somebody's Triple-A roster in 1996.

RUSTY MCGINNIS—The veteran utilityman went 0-for-5 for the Royals, which will probably turn out to be the end of his short major-league career.

HENRY MERCEDES—Brought up to be the Royals' backup catcher when Pat Borders was traded, Mercedes hit .256 in 43 at-bats and performed better than previous reports had indicated he would. Mercedes might get a chance to be a backup in '96.

KEITH MILLER—Batted .333 (5-for-15) with Kansas City. He could have been a good player five years ago or so, if he could have stayed healthy, but he didn't and wasn't.

JOSE MOTA—Began the year as a replacement player and ended it on the DL after tearing a groin muscle. Was 0-for-2 with Kansas City. Career probably over.

DENNIS RASMUSSEN—Inconceivably, was asked back yet again by the Royals. Conceivably, allowed 10 earned runs in 10 innings.

Milwaukee Brewers

JEFF BRONKEY—Returned slowly after missing most of 1994 due to elbow surgery, pitching just eight games for Milwaukee, working 12 innings with a 3.65 ERA. Could still be a long reliever in the majors, but has been released by the Brewers.

ROB DIBBLE—Didn't show anything with his 21 games with the White Sox and Brewers that would lead anybody to think he could pitch effectively again in the majors. Walked an almost unbelievable 46 hitters in just 26.1 innings and allowed 14 runners to steal!

CAL ELDRED—Eldred's several years of hard usage came home to roost as the righthander made four starts (3.42 ERA in 23.2 innings) before landing on the disabled list with right elbow ligament damage that required season-ending—and career-threatening—surgery.

MIKE IGNASIAK—Spent much of the season in the Brewers' bullpen, posting a 4-1 record in 25 games, but had a horrid 5.90 ERA in 39.2 innings, allowing 51 hits and 23 walks. He'll be back but whether he can be effective again is another question.

JAMIE MCANDREW—McAndrew, who was a replacement player, pitched in ten games for Milwaukee, posting a 2-3 record and a 4.71 ERA, but strained his right knee and was finished for the season. He's a borderline prospect at best.

OTHER VETERAN PLAYERS

JOSE MERCEDES—Mercedes pitched seven innings for Milwaukee, walking eight. He missed most of the year with a nerve problem in his pitching elbow and is years away from being ready to pitch effectively in the majors.

AL REYES—Reyes was a Rule V draftee from the Expos' system and pitched quite well for the Brewers in the first two months of 1995, fashioning a 2.43 ERA and 29 strikeouts in 33.1 innings before tearing an elbow ligament. The resulting surgery finished him for the year and he may not pitch in 1996.

JOE SLUSARSKI—The former Athletics righty had a good outing or two with the Brewers, and was suddenly being loosely talked up as a future closer. By the end of the year, he had pitched 12 games (15 innings) and had allowed 21 hits and 9 earned runs. Slusarski is, and has always been, incapable of pitching effectively in the majors.

TURNER WARD—Ward is a fifth outfielder at best and barely hits enough to fill that role. He missed most of 1995 with a hamstring injury, batting .264 with 4 homers in 129 at-bats when healthy.

Minnesota Twins

BERNARDO BRITO—Brito, 32, has now hit over 300 homers in the minor leagues. His only hit in five at-bats with Minnesota in 1995 was—a home run. Brito has no speed or defensive value, and would probably strike out enough that he couldn't play in the bigs, but he's earned a shot by now.

KEVIN CAMPBELL—A veteran righthander without great stuff or good control, he had a 4.66 ERA in 9.2 innings with the 1995 Twins. He's not going to get a foothold.

GREG W. HARRIS—He looks nothing like the pitcher who was effective with the Padres a few years ago. After going 0-5 with an 8.82 ERA in 7 games (6 starts) with the Twins, allowing 50 hits in 32.2 innings, Harris sure looks done.

VINCE HORSMAN—The veteran lefty couldn't even stick around with the Twins, being bombed back to Triple-A after AL hitters pounded out 12 hits (including two homers) against him in just nine innings.

KEVIN MAAS—Started the season as the Twins' lefty DH, but provided just one homer in 57 at-bats and a .193 average before the Twins pulled the plug. It may be over for him.

MO SANFORD—He has a terrific curve but little else, and a 5.30 ERA in 18.2 innings (16 walks) punched his ticket from Minnesota back to Triple-A.

CARL WILLIS—Willis is probably finished after giving up seven earned runs in just ⅔ of an inning for the Twins.

New York Yankees

SCOTT BANKHEAD—Battled injury over the last few years, and pitched ineffectively with the Yankees (6.00 ERA in 39 innings, nine home runs allowed), who released him over the summer. Could conceivably come back since he's returned from serious injury before, but it's unlikely.

ROBERT EENHOORN—The Dutch Treat has a terrific glove at shortstop but has been bypassed on the Yankee org chart because he can't hit a lick. Was 2-for-14 with New York in 1995.

DAVE EILAND—The Yankees brought him into four games in 1995, and he responded by allowing 16 hits in 10 innings, including five doubles. He's past done.

JIMMY KEY—The talented lefthander followed up his great 1994 season by tearing up his rotator cuff, which led to season-ending (and career-threatening) surgery. Key, who is now 34, made just five appearances for the 1995 Yankees, going 1-2 with a 5.64 ERA. Look for a comeback sometime this summer, but proceed with caution.

JOSIAS MANZANILLO—Starting the season with the Mets, he showed little of what made him effective in 1994. He appeared in 12 games, throwing 16 innings, and racked up a 7.88 ERA before being placed on waivers June 5. Moving across town to the Yankees, Manzanillo pitched effectively in 11 games before going on the disabled list in early July with a sore elbow that sidelined him the rest of the season.

JEFF PATTERSON—The veteran righty pitched three times for the Yankees, allowing a run in 3.1 innings. Not a prospect.

DAVE PAVLAS—A Cub in 1990 and 1991, Pavlas came to New York as a replacement player. His recall in July rankled many, but Pavlas was forgotten quickly after pitching just 5.2 innings, allowing eight hits and two runs. Won't ever be back.

Oakland Athletics

SCOTT BAKER—Baker, a 25-year-old lefthander, is a finesse pitcher with control problems who went 4-7, 5.28

OTHER VETERAN PLAYERS

at Triple-A in 1995. He also pitched once for the Athletics, allowing four runs in a 3.2 inning relief stint. He's not likely to cash many more big-league paychecks.

RON DARLING—Oakland finally disconnected life support on Darling in August, after he had made 21 starts and racked up a 6.23 ERA in 104 innings. AL batters, who had socked 16 homers off him in 1995, were sorry to see Darling go.

BRIAN HARPER—Retired in May after going just 0-for-7 for Oakland.

STEVE KARSAY—Former top prospect who missed the whole year because of a sore elbow. Might come back, might not.

DAVE STEWART—He was still throwing hard in August, but couldn't pitch effectively and decided to retire after Oakland cut him loose. Was just 3-7 with a 6.89 ERA in 81 innings, but won't be remembered for that. Stewart, a class guy, was deservedly popular with Oakland fans.

BILLY TAYLOR—After a good debut in 1994, Taylor tore ligaments in his knee and missed all of last season. Will pitch again in the bigs if healthy.

ANDY TOMBERLIN—A minor-league veteran outfielder with some line-drive power, defensive skill, and speed, Tomberlin hit .212 with four homers in 85 at-bats for the Athletics before he was shipped back to Triple-A. Tomberlin could get a few more cups of coffee before he's through.

STEVE WOJCIECHOWSKI—"Wojo" (of course) was 2-3, 5.18 in 14 games for the Athletics, including seven starts. He's got no fastball, and walked 28 men in his 48.2 innings for Oakland. Wojciechowski is highly unlikely to be back.

Seattle Mariners

LEE GUETTERMAN—Guetterman's unexpected return to the majors with Seattle (23 games, 17 innings pitched) wasn't particularly successful, as his ERA was 6.88 and AL hitters had a .300 average. There is almost no chance he will continue to hang around.

GREG HIBBARD—A torn rotator cuff kept him out all season and will likely be the end of his effectiveness if he does come back.

KEVIN KING—King, a marginal lefthander, pitched in 3.2 innings for Seattle, allowing five runs, before being shipped out. Unlikely to have a big-league career.

CHAD KREUTER—His 1994 hitting prowess now appears to have been a mirage: he hit .227 in 75 at-bats before the Mariners dumped him, obviously not feeling his bat would recover. Kreuter will probably return to the majors with some club in 1996.

BILL KRUEGER—Krueger should have retired several years ago, but pitched 27.2 innings with the Mariners and Padres in 1995 to prove the point. He allowed 50 hits in his thankfully short tenure.

GARY THURMAN—Still runs well, but couldn't stick in Seattle despite hitting .320 in 25 at-bats and swiping 5 bases. Might get another shot with somebody this year, and could be a decent reserve outfielder.

Texas Rangers

STEVE BUECHELE—The veteran opened the season as the Cubs' third baseman, but continued to hit so poorly (.188 with 3 extra-base hits in 32 games) that Chicago cut him loose shortly after acquiring Todd Zeile. Texas picked up the popular Buechele later in the summer, but quickly recognized he wouldn't solve their third base problem and jettisoned him almost immediately. Highly unlikely to return.

TERRY BURROWS—Burrowed his way into the Rangers' bullpen in 1995, but quickly tunneled his way back to Triple-A with a 6.45 ERA in 44.2 innings spread over 28 games. He allowed an almost unfathomable 11 home runs in Texas. Underwent shoulder surgery this winter.

JOHN DETTMER—A fairly good prospect, Dettmer pitched a third of an inning for Texas before being traded to the Orioles in July for Jack Voigt.

HECTOR FAJARDO—Placed on the disqualified list by the Rangers after he refused to go to Triple-A. He had allowed 13 runs in 15 innings for Texas. The Expos wound up with him by the end of the season. For years, we've been hearing about this guy's potential, but . . .

ERIC FOX—The veteran flychaser can play good defense and has flying feet, but doesn't hit enough to stick around. 0-for-15 for the 1995 Rangers.

SHAWN HARE—Has been with the Tigers, Mets, and Rangers in the last two years. After hitting .250 in 24 at-bats for Texas in 1995, he's going to keep moving.

BILLY HATCHER—The longtime semi-regular outfielder began the season in Texas but was cast out after a 1-for-12 performance. Probably finished.

OTHER VETERAN PLAYERS

SAM HORN—Came to spring training as a replacement player and got nine late-season at-bats with Texas, collecting one hit. Finished.

CHRIS HOWARD—An undistinguished but potentially decent lefthanded reliever, Howard pitched four innings in four games for Texas, allowing no runs. Has been a member of four organizations in a 10-year career that began as a first baseman.

JOHN MARZANO—Former Red Sox catcher played two games for the Rangers, collecting two hits in six at-bats. Might have a chance to come back in 1996 if someone's desperate.

CHRIS NICHTING—The hard-throwing former Dodgers' prospect had three stints with the Rangers, racking up a 7.03 ERA in 24 innings. Might still have a career, as he pitched extremely well at Triple-A.

DAN SMITH—The Rangers' lefthander missed the season with left elbow trouble. He was the team's #1 draft pick in 1990 and has been regarded as a good prospect, but has had very serious shoulder and elbow problems over the last three years.

JACK VOIGT—Voigt hit .175 in 63 at-bats for the Rangers. If he doesn't hit, he won't play, and is looking for a new organization for '96.

CRAIG WORTHINGTON—Batted .278 in 18 at-bats for the Reds, then went back to Triple-A before the Rangers, desperate for someone to play third base, summoned him. The incredibly slow Worthington got 68 at-bats for Texas, hitting .221 and convincing Johnny Oates that another solution was needed.

Toronto Blue Jays

GIOVANNI CARRARA—The desperate Blue Jays plucked the undistinguished righthander out of Triple-A, where he had been 7-7, 3.96. He was bad with Toronto, compiling a 2-4 record and a 7.21 ERA in 12 games, seven of them starts. He allowed ten homers and 25 walks in 48.2 innings.

BRAD CORNETT—Pitched just five innings with the Jays due to elbow problems. His season ended in July after surgery to repair the ulnar collateral ligament.

DARREN HALL—Underwent right elbow surgery after pitching just 16.1 innings in 17 appearances and notching three saves for Toronto. Hall will try to come back this spring, but he didn't have great stuff before his injury.

RICO JORDAN—A promising lefthanded reliever, Jordan fashioned a 6.57 ERA in his first 12 innings of Triple-A experience in 1995 before being brought to Toronto, where he walked 13 in 15 innings and compiled a 6.60 ERA for the Blue Jays. To say he's not ready would be an understatement.

JIMMY ROGERS—A big righthander who missed all of 1992 after elbow surgery, Rogers made the Jays' staff for 19 games in his eighth season in the system. Control has always been a problem for him, and he walked 18 in 23.2 innings for Toronto. Rogers strikes out a lot of hitters and could conceivably be a 10th man.

DUANE WARD—Ward returned to the Jays bullpen in 1995, allowing eight earned runs, five walks, and 11 hits in 2.2 innings. He then headed back to the DL to rest his aching shoulder. If he comes back successfully, it'll be the story of the season.

NATIONAL LEAGUE

Atlanta Braves

STEVE BEDROSIAN—The 14-year veteran made the Braves staff out of spring training, but pitched poorly when used in long relief, allowing 40 hits (including six homers) in 28 innings and was released in August. He has announced his retirement.

EDDIE GIOVANOLA—Went just 1-for-14 with the Braves, but ended up on the World Series roster when Jeff Blauser went down. Utility infield prospect at best, but he did hit .321 at Triple-A.

BRIAN KOWITZ—Hit .167 in 10 games for the Braves. Kowitz is an interesting prospect who might be a decent reserve outfielder in the majors, but is unlikely to break through with Atlanta.

ROD NICHOLS—Called up for a short time during the summer by Atlanta, Nichols pitched 6.2 innings and allowed 14 hits and five walks. He's now 31, has a career record of 11-31, and is highly unlikely to ever get another prolonged shot at the major leagues.

EDDIE PEREZ—In his ninth year of pro ball, he finally made the majors, going 4-for-13 with the Braves in September before making the postseason roster. His hitting record is very, very poor, but his defense is said to be quite good. Could be the backup if Atlanta doesn't re-sign Charlie O'Brien.

THE SCOUTING REPORT 1996

OTHER VETERAN PLAYERS

MIKE SHARPERSON—He's been stuck at Triple-A for the last few seasons, but can hit, runs fairly well, and is as good as many utility men in the majors. Sharperson, now 34, had one hit in seven tries with the 1995 Braves but needs a big break to get anything more than that this year. May go to spring training with San Diego.

TOM THOBE—The lefty has pitched very well as a middle reliever in the Braves' chain and got into three games in the majors during September. Could break through.

BRAD WOODALL—Looked to be a very good prospect for Atlanta a year ago, but the lefty had a miserable, injury-ridden season at Richmond in 1995. Went 1-1 with a 6.10 ERA in 10 innings with the Braves.

Chicago Cubs

TOM EDENS—Got into five games with the Cubs but finished the year at Triple-A and was released in late September. He could resurface somewhere, as he's just as good as some of the 10th and 11th pitchers in the major leagues and has a fairly good track record. Edens is 34.

RICH GARCES—Chicago claimed him from the Twins in 1994 on waivers and gave him a chance in Chicago. However, he failed to impress in seven games and was again waived, this time being claimed by Florida where he got hit hard but did strike out 16 in 13 innings. He's got a good mix of stuff but inconsistent control and still may not be ready to contribute yet.

JOSE GUZMAN—Has not pitched since early 1994 due to lingering shoulder problems. Guzman is signed through 1996, which is why he is in this book. The Cubs say he'll try again this spring.

JOE KMAK—The veteran minor-leaguer played reasonably well in a backup role for the Cubs, hitting .245 in 19 games and playing good defense. However, he's a marginal player who is 32 years old and ended the year on the disabled list after undergoing knee surgery. The Cubs have at least three catchers they like better than Kmak.

CHRIS NABHOLZ—Pitched 34 games for the Cubs, working just 23 innings as a one-out lefty. Had a 5.40 ERA for the Cubs and struggled with control before going back to Triple-A Iowa, where his ERA was a keen 6.41. Nabholz really belongs in somebody's starting rotation rather than the bullpen, and someday might get another shot. Really not that bad a pitcher.

TODD PRATT—Expected to fill the backup catching role in Chicago, Pratt instead bombed miserably. He played awful defense and batted just .133 in 60 at-bats stretched over 25 games, striking out 21 times. The Cubs released him from his Triple-A contract late in 1995. Career in certain jeopardy.

KEVIN ROBERSON—The switch-hitting outfielder couldn't break out of a reserve role with the Cubs despite good power (four homers, three as a pinch-hitter, in just 38 at-bats in 1995). He was waived in July and claimed by Seattle, then sent to Triple-A where he hit six homers in 157 at-bats but again showed his main weakness, striking out 51 times. Has to either improve his defense or his knowledge of the strike zone to be a fifth outfielder in the big leagues.

RYNE SANDBERG—Decided in October that he wanted to come back to the Cubs, who he perceived were now going in a good direction on and off the field. While it'll be nice to see him back, his talents appeared to have deteriorated in 1993-94, and his future success is far from guaranteed. He will apparently be playing second base and could hit .270 with 18 homers, or he could be hitting .195 at the end of May and decide to quit.

DAVE SWARTZBAUGH—His callup to the Cubs was surprising since his minor-league record has been mediocre. However, he didn't give up a run in his seven appearances for Chicago and could sneak into the bullpen this year. Long relief is his best hope.

Cincinnati Reds

DAMON BERRYHILL—Did not contribute much to the Reds' success, batting .183 with two homers in 82 at-bats. It's hard to see what he brings to a ballclub, since he can't hit and doesn't play good defense anymore, but he continues to stick around. Now 32 years old and a third catcher at best.

MATT GROTT—Grott, a mediocre six-year lefty who doesn't throw hard, was a Rule V pick by the Reds from the Expos' system. He allowed four runs in 1.2 innings for Cincinnati and was 7-4 for Triple-A Indianapolis. Not a prospect.

BRIAN R. HUNTER—He's not able to find any playing time with the Reds and has become injury-prone in the last couple of years. Hunter hit just .215 with one homer in 79 at-bats last season, but if he is healthy, could still hit 20-25 homers somewhere if given 300 platoon at-bats. He doesn't run well and hasn't any defensive value.

BRAD PENNINGTON—He still throws an outstanding fastball with great movement and still hasn't got the slightest bit of control. Walked 11 in 9.2 innings for the

OTHER VETERAN PLAYERS

Reds and another 21 in 14 innings at Indianapolis. Now Boston property.

RICK REED—Reed came to spring camp as a replacement player. Upon his mid-July callup to Cincinnati, he made one good start but the move caused some clubhouse disharmony. When Reed pitched poorly in his next three appearances, he was shipped right back to Indianapolis. Allowed five home runs in 17 major-league innings.

MIKE REMLINGER—Even being lefthanded couldn't keep Remlinger around for long. The Reds got him on May 11 from the Mets, but they said goodbye within days. Pitched seven times in the NL in 1995, allowing nine hits and five walks in 6.2 innings. Hasn't ever pitched well in the majors despite once being a top prospect.

JOHN ROPER—Sent to the Giants in the Deion Sanders trade but never actually pitched for them. With the Reds, he worked just eight innings, allowing 11 earned runs. Roper underwent surgery on both shoulders in September and is questionable for 1996.

JOHNNY RUFFIN—Spent most of the year on the disabled list following serious knee surgery. He struck out 11 and allowed just four hits in 13 innings, but also walked 11. If he's healthy, he'll come back and be a big part of the Cincinnati bullpen. One note of caution: power pitchers rely heavily on their knees.

PETE SMITH—The formerly promising righthander has been plagued by shoulder problems most of the last six years and is now a batting practice-level pitcher. He worked in 11 games (24 innings) with the 1995 Reds, allowing 30 hits—including a monstrous eight homers—and fashioning a 6.66 ERA. Only a desperate team would give Smith a look in 1996, but there are a lot of desperate ballclubs.

FRANK VIOLA—After tearing his elbow up in 1994, Viola came back last summer and got three starts with the Reds. He was rusty, to put it kindly, giving up 20 hits in 14 innings, and was quickly re-disabled by Cincinnati. Could come back this spring but is very unlikely to be any good.

Colorado Rockies

JORGE BRITO—Brito spent nine years in the minors before getting a shot with the Rockies last spring. He has some defensive ability but hit just .216 with three doubles and 17 strikeouts in 51 at-bats in Colorado and isn't very likely to return to the big leagues.

PEDRO CASTELLANO—Now appears to have lost all prospect status. Was 0-for-5 for the Rockies and batted just .266 at hitter-friendly Colorado Springs.

ROBERTO MEJIA—Attitude and bat problems have moved him from top second base prospect in Colorado to second-stringer at Colorado Springs. Hit .294 in Triple-A after going 8-for-52 with the Rockies. It's too early to give up on him, but Don Baylor may not agree.

DAVID NIED—Elbow problems have thrown a wrench into Nied's career. Expected to be the club's #2 starter, he instead pitched just 4.1 innings for Colorado, allowing 10 earned runs. In a minor league rehab at Triple-A, Nied walked 25 in 31 innings. Nied won't be back at 100% this season, and whether he can ever fully rely on his impressive hard sinker again is in question.

MATT NOKES—Signed by the Orioles, he quickly chafed at his bench role and asked for his release. Nokes then signed with Colorado and got only two hits in 11 at-bats when promoted in September. He can still hit for power, but has precious little value outside of that.

HARVEY PULLIAM—The former Royals' outfielder resuscitated his career by hitting .327 with 25 homers at hitting-happy Colorado Springs and got two hits in five at-bats (including a homer) for the Rockies in September. He's not bad and could be on somebody's bench in 1996.

A.J. SAGER—After being cut loose by the Padres in 1994, Sager signed with the Rockies and got into 10 early-season games in Colorado without showing much. A 7.36 ERA in 14 innings will probably scare off most suitors this year.

JIM TATUM—Nosed out of the Rockies' #1 pinch-hitting spot by John VanderWal, Tatum got his release in mid-season after hitting .235 in 34 at-bats. He couldn't immediately hook on anywhere and instead signed a Triple-A contract with his old employers. Tatum batted .323 with six homers in 98 at-bats in Colorado Springs and was snapped up by the Red Sox this winter. Could still be a useful bat in the big leagues.

MARK THOMPSON—Thompson, a second-round pick in 1992, hasn't pitched well since 1993, when he was skipped from the California League to the PCL. He compiled a 2-3 mark for the Rockies in 1995 with a 6.53 ERA in 51 innings, making five starts and 16 relief appearances. He's stalled, and may need to go all the way back to Double-A to regain his confidence.

OTHER VETERAN PLAYERS

Florida Marlins

RYAN BOWEN—After missing most of 1994 with torn knee ligaments, he returned for three starts in September. Bowen appears to be the same pitcher as before: he struck out 15 batters in 16.2 innings, walked 12, and allowed 23 hits. Expect him to contend for a rotation spot this spring even though he really needs more time at Triple-A.

MARIO DIAZ—The itinerant utilityman got into 49 games with the Marlins, batting .230 in 87 at-bats with one home run and one walk. He's a decent defensive infielder, but he's also 34, slow, and has little offensive value.

MATT DUNBAR—The lefty started the year on the Marlins' roster and pitched in eight games, but spent most of the 1995 season on the disabled list. Has been a middle reliever his entire six-year pro career.

BUDDY GROOM—After getting into 23 games with the Tigers, posting a 7.52 ERA (and his first big-league win), Groom was waived and claimed by the Marlins. He pitched 14 games there, notching a 7.20 ERA and allowing 26 hits in 15 innings. If he were righthanded, he'd be sitting in the stands instead of the dugout.

BRYAN HARVEY—Harvey pitched to three batters last year, allowing two hits and a walk, before undergoing elbow surgery that ended his season and put his career in jeopardy. He has missed large amounts of action in three of the last four seasons because of that aching elbow. For a pitcher who throws as hard with as much movement as Harvey did, elbow injuries are about the worst thing that can happen. He'll try to make a comeback, but little can reasonably be expected.

JEREMY HERNANDEZ—The reasonably promising Hernandez missed most of 1994 with a herniated disc in his neck and only pitched in seven games in 1995 as he recovered from surgery to repair the disc. Hernandez is expected to be healthy in 1996 and could contend for a spot in the Florida bullpen. Control has been a problem at times.

JOHN JOHNSTONE—Pitched 4.2 innings with the Marlins, allowing seven hits and two walks, then was disabled most of the rest of the season with an elbow problem which required surgery.

RUSS MORMAN—Morman got into 34 games with the 1995 Marlins when injuries felled some of their regular outfielders. He didn't do badly, hitting .279 with three homers in 72 at-bats, but at age 34 has no future as a major-league regular and little hope of even sticking around as a reserve.

ROB MURPHY—At one time, Murphy was a durable and talented reliever. Now, he's 35 and hanging by a thread. He got into 14 games with the Dodgers and Marlins last year and pitched about as badly as he could, allowing 18 hits and eight walks (three homers) in 12 innings.

BOB NATAL—He has played fairly well at times as a backup in the majors, but last year appeared in only 16 games for Florida in 1995. His future is, obviously, limited after he batted just .233 in 43 at-bats.

RICH SCHEID—Scheid, a minor-league veteran, pitched surprisingly well for the Marlins in 1994 but could not get an extended audition last season. After hurling just 10 innings and allowing 21 baserunners, he may not get back to the majors again.

Houston Astros

MIKE BRUMLEY—The 33-year-old Brumley got one hit in 1995 in 18 at-bats with the Astros. The fact that it was a pinch-hit homer in a key September game won't prevent him from again trudging back to Triple-A.

JERRY GOFF—It was a surprise when Goff spent a few weeks as a backup with the 1995 Astros, but it wasn't a surprise that he hit .154 in 26 at-bats.

PEDRO A. MARTINEZ—Acquired from San Diego in December 1994's Padres-Astros megadeal, Martinez was expected to be Houston's key lefthanded reliever. Unfortunately, his earlier control troubles worsened, leading to a 7.40 ERA in 21 innings for the Astros. Dealt back to the Padres this winter, he'll try again in 1996. Not yet out of chances.

CRAIG MCMURTRY—McMurtry's presence caused serious harm to the Astros' pennant chances, both on the mound where he pitched 11 games and allowed 24 baserunners over 10 innings, and in the clubhouse, where he was far from welcome due to his status as a springtime replacement player. It's hard to see why owner Drayton McLane thought that making this sort of statement was appropriate with his team in the middle of a pennant race, but McMurtry's career appears to be over.

ANDY STANKIEWICZ—Stankiewicz is a moderately gifted, overachieving utility player with some speed, a fair glove, and decent strike-zone judgment. He could stick in 1996, but didn't help himself by batting .115 in 52 at-bats spread over 43 games last season. Nagging injuries have been a problem.

OTHER VETERAN PLAYERS

Los Angeles Dodgers

JIM BRUSKE—A converted outfielder, Bruske made his big-league debut at age 31 for the Dodgers. He pitched in nine games, allowing five earned runs in 10 innings. Has good stuff, but isn't likely to do anything special.

OMAR DAAL—The Dodgers have been desperate for lefthanded relief for several years, and Daal hasn't taken advantage of the opportunity. Last year, he pitched 28 times but totaled only 20 innings. Daal was miserable, notching a 7.20 ERA and walking 15.

NOE MUNOZ—Served as the Dodgers' third catcher when Mike Piazza was injured, getting one at-bat. Has good defensive skills, but is a weak hitter and needs lots of time in the minors.

RICK PARKER—Parker got into 27 games with the Dodgers, hitting .276 in 29 at-bats. He's not really good enough to be even a fifth outfielder, but Tommy Lasorda frequently keeps veterans around even if they're not producing.

TOM PRINCE—When Mike Piazza got hurt, Prince played 18 games as a backup until he, too, got hurt. Prince can throw and has a little power, but he's not going anywhere.

EDDIE PYE—Pye has now spent the last five years at Triple-A Albuquerque, where he consistently hits .300 without convincing the Dodgers that he can play in the majors. He went 0-for-8 for L.A. last year.

RUDY SEANEZ—He finally wore out his welcome in L.A. by giving up one too many game-winning hits. Seanez has a terrific arm but can't get much over the plate. In 1995, he pitched in 37 games with three saves, but was 1-3 and fashioned a 6.75 ERA, walking 18 and allowing 39 hits in 35 innings.

REGGIE WILLIAMS—The 30-year-old flychaser opened the year with the Dodgers but went 1-for-11 and was quickly packed off to Triple-A. He can run, but just doesn't hit enough to stick.

Montreal Expos

TAVO ALVAREZ—Alvarez missed all of 1994 with a torn rotator cuff. He fared well in short stints at Double- and Triple-A in 1995 before coming to the Expos, where he was 1-5 in eight starts with a 6.75 ERA. He has lost velocity and can't afford the bouts of poor control he experienced in Montreal.

LUIS AQUINO—Aquino pitched terribly in 1995, becoming a boo-bird target in Montreal before moving on to San Francisco and not winning many friends there. He allowed 57 hits (including six homers) in 42 innings, and finished 0-3 with two saves and a 5.10 ERA. Can probably pitch Triple-A as long as he wants and may be better off there for awhile where he can work on recovering his effectiveness.

JOSE DELEON—An occasionally effective reliever who throws screwballs almost exclusively, DeLeon allowed a 5.19 ERA in 38 games with the White Sox before the Expos acquired him late in August. In Montreal, DeLeon struck out 12 in eight innings but also allowed seven earned runs. He's no sure bet to be pitching anywhere in 1996.

BRYAN EVERSGERD—Felipe Alou finally got a lefty for the bullpen, but Eversgerd was terrible: 25 games, 21 innings, 5.14 ERA, eight strikeouts. Eversgerd isn't really that bad and could get another trial.

TOM FOLEY—The veteran utility infielder had a very long career but has retired to move into player development.

WILLIE FRASER—The 32-year-old Fraser didn't impress by allowing six home runs in 25 innings. In 22 games, he was 2-1 with a 5.61 ERA and two saves. Probably finished, but who knows?

TIM SPEHR—In August, he was sidelined when a testicular tumor was discovered and removed via surgery. Spehr should be able to return in 1996, but will again have to battle Tim Laker for reserve at-bats. Last season, Spehr hit .257 in 35 at-bats with one homer.

JOE SIDDALL—Came up to be the Expos' third-string catcher last fall when Tim Spehr went down. He got three hits in 10 at-bats. Siddall has now had two cups of coffee in the majors, two more than anticipated.

New York Mets

JEFF BARRY—Barry is an outfielder owned by the Mets who doesn't have overpowering skill or performance in any category but got 15 at-bats with the Mets anyway, collecting two hits.

MIKE BIRKBECK—The 34-year-old veteran made four early-season starts (27 innings) with the Mets, walking only two and ending 0-1 with a nice 1.63 ERA for New York. He was then sold to the Yokohama Bay Stars.

DON FLORENCE—He earned his ticket to New York by compiling an 0.96 ERA in 41 games as a middle reliever at Triple-A Norfolk. With the Mets, Florence was 3-0 in 12 innings, allowing just one extra-base hit but

OTHER VETERAN PLAYERS

walking six. He spent seven years in the Red Sox organization before 1995 but might surface in the big leagues again.

KEVIN LOMON—After a few unspectacular years in the Braves' system, Lomon was drafted by the Mets and began the 1995 season in the major leagues. He pitched six games for New York, allowing 17 hits in 9.1 innings before being sent back to the Atlanta organization.

DAVE TELGHEDER—Short on stuff, Telgheder got into six games last year and was 1-2 with a 5.61 ERA in 26 innings. He allowed 34 hits, four of them homers. He'll probably get a few more trials in the majors but isn't likely to stick anywhere.

Philadelphia Phillies

KYLE ABBOTT—He didn't show much after coming back from Japan. Abbott, pitching entirely in middle relief, was 2-0 for the Phillies with a 3.81 ERA in 18 games. He fanned 21 in 28 innings but also walked 16. Abbott could be a tenth pitcher but shouldn't be asked to do more than that.

GARY BENNETT—Got one at-bat for the Phillies while serving as a third catcher in September. Hasn't hit above the .230s since the Florida State League.

JIM DESHAIES—After pitching nearly as bad as possible in 1994, he made it back to the majors in 1995. He made two starts for Philadelphia and allowed 12 earned runs—and three homers—in five innings.

PAUL FLETCHER—For a few minutes a couple of years ago, he was a phenom. Fletcher had a 5.40 ERA in 13 innings with the 1995 Phillies. Judgment is best reserved.

STEVE FREY—An encouraging late-season performance (2.12 ERA in 18 games, 17 innings) could keep the veteran lefty pitching somewhere this season. However, he did bomb out in Seattle last spring, pitched badly in 1994, and is 32.

BOBBY MUNOZ—Munoz is yet another talented pitcher who had a serious injury that was initially thought to be minor. Munoz made three starts in 1995 amidst denials of serious medical problems, endured some criticism from his manager, and finally was shut down for elbow surgery. No way to be sure if he'll come back.

OMAR OLIVARES—Olivares was terrible for the Rockies and, later, the Phillies in 1995, with 1-4 record and a 6.91 ERA. He walked 23 and allowed 55 hits in 42 innings.

RANDY READY—The star of one of MLB's best 1995 commercials, the much-traveled Ready got into 23 games for the Phillies, batting .138 in 29 at-bats before being released yet again. His career is probably over.

KEVIN SEFCIK—Sefcik, who played shortstop for Double-A Reading in 1995, has some skills but needs more development. Has hit for average in the minors.

DENNIS SPRINGER—The Phillies gave the former Dodgers' knuckleballer, a nine-year pro, his first major league action in 1995. He made four starts, going 0-3 with a 4.84 ERA in 22 innings. Pitched decently at Scranton last summer and may get some more big-league starts to see what he can do.

DAVID WEST—After just eight starts and a 3-2 record, shoulder problems shut West down. His injury required surgery and is serious enough that pitching in 1996 is questionable. Shoulder injuries mainly affect velocity, and throwing hard was West's only real strength.

Pittsburgh Pirates

STEVE COOKE—He sat out the entire 1995 season with a sore left shoulder. Cooke, an anomaly among left-handed finesse pitchers (he gets most of his outs on fly balls) was never a sure bet to be effective, and he's even less likely to be a winner now. However, Pittsburgh is thin on pitching and Cooke will get every opportunity to come back in 1996.

JIM GOTT—Gott was expected to be Dan Miceli's mentor in 1995, but the veteran righthander went down with elbow problems in early August. The resulting surgery will keep him out of action until sometime this spring and possibly for most of 1996. He was just 2-4 with a 6.03 ERA in 25 games with three saves when he was disabled. He's got a limited future even if healthy.

LEE HANCOCK—Made the majors in his eighth pro season, pitching in 11 games for the Pirates. He wasn't bad, allowing just 12 baserunners in 14 innings and posting a 1.93 ERA, but will be hard pressed to escape the "organization pitcher" tag. Hancock has spent the last six years at Double and Triple-A.

DENNIS KONUSZEWSKI—The hard-throwing Konuszewski was in the Carolina League in 1994, but made it to Pittsburgh for one game last season. He allowed three hits and a walk in $\frac{1}{3}$ of an inning. He was 7-7 at Double-A and was on the 40-player winter roster.

RAVELO MANZANILLO—After a surprisingly good, but still walk-filled, 1994 season, the Pirates sent him down to Triple-A after just 3.2 innings in 1995. He didn't

OTHER VETERAN PLAYERS

find his control at Calgary, allowing 10 walks in 12 innings there. A long shot to ever make it back.

ROSS POWELL—Neither Houston nor Pittsburgh got much out of Powell, a diminutive lefthander with a funky motion but below-average control. He pitched in 27 games in 1995, totaling 29.2 innings, walking 21 and allowing six homers. Final record was 0-2, 6.98. He'll be back sometime.

MACKEY SASSER—Apparently retired after being released by Pittsburgh in May, after he had batted .154 in 26 at-bats.

GARY WILSON—Wilson, a durable righthander with marginal stuff, rarely walks anybody and got into ten games (14.1 innings) with the Pirates last summer. However, he missed most of the season due to injury.

St. Louis Cardinals

RAMON CARABALLO—The former Braves' middle infield prospect surfaced in St. Louis last season because of injuries to other players. He smacked two homers within his first two weeks after coming up, but that was about it as Ramon batted .202 with only three RBI in 34 games. His defense is pretty good, though.

DARNELL COLES—Was dumped without ceremony in August after batting .225 in 138 at-bats with three home runs. Coles can probably come back and sign a Triple-A contract with somebody if he wants, but he has no defensive value and hasn't been a productive hitter for two years. He turns 34 in June.

DOUG CREEK—Creek, a former starter, moved to the bullpen in 1995 and pitched very well at Double-A and pretty well at Triple-A before joining the Cardinals for six games, during which he fanned 10 and didn't allow a run in 6.2 innings. Could come on, but control has been a problem.

RAY GIANNELLI—Giannelli got in a few at-bats with the 1991 Blue Jays, and after hitting .295 with 16 homers at Louisville, he got the call to St. Louis and collected one hit in 11 times up. He could be a decent utility man/lefty pinch-hitter in the majors, but doesn't play great defense and needs a serious break.

TIM HULETT—Released in May after getting just 11 at-bats with the Cardinals. His career is probably over.

MANUEL LEE—Lee went 1-for-1 for St. Louis before hitting the DL on April 28 with a severe ankle sprain. After that, he went on a rehab assignment to Triple-A but didn't resurface. He could come back this spring, and with a needy team, he could play a role.

VINCENTE PALACIOS—A fringy pitcher even if healthy, Palacios appeared in 20 games, pitching 40.1 innings for the Cardinals, going 2-3 with a 5.80 ERA. He sat out from June 22 through the end of the season with tendinitis in his shoulder and looks to be bound for Triple-A again.

RICH RODRIGUEZ—Rodriguez had been a bullpen workhorse for several years, but pitched just one game with the Cardinals before shoulder tendinitis forced him to the sidelines for the rest of the season. Uncertain future.

CHRIS SABO—His miserable performance as the White Sox' DH (.254, one homer, five RBI in 71 at-bats) and his whining at being platooned punched his ticket out of Chicago. St. Louis signed Sabo and gave him 13 at-bats, in which he collected two hits, then sent him packing. Sabo might come back in 1996 and, if he accepts that he's 34 and no longer capable of playing every day, he could be a righthanded role player. Don't bet on it.

San Diego Padres

BILLY BEAN—Went 0-for-7 with the Padres. His short major-league career was never impressive and may be finished. He hit .290 with 15 homers as a regular outfielder in Las Vegas, which translates to a lot less in any normal-sized, normal-altitude park.

DONNIE ELLIOTT—Elliott pitched two scoreless innings for San Diego before being sent to the sidelines April 24 with a "sore shoulder"; he was released after the season. Middling prospect if healthy, his career could be over.

TIM HYERS—He was a Rule V pick in 1994 and spent the whole year rotting away on the Padres' bench. Last season he went 0-for-5 with San Diego and batted .290 with one homer at hitter-happy Las Vegas. Not an impressive player in any way, although his defense is pretty good.

LUIS LOPEZ—Tore elbow ligaments in his right elbow during spring training and missed the whole year after undergoing surgery. If he can throw, he'll vie for a utility spot this spring.

TIM MAUSER—Mauser did not pitch well with the Padres in 1995, walking nine in just 5.2 innings, but also struck out nine. He has done well in the recent past and could be a useful middle reliever: he's durable and has pretty good stuff.

OTHER VETERAN PLAYERS

San Francisco Giants

TODD BENZINGER—After going 2-for-10 with the Giants, he was cut so that J.R. Phillips could play every day. Benzinger then signed with the Yankees' Triple-A team at Columbus and batted 50 times, collecting four RBI. He ought to be done by now, but there's no telling how desperate somebody might be this spring.

ENRIQUE BURGOS—Acquired from Kansas City, Burgos has a great fastball but poor control, and showed it with the Giants. In 8.1 innings, he struck out 12, walked six, and allowed 14 hits. Back to the bushes.

PAT GOMEZ—A thoroughly mediocre lefty, Gomez pitched racked up a 5.14 ERA in 14 innings. He could be just about anywhere this year, but won't ever hang around long enough to buy a house in the city he's playing in.

KENNY GREER—Garden-variety righthander who was 0-2 in eight games with the Giants. No upside.

MARK LEONARD—After another productive year at Triple-A, Leonard got another call to San Francisco, where he went 4-for-21. He can hit but can't run or play defense, and it doesn't look like he's ever going to get more than a few swings here and there.

STEVE MINTZ—Unfortunately not nicknamed "Junior." The righty reliever saw some action with the Giants when injuries depleted their pitching staff and went 1-2, 7.45 in 19.1 innings, walking 12. The Giants didn't recall him in September, which doesn't speak well for his future.

KEVIN ROGERS—Missed all season with a blood clotting problem in his left shoulder which first surfaced in 1994. Claimed off waivers by the Pirates this fall. Rogers had tremendous potential before the malady struck, but will likely need at least a year to get back to any sort of competitive level.

Off-Season Player Moves

This section contains updated information on significant player moves through the end of December (trades, signings, waiver claims, Rule V drafts) for all major-league players and prominent prospects. Some of this material was incorporated into the 1996 sections of the player essays, depending on which team a particular player was on and when that team's part of the book went into production.

RICK AGUILERA—Signed with the Twins again in December, where he will supposedly start. Aguilera has never pitched more than 142 innings in a season, making this a risky move for the righthander at this age.

ROBERTO ALOMAR—His signing by Baltimore this winter is perhaps the critical piece in a team now favored to win the AL East. Bret Barberie will, obviously, hit the bench.

LUIS AQUINO—Sold by the Red Sox to the Kintetsu Buffaloes of Japan in October.

JOE AUSANIO—Moves across town this year, signing a Triple-A deal with the Mets in December.

HAROLD BAINES—In mid-December, the White Sox brought him on board for a year to "protect" Frank Thomas.

WILLIE BANKS—The Phillies claimed him off waivers during October.

JEFF BARRY—Barry, an undistinguished Mets outfielder, was traded to the Padres in December. Fifth OF at best.

KIMERA BARTEE—Is this something fishy, or do the Twins really think they have enough quality prospects to leave guys like Bartee unprotected? (Veteran 3B washout Tom Quinlan was on the Minnesota winter roster, while Bartee was left unprotected.) Traded to Minnesota this past summer, the speedy outfielder was reacquired by the Orioles in the December Rule V draft. Likely to spend the whole season with the Birds.

KIM BATISTE—The former Phillies infielder was selected by the Giants from Baltimore during December in the Rule V draft.

HOWARD BATTLE—Philadelphia acquired him from Toronto in the December Quantrill deal as insurance in case the Phils didn't acquire a veteran third baseman.

ANDY BENES—Joins the Cardinals after signing a two-year deal with a club option for a third.

MIKE BENJAMIN—Acquired by the Phillies last October for Jeff Juden, in one of the odder trades of the year.

ERIK BENNETT—Inked by the Twins in December to a Triple-A contract.

SEAN BERRY—Traded to Houston in December for Dave Veres, he will be the Astros' regular third baseman this season.

MIKE BLOWERS—Traded in late November from the Mariners to the Dodgers in a straight salary dump; Blowers, 30, is eligible for arbitration and Seattle didn't want to pay him. Blowers will replace the departed Tim Wallach, while the M's will use the newly-acquired Russ Davis at the hot corner.

JOE BOROWSKI—The righty relief prospect was sent to Atlanta in December as part of the payment for Kent Mercker. Borowski is likely to get a good shot at a bullpen job.

BILLY BREWER—The Royals shipped the erratic lefty to the Dodgers in December for erratic shortstop Jose Offerman.

KEVIN BROWN—Signed a three-year deal with the Marlins, for whom he could be outstanding.

MIKE BUTCHER—Given up for by the Angels, he signed with Seattle in December.

RAMON CARABALLO—He was let go by St. Louis, and signed with Boston in November.

PAUL CAREY—Traded to Boston over the winter.

CHUCK CARR—Made expendable by the signing of Devon White, Carr was dealt to Milwaukee in December for a Class A pitching prospect.

JHONNY CARVAJAL—A good prospect dealt by the Reds to the Expos for Gabe White in December.

PHIL CLARK—Dumped by the Padres, Clark was signed by Boston to a Triple-A deal in December.

ROYCE CLAYTON—Clayton, traded to St. Louis in December, becomes the everyday shortstop, implying that Ozzie Smith is nearing the end of the line.

DOUG CREEK—Creek, part of the December trade for Royce Clayton, will get a shot at being one of the left-handers in the Giants' bullpen.

OFF-SEASON PLAYER MOVES

MILT CUYLER—Dumped by Detroit, he has been signed by the Red Sox and will be given a look in the spring.

OMAR DAAL—The Expos have decided to offer Omar a chance to be their mediocre lefthanded reliever in 1996, acquiring him from the Dodgers in December.

DOUG DASCENZO—The diminutive outfielder will try to pull a Cangelosi and restart his career this year; he signed in December with San Diego.

MARK DAVIS—Believe it or not, he will try to come back this spring. Florida signed him.

RUSS DAVIS—Davis comes to Seattle with the opportunity to play 130 games or more at third base.

JEFF DARWIN—Acquired by Chicago in October as the Player to Be Named Later for Warren Newson, Darwin was added to the 40-man roster this winter.

ROB DEER—San Diego signed him in December and will bring him to camp this spring. True.

RICH DELUCIA—Traded to the Giants in the December Royce Clayton deal, he'll pitch early and often for San Francisco.

ROB DIBBLE—His December signing by the Cubs shows that nobody is ever really "finished" in baseball.

CHRIS DONNELS—Sold by the Red Sox in October to the Kintetsu Buffaloes.

MARIANO DUNCAN—Will travel to the Bronx this year and fill in all over the place for the Yankees.

DAVE EILAND—For some inexplicable reason, St. Louis signed him to a Triple-A deal in December.

DONNIE ELLIOTT—Signed in December by Philadelphia, he will try recover from serious arm problems.

RIKKERT FANEYTE—Had no future in San Francisco with Deion aboard, so Rikkert became a Ranger in December. Unfortunately for him, he won't get a chance at a job in Texas, either.

PAUL FLETCHER—Oakland signed him in December as a six-year free agent.

KEVIN FLORA—Signed by the Angels in November to a minor-league contract.

DON FLORENCE—A free agent, he signed with Baltimore in November.

BROOK FORDYCE—Signed a minor-league contract with the Reds during December.

JULIO FRANCO—After a year in Japan, he returns this year and will DH for the Indians.

WILLIE FRASER—Signed this winter by the Angels.

GARY GAETTI—Kansas City will enter 1996 with an entirely new infield; Gaetti has gone to St. Louis, and...

GREG GAGNE—Gagne, apparently too pricey for the Royals, signed with a one-year deal with the Dodgers in early December.

RON GANT—The Cardinals signed him to a five-year deal this off-season, and will presumably use him in left field.

RICH GARCES—Boston inked him in December.

JOE GIRARDI—Colorado dealt him to the Yankees in late November for minor-league pitching prospects Mike DeJean and Steve Shoemaker.

DWIGHT GOODEN—Signed by the Yankees to a one-year contract in November.

CURTIS GOODWIN—The fleet center fielder will be patrolling the garden for Cincinnati this year, as he was sent to the Reds in December for David Wells.

TOM GORDON—Signed a two-year, free-agent deal with the Red Sox, for whom he is likely to make at least 30 starts this season.

CRAIG GREBECK—Signed a minor-league deal with Florida in December.

BUDDY GROOM—Last December, he signed with Oakland.

MATT GROTT—Inked a Triple-A contract with Philadelphia in November.

DARREN HALL—Presumably recovered from injury, he signed with the Dodgers in November.

JOE HALL—Signed a Triple-A deal with the Orioles in November.

DARRYL HAMILTON—Texas was desperate for a center fielder, and signed Hamilton in December for a year. Whether Darryl's shoulder is healed sufficiently for him to throw from center is another question.

ERIK HANSON—Signed by the Blue Jays in December, he becomes their #1 starter if he is at all healthy.

BRYAN HARVEY—The oft-injured reliever signed a one-year, incentive-laden deal with the Angels. If healthy, Harvey is likely to work as a bridge reliever to Troy Percival.

OFF-SEASON PLAYER MOVES

CHARLIE HAYES—After being spurned by Philadelphia, Charlie signed with the Pirates for a year.

ERIC HELFAND—Removed from the Athletics' roster this winter, he signed with the Indians and could be a third catcher this season.

RICKEY HENDERSON—Signed a two-year deal in December to play left field and lead off for San Diego.

MIKE HENNEMAN—Opted not to retire; will close for the Rangers this season.

BUTCH HENRY—He underwent "Tommy John" surgery late in 1995 and probably won't pitch until late this season, if at all. The Expos tried to sneak him off the 40-man roster in October, but the Red Sox snapped him up.

KEN HILL—The probably-healthy righthander signed a very lucrative deal with the Rangers this year, where he could be a valuable starter or he could be another Kevin Gross.

STERLING HITCHCOCK—Left New York in the mid-December Tino Martinez deal, and will be in the Mariners' rotation this season.

RAY HOLBERT—Dealt from San Diego to Houston last November, he joins an already voluminous crew of Astros middle infielders, but is still a prospect.

DAVE HOLLINS—Minnesota signed him this winter, and will give him a shot at first base.

RICK HONEYCUTT—Sold by the Yankees to St. Louis, so he can continue to work with Tony LaRussa.

JACK HOWELL—Signed with the Angels in November after several years in Japan. Expected to platoon at third base with Tim Wallach, Howell is a shot in the dark.

EDWIN HURTADO—The promising but unready pitcher was sent to Seattle this winter for Bill Risley and could get a chance to start.

TIM HYERS—Packed off to Detroit in November for a stiff to be named later.

PETE INCAVIGLIA—Signed with the Phillies in December after two years in Japan. Unlikely to make a big impact.

RICCARDO INGRAM—In November, he was invited to spring training by the Padres.

JOE JACOBSEN—Selected in the December Rule V draft by Minnesota.

STAN JAVIER—Moves across the bay this year, signing a two-year deal with the Giants.

LANCE JOHNSON—Inked a new deal with the Mets in December. He will play center field and, most likely, lead off. Despite his protestations, Lance isn't best used in the top spot.

JOHN JOHNSTONE—Florida decided to give up on him and his injury troubles. Johnstone signed a minor-league deal this winter with Houston.

DOUG JONES—Signed by the Cubs in December, he is expected to be their closer. At least as long as his ERA is under 5.00.

RICO JORDAN—Part of the return on Paul Quantrill, Jordan could fit into the Phillies' bullpen, which currently lacks a lefthander, but really isn't ready to pitch in the major leagues.

WALLY JOYNER—In December, the Royals swapped him to San Diego in exchange for Bip Roberts.

JEFF JUDEN—Couldn't get out of Jim Fregosi's doghouse, and was basically donated to the Giants in October. The Phillies got Mike Benjamin in the deal, who will presumably be their utility infielder.

GREG KEAGLE—Joins his third organization in less than a year, moving to Detroit via the December Rule V draft.

JOE KMAK—After a decent short stint with the '95 Cubs, Joe inked a minor-league deal this winter with the Reds.

MIKE KINGERY—Pittsburgh signed him to a two-year contract in December. Kingery may be the everyday center fielder this season.

CHAD KREUTER—Signed with the White Sox this winter.

AL LEITER—Despite offering good money and having been loyal to Leiter in the past, Toronto couldn't keep him, losing him to Florida in December. He signed a three-year deal with the Fish.

DARREN LEWIS—After submitting a contract demand the Reds saw as outrageous, Lewis was waived by Cincinnati in early December and was claimed by Texas. However, Lewis rejected the claim and then signed with the White Sox for two years at $2.8 million. He'll play center and probably lead off for Chicago.

THE SCOUTING REPORT 1996

OFF-SEASON PLAYER MOVES

MARK LEWIS—Sent from Cincinnati to Detroit in November as the player to be named later in the David Wells trade. He will contend for a starting job.

RICHIE LEWIS—San Diego inked him to a minor-league deal in December.

BOB MACDONALD—Signed with the Mets this winter. Could be a lefty in the bullpen.

MIKE MACFARLANE—Returns to Kansas City this year after signing a two-year contract.

DAVE MAGADAN—The Cubs brought him on board this winter, and he may be their everyday third baseman in '96.

PEDRO A. MARTINEZ—After the season, he was back to the Padres for Ray Holbert. Then, in December, San Diego traded him to the Mets for Jeff Barry. Martinez could be the Mets' lefthanded setup guy this year, but only if he buys a map of home plate.

TINO MARTINEZ—Dealt to the Yankees in December, he'll fill the hole left by Don Mattingly's departure.

JOHN MARZANO—Seattle signed him to a minor-league deal in December.

BRENT MAYNE—Amazingly, he wasn't worth more than minor league outfielder Al Shirley (who struck out over 200 times in 1994) when dealt to the Mets in December. Will be Todd Hundley's backup.

JEFF MCCURRY—Claimed by the Tigers from Pittsburgh off the waiver wire in November. Could pitch 70 times.

RAY MCDAVID—Formerly the jewel of the Padres' system, Ray was waived in December and claimed by Montreal. He's still just 24.

BLACK JACK MCDOWELL—Will make over $10 million in the next two years for the Indians, as a result of inking a new deal in December.

ROGER MCDOWELL—Baltimore brought Roger on board for this year and Davey Johnson, his old manager in New York, will use him often.

WILLIE MCGEE—Signed with the Cardinals in December. It's hard to see where he fits.

MIGUEL MEJIA—The Royals took him in the December Rule V draft.

PAUL MENHART—Came to Seattle in the deal for Bill Risley. He could make the Mariners' staff as a long reliever.

KENT MERCKER—Traded to the Orioles in December, he will move into the rotation.

PAUL MOLITOR—Will play for his hometown Twins this year, signing a one-season deal in December.

JAMIE MOYER—Inked by the Red Sox to a one-year deal in December.

OSCAR MUNOZ—The former Twin was claimed on waivers by the Orioles in December.

GREG MYERS—Minnesota signed him this December to platoon with Matt Walbeck.

RANDY MYERS—In December, he inked a two-year deal with the Orioles.

CHRIS NABHOLZ—New York has signed him this winter, and the Mets will give him a chance at the bullpen.

TYRONE NARCISE—Drafted by Milwaukee in the Rule V process, he was immediately shipped to Florida as partial payment for Chuck Carr.

JEFF NELSON—Traded to New York in the Tino Martinez deal, he'll do setup work for the Yankees.

WARREN NEWSON—Signed a free-agent deal last December with Texas, who needed lefthanded bench strength.

OTIS NIXON—Signed a two-year deal in December with the Blue Jays, who were desperate for a center fielder.

MATT NOKES—The former Tigers, Yankees, Orioles, and Rockies catcher will start this season in Milwaukee.

CHARLIE O'BRIEN—Toronto signed him in December.

JOSE OFFERMAN—Acquired for Billy Brewer in December, Jose will be the Royals' starting shortstop this year.

JOE ORSULAK—Inked in December by Florida, he will fill the fourth outfielder spot, which has been a source of trouble for the club.

RICKY OTERO—Traded in December by the Mets to the Phillies for failed prospect Phil Geisler, Otero could be a fifth outfielder in the majors this season.

BALTIMORE ORIOLES

CAREY PAIGE—Drafted by Toronto in the December Rule V process.

MARK PARENT—Signed with Detroit in December, where he could end up hitting a bunch of home runs.

STEVE PEGUES—Seattle signed him to a minor-league deal in December and will bring him to spring training.

RUDY PEMBERTON—The Tigers farmhand signed a Triple-A deal with the Rangers this past December.

ALEJANDRO PENA—Back with the Marlins, who signed him in December.

BRAD PENNINGTON—He will try to find it with the Red Sox, who inked him in November.

PHIL PLANTIER—Signed to a one-year deal with Detroit in December, he will play outfield and DH.

PAUL QUANTRILL—Dealt to the Blue Jays in December, he will become the club's fourth starter.

TIM RAINES—Dealt to the Yankees over the winter in a cost-cutting move by the White Sox. His acquisition means Ruben Rivera will probably spend another season at Triple-A.

JON RATLIFF—The former Cubs #1 pick was selected by the Tigers in the December Rule V draft.

JEFF REED—The former Giants' backup was signed by the Rockies, and is being considered to fill a platoon combination with Jayhawk Owens.

RICK REED—The former Cincinnati replacement player signed a Triple-A deal this past winter with the Mets.

MIKE REMLINGER—Went to Kansas City in a three-way December deal revolving around some Rule V picks.

TUFFY RHODES—Sold by the Red Sox to the Kintetsu Buffaloes last October.

CHUCK RICCI—Inked a Triple-A deal with the Red Sox in December.

BILLY RIPKEN—Signed by Baltimore in the winter to a Triple-A contract.

BILL RISLEY—Dealt to the Blue Jays this winter, he will be thrown into the relief mix and could emerge as the closer.

KEVIN ROBERSON—Joined his fourth organization in less than a year in December, inking a Triple-A deal with the Mets. Can hit a little.

BIP ROBERTS—Traded to Kansas City for Wally Joyner, Bip will lead off and play left field for the Royals.

KENNY ROGERS—Signed with the Yankees this winter and will move into the forefront of their rotation.

KEVIN ROGERS—Claimed off waivers by Pittsburgh in October.

JOHN ROPER—Once again belongs to Cincinnati; the Giants decided his health wasn't work the risk and dumped him in November.

RICH ROWLAND—Signed by Toronto in December, he will contend for a backup job.

CHRIS SABO—Improbably, re-signed with the Reds in December, where he may get some time at first and third.

MO SANFORD—Will take his sweeping curve to Texas, where he signed in December.

KEITH SHEPHERD—Baltimore signed the veteran reliever to a Triple-A deal this winter.

PETE SMITH—After several poor seasons, he'll try to claw his way back this spring with the Padres.

MATT STAIRS—Oakland signed him (in December) to a minor-league deal.

ANDY STANKIEWICZ—The veteran infielder signed with Montreal this winter.

MIKE STANLEY—Left the Bronx Zoo in December for the greener pastures of Fenway. Boston signed him for one year.

KURT STILLWELL—Texas signed him over the winter and will bring him to camp in the spring.

B.J. SURHOFF—Went to the greener pastures of Baltimore, where he will probably work in a utility role but could end up the everyday third baseman.

JIM TATUM—Released by Colorado, he hooked on with the Red Sox in October.

DAVE TELGHEDER—Had no future with the Mets, so he signed with the Athletics in December.

BOB TEWKSBURY—The soft-tossing vet was signed by the Padres over the winter.

J.J. THOBE—The Expos waived him, and Boston claimed him in October.

OFF-SEASON PLAYER MOVES

GARY THURMAN—Signed with the Mets over the winter, he could end up their fifth outfielder with a good spring.

RON TINGLEY—Inked a minor-league contract with California in December.

SCOOTER TUCKER—Kansas City signed him to a Triple-A deal in December.

RANDY VELARDE—Signed a three-year deal with the California Angels last December.

DAVE VERES—A workhorse in Houston, he will pitch early and often in Montreal this season. Veres was sent north in December for Sean Berry.

B.J. WALLACE—Missed all of 1995 due to injury, and then was drafted by the Phillies in the December Rule V procedure.

TIM WALLACH—Signed in December with the Angels, and will share third base with Jack Howell. Had elbow surgery over the winter.

ALLEN WATSON—In December, he was sent to the Giants as part of the booty for Royce Clayton.

DAVID WELLS—Dealt to Baltimore in December for Curtis Goodwin, he will move into the rotation.

DEVON WHITE—Florida signed him to a three-year contract in November.

GABE WHITE—The Expos never seemed to have much confidence in him, and in December dealt him to the Reds for minor-league infielder Jhonny Carvajal.

TREY WITTE—Montreal took him in the December Rule V draft.

TODD ZEILE—Signed by the Phillies to a one-year, $2.5 million contract over the winter to replace Charlie Hayes.

Index

This index is an alphabetical list of more than 1800 players who are included in *The Scouting Report: 1996*—the 1133 players who played in the majors in 1995, over 300 top prospects, and over 400 lesser prospects and veteran minor-leaguers.

Players shown in **boldface** are major-leaguers who have been given either the standard full-page or half-page coverage. Players shown in SMALL CAPS are found in the Top Prospects sections for each team; players shown in *italics* are found in the Others to Watch sections for each team; and players shown in normal type are found in the Other Veteran Players section at the end of the book.

ABBOTT, JEFF	93	*Arnold, Jamie*	*344*	**Bautista, Jose**	634	Bielecki, Mike	67
Abbott, Jim	51	**Arocha, Rene**	588	*Bautista, Juan*	*25*	**Biggio, Craig**	439
Abbott, Kurt	415	*Arteaga, Ivan*	*414*	BEAMON, TREY	572	Birkbeck, Mike	655
Abbott, Kyle	656	**Ashby, Andy**	598	Bean, Billy	657	Black, Bud	647
ABREU, BOB	459	*Ashby, Chris*	*230*	BEAUMONT, MATT	72	**Blair, Willie**	600
ACEVEDO, JUAN	525	**Ashley, Billy**	476	**Beck, Rodney**	622	*Blanco, Alberto*	*461*
Acre, Mark	244	ASHWORTH, KYM	482	**Becker, Rich**	186	*Blanco, Henry*	*484*
ADAMS, TERRY	364	**Assenmacher, Paul**	111	*Beckett, Robbie*	*621*	**Blauser, Jeff**	323
ADAMS, WILLIE	249	**Astacio, Pedro**	476	Bedrosian, Steve	651	*Blosser, Greg*	*50*
ADAMSON, JOEL	434	*Atwater, Joe*	*527*	*Beech, Matt*	*551*	**Blowers, Mike**	255
Aguilera, Rick	26	*Aucoin, Derek*	*506*	**Belcher, Tim**	253	*Blum, Geoff*	*506*
Ahearne, Pat	*647*	**Aude, Rich**	564	*Belinda, Stan*	*39*	BLUMA, JAMIE	159
Alberro, Jose	*298*	AURILIA, RICH	642	BELK, TIM	388	BOCACHICA, HIRAM	504
ALCANTARA, ISRAEL	504	**Ausanio, Joe**	221	**Bell, David**	589	**Bochtler, Doug**	611
Aldrete, Mike	66	**Ausmus, Brad**	599	**Bell, Derek**	438	BOEHRINGER, BRIAN	228
Alexander, Manny	2	*Aven, Bruce*	*118*	**Bell, Jay**	552	**Boever, Joe**	131
Alfonseca, Antonio	*436*	**Avery, Steve**	322	Bell, Juan	645	**Bogar, Tim**	520
Alfonso, Edgardo	507	*Avrard, Corey*	*597*	BELL, MIKE	296	**Boggs, Wade**	208
Alicea, Luis	27	**Ayala, Bobby**	252	**Belle, Albert**	98	**Bohanon, Brian**	131
Allanson, Andy	646	*Badorek, Mike*	*597*	**Belliard, Rafael**	337	Bolton, Rod	646
Allen, Cedric	*390*	**Baerga, Carlos**	97	*Belliard, Ronnie*	*185*	*Bonanno, Rob*	*74*
ALLENSWORTH, JERMAINE	572	**Bagwell, Jeff**	437	**Beltre, Esteban**	289	**Bonds, Barry**	623
Allison, Chris	*50*	*Bailey, Cory*	*597*	*Benard, Marvin*	*644*	**Bones, Ricky**	162
Almanzar, Richard	*138*	**Bailey, Roger**	406	BENES, ALAN	595	**Bonilla, Bobby**	5
Alomar Jr., Sandy	96	**Baines, Harold**	4	**Benes, Andy**	254	BONNICI, JAMES	272
Alomar, Roberto	299	Baker, Scott	649	**Benitez, Armando**	17	BOONE, AARON	388
Alou, Moises	485	*Baldwin, James*	*95*	BENITEZ, YAMIL	504	**Boone, Bret**	367
Alston, Garvin	*414*	Bankhead, Scott	649	**Benjamin, Mike**	635	Borbon, Pedro	337
ALVAREZ, GABE	619	BANKS, BRIAN	183	Bennett, Erik	646	**Borders, Pat**	452
Alvarez, Rafael	*207*	**Banks, Willie**	428	Bennett, Gary	656	**Bordick, Mike**	232
Alvarez, Tavo	655	*Baptist, Travis*	*320*	Bennett, Joel	50	**Borland, Toby**	543
Alvarez, Wilson	75	BARBER, BRIAN	595	BENNETT, SHAYNE	48	BOROWSKI, JOE	23
Amaral, Rich	266	**Barberie, Bret**	16	*Benz, Jake*	*506*	**Bosio, Chris**	256
Amaro, Ruben	647	BARCELO, MARC	205	Benzinger, Todd	657	Boskie, Shawn	67
Anderson, Brady	3	Bark, Brian	645	BERBLINGER, JEFF	595	*Boston, D.J.*	*320*
Anderson, Brian	66	*Barker, Glen*	*138*	**Bere, Jason**	76	**Bottalico, Ricky**	528
Anderson, Garret	52	*Barrios, Manny*	*461*	**Bergman, Sean**	120	BOURGEOIS, STEVE	642
Anderson, Jimmy	*574*	Barry, Jeff	655	*Berrios, Harry*	*25*	*Bovee, Mike*	*161*
Anderson, Scott	648	BARTEE, KIMERA	205	**Berroa, Geronimo**	231	Bowen, Ryan	653
Andrews, Shane	498	**Barton, Shawn**	634	**Berry, Sean**	486	*Bowers, Shane*	*207*
ANDUJAR, LUIS	93	**Bass, Kevin**	16	Berryhill, Damon	652	*Boze, Marshall*	*185*
Anthony, Eric	381	**Bates, Jason**	391	BERTOTTI, MIKE	93	BRADSHAW, TERRY	595
Apana, Matt	*274*	BATISTA, TONY	249	**Berumen, Andres**	611	Brady, Doug	646
Appier, Kevin	139	**Battle, Allen**	588	*Betzsold, Jim*	*118*	**Bragg, Darren**	266
Aquino, Luis	655	BATTLE, HOWARD	318	*Beverlin, Jay*	*230*	BRANDENBURG, MARK	296
Arias, Alex	428	*Bauer, Matt*	*138*	*Bevil, Brian*	*161*	BRANDOW, DEREK	318
ARIAS, GEORGE	72	**Bautista, Danny**	119	**Bichette, Dante**	392	**Branson, Jeff**	368

THE SCOUTING REPORT: 1996 665

INDEX

Brantley, Jeff	369	*Byrdak, Timothy*	*161*	**Clontz, Brad**	338	**Cuyler, Milt**	132
Branyan, Russ	*118*	*Cabrera, Jolbert*	*506*	*Cloude, Ken*	*274*	D'AMICO, JEFFREY	183
Brewer, Billy	152	**Caceres, Edgar**	152	CLYBURN, DANNY	23	*Daal, Omar*	*655*
Brewington, Jamie	635	CAIRO, MIGUEL	482	**Colbrunn, Greg**	418	*Dale, Carl*	*597*
Bridges, Kary	*461*	CAMERON, MIKE	93	**Cole, Alex**	198	*Dalesandro, Mark*	*74*
Brito, Bernardo	649	**Caminiti, Ken**	601	*Cole, Jim*	*185*	**Damon, Johnny**	140
Brito, Jorge	653	Campbell, Kevin	649	*Coleman, Michael*	*50*	*Danapilis, Eric*	*138*
BRITO, TILSON	318	**Candiotti, Tom**	463	**Coleman, Vince**	258	*Darensbourg, Vic*	*436*
Brocail, Doug	452	**Cangelosi, John**	453	Coles, Darnell	657	*Darling, Ron*	*650*
Brogna, Rico	508	CANIZARO, JAY	642	COLLIER, LOU	572	*Darr, Mike*	*138*
Bronkey, Jeff	648	**Canseco, Jose**	28	*Colmenares, Luis*	*414*	**Darwin, Danny**	290
Brooks, Wes	*50*	*Cappuccio, Carmine*	*95*	COLON, BART	116	*Daspit, Jim*	*251*
Brosius, Scott	233	*Carlson, Dan*	*644*	**Cone, David**	209	**Daulton, Darren**	529
Brower, Jim	*298*	CARMONA, RAFAEL	272	*Conger, Jeff*	*574*	DAVIS, BEN	619
Brown, Brant	*366*	CARPENTER, CHRIS	318	**Conine, Jeff**	419	**Davis, Chili**	53
Brown, Jarvis	645	**Carr, Chuck**	417	*Conner, Decomba*	*390*	DAVIS, JEFF	296
Brown, Kevin	6	Carrara, Giovanni	651	*Converse, Jim*	*648*	*Davis, Kane*	*574*
BROWN, KEVIN	296	**Carrasco, Hector**	381	*Conway, Keith*	*597*	*Davis, Ray*	*597*
Brown, Mike	*574*	**Carreon, Mark**	624	**Cook, Dennis**	289	**Davis, Russ**	221
Brown, Randy	*50*	*Carter, Andy*	*551*	*Cooke, Steve*	*656*	DAVIS, TOMMY	23
Brown, Ray	*390*	**Carter, Joe**	300	COOKSON, BRENT	48	DAVISON, SCOTT	272
BROWNE, BYRON	183	*Carter, John*	*118*	**Coomer, Ron**	199	*Dawson, Andre*	*429*
Browne, Jerry	429	*Carvajal, Jhonny*	*390*	**Cooper, Scott**	575	**Decker, Steve**	430
Browning, Tom	*648*	*Carvajal, Jovino*	*74*	COPPINGER, ROCKY	23	*Declue, Jon*	*74*
Brumbaugh, Cliff	*298*	CASANOVA, RAUL	619	**Cora, Joey**	259	*Dedrick, Jim*	*645*
Brumfield, Jacob	553	**Casian, Larry**	359	**Cordero, Wil**	487	*Dejean, Mike*	*230*
Brumley, Mike	654	Castellano, Pedro	653	**Cordova, Marty**	187	*Deleon, Jose*	*655*
Bruno, Julio	*621*	**Castilla, Vinny**	393	**Cormier, Rheal**	39	DELGADO, CARLOS	318
Brunson, Matt	*138*	*Castillo, Alberto*	*527*	*Corn, Chris*	*230*	*Delgado, Wilson*	*644*
Bruske, Jim	655	**Castillo, Frank**	346	**Cornelius, Reid**	521	**DeLucia, Rich**	589
Bryant, Pat	*118*	*Castillo, Luis*	*436*	Cornett, Brad	651	DELVECCHIO, NICK	228
Buchanan, Brian	*230*	**Castillo, Tony**	301	*Corps, Edwin*	*644*	*Dennis, Shane*	*621*
Buckles, Bucky	*298*	CASTRO, JUAN	482	Correia, Rod	646	Deshaies, Jim	656
Buddie, Mike	*230*	*Castro, Ramon*	*461*	**Corsi, Jim**	244	**DeShields, Delino**	464
Buechele, Steve	650	**Cedeno, Andujar**	602	*Costo, Tim*	*118*	*Desilva, John*	*645*
Buford, Damon	520	**Cedeno, Domingo**	312	COUNSELL, CRAIG	412	DESSENS, ELMER	572
Buhner, Jay	257	CEDENO, ROGER	482	*Courtright, John*	*207*	*Detmers, Kris*	*597*
Bullett, Scott	359	*Cepeda, Jose*	*161*	**Cox, Danny**	312	Dettmer, John	25
Bullinger, Jim	345	Chamberlain, Wes	645	COX, STEVE	249	Dettmer, John	650
Bullinger, Kirk	*506*	**Charlton, Norm**	267	**Crabtree, Tim**	313	*Devarez, Cesar*	*25*
Bunch, Mel	*161*	CHAVEZ, CARLOS	23	*Cranford, Jay*	*574*	**Devereaux, Mike**	338
Burba, Dave	370	*Chavez, Eric*	*25*	*Crawford, Carlos*	*118*	**Dewey, Mark**	636
Burgos, Enrique	658	CHAVEZ, RAUL	459	Creek, Doug	657	**Diaz, Alex**	267
BURKE, JOHN	412	*Cholowsky, Dan*	*597*	CREEK, RYAN	459	*Diaz, Eddy*	*274*
Burkett, John	416	*Chouinard, Bobby*	*251*	CRESPO, FELIPE	318	DIAZ, EDWIN	296
Burks, Ellis	406	**Christiansen, Jason**	564	*Croghan, Andy*	*230*	*Diaz, Einar*	*118*
Burnitz, Jeromy	*118*	**Christopher, Mike**	132	**Cromer, Tripp**	576	Diaz, Mario	654
Burrows, Terry	650	**Cianfrocco, Archi**	612	CROWTHER, BRENT	412	Dibble, Rob	648
BURT, CHRIS	183	**Cirillo, Jeff**	163	CRUZ, FAUSTO	249	DICKSON, JASON	72
BURTON, DARREN	364	**Clark, Dave**	565	*Cruz, Ivan*	*138*	**DiPoto, Jerry**	521
Burton, Essex	*95*	**Clark, Jerald**	198	CRUZ, JACOB	642	**DiSarcina, Gary**	54
Busby, Mike	*597*	**Clark, Mark**	99	CRUZ, JR., JOSE	272	**Dishman, Glenn**	603
Busch, Mike	*484*	**Clark, Phil**	612	*Cumberland, Chris*	*230*	**Doherty, John**	133
BUSH, HOMER	619	**Clark, Terry**	17	**Cummings, John**	477	*Donato, Dan*	*230*
Butcher, Mike	68	CLARK, TONY	136	**Cummings, Midre**	565	**Donnels, Chris**	40
Butler, Brett	462	**Clark, Will**	275	*Cunnane, Will*	*436*	*Doolan, Blake*	*551*
Butler, Rob	*551*	**Clayton, Royce**	625	**Curtis, Chad**	121	DOSTER, DAVE	549
Byrd, Anthony	*207*	**Clemens, Roger**	29	*Curtis, Kevin*	*25*	**Dougherty, Jim**	453
Byrd, Paul	*527*	*Cline, Pat*	*366*	*Curtis, Randy*	*621*	**Drabek, Doug**	440

666   THE SCOUTING REPORT: 1996

INDEX

Dreifort, Darren	484
Drews, Matt	228
Dreyer, Steve	298
Drumright, Mike	136
Dunbar, Matt	654
Duncan, Mariano	382
Dunn, Steve	207
Dunn, Todd	185
Dunston, Shawon	347
Dunwoody, Todd	436
Duran, Roberto	484
Durant, Mike	207
Durham, Ray	77
Dye, Jermaine	342
Dyer, Mike	566
Dykstra, Lenny	530
Easley, Damion	55
Ebert, Derrin	344
Echevarria, Angel	412
Eckersley, Dennis	234
Eddy, Chris	648
Edenfield, Ken	74
Edens, Tom	652
Edmonds, Jim	56
Edsell, Geoff	74
Eenhoorn, Robert	649
Eichhorn, Mark	645
Eiland, Dave	649
Eischen, Joey	484
Eisenreich, Jim	531
Elarton, Scott	461
Eldred, Cal	648
Elliott, Donnie	657
Ellis, Robert	95
Elster, Kevin	543
Embree, Alan	116
Encarnacion, Angelo	566
Encarnacion, Juan	136
Ericks, John	567
Erickson, Scott	7
Erstad, Darin	72
Eshelman, Vaughn	40
Espinoza, Alvaro	111
Estalella, Bobby	549
Estes, Shawn	642
Etler, Todd	390
Eusebio, Tony	441
Evans, Bart	161
Evans, Tom	320
Everett, Carl	509
Eversgerd, Bryan	655
Fabregas, Jorge	57
Fajardo, Hector	650
Falteisek, Steve	504
Faneyte, Rikkert	636
Farrell, John	647
Fasano, Sal	159
Fassero, Jeff	488
Felder, Ken	185
Fermin, Felix	268
Fermin, Ramon	251
Fernandez, Alex	78
Fernandez, Jared	50
Fernandez, Osvaldo	274
Fernandez, Sid	544
Fernandez, Tony	210
Fesh, Sean	621
Fetters, Mike	164
Fielder, Cecil	122
Figga, Mike	228
Finley, Chuck	58
Finley, Steve	604
Flaherty, John	123
Fleming, Dave	153
Flener, Huck	320
Fletcher, Darrin	489
Fletcher, Paul	656
Fletcher, Scott	133
Flora, Kevin	544
Florence, Don	655
Florie, Bryce	613
Floyd, Cliff	498
Foley, Tom	655
Fonville, Chad	477
Fordham, Tom	93
Fordyce, Brook	647
Forkner, Tim	461
Forney, Rick	25
Fortugno, Tim	646
Fossas, Tony	590
Foster, Kevin	348
Foulke, Keith	644
Fox, Andy	228
Fox, Chad	388
Fox, Eric	650
Franco, John	510
Franco, Julio	647
Franco, Matt	364
Franklin, Micah	572
Frascatore, John	595
Fraser, Willie	655
Frazier, Lou	290
Freeman, Marvin	407
Freire, Alejandro	461
French, Anton	342
Frey, Steve	656
Frye, Jeff	291
Fryman, Travis	124
Fullmer, Brad	506
Fultz, Aaron	207
Fussell, Chris	25
Gaetti, Gary	141
Gagne, Greg	142
Galarraga, Andres	394
Gallagher, Dave	68
Gallaher, Kevin	459
Gallego, Mike	245
Gandarillas, Gus	205
Gant, Ron	371
Garces, Rich	652
Garcia, Al	366
Garcia, Carlos	554
Garcia, Frank	597
Garcia, Freddy	572
Garcia, Karim	482
Garcia, Luis	138
Garcia, Omar	525
Garcia, Vincente	414
Garciaparra, Nomar	48
Gardiner, Mike	647
Gardner, Mark	430
Gaspar, Cade	136
Gates, Brent	235
Geeve, Dave	298
Geisler, Phil	551
Gentile, Scott	504
Giambi, Jason	245
Giannelli, Ray	657
Gibralter, David	48
Gibralter, Steve	388
Gibson, Derrick	412
Gibson, Kirk	647
Gil, Benji	276
Giles, Brian	116
Gilkey, Bernard	577
Giovanola, Eddie	651
Girardi, Joe	395
Giron, Emiliano	390
Givens, Brian	165
Glanville, Doug	364
Glavine, Tom	324
Glinatsis, George	274
Goff, Jerry	654
Gohr, Greg	647
Gomes, Wayne	549
Gomez, Chris	125
Gomez, Leo	18
Gomez, Pat	658
Gonzales, Rene	646
Gonzalez, Alex	302
Gonzalez, Juan	277
Gonzalez, Luis	349
Gonzalez, Raul	161
Gooch, Arnold	527
Goodwin, Curtis	8
Goodwin, Tom	143
Gordon, Mike	320
Gordon, Tom	144
Gorecki, Rick	484
Gott, Jim	656
Grable, Rob	551
Grace, Mark	350
Grace, Mike	549
Graffanino, Tony	344
Grahe, Joe	407
Granger, Jeff	161
Graves, Danny	116
Grebeck, Craig	88
Green, Shawn	303
Green, Tyler	532
Greene, Charlie	527
Greene, Rick	138
Greene, Todd	72
Greene, Tommy	545
Greene, Willie	388
Greenwell, Mike	30
Greer, Kenny	658
Greer, Rusty	278
Gregg, Tommy	431
Grieve, Ben	249
Griffey Jr., Ken	260
Grigsby, Benji	251
Grijak, Kevin	342
Grimsley, Jason	647
Grissom, Marquis	325
Groom, Buddy	654
Gross, Kevin	279
Grotewold, Jeff	648
Grott, Matt	652
Grudzielanek, Mark	499
Grundy, Phil	161
Guardado, Eddie	199
Gubicza, Mark	145
Guerrero, Vladimir	504
Guerrero, Wilton	482
Guetterman, Lee	650
Guevara, Giomar	274
Guiel, Aaron	74
Guillen, Jose	574
Guillen, Ozzie	79
Gulan, Mike	595
Gunderson, Eric	645
Guthrie, Mark	478
Gutierrez, Ricky	454
Gutierrez, Ricky	118
Guzman, Jose	652
Guzman, Juan	304
Gwynn, Chris	478
Gwynn, Tony	605
Habyan, John	69
Hackman, Luther	414
Hajek, Dave	459
Hale, Chip	200
Hall, Billy	621
Hall, Darren	651
Hall, Joe	647
Hamelin, Bob	153
Hamilton, Darryl	166
Hamilton, Joey	606
Hammaker, Atlee	647
Hammond, Chris	420
Hammonds, Jeffrey	18
Hampton, Mike	442
Hancock, Lee	656
Hancock, Ryan	74
Haney, Chris	154
Haney, Todd	366
Hansell, Greg	207
Hansen, Brent	50
Hansen, Dave	479

INDEX

Hansen, Jed	*161*	**Hickerson, Bryan**	**408**	**Ingram, Garey**	**480**	**Juden, Jeff**	**545**
Hanson, Erik	**31**	Hidalgo, Richard	459	*Ingram, Riccardo*	*207*	**Justice, Dave**	**327**
Hardge, Mike	*50*	**Higginson, Bob**	**126**	**Isringhausen, Jason**	**522**	**Kamieniecki, Scott**	**223**
Hardtke, Jason	*527*	*Hiljus, Erik*	*527*	Jackson, Damian	116	**Karchner, Matt**	**88**
Hare, Shawn	650	**Hill, Glenallen**	**626**	**Jackson, Danny**	**579**	**Karkovice, Ron**	**82**
Harikkala, Tim	*274*	**Hill, Ken**	**101**	**Jackson, Mike**	**384**	**Karl, Scott**	**169**
Harkey, Mike	**59**	*Hill, Ty*	*185*	*Jackson, Ryan*	*436*	*Karp, Ryan*	*551*
Harkrider, Tim	*74*	**Hitchcock, Sterling**	**211**	*Jacobs, Frank*	*506*	**Karros, Eric**	**465**
Harnisch, Pete	**511**	Ho Park, Chan	483	*Jacobs, Ryan*	*344*	Karsay, Steve	650
Harper, Brian	650	Hocking, Denny	205	*Jacobsen, Joe*	*484*	*Keagle, Greg*	*274*
Harris, Greg A.	**499**	**Hoffman, Trevor**	**607**	*Jacome, Jason*	*146*	*Keling, Korey*	*74*
Harris, Greg W.	649	**Hoiles, Chris**	**9**	**Jaha, John**	**168**	**Kelly, Mike**	**339**
Harris, Lenny	**382**	Holbert, Aaron	596	**James, Chris**	**43**	**Kelly, Pat**	**224**
Harris, Pep	*118*	**Holbert, Ray**	**613**	**James, Dion**	**223**	**Kelly, Roberto**	**466**
Harrison, Tom	*344*	*Holdridge, David*	*74*	**James, Mike**	**70**	Kendall, Jason	573
Hart, Jason	364	*Holifield, Rick*	*551*	Janicki, Pete	73	Kennedy, David	413
Hartgraves, Dean	**454**	**Hollandsworth, Todd**	**480**	*Janzen, Marty*	*319*	*Kennedy, Gus*	*344*
Hartley, Mike	645	Hollins, Damon	342	*Jarvis, Jason*	*320*	**Kent, Jeff**	**514**
Harvey, Bryan	654	**Hollins, Dave**	**41**	**Jarvis, Kevin**	**384**	*Kester, Tim*	*461*
Haselman, Bill	**41**	*Hollins, Stacy*	*251*	**Javier, Stan**	**237**	Key, Jimmy	649
Hatcher, Billy	650	**Holmes, Darren**	**396**	**Jefferies, Gregg**	**534**	**Keyser, Brian**	**89**
Hatteberg, Scott	*50*	Holt, Chris	460	**Jefferson, Reggie**	**43**	**Kiefer, Mark**	**177**
Hawkins, Latroy	205	Holzemer, Mark	646	Jenkins, Geoff	183	Kieschnick, Brooks	365
Hayes, Charlie	**533**	**Honeycutt, Rick**	**222**	Jennings, Robin	365	**Kile, Darryl**	**455**
Haynes, Jimmy	23	**Hook, Chris**	**637**	Jensen, Marcus	642	*King, Andre*	*95*
Hazlett, Steve	*207*	Hope, John	573	Jeter, Derek	228	**King, Jeff**	**556**
Heberling, Keith	*95*	Horn, Sam	651	*Jimenez, Miguel*	*251*	King, Kevin	650
Heflin, Bronson	*551*	Horsman, Vince	649	*Jimenez, Oscar*	*161*	**Kingery, Mike**	**397**
Heiserman, Rick	*597*	**Hosey, Dwayne**	**42**	**Johns, Doug**	**246**	**Kirby, Wayne**	**112**
Held, Dan	*551*	*Houston, Tyler*	*344*	*Johns, Keith*	*597*	Kirkreit, Daron	116
Helfand, Eric	**246**	Howard, Chris	651	**Johnson, Brian**	**614**	Klassen, Danny	183
Helling, Rick	*298*	**Howard, David**	**154**	**Johnson, Charles**	**421**	**Klesko, Ryan**	**328**
Helms, Wes	*344*	**Howard, Thomas**	**383**	**Johnson, Howard**	**360**	Kline, Steve	117
Helton, Todd	*414*	**Howe, Steve**	**222**	*Johnson, J.J.*	*207*	**Klingenbeck, Scott**	**200**
Hemond, Scott	**590**	Hubbard, Mike	364	*Johnson, Jason*	*298*	Kmak, Joe	652
Henderson, Kenny	*621*	Hubbard, Trenidad	412	Johnson, Jon	296	**Knoblauch, Chuck**	**188**
Henderson, Rickey	**236**	*Huckaby, Ken*	*484*	**Johnson, Lance**	**81**	**Knorr, Randy**	**314**
Henderson, Rod	*506*	**Hudek, John**	**455**	**Johnson, Mark**	**555**	*Koelling, Brian*	*551*
Henke, Tom	**578**	**Hudler, Rex**	**69**	**Johnson, Randy**	**261**	Konerko, Paul	483
Henley, Bob	*506*	Hudson, Joe	42	*Johnson, Russ*	*461*	Konuszewski, Dennis	656
Henneman, Mike	**443**	**Huff, Mike**	**313**	Johnston, Joel	645	Kowitz, Brian	651
Henriquez, Oscar	*461*	*Hughes, Bobby*	*185*	*Johnston, Sean*	*527*	Kreuter, Chad	650
Henry, Butch	**500**	*Huisman, Rick*	*161*	Johnstone, John	654	**Krivda, Rick**	**19**
Henry, Doug	**522**	Hulett, Tim	657	Jones, Andruw	342	Kroon, Marc	619
Henry, Dwayne	647	**Hulse, David**	**167**	**Jones, Bobby**	**513**	Krueger, Bill	650
Hentgen, Pat	**305**	**Hundley, Todd**	**512**	*Jones, Bobby*	*414*	Kruk, John	647
Heredia, Gil	**490**	**Hunter, Brian Lee**	**444**	**Jones, Chipper**	**326**	*Kusiewicz, Mike*	*414*
Heredia, Julian	72	*Hunter, Brian R.*	*652*	**Jones, Chris**	**523**	Lacy, Kerry	297
Heredia, Wilson	434	Hunter, Rich	549	*Jones, Dax*	*644*	*Ladd, Jeff*	*320*
Hermansen, Chad	*574*	*Hunter, Torii*	*207*	**Jones, Doug**	**10**	*Ladjevich, Rick*	*274*
Hermanson, Dustin	619	Hurst, Jimmy	93	*Jones, Ryan*	*320*	**Laker, Tim**	**500**
Hernandez, Carlos	**479**	**Hurtado, Edwin**	**314**	*Jones, Terry*	*414*	**Lampkin, Tom**	**637**
Hernandez, Jeremy	654	Huskey, Butch	525	**Jones, Todd**	**445**	Landry, Todd	184
Hernandez, Jose	**360**	**Huson, Jeff**	**19**	**Jordan, Brian**	**580**	*Lane, Ryan*	*207*
Hernandez, Roberto	**80**	*Hust, Gary*	*251*	Jordan, Kevin	549	**Langston, Mark**	**60**
Hernandez, Xavier	**382**	*Hutcheson, David*	*366*	Jordan, Rico	651	**Lankford, Ray**	**581**
Herrera, Jose	249	Hyers, Tim	657	*Jorgensen, Randy*	*274*	**Lansing, Mike**	**491**
Hershiser, Orel	**100**	Ibanez, Raul	272	*Jorgensen, Tim*	*118*	Larkin, Andy	434
Hiatt, Phil	648	*Ibarra, Jesse*	*644*	Jose, Felix	648	**Larkin, Barry**	**372**
Hibbard, Greg	650	Ignasiak, Mike	648	**Joyner, Wally**	**147**	*Larocca, Greg*	*621*

INDEX

Larocca, Todd	*25*	*Lucca, Lou*	*436*	Mauser, Tim	657	Miller, Kurt	434
LaValliere, Mike	**89**	Ludwick, Eric	525	**Maxcy, Brian**	**134**	**Miller, Orlando**	**447**
Lawton, Matt	205	*Luke, Matt*	229	*Maxwell, Jason*	*366*	Miller, Travis	206
Leary, Rob	*574*	*Luzinski, Ryan*	*484*	May, Darrell	342	*Miller, Trever*	*138*
Ledee, Ricky	*230*	*Lydy, Scott*	*251*	**May, Derrick**	**456**	Milliard, Ralph	435
Ledesma, Aaron	*527*	**Lyons, Barry**	**90**	**Mayne, Brent**	**149**	*Million, Doug*	*414*
Lee, Carlos	*95*	*Lyons, Curt*	*390*	McAndrew, Jamie	648	Mills, Alan	645
Lee, Derrek	620	Maas, Kevin	649	*McCall, Rod*	*118*	**Mimbs, Mike**	**535**
Lee, Manuel	657	**Mabry, John**	**582**	**McCarty, Dave**	**638**	**Minor, Blas**	**523**
Lee, Mark	**20**	**MacDonald, Bob**	**225**	**McCaskill, Kirk**	**91**	Mintz, Steve	658
Leftwich, Phil	73	*Macey, Fausto*	*644*	McClain, Scott	24	**Miranda, Angel**	**179**
Leiper, Dave	**501**	**MacFarlane, Mike**	**32**	*McConnell, Chad*	*551*	*Mitchell, Tony*	*461*
Leiter, Al	**306**	*Macon, Leland*	*298*	McCracken, Quinton	413	**Mlicki, Dave**	**515**
Leiter, Mark	**627**	**Maddux, Greg**	**331**	**McCurry, Jeff**	**568**	Mlicki, Doug	460
Leius, Scott	**189**	**Maddux, Mike**	**44**	McDavid, Ray	620	*Moehler, Brian*	*138*
Lemke, Mark	**329**	Maduro, Calvin	24	**McDonald, Ben**	**20**	**Mohler, Mike**	**247**
Lemp, Chris	*25*	**Magadan, Dave**	**446**	*McDonald, Jason*	*251*	*Moler, Jason*	*551*
Leonard, Mark	658	*Magdaleno, Ricky*	*390*	**McDowell, Jack**	**213**	**Molitor, Paul**	**308**
Lesher, Brian	250	Magee, Wendell	550	**McDowell, Roger**	**292**	**Mondesi, Raul**	**468**
Leskanic, Curt	**398**	**Magnante, Mike**	**155**	**McElroy, Chuck**	**385**	*Monds, Wonder*	*344*
Levis, Jesse	647	*Mahay, Ron*	*50*	*McEwing, Joe*	*597*	Monteleone, Rich	646
Lewis, Anthony	*597*	**Mahomes, Pat**	**201**	*McFarlin, Terric*	*621*	**Montgomery, Jeff**	**150**
Lewis, Darren	**373**	*Maksivish, Joe*	*574*	**McGee, Willie**	**44**	Montgomery, Steve	596
Lewis, Jim	*118*	Malave, Jose	48	McGinnis, Rusty	648	*Montoya, Wil*	*118*
Lewis, Marc	*344*	**Maldonado, Candy**	**291**	**McGriff, Fred**	**332**	*Moody, Eric*	*298*
Lewis, Mark	**385**	Mantei, Matt	434	McGuire, Ryan	48	Moore, Joel	413
Lewis, Richie	**431**	**Manto, Jeff**	**11**	**McGwire, Mark**	**238**	*Moore, Kerwin*	*251*
Lewis, T.R.	*25*	**Manwaring, Kirt**	**628**	*McKeel, Walt*	*50*	*Moore, Marcus*	*390*
Leyritz, Jim	**224**	Manzanillo, Josias	649	**McLemore, Mark**	**280**	Moore, Mike	647
Lieber, Jon	**567**	Manzanillo, Ravelo	657	**McMichael, Greg**	**333**	Moore, Trey	273
Lieberthal, Mike	550	Marquez, Isidro	647	McMillon, Billy	434	*Moore, Vince*	*621*
Lilliquist, Derek	645	**Marsh, Tom**	**546**	McMurtry, Craig	654	*Mora, Melvin*	*461*
Lima, Jose	**127**	**Martin, Al**	**559**	*McNair, Fred*	*551*	**Morandini, Mickey**	**536**
Lind, Jose	646	**Martin, Norberto**	**90**	McRae, Brian	351	**Mordecai, Mike**	**339**
Linton, Doug	648	**Martinez, Angel**	**307**	**Meacham, Rusty**	**155**	Morel, Ramon	573
Lira, Felipe	**128**	Martinez, Carlos	646	*Meadows, Brian*	*436*	**Morgan, Mike**	**583**
Liriano, Nelson	**557**	**Martinez, Dave**	**83**	**Meares, Pat**	**190**	*Morman, Alvin*	*461*
Lis, Joe	*320*	**Martinez, Dennis**	**103**	Mecir, Jim	272	Morman, Russ	654
Listach, Pat	**177**	*Martinez, Eddy*	*25*	*Medina, Rafael*	*230*	*Morris, Bobby*	*366*
Little, Mark	*298*	**Martinez, Edgar**	**262**	*Mejia, Miguel*	*25*	**Morris, Hal**	**374**
Livingstone, Scott	**614**	Martinez, Felix	159	Mejia, Roberto	653	*Morris, Matt*	*597*
Lloyd, Graeme	**178**	*Martinez, Gabby*	*185*	*Melo, Juan*	*621*	*Morrison, Keith*	*74*
Loaiza, Esteban	**558**	*Martinez, Greg*	*185*	*Mendez, Rodolfo*	*161*	*Morrow, Nick*	*390*
Lockhart, Keith	**148**	*Martinez, Javier*	*366*	Mendoza, Ramiro	229	Mosquera, Julio	320
Loewer, Carlton	550	*Martinez, Jesus*	*484*	*Mendoza, Reynol*	*436*	*Moss, Damian*	*344*
Lofton, Kenny	**102**	*Martinez, Jose*	*621*	**Menhart, Paul**	**315**	Mota, Jose	648
Loiselle, Rich	*461*	**Martinez, Pedro J.**	**492**	*Mercado, Hector*	*461*	Mottola, Chad	388
Lomon, Kevin	656	Martinez, Pedro A.	654	**Merced, Orlando**	**560**	Mounce, Tony	460
Long, Terrence	*527*	**Martinez, Ramon**	**467**	Mercedes, Henry	648	**Mouton, James**	**448**
Longmire, Tony	**546**	*Martinez, Ramon*	*436*	Mercedes, Jose	649	**Mouton, Lyle**	**84**
Looney, Brian	*50*	**Martinez, Tino**	**263**	**Mercker, Kent**	**334**	**Moyer, Jamie**	**12**
Lopez, Albie	*118*	Marzano, John	651	*Merloni, Lou*	*50*	Mueller, Bill	643
Lopez, Javier	**330**	*Mashore, Damon*	*251*	**Merullo, Matt**	**202**	**Mulholland, Terry**	**629**
Lopez, Johann	*461*	*Mashore, Justin*	*138*	**Mesa, Jose**	**104**	*Mulligan, Sean*	*621*
Lopez, Luis	658	**Masteller, Dan**	**201**	Metcalfe, Mike	483	Munoz, Bobby	656
Lopez, Mendy	*161*	**Matheny, Mike**	**178**	**Miceli, Dan**	**561**	**Munoz, Mike**	**408**
Loretta, Mark	184	**Mathews, T.J.**	**591**	**Mieske, Matt**	**179**	Munoz, Noe	655
Lorraine, Andy	94	**Mathews, Terry**	**432**	*Millar, Kevin*	*436*	Munoz, Oscar	206
Lowe, Sean	*597*	**Mattingly, Don**	**212**	*Miller, Damian*	*207*	**Munoz, Pedro**	**191**
Lowery, Terrell	297	*Mattson, Rob*	*621*	Miller, Keith	648	Murphy, Rob	654

THE SCOUTING REPORT: 1996   669

INDEX

Murray, Calvin	*644*	**Orellano, Rafael**	49	**Perez, Yorkis**	**432**	*Randa, Joe*	*161*
Murray, Eddie	**105**	*Orie, Kevin*	*366*	**Perry, Herb**	**113**	**Rapp, Pat**	**424**
Murray, Glenn	49	**Orosco, Jesse**	**21**	Person, Robert	526	Rasmussen, Dennis	648
Murray, Heath	620	**Orsulak, Joe**	**516**	**Petagine, Roberto**	**616**	Rath, Gary	483
Murray, Matt	49	**Ortiz, Luis**	**293**	*Peters, Chris*	*574*	Ratliff, Jon	365
Musselwhite, Jim	229	Ortiz, Luis	297	*Petersen, Chris*	*366*	*Raven, Luis*	*74*
Mussina, Mike	**13**	**Osborne, Donovan**	**584**	Peterson, Charles	573	Ray, Ken	160
Myers, Greg	**70**	**Osuna, Antonio**	**481**	**Petkovsek, Mark**	**586**	Ready, Randy	656
Myers, Mike	*138*	Otanez, Willis	483	Pett, Jose	319	**Reboulet, Jeff**	**203**
Myers, Randy	**352**	Otero, Ricky	526	**Pettitte, Andy**	**215**	*Redman, Mark*	*207*
Myers, Rod	159	**Owen, Spike**	**71**	**Phillips, J.R.**	**639**	*Reed, Brandon*	*138*
Myrow, John	*414*	Owens, Billy	24	**Phillips, Tony**	**62**	*Reed, Chris*	*390*
Nabholz, Chris	652	Owens, Eric	389	*Phoenix, Steve*	*251*	**Reed, Jeff**	**639**
Naehring, Tim	**33**	**Owens, Jayhawk**	**409**	**Piazza, Mike**	**471**	**Reed, Jody**	**609**
Nagy, Charles	**106**	**Pagliarulo, Mike**	**293**	**Pichardo, Hipolito**	**156**	Reed, Rick	653
Narcisse, Tyrone	460	**Pagnozzi, Tom**	**585**	Pickett, Ricky	643	**Reed, Steve**	**399**
Natal, Bob	654	*Paige, Carey*	*344*	*Pickford, Kevin*	*574*	Reese, Pokey	389
Navarro, Jaime	**353**	**Painter, Lance**	**409**	Pierce, Jeff	645	**Rekar, Bryan**	**410**
Neagle, Denny	**562**	Palacios, Vincente	657	*Pincavitch, Kevin*	*484*	Relaford, Desi	273
Nelson, Bry	*461*	*Palmeiro, Orlando*	*74*	*Pirkl, Greg*	*274*	Remlinger, Mike	653
Nelson, Jeff	**268**	**Palmeiro, Rafael**	**14**	*Pisciotta, Marc*	*574*	Renteria, Edgar	435
Nen, Robb	**422**	**Palmer, Dean**	**282**	Pittsley, Jim	159	*Resz, Greg*	*230*
Nevin, Phil	136	*Paniagua, Jose*	*506*	*Pivaral, Hugo*	*484*	*Revenig, Todd*	*251*
Newfield, Marc	**615**	**Paquette, Craig**	**247**	**Plantier, Phil**	**608**	Reyes, Al	649
Newson, Warren	**269**	**Parent, Mark**	**361**	**Plesac, Dan**	**569**	**Reyes, Carlos**	**248**
Nichols, Rod	651	Parker, Rick	655	**Plunk, Eric**	**114**	**Reynolds, Shane**	**449**
Nichting, Chris	651	**Parra, Jose**	**202**	Poe, Charles	94	**Reynoso, Armando**	**410**
Nied, David	653	**Parrett, Jeff**	**592**	*Polcovich, Kevin*	*574*	**Rhodes, Arthur**	**22**
Nieves, Melvin	**615**	**Parris, Steve**	**568**	**Polonia, Luis**	**341**	Rhodes, Karl "Tuffy"	645
Nilsson, Dave	**170**	**Parrish, Lance**	**315**	**Poole, Jim**	**114**	*Ricci, Chuck*	*551*
Nitkowski, C.J.	134	**Patterson, Bob**	**71**	**Portugal, Mark**	**375**	*Richardson, Brian*	*484*
Nixon, Otis	**281**	Patterson, Jeff	649	Posada, Jorge	229	Ricken, Ray	229
Nixon, Trot	49	**Patterson, John**	**638**	*Powell, Dante*	*644*	Rigby, Brad	250
Nokes, Matt	653	*Pavano, Carl*	*50*	Powell, Jay	435	*Riggs, Adam*	*484*
Nomo, Hideo	**469**	Pavlas, Dave	649	*Powell, John*	*298*	**Righetti, Dave**	**92**
Norman, Les	*161*	**Pavlik, Roger**	**283**	Powell, Ross	657	**Rightnowar, Ron**	**180**
Norton, Greg	94	Payton, Jay	526	Pozo, Arquimedez	273	**Rijo, Jose**	**386**
Nunez, Clemente	*436*	*Pearson, Eddie*	*95*	*Prado, Jose*	*484*	Riley, Marquis	73
Nunez, Ramon	*344*	Pecorilli, Aldo	343	Pratt, Todd	652	*Rios, Armando*	*644*
Nunez, Sergio	*161*	*Peever, Lloyd*	*414*	*Presley, Kirk*	*527*	*Rios, Danny*	*230*
Nunnally, Jon	**151**	**Pegues, Steve**	**569**	Pride, Curtis	505	*Rios, Eduardo*	*484*
Nye, Ryan	550	*Pemberton, Rudy*	*138*	**Prieto, Ariel**	**248**	Ripken, Billy	647
O'Brien, Charlie	**340**	**Pena, Alejandro**	**340**	Prince, Tom	655	**Ripken, Cal**	**15**
O'Leary, Troy	**34**	**Pena, Geronimo**	**593**	Pritchett, Chris	73	**Risley, Bill**	**269**
O'Neill, Paul	**214**	**Pena, Tony**	**113**	**Puckett, Kirby**	**192**	**Ritz, Kevin**	**400**
Obando, Sherman	*25*	**Pendleton, Terry**	**423**	**Pugh, Tim**	**386**	**Rivera, Mariano**	**226**
Ochoa, Alex	525	*Penn, Shannon*	*138*	Pulliam, Harvey	653	*Rivera, Roberto*	*366*
Offerman, Jose	**470**	Pennington, Brad	652	**Pulsipher, Bill**	**517**	Rivera, Ruben	229
Ogea, Chad	**112**	Percibal, Billy	24	*Pyc, Dave*	*484*	Roa, Joe	117
Olerud, John	**309**	**Percival, Troy**	**61**	Pye, Eddie	655	*Robbins, Jason*	*390*
Oliva, Jose	**591**	**Perez, Carlos**	**493**	**Quantrill, Paul**	**537**	Roberson, Kevin	652
Olivares, Omar	656	*Perez, Danny*	*185*	*Raabe, Brian*	*207*	**Roberson, Sid**	**180**
Oliver, Darren	**292**	Perez, Eddie	651	**Radinsky, Scott**	**91**	**Roberts, Bip**	**610**
Oliver, Joe	**171**	Perez, Eduardo	73	**Radke, Brad**	**193**	*Roberts, Brett*	*207*
Olmeda, Jose	*344*	*Perez, Jhonny*	*461*	*Rain, Steve*	*366*	*Roberts, Chris*	*527*
Olson, Gregg	**156**	**Perez, Melido**	**225**	**Raines, Tim**	**85**	*Roberts, Lonell*	*320*
Ontiveros, Steve	**239**	**Perez, Mike**	**361**	*Raleigh, Matt*	*506*	*Robertson, Jason*	*230*
Oquendo, Jose	**592**	Perez, Neifi	413	Ralston, Kris	159	*Robertson, Mike*	*95*
Oquist, Mike	**21**	Perez, Robert	319	*Ramirez, Angel*	*320*	**Robertson, Rich**	**203**
Ordonez, Rey	525	**Perez, Tomas**	**316**	**Ramirez, Manny**	**107**	*Robinson, Ken*	*320*

670   THE SCOUTING REPORT: 1996

INDEX

Name	Page	Name	Page	Name	Page	Name	Page
Robledo, Nilson	95	Scanlan, Bob	181	Smiley, John	379	Surhoff, B.J.	174
Rodriguez, Alex	270	Scarsone, Steve	640	SMITH, BOBBY	343	SUTTON, LARRY	160
Rodriguez, Carlos	646	SCHALL, GENE	550	Smith, Brian	320	Suzuki, Mac	274
RODRIGUEZ, FELIX	483	Scheid, Rich	654	SMITH, CAM	137	Swann, Pedro	344
Rodriguez, Frank	194	Schilling, Curt	538	Smith, Dan	298	Swartzbaugh, Dave	652
Rodriguez, Frank	185	Schlomann, Brett	230	Smith, Dan	651	SWEENEY, MARK	596
Rodriguez, Henry	501	SCHMIDT, CURT	505	Smith, Demond	251	SWEENEY, MIKE	160
Rodriguez, Ivan	284	SCHMIDT, JASON	343	Smith, Dwight	341	Swift, Bill	402
Rodriguez, Rich	657	Schmidt, Jeff	74	Smith, Lee	64	Swindell, Greg	450
RODRIGUEZ, STEVE	136	Schmidt, Tom	414	SMITH, MARK	24	Tabaka, Jeff	457
Rodriguez, Victor	436	SCHMITT, TODD	620	SMITH, MIKE	297	Talanoa, Scott	185
Rogers, Jimmy	651	Schofield, Dick	646	Smith, Ozzie	594	Tam, Jeff	527
Rogers, Kenny	285	Schourek, Pete	378	Smith, Pete	653	Tapani, Kevin	472
Rogers, Kevin	658	Schuermann, Lance	298	Smith, Zane	46	Tarasco, Tony	496
Rojas, Mel	494	Schullstrom, Erik	204	Smoltz, John	335	Tartabull, Danny	242
ROLEN, SCOTT	550	SCHUTZ, CARL	343	SNOPEK, CHRIS	94	Tatis, Fernando	298
Roper, John	653	Schwab, Chris	506	Snow, J.T.	65	Tatum, Jim	653
Roque, Rafael	527	Scott, Tim	503	SODERSTROM, STEVE	643	Taubensee, Ed	387
Roskos, Johnny	436	Seanez, Rudy	655	SODOWSKY, CLINT	137	Taulbee, Andy	644
ROSSELLI, JOE	643	Sefcik, Kevin	656	Sojo, Luis	264	Tavarez, Jesus	433
Rowland, Rich	646	Segui, David	495	Sorrento, Paul	108	Tavarez, Julian	115
RUEBEL, MATT	573	Seguignol, Fernando	506	Sosa, Sammy	356	Taylor, Billy	650
Rueter, Kirk	502	Seitzer, Kevin	172	Sparks, Steve	173	Taylor, Brien	230
Ruffcorn, Scott	95	Selby, Bill	50	Spehr, Tim	655	Taylor, Kerry	621
Ruffin, Bruce	411	Sele, Aaron	45	Spencer, Shane	230	Taylor, Scott	298
Ruffin, Johnny	653	SERAFINI, DAN	206	Spiers, Bill	524	TELEMACO, AMAURY	365
Rumfield, Toby	390	Servais, Scott	355	SPIEZIO, SCOTT	250	Telgheder, Dave	656
Rupp, Brian	597	Service, Scott	640	Spoljaric, Paul	320	Tettleton, Mickey	286
RUSCH, GLENDON	160	SEXSON, RICHIE	117	Sprague, Ed	310	Tewksbury, Bob	287
Russell, Jeff	294	Sexton, Chris	414	Springer, Dennis	656	Thobe, J.J.	50
Russo, Paul	621	Sexton, Jeff	118	Springer, Russ	547	Thobe, Tom	652
Ryan, Jason	366	Sharperson, Mike	651	Stahoviak, Scott	204	Thomas, Frank	86
Ryan, Ken	45	Shave, Jon	298	Stairs, Matt	46	Thomas, Juan	95
RYAN, MATT	573	Shaw, Jeff	92	Stankiewicz, Andy	654	Thomas, Larry	95
Rychel, Kevin	574	Sheaffer, Danny	593	Stanley, Mike	217	Thome, Jim	109
Saberhagen, Bret	401	Sheets, Andy	274	Stanton, Mike	47	THOMPSON, JASON	620
Sabo, Chris	657	Sheff, Chris	436	STEENSTRA, KENNIE	365	THOMPSON, JUSTIN	137
Sackinsky, Brian	25	Sheffield, Gary	425	Stefanski, Mike	185	Thompson, Mark	653
SADLER, DONNIE	49	Shepherd, Keith	646	Steinbach, Terry	240	Thompson, Milt	458
SAENZ, OLMEDO	94	Shipley, Craig	456	Stephenson, Brian	366	Thompson, Robby	631
Sager, A.J.	653	Shores, Scott	551	STEPHENSON, GARRETT	24	Thompson, Ryan	518
Sagmoen, Marc	298	SHUEY, PAUL	117	Stevens, Dave	195	Thomson, John	414
SALKELD, ROGER	389	Shumpert, Terry	646	STEVERSON, TODD	137	Thurman, Gary	650
Salmon, Tim	63	Siddall, Joe	655	Stewart, Andy	161	Timlin, Mike	316
Samuel, Juan	157	Sierra, Ruben	216	Stewart, Dave	650	Timmons, Ozzie	362
Samuels, Scott	366	Sievert, Mark	320	Stewart, Rachaad	25	Tingley, Ron	135
Sanchez, Jesus	527	SILVA, JOSE	319	STEWART, SHANNON	319	Tinsley, Lee	35
Sanchez, Rey	354	Silvestri, Dave	503	Stinnett, Kelly	524	Tollberg, Brian	185
Sandberg, Ryne	652	Simas, Bill	95	Stocker, Kevin	540	Tomberlin, Andy	650
Sanders, Deion	630	Simmons, Scott	597	Stottlemyre, Todd	241	Tomko, Brett	390
Sanders, Reggie	376	Simms, Mike	457	Stovall, Darond	506	TORRES, DILSON	160
Sanders, Scott	616	Simons, Mitch	207	Strange, Doug	270	Torres, Jaime	230
Sanderson, Scott	646	Simonton, Benji	644	Strawberry, Darryl	226	Torres, Salomon	271
Sanford, Chance	574	Singleton, Chris	644	Strittmatter, Mark	414	Trachsel, Steve	357
Sanford, Mo	649	SINGLETON, DUANE	184	Stubbs, Franklin	135	Trammell, Alan	129
SANTANA, JULIO	297	SIROTKA, MIKE	94	STULL, EVERETT	505	TRAMMELL, BUBBA	137
Santana, Marino	274	Slaught, Don	570	Sturtze, Tanyon	366	Trombley, Mike	196
Santangelo, F.P.	502	Slocumb, Heathcliff	539	STYNES, CHRIS	160	Tucker, Eddie "Scooter"	647
Santiago, Benito	377	Slusarski, Joe	649	SULLIVAN, SCOTT	389	Tucker, Michael	157
Sasser, Mackey	657	Small, Aaron	436	SUPPAN, JEFF	49	Turner, Chris	646

THE SCOUTING REPORT: 1996

671

INDEX

Tuttle, Dave	*138*	WALL, DONNE	460	Williams, Gerald	227
Unroe, Tim	*185*	*Wallace, B.J.*	*506*	*Williams, Glenn*	*344*
Urbani, Tom	**594**	*Wallace, Derek*	*527*	*Williams, Harold*	*95*
URBINA, UGUETH	505	**Wallach, Tim**	**474**	WILLIAMS, JUAN	343
Urso, Sal	*274*	*Walls, Doug*	*414*	WILLIAMS, KEITH	643
Valdes, Ismael	**473**	**Walton, Jerome**	**387**	**Williams, Matt**	**633**
VALDES, MARC	435	*Ward, Bryan*	*436*	**Williams, Mike**	**548**
VALDES, PEDRO	365	WARD, DARYLE	137	Williams, Mitch	646
VALDEZ, CARLOS	643	Ward, Duane	651	Williams, Reggie	655
Valdez, Sergio	**641**	Ward, Turner	649	WILLIAMS, SHAD	73
Valentin, John	**36**	WARE, JEFF	319	*Williams, Todd*	*251*
Valentin, Jose	**175**	*Warner, Mike*	*344*	**Williams, Woody**	**317**
VALENTIN, JOSE	206	WASDIN, JOHN	250	WILLIAMSON, ANTONE	184
Valenzuela, Fernando	**617**	*Washburn, Jarrod*	*74*	Willis, Carl	649
Valle, Dave	**294**	*Waszgis, B.J.*	*25*	*Wilson, Craig*	*95*
Valrie, Kerry	*95*	WATKINS, PAT	389	**Wilson, Dan**	**265**
VanderWal, John	**411**	WATKINS, SCOTT	206	WILSON, ENRIQUE	117
Vanderweele, Doug	*644*	*Watkins, Sean*	*621*	Wilson, Gary	657
Vanegmond, Tim	646	**Watson, Allen**	**587**	WILSON, NIGEL	389
VanLandingham, Bill	**632**	*Wawruck, Jim*	*25*	WILSON, PAUL	526
Van Poppel, Todd	**243**	**Weathers, David**	**427**	WILSON, PRESTON	526
VanRyn, Ben	*74*	WEBB, DOUG	184	**Wilson, Trevor**	**641**
Van Slyke, Andy	**541**	*Weber, Neil*	*506*	*Wimberly, Larry*	*551*
VARITEK, JASON	273	**Webster, Lenny**	**548**	*Wimmer, Chris*	*644*
Varsho, Gary	**547**	**Webster, Mitch**	**481**	**Winfield, Dave**	**115**
Vaughn, Greg	**176**	WEGER, WES	184	*Winslett, Dax*	*366*
Vaughn, Mo	**37**	**Wegman, Bill**	**182**	WITASICK, JAY	596
Vazquez, Archie	*95*	**Wehner, John**	**570**	**Witt, Bobby**	**288**
VELANDIA, JORGE	620	*Weinke, Chris*	*320*	*Witt, Kevin*	*320*
Velarde, Randy	**218**	**Weiss, Walt**	**404**	*Witte, Trey*	*274*
VELAZQUEZ, EDGARDO	413	*Welch, Mike*	*527*	**Wohlers, Mark**	**336**
Ventura, Robin	**87**	**Wells, Bob**	**271**	Wojciechowski, Steve	650
Veras, Quilvio	**426**	**Wells, David**	**380**	WOLCOTT, BOB	273
Veres, Dave	**451**	**Wendell, Turk**	**363**	*Wolfe, Joel*	*251*
Veres, Randy	**433**	*Wengert, Don*	*251*	*Wolff, Mike*	*74*
VESSEL, ANDREW	297	*West, David*	*656*	Woodall, Brad	652
VIDRO, JOSE	505	**Wetteland, John**	**219**	*Woodring, Jason*	*506*
Villalobos, Carlos	*274*	WHISENANT, MATT	435	*Worrell, Tim*	*621*
Villone, Ron	**617**	**Whitaker, Lou**	**130**	**Worrell, Todd**	**475**
Vina, Fernando	**181**	*Whitaker, Steve*	*644*	Worthington, Craig	651
Viola, Frank	653	*White, Derrick*	*138*	WRIGHT, JAMEY	413
Vitiello, Joe	**158**	**White, Devon**	**311**	*Wright, Jaret*	*118*
Vizcaino, Jose	**519**	WHITE, GABE	505	*Wright, Ron*	*344*
Vizquel, Omar	**110**	*White, Jason*	*251*	*Wright, Terry*	*390*
Voigt, Jack	651	*White, Jimmy*	*390*	*Wunsch, Kelly*	*185*
Vosberg, Ed	**295**	**White, Rick**	**571**	*Yan, Esteban*	*506*
Wachter, Derek	*185*	**White, Rondell**	**497**	*Yocum, David*	*484*
WADE, TERRELL	343	**Whiten, Mark**	**542**	**Young, Anthony**	**363**
WAGNER, BILLY	460	**Whiteside, Matt**	**295**	YOUNG, DMITRI	596
WAGNER, BRET	596	Whiteside, Sean	647	**Young, Eric**	**405**
Wagner, Joe	*185*	WHITMORE, DARRELL	435	YOUNG, ERNIE	250
Wagner, Matt	*274*	WHITTEN, CASEY	117	**Young, Kevin**	**571**
Wagner, Paul	**563**	**Wickander, Kevin**	**182**	**Zaun, Greg**	**22**
Wakefield, Tim	**38**	**Wickman, Bob**	**227**	**Zeile, Todd**	**358**
Walbeck, Matt	**197**	WIDGER, CHRIS	273	*Zorrilla, Julio*	*527*
Walker, Larry	**403**	**Wilkins, Rick**	**458**	*Zosky, Eddie*	*436*
Walker, Mike	**362**	**Williams, Bernie**	**220**	*Zuber, Jon*	*551*
WALKER, PETE	526	**Williams, Brian**	**618**		
WALKER, TODD	206	**Williams, Eddie**	**618**		
Walker, Wade	*366*	WILLIAMS, GEORGE	250		

ABOUT THE BASEBALL WORKSHOP

The Baseball Workshop conducts continuing research on the performance of major-league baseball teams and players through a network of correspondents who record games play-by-play and pitch-by-pitch. These records are computerized and compiled into a unique and comprehensive data base containing detailed information and statistics on every major-league player and team.

As a result of this research, The Baseball Workshop manages an extensive data base dating back to the start of the 1984 season. A source of boundless discovery, these data are far more complex and revealing than the official statistics and contain a wealth of insights into how major-league players and teams perform.

The Baseball Workshop produces books, specialized computer data bases, and customized reports for the media, baseball analysts, player agents, major-league teams, insurance companies, and baseball researchers and fans. The Baseball Workshop's clients have included *USA Today Baseball Weekly*, *The Baseball Bluebook*, *Bill Mazeroski's Baseball*, *Inside Sports*, *Total Baseball IV* (the official encyclopedia of major-league baseball), USA Today Sports Center, SportSource, Inc., Publications International Limited, and the DCT Corporation—producer of the TAG (Team Advantage Grade) analysis system.

Computer Products include PLAY-BY-PLAY DATA for each season from 1984 through 1995, comprehensive CAREER DATA for all major-league players who have played in the 1980s and 1990s, complete SITUATIONAL STATISTICS for all players from 1984 through 1995, PLAY-BY-PLAY BOX SCORES for every major-league game in the past twelve seasons, SALARY AND SERVICE TIME DATA for all players in the 1990s, and INJURY AND DISABLED LIST DATA for all major-league players and teams since 1980. The Workshop also has developed specialized software to search and analyze its unique data base.

These products are available directly from The Baseball Workshop at very reasonable prices for research purposes, and licenses for commercial use of the data bases are available for professionals and companies.

Gary Gillette is also the author of the *Great American Baseball Stat Book*. He is the president of The Baseball Workshop, a baseball research and consulting firm in Philadelphia which he founded in 1992. He has written about baseball for many national publications and contributed to dozens of baseball books and periodicals as well as served as a baseball commentator for several National Public Radio stations.

The Baseball Workshop is interested in contacting free-lance writers and baseball fans who are available to cover major-league baseball games in 1996. The Workshop pays correspondents in each city to cover each regular-season game, sending their reports in via fax to a toll-free number after the game. The Baseball Workshop compiles its data base from these scoresheets and reports. If you want information on working as a stringer for the Workshop in 1996, please check the appropriate line on the form on the next page and send it in as soon as possible.

If you would like more information on any of The Baseball Workshop's products, please fill out the form on the next page and mail or fax it to The Baseball Workshop. Information will be sent to you promptly.

THE SCOUTING REPORT: 1996 SPRING TRAINING UPDATE

☐ Please send me a copy of *The Scouting Report: 1996* Spring Training Update.

The Update will be sent via first-class mail on March 20, 1996. The Spring Training Update is a 32-page booklet containing the latest information on all major-league players and top prospects. It includes up-to-date information on spring performance, injuries, rehabilitation progress, trades, free-agent signings, other player moves, and analysis of each team's likely opening day roster. It also includes ratings of the top prospects for 1996 for each team and at each position.

The cost of *The Scouting Report: 1996* Spring Training Update is $9.95 postpaid via first-class mail. It can be sent via overnight courier ($15 additional), or via guaranteed two-day delivery ($10 additional), or via Priority Mail ($5 additional) upon request. Sample copies of the 1995 Spring Training Update are available upon request for $3, postpaid.

_____
Name

_____
Mailing Address

_____
City   State/Province Zip Code

_____
Telephone (optional)   Fax

You can help make *The Scouting Report* even better in the future by giving us your opinion:

1. Please rate these features of *The Scouting Report: 1996* from 10 (excellent) to 1 (poor):

    Major-League Players ___   Top Prospects ___
    Others to Watch ___   Other Veteran Players ___
    User's Guide ___   Statistics ___
    Batter Graphs ___   Pitcher Graphs ___

2. Do you use the information in *The Scouting Report* for fantasy league analysis?   ☐ Yes   ☐ No

3. Any comments or suggestions for improving the next edition of *The Scouting Report*?

If you would like further information on any of the items described on the previous page, please check below:

☐ Please send me information about The Baseball Workshop.

☐ Please contact me regarding scoring for the 1996 baseball season.

☐ Please send me information about computer software and data for the 1984–1995 seasons.

Mail form to:
The Baseball Workshop, 619 Wadsworth Avenue, Philadelphia, PA, 19119
FAX form to: 800-905-7866
or CALL: 215-248-9899